Commissioned Gunner RN

Alfred William DAVIS

(1895-1941)

By

Neville Alfred DAVIS

Foreword by

Captain B. H. KENT RN (Retd)

HERITAGE BOOKS

Bernard Durnford Publishing

(An imprint of Heritage Books Limited)

HERITAGE BOOKS

First published 2006 by Bernard Durnford Publishing
An imprint of Heritage Books Limited,
8 The Laurels, Sylvan Hall Estate, Brighton BN2 3GE.
01273 882356.

A catalogue record of this book is available from the British Library.

ISBN 1 904470 06 8

Cover & Jacket by StewART
Typeset in Times and New Century Schoolbook

Printed and Bound in Great Britain by
Antony Rowe Ltd., Chippenham.

Alfred William Davis (1895 – 1941)
Commissioned Gunner RN

The debut of the naval career of Alfred Wm Davis coincided with the development of the all-big-gun battleship (HMS Dreadnought). The tragic end of Alf's career, thirty years later, heralded the demise of warships – even capital ships – when faced with overwhelming air power.

Alf's first draft as a Boy Seaman, in 1912, was to HMS Vanguard, a battleship already representing the third stage of the rapid development of the Dreadnought. His next draft was to the old HMS Russell, a pre-Dreadnought embodying late and unsuccessful attempts to catch up with the Dreadnought concepts. Thus Alf began to appreciate the great technological and tactical changes resulting from Admiral Fisher's radical efforts to modernise the capital ships of the Royal Navy.

During the First World War Alf saw action from the warm waters of the Indian Ocean to the bleak North Sea. Starting aboard the 6-inch cruiser Weymouth he finished, as a Leading Seaman, in the massively armed 15-inch experimental cruiser Courageous. Post-war, rising through the ranks, Alf served mainly in cruisers, though he also had stints as an Instructor at HMS Ganges. Married twice, he had four children by 1939.

Alf's last appointment was as Commissioned Gunner to the 6-inch cruiser HMS Southampton. He was present at her launching in 1936 and after some interesting deployments in the Atlantic it was in this fine ship that Alf went to war for the second time in his life. A life he was to share with the Southampton, for in 1941 she became the tomb of Alfred William Davis. Present at the birth of the ship, Alf was to be forever wedded to her in death.

Neville A Davis MIQA

Neville Alfred Davis ('Nev' as he likes to be known) is the elder son of Alf Davis, killed, aboard HMS Southampton before Nev reached his 11th birthday. Indeed Nev's mother had died when he was only four and he thus never had the chance to come to terms with his parents in an adult relationship. This book, in part, seeks to redress that lack.

Nev's early intention was to follow a Naval Career only to be thwarted – failing the eyesight test for the Gunnery Branch and then being denied entry due to a "heart murmur". This was very strange, for Nev was very fit and like Alf enjoyed Hockey and also Rugby Football. Indeed he continued to play Rugby, as a prop-forward, until the age of 60.

A fascination with Naval and Military history, coupled to a thirst for knowledge about his family history, drove Nev into a programme of intense research. Investigating archives, contacting former shipmates of his father and drawing on their experiences, adding memorabilia, photographs and postcards from his own collection to support those he had inherited from his father, Nev gradually assembled this book. *Commissioned Gunner RN* is a unique combination of social record and a source of naval history in a single volume.

Neville Davis spent his working life with Kodak Limited, becoming a technologist in various fields of quality development; he retired in 1990. Since 1963 Nev has been happily married to Liz. They have had three children, two of whom survive.

The jacket illustration is a photomontage by StewART depicting Alfred William Davis and his three competing loves on land and sea; Olive Mabel (left), Alice Agnes (right) and ships of the Royal Navy.

FOREWORD

By Captain B H Kent RN (Retd)

[Barrie Kent is the Author of
"Signal! A History of Signalling in the Royal Navy".]

This book, *"Commissioned Gunner RN"*, is a real *tour-de-force*. The author has set out to reconstruct the life and long naval career of his father, whom he hardly knew, and who was killed in action in 1941 when the author was not quite eleven. Thus the author had to start from virtually scratch as almost nothing of his Davis family or his father's life was known.

Extensive research eventually revealed much of the family's origins, and has provided us with a fascinating insight into the social life of the country in the early years of the 20th century. The author has built up an enormous amount of information on his forebears, as shown by the extensive family trees in the Appendices. Alf's family led a hard life and it was not a very happy one, especially after the mother died. Alf was then aged eleven. Alf did not get on with his father, and indeed it had emerged that he actually ran away to sea, immediately regretting it but with no practical alternative but to stick it out.

Little was previously known of Alf's long naval career, but again the author has spent years researching relevant naval documents, including in particular the Logs of every ship in which Alf served. The result is a detailed account of each ship and its activities at the time, including the battleship *Vanguard*, his first ship which Alf joined as a boy in 1912, the cruiser *Weymouth* which was involved with the German cruiser *Konigsberg*, trapped in East Africa during the first world war, and the battle cruiser *Courageous* (before she was converted into an aircraft-carrier). Well described is the filthy 'coal ship' routine which Alf experienced right through to the 1930s, much dressing ship and other ceremonial in peacetime, and the never-ending gun drills. Alf served in several other ships and also did time as an Instructor at the Boys Training Establishment, HMS *Ganges* at Shotley. His career culminated in some six years in the cruiser HMS *Southampton*. From all this research the author has assessed the part probably played by Alf, through the First World War and into the Second, when tragically Alf was killed in action in HMS *Southampton* in 1941, not long before he would have been due to retire.

Alf had achieved the rank of Warrant Officer in 1925 at the age of about 30, progressing to the senior rank of Commissioned Gunner, and was thus one of the stalwart commissioned officers who formed the backbone of the Navy. Reaching officer rank from the lower deck was not easy, being by selection from a large number of hopeful contenders, but these men with their specialist expertise and long experience were invaluable members of a ship's company, and a vital link between the command and the lower deck. Alf was clearly one of the best. (The warrant and commissioned ranks were abolished in the 1970s, other ways of direct access from the lower deck to officer rank being introduced. The title Warrant Officer was then adopted by the most senior Chief Petty Officers, lining up with the equivalent ranks in the Army and Air Force.)

The author refers to assessment reports issued to Alf by his commanding officers at the time he left a ship. These 'flimsies' as they are generally known, are brief extracts from the main confidential reports which will be forwarded to the Admiralty for inclusion in the officer's record.

The book is lavishly illustrated, in some part from his father's photo album (almost the only possession of his father to survive) and also from the wider family's collections, in a smaller part from national and county archives, but largely from the author's unique collection of contemporary naval postcards.

Barrie Kent

CONTENTS

Subject   **Page No**.

NOTE 1: Preceding each of the Chapters 3 to 15(a) there are sections on Alf's 'Private Life' when on spells of home leave, etc. (See Pages 76, 113, 137, 190, 252, 263, 313, 319, 332, 388, 392, 430 and 438.) Additional sections on his Private Life also occur part-way through Chapter 11 during his service in *Birmingham* (see Page 374), and in Chapters 15(a) and 15(b) during his very long service in *Southampton*. (See Pages 463, 514, 531, 557, 582, 618 and 656, respectively.)

NOTE 2: If anybody 'out there' feels that he or she can add usefully to the historical data or anecdotes concerning the late Commissioned Gunner Alfred William DAVIS, or to the various lists of names in this book, the author would be only too delighted to hear of it, for possible inclusion in any later editions of this work.

ERRATA: The author would be very pleased to have any errors of fact brought to his attention, so that appropriate corrective action can be taken in any future editions of this work. Please also see comments regarding the illustrations used, as shown on Page 16 and in Appendix B.

ABBREVIATIONS: During Alf's years of service it was customary for abbreviations to have full-stops after each initial letter. Thus, decorations appeared as (say) D.S.O. for *Distinguished Service Order*, ranks as (say) M.A.A. for *Master at Arms*, and duties as (say) O.O.W. for *Officer of the Watch*. In modern style such abbreviations are rendered without full-stops, and nowadays appear simply as DSO, MAA, OOW and so forth. It is this course which has been followed in the book.

It will usually be found that the full wording relating to each abbreviation is quoted the first time that it appears in the book, and, hopefully, the context in which it is used should make its meaning clear.

A Glossary of Abbreviations is given in Appendix H at the end of this book.

'LATE-ARRIVING' PHOTOGRAPHS: Some photographs reached the hands of the author after the writing, compiling and indexing of the book had reached the final 'print-ready' stage. Certain of these photographs were considered to be invaluable as illustrations for the narrative, and they have therefore been included as a cross-referenced portfolio at the end of the book, called 'APPENDIX J'. Fortunately, even at this late stage, it has been possible to include a few very brief notes within the main text. These notes prompt the reader to make reference to Appendix J whenever appropriate to a particular part of the narrative.

A DEDICATION

This book is dedicated to my dearly beloved wife Liz,
for her love, generosity, support, tolerance and
wise suggestions, not only in
the long preparation of this book, but in all things
throughout over forty years of married life.

N.A.D

A TRIBUTE

I am greatly indebted to my dear daughter Rosie
for much technical assistance in the drafting of this book,
(including advice on various computer aspects which completely baffled me),
for her proof-reading of some chapters, and for her checking and advising on the
general layout and comprehensibility of the work.

N.A.D

A PROFOUND THANKYOU

I am also highly indebted to Captain B H KENT RN (Retd),
for his great generosity in checking on my correct use of 'navalese',
and for his proof-reading and checking for illogicalities throughout.
Also for allowing me to refer to his Midshipman's Diary of the period
and for most kindly writing the Foreword.

(It should be noted that, in 1941, as a young Midshipman,
Captain KENT narrowly survived the aerial bombing of HMS 'Southampton'
when she was fatally struck and Alf and eighty others unfortunately lost their lives.)

N.A.D

Commissioned Gunner Alfred William DAVIS, photographed aboard
HMS *Southampton* when the ship was lying off Bilbao in 1937, at the time of the
Spanish Civil War. 'Alf' was then aged 42, and by that time he had become a highly
experienced and very competent officer. The photograph was taken by Sub Lieutenant
Charles MADDEN (later Rear Admiral C. D. MADDEN CB, CBE, LVO, DSC.)
*[Author's Collection. This fine print was inherited from Alf's domestic effects: his
shipboard effects were all lost with Alf and the ship in 1941.]*

INTRODUCTION

This is a biography of Alfred Wm DAVIS ('Alf') who ran away from home in 1911, after a tremendous quarrel with his father. The runaway, then aged just 15, joined the Royal Navy as a Boy Seaman. The training establishment to which he was drafted was renowned for its 'toughness', and Alf (possibly being much-bullied) soon found the life to be far too harsh. He appealed to his father to 'buy him out'. However, his newly-widowed father had felt greatly piqued by Alf's running off at a time when he and his other four children were still struggling desperately hard to keep a new business afloat. The father also reasoned that Alf must learn to 'tough things out' if he were ever to amount to anything in life. He replied that "Alf had made his bed and he could now lie on it!" Family legend is strong that the rebuff went so deep that proud and resentful son and proud and unbending father never spoke directly to each other ever again, albeit that underlying love and respect remained between them forever.

Alf had no realistic option other than to settle down to the life of a sailor, ere long coming to love it. He served throughout the First World War, being in immediate action on the outbreak of hostilities, and 'coming under enemy fire' in various theatres of war before the armistice of 1918 at last dawned. After witnessing the surrender of the German High Seas Fleet, Alf continued to serve, mainly abroad, through the difficult inter-war years, when government policies led to excessive economies being imposed on all the British armed forces. As time sped by Alf had risen well through the ranks, to achieve the coveted status of Commissioned Gunner in 1935. The Second World War broke out just as his retirement had begun to beckon, but, as a highly experienced officer, Alf's skills and leadership were in urgent demand and he continued on active service, by then well-established in the new cruiser HMS 'Southampton'. Once again he was immediately caught up in wartime patrols and actions which were often of the utmost danger, and which ended in tragedy in 1941.

This book covers the deployments of the nine different warships in which Alf served from 1912-1941, as his naval career proceeded. Alf's intervening periods of service in shore establishments are also examined. The account often borders into the interactions taking place at higher command level, and considers the outcomes of various Courts of Enquiry and Courts Martial which related to the most senior officers of the squadrons and fleets in which Alf served, and which would have been the cause of rumour, debate and controversy in every ship. The book is thus something of a selective 'ground floor history' of the Royal Navy from 1912 to 1941.

Also see overleaf regarding Alf's Private Life.

Aspects of Alf's Private Life

In its drive to understand 'what made Alf tick', the book includes the outcome of research into the roots of Alf's parents, and their raising of Alf. At intervals thereafter, through to 1941, the book examines the progression of Alf's private life, including the tragic lingering death of his first wife, the difficulties of his second marriage, the raising of his four children and all his related domestic problems. Those matters were made far more complex and pressing for Alf by the coming of the 2nd World War, the fall of France in mid-1940, the imminent threat of German invasion of England which promptly ensued, and the real possibility of our utter defeat and ruin.

The 'exigencies of the Service' meant that Alf had to leave his family to 'tough it out alone' when his ship sailed for the Mediterranean in November 1940. It was true that the threat of German invasion had temporarily receded, but German aerial bombing by night was rapidly intensifying: Europe was under the Axis yoke, North Africa was a battlefield and 'The Med' was in crisis.

What thoughts were in Alf's mind on the fateful date of 11th January 1941 when his ship was mortally struck, we will probably never know. But this is an attempt to learn what made him act as he did that day.

IN MEMORIAM (HMS Southampton)

Alf's mortal remains have lain in the wreck of the 5th HMS Southampton in the Ionian Deep since the 11th January 1941. Many others lie there too, as part of the same tragedy. Yet, the great majority of the ship's company of 800 men survived, and, though it is known that some men later lost their lives whilst serving in other ships, it is clear that most of the officers and men went on to outlive the 1939-45 war. Indeed some men did so despite being 'sunk' yet again, and one (at least) had two further ships go down under him. The author's research led him to form warm friendships with several of these surviving war-veterans – fascinating men of highly varied ranks - and the accounts of one and all have added enormously to this book. The author owes them a huge debt of gratitude. Sadly, most of these 'grand old men' have since departed this life and the author greatly misses them.

A 6th HMS Southampton is currently serving in the Royal Navy. She is a Type 42 destroyer, and she was first commissioned on 31st October 1981. Over the years which have elapsed since her commissioning, strong links have developed between the men and women who comprise the present fine "Southamptons", and the splendid "Old Southamptons" from the wartime years. A serving officer acts in the liaison role, and the current ship's company provides an excellent 'mise en scene' for reunions and services of commemoration, which usually take place aboard the 6th HMS Southampton. Some of the sons and daughters of the men who lost their lives whilst serving in the 5th HMS Southampton have also attended these ceremonies, to represent their lost fathers and to draw information and comfort from the men who survived. (The author - and his grandfather-less children - are a case in point.) An album, a booklet and a compilation of photographs and statements by survivors of the 5th Southampton are maintained aboard her successor. These documents provide a superb memorial and testimony.

Alf served in the 5th HMS Southampton throughout her operational life and an account of all her deployments runs through the relevant two-part chapter towards the end of this book. A copy of 'The Roll of Honour' of those who died whilst serving aboard the ship on the 11th January 1941 is included. The Roll is supplemented here by the details of men who are known to have become casualties in actions which took place earlier in her career. The well-deserved awards, some posthumous, which were made after the action of 11th January are also detailed. It is thus hoped that this book will serve as something of an 'extra and unofficial memorial' to the cruiser and her company.

Additionally, a 'Master List' has been compiled of all the officers and warrant officers known to have served at any time in the 5th HMS Southampton, from her commissioning in 1937 to her loss in 1941, using the ship's logs as the primary source of information, well supported by the Diary of Midshipman B. H. KENT. (See Appendix C.)

[Note: It is hoped that this book will also help to 'keep alive' thoughts of the other eight ships' companies in which 'Alf' served, from 1912 until 1935, preceding his appointment to HMS Southampton. Those eight ships ranged in scale from humble ocean-going tug to mighty 'Dreadnought' battleship. Their names form separate headings to the chapters of the book in which their exploits during Alf's spells of service aboard are described.]

A Nostalgic Note by the Author

*When, as a part of researching the history of my family, I was gently interviewing
elderly ladies on a one-to-one basis, especially cousins
of my late mother and of my late step-mother,
the mere mention of Alf's name would often have the very strange effect
of causing this or that elderly cousin's face to become for a few miraculous moments
just like that of the lovely young woman that she once was.
Then, as her memories raced further back and she recalled Alf more fully to mind,
her lips would part a little
and a blush would spread up from her neck to suffuse her face,
moments before the carefully 're-stabilised' visage of the 'senior citizen' once more
swam back into my view, obscuring the delightful vision of the long-ago.
The nostalgic tales that would follow would invariably be of the most discreet
and innocent nature –
but always left me slightly tantalised, marvelling, and pondering.*

*Yes, Alf was clearly quite a 'Lady's Man'
as well as undoubtedly being very much a Sailor and a 'Man's Man'.*

N.A.D

A Summary of
ACKNOWLEDGEMENTS *re* THE WRITTEN CONTENTS

Ⓘt will be seen that many sources have been researched and drawn upon for the writing of this book. Most prominent of the 'official' organisations have been the staff and records of:-

    (i) The National Archives (TNA) [formerly The Public Records Office (PRO)],
    (ii) The Imperial War Museum & the National Maritime Museum, Greenwich,
    (iii) The Family Record Centre and various County Record Offices.
    (iv) The British Library (especially in regard to newspaper articles).
    (v) The Commonwealth War Graves Commission.

To these organisations must be added key information provided by the author's 1st cousin, Raymond PENNEY, and by various survivors of the 5th HMS *Southampton*.

Yct there are many other people to whom the author owes a great debt, including his two sisters Joan and Jessica, his (more than) half-brother Richard, the author's son Robert, the author's nephew Andrew Ford, cousins Colin GREEN, Kath WALLER and Margaret AMEY, and other members of the author's wider family, many now deceased. To these must be added various amateur and professional family history researchers and indexers. The author hereby expresses his sincere thanks to the many people and organisations involved. **A more detailed and formalised listing and acknowledgement of the major 'archival' sources appears in Appendix 'A'.** Here, however, is an outline summary:-

a) Personalised 'Living' Memories
- The author's *personal* memories of his father, 'Alf', last seen by the author at age 10, in 1940.
- The author's *conditioned* memories of his father, Alf, as spontaneously given to the author by his elders and siblings over the years since the 1940s and since much supplemented.
- The outcome of the author's interviews with his cousins, some long-lost but happily re-found.
- The outcome of interviews & correspondence with one-time shipmates of the author's father.

b) Written Records and Memorabilia
- Alf's Naval Records from the Admiralty & Ministry of Defence.
- Alf's progress reports as a WO, as issued by his Commanding Officers (kept in-family).
- The Logs of the ships in which Alf served. [Held by The National Archives Office (TNA)].
- The Journals of Surgeons of Ships & Estab's in which Alf was serving (Held by TNA).
- Misc. documents regarding the ships & men with whom Alf served. (Held by TNA).
- Relevant photographs, diaries and other works held by the IWM and the NMM, Greenwich.
- Letters of condolence about Alf's death (as sent to the author's family in 1941.)
- Family photographs, domestic - including an album filled by Alf in the 1920s/early 1930s.
- Alf's collection of photographs taken later during his career, both 'official' & amateur.
- Relevant photographs provided by cousins and friends, including 'Old Southamptons'.
- Illustrated MSS & typed histories of the 5th HMS *Southampton* by certain of her men.
- An account by an RAF 'passenger' caught up in a sea-battle in HMS *Southampton*.
- Archives *re* the Family History of DAVIS *et alia*, held by the Family Record Centre.
- Archives *re* the Family History of DAVIS *et alia*, held by County Record Offices.
- Archives *re* the Family History of DAVIS *et alia*, held by The Society of Genealogists.
- Relevant newspaper articles e.g. marriage & bereavement notices, as held by the Brit Library.
- 'Photographic' Postcards, mostly 'ship-portraits', mainly from the period 1902-1914.
- Documents and photographs from the 'HMS *IMPREGNABLE* Association'.
- Fragments of information related to the RNTE, HMS *GANGES*, some from its Museum.
- "Kelly's" and other Trade Directories of various places and dates, and "Burkes Peerage 1909"
- Relevant Records of the Commonwealth War Graves Commission.

A Summary of
ACKNOWLEDGEMENTS & COMMENTS *re*
The ILLUSTRATIONS

As already indicated, relevant **photographic illustrations** have been used to add interest and to help the reader in visualising the scenes and times described, which range back to the late 19th Century. Each image produced in the book is identified with its source and at least an approximate date of origin, and, wherever appropriate, the name of the copyright owner who has granted permission for reproduction of the image. The sources and copyright owners include the following eight national and county organisations:

1) **The Imperial War Museum.**
2) **The National Archives (Formerly the Public Record Office, Kew).**
3) **The Royal Naval Museum at Portsmouth.**
4) **English Architectural Heritage, National Monument Record.**
5) **The Royal Commission on the Ancient and Historical Monuments of Scotland.**
6) **The Warwickshire County Museum.**
7) **The Lincolnshire County Council, Education and Cultural Services Directorate.**
8) **ECPA at Fort d'Ivry, France.**

Special acknowledgements and thanks are due to the Staff of all the above organisations. Other photographic illustrations have been drawn from:

9) **Various 'DAVIS', 'GOODMAN', 'GREEN' and 'PENNEY' family archives.**

The 'DAVIS' archive includes various amateur and 'official' photographs from Alf's collection. The author is very grateful to his elder sister and cousins for contributing *cartes de visite*, studio portraits and family snapshots. To support and extend the range of images from sources (1) to (9), the author has also added, from his own collection:

10) **A large number of antique and vintage Photographic Postcards.**

In regard to the postcards used as illustrations in this book, special acknowledgements and thanks are due to the following copyright owners:

> **Gieves & Hawkes Ltd.** (*re* postcards sponsored by 'Gieves Ltd.')
> **The British Library** (*re* 'Sunday Pictorial' postcards)
> **The Royal Naval Museum, Portsmouth** (*re* 'Wright & Logan' postcards)
> **The University of St Andrews Library** (*re* 'Valentines' postcards)
> **The World Ship Society** (*re* 'Abrahams' postcards)
> **W.H.Smith Archive** (*re* 'WH Smith' postcards)

Tracing today's copyright owner of a photographic image produced 75 to 100 years ago is often fraught with difficulty. There is no 'central register' to consult. The author apologises if he has failed in his considerable efforts to find every single instance of surviving copyright of the images used from postcard sources. He would welcome any errors or omissions being brought to his attention, so that suitable modifications can be made in regard to any further editions of this work.

N.B. The images which have been reproduced all appear in the book in '256 greyscale', regardless of the toning or tinting of the original. Also, in a very few instances, the images have been cropped, 'repaired', or otherwise slightly modified. (**See Appendix 'B' for further details.**)

About the Author

Neville Alfred DAVIS ('Nev') is the first son (second child) of the four children of the central figure of this book, the late Commissioned Gunner Alfred William DAVIS RN.

Nev hopes that what has emerged in this book will prove to be a 'good read' for 'naval buffs' with an interest in naval operations during the two World Wars, in warship technology of the 1910-1940 era, and in related peacetime deployments and manoeuvres. The practical and emotional difficulties on the 'domestic scene' which his father experienced during his lifetime are also brought to light. Those domestic problems will doubtless find echoes in the marital difficulties still encountered by many sea-going men, even in these enlightened days of far-shorter periods of naval deployment abroad.

Nev had been only ten years old when Alf was killed in action in January 1941. This book is the outcome of the desire of the 'grown-up Nev' to "discover" his dashing and inspirational father on a 'man to man' basis. That is to say, rather than continuing to remember only through the awe-struck eyes of 'the Young Nev of 1940' the same very loving but also highly-demanding and hard-disciplining father who was always a 'semi-stranger' to him. It had become stubborn rebellion against his step-mother, and thus a guilty conscience, which made Young Nev very apprehensive of 'parental retribution' whenever his charismatic father should happen to come home on leave – that is, there would be a phase of physical punishment 'in cold blood' to be anticipated, dreaded and endured before very thoughtful and loving gifts would be handed out. Nearly fifty years later it would be a far more emotionally mature and 'understanding' Nev, by then married and having brought up his own children, who would set about the decade of formal research towards the writing of this book. He hopes Alf's descendents will treasure it.

Nev had always enjoyed an interest in military and naval history. (This had been intensified by his very narrowly missing acceptance to Dartmouth Naval College and then by his disheartening 'medical rejection' at age 18 from any form of military service.) Now that strong life-long interest proved to be of considerable assistance to Nev in writing the book. Very useful, too, was his obsession with the research of family history. And, as stated earlier, discovering former shipmates of his father and becoming an honorary 'Old Southampton' also helped Nev enormously in the research and writing.

Previous works by the same author:

- *"Jumping for Joy: 50 Years of Kodak Rugby"*, written and compiled by the author and published by the Kodak Rugby Football Club in 1986.[1]
- *"The Frightful Fees",* an article serialised in three consecutive issues of 'Family Tree Magazine' in 1994.

---

[1] Despite the 'suspect' heart which had contributed to his medical downgrading at age 18, the author, by nature stubborn, had merrily played Rugby Union Football, mainly battling as a prop-forward, from age 13 until he was 60 yrs old, consuming a great many pints of beer and singing many convivial ditties along the way. He had a quadruple heart-bypass operation in the year 2000 and also has had 'prosthetic' metal and plastic replacements of his right hip joint and right shoulder joint in recent years.

LIST OF ILLUSTRATIONS

(See also Page 16 and Appendix 'B')

TOTAL: 334 illustrations

(A further eight images appear in Appendix J, increasing the overall number of illustrations to 342.)

See Page 16 and Appendix B regarding Acknowledgements of the Sources and Copyright aspects of the Images used.

The Dreadnought battleship HMS *Vanguard,* with her 'Y' turret trained to port, instead of being in its normal 'fore-and-aft' position. At the time Alf joined this ship, a number of modifications were being made to her secondary armament and to her superstructure aft. We shall discuss these modifications later. (*Photograph taken c.1911. Print reproduced by courtesy of The National Archives, Ref ADM176/742.*)

CHAPTER ONE:

ALF's PARENTS & HIS RAISING (Up to 1911)

Preamble

Alf, then aged 16, certainly took a huge leap into the future when he first set foot aboard the inspirational HMS *Vanguard* (Captain A.D. RICARDS, RN). This fine vessel was one of the three battleships which made up the St Vincent class. She was still relatively new, it being just three years since she was first commissioned.

HMS *Vanguard* had paid off from her first-ever commission at 0900 on the 27th March 1912 at No.6 Wharf in the North Keyham Yard, Devonport. At 1600, that same day, 265 ratings from Chatham had joined ship to form the nucleus of her new company for her second commission. Alf was surely one of those 265 ratings, and he must have been overwhelmed by his new posting, which had 'officially' commenced on the 14th March 1912.

One assumes that, once his previous leave was up, he had joined his new draft at HMS *Pembroke* (the Naval barracks at Chatham) and then travelled with his draft to Devonport by train. He may well have thought it was a bit ironic that his first commission after leaving the training ship HMS *Impregnable* should have brought him straight back to Devonport. Still, at least he would know his way about the area when the time came for a bit of a run ashore with his new shipmates, especially those Boy Seamen who had trained solely at HMS *Ganges* and who had never yet set foot in the West Country. This situation might well turn out to be to his advantage in making friends amongst his new shipmates.

Alf's ship was one of the third series of 'FISHER's Dreadnoughts', following hard on the heels of the first and second series. Like them, she represented a totally new concept in ship design, especially (though by no means solely), in terms of her gunnery. Whereas, in Nelson's day, ships had usually fought at very close ranges, exchanging broadsides at almost point-blank range, one of the First Sea Lord 'Jacky' FISHER's many maxims was *'Frappez vite et frappez fort'* and he had foreseen the new ships fighting at *long* range, and needing to have relatively high speeds of manoeuvre to help them to control the range within the limits that would best suit them, whilst, at the same time, putting the enemy at a disadvantage and then maintaining that situation by the Dreadnought's own sheer speed and manoeuvrability.[2] 'Jacky' FISHER's principle was to have these new turbine-powered Royal Navy ships armed with heavy guns, so that they could hit extremely hard at that long range. Accuracy in gun-aiming was going to be of the greatest importance when a war broke out. Indeed, as we shall later observe, Alf was going to become considerably involved in such aspects as his naval life unfolded.

First, however, we should see how Alf came to be standing on the deck of HMS Vanguard in 1912, and to examine something of his parentage and the raising and background which had fashioned him into the stripling that he then was. We should then

---

[2] FISHER's axiom of *Frappez vite et frappez fort'* ('Hit fast and hit hard') came from a favourite saying of Napoleon Bonaparte, which Jacky had adopted.

investigate his strenuous training for naval service at HMS 'Ganges' and at the aforesaid HMS 'Impregnable', before rejoining the young fellow aboard the mighty battleship 'Vanguard', when one might say that his naval career at sea really started.

(Some notes on the difficulties and problem-solving of the family history research on which the remainder of this chapter is based are given in Appendix E. Family Trees appear in Appendix F and may be helpful to the reader in confirming 'who was who'.)

Alf's Birth

Alf had been born in the hamlet of Portley, which has long been absorbed and virtually 'lost' in the northern environs of the modern town of Caterham, in Surrey. The babe was delivered on the 9th July 1895, almost certainly in the stable block attached to imposing 'Portley House', which was the only residence of any size in the hamlet of those days. Alf's birth was registered at nearby Godstone on the 14th August 1895, his name being entered as Alfred William DAVIS. His mother, who was the 'informant of the birth', was a woman who had been 'in service to the gentry' for many years, and she would therefore have inevitably had a certain well-practised 'deference' about her. Nevertheless, there is every probability that she would have spoken out to the Registrar with good diction and self-confidence, as befitted a 'Children's Nurse', even though she clearly knew her place in the structure of society far too well to try to 'soar above it'. Her name was duly recorded by the Registrar as 'Eliza DAVIS formerly ATKINSON'. She gave her address merely as 'Portley, Caterham' and said that her husband, whom she named as 'Alfred Wm DAVIS', was a 'Domestic Coachman' by occupation.

Over one hundred years later, the upstairs room of the stable-block at Portley in which it is believed that 'Baby Alf' first saw the light of day is *still* a delightfully sunlit and airy one.[3] It overlooks the large, brick-walled vegetable garden of the property, the ten-foot high garden-wall having a lovely 'back-drop' formed by the fine and varied trees which still stand beyond.

Very well built in red brick, Portley House itself, which nowadays has cloisters to link the main residence with its former stable block and other outbuildings, still stands strong to this day. It dominates an estate still richly stocked with trees and shrubs, and the parkland surrounding the house is still complete with a deeply ditched 'ha-ha'. However, there are no farm animals to be kept out nowadays, for the estate is now diminished in area and 'developed' all around with housing and schools. Today, Portley House is itself occupied by the staff and pupils of 'Sunnydown' boarding school, and the former stable-block acts as an annexe containing additional downstairs classrooms and upstairs dormitories.

In total contrast, back in 1895, when Alf was born, the whole property was in occupation by Frederick Augustus WHITE J.P., the extremely wealthy Manager of the Marine Insurance Company of the City of London. The WHITE Family lived in the main part of Portley House and the majority of the 'domestic servants' were accommodated in the uppermost rooms of the House. However, the Butler and his family

---

[3] It gave the author quite a *'frisson'* when he first entered this room.

'lived-out' in the comfortable Lodge House (now gone) which stood at the entrance to the property in those days, and Baby Alf's father, who was the only Coachman, evidently lived, together with his wife and two baby sons, in the Stable-Block which still stands near to the main house.[4]

The *rear aspect* of Portley House, photographed in the mid-1870s. The 'gentry' of various ages relaxing here are not of the WHITE Family, but previous residents. The Stable-Block lies off to the left of this view. It gives on to a huge courtyard which runs across the far side of the house and links to its main entrance, which is on that side. The house was rendered in white (leaving just an 'edging' of its red bricks) in those far-off days. Nowadays the whole external structure consists of red brick.

As shown by the 1891 Census, Frederick Augustus WHITE was a married man with a wife and a sizeable family of two sons and five daughters.[5] The older son had

---

[4] The author is much indebted to Mr T.M. ARMSTRONG, the Head of Sunnydown School, for a conducted tour of the buildings in the year 2002. Also for the opportunity to study related old documents and photographs (one of which is reproduced above) and to walk around the fine grounds.

[5] Regular, nationwide, simple 'head-count' censuses had been taken at 10-year intervals since 1801 and localised censuses far earlier in time. However, a great advance had been made in 1841, when *every individual* in the national census of that year was *named*. Ten-yearly censuses of named individuals have been taken nationwide ever since, with the sole exception of 1941 (when the country was *in extremis* due to the war against the Axis Powers). There is a 100-year 'closure' and the latest available census records are thus currently those of 1901. In the census records all the named individuals in each 'enumeration area' are grouped household by household. Also, having started at the census of 1851, each person is shown in their relationship to the 'Head of House' (e.g. 'Wife' , 'son', 'nephew', 'visitor', 'servant', 'boarder', etc.). The age, sex, marital status, occupation and birthplace of each person is also recorded, in some censuses being accompanied by a basic statement regarding any 'inhibiting' physical or mental infirmity. The census records can thus provide 10-yearly *family-images-in-writing* which are invaluable to the family historian. (As we shall see, it can be difficult to trace the whereabouts of 'mobile'

already started his career as an Insurance Broker in his own right and the oldest two daughters were of now of an age where they were actively seeking suitable husbands. Their parents, especially the mother, would have been working on all kinds of socialising and other strategies to aid the girls in finding reputable and well-born young men and hoping thereby to create marital partnerships which would further advance the business and financial interests of the whole WHITE family.

The daughters would have been preoccupied with the thought of not becoming 'old maids', for marriage was the aim of young ladies of any standing in those Victorian days. The earning of their own living, by entering professional life as (say) doctors or lawyers, was viewed by 'Society' as quite unacceptable. It was therefore vital to keep the reputations of all the daughters free from gossip, to ensure that their 'marriage prospects' remained high. Tight supervision and 'chaperoning' were therefore the order of the day.[6]

Every girl was expected to be still a virgin when she came to be married. Indeed, as their daughters grew up, many mothers, themselves raised in virtual ignorance, found it too embarrassing to talk to their daughters even about their puberty, let alone 'the full facts of life', so that the happenings on their 'wedding night' often came as quite a shock to the more innocent of the young ladies – particularly if they had been very closely-chaperoned. Everyday conversation had nothing like the freedom with which 'sex' is so openly discussed in the modern world.

Augustus had a staff of eight servants, headed by his Butler. As we have seen, amongst those servants was Alf's father, named Alfred William DAVIS, who was the sole Domestic Coachman to the WHITE family. Clearly, 'Baby Alf' had been named directly after his father.[7] Baby Alf's mother, Eliza, was a strongly maternal and capable woman. She and her husband had only recently arrived at Portley House, having both formerly worked for the wealthy ORR-EWING family at Newark Castle, in Maybole, near the west-coast town of Ayr, in Scotland. Alfred Wm had been the Coachman at the castle and Eliza had surely been the Children's Nurse there prior to her marriage to Alfred Wm.[8]

It was probably at Ayr that Alfred Wm and Eliza had first met and, where, on 25th April 1893, they had been married at the Church of the Holy Trinity, after Banns and according to the forms of the Scottish Episcopal Church. One of the marriage witnesses bore the name of 'George LLOYD' and it seems to have been no coincidence that this

---

individuals and families, especially as, to date, only the 1881 and 1901censuses have been fully 'surname-indexed'. Moreover, the data-transcription of the 1901census index has some frustrating inaccuracies.)

[6] As a child the author remembers playing a simple card game called 'Happy Families' in which the objective was to build up a little family of man, wife and children (each individual member appearing on a separate card). This was carried out in competition with the other card players, each of whom was also trying (by 'picking-up' and 'discarding' single cards, in turn) to build up one or more of the families (be it of butcher, baker, carpenter, or whatever.) The main priority was to avoid at all costs being left holding the card depicting a withered old crone-like spinster and entitled 'Old Maid'. When play ended the other players would shout out derisively, "Old Maid!" to whoever had the misfortune to be so left. To an extent, the game mirrored real life attitudes of men and women of those times towards unmarried women who were in their later years of life, and whom no man had ever perceived as being sufficiently 'attractive' to be led to propose marriage to her. (And it was totally 'out of court' for a woman to 'take the initiative'.)

[7] This 'begs the question' as to why the first son was named 'Berty John', and not named after his father. 'Berty' is NOT a DAVIS or ATKINSON 'family name'. Seemingly, the recipient came to hate the 'Berty' name and certainly discarded it totally once he 'came of age'.

[8] Their marriage certificate stated her occupation simply as 'Nurse'.

was also the name of the Butler to the ORR-EWING household. It is almost a 'stone-cold certainty' that he was the very same man. This whole matter is examined more closely in Appendix 'E', for it seems that it was the Butler's dominating presence that was the major factor leading to former 'job-seeking' lies having to be *re-told* by both bride and groom on that special day, and recorded for ever on their marriage certificate.

That certificate had therefore become an absolute travesty of 'the truth'. Luckily, both bride and groom had married very far away from their 'native heaths', and no family members were present, for relatives might well have 'given the game away', either by accident or design – and that would have been disastrous for the future job-prospects of the newly-married couple. In fact, it could well have brought about their utter ruin. Seemingly the young couple simply *had* to keep their nerve, remember the lies they had told and thus maintain their 'cover-stories' as they went through the ramifications of the ceremony and subsequent document-preparation in the vestry.

Author's Collection. Photograph by unknown photographer, inherited from Alf.

Alf's parents, Alfred Wm DAVIS and Eliza DAVIS née ATKINSON. Photograph almost certainly taken on their wedding day in 1893, when he was truly aged 26 (though declaring himself to be 31) and she was truly aged 33. Note the 'lucky heather' in Eliza's corsage. She has a wedding ring on her third finger and a twin-hearts brooch on the collar of her wasp-waisted dress. It is believed that both groom and bride were working for the ORR-EWINGs at this time, Alfred Wm as a Domestic Coachman, and Eliza as a Children's Nurse.

It was in the 'Newark Mains Cothouse' at Newark Castle that Alfred Wm and Eliza's *first* child, Berty John, had been born on St Patrick's Day, the 17th March 1894.[9]

---

[9] The child's birth certificate simply quotes 'Newark Castle, Maybole'. The name of Alfred DAVIS appears as the rent-payer of the 'Newark Mains Cothouse' in the Valuation Rolls of Newark Castle for the Financial Year 1894/5, and it is almost certainly in the 'Cothouse' that baby Berty John would have

Little Alf, who was their *second* child, had been conceived around October of that year. In the early part of the following year, 1895, Alfred Wm had been enjoying taking his master, Charles Lindsay ORR-EWING, around the hustings, for Charles Lindsay was campaigning hard for election to Parliament (and, indeed, would later be elected as the Liberal M.P. for Ayr Burghs).

However, in the midst of their master's electoral campaign, Alfred Wm and/or Eliza had seemingly become embroiled in a sensational scandal which had led to Charles Lindsay ORR-EWING reportedly petitioning his young wife for a divorce on the grounds of infidelity. She was the Hon Beatrix Mary ORR-EWING, who was a daughter of Lord RUTHVEN, and it seems that she had fallen overwhelmingly in love with another man and had suddenly made the earth-shattering and last-minute decision to elope with him at a time when she was expected to journey north with her two very young children from the elegant London home of the ORR-EWINGS, to join her husband at Newark Castle, Ayr. All the arrangements were under way for her reception there.

The suddenly 'motherless' ORR-EWING children would thus have been left alone at the main line train station, in the sole care of a children's nurse. It is just possible that Eliza had been sent down from Scotland to accompany mother and children up to Ayr, and that she was the nursemaid who was thus immediately left stranded *in loco parentis*, metaphorically 'holding the baby' (and literally with a three-year old girl and a five year-old boy on her hands). However, Eliza was married and *enceinte* with a second child, and one suspects that a new nurse would have been engaged by that time. Certainly, if it *had* been Eliza, one can well imagine that the ORR-EWINGs might have wished to disembarrass themselves of her as 'distantly and quickly' as possible.[10]

Be that as it may, Alfred Wm had apparently been found another job as soon as the scandal broke, still working as a Domestic Coachman, but now some 500 miles away from Ayr. Supposedly man and wife had been moved far away to reduce the chance of harassment by journalists and the risk of intimate gossip and scandal about the ORR-EWING Family being spread in the locality of Ayr – especially important to avoid, with Charles Lindsey ORR-EWING still campaigning for election as the local M.P. The DAVIS pair (and possibly other servants, too) had presumably been suitably 'recompensed', given good references, perhaps given 'introductions' or even actually found alternative posts, and told to 'lay low and keep quiet'.

The long journey south of the little DAVIS family, with the changes of train which would have been necessary, must have been a rather worrying time, with Eliza in the mid-term of her second pregnancy and Alf's elder brother being then aged only about 14 months and having to be carried almost everywhere. Most of the little family's belongings would have travelled in a trunk or large cardboard box in the guard's van, but there would still have been various of the more 'personal' and valuable items of their belongings to be carried by husband and wife. There must have been considerable relief when they had landed up safely at Portley House and taken up residence in the upstairs

---

bccn born. The author is indebted to professional researchers Andrew ARMSTRONG of Ayr and Alan McLEOD of Edinburgh for this later fact and related information.

[10] The author is indebted to Mrs A LOWES of Taunton, Somerset, grand-daughter of Charles Lindsey ORR-EWING, for some of this information. The ORR-EWINGs owned important property in Scotland, but Newark Castle was actually only under lease to them from the Marquis of Ailsa at this period of time. NOTE: In those days a divorce was regarded as a very serious and significant matter indeed.

floor of the stable block, living above the large coach-house and the loose boxes for the horses.

Their accommodation upstairs was good; indeed, one might almost say 'lavish' in comparison with the 'norm' for servants, and with a laundry-room handily situated on the ground-floor level. It could scarcely have been better for the birth and care of the new baby and for the raising of his still-infant brother.[11]

Photograph taken by the Author in 2002.

Alf's Birthplace. The one-time Stable-Block at Portley House, photographed in 2002. The cloisters running along the front of the building are a modern addition. The façade of the building has also been modified by the installation of various doors and windows, replacing the larger doors at ground-floor level which had permitted the accommodation of carriages and horses. However, the basic dimensions and main structure are unchanged from 1905. The building gives on to the courtyard which runs across the whole frontage of Portley House.

It was on the fine country estate at Portley House that Baby Alf was raised for first two years of his life, doubtless beginning to respond to and imitate the playful overtures of his elder brother Berty John towards the end of that time. Their mother had already reached the age of 36, for she had started her family rather late in life. However, she was soon pregnant again, and the boys' first sister, Nellie Elizabeth, was born at Portley on the 11th January 1897, in the midst of a bitter winter. Meantime, their father continued as Domestic Coachman to Frederick Augustus WHITE J.P., driving that gentleman to Caterham Station on most weekdays, but to the local magistrate's court whenever it was in session.

During the main part of the day, Alfred Wm would be at the service of other members of the WHITE family, but always arranging matters so that he could be present

---

[11] In 1891 the then Coachman had a wife and no less than six young children living in that accommodation.

to collect his Master for the homeward journey from the railway station or the magistrate's court. There would also sometimes be a need for his services to convey family members to evening functions and to collect them as need arose, doubtless having strongly implied responsibilities to meet. These responsibilities could be rather daunting for him in his status as a 'mere servant' – especially if the girls were being skittish and were perhaps being accompanied by 'haughty young bloods' who were 'rather the worse for drink'. However, if matters looked as if they were becoming beyond the ability of any family-appointed lady-chaperone accompanying the girls to control, Alfred Wm would be expected to step in and to aid the chaperone in 'maintaining a decent level of order and decorum'. This could impose huge demands on Alfred Wm's tact and discretion. Evidently, he managed such matters very competently, with a light touch and good humour.

Distinguished guests sometimes stayed at Portley House, including persons of international status. Alfred Wm was often the first representative of the WHITE household whom such persons met on arrival at the railway station, sometimes at the end of a long and wearying journey for these guests. Indeed, some of these people came from as far away as the U.S.A., for, by 1895, ships were rapidly growing in size and power and safety, with steam replacing sail and steel hulls replacing wood.[12] Travel by rail and sea was now relatively safe, and time-tables were beginning to be 'honoured in the strict observance' – whereas, in the days of sail, arrival times of shipping had been hugely dependent on the variables of wind, tide and current, and ships had sometimes found themselves in dire peril through being 'unable to claw their way off a lee shore'. The world was in a period of considerable change, especially in the ability of quite ordinary people to get 'out and about', and in the great distances the wealthier could now encompass.

First impressions count, and Alfred Wm carried a high level of responsibility in always being immaculately dressed in his livery to meet the important and influential guests and in dealing competently and sympathetically with their immediate needs and with any emergencies which might arise on the journey from Caterham Railway Station back to Portley House. There might well be a need for him to take significant initiatives to overcome such emergencies. Moreover, the Coachman might find himself being 'pumped' for information about the WHITE Family, fielding questions which he would have to answer deferentially but very circumspectly indeed. Or he might be expected to act as a 'sympathetic ear with an extremely short memory', when out on a long journey with a passenger who wished to unburden himself (or herself) on some acute and perhaps distressing problem. Thus, whilst it was true that, once back at Portley House, he deferred immediately to the authority of the Butler, whilst out on the road, and in the absence of any senior family member, he 'carried the full weight'. Alfred Wm's responsibilities could also be considerable in regard to basic safety, for there are steep hills in the Caterham district and winter snow and ice, or morning frost, could make the situation very tricky indeed for carriages having iron-shod wheels and only primitive brakes.

Indeed, Alfred Wm's regular journey to the station and back was through the high ground of Caterham-on-the-Hill, so there was always a certain level of risk on the bleaker

---

[12] For example, Percy CHUBB, a 35 year-old Australian-born businessman, who had become an Underwriter in New York, U.S.A, and his American-born wife Helen, had both been staying with Augustus WHITE at the time of the 1891 Census.

winter days. All such risks were liable to increase sharply if the carriage-horses were made restive by some of the heavy clanking and huffing steam-tractors, traction-engines or back-firing automobiles which were now appearing on the roads.

Author's collection. Card marketed by Alec J BRAIN, Stationer, Caterham Valley. Hand-tinted card postally used at Caterham in 1907.

Caterham Valley. Station Approach.

If Alfred Wm continued on past the station, down Station Approach, this is the view of Caterham which he would have seen, with the Godstone Road running off to the right, and the Croydon Road hard off to the left. The Post Office lay just around the right-hand corner and Alfred Wm may often have had to call there to send off or collect parcels.

Author's collection. From a postcard by H.GRINSTEAD, postally used at Caterham in 1911.

The Hangers, Whitehill, Caterham.   H.Grinstead.

Some of the steep hills in the area of Caterham which Alfred Wm may well have had to negotiate as a Coachman, perhaps, at times, under extremely adverse conditions of frost, snow or ice, and sometimes encountering other horsed vehicles sliding dangerously, 'out of control'. There were, of course, compensations on fine-weather days, when the beauty of the scenery was a sheer delight, sometimes emphasised when the sun broke through after a misty morning.

The world of road transport was beginning to change considerably, and the horseman was expected to accommodate to it. For the present the horseman was still the 'primary user' of the roads, and, for his safety and convenience, automobiles were expected to have a man walking ahead of them carrying a red warning flag. However, any thinking man could see that this situation was not going to last for long. Moreover, as the technology of the motor car improved, its convenience was such that it would soon become the favoured conveyance for all who could afford it – although the 'love affair' of 'man and horse' would continue in one 'secondary' guise or another, probably forever.

Fortunately, the experience which Alfred Wm had previously acquired during his service with the ORR-EWINGs in the hills and mountainous passes during Scottish winters would have stood him in good stead, and his natural sympathy, understanding and firm control of his horses would have greatly reduced the risk of their panicking and bolting in the steep hills around the Caterham area.

However, being a coachman on cold and or really wet days could be a cruelly harsh experience, despite scarves and a heavy overcoat and even though a heavy leather apron was customarily tied across one's legs. In freezing cold weather it could be hard even for those *inside* the coach or carriage, protected as they were by the body of the conveyance with its isinglass windows, and with heavy woollen blankets and a packing of straw to keep the passengers warm, sometimes aided by a hot brick or an earthenware hot water-bottle or two. For the coachman on the outside of the coach, matters were very much bleaker and harder.

Also, on arrival at a destination, whilst the passengers could hurry away into the warm shelter of a house, an inn or a hotel, the coachman was duty-bound to take care of his sweat-saturated and thirsty horses before he paid the least heed to his own condition. It could be a very hard life indeed.

As it was, the end of Frederick Augustus WHITE's tenure of Portley House was already in sight, and the household staff was beginning to be disbanded. Maybe this was the trigger which made Alfred Wm re-consider the job he was doing.

It was in 1898 that Alfred Wm moved his growing family to Bletchley, where Young Alf's second sister, Rose Kathleen, was born on 29th May of that year. It is almost certain that Alfred Wm was by then in the employ of an immensely rich London banker and financier, Sir Herbert LEON. Sir Herbert had lost his first wife tragically young. He had re-married, and he and his second wife Fanny had two, by now near-adult, children.

Sir Herbert LEON had stood for Parliament as a Liberal candidate and he was a friend of the distinguished Welsh-born politician, and later Prime Minister, The Hon. David LLOYD GEORGE.

Sir Herbert and Lady LEON were hunting enthusiasts and they regularly rode out with the Whaddon Chase.[13] Alfred Wm had now adjusted his occupation, still working

---

[13] Sir John LEON, the 4th Baronet, who goes under the celebrated stage name of John STANDING, has kindly read through what the author has written about his great-grandfather and found it to be a reasonable reconstruction. Unfortunately no records of the servants who worked in the household have survived, so direct confirmation that Alfred Wm worked for Sir Herbert LEON has not proved possible. However, Sir Herbert LEON is very much in the wealthy 'riding-to-hounds' image of Alfred Wm's previous and ensuing masters, who were all men in their business prime. (N.B. There is another possibility, in that Alfred Wm *might* have worked at nearby Great Brickhill, on the estate of Sir Everard PAUNCEFOOT-DUNCOMBE. However, Sir Everard had succeeded his father at age 10, and was still only aged 13, so the Brickhill Estate was being administered by guardians at that time. This situation fits

very much with horses, but now as a Domestic Groom. Indeed, he was continuing his drive to work ever more closely with horses, but henceforth he should be able to escape more than a little from the considerable exposure to severe weather which he had been experiencing as a Coachman. Now, as a Groom, he would have had several fine hunters in his care at magnificent Bletchley Park as well as the superb horses which drew the family landau and smaller carriages.[14]

It was about two years after Alfred Wm arrived at Bletchley Park that the Prince of Wales, later to become King Edward VII, stayed there for a few days, his visit being manifest of the wealth and status now existing at that residence.[15]

Author's collection. Postcard published by Valentines. (No Series No.) Card postally used in 1905. Image reproduced by courtesy of St Andrews University Library.

The East Front of splendid Bletchley Park, which was surrounded with magnificent grounds and had various outbuildings, including a large stable block.

Doubtless Alfred Wm's young sons were by now beginning to observe and imitate their father's behaviour and mannerisms, and their father was beginning to think ahead to the time when he might reasonably start to utilise their youthful help in caring

rather less well with the scenario of Alfred Wm's previous and ensuing masters, and the author therefore feels that any likelihood of a PAUNCEFOOT-DUMCOMBE 'link' is an extremely remote one indeed.)

[14] Two or three fragments of the factual data concerning Bletchley Park and Sir Herbert LEON have been gained from the booklet "In Search of the Leons" written by D.ASHFORD in connection with a project undertaken by the Leon School at Bletchley, and printed by the Leon Community Printshop in 1991. This data was kindly brought to the author's attention by Buckinghamshire County Record Office. [N.B. Bletchley Park would later become the 'hush-hush' establishment where British scientists deciphered the German 'Enigma' codes during WW2.]

[15] Portley House had been in the forefront in being equipped with gas for heating and lighting during Augustus WHITE's occupation, but Bletchley Park was well ahead of its time in having a large number of fully plumbed-in bathrooms, provided with hot as well as cold water, and easily sufficient to provide for each family member and their guests. This avoided the need for hot water to be carried laboriously in large jugs to a 'wash stand' in each bedroom (as was still the rather primitive 'norm' in most English country houses). Electricity and telephones were not quite yet 'in the offing'. Hence, postcards were being used for 'rapid communication', and postal deliveries were remarkably quick and frequent in those days. Telegrams were used for brief and ultra-rapid distant communication. (As we shall see, young Alf would later become a Messenger Boy for the GPO before he ran away to sea.)

for the horses in his charge. After all, he had started working for his living at a very young age – so why not them too? Alfred Wm greatly hoped that his young sons had inherited his great natural affinity with horses, and he was already nursing plans to teach the growing boys all the related skills of horse-management. Young though they still were, the two boys would also have been beginning to instinctively observe how smartly their father dressed for his official duties and how he modified his behaviour according to the rank of the person he was addressing, for, by now, Alfred Wm was well experienced in the matter of coping 'competently and naturally' with persons of all walks of life. It seems he managed to do so with a considerable outward display of 'rapid response' and of inoffensively cheerful good humour and *bonhomie*, which attracted considerable goodwill from his superiors in life. This learning 'at his father's feet' would stand Young Alf in remarkably good stead many years ahead.

However, true to his basic, restless nature, Alfred Wm had moved on again within two years, probably just before that Royal Visit to Bletchley Park by the Prince of Wales. [That visit would have been an interesting sight to behold, for Sir Herbert LEON favoured the short, dark, 'spade' beard sported by the prince, and he had a similarly balding head and rather square face. Prince of the Realm and subject would have looked rather like brothers, albeit that Sir Herbert was less portly in build than his future King.]

In changing his place of employment, Alfred Wm was apparently continuing to work his way around the well-moneyed 'Hunting Set'. He was probably using personal recommendations about his excellent abilities in 'horse-management', and perhaps even being 'head-hunted' when moving on, this time (it is believed) to become a Stud Groom to Henry STUBBS Esq. at Camp Hill Hall, which lay about two miles out from Nuneaton, on a rise off the road from Nuneaton to Coleshill. [*From Scotland, to Surrey, to Bucks, and on to Warwickshire within the space of six years – Alfred Wm and his wife, with their growing brood, were certainly getting around the mainland of the British Isles. Yet wider travel was soon to come!*]

Camp Hill Hall was another fine place at which to come and work. It was reached by a drive, almost a half-mile long, through an avenue of trees. This drive had a very large ornamental lake (complete with a boat-house), lying off to the right as one ascended the rise towards the Hall. There was a lodge house at the roadside entrance to the avenue. The estate, which was well-furnished with trees, consisted of no less than 300 acres.

Behind the main house there were various outbuildings, which evidently included the stables and a coach-house. Perhaps the only 'fly in the ointment' was that large granite quarries lay about three-quarters of a mile to the north-east, and, doubtless, the noise of blasting would sometimes have intruded into the peace of the surroundings. Wind-carried dust may also have sometimes been something of a problem.

Henry STUBBS had been born in Bowden, Cheshire in 1864. He had evidently inherited this large property through his STUBBS line. As we have seen, Alfred Wm's previous employers had been J.Ps. Henry was not actually a J.P. when he engaged Alfred Wm – but he would become one (for the Atherstone Petty Sessional Division) in the following year.

As a Stud Groom to Henry STUBBS, Alfred Wm would have become even more deeply involved in the buying and breeding of horses. And those horses would have been of high quality, for Henry STUBBS, who was a married man 'of independent means', with a wife and young teenage daughter, was said to be 'a keen Polo player who did a good deal of race riding'. He was also the Chairman of the Wire Committee of the Atherstone Hunt Club of North Warwickshire, working as best he could (against the conflicting wishes of local farmers) to limit the spread and to control the positioning of barbed wire. The task was a vitally important one, since it had serious implications for the safety of Hunt members in their reckless dash and enthusiasm during a keen chase.

Original image a tinted postcard by E.W. Starmer, Stationer, of Nuneaton. This image supplied and reproduced by courtesy of Warwickshire County Record Office, ref PH352/135/130.

Camp Hill Hall, Nr. Nuneaton.

Camp Hill Hall at Tuttle Hill, Nuneaton, Warwickshire.
The DAVIS Family probably lived above the stables in
the complex of buildings lying behind this fine Hall.

Doubtless, Alfred Wm learned a lot more about the 'sporting scene', as well as increasing his knowledge about horse-management and the breeding of bloodstock hunters, racehorses and polo ponies, whilst he was working for Henry STUBBS.[16]

Alfred Wm would also have found out quite a lot more about the 'sharpies' who have always hung around the racing scene for their own nefarious ends. His young children were also probably learning much from these more dubious contacts of their father, some of whom would doubtless have been extremely interesting and engaging 'characters'. The children of some of these men might also have made appealing playmates for Alf and his brother, perhaps leading them into 'exciting pranks'.

By this time Young Alf's elder brother Berty John (alias 'Jack'), now aged six, would have been attending school in Nuneaton, and Young Alf would probably have

---

[16] The author is indebted to professional researcher Terry BIGLEY of Hinckley, Leicestershire for much of this factual information, some of which has been drawn from the 'Warwickshire County Biographies' housed in Nuneaton Library. Camp Hill Hall was the only residence of any size in the neighbourhood, which is why it is believed that Alfred Wm was employed by Henry STUBBS Esq. The author is further indebted to professional researcher Jackie EDWARDS of Coventry for further information about Henry STUBBS, including the discovery of the illustrations in the archives of Warwickshire C.R.O, as reproduced here.

begun to accompany him by the autumn of the year 1900, starting off further experiences in making friends and, perhaps, in coping with bullies and rivals.[17]

Image supplied and reproduced by courtesy of Warwickshire County Record Office. Image Ref. PH625, page 17.

H. STUBBS, ESQ., J.P.,

This 'newsprint-quality' picture of Henry STUBBS appeared in a Photographic Coronation Souvenir Programme of the Festivities at Nuneaton and Chilvers Coton in Honour of the Coronation of King Edward VII and Queen Alexandra on 26 June 1902. Henry STUBBS' portrait appeared beside that of other local dignitaries, who were mostly fellow-JPs.
(Alfred Wm DAVIS had moved on at least a year before this particular event took place – if, indeed, the event *did* take place, for the King had to be operated on for appendicitis, and the Coronation was postponed until August 1902.)

By that autumn of 1900 the family included baby Eva, born on 16th September that year, 'at Tuttle Hill, Nuneaton'. By that time the mother was 41 years old, and Eva would be the last child born into the DAVIS Family of that generation. Eliza had done her level best for her husband in his ambition of building up a small army of potential helpers who might grow up sufficiently fast to help him to further his great ambitions. Eliza had produced five children in six years, starting at the late (true) age of thirty-five, and her health was not recovering as well after this latest birth as she would have hoped.

All the children would have been profiting from the healthy life style of the beautiful country estates in which their father had come to work over the recent years. Moreover, it seems likely that their mother was a good cook who would have had fresh country produce close at hand to aid her, as well as being both naturally loving and professionally trained at protecting her children from illness and nursing them well through any childhood complaints they may have picked up.[18] In those days, all children were expected to 'be seen, but not heard'. Perhaps the only slight flaw in their young lives would have been that *extreme* restraints would have had to be applied to their children by parents 'in service', to prevent the freedom of expression and noise-making

---

[17] Berty John would probably have been attending the Abbey Green School, but the surviving admission records exist only from 1914. There is a log book for 1898-1905, but it lists few names, mainly those of miscreants. Neither DAVIS boy figures in it.

[18] It is notable that none of Alfred Wm's children seemed to suffer serious illness, and there was no known infant mortality in that DAVIS generation. This was in stark contrast to the very high death-rates, in their mother's 'ATKINSON' line and the associated 'DAYKINS' line. (See the Family Trees in Appendix 'F'.)

which is so natural to young children from reaching the ears of the 'Master's Family and his Guests'.

Nuneaton was a strange district in which to live, for it still had much open country surrounding it, but if, for example, one strolled around the delightful Riversley Park, with its bandstand near the river banks, its neatly laid out paths, lawns and saplings, and its many seats - some occupied by proud nannies with perambulators carrying their little charges – one would find oneself overlooked by a medley of tall factory chimneys, some standing quite near and invariably with some of those chimneys steadily smoking away.

Author's collection. A hand-tinted postcard in the 'Glazette' series by Jones, Bradbury & Co., Nuneaton. Postally used in Nuneaton on 7th June 1907.

Market Day in Nuneaton circa 1905. The street is crowded with prospective buyers from miles around, for this is the only town in the area. It would have been to Nuneaton that the DAVIS family came to buy clothes, shoes, underclothing and little luxuries. It was in this town that Berty John would have gone to school, and probably where Alf began his schooling too.

It is probable that Alfred Wm was now approached by an Irish gentleman with connections to the Meath Hunt. One assumes that the gentleman might well have ridden out as a visitor with the Atherstone Hunt, perhaps whilst staying in England on business. It would seem that this gentleman had been highly impressed by Alfred Wm's natural skills with horses, which had become ever better-honed by the experiences he had been gaining in their breeding and care. Accordingly, it is believed that the Irishman talked Alfred Wm into heading for Ireland and putting his skills to work as Studsman to the Meath Hunt.[19]

This was exactly the sort of 'leg up' which the highly ambitious Alfred Wm was seeking. He therefore 'upped sticks' and promptly took his family over to the 'Emerald Isle'. To undertake this family move was a major step for a man with a wife and five young children to support, and, in some ways, it was possibly not of the best, for the job

---

[19] In 1994, Captain J ARMSTRONG, the then Secretary of the Meath Hunt, was unable to *confirm* that Alfred Wm DAVIS had ever been a Stud Groom to the Meath, but he told the author that the records were incomplete and it was by no means impossible that Alfred Wm had held the post 1901-05.

was a seasonal one and it is fairly certain that Alfred Wm soon found himself looking in vain for alternative work to tide him through the three-month unpaid 'close season'. In a Catholic country where there was an overall shortage of work, it was natural that native-born catholic Irishmen would be favoured over an immigrant protestant Englishman, and Alfred Wm would soon have been in crucial difficulty in sustaining himself and his family.

In the end, probably on a suggestion by a certain John DENNIS, who was a wealthy and very remarkable Catholic Irishman connected with the hunting scene and who may well have perceived the family's plight at first-hand, it seems that Alfred Wm's elder son went 'into service' at the farm of the said John DENNIS. This probably provided a small wage, and it would certainly have 'removed a growing lad's hungry mouth to feed' from the DAVIS family home. However, Berty John was still only seven years old, and, though he learned 'in the school of life', his academic education must have seriously suffered thereby.[20] This may well have been the first intimation to the children of a strong and remorseless streak in their ambitious father's character, whereby he would use them as his 'little slaves' whenever the need arose for the general survival and advancement of his career, albeit that, with some measure of justification, the father would have rationalised the matter as being for the overall future good of the whole family unit. And it is, of course, true that they 'sank or swam' as one. If Alfred Wm prospered, he would ultimately leave whatever wealth he might have created to his children, as and when he departed this life. Indeed, if matters worked out as he hoped, even during his own lifetime he might be able to settle some money on various of the children according to their needs. For the present, however, the older children might well have to 'work very hard indeed for a living'. Their father had been put 'into service' at a very young age (possibly as early as his eighth year of life), and he probably felt that where he had gone as a young child others could well follow, the 'social reforms' introduced by modern Education Acts notwithstanding.[21]

Up to now, their mother, who was intensely protective of her children, would have been able to moderate their father's behaviour in such aspects. On the other hand, it was true that she, too, nurtured dreams of gaining a far higher standard of living and would always go along with her husband's ambitions insofar as she considered them 'reasonable'. However, there had always been a line beyond which she would not concede to her husband. Now, however, it was becoming clear that she no longer had the strong morale and courage of her earlier years, perhaps because, as already suggested, she

---

[20] The Author is greatly indebted to James E NORTON, author of '*A History of the South Dublin Harriers*', for much of this information. James NORTON found that the Irish census of 1901 shows a '*Berty DAVIS, aged 14, a Catholic, born in England*', and working as a *Farm Servant* for the said John DENNIS. Although truly aged only seven, and actually a non-practising Protestant, the author believes that this entry was a deliberately corrupted reference to 'our' Berty John, tailored to keep the presence of an 'under-age' worker very 'low-profile' should the census records be scrutinised for official purposes. [No sign of the remaining members of the DAVIS Family have been found in the Irish Census of 1901, despite individual searches by the author and by various professional and amateur researchers. However, it is clear that significant 'gaps' exist in the surviving data, and one or more of the missing documents probably contained an entry about the DAVIS family which may now be forever lost.]

[21] The 1871 Education Act and its amendments were beginning to have significant effects on such matters as setting the earliest permissible age at which children could leave school, and would later lead toward certain basic educational standards having to be attained before leaving school would be countenanced by the authorities. (See matters related to Eva and her education, which follow later.)

was worn down by childbearing and, now she had reached 42 years of age, her health was clearly starting to deteriorate. She could no longer handle high stress levels because sharp pains would start up in her chest. Increasingly, she would 'give her husband his head', and, horse-like he would start to 'gallop ever more freely'.

The family were in Ireland for four years or more, and it seems likely that Alfred Wm successfully served as Studsman to the Meath Hunt during that period and learned a lot about the hunting and sporting scene in that part of Ireland, probably gaining much 'insider information'. (In later years his elder son, Berty John, was given to singing traditional Irish songs, such as *'Danny Boy'* and *'The Mountains of Morne'*, and it would seem that he had learned these songs whilst working for good old John DENNIS.)

Whilst the DAVIS family were in Ireland the Boer War dragged its way to a conclusion and Queen Victoria died, after a reign of 64 years. The Prince of Wales now came to the throne as King Edward VII. He had very different ideas to those of his late mother as to the manner in which a monarch should live life and relate to people. He had always loved country house parties and amorous adventures, playing cards late into the night, sailing his yacht in competition, attending shooting parties and so forth. However, even more to the point in the regard of Alfred Wm DAVIS, the new monarch particularly favoured the 'Sport of Kings', namely, horse-racing. Very soon, Edward VII had greatly re-invigorated the semi-dormant royal stables and stud, and had quickly set out to breed his own 'Derby Winners'. As well as being an 'Owner', the new king was not at all averse to 'having the odd gentlemanly flutter on the horses'. The overall consequence had been that the whole sporting world of 'flat' and 'hunt' racing had blossomed.

On the general subject of gambling, it is *possible* that Alfred Wm had become caught up in a 'sporting coup' in Ireland, in mid-1905, had pocketed his share of the winnings, and left the country quickly, 'for the benefit of his health'. The author's opinion, to some extent backed by his 'feel' of vague family legend, is that this was the way of it.[22] On the other hand, it may just be that Alfred Wm was revelling in his job with the Meath Hunt and its fine horses, and left Ireland with great regret, only driven to do so because the health of his wife was now deteriorating markedly and because she urgently wanted to head for 'home'.

Now, going back in time to 1867-1872, it is a near-certainty that Alfred Wm had been very short of mother-love in his infancy. This seems to have made him rather cold and crabbed in relationships in which he was *closely involved* emotionally. Within his *psyche*, more as an instinct than as a conscious thought, it is believed that he had looked to his wife to be partly a surrogate 'mother-figure' for him, as well as being the co-creator of his 'empire' of little human slaves. In a way, Eliza had thus become the 'mother he had never had when he was small'. He may well have been totally unable to cope with this new situation of his 'formerly strong and wifely mother-figure' failing him – perhaps, in a sense, 'repeating' the terrible trauma which it is believed his birth-mother had inflicted upon him by her abandonment of him when he was a helpless babe-in-arms. We will examine this newly-arisen situation concerning his sick wife more closely soon. First, however, we should perhaps review how it could have come about that Alfred Wm had been deprived of mother-love as a babe and infant all those years ago.

---

[22] Raymond PENNEY, the author's first-cousin, disagrees with the author on this point, Ray believing that lucky and profitable but nonetheless 'plain and simple' gambling was involved.

His real-life mother was Elizabeth DAVIS, born in January 1851, who was the daughter of an Agricultural Labourer. Elizabeth had been only sixteen years old when she bore Alfred Wm on the 18th January 1867, at Market Lavington, Wiltshire. It follows that she was only 15 years old when she was made pregnant. Her pregnancy was evidently a total and unwanted accident. It is believed that she was not at all maternal by nature. Certainly, she never bore another child.[23]

Anonymous Carte de Visite c.1870. Carte kindly donated by R. PENNEY, Esq.

Alf's paternal grandmother, Elizabeth DAVIS.
Born in 1851, Elizabeth was a daughter of an Agricultural Labourer and sometime Carter named Richard DAVIS. Elizabeth was the third daughter of Richard's second marriage, his first wife having died in 1839. Elizabeth had been only 15 years old when she conceived Alfred Wm in 1866. (Her illegitimate child would live on to father 'Alf' and his siblings from 1894 to 1900.) *N.B. Elizabeth's face is very reminiscent of Alf's 2nd son Richard Paul, when in his young prime. Richard Paul, born in 1939, was the youngest of Elizabeth's four great-grandsons.* [Elizabeth probably never met even her *grandchildren*, and she died in 1910, long before any of her *gt-grandchildren* were born.]

It may have been the case that Elizabeth idolised and perhaps, to an extent, imitated her older half-sister Caroline, who had two illegitimate children before eventually setting up home with an older man, apparently as his common-law wife, and bearing further children, presumably by him. Up to that stage the DAVIS family, whose lineage has been traced back to 1588, had been *extremely* respectable. There must have been great unease and a strong sense of shame when Caroline first fell pregnant. In fact,

---

[23] The author is indebted to the 'I.G.I' (and the related computer search programme of the Church of Latter Day Saints) for initially throwing up 'various *possibilities*' for the birth-details of Alfred Wm. Based on vague family rumour, the author was able to prioritise those 'possibilities', so that professional researcher H R HENLEY of Swindon was subsequently able to confirm the true date and birthplace of Alf's grandfather. This was a vital step. Thereafter, using archival parish records in Wiltshire, and with the aid of other amateur and professional researchers, and other indexers, the author was able to investigate related matters, thereafter being able to open up the whole DAVIS Family Tree back to 1588.

her parents had evidently done their best to conceal the illegitimacy of Caroline's first child by taking the babe into their own home and, to an extent, raising it as their own. They had done the same when Caroline fell pregnant for a second time, and they had continued to raise the two children until Caroline moved in with the aforementioned man *in a different village*, which thus reduced the risk of scandal arising on the parents' home patch. (Caroline did not take her man's name when completing census forms, and the further children she bore - presumably by him – retained the 'DAVIS' surname.)

Now, some years after the first 'fostering', the grandfather and (now) his second wife, were doing much the same in raising Elizabeth's illegitimate child as if he were one of their own, again evidently more or less 'on the Q.T' (though the neighbours may have thought it a bit odd that Elizabeth's mother, by then a woman aged 48, had apparently fallen 'pregnant' once again, and that after a lapse of seven years since her previous lawful but 'late-thought' child, young Emily, had been born).

In basic character, it is more than probable that Elizabeth was a 'forward and provocative girl', and that, like many country girls, she had been much more the 'saucy tease and seducer' than the 'youthful innocent' when she had been made pregnant. Suspicion for her pregnancy has fallen on a certain Richard HOPKINS, a married man, who already had two young sons, *and who was a half-brother to Elizabeth's mother Ann DAVIS née HOPKINS.* Richard was a Drayman at that time, which may have given him a certain 'freedom to roam'- perhaps in more ways than one. It is assumed that he had been a trusted 'uncle figure' around the home of Elizabeth's parents until Elizabeth's pregnancy suddenly became obvious and, (probably put under very great pressure), she presumably confessed to her parents the identity of her lover who (if Richard HOPKINS was indeed the father) was 15 years her senior in age.[24]

If this supposition about fatherhood is true, Alfred Wm's parentage had bordered into the realms of incest, which was evidently the main (though by no means the sole) reason why elaborate 'smokescreens' would subsequently be laid and a tissue of lies would be told on official documents, names withheld or 'switched', etc. (See Appendix E.) In 1866/67 Elizabeth's family might well have been immediately 'after the blood of Richard HOPKINS' for his betrayal of their trust.[25]

As already stated, Elizabeth's child had been born at Market Lavington on the 18th January 1867. His young mother was the informant of the birth. No father's name appeared on his birth certificate and, so far as it has been possible to determine, no bastardy papers were ever taken out. In fact, no formal 'declaration' of the father's name ever appears to have been made.

---

[24] Elizabeth's presumed 'role-model', her half-sister Caroline, was 18 years older than Elizabeth. It may well be the case that Elizabeth was fascinated by 'mature' people a half-generation older than herself, and greatly preferred their company to that of 'gawky' youngsters of her own age.

[25] At the time of the 1871 Census, it is known that Richard HOPKINS was working as a servant to a Maltster who was a family relation of his wife's. This meant that Richard was living at least seven miles away from his lawful wife and legitimate children, *possibly* just to learn the craft of a Maltster, but *possibly* having made that move in 1867 to 'escape from the opprobrium' which (if the author is right) may then have existed against Richard HOPKINS in the DAVIS household in Market Lavington. The truth may never be known. The author has tried, unsuccessfully, to trace any of Richard's lawful descendents to see if they can 'add to the facts and reduce the speculation'. (Of the legitimate sons, it is known that James moved to Swindon, where he became a railway shunter and had issue there, and that William moved to London, where he became a police constable, and married, but apparently remained childless.)

So, just as in Caroline's case some years earlier, it seems that the same course in the raising of the illegitimate child by the mother's parents had been followed.[26] Thus, almost from birth, it is probable that Alfred Wm was raised largely by his grandparents, Richard and Ann DAVIS, who themselves had an 11-year age gap, having been aged 59 and 48, respectively, when Alfred Wm was born in 1867.[27]

Now, it seems likely that his young Aunt Emily, the youngest 'genuine' daughter of Richard and Ann, who was only eight years senior in age to Alfred Wm, was often left in sole charge of the infant. To outward appearances she probably performed her duties well enough as an acting unpaid 'nursemaid', but, when neither her mother nor father were around to see what she was doing, it may be the case that she constantly teased the infant in a sly and cruel manner about his illegitimate and 'unwanted' status in life as compared with her own 'legitimate' and 'treasured' standing.

Carte de Visite by Mieli of Salisbury circa 1870.
Carte kindly donated by R.PENNEY, Esq.

Alf's Father, Alfred Wm DAVIS, aged about three. The infant appears to be well-dressed (even if only in carefully kept 'hand-me-downs' from his grandparents' daughters). He also seems well-nourished, but he looks far from happy, perhaps as a consequence of being short of mother-love and possibly borne down by constant teasing about his illegitimacy. He is wearing a dress, but that was fashionable-enough wear for a boy-child of that era. In looks – though not in expression - he has a distinct resemblance to his grandson, Raymond PENNEY, who is the donor of this photograph. (Ray is the son of Nellie, Alfred Wm's eldest daughter. The resemblance to Ray is continued in the ensuing photograph, when Alfred Wm was 13 years old.)

---

[26] The censuses of 1861 and 1871 show these various children as living with their grandparents.

[27] The whereabouts of Alfred Wm's mother at the time of the 1871 Census is unknown. She does not appear to have been living anywhere in Wiltshire. It *may* be that she had gone 'into service' to earn her keep, possibly in London. However, by the time of the 1881 Census, it *appears* that Elizabeth was living in a house in Church Street, Market Lavington as *'Mrs Elizabeth HOPKINS'*, with the 'Head of House' absent, and thus not named. This Elizabeth had no recorded occupation and it is *possible* she was then a 'kept woman'. By 1891 Elizabeth was definitely calling herself 'Miss DAVIS' and had her widowed mother as 'Head of House'. Elizabeth's sister, Mary Ann was also living in that household. They were *possibly in the same house* in Church Street as the 'Elizabeth HOPKINS' of 1881, though numbering of houses had yet to be introduced so one cannot be *absolutely* sure.

Moreover, although this is also sheer conjecture, Alfred Wm may have overheard his mother saying just a little too loudly and openly in 'adult conversation' that he was '*her mistake*'. All this could have led to Alfred Wm becoming very withdrawn into himself, and may well have been the key to much of his future behaviour.

Against this is the interesting fact that the photograph of his mother as a young woman has survived for over a century in-family. Could it be that a part of Alfred Wm always hoped against hope that his mother would eventually change her tune and 'come around' to show him sincere and loving affection? Or has the writer totally misread the whole scenario, and the fact of the matter was that the young mother was *forced* to give up her child and go into service far away to avoid the local scandal and to earn her keep?

Even if that was the case, the infant would still have been deprived of his mother's love. In her absence, it seems that his grandparents did their best to provide love and reassurance to the infant during his earliest formative years. However, his grandfather, who was a one-time Carter and an Agricultural Labourer, died in 1873 at age 65, whereupon his widow (Alfred Wm's grandmother) immediately became a Pauper, dependent on parish relief, and young Alfred Wm, left more or less without financial support at age 7, was evidently soon put 'into service' by the local authorities to earn his keep.

Certainly, we do know that by age 14 Alfred Wm had become a Junior Footman, working for George MILLS, a wealthy bachelor with a domestic staff of just three servants, who had a large farm at Tilshead, a considerable village in the middle of Salisbury Plain.[28] George MILLS' housekeeper was an unmarried Scotswoman in her 60s named Elizabeth SUNDERLAND. She had been born at Stirling Castle, in Scotland.[29] It may well be the case that she had taken the growing boy-servant under her wing to some extent, and taught him much professionally about the best and 'canniest' way to behave as a servant. He would thus have learned how to get the very best 'deal' possible out of every 'transaction' with his superiors in life, by using what would nowadays be called 'cheerful and proactive behaviour' and by taking 'helpful initiatives', often resulting in 'positive recognition', and culminating with a 'tip' or other reward.

Such well-intentioned help as that from Elizabeth SUNDERLAND must have been truly invaluable to the youngster. However, as already implied, the overall effect of his believed lack of mother-love and the teasing about his being an 'unwanted illegitimate' had evidently resulted in Alfred Wm being 'emotionally crippled', and having laid down a 'hard outer shell' to protect his deeply-buried and highly vulnerable inner self. Although he had swiftly learnt to play the role of a very pleasant, outwardly happy and compliant young boy-servant, it is believed that he found *deep* emotional relationships with human beings very difficult.

Shunning the possible pain of such relationships, by his mid-teens he had evidently come to deflect his deepest affections to horses, which had responded well to his instinctive understanding and care. Exactly how he had come to work with horses after being a Junior Footman to the wealthy farmer George MILLS remains something of an unknown. However, George MILLS died in April 1884, and Young Alfred Wm, by then aged 17, would have been out of a job. All we know for sure is that he next turns up

---

[28] As shown by the 1881 Census of Tilshead.
[29] Presumably, Elizabeth SUNDERLAND had been born in the servants' quarters at the castle, and had probably had a lifetime of experience as a servant.

as a Coachman, in Scotland, around 1892, presumably having served some sort of apprenticeship as a 'Tiger' (i.e. apprentice) to a Coachman early on in that significant eight-year gap.

It may be the case that Thomas Longman MILLS and Frederick MILLS, who were the nephews, executors and joint inheritors of the estate of the late George MILLS, had played a part in funding this apprenticeship.[30]

Carte de Visite by T. HAYWARD of Devizes c. 1880. Carte kindly donated by R. PENNEY Esq.

Alf's father, Alfred Wm DAVIS when aged about 13, and already showing an air of rather *gauche* and premature 'worldliness'. As betokened by the multiple buttons on the cuffs, he is wearing livery in the form of a long-sleeved waist-coat under his jacket. He is carrying a handsome Malacca cane as his badge of office, for, at the time this picture was taken, he was junior Footman to wealthy George MILLS a Farmer at Tilstead, on Salisbury Plain. The seated, rather handsome man is *believed* to be Alfred Wm's putative father, *thought* to be Richard HOPKINS. He is wearing a Bandsman's uniform, probably of the Tilshead Town Band. It seems that Richard, who lived in Market Lavington, maintained discreet contact with his natural son and gave him a measure of emotional and practical support.

Another possibility is that his natural father had stepped in, although, with three lawful sons of his own to raise, and only a fairly basic job as a Maltster, one would have thought that he lacked the necessary financial resources. And the third possibility might be that young Alfred Wm had simply dived in to help a Coachman who was in a spot of difficulty, and that he had then 'charmed the birds off the trees' to secure a job as a 'Tiger' (i.e. as an apprentice coachman). Clearly, he had quickly picked up the necessary skills and must have been naturally talented, possibly aided by the 'nature and nurture' he may have picked up from his grandfather (who was a sometime Carter) and his believed natural father (who was a sometime Drayman.)

How Alfred Wm had thereafter ended up in Scotland, working for the ORR-EWINGs is a matter of sheer speculation. There may have been some link through the aforementioned Elizabeth SUNDERLAND, but the most likely scenario is that he had

---

[30] The Will of George MILLS (proved Salisbury 30 May 1884) is preserved in Wiltshire C.R.O.

worked his way from Wiltshire towards London between 1884 and (say) 1890. Then (rather remarkably – perhaps by more 'fast talking', especially in respect of 'inventing' a father to disguise his illegitimacy, and by saying he was older and thus more mature than he actually was) he had gained employment at the London home of the ORR-EWINGS, later being sent up to Scotland to work as the Domestic Coachman at their Scottish home, much (as we shall see) as Eliza had been. However, no means of exploring this part of his life has been found.

By basic nature, Alfred Wm was intensely ambitious, and his experiences in working for the gentry had sharpened his desire to 'pull himself up by his own boot-straps'. He was something of a 'loner', and, as already indicated, he was the sort of young man who liked to frequently change jobs, and to constantly find fresh fields and pastures new. To improve his lot in life, Alfred Wm had strong dreams of founding his own 'personal dictatorship' which he aimed to populate with 'little slaves' of children who would toil just as he willed, the 'slaves' having been bred by a woman who would be prepared to take risks and to support him to the hilt in whatever moves he made to better himself. Being an only child, he hungered to see the next generation as a large group.

Eliza ATKINSON, the woman he had married in 1893, was intensely maternal and keen to bear children. In actuality Eliza was seven years senior in age to Alfred Wm., though, for professional reasons she had been passing herself off as being a couple of years *younger* than her true age, whilst, to increase his air of maturity, Alfred Wm had been claiming to be four years *older* than his true age. Their true 'age-gap' of nearly 7 years had thus, effectively, been narrowed to just one 'admitted' year. This had eliminated the scandalous gossip which would otherwise have flourished in the servants' quarters in those times about their 'age difference'.[31]

Like her husband, Eliza had been almost desperate to advance in the world, for, in 1876, she had suddenly been turfed out of the very comfortable parental home of her craftsman cabinet-maker father at Potterhanworth, Lincolnshire. That home had always been well-provided with books and paintings, and Eliza's late mother had encouraged her children to read everything in it.[32] Importantly, Eliza had loved reading, and she had absorbed a lot of what she had read over the years. Her mother had been well-bred, and it is likely that Eliza had been encouraged to speak out well and to show good deportment.

Tragically, Eliza's mother had died from consumption in 1872, and, a year or two later, Eliza's elder sister, Mary Elizabeth (who was already betrothed) had left home to marry her fiancé, the wheelwright Robert HICKS. Thereafter, the teenage Eliza had been happily operating as 'Mistress of the House' and as a 'Little Mother' to her two much-younger brothers. Eliza had believed that she had looked after her father and her little brothers very well. Indeed, one suspects she had also taken over certain key but 'difficult' aspects of her father's business, chasing up 'late-payers', and introducing other efficiencies, for she was evidently a remarkably forthright and 'go-ahead' young lady.

However, it seems that her rather *dilettante* father was missing the customary pleasures of the marital bed, and Alice BELL, a new wife (and hence newly imposed

---

[31] The author can well remember the sensitivity of his beloved Maternal Grandmother GREEN to the fact that she was three years senior in age to her husband. She would quite frequently raise the matter in a semi-humorous manner as if to test the reactions of people and almost on the 'strike first' principle, before somebody else 'let the cat out of the bag' to her discomfiture.

[32] The father's Will of 1887 makes clear that the house had sundry books and paintings. A copy is held in the Lincolnshire CRO, under ref 1887/II/520.

step-mother to Eliza and her two small brothers) had come on the scene about two years later. Recognising that Eliza, who was by nature outspoken, was becoming a strong critic of the quality of the new wife's 'housekeeping', and thus a rival to authority, it had clearly not been long before the new wife had issued an ultimatum to Eliza's father along the lines of "*Either Eliza goes or I do!*".

Thereupon poor Eliza had suddenly been put out of her comfortable and well-furnished home to go 'into service', swiftly going from *'Riches to Rags'* by becoming a humble Housemaid aged 17. Thereafter, she was at the beck and call of whoever was set over her, and with the prospect of 'dismissal without a reference' if she showed the least adverse reaction to even the most unreasonable and galling demands on her services. The next downward step from showing even a hint of such 'insubordination', and hence getting 'the sack', might well have been 'Hobson's choices' between prostitution, slaving in a dismal workhouse or eking out a desperate life or death existence 'in the gutter'.[33]

Being a sensible and well-organised girl, Eliza had buckled down to a life in service, and she had quickly progressed from large houses in Lincolnshire to even larger houses in London, and was evidently working at a large property in Hanover Square by 1881.[34] From there she had apparently come into the service of the ORR-EWINGs at their London home in nearby Sloane Square. Some time later she had been sent by train to the ORR-EWING's beautiful rented home, at Newark Castle, in Scotland. This journey north was presumably a consequence of the ORR-EWING Family following the *dictats* of 'The Season', whereby the nobility spent a part of their year at their Scottish estates (for the 'hunting and fishing'), another part at Dinard or some other French seaside resort, another part in the Alps, another part in London, or whatever.

During her ten years with the ORR-EWINGs, and thanks to the knowledge she had gained at the village school, well-supported by her earlier extensive reading of her father's books, Eliza had clawed her way up from being a humble Housemaid to attain the much higher status of Children's Nurse, clearly having 'talked fast and well' at some stage to do so, including the 'false promotion' of her tradesman father's occupation from Carpenter & Joiner to the more convincing 'profession' of 'Clerk'.[35] It was probably already in the role of Nurse that she had arrived at Newark Castle. However, for some

---

[33] Raymond PENNEY is the elder son of Nellie, who was Eliza's eldest daughter. Ray says that Nellie used to utter a set phrase, parrot-fashion, whenever some task she was trying to accomplish went adrift, to her great frustration. The phrase, always delivered theatrically, with eyes raised heavenwards, was "*Oh, Emma, how could you do this to me?!*" It is now apparent that this exclamation was in direct imitation of her mother, Eliza, who surely used exactly that phrase during her lifetime, the 'target' of 'Emma' being Eliza's deceased Mother (née Emma DAYKINS), whose passing away had led to the disastrous arrival of a step-mother (the former Alice BELL) and to Eliza being ejected from her comfortable and until then very secure existence in the parental home. (See ATKINSON and DAYKINS Family Trees in Appendix F.)

[34] At the time of the 1881 Census an Eliza ATKINSON aged 23, born 'in Lincolnshire', was working as a Housemaid in a large household in Hanover Square, London. It is believed that this was 'our' Eliza.

[35] It is probable that Eliza, who was a forthright *Leo*, had come to loath and despise her father John ATKINSON after her 'eviction' from the parental home. Probably as signposts to her loathing, she declared his forename to be 'David' for her marriage documentation, and later, when her young husband was required to give the maiden surname of the mother of their new-born son Berty John, to be inscribed on the babe's birth certificate, he told the registrar that it was 'DAYKENS' (sic) rather than the correct 'ATKINSON', probably because Eliza had chatted to her husband almost solely about her mother's 'DAYKINS' line, eschewing her father's ATKINSON line!

time past Eliza had begun to view her long-term prospects with great alarm, for she could see that, as she aged, she would be in danger of becoming an unattractive and unwanted Nanny who would be without income and virtually all alone in the World.

Crown Copyright: Royal Commission on the Ancient and Historical Monuments of Scotland. (Alfred T SCOTT Collection) Photographic image ref AY3461, dating from July 1860.

Newark Castle where Eliza ATKINSON is believed to have been employed as a Children's Nurse. She married whilst in service and her husband , Alfred Wm DAVIS was recorded as being the rent payer at the 'Newark Mains Cothouse' at the Castle for the year 1894/5. The birth of Berty John, who was their eldest son, was registered as having taken place 'at the Castle' (though more probably at the Cothouse there) on St Patrick's Day, 17th March 1894. It seems that this lovely castle remained virtually unchanged externally from 1860 until the 1960s, when significant building extensions were added to it.

Eliza's 'way out' of her situation had been to try to find an ambitious man who offered the potential of an eventual return to the sort of well-furnished and comfortable home which she had occupied in her youth, and the opportunity to bear for him the children for whom she instinctively yearned. In fact, at an admitted 31 years of age, she had seen her chances of pulling off such a union as drifting fast away, for she was a girl who was by nature highly selective about a marital partner, and most of the men she met had the complaisant air of staying forever 'in service' and living forever on something of a pittance. When Alfred Wm came on the scene at the ORR-EWINGs, Eliza instantly recognised that he was the sort of highly-ambitious young man she was seeking and it soon became clear that he wanted to raise children, which twinned with her instinctive needs. True, she soon discovered that he was very seriously 'crabbed' emotionally, but she reckoned that she would gradually be able to 'gentle him' with love and firm understanding, much as he would soothe and control one of his own young colts. She also quickly recognised that he needed a 'mother-figure' as much as a wife, and his need appealed to her strong maternal nature.

Thus it was, as we have seen, that Eliza and Alfred Wm had come to marry whilst in the employment of the ORR-EWINGs at splendid Newark Castle which stood in a very fine estate in the extensive Ayrshire countryside.

In fact, Eliza and Alfred Wm were really quite well-matched in character and ambition, and, to a limited extent, she had succeeded in softening and maturing her husband over the ten years and more of their marriage, and as they roamed from Scotland to England and on to Ireland. Her husband was now rather more emotionally 'human' under his *superficial* veneer of constant cheerfulness – but his ambitious and remorseless streak still burned bright under the contented and competent servant's image that he presented to his superiors in life.

Sadly, when Eliza's health began to fail, it is likely that Alfred Wm found it difficult to find sympathy for his ailing wife and to care devotedly for her. He had always looked to her to be his *strong* mother-figure, in addition to being the co-founder of his 'Little Empire' of child-helpers. He would have felt resentful and almost betrayed by Eliza revealing herself to have human frailty and to be no longer physically capable of continuing in these demanding roles. It was probably through sensing this latent reaction that Eliza may have begun to press her husband to take her back from Ireland to an English port, and from there to travel to Lincolnshire, where her married elder sister, Mary Elizabeth HICKS, was living. Mary Elizabeth was kindly and strongly maternal, and would surely help to care for her.

Whatever the exact facts surrounding their departure may be, there is no doubt whatsoever that the DAVIS family made the return trip across the Irish Sea in 1906 – and promptly ran into an appalling storm. Conditions were so bad that Nellie, the eldest daughter, then aged eight, swore never again to set foot on a boat in her lifetime![36] However, it seems that young Alf, aged 10, gloried in the spume-flecked and raging seas, where so many others were in a terrible state with sea-sickness. Glowing internally over this success, he may have felt a distinct moral advantage over Nellie, this sister who, young as she was, had long begun to try to boss him about. These matters may have stayed close and dear to his heart, and played a major role in the career move he was to make about five years later in his life.

The family headed for Lincolnshire as soon as they landed. In doing so they were 'going against the flow', for Lincoln was then in the grip of an epidemic of typhoid fever, which had made thousands of people seriously ill and had caused over 100 deaths. The problem had been traced to contamination of the city's water supply by the accidental entry of raw sewage at some unknown point or points in the system, parts of which probably dated as far back as Roman times. All piped water supplies had now been cut off, and there was little prospect of piped water being restored for some time and maybe not for years ahead. Instead, water was being brought in daily by steam trains operating on the railway network, and this water was used to top up static water tanks which had been set up at a number of strategically-placed sites around the city. The population had to draw their water from these tanks, using whatever large jugs and pails the members of individual households could muster, before they joined the long queues which formed all

---

[36] She kept her vow until she was a very old lady. According to her son, Raymond PENNEY, Nellie was then persuaded to make a short trip to Capri on a lovely calm day. However, King Neptune had it in for her, and he whistled up a short sharp Mediterranean gale, which caused poor Nellie the utmost distress with acute *mal de mer*. Such is life for us poor mortals.

day at each tank after it had been filled. The inconvenience and disruption to daily life, as contrasted to the facility of using piped water, was enormous.

Lincoln was a very 'go-ahead' city, and, in 1905 it had been one of the first cities to introduce electric trams. It had been a grievous blow to the prosperity of the city when the typhoid epidemic had struck just months later.

Author's collection. A postcard published by 'K & S' in 1905.

LINCOLN ELECTRIC TRAMCARS (G.B. SYSTEM) STARTED NOV. 23ᴿᴰ 1905. FIRST CAR.

Lincoln has its first electric tramcars, replacing the former horse-drawn vehicles. The trams will serve the city well and are a visible token of its increasing wealth.

The consequence of the typhoid epidemic was that some people had begun to move away from the City. Property prices had surely fallen in Lincoln, and Alfred Wm, ever alive to an opportunity, managed to take over the management of a pub called the 'Crown Hotel' in late November 1906, using the limited fund of money he had brought back from Ireland. Alfred Wm quickly made a business agreement with a local brewer, and advertised on the front page of the local paper that 'The Crown' Hotel was *under new management* and that the pub had *'Good Stabling and Loose Boxes'*, and a *'Glass-Covered Yard'*. He called himself *'Late Studsman to the Meath Hunt'* and used the opportunity to extol the pub's good beers and the low-priced 'specials' available on market days.[37] To keep his running costs at rock-bottom, he was going to use his children – the two eldest working full-time 'for their keep' - as his workforce.

'The Crown' public house was at No.8 Brayford Street in the Parish of St Mary le Wigford, near the main railway station. Brayford Street was only about 350 yards long. At one end of it lay the busy High Street, and at the other end lay the waterfront of Brayford Head, with its river-barges and light industry. Brayford Street was rather narrow, but it was straight and direct. (The only other public link between the High

---

[37] Alfred Wm's advertisement appeared in The Lincolnshire Chronicle and General Advertiser of 08 Dec 1906. The above quotations from it appear by kind permission of The British Library.

Street and Brayford Pool was by Swanpool Court, but this was narrower than Brayford Street and far from straight. Hence it was rather restrictive, even for hand-carts, let alone for the passage of horse-drawn vehicles.) The 'Crown', with its good stabling, was thus in a very advantageous position from the local-traffic point of view, be it by horse or foot.

Reproduced from Negative No. LCL 4364, from the Local Studies Collection, by courtesy of Lincolnshire County Council, Education and Local Services Directorate.

Brayford Street in 1960, looking up towards the narrow arched exit which leads out into the High Street. "The Crown" stands at front right, with the entry to its large yard a short distance up the road, on the left. As can be seen, the whole area has gone sadly down (it would shortly be re-developed into a multi-storey car park), and "The Crown" and its once handsome sign now look very time-worn and neglected. However, the picture gives a good idea of the narrow nature of the cobbled road and the nearness of the High Street. Brayford Pool lies at only a slightly greater distance 'behind the photographer'.

The following pictures show the busy waterfront at Brayford Head and the bustling High Street which lies about 350 yards away off to the right of the waterfront scene as depicted. Brayford Street, which connects the two, leads off from the landward edge of the wharf in the extreme right foreground of the upper picture on Page 51. On the way up Brayford Street to reach the High Street, as shown in the above photo, one will have to pass 'The Crown' (then in its heyday) – and perhaps be tempted to call in for refreshment.

Author's collection A postcard by an anonymous publisher. Card postally used in 1910.

The Head of Brayford Pool, busy with barges and surrounded by warehouses and light industry. Lincoln Cathedral dominates the skyline. The entry into the west end of Brayford Street is in line with the cut-back visible in Brayford Wharf East, at the extreme front-right of this view.

Author's collection. Postcard No. 67416 by Valentines. Reproduced by courtesy of the University of St Andrews Library. Card postally used in 1918, but having originated in 1910.

The busy High Street, with the towers of Lincoln Cathedral in the distance. The east end of Brayford Street forms the narrow roadway running off to the left by the shop advertising 'CIGARS'. The 'Crown' P.H. was about 150 yards down Brayford Street.

In summary, 'The Crown' was well-placed to earn a good profit, especially when there was horse-racing on the Carholme or when one of the celebrated Lincoln Horse Fairs was in progress.

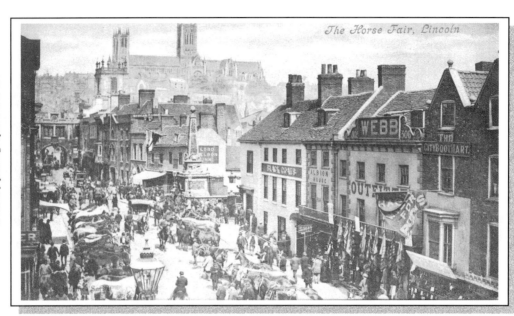

Author's Collection. An anonymous postcard, evidently photographed c.1905.

A Horse Fair at Lincoln. As can be seen from the nearness of the cathedral, this view is well up the High Street, with the celebrated Stonebow Arch at upper left. In this typically busy scene, horses crowd both sides of the street and potential buyers are jogging up and down on horseback, testing the performance of individual animals. Brayford Street lies a good 600 yards 'behind the cameraman's back', but, in the heyday of the horse fairs, virtually all that distance would be filled with horses.

However, although business looked promising, Alfred Wm's problem was that his wife was now very seriously ill, and her problem was diagnosed as being due to heart-deterioration. A busy pub was no place in which to try to care for her. Accordingly, protecting her husband's interests to the last, it is believed that she now begged her husband to transfer her with no further delay into the care of her sister at nearby Metheringham. This was a quiet village, despite its proximity to the City of Lincoln, and it was virtually next-door to Potterhanworth where Eliza had been born. Here, doubtless, Eliza would find a measure of calm and comfort during her now rapid decline in health, and her sister, who was a motherly soul with a fairly well-off husband and a family of near 'grown-up' teenagers already 'leaving the nest', would doubtless take good care of her. This move was therefore carried out.

It seems that Young Alf, then aged 11, saw this 'sending away of his mother' as a betrayal of Eliza by his father. Like most Cancerians, he deeply loved his mother, and, had it been left to him, no matter what the difficulty, one feels that he would never have abandoned her. This 'wound' evidently festered deep in his heart.

Author's collection. A postcard by R.J.Swinton, stationer, Metheringham, c.1906. Postally used 21st January 1908.

High Street, Metheringham

Metheringham, the quiet village adjacent to her birthplace of Potterhanworth, where Alf's mother went to seek quietude and home-nursing from her elder sister, Mary Elizabeth HICKS née ATKINSON. Ere long, Alf's mother would be buried in the churchyard here.

However, it was to Metheringham that Eliza was conveyed and there she died on 4th December 1906. Whether or not any of the family had visited her in the intervening period remains an unknown. They would have been pretty well 'run off their feet' in running the pub, and it is hard to know if visits took place, even though the journey would not have been an arduous or expensive one by train or carter's cart. The 'Informant of the Death' was Eliza's sister, Mary Elizabeth HICKS, which may well imply that no DAVIS family member was present at Eliza's end. Eliza was buried in Metheringham churchyard on the 8th December 1906. (Although headstones would later be raised for Mary Elizabeth and her HICKS Family, it is almost definite that no headstone was ever raised for Eliza DAVIS – indeed, Alfred Wm was in no financial position to afford one at that stage of his career and he seemingly did not see fit to do so later in life when he did have the money – though, by then, it must be said that he was already contemplating a move to a place far away from Lincoln.)

Meantime, back in Lincoln, Alfred Wm would already have been striving with might and main to make the pub a commercial success, running the business on a shoe-string and, as we have seen, using 'Jack' and Nellie, as his main helpers. Under the terms of the 1871 Education Act he might have been forced to let the girl attend school at least part-time, loath though he would have been to do so. Generally, he would have hoped that 'officialdom' would appreciate his difficulty, 'turn a blind eye', and generally let matters lie. Indeed, one does have the feeling that a parent of that period would have found less opposition from the authorities if keeping a girl away from school than if doing the same with a boy. The other children continued at school for the present, but

Alf and his two younger sisters were all expected to work in the pub as soon as they returned home from school each day.

As we have seen, there was no piped water of potable quality, and only limited supplies of drinking water could be withdrawn from the limited number of tanks placed around the city streets and topped up daily by the civil authorities. Rare photographic postcards of the day (now high-priced collectors' items) show the long queues, mainly of working-class women and children, always present at these 'water-stations'. Whether 'impure' piped water could sometimes be obtained for washing and toilet-flushing is unknown, but this seems unlikely, especially at the times when the main system was being excavated and 'explored' in the repeated efforts of the authorities to trace the source(s) of contamination.

It may well be the case that such essential jobs at the 'Crown' as washing down the stable-yard and loose boxes, flushing the urinals and toilets, and perhaps of dealing with the family laundry, sometimes had to be performed with water drawn from the Brayford Pool, some 200 yards away down the road. One assumes that the DAVIS Family would have purchased a small wheeled tank to convey the water they drew – or maybe even have bought a larger version designed to be horse-drawn. Meantime, several times a day, one or more of the children would be going to and from the nearest pure water-tank, and queuing up with the largest containers which they could physically carry when full, ready to be charged with potable water and to be lugged back to the pub for use in preparing food, and for washing-up and drinking purposes. It would all have been sheer, time-consuming, hard labour. A terrible slog for young children to have to endure as the weeks turned to months and the months turned to years with piped water of potable quality still not restored.[38]

Throughout 1906, young Alf (by then aged 11), Rose (aged 7) and Eva (rising 6) would evidently have been going to the school in Free School Lane, which was located near to the centre of Lincoln, not far from the high ground on which the celebrated cathedral stands. It is probable that the children were subjected to some teasing when they started school in Lincoln, because the quicksilver Irish accents and whimsical modes of expression which they would have acquired during the previous five years would have been very different to the slow and deliberately spoken flat brogue of the Lincolnshire-born children. This teasing might well have got young Alf into a few rough and tumbles, for he had the quick temper which often accompanies reddish-coloured fair hair, he was courageous, and he had a high self-pride and a low flashpoint.

As soon as they came home from school, the girls would have been expected to pitch in and help with the washing and cleaning in the pub, and to lend a hand with domestic chores and the preparation of the family meals. Nellie was not slow in coming forward and 'organising' everybody. Young Alf would have been expected to help his brother as a potman, and, especially, as an ostler and cleaner in the stable yard which lay just across the road from the public house. Like his father, Alf seemed to have a natural affinity in handling horses.

It must not be forgotten that, no matter how he managed to 'harden his heart', Alfred Wm would still have been grieving internally over the loss of Eliza, who had been a splendid wife and mother, and surely the peacemaker within the family circle. His children, too, would have been grieving and keenly feeling the absence of their mother.

---

[38] It was not until 1911 that the supply of potable piped water was restored.

Yet, the hectic lives they were all leading to cope with the remorseless demands of running the busy pub would have been preventing them from taking any 'time out' to grieve, and at the same time physically draining them to huge degree. One suspects that the father gave each of his children specific tasks to accomplish, and used a heavy hand to ensure that they did so, yet let them run free once their tasks were fulfilled. Basically, he was concentrating on training his daughters to be good barmaids and domestic servants and his sons to be skilled barmen, potmen and ostlers. And one should remember that Alfred Wm himself was on a 'learning curve' in all this. Life was hard and tiring for them all, yet they had to present a cheerful and welcoming 'hail-fellow-well-met' attitude to the varied mix of people using the pub – only working off any outbursts of weeping or bad-temper 'behind doors', 'within family' and out of the hearing of any customers. There is a hint of evidence that the pub took in paying guests at times, which would have added to the labour and further limited the extent to which emotions could be released.

Family legend strongly suggests that, the father, Alfred Wm, was quickly becoming a very convincing 'Mine Host' figure, and he was building a good reputation locally. Young Nellie, too, was showing considerable dedication and mature skills in supporting her father in a 'front of house' role, and in self-disciplining herself to perform her 'bar maid/manageress function at a high 'social' level. Despite her very young age as measured by her years, Nellie was certainly a very 'organising' girl, with high personal ambitions, and it seems likely that she was already beginning to get the measure of her father and would eventually have him almost 'eating out of her hand'. The fact that they were both born under the same zodiac sign (Capricorn) may well have resulted in much mutual understanding and acceptance of each other's ambitious and money-conscious personalities. Indeed, Nellie was well on the way to becoming a junior 'family matriarch' in her late mother's stead. Perhaps Alf was the only one of her siblings who fought against Nellie's moral dominion.[39]

Eighteen months after Eliza's sad demise, a public event caused great excitement in Lincoln, when, on the 26th June 1907, King Edward VII (whom the family appear to have narrowly missed seeing in 1901, when, as Prince of Wales, he had stayed at Bletchley Park) made an official visit to the City and attended the large Agricultural Show, being conveyed through the city in an open carriage drawn by four horses, with top-hatted grooms astride the leaders.

The carriage had a cavalry escort and soldiers, including men of the City Imperial Volunteers, with rifles and fixed bayonets lined the route, presenting arms as the carriage passed by. A 'triumphal arch' had been constructed near the top of the High Street. It bore the proud words "Lincoln's Wealth 1907" across its broad plinth, the plinth being supported by eight Doric-style columns made in wood and plaster. Two winged horses stood on the plinth, supporting the city's Coat of Arms – and, on a deck constructed above them, majestically, towered a 'real live' steam traction engine provided by a local engineering company. This iron monster had its enormously tall smokestack hinged back

---

[39] In her adult life Nellie became a pub landlady in her own right. She would not eat her 'evening' meal (which usually included Stilton cheese!) until the pub had closed for the night and the clearing-away and washing-up had been completed, ready for opening-up next day. Nor would she let her husband and children eat before that work was done. It is believed that this tight self-discipline had evolved under her father's regime in Lincoln, from 1906 until she left home, circa 1915.

beside its huge flywheel. Flags and bunting and garlands decorated all the shops and buildings along the High Street. Altogether, it was a most impressive sight.[40]

Author's collection. A postcard by an anonymous publisher, issued in 1907.

His Majesty King Edward VII is conveyed through the City of Lincoln in 1907. It appears that all the schoolchildren were given a day's holiday to cheer the King as he passed by. It is thus possible that Young Alf (aged nearly 12) and his younger siblings would have been a part of the enthusiastic crowd of all ages who lined the route, as portrayed in this photographic postcard. However, their father's pub would have been open, and possibly 'rocking', and Alf & Co may have only been allowed very limited 'time off'.

The enthusiastic crowds which had gathered were all good for the business of the pubs and hotels in Lincoln, restored some confidence after the ravages of the typhoid epidemic, and stimulated further progress in the development of the city.[41] Gradually, Alfred Wm began to turn a real profit from the business as the years went by, and as all five of his children continued to grow up and play increasingly adult roles in the running of the pub.[42]

---

[40] Nobody would have foreseen that, within the short space of eight years, the manufacturer of the steam traction engine would be constructing highly innovative and secret caterpillar-tracked armoured fighting vehicles (which later came to be generally called 'Tanks' after their original 'cover name').

[41] This was one of many goodwill visits made by the King around the UK, getting to be seen and also to himself see something of his people, in this, the sixth year of his reign.

[42] After so many unsuccessful searches down the years seeking school attendance records for all and any of the DAVIS children at Bletchley, Fenny Stratford, Nuneaton and Lincoln, it seemed almost ironic to the author to find the name of Eva, the youngest child, recorded as starting to attend Christ's Hospital Terrace Higher Elementary School in Lincoln City on 01 March 1912, '*having transferred there from the school in Free School Lane*'. Her father was correctly shown as Alfred DAVIS of the 'Crown' P.H. at Brayford. Unfortunately, no attendance records have survived for the school in Free School Lane, which all the DAVIS children probably attended pre-1912. [The author is indebted to professional researcher Nigel COLLEY of Lincoln for this and certain other 'Lincolnshire-based' information.]

Berty John, who had by now dropped his 'Berty' and become simply 'John', and was more often known merely as 'Jack', was clearly cut out for life in a hostelry, and was keen to acquire his own pub. Figuratively, if not in actuality, he may well have 'kissed the Blarney Stone' whilst he was in Ireland, and he was clearly growing up to be a very 'social' man - evidently being a totally different person outside his home to what he was when in it.

Author's collection. An anonymous postcard, postally used at Lincoln in 1907.

Another photograph of the royal procession and the crowds in their 'Sunday Best' who had lined the route, which was extremely well decorated with flags and bunting.

However, perhaps partly due to his internal grieving over the death of his mother, and the part-loss of his boyhood and education from having had to help his father all along the way, Jack was a reckless youth. Perhaps Alfred Wm recognised that he owed his elder son a lot, having deprived him of so much, and having relied on Jack for a great deal of assistance in his business enterprises.

If the author's reconstruction of events is anywhere near correct, it could justly be said that Alfred Wm had stolen his son's childhood and he probably recognised that he 'owed Jack, big-time'. The father was therefore prepared to 'forgive Jack his trespasses' to a large extent. However, it seems quite definite that Alfred Wm knew that he and Jack would never be able to make a go of things together as business-partners, long-term, though he probably always intended to help Jack to set up his own pub as soon as could reasonably be managed. Increasingly, although he would always see that Jack at least received his 'fair share', it seems fairly certain that Alfred Wm's thoughts had turned towards making Young Alf, and not Jack, his eventual partner and successor in the business.

For his part, it is to be expected that Young Alf never really got over the loss of his mother, and it is likely that the twists and turns of fate caused this matter to come back to haunt him with a vengeance in later years. But life had to go on, and by the age of fourteen Alf was a Messenger Boy for the Telegraph Service run by the General Post Office in Lincoln, his wages going to help the family budget.

As a Messenger Boy Alf wore a military-style uniform and presumably rode a Post-Office bicycle to speed himself along his route. He could expect to receive a tip as often as not when he delivered his message, especially if he managed to present the 'right' image, outwardly quite cheerful but also restrained and respectful, lest the message he delivered bore bad news.

Author's collection. An anonymous postcard franked at Lincoln, date unclear. Photograph probably dated c.1905.

This is believed to be a photograph of the staff at the General Post Office in Lincoln, but preceding Alf's employment as a Messenger Boy there. He would have had a uniform like that of the fourth figure from the left of this picture.

There was considerable pride in being in the General Postal Service, and postmen were highly regarded by the general public. Indeed, the author has strong boyhood memories of his maternal 'Grandmother GREEN' frequently declaiming a valedictory Edwardian poem which began, "*Hurrah for the Postman who brings us the news - what a lot it must cost him to pay for his shoes!*"

In those days, the boys and men were encouraged to form military-style bands and the bandsmen were expected to march in some style as they played their instruments. The men in the photograph above may look a little 'untidy' to modern eyes, because they tend to have the two bottom buttons of their uniform jackets undone. However, this appears to have been the 'fashion' – perhaps 'led' by the need to permit easy access to the fob-pockets of their waistcoats for access to such things as stubs of pencils and timepieces. (Note the chains of the pocket-watches visible on the 1st and 3rd figures from the left and on the 1st and 6th from the right.)

Seemingly, Alf's father had high hopes of Young Alf, for he was a bright lad and his education had been continued past the minimum standard school leaving-age of 10 years. Unlike Jack, Young Alf seemed to be fairly temperate in his habits. Indeed there appeared to be more that a touch of the Spartan and near-Puritan about him, though, conversely, he did have the beginnings of a latent 'twinkle' in his eye - perhaps not unrelated to the highly-sexed HOPKINS blood which flowed in his veins – probably in 'double-measure'. Father and son were much alike in many respects, with Young Alf having that quick and hot temper and high self-pride, both of which he had probably inherited from his father.

Family legend is strong that there was a monumental quarrel between father and son one day. The cause of their row is unknown, but it may have had several underlying causes, all waiting to burst forth at some time, and that one particular matter came to a sudden head and 'applied the spark to the touch-hole', so to speak.

One underlying cause may have been the fact that Alf was angry that Jack was getting away with 'blue murder', (and perhaps Alf had learned that Jack was to be helped to set up his own pub sooner or later) whilst every little imperfection or lapse on his part immediately received heavy criticism from his father (who probably never said outright that he was 'grooming' Alf for high responsibilities and a share in the business.).

Another underlying cause may have arisen when, after having always told 'fairy stories' about the 'respectability' of his family origins - essential whilst Alfred Wm had remained 'in service', to mask his illegitimacy and to prevent his children from blabbering innocently about the matter - the father, being at last free from the 'bonds of servitude' had let slip to his children that he, Alfred Wm senior, had actually been born illegitimately and to a degree, incestuously. It may have been late-arriving news of the death of his 'remote' mother in faraway Wiltshire, which had taken place on 13th February 1910, which had subsequently led Alfred Wm to make the disclosure, perhaps almost inadvertently.

Justifiably, Young Alf had always taken a pride in his name of DAVIS, and this illegitimacy of his father may have greatly rankled with him, especially if it somehow detracted from the 'purity and innocence' of Elizabeth, his paternal grandmother, whom he had presumably never met, but a woman whom he would probably have instinctively placed on a sort of high mental pedestal, unrealistic though that might have been. To hear that she might have had an incestuous relationship with one of her uncles might have horrified him. (*Certainly, he and his siblings would forever maintain their own versions of 'smokescreens' around this 'shameful' matter, telling their own children virtually nothing. They would have carried on in this way with the very best of intentions, but children almost inevitably ask, at some stage, about their 'roots', and withholding information can become a double-edged sword, actively promoting the very curiosity that the parents so much wish to suppress. Also see Appendices E and F.*)

Another possibility is that Young Alf accidentally happened upon his bereaved father seeking ardent solace in the arms of 'another woman', maybe on a casual basis, and with Young Alf's mother 'not yet cold in her grave' in the lad's eyes – though over four years had actually elapsed.

However, the author feels that the spark which caused the explosion was probably something that was said by the father that was critical about Alf's late mother. Perhaps it was an ill-advised and heavy joke about the 'poor bargain' he had struck in marrying an older woman. Coming on top of what Alf probably conceived as his father's rejection of Eliza from the family home in the run-up to her death, Alf might well have had an extremely adverse reaction to any such critical word or 'heavy jest' concerning his late mother.

Perhaps it was something 'truly monumental' that was quite different to each and any of these matters. Doubtless, Young Alf's adverse reaction was heightened by the fact that, like every family member, he was 'living on the edge' of near-exhaustion and constant tension from the labour, concentration and nervous energy required to run a busy pub when constantly 'short-handed', plus, in his case, from also having to hold down his paid job as a Telegraph Messenger. Be that all as it may, the end result of the argument with his father was that Young Alf stormed out of the house in a great rage.

Young Alf had always liked being in uniform, even if it was only that of a Telegraph Messenger. Now, on a sudden impulse, 'fed up' with his father and having to devote so much of his life towards his father's business, and bitterly angry at whatever had sparked the 'Great Quarrel', he signed on as a 'Boy II' in the Royal Navy.[43]

The crossing of the stormy Irish Sea, in 1906, which Young Alf seems to have survived so well, may have been a factor. Perhaps the lure of the sea had crept into his soul. Perhaps, he just wanted to get away from the pressures and drudgery at home. Perhaps he was so furious with his father that he could not bring himself to slave any longer for his father's pub. Perhaps, at root, he simply craved a 'great adventure'. Perhaps it was all these things and more – perhaps it was quite 'something else' totally unknown, eclipsing all of them. Family rumour was always strong that there had been a terrific argument – but it never revealed a possible cause for it.

One imagines that his father nearly had a fit when Young Alf came home and declared, perhaps rather shamefacedly, what he had done. All the hopes that it is believed Alfred Wm had cherished of having Alf become his partner in the business which had so painfully been built up from nothing, had crashed to the ground in one awful moment. Now Alfred Wm would never have a male inheritor of all that he had striven so hard to set up. The 'little empire' that he had so carefully constructed over the years was falling apart. The father must have despaired and felt utterly heart-sick as, under Alf's impatient urging, he signed his name as 'consenting parent' on Alf's naval recruitment form. Perhaps he tried to get Alf to change his mind - and perhaps he got a very negative response from a very fired-up young man! In the end, what else could the father do? Cases are known where young men had simply forged their father's signature on such documents and the servicemen who were conducting the recruiting were keen 'to make their quotas', and, by tradition, not given to closely examining the 'minutiae' of the signatures on the documentation.

Young Alf was fifteen when he signed on, on 15th March 1911. He was promptly posted to the Naval Training Establishment HMS *Ganges*, at Shotley, Suffolk, presumably having been issued with a railway warrant and a food-voucher to get himself to Ipswich and being taken in charge there by a Petty Officer for the 'last lap' out along the peninsular to *Ganges* at Shotley.

It turned out all to be a bit too much, too soon, for Alf evidently found the life at *Ganges* too Spartan - even for *his* nature - and the discipline too confining, too harsh and too brutal. Moreover, it may well be the case that he had a particular tormentor, who was in a position of petty power and who 'picked on' Alf for every shortcoming. Perhaps Alf

---

[43] It appears that there was no permanent naval recruiting office in Lincoln, so one suspects that Young Alf took a train to somewhere like Grimsby or Skegness to join the Navy, perhaps registering at the coastguard station there. (Lincoln's 'Great Northern' main-line railway station lay within a very short distance of the family pub.)

had never experienced the need to struggle against such a difficult situation before. Nor, one suspects, had he ever been under so tight a discipline, with virtually no means of escape from it.[44]

He must have had a terrible problem in controlling his quick temper and not lashing out instinctively at those who had power over him. Indeed, one could even conceive that he might indeed have lashed out in temper early on, and, instead of being put on Captain's Report as a Defaulter, had been made to suffer an 'informal' and probably rather brutal, demeaning and perhaps on-going physical punishment by the Petty Officer Instructor or whoever else might have been involved.

Whatever the exact situation may have been, family rumour is strong that Alf wrote beseechingly to his father, begging to be 'bought out'. However, his father must have considered matters carefully. Yes, he could buy Alf out, and maybe eventually make the boy his partner in the business. This could solve some of Alfred Wm's personal and practical difficulties in running the 'Crown'. But, would Young Alf ever settle to *anything* if he were allowed to walk away from a problem of his own creation? Would Alf let his father down again in some way, in the future? Deep in his soul Alfred Wm may also have nursed 'innermost feelings' that Alf had utterly betrayed him by 'walking away' from his assigned role as an important 'slave' and potential main inheritor of his father's 'benevolent dictatorship', and that Alf had thus stepped 'beyond the pale'. Alfred Wm looked at the rather dissolute life that Jack, his elder son, was beginning to lead - and made up his mind.

He wrote back to Alf saying that he was simply not prepared to buy Alf out. Alf had *'made his own bed and now he could lie on it'*. It seems that Alf, frustrated and miserable, never outwardly ever forgave his father. Perhaps, had Eliza still been alive, she might have been able to bring about a reconciliation between her proud and unbending husband and their proud and unyielding son. But, in the absence of a catalyst such as Eliza, both men were gripped by their high pride and stubbornness, and neither could ever bring himself to make the first move towards reconciliation. One suspects that Alf had somehow seized a large chunk of 'moral high ground', so that his father would have had to utterly 'demean himself' to rectify things. As a 'dictatorial father', who had been 'totally betrayed', he could never quite bring himself to do that. Left to themselves, and bereft of a skilful and neutral go-between, apologies would never occur - though intense mutual respect and loyalty would always be there, unspoken, between them. It may sound stupid, but family legend is strong that this was the fact.

Yet, future events would show that Alf's father was more right than wrong in refusing to buy Alf out. Perhaps, too, a senior naval man at *Ganges* talked to Alf like a 'Dutch Uncle' and a wise counsellor. For Alf soon came to realise that the only sensible course he could follow was to make the best of things, adapt to what was required of him, get through his training, be responsive and make the Navy his career. Already, he could see the appeal of the uniform for the fairer sex. That nascent 'twinkle' was not in his eye for nothing. In a way he had abandoned what could have become, with luck and hard work, quite a well-off life running a pub with his father, but there might yet be other major satisfactions to be gained. Perhaps he would get to see the world. He'd show them all at home. He began to square his still-young but broadening shoulders.

---

[44] It appears that the number of unhappy and distressed boys desperately managing to escape from Shotley was a matter of concern for the authorities.

CHAPTER TWO:

HMS *GANGES* & HMS *IMPREGNABLE* (1911-12)

At his time of joining the Royal Navy, Alf had been given the Official Service Number 'Chatham J11704'. As we have seen, he was posted to HMS *Ganges* as a Boy II, with effect from 15th March 1911.[45] He was then 15 years and eight months old – just above the minimum permissible age. To join the navy, he had perforce to agree to serve for a minimum of twelve years after reaching the age of 18. (*The Royal Navy was intent on not wasting the time and effort which would be put into teaching Alf how to adapt successfully to a life at sea and how to become a 'useful cog in the wheel'.*)

HMS *Ganges* (dubbed a 'stone-frigate' in Naval parlance), was a brick-built Boys Training Establishment at Shotley, Suffolk. Prior to October 1905, this establishment had been based on a wooden-walled 'hulk' permanently moored in the Orwell Estuary. This hulk was a former ship of the line, which had originally been built as far back in time as 1821. Training aboard the hulk had been very old-fashioned and basic. The boys had learned the age-old standard routines for sailing and fighting a square-rigged sailing ship, but precious little about operating up-to-date equipment ready for the next war.

Author's collection. Postcard No. 39283 published by Valentine's in 1903. Image reproduced by courtesy of St Andrews University Library.

The Training Ship HMS *Ganges* lying in the Orwell Estuary, off Shotley Point, circa 1903. (A traditional 'wooden wall', originally named HMS *Agincourt*, she had been superseded by ironclad battleships and the coming of steam. All-steel warships had soon followed.) Here, her booms are out and boatwork is going on around her. Thames barges and other sailing craft lie nearby.

---

[45] Technically speaking, The Royal Naval Training Establishment at Shotley was not commissioned as 'HMS *Ganges*' until 1927. However, in ordinary conversation old matelots refer to the establishment as 'HMS *Ganges*', and personnel records generally refer retrospectively to the establishment as 'HMS *Ganges*'. It therefore seems easiest to follow the same familiar practice.

However, whirlwind Admiral 'Jacky' FISHER had been appointed Britain's Second Sea Lord in 1902, and, as such, he had become responsible for all Naval training. He had promptly set in hand the most radical reforms ever seen in the history of education for officers and ratings in the Royal Navy. Some of these reforms had related to making the training much more relevant to the modern Navy, with its steel ships and emphasis on steam and mechanisation, which were rapidly replacing 'wooden walls and sail'.

Among his new projects had been the building of schools for ratings at various places around the coast of England. The Royal Navy Training Establishment at Shotley was one such place. The purchase of the land had been completed by 1903, the foundations had been started by February 1904, and the first parties of ratings had marched into the accommodation on 4th October 1905.

HMS *Ganges* had therefore been in operation as a shore establishment for a little over five years when Alf first laid eyes on it, and it was still being enlarged. In fact, by the time Alf joined, there were well in excess of 1,200 boys being trained there, with the number of dormitories, mess halls, drill halls and gymnasia still being expanded, and the establishment already well equipped with school-rooms, kitchens, bathrooms, a hospital of considerable dimensions, a bakery, a swimming pool, a laundry and so on. The famous tall mast (mostly taken from an old frigate) had already been standing for four years and would stand for a great many more years yet. As invariably happens in places inhabited by large groups of human beings, infestation by rats had already become a serious problem and measures were being taken to try to control it.

Author's collection Postcard No. S 7469 by W.H.S & S of London. Reproduced by courtesy of W H Smith Archive. Card postally used in 1911.

HMS *Ganges*, formerly HMS *Caroline*. The minority of Boys who slept in this ship considered themselves to be just that bit more 'nautical' and hence a notch above the far greater number of Boys who slept in the brand-new barracks *ashore*.

Meantime, *Ganges II*, a composite 'steam plus sail' ship had replaced the 'all-sail' *Ganges*. In the early days of shore-development, *Ganges II* provided sleeping quarters for the minority of Boys who could not be fitted into the still-expanding dormitories on land. *Ganges II* would operate (by then mainly as a 'boat pier') during Alf's time at Shotley, and she would have been familiar to him.

After about a year at Shotley or similar establishments, Boys would be sent out in batches to depots, from thence to be posted on to naval ships for further 'on the job' training. New boys like Alf arrived in what one might call 'driblets' (the driblets sometimes being as small as only one or two boys), but their arrival was virtually on a steady 'day by day' basis. Other lads, already 'institutionalised', came in small batches from orphanages. Like all the other new arrivals, Alf would have been put into the so-called 'Nozzer's Mess' where his initial 'induction' would have begun. There he would have stayed, being referred to by the rather derisory generic name of 'Nozzer', until such times as the number of boys in his mess had risen to about fifty, when the boys would have been formed into two classes, each under the charge of a Petty Officer instructor, and their basic training in seamanship (plus a continuation of normal school-room classwork by Naval Schoolteachers) would have begun. By that time, their 'kitting out' would have commenced - and 'kit inspections' would have continued at intervals ever afterwards to check that each boy had his full complement of kit (which was building up progressively at this early stage of his career), and that he laid it out in 'regulation manner' for every inspection - or woe betide him!

Alf's days at Shotley would have begun at 0600 (at the earlier hour of 0530 once Spring arrived), when the buglers would sound 'Reveille', and the dormitory for 50 or so boys in which he would have slept would have come alive as the boys were roused out to have a cold-water wash, to make their beds neatly, and to quickly sup some coffee which would have been served out, maybe with a biscuit. The boys would then have been divided into their various classes for an hour of instruction. This would have been followed by a cooked breakfast at 0800, and then by an inspection by the Captain. Prayers, conducted by the Chaplain would have followed, then marching and running, usually to the accompaniment of the Band. From 0900 to 1200 there would then have been work and instruction, with a short mid-time break. The instruction would have been a mix of formal school-work (conducted by naval school-masters) combined with training in such diverse subjects as boat-pulling and sailing, rifle-practice, the use and dismantling/assembling of heavier weapons, seamanship, knotting and splicing rope, the use of a compass, the use of a log for assessing a ship's speed through the water, the knowledge of the lights which must be carried by a ship at night, a study of what one might call the 'rules of the road' for safety at sea, and so forth.

At 1200 there would have been a break of one and a half hours for lunch (always called 'Dinner' in the Navy) and cleaning up, followed by more work and instruction until 1530. Field sports in the large recreation fields would then take place, and, at 1700, tea (usually of the bread, butter and jam variety) would be taken. That would be followed by 'Evening Quarters' (the final inspection of the day). The Boys would then have free time until 'Pipe Down' (i.e. what soldiers call 'Lights Out') at 2100, a Supper having been served at 1900.

Unlike the academically qualified naval schoolmasters who taught the classical subjects, such as Mathematics and English Grammar, the men who had the job of training these boys in the practical aspects of seamanship and gunnery had been raised in a hard school. In that old 'school', 'starters' (i.e. short lengths of rope with a knot at one end, or canes about 2ft long and made of rattan or similar material), or other *ad hoc* 'weapons', had been freely used to whack the 'slow movers' (and sometimes just whoever had the misfortune to be nearest at hand), almost immediately an order had been given. This was the way of emphasising that immediate and active response to any order was always expected. Even though the more enlightened of the senior officers had realised that the old regime needed to be greatly tempered and moderated, the use of such 'starters' had not yet entirely disappeared at Shotley and a strong vein of rather brutal physical punishment and 'hard knocks' still existed when Alf came on the scene, and would continue, albeit in diminishing degree, for many years to come.[46]

Author's collection. Postcard No. 762 of the W H Smith's 'Suitall Series'. Image reproduced by courtesy of W H Smith Archive. Card postally used in 1909.

SHOTLEY. H. M. Training Establishments. Stripping and Explaining the Rifle. 762.

This photograph, somewhat posed for the camera, pre-dates Alf's time at *Ganges* by at least two years, but the scene is very representative of the type of instruction he would have received on the rifle. Alf probably paid full attention to his Instructors, for he would become a very good marksman during his career, winning a number of trophies.

Old customs have always died hard. Indeed, 'Birching', which had long been used as a means of severe punishment, had persisted until only a few years before Alf joined. [*In 'Birching', all hands had been called to witness punishment, the culprit being brought before them half stripped, and hit several hard strokes with a bundle of birch twigs.*] It is understood that, for the more serious offences corporal punishment still *officially* continued at Shotley, a heavy cane being used by the Regulating PO (The 'Crusher') to apply twelve so-called 'cuts' across the boy's bottom. For somewhat lesser offences one hears that prolonged and exhausting 'doubling' with a rifle held aloft was imposed. And one suspects that 'unofficial' and bullying punishments somehow continued 'discreetly and unofficially' through and well past the time when Alf arrived on the scene. This is not surprising to the author.[47]

---

[46] Some of the 'personal recollections' in papers in the archives of the HMS *Ganges* Museum at Shotley differ in detail but generally confirm this general 'climate' of corporal punishment at that era. (The author is indebted to the HMS *Ganges* Museum for access to their interesting documentation.)

[47] Within H.M Ships and shore establishments flogging men with a cat o' nine tails had been abolished in 1881. Yet, flogging with the birch had officially continued at Training Establishments until around 1905. [It would be retained in H.M. Prisons for young but persistent and serious offenders in

It is not to be wondered at if Alf initially found this life very Spartan and the discipline arduous - and, as already suggested, it may well be that in his earliest days he had a bullying 'tormenter' in a position of petty power over him, who made his life almost unbearable. However, once his father had refused point-blank to buy him out, and thus to free Alf from his misery, Alf had accepted the inevitable and had begun to settle down to the life.

Alf soon realised that if he responded to orders with alacrity, and generally 'kept his nose clean', he was at least as bright as the average new recruit, and a lot quicker in the uptake than most. He was trimly built and the uniform flattered him. Alf had already been conditioned to taking care of his appearance and his uniform whilst working as a Telegraph Messenger for the Post Office, and, although the demands in the Navy were much higher, at least he had a head start over many of the other lads, some of whom came from very impoverished backgrounds and initially had no concept at all of 'cleanliness and smartness'.

Alf learned well, and began to work hard, finding that there were a great many matters involved in becoming a seaman. He also learned how to keep his quick temper in check, using the lower-deck philosophy that 'Orders is orders' and that the time to question them (if ever!) is after carrying them out - and never before or whilst doing so. By the time the order had been executed his initial rage had usually disappeared anyway - for his temper was of the sort that quickly flared and almost as quickly died. His high personal pride, too, became controlled, by always giving immediate respect to the rank (another lower-deck philosophy) and letting time and experience decide what he felt, privately, about the man wearing it. In the fullness of time, relationships could become a lot more sophisticated and subtle.

A very interesting 'game' could then evolve that would take a good many years to hone to a fine art, with the 'Lower Rank' always having to tread very warily in all contact with a 'Higher Rank', so the game had to become as much a 'painstaking science' as an 'art-form'. [There is no reason to believe that Alf himself ever 'stretched matters' very far, but, during his service life he would surely have been witness to situations which even got to the 'transparent' stage where, after the call 'Defaulters to Muster', a rating who had misbehaved and been put in 'The Rattle', would find himself being questioned before the Captain or Commander, and a dialogue ensuing with the situation quickly arising where the rating would be thinking to himself: *That officer knows, that I know, that he knows I am lying in my teeth, but he is playing the game too, has a pretty good idea of what really happened, and he's going to inflict a punishment on me in the end – but he has a lurking respect for my cheek and perseverance and it will not be too hard a 'sentence' when he does eventually find me 'guilty'!"*]

---

civilian life for a round half-century yet to come. Nowadays, as with the case of capital punishment, one rather wonders if it should ever have been totally discontinued.] The author speaks as one who was (more or less 'justifiably' by the rules of the day) hard-thrashed with 'six of the best' across his bottom, sometimes covered only by a linen nightshirt, with objects as diverse as a standard schoolmaster's cane, an Army 'swagger stick' and a steel rapier of ¼-inch square cross-section, all whilst at his charitable boarding school. The cane was administered by the headmaster and the other 'instruments' as clandestine 'endorsing' nocturnal punishment by school prefects - and that was as late as 1942/3. The rapier was easily the most savage and unorthodox instrument of punishment, raising bleeding cuts and weals. The author remembers these punishments with a strange mixture of hurt, dread and pride.]

Whilst one instructor had charge of each party of lads forming a 'mess', other 'Old Salts' also had a hand in their teaching, and many were fascinating characters, with a tremendous fund of experience and anecdotes. Their advice was invariably sound - often pithily so. Some were rather free with their 'starters' ('paying back', in a strange way, for the brutality which they had themselves suffered when young), and sometimes they played rather ponderous games on the new intake. However, Alf found that there was almost always a point to their actions, if one looked hard enough.

In these first weeks, Alf was taught the first essentials of his new life - what was the number of his mess, his hammock, the name of his petty officer instructor, which was his division of port or starboard watch, how to sling his hammock, how to dress himself correctly in the clothes with which he was issued, how to stow those clothes and equipment in his kitbag and how life on board a ship is generally conducted.

Alf may have already learned the rudiments of swimming. If not, it was at Shotley that he would have started to learn, for the Navy was desirous that every boy should swim. The more nervous boys had a hard time of it, as the instructors used rather brutal means of driving them to overcome their fears. In the fullness of time, Alf would become a very powerful swimmer, and one suspects that he did quite well in these early stages. That would have gained him the grudging approval of his instructors.

Author's collection. An image from a postcard by H.R. Tunn & Co., c.1919. Postally used in October 1919.

The Covered Way at Shotley Barracks. Various 'Messes' (i.e. 'Barracks') lay on both sides of this passageway. Other Messes lay on both sides of a second 'open way'. It is regretted that the above image is ill-defined. [It has perforce been magnified from the 4 cm x 2.5 cm print of the original card, which showed five different images of Shotley.] However, it does give a useful impression of the living conditions, with washing hung out to air. There would have been little change in this area since 1911 when Alf was there.

Alf would have begun to overcome his deep disappointment at his father's refusal to 'buy him out', and, almost against himself, he would have begun to get into the routine, to learn something of seamanship, of gunnery, of gymnastics, and also to continue with mathematics and other 'standard' school subjects. He was not exactly a 'happy bunny', but he was beginning to fit in. He was also the sort of boy who had good co-ordination of hand and eye, and he took to 'sports' like a duck to water. It is believed that he was also good at gymnastics which would again have gained the approval of his instructors. (There was a large gymnasium at Shotley, and the youngsters were encouraged to spend some of their free time there, in addition to their compulsory period during the main part of the day). There were also other recreational games such as billiards, draughts and dominoes to while away the free time, apart from reading, writing and studying facilities for periods of reflection. The boys were also allowed out on organised rambles at the weekends.

At that opening stage of his naval life, Alf had little near-contact with officers. However, even from the little he saw, it was obvious that officers were a quite different proposition to the senior ratings and warrant officers, and lived much of their lives in what was virtually a different world. The officers were of many and varying personalities. We shall look at Alf's relationships with officers in a following chapter and at subsequent intervals during his career.

Author's collection. An anonymous postcard, c.1910.

A Dining Hall at Shotley. This was how Alf would have eaten his meals.

Now, with effect from the 27th May 1911 - after only about ten weeks at Shotley - Alf was posted to the Boys Training Establishment which was housed in "HMS *Impregnable"*, at Devonport. It is probable that, despite his slightly rocky start, Alf had nevertheless been chosen as being potentially suitable material for 'fast-track' promotion within the service. It is known that such boys were transferred to the Advanced Class at *Impregnable*. Whereas all Boys could expect to be automatically made up to Boy I status after 9 months, Boys who qualified for the Advanced Class at *Impregnable* would be promoted to Boy I in much less than 9 months. As we shall see, Alf would actually make the transition in 6 months, so it seems almost certain that he had been put in the Advanced Class. It is probable that he suddenly saw the potential rewards, started to 'put his back into things', and never really looked back.

It is a near-certainty that the training establishments were under pressure to find as many promising boys as possible to be put in the Advanced Class, for 'Jacky' FISHER's new Dreadnoughts had brought technological developments, especially in gunnery, which required agile and quite well-educated brains to master, and suitable young men were hard to find amongst the sort of lads who were volunteering for service. Perhaps Alf had made a good impression when he had appeared as a 'Requestman', making enquiries about 'buying himself out', and this had somehow set some semi-official enquiries in motion which had revealed that bullying, at a quite unacceptable level, had been going on. Captain C.S. HICKLEY had taken over command of HMS *Ganges* at around this period of 1911, and one wonders if it came to the attention of this 'new broom' that here was a young man of considerable potential that the Navy was in serious danger of losing. Be that as it may, Alf was posted to *Impregnable* on 27th May 1911, evidently to join the Advanced Class.[48]

Author's collection. Postcard No.7404 by Valentine's, reproduced by courtesy of St Andrews University Library. Card dated 1887.

HMS *Impregnable* on the Hamoaze, with her boats busily clustered around her. Another masted hulk, probably the 'receiving ship' *Circe*, lies in the mid-distance and yet another hulk in the further offing. This fine picture pre-dates Alf's posting to *Impregnable*.

In a way, this transfer was a step into the past, for *Impregnable* was essentially still based on hulks rather than embodying the 'land establishment' concept which had been instituted at Shotley. Indeed, the local businessmen in Devonport had been greatly disappointed when Shotley had been chosen to be developed as a land establishment rather than their own area.

Impregnable was a former battleship of considerable size, for she had previously mounted 110 guns, had a displacement of 6,557 tons, a length of 275 feet and, at her

---

[48] The author is greatly indebted to the HMS *Impregnable* Association for some of the detail which follows.

peak, she'd had a peacetime complement of no less than 1,000 men. She had been built in 1860, had steam as well as sail, and had originally been named HMS *Howe*

As of about 1905 *Impregnable I* had her fore, main and mizzen masts stepped, and her bowsprit still standing. However, by 1911, when Alf joined her, it seems likely that her masts and standing rigging would have been greatly reduced. This would have permitted her main deck to be roofed-over, both to extend her accommodation and to provide better all-weather protection. Way back in 1894, the hulk had been so badly infested with cockroaches that there were standing orders that every Boy Seaman had to turn up for his breakfast with an enamel plate filled with cockroaches that he had killed - otherwise, he was given nothing to eat! Fortunately, matters in regard to fumigation had improved to an appreciable degree during the 17 years which had elapsed before Alf joined *Impregnable*. One could not swear to it, but, so far as we know, Alf never had to make any 'cockroach culls'.

By the time that Alf joined in 1911, the need for accommodation had grown, and there were actually three hulks moored in line, and connected to each other by gangways.

Impregnable III, Impregnable II and *Impregnable I*, moored in line and with an inter-connecting gangway clearly visible between the further vessels. Ships boats are active around the hulks, with further boats in reserve on the falls.

The hulks were known respectively as *Impregnable I, II and III*. Impregnable II was the former *Inconstant* (an obsolete steam-frigate), which had arrived at Devonport in 1906, and Impregnable III was the former *Black Prince*, which had arrived just the previous year. There was another hulk, called the *Circe*, built in 1827, which had long acted as a 'receiving ship', and would, years later, become known as Impregnable IV. All these hulks were, at that time, moored in Mutton Cove.[49]

Having already spent ten weeks at *Ganges*, Alf *may* have short-circuited some of the normal acceptance procedures at *Impregnable*. However, if he had followed the

---

[49] At a later date they would be moved upstream, to give them better protection against wind and tide.

standard routine, Alf would first of all have been taken aboard the *Circe* for up to two weeks, having any deficiencies in his kit made up, being given a hammock, and continuing with gymnastics, swimming lessons and so forth, whilst being observed medically for any sign of infectious disease.[50] All being well, he would then have been transferred to *Impregnable I*, placed in a division of either port or starboard watch, and been given a ticket with his ship's number, the number of his mess, his hammock, the name of his petty-officer instructor and so forth. His life at *Impregnable* may now be said to have properly commenced, as one of a 'mess' of 20 boys, all under one instructor.

As a daily routine, Alf would have been roused out of his hammock at 5.00 a.m., to lash up his hammock, stow it away in the nettings on the bulwarks of the upper deck, wash himself, have a cup of cocoa, and fall in for cleaning ship and scrubbing decks.[51] At 7.00 a.m., he would have had gymnastics and/or 'boat pulling' (i.e. rowing), before taking his breakfast. After breakfast he would have been fallen in for inspection and to attend church service under the ship's chaplain. He would then have attended school.

Author's collection. A postcard by Gale & Polden, being No. 6021 in their Nelson Series. Card of date c.1905.

The Schoolroom of HMS *Impregnable*, with its blackboards, school desks and benches, but in the almost Nelsonian setting of a large 'wooden-wall' man-o'-war, with its deckhead beams and their supporting 'knees', steel stanchions, deckhead lanterns, solid masts and, doubtless, the gentle but constant movement of a ship floating in sheltered waters. It was the land which would now feel strangely 'immobile' to Alf, on stepping ashore and starting to walk with his rolling sailor's gait.

---

[50] In those pre-inoculation, pre-antibiotics days, infectious diseases were a very serious problem in the confined living spaces of a ship, where they could spread with distressing speed.

[51] The practice of stowing the lashed-up hammocks in the 'nettings' was an old one. In Nelson's time, during a naval battle, the 'wall' made by the hammocks (coupled with protection by netting spread overhead) had provided men who were in exposed positions on the upper deck with some protection against musket-balls, flying splinters and also shot-away 'blocks', spars and rigging falling from overhead. Also, a properly-lashed hammock would float for a considerable time, and could act as a life-preserver should the ship founder. Finally, being exposed to the air served to keep the hammocks 'fresh' and thus, if scrubbed and washed at intervals, reasonably free from body-odour and infestation.

School was both for everyday subjects and for the more specialised naval lessons in seamanship, gunnery and gymnastics, the lessons being interrupted at 1.00 p.m. for a 'meat and veg' dinner, perhaps followed by 'figgy duff' or some such pudding.[52] This meal would have been followed by field sports on the recreation field on the Cremyll (i.e. Cornish) side of the Hamoaze River.

Author's collection. Postcard by Valentine's, manually-numbered 48714 and dating from 1905. Image reproduced by courtesy of St Andrews University Library.

Cremyll, near Devonport

Cremyll, just across the river from Devonport where HMS *Impregnable* was moored during Alf's time there. One of the ship's boats is at the landing steps in the foreground of this photograph, and other boats are rowing and sailing in the mid-distance. A crowd watches.

The recreation grounds on the Cremyll side were extensive and they included facilities for gymnastics, cricket, football and hockey. Tea would follow on afterwards. When the summer months arrived, with their longer hours of daylight, tea would be taken as a mid-afternoon break, from 3.30 to 4.00pm, and sports continued afterwards. Tea consisted of bread and jam. Supper, at 7.00 p.m., was of bread and butter and jam, or dripping. There would then have been a spell of free time for writing letters, reading, etc., before hammocks were slung at 8.00 p.m. Pipe Down would have been at 9.00 p.m.[53] This, then, would have been Alf's more or less daily routine at *Impregnable*.

On 14th September 1911 Alf passed for First Class Boy, gaining an immediate increase both in privileges and in his pocket-money. (The latter would have risen from 6d a day to 9d a day - quite a difference in those days – although there were always 'charges' which were levied on pay by authority, so Alf saw only a small proportion of it.) His kit would also have been augmented at that time. He would have learned a tremendous amount in the 3½ months leading up to that September (six months if one

---

[52] 'Figgy Duff' was a suet pudding containing raisins or other stewed fruit.

[53] It will be noted that this schedule differs slightly from what was shown to take place at Shotley. Some of this was driven by the fact that *Impregnable* was still a ship, albeit a hulk, whereas *Ganges* was a land-based 'stone frigate'. Other minor departures in procedure may be attributable to fading memories by various writers of that now-distant era. The general thrust is, however, in very good agreement.

includes his time at *Ganges*), especially in subjects such as seamanship. The groundwork had also been laid by which he would become a very enthusiastic sportsman, his naturally good co-ordination of hand and eye helping him to become particularly good at musketry and field hockey. He would go on to hone those skills to a high standard. By now, thanks to training in the so-called 'bathing-trays' - large tanks 50 ft long floating beside the ship - he had long passed the initial qualification test of being able to swim four lengths of the tray in loose 'duck' clothing, and he would have graduated to free swimming in the river.[54] He was thus on his way to becoming an exceptionally strong swimmer, and he would go on developing himself at it during his service career, up to life-saving standard and beyond.

Becoming a First Class Boy meant that he would have started to have responsibilities laid on his shoulders, such, perhaps, as marching the Boys of his mess from class to class and generally being expected to exert minor 'leadership' roles.

Alf received further, more specialised training in seamanship, gunnery and mechanical work in the following months. The gunnery training included not only the laying and firing of guns (including some aspects of deflection shooting), but also the stripping of weapons, which ranged from light Maxim guns up to much-heavier 4.7 inch guns. To some extent, under the guidance of an armourer rating, he would also have learnt something of the cleaning, repair and replacement of any damaged components of this equipment. The mechanical work included experience in using various tools, aimed at being able to provide some assistance as engine-room auxiliaries, and in effecting minor ship-repairs (such as might be made necessary by weather or battle-damage), doing so under the guidance of engine room artificers.

Also at this time, the signalling branch of the Navy was beginning to come into its own, wireless transmission and receiving having by now become a reality and thus utterly transforming the distance over which ship-to-shore and ship-to-ship signalling (formerly only by the visual means of signal flag and semaphore) could ensue. Already, the intakes of boys were being questioned as to which branch they wished to specialise in, and, based on aptitude, some selection of boys to particular branches was coming about.

In the general context of gunnery, some of the exercise-work was now becoming inter-related with 'reality', with (for example) a strange set-up in the gymnasium (called a 'Dummy-Loader') which simulated the sheer hard work, co-ordination, team-work, and rhythm required of a gun-crew firing a weapon at a high repetitive rate, and using a realistic weight of shot (usually 100 lb., which was on the limit that a robust boy could handle). Role-changing was practised within each gun-crew, to widen the skills of each boy. [*The use of the 'Dummy-Loader' would continue deep into Alf's future career. The machine was regarded as invaluable in training gun crews to very high levels of skill and speed. When one considers a six-inch gun, firing shells weighing 100 lb and getting off 10 rounds per minute, or a four-inch gun achieving 20 rounds per minute with shells of 25 lb. weight, the need for co-ordination and rhythm becomes very apparent. The need*

---

[54] For reasons of safety, these 'trays' had bottom boards spaced close enough to prevent a boy's body slipping through between them, but wide enough to permit free circulation of the river water. The boards were barnacled and weeded and generally unpleasant to actually stand on - apart from being deliberately set so low that all but the taller boys were out of their depth. Boys who were terrified of the water and could not bring themselves to swim were spurned both by their peers and by the instructors.

for precision in every movement, to prevent the possible risk of serious human injury and/or damage to the weaponry, also becomes evident.]

Other work in the gym was also designed to generally raise levels of strength and hand-to-eye co-ordination, as well as fitness, and also to bring out a certain amount of aggression. For example, field sports were encouraged and boxing particularly so. Pride in the Royal Navy was also engendered in many ways, such as by doubling smartly when moving from one task to another in the daily round, by marching smartly behind bands when going to this or that entertainment ashore (e.g. the local theatres), by having bands playing on some evenings, by having concerts and magic-lantern shows on board ship, and so on.

Boys were also encouraged to take a pride in their personal appearance, to 'dhobi' (i.e. wash) their clothes regularly and to iron and press their trousers, tunics and other items to bring them up 'just so'. Bad or careless behaviour was punished - severely so when merited - but good behaviour, in effect, earned group rewards.

Author's collection. Postcard No. 6018 by Gale & Polden Ltd. Card postally used in 1908.

Firing by Lanyard. Boys from HMS *Impregnable* in training with a light field-gun on the banks of the Hamoaze River. This photo slightly precedes Alf's time.

It is worth adding that Devonport was then a busy shipyard as well as a naval base, leading to opportunities for other co-operative enterprises. In this regard, it may be noteworthy that, during Alf's training period at *Impregnable*, the battlecruiser HMS *Lion* (later to be Admiral BEATTY's famous flagship at the Battle of Jutland and to become quite well-known to Alf in 1917-19) was being completed at Devonport.[55] Also during Alf's time, the hull of the battleship HMS *Centurion* was launched there. *(She had been laid down in January 1911 and would also be present at the Battle of Jutland in 1916. She would then have a very varied, unusual and very useful career, for she would become a 'semi-indestructible and constantly-repaired target ship' in her middle age, would be disguised in her old age in 1939/43 as a 'modern battleship', to tempt German bombers*

---

[55] She was commissioned in June 1912.

away from the 'genuine articles' at Scapa Flow and, later, in the 'Med', and, in her 'geriatric years', she would be sunk as a protective blockship for the celebrated 'Mulberry Harbour' at Arrowmanches, off the Normandy landing beaches of 1944 – helping to save the Harbour from a severe storm which virtually destroyed its American 'twin' a few days after the assault landings.)

Alf left *Impregnable* on 13th March 1912, with a year of naval training completed, including six months at Boy I level. This first promotion meant that, all continuing well, he was already 'earmarked' to become an Able Seaman soon after he achieved the age of eighteen years. It seems quite clear that the high standards of the Navy, and some of its tradition, were already becoming absorbed into his soul. He was fit and 'bouncy' and becoming quite confident within himself and his abilities, though he knew he still had an enormous amount to learn, especially in 'seamanship'.

Author's collection. Postcard in the 'Wellington Series', published by Gale & Polden Ltd. C.1912.

A 'C' Class destroyer enters dock at Devonport Dockyard circa 1912. A line of washing hangs from her fore-stay. Examination with a magnifying-glass reveals no 'holidays' (i.e. gaps) along the line. The hulks of *Impregnable I* and *Impregnable II* can be seen in the distance, beyond the two-funnelled troopship lying at the mole in the middle-distance.

Alf had also acquired some knowledge of the specialised vocabulary (formal and informal) which is a rich part of Naval Life, and his everyday speech was probably already well 'larded' with it. As a parting gift he was given a small bible with a 'presentation panel', signed by the Chaplain of HMS *Impregnable*.[56]

Let's take a peek at Alf's private life.

---

[56] This bible is still held in trust by the author.

Private Life

Author's Note:

I feel that I should preface what I propose to write about Alf's private life by stating that some of it is inevitably based on conjecture on my part. I have done my best in trying to 'cobble together' little bits of 'Family Legend', stitching in this and that 'known fact', and trying to create some sort of 'logical progression' out of it all. I am very conscious that 'accuracy' and 'depth' are in rather short supply in the early years. There is no doubt that both these aspects improve considerably as the story reaches the 1930s, since my own memories of events become personal ones from that time on. [It is fortunate that I have been able to garner other 'personal' memories from my siblings and cousins to help to span the gap from the late 1920s into the 1930s. Also that Alf's carefully annotated photographic album, which I inherited, 'begins' in the early 1920s – and also that my maternal grandmother frequently told me legends about our 'family history', albeit mainly on the distaff side.]

Should a family member wish to raise and validate a different view regarding any aspect bearing on Alf's private life and indeed on those of his siblings (and perhaps on the children of the ensuing generation), I will be very pleased to consider the insertion of a 'qualifying comment' in any further printings of this work. It must be borne in mind, however, that one child's trauma are not necessarily akin to those of another child of the same family, and also that the mind of one person may totally 'block' certain highly uncomfortable memories, for the sake of sheer sanity, whereas another sibling may nurse forever what amounts to those same memories and keep them very much alive and vital in their minds. Perhaps the most remarkable thing is the high degree of <u>congruity</u> of memory which my research has shown to clearly exist between the siblings in so many instances, and which has been written into this book.

Well, let's now get back to the Great Britain of mid-1912. Their Majesties King George V and Queen Mary, who had been crowned on 22nd June 1911, were the new monarchs. Queen Alexandra had become the Queen Mother, the Boer War was already fading into the past, and Germany was showing signs of creating a sizeable Navy, now including 'Dreadnought' types, under the ambitions and urgings of the Kaiser. For the moment however, Great Britain was secure. She had a vast Empire and, especially with the introduction of her series of revolutionary 'Dreadnought' battleships since 1906, looked to her large Royal Navy and her small but very professional Regular Army to protect all the related activities of world-wide trade and expansionism. There was no Air Force as such, though the first crossing of the English Channel by an aircraft piloted by the Frenchman Blériot had just occurred and the British Army had been experimenting with man-carrying kites and balloons for a decade and more – and had, indeed, used man-carrying balloons for observation purposes during the Boer War.

Alf may have had a brief leave when he left *Ganges*. He certainly had a home leave when he was at *Impregnable*, for he appeared in the interesting family photograph which is reproduced on the following page. As this inset taken from that photograph reveals, his cap-band bore the legend HMS *Impregnable*. This would date the photo at around mid-March 1912, when he was four months short of his 17th birthday. *This is the first known image of Alf.*

As clearly shows in Alf's face, his 'feathers were still definitely ruffled' and he was far from being a 'happy bunny'. He was still upset at whatever had been the basis of the great row with his father, and he still greatly resented the fact that his father had not 'bought him out'. Their first encounter on Alf's return home on leave would have been difficult and 'frosty' for them both. As we have already seen, very harsh words must have been exchanged during the quarrel and the hurt was so grievous on both sides, that neither father nor son could unbend enough to make the first move towards a possible reconciliation. There is also the possibility that Alf may have seized a high moral ground, adding to the difficulty his father would have experienced in 'humbling himself' to reach amity between them. Moreover, the father's hurt probably went very deep into his *psyche*, and his innate feeling of 'betrayal' by Alf would doubtless have continued to run very strongly indeed. The father may also have sensed that Alf was already settling quite well into 'naval life', and, perhaps with some justification, have felt that Alf was taking a rather 'dog in the manger' attitude about not having been 'bought out'

With Alf's mother now dead and departed, it seems that, *faute de mieux,* Nellie, as the *de facto* woman of the house, was relied upon to act as a sort of 'go-between' betwixt father and son. However, she probably felt that she lacked the necessary age and status to perform that conciliatory role. Moreover, her nature was not well-suited to the qualities required of a neutral conciliator. Instead, her orientation may well have been to 'divide and rule', filtering and de-humanising the words submitted to her by the father to pass on to the son, and *vice versa*, so that the verbal exchanges may well have remained more impersonal and bleak than the participants themselves may have realised.

One has to remember that Alf's impetuous departure would have added significantly not only to the loading on Alf's father, but also on each of the four children who had stayed. Nellie and her older brother, Berty John (alias 'Jack'), might, with considerable justification, have heartily resented the fact that Alf had escaped from the domestic drudgery in which his elder brother and three sisters were perforce involved six days a week in helping their father to run the pub, with Berty John and Nellie having to do so full-time. It must have been a mercy for them that pubs were generally shut on Sundays in that era.

However, it seems likely that Nellie, probably with some help from Rose, would have been expected 'to cook Sunday lunch', on what 'by rights' should have been her day off! And Rose and Eva would probably have been looked-to to do the washing-up. There would also have been the need to deal with the family's laundry, the task probably again descending on Nellie's shoulders, with some aid from Rose. (One might hope that their father used a local 'bagwash' service for much of it – though Alf no longer bringing in his wage as a Messenger Boy for the GPO may have necessitated further economies on the 'Home Front'.) One bright spot was that the supply of piped water had at last been restored, greatly easing the family's day-to-day toil.

Author's collection. Photographer unknown. Print kindly donated by Raymond PENNEY Esq.

Alf (aged 16) on home leave from HMS *Impregnable* circa March 1912. Alf and 'Jack' (just turning 18) stand behind the seated Rose (13) and Nellie (now turned 15). Little Eva (11) stands between her elder sisters. Note the mature air of Nellie, despite her young years. It seems that this picture was taken in the back yard of their pub, 'The Crown'.

Probably driven by the hard responsibilities as 'barmaid' and 'homemaker' which had been thrust upon her, the photograph above shows that Nellie already had the air of a quite mature woman, though she was still only just turned 15, having had her birthday in mid-January. As the older sister, and by virtue of her strong personality, Nellie was clearly 'in charge' of the female side of the family and would continue to dominate them as the years sped by. She was well-dressed for the photograph, perhaps showing to the world at large that she had finished with school and become her own woman.

In contrast, her two younger sisters were still attending school, and they were dressed in matching 'petticoat dresses', evidently as a form of rather unflattering uniform. Whether or not the two younger girls had also specially dressed for the photographer is unknown, but they certainly looked clean and neat, despite the pressures they would have been under in helping their father to run the pub, with Nellie working 'full-time' and her sisters toiling during their out-of-school-hours. One might well say that their clean appearance was a credit to their father's and Nellie's supervision and management.

The other feature which strikes home is the strong and capable look of Rose, then still two months short of her 14th birthday. Note her solid-looking boots and the large size of her hands. It seems that she had inherited those large 'coachman's hands' from her father. Eva, her 11 year-old sister looks quite fragile beside her.

Jack may look just marginally less neat and clean in appearance, but his multi-functional job as potman, barman, ostler and carriage attendant 'rolled into one', may have detracted from his smartness. None of the youngsters looks happy, although the need to hold a pose for the required long exposure would have inevitably led to their expressions being somewhat 'set'.[57]

Family legend suggests that Eva, the least 'put-upon' by family chores, was very taken by Alf's uniform and perhaps the one person who seemed to be interested to learn something of Alf's adventures away from home. For his part, one understands that Alf was becoming much more settled in his naval career by the time he left *Impregnable*, and, sailor-like, quite prepared to do his bit on the 'home front' whenever he returned on leave. Perhaps he tried to 'get himself in Nellie's good books' by assuming some of her many chores and trying to persuade her to take a few hours off, to give her a break from the endless work.[58] Whether his help would have been welcomed is, however, uncertain.

On the whole, one imagines that Alf would have been quite pleased when his leave was up and that, after all his 'basic training', he was off to sea at last. His 'Grand Adventure' was about to begin.

---

[57] It would take a great many years of dedicated development and experimentation before truly 'high-speed' photographic emulsions came into general use. Early emulsions required relatively long periods of exposure - several seconds as opposed to tenths, hundredths or thousandths of seconds. However, camera lenses (not yet needing to be 'colour-corrected') were quickly improving. Indeed, the sharpness of the image above is a credit to the apparatus and to the photographer who was using it.

It would be interesting to know the circumstances under which the photo was taken. e.g. whether the motivation arose from a sales opportunity taken by a peripatetic photographer who was staying at 'The Crown', perhaps to part-pay for his accommodation, or whether it was Alfred Wm himself who was motivated by Alf's return home on leave to arrange for a joint portrait of his teenage children to be taken. However, we have no information on that score.

[58] We will consider some of those many domestic chores – the cleaning of ashes from the grates, the laying and lighting of coal-fires, the maintenance and lighting of oil-lamps and gas mantles, the heating of water for washing-up of glasses and of dishes, and for personal bathing, etc., etc., at a later stage.

CHAPTER THREE:

HMS *VANGUARD* (1912)

Having left the old hulks which made up the Devonport-based HMS *Impregnable,* Alf certainly took a huge leap into the future when he first set foot aboard the inspirational HMS *Vanguard* (Captain A.D. RICARDS, RN). This fine vessel was one of the three battleships which made up the St Vincent class. She was still relatively new, it being just three years since she was first commissioned.

Author's collection. An anonymous postcard c.1910.
(A Serial No. 3410 appears where postage stamp was to be applied.)

"Brand New": HMS *Vanguard* leaving the Vickers Shipyard at Barrow-in-Furness in 1910. She is riding quite high, and clearly has yet to take her normal complement of stores, fuel and ammunition on board.

HMS *Vanguard* had paid off from her first-ever commission at 0900 on the 27th March 1912 at No.6 Wharf in the North Keyham Yard, Devonport. At 1600, that same day, 265 ratings from Chatham, 55 Royal Marines and a handful of RN and RM officers had joined ship to form the nucleus of her new company for her second commission. Alf was surely one of those 265 ratings, and he must have been overwhelmed by his new posting, which had 'officially' commenced on the 14th March 1912.

One assumes that, at the end of his leave, he had joined his new draft at HMS *Pembroke* (the Naval barracks at Chatham) and then travelled with his draft to Devonport by train. He may well have thought it was a bit ironic that his first commission after leaving *Impregnable* should have brought him straight back to Devonport. Still, at least he would know his way about the area when the time came for a bit of a run ashore with his new shipmates, especially those Boys who had trained solely at *Ganges* and had never yet set foot in the West Country. This situation might well turn out to be to his advantage.

Author's collection. A postcard by Gale & Polden Ltd., Nelson House, Portsmouth, issued c.1904.

Sailors Mustering at Divisions on the Parade Ground at the Royal Naval Barracks, Chatham, then newly-built. A near-decade later, the 265 Chatham-based ratings (including Alf), who joined HMS *Vanguard* at Devonport on 27th March 1912, would have been very familiar with this almost unchanging scene at the 'stone frigate' called "HMS *Pembroke*".

Alf's new ship was one of the third series of 'FISHER's Dreadnoughts', following hard on the heels of the first and second series. Like them, she represented a totally new concept in ship design, especially (though by no means solely), in terms of gunnery. Whereas, in Nelson's day, ships had usually fought at very close ranges, exchanging broadsides at almost point-blank range, one of the First Sea Lord 'Jacky' FISHER's many maxims was *'Frappez vite et frappez fort'* and he had foreseen the new ships fighting at long ranges, and needing to have relatively high speeds of manoeuvre to help them to control the range within the limits that would best suit them, whilst, at the same time, putting, and maintaining, the enemy at a disadvantage.[59] His principle was to have these new turbine-powered Royal Navy ships armed with heavy guns, so that they could hit extremely hard at that long range. Accuracy in gun-aiming was going to be of the greatest importance when a war broke out. As we shall see, the Royal Navy was experiencing great technical difficulties (and considerable problems in changing 'mind sets') in meeting the aspirations which 'Jacky' FISHER cherished for this radically new concept of combat at long range.

We shall look more closely at this huge ship, HMS *Vanguard*, shortly. First, however, let's look at her complement. When her establishment was full, there would be over 750 men aboard, made up of 50 Officers, 315 Seamen and Boys, 90 Royal Marines, 225 'Engine-Room Establishment' and 75 'Non-Executive' Ratings.

---

[59] *'Frappez vite et frappez fort'* was an axiom ('Hit fast and hit hard') once used by Napoleon Bonaparte, which Jacky FISHER had adopted.

Discipline was clearly likely to be tight in this huge 'floating barracks and gun-battery'. For the moment, however, the ship was in a strange state of comings and goings, for she had other drafts joining and no less than 350 ratings were about to be drafted out of the ship to go to the Naval Barracks at Chatham. There, depending upon the career-status of each individual concerned, they would either attend for courses and re-qualifying examinations, or, hopefully (rather than 'rotting' in barracks), be re-drafted to other ships almost as soon as any accumulated 'long leaves' had been granted and 'savoured' by the individuals concerned.

Photograph reproduced by courtesy of The National Archives, Ref. ADM 176/742, dated 1911.

HMS *Vanguard*, as originally completed, and now with her normal complement of stores aboard. Thus she is lying at her normal draught, and not 'riding high', as shown in the photograph two pages previously.

Currently, in addition to her complement, *Vanguard* had at least a hundred dockyard men working on board, because she was undergoing appreciable modifications. In fact, the dockyard men had started working aboard on 19th March, eight days before Alf joined and shortly after the ship had returned from the Mediterranean. The numbers of dockyard men had built up steadily over those days. The most visible modification which had taken place since she was first completed was an increase and re-disposition of the ship's installation of small-calibre guns for close-range protection against torpedo boats and their like, and a modification of her aftercastle, evidently to facilitate the installation of twin port and starboard searchlight platforms towards the same defensive end. It is believed that these changes were taking place during the refit which was in progress when Alf joined the ship.

It seems that these increases in the short-range weaponry of *Vanguard* were in response to information gained about German manoeuvres. Contemporary photographs of such manoeuvres showed flotillas of fast German destroyers delivering torpedo-attacks on a 'hostile' fleet on the opposite flank of their own fleet. To do so, they were performing the highly dangerous act of racing across the bows of 'friendly' battleships which were manoeuvring in multiple columns. The hazard was greatly increased because the battleships were 'pre-occupied' in firing and 'spotting' broadsides from their main guns which were in mock but realistic action against that same 'hostile' fleet.

If the Germans were practising hard at such fast, close-range, bold and hard-hitting attacks, it clearly behove the British Admiralty to take appropriate counter-measures by greatly increasing the defensive close-range armament of their heavy warships to give them a high chance of crippling or sinking the speedy German destroyers before they could close to effective torpedo-launching distance.[60]

Photograph reproduced by courtesy of The National Archives, Ref. No. ADM 176/742, dated 1911.

A fine stern view of HMS *Vanguard*, taken during her first commission, a year before Alf joined her. Note the two close-support small-calibre guns mounted on top of her 'Y' Turret. These guns would later be moved forward to her 'X' Turret, and further small-calibre guns would be added elsewhere, most notably atop her 'A' Turret. The single searchlight tower between 'Y' and 'X' Turrets would later become a twin-tower structure. Her very tall foremast and mainmast carry wireless aerials. The Admiralty were rapidly expanding their ability to exchange long-range wireless transmissions by means of relay stations set up strategically around the globe. Soon the Admiralty would be seeking to control 'far-flung' operations on an 'hour-by-hour' basis – not always to the advantage of the senior officer 'on the spot', as we shall later see.

It would quickly have become apparent to Alf and the Boys who joined with him that the officers were appreciative of the modifications to their ship, but nevertheless anxious to be clear of the dockyard 'maties' and all their clutter as quickly as could be managed, so that the ship's company could quickly be set to restoring *Vanguard* to her normal state of pristine beauty.

---

[60] It is interesting to reflect that Admiral JELLICOE would be criticised in certain quarters because (in order to 'comb' incoming torpedo-tracks) he turned his battleships *away* following an attack by German destroyers (i.e. rather than turning *towards* them) at the subsequent Battle of Jutland – thus losing an important and fast-fleeting opportunity to close with the German battleships and battlecruisers. However, it may be that he ordered his battleships to turn away because he knew what a real threat the German destroyers posed at close quarters. (See later comments ref. Admiral JELLICOE.)

For the Boys newly joined, remembering their way around this large and complex vessel must have been quite difficult at first. And they may well have found a disconcerting measure of scorn and derision from the older hands if they attempted to ask for directions. At least the Boys would have had the consolation that the ship was stationary and semi-inactive for their first few days aboard, rather than being immediately at sea, perhaps rolling and pitching in rough weather. On the other hand, the ship was only half-alive, and the presence and equipment of the dockyard men, perhaps with the 'tween-decks lighting being reduced at times, and sometimes with considerable riveting and other noises being generated, must have added its own level of confusion to the new hands.[61]

One feature the Boys would have found straightaway was that was that the ratings, by long tradition confined to the cramped forepart of a ship, were now accommodated in the *after*part of this new ship. (The officers, who had previously enjoyed the more spacious accommodation in the afterpart of older ships, were now housed amidships.)

The Boys were immediately divided into Port and Starboard Watches, each broken down into four 'parts of ship', namely Fo'c'sle, Fore-Top, Main-Top and After Castle - (abbreviated to 'F.X', 'F.T', 'M.T' and 'A.X'). They were shown their messes, allocated lockers for their kit, shown where to sling their hammocks and where to take up their varied 'Action' and 'Cruising' stations. And they would soon have been receiving instruction about the structure and history of their new home.

The Boys would have learned that *Vanguard* had been laid down by Vickers, Sons and Maxim at Barrow-in-Furness on 2nd April 1908, launched on the 22nd February 1909, and completed on 10th February 1910, i.e. in the very short time of only 22 months. She had broken a record at her launch, for, due to her heavily armoured barbettes being near-completed *whilst she was still on the stocks*, she had weighed no less than 10,250 tons when she went down the slipway – some 3,250 tons more than her two slightly 'elder' sisters, *St Vincent* and *Collingwood*, and a record weight for any battleship launched up to that time.

When completed, like her sisters, *Vanguard* had a displacement of 19,250 tons (and of about 23,000 tons 'deep load'). She had cost £1.76 million - almost twice the cost of a 'pre-Dreadnought' battleship. Her length was 536 feet, and her beam was 84 feet. Her designed mean load draught was 27 feet, but (as of 1912) she had a draught of 29' 3" forward and 31' 9" aft. [By way of giving scale to this, it took no less than 73.45 tons to increase her draught by just one inch. The difference in draught between her *designed* mean load displacement and her *actual* mean load displacement was in excess of 3ft - or, say, the equivalent of at least 2.6 thousand tons. She really was quite a beast!]

The ship was driven by eighteen Babcock and Wilcox boilers linked to eight Parsons Turbines, and developed 24,500 shaft horsepower to give her an official maximum speed of 21 knots, though it is probable that she could actually exceed 22 knots. Propelled by four three-bladed screws of manganese bronze made by the specialist firm of J. Stone & Co., her cruising speed was of the order of 10 knots, at which she had a range of about 7,000 miles.

---

[61] The standard system adopted by the Royal Navy in clearly numbering every compartment in a logical and sequential manner would undoubtedly have been a positive help. The Boys would already have been taught the basic system at *Ganges* or *Impregnable*.

A postcard by Sankey Photo, postally used at Barrow 08 Mar 1909.

The launching of HMS *Vanguard* at Barrow by Mrs McKENNA, on 22nd February 1909. There had been considerable relief when her 10,250 tons had slid gracefully down the ways.

Vanguard's main armament consisted of ten 12-inch Breech-Loading Mk XI* guns.[62] These big guns were in twin turrets, one mounted on the F'c'sle, and two on the Quarter-Deck (all placed along the centre-line), plus two twin 'broadside' turrets mounted amidships, one on the port side and one on the starboard. These guns were so arranged as to also have forward-firing capability. The individual shells weighed 850 lb each, and *Vanguard* could hurl a 'broadside' of 6,800 lb. of shell (i.e. a little under three tons) as far as 20 miles, and make at least six such broadsides in each ten minutes of rapid fire. However, as we shall see, it would be more usual to fire half the armament, and then the next 'half' (whilst the first 'half' re-loaded), and thus to increase the frequency of the 'salvoes' falling on the enemy, giving him precious little respite and hopefully keeping him off balance.[63] The ship had an unusually long forecastle and a freeboard of almost 30 feet at the bow. This kept her deck reasonably dry in bad weather and thus helped to

---

[62] According to 'Hamilton's Papers'† at the NMM, Greenwich (ref HTN/219) two of the guns were actually of the former Mk XI version, which had the same inner 'A' tubes as the 'Mk XI*', but differed slightly in their outer tubes. This same source states that, to protect the gun-crews, the gun-ports were as small as possible consistent with the required 'travel' for the guns, and that the gunlayers were further protected by 2-inch splinter screens secured to the front of the gunhouse and fitting very closely over the guns. [†Louis Henry Keppel HAMILTON, then a young naval officer (and the son of Admiral Sir F T HAMILTON, GCVO, KGB), was fated to also be knighted and to become an Admiral in his own right.] The author is indebted to professional researcher Robert O'HARA of Kew for finding a number of interesting personal papers at TNA, such as these of Louis HAMILTON, and also several relevant photos.

[63] A 'broadside' involved the firing of both guns in every twin turret which would bear on the target. A 'salvo' involved only one gun per twin turret firing, those guns then being reloaded whilst the next salvo was fired from the guns which had remained unfired during the first salvo, and so on. The intervals at which fire fell on the target was clearly much shorter when firing salvoes than when firing broadsides, though the volume of fire per incident of fall-of-shot was correspondingly less.

enhance the quality of her gunnery. This 'dryness' held good despite the fact that she tended to drive 'through' waves almost as much as to 'ride' them.

By the time Alf joined the ship, in addition to her main armament, *Vanguard* had a secondary armament of eighteen 4-inch Mk VII quick-firing guns on P II mountings.[64] Each 4-inch gun fired a shell of 25 lb. and could get off 20 rounds per minute.[65] The guns were sited at various points to give all-round short-range defence against such light, fast and highly manoeuvrable enemy forces, (e.g. torpedo-boats) as might manage to penetrate the long-range fire of *Vanguard's* heavy 12-inch guns.

Author's collection. Postcard No. 7264 A, as printed by the Rotary Photo Company c.1914.

HMS *Vanguard* undergoing a refit, as denoted by the cranes on the dockside and the fact that the ship is floating high in the water, most of her stores having been removed. (Visual comparison with the waterline of *Vanguard* when at sea – as shown in the previous photographs - suggests that her draught has been reduced by a good five feet – the equivalent of 4.3 thousand tons.) The two 4-inch guns mounted on the roof of 'A' Turret are a part of the additional weaponry added for close-range protection since her original completion by Vickers Ltd. (The pair of 4-inch guns formerly mounted on her 'Y' Turret is now on her 'X' Turret.) Her superstructure aft has also been revised.

Some of the 4" guns were mounted on her main gun-turrets and others elsewhere in her superstructure. (The siting of some of these guns above the turrets meant that their crews certainly had commanding viewpoints, but they would be highly vulnerable to incoming enemy shell-fire. (They would also have been vulnerable to blast effects from their own main guns, which would therefore have been inhibited from firing.) This matter was a cause of concern to certain thinking minds. One presumes that 'higher

---

[64] The modifications she had been undergoing evidently included an addition of six 4" guns.

[65] 'Hamilton's Papers' at the NMM, Greenwich, dated around 1911, (ref HTN/219) slightly disagree, and state that there were 20 'anti-destroyer' guns, on P2* mountings, firing 31 lb projectiles, & using a charge of 9lb 15 ozs. The ammunition allowance was of no less than 650 rounds, the predicted 'expenditure' including 160 rounds for 'night-firing' practice.

authority' viewed the matter as a case of 'when the Devil drives', and felt that they simply had to 'bite on the bullet'.)

HMS *Vanguard* also had a number of yet smaller-calibre close-defence guns, including two 3" guns in the newly established anti-aircraft role, which could hurl their shells to a height of 25,000 ft.[66] Moreover, the ship mounted two 18" torpedo tubes on the broadside and one at the stern, all mounted below the water-line in what were called 'flats'. (Her total 'outfit' consisted of 20 torpedoes.)

Her massive gun turrets had strong barbettes (i.e. supporting cylindrical trunks on which the turrets, powered by electric motors, could be rotated by means of supporting ball-bearings and the use of teethed gearing). The barbettes linked each turret with its magazine-supply, which was sited well below the water-line. These barbettes had 10-inch armour-plate protection, as did her conning tower.[67] Belts of 10-inch armour plate sheathed her hull amidships along the water-line. Wing bunkers, holding much of her total load of about 2,800 tons of coal formed another protection against the explosion of a torpedo-hit amidships.[68] Transverse watertight bulkheads divided the ship into eighteen sealable sections.

Profiting from hard-won experience with HMS *Dreadnought*, which had been the revolutionary first ship of this radically new type, the foremast of *Vanguard* was placed ahead of the first funnel rather than in rear of it. A second mast was fitted ahead of the second funnel.[69] Both masts were of tripod design, to provide a sturdy platform for the control towers and maintop, which contained rangefinders and 'fire-control teams'.[70] The tripod construction of the masts meant that they suffered less from vibration when the ship was at speed, and were better able to withstand battle-damage from enemy shell-fire than would have been the case for single (or 'pole') masts.

Vanguard had an array of twenty-six massive booms mounted along her sides, designed to carry anti-torpedo netting. The netting was made of heavy wire.[71] Some of

---

[66] Aeroplanes were a relatively new invention. Training of the first naval airmen had begun in 1911. The 'planes were not yet armed with guns or bombs, but carried out scouting missions. Airships and man-carrying balloons were also in use.

[67] Starting with the '*Canopus*' class of 1896, the armour-plate being used in battleships of the Royal Navy had been made by Krupps of Essen, Germany, 5¾ inches of Krupps armour giving equivalent protection to 7½ inches of the best British-made product at that time (Source: Hamilton's Papers, ref HTN/219 at the NMM, Greenwich). Clearly, this critical supply-situation could not long continue in the increasingly difficult political situation with the Kaiser's Germany, and a suitable British manufacturer would soon have to be firmly established.

[68] Later, she would be converted to burn oil. Oh! The blessing to be free from the filthy and arduous job of 'coaling ship', though, after her conversion, it was said that the movement of the heavy liquid load introduced a sort of 'double-kick' to the ship's roll in a seaway. This had nauseous effects for motion-sensitive members of her company, which were heightened for some of these unfortunate men by the pervasive smell of the oil fuel itself.

[69] In HMS *Dreadnought* it had been found that the funnel-smoke sometimes obscured vision from the maintop, and that the heat from the funnel made the tripod tubing of the mast very hot - sometimes so much so, as when steaming into a head-wind, that it was impossible for men to either climb the ladder mounted inside the tripod-tubing which led aloft to the maintop, or, having got there earlier, to go back from there down to deck-level.

[70] 'Fire-control' meaning 'gunfire-control' (rather than what might be called 'anti-combustion precautions').

[71] This defensive measure was found to be less than effective in World War One, and was abandoned.

these booms were swung out whilst *Vanguard* was in harbour and such boats as she hoisted out each day would then be secured under them when not in actual use. Midshipmen and ratings became expert in walking back and forth along these narrow booms, and swarming up or down the 'Jacob's Ladders' which hung down from the booms to the ship's boats. Even so, in a lively sea, with a ship's boat rising and falling erratically, and possibly 'surging' and 'broaching', the young officers and boat's crews had to keep their wits about them and to 'stay sharp and alert' physically. [*Vanguard's* full complement of boats consisted of two 50ft steam boats, one 42ft sailing launch, one 36ft sailing pinnace, three 32ft sailing cutters (prized for their sailing qualities), one 30ft gig, three 27ft whalers, one 16ft sailing skiff and one 13½ft balsa raft. As would have been stressed to Alf and the other Boys, the condition of a ship's boats were regarded as a pointer to her overall level of efficiency and smartness - probably just before they were told off to scrape and paint one or more of them, just to emphasise the matter.]

Whilst on the subject of boats, on the basis that a 42 ft launch could hold 130 men, a 32 ft cutter 59 men and a 27 ft whaler 27 men, it has been calculated (with the aid of the 'Manual of Seamanship'), that *Vanguard's* boats could hold rather less than 660 men out of her full complement of 750 should the order 'Abandon Ship!' ever have to be given as a full emergency.

During his long career Alf would come to serve on ships which ranged from this massive 'battle wagon' at one extreme, down to a small but sturdy 'ocean-going tug' at the other. To give us a means of readily comparing and contrasting one ship against another, and estimating how each new ship might have struck Alf in regard to his earlier experiences, we shall lay out tables which illustrate the main characteristics of each ship. Starting with this great vessel we shall add progressively, line by line, to these contrasting tabulations, from chapter to chapter of this book.

Basic Details

Name of Ship	Type Of Ship	Displacement (tons)	Year Completed	1st Year Alf srv'd (ship age)	Complement	Max. Length (feet)	Max. Beam (feet)	Draught (feet)	Shaft Horse-Power	Max. Speed (knots)
Vanguard	Dreadnought	19,250	1910	1912 (2)	823	536	84	31.75	24,500	22

Name of Ship	Guns				Torpedo-Tubes		Armour			
	Main		Secondary		A.A		Deck	Side	Turr't	D.C.T
	Calibre	Number	Calibre	Number	Capability	Calibre	Number	(ins)	(ins)	(ins)	(ins)
Vanguard	12"	Ten	4"	Twelve	2x3"	18"	Three	1.5 - 3	10	11	8 – 11

Although the table shows 11 inches of armour for the turrets, the turret structure was relatively complex, certainly with 11 inches on the turret sides, *but only 4½ to 5 inches of armour on the roof.* The roof was actually spanned fore to aft, by three plates (each extending over the full width of the turret), slightly overlapped where they joined and supported by struts at those points. The roof-plates were "*not pierced at all, the securing bolts being screwed in from the outside, so that any fragments flying off, when hit, would fly outwards.*"[72]

Put this in context with the armoured deck having a thickness of only 1.5 to 3-inches, as compared with the ship's sides having 10-inches of armour-plate over her 'vitals', and one can see that the designers had been anticipating close-range fighting with shells impacting almost horizontally against the more or less 'vertical' surfaces (such as the turret-walls and the ship's sides. Whereas, due to arriving at shallow 'glancing angles', it was anticipated that incoming shells fired at close range would tend to ricochet off 'horizontal' surfaces, even if their armoured surfaces were of only of moderate 'solidarity', (such as the turret-roofs and the upper-deck). In other words, the designers were protecting against mainly low-trajectory incoming fire rather than 'plunging, near-vertical, long-range fire'.

Indeed, when the main armament was being calibrated by practice firing, a range of 5,000 yards was kept, and the guns were graduated for a range of 5,000 yards.[73] (Battle-practice, even after the 1914-18 War broke out, seldom, if ever, seems to have been conducted at ranges in excess of 10,000 to 15,000 yards.) This all seems to run counter to 'Jacky' FISHER's concept of Dreadnoughts firing at very long ranges.

We'll come back to the subject of the ship, her construction, and her weapons systems a bit later. So far as Alf's life on board was concerned, we know that the ship's company were paid their wages on 30th March 1912.

Author's collection. A postcard in the 'Valentines Series', photo by Crockett. Image reproduced by courtesy of St Andrews University Library. Card postally used at Invergordon on 23rd August 1906.

Ship unknown. Sailors receiving their pay. This picture precedes Alf's time, but little change had occurred and, as here, Alf would have had to learn exactly how and when to remove his cap and present it, crown uppermost, to have his pay laid upon it.

---

[72] These details about the turret roof are taken from 'Hamilton's Papers' at the NMM, Greenwich, Ref HTN/219.

[73] See 'Hamilton's Papers' at the NMM, Greenwich, ref HTN/219.

One Watch of the Boys was then given a brief leave to have a short run ashore in Devonport. The other Watch of Boys had their turn on the next day, the 31st March. Doubtless, Alf would have known the best haunts to which to take any of his young shipmates who were strangers to Devonport, and who might have cared to 'tag along' with him when his turn came – if, that is, the Boys were allowed ashore at any time without a Petty Officer being in charge of the party and directing events. There was always the respected establishment of 'Aggie Weston' for inexpensive 'tea and buns' if they started to run short of cash.

By the end of March, the number of Dockyard 'maties' on board had fallen to about 30, and the opportunity was taken to scrub and wash clothes. Also, preparatory to going to sea, the ship was beginning to take substantial quantities of food aboard. For example, Alf and his young shipmates might well have been involved in some of the heavy handling on the 1st April, when she took in 5,000 lb. of vegetables and 2,515 lb. of beef. And, on the lines of 'give us our daily bread' - well, reduced in numbers though they were, the company was consuming 600 lb. per day of it - say 1¼ lb. per man - taken aboard fresh whilst she was alongside the dock.

On 10th April a further 250 ratings joined from Chatham. By the next day, the 11th April, the Dockyard workers had completed their work, and the ship coaled – presumably from a collier which had come alongside.

This would probably have been Alf's first experience of the heavy and filthy task of coaling, in which it was customary for all ranks to be closely involved up to the level of the Senior Lt-Commander and the Captain of Marines, and with the Executive Officer (The Commander) personally inspecting all leads and safety of gear.

Only the bare minimum of the Ship's Company were left to attend to the other essential needs of the ship in regard to guarding the gangways, maintaining a watch on deck, performing signalling duties, maintaining guards for men in cells, covering for any needs of the Sick Bay, providing of electrical and steam power (for lighting and working derricks, etc.), and for regular sustenance with food and drink of the men toiling for the hours ahead at the task of coaling.

Alf was a Boy Seaman, but a 'Seaman' none the less. If the procedures laid down in the 'Manual of Seamanship' were being followed, at least in principle, Alf would thus have found himself working in one of the holds of the collier rather than remaining on *Vanguard's* upper deck to cope with the coal coming aboard. Once in the collier's hold, Alf might well have been one of many engaged in the heavy task of breaking into the coal-stack with round-ended shovels and filling large hessian sacks. As each sack was loaded it was immediately hoisted aloft by a derrick or other lifting gear and transferred across to *Vanguard's* deck, where CPOs, Boatswain's Mates, Artisan POs, Writers and others 'unhooked' the bags, and her stokers, and 'spare' artisans, telegraphists, signalmen, cook's mates and victualling staff were waiting with barrows, to transfer the sacks to positions where 'tippers' were waiting to propel the coal down into the bunkers via hatches and chutes, liberating the sacks so that the empty bags could be re-cycled back to the hold of the collier where Alf and the other Seamen were continuing to toil away.

The organisation was intended to bring system, control, motivation, competition between groups *and a high level of safety* into a situation where many people were working under pressure and steadily increasing fatigue, with heavy loads swinging 'aloft and alow' all the time.

Author's collection. A postcard in the 'Star Series' by G.D & D., London, printed in Bavaria. Issued c.1907.

Ship possibly *HMS 'Dreadnought'*. Some of these sailors are completing the taking of coal on board and others are beginning to clean ship. This photo precedes Alf's time, but gives an idea. The exact methods used depended on prevailing circumstances, but coal-sacks, shovels, sack-trucks and wheelbarrows, plus derricks and other hoisting devices and a huge amount of physical labour were invariably required to get the coal on board and down into the ship's bunkers. This would all be followed by hosing down with water, rubbing down with sandstone blocks, and much 'elbow grease' generally, to clean ship afterwards. Then came the tasks of washing *oneself* and *one's clothes*.

As a Boy, if Alf were lucky, he might have been one of those ordered to hold empty bags, one by one, for the men to shovel the coal into. This demanded less physical labour than shovelling, but also needed skill, to present the bag low down initially, so that the men only had to lift their shovels to the height of the growing load within the bag. The bag-holder then had to progressively raise the sides and 'shuffle' the bag at intervals to even-out the load and to fill the bag fully and appropriately as it grew towards a full hundredweight (112 lb.). As a bag-handler Alf would also have had to 'keep his fingers clear', to avoid the sharp edges of the heavy shovels – for the men were sometimes a bit 'free' in the manner they swung the shovels, and, as their tiredness grew, bag after bag, and load after load, they could become, almost inevitably, even more 'clumsily careless'. The expected rate of working was one ton per man, per hour. To introduce a spirit of competition, the 'parts of ship' were often set against each other, 'FX' against 'F.Top': 'M.Top' against 'Q.Dk'.

No less than 1,165 tons of coal were brought aboard and shovelled down into the bunkers. Despite the welcome presence of the new batch of 250 ratings, it still took the ship's company six and a half hours of hard toil to complete the coaling operation (from 0635 to 1305).

There would have been short breaks for 'char and a wad' at intervals, but 1,165 divided by (say) 3.5 hrs (to cover for 'Breakfast', 'Dinner' and 'smoke-breaks' out of the nominal 6.5 hours), would indicate about some 330 men being involved in the collier's holds alone. (This would be in good agreement with 'The manual of Seamanship'.) On the ship herself, at least 100 specialist ratings, artificers, POs, CPOs etc., were probably at work and perhaps 40 officers overall.

Author's collection. A postcard entitled 'Jack at Play: An interval in Coaling', by C Cozens, Naval Photographer, Portsmouth, c.1913.

Ship unknown. 'An Interval in Coaling'. As shown here, 'progressive relaxation' in the clothing permitted to be worn for coaling took place after about 1912/13. Moreover, it seemed that every ship's company had a number of extroverts who were prepared to 'play the fool' at the drop of a hat. Here whilst 'playing' on his 'banjo-shovel' and doubtless singing a merry little ballad to the photographer, one 'Jack me Hearty' sits atop two willing shipmates. Such jokers – so long as they didn't overplay their hands – could lift the spirits of the men enormously, especially when there was a really hard day's work in progress. One can see the heavy coal-stains on the once-white trousers of the men on the right – and on some faces, too - perhaps sportingly 'blacked-up' as would-be 'nigger minstrels', which were then 'all the rage'. Doubtless, there's plenty more coal yet to be embarked. After that will come the heavy task of 'cleaning ship', etc., etc.

They would then have had to clean ship and, later, themselves. And, as soon as chance offered, to wash clean the filthy clothes they had removed.[74]

Next day, *Vanguard* took in ammunition (another task requiring heavy labour, but again coupled with systematic discipline and rigid, pre-planned control, to route each calibre of shell to its appropriate shell-room, and then to convey each cordite charge to its proper magazine, never crossing the path of the one with the other). *Vanguard* then shifted to No.7 berth. We can now begin to see the total of 3.75 thousand tons between her 'standard' and 'deep' draughts 'come to life', with 1.2 thousand tons of coal being taken aboard to supplement any remaining stock, plus (say) 1,000 tons of ammunition and (say) at least some 100 tons of provisions and (say) 200 tons of water, totalling about 2.5 thousand tons.

---

[74] There is a rather confusing naval expression concerning 'cleaning' into a different rig - meaning to change into a different type of uniform. Here, however, 'cleaning' means 'dhobying' (i.e. washing) one's gear.

On the 14th *Vanguard* 'slipped and proceeded', with tugs assisting her, down the Hamoaze River, to come to moorings at No.9 buoy, well down towards the estuary. At 0415 on the 15th she slipped and proceeded down the Hamoaze Estuary to the sea, heading for Portland and carrying out various trials on the way. Apart from any short sea-trips Alf may have had whilst at his training establishments, this would have been Alf's first naval voyage out to sea. It was a comparatively short one, which would end in Berth C.3 at Portland.

The order to weigh and proceed having been given, one can imagine that Alf and any other raw young sailors who might have been present would have tended to 'stop and stare' at all that was going on, with their jaws hanging open in wonderment, only to be immediately bawled out and sent about their duty.

The flurry of activity one might see as such a large ship put to sea was wonderfully described in 1913 in the diary of the (then) Midshipman Roy STRUBEN, as shown below his photograph.[75]

Photograph reproduced by courtesy of the Imperial War Museum. The original is in Pt 1 of the Diary of Commander R.F.C. STRUBEN RN, Ref 86/60/1.

A photographic portrait of Roy STRUBEN as a Midshipman, taken c. 1913. As shown by the long extract quoted in the following text, the young Roy STRUBEN had very good powers of observation and a great ability to describe very graphically the things he saw. His diary therefore makes very interesting reading. In the early 1920s, when Roy STRUBEN was serving as a Lieutenant in the cruiser *Lowestoft*, his diary achieves great significance, for Alf was serving in the same ship.

As young Roy STRUBEN wrote: *"...sailors emerging from every hatchway, bugles blaring, Bosuns' pipes wailing and trilling, Bosuns' Mates bawling orders all round the ship, on deck and below. Officers hurrying to their stations to supervise operations, and the Commander seeming to be in every part of the ship at once, checking every detail. Boats' crews, headed by their midshipmen, would dash out along the booms and swarm down the swaying Jacob's Ladders into the picket-boats and motor-launches,*

---

[75] We shall see more of the work of Roy STRUBEN further into this book. His excellent diary is preserved in the Imperial War Museum. (See Appendix A for further details.)

cast off mooring ropes and await their turn for hoisting by the huge main derrick now swinging outboard with its ponderous great hook.[76] Hooking on to the slings was always a ticklish job in rough weather. Meanwhile, sailors would be laying aft the boats' booms, lashing them securely at the ship's side and hoisting inboard the heavy gangways."

And, (if wartime conditions were being simulated), *"...some of the foc'slemen would unstow and rig the complicated gear for hoisting out and running the mine-sweeping paravanes, for those ingenious and protective devices would have to be ready for lowering the moment the ship should clear the harbour entrance - lest an enemy submarine should have laid mines....."*

Author's collection. A postcard in the 'Nelson' series by Gale & Polden Ltd. Issued c. 1910.

Ship unknown. Hoisting in the Pinnace, using *"the huge main derrick with its ponderous great hook"*, as Midshipman STRUBEN wrote in his diary. Note the use of two pulleys to obtain a 'mechanical advantage', and the easy confidence of the men standing in the pinnace. However, note, too, the lifebuoy ready to hand for any emergencies. Also, the gun in its casemate in the side of the ship. Alf would have been learning a huge number of routines and 'tricks of the trade' by a mixture of instruction, observation and hands-on experience in many fields.

As young Alf would doubtless have had dinned into him, *Vanguard* was the 8th naval ship to carry the name. Behind this numbering lay more tradition, and we can well imagine that Alf would have been expected to learn something about all the former holders of that name. For example, the hull of the 7th *Vanguard,* which was completed in the early 1870s, had been of composite iron and steel construction, protected by armour

---

[76] The reader will by now have noted that various photographers of the day enjoyed surprisingly free access to photograph life *on board* ship. The firm of Gale & Polden, which had an enterprising senior executive who was a former naval officer, perhaps had more access than most. It seems that this freedom of access was a privilege granted by the Admiralty with a view to publicising and promoting the Royal Navy and in the belief that the sale of such postcards would provide a stimulus for recruitment of the many young men it needed. It will be observed that this freedom of access declined after the introduction of the revolutionary 'Dreadnought-Class' of battleships, and virtually ceased immediately after the outbreak of war in 1914. It picked up again, though to a less 'intimate' extent, between the two world wars.

all along the water-line, but using armour above the water-line to protect only the vital central gun-battery. Direct ahead and astern fire was made possible from the guns of this battery by constructing it to extend *outboard* to port and starboard by a few feet. The ship had a powerful ram bow, still then regarded as a potentially useful weapon of war, and could probably have made 14 knots flat out. Her range was limited because she had only relatively small coal bunkers. She was rigged to enable her to continue sailing in the event of engine breakdown or of running out of coal, but she was basically designed as a powered vessel, and, being a compromise, her sailing qualities were not very good.[77]

On the other hand, her predecessor, the 6th *Vanguard*, had been designed as a wind-powered line-of-battle 'wooden wall', with good sailing abilities. She had been constructed a good half-century before the 7th *Vanguard*, and she had mounted 74 muzzle-loading cannon. She had been fully rigged, and, whilst to some extent she had been at the mercy of wind and weather, and might thus have sometimes become becalmed for long periods or been driven far off-course by heavy storms - and always in mortal peril of being unable to claw her way off a 'lee shore'- her range would usually have been limited more by the period of time her food and drinking-water provisions could have been made to last than by any other considerations. Further, it was sometimes possible to replenish stocks, especially of water, by making a suitable landfall - whereas, for the boiler-driven, coal-burning ships which succeeded her, deposits of coal could be very hard to come by, sometimes drastically reducing a ship's potential range.....and matters were even worse for oil-burning ships. To a considerable extent, the 6th *Vanguard* could have re-rigged herself and repaired quite severe battle-damage, particularly if she were able to find a sheltered stretch of water. Careening the ship (i.e. heeling her over) to enable repairs to be conducted on her bottom, might even have been possible. Total replacement of her masts and yards by making a 'jury rig' from spare spars and cut-down trees might also have been possible.

Her ability at self-repair was thus proportionately much greater than that which a modern, steel-built vessel could achieve. Moreover, an enterprising captain, often well-aided by a skilful master, could modify his ship's trim, change the rake of her masts, alter her yards and make other refinements to improve her sailing ability, whereas an iron or steel ship was very limited in how much she could be so changed. *In extremis,* as when overwhelmed by an exceptionally severe storm and in imminent danger of capsizing or foundering, it was even possible with a 'wooden wall' battleship to cut away the rigging and stays and to let the masts 'go by the board', so that the ship, with greatly reduced 'windage', and perhaps riding with a 'sea-anchor' out to keep her bows-on to the wind, swam rather like a relatively stable log of wood. As the storm abated, a jury rig could be constructed from spare spars, cordage and sails, to bring the ship to a place of safety where full repairs could be carried out. This procedure was simply not practical with a steel ship. *All* things considered, it was not surprising that many older admirals preferred sail to steam.

A typical day in the 8th *Vanguard's* peacetime routine might have been much as listed in the tabulation which follows. As can be seen, development training in *Vanguard*

---

[77] Her life was short, for during 1872, in a fog-shrouded Irish Sea, she was accidentally hit amidships and sunk by her sister-ship, *HMS Iron Duke*, the ram bow of *Iron Duke* causing fatal damage to *Vanguard*.

continued for the Boys and the Men, mixed with work tasks and entertainment, some of the entertainment also being slanted towards further personal development. For a 'new boy' like Alf, still learning the ropes, the whole business must have been daunting. Yet, overall, his feelings must have been mixed with a certain considerable pride, especially as he began to find his feet and to experience a level of fellow-suffering with other new lads, leading towards 'comradeship in adversity'. The odd gesture of kindness by one or another of the older sweats would certainly have been very welcome.

Note: For convenience, the times in the table are quoted in 'modern' naval fashion. However, until post-WW1, the Navy used the 12 o'clock system, so that 1555, for example, would actually have been shown as 3.55 pm.

0355	Morning Watch Men to Muster	1600	Quarters. Port Watch to Tea
0530	Call the Hands ('Lash Up & Stow')	1620	Starboard Watch to Tea
0535	Cooks to the Galley for Cocoa	1630	Cinema Show for Red Watch of Engine
0600	Hands Fall In. Scrub Decks/Clean out Boats		Room Department. Fo'c'sle & Torpedo
0705	Starboard Watch to Breakfast		Divisions to Deck Hockey
0725	Port Watch to Breakfast	1645	Tombola in Main Dining Hall
0755	Forenoon Watch Men to Muster		Miniature Rifle Range Open.
	Both Watches of Hands Fall In.	1755	Last Dog Watch Men to Muster
	Prayers. Detailed for Work	1815	Cooks to the Galley
0900	Divisions. Training Classes to Instruction	1825	Hands to Supper
1155	Grog Issue	1930	Cinema Show for Starboard Watch RM
1200	Starboard Watch to Dinner	1955	First Watch Men to Muster
1225	Afternoon Watch to Dinner	2000	Port Watch Fall In. Clean Up Mess Decks
1230	Port Watch to Dinner		and Flats. Concert.
1315	Both Watches of Hands Fall In	2030	Rounds
	Detail for Work.	2130	Pipe Down
	Training Classes to Instruction	2145	CPOs and POs Pipe Down
1555	First Day Watch Men to Muster	2355	Middle Watch Men to Muster.

Seeing the second-listed item at 1645, one is drawn to comment that Alf probably frequented the ship's miniature rifle range, for he became a qualified marksman and was a keen shot. He might well have also played at deck hockey, to keep his eye in for hockey matches ashore, when opportunity offered. His personality was probably beginning to emerge more strongly, as he found his feet, albeit knowing that he still had a great deal to learn.

It is clear that Alf took a positive interest in gunnery from early on in his career, and it is worth having a closer look at this matter of gunnery and the 'aiming off' (or 'deflection') which was necessary by the 'gunlayer' to compensate for the relative movements of the firing ship and its target, which, if another ship, was likely to be moving at a comparatively high rate.

The following photograph shows something of the sort of drill which was in use at the turn of the 19th and 20th centuries, prior to the coming of the 'Dreadnought' Class of battleships. Finding that some gunlayers were much more naturally gifted than others in compensating for the roll of their ship and other effects when manually working guns of small to moderate calibre, and thus in keeping their gun constantly 'on target' as round after round was fired, a Captain Percy SCOTT had carefully studied the techniques *instinctively* used by these naturally talented men. Right at the end of the 19th Century, this had led him to invent his so-called 'Dotter' trainer.

Captain SCOTT's 'Dotter Trainer' could greatly improve the 'average' man's skills at the art of gun-laying, and thus greatly improve the accuracy of fire of every gun in a ship. The 'Dotter' employed a miniature rifle which fired a shot weighing less than a ½ ounce (about 14 grams), to represent a shell of (say) 850 lb. The outcome was a series of pencilled 'dots' on a recording paper which showed the level of accuracy of the gunlayer concerned. The 'Dotter Trainer' was very successful in training gunlayers and it continued in use for many years.

Author's collection. A postcard from the 'Wellington' series by Gale and Polden, probably dating from 1904. The card was postally used on 15th April 1908 (See postmark).

Gunlayers practising their skills at a 6-inch gun, by using a long spar projecting outboard. This spar carries a circular paper target fixed to a vertical board sited just short of the muzzle of the gun. Evidently, the spar could be rotated in a flat horizontal arc by the rating standing on the right by the breech, to simulate the changing bearing of a moving enemy ship. The gunlayer, eye 'glued' to his telescopic sight on the left of the breech, would try to 'follow' the moving 'sweep' of the target by using the gun-controls, loosing off 'aiming rifle rounds' which punctured the target and demonstrated his level of skill and aptitude in 'laying' the gun. In this scene, other gunlayers, some holding spare paper targets, stand by at the rear of the gun. A small stack of target-papers, showing the black 'bulls-eye', can be seen at bottom left of the photo. This system was soon to be replaced by Captain Percy SCOTT's 'Dotter' trainer which combined the horizontal 'laying' with the vertical 'training' element necessitated by the rolling and pitching of the vessels.

However, the coming of the Dreadnought, with the concept that battles at sea should be fought at long range, meant that individual gunlayers, sited comparatively low-down in the ship, would not be in a good position to observe the enemy and to distinguish whether their own fire was falling short, on, or over the enemy, or to the left, on, or to the right of him. Hence, amongst the more clear-thinking officers, it was generally accepted that rather than having individual gunlayers aiming and firing each individual gun, it would be much better if all the main guns could be aimed and fired by one man in control of a small spotting team, well-protected by armour, helped by powerful telescopes and sited high up in the ship (the latter to provide the team with good all-round long-range visibility). Absolutely key would be the matter of deciding the 'Deflection' to set – to decide how far to 'aim off' ahead of the target to have the greatest chance of making the shell and the 'jinking' enemy ship reach the same point in space at the same moment in time.

The 'fire-control' team (as it came to be called) would need reliable and immediate two-way communication with each gun and to be equipped with the best optical systems which could be made available, not only for 'spotting', as such, but also for the essential 'range-finding', etc. In fact, it would be better to have more than one fire-control team, in different positions, and each with its own communications system, lest the 'master' team be put out-of-action by incoming shell-fire early on during an engagement. And, the next finding was that it would be best to have a co-ordinating team, in a 'transmitting station', placed below the waterline of the ship, in a more or less 'impregnable' position, where optimal 'Deflection' could be decided salvo by salvo and matters could be kept going tactically, with all the incoming data being coolly worked upon and contrasted and co-ordinated, so that the guns could be continually fed with the optimal 'range' and 'bearing' to set, even if one or more of the relatively exposed 'spotting positions' were to be put out of action. Only in the last resort would the individual turrets revert to 'local control', performing their own spotting, etc.

The years from about 1904 to 1911, when Alf first set foot on HMS *Vanguard*, had been hectic ones behind the scenes, as the Admiralty and its advisors and specialists tried to bring this concept of centralised 'fire-control' towards some sort of reality. How deeply a Boy Seaman like Alf would have been brought into the picture, where some of the evolving techniques and machines were a closely-guarded secret, is hard to evaluate. One suspects that he would have been well-primed at any particular duty to which he was assigned, but that he would have been given only a broad idea of the totality of the system in the 'state of the art' to which it had by then developed. He possibly came to hear about such things as 'The Argo Clock', 'The Gun-Corrector' and 'Plotting Tables'. But he may well never have had a sight of such things at that stage of his career. We will have a bit more of a look at the situation prevailing in 1911 in a slightly later page, but we will take a broader look at some of the surrounding matters and controversies when we get to 1917/18, by which time Alf would be in a higher rate in gunnery, and more likely to have been fairly well 'in the know'.

Let's look at another aspect. As already said, when firing the main guns, it would be usual for each salvo to consist of only half of the main armament, so that the second half could fire (to keep up the pressure on the enemy), whilst the first half were re-loading after firing. Keeping the range open, *and using only the main armament*, would also make the 'spotting' of 'splashes' and hits easier to control than might have been the case of a vessel with heavy, medium and light weapons all in action at once, fighting at an intermediate range, with all guns creating a localised fog of 'muzzle smoke' and with far more splashes and hits (some 'non-penetrating) around and on the target and all interfering with vision. [Many lessons had been learnt from the defeat of the Russian fleet by the Japanese at the Battle of Tsushima on 27th May 1905, where the overwhelming importance of long-range, powerful-hitting 12-inch guns mounted in fast-moving ships had really struck home to the more clear-thinking of the naval observers who were privileged to be present. Amongst those distinguished observers from the World Powers was a British Naval Officer bearing the name of Ernest Charles Thomas TROUBRIDGE, of whom we shall soon hear more.]

Jacky FISHER had always been a man to seize on 'newfangled ideas', and, as Commander in Chief of the Mediterranean Fleet in 1899/1902 he had introduced tactical exercises and new gunfire-control techniques which had brought about huge increases in the accuracy of the gunnery of that fleet.

However, at that time he had not been wedded to the idea of having only the main guns in action and firing from comparatively long range. Certainly, 'Jacky' FISHER had long cherished rather vague ideas of somehow or other 'overwhelming' enemy ships by concentrated and accurate gunfire, but the ideas behind the new 'Dreadnought' 'all big gun' ships which he came to so vigorously promote in 1904/05 were not entirely Jacky FISHER's own, for he owed much of the basic design to Mr W H GARD the one-time Chief Naval Constructor at Malta who later came to work at Portsmouth.

Author's collection. A postcard in the Rotary Photographic Series, reference number '88 A'. Produced in or shortly after 1913.

Admiral Lord FISHER. From 1899 to 1902, as C-in-C of the Mediterranean Fleet, he had brought about great improvements in the accuracy of the gunnery of the Fleet. He would go on to introduce the 'Dreadnoughts' – the 'all big gun battleships' - and he would later set about drastic improve-ments in the training given to both officers and men. He did enormous good, but some harm, mainly through his ruthlessness to impose his will and his long feud with Admiral BERESFORD.

Moreover, the work of Mr GARD may well have been previously stimulated from observing ideas being put about various inventors on the international scene. Over and beyond that, the Battle of Tsushima had surely been a turning point, leading to much re-thinking of tactics and strategies.

Be that as it may, in December 1904, less than three months after being appointed as First Sea Lord, Jacky had appointed a 'Committee on Design', which he had himself chaired, and which had been packed with some of the finest naval and civilian brains in the country.

Jacky FISHER's 'Committee on Design' had included such distinguished figures as the mathematician and physicist Lord KELVIN, Sir Philip WATTS, who was the then Director of Naval Construction, Rear Admiral Prince Louis of BATTENBERG and Captain John JELLICOE. Doubtless, the varied contributions of all these people had been vital in drawing up the basic specification for the innovative 'all big-gun, heavily-armoured, battleship'.

However, the driving force had undoubtedly been that of Jacky FISHER himself. Importantly, 'Jacky' FISHER had the ear of King Edward VII who took a close and powerful interest in all affairs naval. Admiral FISHER was a controversial man with ruthless drive, who brooked no opposition. In general he was right, and very innovative - but in a few matters history has shown that he was quite wrong, and his sheer pugnacity prevented debate and held back rectification during his 'reign'.

It also has to be said that the petty feud which sprang up between the admirals Lord FISHER and Lord BERESFORD was highly divisive and damaging for the Navy.

Author's collection. A postcard in the 'Dainty Series by an anonymous publisher. Photo by the London Stereoscopic Society. Issued c. 1904.

The then Vice-Admiral the Right Hon. Lord Charles W.D. BERESFORD, KCB., KCVO. As captain of a small gunboat armed only with so-called 'popguns', he had 'won his spurs' at the Siege of Alexandria in 1882, by taking on a fort armed with 'huge' 10-inch guns. He had thus deliberately drawn off the enemy fire from several British battleships which were in real danger of being overwhelmed. Justly, Lord BERESFORD was greatly admired in many quarters. It was a great pity that he could not let his feud with Lord FISHER simply drop.

In particular the feud was sometimes highly destructive for the future careers of some of the rising young officers in the Royal Navy, who were all-too-liable to find themselves having to choose sides – and who sometimes became caught out by having made the 'wrong' choice. It seems a great shame that these two otherwise fine senior men could not have somehow reconciled their differences for the 'greater good of the Service'.

As already stated, the building of HMS *Vanguard* had followed hard on the heels of the first of the revolutionary new line, HMS *Dreadnought*. So far as practicable, FISHER and his design committee had arranged for all these ships to be made in standardised steel sheet sizes, for making up rectangular box-like structures. The number of *specialised* sheets and parts was kept to a minimum. Thus, one pre-cut sheet arriving from the steel mills was usually as well-suited as the next, so that the construction process was seldom held up due to 'waiting for parts'. This had helped to make the speed of building of the new ships revolutionary for vessels of such size, and HMS *Dreadnought* had been sprung on the naval world as a *fait accompli* before the secret about her design and construction had been in any way 'leaked'. This was all a remarkable achievement.

Still, let's get back to our main story about this particular 'floating gun-battery' of a Dreadnought, HMS *Vanguard*. Her refit of 1912 completed, and verification tests of the dockyard work appearing satisfactory, at 1315 on 17th April 1912, the 8th *Vanguard* slipped from Berth C.3 at Portland, and headed out into the English Channel.

Author's collection. A postcard in the "Dainty" Series by 'FTWD', c.1902. Postally used on 14th May 1905.

> This card pre-dates Alf's first sight of Portland Harbour by at least seven years, but the facilities, including the six large dockyard cranes (at what appears to be the coaling wharf), were unlikely to have changed very much in the interim. However, note that a new mole is under construction in this scene. One of the long breakwaters which protects the roadstead is *just* visible as a long, low white line just beyond the farthest ships at right-centre and off to the right. *Most* of the naval ships moored in the roadstead appear to have black hulls, white upperworks and buff funnels, which probably dates the photograph at about 1902.

Soon, the bugler was ordered to blow the stirring "Call to Arms", and the company quickly closed up to their Action Stations. Thus 'manned and armed', the ship then took part in repelling 'mock' attacks made on her from port and starboard sides by destroyers. This would have been a thrilling sight for those of the Boys who were fortunate enough to be in positions where they could see what was going on. Already, the ship's company were practising for war.

Next day, a thick fog had developed by 2200, and the ship reduced her speed down to 7 knots, and then down to 6 knots, creeping through the darkening water at little more than that of a man at jogging pace and so continuing through into the night, until 0115, when the fog suddenly lifted. Next day the turret gun crews were put to 'aiming rifle' practice at towed targets, to 'get their eyes in' at 'deflection shooting'. Work was also done at testing the gun sights, and the ship's searchlights were 'burnt' that night. [The term 'burnt' evidently relating to the fact that the searchlights used 'carbon arcs', which gave a brilliant light. The points of the carbon electrodes gradually 'burnt away' during use. Manual re-adjustments were therefore needed at frequent intervals to keep the carbon points at optimal separation. Eventually, mechanical means were introduced to progressively and automatically 'wind-in' the electrodes, to compensate for the burning away, so that manual adjustments would be required much less frequently.]

On 20th April, the company busied themselves with various activities, namely, (i) a range party was landed at Berehaven, in Bantry Bay (which had a good anchorage), (ii) a working party was put to transferring 45 tons of coal to the destroyer *Greyhound*, which had come alongside, (iii) boats were sent away to exercise under sail in the bay, and (iv) the Starboard Watch of Boys, Alf perhaps included, was given a short leave ashore to explore Berehaven, which would have been new to their experience.

From Berehaven the ship proceeded to Portland, and next day to Weymouth Roads, where she dressed ship with masthead flags to mark 'St George's Day', and made rendezvous with the 2nd and 3rd Battle Fleets and with the 1st and 2nd Cruiser Squadrons. The turret gun crews were then put to divisional drill. On 9th May, the ships proceeded for squadron firing. However, when *Vanguard* came to start her own run there was disappointment aboard, for the visibility closed right down and she had to break off at 1340. She anchored astern of *Orion* in 12 fathoms (72 feet), which was more than ample for her large draught of about 32ft. They were in position N 50° 32', W 2°19', about twenty miles to the north of Alderney in the Channel Islands - itself an area of dangerous reefs. Subsequently, the visibility improved to everybody's relief, and *Bellerophon* and *Lord Nelson* proceeded with target-firing, whilst *Vanguard* assumed the duties of 'intermediate ship', spotting their fall of shot.

On 10th May they were back at Portland, where *Vanguard* immediately prepared herself for further possible action by coaling (1,000 tons), embarking cordite and projectiles and drawing stores from the dockyard. This sounds simple enough to say, but it meant that, in effect, almost every man aboard had to shift nearly 1½ tons of coal, more or less twice over, and then clean the ship and himself. Getting in and striking down 12-inch projectiles and charges was also a heavy task, especially when much ammunition had previously been expended. (Perhaps, in this case, the men involved in the hard work rather blessed the fact that their practice firing had been cut short by the poor visibility of 9th May.) With a view to ever-improving her gunnery performance, the ship also sent her turret-firing groups ashore to attend deflector training at this time.

One presumes that young Alf was by now learning more about the fire-control system in *Vanguard*. He would probably now have been aware that she had three 'Spotting Officers', each with his own small team of officers and key ratings. The 1st Spotting Officer was located in the Forward Control Tower (FCT), the 2nd in the Main Top (MT) and the 3rd in the After Control Tower (ACT). These positions each had one of the new 9 ft 6 ins Barr & Stroud rangefinders, which were a great improvement on the

4 ft 6 ins instruments formerly in use. These new rangefinders were equipped with 'bearing plates', so that both the range and bearing of a target could be read off. Whether Alf would have known that each rangefinder was mounted on a 'gyroscope' (a mechanism only recently brought to fruition as a practical proposition, and hence perhaps still 'classified'), is an unknown. The gyroscope was invaluable in virtually eliminating the effects of the pitch and roll to which the ship herself was subject.

The ship was equipped with two Transmitting Stations, one forward (the FTS) and one aft (the ATS). These positions were placed deep in the hull, below the water-line, and were regarded as being more or less 'impregnable.' The FTS was equipped with various devices to aid in fire-control. One suspects that Boy Seamen like Alf would not have set foot in these places, where the equipment and techniques were probably kept highly confidential.

In broad terms, however, Alf was probably well aware that the combined effect of the data input from the Spotting Officers high up in the ship, watching the fall of shot relative to the target and applying corrections ready for the next salvo to be fired, would be absorbed, filtered and perhaps modified by officers and key ratings working in the Transmitting Stations, who worked out the optimal 'Deflections' (and, when relevant, fuse-settings) to apply, depending on a whole raft of attributes regarding wind speed, barometric pressure, time of flight of the shell over the range involved, perhaps the last 'jinking moves' of the target, the 'jinking' of their own ship, and so forth.

Alf might well have 'caught on', from some of the practice exercises, that it was possible for the After Transmitting Station to take over if the Forward Station was put out of action, and so forth. And some of his training would doubtless have involved him in localised firing by the crews of individual turrets, doing their own spotting, range-taking, deflection-setting, gun-laying and gun-training, as would come about if the ship were *in extremis*, with all the centralised fire-control positions out-of-action. This may have made him aware of a 'magic instrument' called a *Dumaresq* which, in modified form, could aid in deciding the optimal 'deflection' to use.[78]

Practice actions such as the one they had recently experienced, in which a fleet was manoeuvred in battle-formation, with each ship practising station-keeping on her 'next ahead', changing course, zig-zagging, etc., without running foul of each other, were impressive to observe. Great attention was being paid at this time to 'crossing the T', a tactic aimed at being able to bring fleet broadsides to bear on the enemy, whilst the enemy ships could only hit back with their forward turrets. The sight of these ocean leviathans manoeuvring at speed in close company with each other must have been not only awe-inspiring but also demanding of considerable nerve by the key players in each ship who were responsible for her navigation and steering. The Navy had suffered from too many catastrophic disasters in Victorian times when ship had accidentally rammed into ship, because the turning circles, stopping distances, the forces of attraction caused by turbulence, and the loss of power when cutting through the disturbed and turbulent wake left by another ship, were not properly understood and appreciated. Now, all this

---

[78] Some of the background to this writing can be read, in much more detailed form, in 'Hamilton's Papers', ref HTN 219, at the National Maritime Museum. Hamilton's Papers are a reflection of the teaching which would have been given to *young officers*, with its much greater attention to the theory and logic involved, as compared with the less-sophisticated training of *'other ranks'* such as Alf.

complex learning was in the forefront of people's minds - sometimes almost 'mentally crippling' and 'inhibiting' them. People might sometimes either 'freeze' or over-react....and 'steering engines' did not always 'behave' quite as expected. Moreover, going 'hard astern' sometimes took an extraordinarily long time to get the way off these huge vessels.

The more practice the better - but the high financial cost of operating these huge ships was constantly in the mind of 'authority', headed by a parsimonious peacetime government. Jacky FISHER's rather contentious approach had been to scrap a great many of the smaller and more obsolete ships to save manning and operating costs - but this was a dangerous policy should war break out, and with so many far-flung 'outposts of Empire' and all our shipping trade to defend. The need would then be for ships and yet more ships, especially cruisers.

Still, let's get back to Alf's experiences aboard this Dreadnought. On 16th May *Vanguard* was at sea again, manoeuvring in company with other warships just off Portland. When they were at 50° 33' N, 2° 24' W, they sighted the 'Blue Fleet' approaching them from the west. (This fleet was their enemy for the purpose of the exercise). The Blue Fleet saw them at much the same time, and immediately reversed their course, whereupon *Vanguard* and her consorts *'commenced the tactical exercise as ordered'*. In chase of the Blue Fleet, they headed westwards, rounding Land's End, and then heading north up the west coast of England. (They were now engaged on what would prove to be a long stern chase, reaching to the anchorage at Lamlash on the Isle of Arran, Scotland and, indeed, beyond.)

On the 18th the ship was ordered to haul out of line, and to shift to emergency Control Tower steering (i.e. as if a gun-battle against the Blue Fleet was raging, and *Vanguard's* normal conning position on the bridge had been destroyed by enemy action.). Fifteen minutes later she resumed her station, whereupon Captain RICARDS suddenly said to the Officer of the Watch, *"For the purpose of this exercise I've just been killed by an enemy shell-burst"*, (or some such words), whereupon the Commander was immediately informed and requested to take charge in the "late" Captain's stead.[79] This all took place at around N 54° 26', W 5° 13', shortly before the ship entered Lamlash Bay on the east coast of the Isle of Arran.

The 4" gun crews of the secondary armament were now sent to practice with the Dummy-Loader (See following photograph) and the 12" gun-turrets of the main armament practised firing sub-calibre ammunition at towed targets.[80] The company also practised firing torpedoes. Then firing with the 4" guns. The gunlayers of both the heavy and lighter guns were tested.

Whilst at Lamlash the ship practised getting out the heavy steel anti-torpedo nets, first in 'slow time' to get the men practised at the evolution, and then again, in 'quick time'. Care needed to be taken for the nets were very heavy, and if the operation was not done correctly and in unison along the full length, the net could 'take charge' as it

---

[79] By 'custom and practice' the Commander and Captain would always be in different parts of the ship from each other, to prevent the risk of one enemy shell killing both the Captain and his 2nd in Command in one fatal blow.

[80] The use of sub-calibre ammunition for 'practice shoots', (employing reduced-size Cordite charges) cut down on the rate of wear of the rifling in the guns. Such wear would ultimately lead to the expensive gun-barrels having to be hoisted out by a heavy dockyard crane and replaced with new or reconditioned ones.

unrolled, possibly breaking its restraining wire 'brails', sending the ruptured ends flying dangerously and creating an unwieldy mass which was hard to rectify.

Author's collection. A postcard by an anonymous printer, but having a photograph attributed to Gale & Polden, ref. 7757. Issue date c. 1904.

Gunners training on a Dummy-Loader. It seems that several variants of the Loader existed, and the one used in *Vanguard* may have differed significantly from this earlier model in a different ship.

On 6th June the fleet put to sea for fleet torpedo firing, *Dreadnought, Gloucester, Témeraire* and *Vanguard's* sister-ship *Collingwood* being in company with *Vanguard*. They cleared for action at 55° 07' N, 05° 08' W, off Corsewall Point, in the North Channel, and each ship loosed torpedoes at towed targets as and when ordered. Their accompanying destroyers were then tasked with finding and recovering the torpedoes fired by the fleet, as the Dreadnoughts proceeded majestically northwards towards the Firth of Clyde.[81] *Vanguard* came to anchor at Greenock later that day, in glorious weather, and spread her awnings. The hands were engaged in mending targets and reeving a new topping lift for the main derrick. A Bosun's party were turning the main derrick purchase 'end for end'.[82]

On 10th June, *Vanguard* proceeded out to sea again, exercising her 4" guns crews at 1" 'tube' aiming practice, before arriving at Lamlash. Once there, her hands were put to cleaning and scraping her boats, whilst her 'A', 'P' and 'Q' main turret crews, and the related magazine and shell room parties, were drilled as teams, in conjunction one with

---

[81] Torpedoes were expensive. They were designed to float on the surface once their motors had run down, and torpedoes were always recovered for further use if this was feasible. Time and time again we shall see the great efforts made to recover torpedoes fired by the various ships in which Alf would come to serve, and to hoist them back on board to be refurbished for further use.

[82] A 'purchase' is a device consisting of pulleys in blocks, combined with ropes, and arranged in various numbers and configurations, but always with the principle of obtaining a 'mechanical advantage', so that the force applied by the purchase is greater (sometimes by a factor of two, three or more) than the effort being put in.

another. A couple of days later the Boys, presumably including Alf, were under practical training at 4" gun drill, and a shell room party were fusing Lyddite shells.[83]

Next day the ship carried out a Full Power Trial in the Firth of Clyde, and then proceeded south, arriving at Portland on 22nd June. There, she dressed ship 'rainbow fashion' and fired a royal salute of 21 guns in honour of the Birthday of King Edward VII. This fine naval spectacle was virtually Alf's last experience aboard *Vanguard*, for his service in the ship terminated on the 30th June 1913. He must have wondered what would come up next.

He may also have reflected on the places he had been, and wondered to what corners of the globe his career might take him in the future. Was it true that one could *'Join the Navy and See the World'*? How far might his voyages reach, to north, south, east or west? It is therefore intended to add a rough sketch-map at the end of each deployment, and a short tabulation of the 'geographical extremities' Alf had attained.

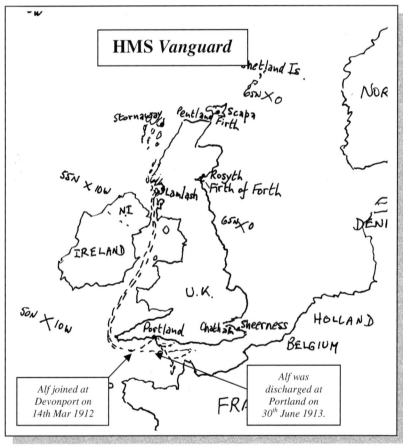

Farthest North	Lamlash	**56 N** 05 W
Farthest South	Off Channel Islands	**49 N** 02 W
Farthest East	Mid-Channel	50N **02 W**
Farthest West	Off Land's End	50N **07 W**

---

[83] Lyddite was an explosive made from potassium pirate, which the British had introduced during the Boer War. It was named after Lydd, in Kent, where it was manufactured.

As further deployments come Alf's way, we shall keep a progressive watch on the 'Farthest Geographic Points Ever Reached by Alf, along each of the axes, North, South, East and West.'

By now, Alf would surely have begun to have more contact with officers, and it is worth examining this matter to some extent.

Nearly all officers came from moneyed backgrounds - indeed, it was clear that it was virtually impossible for a young naval officer to live, to pay his mess bills, and to equip himself with dress and undress uniforms and equipment, (including an expensive dress sword), unless he had a private income to supplement his pay. Alf would doubtless learn that officer-cadets (or their families) were expected to stump up £75 a year as an annual tuition fee for their education at Osborne and Dartmouth. The fee was reduced to £40 for the sons of military and naval officers, but, in terms of the value of money in these days, even £40 was a considerable financial barrier that had to be surmounted.[84]

Author's collection. A postcard by Davidson Brothers, of London, probably printed in or about 1912.

HMS *Vanguard* as Alf would have remembered her, with additional short-range guns mounted high on her 'A' main gun turret (and also, in fact, on her 'X' turret), and a truncated but two-tower rear superstructure carrying reduced masts, as compared with her original design.

A decade earlier Jacky FISHER had proposed scholarship schemes, but only now were they being seriously considered. Most officers had come through the public school system of education, in many ways an admirable introduction for a boy to learn to stand on his own two feet and to find out how to mix, cope and live with many other male personalities. However, having to live in the 'closed society' of a public school led to some boys who had deeply-buried feelings of inferiority soon either learning to acquire hectoring and bullying attitudes by which they managed to survive in such establishments or to some of the overtly weaker characters among them remaining forever 'the bullied', [with a small minority totally cracking-up under the unremitting stress.] The 'bullies'

---

[84] By way of scale, a tradesman probably earned about £100 per annum at that time.

carried these aggressive and yet often craven behaviours through into their adult lives, usually under a veneer of outward competence, but with erratic behaviour always liable to re-surface adversely in a crisis. And the bully prevalent in such people often became only too apparent when they were in a position of power over those of lower rank, especially when nobody of more senior rank happening to be looking on.

Happily, the great majority of the officers had survived their schooling well and most were decent and honourable men - but there were unfortunate exceptions. 'Toadying' was also too-often present, the 'respect for rank' sometimes being overdone in the Royal Navy. Yet it took great courage and resolve for an officer of junior rank to approach a senior rank to 'make a positive suggestion' (say) of a possibly better way to deal with a problem. To have such 'brazen effrontery' might well hazard his future career. Progressive young officers had to 'find their best way' to handle such matters with the most enormous tact and discretion.

There tended to be considerable reliance by the younger and inexperienced officers upon the practical experience of the older warrant officers and chief petty officers, though some young officers took great pride in learning exactly how each task should be tackled, and thereafter coming to know every 'wrinkle' of the way a professional job should be properly done.[85] Again, some young officers who were short of natural ability and unsure of themselves would sometimes impulsively 'seize the initiative' and make command errors leading to a sudden crisis - even to a threat to lives - when it might have been better to have left an old and experienced ranker to 'sort out the detail'. However, there were also some young officers who became over-reliant on an old petty officer or leading seaman who then 'cynically took advantage', to the detriment of the men under command. This could lead to sloth and, potentially, to accidents. Alf soon began to realise that it would take many years before one would gain any sureness in the way to respond to any particular officer. Some might be firm but fair, some might be indulgent, some might be razor-sharp and some might be highly unpredictable, having 'good days' and 'bad days'. Some might want to be both respected and loved by their men, whereas others, harder and stricter by nature, wanted only respect.

There was a great deal to learn - and some of it was far from straightforward. It would be nice to think that Alf might have read a book printed in 1902, (and available at that general period through W. H. Smith & Son's Subscription Library), entitled 'The Passing of the Flagship and Other Stories' by Major W. P. Drury, RMLI.[86] In a humorous way, this book says quite a lot about the delicate relationships between officers and men.

Thus, one of its central figures, an old Private in the RMLI, is talking about having been 'cabin-door sentry' whilst a Dutch Admiral dined heavily and not too wisely with the 'Skipper' of the British 2nd class cruiser HMS *Duke of York* which was moored overnight in the Harbour of Batavia.[87] The sentry had strained, most illicitly of course, to

---

[85] One of 'Jacky' FISHER's maxims was that young officers should not be frightened of getting their hands dirty, and that they should be prepared to handle machinery of all sorts.

[86] RMLI signifying the Royal Marine Light Infantry. The book was published by A. H. Bullen, London.

The newly re-surfaced island turned out to have a skeleton of a long-dead marine and to be a very uncanny place! (Its position, as quoted in the story, lies off to the north-west of Christmas Island, in the Indian Ocean.)

[87] The *Duke of York* appears to have been a fictitious name for the warship.

overhear the substance of the heavily-lubricated conversation between Dutch Admiral and British Captain, the sentry even ceasing his endless marching back and forth, at times, to do so.[88]

The sentry was sent for by the Captain next morning and interrogated. The Marine describes this as follows: *"'You had the first watch on the cabin door last night?" "I 'ad, Sir." says I. "I misremember," says the Captain, "The exact longitude and latitude of that secret new island which has arisen out of the sea, to which the Dutch Admiral injudiciously referred, and to which he plans to shape his course today, to raise his country's flag and officially take possession." "Nine thirteen south", says I, "by one hundred and four east." "How do you know?" says he. "I wrote it down on the aft-deck paintwork," I says, "with me trigger finger dipped in some corfy your sto'oard was carrying into the cabin at the time". "Then you'll probably get fourteen days from the first lieutenant," says the Captain, "for spoiling his paint, and fourteen more from me for listening to international con'frences. Now you can go."'*

[As a postscript, when the island - not much more than a small area of shallow rock peeping above the waves - was duly found at the said position, and bang athwart the course the Captain had shaped to reach it, the Marine was sent for again, and rewarded by restoration of his lance stripe, instead of receiving the said 28 days punishment.[89]]

Of such fine tuning was the relationship of officer to marine (or rating) balanced. One hopes that, even if Alf had not read such stories, he may have picked up similar accounts of 'goings on', from the lips of some of the 'Old Salts' aboard *Vanguard*.

So far, we have scarcely considered the more personal aspects of Alf's life aboard ship. How he was dealing with matters of personal hygiene, how well he was coping with living 'cheek by jowl' with many different personalities, how his daily life went on 'off-duty'. We'll have a bit of a look at this in the next chapter.

As already said, Alf had left HMS Vanguard on 30th June 1912, and had been posted to HMS Pembroke, the Royal Naval Barracks at Chatham until 12th August 1912. He would have gone there to 'requalify', but the seven weeks which elapsed there until his next posting may have been the most flat of his career up to that time, albeit that some useful educational courses and important examinations would have taken place whilst he was there. He also could have managed to get in some home leave at this period.

---

[88] He was, of course, keen to transmit to his shipmates the likely next sailing and destination of the ship.

[89] Almost needless to say, the Marine was destined to lose his stripe, for misconduct, a few months later.

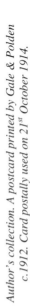

Author's collection. A postcard printed by Gale & Polden c.1912. Card postally used on 21ˢᵗ October 1914.

Gunners training with field guns in the Drill Shed at the Royal Naval Barracks, Chatham. Alf might well have found himself being tested by having to give orders as well as receive them.

Postscript. *Even though he had by then moved on, one supposes that Alf might have kept half an eye on the 'occasions' of the various ships in which he served during his career. Thus he might have learned of HMS 'Vanguard' that, although her part in the action was limited due to poor visibility, 'Vanguard' went on to fight successfully at the Battle of Jutland in 1916, firing 67 rounds from her 12-inch guns, with the result of hitting and probably disabling two German light cruisers and sinking a German destroyer. All that target practice had not been in vain. She would take no hits herself and suffer no casualties*

The following photographs, which were taken of an informal visit by a bishop wearing gaiters and a long coat, perhaps in 1916 in the aftermath of the Battle of Jutland, give us the opportunity to 'stand aboard' HMS 'Vanguard' for a moment in time and to see something of her officers and men, some of whom Alf might have known, though she would surely have re-commissioned with a largely fresh company during the three years which had elapsed since Alf's time on board.

Author's collection. These are both anonymous postcards. The two cards have similar printed backs with the Ref No. 0431 appearing in the pre-printed panel reserved for the postage stamp.

One cannot help but wonder how many of the officers and men depicted in the photographs were fated to meet a very sudden death on 9th July 1917. For on that tragic day, whilst lying at anchor in Scapa Flow, one of 'Vanguard's magazines would suddenly blow up, probably due to the limits for the safe period of storage of cordite having been exceeded. The spontaneous explosion of one magazine led to the immediate detonation of her other magazines, and the ship, torn apart, would immediately founder, costing the lives of all but two men out of the 804 of those aboard.[90]

---

[90] By that time *Vanguard* was under the command of Captain James DICK RN, who was amongst those who died. The two men who survived the explosion, Stoker 1st Class F.W. FOX and Private J. WILLIAMS RMLI, had been standing near 'Y' Turret (i.e. well aft) at the moment of detonation. Lt-Commander A.C.H. DUKE had also been picked up alive but terribly injured, and he had died soon afterwards. According to the Court of Enquiry into the loss of *Vanguard*, which was held in Sept 1917 under the Presidency of Rear Admiral Roger KEYES, 240 cases of Cordite were about to be 'returned' in accordance with an Admiralty Weekly Order. [Although not so stated at the Court of Enquiry, this might imply that the Cordite was approaching its 'expiry date'. It was being widely rumoured that, due to the

The water was full of floating wreckage, including broken and seared woodwork and a lot of hammocks. Everything was covered in black fuel oil. Bobbing around in this débris were a number of bodies, some shattered and many horribly scorched. The nearby coast was a horrific sight in the aftermath of that terrible day, being traumatic in the extreme for the men who were sent to collect up the shattered human remains which were being cast ashore. The 24 officers and 71 men of her complement who were not aboard at the time, and who thus escaped the holocaust would surely have counted themselves as being incredibly lucky. Doubtless, some would have lost close friends and 'oppos', and some would have been haunted by the incident for the rest of their lives.

Alf had left 'Vanguard' five years before the catastrophe which overwhelmed this fine ship. He was young, and the five-year gap was probably sufficient to insulate him from experiencing too much of a shock about the fate which had overtaken 'Vanguard' and her complement. Moreover, by 1917, Alf had seen his fair share of sudden death at first hand, as this book will reveal. Certainly, the author has no remembrance of his father ever talking specifically about the loss of 'Vanguard', whereas, for example, he can well remember overhearing adult conversations in the late 1930s, in which his father held forth, concerning entire ships' companies, each of 1,000 men and more, being wiped out 'left, right and centre', (as the big battle-cruisers 'Indefatigable', 'Queen Mary' and 'Black Prince' blew up), each ship in just a few agonising moments of time after being hit by the highly-effective German armour-piercing shells at the Battle of Jutland.

Alf had not been present at Jutland, and one supposes that these conversations, (which often involved Alf's father-in-law Joseph Walter GREEN, who had been an artilleryman on the Western Front in WW1) were about the generality of the situation as seen from the viewpoint of a man who was a Gunner and a naval professional talking to another 'Gunner', albeit an Army man, but one who could appreciate a lot of the finer points involved.

---

huge wartime consumption of ammunition on the Western Front, there was a shortage of cordite and chances were being taken by prolonging its storage-times beyond normal safety limits, instead of safely destroying the 'over-expiry' stocks.] Cordite can give off gases which must be vented away. Any incipient deterioration might have been accelerated by such factors as 'hot spots' in the magazines due to inherent poor ventilation, limited circulation of air, and the possibility of ventilation being reduced by the stowage of bulky stores in places which hindered the free flow of air into and out of the ventilation shafts linking to the magazine spaces. These adverse factors had certainly existed to some degree in *Vanguard*. The poor placement of measuring thermometers, possibly causing 'hot spots' to remain undetected was also reported to the Court. Certain recommendations were made, but one feels that a lot of 'head-scratching' had failed to establish a definite cause of the disaster, and considerable unease must have remained. [The earlier losses of the cruisers *Bulwark* (in 1914) and *Natal* (in 1915) also through internal explosion, had merely served to underline that unease. The French Navy, albeit that they used a slightly different and probably more volatile explosive, had experienced similar disasters.] The Court raised (and more or less dismissed) the possibility of deliberate sabotage by dock workers. Nevertheless, it was revealed to the Court that two men had worked on both *Natal* and *Vanguard*, in each case leaving only a short period before first one ship, and then the other, had blown up. One suspects that these two unfortunate men had been 'very severely interrogated' by MI.6 to the point that Naval Intelligence was *'now quite sure that they were innocent'* and the members of the Court of Enquiry were therefore told to disregard sabotage as a possible factor. [See ADM 116/1615A at TNA (formerly the PRO).]

Private Life

Assuming that Alf, who was now approaching his 18th birthday, did go home on leave in mid-1913, he would have found that little had changed in Lincoln. Alf's brother Jack was now 19, his sister Nellie 16, Rose 15, and Eva three months short of her 13th birthday. All four were still helping in their father's business at 'The Crown Hotel'. It was hard work, but the pub was thriving under their father's management and with his children's support. However, 'outside his working hours', it seemed that young Jack had managed to get involved in some quite heavy drinking and some serious 'scrapes', to his father's despair.

For his part, Alf was probably beginning to feel that he belonged to another world. However, he would have pitched in and helped. Already, his Naval training was beginning to drive him to create order out of chaos, by now almost as 'second nature', and it is to be expected that he may have had a few rebuffs for 'interfering' too much with the routines that had been set up, especially by Nellie, who already saw herself as *mater familias* and as a future publican in her own right. There was still a great coolness between Alf and his father, with Nellie continuing to act as a 'go-between' - though, as we have already reasoned, probably as a rather biased one.

England was enjoying days of peace. For those with sufficient wealth and good health it was a magnificent time. In fact, many people were managing to survive quite well, and those in reasonable jobs were furnishing their houses well, dressing themselves in some style, going out to Music Halls for entertainment, and acquiring little luxuries, such as bicycles (which gave them a level of 'mobility and freedom' quite unknown to earlier 'working-class' generations). It is interesting to reflect that those bicycles had only 'acetylene' lamps if they were to be used at night. Indeed, homes were still lit by oil lamps or 'gas mantles' as darkness fell and most people went to bed by candlelight. Even the stages of music halls and theatres were still lit by 'limelight'. All these forms of illumination had to be individually lit, adjusted and maintained. There was no simple 'flick of a switch' in those days and the quality of the lighting, though it had a certain intimacy and romance about it, fell vastly short of modern standards. Domestic fuels were of wood, coal or coke. Every morning, after the dusty ashes of the previous day's fires had been removed, fresh fires had to be skilfully 'laid' with paper and 'kindling', and then lit, to start combustion of the main fuel which had to be added very carefully at the start – otherwise it would 'kill the fire', and, heartbreakingly, the whole process would have to be recommenced. Hot water for washing oneself and household tasks was not available 'on tap', but came from kettles boiled on fires or kitchen ranges.

For these and other reasons, there was considerable toil in running a home, and proportionally more for pubs, such as the one being run by Alf's father and his children. Yet they were beginning to make some money, which the DAVIS Family certainly appreciated, for stark poverty existed in some parts of Lincoln just as in most other cities and towns. And poverty was widespread in country areas, with very many labourers living on short commons' food-wise and having great difficulty in adequately clothing themselves and their families.

On the whole, it seems probable that Alf would have been quite happy when his leave was up, and he could get back to Naval Life - and the prospect of another ship, and, who knows, perhaps of a posting to some exotic place abroad.

CHAPTER FOUR:

HMS *RUSSELL* (1912-13)

I f Alf had headed 'into the future' when he first set foot on HMS *Vanguard*, he stepped a bit 'back into the past' when he boarded his next ship, HMS *Russell,* to which he was officially drafted on 13th August 1912. When first commissioned, she had been called a 'First Class Battleship', allegedly costing £1,000,000 to build. But she had now become re-classified and downgraded as a so-called '*Pre*-Dreadnought'. Not that she was really old, for she had been laid down in 1899 and completed early in 1901. It was more that, within much less than a decade, she had been totally superseded and out-moded by the 'Dreadnought' Class of battleships, such as HMS *Vanguard*.

Author's collection. Postcard No.187 in the Empire Series, London, printed in Leipzig, probably in 1901/02.

HMS *Russell*, as built. A cutter pulls around her bows: men are busy on her foredeck. Note the round 'fighting-tops' in the lower parts of her masts and the forward-firing gun-battery inset in the hull near to her bows. These will be removed later in her career.

There is a gap in the sequence of logs for HMS *Russell* which nowadays survive at The National Archives, for one log ends on 11th August 1912, and the next log does not commence until 4½ months later, on 1st January 1913. When the former log ends, we find that the ship was at No 16 buoy on the River Medway, and her company were being paid off at the end of a commission. Officially, Alf joined the ship just two days later, on 13th August 1912, presumably as a member of a draft from HMS *Pembroke* making up a part of the new company for the ship's next commission. This sort of situation would have been more or less the 'norm'.

Author's collection. A postcard in the 'Eastgate' Series by 'W.N Real Photographic'. Postally used on 17ᵗʰ August 1912.

A fine view of Garrison Point on the River Medway, with Sheerness Dockyard on the extreme right. HMS *Russell* was anchored here when her log ended on 11ᵗʰ August 1912. Alf had been drafted to join her two days later. *Russell* is not evident in this photo which was probably taken earlier in 1912. Instead, the 14,900 ton Pre-Dreadnought battleship *Hannibal* of the Majestic Class is in the foreground, with her sister-ship *Ceasar* moored beyond her, both ships bows-on to the incoming tide. A 7,350 ton Edgar Class cruiser, probably the *Endymion*, is proceeding upriver. A steam pinnace surges busily past the viewer and other pinnaces are to be seen in the background taking officers and men, or light stores and equipment, between ship and shore, or ship and ship.

However, the absence of a ship's log at this time, and for the ensuing 4½ months, suggests to the author that the ship may have been left in reserve for a few weeks before being taken out to Gibraltar to be given a refit. If so, Alf would have found himself having a quiet initial period, and then being busily occupied as part of a 'navigating company' as the *Russell* made her southward voyage. It may even be that she was towed out to 'Gib'. Had it been altogether otherwise, one would have expected a log to have existed for this period.

Certainly, when the next available log does commence, on 1ˢᵗ January 1913, HMS *Russell* (Captain G.W. SMITH) has *somehow* made her way out to Gibraltar, and is alongside the South Mole, having evidently just undergone a substantial refit there. Indeed, she is just about to get herself back into operational status, with fore topmast about to be swayed, her wireless yards then to be 'crossed', chain cables soon to be drawn from the dockyard, her magnetic compass soon to be 'swung', and the ship, which is 'riding light', then to be coaled and provisioned ready for sea. This is where we will re-join Alf and his career, so to speak. This is probably the first time he has laid eyes on the 'Med' - though it certainly will not be his last chance to do so.

One suspects that Alf's morale may have sagged a bit the first time he had laid eyes on HMS *Russell,* though, to tell the truth, she did have a certain old-fashioned charm, and it appears that she handled well and was a reliable steamer.

Author's collection. A postcard by Gale & Polden printed c.1910.

HMS *Russell* as she would have appeared when Alf served in her. By this time, a fire-control position to 'unify' her gunfire had been added high up on the foremast and a smaller-scale one on the mainmast. The circular 'fighting top' which was previously fitted to the lower part of her foremast had disappeared, and the fighting-top on the after-mast had been reduced and reconstructed. The gun-battery in the hull near the bows had been eliminated and plated-over. Where the battery once existed, men, seated on stages, are now painting the ship's port side.

HMS *Russell* was of the 'Duncan' Class, and built by Palmers.[91] Her displacement was of 14,000 tons. She had a length of 418 feet and a beam of 75½ feet. Her draught was considerable, at 27½ feet forward and 28 feet aft. Her triple expansion engines gave her 18,220 shaft horsepower and a nominal speed of 19 knots. As we shall see, she could pretty well attain this speed, but it seems doubtful if she could exceed it, and this would be something of a problem when she was exercising with the more modern 'Dreadnought' battleships which could go a full three knots faster. Alf would also have found that she vibrated considerably more, even at her 'most economical speed', than did the turbine-driven *Vanguard*. Vibrated more, probably, than *Vanguard* vibrated, even when *Vanguard* was being driven at comparatively high speed.

Russell's maximum load of coal was 2,200 tons and her range was of 7,200 miles at 10 knots. She carried 80 tons of water for her boilers and 85 tons of water for drinking, etc. Her complement was of 718 men. (It was made up by 45 Officers, 36 Petty Officers, 280 Seamen and Boys, 73 Royal Marines, 192 Engine Room Establishment and 92 Non-

---

[91] At one time the Class Leader, HMS *Duncan*, was a 'Chummy Ship' to the Ship's Company of HMS *Russell*, the author having found an old photographic postcard to that effect. [The photo is of the artistically-produced cover of a programme for a Concert whilst the two ships were at Berehaven. The programme depicts the 'Cockerel' from the ship's badge of *Duncan* welcoming aboard the Lion from the badge of *Russell*. This concert does not appear to have taken place during Alf's year aboard *Russell*, but must have been very near to that period.]

Executive Ratings.) In what had long been the traditional way, her ratings lived in the fore-part of the ship and the officers aft.

Russell's main armament consisted of two twelve-inch B.L (i.e. breech-loading) Mk IX guns in each of two turrets, both on the centre-line, one on the f'c'sle and one aft, the former being forward-firing and the latter aft-firing, and both having wide arcs of fire round to the broadside and beyond. She also had twelve six-inch B.L Mk VII guns in turrets and casemates, mostly firing 'on the broadside', but some also with limited forward and aft firing capability. For close-range defence she also had ten 12 pdr (12 cwt) quick-firing guns, six 3 pdr Hotchkiss guns, two 12 pdr (8 cwt) guns and two 0.303" Maxim machine-guns. And she had four torpedo tubes for which she carried an outfit of eighteen 18" Long Whitehead torpedoes and six 14" standard torpedoes.

She had an armour belt varying from 5" to 7" in thickness, with 11" to 12" over her barbettes and conning tower, and, nominally, 6" for her main gun-turrets. She was certainly no slouch from that point of view.

Russell carried no less than fifteen 'ship's boats'. They were comprised of 2 x 56ft steam pinnaces, 1 x 40ft steam pinnace, 1 x 42 ft launch, 1 x 36 ft pinnace, 2 x 34 ft cutters, 1 x 30 ft cutter, 1 x 27 ft whaler, 1 x 32 ft gig, 1 x 28 ft gig, 2 x 24 ft gigs, 1 x 16 ft dinghy and 1 x 13½ ft balsa raft. For 'Abandon Ship', each 56 ft pinnace could accommodate 80 men, the 42 ft launch 130 men, each 34 ft cutter 66 men, the 32 ft gig 28 men, and so forth, so that her boats were more than sufficient to carry every man-jack of the 718 men of her ship's company.

She had a 'flying' type bridge, which would have been ideal for observation by the Captain and Navigating Officer when conning her alongside low-standing dock walls or low-lying 'camels'. During her career, two large searchlights came to be fitted to the extremities of this flying bridge. As built, another open bridge had also spanned her beam just aft of the mainmast. The span of this bridge was reduced later, and it was also modified to mount two searchlights.

HMS *Russell's* basic details run along the bottom line of each of the two tables below (which are really one continuous table which would have been far too wide to 'fit the page'). The details are compared with the equivalent details for HMS *Vanguard*. [Within each column, starting with 'Displacement', the **bold** type indicates the 'maximum' (or 'preferred') value, characteristic by characteristic.]

Name of Ship	Type Of Ship	Displace-ment (tons)	Year Completed	1st Year Alf srv'd (Ship's age)	Comple-ment	Max. Length (feet)	Max. Beam (feet)	Draught (feet)	Shaft Horse-Power	Max. Speed (knots)
Vanguard	Dreadnought	**19,250**	**1910**	1912 **(2)**	**823**	**536**	**84**	**31.75**	**24,500**	**22**
Russell	Pre-Dreadnought	14,000	1903	1912 (9)	718	418	75.5	28	18,220	19

Name of Ship	Guns					Torpedo-Tubes		Armour			
	Main		Secondary		A.A			Deck	Side	Turr't	D.C.T
	Calibre	Number	Calibre	Number	Capability	Calibre	Number	(ins)	(ins)	(ins)	(ins)
Vanguard	12"	**Ten**	4"	Twelve	**2x3"**	18"	Three	1.5 - 3	**10**	**11**	8 – 11
Russell	12"	Four	6"	Twelve	-	18"	**Four**	2.5	3-4	6	**12**

As indicated by the general lack of **bold** type in the two 'bottom lines', *Russell* was considerably out-rated by the newer battleship HMS *Vanguard* in virtually every particular, except in *calibre* of secondary armament and in the *number* of her torpedo tubes. However, it will be remembered that, insofar as the Dreadnought battleships such as *Vanguard* were concerned, 'Jacky' FISHER had changed the role of secondary armament to be almost solely for close-range defence and no longer to be used as a support for longer range firing by the main armament (due to the risk of confusing 'spotting of the fall of shot' and hence confounding corrections in 'gun-laying') – and the prospects of any battleship firing torpedoes in anger was, to say the least of it, 'remote'.

It was very significant that centralised fire-control stations for *Russell's* main armament had been retrospectively fitted in 1906, to bring her towards some sort of parity with the modern 'long range' gunnery principles embodied in the Dreadnoughts.

Author's collection. A tinted postcard by Bean, Malin & Co., of Gibraltar, printed in Saxony c.1912.

HMS *Russell*, identifiable by the twin white bands on her two funnels, in Queen Alexandra's Dock No.1 at Gibraltar. She is well-secured with large wooden 'shores'. Painting stages are rigged well forrard near her port bow. A large party of sailors is going aboard over her brow. The two 12"guns in her 'A' Turret show to advantage, and the two forward-firing 6" guns of her port-side secondary armament can also be distinguished both on and immediately below her upper-deck level. A 14,000 ton cruiser of the 'Drake' Class lies in No.2 Dock. Two other vessels lie alongside the New Mole, but the large 'Med' Fleet is 'notable by its absence'.

Russell's masts went through various modifications in her career, basically to improve her maintops in respect of gunnery spotting and control. However, the masts remained of 'single pole' construction, never attaining the more stable 'tripod' construction used in the Dreadnoughts. This meant that her fire-control crews would have had considerably more vibration with which to contend than did their equivalents in the more modern ships, with their tripod masts.[92] By the end of *Russell's* career, her pole masts had grown to a considerable height, evidently to as much as 190 feet. This was to

---

[92] To say nothing of the triple-expansion engines having been superseded by turbine power, which caused much less vibration in the Dreadnoughts when at speed, as in a gun-action.

aid in wireless transmission and receiving but must surely have added to the roll of the ship.

As indicated in the earlier note about her 'chummy ship', *Russell's* badge showed a lion rampant. Early in her life *Russell* had been given buff funnels and masts, but during the time of Alf's service aboard she was painted grey overall. The twin white identifying bands around her funnels, as in the above photograph, were intended to distinguish her from her sisters, who were *Albermarle, Cornwallis, Duncan* and *Exmouth*. (Each ship had different combinations of identifying funnel-bandings.)

Alf could not have known it, but he was going to gain a great deal of practical experience in *Russell*, pre-Dreadnought or not. So, let's get back to the life of Alf and his shipmates in January 1913.

On 3rd January that year, following her refit, the ship came out from dock and was towed to No 7 buoy at Gibraltar, so that she could be 'swung' (with the assistance of a tug), to check the variation of her magnetic compass. During this 'swinging' operation, the wire 'bridle' which secured her to the buoy suddenly and dramatically parted under the strain, though, luckily, nobody was hurt by the dangerously flying ends of the broken bridle. Fortunately, the underwater pendant to the buoy held, despite the wild gyrations of the buoy due to the abrupt removal of the strain, and *Russell's* company were able to quickly set up a new bridle. There must then have been distinct sighs of relief all round, for, until that moment, the ship, which had no steam raised, had been completely out of control and, despite the presence of the tug, *Russell* might have drifted dangerously off station at great risk of collision or grounding, had it not been possible to re-secure her to the buoy immediately.[93]

On the 5th January 1913, the ship, now provisioned and coaled, lit fires in three of her boilers, and, all seeming well, two hours later she lit nine more. She unshackled from the buoy, rove a slip rope, hoisted in her picket boat, then slipped and proceeded out of harbour working up for trials of her machinery following her major refit.

No serious problems being found, she shaped course for England, going to her normal routines on board, and exercising her sea boat's crew.

On 7th January, she sighted Cape Finisterre on a bearing of N38°E, exercised at General Quarters, and, during that day and the next, inspected small arms, exercised at Collision Stations, exercised a training class at gunnery, employed hands at cleaning the ammunition passages, and so on.

On 10th January she 'came to' at Sheerness, setting out her many booms and exercising her net defences, whilst her fires were banked up, and some subsequently let go out. Her boys were put at physical drill, and further training classes were held at gunnery. A working party was set to holystone the decks, to bring them back to sparkling whiteness after the 'tribulations' of her refit. Long Leave was granted to the Port Watch.

Before the end of the month, six POs and 44 men and boys had been discharged to the depot. Meantime, the ship had entered Sheerness Harbour, securing to No 7 buoy,

---

[93] The 'pendant' runs down from the buoy to the sea bed where (in the 'three-arm system') it is shackled to a central ring from which three very heavy 'ground chains' radiate out horizontally (at angles of about 120° to each other) to the three 'mooring anchors'. A more sophisticated arrangement, involving four mooring anchors and used when there is a need to keep the fairway clear, is known as the 'span-mooring' system. Whichever system was in operation for No.7 Buoy at Gibraltar, a failure of the pendant would have left the buoy drifting free and thus useless.

where her slightly reduced company coaled ship from a lighter (taking in 820 tons). They cleaned ship after this heavy and grimy task, and, next afternoon, washed clothes.

An intensive period of activity followed, with a detachment at infantry drill, gunlayers exercising at the Deflection Teacher, the Gunnery Training Classes put at small arms drill and a training class practising at the 6" 'Dotter' of Percy SCOTT fame. Quarters were practised, and hammocks were scrubbed. By now the Port Watch had returned from its Long Leave, and the Starboard Watch now went off in their turn on Long Leave. Doubtless, Alf went off with one watch or the other. Some 'Friday whiles' and 'Saturday whiles' were also granted during this period.

On 11th February 1913 the company provisioned ship and took in torpedoes, and on the 12th they coaled again, taking in 378 tons from 0730 to 1230, and then cleaning ship. On 16th February the colours were half-masted, and a Memorial Service was held aboard in tribute to the late Captain Robert Falcon SCOTT RN and the members of the British Antarctic Expedition who had lost their lives in a vain but valiant bid to be the first to reach the South Pole. The heroism displayed in this endeavour had made a huge impression on the British Nation at that time. Indeed, these unfortunate men, especially the self-sacrificial Captain OATES, became role-models in heroism for the youngsters of that era - and, to some extent, even to their sons, such as the author of this book.[94]

Author's collection. A postcard by J Welch & Sons, Photographic Publishers of Portsmouth, Series No.339. Card printed in Saxony, Germany, circa 1911.

Sheerness Dockyard. Within its one, small basin lies a 7,700-ton 'Crescent' Class cruiser, with a set of sheerlegs towering high above her. Smoke streams from the tall stack of the steam-engine of its heavy lifting gear. A Thames barge is berthed on the near side of the mole.

During the remainder of February, and well into March, *Russell* continued training her company, and participated in various fleet exercises in the Irish Sea, and around the north coast of Ireland as far west as Malin Head. As a part of the fleet, she

---

[94] In modern times, cold-blooded and retrospective analysis has demonstrated some of the very serious errors which were made – one might even call some of them 'follies' – and this has rather debunked the heroism of the great endeavour. However, for the purpose of this book one needs to look at these matters in the context of the attitudes and knowledge which then prevailed.

also roved eastward into the Firth of Clyde and around the Isle of Arran, entering various anchorages which would have been new to Alf, sometimes putting out her booms and extending her anti-torpedo nets from them. At sea, her company practised going to 'Action Stations', and *Russell's* men became expert at 'streaming paravanes' (to sweep mines), at night-firing of her main armament at moving targets, at the use of her searchlights, at firing torpedoes (and evading torpedoes fired at the ship by other vessels), at coping with simulated battle-damage (including the loss of power in one engine or propeller), and at suddenly transferring command from her Captain to her Commander (her Captain having suddenly announced in the middle of some complex evolution that he was '*temporarily dead*' by enemy action).

They practised meeting up with the other ships of the fleet at one pre-ordained point in the 'ocean', at a pre-set time. They practised 'Out Fire Engine' and 'Out Kedge Anchor'. They trained at landing *Russell's* Marines for infantry drill. They put their battalion of seamen to small arms training. They carried out 'Full Power Trials' and 3/5ths Power Trials. All this they did, and much more, including all the 'normal training' in seamanship and gunnery for her Boys, like Alf.

Alf would have played his part in certain aspects of the various exercises, and must have learned a lot from them. One wonders if he may even have 'borne an *extra* hand' at times. For example, during the 'Full Power' engine trials, in *Russell's* case pounding along at a speed of 18.5 knots, her stokers would have been working extremely hard, for she was consuming coal at the tremendous rate of very nearly one ton per mile, as compared with only 0.44 tons per mile at their 'ordinary speed' of 12 knots and significantly less than that at their 'most economical speed'.[95] Yet, during the Full Power Trial, the Bridge would probably have been imploring the Engine and Boiler Room staff for yet more speed, because the 'pre-Dreadnoughts' like *Russell* would have been struggling hard to 'keep up' with the much higher-powered and turbine-driven 'Dreadnoughts' like *Neptune*. The smooth-running turbines of *Neptune* and her sisters provided a potential speed in excess of 20 knots, and the pride 'against the odds' of the captains of the pre-Dreadnought ships with their slogging 'triple-expansion' engines, would doubtless have been at stake. Under these circumstances the Boiler Room may well, in response, have begged the Executive staff to send working parties of seamen to help out the stokers in the very hard labour of 'shovelling coal at high speed' – probably more by bringing coal from the bunkers to the stokehole, and by clearing away and disposing of the ash, than by the actual feeding of the fire bed, which was very skilled, hot and heavy work.

Alf would have been beginning to be able to identify ships of the fleet at some distance off by now. Thus *Albemarle* and *Duncan*, which were sister-ships of *Russell,* had profiles which would have looked very familiar to Alf, and, closer to, as already said, they would have been nicely distinguishable from each other, because each ship had a different pattern of banding on her funnel. However, *Africa*, another Pre-Dreadnought, could have caught youngsters like Alf out, for, although of a later class, her profile was not dissimilar to the Duncan class - that is, until a detailed comparison was made. On the other hand, the Dreadnought *Neptune*, which was often in company at this time, would

---

[95] The log does not give details regarding the measurement of 'Most Economical Speed' for this time-period.

have had a very different profile to the pre-Dreadnoughts. In fact, though a Dreadnought like Alf's previous ship *Vanguard*, she would not have looked at all familiar to Alf because she had a very different spacing of her funnels and masts to that of *Vanguard*. All in all, the data of all kinds which Alf would have been striving to fix in his brain at this time of his career was vast.

On 8th March *Russell* and her consorts were moored at Lamlash, on the south-east coast of the Island of Arran, when, for the first time in his life, Alf would have heard a Court Marshal Gun fired and probably seen the senior officers who filed solemnly aboard to sit in judgement in the court.

On 10th March, Vice-Admiral BRIGGS inspected the ship's company and the ship herself. That evening they towed a target out of harbour, and later themselves carried out two runs of 1" aiming rifle firing at a target towed by *Albemarle*, before proceeding to Whiting Bay. Leaving there the next day on the way to a fleet rendezvous, they were subjected to a dummy torpedo attack by submarines. Then Vice-Admiral BRIGGS came aboard from *Albemarle*, and they proceeded with another night-firing exercise, this time with their 12-inch guns, and using sub-calibre ammunition, before returning to Lamlash Harbour. 'Night-firing' is easily said, but, on a pitch-dark night, with one's eyes being 'blinded for several moments' from time to time, by one's own and nearby gun-flashes, and with the ships in company manoeuvring at speed and possibly changing courses the while, the whole operation could be very exciting and stimulating, but also seriously fraught with great danger. One wonders if Alf leant the trick of keeping one eye closed when bright flashes were to be anticipated, thus preserving some of his night vision.

Author's collection. An inset photo from a postcard in the 'Reliable Series' by 'W R & S', ref 545/204, marketed by R S McNEISH, General Merchant, Lamlash. Printed in Saxony, Germany c. 1910.

A photograph of the anchorage at Lamlash on the east side of the Isle of Arran. Note the very rocky foreshore. The nearest dreadnought battleship is HMS *Neptune*, the only one of her class. To Alf, her profile would have seemed very different to that of his former dreadnought, the *Vanguard*, mainly because *Neptune's* mainmast was set so far abaft of her second funnel. She was also unusual in having a long, raised superstructure running between her two masts, and she had 'X' turret placed high up, to 'super-fire' over her 'Y'.

It was whilst they were at Lamlash, on 14th March, that they had a boat handling accident in which their 30 ft cutter was swamped, losing its awning and cover overboard.

Luckily, it seems that the boat's crew came to no harm. That same day the ship's company coaled ship (550 tons), and, on St Patrick's Day, the 17th March (Alf's brother Jack's birthday), the fleet left for Portland, working up to a further Full Speed Power Trial in response to orders received from the C-in-C whilst en route.

On 20th March 1913, at Portland Harbour, Captain H.A.S FYLER RN took command of the ship, and Captain G.W. SMITH RN was 'discharged to the shore'. Commander C.C. WALCOTT joined the ship as her second in command, and Commander G.P. BEVAN was discharged to the shore. That same day they coaled ship again (650 tons).

Author's collection. A postcard in the 'Royal' series, No.4429, 'Life in the Navy', by M. Ettlinger & Co., London. Card issued c.1905

A Holland-type submarine of 1904 vintage. There is much more of this bulbous vessel beneath the surface than her limited upperworks would suggest. The submarines with which *Russell* and her consorts were manoeuvring in 1912 were probably of later marks than this, were already capable of 12-16 knots on the surface (8-10 knots submerged) and were fitted with two or more torpedo tubes. Some 'subs' could also lay mines. They were being rapidly & progressively developed in all major navies. As we shall see, when WW1 broke out surface ships were very vulnerable to submarine attacks, and the range of offensive or defensive counter-measures which could be adopted was very limited.

On 24th March the ship's divers were down below, examining her underwater fittings. Evidently, all appeared well, for she then proceeded to sea in company with her class leader, *Duncan*, and they engaged in one-inch aiming rifle practice, taking it in turns to veer and tow targets for one another, before arriving at Sheerness. Whilst there, they took the precaution of getting out cordite charges for inspection and testing. They then coaled again, and provisioned ship, subsequently having to report the loss of a small hazelwood fender, '*lost overboard by accident between the ship's side and the provisioning lighter alongside*'. It has to be said that small losses of equipment to Father Neptune occurred quite frequently, shovels and coalbags being particularly vulnerable, their tumbling overboard doubtless aggravated by the large numbers of men involved and the fatigue which tended to occur when coaling ship. This tiredness and over-exertion could be magnified if the C-in-C had set one ship in competition with another, and the men were thus being driven to some extent by keen officers - but mostly by their pride in their ship and their own determination not to be last!

On 12th April 1913 the light cruiser *Weymouth* arrived at Sheerness, and one wonders if Alf laid eyes on her at this time, because she was going to be of very considerable significance to him during the next three years.

Russell's company remained active, the ship putting back to Portland for a while, and then with all the ship's boats being away sailing in Weymouth Bay on the 21st of April. Her gunners were continuing their training with 1" aiming-rifle firing, her torpedomen were practising in the flat which housed the submerged torpedo tubes, and one of the gun-crews of the secondary armament was authorised to fire off just one round of 6" ammunition. This was all a preliminary for another fleet exercise under the C-in-C, involving squadron firing of torpedoes, and of 'counter-firing' against a mock daylight attack by destroyers. On May 1st the practice was extended to include squadron firing at targets towed, in turn, by the various ships of the squadron, including *Russell* herself.

On May 6th the ships were dressed overall in honour of the Accession of H.M. King George V. The short Edwardian era was over, probably to the regret of many people. Despite his rather notorious years when Prince of Wales, Edward VII had striven to be a good king who had paid considerable (and badly-needed) attention to naval affairs. Admiral FISHER and many other officers would greatly mourn his passing. The reign of George V now lay ahead, like an as yet unwritten book.

During the ensuing days after the new monarch's accession the crews of *Russell's* main turrets fired sub-calibre ammunition at towed targets, and, later, the gunners fired both their 12" guns and their 6" guns at a target towed by the light cruiser *Active*. In terms of defensive measures, they also practised 'out collision mats' and 'out fire engine', as well as connecting up the after conning tower steering gear and employing it for a while, before reverting to the use of the normal fore-bridge steering gear. On the 8th they again carried out gunnery practice on their 12" and 6" guns, again firing at targets towed by *Active*. On the 13th they prepared the ship 'as for war', and, two days later, Rear-Admiral BRIGGS came aboard to inspect the ship and her company. They then put to sea, and practised 'special firing' with sub-calibre ammunition at a target towed by HMS *Africa*, did some target-towing themselves, and eventually handed over the target to the care of a dockyard tug, leaving *Dreadnought* herself, the pre-Dreadnoughts *Hindustan* and *Africa*, and the light cruiser *Active* to continue the exercise.

On 21st May 1913 they were at sea again, when a submarine made a practice attack on the squadron. [It is unfortunate that we neither know what counter-measures (if any) were adopted, nor how successful (or otherwise) the tactics followed by the submarine were deemed to be, nor what lessons may have been learned.] Then *Russell* and the others ships in company moved on to a range-keeping exercise, followed by an exercise at 'preparing to be taken in tow'. They were 'streaming paravanes', with the Lizard on their starboard beam, when they ran into thick fog, causing them to reduce speed and stream a fog buoy. This would have been a tense time, with so many large vessels manoeuvring in close proximity to each other, with each ship in column anxiously following the 'Will o' the Wisp' of the fog buoy of the preceding ship and trusting that the lead ship was holding to a safe course. The fog eventually dissipated, but it had delayed the squadron for a while as they shaped course northward for Stornaway, later returning to Lamlash.

On 26th May, the Squadron, with a destroyer escort, proceeded out of Lamlash harbour to practice long-range torpedo-firing. The destroyers subsequently made two dummy attacks on the battleships. More practice, but this time involving the various gun-crews ensued in the next few days, interspersed with coaling, 'cable-surveying', painting ship, practising 'Abandon Ship' drill, connecting up the emergency 'handwheel steering gear', going to 'Collision Stations', landing their Marines in full marching order, etc., etc.

On 3rd June, they dressed ship in honour of King George V's birthday and fired a 21-gun salute. More mundanely, working parties were cleaning out the port and starboard chain-lockers at this time - an important task, designed to minimise the foul smells from the mud residues brought in on the anchors and cables. The cables were always hosed down as they came inboard, but some mud always managed to cling on.

Author's collection. An anonymous postcard, entitled 'Abandon Ship'. Pencilled on reverse, 'HMS Emperor of India'. Date of issue c.1914.

In late May of 1913, Alf would doubtless have been one of the crew of *Russell* who took part in an 'Abandon Ship' exercise. This photo evidently relates to the training of the crew of the Dreadnought *Emperor of India*. However, the photo gives some idea of the experience which Alf and his shipmates would have gone through, with some men in boats (perhaps being towed by the steam pinnace), and with others staying afloat by means of clinging to the lifelines of rafts. There are about 80 men visible in this picture. One can imagine what a daunting sight *800 men* would make to the eyes of would-be rescuers. It should be noted that this photo shows 'Carley Floats' in use. They had evidently been introduced c.1914. In 1913, the crew of *Russell* might have had to manage without their aid.

At times, Vice-Admiral BRIGGS came aboard, presumably to 'sharpen things up', and to have his 'Very Important Person' safely transferred from ship to ship whilst at sea. By way of lighter relief, a 'Sailing Regatta' was planned for 20th June - but had to be postponed because there were only fitful airs that day. Luckily, on the next day winds of 1-2 knots held fair, and the regatta went ahead. Then it was back to more 'standard training' of the men and boys at gunnery, at landing the small arms companies, at getting up the field guns, and at the prosaic but skilled and painstaking task of painting (this time painting the ship's boats). The ship also put to sea for 'rate of change' exercises with *Cornwallis* and other ships, designed to improve gunnery control.

On 1st July they were back at 'Full Power' trials and 4/5ths Power trials, and other 'listed manoeuvres', followed by a second FP trial. Next day, the Squadron left harbour, formed up, and headed south for Portland. They arrived there on the 5th, and coaled on the 8th, *Russell* taking in no less than 1,465 tons! This sounds like really hard and filthy work. Perhaps it's not surprising that 28 coal bags were accidentally lost overboard in the process![96] *Russell's* bunkers must have been getting unusually low, though far from being so low as to be critical. (She could carry up to 2,200 tons at her maximum capacity.)

Alf attained his 18th birthday on 9th July 1913. This was a significant event in his career, for, by virtue of already holding the status of Boy I, his age of 18 years now immediately qualified him for the rank of Ordinary Seaman, though one presumes that he had to formally attend as a 'Requestman' to obtain it. He then officially became 'a man', and his naval service proper began from that date. His pay immediately leapt from a substantive rate of 7d a day to the Ordinary Seaman's substantive rate of 1s.3d a day, and with the prospect of earning more when he attained the rank of Able Seaman (and then more still if he worked his way up through the various rates in 'gunnery', which he had selected as his specialisation). [Note: These rates of pay had prevailed since c.1895.]

Author's collection. A postcard in the 'Wellington' series by Gale & Polden, probably dating from 1904. Card postally used 16th November 1904.

Ratings practising at loading a 6-inch gun. First man on right is holding a 6-inch shell weighing about 100 lb. (regarded as the limit able to be manually-handled repetitively). A charge is being loaded into the breech, with two men in the rear holding further charges. A rammer lies on the matting. Only the gunlayer and the gun-trainer, seated inside the shield, have any protection from incoming enemy fire. The other members of the gun-crew would be very exposed indeed.

Alf had confirmed Chatham (HMS *Pembroke*) as his Port Division. This '*Pembroke*' decision would hold good for the rest of his service life. Moreover, by virtue of having already signed on for his 'twelve' (i.e. for twelve years), he had become a

---

[96] As a matter of interest, 28 bags represent less than 3% of the 1,000 or so bags which would have been in use. One imagines that there must have been a certain level of wear and tear on the ship's stock of bags, and one wonders if some of these 'losses from the ledger' might just somehow have been of the 'worst-deteriorated' bags.

'continuous service man'. This meant that, provided his conduct was satisfactory, and should he subsequently sign on for a further ten years, making 22 years in all, he would then become eligible for a pension, for which his first twelve years would 'count'. (In stark contrast, had he signed on for spells of only five years at a time, he would not have become eligible for a pension. The thinking behind this was that the Navy wished to encourage long spells of service, rather than to train men up only to risk having them leave.)

Another bonus Alf would have noted immediately was that, as a 'man', he now qualified for longer 'runs ashore' than the limited hours (usually from 1315 to 2100), to which he had been restricted as a Boy. Now, he would often not be required to be back aboard before (say) early the next day. Moreover, he had more money in his pocket to last him through such longer hours. One therefore assumes that Alf would have enjoyed the greater freedom of the one or two new short runs ashore which he was permitted in the remaining time available. There was another privilege which was still denied to him – that was a daily 'tot' of rum. He would not be entitled to it until he attained his 20th birthday. He would then be able to use the well-established principle of 'sippers' and 'gulpers' to solicit little favours from his shipmates. And what was left of his tot after paying off his dues could then be a wonderful comfort, especially when coming off watch chilled through on miserable, cold, wet days.

The question of money was certainly a real one. A sailor's pay was far from lavish, and a 'matelot' could find that several hands were reaching out to him for payment almost as soon as he stepped away from the paymaster's table, fortnight by fortnight.[97] Amongst others there could be the 'Jewing Firm', who were always in demand to 'improve' the issue uniform to a flattering degree, and there could also be the 'Dhobying Firm', the 'Barber', the 'Bookstall', past loans to repay of Soap and Tobacco, purchases to do with 'Slops' (items of clothing), and perhaps a 'Sweepstake' ticket to be paid for….and, always, the Mess Bill to be paid off. One had to watch one's commitments carefully, if anything at all was to be left for the odd 'run ashore'. The 'pressure' by shipmates to join in all kinds of social activities afloat and ashore, and their begging for loans, had to be gently resisted at times, but without coming over as a 'spoilsport' or driving the others 'Up the Pole' in frustration.

---

[97] When serving abroad, sailors were paid monthly.

Author's collection. A postcard in the Rotary Photographic Series, Ref. 6776 B, postally used at Chatham, on 6th December 1910.

This card, posted from 18 Mess, A2, RN Barracks at Chatham, was sent from a rating to his brother. The photograph shows a one-man 'Jewing Firm' at work. In true tailoring tradition, this Leading Torpedo Man is seated cross-legged as he goes about his 'Jewing' work, with his cotton-reels and tape-measure ready for use beside him. The other 'Stripey' appears to be earnestly asking a favour of him, though the cameraman may have helped to pose this shot. Men with good tailoring skills were always in great demand to 'improve' to a flattering degree the fit of the uniforms which were issued.

Now, however, it was back to sea for more exercises with the Squadron, including one in which *Cornwallis* took *Russell* in tow. Unfortunately, the port hawser parted under the strain (apparently without the ensuing 'whiplash' causing any human casualties), and then, when *Cornwallis* cast off the restored tow five hours later, the hawser somehow became caught under the bottom of *Russell*. [The upshot was that 52 fathoms of 6" Manilla rope, 88 fathoms of 5" Coir rope, and another 48 fathoms of 5" Coir rope, were accidentally lost.[98]] The Squadron sailed on for Bantry Bay, in south-west Ireland, leaving *Russell* to 'sort herself out as best she could', before catching up. This task duly accomplished, she took station astern of *Dreadnought*, just in time to practice 'streaming paravanes'.

In the next few days, operating from south-west Ireland and playing the part of a 'hostile fleet', the Squadron practised the 'capture' of numerous of the merchant ships which were innocently plying that part of the ocean. The squadron then headed out into the Atlantic for further manoeuvres, *Russell's* Captain 'communicating' with *Dreadnought* by boat when in mid-Atlantic, at 50° 30'N, 30° 5'W, about 300 miles south of the Denmark Strait.

By 1st August the Squadron had returned eastwards via the English Channel into the North Sea, again on manoeuvres, passing through a fleet of drifters and having to keep altering course to avoid one drifter after another.[99] Whilst busily so doing, heading

---

[98] Coir rope, having good extensibility and being sufficiently light to float on the surface of the sea, was often involved in towing work. (The total length of the various ropes lost on this occasion was about 188 fathoms (or 376 yards.)

[99] Fishing fleets always caused something of a problem due to the need to keep well clear of the nets, which were often paid out far from the position of the fishing boats themselves. As *Russell* was not so very long back from 'The Med', one wonders if this need for careful circumvention might have caused

ever northwards, they nevertheless 'kept an eye on the ball', and sighted the 'hostile' Red Fleet off their starboard bow, themselves advancing to engage the 'enemy's' battle cruisers off the mouth of the River Tyne, at 55° 51' N, 1° 34' W.

Subsequently, the two fleets of battleships 'came into action' against each other, and one assumes that the umpires had a busy time deciding which ship had sunk or damaged which, and to whom victory should be awarded. The battle over, *Russell* 'parted company from the Flag', and headed into the Thames Estuary - coaling with 1,265 tons, as a reflection of the many miles she had been sailing, and losing overboard 24 coal bags and two shovels, for good measure. Whilst in the Estuary, Alf might well have seen his former ship *Vanguard*, as she headed upriver with the pre-Dreadnought battleship *Hibernia* in company. If so, one wonders what his thoughts might have been. Were they perhaps a little nostalgic for *Vanguard*, or was he feeling so well-settled in the good old *Russell* that he now had no time for such thoughts?

During the next few days at the Nore, the company re-provisioned ship, with the Boatswain's, Carpenter's and Gunner's Torpedo parties all actively drawing stores at Chatham. On 23rd August the company dressed ship and fired a royal salute of 21 guns as the splendid old Royal Yacht *Victoria and Albert* sailed from the Nore, and on the 28th they themselves slipped and proceeded to Portland.

It is understood that *Russell* was re-commissioned at Portland. Certainly, Alf was discharged from her on 30th September 1913, carrying his bag and lashed-up hammock down the brow, and being drafted to HMS *Pembroke* from 1st October, presumably for training and requalifying examinations towards his hoped-for promotion from Ordinary Seaman to Able Seaman.[100] He was also due some leave, which was given on the scale of 7 days in every four months, plus, hopefully, some weekend leaves - which would be a mix of (short weekend) 'Saturday whiles' and (long weekend) 'Friday whiles'. One way and another, he would probably have headed home for a time, on at least one such occasion.

Alf had learnt a lot - some of it 'ex-officio' in absorbing the many human lessons of how to live acceptably 'cheek by jowl' with his shipmates. We have not dwelt on that basic but vitally important aspect of lower-deck naval life. Perhaps we should now take another glance at it, aided by the following photographs.

By now Alf would long have become adapted to hoisting himself into his hammock, even when other hammocks, each filled with a sleeping shipmate, were crowded all around, perhaps giving less than the regulation 14" of space, so that, coming off watch at night, Alf would have had to push his neighbours gently aside as he settled

---

some jocular comments on the bridge about the parallels with the so-called 'herring fleet' of ladies in search of matrimony who descended on 'Gib' and Malta every spring, at the time of the combined manoeuvres of the Home and Mediterranean Fleets - and which 'dainty craft' also needed careful 'evasive action' to avoid their 'matrimonial nets', albeit also sometimes allied with a little dashing and skilful 'risk-taking'.

[100] Throughout this book, *with one important exception*, it has not seemed worthwhile to create separate chapters for Alf's sessions 'between-ships', at *Pembroke* Naval Barracks. Mostly, his sojourns there were brief. [One hears that these barracks were seriously run-down, having been consistently neglected over the years by a parsimonious Admiralty. Most men drafted to these barracks longed to get a prompt posting to a ship, to escape from the dreariness of life at *Pembroke*. Only men whose homes were in the locality, or who had some kind of 'racket' going on, 'kept their heads down' and hoped to be overlooked.]

comfortably into his hammock, whilst the whole array of hammocks and sleeping figures swung in harmony with the roll of the ship.

Author's collection. Postcard entitled "Jack in his Hammock", by C. Cozens, Photo, 168 Queen Street, Portsmouth. Issued c.1912.

A crowded mess-deck, with sleeping and dozing figures swaying side by side. Unfortunately, the abnormality created by the bright lighting for the camera-exposure has created an unusual level of alertness and, doubtless, banter in some of the men. By now Alf would have become well-accustomed to such living conditions and to having the bare minimum of storage space for his possessions, demanding great neatness and control.

We should note that three months before leaving HMS *Russell,* Alf would have 'graduated' from being in an all-Boy mess, with an adult PO controlling behaviour, to become part of a 'man's mess' under a 'Killick' (a Leading Seaman), where Alf would have had to learn to live and mix with adults of widely varied ages, experience and character. He would have had to recognise the subtle variations in 'accepted status' of each member of the mess, which was biased by personality, coupled with physical and mental toughness, and or cheerfulness and good humour, and far more complex than just the 'official status' denoted by the badges each man wore, especially when no officer was present, and quite different again when a warrant officer (by definition highly experienced in all matters affecting the lower-deck), was on hand. [Many years later in Alf's career, we shall see an interesting example of a suspected 'play' on this highly involved interaction with a warrant officer, where conflicting evidence given in the court martial of a rating who went by the name of DAVIS is concerned.[101] We shall also see that 'officialdom' would probably have been better to have kept their noses well out of it!]

When a sailor had received a 'Green Rub' (a 'rebuke' from a senior rank for a misdemeanour which had actually been committed by a *different* rating) it was almost the 'norm' for the shipmates of the innocent man to say, by way of scant comfort, but in a sense consolingly, "If *you can't take a joke, you shouldn't have joined!*" Whether this became Alf's favourite philosophy at that period of his life is unknown, but there must have been some measure of it in his thinking, especially when one remembers the plea he

---

[101] Although happening to bear the same surname of DAVIS, this rating was unrelated to Alf and his family.

had once made in vain to his father, to be bought out, because things had looked so unfair and bad. Certainly, one gets the feel that along the three eventful years which had since elapsed Alf had rapidly matured, and that he was already becoming keen and alert to learn all he reasonably could and to set about developing his skills to a high degree. Perhaps, rather like his once-impoverished but ambitious father before him, he saw the much more comfortable life being lived by 'the officers', and it was now that he started on the long, long road to try, eventually, to emulate their life-style insofar as that was available to a ranker. One feels that, like his Dad, he consciously 'put himself about' to become visibly 'cheerful, optimistic, willing and constructively helpful', but not so much so as to appear priggish and hence not to become repugnant to those of the men around him who were happy to 'obey orders' but who otherwise wanted to 'keep their heads down'. One needed to remember that there was comfort and sociability in simply being a member of the lower deck, and loyalty to an understood but unwritten code of 'them and us' needed to be kept. There was a very fine line to be drawn by the more ambitious man.

So far, Alf had served only in large vessels, where accommodation was crowded, but generally quite well protected from the elements and reasonably 'dry' even when the ship was experiencing heavy weather.[102] So-called 'Canteen Messing' prevailed in these ships, so Alf would have had to take his turn to be the so-called 'Cook', usually working with an 'oppo'.

The job of Duty Cook involved the collecting of the main provisions of (say) Meat, Potatoes and a fresh vegetable from the galley, and using an allotment of the 'Canteen Messing' money (as doled out by his Leading Hand), to buy little extras, as necessary, such as pickles and proprietary sauces. Then preparing the meat in a lidded metal pan, arranging peeled potatoes around and under it – a so-called 'Straight Rush' - and taking it to the galley to be inspected by the PO Cook. If 'passing muster' it would then be handed over, to be cooked in the galley, accompanied by any prepared fresh vegetable, all in the one metal pan. Later, the Duty Cook would have to collect the cooked dishes, and, after the meal had been served and eaten, wash the pans, plates and utensils, clean the table and sweep out the Mess. The following photo was taken about eight years before Alf's time at sea began. However, matters would not have changed very much in the interim.

It would be interesting to know how Alf had coped with having 'graduated' to being in a 'man's mess' whilst he was in *Russell*, but, unfortunately, though knowing that he certainly 'survived', we do not know whether his transition was relatively rough or smooth. Later indications are that it was quite smooth, perhaps with his performance being greatly aided by the manifold experiences he had already gone through in life in dealing with adults of every type and persuasion, including Alf's working as a ten year-old at the 'Crown' in Lincoln before launching into his 'eye-opening' naval career. This had already spanned three years, albeit, until recently, as a Boy Seaman.

---

[102] Condensation could still, however, impose serious problems under certain weather and atmospheric conditions, particularly if the ship was at action stations with all watertight doors closed and/or 'battened down' against heavy weather, and the air circulation thereby greatly restricted.

Author's collection. A postcard from the 'Wellington' series by Gale & Polden Ltd. Date of issue around 1904.

'Dinner' (the midday meal in a Seamen's Mess), always prepared by the 'Cooks of the Day' in time for the afternoon watch to eat before they go on duty. There are various items of gear on the table, including a large metal 'fanny' in the foreground. Matting is being used to reduce the risk of gear sliding off the table due to the rolling of the ship. After the meal has been cleared away, the area will be cleaned and used for relaxation until Supper is taken and cleared away. At 'Pipe Down', hammocks having been slung, men who are off watch will take their rest. The horizontal bars set in the deckhead assist men to climb into the hammocks which will swing from hooks set in the deckhead.

By now, Alf probably felt that he was really beginning to know his way around, and to be able to gauge fairly well the boundaries of discipline to which he must conform. He would have been constantly joining in with all kinds of activities to do with day-to-day living with his fellow-ratings, and this would have been steadily working away on his personality and leading him to adopt certain roles and behaviours to help him to fit as comfortably as possible into his mess and to be well-accepted into the team. He would have been learning to keep certain 'characters' at 'arms length' and also further honing his ability to work each situation as much as possible into his own 'comfort zone'.

Many situations required 'team-working', as in 'washing hammocks' (See following photo).

Alf was probably walking with a sailor's roll in his gait - partly unavoidable after a long spell at sea, but partly exaggerated for effect and to show how 'springy' and fit he felt. His spells aboard *Vanguard* and *Russell*, relatively brief though they may have been, had seen much in the way of training, exercises and manoeuvring, often as a squadron or a fleet, and as a preparative for war. There had been a tremendous amount of data to absorb, and much food for thought for a 'thinking man' to reflect upon. Alf had also now learnt to 'survive' and to 'accommodate' to others, as an adult, on the lower deck.

Author's collection. Postcard by an anonymous publisher c.1913.

Scrubbing and Washing Hammocks. Alf would by now have become well-accustomed to such necessary tasks, usually conducted 'mob-handed', as here. This particular card is said to relate to the ill-fated cruiser HMS *Natal*, which would spontaneously blow up in 1915 with the loss of all on board. The sailor who sent it to his home stands in the back row. He has marked his image with a triple ink-dot.

Probably without even realising it, Alf was now speaking fluent 'navalese'. To him, every man with the name ADAMS was now automatically called 'Daisy', every man with the surname BELL was called 'Dinger', every CLARK was called 'Nobby', every DAY called 'Happy', every GREEN called 'Jimmy', every MILLER called 'Dusty', every WALLACE called 'Nellie', every WHITE called 'Knocker', every WILLIAMS called 'Bungy', every WILSON called 'Tug' and so on and so forth. One presumes that this practice had grown up because the bigger warships carried large ship's companies and there was a need for the men to get to know one another quickly at the start of a commission. Hence, knowing that any man called by the soubriquet 'Dusty' had the surname MILLER, (especially when coupled with the badges of rank and specialisation which he wore), was a positive help towards swift memorisation and subsequent quick recognition of that man in watch bills and other ship's records.

There would be comings and goings during the two to three years of a commission, and probably a total break-up of the ship's company at the end of that time. The whole process of 'getting to know each other' then had to be repeated by the next ship's company in which a given individual was involved. Inevitably, men who had not met for some years might suddenly be thrown together again in a new company – and it was very handy if the nickname was remembered for then the surname, too, would immediately be a 'known'.

There was no 'automatic' nickname for 'DAVIS', so Alf was generally called 'Alf', though, as we shall much later observe, some called him 'Dave' as a nickname.

Author's collection. A postcard from the 'Nelson' series by Gale & Polden, issued c.1904.

This picture pre-dates Alf's service in *Russell* by eight years or so. Here, sailors are re-fitting the clews, lanyards and lashings to newly-washed and aired hammocks. (Like Alf, every Boy Seaman was issued with two hammocks on leaving his training ship – *but only one set of the clews, lanyards and lashings.*) The 'Manual of Seamanship, Vol I' devoted several pages to the importance and care of the Sailor's Hammock. Clean hammocks were to be slung once a fortnight. Contrary to the previous photograph, when being washed they were *supposed* to be scrubbed only with hand scrubbers – NOT with deck scrubbers!

Alf also had a fine grasp on the slang names for the various ranks of officers, with the Commander being called 'The Bloke', the Navigator called 'Pilot', the Gunnery Officer called 'Guns' and the Ship's surgeon called 'Doc'. The Doc's SBAs were called 'Poultice Wallopers', any Supply Assistant was called 'Jack Dusty', any Warrant Cookery Officer a 'Custard Bos'sn, and so on. Chatham was 'Chatty', Portsmouth was 'Pompey', and Plymouth was 'Guz'. Whale Island was 'Whaley'. A 'Bootneck' or a 'Royal' was a Royal Marine. A 'Bottle' was a fierce telling-off or verbal reprimand. A 'Gannet' was a constantly hungry man, who devoured every available scrap of food. A 'Holiday' was a gap inadvertently left when painting (or when setting out washed items to dry on a line rigged on the ship). A 'Snob' was a shoe-repairer and, as we have seen, a 'Jewing Firm' was a rating skilled in tailoring and garment-repairs. Fore and aft rig was a uniform consisting of a peaked cap, a jacket and trousers having conventional creases (rather than the creases down each side of the leg as given to a rating's 'bell-bottoms').

A 'Pier-Head Jump' was a draft chit giving very little time before having to join a ship. Perhaps almost inevitably, we shall see Alf being put very much into such a 'tight' situation later in his career. By 'Murphy's Law', Alf's turn to encounter that particular Pierhead Jump would come at a very tricky time in his private life.

And, talking of travel and ships, here's Alf's 'voyaging to date', shown in map and table.

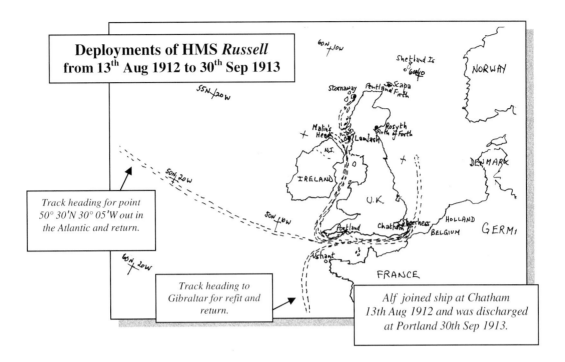

**Deployments of HMS *Russell*
from 13th Aug 1912 to 30th Sep 1913**

Track heading for point
50° 30'N 30° 05'W out in
the Atlantic and return.

Track heading to
Gibraltar for refit and
return.

Alf joined ship at Chatham
13th Aug 1912 and was discharged
at Portland 30th Sep 1913.

VOYAGES DURING THIS DEPLOYMENT: PERSONAL RECORD of Alfred William DAVIS RN					
Farthest North	Stornaway	**57 N** 06 W	*Fa/North (ever)*	*Stornaway*	**57 N** 06 W
Farthest South	Gibraltar	**34 N** 05 W	*Fa/ South (ever)*	*Gibraltar*	**34 N** 05 W
Farthest East	In North Sea	57 N **02 E**	*Fa/East (ever)*	*In North Sea*	57 N **02 E**
Farthest West	In Atlantic Ocean	50 N **30 W**	*Fa/West (ever)*	*Atlantic Ocean*	50 N **30 W**

Now, however, discharged from *Russell* and back at *Pembroke* 'between drafts', it was a return to basics in a subtly different naval world, with Alf being bereft of most of his shipmates. Allocated to a new mess, he would have to start all over again in finding good 'oppos', and creating new relationships. He may have found himself having to 'create something of his own niche', perhaps having to look around for a bunk, or a bed, or just somewhere to sling his hammock, in which he could relax. He may even have had to keep a tight watch on his meagre possessions.

Perhaps Alf was also thinking about going on leave, perhaps to head northwards for a few days. There he could enjoy a little 'home cooking' if he plotted a course back to 'The Crown' at Lincoln and stayed with the family. We'll see what had been happening at Lincoln in just a moment.

Author's collection. A postcard in the 'Wellington' series by Gale & Polden Ltd. Postally used at Chatham 7th November 1904.

Men preparing for a Kit Inspection. This photo precedes Alf's short spell at the Barracks by several years, but the 'feel' and surroundings look very relevant. Note the wide-brimmed Sennit hats in the kit. As we shall see, Sennit hats would have their uses during Alf's deployment under his next draft chit. Note, too, the raised boxing ring. Boxing was a sport which was greatly encouraged in the Royal Navy. (A century ago, the sender of this postcard had been "…*told off for draft to the battleship 'Rodney'*.")

Author's collection. A postcard by Gale & Polden, Nelson House, Portsmouth. Date of issue c. 1904.

The Guard House at Chatham Barracks, with a line of ratings going on leave. Nine years later, this would still have been a scene familiar to Alf. Some of the men are carrying small bags and parcels which probably contain little gifts and souvenirs for their girl friends or families. A few of these parcels will doubtless contain illegal 'rabbits' which the men are hoping to sneak past the sharp-eyed naval police.

Private Life

Whether or not Alf actually headed for home in October 1913, during the 13 days he was nominally at *Pembroke* is unknown. If so, he would have found the domestic situation little different from his previous leaves, though it seems that the pub would have been showing an increasing profit, with Nellie, aged 16, playing an increasingly adult 'bar-manageress role', whilst her father acted as 'Mine Host', and having Rose, who was 15 and had by now left school, available to help out as a regular Bar-Maid. One suspects that, outside 'opening hours', Rose would also have been coping with a lot of the 'backstage' household duties of cooking, cleaning and washing. Eva, now just turned 13, was still attending school, but helping out between-times.

For his part, Jack, now 19½ years old, was evidently still acting as Barman, Potman and Ostler rolled into one, but becoming wilder in his behaviour away from home, to his father's despair. One family legend tells how, 'behind his father's back', Jack 'borrowed' his father's favourite pony and highly-polished gig, and went out carousing one evening. By the time he started back, he was well drunk and night had long fallen. Swinging round near Brayford Pool, far too fast, he totally misjudged his turn into narrow Brayford Street and Jack, pony and gig ended up in the river in a state of total confusion, with Jack and the pony thrashing about in the shafts and in the confused reins and harness of the gig to little good effect, and at serious risk of drowning, for the Pool was deep. It was also dangerously steep-to, so as to allow the deep-draught river-barges to come close alongside the wharf. Jack was very lucky that some pedestrians were nearby, and that they were brave and resolute enough to rescue man, beast and vehicle. Jack's father was furious with him, though glad that the crestfallen and apologetic young man had survived and that the pony had come to no real harm. In the fullness of time, though the matter would always live on in 'family legend', Jack was forgiven by his father.

On the other hand, this same father and Alf were *still* hurt and distant in their behaviour to each other, and neither was yet willing to 'humble himself' by making the first move towards an apology and a possible reconciliation. Nellie was still expected to act as a 'go-between'. As already suggested, it is possible that, with a woman's subtlety, she sometimes even gently invoked the 'divide and rule' principle to the active detriment of the father-son relationship.

Nellie, who had considerable ambition and self-reliance, was probably the only one of the three daughters who was brave enough to stand up to a father who was becoming increasingly dominant and demanding within the family circle. Her strong position as *'mater familias'* would have been of considerable help to her in this regard.

Alf's tales of 'Gib' and other places apparently aroused only limited interest. He would doubtless have been happy enough to go back to his ship at the expiration of his leave. Back to a world where relationships were more regulated and controlled, and much easier to deal with. *He certainly knew he might well be heading somewhere abroad, but whether he fully realised that he might be going off to fight in a war, and that this might be the last time he would ever see his 'parental family' remains unknown.*

As it turned out, his next 'draft chit' was not long in coming.

CHAPTER FIVE:

HMS *WEYMOUTH* (1913-16)

Until now, Alf had served only in a battlecruiser and a battleship, in both of which the hierarchy of command and discipline would have been quite rigidly enforced and formal. However, Alf's life was about to go through something of a sea-change, for his next posting was to HMS *Weymouth*, a so-called 'Protected Cruiser'. Here (in a ship which was considerably smaller and mustered only half the number of men to which he had become accustomed), the lines of demarcation and discipline would be rather less rigid, but likely to be far more fine-tuned and subtle.

A photograph reproduced by courtesy of the Royal Naval Museum, Portsmouth.

The 'long and lean' cruiser, HMS *Weymouth*, much as she would have looked (once out of dock) when Alf, then aged 18, joined her at Chatham, in mid-October 1913.

Officially, Alf joined *Weymouth* (Captain W.D.CHURCH) on the 15th October 1913, which was the day of her re-commissioning, at Chatham, ready, as her Log put it, *'for further service in the 2nd Light Cruiser Squadron'*. At 0730 the 'old' Ship's Company had filed ashore to head by rail for the Portsmouth Depot, and by 0900 a 'new' draft from the Chatham Depot (doubtless including 18 year-old Alf), had come aboard and the ship, which was lying in No.3 Basin of the North Dockyard, had immediately been re-commissioned.

That very same day, Alf's promotion to Able Seaman had become effective, whereupon his substantive pay had increased from 1s.3d to 1s.8d a day, with the prospect of a further increase to 1s.11d if his conduct remained satisfactory. In those days, having just a few more coppers in his pocket made quite a difference to what a sailor could buy as 'little extras' to improve his quality of life.[103] [Moreover, having become an AB, Alf had now qualified to have opportunities for further allowances of pay to be added on, if and when he progressed sequentially through each of the 3rd and 2nd Class rates in gunlaying. Should he eventually achieve a 2nd Class rating, it would lead on to his pay as an AB reaching as much as 2s.2d a day. *(The '1st Class rate', with its yet higher pay allowances, would be closed to him until such times as he managed to attain the higher rank of Leading Seaman.)* Note: The above rates had increased by 5.25 % since 1895.]

It would turn out that *Weymouth* would provide Alf with much invaluable experience, a certain amount of boredom, suffering and deprivation, and more than a little spice of excitement and danger. Perhaps he would always be a cruiser man at heart, from this posting on.

Weymouth was the Class Leader, completed by the Elswick Yard on the Tyne in 1911, and thus still comparatively new. [True, this was her second commission, but the first had started on 31st October 1911 and had been for a period of only two years.] Her sister ships were *Dartmouth, Falmouth and Yarmouth*. Her displacement was of 5,250 tons, and she was armed with eight six-inch B.L. Mk XI guns, and two twenty-one inch submerged torpedo tubes. In the near future she would also be armed with one three-inch anti-aircraft gun (the number later being increased to four). Aircraft, at that time made from low-density wood and canvas, fixed together with glue, string and bracing wires, and painted with dope to protect the assembly from the elements, were still in little more than their 'infancy'. However, aircraft would soon begin to play a significant and innovative part in the career of this ship and in that of some of her consorts - one might even say that a cornerstone of 'naval aviation' would be laid in a prolonged action in which *Weymouth* would play an important part ere long.

Her boilers were of the Yarrow type, manufactured by Hawthorn, Leslie & Co. at Hebburn, Newcastle on Tyne. She was propelled by Parsons Turbines, at 23,500 shaft horsepower, the turbines driving 4 x three-bladed screws manufactured by J. Stone & Co. of Deptford. With the considerable power thus being produced *Weymouth* could work up to 25½ knots. This would be an appreciably faster speed through the water than Alf had as yet experienced. Four-funelled, *Weymouth* had a ram bow, and a distinctive (and graceful) 'cruiser' stern. Although she had quite a good freeboard (which would help her gunnery in broken water), she was long and low to look at - that is, if one disregarded her exceptionally tall pole masts with their wireless aerials. (Wireless communication from the Admiralty was now gradually expanding its range and would ultimately become world-wide. Tall aerials, to improve reception, were the order of the day. Admirals and Captains were beginning to lose the great freedom of action which a foreign deployment had previously provided. Whilst there were obvious advantages in speeding-up 'communications with base', there would be some instances where the tighter control from far away would prove to be a positive curse for the 'man on the spot'. We shall see just such a situation unfold ere long.)

---

[103] There were 12 pennies in a shilling and 20 shillings in a pound. When writing amounts, the penny was abbreviated to'd' and the shilling to's'. Then, as now, the pound was abbreviated to '£'. At the time that decimal coinage was introduced in the year 1971, the shilling was worth 5 new pence. However, in 1913 a shilling was worth a lot more than 5p would nowadays suggest, and a quite good evening's entertainment (e.g. having a pint or two whilst enjoying an evening of entertainment at a small Music Hall) could be had for 2s. 6d., nominally equivalent to today's 12½p! Looked at as a 'day's pay', 2s in old money in 1913 was probably the equivalent of today's £20 or more!

Here (along the 'bottom lines') are *Weymouth's* basic details, as compared with Alf's earlier Ships:-

Name of Ship	Type Of Ship	Displacement (tons)	Year Completed	1st Year Alf srv'd (Ship's Age)	Complement	Max. Length (feet)	Max. Beam (feet)	Draught (feet)	Shaft Horse-Power	Max. Speed (knots)
Vanguard	Dreadnought	**19,250**	1910	1912 **(2)**	**823**	**536**	**84**	**31.75**	**24,500**	22
Russell	Pre-Dreadnought	14,000	1903	1912 (9)	718	418	75.5	28	18,220	19
Weymouth	Armour'd Cruiser	5,250	**1911**	1913 **(2)**	392	453	48.5	18	22,000	**25.5**

Name of Ship	Guns					Torpedo-Tubes		Armour			
	Main		Secondary		A.A			Deck (ins)	Side (ins)	Turr't (ins)	D.C.T (ins)
	Calibre	Number	Calibre	Number	Capability	Calibre	Number				
Vanguard	**12"**	**Ten**	4"	Twelve	**2x3"**	18"	Three	1.5 - 3	**10**	**11**	**8 – 11**
Russell	12"	Four	**6"**	Twelve	-	18"	Four	2.5	3-4	6	12
Weymouth	6"	Eight	3"	One	1x3"	**21"**	Two	1-2	Nil	1	2

The **bold** figures show the 'maxima' for each of the characteristics. From the bottom strips it can thus be seen that *Weymouth* was the most recently constructed of the three ships, that she had the highest speed of the three ships on which Alf had so far served, and that she also carried the most powerful torpedoes.

In all other respects she was inferior to the *Vanguard* and the *Russell*, and could not stand in the direct 'line of battle' with them, generally reflecting her quite different role in naval warfare. That is to say, her normal task would be the protection of Britain's world-wide trade against enemy commerce raiders, or in scouting ahead of fleets of battlecruisers and battleships in operations against enemy fleets of various combinations of warships. In either role, should she encounter enemy units which greatly out-gunned her, her normal role would be to stand off, observe and report back on the movements of those enemy ships until our heavy units could close with them and bring them to battle - rather akin to the *modus operandi* of a frigate in Nelson's time.

Only *in extremis* would she be likely to take on an enemy battleship or battlecruiser. To do so she would probably make a lightning 'hit and run' strike with her torpedoes - perhaps by dashing out briefly from a smokescreen laid by herself or any of her sister-cruisers which might happen to be in company with her - and praying that the enemy battleships or battlecruisers would not anticipate her movements and blow her out of the water as soon as she emerged into view! Generally speaking such 'hit and run' strikes against battleships and battlecruisers were better left to torpedo-assaults by destroyers and torpedo-boats, which were more nimble and faster-moving, and which also presented much smaller targets.)

Weymouth's length was 453¼ feet and her beam 48½ feet. In basic shape she was thus not unlike a medium-length pencil which was swollen slightly towards its centre, and, despite her bilge keels, her rolling in a sea would be much more lively than Alf had experienced in the far heavier and beamier *Russell* and *Vanguard*. Her pitching in a sea would also be different, certainly much livelier than in *Vanguard*, which was 83 feet longer and a much more stable gun-platform by comparison. The pitching, combined with the rolling, would be quite different in character from that of the *Russell*, but more difficult to evaluate, for although the *Russell* was much heavier and beamier, she was actually 35 feet *shorter* than *Weymouth*. This single statistic gives an interesting perspective on *Weymouth's* considerable length.

Author's collection. A postcard by W.H. Smith, c.1916. Reproduced by courtesy of W.H.Smith Archives.

HMS *Weymouth* wearing disruptive camouflage, as she appeared later on during the Great War of 1914-18. Alf was about to undergo a progression of highly varied experiences of peace and war aboard this ship from 1913-1916, greatly honing his character.

Of the eight six-inch guns which formed *Weymouth's* main armament, two single guns were mounted on the centre-line, one forrard on the fo'c'sle, and one aft on the Upper Deck. Two more guns were also mounted on the fo'c'sle, one on each beam, just abaft the bridge. Four more guns were also mounted on the Quarter Deck, one pair amidships and another pair further aft, two on the port side and two on the starboard. All eight guns were on mountings which permitted them to train round to various arcs, outboard of the ship. She thus had three guns which could bear directly forward, and three which could bear directly aft. She could also fire broadsides of up to five guns.

Every gun had a rounded frontal shield, which was fixed to the gun and rotated with it. These shields thus gave limited protection to the gunlayer and the trainer, and any other members of the gun crew who were closed up near the breech, insofar as any incoming fire coming from near the bearing on which the gun happened to be aimed at any particular time was concerned. However, the shields gave only limited cover at the 'flanks' of the gun (and none 'in its rear', or from splinters and débris from shells bursting behind). There was thus very little protection for any supervising Officer and Warrant Officer, nor for the ammunition-supply parties working in the area of deck behind each gun. It will be noted that this was a very different situation from that which existed for the *fully-turreted* main guns of *Vanguard* and *Russell*, and for which the ammunition supply came up through the supporting, well-armoured barbettes. Draughty though full turrets could be, the accompanying difference for guns with frontal shields only, in their limited degree of protection from extremes of weather, will also be noted.

Weymouth had an armoured deck, varying in thickness from ¾ inch to 2 inches, which offered a certain amount of protection from 'plunging fire'. However, she had only limited thickness of armour over her other 'vitals', such as her Director Control Tower, and she had no side-plating to her hull. This made her vulnerable to close-range (i.e. flat-trajectory) enemy fire, and also to torpedoes and floating sea-mines striking on her beam.

With standard load, her draught was 15 ft 9 inches forward and 18 ft 2 inches aft. *[As we shall see, this comparatively deep draught was to prove to be to her disadvantage in 1915 when she was trying to penetrate the inland reaches of an African River in pursuit of a German cruiser of shallower draft.]*

Weymouth's draught was increased by one inch for every 36.2 tons carried aboard beyond her 'standard load'. In terms of that 'standard load', she could accommodate 1,290 tons of coal in her bunkers, giving her an estimated range of 5,600 miles at a speed of 10 knots. At her 'ordinary speed' of 15 knots that range would have dropped to under 4,000 miles. She also carried 274 tons of oil fuel (for 'making smoke', etc.) plus 94 tons of water for her boilers and 34 tons of drinking water for her company.

When Alf joined *Weymouth* she was carrying a considerable range of boats, comprising 1 x 35' steam cutter, 1 x 34' cutter, 2 x 30' cutters, 2 x 30' gigs, 3 x 27' whalers, 2 x 16' skiffs and 1 x 13½' punt. Should hostilities break out, she would reduce the number of boats she carried, and thus minimise the risk of a fire being ignited among them from incoming shell-hits. [*Carley floats - then still a new lifesaving device - would be added later, and would then adorn the sides of her superstructure aft.*]

On joining *Weymouth*, Alf may well have heard one of the braggart 'Jack-me-Hearties' in his draft, (on seeing *Weymouth's* considerable length and narrow beam), commenting in a lordly and dismissive manner that *Weymouth* "*would probably roll on wet grass*", and receiving his 'Acid Drop' shipmate's pessimistic assent "*Sure as eggs is eggs she'll roll - Gawd 'elp us honest Jacks!*" They were not wholly wrong, but, as we shall see, *Weymouth* would prove to be a good sea boat, for in this commission alone she would survive a 'Force 11' gale with a sea which had a conflicting swell, and was sufficiently whipped up by that swell and the strong wind to carry away three of her boats. Nor, in the course of their long careers, did she or any of her three sisters end up by capsizing or foundering, despite meeting a great range of weather conditions.

The full complement of *Weymouth* would total 392 souls, made up of 20 officers, 112 seamen, 14 boys, 29 Marines, 177 engine room establishment and 40 non-executive ratings. However, when Alf joined in October 1913, he found that she was less than 2/3rds manned. Further small drafts and individual officers would be arriving during the ensuing weeks, but, as it turned out, the full complement would not be attained until as late as the 6th January 1914, just days prior to her sailing abroad. It is doubtful if the ship's company would have been aware of the comparatively long term that the initial short-manning was going to last, though they would have been only too well aware that they were short-handed for the present time, and this would certainly have made itself felt for such labour-intensive tasks as coaling and ammunitioning ship. Like 'Saturday's Child', Alf (and his new shipmates) were going to have to '*work hard for a living*', and exceptionally so for some eight weeks to come.

This then was the cruiser *Weymouth*, the ship in which young Alf, now an Able Seaman aged 18, was to serve, initially in a period of peace, but whilst busily exercising for the war which was well foreseen by the Admiralty, and regarded by them as inevitable. The ship's log indicates that this mind-set had filtered down to the junior officers, and, knowing how quickly 'buzzes' generally found their way down to the lower deck, one has to believe that there would have been a general awareness that serious matters were afoot from the start of the year 1914, if not even earlier. The intensity of the training, which we shall soon witness, would have of itself been manifest to the potential seriousness of the situation prevailing.

As Lt C.H.G. BENSON, the ship's new Navigating Officer, wrote in the log, "*At 0900 on 15th October 1913 the ship re-commissioned with an Active Crew.*" His reporting made clear that, in accordance with regulations, 'Fire Stations' were exercised almost immediately the first draft was aboard. Also that, next day, the hands were put to work in refitting and overhauling the boats' gear and surveying the boats' stores. Her Captain and 'No.1' were ensuring that, should the ship put to sea and disaster subsequently strike, the lives of the company would be protected as well as could be.

However, much other work also needed to be done to make the ship fit for her new commission, and, by Saturday 18th October, the ship had six Dockyard Shipwrights and one Dockyard Driller working aboard. The number of Dockyard 'maties' considerably increased during the following days, with the noise of drilling rising, and the disturbance throughout the ship increasing as more and more dockyard 'trades', to say nothing of their masses of associated equipment, came on board. On Saturday 18th October, weekend leave was given to one watch, the Boy Seamen were given leave until 7 pm on the 19th, and, on the 20th many of the hands were sent off as 'Dockyard Parties' to work 'as requisite'. One presumes that all such 'escapes' from the noisy racket and apparent confusion aboard *Weymouth* would have been most welcome to the ship's company.

On 21st October (Trafalgar Day), the company were exercised at General Quarters and Commodore NAPIER carried out an inspection of the ship. Possibly as a result of his inspection, two days later, *Weymouth* was moved into No. 5 Dry Dock, with Dockyard People still busy aboard, and she was then put on blocks, and well-shored with stout beams of wood, as the water drained away. By 29th October she had no less that 55 Shipwrights, 30 Drillers, 45 painters, 15 Bricklayers, 13 Labourers, 12 Fitters and 3 Plumbers working aboard - to say nothing of a working party of 38 Stokers from the depot.

An experienced Gunner, Mr J.L.BROWNE, had joined the ship by this time, and, perhaps as a consequence of his arrival, (and adding to the apparent confusion), by 3rd November, the 'Gunners' Party' were dismounting the 6" guns on the fo'csle, and had moved on by the 5th November to temporarily dismount the remainder of the 6" guns. Then it was a question of re-mounting all the guns. This required hard physical work, despite the use of 'purchases', derricks and cranes to ease the heavy lifting involved. By 11th November the 'Dockyard Swarm' had increased to no less than 160 Shipwrights and 20 Caulkers. Moreover, ten Painters were active. It is easy to imagine how ardently the ship's officers must have been longing by this time to get the ship back to a normal, quiet, 'shipshape' condition and out of dockyard hands.

Yet, there was 'a light at the end of the tunnel', for, on the 13th, the dock was flooded, and the ship was warped out. By the 17th the Carpenter's and Gunner's parties were drawing stores and the hands were filling coal bags from the coal-heap, with a working party of no less than 68 Stokers from the depot giving welcome assistance to the still short-handed company.

Author's collection. A postcard in the 'Nelson' series, ref. No.4291, by Gale & Polden, issued c.1904.

Ship unknown. A working party dismantling a 6-inch gun for examination. Note the heavy-duty handling trolley and the 'purchases' by which the sailors are gaining a 'mechanical advantage', whereby the force applied is much greater than that which merely pulling together on a simple line would have imparted. There is a very large mass being handled here, demanding carefully controlled teamwork and all the proper precautions being taken. This photograph precedes Alf's time aboard Weymouth by almost a decade. However, the principles involved in dismounting her 6-inch guns would have been much the same even though derricks and cranes might have been brought more into use.

On Monday 18th November the company began coaling ship with a vengeance, again with a large working party from the depot helping, and taking aboard 220 tons. Then a further 240 tons next day, 220 tons the day after, and a final spurt of 200 tons to make a grand total of 980 tons. *Weymouth's* draught, after coaling, was 15'10" forward and 17' 6" aft. Whether the company had been expected to clean ship (and themselves) after each spell of coaling is unclear. Perhaps some sort of compromise was reached, but cleaning down thoroughly would certainly have been demanded of the company after the final spell, then thorough washing of themselves and then washing of their 'coaling rig'.

More periods of leave, including weekend leaves, were being given during this time, efforts evidently being made 'within the exigencies of the Service', to bring the members of the ship's company to a state where their leaves were, so far as practicable, 'up to the full allowance'.[104] However, the work of readying the ship for sea continued unabated, with stages now being rigged for touching up the paint on the ship's side. She was then given a 'basin trial', and her compass (which was of the traditional 'magnetic' type) was 'swung', magnetic 'correctors' being installed to bring back within limits the

---

[104] Ratings joining a ship commissioning for 'foreign service' were normally allowed ten days of leave before she sailed.

slight deviation which was found.[105]   This deviation was due to the changes in the naturally-induced magnetic fields of the ship's steel hull and fittings which had taken place subsequent to the previous set of adjustments to 'zero' her compass.

On 25th November she finished oiling (249 tons), ammunitioned from a lighter which came alongside, and sent her steam cutter for urgent 'last-day' dockyard repairs. Three days later, her Marines were inspected and her lifebuoys were checked. Her painting was continued - but ceased in time for the ship to be dressed overall on the 1st December in honour of the birthday of Queen Alexandra, a guard being paraded and a Royal Salute of 21 guns being fired at noon.

On 3rd December the company provisioned ship with the 'necessities of life', stowing cases away in the holds. Painting of the ship and her boats continued under increasingly hostile conditions, and an anchor watch was set because the wind and sea had got up, the wind increasing to Force 6 or 7 by 2000, before 'blowing itself out'. On the 7th December they cleaned the guns, and then there was 'a bit of a sensation', for HMS *Actaeon* was observed to be on fire. *Weymouth* promptly sent boats to her assistance, the boats returning a little over two hours later, by which time the fire had been brought under control.

Next day the company tested all *Weymouth's* flooding arrangements, and painted her guns. On the day after that they began to get up and range her cables for survey, the very comprehensive survey (and the careful oiling and 'flaking down' which would have followed) taking up the ensuing four days. Between whiles they exercised the ship's divers.

NOTE: As throughout this work, the majority of this Chapter has been built up on the basis of the Ship's Logs, which are held at The National Archives, in Kew, London. However, the informal journal of an Unidentified Stoker who served in this Commission of Weymouth is held in the Imperial War Museum, London. Data drawn from that document has been used with the kind permission of the IWM, to supplement and provide additional 'colour' for the narrative which now follows right on through to the end of this Chapter. As we shall see, an Officer's diary will also come to play an important part further on, so that we shall then have had invaluable 'eye-witness contributions' from both the Lower and Upper Deck.

An unusual and tragic event took place on 2nd January, for a Petty Officer, aged 33, was reported missing from a working party engaged in painting the Messdecks. His body was subsequently discovered in the 'chest flat', his death being attributed to strangulation from having hanged himself. His body was sent to Sheerness mortuary, and a Court of Enquiry was held aboard next day. Evidently, it was decided that this was a clear case of suicide and no foul play was suspected.[106] A funeral party was landed next day, the burial being at sea, presumably taking place from a smaller vessel arranged by the dockyard authorities.

---

[105] The aim was to keep the deviation well below the permitted maximum of 2° on each and any bearing of the compass, a specified selection of bearings being checked around the compass rose.

[106] This unfortunate man is named and his death is confirmed as 'Suicide by Hanging' in Admiralty file ADM 104/110 at TNA. Nobody seems to have enquired more than superficially into the dire circumstance and/or 'mind set' which had led him to take this drastic and fatal step.

Matters really began moving on 6th January, when a party of 125 ratings and 18 Marines joined the ship, bringing her up to full establishment at last. The ship coaled again on the 8th - taking nearly 7½ hours to embark a further 300 tons. She took in further ammunition from a lighter, and holystoned her upper deck, striving to get back towards her 'full glory'. She also got in some more messtraps.[107]

At last, on the 17th January 1914, at 1440, *Weymouth* slipped and proceeded, leaving Sheerness, heading out westward through the English Channel and then changing course southwards for the Mediterranean and Malta. Interestingly, the suicide of the Seaman PO does not seem to have been regarded as an unlucky omen for this deployment.

Weymouth had a good crossing of the infamous Bay of Biscay and called at Gibraltar on the 21st; saluting the flag with 13 guns, securing alongside the North Mole, and taking the opportunity to coal ship (300 tons). She stayed overnight and, early next morning she endured a violent electrical storm with heavy rain. As the storm died away, she left harbour to make a short 1/5th power trial, then reduced to 10 knots and continued direct to Malta, running eastwards across the Mediterranean Sea. She reached Malta on the 24th. This appears to have been Alf's first experience of getting out into 'The Med' beyond Gibraltar, and would thus have been his first sight of Grand Harbour at Malta, which was one of the most famous places in 'lower-deck legend'. Once there, the ship promptly coaled again.

During the next few days *Weymouth* was involved in a range of various duties, with her seamen and stokers each having parties at field gun practice, her 6" gun crews (both seamen and Marines) practising at the 'Dummy-Loader', her higher gunnery ratings practising at targets with the 0.303 aiming rifle, her searchlight crews exercising by night, and so on. She also landed her portable wireless gear, sent boats away at sailing practice, and underwent an inspection by the C-in-C.

A court of inquiry was also held on board, regarding the loss of a torpedo fired by another ship. Meantime, her Divers were checking her underwater fittings. She made a short voyage to Marsa Sirocco, where she landed a Picket, underwent successfully a practice attack by torpedo-boats B9 and B11, exercised 'Night Defence Stations' and 'Away All Boats' and landed her Marines for infantry drill. Meantime, 'normal life' went on, with, for example, her boys being kept at seamanship instruction.

By 7th February she was back at Grand Harbour, where she landed a range working party and her stokers' field gun crew, whilst she exercised on board ship the No 2's of all her main guns (evidently to cover the eventuality of their No1's becoming casualties in battle), and also practised 'General Quarters'. She then proceeded to Saint Paul's Bay, carrying out 1" aiming practice during the passage at a target towed by TB 063, and exercising her field gun crews on arrival in the Bay. Then, back to Marsa Sirocco, where she again landed her portable wireless party - and a sports party - and then exercised sub-calibre firing out at sea. Next day she proceeded to Grand Harbour, conducting gunlayers' tests at a target towed by HMS *Gloucester* (of whom more later) whilst in transit.

---

[107] 'Messtraps' signifying cooking utensils, crockery and cutlery of all descriptions necessary for day to day living throughout the commission.

147

'Grand Harbour' at Malta. A 19,000-ton battlecruiser of the 'Indefatigable' Class – probably *Indefatigable* herself - is moored near to Fort St Angelo. Beyond her lies a cruiser, *possibly* of the 5,500-ton 'Weymouth' Class, and maybe *Weymouth* herself. Small craft, known as 'dghaisas', hover around as the Maltese seek to ply their wares to the naval officers and men.

Here, in HMS *Weymouth*, was a ship definitely preparing for war - but with more than half an eye on the 'fleet regattas' and 'field gun competitions' which would soon be coming about if peace were to hold on a little longer! Short leaves were given, including 'canteen leaves', and shore patrols were also landed on occasion. On 16th February, *Weymouth* coaled (275 tons), and sent parties ashore to fulfil duties regarding 'stores', 'provisioning', 'recreation ground' and 'hospital' needs - followed by landing her field gun crews, a ground party, a portable wireless party and a sports party. She also returned her empty cordite cases ashore, following her sub-calibre firing exercises. Her steamboat was especially busy that day, not drawing its fires until 1925.

On the 18th *Weymouth* ammunitioned from a lighter which came alongside, prepared for sea, slipped and proceeded. At 1155 she sighted the 2nd Battle Squadron, and took station astern, initially at 11 knots but working up to the maximum speed for the battleships of 22 knots. This would have been a great and stimulating sight for the men of the ship's company who were in a position to look around on the appropriate bearings. Subsequently, in company with destroyers, she made a practice attack on the squadron, firing a torpedo for which she subsequently searched and later recovered. Parting company with the destroyers, she practised letting go and recovering lifebuoys, and then proceeded eastwards across the Ionian Sea, passing well south of Mount Etna, which was semi-active, and heading for the Island of Platea. On arrival, *Weymouth* anchored in 13½ fathoms, veering 5 shackles, in No.1 Berth. So far as the ratings were concerned, this island was found to be small and destitute, though marginally enlivened by having a wet canteen. The ship landed her signalmen for an exercise here, and also a Marine detachment, whilst training classes continued aboard and an 'hygienic' lecture was given to the men (probably about the risks from sexually-transmitted diseases), just before the seamen ratings were medically inspected. Further communication exercises followed, both 'morse-transmitting' and 'voice control' parties being landed.[108] A kedge anchor was also laid out as an exercise in seamanship, and subsequently recovered.

Other ships came and went, including the torpedo boat destroyers *Basilisk* and *Harpy*. *Weymouth* herself put to sea, and commenced a torpedo test run, hoisting torpedoes in and out as requisite, before heading for Seagamento Bay. Once secured there, physical drill followed, then exercising 'Fire Stations', then exercising 'Collision Stations' and then exercising 'Defence Stations'. Captain CHURCH was clearly set on getting his ship onto 'top line', where the company would be able to do standard drills and manoeuvres almost 'in their sleep'.

During March the company saw some of the highly celebrated parts of the 'Med', including Elba, with its then-dormant volcano. A fleet torpedo exercise took place at Elba, which involved *Weymouth*. Meantime she was exercising her small arms companies, her diving party was away searching for a lost stanchion and an Engineer Captain inspected her engine room to ensure that everything was 'on the top line'. *Weymouth* also visited the world-famous and beautiful Bay of Naples, spreading her awnings against the hot sun. Her Marines were inspected by a senior Marine Officer, and she coaled ship at the harbour there, before returning to Malta. Once at Malta, she sent a shooting party to the rifle range and put her Gunlayers and Sightsetters to Control Drill.

On 30th March, a part of the French Fleet arrived at Malta. The French fleet included the five-funelled and strange-looking 'Semi-Dreadnought' *Diderot,* and the slightly older three-funnelled battleships, *Justice* and *République*. A photograph of the *Diderot* appears overleaf. All three of these battleships mounted 12-inch guns. (Their arrival was a practice exercise for a more substantial deployment by French ships should the expected hostilities with Germany and/or Austria eventually break out.)

The French Squadron left Malta on 3rd April 1914, and the hands on the British ships manned and cheered ship as the French proceeded out of the harbour. This alliance with France, although having a precursor in the Crimean War of 1856, must still have seemed strange to the officers and men of the Royal Navy, reared as they were in the Nelsonian tradition of a prolonged history of combat at sea against French vessels. By way of contrast, some visits had recently been exchanged between the ships of the Home Fleet and the ships of the German Navy, and a few of the more senior officers were on quite good social terms with their German equivalents.

---

[108] This 'voice-transmission' showed the technical development which was going on in wireless-telegraphy, which, at the outset, had been able to transmit and receive only in the 'dots and dashes' of the Morse Code. . The field of signalling is only touched upon here and there in this biography, which concentrates mainly on Alf's specialisation of gunnery, but the accurate and reliable giving and receiving of signals was a vital matter and we shall see how the sad effects of shortcomings in certain signalling and 'RDF' fields intrude into our story at various points. [The book *"Signal. A History of Signalling in the Royal Navy"* by Captain Barrie KENT, published by Hyden House in 1993, is a classic on all signalling matters, extending from the 1660s through to the 1990s. Its coverage includes 'RDF' (i.e. Radar), from the late 1930s, the introduction of computers, the use of satellites, etc., etc.]

Author's collection. A Raphael Tuck "Photogravure" postcard, No. 4312. Photo by Cribb of Southsea, probably taken when the French ship made a pre-war visit to the UK.

The strange-looking 18,400-ton French 'Semi-Dreadnought' *Diderot*, with four 12"guns, twelve 9.4" guns (in six twin turrets) and sixteen 3" guns. Her Parsons turbines were of 22,500 horsepower but it was said she could only attain 19 knots.

During April, *Weymouth* was based at Valetta for duties in towing targets, and for gun practice around the Island, sometimes in company with the heavy battle-cruiser *Indefatigable*, a 19,000 ton Devonport-built ship mounting eight twelve-inch and sixteen four-inch guns. *Weymouth* continued the training of her company on the lines already described, adding further evolutions and variants to them, as when she connected up 'Conning Tower' firing, before sponging out her guns and then engaging in torpedo firing, all whilst making short passages to Mellick Bay and St Paul's Bay. On the 18th April *Weymouth* had the honour of being Scoring Ship for the Fleet during a gunnery exercise. [At that time the Mediterranean Fleet, which was under the command of Admiral Sir Archibald Berkeley MILNE, included the battlecruisers *Inflexible* (flagship), *Indomitable* and *Indefatigable*, the armoured cruisers *Defence, Duke of York, Black Prince and Warrior*, the light cruisers *Dublin, Gloucester, Chatham* and *Weymouth* and sixteen *Beagle* Class destroyers.]

Late in April *Weymouth's* 6" guns were given their quarterly examination, and, presumably based on the findings, on 1st May 1914 their bores were lapped and milled. *Weymouth* then visited Venice, acting as target ship for 'torpedo control' astern of *Dublin* whilst on passage there. The ship was dressed overall on arrival at Malamoccio, in honour of Accession Day, and a 21-gun salute was fired. Her divers were active around this time, cleaning her main inlet, (and losing a knife, belt and case, by accident, in so doing). Meantime she had her boats' crews refitting gear, a torpedo class under instruction and her Marines at pulling exercise. She then proceeded to Triest at the head of the Adriatic Sea, which she reached on 9th May.

A tragedy occurred at Triest, for a seaman in the battle-cruiser *Indomitable* was killed by a misfire when a salute was being fired. On the 11th, the seaman was buried at a ceremony in the English quarters ashore, *Weymouth* being one of the ships which landed a burial party. Alf was beginning to see at close hand some of the dangers of his profession.

On the 13th, *Weymouth* visited Fiume, picking up an Austrian Pilot to guide her in safely, securing with her stern to the mole, and coaling for over eight hours. Her ship's company was treated well by the Austrians and a good visit transpired. For example, one evening, a military band came aboard and played, and many visitors were entertained on board during *Weymouth's* short stay. During the 900-mile return voyage to Malta, a steam trial at three-fifths power was carried out, with *Weymouth* running swiftly through the water abeam of *Chatham*. (This was probably another rather thrilling 'preparative-for-war' exercise - indeed at 2000 the Ship's Company were put into 'War Routine' overnight.)

On 19th May 1914 the ship conducted another Power Trial, subsequently again coaling (530 tons), and scraping and painting her funnels, of which the existing paintwork had become blistered by her prolonged high-speed runs. Meantime her gunners were obtaining useful practice at the Deflection Teacher. The Austrian battleships SMS *Tegetthof*, *Viribus Unitis* and *Zrinyi* arrived at Malta at this time, returning the courtesy visit by British ships to Fiume. On 20th May, the British ships were spectacularly dressed overall in honour of H.M. King George V's actual birthday, and a 21-gun salute was fired. Taking advantage of the warm water, the hands were frequently sent to bathe during this whole period, and non-swimmers were put under instruction. Alf would have been in his element.

The Austrian ships left Malta on the 30th May, and the hands 'manned and cheered ship'. Aboard *Weymouth* at least, this evolution was not carried out smartly enough, and, certainly, next day, the company were exercised again by the Captain in manning ship. This was a strange time, for, although there seemed to be little doubt that a war would shortly break out, such matters as to whether the Austrians and Italians would be hostile, friendly or neutral, had not yet become at all clear. Perhaps the lower deck, with its sturdy common-sense, had already decided that the Austrians were going to be our enemies. Perhaps the officers thought so too – but had to maintain the 'right' protocols!

In June, the ship went into dry dock at Malta for a four-day temporary refit, the hands 'staging her down' and scrubbing the ship's bottom clear of weed. Her company still dressed ship with masthead flags on 4th June in honour of the King's 'official' birthday, and continued training by sending her signalmen ashore for heliograph exercises, before the dock was flooded and the ship emerged from it, under steam, but with tugs assisting, to secure to No5 and 5A Buoys. She then went out with *Chatham* for a day of long-range torpedo-firing practice, later recovering, hoisting in and striking down the torpedoes she'd fired, then clearing away her guns for night defence, proceeding for night practice with the 1" aiming rifle, and later returning to Malta. Somewhere along the way, she also took time out to swing ship, to re-check her compass variation. On 10th June she provisioned ship, coaled (360 tons), took in 56 tons of oil, and then sent her hands for a welcome bathe in the clear blue Mediterranean Sea. She then voyaged the 400 miles north-east to Corfu, again practising long-range torpedo-firing en route.[109] During the night she exercised 'searchlight control' with her

---

[109] It is assumed that one of the destroyers was charged with recovering the torpedoes fired by *Weymouth*.

accompanying destroyers, at the steady pace of 7 to 9 knots, adjusting her course and speed as requisite for 'taking station on the beam' of *Chatham.*

From Corfu she cruised around the south of Greece and up the east coast to Phaleras Bay, Athens, and on to Volos by the end of the month. There was another tragedy in departing from Volos, for the destroyer HMS *Savage,* which was in company, lost three men drowned from an accident whilst lowering a boat.

The company of *Weymouth* then participated in the Fleet Regatta at Marmarice, which was a great occasion for much hearty effort and 'letting off a great deal of pent-up steam', before proceeding to Limassol, in the south of the Island of Cyprus. This was reached on the 10th July. They then proceeded south-south-east to Haifa and thence southwards down the coast to Jaffa. From Jaffa a part of the ship's company went on a two-day trip to Jerusalem. We can be reasonably sure that Alf went on this trip to the Holy City, for, after his return to England, he gave his sister Rose a fine souvenir book with polished wooden covers containing pressed flowers from the Garden of Gethsemane, beautifully mounted on skilfully hand-decorated pages. (See F/Note, Page 192.)

As we shall see in a moment, it could be said that this was the last peace-time 'junket' for the company of *Weymouth.* What had befallen *Weymouth* since her re-commissioning, for good or ill, would have more or less befallen Alf, either directly, or as a spectator, or as a listening ear with a close interest in what was going on. Alf had certainly seen vast areas of the blue Mediterranean Sea by now, and many of the principal ports which lie around its basin, including some of the most celebrated 'beauty-spots'.

At the same time, the men of the ship's company, especially those involved with observation and navigation, had been given invaluable opportunities to come and go into harbour-installations which, should war break out, they might have to 'feel their way into (or out of)' by night, probably under 'blacked out' conditions, and perhaps against hostile defences. There had been the chance to see something of their potential enemies (and potential allies), in terms of the quality of their men, their ships, their guns and their fortifications.[110] There had also been the chance to practice with the Royal Navy's own weapons and to join, to some extent, in British ship to ship co-operation and in Fleet manoeuvres. And they had made useful exercises in communication, including wireless transmissions. They had also practised a long run at comparatively high speed, which might well be a wartime need from time to time. *Weymouth's* increase in fuel-consumption under such circumstances had been evaluated to some degree, as was essential if realistic estimates of her range with a given tonnage of coal aboard were to be computed for battle conditions.

From Jaffa, *Weymouth* then proceeded south and then westwards to Alexandria, via Beirut. Her company found that most of the Mediterranean Fleet was by then at Alexandria, including *Inflexible, Indefatigable, Warrior, Black Prince, Chatham, Dublin, Gloucester* and nearly all of the sixteen destroyers. Rumours of war between Austria and Serbia were rife, and 'War Routine' was carried out whilst *Weymouth* was at Alexandria, being actively continued as she voyaged back to Malta, evidently as a part of virtually the whole fleet. Being half 'closed down' probably made the ship considerably more hot and stuffy than she would normally have been, and would probably have caused some quiet

---

[110] As indicated above, making for difficulties all round, it was hard to know who would become 'allies', or 'neutrals' or 'enemies' in the undoubtedly pending conflict. We shall see this problem become even more acute.

'griping' by the 'troops'.[111] On arrival at Malta on the 30th July, rumours of European involvement in war were even stronger. The ship was now readied for war, all her disposable furniture and woodwork being sent ashore, to reduce the risk of fire should she receive incoming shell-hits. This must have been a telling time, reducing the comfort of the accommodation aboard and showing that matters really were becoming 'serious'.

Thus it was that, on Saturday 1st August 1914, whilst in harbour at Malta, *Weymouth* (still under her Captain R.('Bob') CHURCH) provisioned ship and prepared to go onto a full war footing. Next day, all men on leave were recalled aboard. They would have found that the anchorage was suddenly and dramatically almost empty, for virtually the whole fleet, save the battle-cruiser *Indefatigable* and the cruisers *Chatham*, *Dublin* and *Weymouth*, had already left harbour. Very early on Monday, the 3rd August, W*eymouth* and *Dublin* were ordered by Admiral Sir Archibald Berkeley MILNE to make a full-speed 900-mile dash to Sicily, duly arriving there at 0900 the next morning, the ships having been hard-driven in calm seas. In some senses their war had started, for they had been sent to check for the possible presence of two German warships in the Straits of Messina. In the event, they just missed their dangerous quarry.

This movement by *Weymouth* and *Dublin* (the latter being a *Chatham*-class cruiser and thus slightly larger than *Weymouth*), was a part of other operations being co-ordinated by the British Admiralty and executed by Admiral MILNE. The Admiralty had sent orders that German warships, which were known to be present in the Mediterranean, were to be shadowed *but not engaged* until war was declared. One major fear was that the German warships might attack vulnerable French troopships conveying men from the Algerian ports northwards to Marseilles, as reserves for the expected heavy fighting on the borders of France and Germany.

An Admiralty signal to Admiral MILNE of 30th July 1914 had said "......*it is especially important that your squadron should not be seriously engaged with Austrian ships before we know what Italy will do. Your first task should be to aid the French in the transportation of their African Army by covering and if possible bringing to action individual fast German ships particularly 'Goeben' who may interfere with that transportation. You will be notified by telegraph when you may consult with the French Admiral. Do not at this stage be brought to action against superior forces except in consultation with the French as part of a general battle. The speed of your squadrons is sufficient to enable you to choose your moment. We shall hope later to reinforce the Mediterranean and you must husband your force at the outset.*"

In view of subsequent events, the above Admiralty telegram would go on to assume colossal importance. Right from the outset, for anybody who was 'in the know', the telegram contained several potentially contradictory elements. It was by nature something of a 'poisoned chalice' for the senior men on the spot.

Moreover, the Admiralty telegram had commenced: "*Should war break out, and England and France engage in it, it now seems probable that Italy will remain neutral and that Greece can be made an ally. Spain will be friendly and possibly an ally. The attitude of Italy in however uncertain....*" Since the manner in which these countries actually went on to become friends, foes or neutrals in British eyes, turned out to be so

---

[111] 'The troops' is a soubriquet which is not to be confused with a plurality of soldiers, but is an informal naval term for the ratings, sometimes also called the 'Lower Deck'.

different from this Admiralty speculation, one can appreciate the dilemmas in which Admiral MILNE found himself on the eve (and opening days) of the war.

Author's collection. A postcard by 'G.D. & D of London'. Photograph by 'Elliott & Fry'. Card postally used in England on 24th May 1915, the writer saying that "George was wounded", evidently in the land fighting in France, and asking if the addressee "had any news of Will".

Rear Admiral Sir Archibald Berkeley MILNE had rubbed shoulders with the highest nobility in England, and he had figured strongly in 'Queen Alexandra's Book of Photographs'. Now, as C-in-C (Mediterranean), the rather conflicting orders to him from the Admiralty, regarding the actions to be taken on the outbreak of war, would prove to be something of a 'poisoned chalice'. The Admiralty would impose tactical orders from afar, over-ruling 'the man on the spot'. Admiral MILNE's rather inadequate response to the *totally unexpected* strategy and tactics of the German warships *Goeben* and *Breslau*, would lead to his previously fine career becoming forever ruined.

It is clear that Admiral MILNE passed some of the substance of his orders on to his next-in-commands, such as Admiral TROUBRIDGE, though only on what he perceived as a 'need to know' basis. The most senior of the officers must have been 'treading on eggshells' in trying to avoid upsetting any country around the Mediterranean rim. The Captains of the various ships, such as Captain CHURCH of *Weymouth*, would also have each received a certain amount of 'priming' in these matters, and been told to 'watch their step' in 'international matters'.

As we have seen, the Admiralty had told Admiral MILNE to be particularly watchful for the German cruiser *Goeben*, and, if possible, to bring her (and any other 'fast German ships') to action. [*Though his 'first task' was clearly stated to be the protection of the French troop transports.* N.B. Nowhere was it suggested that *Goeben* or her consorts might head 'permanently' for the far 'eastern end' of the 'Med'.]

Goeben was a modern battle-cruiser of 22,640 tons, mounting ten 11" guns and allegedly 'normally capable' of the high speed of 25.5 knots.[112] In the event, she was accompanied by the cruiser *Breslau* of 4,550 tons, mounting twelve 4.1" guns, and capable of the even higher speed of 28.5 knots.

Author's collection. A postcard bearing the inscription 'Deutches Marineheim – Konstantinople Jenikoi'. The photograph was probably taken in late August 1914.

The fine German battlecruiser SMS *Goeben,* completed in 1911. Her penetration into the Mediterranean just before war was declared certainly 'put a cat amongst the pigeons'. She was accompanied by the cruiser *Breslau*, and the combined gun-power, speed, tactics and underlying strategy of these two warships caused the Royal Navy very serious problems indeed.

These ships had, in fact, slipped through the Straits of Messina a few hours before *Dublin* and *Weymouth* had made their investigation. At 0500 on the 4th August, immediately following the declaration of war between Germany and France, *Goeben* had shelled the port of Philippeville, and *Breslau* had shelled the port of Bône, both lying on the Algerian Coast. *[They may well have done so to create the impression that they were going to continue through the Sicilian Channel to the south of Sicily, rather than attempting the narrow Straits of Messina to the north of the island.]* Their bombardments were unopposed but, fortunately, did little damage.[113]

As the German ships had headed through the Straits of Messina they had been observed by the British battlecruisers *Indomitable* and *Indefatigable*. However, Britain and Germany were not then officially at war, and, although a high degree of tension had

---

[112] In fact, some sources claimed that *Goeben's* speed was down to about 22.5 - 24 knots, due to boiler defects which the imminence of the declaration of war, and the consequent need to be at sea, had prevented from being repaired. This was probably a false rumour deliberately created by the Germans. Had it been anywhere near true, it seems surprising that *Indomitable* and *Indefatigable*, both rated at around 27 or 28 knots, could not keep up with *Goeben*, even though they were probably short of stokers for a prolonged chase and the hulls of both British ships were said to be rather foul with weed. One way and another, their problem with *Breslau's* speed was clear enough. She was probably doing *at least* 26 knots at times, and possibly as much as 28 knots! (Also see overleaf.)

[113] Just to add a little further confusion, a signal reporting these bombardments had been miss-interpreted, the name 'Bône' having been wrongly recorded as 'Dover'!

existed, none of the four ships had fired on the other. In fact, the British ships had not even fired the customary salute, lest their intentions be misunderstood.

The British ultimatum to Germany did not expire until midnight on that day, and the Admiralty (who were kept *au courant* by wireless signal) 'bit their lips' but held back from giving approval for hostilities to begin prematurely between the ships. Receiving no Admiralty signal to engage the enemy, the British battlecruisers had simply turned and followed the German warships, the British proceeding at their highest speed. However, only the cruiser *Chatham*, rated at 25½ knots, which had arrived on the scene from Bizerta, could anywhere near keep up the hot pace (she must have really been excelling herself!) – and, unsurprisingly, she, too, had lost sight of the speeding German ships about three hours before the midnight deadline for the commencement of hostilities.

Author's collection. A postcard by Russell & Sons of Southsea, postally used at Portsmouth 5th June 1905.

HMS *Indomitable*, 'at full speed'. She could probably make in excess of 27 knots – but she could not keep up with the *Goeben* and the *Breslau*.

It was later learned that the German ships had then taken advantage of restraint by the Italian Navy, and had been allowed to replenish their coal-bunkers from a German collier in Messina Harbour, before being asked to leave. (*This collier may well have been the German ship subsequently captured by Chatham, on the 5th August.*) Interestingly, the C-in-C would now send a signal to the *Gloucester* that *Goeben* and *Breslau* had been steaming '*at 28 knots*' on the 4th (Presumably assessed as such by the British battlecruisers.) See ADM137/3105 at TNA.

No doubt influenced by the Admiralty orders, Admiral MILNE had then ordered a patrol line to be established to the west of Sicily, lest the German ships made an attack upon the route being used by the many French troopships conveying soldiers to mainland France, for the fighting on what would soon become called the 'Western Front.' Three British battlecruisers, and the cruisers *Chatham* and *Weymouth* were tasked with making up that screen. Aboard *Weymouth*, as on the other ships, considerable excitement and a certain amount of nervous tension prevailed, especially when the 'buzz' around the ships was that the fleet expected to make an attack on the *Goeben* and the *Breslau* at 0400 next day, the 6th August.

There was then great disappointment when the two German ships '*failed to appear*'. What had happened was that they had not headed west at all, but *eastwards*. Wisely, Admiral MILNE had taken the precaution of stationing the cruiser *Gloucester* to watch the southern approach to Messina, and she duly spotted the German ships. Captain KELLY of the *Gloucester* signalled the sighting by wireless, and hung on to his quarry for 24 hours whilst various British warships strove to close with them.

Using his initiative (and seriously risking his ship in so doing) Captain KELLY did his best to slow down the German ships by firing on the *Breslau* from 1335 to 1345 on the 7th August. He succeeded in hitting her at a range of 11,500 yards, which provoked the heavier *Goeben* to turn to the aid of *Breslau*, and to very nearly hit the 'jinking' *Gloucester* with at least two well-directed salvoes.

Author's collection. A postcard by the Photochrom Co., Ltd., in its Photogravure Naval Series, No.11. Card postally used in December 1914.

HMS *Gloucester* (Captain KELLY), a cruiser of similar overall dimensions to *Weymouth* but armed with only two 6-inch guns (and ten 4-inch guns), as compared with *Weymouth's* eight 6-inch guns. The 'Gallant Little *Gloucester*', as she came to be called, often going 'flat-out', hung on to her lone eastward chase of *Goeben* and *Breslau* for many hours, at times opening fire and being 'near-missed' (by 11-inch shells!) in return, before receiving *unequivocal* orders from Admiral MILNE to desist.

Some contemporary reports stated that shortage of coal forced Captain KELLY to give up the hot pursuit. This was untrue: he was *ordered* to forbear.[114]

---

[114] An anonymous article in the 'Naval Review' of 1918 (To be found in ADM 178/158) stated that the C-in-C (Admiral MILNE) ordered *Gloucester* not to go past Cape Matapan, but to turn back and rejoin Rear Admiral TROUBRIDGE (who was evidently by then again guarding the approach to the Adriatic, lest the Austrians broke out into the 'Med'). In ADM137/3105 one reads that Admiral MILNE had initially ordered *Gloucester* to retire soon after daybreak on the 7th, 'to avoid capture' (a signal which Captain KELLY, as 'the man on the spot', had decided to ignore - since both German ships were ahead of him at the time), but Admiral MILNE then gave definite orders to Captain KELLY not to pass Cape Matapan. In response to an enquiry sent by WT from Rear Admiral TROUBRIDGE (1st CS), *Gloucester* reported that she still 'had 723 tons of coal aboard' (i.e. when she reluctantly gave up the chase at 1700,

For their part, the two German warships subsequently succeeded in coaling at the Aegean island of Denusa on the 8th August, not leaving until dawn of the 10th and clandestinely heading for the Dardenelles.

Weymouth had re-entered harbour at Malta on the 7th, to take aboard 650 tons of coal, as always a back-breaking and filthy task, and now carried out just as quickly as could be managed. She had slipped out at midnight and headed for the Greek Archipelago. There she had made rendezvous with a collier, and awaited the arrival of some destroyers. All these ships had then cruised around the Adriatic on the lookout for the two German ships, but in vain, for on the 11th a signal was received that the *Goeben* and the *Breslau* had entered the Dardenelles. The 'squadron' had immediately headed there, with the fleet following on some hours behind.

When the squadron arrived at the Dardenelles, the Turks promptly refused permission for them to enter. Captain CHURCH attempted to force the entrance with *Weymouth*, but the Turks fired warning shots from their coastal batteries which pitched close alongside. Rather than create a diplomatic incident with a neutral country, Captain CHURCH decided to await the arrival of the fleet. But the next day, the 12th, before the fleet arrived, a representative of the Turkish government requested permission to come aboard *Weymouth*, and then reported that the Turks had purchased the German ships for £4 million. This was a very neat trick by the Germans. It was understood at the time that the companies of the German ships had been interned by the Turks - though it was later established that most of the ordinary rankers had been put aboard railway trains and had travelled straight back to Germany to carry on with the war.

The majority of the German officers, and the seamen with technical roles, had adopted the 'fez' as headgear, and were now, effectively, German advisors to the Turkish Navy. [*The Goeben and the Breslau, albeit now nominally in neutral Turkish hands, and re-named the 'Sultan Jevus Selimand' and the 'Midhili', remained a potential threat to Allied shipping in the eastern Mediterranean. Later, they would become a serious threat 'in being' to the British Dardenelles Campaign of 1915. Virtually here and now, they sailed into the Black Sea and shelled the Russian port of Odessa. When Russia entered the war, the Dardenelles was closed to her extensive trade in wheat, due to the presence of these two Turko-German warships. The Dardenelles were also closed to subsequent British and French efforts to supply the Russian Armies with war munitions. The escape of the 'Goeben' and the 'Breslau' from the British Mediterranean Fleet in the opening days of the war had certainly had the direst of consequences, and was a major success for the German Navy.*]

Frustrated, and chastened by their failure to intercept *Goeben* and *Breslau* before they had entered the safety of the Dardenelles, the British ships withdrew. The C-in-C ordered *Dublin* and *Weymouth* back to Malta, and *Weymouth* re-entered harbour there late in the afternoon of the 14th, and again coaled ship, this time taking aboard no less than 1,150 tons. Her bunkers must have been very nearly empty. Hostilities against Austria commenced that same day, though the full Austrian Fleet did not immediately *débouche*

---

with Cape Matapan then abeam.) It is true that she would embark 850 tons of coal, at Malta, on the 9th August, to 'top up' her bunkers, and that this may have led to a general belief that she had been getting short of coal on the 7th. However, she'd done many more miles of steaming by the time she coaled at Malta. (See her Log under ADM 53/43057 at TNA.) Perhaps Captain KELLY had let the rumour about 'shortage of coal' stand – rather than to have to explain to his highly motivated and enthusiastic ship's company that the exciting chase had simply been called off.

into the 'Med' as had been half-expected. On Saturday 15th August 1914, all hands were stood off. They would surely have been in real need of a relaxing run ashore, savouring the delights of Malta. Doubtless a great deal of the local brew was consumed, as 'Jack' drowned his sorrows at the anti-climax. Whether Alf was heavily involved in this or not, is uncertain, but he must certainly have been in need of 'liberty' of some kind.

AUTHOR's NOTE: For reasons which need not be gone into too deeply here, none of the British ships, apart from the 'gallant little *Gloucester*' had managed to bring the German warships under their gunfire. Reading between the lines of all that I have been able to find which was written and given in evidence, I have formed the opinion that everybody in higher command, from the Admiralty downwards, had initially believed that the 'escape' of *Goeben* and *Breslau* had only been in the nature of a respite for the two German ships, and that they would almost inevitably be caught and destroyed by the RN within a matter of days or weeks. After all, the Navy had three battlecruisers and other smaller warships to set against just one battlecruiser and one cruiser, when (as was then generally believed) the German ships would 'inevitably' come to make their exits from the 'Med' to regain Germany. Meanwhile, much defensive attention was being focused on possible operations by the Austrian Navy. Nobody in British high command had anticipated that the German ships were destined to become a key and inspirational part of the Turkish Navy.

As we shall now see, these failures led to a Court of Enquiry being held, and to Admiral TROUBRIDGE, who had been in command of the four armoured cruisers under MILNE's command, subsequently being court-martialled that he, 'through negligence or through other default, did forbear to chase SMS *Goeben,* being an enemy then flying'. Also, Admiral MILNE did not get the appointment to the Nore Command, which he had been promised before the war broke out, and he languished with *no other appointment*, despite his pleas for employment. [Years later the Admiralty would say this was due to 'other exigencies of the Service' (see ADM 156/184), but, in my opinion, their words still had a very hollow sound.]

Ironically, it seems that, initially, the Admiralty had been well satisfied with MILNE's 'success' in meeting 'his first task' of preventing the German ships from making any attacks on the French troop transports. He was returning to England in any case, since the French Admiral LAPEYRERE was, by prior Anglo-French governmental agreement, becoming C-in-C in the Mediterranean. It appears that it was some days before all the potential implications of the German ships having reached Turkish waters began to really dawn on the Admiralty. It is not surprising that the Admiralty had then been greatly nettled by the opprobrium from the British Government and press alike, which quickly began to descend around their ears. Very soon every man-jack in higher command 'was trying to clear his own yardarm' and it seems to me that an element of ruthlessness quickly crept in, the highest against the less high.

A seemingly furious minute of the First Sea Lord dated 7th September 1914 said such things as "...*superior speed in a single ship can be nullified by proper tactical dispositions of four units.....the escape of the 'Goeben' must ever reside a shameful episode...the Flag Officer who is responsible cannot be entrusted with any further command afloat.....*"

On 23rd September a Court of Enquiry was held under Admirals H. MEUX and G.A. CALLAGHAN. They found that Admiral E. C. T. TROUBRIDGE had *"....long been obsessed with, in his opinion, the superiority of the battle-cruiser 'Goeben' against any number of non-battlecruisers, if meeting them in the open sea...*

Author's collection. Two postcards in the Rotary Photographic Series, c.1914. (MEUX under Ref. 9610 B.)

The two highly-decorated admirals Sir Hedworth MEUX and Sir George A CALLAGHAN, both photographed shortly before the Great War. The 1914 Court of Enquiry under these highly renowned naval officers (who were themselves almost certainly under great pressure and very much in a 'No Win' situation) had found that Rear Admiral TROUBRIDGE had *"…long been obsessed with, in his opinion, the superiority of the German Battle-cruiser Goeben against any number of non-battlecruisers, if meeting them in the open sea. We do not admit this superiority…etc., etc."* This finding by the court led to Admiral TROUBRIDGE being court-martialled, and to the many consequences stemming therefrom, including much ensuing debate and rancour throughout the Royal Navy.

…We do not admit this superiority, as the weight of broadside fire from the four British cruisers concerned is at least equal to that of Goeben....we cannot accept that the fire of Goeben would be of overwhelming accuracy...until it has been proved.[115].

---

[115] This seems a quite remarkable and 'old-fashioned' statement in view of all the pronouncements of Admiral FISHER (then about to be recalled from retirement) on the overwhelming superiority of 'his' new-fangled heavy-gunned fast-moving battlecruisers (of which *Goeben* was an excellent German copy), with their ability to control the battle, keeping the range open just as wide as they pleased, when engaging shorter-ranged guns mounted in slower, less well-armoured ships. This is to say nothing of the probable ability of the former to bring broadsides to bear on opponents who were not only outranged but also likely to be caught more or less bows-on, or stern-on, and then most unlikely to be able to fire effective

In 1914 the findings of the Court of Enquiry continued: *In our opinion Rear Admiral TROUBRIDGE made the correct initial signal to engage on 7th August - that he should have reversed his decision we consider deplorable and contrary to the tradition of the RN....Although through superior speed the Goeben might have declined action, if she had accepted it the four cruisers, possibly assisted by the two light cruisers with long-range torpedoes, and the two TBDs, might have had a chance of at least delaying Goeben......"* (and, shown ONLY in the body of their report), *"....even if at the cost of one of the cruisers."*[116]

From all of the foregoing one would have thought that the fate of Rear Admiral TROUBRIDGE was well and truly sealed. Yet the Court Martial, held some six weeks later, the board of which consisted of nine senior officers with Admiral Sir George EGERTON as its President, found the Charge against the Accused not proved and fully and honourably acquitted him of the same! The main basis for this decision appears to have been the Accused's orders from his C-in-C that *'it will be important at first to husband the Naval force in the Mediterranean and, in the earlier stages, to avoid being brought to action against superior forces.* Also, TROUBRIDGE had been told by his C-in-C, *'Goeben must be shadowed by two battle cruisers: the approach to the Adriatic is to be watched by (your) cruisers and destroyers....*the Court found that the Accused was justified in considering that he must not abandon his watch on the Adriatic, having regard to the possibility of the Austrian Fleet coming out and attacking the French transports....the fact that his destroyers were short of coal... that the C-in-C's orders were that the 1st Cruiser Squadron were not to get seriously engaged with superior forces... that the Accused would receive no support for his squadron.... *The Court are of the opinion that the Goeben was a superior force if met in the open sea, and, though he tried to do so, the Accused could not cross her path soon enough to attack Goeben in the hours of darkness (and/or in shoal waters), which would have allowed the range to be closed and would at least have given him some measure of protection and a chance of inflicting real damage.....*

---

broadsides in return. This even with skilful and self-sacrificial manoeuvring to try to get one or more of their number within effective range. [In more modern times adverse comparisons have sometimes been made with the British heroism and success at the Battle of the River Plate early in WW2, but the three British cruisers involved all had good speed and manoeuvrability on their side. Surely anybody will admit that Commodore HARWOOD, who led by excellent forward planning with his captains, and set a tremendous example by his superb personal courage, dash and élan, was still incredibly lucky. *Graf Spey* could, and, indeed, should in all logic have destroyed all three of the British cruisers, despite their successful division of her fire. What if *Graf Spey* had managed to hold off and keep the range constantly open, picking off the British ships at leisure? And what would HARWOOD have done if, *like TROUBRIDGE*, he had been ordered to keep his three ships more or less 'intact' for the 'next' battle against a larger hostile squadron? In 1939 *Exeter* would have been in no state at all to continue in action afterwards, and *Ajax* also had very significant damage, with her 'X' turret totally out of action and her 'Y' turret jammed on an extreme forward bearing. Surely, like TROUBRIDGE before him, given such 'conserving' orders, Commodore HARWOOD would have held off and shadowed *Graf Spey* until either nightfall, or low visibility, or shoal waters intervened to provide some 'cover' or 'range-narrowing' for his attacks, possibly then going in close to launch torpedoes. Meantime, he would doubtless have been constantly hoping that heavier units would arrive on the scene – exactly as per the spurious 'leaked' messages that were actually and successfully created of a battlefleet swiftly converging on Montevideo.]

[116] *Author's note*: Which loss would, of course, have been against the direct orders of his C-in-C and the Admiralty, to 'husband' his squadron.

Rear Admiral TROUBRIDGE must surely have considered himself very fortunate to be exonerated.[117] However, as Shakespeare said, '*What great ones do the less will prattle of*', and the general word around the Mediterranean Fleet was that TROUBRIDGE had allowed himself to be swayed not to engage the *Goeben* by his Flag Captain Fawcett WRAY who was a gunnery expert, and who was called to give evidence at the Enquiry. At the time of the incident, WRAY is alleged to have said something to the effect that "*The Goeben can manoeuvre around us, keeping herself well outside the range of our guns, but keeping us well inside hers. This may mean the total destruction of our Squadron which, you tell us, you have orders to maintain intact.*" TROUBRIDGE denied that he was unduly swayed by any such conversation. He claimed that to put one's life on the line was but a small affair, and that to engage '*at all costs*' would have been a simple and straightforward matter. It was his orders not to engage a superior force, and to keep his ships intact pending the arrival of reinforcements, which went completely 'against the grain' for him and led to his 'emotional distress'.

The findings of the Court Martial implied some level of criticism of the Admiralty, which was greatly unwelcome in high places. Admiral MILNE also received some implied criticism. Sadly, the careers of Admiral MILNE and Rear-Admiral TROUBRIDGE were forever blighted.[118] In private at least, the Admiralty surely had to do some serious self-analysis, for they had tried to exercise too much control, from too far away and, in the author's opinion, the Admiralty orders had indeed been ambiguous, much as 'official' efforts were made to deny this.

A high-level Court Martial such as the one of TROUBRIDGE knocks the morale of a fleet from top to bottom. Inevitably, the 'truth' can never come fully out, and rumours, often unjust, highly speculative and wildly inaccurate, are bandied about from mouth to ear and ear to mouth. One is left with deep sympathy with both senior officers concerned and with considerable admiration for the relatively diplomatic skill with which Rear Admiral TROUBRIDGE defended himself. It is sad that his career was savaged, and that he was never given another seagoing command. His Flag Captain also suffered the virtual destruction of his career, partly from 'spontaneous condemnation' from his peers within the Navy itself, where it seems that 'dog ate dog' with complete abandon. The thought that '*there but for the Grace of God go I*', would surely have been a much more appropriate dictum to live by. Whatever may or may not have been debated on the

---

[117] See the files ADM 156/76,156/110 and 156/159 at TNA. HMS *Gloucester's* log also makes interesting reading for the dates concerned - see ADM 53/43057 - as does ADM 137/3105 which gives Captain KELLY's report to his C-in-C, later forwarded to the Admiralty.

[118] Admiral MILNE's letters to the Admiralty in 1918 make moving and interesting reading. In them he is hoping against hope for some employment to show that he 'retained the confidence of their Lordships', or for at least the publication of an official notice to that effect - or for a trial by Court Martial, so that he could clear his name. It seems that the Admiralty simply 'stonewalled' his appeals in this direction. One imagines that there was too much 'dirty linen' which might come out. The Admiralty continued to ask him to retire voluntarily, 'to make way for the promotion of younger officers', as ultimately occurred after what one might call 'a bit of rather unsatisfactory bartering on both sides'. (See ADM 156/184). Perhaps Admiral MILNE *should* have stopped 'playing with such a straight bat' and 'taken a leaf out of Admiral JELLICOE's book', and sooner or later (like JELLICOE in the contentious aftermath of the Battle of Jutland) published *his own version* of events, 'Official Secrets Act be (more or less) damned'. (See ADM 178/158.) The documentation suggests that Admiral MILNE had very seriously considered taking this option, but had a strong sense of 'duty and loyalty' - and may also have felt that he did not have quite sufficient 'national clout' to get away with it!

fatal day in question, the decision as to whether or not to risk the destruction of some or all of his cruisers always had to be the responsibility of Rear Admiral TROUBRIDGE and never that of Captain WRAY. In the author's view Captain WRAY did no wrong, and one has to say that he may well, in all logic, have been quite correct. The British *could* easily have had a total disaster on their hands.

Comparison with the concurrent behaviour of Captain KELLY of the *Gloucester* is interesting. Admiral MILNE had signalled him to cease the chase lest his ship be sunk or captured by her two powerful opponents. Yet KELLY still had the temerity to fire some 18 rounds of 6-inch and 14 rounds of 4-inch at them, despite being very near-missed twice out of two 11-inch salvoes fired by *Goeben* in return, with some shells falling only 20 yards away. Had one of those heavy shells hit, and had this led to the loss of his ship, Captain KELLY would surely have been court-martialled and undoubtedly found guilty for refusing to follow orders. The line between hero and victim is often a very fine one. One needs luck as well as judgement.

In the immediate aftermath, Rear Admiral TROUBRIDGE had signalled Captain KELLY, "My congratulations on your fine piece of work with *Goeben*." As it was, the Admiralty response to Captain KELLY's written report (seemingly, and understandably, forwarded to the Admiralty without comment by Rear-Admiral TROUBRIDGE), was to say: *"Captain KELLY to be apprised that his conduct has met with the marked approbation of Their Lordships."* Perhaps the Nelsonian tradition that, *"No Captain can go far wrong who lays his ship alongside that of an enemy"* still held good in Naval eyes, even when to do so might mean instant immolation for ships' companies each of up to a thousand in number. Seemingly it was a matter of sooner be thought a 'dead hero' than be thought a 'live coward', no matter the cold logic of fighting on one's own terms, of the carefully predicted 'unfortunate outcome' of a given battle-situation - no matter the need to meet the longer-term objectives of the overall strategic plan of conserving ships until reinforcements arrived in the 'Med'. Old FISHER had certainly 'set a cat amongst the pigeons' with his long-range, hard-hitting, fast-ship concept – which had been more than ably copied by the Germans. The minds of some senior people were simply not in tune with this concept, which had now become a reality of war.

Doubtless Alf heard many of the rumours and debates which were sweeping around the fleet after all these events. So far as his immediate service life was concerned, for the rest of the month of August and into September, there were various passages for *Weymouth* and he played his due part. She took the opportunity of clearing her guns by discharging them at sea, on the 19th August, during a short passage out from Malta, and she then criss-crossed the Mediterranean, making landfalls at Syracuse, Sliema Bay, Port Said and such places.

By 18th August the French under Admiral LAPEYRERE as the new C-in-C had taken over command of the dockyard at Malta, and the French fleet arrived there two days later (Remember that pre-war visit on 13th March 1914?). As previously intimated, the French Navy were particularly anxious to safeguard the movements of their North African troops across the Mediterranean, to the battlefields of the Western Front - exactly as Admirals MILNE and TROUBRIDGE had sought to do, in full compliance with their orders.

Whilst at Port Said near the end of August, news was received of a Battle off Heligoland in which five German ships were reported sunk, and the *Laertes* and the *Amethyst* damaged. Also, again whilst *Weymouth* was at Port Said, there was a flurry of activity after a German merchant ship which had been captured was suddenly found to be ablaze, perhaps as an act of sabotage.

Author's collection. Postcard No.69 from a booklet printed by Levy et Fils of Paris, France, around 1914.

A General View of the Town and Canal at Port Said.

Whilst at El Arish, the cutter's crew of *Weymouth* practised a landing in full marching order, in blazing heat. On leaving El Arish, four days later, *Weymouth* carried two English lady-missionaries to Port Said. There, the company again coaled ship, and left for Alexandria.

At Alexandria *Weymouth* made rendezvous with nineteen troopships carrying Gordon Highlanders and Devonshires, and escorted them safely to Port Said, joining up *en route* with the battle-cruiser *Indomitable*, which had a further five troopships under her protection.

On the 21st September 1914, Russia declared war on Turkey. The battlecruiser *Indomitable* left for the Dardanelles. But *Weymouth* received orders to report to the C-in-C East Indies after finishing her duty of escorting thirteen troopships to Alexandria, these ships having been handed-over to her by the *Minerva*. The troops being carried were Territorials. One soldier, recorded in *Weymouth's* log as Private BRIDGES, died in passage aboard the SS *Aragon* and was buried at sea with full military honours – a rather unusual circumstance for a soldier.[119]

On the 23rd September the fleet received the distressing report that the 12,000 ton armoured cruisers *Aboukir, Cressy* and *Hogue* had each been sunk in the North Sea, all

---

[119] Evidently this was Private John BRIDGE of the 1st/9th Btn of the Manchester Regiment, who appears in the records of the Commonwealth War Graves Commission as having died on the 24th September 1914, and as being commemorated on the Chatby Memorial at Alexandria. He appears to have had no next of kin.

on the same day, by a single German submarine. There had been heavy loss of life. Apparently the Captain of the first ship to be hit initially believed he had hit a mine and had not thought of the possibility that he might have been torpedoed. Whilst more alert ship-handling, common sense and forethought, (perhaps coupled with the precious gift of hindsight!), might have prevented the second and third sinking, the Navy had yet to come to grips with ways of countering submarine attack, and this triple sinking was worrying news indeed. The Navy had also to learn that common humanity and the unwritten laws of the sea concerning the rescue of drowning men now had to take second place to cold logic and 'total war', where ships engaged in rescue work might find themselves attacked whilst hove-to and thus very 'soft' targets.

Author's collection. A postcard identified 'Ala.44' (perhaps for 'Alexandria') and the reference number 08 59635'. Dated c.1914.

A View of the Port at Alexandria, busy with merchant shipping and with robed Arabs at work in the immediate foreground. It was to and from Alexandria that *Weymouth* came to escort two large military convoys in August and September 1914.

Continuing southwards, *Weymouth* left Aden on the 2nd October for Mombassa, crossing the Line on the 5th October. This was surely Alf's first crossing of the Equator, but it is clear that no ceremony was held for the 'noviciates' in this time of war. *Weymouth* arrived at Mombassa on the 6th, finding there the light cruiser *Fox* and the cruiser *Chatham*, the latter being of similar force to *Weymouth*, but with an armoured belt. This slightly increased her displacement but gave her greater protection against a torpedo-hit or when engaged in close-range surface action. It is not known if shore leave was granted at Mombassa. If so, it would have been strictly restricted to the Kilindini Recreation Ground, where an Indian-run canteen existed

From Mombassa, *Weymouth* proceeded to Zanzibar. Here, natives, mainly women, coaled ship, putting some 850 tons into her bunkers. This coal had been previously captured from the Germans by *Pegasus*, an obsolete light cruiser.

It was most unfortunate that *Pegasus* (Captain INGLIS) had subsequently been surprised and overwhelmed by the German cruiser *Konigsberg* whilst *Pegasus was* at anchor effecting boiler repairs off Zanzibar. Hard-hit by accurate shell-fire coming at them from a range of some 7,000 yards, and following a 'last-resort' beaching attempt, *Pegasus* had sunk after sliding off a steeply-shelving mud-flat into deep water. She had lost 27 of her company killed and 55 wounded (seven of whom later died of their wounds).[120] This attack had occurred on 20th August.

Author's collection. An anonymous postcard, c. 1910

The obsolete HMS *Pegasus* (2,135 tons, eight 4-inch guns). She was fated to be overwhelmed and sunk by the German cruiser *Konigsberg*.

The hunt was now well on for the *Konigsberg,* which seemed to have 'gone to ground'.[121] The Royal Navy was thirsting to avenge the fate of *Pegasus*. For the next five days *Weymouth* searched the coast, receiving a signal by wireless that *Konigsberg* was in neutral Portuguese waters, but failing to find her. The Gunner's working party on *Weymouth* had been busily scraping and gauging projectiles for their guns, but, so far, with no reason to fire them at anybody in anger. Indeed, so far as *Weymouth* was

---

[120] At his Court Martial (discussed earlier) Admiral TROUBRIDGE had quoted this incident as being testament to the accuracy of what was comparatively long-range fire from a German warship. He claimed that British guns were much less accurate than the German guns, the latter all being precision-manufactured by Krupps of Essen. He commented in contrast on a British Fleet-firing exercise at 7,000 yards, which he and Winston CHURCHILL had attended pre-war, and in which *not one shell* had hit the target, most falling at least 1,000 yards away, and *"in all directions away from the target"*. [We shall find a C-in-C on the Africa Station making very similar critical comments in the 1920s and getting precious little positive response from the Admiralty.]

[121] She had actually headed straight back for the Rufuji River, and was well hidden at least six miles upstream.

concerned, the hunt for *Konigsberg* was then broken off, for *Weymouth* made rendezvous with the cruiser *Dartmouth* on the 16th October and the two ships made their way to German East Africa, hunting for *another* German cruiser, the *Emden*, which had been making depredations at Penang, Malaya. *Weymouth's* men must have wondered if they would have any more luck in tracing *her*, or whether further frustration awaited them. The Indian Ocean is a very large expanse of water.

Weymouth and *Dartmouth* went via Myotta, where they met up with the collier *St Bronwen, Weymouth* filling her bunkers with some 960 tons of *St Bronwen's* coal. The two cruisers then searched the Indian Ocean, separately, but in vain, returning to make rendezvous at Myotta on the 30th October 1914. Whilst there, *Weymouth* re-coaled with 975 tons of coal - a tribute to the great distance which had been traversed. The heat had been tremendous and the anonymous stoker's diary assures us that the pint of beer that had been served out to every man on the 27th had been greatly welcomed! *[The 'Emden' had, in fact, left the Indian Ocean and headed for the Cocos Islands, where HMAS 'Sydney' would be fated to intercept and destroy her on the 9th November 1914, in a ship versus ship action which became famous around the world.]*

However, by the 1st November *Weymouth* was on her way back to rejoin the *Dartmouth* and the *Chatham* off the East Coast of Africa. These two latter ships had eventually tracked down the *Konigsberg,* which had a relatively shallow draught, (significantly less than that of *Weymouth, Chatham* or *Dartmouth*). Like them, *Konigsberg* was limited to crossing the sand-bar at the river-mouth *only* at high water springs, but she could proceed significantly further upriver. *Konigsberg* was now moored about six miles up the Rufuji River, together with a German storeship, the *Somali*. At 1030 *Weymouth* and *Chatham*, having crossed the sand-bar and made their way a short distance upriver, began bombarding the *Konigsberg, Dartmouth* joining them initially, but having to depart later in the day to coal at Mombassa. *Weymouth* and *Chatham* continued with the bombardment next day. However, it was apparent that their shells were wide of the target and generally falling short. The winding nature of the river and the prolific mangrove swamps which lined its banks were making 'spotting' of the fall of shot extremely difficult to master. To run aground, either on the sand-bar, or further upstream, would be highly dangerous, as it would expose the ship to harassing fire from the river-banks and even the possibility of direct assault. The Germans had laid an improvised minefield to further complicate matters, and there was a definite limit to the distance the British ships could get upstream, owing to their substantial draught and the winding and shallow nature of the river.

Other tactics were indicated. Hence, on the 6th November, a steam-powered cutter and a whaler, with *Weymouth's* First Lieutenant leading a landing party, went up-river to reconnoitre, returning safely, and with a native dhow in tow.

Next day, the *Dartmouth* returned from coaling at Mombassa, and the steamboats from *Weymouth* and *Chatham* went up-river together in an attempt to torpedo the *Konigsberg*. (One assumes they were rigged to fire torpedoes as shown in the following photograph.) However, the Germans had by now unshipped some of *Konigsberg's* guns and installed them on the river bank some way down-river, protecting these guns with machine-gun and rifle-fire. It seems likely that their artillery had also been supplemented with some field-guns from German Army personnel in the area. In the face of heavy fire from these positions on the river-banks, the British steamboats withdrew.

On the 10th, landing parties made up from all three cruisers, in three steamboats and one picket-boat, together with the cable-ship *Duplex*, tried again, this time taking the collier *Newbury* with them and sinking her in the river-mouth as a blockship to make the channel unusable.

This was achieved, although two ratings were unfortunately killed and several men wounded. One of the men who died that day was from the *Weymouth*. He was 26 year-old Leading Seaman Walter George FITZJOHN who came from Walworth, London. *Weymouth's* steamboat was quoted as having been 'riddled with bullets' and there were many 'narrow escapes'. A burial service for the two ratings was conducted out at sea. Our anonymous stoker reported this as having been *'very impressive'*. We do not know how deeply Alf was involved in the actual landing parties, but it must have been a tense time for all concerned, in or out of the ship.

Author's collection. A photographic postcard in the 'Nelson' series by Gale & Polden, c.1905.

A Picket Boat, rigged for firing torpedoes, proceeding at speed.

A collier had arrived from Mombassa on the 9th November, but her load of coal had been found to be smouldering dangerously and to be more or less unusable. It was clear that, as time went on, and as their coal supplies became low, each cruiser would have to depart from the scene, in turn, to seek replenishment at Mombassa or elsewhere. Meantime, at least one and preferably two or more cruisers would have to remain on patrol off the river mouth, lest *Konigsberg* should 'make a run for safety', or should another German warship come to her aid.

We do know that some officers and men were having experiences of different ships at this time. For example, Sub-Lt N.A. MacQUEEN RNR was lent to the *Duplex*, and Sub-Lt W.R.F. GREGORY had earlier been lent to the ill-fated *Pegasus*.[122] The

---

[122] It appears that he had survived her sinking, for his name does not appear in the Commonwealth War Graves Commission listings for the period.

likelihood is that these officers took small parties of men and side-arms with them - probably also Maxim guns. Whether Alf was involved in any such temporary transfers is not known. On the whole it seems unlikely.

Konigsberg, which the *Weymouth's* ratings were by now colloquially calling '*The Connig*' was proving to be a tough nut to crack. True, she was blockaded, but she was still very much an enemy warship in being, she and might yet effect a breakout. In view of their manifold duties, the Royal Navy needed every one of their cruisers to be fully operational, and they simply could not afford to have cruisers engaged long-term in bottling up the *Konigsberg.* Her destruction was becoming a matter of priority. The need was for heavy-gunned ships of shallow draught, viz, monitors, and for a means of observation of the target, viz balloons or, better, aircraft. None of these was immediately available. Moreover, the cruisers present needed relief.

On the 11th November, *Duplex* ran aground, but *Weymouth* managed to tow her off, before proceeding to Zanzibar, and thence to Mombassa, where she coaled with over 790 tons, before leaving Mombassa at 1000, heading for Simonstown. However, *Weymouth* first coaled at Durban on the 19th, where a popular young man familiarly called 'Kitty' WELLS, who had fallen seriously ill and was now a cot case, was put into hospital. [*Sadly, it would later be learned that Able Seaman WELLS, W.J., aged 23, had died of pneumonia at Durban Hospital on the 25th November 1914.*[123]]

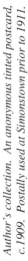

Author's collection. An anonymous tinted postcard, c.1909. Postally used at Simonstown prior to 1911.

HMS *Hermes* lying off Simonstown in pre-war days. She was a *sister-ship* of HMS *Hyacinth* (in which Admiral KING-HALL was now flying his flag). This photograph is very much akin to the view Alf would have had of *Hyacinth* and the shore-line from HMS *Weymouth.* The obvious obsolescence of this ship, her low speed of 19 knots, and her relatively small armament of eleven 6-inch guns (all of early marks), are testament to the lack of force of the ships on the Africa Station. *Weymouth* and *Chatham* were the best 'fighting machines' currently available to Admiral KING-HALL.

---

[123] In the Royal Navy men named WELLS are invariably nicknamed 'Kitty', presumably from the nursery rhyme 'Ding dong bell, Pussy's in the Well'. This unfortunate young man was buried in Durban Cemetery.

At Durban, the *'people ashore'*, clearly knowing the ship had been in action, treated the ship's company well, giving them *'fags, books and meat'*. The ship then left for Simonstown (see above photo), arriving off the port on the 21st, although the sea state was too rough for communication with the shore that day. The *Dartmouth, Albion, Astrea* and *Hyacinth* (Flag) were all present at the port.

On the 24th November, the weather moderated, and leave was given to the company by alternate watches. One assumes that Alf then stepped ashore at Simonstown for the first time. (It would be far from also being his last time there.) During the ensuing days, *Weymouth* coaled and provisioned ship, leaving on the 7th December for Capetown.

Weymouth left Capetown on the 8th, escorting three troopships up the west coast as far as Ludowitzbacht, a port which had been captured from the Germans. It was rumoured that a German aeroplane had been seen in the vicinity.

Weymouth arrived back at Capetown on the 14th December 1914, and 32 bags of mail came aboard – evidently the first mail the company had received since September! This event must have been greeted with much joy. The ship went into dry dock at Simonstown on the 15th, emerging on the 19th, and coaling, before leaving for Durban. Arriving there at 6am on the 23rd December, they coaled ship, and then (according to 'our' ship's stoker) the Caterers of Messes went ashore to buy Christmas Dinners, all allegedly *'coming off drunk'* - so they, at least, had a good time. Even if the rest of the company perforce remained sober, they were by no means ignored, for the Women's Patriotic League sent them most welcome gifts of fruit and tobacco.

Weymouth sailed at 6pm and Christmas Day 1914 was spent at sea. It was reported that the company had a 'fairly decent time', and they had 'a good sing-song on deck' after darkness fell. They were heading back to their part of the War.

Weymouth coaled at Zanzibar, and arrived back at the Rufuji River Mouth at 8.30 am on the 30th December. On the 1st January 1915, *Weymouth*, evidently 'feeling festive and jocular' - and perhaps more than a bit frustrated and curious, sent a wireless message to the *Konigsberg,* saying*: "A Happy New Year. When are you coming out?" Konigsberg* replied: *"Same to you. I am always at home when you want to see me!"* Clearly, the Germans were not devoid of an ironic sense of humour - nor were they exactly giving anything away about their intentions!

On the 5th January *Weymouth* risked landing a bathing party on a quiet patch of the delta, probably to provide just a little by way of a diversion and relief for the company from the oppressive heat. On the 9th January, *Weymouth* was relieved from her 'guard duties' at the river mouth, and went to give some assistance to the *Kinfauns Castle*, an armed merchant cruiser, which was carrying an invasion force of 700 Burmese troops to assault the Island of Nioroco.

The *Kinfauns Castle* made a bombardment, landed her men and captured the island, at a low cost in casualties. The enemy prisoners were sent to Zanzibar, and *Weymouth* returned to the Rufuji River.

However, *Weymouth* soon again left the Rufuji River estuary, this time for Hori Vanga, where our troops were attacking German forces but being cut up by a 4-inch gun, which they were having difficulty in locating. *Weymouth* began bombarding the believed position of this gun on the 29th January, continuing throughout the day and through the night. This bombardment was reportedly of great help to the troops, who made good progress. Men of the East Lancs, and units of Mexican volunteers and Indian troops were landed, to add to the invasion force. However, the force received a hostile reception, and had to retire from Hori Vanga on the 11th February.

Author's collection. An anonymous postcard, bearing the serial number '133' on its face and '119702' on its reverse. Card issued c.1912.

RMS *Kinfauns Castle* of the Union Castle Line, prior to her conversion to an armed merchant cruiser. It was from the relatively airy and spacious accommodation in the captain's cabin of this ship that Captain CRAMPTON would transfer to the command of HMS *Weymouth* in March 1915, thereupon finding *Weymouth* to be '*uncomfortably hot*'. Nevertheless, Captain CRAMPTON would make an excellent successor to the very capable Captain CHURCH.

By that time *Weymouth* was back at Rufuji, where she shelled the by-then derelict *Adjutant*. This former German tug had been captured by *Dartmouth* on 9th October. After being armed with three 47mm guns and two Maxims, she had gone up-river to make a reconnaissance, but had come under a devastating storm of fire from the river-banks, which had led to her being recaptured by the Germans. The company had surrendered to the Germans after one AB had been killed and another wounded. This wounded man was reported to be in the care of the wife of the Captain of Marines from the *Konigsberg*. Once again, the *Konigsberg* and her company had shown their mettle. Moreover, the guns from *Adjutant* had now been added to the German defences along the river-banks.

For *Weymouth* there now followed a period of short voyages interspersed with 'guard duties' off the Rufuji River entrance, and breaks at Zanzibar for coaling. One mission was to Dar-es-Salaam (see following photograph), where the German Governor came aboard under a white flag of truce, for certain negotiations, including being told details of the Blockade which was being imposed by the British on German East Africa, the situation regarding neutral vessels, and coming to an agreement on such matters as the treatment of prisoners of war.

Weymouth then headed back for a further spell of duty at Rufuji. By that time, two Sopwith 807 seaplanes had materialised in the general vicinity, with accompanying RNAS personnel. Whilst *Weymouth* was at Nioro Island (which lies about 20 miles north-east of the Rufuji Delta), these planes were seen by the company to be making trial flights there. Back at Rufuji on the 25th February 1915, *Weymouth* turned over 6 rifles and a Maxim gun to the company of *Fly,* a steam whaling vessel which had been engaged for patrol duty at the river entrance.

Author's collection. A postcard published by A Montiero, Photographer, Dar-es-Salaam, Serial No. 14 679, c.1914.

A view of Dar-es-Salaam, where the German Governor came aboard under a white flag of truce, for various negotiations with Captain CHURCH.

Weymouth was suffering from navigating in the shallow and muddy waters within the vicinity of the Rufuji River, and on the 26th February, whilst she was at Nioro, divers went down and cleared her main inlets. Presumably they reported that the ship's bottom was very foul, for the following day she went to Mafia, where divers cleaned her bottom. She then proceeded to Rufuji, which she reached after dark. The following day she proceeded to an island close to the river mouth shortly after her armed cutter, which was patrolling the estuary, had chased a dhow ashore there, but by that time the occupants had managed to escape. Clearly, various clandestine operations were in hand by both sides, and, on the 9th the whaling vessel *Fly* was attacked by an armed dhow, the latter being driven off with the help of the light cruiser *Pyramus.* The automatic weapons provided by *Weymouth* had found almost immediate use.

On the 6th March, the steamer *Kinfauns Castle* arrived with the two Sopwith flying boats aboard. And, on the 7th, Admiral KING-HALL arrived on the scene, now temporarily flying his flag in *Goliath.* On his way in he was met by *Weymouth* off Mafia Island, and he had a long conference with Captain CHURCH.

In flying trials one of the seaplanes made a crash landing and was damaged beyond repair. It was then found that the other machine was becoming unsafe to fly because the hot and humid climate had attacked its component parts and structure.

Photograph reproduced by courtesy of the IWM. The original print is taken from Page 148 of the Diary of Vice-Admiral D.B. CRAMPTON, Museum Ref. 71/29/1

Seaplane No.920 which was practising at Nioro Island.   Men on the beach are working with stores for her.   The *Kinfauns Castle* lies in the offing.

There must have been steadily mounting tension in high places by this time, as one problem after another presented itself and the Navy appeared incapable of destroying one light German warship which was tying down several of their own vessels.   The World was looking on in some amazement, not recognising the tactical and technological problems involved.   Admiral KING-HALL did not have an enviable task to accomplish.

On the 26th March *Weymouth* proceeded to Zanzibar to discharge Captain CHURCH who was suffering with a large carbuncle, and whose state of health in the adverse climate was becoming a matter of concern to Temporary Surgeon P.W. CARRUTHERS M.B.   The ship experienced a delay en route due to the breaking down of her steerage gear, but the problem was remedied by her Engineering Staff.   She returned to Rufuji, off and on, with short breaks for coaling and re-provisioning at Zanzibar.

It is unclear as to whether any shore leave was granted at Zanzibar.   If so, tight restrictions would have been imposed, the ratings only being allowed to go to the Cooper Institute (though the POs and CPOs could visit the town).   Sports facilities lent to the RN by courtesy of the Sultan of Zanzibar existed at this institute.   However, Martial Law had been imposed by the authorities and it was a punishable offence for spirituous liquor to be sold to any PO or man of the RN or RMs.   All leave expired at sunset, and shore patrols were mounted to prevent any entry to the districts where native bars and brothels existed.

During this time, Captain D.B. CRAMPTON transferred from command of the *Kinfauns Castle* to that of the *Weymouth,* finding her '*damnably hot*' after the larger and airier spaces of the intermediate liner.   He seems to have been a very determined and progressive captain.   He was later promoted, and he has left his diary and papers for posterity. *NOTE: The author has thus been able to draw from the 'Diary of Vice Admiral CRAMPTON', which is preserved in the Imperial War Museum, London, to supplement and give colour to what follows of the remaining commission of Weymouth.   The main content continues, however, to be drawn from the Ship's Log, with additional material still coming from the Diary of the Anonymous Stoker.*

Photograph reproduced by courtesy of the IWM. The original print appears on Page 145 of the MSS Diary of Vice-Admiral D.B. CRAMPTON, Museum Reference 71/29/1.

A wrecked seaplane being hoisted aboard HMS *Weymouth*. Its torn-off floats hang forlornly down, and are visible just beyond the shield of one of *Weymouth's* 6-inch guns. Note that the ratings are wearing semi-obsolescent 'Sennit' hats against the strength of the sun. The flying officer in the foreground favours a pith helmet.

Captain CRAMPTON dealt with 20 defaulters the day he joined. He also left for posterity a list of the Officers of the *Weymouth* at the time he assumed temporary command. These gentlemen are listed below. Some we have already encountered as names written in the Ship's Log (or more or less 'indistinguishably' as initials inscribed when they were on duty as Officers of the Watch), but most have been anonymous up to this point.

List of Officers and Warrant Officers of HMS *Weymouth*.
(March 1915)

Rank	Name	Seniority
Captain	D.B. CRAMPTON	07 APR 1915
Commander	G.H. LANG	31 OCT 1911
Lieut	H.W.K YOUNG	01 JAN 1914
Lieut (G)	A.F. PECOLLICUM	13 AUG 1913
Lieut (N)	H.M. SPRECKLEY	13 DEC 1913
Lieut	A. KIMBLEY	12 JAN 1914
Lieut	A.G. MURRAY	08 JUN 1914
Lieut RNR	W.R. CULDER	08 AUG 1914
Eng Commander	J.W. MILNE	30 SEP 1913
Eng Lt Commdr	S.R. DIGHT	06 JAN 1914

Staff Surgeon	W.H. HARRIS	- - JAN 1914
Staff Paymaster	E.A. COUPER	15 OCT 1913
Temp Surgeon	P.W. CURRUTHERS M.B.	29 DEC 1914
Sub Lieut	W.R.F. GREGORY*	- - SEP 1914
Sub Lieut RNR	N.A. MacQUEEN**	02 DEC 1913
Gunner	J.L. BROWNE	15 OCT 1913
Gunner (T)	W.T. SKINNER	16 OCT 1913
Bosun	W.J. WAKEFORD	08 JAN 1914
Sig Bosun	A.A.P. HATCHER	- - JAN 1914
Carpenter	A. HITCHINGS	22 DEC 1913
A. Eng	J.C. SMITH	31 OCT 1911
A. Eng	A.T. BIRCH	06 JAN 1914
A. Eng	C.W. EVANS	01 SEP 1914
Clerk	W. McBRIDE	15 OCT 1913

[* = Temporarily Lent to *Pegasus*. ** = Temporarily Lent to *Duplex*. It seems probable that small parties of armed Ratings (the arms including machine guns), had been told off to accompany these two officers. Seemingly, the officer and men lent to *Pegasus* had survived her sinking by *Konigsberg* at Zanzibar, though they had evidently not yet rejoined *Weymouth*.]

On the 22nd April 1915, Captain CRAMPTON's former ship the *Kinfauns Castle* left for Simonstown and the liner *Laconia* arrived with three replacement flying boats - machines made by the Short Aircraft Company. These had been brought out from the UK in the *Dunvegan Castle* and assembled at Durban. It was clear that these machines had already seen hard service with the RNAS. Nevertheless, one of the aircraft flew upriver successfully on the 24th April, albeit at an altitude of only 800 feet, and observed the *Konigsberg,* apparently in a seaworthy condition. This aircraft had been piloted by Flight Commander CULL, who reported that he had been heavily fired upon, the wings being perforated and the engine also struck.

At last supplies of coal arrived on the scene on Sunday 25th, when the collier *Centro* came alongside and *Weymouth* coaled from her, then washed down, and held divine service. One of the planes made a further reconnaissance flight and obtained a good photograph of *Konigsberg* in its 'lair' in the meandering and densely tree-lined river. This photograph was invaluable, for it revealed that *Konigsberg* was in a different position to that previously supposed.

On 1st May, the cruiser *Chatham* arrived at Rufuji after a refit at Bombay, relieving *Weymouth,* who was thus free to proceed to Zanzibar to undergo a very quick refit, albeit of a temporary nature. However, there was a hitch on the 2nd, for the armed tug *Duplex* 'lost her bearings', and *Weymouth* was sent to look for her, finding her that evening, before herself being able to proceed.

On 7th May, at Zanzibar, during the ship's refit, the Signal Boatswain was court-martialled aboard *Weymouth*. Apparently, two urgent signals had come in during the night of 17th/18th April, and had not been decoded and reported to Captain CRAMPTON until 0800 the following morning. This was regarded as a most serious matter which might have upset the plans being made aboard *Hyacinth*, which was now the flagship.

A peacetime photo of HMS *Hyacinth*, which had been completed in 1898. A cutter is pulling around her stern. By 1914 she was the Flagship of Admiral KING-HALL.

As a result, the 'Signal Bosun' (sic) had been logged for neglect of duty. His case was heard by a board of ship's captains, with Captain CRAMPTON as its President. The Signal Boatswain was found guilty of leave-breaking and desertion and sentenced to lose two years seniority, being severely reprimanded and dismissed his ship.

All too soon, *Weymouth* was back off the Rufuji River mouth. This was a tense time. The rainy season was at its height, it was unbearably hot and humid, and tempers were becoming frayed, even at the highest level of command. For some obscure reason, orders were given from top level that there was to be no singing at night - which had been one of the little pleasures of the men. The frequency of issue of their fresh meat ration had fallen below the regulatory level of twice a week - and two cases of beri-beri had arisen. Captain CRAMPTON felt that a change of climate was urgently needed - but first, it would be necessary to destroy the *Konigsberg*. The arrival of a bag of mail on the 19th May was a help to morale, and the men received Princess Mary's *Christmas* gift! - reportedly a pencil case. Alf would have been suffering with the other men, but the manifold experiences he was gaining would have been leading him to mature rapidly.

For the rest of the month and into early June, *Weymouth* moved back and forth between Rufuji and Mafia Island, the latter having recently been captured from the Germans and made into an airfield and a coaling station. During this period *Weymouth* re-provisioned from both the *Laconia* and the *Lorentic*. On the 11th June Captain CRAMPTON had to sentence a man to 7 days in the cells, for being found asleep on watch. It was the man's second offence. This made the seventh case in two months, and was probably another portent of the decline in both the health and the morale of the company. Captain CRAMPTON could not allow this dangerous situation to continue, and ordered that, until further orders, there were to be two lookouts on each gun.

At last, on the 10th June, the SS *Trent* arrived with the monitors *Severn* and *Mersey* which had been withdrawn from operations in the North Sea. These ships were each of 1,270 tons, had two 6-inch guns and two 4.7-inch howitzers, had companies of about 100 men and drew only about 5 ft 10 inches (as compared, for example, with *Weymouth's* 15 feet). Their maximum speed was about 12 knots, but it is believed that their 'economical speed' was only about 9 knots. They had been towed for a considerable part of their long passage out from England.

The fleet now consisted of six commissioned ships, namely the *Weymouth, Laconia, Severn, Mersey, Hyacinth* and *Pioneer.*[124] There were also four steam whalers, *Pickle, Echo, Fly* and *Childers,* and the *Trent,* which was a tender to *Severn* and *Mersey.* There were also four tugs, *T A Joliffe, Sarah Joliffe, Revenge* and *Blackcock,* to say nothing of three colliers and a transport, making a total of 19 ships. [Four further steam whalers arrived a few days later, making eight whalers in all.]

Author's collection. An anonymous postcard, issued shortly after 21ˢᵗ October 1914.

The monitor HMS *Severn* (Captain FULLERTON) 1,270 tons, two six-inch guns and two 4.7-inch howitzers. In company with her sister-ship *Mersey*, the *Severn*, well-supported by *Weymouth*, would soon write '*finis*' to the *Konigsberg* – though not without taking casualties, for *Konigsberg* 'had teeth' to the end. For the first time in Royal Naval history, spotter aircraft, using wireless communications, would play an important role in battle.

Perhaps as a slightly retrospective 'treat' for Captain CRAMPTON's birthday (which had fallen on 14ᵗʰ June), *Weymouth* now had the honour of taking Admiral KING-HALL, and the captains of the monitors aboard, and showing them the Rufuji delta and the heavily tree-lined nature of its banks - presumably tempering risk with prudence.

As a consequence of the ensuing discussions between Admiral and Captains, the Navigator of the *Weymouth,* Lieutenant H.M. SPRECKLEY, went aboard one of the whalers on 22ⁿᵈ June, and took soundings off the river entrance. Probably in connection with the same exercise, the Australian light cruiser *Pioneer*, which drew about 17 ft,

---

[124] Prior to the arrival of the monitors, Admiral KING-HALL had reported to the Admiralty that, with the exception of *Weymouth*, all his 'men o' war' were 'old or worn in every direction' and quite incapable of chasing or engaging the *Konigsberg*. If *Hyacinth* or *Challenger* could get within range, they could deal with *Konigsberg*, but neither *Pioneer, nor Pyramus, nor Laconia nor Laurentic* would have any likelihood of success. He said that a second Town Class cruiser was therefore required, to enable one cruiser to leave for short refits whilst the other stayed on patrol. (See ADM 137/702 at TNA.)

grounded on a reef at 1730 on the 23rd. *Weymouth* went to her assistance, and *Pioneer* came off with the tide four hours later. *Weymouth* coaled ship on the 24th seeing rockets fired from ashore, apparently by the Germans.

Then, preparatory to an attack on the *Konigsberg,* the *Weymouth* took aboard sandbags from a dhow. Once filled with sand, these were built up in walls to provide additional protection from enfilading fire from the river-banks. (The monitors and other ships were similarly protected, the monitors also being given some steel plates to supplement the sandbag walls.) After coaling, *Weymouth's* trim was checked to make it optimal for manoeuvring in shallow waters. This was achieved by moving some of her coal further aft. Divers had been down a few days before that, to check on the doors of the submarine torpedoes and clean them of barnacles. *Weymouth* also gave herself some extra teeth by taking aboard two Maxim guns, plus 4,000 rounds in filled belts, and six men to operate them. These all came from the cruiser *Hyacinth. Weymouth* also installed two 3-pounder Hotchkiss guns from the Australian light cruiser *Pioneer.* The needs of the 'inner man' were also met to some degree, when the trawler *Fly* came alongside, bringing badly-needed fresh meat.

The aeroplanes were also active in the overall preparations. Their performance was improving, a height of 4,500 ft being attained in 30 minutes from take-off.

In his personal diary Captain CRAMPTON confided, *"I gather that the Admiralty orders are that on no account is the 'Weymouth' to be risked by going up the river, because she is needed in the 'Med'. So we are to anchor at the mouth of the river, where the soundings recently taken by Lieutenant SPRECKLEY end."* On Sunday the 4th July he added, *"After Prayers I described the Plan of Operation to the Ship's Company, with the aid of a blackboard."* It is clear that Captain CRAMPTON was not only forthright, tough and progressive, but also a thoughtful commander of men, who was constantly showing considerable initiative.

On the 6th July 1915, at dawn (0500), the two monitors entered the Rufuji River with the *Weymouth* weighing and following as soon as the C-in-C had come aboard. Heart-stoppingly, despite having adjusted her trim, *Weymouth* stuck on the sandy mud of the bar at the river-mouth for ten minutes, but got off and over with the flood tide. She then proceeded upriver, with the trawlers *Echo* and *Fly* sweeping ahead for mines and with the trawler *Childers* sounding, until *Weymouth's* pre-agreed bombarding position was reached. Aided by their shallower draught, the monitors were moving yet further upriver. *Weymouth* and her escorting ships were all fired on very heavily by what were judged to be 3-pounder guns on both banks of the river. *Fly* was hit, and *Weymouth* had at least two shots which screamed between her funnels before pitching 100 yards 'over'. *Weymouth* and the others returned this fire, *Weymouth* using Lyddite to good effect, and virtually silencing the enemy guns. Meantime, the aircraft had arrived overhead and continued upriver, spotting the fall of shot from the monitors, which continued in action. They were engaging the distant *Konigsberg* whilst *Weymouth* concentrated her fire on the river banks and also, at long range, on the town of Pemba. It would seem reasonable to suppose that Alf was engaged in the thick of all this exciting, hot-blooded, noisy, smoke-bound and hectic work.

Weymouth was ordered to withdraw at noon, having fired off 78 rounds from her main armament. The monitors did not withdraw before about 1600, the *Mersey* having had her forward six-inch gun put out of action. She had lost four men killed and three wounded.   By that time *Weymouth* had returned the Admiral to *Hyacinth,* and *Weymouth's* deck-officers and men were able to watch the monitors coming out, apparently under fire and both firing hard left and right at the river-banks as they came. *Weymouth* lined ship and her company gave the monitors a cheer.   *Weymouth* also signalled her congratulations to them. The *Konigsberg* had been hit several times. She had been damaged, but she was certainly far from being destroyed. The spotting and correction of the fall of shot, as reported by the aircraft, had been less than satisfactory, mainly due to difficulties caused by both monitors firing in unison, instead of one after the other. However, valuable lessons had been learned.

Weymouth* coaled at the new station on Mafia Island, taking aboard 300 tons. It was learned that the two aircraft had flown a combined distance of almost 1,000 miles during the action, with a gap of only ½ hour in their patrol, in which otherwise one aircraft or the other had been over the *Konigsberg* continuously from 6am to 3.30 pm. This was a considerable feat. Their crews, each at this time consisting of an officer with a rating as his observer, had become very stiff and chilled from the long exposure and reduced oxygen level at almost 5,000 feet, to such a degree that some of the men had to be lifted out of the respective cockpits. One pilot reported that the *Weymouth* had twice *'saved his bacon'* after a German gun had got his range with shrapnel shells - *Weymouth* having seen the air-bursts and fired blindly some 14,000 yards at the presumed position of the gun. Evidently she had been rewarded with some luck, the pilot having been pleased to see *Weymouth's* shells bursting near to his harasser.[125]

Commander FULLERTON, who was in command of the *Severn*, came aboard *Weymouth* on the 8th July, and told how, during the action of the 6th July, the monitors were being straddled all the time by the 4.1 inch guns of the *Konigsberg,* and it was *'only by Providence'* that they were both not more seriously damaged. It was Alf's twentieth birthday on the 9th July, and he may have wondered if he would see his 21st, in view of the hot reception which their efforts to destroy the *Konigsberg* had so far brought about their ears. Clearly, there was more yet to do. It also appears that the monitors had both strained their hulls slightly by the intensity of their volley-firing, perhaps aggravated by the sheer weight of the protective sandbags and steel plates they had temporarily mounted. If this news of hull-straining had somehow percolated to the 'Lower Deck', Alf may have reflected about the matter a couple of years later, when events took a rather similar 'twist' (no pun intended) in the next ship in which he was to serve.

On the 11th July, the monitors tried again, once more with *Weymouth* carrying the Admiral aboard, and staying near the river-mouth. The monitors this time fired one at a time. This made the spotting by aircraft, and their wireless signalling of the appropriate correction of fall of shot by each ship, much more successful, and this time the *Konigsberg* was observed to be hit at least nine times, with two very large explosions being heard and seen, one at 1250 and an even heavier one at 1315. *Konigsberg* was subsequently observed to be on fire.

One of the spotting aircraft had been forced to make an emergency crash-landing due to engine-failure. The two crew members, Flight Commander CULL and Flight Sub-Lt ARNOLD, were extremely lucky to survive, as the aircraft had quickly foundered. The airmen were picked up by the *Severn* around 1310. At 1335 there were two more

---

[125] This would indeed have been a matter of luck combined with a 'good eye', for none of the British guns would have been 'ranged in' at anywhere near such a very long distance.

massive explosions in the *Konigsberg*, and it was thought that the Germans were blowing her up to prevent her capture. The *Severn* reported that she could see the *Konigsberg* from her masthead, that *Konigsberg's* funnels appeared to be gone, that she was burning fiercely from bow to stern and that her foremast was leaning over.[126]

Mersey had three men wounded in the action, Able Seaman CARTER very slightly, and ABs THORPE and WILLIAMS slightly: *Severn* had suffered no casualties at all. The second aircraft crashed on landing on her return, but the crew were unhurt.

So ended the long drawn-out *Konigsberg* affair. To the great pleasure of the company, who were heart-sick of Rufuji, *Weymouth* was immediately put under orders to proceed to Zanzibar, and, from there for a re-fit, *'probably at Malta'*. This was something to really look forward to. However, there was a sting in the tail, for the C-in-C ordered them to off-load at Zanzibar 200 Lyddite shells and 100 shrapnel shells (with the related charges for them), for the use of the monitors. The C-in-C also retained three signalmen, and a wireless-operator of *Weymouth's* company, plus 14 rifles from her weaponry. Privately, Captain CRAMPTON was not best pleased. Nor were the crew, who may have muttered *very* discreetly when they were ordered from on high *to re-embark* the 200 Lyddite shells just five days later!

On the 13th July 1915 the C-in-C, Admiral KING-HALL came aboard and made a pleasant speech of farewell to the men, saying that he was sorry to lose them and giving them his congratulations *'for their good services in such a tedious task'*. Mail was also delivered, making for a very happy day. Commander FULLERTON also came to say goodbye.[127] *Weymouth* then sailed for Aden at 1300, crossing the Line at 2010, but again with no ceremonial to King Neptune during this time of war.

On the 14th they overtook a French Mail ship on the same heading, whilst at 01° 47' N, 42° 30' E. A week later they were at 08° 24' N, 50° 39' E at noon, and, on 23rd July they arrived at Aden, finding it *'a deadly place of yellow sand and rock'*. (See photo overleaf.) Coal was in short supply, and poor stuff, but they got 380 tons on board, before proceeding through the Red Sea to Suez.

---

[126] In the first attack *Konigsberg* had suffered 2 killed and several wounded including her Commander, Captain LOOF. In the second attack she suffered 9 killed and 45 wounded (21 seriously). So far as the Germans were concerned, the ship was by no means a 'dead loss', for her guns would be recovered by the Germans and used in their long holding action against the British land invasion of German East Africa. [Tipped off by British intelligence, Admiral KING-HALL, flying his flag in *Hyacinth*, had previously intercepted the supply-ship *Sperrbrecher*, sent out from Germany to sustain *Konigsberg*. By means of an overland bombardment, *Hyacinth* had severely damaged *Sperrbrecher* and set her on fire, to the extent that the Germans had scuttled the ship. However, the Germans subsequently salvaged shells from the wreck to feed Konigsberg's salvaged guns in the land war - to say nothing of recovering other useful weapons from the *Sperrbrecher*. One has to say that the German commanders in East Africa were remarkably resourceful, self-sustaining and resilient.]

[127] His ship, HMS *Severn*, and her consort, HMS *Mersey*, would stay on the Africa Station for some time, to provide valuable shore-bombardments in support of the land forces. *Mersey* would later provide similar support for the troops involved in the ill-fated Gallipoli Campaign.

Author's collection. A postcard by Pallonjee, Dinshaw & Co, Aden, dating from about 1910.

A pre-war photograph of Steamer Point at Aden, taken from one of the tortured and spectacular volcanic peaks which tower above the port. The two warships lying off the point have white hulls and buff funnels and are evidently cruisers of the 'Astrea' Class and the 'Royal Arthur' Class. They are already obsolescent. When *Weymouth* called at Aden in July 1915, to take in coal, her crew found the port to be '*a deadly place of yellow sand and rock*'.

Weymouth's company found the passage through the Red Sea 'terribly hot', and men were collapsing with heat-exhaustion. A Pilot came aboard at Suez, and they entered the Sweetwater Canal, passing through the Bitter Lakes and on through to the famous Suez Canal itself. British troops, who one assumes, had heard of the destruction of the *Konigsberg*, lined the bank of the Suez Canal and gave *Weymouth* a 'hearteningly warm reception' as she headed northwards towards Port Said.

Weymouth left Port Said after coaling there, having taken aboard almost a full load, namely 1,075 tons - a back-breaking and exhausting job in the great heat. She was now in the 'Med', and hostile submarines were rumoured to be active. Accordingly, *Weymouth* zig-zagged for three hours of her voyage, then increased to 18 knots. She had three of her guns manned day and night against possible submarine attack, but reached Malta without incident - save that one of her boilers by now appeared to be burnt out. She was definitely going to have to go in for her badly-needed refit, estimated now to take five weeks to complete. The company probably cheered at the news, and certainly did so when the ship was put into Dockyard Hands at Malta, and general leave was given.

We do not know how Alf and his closest shipmates spent the time that followed - but we can imagine the various ways in which 'Jack' spent his periods of shore-leave during those five weeks on the famous island. After the extreme boredom, enlivened by periods of intense excitement and danger, which they had been going through under tropical heat and humidity, the fresher heat, sunshine, entertainment and safety of Malta must have come as a positive delight. We can be assured that the company did their level best to use the facilities of Malta to the full, ranging from swimming parties in Bighi Bay by day to the fleshpots of Valetta by night. And, in a way, their luck held good, for the refit took a great many weeks to complete.

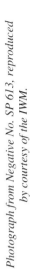

HMS *Lowestoft* at Malta c. 1915. A photograph evocative of *Weymouth's* arrival at Malta for her urgently-needed refit. *Weymouth's* crew were also in dire need of 'rest and recuperation'.

But all good things have to come to an end, and the 24th November 1915 found *Weymouth* emerging from the dockyard, to carry out a two-hour steam trial. This proving satisfactory, she left Malta at 3.30 pm, bound for Taranto. The Italians had now become our allies in the war against Germany and Austria. *Weymouth* departed from Taranto on the 26th being met off Cape Santa Maria de Leuce by an Italian destroyer escort, which conducted her into the harbour at Brindisi on the afternoon of the same day. An Italian naval officer, Commander SENGIETO, then visited the ship and was shown round.

At this time the weather, in stark contrast with the very hot conditions they had been going through for many months past, had become intensely cold, with snow an inch deep on deck, and bitter squalls. *Weymouth*, coaled ship on the 27th, was guard ship for two days, and then went out on patrol on the evening of the 30th November, in company with the Italian ships *Epiro* and *Pepe*. The sea turned rough, and the ships became separated. *Weymouth* continued on her course for a time, but the weather became severe, and she turned back to Brindisi, still finding no sign of her consorts. She therefore headed at full speed for St Giovanni Dimedua. Off there she found *Pepe* who reported that *Epiro* had already entered port. Matters then became hectic, for *Weymouth* spotted an Austrian submarine on the surface and managed to get in just one shot from her forrard gun at the submarine before it dived.

It was believed that three hostile submarines were active in the area. The main protection for *Weymouth* and her consorts was to travel at high speed, but this meant frequent hard and filthy work in coaling and higher than normal wear and tear on their machinery. Convoys were being moved, so far as possible, under cover of darkness. On the 4th, a submarine fired a torpedo at HMS *Topaze*, which, fortunately, missed.

Author's collection. A postcard by Gale & Polden, evidently taken in 1915/16.

H.M.S. Topaze.

The light cruiser HMS *Topaze,* 3,000 tons, twelve 4-inch guns, here seen with wartime camouflage intended to confuse enemy gunlayers and torpedo-men. As in the case of *Weymouth* and other British and Italian warships, the crew of *Topaze* were struggling to deal with underwater threats from torpedo and mine, which were totally new to their experience.

On the 7th *Weymouth* left harbour with an Italian light cruiser, the *Rixio*, and four destroyers, but lost contact with *Rixio* in fog which suddenly came down, later learning that *Rixio* had spotted a mine, which she had sunk by gunfire. (It is probable that these highly dangerous mines were being laid in the shipping lanes by the Austrian submarines.) *Weymouth* returned to Brindisi at 11.00 and coaled ship yet again, leaving harbour at 1800 to patrol off the Albanian coast, returning next day. On the 13th six stoker ratings joined the ship. One imagines that they were very welcome, for the engine room had been working flat out during this period.

Again, on the 17th, having been joined by *Nievo* and *Ardente*, *Weymouth,* whose captain was now in command of what the company called 'our usual fleet', sighted a submarine on the surface, though out of range of her guns. The submarine dived. By now, everybody was on the *qui vive*, and submarines were being recognised as a real threat against which defensive tactics had yet to be properly resolved. Understandably, there was a certain degree of 'jumpiness' in the surface ships about their foes beneath the waves.

After leaving Brindisi on the evening of the 21st December, *Weymouth* again saw a submarine on the surface at 8.30 p.m., which she challenged. No reply being seen, *Weymouth* promptly opened fire with her six-inch guns (the French destroyers which were in company also opening up with their quickfirers). As a tribute to their marksmanship, it was later discovered that a hit was scored, which had made a large hole - but, unfortunately, their target was found to be a French submarine! Luckily, there were no casualties and the submarine survived. The surface ships must have had mixed feelings about this, for the fact that they had 'seriously hurt' a submarine must have made them feel, to an extent, capable of striking back at the threat that a *hostile* submarine would pose.

On the 23rd December 1915, *Weymouth* escorted two store ships with provisions for Serbian refugees in Albania. A previous sally by other ships to do so had been intercepted and attacked by Austrian cruisers, and this must have added a certain tension to the voyage. However, all went well and *Weymouth* arrived back at Brindisi at noon on the 25th. As our stoker noted in his diary, '*we had a very quiet time (on the rest of) Christmas Day*'. But, come Boxing Day, they were back at the filthy task of coaling ship yet again.

It was just as well they had full bunkers, for there was what the company called '*a sudden spasm*' on the 29th December, in fact after a report had been received by Captain CRAMPTON (who was now the British SNO at Brindisi) that an Austrian Cruiser with attendant destroyers was bombarding Durazzo. *Dartmouth* was shadowing them, and believed that she had remained undetected. Steam was promptly raised. Rear-Admiral BELLINI hoisted his flag in the cruiser *Rixio*, and, with *Weymouth* and the Italian destroyers *Abba, Niero, Nosto* and *Pilo*, set off at full speed for Cattaro. When the enemy fleet was sighted, two Italian TBDs were sent to cut off an enemy destroyer lagging behind the main group, *Weymouth* holding to a northerly course and *Dartmouth* more southerly, with the objective of catching the enemy between them. The enemy ships were thought to be one light cruiser with 9.2 inch guns, two light cruisers and two destroyers. They were therefore a superior force to the Allied fleet.

Aided by a smokescreen, the enemy evaded the opening movement of the Allied ships, and, after 1300, a high-speed chase developed, in which *Weymouth* attained as much as 27.7 knots for a short time. Visibility was difficult against the setting sun, but fire was opened at a range of 7,000 yards. Unfortunately, the fall of shot could not be well seen, but it was believed that at least two hits were scored. By 1630 the sun had set behind the enemy, who subsequently escaped under cover of darkness. The enemy ships had replied to the Allied fire, and the Italian destroyer *Nino* had been struck twice. Several salvoes had been fired at *Weymouth* but the evasive tactics used by Captain CRAMPTON had proved very successful. And, as Captain CRAMPTON wrote a little later, the high speeds maintained by *Weymouth* during four hours to reach the scene, and then in four hours of pursuit of the enemy, were "*a great credit to her Engine Room Departments.*"

According to 'our' stoker, the 'buzz' on the lower deck was that a French destroyer had sunk an Austrian one, that another Austrian destroyer had hit a mine and sunk, and that another mine had severely damaged yet another Austrian destroyer. The company of *Weymouth* were very elated at the whole affair. Four days later they would take in 100 rounds of ammunition as a testament to the number of salvoes they had fired during the action. And in the interval of time, they would escort more storeships to Albania and coal their own ship twice. They did not lack for work.

However, danger lurked all around. On the 2nd January 1916, the *Jean Bart*, a chalutier, had blown up off Durazzo, supposedly after striking a mine. On the 8th January the *City of Palermo*, an Italian armed merchant cruiser, struck a mine just outside Brindisi harbour at 0836. Amongst other passengers, she had on board some 140 British Army Service Corps personnel bound for Salonika. Tugs, TBDs and other ships went to her assistance. Amongst the would-be rescuers were two drifters, the *Freucheney* and the

Morning Star, one of which also struck a mine. The resultant explosion completely destroyed both ships, with only three men being saved from the two of them. Seventeen men were thus lost in these drifters, including all the officers. Fifty-four men drowned in the sinking of the *City of Palermo*. The survivors were taken aboard the *Weymouth* and *Topaze*, and were clothed and fed. Whether the mines were Allied ones which had broken adrift, or Austrian mines sown by a submarine or surface vessel, remained unclear. The latter seems much the more probable. On the 9th January 1916 the SS *Benedini* was also blown up on a mine, only 100 people being saved out of 500 on board.

On the 12th fifteen ratings arrived from Devonport and joined the ship. On the 17th, at 0830, HRH King Victor EMANUEL of Italy came aboard and decorated Captain CRAMPTON for his meritorious services. At 0010 Admiral THURSBY inspected the ship. Three days later, Admiral TROUBRIDGE (whom the company had last 'encountered' in the abortive chase of *Goeben* and *Breslau*), arrived in Brindisi from Albania, aboard a French destroyer. He came aboard *Weymouth* in the afternoon. (His conversation with the senior officers aboard *Weymouth* might have been very interesting, that is, if any 'levelling' was taking place. However, those concerned may have considered such 'verbal territory' about the chase of '*G*' and '*B*' simply too dangerously controversial to enter into.)

There then followed more days of patrolling. One such patrol, on the 30th January, led to the detection of three Austrian submarines and thence to the identification of a submarine base, which was successfully bombarded. On the 6th February, at 1100, *Weymouth*, escorted by the French destroyer *Bouclier*, set off on patrol from Brindisi, speed 20 knots. At 1423 *Liverpool* reported enemy ships in sight, her position then being 41° 40' N, 18° 40' E. *Weymouth* was in that general vicinity and she set an interception course, raising her speed to 22 knots. However, in less than an hour *Liverpool* reported that the enemy ships had entered Cattaro. *Weymouth* therefore resumed her patrol, and, at 1930 discovered a superior force of three enemy destroyers on her port bow, heading south. She increased speed to 22 knots, came round onto a southerly course, and opened deliberate fire when the enemy had closed the range to 7,000 yards. Having fired nine rounds, *Weymouth* ceased firing, changed course again, and made her escape.

Next day, at 7.40 a.m., a torpedo fired from the starboard beam passed close under *Weymouth's* stern, breaking water in the wash of the screws. *Bouclier*, which was nearby, immediately increased speed, and, having gone out to starboard, dropped three bombs 250 metres distant, at the place where the submarine responsible had been sighted. The company of *Bouclier* believed they sank it. Another submarine was sighted at 11 a.m., about five miles off. Captain CRAMPTON tried to lure it closer by hoisting the Austrian Ensign, but the submarine made off after an intense (but distant) inspection. At 1500 a submarine surfaced unexpectedly, close at hand, and the Captain of *Weymouth* attempted to ram it, but without success.

The ship returned to Brindisi at 1700, after an eventful and stressful two-day patrol - and her company coaled ship again. More patrolling followed, relieved by the Fleet Regatta on 11th March 1916, where, one might be forgiven for supposing that near-hysterical enthusiasm prevailed as some of the men's mental and emotional tension was released whilst the competition proceeded. Condenser trouble cut short a patrol with an Italian destroyer on the 12th March.

Alf was maturing and rapidly gaining in experience. He became a Leading Seaman with effect from 1st April 1916. The non-substantive rate of 1st Class Gunlayer was now open to him, which would add 8d a day to his now-increased substantive rate of pay of 2s. 2d. per day, which could increase to 2s. 4d if he continued to give satisfaction to his superiors. He could now begin to hope that he might make the non-substantive rate of 'Gunner's Mate' – so long as he survived the next phase of this hectic warfare.

Weymouth ended up in Malta in April, being assisted into dry dock by tugs on the 10th April, her hands cleaning out the magazines and shell rooms whilst repairs proceeded. She emerged into the basin on the 14th. They drew stores, discharged three privates of the RMLI to the Detention Barracks ashore and placed Leading Seaman McBANF under arrest for being drunk. He must have been an extreme case amongst many who were more or less 'under the influence', for one understands that some 'Friday Whiles' and 'Saturday Whiles' had been granted at this time and well celebrated.

Author's 'inherited' collection of Family Photographs. An anonymous postcard portrait, studio unknown. Evidently postally-used, but inside an outer cover, since lost.

Leading Seaman Alfred Wm DAVIS.
Alf wrote on the back of the original print (from which this image was copied) *"Your loving brother, Alf"* and presumably sent it off in an envelope (perhaps with a covering letter) to his three sisters at Lincoln.
It seems unlikely that he sent a copy to his father, with whom it seems he was still not communicating directly.
(This image of Alf is very reminiscent of his grandson David GOODMAN.)

Alf, wearing his Leading Seaman badge above a three-year Good Conduct badge on his left arm, and his so-called 'non-substantive' qualification, as a Seaman Gunner, on his right arm. His cap-ribbon is that of HMS *Weymouth*. This photographic portrait was evidently taken soon after his return to England in May 1916, aged 20. He has seen various parts of the world, endured many varied wartime experiences, some very harrowing, and frequently had brushes with death.

As we can see from the above photograph, for one who had already come through a lot of wartime experiences and survived both tropical and wintry climes, Alf still looked remarkably young – though his left eye has developed a mature and appraising look.

A tremor ran through the ship on the 19th when the S.S. *Tantallon* struck their stem, slightly bending one plate. This was followed by further 'excitement' next evening when the sentry based on the Power Station roof raised the alarm for an aerial attack - which fortunately did not manifest itself. His raising of this alarm may well have been the result of a hallucination from an over-stressed imagination – though this matter does not seem to have been investigated.

Then, on the 24th, they coaled ship, using native labour, and taking aboard 348 tons, before proceeding to Port Said at 1525 on the 26th, being escorted by the destroyer *Minstrel* until 1800. They manned their fo'csle and 'submarine' guns on the 27th, and arrived in a rain-squall, on the evening of the 28th April - only to coal again with 580 tons. A sub-division of Russian TBDs arrived from Suez shortly afterwards - and the Aeroplane Attack Alarm was sounded off at 1130, though, again, nothing transpired.

On the 1st May 1916, HRH the Prince of Wales came aboard with Lord HAMILTON and Lt Commander MURRAY, who all took passage in *Weymouth* to Spezia. On arrival there, General BIRDWOOD and an Italian admiral came aboard to greet the Prince of Wales, who left the ship at 1930. *Weymouth's* bunkers were nearly empty by then, so they took aboard 800 tons on the 5th - and a further 800 tons on the 6th! The company must have been shattered by the time they had twice 'cleaned ship' - and twice themselves.

On the 10th they left Spezia, passed through the Straits of Messina on the 11th and arrived at Taranto on the 12th, coaling on the 13th, before proceeding to Gibraltar which they reached on the 19th May. Having taken aboard 640 tons of coal, they then proceeded to Plymouth, arriving on the 23rd, and from thence to Sheerness and on to Chatham, which they reached at 1800 on the 25th May 1916. England, home and beauty. They had come through many close shaves and were due a little 'R & R'- for now, at least.[128]

One matter that we have not mentioned was that Alf had qualified for his 'tot' on 9th July 1915. This had come about on the eve of the final and decisive attack on the *Konigsberg*. Doubtless, a tot could help to steady nerves when a ship was involved in war – but the real benefit would come about when Alf returned to freezing northern climes and there would be times when he would come off watch chilled to the bone. He also now had the marvellous facility of offering 'sips' and 'gulpers' from his tot, in order to elicit little favours from shipmates with particular skills or money to loan.

So far as his immediate future was concerned, Alf was posted to HMS *Pembroke* from 29th May 1916 to 3rd November 1916, presumably for re-qualifying and further training. Whilst there he would be awarded his first Good Conduct badge, on 18th July 1916. This would bring him an extra 1d. a day - not a lot, but by no means insignificant in those days, and, as the Old Lady murmured philosophically when she relieved herself into the sea: "*I'm sure that every little helps.*"

---

[128] 'R & R' meaning 'Rest and Recreation', due to them after the rigours of a spell of 'Active Service'.

Photograph reproduced by courtesy of the IWM.
The original has the negative reference Q.40572.

A splendid picture of HMS *Weymouth*, wearing camouflage paint, possibly at the start of her next commission. By that time Alf had left her, but he would have had a great many enduring memories of his service aboard this fine ship. She would survive the war and continue in use until 1928.

One suspects that Alf would have found HMS *Pembroke* to be considerably changed. The barracks attended to the manning of about one-third of the number of ratings who formed the Royal Navy. Even before the outbreak of World War One their ranks had been growing. Since that time the growth had been vast, and the total of ratings now numbered some 200,000. Of these men, *Pembroke* was now controlling the lives of some 65,000 individuals, with Portsmouth and Devonport looking after the remainder. Whilst, at any time, the great majority of these men would have been serving at sea, there would always be groups of ratings who had been discharged from a ship at the end of a commission, and who were attending courses ashore and/or awaiting their next draft chit to go to another ship which was soon to be commissioned or re-commissioned. All the depots were, in fact, swamped by the numbers of men passing through – *Pembroke* perhaps the most so.

Moreover, these men were not the 'tightly disciplined professional sailors' of the peacetime Navy, but 'diluted' by 'Hostilities Only' men, and men from the RNVR and RNR. Some of these were quite 'free' in their attitudes to the discipline of the 'Old School', and the overall climate had softened to a certain degree. It might even be that a certain level of chaos reigned, not helped by the overcrowding and the deterioration in the fabric and amenities at *Pembroke*, where a parsimonious Admiralty had spent precious little on maintenance over the 15 or so years since the buildings were erected.

Alf might thus have found himself having to 'put himself about a bit' to get himself suitably accommodated in a decent mess in a reasonable barrack-environment.

Let's break off for a moment to take a look at Alf's voyaging in HMS *Weymouth*, which had considerably extended his Farthest Points South and East.

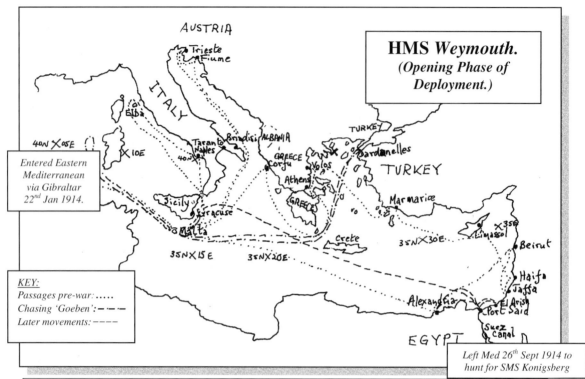

HMS *Weymouth*.
(Opening Phase of Deployment.)

Entered Eastern Mediterranean via Gibraltar 22nd Jan 1914.

KEY:
Passages pre-war: .....
Chasing 'Goeben': —·—·—
Later movements: ————

Left Med 26th Sept 1914 to hunt for SMS Konigsberg

VOYAGES DURING 1st Pt. of DEPLOYMENT: Pers. RECORD of Alfred William DAVIS RN					
Farthest North	Trieste	**46 N** 13 E	*F/North (ever)*	Stornaway	**57 N** 06 W
Farthest South	Port Said	**31 N** 32 E	*F/ South (ever)*	Port Said	**31 N** 32 E
Farthest East	Beirut	34 N **35 E**	*F/East (ever)*	Beirut	34 N **35 E**
Farthest West	Gibraltar	36 N **05 W**	*F/West (ever)*	Atlantic Ocean	50 N **30 W**

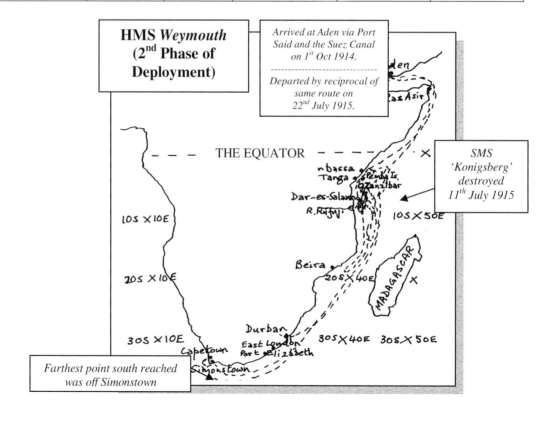

**HMS *Weymouth*
(2nd Phase of Deployment)**

Arrived at Aden via Port Said and the Suez Canal on 1st Oct 1914.

Departed by reciprocal of same route on 22nd July 1915.

THE EQUATOR

SMS 'Konigsberg' destroyed 11th July 1915

Farthest point south reached was off Simonstown

VOYAGES DURING 2ⁿᵈ Pt .of DEPLOYMENT: Pers. RECORD of Alfred William DAVIS RN					
Farthest North	Aden	**13 N** 44 E	*F/North (ever)*	Stornaway	**57 N** 06 W
Farthest South	Simonstown	**36 S** 18 E	*F/ South (ever)*	Simonstown	**36 S** 18 E
Farthest East	Ras Asir	54 N **54 E**	*F/East (ever)*	Ras Asir	54 N **54 E**
Farthest West	Simonstown	36 S **18 E**	*F/West (ever)*	*Atlantic Ocean*	50 N **30 W**

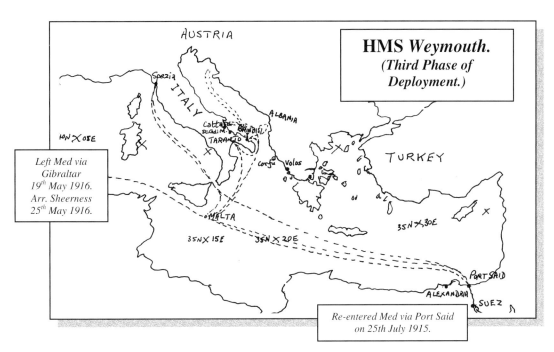

VOYAGES DURING 3ʳᵈ Pt .of DEPLOYMENT: Pers. RECORD of Alfred William DAVIS RN					
Farthest North	Off Trieste	**45 N** 14 E	*F/North (ever)*	Stornaway	**57 N** 06 W
Farthest South	Port Said	**31 N** 32 E	*F/ South (ever)*	Simonstown	**36 S** 18 E
Farthest East	Port Said	31 N **32 E**	*F/East (ever)*	Ras Asir	54 N **54 E**
Farthest West	Spezia	44 N **10 E**	*F/West (ever)*	*Atlantic Ocean*	50 N **30 W**

As shown in the above three tables, HMS *Weymouth* had carried Alf to points further south, and east, than he had ever been before. He had 'crossed the line' twice.[129]

NOTE: If the author is correct in his assessment about Alf's spell at HMS Pembroke, Alf would NOT have been a 'happy bunny', and he might well have nursed certain frustrated feelings and desires in his breast to restore a substantial measure of the high quality of discipline and control of the past. It may have been the memories of such thoughts that evidently prompted him to take action a few years later, when he was once again at Pembroke, by then at a higher rank.

---

[129] It would be discourteous to 'sign off' from HMS *Weymouth* without saying a goodbye to 'our' anonymous stoker. He has provided invaluable 'colour' to our narrative, and the author would like to thank him very much for it. The author would also like to express his great appreciation of the Diary of Captain CRAMPTON. The author owes grateful thanks the staff of the Imperial War Museum (and to the original contributors), who have preserved both these diaries, thus enabling the author to draw data from them.

Private Life

One assumes that Alf had his standard spells of accumulated leave during the six months he would spend at *'Pembroke'*, starting in May 1916, and that he may well have headed for home – perhaps more than once. The manifold experiences and extreme dangers he had been going through since the family had last seen him would have developed and matured him enormously and his father and sisters would undoubtedly have found him considerably changed. Physically, he was probably far more bronzed and somehow more 'filled-out', though still lean and compact, than when they had last seen him. He was also more self-assured in his manner. His blue eyes had just begun to develop the thin 'Crow's Feet' in their external corners which are the hall-mark of a seaman, from gazing into the distance, often 'against the sun and the dancing reflections of light off the sea itself".

Alf celebrated his 21st birthday on 9th July 1916, and one wonders if the family might have held some sort of celebration for him. If that had come about, his brother is most unlikely to have been present.

That is to say, Berty John, normally called 'Jack', had enlisted in the Army on 1st September 1914 as 'John DAVIS', probably being just one of the thousands of fine young men anxious to be promptly involved in the 'great adventure', because it was 'on every tongue' that the 'fighting would be over by Christmas', and he did not want to miss the excitement. He was now in the 7th Battalion of the Lincolnshire Regiment, with the regimental number 11462, and he had been out in France and Flanders since the 14th July 1915. Jack had swiftly learned that the war was likely to drag on for a long, long while. The war on the so-called 'Western Front', had settled down into static trench warfare - an affair of mud and blood and misery for all concerned, made bearable only by the comradeship and humour in adversity of the front-line troops.

To be more specific, by 1916 his battalion had become a part of the 51st Brigade, itself a part of the 17th (Northern) Division, and, during Alf's long stint at HMS *Pembroke*, at Chatham, (whilst Alf was re-training and waiting for his next ship), Jack's battalion became heavily embroiled in the Battle of the Somme. The British offensive was unleashed on the 1st July 1916. The Army took 60,000 casualties on that terrible day, easily the worst in their history, and they suffered a wastage rate of 20,000 a day for days thereafter, continuing at about 10,000 a day for months on end.

Jack's battalion had been involved as early as the 2nd July 1916, the second day of the catastrophic battle. His battalion had advanced against German machine-gun fire in the area of Fricourt Wood, taking numerous casualties and making only slow progress. A week later they were involved in the costly fighting around Mametz Wood. In early August, his battalion was engaged in the fighting around Delville Wood, which was already well-carpeted with dead and rapidly becoming one of the most dreaded places on the Western Front.

In early November Jack would almost certainly have been involved in the bitter fighting around Beaumont Hamel, in which the 7th Lincolns, by then occupying hotly-contested 'Zenith Trench', repulsed a determined German counter-attack over an open killing-ground. Despite their heavy losses, the Germans succeeded in seizing a part of the extensive Zenith trench system, but, counter-attacking in their turn, that evening, the Lincolns and the dour, tough, Yorkshiremen of the 7th Green Howards drove the Germans out again with bombs, bullets and bayonets. The battlefield was littered with their own casualties and the dead and wounded of their foes, but all this was just a microcosm of the overall action in the huge area of the battle. By that time, the Battle of the Somme was drawing to a close. The British had made little ground and had suffered appalling casualties. The Germans, exceptionally well dug-in, had taken *relatively* few casualties in return, until, that is, they set about desperately trying to wrest back the little ground they had actually lost.

Somehow, Jack had come through, to fight again. Before the War was done, 'John' would attain the rank of sergeant and he would reportedly gain a Mention in Despatches. He, too, would be becoming greatly changed by his experiences, some of which would have been harrowing in the extreme.

Hardly surprisingly, a manpower shortage would loom in the UK. [Later, when it seemed that the German High Seas Fleet was rather loath to come out and meet the British Grand Fleet in open combat, the Navy would be urged to provide fighting men to help out at the Front. The immortal and superb Naval Division would then be formed, and would play a full part in the land war. Alf, however, would not be directly involved in that aspect.]

Meantime, all three of Alf's sisters would have still been at home in Lincoln, helping their father to run his pub.[130] They would have been finding increasing difficulty in so doing, for serious shortages of food and other commodities were now prevalent, priority being given to sustaining the Armed Forces. It seems likely that Nellie had been strengthening her hand, fostering a bargain with her father (who was surely highly dependent on her) that she would stay on the scene until her two sisters were sufficiently grown up to take over. Nellie would then consider whether she wanted to branch out to lead a life of her own for the first time, having perforce been 'The Little Mother' since the age of nine or so. She felt that her father 'owed her a life' and probably told him, in her Capricorn way, that he should give her some sort of financial allowance now that the pub was making a reasonable return.

Tragically, both Alf and his father continued to be unbending and 'distant' in their relationship. The depth of the hurt in their joint self-pride must have been incredibly deep. For Alf to have been at sea, often with his life at the greatest risk, and for this sort of behaviour to be still ongoing between father and son seems quite amazing. Did the father simply not understand the dangers being run?

Had Jack perhaps 'queered the pitch' by debunking the role the Navy were playing, especially after all the 'negative rumours' which swept the Country following the Battle of Jutland? Had Jack's letters home claimed that it was the Army who were 'taking all the dirty end of the stick'? Seemingly, Nellie continued to act as a sort of 'Go-Between', probably still picking and choosing what she passed on, and how she expressed it, with her own 'hidden agenda' intruding now and again. Her way of proceeding may well have done more harm than good to the relationship of father and son, had they but known.

---

[130] There is a *possibility* that Alfred Wm had moved on with his family to some place as yet unknown, because, although the Kelly's Directory of 1913 shows him as still in residence at 'The Crown' P.H. at Brayford Head, it also shows a Wm SCOTT in residence at 'The Crown and Woolpack' in Brayford Street – which is surely the same address. (However, it seems more likely that Wm SCOTT was a long-term tenant at Alfred Wm's premises, perhaps running some sort of business from the same building.)

Perhaps Alf enjoyed the familiarity of being back in Lincoln, and helping out on the 'Domestic Front' for a while. However, as was the case with many servicemen who returned home on leave, he may have found the people far too jingoistic and uncomprehending of what the war was all about. This may have steadily gnawed away at him. However, the people were beginning to have the scales lifted from their eyes to an enormous degree as the lives of their husbands and sons, their brothers, their cousins and their neighbours' husbands and sons were squandered in their tens of thousands on the Western Front. This process may well have accelerated as Alf's stay at *Pembroke* continued. When in uniform he may have found himself being quizzed by strangers as to why he was not at sea fighting, and, if in mufti, being quizzed as to why he was not in the Forces. (There were often ladies around who were well-provided with 'white feathers' to dole out to men whom the ladies judged to be dodging the fighting and promptly condemned - merely 'on sight'.)

A 22 year-old acting-corporal named Walter Wilfred GREEN, a very fine young man, had been amongst the hundreds of thousands of men killed in the Battle of the Somme. He had lost his life whilst serving with the 9th Btn of 'The Green Howards' in the vicinity of Thiepval on 6th October. His unit was not in the front line that day and he had probably been killed by shellfire, for he was one of the many thousands who had no known grave. Alf would surely come to know of him later.

One wonders if any vague rumours had been sculling about the pubs in the City of Lincoln during Alf''s leave in May, concerning the development of 'hush-hush' caterpillar-tracked steel monsters at the works of William Foster & Co. (See following photos.) This new secret weapon of enormous potential, the so-called 'Tank', was unleashed, though only in 'penny packets' and under totally unsuitable conditions, on the 15th September 1916, at the peak of the horrendous Battle of the Somme. However, by that stage General HAIG was becoming desperate to see a positive outcome from the battle which was costing so dear in lives lost in fruitless frontal attacks against strongly-defended and deeply-entrenched positions. The French would surely have cursed him, for their idea had been to keep the new weapons a total secret, to build up an enormous force of their secret two-man light Renault tanks, and then to launch a colossal assault, synchronised with an attack by the (previously secret) British tanks, in a devastating surprise bid to break through the German lines and win the war in one fell swoop. General HAIG had ruined any such surprise, though one can appreciate the desperation from which his action had come about.

All things considered, it would seem likely that Alf would have been glad to get away from home and back to the ordered naval life amidst the rather dilapidated buildings at HMS *Pembroke*. Who can say? His next draft chit would come to hand as the Battle of the Somme was being wound down in early November 1916.

Footnote. Alf had brought home various souvenirs, including the aforementioned book of pressed flowers from the Garden of Gethsemane, which he gave to Rose. In much later years Rose would pass this handsome book to Dorothy (the wife of Rose's nephew Ray PENNEY), who had always admired it. In February 2006 Dorothy kindly showed the by then 90 year-old book to the author, thus adding another valuable fragment of data to this biography.

FIRST TANK tested at Lincoln, August, 1915.

FIRST TANKS in action 15th Sept., 1916.

THE "FOSTER" FIGHTING TANK.

With the Compliments of WILLIAM FOSTER & CO. LTD., ENGINEERS, LINCOLN.

'Mother', the first type of tank to see action. The particular model shown is a so-called 'male' version, having cannon mounted in her sponsons rather than the machine-guns of the 'female' version. This 'Mother' has broad so-called 'spud' track-plates at intervals along her tracks, and an 'undyitching beam' on the rear part of her roof (which can readily be attached to her tracks), all being designed to help her to claw her way out from broken or muddy ground. Winston CHURCHILL and his 'Landships' Committee had much to do with her successful inception.

DON'T YOU THINK

THAT

William Foster & Co., Ltd.,

ENGINEERS, LINCOLN,

the Originators and Designers of the famous Fighting Tank, are just THE People to assist you with your Machinery problems? If so, write, 'phone or wire them for advice.

Makers of

TRACTION ENGINES, ROAD LOCOS, STEAM TRACTORS, STEAM WAGONS, THRASHING MACHINERY, TRACTION WAGONS, TRAILERS, &c., &c.

Telegrams: "FOSTER, LINCOLN."　　　　'Phone: 18 LINCOLN.

The reverse of the trade card. At the peak period in the wartime production of tanks, the firm of William Foster, which had an excellent reputation, was employing about 2,000 of the local people.

CHAPTER SIX:

HMS *COURAGEOUS* (1916-19)

I t was on the 4th November 1916 that Alf joined this huge ship. This was the day that HMS *Courageous* was commissioned by Captain A BROMLEY RN, and had her colours hoisted for the very first time.

Photograph reproduced by courtesy of
The National Archives, ref. ADM 176/163.

HMS *Courageous* fitting out in Armstrong Whitworth's shipyard, and probably completed, for she has steam up and a white ensign flying at her gaff. Note the considerable flare-out of her bows. She is an elegant-looking warship, but many questions hang over her, not least the fact that she has only four main guns, two forrard and two aft. To save weight, by design, the thickness of her deck-plating and side-plating is reduced forward of 'A' gun-turret. This has had the effect of reducing her 'stiffness' for'r'rd , as compared with the great stiffness of her mid-section between 'A' and 'Y' turret.

Albeit now battle-hardened and much more sure of himself, Alf would have been just one small human 'cog' of the detachment of 789 officers and men who had filed aboard in time for the commissioning ceremony. Like his new shipmates, Alf would have anticipated staying aboard this ship for the next two and perhaps even three years, as the war at sea continued. The ground fighting on the 'Western Front' seemed to be locked in stalemate, with endless lists of casualties being published as one seemingly futile frontal attack followed another, be it German, French or English. In fact, the French seemed to be almost on their knees. It was hard to see how it would all end.

Doubtless, the men would have been wondering how *Courageous* would fare in whatever tasks would confront her in the war, and perhaps we, too, should start off this chapter by having a quick look at the details of this brand-new but slightly anachronistic vessel, which, in boxing parlance, '*Packed a mighty punch*' but was believed to be somewhat suspect for '*having a glass jaw*'.

HMS *Courageous* was the class leader of three huge cruisers which had been laid down in 1915 as a part of the War Emergency Programme. Although they mounted huge guns, the matter as to whether or not they really qualified as 'Battlecruisers' has been argued ever since.[131] Built by the Armstrong Whitworth Company in the Elswick shipyard, Newcastle-upon-Tyne, and launched on the 5th February 1916, *Courageous* was now officially all but complete, and *should* need only minor amendments now that she was being commissioned. However, in practice, it will be found that she needs significant follow-up modification to strengthen her hull before she is ready to go to war.

Photograph reproduced by courtesy of The National Archives, Ref. ADM 176/163.

HMS *Courageous* fitting out in the Armstrong Whitworth shipyard. (Note the cranes and girder-work of the slipways in the background.) This shot shows the massive 15-inch guns of her 'Y' Turret to advantage, but somehow emphasises the fact that there are only two of them facing directly aft. Her deck looks well-made, but much of her upper deck armour was only 1-inch thick, and she had only 1.5-inches on her lower deck aft, except over the area of the rudder, where it was a 'respectable' 3-inches thick.

In terms of ship-building of this class, HMS *Courageous* already had a 'sister-ship', HMS *Glorious*, which was being constructed by Harland and Wolf, at Belfast. HMS *Glorious* was virtually identical to *Courageous*, and both ships were nominally

---

[131] In his fine book 'The Navy and Defence', Admiral of the Fleet Lord CHATFIELD calls *Courageous* a '15,000 ton <u>Cruiser</u>', which became the '*Flagship of the Light Cruiser Force....of 1917*'. In another chapter he refers to the '*three freak cruisers built by Lord FISHER*'. On the other hand, in his very authoritative book 'Cruiser: A History of British Cruisers from 1889 to 1960', Mr S.L. POOLE gives no mention at all *of Courageous or Glorious,* and refers to *Furious* in one *throwaway phrase* only, calling her a '*hybrid curiosity*'. It would seem clear that *he* did not regard these three ships as cruisers but, by implication, as '<u>battlecruisers</u>' and therefore not within the scope of his book. A post-war note which the author has happened across, written between two anonymous cash-strapped naval brother-officers, calls *Courageous* and *Glorious* "The first light battlecruisers (Experimental)" – and says they are "in the Reserve Fleet now." (See later portrait of *Courageous* and its footnote.)

completed in the same month. It appears that they each cost approximately £2,000,000 to build, which compared well with the estimates which had been made beforehand.

A third 'sister-ship', HMS *Furious*, was following not far behind them. In fact, *Furious* was being built on a different slip of the same huge shipyard at Elswick where HMS *Courageous* was now being commissioned. (Presumably, she is hidden somewhere in the forest of cranes and girders in the background of the above photograph.)

Furious would be launched about six months after the hull of *Courageous* had first taken to the water. *Furious* would be of slightly greater displacement than her two slightly older sisters and would vary in detail, particularly in her armament. Her construction would take advantage of important lessons gained from building and operating her two sisters and she would not be completed before mid-1917.

As we shall see, *Courageous* and *Furious* would be in action side by side against German warships in mid-November 1917, and all three sister-ships would be operating together, at times, in 1918.   In doing so they would have become part of the 'Light Cruiser Force' under the command of Vice-Admiral NAPIER, who would fly his Flag in *Courageous*.

The lowest lines in the following tables show the basic details of *Courageous* as compared with Alf's earlier ships. The **bold** entries show the maxima for each of the 'characteristics', column by column, starting with 'Displacement'.

Name of Ship	Type Of Ship	Displace-ment (tons)	Year Completed	1st Year Alf srv'd (diff.)	Comple-ment	Max. Length (feet)	Max. Beam (feet)	Draught (feet)	Shaft Horse-Power	Max. Speed (knots)
Vanguard	Dreadnought	**19,250**	1910	1912 (2)	823	536	**84**	**31.75**	24,500	22
Russell	Pre-Dreadnought	14,000	1903	1912 (9)	718	418	75.5	28	18,220	19
Weymouth	Armour'd Cruiser	5,250	1911	1913 (2)	392	453	48.5	18	22,000	25.5
Courageous	Battle Cruiser	18,600	**1916**	1916 **(0)**	**829**	**786.5**	81	26	**90,000**	**35**

Name of Ship	Guns					Torpedo-Tubes		Armour			
	Main		Secondary		A.A			Deck	Side	Turr't	D.C.T
	Calibre	Number	Calibre	Number	Capability	Calibre	Number	(ins)	(ins)	(ins)	(ins)
Vanguard	12"	**Ten**	4"	Twelve	**2x3"**	18"	Three	1.5 - 3	**10**	**11**	8 – 11
Russell	12"	Four	6"	Twelve	-	18"	Four	2.5	3-4	6	12
Weymouth	6"	Eight	3"	One	1x3"	21"	Two	1-2	Nil	1	2
Courageous	**15"**	Four	4"	**Eighteen**	2x3"	21"	**Fourteen**	1-3	3	7-9	10

As can be seen from the **bold** entries along the lower line of the upper table, *Courageous* was not only the most modern, but also by far the longest ship in which Alf had ever served. She also had *by far* the greatest Shaft Horse Power, and could attain the highest speed. (She could certainly attain her designed speed of 35 knots – and (as we shall see) she *may* have even attained over 40 knots at certain times!).   Moreover, although she was only a Battlecruiser (and arguably not even that) her displacement was almost the equivalent of that of the Dreadnought HMS *Vanguard*. And the number of her ship's company marginally *exceeded* that of *Vanguard*.

As can be seen from the bolding in the second part of the Table, *Courageous* carried very heavy guns indeed. Their 15-inch calibre was easily the largest of any ship in which Alf had served. HOWEVER, there were only four of these guns when firing broadsides, and *only two* for direct ahead or astern fire. [The so-called 'A-arc' for maximising the fire of *Courageous* in a basically forward direction, was also limited to four guns, and the arc had to be a very broad one indeed!] We shall explore these serious potential deficiencies later.[132] To compensate for this 'numerical shortfall' in her main armament, *Courageous*, mounted a huge array of 4-inch guns as her secondary armament against the risk of TBDs getting through her heavy-calibre but rather sparse long-range main-gun fire. Some said that she carried *too many* 4-inch guns, because there was insufficient space for the gunners to work without each gun-crew seriously jostling the neighbouring teams, and itself being jostled by its neighbours.

This large outfit of secondary armament was probably also an acknowledgement that, as the war had developed, German TBDs had well-demonstrated their speed and agility, and the bravery, determination and practised dexterity of their ships' companies in penetrating the defensive fire of the main armaments of our heavy warships. In doing so they courted the risk of near-instant annihilation from a single massive shell-hit, but that was a risk that they always seemed willing to run. Indeed, naval thought was beginning to favour 6-inch guns rather than 4-inch against this threat, meaning that the calibre of the secondary armament of *Courageous* might soon be regarded as inadequate.

Courageous also carried a very heavy outfit in regard to torpedo-tubes. These could provide good back-up should she become too closely involved in actions against the Dreadnought-type battleships of that era. In any such engagements, *Courageous* would hope to use her superior speed to keep the range well open, so that the enemy could be maintained near the extreme range of the 15-inch guns of *Courageous*, with the enemy not being able to reply effectively with their slightly shorter-range, 11-inch or 12-inch calibre guns. Then, should the enemy somehow manage to close the range, *Courageous* (in accord with standard 'cruiser' tactics) would hope to loose off torpedoes at the opposing ships, and then to 'cut and run' (perhaps with the aid of a smoke-screen) as the enemy battlefleet turned 'end-on' to 'comb' the torpedo tracks heading for them, thus temporarily losing the ability to fire broadsides.

The thickness of the armour of the deck, turret and DCT of *Courageous* was a compromise (note lack of bolding in the above table, except for a part of her deck), and meant that she was not well-equipped to 'slog it out' with a heavily armoured Dreadnought. Hence the analogy of her being like a Boxer with something of a 'glass jaw'. She certainly ran a serious risk of being 'knocked out' if she tried to stand around and fight a heavy opponent - and she would always be vulnerable to disablement (or even annihilation) from a single lucky but telling shell-hit. Low-trajectory, close range heavy shell fire, hitting her on or below the water-line could also be a serious matter, for she had extremely limited thickness of side-armour. For the same reason, she was vulnerable to torpedo attack or sea-mines.

---

[132] In his remarkably erudite little book "The Navy Shown to the Children", Percival HISLAM wrote, regarding the battlecruiser, *"It can fight an enemy or avoid it as it pleases...engines of much greater power are a pre-requisite.....larger space has to be occupied by boilers... a great number of men needed to keep the furnaces going... but in a stand-up fight it must be inferior to the battleship because of the sacrifices in guns and armour which have to be made to reach its high speed."* Tellingly, he also added, *"needs to be able to fire four heavy guns straight ahead when in chase of an enemy."*

From his immediate impressions, Alf would have been finding that *Courageous*, was easily the largest vessel in which he had served. It's time we had a look at a side-view illustration of this huge vessel. The illustration comes from a 'used' postcard with a message on the back evidently written from one naval officer to another – who may well have been his brother - in a different ship or establishment, and presumably sent under an outer cover (now lost) which would have borne the postage stamp.[133]

Author's collection. A postcard by Abrahams of Devonport, No. 969, c.1919. Image reproduced by kind permission of the World Ship Society.

HMS *Courageous*. There is a message on the back of the postcard in the author's possession, evidently written by a naval officer, which confirms this ship as having four 15-inch guns, but quotes only seventeen 4-inch guns, as against the 'official' eighteen. This may have relevance, for some sources claim that her eighteen 4-inch guns were placed too closely together for satisfactory operation. Most interestingly, the message also quotes *Courageous* as having speed ranging from 35 knots to no less than 42 knots!

Her standard displacement of 18,600 tons increased to about 23,000 tons at full load.[134] The four massive 15-inch guns which formed her main armament were paired in turrets, one turret being placed forward and one aft. Her complement would be gradually built up until it approached 1,000 men. It could be argued that she was the epitome of Admiral FISHER's dictum of being 'hard-hitting, fast and highly manoeuvrable'. *['Hit*

---

[133] The message is rather endearing. After giving the technical details as quoted under the above 'ship-portrait', the writer continues, *"Hope you have a topping leave old Scrap. May see you. Broke, to put it mildly. Have had millions of letters for Xmas. Presents; a box of Guava Jelly from Miss Lea (to whom I sent nothing); a box of Bath Salts from Rhona (to whom I sent nothing); a box of Sweets from K.B.M (Don't know who the hell that is!), a pair of socks from Scraps; £1 from Pater; a large photo from Joan, and a wee calendar from Judy. Heard from Hecky today. He sends you his love and wants you to write. Also sends his regards to Pater & Mater. Have had a hell of a lot of work to do these last few days. Was ill for a few days a little while ago. Rest cure. Heard a horrible rumour that I am to be sent to hospital some time. Love, yours, Erb."* (One key point to note is the relative impoverishment of this young officer. As we shall see, under pressure from the government for post-war financial cuts, the Admiralty would soon make matters worse for Naval Officers' pay – and even worse still for the pay of their men! Herein would lay the seeds for a post-war mutiny!)

[134] Her 'legend displacement' was 19,171 tons.

first! Hit hard! Keep on hitting!'] However, as already indicated, there were some important 'qualifiers' to add to this - especially in regard to the very limited number of heavy guns she mounted.

The nearest ship in Alf's past experience, against which he could have compared *Courageous*, would have been HMS *Vanguard*. However, in a way, this was to compare 'chalk with cheese'. For one thing, *Vanguard* had been laid down seven years earlier, at a time when a huge re-think had just occurred, and a vast programme of building of large 'Dreadnought-style' warships was under way. Rapid technological developments were taking place from one class to the next, and these developments had become yet faster-accelerated by the coming of war and practical experience in battle. Progress in many fields had been swift, and, for example, the Parsons turbines which would now drive *Courageous* developed 90,000 shaft horsepower, as compared with the 'mere' 24,500 horsepower of the turbines which drove *Vanguard* - albeit that, in part, the huge increase reflected the need for *Courageous* to develop very high speed if she were to enjoy any sort of safety in battle.

Moreover, *Courageous*, was a battle*cruiser* (more correctly, one might say a 'heavily armed armoured cruiser') which certainly packed a heavy punch in terms of its armament, but was a ship in which armoured protection had been sacrificed, to a very considerable degree, to gain in speed and manoeuvrability. It should, however, be noted that she carried reasonable deck-armour over her vitals, to guard against *long-range* gunfire of which, due to their trajectory, the shells would strike at angles approaching the vertical. Her Control-Tower was also well-armoured, because a failure of her long-range gunnery control in an action would be devastating to her tactics. Clearly, thought had gone into her armour-reduction.[135]

In contrast to these 'battlecruiser' ideas, *Vanguard* was almost the antithesis of this 'hit hard *but stand off*' concept, for she was a battle*ship*, designed not just to dish out heavy punishment, but to a considerable extent, *to be able to take it, too, in a slogging match*, especially at quite close range. Hence, although *outwardly* rather similar, *Vanguard* was much more heavily armoured, which (even had her turbines been of such high power as those of *Courageous*,) inevitably meant that her greater weight would have reduced her speed and manoeuvrability in comparative terms. [It should also be noted that *Vanguard* carried yet further weight due to having a larger number of heavy guns than the more 'economically-armed' *Courageous* mounted, albeit that those of *Vanguard* were individually of smaller calibre, being 12" as opposed to the 15" guns of *Courageous*.]

In the event, *Courageous*, at 81 feet, was very nearly as broad in the beam as *Vanguard*, but, significantly, she was *250 feet greater in length*.[136] Compared with the

---

[135] It could be argued that she was little more than an armoured cruiser - albeit a very large one, with remarkably large-calibre guns. Perhaps 'an armoured cruiser *destroyer*' might have been a better term, though she had limitations for that role due to the small number of forward-firing main guns she could bring to bear in a chase against a rapidly-retiring and 'nimble' opponent. Mr POOLE's term '*Hybrid curiosity*' does seem remarkably apt.

[136] The size limitations of the docks around the British Isles meant that the beam of British capital warships had to be constrained to a maximum of about 90 feet. In his visionary way, Admiral FISHER had proposed widening the principal docks, so that our ships could be made beamier. (He had also proposed greatly widening the Caledonian Canal which traversed Scotland on an east-west axis. Had this been done, it would have permitted quick passage of heavy warships between the Irish Sea and the North Sea.)

way that *Vanguard*, with her 25 foot draught and displacement of 19,250 tons, would have seemed to 'plough through the waves', *Courageous*, at 23¼ foot draught and 18,600 tons would have seemed to make at least *some* positive response to them.[137] And her top speed was designed to be *at least* 32 knots as compared to only 21 knots for *Vanguard*. Alf would certainly have felt these differences when she was at sea, and it would have been a thrilling experience to be out on deck during operations involving *Courageous*, when it was found that she was quite nimble and could easily attain her 35 knots! On the face of things, she was an incredibly 'symmetrical' and beautiful ship.

In terms of the actual thickness of their armour plate, *Vanguard* had a belt of 7" to 10" and bulkheads of 4" to 8", whereas *Courageous*, had a belt of only 2" to 3" and bulkheads of only 2" to 3". Similar 'economies' applied to the armour plate of the turrets, and other 'vitals'. These were very real differences, but their significance would only really have become apparent under combat conditions and then only if *Courageous*, were to have had the misfortune to suffer 'direct hits' from armour-piercing shells, or to suffer strikes by torpedoes or mines.

Yet, there were shrewd and analytical minds on the lower deck as well as in the wardroom, and the men of the fleet thought about the potential inadequacy of the thin armour plate in terms of incoming enemy shellfire, particularly at close ranges. Rumours about the high vulnerability of all our battle-cruisers to German shells were already on many lips. The gunners also thought about the very limited number of heavy guns (making only two or at best four rounds per salvo) with which to 'straddle' an enemy ship - so that fast and accurate range-finding was going to be difficult. [There were 'reasons why', but it would be worse in the case of *Furious*, for she would end up with only one, huge, 18" gun in her 'Y' turret, with a very slow rate of fire, and *nothing* forward. It was not long before *Furious, Glorious* and *Courageous* were nicknamed 'Curious', 'Spurious' and 'Outrageous' by their critics - though the ratings serving in those ships would probably still have 'blacked the eye' of any ratings from other warships who might have had the temerity to thus 'poke fun' at their ships, to their faces!]

The frightening lessons of the Battle of Jutland were still being absorbed as *Courageous* and her sisters were being completed. It was already clear, however, that better means of 'insulating' the magazine from the lightning-quick spread of a cordite fire [as might arise should a turret or its barbette (i.e. supporting armoured trunking) be penetrated by an incoming enemy shell], was an absolute and over-riding necessity. At the same time, the functional ability to keep passing the ship's own shells and charges from magazine and shell-room to the turret via that same trunking was a vital requirement. Many brains were working on this 'insulation' problem, and this quickly led to the development of a complex system of interlocking screens and shutters. One assumes that the lighter armour employed in battlecruisers *vis-à-vis* battleships, would have made this whole matter of very great significance in the building of *Courageous* and her sisters, and that Alf, whom one suspects was beginning by now to take the keenest

---

However, these expensive ideas had been turned down, despite his forceful urging. This was quite different to the attitude in Germany, where the Kiel Canal and the main docks had been reconstructed to accommodate warships of up to *97 feet* in the beam. Making the German warships so much beamier allowed greater side-protection and considerably improved the basic stability of each such ship. This was invaluable should she suffer flooding of her side-compartments from battle-damage, collision or grounding. The risk of the ship capsizing was greatly reduced.

[137] Though more on this aspect shortly.

interest in Gunnery, would probably have been very aware of certain aspects of this overall situation.[138] It was well-known that the thickness of certain parts of the armour of *Courageous* and her sisters was added-to beyond the original specification, more or less 'on the fly', during their construction.

Alf was probably also well aware of the associated debate concerning the effectiveness and reliability of the armour-piercing shells then in use by the Navy *vis-à-vis* their German equivalents. The latter had far out-performed the British shells at Jutland, showing high powers of penetration and carefully-timed delays in their fuse-settings, so that they exploded immediately *after* penetration rather than at *the moment* of impact. In the event, these matters would be quite quickly resolved in the Royal Navy, and appropriate modifications made.[139] However, 1917 would be a critical year, when the fleets would have to subsist on inferior-quality shells pending their gradual exchange by improved types. All these matters were kept secret from all but the highest-ranking officers.

How much Alf would have been aware of another controversy is unknown, though memory suggests that he was certainly aware of the fact that the Germans tended to gain a strike with their opening salvo in an exchange of fire, whereas the British tended to expect little better than 'coming near' with their opening salvo, and (if by then not knocked out or sunk) would seek to 'home in' from there in successive salvoes. Indeed they often used a so-called 'ladder' method of 'walking up' to the target until they began to get 'straddles'. Clearly, this did not fit in with Lord FISHER's maxim of 'Strike First!' - nor did it accord well with sheer common sense when, from his side, the enemy aimed to hit hard and accurately with his opening shots! Hence it was far from satisfactory.

In this general context, Alf also seems to have been well aware that the optical quality of the German rangefinders was significantly better than that of the Barr & Stroud equipment in general use in the Royal Navy.[140] A general controversy surrounded the 'fire-control system' which had been invented by a civilian-inventor, Arthur POLLEN, in an effort to overcome the age-old nautical problem of one highly mobile gun-battery (a warship) trying to hit another mobile warship, in an exchange of fire, where the sort of

---

[138] The author (then aged about eight) has a clear memory of his father holding forth to family adults in 1938 about the battlecruisers which blew up at the Battle of Jutland (the *Queen Mary*, *Invincible* and *Indefatigable*), each with the immediate loss of 1,000 or so men - and the near-detonation of BEATTY's ship, the *Lion*, immediately after her Q turret was penetrated with the immediate 'localised effect' of the loss of eighty men. It may well be that his father was speaking from the heart, for he would have known only too well how vulnerable *Courageous* would have been to 'incoming' armour-piercing shell or bomb, or to torpedo or sea-mine. The lives of the men on board would often have been 'hanging by a thread' throughout 1917/18, as we shall see.

[139] As spelt out in Admiral CHATFIELD's book and reinforced by files ADM 137/3834-39 at TNA, and other sources, it took considerable persistence by high-ranking 'front line' officers such as himself, backed up by Admiral BEATTY, to convince the Admiralty that there was anything at all wrong with the British shells. The Admiralty had become complacent because their proving tests had been 'satisfactory'. They had failed to recognise that their standard tests *had become obsolete* because they were made at ranges which were too short and had thus failed to reproduce the 'near-vertical angles of attack' and reduced velocities of shells nearing the end of their extreme range. [The latter factor aggravated the problem that the British shells exploded on impact, before penetrating the armour, making impressive flashes and smoke bursts, but actually causing relatively little damage. It seems that the shape and structure of the metal casing, the quality of the explosive and the fusing arrangements all needed significant change.]

[140] This is based on the author's memory of his father's discourses with other adults in the 1930s.

'stationary reference points' normally involved on land are non-existent and when both ships are doing their best to 'dodge and weave' to avoid being hit. This fundamental problem had become far greater with the introduction of the long-range naval gun.

Arthur POLLEN's system appears to have used as its basis the actual plots of the tracks of both vessels engaged, whereas the system which came to be used by the Admiralty apparently worked off two graphs, the one showing the sequence of observed ranges and the other the related bearings of the target. The former method was called the 'True Plot' and the latter 'Rate-Plotting'. In effect, POLLEN's system came to use a form of mechanical computer (The 'Argo Clock', sometimes known as the Argo Training Gear) to cope with the large number of variables which had to be fed into the system.

It was claimed by POLLEN's supporters that the 'True Plot' system could maintain the ship's guns on target when the ship was 'under heavy helm', whereas the 'Rate-Plotting' system could not. Since ships in combat usually zig-zagged irregularly and near-constantly to (hopefully) dodge each next incoming salvo of hostile fire, such an advantage would have been very significant indeed.[141] The author does not aspire to understand all the technical aspects involved, nor to know the rights and wrongs of the controversy. Further, this is not the place to go into all the details concerning the introduction of gyros to stabilise the rangefinders in use, nor the optical quality of the rangefinders proposed by Arthur POLLEN, which he claimed to be much superior to the rangefinders in use by the Admiralty, and also to have a form of image-intensification to give them improved performance in low light-levels.[142]

It seems clear that some of Arthur POLLEN's ideas and equipment did come into use in the Royal Navy in one guise or another, though, apparently, with only limited acknowledgement to him and evidently not to the full magnitude of which POLLEN's methods appear to have been capable. It would be interesting to know whether the Gunnery Branch in general, and Alf in particular, were aware of this general situation. Also to know whether Alf ultimately became more of the school who strove to make the Dreyer Table and the other 'spotting and plotting' equipment work to its full extent - or whether his disposition as he rose in rank was more to revert to 'first basic principles', to

---

[141] It seems strange to read in Admiral Lord CHATFIELD's book that, in his strong-minded way, he kept his battle-cruiser HMS *Lion* 'steady on her course' at the Battle of the Dogger Bank, to *'make it easier for the gunlayers'*. He meant the British GLs, but maybe in so doing he made it easier for the opposing *German* GLs, too, for *Lion* received nine heavy-calibre hits, to say nothing of several smaller-calibre hits. One of the heavy calibre shells penetrated the hoist to the 13.5 inch magazine, and it was only by the greatest good fortune that the shell failed to explode! As it was, by the end of the battle 3,000 tons of seawater had entered the ship due to very heavy hits *on her armoured belt* which had led to the partial-collapse of the hull behind it. [This, of itself, would indicate that the British battlecruisers were fighting at too short a range, being forced to do so because the visibility was poor and their own shooting too inaccurate.] The artist W E WYLIE, R A, produced a superbly evocative picture of the *Lion* under tow and approaching the Forth Bridge after the battle. If this work was accurate, she had a list to port of some 25°!

[142] Albeit, one feels, putting only one side of an argument strongly and thus perhaps inevitably with a measure of bias, the book 'The Great Gunnery Scandal: The Mystery of Jutland' by Anthony POLLEN, gives a great deal of chapter and verse on this whole technical topic. (Miss A POLLEN, daughter of Anthony POLLEN, is the copyright holder and has kindly permitted the author to use the above information from the book.) One wonders if the inventor Arthur POLLEN (Anthony's father) might have been better-advised to have been less trusting of others and to have followed the more hard-headed and commercial route used by Robert WHITEHEAD, the inventor of the modern torpedo - though Robert WHITEHEAD did have some 'lucky breaks' which set him on his successful road. (See the book 'The Devil's Device' by Edwyn GRAY.)

switch off the 'sophisticated electrics', and, as a natural marksman, to use the simple co-ordination of hand and eye in the hectic moments of combat.[143]

Be that as it all may, in day-to-day operation of the ship, the most outstanding difference that Alf would have detected was that, unlike any ship in which he had so far served, *Courageous* was *oil-fired*. No longer was the filthy and heavy work of coaling ship awaiting the company, as virtually their first task when they came into port at the end of each voyage. No longer would cleaning ship, and then themselves, have awaited the by then often almost exhausted company. This must have been a colossal relief, for a coal-fired ship of the magnitude of *Courageous* would have taken on board anything up to 3,000 tons of coal at a time, requiring up to twelve hours of hard physical labour by every man-Jack aboard, bar the bare minimum who were covering the essential needs of the ship - often with ship working in contest against other ships in the fleet at the admiral's behest - with the laudable view that quick turnaround might be vital should battle need to quickly recommence! Cleaning-down the ship afterwards (and oneself, and one's clothes!) was a major task after coaling a ship. In complete contrast, refuelling from an oiler was a quick process, the need for subsequent cleaning-down was minimal, and an oil-fired ship was very soon ready for operational use again. This was luxury indeed. One reflects that the companies of the coal-fired *Vanguard* and her like must have been very pleased when, starting in 1916, their ships were being converted, one by one, from coal to oil-fuel![144]

---

[143] There is an interesting document in TNA under ADM 1/8391/286, which is a report from Captain (later Admiral) CHATFIELD of the battlecruiser HMS *Lion* on his experiences in the Battle of the Heligoland Bight on 28th August 1915. He said: *"The Guns and 'Argos' were kept trained on the enemy by bearing, but it was impossible to take ranges due to poor visibility. (The gunnery officer in the DCT simply opened fire on the rapidly closing enemy without that data...")* Author's Note: Presumably increasing the range of successive salvoes of 'shorts' until he began to get 'overs' and then concentrating on getting 'straddles'. Captain CHATFIELD continued: *"Even greater difficulty was experienced by the men in the turrets when local firing was resorted-to, due to the periscopes getting damp with humidity, which problem became aggravated by sea spray contamination,....,"* (Author's Note: Doubtless aggravated by the 'splashes' of near-misses) *". .. and the smoke of their own guns. After firing a round it was difficult to find the target again. The Argo training gear having broken down with the first salvo, its 'Evershed' could not be used to direct the guns, 'otherwise it would have been invaluable'. The Evershed bearing receivers were of little or no use to the turret trainers. Smoke from enemy and our own shell bursts soon made it difficult to aim at anything but the enemy gunflashes"*. He recommended that *"...turret officers should have some form of open sight to get their gunlayers on to the enemy quickly. (Author's Note: This seems rather retrograde in concept, but was taken up by the Admiralty.)* Captain CHATFIELD went on to say that *"Bearing Plates in the Conning Tower are also essential even when Eversheds are fitted, as the latter are disappointing in thick weather."* [He added a rider that *'German shells always burst on hitting the water'*, evidently to indicate the great sensitivity of their contact fuses.]. (Author's Note: The overall thrust of Captain CHATFIELD's document would indicate that the centralised Gunnery Control System was virtually useless at that stage of its development. It also begs the question as to why such deficiencies had not become apparent in practice and manoeuvres. Could it be that the Navy had never practised gunnery 'under stress', in conditions of inferior visibility, and with ships making rapid alterations of course headlong against each other? [Reading the *book* which was written by Captain CHATFIELD in the 1940s (he was by then Admiral of the Fleet), this surmise would seem to be correct.] The author has formed the impression that the Germans had made much more 'realistic' and demanding pre-war exercises.

[144] *Courageous* was not entirely 'coal-free'. Thus, she took in 58 tons of coal on 21st December. However, this was 'chicken feed' in comparison with a fully coal-fired ship, and intended for what one might call 'domestic purposes' aboard, in wardroom and galley, and for fuelling her steam-pinnace, etc.

Still, let's revert to the day that Alf joined *Courageous*. Following the Commissioning Ceremony, her hands were soon employed in drawing stores as requisite, and taking onboard no less than 1,537 lb. of meat, 8,000 lb. of vegetables and 2,500 lb. of bread. The company went to evening quarters at 1630 and 'B and C doors were closed at 2015'. This great ship was quickly coming to life as a naval vessel and her first-ever company were swiftly 'taking up residence'.

During the next few days, she took in ammunition for her huge 15"guns (which would have been heavy work, requiring various mechanical aids to handle each 1,925 lb. projectile – see illustration below). She also took in shells for her secondary 4" armament, weighing only 25 lb. apiece, but presumably cased in multiple lots. Her guns crews were put to drill - as were her sight setters, her magazine and shell room parties, and the various control groups. Her hands were exercised at General Quarters and at Night Defence stations. As a relief from such activities, short periods of shore leave were given to the various watches, Blue one day, White the next, Red the next.

Author's collection. A postcard by the Pictorial Newspaper Co. (1910) Ltd. Issued c. 1915. Reproduced by courtesy of the British Library.

This photograph shows 13.5-inch shells being taken aboard the battlecruiser HMS *Lion*. The scene would have been very similar aboard HMS *Courageous*, with long-handled lifting dollies and wire 'slings' being employed (as here) to 'encourage' the very heavy shells on to the very strongly built flat wooden trolleys which are being used to carry the shells to the hoists which will convey them down to the magazines deep within the ship. Note the copper 'driving bands' on the shells. Once the shells are embarked the ammunition lighters will come alongside to off-load their heavy cardboard cases of cordite. Despite the apparent confusion, organisation and discipline are being carefully exercised to avoid the least possibility of a mix-up or handling 'accident'.

Courageous was not yet fully out of dockyard hands - indeed a dockyard worker was accidentally injured in her 'Engine Room' lift during this time and had to be evacuated off the ship under medical attention - but she was now well on her way to becoming 'home' to her company, who were anxious to take her over for their exclusive use, just as soon as possible.

One imagines that Alf learned a lot about the intrinsic construction of this great ship in those early days. There would undoubtedly have been sundry teething problems to overcome, and some totally new ones evidently began to manifest themselves on 14th November. On that day, by the hour of 1000, all those officers and men who had been on leave had come back on board, some of the more senior and experienced 'contractor's officials and men' had joined the ship as observers, her boilers had been lit and she had cast off at 1610 for her acceptance trials. She was taken in charge by tugs as she proceeded slowly to the harbour entrance in what her log called 'calm seas and light airs'. At 1750 she passed the breakwater and, having cast off her tugs, headed north up the East Coast. She was accompanied by four destroyers which formed an anti-submarine screen ahead. Soon she began to work up for her speed trials, and by 1800 she had increased to 22½ knots.

At 2000, 'Courageous' began gun trials of all her guns, but her log indicates that she did not at any time increase her speed and work up to the 32 knots for which she had been designed. This suggests that something had gone wrong, though no details of the problem are revealed in her Log. She passed under the great railway bridge over the Firth of Forth at 2350, stopped engines, came to with both bower anchors, and carried out capstan trials. But, clearly, all was not exactly well.

Author's collection. A postcard by Valentines, c.1912. Postally used on 4th September 1933. Image reproduced by courtesy of St Andrews University Library.

The massive steel railway bridge over the Firth of Forth, with its highest part towering 360 feet above sea level, and its two widest spans being of 1,710 feet. The single-funelled coasting vessel at extreme left gives a visual scale of the sheer size of the bridge. Opened in March 1890, the bridge would remain virtually unchanged right through into the 21st Century – apart from being given countless coats of paint! Alf first laid eyes on this 51,000-ton monster on 14th November 1916, when *Courageous* passed under it on her way to Rosyth naval base. Alf would see plenty more of the bridge during the next two years – and, as we shall later see, his 9th ship was fated to experience highly accurate aerial bombing in its shadow in 1939.

Next day *Courageous* entered No.3 dry dock at Rosyth. Presumably the prompt detection of some problem or other, by the various experts being carried aboard, was the reason why her speed trials had not been 'stretched' to her designed speed of about 32 knots. One wonders if the problem was related in some way to the firing of salvoes from her massive 15" guns. [Had the concussive effects perhaps led to rather more than the customary flaking-off of paint in compartments surrounding the barbettes? Had some minor opening-up of joints appeared? Did this perhaps lead Alf to reflect about the hull-straining said to have been experienced by the two monitors *Severn* and *Mersey* following their heavy firing during the Rufuji River action of 1915?][145]

Discussion on whatever problems had arisen may have been the reason for a visit paid to the ship by Vice-Admiral PAKENHAM, commanding the Battle Cruiser Force (accompanied by Rear-Admiral NAPIER), on 16th November. *Courageous* was already in dry-dock, and it seems that the required emergency work was speedily carried out. Meantime, the training of her gun crews, sight setters, Spotting Top and Transmitting Station crews continued 'as normal'. As she emerged from dry dock on the 20th, her hands warped the ship to the west wall, and active training continued aboard. Meantime she had taken in 2,467 tons of oil fuel, and, on the 22nd, she (rather belatedly) discharged the empty ammunition cases accrued from her firing trials of the 14th November.

Author's collection. A Kingsway Real Photo Card, Serial No. S 13141, printed by W H Smith & Co. c. 1913. Image reproduced by courtesy of W.H. Smith Archive.

Telescope under arm, Admiral Sir John R. JELLICOE, KCB, KCVO, when in Supreme Command of the Grand Fleet.

This officer had been told that he could 'lose the war in a day'. Perhaps he *should* have been told that he could TURN the war in a day, but *he would have to take calculated risks*. As it was, caution was his watchword at the Battle of Jutland. Hence, he turned his battleships *away from* (rather than *towards*) a torpedo-attack by German destroyers, and he did not to continue the fleet combat by night (only to find that the enemy had slipped away from his clutches by daybreak.) There also seems to have been a lack in overall preparation of his fleet, so that (i) his cruiser captains did not communicate enough to him *re* enemy movements (ii) the gunnery control teams could not cope with poor visibility aggravated by gun-smoke and funnel-smoke, and (iii) the searchlights and their control systems were of poor quality. One feels that all these matters should have been brought under control long before, by *realistic* exercises and further technological development.

---

[145] It must be said that this '*hull straining due to the concussive effects of firing the main guns*' is pure speculation on the part of the author. He has found no documentary evidence to confirm his suspicions. But please read on.

On the 27th November Admiral Sir John JELLICOE had visited the ship. Admiral JELLICOE was undoubtedly a great but somewhat reserved and withdrawn man, who was known to sometimes talk, quite spontaneously and naturally, with men of even the humblest rank. Generally, he seems to have commanded both love and respect in the Navy. He made a great many perfectly sound decisions in his career, but being human, he also made a few quite poor judgements. Some say that his greatness lay in the fact that (unlike far too many men and despite his high rank), he was not totally averse to changing his mind if he became convinced of the justification for such amendment.

Unfortunately, (as mentioned earlier) Admiral JELLICOE had become a rather controversial figure immediately after the Battle of Jutland, and, in retirement, he would be driven to defend and justify his actions publicly. In doing so, it could be argued that he breached what might have been regarded as the 'Official Secrets Act', but had just about enough 'pull' to get away with so doing.[146]

As a child, the author can remember Alf talking to other adults about the respective merits of the dignified and quietly determined Admiral JELLICOE and the ebullient and extrovert Admiral BEATTY, but the author's memory is not sufficiently good to remember which leader (if either) Alf preferred.

Author's collection. A postcard by J Beagles & Co, London, ref 430S. Photo by Speaight Ltd., dated c.1919.

Admiral Sir David BEATTY, photographed just post-war, with his cap still worn at its customarily 'jaunty' angle. Evidently a very extrovert and forthright man and a taker of calculated risks. He had handled the 'surrender' of the German High Seas Fleet extremely well. Not an intellectual man, by all accounts, and not a man to give out warmth to the men he commanded. He was after their instant obedience and respect rather that their love. Yet, those eyes have a slightly haunted look. Was that totally due to the long and fretful illness of his deeply beloved but very demanding wife – or did he sometimes reflect inwardly about the three British battlecruisers under his direct command and the 3,300 of their men (and 80 from his own ship) who had been blasted into eternity at the Battle of Jutland, causing him to growl, *"There's something wrong with our bloody ships today!"*

---

[146] See earlier notes concerning Admiral MILNE and the abortive hunt for the *Breslau* and the *Goeben* in 1914. In his pleas to the Admiralty for further employment, Admiral MILNE stated that he had deliberately refrained from following Admiral JELLICOE's lead in using and publishing Admiralty and other confidential signals in his own defence.

Perhaps there were 'pros and cons' from Alf's point of view regarding the merits of the two admirals. One suspects that Alf would have liked the 'obey orders', 'stick fast to Admiralty Regulations' and 'law and order' attitude of JELLICOE, but that Alf would also have veered towards Admiral BEATTY as being less cautious and more the taker of 'calculated risks', even though BEATTY might thus be gambling with a great many human lives. As we have already seen, the Admiralty generally seemed to favour the Nelsonian tradition that *"No Captain can go far wrong who lays his ship alongside that of an enemy"*, but a 'dashing action' resulting in (say) the loss of one's ship, would almost certainly bring 'coals of retributive fire' around the would-be hero's head from that same Admiralty!

As he grew in confidence and experience, Alf was becoming something of a 'dashing man' himself, as suited his mercurial temperament – even though, as a strict disciplinarian, he was also probably beginning to nurse the rather conflicting idea of eventually becoming something of a 'brassbound GI'. Certainly, in terms of his personal development, Alf, who had been a Leading Seaman for seven months when he joined *Courageous*, must have been hoping that Petty Officer rank was now in his sights, especially under the wartime conditions then prevailing. As we shall see, his wish would be granted during this commission.

The author has a childhood memory of his father talking of his time in *Courageous* with pride and affection. One imagines that she was a happy ship, and there may be a pointer to this in terms of a programme which survives of on-ship entertainment just post-war, of which more later.

On 6th December 1916, the Dreadnought HMS *Vanguard* arrived at Rosyth, and went into dock. One wonders if Alf felt any stirring of nostalgic affection for this, his first ship, or whether he had mentally 'moved on'. Certainly, in *Courageous*, the training of the crews of 'A' and 'Y' turrets, and the 4" secondary armament was continuing actively and, though we do not know Alf's exact station, some part of this was surely keeping him busy. It is worth reminding ourselves that each main gun-turret required at least 80 Seamen and artisans, under one or more officers, with further parties of men in the Spotting Tops, in the Transmitting Station and at the Plotting Tables. The training of these men was not just in terms of the basic operation of their equipment, but also in coping with various aspects of potential battle-damage, and finding ways of somehow keeping the guns in action. For example, by putting 'A' turret into 'local control', as if the Spotting Top or TS had been destroyed, and, for example, by putting each of the 4" guns into individual control, as if both their forward and aft Director Control Towers had been wrecked.[147]

On 5th January 1917, having taken on board some sub-calibre 4" ammunition and provisioned ship, *Courageous* proceeded for a 'Special Trial' between the mid-channel buoy and May Island, during which she attained a speed of 28 knots before heading north and west into Scapa Flow. One suspects that her captain was being careful and not yet taking her up to her full power capability. Then, on 8th January, having 'oiled', she passed through the Oxcars Gate, and commenced to zig-zag two points each side of her

---

[147] The epic performance of the mortally-wounded Boy Seaman Gunner CORNWALL in keeping his gun in action at the Battle of Jutland, with all the other members of its crew lying dead around it, was archetypal of Naval discipline and training. He was used as a role model at *Ganges* and similar training establishments. Boy Seaman Gunner CORNWALL well deserved his posthumous VC.

mean course. She was heading out to sea, in a chill rising wind coming from N E by North and freshening to Force 5, with a sea which was getting up from moderate to 'rather rough'. On the face of it, such weather was really 'quite normal'. In these conditions *Courageous* was driven at up to 290 revolutions, that is, at a speed approaching 30 knots, and it seems likely that it was at this time that she (again?) strained her hull (*possibly* already weakened by the firing of her guns, as implied earlier). Certainly, the strain was located in an area just forward of 'A' Turret. She returned to Scapa Flow where she came to anchor at 1100 on the 9th.

On the 10th a Court of Enquiry convened on board, continuing for two hours that day, and reconvening the next day for a further two hours before reaching its decision. The Court Members were Rear Admiral W.E. GOODENOUGH (2nd Battle Squadron), Captain J.A. FERGUSSEN (HMS *Thunderer*), Engineer Cmdr H.S. GARWOOD (HMS *Thunderer*) and Assistant Constructor V.G. SHEPEARD (HMS *Agincourt*). Their report was dated 11th January 1916.[148] They found that the structural damage had occurred on Monday 8th January, about 2330-2340, when the ship was at 56° 14' N, 2° 00' W, course 90° speed 29½ knots. The wind was from the north-east at Force 4 to 5. The sea was moderate, short and sharp. It had been logged as 4 by *Courageous*.

No heavy seas were shipped, and the court formed the opinion that "*the damage was due to the pressure of water from the outside, and not due to the weight of water coming aboard.*"

The court considered that the damage was principally due to the longitudinal weakness in the fore part of the ship. It seemed that she was stiff longitudinally between 'Y' and 'A' turrets, but that she became less stiff from 'A' turret forward, 'A' turret being about 270 feet from the stem. The court found that "*This great length, insufficiently stiffened, combined with the effect of the sea on her flare, is a source of serious weakness.*" They went on, "*…we are of the opinion the ship is structurally weak, as evidenced by the leaks into the oil tanks and at other places, extending to a considerable part of the whole length of the ship.*" [However, they also had to add a note that the Assistant Constructor, Mr SHEPHEARD, did not concur about the ship being structurally weak, "*…except at the fore end, ahead of 60 Station.*"] No blame was attached to Captain BROMLEY or anyone on board. The ship had been handled in a proper and seamanlike manner. "*The ship should be docked and repaired at once.*"

An attached report gave further detail, including a short tabulation of the local weather assessments on the 8th January as made respectively by the 'Met' Office, by 'HMS *Renown*', and by 'HMS *Courageous*'. These three 'sources' pretty well agreed about wind direction as being N.E or N.N.E, but disagreed about its force, rated as '6-8, squally' by the 'Met Office, and as '8' by *Renown*, but as only '4-5' by *Courageous*. Similarly, the state of the sea was rated respectively as '*Rough*', as '6' and as only '*Moderate*', '4'. From this one might strongly suspect that those aboard *Courageous* might well have underestimated the strength of the wind and the roughness of the sea on the night of the 8th January 1917. In that regard, play was made of the fact that the design of *Courageous* was in several ways 'unprecedented'. The nearest 'comparatives' were

---

[148] The report survives at the National Maritime Museum, Greenwich, under reference DEY/29 (The Papers of Sir James D'EYNCOURT, DNC 1868-1951), where professional researcher R. O'HARA came across it whilst conducting a 'broadly targetted search ref maintenance/repair of *Courageous* during WW1' on behalf of the author of this book.

the battlecruisers *Renown* and *Repulse*, but these ships were 7,000 tons heavier and only 8 feet longer overall than *Courageous*. The behaviour of *Courageous*, even in comparatively severe weather, might be such that her tendency to pitch and roll, especially at fairly high speed, would be much less than experienced serving officers would have come to expect of a 'big ship' when at sea. And the implication of the report was indeed that, *on a dark night*, her officers might have underestimated the severity of the weather – rating a Force 8 gale as being only a Force 5 one. The report referred to the fact that the fore end of the seaplane platform was buckled and distorted during the storm (presumed to have been due to seas breaking unseen on the forecastle deck) as possibly endorsing this belief.

Stress was laid on the fact that the Captain had reported two seas as having struck the ship on the weather bow well forward under the flare, which had '*shaken the ship a good deal*'. She was then doing 29.6 knots. The navigating officer, Cmdr HEWETT, had said in his evidence to the court that these blows had made the ship "*quiver tremendously*", so much so that, at his post in the upper charthouse, he had been "*unable to use his dividers with any certainty for some seconds.*" The report went on to conjecture that the damage had been due to two particularly heavy blows of the sea on her bow (as distinct from wave pressure lifting her by the head), and somehow deduced from this the desirability of additional plating on deck and topside in the vicinity of the sick bay near to the point where the top edge of the thick protective plating dropped from the forecastle to the upper deck level. The report said that the need for this had been demonstrated on the night of 8th January – despite the calculations which had previously been made for her design and which had '*made her the equal of fast Atlantic liners*'.

The report went on to say that, when the ship was docked, "*it was seen that the lower part of the structure had withstood the strain very well. Caulking the leaks had put matters sufficiently right for her to proceed to sea after a certain amount of repair to the upper structure*". Although not directly stated, the clear implication was 'With the upper structure well shored-up, and in order to reach a dock where the plating on deck and topside can be 'thickened-up.' (As we shall see, the damage to the lower part of the structure was rather greater than superficial examination had revealed.)[149]

---

[149] Author's Note: I am reminded of the dramatic failure of certain all-welded Liberty Ships in and soon after WW2, which were neither sufficiently 'stiff' (nor sufficiently 'flexible'), to cope with the repeated flexing of the ship under certain large/long wave conditions. It took some time for 'Authority' to accept that there was a serious flaw in the ships. In regard to *Courageous* I gain a feeling of strong behind the scenes disagreement within the Court of Enquiry, and I feel that there is a certain lack of logicality in their findings. Did *most* of the members of the Court of Enquiry into the damage to *Courageous* feel that the problem was actually due to the very flared bow section being strongly lifted as it met a freak large wave, and then the fore-part not being 'man enough' to raise the very heavy main section before the wave reached it, so that the ship 'folded' at the weakest point of its 'box-section' – which was just forward of 'A' turret?

Were those two, close-spaced, extraordinary 'quiverings' and 'heavy vibrations' reported by 'Pilot' and Captain not heavy waves 'hitting' the ship *per se*, but *actually* the ship bending slightly upwards forward of 'A' turret as a very large wave passed under it, and then, as the wave continued under the mid-part of the ship, the forepart dropping, unsupported, down into the deep following trough (cracking the upper deck as it did so), and then the whole structure settling back, somewhat crumpled and distorted ,as the lesser ensuing waves restored a reasonably 'cradling' support for the whole length of the ship? Could not the 'crumpling-up' damage to the Flying-off Platform forward of 'A' turret have been caused by that momentary bending and straightening of the hull?

On the 12th four shipwrights from each battleship present at Scapa Flow came aboard and were employed in what the log calls simply 'shoring up' (evidently of the weakened and distorted compartments). A letter from R.J. PRENDERGAST (on board HMS *Orion*) addressed "My Dear Sir James" and dated 12th January, says that he had seen the buckling on HMS *Courageous* and that he considered it serious. He had '*sent off the timber as requested and some dockyard drillers.*' He also confirmed that 40 shipwrights 'from the Fleet' were busy '*shoring up the decks*' – but that the sooner *Courageous* was in dock, the better.[150]

At 1815 on the 13th January *Courageous* slipped and proceeded, having the consideration, incidentally, to release her prisoners at 2030 from confinement in their cells.[151] By that time she was making 20 knots in a wind of Force 5 to 6, and a 'moderate' sea. The destroyers *Sorcerer* and *Sable* formed up astern at 2116. *Courageous* commenced zig-zagging at 0030, and anchored at Rosyth at 0838. Her hands were soon busy at disembarking ammunition into a lighter which had come alongside. The lighter was still there when a Dockyard party and various Constructors came aboard. A subsequent report by W.J. BERRY to the DNC (Director of Naval Construction) expressed inability to deal with the problems besetting *Courageous* due to shortage of staff and the fact that he already had *Repulse* 'with a hole in her side' in one dock, *Tiger* 'having a refit and damaged armour plate replaced' in another dock and with the third and last dock (in which *Courageous* was temporarily sitting) being required for the '*ordinary work of the yard.*" Further, the C-in-C Grand Fleet did not want this dock filled with a lengthy repair job '*when it might be required at any moment for dealing with fleet damage after action, etc.*' Rosyth therefore planned to refloat *Courageous* as soon as the examination of her bottom was complete, and then to keep her out in the basin until her destination was decided.

As matters stood, therefore, tugs assisted *Courageous* into No.1 Dock on the 15th, and she did not re-emerge until the 17th. The exact findings of the examination are not known, but it had been confirmed that there were leaks in many of her oil tanks, some of the tanks directly under the damaged decks having been completely full of water when the ship had arrived. Her draught was re-checked after she had been refloated, being assessed at 22 ft 4 ins forward and 24 ft 8¾ ins aft.

The *effect* of the changes the board were proposing would be to strengthen the box-section of the whole ship forward of 'A' turret (i.e. to make her more 'stiff'), which would seem to be just what was required. However, the Assistant Constructor (or his boss behind the scenes) was clearly 'in denial' that the ship was insufficiently stiff to any real degree. Could it just be that 'Barge' GOODENOUGH (who was a great 'character') was being politically subtle by 'resolving the problem' without causing the Assistant Constructor to lose face? That is, by deliberately excluding the concept of 'wave pressure tending to lift her by the head', and talking 'smokescreen stuff' about the lack of inherent 'strength' in resisting the 'pressure' of waves battering the bows.

[150] Tellingly, he also said, "*I think it would be safer to shore up 'Glorious' before she starts buckling. She has already shown signs of weakness, as they have asked me to make them a lot of steel brackets, etc.*" (See DEY/29 at the NMM.)

[151] A merciful act, since the hull had clearly been strained and there was the risk of the ship being torpedoed, or of hitting a mine, etc., with these men being incarcerated in their cells low down in the ship. [On the debit side of that equation, there were, of course, at water-line level or below, many 'good men and true' sealed in compartments behind watertight doors who were duty-bound to stay at their cruising or action stations, and for whom no such 'release' could possibly be granted.]

Vice-Admiral CHOCKEPRAT of the French Navy visited the ship on 23rd January, and one wonders if his visit was to appraise this new venture in cruiser construction, and, if so, whether her rather embarrassing damage was screened from him. Be that as it may, over the next two days she took in ammunition, embarked stores and re-oiled. On the 27th, it was another 942-mile voyage from Rosyth, which ended with the ship back at Scapa Flow once more (but evidently merely as a 'staging post' on a journey which would soon take her round the north of Scotland and down the west coast of England to Portsmouth). During this initial journey the company used their sounding machine, which had been pre-tested and found correct. They ran at up to 28 knots in a 'smooth' to 'light' sea, though at the shallow draught of 23 ft 5 ins forward (25 ft 6 ins aft) and with not much more than a half-load of oil fuel. By 1st February they had proceeded to Greenock, and on Monday the 5th they proceeded all the way down the west coast and round to Portsmouth, again in a smooth to light sea, with a screen of torpedo boat destroyers in company, zig-zagging at times, and generally making 20 to 21½ knots, sometimes increasing to 25 knots. They covered the 552 miles without incident, arriving on the 6th.

Once at Portsmouth, they discharged their oil into a lighter for testing, and to enable the tanks to be cleaned. Starting on the 6th, and continuing all day on the 7th, they disembarked ammunition.

The hands must have been exhausted by the time they had finished. It would appear that they had cleared the forward 15" and 4" magazines and shell rooms completely, and also 'cleared' (in naval parlance 'cleaned') the adjacent compartments 'as requisite to the Dockyard instructions', evidently to enable the dockyard workers to work unencumbered in those areas.

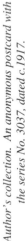

Author's collection. An anonymous postcard with the series No. 3037, dated c.1917.

HMS *Courageous*, exact date and place of photograph unknown but *possibly* on her arrival at Portsmouth in February 1917. N.B. The Admiralty officially 'discouraged' the taking of photographs of ships in wartime.

The confidential signal books were withdrawn from use, and secured. On the 8th February, the ship secured in Dry Dock, the after 15" and 4" shell rooms then being sealed up for safety purposes and the keys being handed over to the Dockyard Police. It would not be until 3rd April (eight weeks later) that the dock would be flooded preparatory to warping the ship out.

It is believed that a significant amount of internal strengthening and repair work was carried out in the compartments athwartships and just ahead of the barbette of 'A' turret, and probably in its associated shell rooms and magazines, during those two months, this work presumably being additional to 'double-plating' the deck and topside forward of 'A' turret. During that time Admiral BEATTY, the C-in-C, visited the ship, later followed by Admiral ORRERY the Director of Naval Operations. Admiral BEATTY re-visited the ship in late March, this time accompanied by General Sir A. HUNTER. Admiral ORRERY would make a further visit on 4th April, by which time the dockyard work was apparently complete. [As a precaution, *Glorious* would also eventually have her hull "double-plated" in the vicinity of 'A' turret and just ahead of it.[152] It seems probable that *Furious* was sufficiently far behind in her construction to have suitable modifications introduced as an *integral part* of her initial building.]

In the meantime, the men of *Courageous* were exercised at their weapons and control equipment, and parties were sent to the training establishments at Whale Island and at HMS *Vernon* for courses of instruction. Five Torpedo Ratings were sent to Immingham on a mining course, and the Wireless Telegraphist Ratings were sent to the Royal Naval Barracks for further instruction. Some 'long leaves' were also granted during this period.

On 4th April the hands were engaged in drawing and embarking torpedoes and, on the 5th, as the ship undocked, the hands promptly coaled ship and then, next day, started to embark oil from a lighter which came alongside. An ammunition lighter also came alongside and oiling and ammunitioning continued through into the evening. Provisioning ship was also in progress, and, on the 10th, a lighter carrying sea-mines came alongside, the sinkers for the mines having arrived on board a day earlier. Next day they commenced basin trials which were completed satisfactorily, drew more stores and 'got up' paravanes. On the 13th they tested their paravane and mining gear, and on the 14th they checked their draught, which had now increased to 25 ft 10 ins forward and 25 ft 10½ ins aft, partly due to their load of oil, ammunition, mines, etc., and now permanently augmented by the (believed) internal strengthening and the double-plating. At 2137 they left their berth with a Pilot on board, to oversee them out of harbour, dropping him off at 2020. They then proceeded to carry out mining trials, later coming to anchor in Stokes Bay. Next day they carried out a paravane test. On the 16th April they exercised at General Quarters, had the various gun-crews at sundry drills, and exercised Night Defence Stations on a watch by watch basis. Mr ASTON (Gunner) joined the ship.

On the 19th April they proceeded from Portsmouth to Plymouth, conducting steam trials on the way, with a Full Speed Trial which started at noon on the 20th, and finished at 1610 the same day. They secured to No.2 Buoy at Plymouth at 1740. Next day the

---

[152] Jane's 'Fighting Ships of World War One' talks only of 'double-plating', but the author suspects that internal bracing and strengthening also took place on a significant scale. The letter by R.J. PRENDERGAST to Sir James D'EYNCOURT of 18th January mentioned a request for 'a lot of steel brackets' for *Glorious* which had 'already shown signs of weakness', and would thus seem to confirm this.

crews of 'A' and 'Y' turrets got out cordite ammunition (presumably nearing its 'safe storage' time-limit). This ammunition was discharged into a lighter alongside, and replaced by getting in fresh stocks of cordite. As we shall soon see, the ship would shortly be heading north again, sometimes being stationed in the vicinity of Rosyth, and sometimes at Scapa Flow. She would fall into a routine and it seems worthwhile to try to recapture something of what the actual living conditions were like for Alf and his shipmates aboard this huge ship.

Now, in the early 1920s, Alf would come to serve with a very go-ahead young Lieutenant, Roy STRUBEN by name. As 'Midshipman R.F.C. STRUBEN', this young gentleman had served in the battleship *Canada* when she was a part of the Grand Fleet. HMS *Canada* had fought at the Battle of Jutland, but Roy STRUBEN's service in her took place in the immediate 'post-Jutland' period, when the British Navy were still 'trailing their coats' in an effort to lure the German High Seas Fleet to head out into the North Sea again, and to meet them in renewed combat. Midshipman STRUBEN has left us some superb written images of life aboard these great ships at that time. They are indicative of his humanity and his fascination with the interplay within the Royal Navy of pragmatism, personality and rank. His MSS diary, ending in the peace-time period following WW1 (by which time he had attained the rank of Commander), is held in the Imperial War Museum.

From Roy STRUBEN's diary we can judge quite a lot about the life that Alf would have led in *Courageous*, at that same general period of time. For example, Alf would have been appointed to one of the four Divisions of Seamen - Fo'c'sle, Foretop, Maintop and Quarterdeck, and it is a little unfortunate that we do not know in which one he served. The division to which he was appointed would have automatically decreed which gun-turret he helped to man. [As indicated by the aforementioned losses in HMS *Lion* at Jutland, when her Q Turret - manned by Royal Marines in that instance - was hit and penetrated, each gun-turret required 80 Seamen and artisans, (or Marines and artisans) under one or more officers.]

Roy STRUBEN tells us: *"Every morning in harbour at about 0715, the Seamen and Marines would be piped to 'clean guns'. [Their day would have started some two hours earlier, and by 0715 the men would have rolled up their hammocks, had a mug of piping hot cocoa and a wash. The hands would have been fallen in, decks hosed down and scrubbed, and the duty boat would have been cleaned and made ready for the day's work. The men would then have been fallen in again.] On hearing the pipe, 'Quarters, clean guns', every man would then have gone to his action station, be it in main turret, secondary armament battery, torpedo flat, searchlight platform, spotting top high up on the fore-mast, transmitting station far below the waterline, or wherever. In each position, every piece of equipment would be cleaned and, if appropriate, oiled, then tested and reported correct (or otherwise) via voice-pipe or telephone, to the Gunnery Officer or his delegate. 'Dummy Runs' might then well ensue, imaginary targets being engaged. The rangefinders, plotting table, order transmitters, sights, gyro-controlled director telescopes and firing pistols would be brought into play as the guns were trained and elevated to bear on the selected targets.*

Meantime, at about 0730, a bugler would have sounded 'Cooks to the Galley', followed by 'Secure', meaning that everything must be made fast and stowed away. Then, at 0800, the men would hear the welcome pipe, 'H-a-a-nds to breakfast'. At 0845 would come the order 'Out Pipes', signalling the end of breakfast and relaxation, the flagship would 'make' 0900 by hoisting a signal, and all hands being mustered, the ensign would be raised. The ship's company would face aft, towards the ensign, the officers would salute and the band would play 'God Save the King'.

If leaving harbour, the blacksmiths would be striking off the cable stoppers and slips and manning steam capstans. Soon the huge chain cables would begin to come clanking inboard through the hawse-pipes and thence down into the cable lockers below. Shipwrights would have opened up pressure to the salt-water mains so that sailors could scrub the often odious mud off the chains and anchors, to prevent the foul smells which might otherwise contaminate the cable lockers and seep into the forrard mess decks. Down in the cable flat under the fo'c'sle men with steel hooks would be carefully 'flaking down' the heavy chain into the lockers, to ensure it would run out smoothly next time the anchors were let go.

Meantime, all over the ship, all port-holes, deadlights, water-tight doors and hatches, (many of the latter heavy pieces of equipment), would be clanging-to under the organised efforts of other men. Checks would also be in progress to make sure that all was secured and shipshape against the most violent rolling of the ship, or the heaviest sea breaking aboard.

The hands would then fall in by Divisions, Fo'c'sle men on the fo'c'sle, Foretopmen and Maintopmen in the waist and Quarterdeck men on the scrubbed and gleaming teak planking of the quarterdeck, with all ranks smartly aligned and standing at ease, and with the officers out in front of each Division. Meantime, the Commander would march aft to report to the Captain that 'the ship was ready for sea, and the cable shortened in to three shackles'.

If leaving in company with other ships, say as part of a squadron or a fleet, the flag signal 'Weigh and Proceed' would follow, and the ships would leave in a pre-set sequence. Usually, fleet minesweepers would be working ahead of the warships. If not, or if leaving independently, some of the fo'c'slemen would already have unstowed and rigged the complicated gear for hoisting out and running the mine-sweeping paravanes, which would be lowered the moment the ship cleared the harbour entrance. This was a precaution against the risk that German submarines might have laid mines since the channel was last swept.

Immediately on leaving, the anchors would be secured and all would be quiet except on the bridge, where the crisp orders of the Captain regarding engine speed and helm, would be heard, as his orders went down the voice-pipe to the Chief Quartermaster in the wheel house below. After all the noise and bustle of getting under way, the impression would be of a vast quietude, somehow emphasised by the steady hum of the ventilators, the low roar of the funnels under forced draught and the swish of the bow wave.

This would last for only a short time, for the bugles would suddenly bray out, 'General Quarters', and the ranks on deck would promptly dissolve to the stirring call, as men rushed to their action stations. There, they would test the powerful hydraulic equipment for training the massive turrets, elevating the huge guns, raising the ammunition cages and working the great rams. At the same time every item of the complicated electrical control system and telephone network would be checked, from lofty spotting top down to the shell rooms and torpedo flats in the depths of the ship.

When the Captain had received all reports and was satisfied that his ship was ready for instant action, he would order, 'Hands to cruising stations', and the Commander would call, 'Bugler, Sound off Port Watch to Cruising Stations'.[153] This order would be repeated to all parts of the ship by telephone or voice-pipe. In practice, during wartime, at least one watch of officers and men were always at action stations, day and night, whilst the remainder had their meals, rested, or did the necessary work about the ship - the minimum required for efficiency and cleanliness.

Much of that work was repetitive and boring, but essential to keep the ship in perfect order. Much of the drilling at action stations was also repetitive and boring, but needed to be done time and again, day after day, swapping posts, and learning to work in rhythm, until each movement of each man became as near to automatic as could be and he was in a position to 'swap' roles with any of his shipmates who became disabled in action.

Morale in the ship, which was crowded and uncomfortable, could be difficult to maintain. Principally, it depended upon the quality and behaviour of the officers, (be they of commissioned, subordinate or warrant rank), and also on the petty officers. The valued traditions of the Royal Navy and the pride of the officers and men in those traditions was a very important factor in this. The officers needed to do all they could to earn the trust, respect, and, if possible, the affection of their men - though by no means all officers sought affection and some preferred to act more as ogres. Trust and respect were the crucial factors. The best clue to morale was often the appearance of the ship. If she was ill-kept, with gear all awry, ropes dangling, guns askew, etc., it was very probable that the morale of her officers and men was at a low ebb. The condition of a ship's boats was often a very good 'indicator'. A smart ship nearly always meant a fine company.

Within the main gun-turrets, the physical conditions often became appalling, especially in heavy seas. With a thick fug developing in the turret, and perhaps with the ship having a slow corkscrew roll and slow pitch, promoting seasickness and leading to the large iron sanitary buckets becoming ever more full of foul-smelling urine and vomit, and perhaps with young sailors pitiably ill and sprawled out helpless on the steel decks - a considerable feeling of mutual suffering could exist between officers and men. Nightfall made the whole situation more nightmarish, increasing the sense of fuggy odour, and, if positioned in 'Y' turret aft, making one even more conscious of such things as the intermittent rattle of the steering quadrant in the tiller flat below, and the rumble of the great propeller shafts in their tunnels. This noise would increase to a vibrating roar as the stern lifted and the propellers raced, and then slowed as the stern subsided deep into the sea, only to rise in speed again, on and on.... Meantime, the gun's crews would have found such odd corners as they could, in which to yarn and doze in the dim red light of the darkened ship: it was only the gun-layers and the sight-setters who had small stools to crouch upon, though precious little was the comfort the sheer hardness of the stools offered. Every metal surface would be saturated in condensed moisture from the foul air.

The magazine crews below were quite pampered in comparison, having wooden deck planks to stretch out upon. And those in the shell room had the luxury of more space than was available in the machinery-packed gun-house - though the noise from the

---

[153] Or 'Starboard Watch', etc., depending on the duty sequence.

propeller-shafts was absolutely deafening in the aft shell room. Meantime, the crews in the 4-inch guns in the batteries outside were free from such intense fug and stench as those in the gun-house suffered, but were at risk of having cold sea-water coming in through the gun-ports. This then washed about in the vomit on deck, in which lay the inert and chilling bodies of the lads suffering most acutely from sea-sickness.

It was a relief if the long, long hours at action stations were broken by a 'dummy run', with an order such as, 'For exercise. Enemy bearing green four five...', passed by telephone from the spotting top, followed by the rapid ticking of the electric repeaters from the revolving tower at the masthead, as the director layer came onto target, accompanied by the swishing of the powerful hydraulic swash plate engine and the elevating rams, as the two trainers and the two gunlayers followed the pointers on their dials. Otherwise it was a matter of dozing or yarning, and if one could not avoid it - thinking, perhaps too much, of what fate might have in store at any moment by devastating explosion of mine or torpedo or the sudden searing hit of an incoming shell.. Being relieved, to stand down from such turret duty, was always good.....but it seemed no time before one was back at it again." [End of quotation from Roy STRUBEN.]

Now, before this remarkable insight into living conditions aboard, we had left the ship at Plymouth. From there, on 22ⁿᵈ April 1917, she proceeded round Lands End and proceeded north to Scapa Flow, not via St George's Channel, but taking the longer route around the west coast of Ireland. She had a destroyer screen ahead, and generally ran at 22 knots, with frequent spells of zig-zagging. On the 23ʳᵈ the ship spoke various steamers and one sailing ship which was bound south. Shortly after speaking with a second sailing ship at 50° 20' N, 17° 34' W (on the latitude of Land's End, but far to the west of it), a 'swirl' of water was detected about six points on the starboard bow, bearing 60°, distance 1200 yds, and the tracks of two torpedoes were observed heading in for the ship. Action was immediately taken, steering hard a'port and going to full speed, soon followed by steering hard a'starboard.[154] This had the happy result of the torpedoes missing.

A derelict schooner which was on fire was passed at position 50° 22 N, 19° 00 W, and, next day, some wreckage was passed at 1430. Clearly, German 'U-boats' were active in the area. Moreover, they were by no means reluctant to 'have a go' at a major British warship, even if she were screened by destroyers. Sure enough, at 2031 on the 24ᵗʰ April, the track of a torpedo was reported, heading in on the Port Bow, the Officer of the Watch immediately ordering full speed, with the helm being put hard a'port (evidently to 'comb' the track of the torpedo). This 'turning towards' (rather than 'away') would almost certainly have been a better response to the attack of the previous day. Perhaps the ship's officers had mulled things over together. Clearly, they were gaining in experience. Again, fortunately, the torpedo missed. It was clear that their escorts needed to be 'quick on their toes' too, with *Courageous* making violent and unheralded changes of helm to avoid incoming torpedoes and therefore liable to accidentally ram an escort, particularly if the escort also suddenly altered course.

On 25ᵗʰ April *Courageous* made rendezvous with two more destroyers, and, five hours later they entered the outer gate at Scapa Flow, anchoring at 2154 after a run of

---

[154] Presumably the second order was to 'swing the ship's stern clear' (i.e. clear of the torpedoes boring in from an angle to starboard and liable to hit the ship near her stern if she had simply maintained the first change of course and continued to accelerate. This was clearly 'a very close thing'.

2,082 miles and probably with a combined, if muted, sigh of relief. An oil tank lighter secured alongside just over an hour after their arrival, and cast off 15 minutes later, her task completed. By that time, *Courageous* had 3,040 tons of oil aboard.

HMS *Courageous*. Exact time & place of photograph unknown, but evidently prior to March 1918.

More training followed through into May, with the crews of the 'submerged' torpedo tubes working in the flat deep down in the ship, the 4-inch guns crews at practice on the Dummy-Loader, the 15" Director party at exercise, the Spotting Tables crew and the Transmitting Station crew both at drill, and so on. The ship had left harbour briefly, for sub-calibre firing, on 1st May and she proceeded into the Pentland Firth next day for full-calibre firing, returning to Scapa to re-ammunition from a lighter. Later that same day, the ship passed through the outer gate and set course as requisite for torpedo-firing and range-taking exercises, before again returning to Scapa. The company then unshipped her mining rails, evidently as a conclusion to an exercise in mine-laying. On 4th May, the ship again proceeded for sub-calibre firing and for practice with the 1" aiming rifle, followed by the crew of 'A' Turret practising with the .303" aiming rifle and the 4" crews being at work 'towing targets'. On 6th May the oil lighter *Limmerol* came alongside, evidently rather unhandily, and carried away a '*porthole cover, port side, aft*'.

There was more sub-calibre firing practice on the 8th May, accompanied by paravane trials. A 'Rake party' were away in a tug with a practice target on the 12th, and the ship proceeded to full-calibre 4" practice firing that same day. On the 15th they proceeded to the Pentland Firth for full-calibre 15" and 4" firing, next day getting up shell for examination and receiving four boxes of what the log called 'Delay Action Fuses'. One wonders if these were of an improved type, following the adverse experiences with British shells at the Battle of Jutland, and the urgent need for technological developments to 'catch up' with the quality of the German shells. It is clear that the Admiralty were in some difficulty in quietly replacing stocks of the inferior and now-obsolete 'standard' armour-piercing shells with better quality shells (now appearing in limited quantities), whilst not letting it become generally known that the main run of AP shells were of limited value except at what might be regarded as 'suicidally' close ranges. Knowing the shrewdness of naval ratings, one wonders how quickly the significance of the colour-coded new shells crept into their combined 'scuttle-butt' consciousness. [It seems that navalese slang terms for the shells of each new colour code were already evolving!]

The ship left harbour again on the 17th May, firing (and subsequently recovering) two torpedoes, before again carrying out sub-calibre firing and then returning to Scapa. On the 19th she was out at sea again, this time four cables astern of her sister-ship *Glorious*, both ships zig-zagging at times, initially a one-point zig-zag every ten minutes, then two points every ten minutes, and then three. The speed of advance of the ships varied between 15 knots and 17 knots. They both carried out paravane exercises this day.

Author's collection. A postcard by Abrahams of Devonport, Ref. No. 861. Postally used 2nd November 1924. Image reproduced by kind permission of the World Ship Society.

A paravane being hoisted outboard by means of a small, powered, crane, by which it will be lowered alongside and into the sea. The towing-wire hanging down at the front of the paravane will run through an 'easing out hook' and tripping wire, to run down to a swivelling tow connection set well down below the waterline in the bows of the ship. Once launched, the paravane will veer out at an angle of about 45° from the ship, drawn along by the pull coming from the bows as the ship runs through the sea. The towing wire will snag the cables of any sea mines floating above the depth at which the tow-line is set, hopefully cutting the mine-cable. A cut mine, being buoyant, will float to the surface, where it can be destroyed at a safe distance by means of rifle-fire.

Courageous had a wire which parted under the strain, and she consequently lost '*Paravane No.1928, one shackle and one towing wire.*'[155]

On return to Scapa, *Courageous* took in 2,564 tons of oil, increasing her draught by 9" forward (to 25' 11") and by 2" aft (to 26' 1") - apparently an average increase of only one inch of draught per 466 tons embarked. This is an incredibly low ratio of increase in draught, though she had been going through a lot of structural changes which must have affected the 'baseline figure' to some extent. None the more for that *Courageous* was certainly a massive ship with enormous buoyancy.

---

[155] All paravanes were 'handed' and serially-numbered, paravanes with even numbers being for use 'port side only', and vice-versa.

On the 23rd the ship again carried out a full-calibre 4" firing exercise and a 15" sub-calibre one. Next day, whilst her 4" sight-testing party were at drill, divers examined her propellers. Perhaps there was concern that a length of the lost paravane wire might have become entangled in them. However, all appears to have been well. Mr REET, Gunner, joined ship that day - a man who may well have been very significant in Alf's career.

Author's collection. An anonymous postcard, c.1915.

SCAPA FLOW from LONG HOPE.

"Scapa Bloody Scapa!", as this windswept anchorage soon came to be called. About half-a-dozen warships and their funnel-smoke can *just* be distinguished in the distance, beyond the two necks of land. This photograph, taken c.1915, is evocative of the barren nature of the area. The Admiralty would eventually install a rather primitive canteen, and a handful of football pitches for exercise, but the sheer isolation from the Scottish mainland and general lack of human habitation were extremely depressing for men of ships stationed here long-term.

On 1st June, 200 ratings were landed for recreation, although the 'delights' of Scapa were still very limited at that time and steps were being taken to try to improve things to some degree. Next day, throat-spraying of the whole company commenced. This would be done on a watch by watch basis. The ship's log defines neither the type of spray nor the illness (or symptoms) which it was intended to stave off. [From his own long-past experience, the author suspects that the spray would have been iodine-based and intended to minimise sore throats such as might arise from the common cold, influenza, tonsillitis, etc. It would have been an unpleasant procedure to undergo, though probably better that the use of a swab, which made one want to 'gag'.] That same day the ship received detonators, primers and 4" charges from the S.S *Arkwood*, frozen meat from a meat ship which subsequently came alongside, and sundry goods from a canteen ship which secured alongside shortly afterwards.

On the 5th June '17, a winch was taken aboard and installed, ready for securing a kite balloon. The balloon itself arrived next day, and was duly secured. *Courageous* then proceeded to Ophir Bay for sub-calibre firing, and then continued on to full-calibre firing. Further practice 4" and 15" full-calibre firings were carried out in Pentland Firth on the

9th, an attempt to do so on the 8th having had to be abandoned due to poor visibility.[156] The ship weighed and proceeded from Scapa to Rosyth in the evening of the 9th, arriving at 2100. Evidently she had streamed her paravanes during the voyage, for two paravanes had been lost, each complete with their shackles and towing wires. These losses were becoming rather frequent, and it would appear that a serious technical problem existed which needed to be resolved. It was evident that paravanes were regarded as vital accessories to protect the ship and both the lost paravanes were replaced shortly after the arrival of *Courageous* at Rosyth.

On 14th June the Admiral's staff joined from *Glorious*. The Log shows that 'A' and 'Y' turret crews had been sponging out on 12th June, presumably following from the firing on 9th June. Apparently, some problem had been experienced in that 15-inch firing, for eight ordnance workers came aboard on the 17th to effect repairs. Meanwhile, training classes continued in seamanship, gunnery and torpedo instruction, lecture parties from *Galatea, Phaeton* and *Inconstant* came aboard, and other parties from *Birkenhead* and *Chatham* were given instruction in the use and maintenance of 'Hanison' Lights. Recreation and football parties were also landed. Then, as the days went by through June, the 15" Transmitting Station and Spotting crews were exercised at the Spotting Table, before, on the 22nd, the ship proceeded out of the gates for 4"and 15" sub-calibre firing practice.

An ammunition lighter came alongside with sea mines on the 25th, before, on the 26th June, the ships companies of *Birkenhead, Chatham, Chester, Glorious* and *Yarmouth* came aboard at 0900, and then, memorably, at 1205 His Majesty King George V officially visited the ship, not leaving until 1535. The visiting ships' companies had left at 1245, and now all the warships 'manned and cheered ship' at 1555, as the King departed.[157]

On the 28th *Courageous* re-ammunitioned and took in water, before proceeding next morning to 40 minutes more of sub-calibre firing practice, followed by range-taking exercises. By 1247 the ship was at anchor just below the famous railway bridge, the gun-crews of 'A' and 'Y' turrets were 'sponging out' again, and the 4" gun crews, acting gunlayers and seamen gunners were practising at the .303 target. Next day, further .303 practice continued, but with a towed target, and, much later, at the ungodly hour of 0110, the ship suddenly exercised Action Stations. One can almost feel the gut-wrenching shock to men sound asleep as the 'Call to Arms' was sounded by bugle, springing them into immediate, dazed and half-comatose haste to somehow 'grab their boots and gear' and rush to their action stations.

Throughout all this period, if proceeding to sea as part of a fleet, there was always the possibility, to far as the lower deck were concerned, that the fleet might be engaged on a sweep to try to catch the German High Seas Fleet and to inflict a heavy defeat on them. 'Buzzes' were always rife, and disappointments frequent. The companies were

---

[156] Bearing in mind the poor visibility which so often prevailed in the North Sea, one wonders whether good value might have been obtained from persisting with this trial. See earlier comments concerning the inadequacies of gunnery practice.

[157] H.M. King George V and his advisors well-recognised the need for such morale-boosting visits. A series of photographic postcards depicting a Royal Visit to the troops on the Western Front was issued around this time. The lively presence of Edward, the Prince of Wales, who was attached to one of the military headquarters in France and sometimes made his way into the forward areas, was certainly appreciated by the front-line soldiers.

more than ready to put their lives 'on the line' to get a result and, above all, to break the boredom. One can get to a point where further training becomes almost negative in its effect.

Yet, throughout July they continued their training and exercising. By now, examinations for wireless ratings were being held, as that branch began to expand and the range and reliability of the transmitters/receivers increased.[158] Again, *Courageous* went to sea briefly, thrice, for sub-calibre firing, for reduced charge firing and for torpedo practice. And, once again, the paravane chains fouled the ship. This time she had to go astern to free them. Perhaps inspired by thoughts of the damage that the chains might have done, as well as by the usual thoughts of possible battle-damage scenarios, the company exercised at all 'steering breakdown' positions. Meantime the usual routines went on, (i) with torpedo ratings being sent on courses to Roehampton, (ii) with the regular flow of ratings to the RN Barracks at Chatham for qualifying courses and re-posting being kept up (iii) with standard maintenance of the ship continuing, such as inspecting and oiling wire hawsers, and checking and repairing the rigging screws and stays, (iv) with inspection of the condition of ammunition - including the despatch of samples for expert testing and appraisal - and (v) with the usual provisioning with oil, coal, water, meat, vegetables, etc., all going on. In the interim, occasional periods of leave were being granted, on a watch by watch basis. Once again, Dockyard workers came aboard (on 14th July) to effect some minor but specialist repairs.

On 9th July 1917, as recounted earlier in this book, Alf's former ship, the dreadnought HMS 'Vanguard' was devastated, apparently by the explosion of unstable cordite, with the loss of life of all but two of the men aboard. One assumes that it did not take long for the news of this tragedy to filter through to the troops. However, by this time one imagines that Alf was becoming inured to the losses of ships and men, and Vanguard was not the first ship to perish in this manner, for 'Bulwark' and 'Natal' had also blown up in 1914 and 1915, respectively, due to catastrophic internal explosions. Indeed, Alf's second-ever ship, the old 'Russell', had hit two mines off Malta in May 1916, which had set her on fire, and this had been followed by partial explosion of her 12" Magazine, despite the flooding effect of the inrushing water from the mine-damage.

However, Alf had been under fire, and, having been out of 'Vanguard' and 'Russell' for four or five years, and still aged only 22, he probably did not 'personalise' these disasters by reflecting too much upon his 'lucky escapes'. Indeed, his emotions may well have been becoming 'blunted' by this time, and he may not have been hit as hard by such news as one might have supposed. However, spontaneous explosions such as these certainly had great relevance from the professional viewpoint, and there may

[158] File ADM 1 8380/151, entitled 'The Empire's Wireless Communication' and dated 15th June 1914, states: "*A service Mk II set, with special masts adapted for shore work and employing a wave suitable for reception by ships could be received by men-o'-war at 800 miles*". The report went on to promote the idea of '*onward transmitting*' stations at suitable intervals all round the world, *such as Gibraltar, Ascension Island, the Cape of Good Hope, Aden, Ceylon, Singapore, Hong Kong, Fiji*.....Already, it was clear, that over the three years of war, considerable further improvements in wireless technology had occurred. [The Germans were also 'in on the act'. During the *Konigsberg* affair of 1914/15, it was known that they had a transmitting station at Dar-el-Salaam, with a 600-mile range, and a main transmitting station at Windhoek, with a 1,000-mile range. They could thus communicate with Berlin. Both sides were listening-in on each other's communications and constantly working to break each other's secret codes. That was how (as previously mentioned) the British had come to successfully intercept the German supply ship *Sperrbrecher*, on her way to sustain the *Konigsberg*.]

have been much discussion on board as to the possible causes of the disasters, and debate as to whether any tightening up should be made in their own ship pending whatever information might filter down to lower levels regarding any Admiralty notices which might follow from the findings of the various Courts of Enquiry.

Mid-month, *Courageous* put to sea for manoeuvres with other ships, the warships evidently operating as two opposing fleets, and with *Courageous* 'opening fire' on the seaplane-carrier HMS *Campania* when about 100 miles due east of Rosyth, and then 'opening up' on the leading 'enemy' battleship and a submarine. At this time they were making about 220 revolutions (say 22 knots). They continued in gunfire action for 72 minutes, returning to Rosyth and mooring below the bridge at 0800 next day, having steamed 440 miles. Next day, it was back to further reduced-charge firing in the Firth of Forth, followed by re-ammunitioning.

On 25th July a Confirmation Service was held on board by the Bishop of Edinburgh. On 27th July, a Balloon Party were landed for instruction. The balloons which were carried by the ships were man-carrying and each was linked to the ship by means of a wire cable. Each balloon was attached to the cable by a system of guys. The balloons were sausage-shaped, with pointed noses and fitted with tail-fins and stabilisers, to make them reasonably aerodynamic. However, strong gusts of wind could make them veer, dive or rear-up as they fought against the restraint imposed by the cable. A sudden change of course by the parent ship could also cause considerable reactions if it brought a strong wind on to play on a different quarter of the balloon.

Suspended in a basket below the floating balloon itself, observers equipped with binoculars could search the various sectors around the ship for any signs of shipping, especially hostile submarines, torpedo-tracks, floating mines, wreckage, etc., and communicate directly by telephone to the officers on board the ship. They could also observe and report the fall of shot in a naval engagement. If necessary, the balloon crews could also make signals by Aldis Lamp or by semaphore flag, not only to the ship to which they were secured, but also to other ships. For the larger part of the time, however, the balloons were flown with no crewmen aboard, being readily winched down to enable crewmen to clamber into the basket as and when need arose. Keeping the balloons aloft kept the ship clear of a physical encumbrance which was, moreover, a significant fire hazard, for the balloon contained a considerable volume of hydrogen gas. Special precautions against fire needed to be operated by the ship, especially when the balloon was at low altitude or actually on deck. The Navy were still learning lessons about flying kite balloons, and it would have been interesting to have been 'a fly on the wall' to hear what was put across at this course of instruction. (We'll have a further look at balloons presently.)

The 1st August found the ship moored below the great Forth Bridge, with drilling continuing, the company being paid their monthly money and 25 ratings making up an advance party for leave. They oiled next day (153 tons), and were honoured by a threequarter-hour visit from the Duke of Connaught on the 3rd. The 4th saw the gunlayers at the Deflection Teacher, the 4" crews at drill and at the Loader, with the 4" gunlayers practising at Director Laying. Much the same was going on during the 7th, together with the 15" Spotting Table crew being at drill and the 4" gunlayers of the P1 Group at drill. Training classes were at instruction, the Carley floats were being refitted and the boats were all being hoisted out. They exercised Action Stations on the 8th, gave a 4-hour leave to Blue Watch and discharged empty 4" ammunition cases (together with four filled cases for test.)

On the 9th they broke the flag of Vice-Admiral Trevylan J.W. NAPIER and carried on drilling their gunlayers and Spotting Table crews. Meantime, they'd been re-provisioning ship. The 11th saw them receiving a kite balloon on board before weighing and proceeding at 0750, in company with *Furious*, for sub-calibre firing, torpedo-firing and range-finding exercises in the Firth, returning at 1255 and letting go both anchors, with 5 shackles on each in 9 fathoms. The ship then discharged her balloon to a drifter.

On the 13th she was out in the Firth again, engaged in further range-keeping exercises, now with *Glorious* in company. Then, on the 15th, presumably to 'liven things up', the order (presumably from Admiral NAPIER) was received at 1110, 'Away All Boats - Pull Round the Fleet!', followed by Divisions, and then by the heavy exercises of getting out the bower, kedge and starboard anchors. The hands were then set to cleaning out the boats and overhauling the stream anchor gear.

It was back to drill again on the 16th for the 'Y' turret and shellroom crews, with Action Stations being practised on the 17th, with more drill for the acting gunlayers. On the next day, they discharged their remaining torpedoes to the Dockyard, exchanging them for new ones.[159] Subsequently, the minelayer HMS *Abdiel* came alongside for 2½ hours with a delivery of mines. More pleasing for the 'Custard Bos'n', the beef boat *Griffin* also came alongside.

On the 20th they were busy oiling the main derrick wires, with the associated purchase, topping lift and guys, the spare hands being used to 'paint ship'. Meantime, a 4" and 15" Director Test was in progress, the 'A' and 'Y' turret crews were at drill and the 4" trainers were practising. A munitions party had also left the ship and entered the Dockyard. Another provision ship had secured alongside and, subsequently, telephone and telegraph cables were secured to the ship after her hands had changed her berth to the 'F1' buoy. (This was evidently to provide Admiral NAPIER and his staff with immediate communication with the Admiralty.)

So matters continued, with kite balloons coming and going, further gunnery and director drills of all sorts, seamen heading for the RNB at Chatham 'for examinations for rate', provisioning, refuelling, short leaves being granted, football parties being landed and Marines being put ashore for exercises, whilst, all the time, other ships and squadrons were arriving and departing. It was notable that the weather had been kind for this whole period.

On 1st September, whilst still at Rosyth, they once more received a kite balloon aboard before proceeding beyond the outer gate to make two runs of sub-calibre firing and carry out range-taking exercises in company with *Glorious*. On the 8th they proceeded to Scapa Flow, again in company with *Glorious*, zig-zagging at times *en route*, and accidentally losing overboard two of their 4" sponge rammers, presumably in the course of an exercise. The wind was from the north-west and was of a brisk and rather chill Force 4 to Force 5 at the time, so the ship had probably been quite 'lively' whilst the drill was in progress.

---

[159] The new stocks were probably of an improved type. Sundry modifications to increase the speed, direction-keeping, running at constant depth, explosive power, and reliability to remain afloat at the end of a run were constantly on-going.

On the 10th September, *Courageous* took in provisions from the store-ship *Gourka* which had come alongside, before *Courageous* and *Glorious* proceeded out to the firing range in the northern sector of the Flow. *Courageous* then made range-taking runs in company with her consort, went to Action Stations, and carried out sub-calibre firings and 1" aiming runs, first in daylight and, later, by night. She was flying her kite balloon for observation and hauling it down '*as need arose for re-filling*'. This implies that *Courageous* would have been carrying cylinders of liquefied compressed hydrogen aboard and also that some hydrogen would have been gradually leaking from the envelope. Such leakage could be a significant fire-hazard and constant attention was necessary to prevent any generation of sparks or burning embers around the ship or on the deck or superstructure coming anywhere near the balloon.

On the 13th *Courageous* again put to sea, and, after cruising around whilst waiting for a fog to lift, she carried out full calibre 15" and 4" firing. During this time she lost overboard by accident one boat's wallet, complete with flags. Next day, she again put to sea with *Glorious* in company, to carry out practice torpedo-firing exercises against the light cruiser *Birkenhead*. The company of *Courageous* successfully recovered the two torpedoes they had fired. Such recovery was regarded as important, for, by that period, it was understood that the cost of each torpedo had risen to about £900. Moreover, after only a short (though vital) period of maintenance, each torpedo was suitable for re-use. (By this time it had been discovered that a small heater fitted into the torpedo would add significant force to the compressed air fed to the power-unit driving the propellers. This heater would have added significantly to the manufacturing cost of each torpedo.)

On the 16th September *Courageous* and *Furious*, with four escorting destroyers, proceeded to Rosyth, leaving their berths at Scapa Flow at 2245, and soon beginning to stream their paravanes. *Courageous* was flying a kite balloon for observational purposes. She was also streaming her Trident patent log, but her log line parted and both the log and the rotator were lost. The *Lion* (Captain R BACKHOUSE) was in company for a while, as part of a battlecruiser and light cruiser force which departed from Scapa at the same time, but the distance between the two squadrons soon opened up and the other ships were gradually lost to view, leaving *Courageous, Furious* and their four escorting destroyers zig-zagging on their course, at 22 knots, to reach Rosyth safely on the 18th.

On the night of the 20th/21st September the wind got up to Force 4 or 5 and an anchor watch was set as a precaution, until the wind abated. A pulling regatta was held on the 24th, in what turned out to be a small window of opportunity in the weather, for the sea got up again on the 27th, it being deemed wise for an anchor watch to again be set.

On 1st October 1917 Alf became a Petty Officer. His substantive pay would have immediately increased to 3s per day, with the prospect of a further increase to 3s. 4d per day, and his non-substantive pay would have remained at 8d per day. There was the further prospect of his substantive pay going up to 3s. 9d per day if he qualified as a Gunner's Mate. His responsibilities over other men had now significantly increased and he would have moved into a Petty Officers' Mess. This would have given him the luxury of a modicum more personal space.

In early October, football parties were landed, and the ship put to sea for torpedo practice as part of the 1st Cruiser Squadron (made up of *Courageous, Furious* and *Glorious*). Evidently one torpedo was lost (it sank at the end of its run) but *Glorious* managed to mark its position (presumably with a Dan buoy or similar), and a working party of divers from *Courageous* which was subsequently sent away on the drifter *Stebba*, to hunt for it, returned in triumph on the next day bearing the 'lost' torpedo.

In November 1917, exercises continued as usual, including practising 'Abandon Ship' stations. *Courageous* also put to sea in company with *Glorious,* with four destroyers (*Nepean, Nereus, Pigeon* and *Vanquisher*) as escort, and with the 1st Light Cruiser Squadron manoeuvring out on their port beam. 'Action Stations' were practised before the detachment returned to Rosyth. This was all useful practice, for, on the 16th November, still flying the Flag of Vice-Admiral NAPIER, *Courageous* with *Glorious* and their four attendant destroyers in company, plus the 1st Light Cruiser Squadron and the 1st Battle Cruiser Squadron, proceeded from Rosyth and headed out towards the Dogger Bank. Subsequently, they were joined by the 6th LCS.

Photograph reproduced by courtesy of the IWM. Negative has Museum Serial No. SP 727.

Courageous and *Glorious*, the latter 'flying' a kite-balloon, head swiftly through the North Sea. An escorting 'W' Class destroyer speeds along on the port beam of the two battlecruisers. Two other heavy units make tell-tale smudges of smoke as they pound along near the horizon. Another ship creates considerable wash in the foreground. It is not known if this exciting scene specifically relates to the action of 17th November 1917, but, for atmosphere, it must have strong kinship with it.

The detachment now joined a Battlecruiser Force, which included the battlecruisers *Repulse* and *Renown,* and which was under the command of Admiral PAKENHAM. This combined force accompanied the 1st Battle Squadron under Admiral MADDEN into the Heligoland Bight. The mission which the senior commanders had been given by the C-in-C, Admiral BEATTY, was to intercept a German Fleet which was known to be at sea. This fleet was engaged in covering German minesweepers (themselves directly escorted by light defence forces), which were sweeping the extensive British minefield which had been laid off Heligoland. (The numerous German wireless transmissions involved in this operation had been picked up and interpreted by

British intelligence, for the Germans had not, at that time, fully learnt the need to preserve wireless silence.)

At about 0730 on the 17th November, there would have been some excitement aboard, for *Courageous*, *Furious* and the 6th Light Cruiser Squadron sighted and opened fire on the German minesweepers and their escorting light cruisers and submarines. The submarines immediately dived, but hits were scored on the surface ships, which promptly made smoke. The minesweepers immediately slipped their gear, and fled south-east towards the protection of their covering fleet of five German battlecruisers of the 2nd SG.

This German fleet was under the command of Rear-Admiral Von REUTER, who was flying his flag in a totally new *Konigsberg*. (Alf may have thought the presence of this ship rather ironic, since he had already played his part in the great pains which had been taken, two years earlier, to destroy her predecessor!)

At 0756, *Courageous* passed an enemy armed trawler which was apparently disabled, but, gallantly, still firing at the British destroyers. The 6th LCS (*Cardiff, Ceres, Caledon* and *Caradoc*) were crossing ahead of *Courageous* at this time. At 0935 *Courageous* passed down the outer boundary of the minefield, Admiral NAPIER considering the risk too great to penetrate the minefield, especially as the visibility was steadily worsening. He signalled the other British ships to withdraw.[160] However, it seems that 'blood was up' (presumably from all the many months of exercising and frustratingly empty patrolling) and it was not until twenty-five minutes later that the company of *Courageous* observed the *Repulse* apparently retiring, accompanied by the 1st and 6th LCS. In fact, they were trying to lure the heavy German ships on to the heavy guns of the concentration of English and American battleships and battlecruisers, including *Courageous* and *Furious*.[161]

That is to say, during the interim of time from 0930 to 1000, the German battlecruiser force had come forward to protect the minesweepers, until fired upon by the then advancing *Repulse*, whereupon the German battlecruisers had reversed course, and, under cover of a smokescreen, headed for the protection of the powerful German dreadnoughts *Kaiser* and *Kaiserin*. (See photo overleaf.)

A stern chase and gunfire exchange had then ensued with the German battlecruisers, but a fight in which the gunnery conditions were too poor for either side to make many hits. Flying his flag in *Repulse*, Rear-Admiral PHILLIMORE, had pressed on, accompanied by the 1st and 6th Light Cruiser Squadrons – until, that is, they came upon the *Kaiser* and *Kaiserin*, each of 24,333 tons and armed with ten twelve-inch guns. Rear-Admiral PHILLIMORE had then quickly swung his ships away to the north-west, thereby hoping to draw the German ships towards Admiral PAKENHAM's other

---

[160] It seems utterly amazing, but ADM 137/4528 makes clear that the amount of data (about the 'residual lethality' and extent of the British and German minefields) which had been given to the various senior officers differed considerably from one SNO to the next. The distribution of the available information had been both too laconic - and yet too restricted. Thus the level of knowledge varied from squadron to squadron concerning the extent of the minefields and the expectation (or otherwise) that certain long-laid mines were now 'safe', due to nullifying devices which automatically came into force after a certain period of time. Hence another reason why some ships plunged jauntily on, gaining in confidence by being in nominally 'mined waters', but where the Germans were fleeing with apparent impunity. Admiral PAKENHAM might have had 'more of the action' had he advanced at 30 knots rather than 25 knots only - but he may have been short of the 'full picture' and unduly concerned about the risks from mines.

[161] The U.S.A had entered the War in 1917, with her Navy immediately becoming actively involved.

battlecruisers and Admiral MADDEN's battleships, but the Germans had preferred to stay behind the safety of the German minefields.

So, the action came to an unsatisfactory end, with a handful of German minesweepers sunk, and with damage to the new cruiser *Konigsberg,* which was hit by two 15-inch shells, significantly reducing her speed. (One wonders if Alf had the satisfaction of having any hand in this, though it seems more likely that the gunners in *Repulse* were responsible.) On the British side, the cruiser HMS *Caledon* was '*severely shaken*' by a 12-inch shell-hit, and the *Cardiff* and the *Calypso* were slightly damaged. *Courageous* had fired several salvoes, but had herself remained unharmed from the German gunfire.

The 24,333 ton Dreadnought SMS *Kaiserin* (and her sister, the *Kaiser*) each packed quite a strong punch, with ten 12-inch guns and fourteen 6-inch as secondary armament. Their armour included a hefty 14-inch armour belt amidships and 12-inch of armour over their gun-turrets. They could do at least 20 knots.

This operation, in which British ships had penetrated deeply into 'German waters' did have the positive effect of denting German morale, and led to some recriminations and dismissals in the ranks of the German Naval Command. One wonders whether it was shells of the improved type which had hit the *Konigsberg.* If so, that too might have dented German morale, for, according to a Swedish source, the German officers had laughed at the rather poor performance of the British heavy-calibre AP shells at the Battle of Jutland - but they would no longer have laughed on seeing the damage the *new* British shells could do. In some ways it seems unfortunate, but, for various politico-strategic reasons, no further similar operation was mounted by the British Navy before April 1918.

The log of *Courageous* is fairly non-committal about this whole affair, their only 'damage' being a mention that one lifebuoy, and one wallet containing an armourer's tools, were each lost overboard during the action. The log continues that the ship zig-zagged as they headed north-north-west away from the area, later ran into a fog bank for a while, and so made their way back to D9 buoy at Rosyth, passing through the series of four protective 'gates', and then under the vast bridge with its red and green signal lights indicating whether or not the gate immediately beneath the bridge was open.[162] (This 'gate' consisted of a heavy wire net which could be raised from, or lowered towards, the bed of the estuary.)

Flag Commander THURSFIELD (who later became an authoritative writer of Naval books) joined the ship for a few days at this time, whilst *Courageous* sent a working party to the dockyard to unload mines, leave was given to a football party, qualifying examinations were held aboard for men from various ships, and the ship herself participated in firing and range-taking exercises in company with *Glorious*. On 16th December 1917 Commander THURSFIELD returned to the battlecruiser *Lion*. Soon afterwards a floating crane secured alongside for embarking torpedo tubes. Exercises continued unabated, eight rounds being fired from 'Y' turret one day, three runs of 15" and 4" sub-calibre firing being made on another day, followed by a further three runs the next day. A kite balloon was sometimes in use, the 4" control parties and gun crews regularly being drilled, the gunlayers put at the Deflection Teacher, and so on.

On 28th December some of the men were sent on long 'New Year's leave (perhaps including Alf), and, next day, the remaining men of her company set about de-ammunitioning the ship preparatory to her entry into dry dock on the 31st. She was refitting there until 23rd January.

On 26th January 1918 a Chief Stoker Petty Officer was unfortunately found dead in 'B' Boiler Room. Seemingly, foul play was not suspected and he was duly recorded in the log under the long-traditional entry, 'D/D' ('Discharged Dead'). For the ship's company, life went on, and, having re-ammunitioned on the 26th, *Courageous* slipped and proceeded to sea on the 28th for Full Power Trials, losing her Patent Log Governor, Rotator and Line in the process.

On the morning of the 31st she received aboard 18 cylinders of hydrogen gas, followed by the kite balloon itself during mid-afternoon. She slipped and proceeded for fleet exercises, almost immediately streaming her paravanes. She sighted the 3rd LCS and attendant destroyers on her starboard bow, (evidently units of the fleet of which she was herself a part) soon after proceeding from Rosyth, and now, on the 1st February, at around 55° 47'N, 1° 47E (i.e. about 110 miles East of Rosyth) zig-zagging, paravanes streaming and at the good speed of 28 knots, as part of the "friendly" fleet, she sighted and 'opened fire' on the "enemy" fleet, increasing to full ahead as she did so. *Courageous* and the accompanying ships must have made an impressive sight.

She continued 'in action' for three-quarters of an hour, then took in her paravanes and reduced to 25 knots, at which time her Trident Patent Log and its Rotator were noted to have carried away (yet again!), though the Forbes Log continued in operation. *Courageous* then re-streamed her paravanes, and took station as ordered, 2.1 miles and 90° from *Lion*, the accompanying Battlecruiser force shaking out into line-ahead formation. The Battleship force was then sighted, whilst paravanes were being taken in, and course set for Scapa Flow.

During the next days it was back to yet more training, 1" aiming rifle practice, searchlight drill, 15" and 4" sub-calibre firing, torpedo firing, rangefinder practice, night action exercises (some with the use of star shell), High Angle sight testing, 4" Director

---

[162] It seems that the colours and combinations of lights were changed from time to time, sometimes, for example being red and white in colour.

testing and so forth, followed, on the 15th February, by full-calibre night firing in company with destroyers. Then, on the 16th, *Courageous* slipped and proceeded to sea, taking station astern of the 5th Battle Squadron and with the 3rd Light Cruiser Squadron out on her port bow. By now her paravanes were being streamed and she was zig-zagging in a rising sea, which was getting up to rough and with a SSE wind increasing to Force 6. Perhaps it was not surprising that her Trident electric log was lost overboard, complete, though her Forbes held, and showed 240 miles steamed by the time that the exercise was complete and *Courageous* snug back in her berth at Scapa Flow.

Next day it was back to training, with the turrets crews at drill and the gunlayers at the Deflection Teacher. On the more basic side of naval life, the Beef Ship *Gourka* came alongside, followed by an oiler. The weather was chill at this time, with generally blue skies and clouds, but occasional squalls and an air temperature of only 35° to 37° F (approx 1.6°C) accompanied with a wind of Force 5 from the NNE making the temperature seem much lower. Scapa must have seemed very desolate indeed. Although not spelt out in this account, Divisions and Prayers (and Captain's inspections) were held regularly, and it would often have been a very cold business indeed to be standing out on the open deck for such ceremonies.

On 1st March, having exercised Action Stations the day before, *Courageous* proceeded from Scapa Flow to Rosyth, taking up a 1-point zig-zag, at 19 knots, accompanied by destroyers and having the TBD *Maynard* in close company on her port bow. At 1728 a torpedo was reported by the lookouts as crossing the bow from port to starboard, whereupon *Courageous* immediately increased to full ahead, the destroyers taking station astern. Clearly, German submarines were still active and prepared to take a shot whenever chance offered. [*For their part, the destroyers were gradually 'getting teeth' to deal with enemy submarines. Hydrophones were in use for underwater detection of submarines, and the latest depth-charge, the so-called 'Type D' with its hydrostatic firing pistol, was a distinct improvement over earlier efforts at grenades, etc. Special chutes and hydraulic releasing gear were being constructed and fitted to destroyers. The latest throwers were capable of projecting the Type D charges 40 yards out from the ship's side, and thus to create a 'spread' when allied with the charges dropped directly astern. (Surely over-optimistically, the destructive effect of a Type D charge was reckoned to extend 70 yards from the point of detonation. Electrical artificers were being specially trained in England for this new form of warfare. Already, the need to strongly secure all charges against the risk of their breaking adrift in heavy weather and then hazarding friendly vessels (including one's own) as they detonated on reaching their pre-set depth, had become very evident. (See ADM 137/4173 at TNA.) Thinking minds were also realising the need to set depth-charges to 'safe' should the ship on which they were carried be foundering, leaving men, boats and lifebuoys, etc., at great risk in the water nearby should the depth-charges detonate.*]

Again, there would have been a sigh of relief when *Courageous* and her escorts arrived safely at Rosyth on the 2nd March after a voyage of 302 miles. *Courageous* oiled almost at once, taking in 2,352 tons. Brief afternoon runs ashore were given, alternately, to her red, white and blue watches at this time, and her Marines were landed for a lung-clearing route march. Mr BRADLEY, Gunner, who had been discharged to hospital early in February, rejoined the ship on the 5th March and, that same day, *Courageous* received an aeroplane platform. Her carpenters would have been busy in the next days in rigging the aeroplane platform and securing the aircraft upon it, ready to be flown off. The advantage of mounting the framework on the turret was that the turret could be rotated over a wide arc, giving a good prospect that the aeroplane could be 'turned into the wind' for takeoff, with the ship not necessarily having to steam directly into that wind. Indeed, even when the ship was moored, if there was a good wind blowing, take off was often possible with a light aircraft.

Author's collection. A postcard by an anonymous printer, probably issued circa 1917.

A Sopwith 'Pup' takes off from a wooden staging fitted above a gun-turret. The ship shown here is HMS *Barham*, but the scene is very representative of the situation which was now evolving aboard HMS *Courageous*. As we shall see, the heroic men who flew these machines risked their lives every time they attempted a take-off like this.

In the meantime, it was back to some seamanship training for the company, as they exercised 'Collision Stations' and 'Prepare to Tow Forward'. They also oiled some of the wire hawsers and painted ship. The 2nd Battleship Squadron and the 3rd LCS both proceeded out from Rosyth at this time. On the 11th March it was the turn of *Courageous* to head out to sea, for a short exercise with the 1st and 6th LCS in company, before returning to Rosyth. There she exercised her searchlight and anti-aircraft gun crews, whilst the oiler *Sea Nymph* came alongside. On the 14th, some restricted afternoon leave was granted and football parties were allowed ashore, whilst the turret crews were getting in ammunition.

Further exercises were conducted next day - steering breakdown, gunnery, and torpedo - together with seamanship training classes - before they put to sea on the 16th March, with the cruiser *Penelope* and the 1st LCS in company, passing the Oxcars Gate and commencing a one-point zig-zag before altering course to join with the battlecruiser *Lion*. At 1250 they went to Action Stations for 2½ hours, before reducing to Cruising Stations. The air temperature was a modest 40°F (4.5°C) but the sea was only smooth to slight and the ship would have been cruising easily with the 1st LCS now following astern of them. However, the calm was deceptive, for, next morning, shortly after passing a

Dutch topsail schooner, a submarine periscope was spotted and reported by the cruiser *Penelope*, and the whole squadron increased to full speed with a considerable alteration of course. At 1445 *Courageous* took station five cables ahead of *Lion*, before, at 1704, *Lion* with the 1st BCS and *Penelope* in company, proceeded north-westwards to Scapa Flow. *Courageous*, with the 1st LCS in company, made her way eastwards to Rosyth, running through a patch of fog at 1910, then, in the darkness at 0405 hearing the May Island fog signal, passing the Black Rock lighthouse at 0651, going through the security of the Oxcars Gate at 0716 and stopping engines at 0719 after a run of 928 miles. Meantime, the 1st LCS continued up-harbour to their anchorage.

Author's collection. A postcard by an anonymous publisher. Photo ref H124A by Cribb of Southsea. Issue date c.1914.

The 1st Battlecruiser Squadron under Vice Admiral Sir David BEATTY, led by his flagship HMS *Lion*, and photographed just before the War. This scene is evocative of what Alf would have seen on the 16th March 1918. However, post-Jutland, BEATTY had become a full Admiral and was now in overall command of the Grand Fleet. The 1st BCS was now commanded by Admiral PACKENHAM. Those ships which had survived Jutland would have had certain modifications since 1916. Moreover, they were probably painted in camouflage colours designed to confuse enemy gunners and torpedo-men, and some ships might have had kite-balloons aloft and aircraft standing on platforms fixed to the roofs of gun-turrets.

Courageous immediately oiled, taking in 1,975 tons. She also discharged Sub-Lt MOORE of the RNAS to the Balloon Station at North Queensferry. One assumes that he was a pilot for the aircraft which had been taken aboard early in March. Whether this aircraft had yet flown off from its wooden platform, and, whether, if so, Sub-Lt MOORE had been in it, remains a matter of conjecture. Since the aircraft were primarily intended to attack any zeppelins scouting British ship movements, and no zeppelins had been sighted, it may well be that the aircraft had not yet been launched.

Be that as it may, on 2nd April, in the early-morning dark at 0436, *Courageous* slipped and proceeded under the signal lights of the huge railway bridge over the Forth, before passing through the Oxcars Gate, and sending her hands to day cruising stations at 0715. At 0930, 'General Quarters' was exercised whilst the 6th LCS took station four cables ahead of *Courageous* and the 5,400-ton minelayer *Princes Margaret* (a converted liner), which was evidently in company. By midday they were at 56° 10' N, 0° 4' E, not far from the 'Devil's Hole' in the North Sea, about 120 miles to the east of the Firth of Forth, and still heading east. At 0815 a horned mine was sighted on the port bow, the ship promptly altering course to avoid it and starting to zig-zag (presumably as a precautionary measure lest a submarine be releasing mines in her path and possibly be trying to get into position to fire a torpedo). Thirteen minutes later a spar buoy with a white top was sighted on the starboard beam, at 1000 yds, and at 2115, night having closed in, the North Dogger Bank light was sighted on a bearing of 129°. Three vessels bearing lights were passed at 2330 and the 6th LCS now changed their position, taking station astern during the night. At dawn the ships were heading for home, zig-zagging at times. *Courageous* sighted another mine at 0626 and again commencing to zig-zag as a precautionary measure. At 1500 the *Princess Margaret* (presumably having sowed her mines overnight) and the attendant destroyers took station astern. The sea was smooth but the wind was veering fitfully and erratically at Force 2 in the chill air temperature of 40° F. Some 525 miles had been covered by the time they returned to Rosyth, and they oiled almost immediately, taking in 2,290 tons and then topping up further next day.

On Saturday 6th April they received a kite balloon aboard and then proceeded for 15" sub-calibre and 4" and 3-pdr full-calibre firing exercises, together with range-keeping exercises. This was clearly to get everybody on to 'top form'. At 1513 on Monday the 8th April they again proceeded, this time with destroyers astern, with the 1st LCS on their starboard beam and the 1st BCS about 11 cables astern. Next morning they sighted the 5th Battle Squadron.

Just after noon, the lookouts on *Courageous* sighted a mine. By this time the force were at 56° 54' N 5° 44' E, well across the North Sea and only about 110 miles from the Danish Coast. The hands went to Action Stations at 1230, and they then began to run in and out of patches of fog, sighting the British submarine J5 (which was providing 'cover' for the surface forces) during one intervening clear period. Next morning they again sighted this British submarine J5,[163] then, at 1115, they sighted a horned mine, and another mine 5 minutes later and yet another 17 minutes later. Then (*Courageous* having taken station at 258° from *Lion*, at a distance of 4 miles), their escorting destroyer *Cassandra* reported yet another mine in her sight. Seemingly, a minelaying enemy submarine was 'having a go'. By the morning of the 11th April they were well into their return leg, and, at 1205 they sighted St Abbs Head, seeing May Island right ahead at 1225 and entering harbour soon thereafter after a voyage of 874 nautical miles.

They promptly oiled again, with 1,960 tons, turned and proceeded out to sea once again at 2221. At midday on the 12th they sighted the airship C1A on the starboard beam, and then sighted their sister-ship *Glorious*, which took station on them, as the two ships zig-zagged back to Rosyth. This time *Courageous* took aboard 2,500 tons of oil, filling her bunkers from the RFA *Burma*. Next day, at 1105, they were off on yet another sweep, again heading east but with a slightly more northerly component. On the 14th April, their escorting destroyers and the 1st LCS were astern, with all the ships zig-zagging. The hands went to Action Stations at 1335, reducing at 1530 to Cruising Stations. At 1920 they sighted the coast of Norway, bearing 16°. At noon on the 15th they were at 57° 12' N, 7° 29' E, closing the hostile waters of the Skaggerak between

---

[163] J5 survived the war and was presented to the Australian Navy late in 1918.

Denmark and Norway, at which tense moment both navigational gyros suddenly chose to fail!

Author's collection. A postcard by Gale & Polden, c.1914

HMS *Iron Duke* leads a Squadron of British 'Super-Dreadnought' Battleships. At the time this pre-war photograph was taken, *Iron Duke* was the Flagship of Admiral Sir John JELLICOE. Now, on 8th April 1918, as part of the 1st BS, she is the Flagship of Admiral MADDEN. Alf might well have seen this heavily-armoured battle-wagon and her consorts providing cover for the provocative movements of the less well-armoured ships, such as *Courageous*, as the Fleet 'trailed its coat', trying in vain to 'entice the Germans out for decisive combat'.

As if to confirm the seriousness of their position, the coast of Norway was sighted on a bearing of 34½° just over a half-hour later. However, there was no apparent reaction from the enemy, and the British ships commenced their return voyage, passing BE mines at 1735, 1915 and 1950. At 0900 on the 16th they took station astern of the 1st BCS, and by 1042 they were back in their F9 berth at Rosyth, in 13 fathoms and with 6 shackles on each anchor. They had run 928 miles - and promptly refuelled with 2,034 tons. [The figures in the above paragraph would suggest the considerable oil consumption of 2.2 tons per mile under wartime conditions.]

On the 17th April the hands were 'rigging a stay' for an aeroplane, and a Sopwith *'Camel'* was subsequently taken aboard. Next day, they proceeded to sea for 15" and 4" sub-calibre firing practice - and the aeroplane successfully took off from 'Y' turret.

The ship was a hive of activity on the 19th, with the extra 4" gun crews at drill, the 15" and 4" Sight Testers at drill, a 4" Director Test in progress, the 4" Control Officers at the Spotting Table, the 4" Gunlayers and Trainers at exercise, Training Classes at instruction, and, on the maintenance side, painting in progress. Moreover, Divisions had been held at 0925!

Having ammunitioned from a lighter on the Saturday (at which time the Reverend ALLEN RN joined from HMS *Superb*), the ship celebrated Holy Communion early the next morning, before taking aboard one *'Camel'* aeroplane (evidently to be mounted on 'Y' Turret), followed, in the evening, by taking aboard another *'Camel'* for the forward turret. To fly one of these aircraft Lt MURRELL RAF joined ship, and to help maintain them, one 'rating RAF' joined ship.

Next day, the 22nd, *Courageous* proceeded 'in company' with other warships, in light airs and a calm sea. At 1205 the cruiser HMS *Caledon* reported a mine in sight, and further mines were sighted at 1209, 1603 and 1943, one at one cable distant, the others at three. Fog developed during the night, increasing the hazard of striking a mine. Sure enough, as dawn broke, and the fog began to disperse, further mines were sighted at 0910 and then at 1000, the ship having commenced to zig-zag at 0930. Divisions were held at that time, followed by exercising Action Stations and then reducing to Cruising Stations. *Courageous* entered Rosyth, but only to refuel, promptly proceeding in company with the 2nd, 3rd and 6th LCS and taking up a zig-zag course. At 0500 the next morning they went to Action Stations with a slight to moderate sea running and a wind from the ENE of Force 4 to 5. Again, a mine was sighted, 5 cables off. By the 26th April, both *Glorious* and *Furious* were in company with *Courageous*, making the first occasion on which the three sisters were at sea together. That morning they re-entered Rosyth, and *Courageous* refuelled, taking in 2,275 tons from the RFA *Unio*. She also received one aeroplane, and one 'left', presumably flying off from a turret to land at an airfield, possibly at Carlinghouse.

The ship was off to sea again, briefly, on the 30th April, at 1750, for a range-keeping exercise with *Glorious*, following which they again proceeded, at 1830 on the 7th May, their attendant destroyers forming an anti-submarine screen. The 8th May found them at 22 knots, and zig-zagging. On the next day, at 0315, heavy gunfire was heard on a bearing of 200° (i.e to the WSW of their position). The cause of this was unknown. They passed a mine 3 cables off at 0648, and another at 1250, which was reported 5 cables off their port beam. By that time they were at 56° 24' N, 2° 35' E, half way across the North Sea, and roughly at the latitude of Rosyth. At 1600 they passed yet another mine. On their return leg they commenced a one-hour 'inclination exercise' with *Glorious*, during which they happened to pass the British submarine K7. [*She was classified as a 'Fleet Submarine', designed for working with the Grand Fleet, but viewed by naval men as being something of an oddity, for she was driven when on the surface by a combination of steam turbine and diesel engine, but by electricity when submerged. Her diving procedure was inevitably complex, albeit that it would often have to be carried out under the pressure of 'emergency dive' conditions. The 'K Boats' were developing an unfortunate reputation, three being lost in the war and one, K13, foundering with all hands, later to be salvaged and recommissioned as K22.*] This particular submarine, K7, would survive the war, but one imagines that the deck officers and ratings on board *Courageous* might well have regarded her with some uneasy fascination. For her part, *Courageous* completed her voyage safely and re-entered harbour at 2332.

More drilling and training, accompanied by very brief runs ashore for recreational parties and 'housekeeping activities', such as slinging clean hammocks and airing bedding, ensued during the next few days. Then, on the 16th May, the Admiral and his staff transferred to *Glorious* for a couple of days, before he re-hoisted his flag in *Courageous* on the 18th May. On 20th May the hands were engaged in rigging gear for a ship's concert, which (judging by a later event) would have been a very welcome diversion. Meantime, their sister ship HMS *Furious* sailed. On the 26th May they proceeded to sea briefly, fired a practice torpedo, flew off an aeroplane from 'A' turret, picked up the torpedo which had been fired, exercised their gunnery, and returned to harbour where they hoisted-in a replacement aeroplane.

Through to the end of the month they drilled their gun-turret and Director crews, put their Acting Gunlayers to practice on the Deflection Teacher, received a kite balloon aboard, let go the ship's sheet anchor and went through the arduous procedure of weighing it by hand, landed their Marines for a field exercise, and so forth. They also checked the ship's draught and trim (25' 7" forward and 25' 9" aft, as compared with 25' 9" forward and 25' 10" aft on 5th May, when she'd had 2,592 tons of fuel aboard.)

The 1st June found *Courageous* at sea, about 150 miles off Heligoland, passing floating mines at 0510, 0628, 0745, and 0936. She was in company with the Battle Cruiser Force, 'looking for trouble' and, sure enough, at 0943 German seaplanes attacked the British ships with bombs. Here was a new experience for Alf and his shipmates. Their High Angle firing practice had not been in vain. Seemingly, however, neither side caused any significant damage to the other. At 10.22 and 1140 they passed more mines, sighting an unidentified submarine (which might have been the source of the mines) between-times. *Courageous* returned to Rosyth in the evening of Sunday the 2nd June, refuelling with 2,738 tons of oil and returning the kite balloon they had been flying.

On 4th June, they received a two-seater aeroplane, and, on 8th June, having proceeded to sea, they successfully flew off aeroplanes from both their forward and after turrets. They then assumed the role of target ship for practice torpedo attacks by the 1st LCS, following which *Glorious* took station astern and the two ships commenced 4" calibration firing before, in their turn, making torpedo attacks on the 1st LCS. They then returned to harbour after a busy day, taking in 2,743 tons of oil and receiving on board two replacement aeroplanes.

Next day, they watched as the 2nd and 7th LCS sailed, followed by the great sight of the Grand Fleet on the move. *Courageous* then shifted her moorings downstream to the D9 buoy, and from this position she sent away her whaler with an emergency party aboard, to discover the whereabouts of a balloon which was reported to have descended on the North Shore.

On the 13th June she exercised in the Firth, flew off her two aircraft when she was abeam of the island of Inchkeith, and proceeded to torpedo and 4" full-calibre firing practice. She was at sea again, briefly, on the 19th, exercising with the 1" aiming rifle and her 3 pdr guns at towed targets, and making two runs of 15" sub-calibre firing. On return that evening, her balloon was hauled down, re-filled with hydrogen, and let up again. On the 25th she again proceeded into the Firth to fly off her forward aeroplane and practice HA gun-firing. Next day, she was again at sea, in moderate weather conditions, when her port and starboard paravane chains both carried away. (It would seem likely that they had 'crossed' under the ship, a problem to which paravanes were sometimes prone.) In consequence, she lost overboard *"one paravane, one lifting hand, two shackles, 56 yards of towing wire and two towing sleeves"* - to say nothing of 90 fathoms of log line and one rotator. Perhaps the latter had become embroiled in the *melée*. Unsurprisingly, her divers would be down on the 29th June, examining her propellers and underwater fittings - but by that time she was in G5 berth at Scapa Flow, having practised with her 1" aiming rifle *en route* the previous day.

On the 1st June she was at sea, exercising in company with *Glorious*, both ships engaging in sub-calibre 15" firing, and practising with the 1" aiming rifle. Next day both ships again put to sea, for torpedo practice one against the other. On the 4th, (having taken the Carley floats off 'A' and 'Y' turrets and removed the aeroplane from 'Y' turret the previous day), *Courageous* yet again went to sea with *Glorious* for further exercises in which a Directing party from HMS *Centurion* came aboard *Courageous*, her forward aeroplane was flown off, and she opened full-calibre fire with her 15" guns. During this time, *Glorious* also attempted to fly off her aft aeroplane, but it '*came to grief*' as the log put it, demonstrating how close the safety margins lay in these 'turret takeoffs'. The RAF pilots who flew them were very brave men, and they sometimes paid for their intrepidity with their lives. One suspects that the pilot 'got away with nothing worse than a shaking' on this occasion, though the log is non-specific on the matter. *Courageous* was still flying a kite balloon, which was transferred to the RFA *Kite* on return to harbour at Scapa Flow, the forward aeroplane being received back on board at much the same time. (Presumably it had landed safely, probably at nearby Houton Air Station.)

Author's collection. An anonymous postcard-sized print, with the inked legend HMS 'Glorious'.

This photograph of HMS *Glorious* shows aircraft perched on wooden flight-decking mounted on her 'A' and 'Y' turrets. This mirrors the arrangements which would have existed aboard HMS Courageous. Both ships evidently bore camouflage paint at this time, designed to break up their outlines and thus to confuse German gunnery spotters.

Courageous again put to sea briefly in the next two days, zig-zagging at times, and having to stop the starboard inner engine for 14 minutes at one time whilst a defect was resolved. They had their kite balloon aloft for all-round observation, but the fourteen minutes may well have been rather nerve-wracking ones as they limped along at slow speed, lest an enemy submarine was being brave enough to close the coast off Scapa Flow. On the 11th and 13th July they were again at sea with *Glorious*, exercising sub-calibre firing with their 15" guns and full-calibre firing with their 4" guns. On the 14th they proceeded to Rosyth, flying off their forward aeroplane *en route*, only to see it have to make an emergency landing on the sea minutes later. (The planes were normally equipped with floatation bags for such emergencies, and one assumes the pilot would have been picked up by an escorting destroyer. The aircraft may well have been recovered too.)

On arrival at Rosyth, the ship was taken in tow by two tugs for berthing, preparatory to going into Dry Dock on the 18th July. The majority of the ship's company, who were about to proceed on long leave (Alf perhaps among them), had been paid on the 16th, and Captain NOBLE left the ship on the 24th. On the 30th July leave was given to the starboard watch of the 'skeleton ship's company' who had remained aboard, so that they could attend the Grand Final of the Fleet Boxing Tournament. Next day, the ship's refit completed, the dry dock commenced to be flooded, and *Courageous* was towed out on the 1st August, to be secured against the west wall of the basin. She was still there when the ship's company returned from their three-week long leave, and they were promptly employed over the next few days in restoring the ship to her active state, by 'painting down aloft', and by embarking ammunition, cordite charges, torpedo warheads and stores of all kinds. As a precautionary measure (perhaps prompted by the *Vanguard* disaster, where, at one time, suspicion had fallen on possible sabotage by dockyard workers), the compartments adjacent to the magazines were thoroughly searched before the ammunition and charges were stowed away. On the 17th *Courageous* received her forward aeroplane aboard, and next day she went to sea briefly, working up for a full speed trial to check that all was well following her refit. Two days later she embarked new paravanes, disembarking her old ones. (It seems probable that the replacements were of an improved type. Bearing in mind the problems which she had been experiencing with the former ones, an improved version would doubtless have been most welcome!) That same day, the RFAs *Teal* and *Griffin* came alongside with meat and vegetables for the ship, and torpedoes were also embarked (their warheads having been taken aboard five days earlier.) Meantime, the 4" Director Testing party were closed up for drill.

On the 22nd *Courageous* received a kite balloon aboard and, at 1431 she proceeded to sea, her hands going to Day Cruising Stations at 1600. *Glorious* and *Furious* took station on her starboard beam, and they commenced to zig-zag at a mean speed of 15½ knots in a wind which was increasing from Force 4 to 5 and up to 6. The sea was getting up and worse was yet to come. The hands went to Night Defence Stations at 2210 and dawn came with the wind at Force 8 and the sea at State 6 (i.e. in naval parlance, 'rough'). By noon they were at 57° 35' N, 3° 11½' E, that is, about 40 miles east of the Devil's Hole and approaching the SW corner of the Great Fisher Bank. At 0140 their kite balloon, gyrating madly on its cable, carried away their starboard wireless aerial. At 0200 it carried away the helm indicator, and at 0205 it carried away the *port* wireless aerial! The 'bullet was at last then bitten' and the balloon was cut adrift before it caused any more mayhem!

It seems that there was great reluctance to sacrifice these balloons, due to the prevailing shortage of balloon fabric. As ADM 12/3727 at TNA makes clear, the balloons were something of a mixed blessing, being liable to go on fire if struck by lightning.[164] They might also burst into flame if accidentally torn, thus allowing gas to escape, perhaps with a spark or ember nearby. Or they might go out of control if their stabilisers, guy-ropes or other fittings became damaged against any part of the ship's superstructure.

---

[164] There was an Admiralty Instruction that the Observers should be landed in thunderstorms. It also detailed the procedure by which the balloon cable should be 'sufficiently earthed' to the 'final lead block to the bare metal' of the ship's deck.

They veered and plunged in high winds, or if the parent-ship went from moderate to high speed, and it was not for nothing that the expression 'kiting about' came into naval parlance for this kind of spectacular behaviour.

Their crews were 'winched up' to altitudes in excess of 1,500 feet with the ship proceeding at perhaps 15 to 20 knots (sometimes more). They were brave men.

It is scarcely surprising to learn that, although not reported in the log this day, it appears that an aeroplane which they were carrying was also damaged by the extreme weather conditions. It is a tribute to the skill of the men who secured it on the turret platform that this 'plane was not swept completely away.

Despite the severe conditions paravane exercises were carried out with the new equipment, and apparently with success. At the end of the day the log recorded losses of an *Aldis Lamp and battery, a Mk II telephone (complete), a crossover cable attachment (complete), with two cable clips, a box spanner and a 278 ton shackle* - all presumably related to the cut away balloon - and a *Patent Log Rotator with 95 fathoms of log line carried away* – but, surprisingly, nothing lost in regard to paravanes.

By 2045, when *Glorious* and *Furious* resumed station astern, the wind had reduced to Force 6 and the sea to State 5 (or officially 'rather rough'). The worst of the storm was over, and *Courageous* re-entered harbour at 0916 on the 24th, promptly re-oiling with 418 tons to make up for the 196 nautical miles she had run (at an average of 2.1 tons per mile). The aircraft which had been damaged was discharged into a lighter and a new aeroplane was embarked in its place. On the next day, a replacement kite balloon was also received on board. (One assumes that the wireless aerials and helm indicator had been replaced whilst the ship was at sea, and immediately the weather had begun to ease.)

On the 28th August they put to sea briefly, with *Glorious* and *Furious* in company for an exercise, and, on their return, immediately prepared for setting out again, topping up their balloon with gas, before leaving harbour. By midday on the 29th they were at 56° 17' N, 0° 12' W, about 90 nautical miles east of the Firth of Forth, heading for the Dogger Bank. At 1813 a mine suddenly came to the surface on the starboard quarter, but they ran through the night with no further alarms. Next morning they passed fleet minesweepers and the submarine E42.[165] They also observed a kite balloon being towed by a light cruiser. At 1351 *Courageous* attempted to fly off her forward aeroplane, but, unfortunately, it immediately crashed on the fo'csle, again demonstrating the acute hazards faced by the airmen. It would seem that the pilot was unfortunately killed, for the ship would put a funeral party ashore on the 3rd September.[166]

One of the escorting destroyers managed to damage the patent log rotator of *Courageous* before the cruiser regained her berth, where she promptly refuelled and took on stores from the RFA *Faun* which came alongside next day. The draught of *Courageous* was re-checked at this time, when she had 2,570 tons of oil aboard, being found to be 25' 9" forward and 25' 10" aft.

On the 2nd September she slipped out into the Firth and carried out 15" sub-calibre firing, practising with the 1" aiming rifle and exercising with sub-calibre 15"

---

[165] E42 would survive the war.

[166] No name or other details of this brave man have been found. One assumes that such details exist only in RAF records.

'concentration' firing in company with *Glorious*.[167]   Both ships also fired (and subsequently found and re-embarked) torpedoes. Next day *Success II* secured alongside, delivering 'Henderson' firing gear. A replacement aeroplane was also embarked from a lighter, and fresh meat was taken aboard from a drifter. A Flight Observer joined the ship, presumably indicating that the new aircraft were becoming sufficiently nimble and powerful to carry two men aloft, despite their highly restrictive take off facilities from the ship.[168]

During the 5th September *Courageous* was again at sea, in the vicinity of the Devil's Hole, heading towards the Dogger Bank, zig-zagging and with the company at Action Stations. Next morning they sighted the 'Fleet Submarine' K6 [169], shortly before an escorting destroyer carried away their patent log, yet again! Perhaps the destroyers were a little *too* keen in dashing around the sterns of their larger consorts. On the return leg of this foray in the North Sea, the company of *Courageous* sighted a 'special destroyer patrol' (HMS *Valkyrie*), re-commenced their zig-zag, and then heard firing from the 1st LCS which was directly ahead of them. They increased to full speed, but no more alarms took place and they re-entered harbour safely on the evening of the 6th. They immediately refuelled, with 410 tons, having run 529 nautical miles.[170]

More training followed, with classes at Lewis Gun instruction, at First Aid, at the Spotting Table, Submarine Lookout drill and so on. On the 13th September a lighter came alongside and embarked the 1st cutter and the 1st whaler, both of which had been damaged. Next day the ship headed out into the Firth for 15" sub-calibre concentration firing and torpedo running exercises, both operations being made in company with *Glorious*. The ship also successfully flew off her after aeroplane. Back in harbour, gas masks were issued, starting with the 4" Magazine and Shell Room crews, the RFA *Maggie Purvis* embarked random samples of 15" and 4" cartridges for the half-yearly tests which had become due, and a lighter secured alongside with their after aeroplane, which had landed safely. Next day, another lighter arrived with a forward aeroplane. On the 16th a snap inspection and test was made of the gas masks which had been issued, and this was followed next day by a test of the flooding arrangements for the Magazines and Shell Rooms.[171]

---

[167] 'Concentration' firing was intended to represent the situation where the whole main gunfire of a squadron was to be directed at (say) just one or two *specified* ships in an enemy formation, rather than (say) each ship taking on her 'opposite number'. The basic intention would be to utterly destroy and *sink* a number of the hostile ships, albeit perhaps only a small number (but such ships thus being totally lost to the enemy), rather than have all or nearly all of the enemy ships return to their base, perhaps nearly all battle-damaged to some degree, but able to be repaired and to thus be able to stand in the line of battle again at a later date.

[168] The purpose of Henderson Firing Gear is unknown to the author. He conjectures that it may have been a means of accelerating the take-off speed of the aircraft, rather like the 'Rocket Assisted Take-Off' (R.A.T.O) system of WW2.

[169] K6 also survived the war.

[170] It should be noted that the German mine-laying cruisers *Bremse* and *Brummer*, each capable of at least 28 knots, had made a foray in October 1917 to successfully attack one of the British Lerwick - Bergen convoys, and the Germans had followed this up by an attack by four large torpedo-boats on another of these convoys in December 1917. There was always the possibility of further attacks of this nature, let alone the constant U-boat menace.

[171] For some reason (almost as a hope against hope in certain quarters) the Admiralty seemed to expect a *Gotterdammerung*-like attack by the Germans as a kind of last, desperate fling, and, who knows, possibly involving the use of gas amongst other 'terror weapons'.

Yet again (on the 20th September), *Courageous* put to sea briefly for sub-calibre 15" firing and drill with the 1" aiming rifle at a towed target, again in company with *Glorious*. Both ships also went out in the gathering darkness for similar firing trials, but this time at a moored target, above which Star Shells were fired for illumination.[172] Next day *Courageous* (and her 'submarine screen of destroyers') proceeded to sea again after she had received on board a kite balloon and two Flight Officers. The ship streamed paravanes and commenced zig-zagging, the 1st LCS and *Furious* by then being in company. During the paravane exercise they sighted a horned mine painted red and a spherical, green-painted mine with a white 'T' painted on it. At midday they were well out into the North Sea, at 58° 52' N, 3°12½' E - say 110 miles off the southern coast of Norway - in a wind of Force 4 rising to 5, and a sea which was becoming 'rather rough', as it increased from State 3 to 4 to 5. No enemy opposition was brought against them and they returned safely to harbour at Rosyth.

Four days later they proceeded to sea with *Glorious* for an exchange of full-calibre 15" firing and with both ships using their 4" guns in practising defence against destroyers which were making dummy attacks on them with torpedoes. *Courageous* oiled on return to Rosyth, taking in 208 tons, bringing her total on board to 2,742 tons. She slipped out again on the 30th September, but only to fly off her after aeroplane.

Much the same pattern of activities continued right through October, over and over again, with 4" full-calibre 'concentration firing' in concert with *Glorious*, and with 15" sub-calibre firing, some of it by night. Sometimes *Courageous* acted as a target ship for torpedo attacks by the 1st LCS, and sometimes she made torpedo attacks in her own right. She flew off her aeroplanes, and frequently she carried a kite balloon.

November, however, brought something of a change, for it was clear that the war was dragging to a close. On 4th November the Japanese Admiral Prince Yorchito Higashi Fushimi and his staff visited the ship for about an hour. Early next morning the wind got up dramatically, from Force 6 to Force 8, with rain squalls, and, at 0345, the 2nd Picket Boat, which had been left alongside, broke loose from the port lower boom.....and sank. At 0410, it was deemed wise for the ship to ease the strain on her anchors and cables by raising steam for slow speed against wind and tide, and to set an anchor watch. Next day, the ship's cutters were employed in sweeping for the sunken Picket Boat, but without success. The weather cut up rough on the 8th and 10th, again leading to steam being raised for slow speed into wind and tide, and to anchor watches being set. Next day was calmer, and divers were sent down early to search for the sunken Picket Boat, but in vain.

However, on this fantastic day came the famous armistice 'of the 11th hour of the 11th day of the 11th month'. The period of greatest danger was past. However, so far as the navy was concerned, hazards from floating mines, from moored mines that had yet to be swept, from unexploded bombs and shells and charges of myriad kinds would continue to pose fatal risks for years to come. [Mines which broke loose from their moorings were supposed to have an automatic safety feature to prevent explosion, but the 'interrupter' sometimes failed to operate, with potentially lethal consequences.] In addition to these potential problems with *matériel*, there was also the question as to whether individual units of the enemy would want to continue to fight, perhaps to the death. And over-riding everything was the question as to whether the armistice would

---

[172] Admiral JELLICOE had held back from committing his ships to a night action at the Battle of Jutland. The new mood in the Navy was to fight by day *or* night, and they were training to do just that.

last, and lead to peace - or whether the war would somehow break out all over again. There was therefore a limit as to how far men could 'stand down' their personal 'mental' defences as yet. Many found the 'cessation of hostilities' to be neither 'fish nor fowl nor good red herring', and almost unbearable. It was unbelievable that they had survived thus far, and too incredible to take on board that the imminent risk of sudden death had now vastly diminished. It was all too much to hope for.....and, especially for those who were a little bit superstitious, simply too dangerous to relax.

So far as immediate life aboard *Courageous* was concerned, well, her divers continued the search for the lost picket boat at intervals during the ensuing three days, but unavailingly. It would seem that the boat had 'planed' as it sank, and had probably ended up a long way out from the ship's position at the time. It seemed best to simply 'cut their losses' and 'give it up as a bad job', even though such loss would undoubtedly lead to a Court of Enquiry being held and perhaps to personal reputations being sullied to some degree.

Author's collection. A postcard in the 'Wellington' series by Gale & Polden, issued c. 1904

Although this photograph dates from about 1904, the equipment was still basically still the same in 1918. These divers had to wear extremely heavy boots and clumsy helmets with only small vision panels. The divers were tethered to hemp lines carrying the hoses which provided the vital, life-sustaining, air, pumped down to them by the ratings turning the wheels on the 'box pump'. The period of time the divers could stay underwater was very limited. Under all these circumstances their prospects of finding the lost picket-boat were small indeed – especially if the boat had 'planed' away from the ship's position as it sank.

On the 20th November at 1130, HMS *Royal Oak*, with HM King George V and the Prince of Wales on board, passed between the lines of warships at Rosyth whilst the hands manned and cheered ship in huge relief. Here, surely, was a real token of the peace to come.

Then, on the 21st, at 0237, *Courageous* slipped, turned and proceeded out of the Firth as one of many ships, with her watch at Night Defence Stations. Everybody on board was tense, and her Captain sent them to Action Stations at 0837. *Courageous* had all her guns loaded well before her company caught a tantalising glimpse of the German Fleet well off on the starboard bow, just before the morning mist closed in again. At that moment - about 0912 - *Courageous* was steering at 087½° at 122 revolutions, heading almost due east into the North Sea at around 10 knots. And she was far from being alone.

Although the author has no memory of 'Alf' ever talking about it, there seems to be no reason to doubt that Alf was aboard *Courageous* on that morning of the 21st November 1918, when virtually the whole of the Grand Fleet was at sea, formed into two long single lines, steaming on parallel courses, and about six miles apart from each other. The weather was rather misty, with a fitful sun having risen ahead of the Fleet. A gentle breeze was blowing from nearly aft, actually from W.S.W. The Fleet was steaming due east, at almost exactly 090°, at ten knots, with such sea as there was coming from nearly aft and causing just a slow gentle corkscrew roll. As on *Courageous*, all the companies on every Allied ship were closed up at action stations, with the gun crews in anti-flash gear. The ships' masthead ensigns were flying.

Courageous was the 9th ship in the port column, being preceded by a squadron of eight cruisers, and followed by her sister-ship *Glorious*. Following *Courageous* and *Glorious* were seventeen battleships in three squadrons, then the battleship HMS *Queen Elizabeth* flying the flag of the C-in-C Admiral BEATTY, followed by five battlecruisers and six cruisers, all in line astern. Six or seven torpedo-boat destroyers flanked the line to port, at intervals, as protection against possible surprise submarine attack. A couple of cruisers flanked the line to starboard.

A hand-written note on the back of this card says, "*5th Battle Squadron headed by Queen Elizabeth March 1918.*" Although the photograph was taken eight months earlier, the image is surely very evocative of the unfolding scene in the North Sea which would have met Alf's eyes on the 21st November 1918.

Much further away over to starboard it was known that a similar long line of cruisers, battleships, battlecruisers and yet more cruisers was steering, though they were generally out of sight due to the rather poor visibility, which was often down to about 5,000 yards. [In fact, all told, there were over seventy ships of the Grand Fleet, not counting the smaller vessels, such as torpedo-boat destroyers. They were supported by five U.S. battleships and one French battleship, all standing in the line.]

At about 0945, suddenly, looming again out of the mist and weak sun ahead, off the starboard bow of *Courageous*, and westbound on the opposite course, exactly on 270°, came the British cruiser *Cardiff*, flying the flag of Rear-Admiral SINCLAIR, and, following her, the German battlecruiser *Seydlitz* in the van of a line of other German warships now emerging into view.[173]   In accordance with the orders of Sir David BEATTY GCB, GCVO, DSO the German ships were meeting the British Grand Fleet at position 56° 11' N, 1° 20' W, well to the north-west of the Dogger Bank, preparatory to being interned in the anchorage of Scapa Flow.

Everybody remained very much on the *qui vive* lest the German ships, heavily outnumbered though they were, should suddenly decide to start a *gotterdammerung* 'death ride' assault on the British ships and their allies. True, they were supposed to have unloaded all their ammunition before sailing, but one could not be too sure. It was a very strange and tense moment in time. There, eighth and ninth in the line of German ships, were the imposing *Kaiser* and the *Kaiserin* with which *Courageous* and *Furious* and other British ships had been in a fire-fight just over a year earlier. All told, there seemed to be twenty-one German ships. Where, the British might have wondered, was the 'new' cruiser *Konigsberg* (of such a memorable name to Alf) which they had hit and severely damaged with a couple of 15" shells in that skirmish? There were no signs of her presence. Was she still in dock, disabled? Men who had been present at the Battle of Jutland back in 1916 began to recognise some of the ships they had fought against.

Even as Alf and his shipmates watched this fantastic sight, they felt the slow heel of *Courageous* as her helm was put over, and she made a 16 point (or 180°) turn to port, continuing round until she had steadied on 270°, exactly reversing her course. *Glorious* had continued briefly on her original course and had made her turn at the same position as had *Courageous,* and was now coming round to follow in the wake of *Courageous.* The cruisers which had been ahead of *Courageous* had made a similar 'follow my leader' turn in succession, and were now coming up astern of *Furious.* Meantime, the battleships which had been astern of *Furious* on the previous course had made similar turns in succession behind the leader of each division. The whole line had done an 'about face', and the ships were now working up speed to steam at 16 knots until they were abreast of the German High Seas Fleet, which was continuing steadily at 10 knots.   In the meantime, what had been the starboard line of the British Fleet, had also made a 180° change in course, and were running parallel to the line of the German ships, far off to port.

The formation 'on the right of the line' had now become six British cruisers preceding five British battlecruisers (led by the *Lion*, in which Admiral BEATTY had flown his flag at the Battle of Jutland), followed by the battleship *Queen Elizabeth* flying

---

[173] According to Ludwig FREIWALD's Book, 'Last Days of the German Fleet', *Cardiff* had a kite balloon aloft, and British aircraft were 'buzzing' the German ships. He says that the total of ships to be surrendered were 10 Dreadnoughts, 6 battlecruisers, 6 light cruisers, 100 submarines and 50 TBDs. The remaining warships left in Germany were to be disarmed. He refers to the dismay in the seaports, looming starvation for the dockyard workers, ruin to the careers of the thousands of POs, warrant-officers and commissioned officers in the Kriegsmarine.......

the flag of Admiral BEATTY this day, and leading nine British battleships, followed by the U.S. squadron of five battleships and yet four more British battleships, then the battlecruisers *Courageous* and *Glorious*, followed by eight cruisers.

The formation on the left of the line was similar, with the battleship *Revenge* flying the flag of Admiral C.B. MADDEN in the equivalent position to Admiral BEATTY. *Furious*, the sister-ship of *Courageous and Glorious,* but mounting a massive 18-inch gun, was 25th in that line. Leading the nine cruisers at the end of the line was the *Birmingham*, which Alf was to get to know much more closely ere long.

Between the two lines was the column of German ships, with five battlecruisers leading, followed by nine battleships, of which the leader, the *Freidrich der Grosse*, flew the flag of Rear-Admiral Von REUTER. They were followed by seven cruisers. Somehow, they all looked deteriorated and careworn, especially when compared with the smartness of the British ships.[174]

Author's collection. A postcard by Valentine & Son Ltd., issued c. 28th November 1918. Postally used 30th November 1918. Image reproduced by courtesy of the University of St Andrews Library.

The German ships proceeding in line to surrender, as seen from a ship of the Royal Navy. The nearest German Dreadnought is of the Nassau Class, with a main armament of twelve 11-inch guns. This is just the sort of view that Alf might have had on the day, albeit that it is from the 'port' column. The writer of the card, posted two days after the event, said: "*Many thanks for your letter and the enclosure from the Grand Fleet*".

It was Von REUTER, then flying his flag in the *Konigsberg*, who had led the German squadron which had engaged the *Courageous, Furious* and other British ships the previous November, and who would have seen and felt the massive shock of two 15" shells hitting his ship. His presence might well have been a talking-point amongst the officers and men of *Courageous* on this strange and momentous day.

---

[174] According to Ludwig FREIWALD's book, 'Last Days of the German Fleet', the German ships had already been stripped of their rangefinders, transmitters and other gunnery instruments. He makes it sound as if they had been 'raped', and thus implies that one or other of the Allies had taken possession of this fine equipment. If true, one just hopes it was by representatives of the RN - but rather fears it was not.)

To the relief of all concerned, everything went well. The German ships duly took up their *'pro tem'* places in the anchorage of Scapa Flow, as instructed. The German ensigns were lowered. The ships were ordered not to raise them again until further notice.

Author's collection. An anonymous postcard, probably of date c.1914.

A former owner of this card wrote on the back, *"Us, looking aft from the fore-bridge."* 'Us' was a Queen Elizabeth-class battleship of 27,500 tons, armed with eight 13.5-inch guns and sixteen 6-inch guns. This may be HMS *Queen Elizabeth* herself – who had become Admiral Sir David BEATTY's flagship at the time of the German surrender. This most unusual view shows how the ship would have looked from on high, with her four tall searchlight towers surrounding the after funnel and, at deck-level, her officers and men looking very small indeed. Four dockyard workers can be seen on board. A picket boat is coming alongside with 'dash and daring'.

[*It should be explained that, soon after the declaration of the Armistice, the German Admiral MUERER had visited the Firth of Forth in the cruiser 'Karlsruhe', to discuss surrender terms. He had been accompanied by delegates of the seamen's 'soviets', but Admiral BEATTY had agreed to see Admiral MUERER and his staff only. A meeting was then held by BEATTY on board his flagship the 'Queen Elizabeth' on 16th November 1918, at Rosyth, at which, with a concise, forthright and 'no nonsense' attitude, he clearly laid down to the German Admiral the terms under which the German ships would be detained. Those terms had been accepted, though the German officers indicated that they might not be in full control of all their ships due to the rebellious and bellicose state of some of the companies. The momentous meeting was immortalised in a painting by Sir John LAVERY, A.R.A.*]

It was this surrender which had now been brought to uneasy fruition. Admiral BEATTY fully deserved the ovation which he received when the companies of each battleship manned and cheered ship as they passed the *Queen Elizabeth* on their way to anchor in the Firth of Forth at the end of this momentous day.

So far as Alf's immediate life was concerned, *Courageous* promptly refuelled with 280 tons of oil, as soon as she returned to Rosyth, late on the 21st November. For reasons which are unclear, Mr R. BRADLEY (Gunner), whom Alf would undoubtedly have known, was discharged to the RFA *China* at that time. [He would rejoin on the 29th, accompanied by Mr F.H. PERT (Gunner). Perhaps they had been making some investigations of the German warships.]

On the 27th, as had been expected, a Court of Enquiry was held into the loss of the aforementioned 2nd Picket Boat during the gale conditions which had prevailed on the 5th November. The outcome does not seem to have been preserved for posterity. Meantime, albeit that the sense of danger to life and limb was receding, matters naval went on much as before the German surrender. Thus, *Courageous* regularly held Divisions and Divine Service, drilled her turret crews, practised 4" full-calibre firing and torpedo firing, flew off her aircraft, practised going to Evening Quarters, paid her company, sent some men off on a few hours leave, oiled, took in provisions, ammunitioned ship, sent recreation parties ashore to play football and worked her main derrick to hoist out and in her boats. She also lost three buoys, six ½-hundreweight iron sinkers and an Admiralty-pattern anchor whilst practising at torpedo-recovery, to say nothing of a boat hook. The torpedo involved was also lost.

This took her up to the 12th December, when the wind increased to Force 5, leading her Captain to set an anchor watch and to raise steam for slow speed. More exercises of her gunners and control groups ensued, before the Court of Enquiry was held into the loss of the torpedo.

There seems to be no hint of it in the log at all, but, at Christmas 1918, a variety performance was mounted by the ship's company. A well-printed copy of the programme survives amongst the author's souvenirs, complete with boar's head crest and motto '*Courageux et Fougueux*' (Courageous and High-Mettled). It is headed '**Coliseum (The *coolest* theatre in the North) HMS "*Courageous*"**', indicating that the ship was stationed at Rosyth at the time. The programme, 'printed on board', is priced at 2d, '*the profits derived from which devoted entirely to the "Courageous" Cot Fund*'. It is full of innuendo and what are obviously 'in-jokes'. However, some of the 'advertising' is understandable enough, such as ['*To the Ladies: Wear the famous 'Seymore' blouses. They are a sure attraction...*'], and, ['*Beds! Accommodation for all. Try our Cable Locker Shakedowns....*'], and, ['*Would you like to learn COOKERY? Practical attempts given daily - Apply Ship's Galley. Come and learn the gentle art of camouflage. Dripping a speciality.[175]*'], and, again, ['*WHY NOT TRAVEL? See the World in Luxury & Comfort? Apply the RN Recruiting Bureau. A recent Testimonial: "Can highly recommend these tours of yours to all who are contemplating suicide!" - HO.]*'[176]

---

[175] Probably also a pun, for 'dripping' is naval slang for what the Army call 'grousing' (i.e. endlessly grumbling about things in a lugubrious and 'semi-therapeutic' manner.)

[176] These initials of 'HO' may be genuine - but are more likely to be a jocular reference to '**H**ostilities **O**nly' ratings.

The programme lists fifteen different acts, including 'The Humming Birds', A Burlesque of a Music Hall Performance', which it says is *the latest screaming absurdity of Messrs Clayton, Weller and Oliver.*' This has a cast of six and five 'turns'. One assumes that the thirty names listed are basically genuine - even the three 'ladies', *Miss Sidnee HIBBARD, Miss Gluie STICKINGS* and *Miss Queenie FLORENTINE.* Clearly, a huge effort had been put in by the lower deck, and one suspects that a rip-roaring and probably almost hysterical time was had by all, probably 'laughing till they cried', and letting off a mighty lot of pent-up steam.

Still under Captain Arthur BROMLEY, *Courageous* carried on into the New Year of 1919. On the 2nd January she prepared to enter the Basin, and from thence she went into Dry Dock. There, her hands ranged her cables for survey and began to paint ship. Momentously, on the 25th January she demobilised and discharged 205 of her ratings, with further discharges to follow to the RNB at Chatham, so that the ship herself was undermanned and 'reduced to complement for the 3rd Fleet'. She discharged her 'demobilised officers' on the 31st, whilst such of her company as were left continued to clean ship, practised at fire stations, completed with coal, (so that there could be a little creature comfort aboard), and worked her boats insofar as that was necessary. In doing so they somehow lost overboard from the picket boat, which was coal-fired, one *'bunker lid'*. This was probably 'a first' in the history of the ship and her company.

On 4th March, *Courageous* 'discharged 50 ratings to leave and to the depot'. It is virtually certain that Alf was one of these men. His war service was over, but he ardently hoped to be able to continue his service career.

For the present, his draft ticket was to *Pembroke*. As per her motto, *Courageous* had certainly 'tested his mettle', and she had slightly extended his record for 'voyaging'.

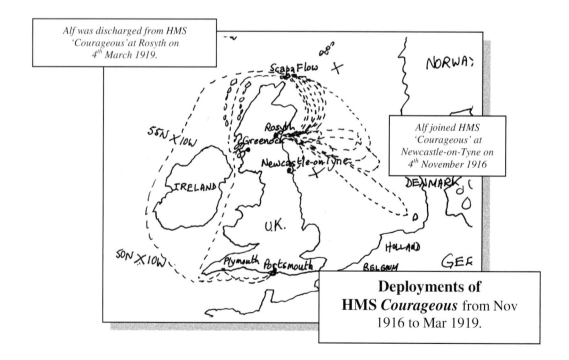

Alf was discharged from HMS 'Courageous' at Rosyth on 4th March 1919.

Alf joined HMS 'Courageous' at Newcastle-on-Tyne on 4th November 1916

Deployments of HMS *Courageous* from Nov 1916 to Mar 1919.

VOYAGES DURING DEPLOYMENT: Pers. RECORD of Alfred William DAVIS RN					
Farthest North	Off Scapa Flow	**59 N 02** E	*F/North (ever)*	Off Scapa Flow	**59 N 02** E
Farthest South	English Channel	**49 N** 04 W	*F/ South (ever)*	Simonstown	**36 S** 18 E
Farthest East	Off Heligoland	55 N **07 E**	*F/East (ever)*	Ras Asir	12 N **51 E**
Farthest West	Off Irish Coast	52 N **11 W**	*F/West (ever)*	*Atlantic Ocean*	50 N **30 W**

During this commission in *Courageous* Alf had travelled farther north that ever before – though, as we shall later find, he hadn't seen anything yet!

Alf would have found *Pembroke* in even more of a ferment this time around. Basically this was because the Navy was reducing itself enormously, so that its 200,000 ratings would be down to (say) 130,000 inside a year and down to perhaps 100,000 by the following year. A lot of the men at *Pembroke* would have been desperate to gain priority in being 'demobilised' and to get back as swiftly as possible to the civilian life from which they had volunteered or been conscripted. On the other hand, many men, like Alf, would have been most anxious to be retained in a Navy which was shrinking around them.

As we shall see, many of the men were in an abnormal state of mind due to the experiences they had undergone and the sheer nervous strain of being at sea under near-constant threat from mine, torpedo or bomb. The numbers of these men passing through *Pembroke* would have been very high and their attitudes vastly 'jumbled'. The strain on the Administration would have been terrific. The quality of the organisation would doubtless have suffered, and Alf probably found it was even more necessary to 'put himself about', even as a Petty Officer, to gain suitable mess accommodation and to have his essential 'survival' needs met. He, too, had been under a lot of continuous strain.

Footnote:

In view of what later transpired, which would have dramatic effects throughout the whole World, it seems well worthwhile to have a quick look at what was going on at Scapa Flow following the 'pro tem' internment of the German Fleet. For good or ill, the British Admiralty had considered it unwise to allow the German sailors ashore at all, and their skeleton companies perforce remained on board, evidently bored out of their wits and with all the emotions and depressions of men who had staked their lives for their country and ended up in bitter defeat. ADM 137/4702 indicates the tight control exercised even in normal movements of men for compassionate postings, ship to ship officer-exchange, sick leave, attendance at courts martial, etc. Every docket, no matter how trivial, had to go to the British C-in-C for a decision.

For the men of any nation cooped up in ships at Scapa Flow, the conditions would have been very far from ideal. For German officers and men in their demoralised state of mind it must have been an appalling situation. It was soon apparent that the state of morale of the men was generally poor, with the ratings of some of the German warships having already formed action committees on Bolshevik lines (sometimes known as 'Soviets') even before they had reached Scapa, and with their officers all-too-often then being virtually powerless to issue direct orders to the men. It was clearly desirable that the fate of the German ships should be agreed as quickly as possible so that these men could be sent back to Germany. In the meantime, British admirals, each with a battle squadron and destroyers, and numbers of smaller naval craft, took it in turns for a month at a time to see that the terms of the armistice were complied with. [As we have seen, 'Courageous' was not directly involved.]

Author's collection. Postcard No.2, published by T. Kent. Postally used at Christmas 1918.

The German Fleet in Scapa Flow on 28th November 1918. The sender of this card wrote to his wife Edith: *"Well, it's all over and it's not so far to Tipperary. ' Woodbines' have gone up to 4d for 50, and bloomers have come down all over Blighty. Flew over the Channel yesterday, very tiring. Must get an aeroplane next time. As Noel Coward would say; "I'll see you again when the springs burst through again." I still love you: Prune."*

However, negotiations amongst the Allied Powers concerning the ultimate share-out and dispersal of the German naval units between the various Allied navies became protracted, and it remained unclear whether or not the Germans would ultimately accept whatever proposals eventually emerged. Indeed fears of a Gotterdammerung 'death ride' by the Germans against the British Fleet were again regarded as a real prospect at one time. The mood of the skeleton companies on the German ships was very hard to gauge. Generally, there seemed to be steadily increasing tension as the months rolled by.

Somehow it did not come as a great surprise when the German Fleet decided to scuttle itself on 21st June 1919, when their surrender and sub-division amongst the Allies was at last about to be declared under the negotiated peace terms following the Armistice. The German Fleet deliberately chose a moment when the majority of the British Fleet which was overseeing them was temporarily at sea. Alf had already been drafted out of 'Courageous' by that time.[177] In fact, he was by then at 'Pembroke', so he was never at risk of having to meet the dangers faced by those British sailors who had the unenviable task of trying to stop the German companies from scuttling their own ships,

---

[177] During the inter-war years, *Courageous*, and her two sisters would all be converted into more or less 'fully flight-decked' aircraft-carriers, which turned out to be vitally-needed in WWII. We shall encounter *Furious* and *Glorious* again later, and also note the early passing of *Courageous* in 1939, which was followed only months later by *Glorious*.

and to attempt to save those ships which the German ship's companies had abandoned and which were already in process of foundering after being scuttled.

The British found it very hard to come to terms with the German mentality which had led Germany's naval men to scuttle their ships. The British Navy and Nation saw it as a dishonourable act. World opinion seemed to more or less agree. Yet, the Germans had played something of a trump card, for they had ensured that there were virtually no German Naval surface ships for the Allies to add to their own navies. Only a limited number of the German ships were subsequently raised from the depths of Scapa Flow. Rather than the navies of the Allies profiting, it was more the case that civilian salvage companies made a profit by realising the scrap value of the steel and other more valuable metals they gained by breaking up the sunken German ships 'in situ' throughout the nineteen-twenties and thirties.

Private Life

Alf may have had some short leaves during his time with *Courageous*. 'Friday Whiles' were too short to risk wartime transport from Rosyth back to Lincoln, for fear of being adrift on the Monday morning and getting a 'Bottle' - or even of being arrested for being absent without leave.[178] So, he must have awaited longer periods of leave, which were rare, and it must be doubtful if he was able to get home much, if at all. One imagines he failed to get to his eldest sister's wedding - even if he knew about it in advance, that is. This wedding took place at Chelsea Register Office in London, by Licence, on 24th February 1918, when Nellie, then aged 21 (but calling herself 19), and a Barmaid by occupation, married Wilfred George PENNEY, aged 21, then a Private in the Royal Naval Air Service, and a Farmer by civil occupation. Wilfred was a nephew of the landlady of the pub where Nellie had found a job.

It is a good question as to whether any other members of the DAVIS Family were present at this 'wartime wedding'. Certainly, none signed as Witnesses of the marriage. One even wonders if Nellie only told her father after the event.

Seemingly, Nellie had at last escaped from the drudgery of being a 'barmaid and little housewife', working for her father in Lincoln, and had headed for the Metropolis. Maybe her move away from home was to do with the liberating aspect of the war, which had improved the status of women in the social structure. As already indicated, she may have set up a sort of agreement with her father well in advance, saying that once Eva was old enough to really help out Rose, she (Nellie) would depart - and would expect him to accept that situation and even to give her a small regular allowance.

Once in London, Nellie had found herself a Barmaid's job, which she well knew how to do, of course, and then also had free time in which to 'be her own person', probably for the first time in her life since her mother had first fallen ill in 1905. One could hardly blame Nellie for wanting a life of her own.

Nellie's husband Wilfred, who was the son of a Farmer, had inherited quite well following his father's recent demise. Nellie had thus met the 'Prince Charming' with a 'substantial nest egg' of whom she had dreamed. Wilf and Nellie would set up their own pub when Wilf was demobbed. Like many people born under the sign of Capricorn, Nellie was an industrious, money-conscious and ambitious worker, and she was determined that she and Wilf would then 'go places' financially.

Thus, if Alf had gone home to Lincoln in the winter of 1917/18, he would have found only Rose, now aged 19, and Eva, now aged 17, still working in their father's pub at Lincoln, with Rose having fallen somewhat into Nellie's former role of 'housewife' and 'big sister', although her character was softer and she did not have Nellie's skill in 'managing' their father. She was, however, a relatively hard worker with quite a shrewd brain by that stage of her life. The two younger girls would continue to stay with their father for some time ahead. By now, 'The Crown' was

---

[178] 'Friday Whiles' were periods of weekend leave which stretched from Friday until early on Monday, as compared with the shorter 'Saturday Whiles', which started a day later and also ended early on Monday. A 'Bottle' was a very severe verbal reprimand indeed: one might almost say a 'tongue lashing', Navy-style.

doing a good trade, and their father could afford to employ some paid staff, including a man to work in the yard.

However, cars were beginning to replace horses and carriages for moneyed people, and the effects were beginning to become noticeable down through 'society' to the middle classes. There were fewer demands for stabling at the pub nowadays. The famous Lincoln Horse Fairs were in steady decline. Perhaps Alfred Wm could see 'the writing on the wall' and was already thinking of yet another career move.

At least all the DAVIS Family had escaped any serious effects from the influenza epidemic which ravaged the country towards the end of the War, causing a great many deaths in the under-nourished population. Had Alf managed to get home, he would probably have found more of an 'acceptance' there, for Rose was of a much less tough nature than Nellie. However, he and his father were STILL not on speaking terms, though there would always remain that deep underlying respect between them.

Author's collection. A postcard by an anonymous publisher, postally used 25th September 1919.

High Street, Lincoln

A familiar scene to Alf, with Brayford Street leading away off to the left by the 'CIGARS' sign. His father's pub, 'The Crown', lies just 150 yards down that road. Perhaps those two straw-hatted chaps are heading for it. There are more bicycles on the streets than in 1910, and a telephone facility is now advertised above the CIGARS sign. No cars are visible: carts are still horse-drawn. The tram service is flourishing. Superficially, little seems to have changed 'on the ground'– but the mood within the population has been totally transformed by the colossal losses in the ranks of its young men.

The war had already greatly changed many attitudes and values. The German naval bombardments of the East Coast and the bombing by Zeppelins and *'Gotha'* bombers, particularly on the East Coast but also on London and elsewhere, had brought war to the British homeland in a way never before seen. And the German U-boat campaign had caused severe deprivation in regard to supplies of various foodstuffs.

The relief felt by the population when the Armistice was declared was enormous. But those returning from the war expecting to find '*A Land Fit for Heroes to Live In*', were doomed, by and large, to be sadly disappointed.

The main feeling which would sweep the country in 1919 and the early 1920s would be enormous sadness at the colossal wastage of young male lives which had occurred, and the barren lives that so many young women would have to endure because their potential spouses had been obliterated. There would simply not be enough men to go round. In its grief the Nation would soon start to erect 'War Memorials' in virtually every town and village, commemorating the millions of young lives so sadly and wastefully lost.

As an escape from these sad thoughts and from the knowledge of the ever-increasing horrors of 'modern warfare', a strange and artificial gaiety – almost a madness - would ensue. A total disbelief that they were still alive when so many of their comrades had died seriously affected many of the returning servicemen, leading to strange behaviours. We shall examine all these matters in a later chapter. We will also see how Jack had been getting on after being demobilised.

For his part, Alf, still adjusting to no longer being 'shot at' by shell or torpedo, was just hoping for a draft to another ship.

CHAPTER SEVEN:

HMS *PEMBROKE* & HMS *GANGES* (1919-21)

Alf was at HMS Pembroke from 5th March 1919 until 21st July 1920, 're-qualifying' during some of this sixteen-month period of time. He was nearing his 24th birthday when he arrived at *Pembroke*, and one understands that in addition to receiving training he was also involved, as a Petty Officer, in giving training to men who were of lesser status and experience to himself - youngsters coming from the influx of men who had entered the Royal Navy just as the war reached its conclusion or in the few months which had now elapsed since the Armistice of November 1918.

Author's collection. A postcard by Ive & Lowe Ltd., Chatham. Postally used in September 1914.

This is a pre-war photograph of Chatham, taken from the Great Lines and looking out over the River Medway. The docks extend from the centre of the view to the far right. Considerable industrialisation is evident to left of centre. By now there was more, for Chatham had been a very busy place throughout the war.

These would have been strangely anti-climatic days, now that the fighting was over except for a few 'grass-fire wars' continuing here and there. A general air of unreality and perhaps even of demotivation probably existed. There might well have been spells where there was little activity, for the Navy was still shrinking overall.

Alf would have found it difficult to 'take this lying down'. 'Fatigue-dodging' and idleness was not his style and, consciously or subconsciously he would still have been carrying considerable mental and emotional tension from his wartime years, which would have heightened his reactions. He must have pined for a posting to a ship, but known this was running against the odds in a climate where 'demobilisation' was rife, the Government was looking to bring in 'economies' of all kinds, and large numbers of ships were already being taken out of service. However, instead of caving-in to any such 'negative' thinking, it seems that Alf rose to the difficult challenge quite brilliantly. The exact circumstances remain unknown, but it is a fact that, when he left *Pembroke*, the men of his mess presented him with an attractive silver cigarette-case inscribed with his '*AWD*' monogram on its face and, on its back, with the legend '*Presented to A.W. Davis by his Messmates of 7L, July 1920, "A Jolly Good Fellow"*'.[179]

The author believes that Alf had stepped in, taken some initiatives to get his mess as near as possible to 'top line', shown great personal example and inspiration, and restored a high measure of smartness, discipline and self-pride into his messmates, when much 'sloth' was evident in various other messes all around and the whole establishment was visibly run down.

Alf had received his second Good Conduct badge in 1919, whilst he was at *Pembroke*, bringing him another penny a day. And he would have had at least three seven-day spells of 'Long Leave' in that time, plus, doubtless, a number of weekend 'Friday Whiles' and 'Saturday Whiles'. These leaves would surely have been very welcome to 'get far away from it all, and to have a total change of scene'.

By the early 1920s, as people sought to expunge their grief, the erection of memorials to the war dead was in full swing in many a town and village, and the pendulum had swung away from war and armaments and strongly towards peace and 'idealism'. Great faith was being placed in the creation of a 'League of Nations'. To a considerable extent, investment in 'National Defence' was going 'out of the window' - far too much so, as would become apparent a decade later. Like the Army and the Air Force, the Navy was about to be drastically 'pruned'.....

In the event, it was to the Training Establishment HMS *Ganges* that Alf was drafted, with effect from 22nd July 1920. In many ways, this would have been a satisfying return for him, and an opportunity to 'lay some of his ghosts', when one remembers that the last time he had been there he had been very much a raw recruit having great difficulty in settling-down to Naval Life. Now, nine eventful years had rolled by and he was a veteran of the war and a well-established Petty Officer, though not yet of 'confirmed' status. His self-confidence had soared. It could be said that 'the boot was now on the other foot' so far as his arrival at *Ganges* would be concerned, perhaps with a vengeance, for, as well as being inspirational, Alf could also be a hard taskmaster if the need arose. In recompense, he also had a strong fellow-feeling and a lurking paternal streak, and his first instinct would have been very much to try to 'buck up' any boy who was unhappy and not pulling his weight.

HMS *Ganges* was still growing as a shore training establishment. Its most prominent feature was still the huge mast, towering over 140 feet above the parade ground. It was a massive structure, made up in three sections, the lower part being of steel, and the whole weighing over forty tons. There were now more buildings than when Alf had been a Boy Seaman there. Where there had been thirty messes, there were now thirty-five. Instead of messing with the boys, as formerly, the instructors had been allocated two messes as their own separate accommodation. The dining halls and drill halls were larger than in 1911, and two more gymnasia had been built.

---

[179] This interesting little heirloom, of which the author had no prior knowledge at all, was very kindly passed on to him in 2004, by his half-brother Richard DAVIS, Alf's son by his second marriage.

Author's collection of inherited family photographs.

Alf as a Petty Officer Instructor at HMS *Ganges*, 1920/21. A CPO. in No.1 dress stands to his right, and a PO (confirmed), in working dress to his left. Their badges show that these men are skilled Gunlayers. The CPO has an impressive array of medal-ribbons, and it would be interesting to know the conflicts in which he was involved during WW1 and perhaps before it. Alf's WW1 medal ribbon can just be distinguished under his silk. Alf is evidently in his element in instilling discipline and instruction into the Boy Seaman, and there seems to be a good understanding between all three of these war-veterans.

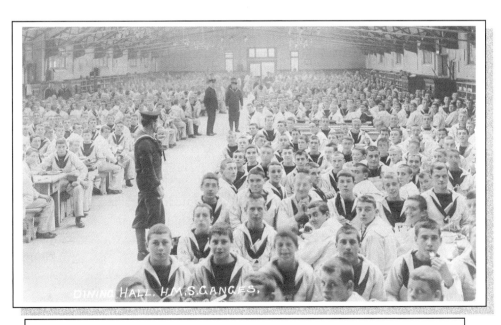

Author's collection. A postcard by H R TUNN & Co. of Ipswich, c.1920.

DINING HALL. H.M.S.GANGES.

One of the new Dining Halls at HMS *Ganges*, evidently catering for about 700 Boys. The gaitered Instructor standing next to the Warrant Officer in the centre of the aisle has every appearance of being Petty Officer Alfred Wm DAVIS.

The former dining hall had become a recreational hall and library. A wooden canteen now existed. An indoor rifle range had been built, to go with the swimming pool and large sports field. On the river estuary there was now a pier with a very well-equipped boat deck which had replaced the old wooden hulk. (See below.) The batteries of guns, most of which had been 'afloat' in *Ganges II* during Alf's spell at the establishment in 1911, were now all well-established ashore.

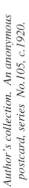

Author's collection. An anonymous postcard, series No.105, c.1920.

The smart new Boat Pier at HMS *Ganges*, replacing the former hulk. The Boy Seamen are wearing their white working dress, the Leading Hand Instructors their blue No.1 rig with gaiters, and the CPO his No.1 Dress.

Alf promptly settled in as a Gunnery Instructor. He enjoyed this role. He liked to teach and he liked to exert discipline, showing the boys the 'right and seamanlike' way to do any task. He stood no nonsense but he was always fair and square. He was fit and alert, smart and neat and he expected the same of the boys in his squad. Where there was a cup to be won, he did his level best to work with the officer in charge of his squad to achieve a win. He loved being in his 'No 1' uniform and he revelled in 'Open Days' when 'The Navy' showed itself off to the local dignitaries and populace.

Being at *Ganges* for what turned out to be almost ten months, meant that he had plenty of opportunities to play sport, and he grasped them with both hands. He particularly enjoyed field hockey. He practised hard at swimming, rowing and shooting, too, constantly trying to improve his performance at all these sports. As a part of being fit he had developed the habit of having a cold shower every morning. It could truly be said that he was 'Spartan' in his lifestyle, working hard and playing hard. Yet, very soon now, his private life would go through a massive 'sea change' which would temper his character considerably and make him a much more 'rounded' personality.

Author's collection. An anonymous postcard, c.1920.

CAPTAIN WIGRAM INSPECTING 3RD DIVISION. H.M.T.E. SHOTLEY. N°1.

The date of this photograph is uncertain, but Alf may well have been one of the Instructors who were present. Captain WIGRAM was a most imposing man with a very strong-looking face. He had a considerable entourage in his wake this day.

As shown by these images, the staff at *Ganges* certainly 'did their bit' to promote the Royal Navy to the citizens and, especially, the youth of Ipswich and its environs.

Author's collection. A postcard by Edith F. Driver, of Ipswich, issued c.1920.

A spectacular display at Ipswich, with much noise, movement, gunsmoke and the rattle of blank rifle-fire. These displays always attracted large crowds of spectators, as evidenced on the right of Edith's photograph. Whether Alf played a part in this particular display is not known.

The staff at *Ganges* had cause to be grateful to Edith F. DRIVER, for she was a good photographer and took numerous studies of the training establishment. Converted into postcards, these advertised the Navy well and doubtless stimulated recruitment. Presumably, the sales to the public also earned her business a good profit.

Author's collection. A postcard by Edith F. Driver of Ipswich, issued 1922.

Boys at Assembly on Empire Day, 24th May 1922. At a rough count, it would appear that at least 1,300 Boys are in training. The strongly-anchored wire stays in the foreground run up to the great mast which is towering high above the parade ground. The banks of the River Orwell form a backdrop. A Thames barge can be seen on the river, heading upstream.

Alf had moved on a year before the above photo of Boys at Assembly was taken, but it does give a good idea of the sheer scale of the training which was in progress.

Author's collection. A Postcard by an anonymous publisher, issued c.1920.

It seems wrong to leave HMS *Ganges* without a peek at its huge mast. Here, Boy Seamen in sports gear are clambering freely all over it. It dominated the skyline over Shotley. The lads who became 'Button Boys', and stood on the cap of the mast during parades, achieved a well-merited level of fame. Did boys ever fall from it? Yes, they did. There was a so-called 'safety net' tightly stretched around the base of the mast about twelve feet above ground level and radiating out for some 25 feet. Did it save the life of any Boy who fell? H'mm, well, sometimes. (See Alf's next term as an Instructor at *Ganges*.)

Author's inherited family collection. A portrait by an anonymous studio c.1921.

Alf as a Petty Officer at HMS *Ganges*, with two Good Conduct badges, WW1 medal ribbon, and Gunlayer badge (just visible) on right arm. He also has the badge of a Coxswain on his left breast. As would be expected, he also wears a *well-faded* silk – the envy of every 'Nozzer'.

He sent this print to his newly-beloved, Olive GREEN, in January 1921. By the time Alf left *Ganges*, in May 1921, his romance had quickly blossomed. (*Alf's younger son, Richard, bore a considerable resemblance to this image of his father, when at the equivalent age of 25.*)

Photograph reproduced by courtesy of the Royal Naval Museum, Portsmouth.

GENERAL VIEW, SHOWING QUARTER DECK, H.M.S. GANGES.

A general view of HMS *Ganges*, pre-dating Alf's service there as an instructor by about five years. The construction of further buildings had taken place by 1920.

It would be interesting to know what kind of reputation Alf earned at *Ganges*, always renowned for its tough discipline, and whether he came to the attention of Captain WIGRAM during his period of office – for we shall encounter Captain WIGRAM again.

NOTE: Picture (i) in Appendix J, page 749, is a group photograph of Gunnery Officers and Staff at HMS 'Ganges', taken in June 1921. Alf appears in it.

In mid-May 1921, Alf had again been posted to HMS *Pembroke*, though this time for just a month, before briefly returning to *Ganges* and, as we shall next see, then being sent on Foreign Service for three years. It was around this time that the infamous and cruel 'Geddes Axe' fell on a large proportion of Naval Officers, many thus being 'retired early' from a profession they loved. This did not bear *directly* on Alf. However, the rapid reduction in the size of the fleet from its large wartime strength, and this clear evidence that the Government was actively looking to reduce its Defence Expenditure, was leading to great unease from the very highest to the very lowest ranks within the Royal Navy.

In 1919, there had at last been some small increases in service pay to make up for the huge shortfall relative to the increased cost of living being experienced by naval wives and families. This had been intended to compensate them, in some degree, in relation to the large increases which had come about in civilian war-workers' take-home pay relative to that of servicemen. However, less than three years later, strong rumours now abounded of pending *cuts* in pay for all ranks.

The author has vague memories that Alf's main concern at this period had been his desire to stay in a life he loved, so that his primary concern was the dwindling number of ships and reducing numbers of posts to be filled at all levels of rank. However, in view of what was happening in Alf's private life, these rumours of pay cuts would soon have also been becoming of increasing significance for him, and, indeed, ere long very disturbing for him too.

As already mentioned, Alf was posted to *Pembroke* for a month, but it is highly probable that he managed to get at least some 'Friday While' weekend leaves, for he was rapidly falling 'head over heels' in love with a girl he had met. Indeed, he probably became something of a 'driven man', for, from *Pembroke*, he was quickly drafted to a steamer about to leave for the South Africa Station, where Alf was to join his next warship and begin those aforementioned three years of Foreign Service. There was a 'sea-change' in his life, and, for the first time ever, he would surely have been desperately torn between love and duty.

However, his steamer, the SS *Cluny Castle*, would proceed in early July 1921, and he would be aboard.

<u>Private Life</u>

By now Alf had entered the Masonic Order, having been initiated into the Essex United Services Lodge at Harwich on 4th November 1920. There is no evidence to suggest that Alf's father or brother were Freemasons, and it seems probable that Alf had allowed himself to be persuaded to join by naval friends he had made at *Ganges* – maybe one of the two Instructors shown in the photograph six pages previously. Alf may well have joined the organisation in the belief that the Masonic movement could increase his 'contacts', 'expand his horizons' and help to further his career.

Sailors were encouraged to dance (even if it had to be with each other!), and, as a part of his 'rounding', Alf had also become good at the social accomplishment of Ballroom Dancing. He was thus present at a ball held in Ipswich, early in 1921. This was attended by some of the loveliest flowers of the local womenfolk. Amongst those women was fine-looking Alice Agnes GREEN, aged 21, who was accompanied by her very attractive and vivacious younger sister, Olive Mabel GREEN, aged 18. They were the daughters of an Ipswich-based House-Painter and Carpenter, called Joseph Walter GREEN and his wife Agnes Sarah GREEN née ENGLISH. The girls had two brothers, aged 19 and five.

Like the vast majority of men of his generation and especially of the half-generation which had followed it, Joseph Walter GREEN (born in 1876) was a veteran-soldier of the Great War. He and his wife Agnes Sarah regarded themselves as 'upper working class' and as 'very respectable'. Their daughters had been well brought up, and were expected to have paid jobs to earn their keep. In her free time, Alice, the older of the two girls was a member of a small amateur string band, in which she played the violin. Her younger sister, Olive, often accompanied Alice to events, each girl 'chaperoning' the other, so to speak, though one suspects that Alice, who could be very sharply outspoken, was the more moderating influence.

On this particular evening at Ipswich, Alice was not there to play her instrument for the entertainment of others, and both girls were free to simply socialise and enjoy themselves. It is more than possible that they had gone along as members of an outing organised by a local Business Association, stemming, perhaps from wartime charity-raising.

The war had introduced many changes in society. Before the war, whilst what were called the 'lower classes' certainly had their 'knees-ups', often in quite riotous fashion, the dances, hunt balls and other events held in the 'middle' and 'upper classes' of society had been very segregated, stately and strictly-controlled affairs, and with only limited mixing of people even when they came from exactly the same social level.

Nowadays, social functions like this dance at Ipswich extended over much wider strata of society, and were much more spontaneous. They expressed the prevailing mood of freedom and, under a surface layer of nonchalance, a sort of near-madness. This arose from the relief and, indeed, disbelief, felt by men coming back alive from the holocaust of the war, in which so many of their pals had died. Many of them still had difficulty in coming to terms with the fact that they, by sheer chance, were still alive. The former soldiers had near-constant reminders of just how close death or grievous wound had been, because shell-shocked men lurched and muttered incomprehensibly among them in the towns and villages, and there were many men minus an arm, with an empty sleeve pinned across their chests, or minus a leg and getting about on crutches. Other men had been blinded and tapped their way along the road with white sticks. There were also a multitude who had been 'gassed', albeit less-than-fatally (and who would forever cough every few moments in a shallow, dry way, and who would suffer with bronchitis in the winter months, right through until their dying day.)[180]

In some ways the naval veterans had gone through a more comfortable war than their soldier equivalents. That is to say (apart from the celebrated 'Naval Division' who had fought as infantry on the Western Front), naval men had not had to endure the fighting in the mud, filth, stench and misery of the trenches - where safety lay in digging deep, but death was waiting if the dugout should happen to be overrun (when a stick-grenade would like as not come hurtling in) or should its entrance be crushed by the explosion of a heavy shell (when they were likely to remain entombed) - and where 'Going Over the Top' meant advancing into a deadly storm of shrapnel and machine-gun bullets. Nor had the war of naval men been like that of their air force fighting equivalents, who had lived reasonably well and safely when on the ground, but who had been kept devoid of parachutes (until the later stages of the war), and thus had the dreadful choice of 'jump or burn' when out-fought in the air, with their aircraft then all too likely to catch fire.[181] However, for the naval men, the strain whenever at sea of constantly waiting for sudden and catastrophic explosion of mine or torpedo, coupled with the knowledge that one shell hit in the wrong spot could lead to immediate immolation of every man-jack aboard, had told deeply on the nerves of many of them. The isolation and boredom of naval bases like Scapa Flow had done nothing to dispel their nervous tension when their ships had returned from the open sea. Many were the hands which still had slight but constant trembling of the fingers and many the faces with slight and involuntary nervous tics and twitches.

As a 'mental defence mechanism', some men of all the three services had managed to develop a fatalistic attitude where 'nothing mattered'. They had come through so much that there was simply nothing more that Life could possibly hurl at them that would be 'unhandleable'. Some saw Death almost as a friend of last-resort, who would finally put an end to all their struggles. They found themselves easy jobs, had 'contacts', sometimes illegal ones, and freewheeled through the rest of

---

[180] There were numbers of men who had been more severely gassed, who were held in hospitals around the country, living on oxygen-support, and most with but short lives left to live out. There were also many men who were too terribly disfigured to be 'let out' into the world, or too badly damaged physically to survive without constant medical attention. There were also numbers of men who were too mentally unstable to be released. However, though individual families certainly knew of these tragic cases, the relatives of these men were often too embarrassed to talk about them and the 'public at large' remained in virtual ignorance of their existence.

[181] Only the men who had been given the extremely dangerous task of manning hydrogen-filled observation balloons over the trenches had been given parachutes right from the very commencement of hostilities. Aircraft pilots had not been given parachutes until relatively late in the war, because the 'authorities' had believed they would abandon their aircraft 'too readily'. Many airmen had therefore been condemned to die a terrible death who could otherwise have 'taken to the silk' – and lived to fight again.

their lives. Such men often had great charm and attractiveness, and would light-heartedly 'play the fool' to entertain others at gatherings and parties. However, the responsibility and emotional ties of matrimony and fatherhood were 'dangerous waters' which they would instinctively avoid. They, too, had been 'crippled' by the war, their emotions 'mortally wounded'.[182]

The amazing feature was that so many men had somehow 'come through' the trauma, and, overtly, had made a reasonable return to civilian life. Even these men, however, were sometimes haunted in their dreams by the most appalling trauma, which would not fade, but sometimes became even sharper-defined as they entered their old age. (To some extent, this would be the case with Joseph GREEN, aforementioned, who certainly suffered at times from 'night horrors'.) Some men talked endlessly of their more traumatic battle-experiences, to the extent of being at risk of boring their listeners, though repeatedly 'talking out' their experiences was probably the very best way of gradually 'laying their ghosts'.[183] However, many men could not talk at all, partly because of the *'devils which talk would then again unleash in their nightmares'*, and partly because their wives and 'civilian' listeners simply could not comprehend the background situation and the trauma of a battlefield, or of an aircraft crashing or of a ship foundering, and it was far too difficult to try to explain the multitudinous factors involved, for one really *'had to have lived it to know it'*. The constant refrain: *"They just don't understand!"*, as so often uttered by veterans (of both World Wars), still lurks in the author's brain.

The trauma remained constantly in the inner *psyches* of these men. In some households, the wives were scared out of their wits in the middle of the night by the screaming, moaning and threshing about of their wildly-dreaming husbands. Some of these men sometimes *'laid violent hands on their wives, as if they were an enemy in hand-to-hand combat'*. The wives of such men had long since started to sleep in separate rooms. This sort of thing was something that was seldom talked about in those days, so its real extent remained unknown.[184] Lucky indeed was the wife whose husband had managed to remain comparatively 'well-adjusted and normal'.

---

[182] As a child of eight or nine the Author came to know one such family friend, always called just 'RIGDEN', and remembers him with great affection. He had become the chauffeur to a wealthy but single lady. RIGDEN treated children like young adults and his *blasé* attitude to 'Authority' was refreshing and inspirational. He was well in with the fishermen who were the covert smugglers on the East Coast.

[183] The Author's phlegmatic 'Uncle Bill', and some of the Old Soldiers the author later worked with in industry, fell into this category. The author listened avidly and somehow enviously to their fantastic and often horrific tales of the Boer War and WW1.

[184] Indeed, such matters would still tend to remain 'hidden under the carpet' when the whole sad cycle was repeated a quarter-century later, with soldiers who had returned home from the trauma of WW2, especially those who had been 'out East', fighting the Japanese and their 'Bushido Culture' of 'pitiless war to the death'. In Europe, some of the men who witnessed the aftermath of the appalling 'air-strike' slaughter and semi-cremation of tens of thousands of German troops, their bodies spread over mile after mile in the 'Falaise Gap' of 1944, never really recovered from the experience. The 'Free Poles' – who, armed with anti-tank guns, were placed on rising ground as a sort of 'cork in the eastern bottle-neck', and thereafter reaped a terrible harvest to prevent themselves being overrun by sheer weight of numbers of frantically retreating Germans flowing back towards the Rhine on both sides of them, with the rising human tide threatening to simply engulf and murder them – also carried dreadful memories. Nor were these the only horrors. And, as for the truly nightmare

The varied emotional and nervous states disguised to greater or lesser degree amongst the men from the 1914-18 war were linked with the certain knowledge amongst young women that their chances of ever finding a male life-partner were enormously reduced as compared with the high probability of doing so which had existed pre-war - indeed hundreds of thousands of young British women had already lost the first great love of their life to bayonet, bullet, bomb, gas, shell, mine or torpedo, and would spend the rest of their lives grieving for their young men. Hundreds of thousands of other young women were doomed never to meet a 'life-partner', for many young men had died innocent of any love-affair at all. Never before had there been a generation where such a high proportion of young women were doomed to live out single lives and never to rear the children for whom they instinctively yearned. Here was another massive facet of the tragic face of war, which facet was, of course, repeated over large parts of the globe, especially in France and Germany.

[*During the war, as young teenagers, Alice and Olive had met many young soldiers who had enjoyed the open hospitality of their parents' home in the garrison town of Ipswich before embarking for France, some never to return to England. Their younger brother, George Neville, born in 1916, had taken his name 'Neville' from one such, a Corporal Neville JENNINGS of the London Regiment.*[185] *Rather than 'let his men down', Corporal JENNINGS had refused point-blank to 'go sick' when his Battalion was ordered to the trenches - and had died of peritonitis in consequence. As already mentioned, Lance Corporal Walter Wilfred GREEN of the Green Howards, a 22 year-old second cousin of Alice and Olive, had been another fine lad lost. Missing, presumed killed on 6th October 1916, almost certainly by shellfire for his unit was not in front-line action that day. His shattered body was never found in the mud of the Somme. His already-widowed mother, her health and spirit broken, and his only sister (who perforce became a full-time carer of the mother), would never recover from the emotional loss, both their lives forever ruined.*]

Nowadays, though *some* sort of initial 'introduction' was still expected, men and women chatted and drank together socially at dances. Many also smoked. Social *mores* were breaking down. Most men had travelled abroad to some extent, even if only under the controlled conditions of military service, and had certainly become 'worldly-wise'. The 'wireless' was coming into its own, expanding world-wide communication. Many people built their own receivers, often starting off with earphones and using a so-called 'cat's whisker' to pick up the emission from a so-called 'crystal', before they moved on to a more sophisticated apparatus of 'valves', 'tuner', 'loudspeaker', storage-battery and wire aerials draped between poles (or an even more sophisticated commercially-built model), around which the family could gather to hear broadcasts.

The coming of 'Prohibition' in America, with its concentrated and illegal drinking bouts in 'speakeasies', and the rather free human 'attitudes' thus created, had also somehow travelled across the Atlantic Ocean 'in mood', to affect the whole behavioural issue. Jazz music had also played a part. A film industry had come into being on both sides of the Atlantic, with much interchange of both films and film-

---

sights of the suffering and filth of the starving victims in the German concentration camps such as Auswich, Belsen and Buchenwald, well, they simply passed beyond belief.

[185] Hence, also, the author's first name.

stars. Gramophones, driven by clockwork mechanisms, played wax-disc recordings of music and song of all kinds. Electrically-powered models called 'radiograms' were coming on the scene.

So far as dances were concerned, whilst semi-formal Waltzes and Polkas still existed, Foxtrots, Quicksteps and exotic 'Latin Dances', such as the Rumba, the Tango and the Paso Doblé, were now on the scene, and the 'Charleston' and the 'Black Bottom' were beginning to come into vogue amongst the 'Smart Set'. People were determined to 'Have Fun', in a way their parents had never known.

We do not know what dances were performed on this particular occasion at Ipswich in 1921, but the meeting between Alf and the two girls was a very fateful and romantic one indeed. Their lives would never be the same again. It seems likely that Alice was a more than a little 'smitten' with Alf. However, it was Olive and Alf who promptly fell in love, the 'chemistry' being overwhelming and the fact that Alf was eight years older than Olive seeming to count for nothing. Although well set-up physically, with strong shoulders and an athletic appearance, Alf was only about 5ft 7ins tall. Olive's 'medium height' of 5ft 4½ins suited him perfectly. Her personality melded wonderfully with his and their romance quickly blossomed.

Author's collection of inherited family photographs.

Olive Mabel GREEN, born on 10th November 1903 at Sudbury, Suffolk. Olive was the second daughter (third child) of Agnes Sarah and Joseph Walter GREEN. Olive was a remarkably attractive girl, with a very engaging and happy personality and many friends. Alf was eight years her senior in age, but they were immediately 'smitten' with each other, and a courtship began. It gave every indication that their personalities were extremely well suited.

All too soon, Alf was posted to *Pembroke* for a month, but it is highly probable that he managed to get at least some 'Friday While' weekend leave to see Olive again. Indeed, he probably became something of a 'driven man', for, from *Pembroke*, he was quickly drafted to a steamer about to leave for the South Africa Station, where, as we have seen, Alf was to join his next warship and begin those three years of Foreign Service.

His steamer, the SS *Cluny Castle*, proceeded in early July. Alf was on board, and he then immediately began a 'courtship correspondence' by letters of increasing tenderness, to which Olive regularly replied, and the couple began to add the exchanging of photographs to the interchanging of 'news' as those three years went on.

Alf's brother Berty John, now generally known as 'Jack', was also in the 'matrimonial stakes', and much further down that track than Alf, for strong feelings had got the better of him and his girl and he would soon be 'hurrying up the aisle' with Kate HOOPER. Kate was the daughter of a Mason's Labourer, her father being by then deceased. The marriage of Berty John and Kate took place at Bristol on 27th August 1921. At that time Alf was far away at sea, and, obviously, he did not attend the wedding. In fact, it seems doubtful if any DAVIS family members at all were present, for the witnesses were two members of the Bride's family.

We do not really know what had been going on with 'Jack'. It is said that he had gained a Mention in Despatches for heroic conduct whilst serving in the Lincolnshire Regiment. However, like many of the front-line soldiers who had endured the terrible conditions and sights of trench warfare, it seems likely that Jack had become very disorientated when he was demobilised, and that he had found his return to civilian life extremely difficult to endure. Perhaps he would never really get over the trauma he had undergone on the Western Front in 1915-18. The loss of that special bond of comradeship which men find in combat may also have been a telling factor in his case.[186]

Seemingly, he had not returned home to Lincoln, but had found employment as a General Mill Worker in Bristol. Perhaps his lack of a formal education had hampered him in finding employment, at a time when hundreds of thousands of demobilised war veterans were desperately seeking jobs, though one would have thought that his status as a Sergeant, with a (believed) Mention in Despatches to his name, should have stood him in good stead. Perhaps he was still slightly 'shell-shocked' and his 'attitude' put off potential employers.

There is a nuance of a rumour within the family that Jack had squandered such money as he had received on his discharge - perhaps in gambling it away. It is possible that he simply could not face going home to Lincoln. Perhaps the thought of having to go on helping his father to run his business was just too much for Jack to endure with the agitated 'mind set' that he had at the time.

Alf's younger sisters, Rose and Eva, were still helping out their father at Lincoln. However, Nellie, now aged 24, was far from that scene, for her young husband Wilf had been demobbed from the Royal Naval Air Service, and the two of them were now running the "Stones Cross" Hotel, at Midsomer Norton in Somerset. Wilf's numerous relations had long been heavily involved in running various Public Houses, so Wilf had plenty of business experience from which to draw helpful tips

---

[186] Jack's Service Number and references to his campaign medals were kindly found for the author by Jack's daughter Margaret and later confirmed by the records at TNA (Kew). However, Jack's main military records appear not to have survived the WW2 bombing which completely destroyed such a high proportion of the War Office documentation which had been stockpiled since WW1. Nor have Jack's records been found amongst the so-called 'Burnt Records', which semi-survived, and are now to be found at TNA (Kew). Nor has it been found possible to locate any reference to his M.I.D in the archives at TNA (Kew). It is known that a framed photograph of fair-haired Jack in his soldier's uniform existed 'in-family' until the 1980s, but that, too, since seems to have disappeared. [It is said that the frame had an interwoven Oak Leaf in token of his M.I.D.] The disappearance of all this data is very disappointing.

and 'back-up' information on the 'financial side' of managing a pub, and, as we have seen, Nellie had years of practical bar-room experience and may well have 'done the books' for her father. She was thus extremely well-versed in the 'grass roots' side. Both husband and wife also had a good knowledge of horses and the sporting life, and knew how to maintain good public relations with their clients generally. The hotel had a Licence, and the couple already looked well set in life. To further the public relations side of the business, Wilf had sought and found a distinguishing 'gimmick' or 'trade mark', for, regardless of the time of year, he always wore a carnation in his button-hole. This was a shrewd move. There was, however, a great sadness at this time, for Nellie lost their first child, a daughter, who died at birth.

Nellie's father, Alfred Wm, did however now become a grandfather, for Jack's wife Kate gave birth to a daughter on 10th November 1921, at Bristol. They called the baby Joyce.

A snapshot from the extensive collection of inherited family photographs held by the author's first cousin Colin GREEN. Picture taken at Felixstowe in mid-1923.

The girl Alf had left behind in England as their courtship developed by the written word. Olive, on left of picture, looks radiant. Her mother 'Nan' is at 'centre-stage' and her sister Alice on the right. Nan, justifiably, looks extremely proud of her two girls. Who could have predicted the twists and turns of fate which would bind their future lives so closely with that of Alf?

Alf and his father were still not on speaking terms. Indeed, Alf was becoming somewhat 'distanced' from his family, in more ways than one. His focus in life was now Olive and he was looking forward to become heavily involved with her parents and relations when he eventually came home on leave - virtually seeking a new family for himself – though he did maintain a level of contact with his three sisters.

CHAPTER EIGHT:

HMS *LOWESTOFT* (1921-24)

Alf joined the light cruiser HMS *Lowestoft* (Captain N. O'NEILL) on 15th July 1921.[187] *Lowestoft* was stationed at Simonstown, South Africa at the time, having just paid off there and been immediately re-commissioned. Only a few of her old company had been retained after the former three-year commission.

The former ship's company seem to have greatly enjoyed themselves over the period of the commission, as is typified by this photograph.

Author's collection. A postcard printed by 'T.I.C', issued in 1921.

Jack ashore, and having a great time in this charabanc, complete with its native driver. (Indeed, the happy 'Lowestofts' may well have found their way into the hearts of the local population during their commission, greatly improving relationships with the South Africans.) Yet the PO who is with them 'amidships' seems rather restrained. Had the lads awarded him that 'informal badge'? Was it a *sincere* gesture or are the experienced 'stripeys' on each side somehow dominating him and making a bit of a fool of him? Had it been Alf who was there at that time, he might have looked more than a little 'sideways' at the caps perched on the backs of certain heads and at the large paper 'rosettes' that some of the ratings are wearing. Fun and merriment can go too far and it is believed that, as a PO, Alf (who had a naturally quick temper) had by now learnt from highly experienced POs and CPOs how to explode in a *controlled* way (but still like a true 'Torpoint Chicken'), if he felt that men were failing to give the King's uniform they wore its proper respect, and neglecting to properly acknowledge a senior rank.

The few members of the former ship's company who had volunteered to stay behind sometimes yarned to the newcomers about the highly memorable night when the men of the old company who were scheduled to go home had been due to embark the

---

[187] Captain Neill O'NEILL was described by the then Sub Lt Roy STRUBEN (see next note) as "*an exceptionally delightful character and a pleasure to serve under.*"

following day in the mail ship for England, and had 'really let their hair down'. That night had witnessed the most extreme revelry after a watch and a part-watch (i.e. about 75% of the company) had been given short leave until midnight.

Sub-Lieutenant Roy STRUBEN was one of the officers who had been retained for the new commission, which retention seems hardly to have been to his 'unmitigated pleasure'.[188] He then had the misfortune to be OOW from 0800 until midnight, faced with the problem that the normal powers of discipline available to him were about to go 'out of the window'. That is to say, short of their having committed murder or some such heinous crime, each and every one of the men with home-postings would be leaving the ship next day almost 'come what may'. In other words, the men knew they had considerably more licence to misbehave themselves than would normally have been tolerated.

In the event, most of the men had come back in very amiable mood, but they were barely manageable and there was much sky-larking going on. S/Lt. STRUBEN soon had the cells *full* and had been continually going the rounds of the messdecks preceded by a bugler blowing ear-splitting 'Stills', with STRUBEN sternly ordering the men to bed - but with only limited success. He must have heaved a sigh of relief when things gradually began to settle down, and an even bigger sigh of relief next day, when the old company left the ship and the new men began to arrive. Though not articulated in his diary, one wonders if he had felt he had been struggling in adversity with the old company, and perhaps not getting all the support he had felt he needed from his immediate superiors in rank. It may well be that he was hoping the new company would prove to be a more tightly-disciplined body of men. If so, petty officers with a mind-set like Alf would have been as 'meat and drink' to S/Lt. STRUBEN.

Author's collection. An anonymous postcard, c.1921.

This card was inscribed: *"Some of the Boys, HMS 'Lowestoft', South Africa, 1919-21."* Although this photo relates to the previous commission, it has been included because it provides a view of the breech and the fitments inside one of *Lowestoft's* 6-inch gun shields. It is thus very relevant to Alf's forthcoming duties.

---

[188] With the kind assistance of the IWM, relevant parts of the MSS diary of Commander Roy STRUBEN (as he later became) have been drawn upon here to supplement the data given in the Logs of HMS *Lowestoft*. (See Appendix A regarding copyright matters.)

Alf was one of a large party which had travelled out from the U.K to reach HMS *Lowestoft* for her re-commissioning. The party had travelled out to Capetown in the intermediate steamer '*Cluny Castle*', of the Union Castle Line. Photographs of what was clearly a very spectacular and memorable 'Crossing the Line' ceremony in the *Cluny Castle* survive in an album which Alf left for posterity. Here are three images from it.

King Neptune comes aboard at the Equator, dressed in all his finery and with a bottle of some concoction clutched in his left hand.

Alf, dressed in a one-piece bathing suit, acts as one of Neptune's acolytes at the traditional lathering, shaving and ducking of the novices.

The happy 'Shellbacks', with 'Old Bill' sitting between King Neptune and the Captain of the SS *Cluny Castle*. Alf's face is framed above the points of Neptune's trident. He is one of Neptune's 'Bears', which accounts for his strange headdress. (Note the well-maned 'Chief Bear' in the front row.). There are many imitation U.S – style 'Keystone Cops' in view. Such 'police-stuntmen' had appeared in a series of hilarious comedy films of the 1920s.

This ceremony would have broken what might otherwise have been a somewhat tedious voyage of very nearly 6,000 nautical miles. Perhaps something of the feeling of the 'day to day' voyage is exhibited in the following photo from Alf's album, which he entitled "Washing Day". It looks as if the ship has a gentle roll on.

As we have said, Alf had acted as one of Neptune's acolytes, and thus been on the 'giving' rather that the 'receiving' end of the traditional physical abuse of the novitiates. It may have been a question that King Neptune was short of 'shellbacks' to carry out the latherings, shavings and duckings, and, under the stress of the moment, it might have been considered that Alf's two wartime crossings of the Equator had at least 'semi-qualified' him as a 'denizen of the deep', albeit that no 'formal' ceremonies had been held by King Neptune in those dangerous days of conflict. [Later, as we shall see, a different 'ocean view' would be taken, whereupon we can be sure that Alf *did* get a lathering and a ducking, for Alf would be given a 'Crossed the Line' certificate no less than *five years later*, that apparently being the first occasion on which he had 'officially' Crossed the Line *aboard a British warship*, in times of peace.]

Let's have a look at the ship that Alf and his party joined at Simonstown, after completing their journey from Capetown to Simonstown by train.

The light cruiser *Lowestoft* was a ship of the *Chatham* Class. Indeed, living up to the name of her class, she had actually been built in the shipyard at Chatham. That was in 1912-14. She was of 5,440 tons displacement. Her designed draught was reportedly only 14 ft 10 ins forward and 16 ft 10 ins aft, but, by 1921, she had a standard draught of 16 ft 6 ins forward and 17 ft 10 ins aft, and a load draught of 17 ft 10 ins forward and 18 ft 3 ins aft. It took 36.9 tons to increase her draught by one inch. At load draught she carried 650 tons of coal. With bunkers full, she carried 1,069 tons of coal, giving her a range of about 4,500 miles at 10 knots. She also carried 230 tons of oil fuel, 85 tons of water for her boilers and 66 tons of water for drinking purposes. Her complement was made up of 546 souls, namely 34 Officers, 152 Seamen and Boys, 31 Marines, 168 Engine-Room establishment and 48 Non-executive Ratings.

Author's collection. A postcard by J. Welch & Sons, Portsmouth. Date of issue probably c.1913.

HMS *Lowestoft. A photograph which was probably taken in the year she was completed.*

A basic comparison of *Lowestoft* as compared with Alf's earlier ships is as follows (See lower lines in the two tables):-

Name of Ship	Type Of Ship	Displace-ment (tons)	Year Completed	1st Year Alf srv'd (diff.)	Comple-ment	Max. Length (feet)	Max. Beam (feet)	Draught (feet)	Shaft Horse-Power	Max. Speed (knots)
Vanguard	Dreadnought	**19,250**	1910	1912 (2)	823	536	**84**	**31.75**	24,500	22
Russell	Pre-Dreadnought	14,000	1903	1912 (9)	718	418	75.5	28	18,220	19
Weymouth	Armour'd Cruiser	5,250	1911	1913 (2)	392	453	48.5	18	22,000	25.5
Courageous	Battle Cruiser	18,600	**1916**	1916 **(0)**	**829**	**786.5**	81	26	**90,000**	**35**
Lowestoft	Armour'd Cruiser	5,440	1913	1920 (7)	546	459.5	49.8	18.25	25,000	25.5

Name of Ship	Guns					Torpedo-Tubes		Armour			
	Main		Secondary		A.A			Deck (ins)	Side (ins)	Turr't (ins)	D.C.T (ins)
	Calibre	Number	Calibre	Number	Capability	Calibre	Number				
Vanguard	12"	**Ten**	4"	Twelve	**2x3"**	18"	Three	1.5 - 3	**10**	**11**	**8 – 11**
Russell	12"	Four	**6"**	Twelve	-	18"	Four	2.5	3-4	6	12
Weymouth	6"	Eight	3"	One	1x3"	**21"**	Two	1-2	Nil	1	2
Courageous	**15"**	Four	4"	**Eighteen**	**2x3"**	**21"**	**Fourteen**	1-3	3	7-9	10
Lowestoft	6"	Nine	3 pdr	Four	1x3"	**21"**	Nine	1-2	3	1	2

As can be seen from the **bold** figures, the battlecruiser *Courageous* remained the newest, longest, most highly-powered and fastest ship in which Alf had served, [and she had carried the largest-calibre guns], though the late battleship *Vanguard* had been the beamiest, the most heavily-armoured overall and had carried *the largest total* of heavy guns. Unsurprisingly, *Vanguard* also had *by far* the deepest draught

Comparison of the data for *Lowestoft* with *Weymouth* shows quite close agreement between these two cruisers, the major differences being that *Lowestoft* was 6½ ft longer, carried nine as opposed to eight 6" guns, a bigger outfit of torpedo-tubes and a larger ship's company. She also had a slightly greater displacement, mainly due to having a protective belt of 3" armour whereas *Weymouth* had no such belt. There was a further difference in that *Weymouth* had only been two years old when Alf joined her (i.e. still almost 'brand-new'), whereas *Lowestoft* was now seven years old. [At nine years of age, *Russell* continued to be the 'oldest' ship in which Alf had ever served. [189] However, it should be noted that the lives of these cruisers and battleships might well be expected to approach to twenty or even thirty years - usually with major refits at intervals, to keep them more or less up-to-date with 'modern developments', as time went on.]

The nine six-inch Mk XI guns were on PVII mountings, two being sited on the foc'sle, four on the upper deck, two in the waist and one on the quarter deck. On the upper deck she also had one three-inch 20 cwt Mk II gun on a high-angle mounting, and, mounted in the waist, four 3-pdr Hotchkiss saluting guns. She also carried two 0.303" Maxim guns, ten 0.303" Lewis guns and one 2-pdr Mk II pom-pom, none of which had fixed mountings. Her offensive armament was completed by two 21" submerged torpedo tubes and seven 21" torpedo tubes on her upper deck. And she had that three-inch armour belt, originally designed as a protection for her magazines against close-range, flat trajectory gunfire, but now become a token of the importance that the threat of the submarine-fired torpedo had generated as WW1 went on.

Effective methods for dealing with submarines had begun to come about, though there was still a long way to go, especially in their detection underwater.[190] Indeed, though not mentioned in the preamble of her details as given in her Logs of this period, *Lowestoft* would come to be fitted with depth-charge rails during this commission, and, as we shall see, she would drop a small number of depth-charges for practice.

Lowestoft was driven by turbines generating 25,000 horsepower (at forced draught) and she could reach a speed of at least 25.5 knots.[191] Her boilers were of the Yarrow small tube type, and made by Fairfields. Her propellers were also produced by Fairfields, being three-bladed and made from manganese-bronze.

She carried a full complement of 11 'ship's boats'. (Namely: 2 x 35 ft Motor Boats (one acting as an Admiral's Barge) , 1 x 34 ft Cutter, 2 x 30 ft Cutters, 2 x 16 ft Dinghies, 2 x 30 ft Gigs, 1 x 27 ft Whaler and 1 x 13 ½ ft Balsa Raft. Note: Prior to the ship becoming a Flagship on 30th April 1921, she had carried only the one Motor Boat, but two 27 ft Whalers instead of just the one.)

---

[189] 'Oldest' in terms of his arrival on board as compared with the date of her first commissioning. [In terms of her year of design and construction, *Russell* was, of course, also the 'oldest' ship in the more usual interpretation of the word 'oldest'. *Courageous* was then still the 'newest' in both interpretations.]

[190] The Admiralty had a research team working hard on this problem. Ultimately, they would come up with 'Asdic' (much later called SONAR) - but that was a very long way ahead at this stage.

[191] 'Forced Draught' implied that the air-locks which were fitted to the Boiler Rooms of a ship would be closed, and the air-supply would then be increased beyond atmospheric pressure by speeding up the fans in the air-intakes. This would intensify the supply of air (i.e. oxygen) to the furnace-flames, thereby improve the heat generated and thus increase the revolutions obtained (as compared with working under standard atmospheric pressure). [N.B. The air-locks would be essential to prevent potentially disastrous and lethal 'blow-back' from the furnaces, should a standard door for the entry/exit of personnel be opened.]

Out on the Africa Station at that time with the light cruiser *Lowestoft* were her sister-ship, *Birmingham*, and her near-sister, *Dublin*. (There were also some sloops and other vessels which were intended for duty up those rivers of Africa which were too shallow to be penetrated by the light cruisers.) Alf would have remembered *Dublin* from working with her during the *Konigsberg* affair – and he would get to know *Birmingham* very well a few years hence – and even one of the sloops in due course...

The ships on the African Station were kept in a state of efficiency by means of the usual drills in harbour and gunnery practice at sea, whilst sailors were brought forward in training classes to qualify for higher ratings.

The Africa Station extended 3,500 miles southwards down the west coast of the Continent, from Accra (on the north coast of the Gulf of Guinea), to the Cape of Good Hope and then round the Cape and northwards up the east coast for a further 2,000 miles and more, up to Beira in Mozambique. That meant nearly 6,000 miles of coastline to be covered, though the cruisers seldom went further north up the West Coast than Lobito in Angola, leaving the sloops and gunboats to show the flag beyond. However, the cruisers also sometimes headed well out north and eastwards into the Atlantic to visit such places as the Island of St Helena, or Sierra Leone, which was on the African mainland well to the north of the Gulf of Guinea. As we shall see, during this commission *Weymouth* would indeed head as far northwards as the Gulf of Guinea.

The ships usually cruised singly, the object being to maintain the spirit of goodwill then prevailing throughout the British Commonwealth and Empire and to establish friendly relationships with the Portuguese Colonies. The ships companies were given warm and overwhelmingly hospitable receptions at all ports of call from little settlements such as the whaling station of Saldahna Bay to the thriving and attractive city of Durban.

The memories which naval men like Lt STRUBEN cherished from those days were '*of blissful peace on a station remote from quarrelling Europe, after the stresses of a long war.*' There were plenty of chances for pleasure and relaxation. The opportunities were very extensive for the officers like Lieutenant Roy STRUBEN and Lieutenant HEAD.[192] However, the opportunities were also wide-ranging for the petty officers, like Alf, and the men. Soccer, hockey, cricket, rugby, athletics meetings, tennis, surfing, picnics and so on, all were available. *Lowestoft* had something of a tradition in rowing events, and there was plenty of practice in boat pulling. In fact, the crew of *Lowestoft's* gig would remain undefeated during Alf's time aboard. There was also some sight-seeing, to places such as the magnificent Rhodes Estate at Groote Schur in South Africa and, at the other extreme of the scale, group visits 'to see how the natives lived', in such places as Songo Town, West Africa.

So far as Alf and his shipmates were concerned, friendships would quickly begin to be struck up with some of the white families round about in Simonstown, Capetown and elsewhere. There was something of a 'flying start' in this, for the previous ship's company had clearly been very go-ahead socially and those men who had been retained for the new commission doubtless acted as 'channels' in fostering and expanding such relationships.

---

[192] Alf's album includes a faded photograph of Lt HEAD and himself out of the ship together. It is probable that Lt HEAD was the Gunnery Officer of *Lowestoft*.

One other feature which should be mentioned was that, thanks to pioneers such as George EASTMAN, the founder of the Eastman Kodak Company in the U.S.A., and his famous slogan "You press the button - and we do the rest!", amateur photography was by now beginning to become relatively simple, reasonably inexpensive and hence popular all around the developed World, and sailors such as Alf were beginning to compile albums which incorporated a mix of 'official', 'civilian professional' and 'amateur snapshot' photographs. Since many of these photographs have survived in the DAVIS family, it is possible to add, post 1920 or so, yet more fragments of the 'jigsaw' to the research which has been conducted on Alf's career - especially as a 'picture is often worth a thousand words'. In this way, images of some of the events and the sight-seeing in which Alf was involved have been preserved for posterity, sometimes having his original descriptive titles, and, as we have just seen in regard to the 'Cluny Castle', they can be juxtaposed into the narrative. Their quality will improve as the years go by.

At the time when Alf joined the ship, in mid-July 1921, it appears that she was undergoing a refit at Simonstown.

HMS *Lowestoft* alongside the Dockyard Wall at Simonstown. Libertymen are going ashore. This photo *may* relate to the time when her 1921 refit was virtually complete. An awning has been rigged to provide some welcome shade. The cruiser looks long, low, lean and exciting.

No ship's log would have been maintained during a refit, and this would go a long way to explain why no log nowadays survives at TNA (Kew) for the months of July and August 1921. However, a log which once covered the latter part of August is surely nowadays missing.

Nevertheless, from the logbooks which *have* survived, we can pick up the account from 11th September onwards, showing the ship having evidently proceeded from Simonstown, and to be now making her way at a steady 10 knots from Port Nolloth to

Walvis Bay, with 366 miles of the voyage already run. That day there was a moderate sea running and a brisk breeze, making the air seem a little cooler than its actual temperature of 60° F. By noon on that day they were at 26° 06' S, 14° 25½' E with their voyage about three-quarters complete.

On the early morning of the 12th September they exercised their seaboat's crew and cleaned ship before they ran into thick fog, leading them to reduce speed to 6 knots from 0750 until 0830, when the fog suddenly cleared. They then dropped a target and carried out a sub-calibre 6" gun practice for 1½ hours before recovering their target and continuing at 12 knots to Walvis Bay, anchoring there in 6 fathoms with 5 shackles on the cable.

Whilst there they coaled (150 tons), a filthy procedure which Alf may well have hoped he would never have to repeat after the relatively 'soft and clean life' he had previously been enjoying aboard the oil-fired *Courageous*. Subsequent to the coaling, the seamen were set to towing the 710-ton gunboat *Thistle*, for practice in the appropriate skills of seamanship. *Thistle* eased the strain on the tow by maintaining revs for about five knots, but this was going to be a mighty long tow, lasting for nearly five days.

HMS *Lowestoft* apparently with a vessel under tow, although the length and strength of the tow-line appears to be inadequate. Possibly the tow-line is still being veered although there are few signs of activity in either ship. Only the fore-part of the smaller ship is visible, but, although she appears to be of the correct proportions, her profile does NOT appear to be that of HMS *Thistle*. The occasion on which this faded photo was taken remains unconfirmed.

On the 14th September 1921, towing *Thistle*, HMS *Lowestoft* proceeded southwards for Capetown, again finding a fogbank which led them to come down to reduced speed for almost three hours, before it was considered safe to revert to 'normal' speed. They put their gun crews to drill on the 16th. Next day, they experienced a condenser leak (whilst they were at the latitude of Port Nolloch, but almost 100 miles out to seaward from it), and had to stop their starboard engine for 2¼ hours, and continue only on the starboard one, until the leak had been repaired by the engine room artificers. At 2000 on the 16th, as night came down, they commenced star shell practice over a moderate sea. On the 17th thick fog came down again, not lifting till 0015 on the 18th, and causing their arrival at Capetown to be made in an early morning mist in which a nasty, oily, heavy swell was getting up from the SSW. It was considered prudent to keep the ship's head pointing towards this swell - otherwise, she rolled most horribly - likewise her tow, still following astern with the catenary of the towing hawser generally slack enough, but sometimes developing some unwanted tension due to the conflicting rolls of the two ships, which certainly kept the quartermasters 'on their toes'. They had run about 708 miles by 0820, when *Lowestoft* again reduced speed, in order to cast off *Thistle* after their marathon voyage. That tow had been requiring constant vigilance both by towing ship and towed ship alike, and casting off at last must have been a great relief as well as a source of pride at a job well done.

Stopping after she had entered Table Bay, *Lowestoft* picked up a Pilot and proceeded into Capetown Docks. Next day, *Lowestoft* landed her small arms companies and her Marines. Meantime, the remainder of the hands coaled ship, from 0815 to 1650, taking in 260 tons. Next morning, coaling resumed, but now using native labour. A further 450 tons was taken aboard from 0715 to 1430. With what must have by then been virtually full bunkers, her draught was rechecked and found to be 18' 3" forward and 18' 0" aft. [As Roy STRUBEN had put it, *'there was the periodical 'Coaling Ship' to restore a little realism to life. And what dusty, broken stuff that Natal coal was - and how choking the hot sun combined with the howling south-east wind!'*[193] At some ports the coaling was done by native stevedores - but at Simonstown, for example, the work had to be done by the officers and men of the ship. As we shall see, they also had to coal ship on a visit they paid to the lonely island of St Helena. Whilst there, Napoleon Bonaparte's tomb would be visited, and Alf would duly keep a snapshot of it.[194]]

Lowestoft was then piloted out of dock and proceeded eastward to Simonstown, streaming her paravanes from 0838 until the order to take them in was given at 1350. However, difficulty in doing so manifested itself, and they had to stop ship at 1402 to clear the starboard paravane, before the task could be completed. At 1442 they again stopped, to embark the King's Harbour Master, before proceeding into harbour at Simonstown.

Their stay there was very short, for at 0930 next morning they again weighed and proceeded, stopping outside the basin to embark the C-in-C, Admiral Sir William GOODENOUGH, before continuing to Mossel Bay. Roy STRUBEN confided to his diary (which, as we have seen, is preserved at the IWM) that Admiral Sir William GOODENOUGH, known as 'Barge', was a 'character', *'strong' certainly, but not 'silent', for he loved to address the ships' companies on any occasion he considered suitable. Standing on the after capstan he would hold forth with great fluency and length, invariably bringing in 'during my forty years at sea' and going on to refer to his father, Captain GOODENOUGH, of whom he would say that he was 'the distinguished Naval*

---

[193] By 1926, when Alf was serving his next commission on the Africa Station, the then C-in-C was arranging that his turbine-powered cruisers were fuelled with higher-grade coal imported from England (despite a shortage due to the Coal Strike back home!), and that the Natal coal, which was indeed poor stuff, was held over for use by his sloops, which had old-fashioned reciprocating engines.

[194] The tomb was empty, the body, dressed in full uniform, having been long transferred to a grand mausoleum at 'Les Invalides' in Paris. There, it is enclosed in a *multiplicity* of coffins within an enormous stone structure in red porphyry. There seems to be little chance of Napolean Bonaparte getting out again.

280

Officer eaten by cannibals in the South Seas' - (*in fact*, said Roy STRUBEN, *massacred with a whole cutter's crew.*)

One suspects therefore that the younger officers always waited for these references to crop up, and risked 'knowing winks and subtle nods' to each other when they duly did! One imagines that some of the wits on the lower deck also risked imitating their Admiral 'below decks' – though with considerable caution.[195]

Author's collection. Inset portrait (by Symonds) in a postcard by J. Beagles & Co., London, c.1918.

Admiral GOODENOUGH, photographed c. 1918, when he held the rank of Commodore. Roy STRUBEN wrote of him: *"He was a great character and loved to address the ship's companies..."*

They arrived at Mossel Bay at 0900 the following morning. Whilst there they shifted berth and somehow managed to lose overboard by accident *one Storeroom Lantern, Pattern 275*. At 1900 the next day there was another accident, which was *potentially* more serious, when their whaler was upset as they came to hoist it in (perhaps through one of the falls failing or being inadvertently let go as the whaler rose towards deck-level, but before the shackles could be slipped on). The wind had been steadily getting up, rising towards Force 5, and it may be that a sudden blast, causing a heavy lurch of the ship, had caught the men by surprise. The log implies that, in consequence, *one case of corned beef and one pair of boots, the private property of one Able Seaman DONNE*, plummeted into the sea never to be seen again. [Whether AB DONNE and other members of the whaler's crew had managed to hang tenaciously on to their lifelines, or whether they had accompanied the corned beef into the 'oggin' is unknown. If any of them had actually dropped into the sea, one assumes that a lifebuoy had been quickly thrown to them and/or that their life-jackets had kept them afloat long enough to be recovered from the deep without any 'song and dance' needing to be made about it.]

The weather conditions continued to worsen. An anchor watch was therefore set at 2200, whilst the wind went on increasing, to reach gale Force 7 by 0100 next morning.

---

[195] Admiral GOODENOUGH was clearly a strong personality who was much respected and warmly regarded by the officers and men on the Africa Station. In 1916, as Commodore GOODENOUGH, he had commanded the 2nd Cruiser Squadron at the world-famous Battle of Jutland, flying his pennant in the cruiser HMS *Southampton*. He had performed with great skill and daring, being the only senior officer in the scouting force who had realised the vital importance of reporting by wireless to the C-in-C of the Grand Fleet, Admiral JELLICOE, to inform him of the complex manoeuvres of the enemy ships in the poor visibility which was prevailing. Seemingly, one reason that others had 'refrained' was that standing orders had been to avoid 'cluttering up' the air waves.

Now, Captain O'NEILL was in hospital at Simonstown at this time and his second-in-command, Commander Roger AKISON, was standing in for him. Perhaps Commander AKISON did not like the feeling of being on a 'lee shore' with the anchor in ground which he may have felt to be of dubious holding characteristics. Be that as it may, in the stormy darkness at 0203 of what had now become the 30th September, *Lowestoft* weighed and proceeded at 6 knots into the wind, exercising her seaboat's crew as she did so. At 1030 she stopped, still off Mossel Bay, and communicated with the shore by signal. By that time the gale was easing. *Lowestoft* then rounded Cape St Blaize, increased from 11 knots to full speed ahead at 1644, and, at 1645 dropped one depth-charge, presumably with the spectacular results to which later generations of the public would become accustomed, as the sea erupted upwards in a great column, to cascade back in a huge surge of foam and sometimes with dead and stunned fish beginning to drift to the surface if a shoal had happened to be in the vicinity. [Sometimes the ship's companies were permitted to harvest such fish, which were perfectly fit to be cooked and eaten, but there is no evidence that any such thing occurred on this particular occasion.]

Lowestoft entered harbour at Simonstown on Saturday 1st October 1921 where, at 0900, she landed a funeral party for the burial of the late Stoker KENNIMUND, aged only 19, who had succumbed to pneumonia at the RNH at the Cape of Good Hope, on 30th September. Meantime, Commander Roger AKISON continued in command. One rather wonders how he was doing, especially as Sub Lt STRUBEN had confided to his diary that Commander AKISON *"was a good man, though he had a tendency to short-circuit his subordinate officers by giving orders directly to the men."* If he was figuratively taking more or less 'the full weight of the ship on his back', he must have been having a very hard time of things as her stand-in Captain.

Surgeon-Commander RICKARD RN now joined the ship (and Surgeon-Commander ADDISON-SCOTT left). Two ratings were discharged to detention but another rejoined. Monday 3rd October was 'Weiner's Day' and the ship 'piped down' at 1045 for this public holiday. Next day, Captain O'NEILL rejoined from hospital and the gun crews were put to drill. The 5th October saw 'business as usual', when, starting at 0900, the tug *St Dogmael* secured astern and the ship was swung for adjustment of her magnetic compasses and also for a Director Test.[196] At 1350 she proceeded into the wide expanse of False Bay for sub-calibre firing followed by making a dummy torpedo attack, and managing to regather both of the torpedoes she'd fired. At 1620 she began to lay out a target for night firing, returning to False Bay very late that evening for sub-calibre night firing practice. On the 7th October she was back there again, for more sub-calibre practice firing, followed by 1" firing at a moored target. She later took her target back on board and returned to Simonstown.

On the 10th she coaled again (412 tons), and next day she returned to False Bay for reduced-charge firing practice. Medical Congress Delegates visited the ship on the 13th, but, next day, it was back to the False Bay firing range again, this time to make a simulated long-range torpedo attack. Then, on the 20th, there was more sub-calibre firing practice before the ship returned to Simonstown. There, on the 24th, they exercised 'Abandon Ship' and 'Out Bower Anchor'. Nor were they yet quite done, for, on the 22nd, they put out to False Bay for full-calibre firing from 0940 to 0953, before heading for Capetown and taking on board a Pilot for the final stage of the journey into the Table Bay

---

[196] *St Dogmael* was a sister of doughty little *St Cyrus*, of which we shall hear more later.

Docks.

On the 24th they were off again. At 0806, as they emerged from their dock, and cast off the tow from their tug, they 'spoke' with the SS *Cluny Castle*, the ship on which Alf and others had sailed out from England to South Africa three months earlier. Six and a half hours later they were securing alongside 'C' Wall at Simonstown. On 27th October they landed their Marines for drill. They also had their divers down in the water at their regular monthly practice. On 2nd November 1921 the Spanish Consul visited Admiralty House, and the ship fired a salute of 7 guns in his honour. On the 4th, an advance party for firing on the rifle range, consisting of 14 ratings in the charge of the aforementioned Sub-Lt STRUBEN, were landed. As is clear from Alf's photo album, this was an open air range which was used for improving the men's skills with small arms. Alf's album shows that there was sometimes also practice with demolition charges at Simonstown.

A clutch of seven midshipmen proceeded on leave at this time, including one by the name of RUCK-KEENE. It is believed that this young man may well have been a relative of another midshipman of that same RUCK-KEENE name, whom Alf would encounter on another cruiser, almost twenty years later.

The ship now entered dry dock. Her 1st Range Party, consisting of 117 ratings in the charge of Lt-Commander BEVAN and Midshipman FORD, then left. At the same time, Lieutenant HOOD and Midshipman BYAS returned from leave. The ship was regularly running a sick-list of about 8 or 9 men at this time, and she had discharged 8 ratings to the hospital on the 7th November. Such discharges, usually of five or six men, were quite regular events when the ship put back into Simonstown after being out at sea on short cruises. Most of the men who were thus discharged would return to the ship after a few days or weeks, but, now and again, a man would succumb to his illness. This had evidently been the case with Stoker KENNIMUND whom, as we have seen, had been buried on the 1st October. Now, on 10th November, the ship was landing another funeral party, this time for the burial of the late AB Hugh TREVIN. She half-masted her colours from 1000 to 1100 as a mark of respect for him.

Next day the ship observed a two-minute silence in honour of the Anniversary of Armistice Day, and, on Saturday the 12th November, the 2nd Range Party (this time of 116 ratings) was landed, the 1st Range Party returning just fifty minutes later, presumably on the return trip by the same ship's boats. Leaves were being given at this time, typically being a mix of 'Saturday Whiles' for one watch (i.e. through to 0745 on the Monday), another watch having only to 0700 on the Sunday, whilst another watch remained on duty. [The Boys would have only until 1900 on the Saturday itself.] The following weekend the watches would 'turn around', in rotation.

Meantime, Alf would have been busy, for it seems that *Lowestoft's* guns were being dismounted and given a complete examination and overhaul. (See overleaf.)

On 19th November 1921, the 3rd Range Party left the ship, and the 2nd Range Party returned. The 1st of two Range Parties made up of the ship's Royal Marines would follow in their turn, a week later, when the 3rd Naval Range Party returned. Thus, everybody was 'having a go' on the range. On the 22nd the Consul General of the Netherlands visited the ship and she was dressed overall on 1st December, which was the birthday of the Queen Mother, H.R.H Queen Alexandra. On 19th December the company watched as the ship's company of the *Dublin*, who had been relieved, marched cheerily out of the Dockyard to Wynberg Camp *en route* for England.

*Snapshots c.1921
from Alf's small
album.*

Lowestoft in the
Selborne Dock at
Simonstown, and
undergoing a
comprehensive gun-
examination as part of
her general refit.

Meantime, *Lowestoft* was re-ammunitioning, getting her boats hoisted back on board from the dockside and being generally cleaned by her company. The dock was flooded, and she was warped out on the 21st. That same day, she assembled a Guard of Honour and set them to drill. They were landed at 1215 on the 22nd to take part in the ceremonies at Capetown arising from the departure of Major-General CARTER.[197]

The ship was inactive over the immediate Christmas period, but on Thursday the 29th she slipped at 0800 and, with the aid of the tug *St Dogmael*, which had secured astern, swung ship for a Director Test. Casting off *St Dogmael* at 1056, she then proceeded the sixty miles to Capetown, embarking a Pilot before continuing into the Docks. There, she coaled, using native labour, who put 747 tons into her bunkers. [Her draught was subsequently checked as being 18' 5" f'w'd and 18' 3" aft.] Meantime, she landed her Small Arms Parties for a route march in the pleasant conditions which generally prevailed at the Cape. Apart from one very heavy shower of rain, followed by a stiff breeze for a couple of days now and again, the wind and sea had been calm and the temperature moderate for weeks. At that time the sick list was very low indeed.

---

[197] The author assumes he was the General Officer Commanding (Cape Peninsular), returning home after completing his appointment.

There was a minor flurry of excitement on New Years Day, when, perhaps as a token of the general absence of rain, a bush fire was observed to have broken out ashore on the hilly 'Lions Rump', and a Fire Party were landed to extinguish it, returning two hours later, duty done. Next day, at 1750, the C-in-C and his staff embarked, and, at 1800, the ship proceeded for St Helena, way out in the Atlantic and some 1,700 nautical miles to the nor'-nor'-west of the Cape, as the crow flies. Although not spelt out in the log, it seems that *Dublin* (now re-commissioned with a new company) and the sloop *Wallflower* were in company. *Lowestoft* (and presumably the rest of the little squadron) arrived at St Helena on the 8th, *Lowestoft* having had condenser trouble twice on the voyage, necessitating her starboard engine being stopped for short periods whilst she went ahead on one engine only. This engine was increased to its full power during the interim, so that a speed of about 12 knots could be maintained by the squadron.

On arrival, the C-in-C and the Captain went ashore to pay a visit on His Excellency the Governor, who responded with a visit to the ship, the usual courtesies being made and salutes being fired. On a more functional aspect, the ship coaled, her company taking in 350 tons and losing overboard a shovel and four coal sacks.

A snapshot from Alf's small album.

A faded snapshot of one of the Working Parties 'coaling ship' at St Helena in 1922. Alf is sitting behind the right arm of the foremost man

The ship stayed only until the 12th, departing eastwards across a slight southerly swell for Walvis Bay on the west coast of mainland Africa. One assumes this southerly swell would have led the ship to roll slowly, her motion being slightly compounded in mid-voyage by a south-easterly wind of Force 5 and waves graded as 'slight'. The weather was halcyon, with blue sky and some white clouds.

The gun's crews were put to drill on the 13th January 1922, as the ship proceeded, and the Lewis gunners were at practice on the 16th. The formal side was not forgotten, with Divisions and Quarters being held in the usual manner. In broad terms, the daily 'fixes' for the 15th to the 17th showed the latitude gently 'rising' from 19° to 21° to 22° S, and the longitude rising from 6° to 10° to 14° E, confirming that they were heading south of east. The haven of the semi-redundant whaling station of Walvis Bay hove in sight on the 18th, and they came to in 5 fathoms with their port anchor veered to 5 shackles, taking one of their triangulation bearings on the chimney of the whaling station itself and another on the chimney of the main settlement building. The temperature was a pleasant 65° F. They had run 1,259 nautical miles and they coaled immediately, taking in 740 tons.

During the next week (though not shown in the log) they put a large landing party ashore at Walvis Bay - where they were severely tormented by sand flies.

Two snapshots from Alf's album.

(Above) The landing party at Walvis Bay, being severely tormented by sand flies, but holding their ranks.
(Left) A 'boating trip' at Walvis Bay, with at least four boats linked together and under tow.

On various days, they put the Boys to sailing in the protected water of the Bay, they drilled their torpedo and torpedo control parties, and they exercised 'Away All Boats Under Oars and Sail'.

They also held a party aboard for the local children and they fired a 13 gun salute as His Honour the Administrator of the South West Protectorate left the ship after a visit on the C-in-C.

From Walvis Bay they proceeded to Great Fish Bay, some 400 miles to the northward, putting their platoons to rifle drill and the remaining hands to physical drill *en route*. The approach to Great Fish Bay was slightly hazardous and the ship sounded her way in for some hours, sighting breakers on her starboard bow as she closed the coastline. Despite this need for alertness in her navigation, shipboard life continued as normal, with

General Quarters being sounded off at 1000 and the magazine flooding arrangements being checked and found satisfactory at 1030. They came to anchor at 1230 on the 27th. Two days later they proceeded to Walvis Bay, against a south-easterly wind which had got up to Force 6 to 7 and a south-westerly swell with a 'rough' and at times 'high' sea running. This must have been invigorating, with the ship pitching and sending sheets of spray flying back over and over again from her bows. By the 31st the swell had decreased, and, scarcely stopping at Walvis Bay they continued on southwards towards Saldanha Bay.

The swell got up again during the 1st February. Their patent log jammed, and they hauled it in briefly, at 0630, to clear it. However, it carried away completely at 1930, and 70 fathoms of their log line were lost, together with the rotator and governor. Next day, the swell had reduced and the wind was only at Force 2, so having to stop the port engine for a while to deal with the re-appearance of its condenser trouble, and hence running only on the starboard engine for nearly two hours before normal running was restored, was not a problem. And all went well on the 3rd, as they began the approach to Saldanha Bay and the C-in-C began to manoeuvre the squadron, calling in *Dublin* and *Wallflower* to take station astern.

All the ship's boats were put to sailing at Saldanha Bay on the 6th, probably with more than one upset, for no less than three oars, five crutches, two boathooks, one mast and one rudder yoke were reported *'lost overboard'*. The boats were away again next day, *'for inspection by the C-in-C'*. They were away again the day after, for further sailing. On the 8th, the ship's Small Arms Companies and her marines were landed, again for inspection by the C-in-C. One assumes that all these activities were being carried out in conjunction with the other ships in the squadron. Certainly, *Dublin* and *Wallflower* were initially in company when *Lowestoft* proceeded at 0510 on the 9th, heading back to Capetown, though *Wallflower* parted company at 0633 to proceed independently to Simonstown. *Lowestoft* was in dock at Capetown and coaling by 0750 on the 10th February, taking in 700 tons and not completing her task until 1810, when a weary company would have set about cleaning the ship, themselves and, subsequently, their clothes.

Saturday, the 11th, found them proceeding the 60 miles to Simonstown where the tug *St Dogmael* secured astern so that a Director Test could be carried out. The Dutch Consul visited Admiralty House on the 15th, a salute of 7 guns being fired as he left, and the formalities continued on the 17th February, when the ship landed a well-drilled Guard of Honour to attend the Opening of Parliament. The necks of the Marines would not have looked too red, as conditions were good, with a moderate breeze from the nor'-nor'-west, blue skies, the odd fleecy cloud and an air temperature of 65°F.

As evidenced by his photo album. Alf had already made a number of friends amongst the civilian population, apparently mainly in Capetown. It is difficult to know who 'fitted in where', but beach parties, picnics and spontaneous family games of cricket figured strongly. This photograph of women and children in a voortreker's cart, drawn by four horses, and with the menfolk standing alongside, ready to head homewards after a day out, seems to typify the general scene.

287

A faded snapshot from Alf's album.

Homeward Bound in Dappled Shade. Alf, in his whites, and wearing a white sweater, stands on the extreme left of the group. Another PO, similarly dressed, but capless and holding a slouch hat, stands on Alf's left. The other two men are evidently permanent residents of South Africa. The family dog looks out over their heads.

On the 21st the ship was at sub-calibre firing in False Bay, for which the company laid out a Pattern VI Target. She had her divers down later, tackling the task of clearing her starboard propeller. Working in spells, this took them until noon next day to complete. Somewhere along the way, there was probably another minor boating accident, for two barricoes, one anchor buoy and one megaphone were reported 'lost overboard'. Meantime, her hands were busily preparing to 'illuminate ship' that evening.

On the 23rd the ship was out in False Bay again, for more sub-calibre daylight firing, returning in the evening for night sub-calibre practice, which she completed at 2156, before returning to harbour. Predictably, she was out again next morning, this time for ten minutes of full-calibre firing at a target towed by *Dublin*, following which, that afternoon, she towed the target for *Dublin* to practice firing upon. The breeze was stiffening as the day wore on, and they hauled in the target to 'short span' for the return to their moorings at Simonstown. However, the wind increased over the next two days, coming from the south-east and rising to gale Force 10, and, as a precaution against the target possibly pounding against the ship's side, they veered the target further astern and set an anchor watch. Along the way they lost overboard one 11" Clump Block.

Having reduced a little, the wind returned with a vengeance on the 27th, but the guns crews nevertheless practised at the Dummy-Loader and the gunnery recorders were at drill. Come the 28th, the weather had moderated, and they dressed ship overall in honour of the marriage of H.R.H Princess Mary, switching on the ship's illuminations from 2000 to 2300. On the 3rd March the hands were at a gunnery lecture and Loader competition and, on the 6th, there were more exercises in False Bay, this time with *Dublin* and *Wallflower*, and being a mixture of dummy torpedo attacks and inclination exercises by day, and full-calibre firing and torpedo-firing by night. More gunnery practice and drilling of the control parties followed on the 7th, with *St Dogmael* target-towing at times. At one point *Lowestoft* sent a working party to this tug to unmoor the target and weigh a kedge anchor. However, the tow parted and the outcome was that the 10 cwt kedge anchor was lost overboard. Meantime, the sub-calibre 'throw-off' practice continued with *Dublin*, followed by an inclination exercise.[198]

On 11th March 1922, after Divisions, a party of eighteen Members of the South African Parliament arrived on board to witness firings out in False Bay. Once there, throw-off full-calibre firing was undertaken in company with *Dublin*, followed by high-angle firing and torpedo-firing practice, the torpedo fired being safely recovered. *Lowestoft* then acted as Target Ship whilst *Dublin* launched a torpedo at her, so it would seem that the M.Ps had their full 'moneys-worth' before they disembarked back at Simonstown, at 1440.

Lowestoft coaled on the 14th , taking in 824 tons, whilst the wind rose again, peaking at Force 8, before slowly dropping to Force 4 on the 17th. At that stage her divers fitted paravane chains to her hull. On the 20th March they proceeded east for Port Elizabeth with *Dublin* in company. However, *Lowestoft* was again struck by her dreaded 'condenseritis' problem four hours after their departure, again having to stop her port engine, this time for three and a half hours before a repair was completed. On the 21st, at 1445, Cape Recife Light House hove in sight off the port bow, and, having rounded the cape, they anchored in 7 fathoms at Port Elizabeth at 1615, after a run of 400 miles. HMS *Wallflower* arrived soon afterwards. RMS *Kinfauns Castle* arrived next day. She had been beautifully transformed from her wartime overall dull grey paint to have the traditional red funnels, white upperworks and light blue-grey hull of the Union Castle Line to which she again fully belonged. Despite her changed appearance, one wonders if she brought back powerful memories to Alf of the long days off the Rufuji River in 1915 and the eventual destruction of the *Konigsberg*.

RMS *Kinfauns Castle* sailed at 2035, at the termination of a spectacular searchlight display which had been mounted by the squadron in the gathering darkness since 1945 that evening. One imagines that her passengers would have had a 'grandstand seat', and thoroughly enjoyed themselves. Next evening, the Squadron carried out the display again, having had the ships open to visitors from 1400 to 1600 that afternoon

Next day they proceeded at the very early hour of 0138, rounding Cape Recife again and working up for an eight-hour Full Power Trial, with *Dublin* in company, running swiftly over a smooth sea which had just a slight westerly swell. All went well, and, easing off speed gradually to 8 knots, they continued back to Simonstown, testing their patent log at the end of the voyage and finding it to have been over-logging by 7%. They anchored at 1036 on the 26th, with 403 miles run. The weather was calm and the hands set about striking the main topmast.

Dublin and *Wallflower* had followed into the anchorage a few hours later. On the 27th March *Lowestoft* proceeded into the basin, coaled with 563 tons, and her hands then warped her into the dock where her mainmast was to be hoisted out. In the next days, she exercised her small arms platoon, and drilled a Guard of Honour. The latter were landed on the 1st April to attend the renaming ceremony for the South African Training Ship

---

[198] 'Throw-off' indicating that the firing ship aimed ('threw') its shots several degrees ahead of ('off') the point in space which would be attained by the target ship by the time the shots arrived at the aiming point.

General Botha. During the next week they provisioned ship, embarked torpedoes, put their field gun crew to drill, carried out a Director Test, had their guns' crews at the Dummy-Loader, and their control parties at drill. The divers were down examining the inlets. The ship also sent a Fire Party to Muizenberg, whence they travelled by motor lorry, to help to fight another bush fire. Alf went ashore to a photographer's during this time and had a studio portrait taken. He sent a copy to Olive with a very loving message.

Author's collection of inherited family photographs. Studio unknown.

Alf in his No.1 rig as a Petty Officer (confirmed). He has qualified as a Gunner's Mate (generally called a 'GI') and he has two good conduct badges on his left arm. As can be seen by the inscription, he posted this photo off to his beloved Olive.

On 11th April *Lowestoft* had eased out of the basin, apparently with no mainmast stepped, and, on the 12th April, at 0852, she proceeded for sub-calibre firing practice. However, a NNW wind was blowing, and this quickly increased from Force 4, to 6 and on to gale Force 7, with ugly-looking, lowering clouds. The practice was therefore abandoned at 0930. However, that afternoon, *Lowestoft* and *Dublin* proceeded into Simons Bay for 2½ hours of 'throw-off' sub-calibre firing. On the 13th, the C-in-C embarked and, *Dublin* being in company (and with the tug *St Dogmael* having preceded them towing a target), *Lowestoft* carried out a dummy, long-range, torpedo attack on *Dublin*, followed by a 50-minute throw-off full calibre firing practice at the target. *Dublin* then reciprocated.

By 1343 they had come to anchor at Simonstown - and at 1800 eighty Members of the S.A. Trades Builders Congress visited the ship. The ship's divers were active again during the next two days, clearing her underwater fittings, whilst the field gun crew were exercised. A dance was held aboard on the 25th.

On the 1st May the port after spring suddenly carried away, luckily without causing any serious damage or casualties. On the 8th a new mainmast was at last shipped and the hands were busy setting up the main rigging, hoisting the topmast, etc. Two days later, just as the job was virtually complete, a crane carried away the fore topgallant mast. One imagines that there might well have been 'a considerable flow of invective'. On the 11th they coaled for six hours (514 tons) - and one of the Warrant Shipwrights was *cautioned as to his future behaviour, he having returned on board for duty under the influence of drink*. Perhaps he had been drowning his sorrows about the prolonged stepping of the masts. Be that as it may, on the 12th they swayed the restored fore topgallant mast, and were 'back to normal'.

Thus it was that they were out again on the 16th for full-calibre firing and torpedo practice. On the 17th, the C-in-C came aboard and the ship proceeded from Simonstown to Port Elizabeth, sighting an abandoned floating torpedo off the starboard bow, and taking it on board, before continuing her voyage, and streaming her paravanes for some hours. However, before completing the 392 miles to Port Elizabeth, she had to stop her starboard engine for an hour whilst its condenser defect was repaired. From Port Elizabeth she proceeded to East London, and, before Cape Recife lighthouse was sighted, at 0355 on the 19th May, the condenser had failed again. Nevertheless, *Lowestoft* gained East London, after a run of 135 miles, putting out to sea again briefly that afternoon (presumably with her condenser repaired), for the dropping of another depth-charge.

On 24th May 1922, at 1800, the ship was dressed overall in Honour of Empire Day, and she landed her Small Arms Platoons and Field Gun crew to take part in the local celebrations which were held at East London that morning. The ship was then opened for visitors during the afternoon. She was dressed overall again, on the 26th May, in honour of the birthday of H.M. the Queen, and the ship paraded a Guard of Honour and her band.

Next day she proceeded to Durban, securing alongside the jetty, opposite to 'D' Shed, after a voyage of 312 miles. The RMS *Kinfauns Castle* arrived at 0700 on the 3rd June – just over 10 weeks since her voyage to England and subsequent return. That same day of June the hands dressed ship overall in honour of the birthday of H.M. King George V. On the 7th they coaled ship using native labour (739 tons). On the 20th they landed their Field Gun crew to take part in a military parade at Maritzberg, and, two days later they dressed ship overall in honour of Coronation Day, parading their Guard and Band and firing a royal salute of 21 guns.

On Saturday 24th June they proceeded for Simonstown, in a sea which had an increasing swell and was getting up from State 1 to a lively State 6, officially classified as 'rough'. However, the conditions had eased by the 26th, and were relatively calm when the ship anchored at Simonstown, at 1034, with some 580 miles run. They promptly coaled ship, taking in 547 tons. They then cleaned ship, and she was presentable in time for Divisions at 0920 next morning.

The 'Exploring Vessel' *Quest* of the Royal Yacht Squadron arrived on the 7th July. She was an object of curiosity and pride for she had been the ship of the Polar Explorer Ernest SHACKLETON who had tragically died whilst leading a recent Antarctic expedition. The ship was now returning under Commander WILD and had put into Simonstown for fuel and stores. According to Roy STRUBEN she had arrived at dusk. Her arrival was expected and eighteen of *Lowestoft's* seamen were standing by to receive her, ready to handle the anticipated heavy wire ropes, to pass the eyes of the ropes over bollards, and to bring her to a snug berthing. In the event, however, *Quest* proved to be tiny, being no larger than a trawler, and just two or three light hemp ropes were all that were required to moor her. The large party of *Lowestoft's* men therefore represented considerable 'overkill', and they departed in some embarrassment. *Quest* was visited by HRH the Governor-General on the 13th, and the hands manned ship and cheered *Quest* when she departed later that day.

On a very different note, on Wednesday 12th July 1922, *Lowestoft* had received three prisoners (presumably deserters) from the newly-arrived *Thistle*, who were to await trial by Court Martial. On Sunday, 16th July, *Lowestoft* landed a party to attend a Memorial Service in Capetown. That same day she put ashore her 1st Range Party, followed, next day, by the 2nd party. On the 18th, her Marines were paraded for inspection by the Fleet Royal Marine Officer, and, on the 28th, her admired Captain, Neil O'NEILL, left ship for passage home to England. *Verbena* arrived that same day. On 31st July the ship's Lewis gun party left '*for the Sanatorium Firing Range*', and, later that day, Captain H.J.S BROWNRIGG DSO joined ship and took command.

Cross-checking through the ship's logs, and noting the names of officers they show as having joined and left the ship since she was commissioned in July 1921, it is possible to make a fair reconstruction of the Officers and Warrant Officers whom Captain BROWNRIGG would have found to be under his command as at 31st July 1922, although it is notable that the Engineering Branch, who tended to be something of 'a race apart', are 'prominent by their absence'. So, too, are some of the Warrant Ranks. However, here are 25 of the 34 who would have made up the full complement of officers.

Captain	H.J.S. BROWNRIGG, DSO.
Commander	R. AKISON
Commander	R.F.U.P. FITZGERALD
Commander (N)	J.M. MACRANE
Lt Commander	R.H. BEVAN
Lt Commander	- SANDFORD
Lt Commander	- JEPSON
Lieutenant	W.A. MOENS
Lieutenant	B.F. JOHNSON
Lieutenant	- HEAD
Sub-Lieutenant	C.K. ARBUTHNOT
Sub-Lieutenant	R.F.C. STRUBEN
Midshipman	N.J. CROSSLEY
Midshipman	RUCK-KEENE
Midshipman	- FORD
Midshipman	- BYAS
Surgeon Commander	- RICKARD
Surgeon Lt Commander	F.C.W. WRIGHT
Surgeon Lieutenant	- HURST
Paymaster Lieutenant	R.H.G. FRANKLIN
Paymaster Lieutenant	- TOWNSEND
Chaplain	Rev. C.G.C. PEARSON
Commissioned Gunner (T)	Mr WYATT
Gunner	Mr G.F. ADAMS
Gunner	Mr W.A.R. IMRIE

On 1st August 1922 the C-in-C, Sir William GOODENOUGH, came aboard to say goodbye to the officers and men and, next day, at 0800, HMS *Verbena* hoisted the flag of Sir Rudolf BENTNICK KCMG, CB, the new C-in-C., who assumed command. At 1808 on 2nd August, *Lowestoft* struck the flag of Sir William GOODENOUGH KCB, MVO, and next day at 0800 *Verbena* struck and *Lowestoft* hoisted the flag of Rear-Admiral Sir Rudolf BENTNICK, the new C-in-C Africa Station. At 1130 the GOC Cape Peninsular visited the C-in-C at Admiralty House and *Lowestoft* paraded her Guard and Band and fired a Salute of 11 guns.

On the 4th, *Lowestoft* landed her No.2 Platoon for drill, and, next day, the new C-in-C came aboard for an hour and a half and inspected the Ship's Company. There still seemed to be a problem with the previously-damaged fore topgallant mast, which was struck yet again, to be swung again next day. During that interval of time, Sub-Lt Roy F.C. STRUBEN left the ship. His career did not 'cross paths' with Alf 's again, so far as is known, but he and the relevant part of his interesting diary have been very important to the telling of this chapter of the book, and we shall miss him.

On 10th August 1922 'every available man' was landed, and, next day, the Control Parties went to drill in the morning and the hands holystoned the Upper Deck in the afternoon. Three days later they were tautening up the securing wires. Those wires would be tautened again on the 15th, and one wonders if the new Captain might have been 'tightening things up' in more senses than one. Admiral BENTNICK was also 'picking up the reins', and, on the 14th at 0800 *Lowestoft* fired a Court Martial gun and hoisted the Jack. The ship went to Divisions and prayers, followed by physical drill and then by the hands going to training as requisite. Meantime, the Court Martial sat in the Dockyard, from 1100 until it was dissolved at 1640. One assumes the trial related to the three men from *Verbena*, but we do not know the subject for sure, nor the finding of the court. During the course of the day, Commissioned Gunner (T) Mr WYATT was discharged to hospital.

On 21st May the ship was warped into Dry Dock and secured, the fire main and flooding arrangements then being checked and found satisfactory.

During next days the Consul General of the Argentine visited the C-in-C at Admiralty House, and *Lowestoft* fired a salute of 11 guns in his honour. Meantime, shipboard life continued, exercising 'Action Stations', exercising the divers, exercising a Fire Party and landing a Small Arms Platoon. At this period her company of about 550 officers and men was consuming 250 lb. of beef a day, sometimes interspersed with mutton. They were also consuming about 700 lb. of potatoes per day, with occasional additions of onions. This works out at a very respectable 0.45 lb. of meat and 1.2 lb. of potatoes per man, per day.

Mr WYATT, the Gunner (T) rejoined from hospital on the 25th and a new Gunner, Mr G.F. ADAMS RN, accompanied by Lt W.A. MOENS, joined the ship on the 28th. Next day, flooding of the dock commenced to 10 ft draught, presumably to check that *Lowestoft* was watertight, before further flooding until the ship floated. She was warped out on the 29th, and secured alongside the West Wall. On the 1st September the Captain read the Articles of War and the 'Court Martial Returns'. On Sunday the 3rd, the C-in-C came aboard at 1030, and left at 1205, but during that time he may well have flung out some orders, for on the next day a whole 'raft' of heavy tasks was set the company, namely 'Let go Bower Anchor and Weigh by Hand', 'Out Kedge Anchor', 'Watch to

Collision Stations' and 'Out All Boats'. During the next few days more tasks followed, signal and WT ratings being landed for a shore signalling exercise, the after-magazine flooding arrangements being tested, the regulation checks being made on the lifebuoys and more mundane routine tasks such as holystoning the decks and airing night clothing undertaken. The order 'Land Every Available Man' followed, before the ship was coaled, taking in 409 tons from 0802 to 1223, with a one-hour break. Then the tug *St Dogmael* secured astern and the ship was 'swung' to check and adjust her magnetic compasses.

On the 19th *Dublin* proceeded for a sub-calibre firing practice, before the C-in-C and his staff embarked in *Lowestoft* which slipped and proceeded at 1345, bound for Durban. At 1458 the ship began to work up speed for a Full Power Trial, which she commenced at 1600, on a very smooth sea with a long slight swell under a blue sky with some cloud. At 1720, whilst still at full power, the company dropped overboard 23 depth-charges, 75 'disconnectors' and 900 detonators, all of which had been condemned. (With the ship travelling at well over 25 knots, should any of these dangerous articles happen to explode, she was going to be as far away as possible from the resultant underwater concussion!) All passed off well and *Lowestoft* finished her eight-hour full power trial at 2400, only to immediately commence a 3/5ths Power Trial. By midday on the 20th she was at 33° 49' S, 26° 45' E, and she came down to 14 knots after she finished the 3/5ths Power Trial at 1600. She then exercised Collision Stations and also exercised her Seaboat's crew. She reduced to 12 knots on the 21st, again exercising her seaboat's crew, at the early hour of 0450, held Divisions at 0915, then prayers, followed by a lecture of Hygiene, before exercising 'Abandon Ship Stations' and exercising her Control Parties, before securing alongside 'I' Shed at Durban with about 900 miles run. She had averaged about 20 knots, despite reducing to12 knots or less over the final half-leg!

She coaled next day, taking in 578 tons in 8¼ hours. Meantime, she had landed her Small Arms Platoons for a route march, and fired individual 7-gun salutes for the Consuls of the U.S.A., Portugal, Sweden, Norway and the Argentine, each and all of whom called upon the new C-in-C during the day. Next day, H.R.H the Governor-General also visited the C-in-C, receiving a 21-Gun salute, both on arriving and when he left, a half-hour later. The ship was open to visitors in the mid-afternoon for this day and the next. She had her awnings spread and the temperature was a pleasant 62°F, though the humidity was apparently a little high, especially at 1800 on the 1st October, when a very violent thunderstorm suddenly passed over the ship, with torrential rain.

On 3rd October 1922 the ship again proceeded, dropped the Pilot she had taken aboard to con her out, made her way round the bluff off the harbour, and exercised 'Man Overboard' before continuing to East London, having to haul in her patent log at one stage to clear it, and exercising her seaboat's crew yet again. Her log showed only 200 miles run when she arrived at East London, which was clearly an underestimate caused by the earlier need to haul the log. Once at East London, her Control Parties and Submerged Tubes crews were put to drill.

On the 11th she proceeded from East London to Port Elizabeth, encountering a heavy swell on the 145 mile voyage. The divers were then put to securing paravane chains, and the related sweeping gear was prepared, before, on the 14th October at 2400, *Lowestoft* proceeded for Simonstown, finding the weather turning rough next day, with the wind reaching gale Force 7 after having veered from NW to WNW to SW.

A southerly swell had also got up, becoming heavy, with waves graded as 'rough'. *Lowestoft* had to progressively reduce her speed, initially down to 10 knots, and later to as little as 6 knots. At one stage she also had to alter course to 240° to secure her accommodation ladders, altering back to 261° a half-hour later - and heading back into the teeth of the gale. The storm eased marginally as the evening came on, and she exercised her inured seaboat's crew yet again, at 2315. At 1320 on the next day, she hauled in her patent log, which recorded 420 miles run and, at 1503 she secured to 'C' Wall. Midshipmen I. JEFFREY and De VILLIERS, plus five ratings joined ship, being just in time to help in coaling the ship on the 17th (607 tons in 6¼ hours). Warrant Shipwright E.J. MUNDAY RN joined five days later.

Whilst at Simonstown *Lowestoft* exercised 'Night Defence' and 'Night Action' Stations, carried out a Director Test, kept her Field Gun crew hard at training (evidently with Alf deeply committed to this), and went out into False Bay for sub-calibre firing, together with putting a training class at aiming rifle practice. She also conducted a manoeuvring exercise with the tug *St Dogmael*. This was a prelude to several days of practical gunnery practice (dummy and sub-calibre) and going on to concentration firing in company with *Dublin*, followed by an inclination exercise and firing two torpedoes in a dummy torpedo attack involving *Dublin*. The two ships also carried out sub-calibre night-firing, followed by full-calibre night-firing. Seemingly, Alf was having a very busy time. This whole programme was then more or less repeated in the ensuing days, ending on the 6th November with General Drill, 'Prepare to be Taken in Tow', and 'Prepare to Tow Aft'.

On 9th November Vice-Admiral YANIQUICHI of the Imperial Japanese Navy visited the C-in-C at Admiralty House and a Salute of 15 guns was fired in his honour. A Guard of Honour had been landed for this visit.[199] That afternoon a party of Japanese Officers and Cadets visited the ship for 2½ hours. On 10th November a Squadron Loading Competition was held in the early morning, the decks were holystoned and a second party of Japanese Officers and Cadets visited the ship. Next day, the 11th November, the Field Gun crew and a Marine Guard of Honour were landed to take part in the Armistice Day Memorial Service ashore. It is a near-certainty that Alf would have played a prominent part in this. A 2-minute silence was held on board at 1100.

On 13th November 1922 the ship proceeded into Simon's Bay for a 1½-hour sub-calibre firing exercise with *Dublin*, repeating the exercise next day and adding to it practice in torpedo-firing. On the 15th a funeral party were landed whilst the hands were provisioning ship. This was presumably in relation to the interment of B.T. HENWOOD, a Chief ERA, who had died at the New Somerset Hospital at Cape Town on 12th November, following a fracture he had unfortunately suffered to the base of his skull. The exact circumstances are unknown, but this appears to have been simply a sad accident.

Next day the ship proceeded for Saldanha Bay, carrying out a tactical exercise with *Dublin, Verbena* and *Wallflower* at the start of the voyage, the ships then continuing in company. Passing through a fog bank in the early morning of the 17th, the ships anchored at Saldanha Bay with 211 miles run. It was there that Lt G.O. LATHAM joined

---

[199] In view of all that would happen a score of years later, it is easy to forget that Japan had been a staunch ally in WW1, and that Japanese soldiers had fought valiantly against the Germans in the trenches of the 'Western Front'. The Imperial Japanese Navy was a proud and significant force.

Lowestoft. The Fleet Regatta was started on the 21st November at 0900, commencing with boat pulling, but was called off at 1430, *'due to the weather'* - presumably because the wind had fallen too light for the subsequent sailing events. Next day the wind was a little more lively, at Force 2 to 3, and the Regatta was continued under blue and slightly cloudy skies.   At 1515, the C-in-C began to present the prizes.   In the early evening Lt-Commander SANDFORD left ship for passage to England.

Next day the C-in-C inspected HMS *Verbena*, and *Lowestoft* paraded her Guard and Band. The day after that saw all the ships' boats being prepared for the Midshipmen's Sailing Race, which took place next day.   The C-in-C inspected HMS *Wallflower*, and *Lowestoft* again paraded her Guard and Band.   That afternoon it was 'Away All Boats' for the Coxswains' sailing race. On the 25th a shooting party left the ship. On the 27th the C-in-C inspected *Dublin* and hoisted his flag in her. A number of signals followed in quick succession, one succeeding another as its predecessor was in the process of being executed, such as 'Send Collision Mat', 'Land Fire Engine', and 'Out All Boats: Pull Round the Fleet'. As a measure of the speed of the activities which ensued, the C-in-C was back onboard *Lowestoft* within less than three hours. Next day, he ordered the ship's companies to muster by ledger (instead of 'by open list') - again causing confusion - then ran through a similar list of successive orders to those of the preceding day.

On the 29th November 1922 the ship prepared for sea, the C-in-C showing his teeth by ordering that the fleet should unmoor by hand, before proceeding in single line ahead, streaming paravanes. At 1827 he ordered an increase from 8 to 10 knots, but that seemed to be a little ambitious for the single-screwed *Wallflower* and *Verbena* which fell out of station *'owing to hot bearings of their triple-expansion engines'*.[200] Speed was reduced to 8 knots for the night exercise which ensued, including the always-dramatic firing of Starshell. The C-in-C left after *Lowestoft* secured at Simonstown, the ship being dressed overall and a 21 gun salute being fired next day, 1st December, in Honour of Queen Alexandra's Birthday. The ship's guard and band were also paraded.

Alf fell sick towards the end of 1922, and he was in the Sanatorium at Simonstown for a spell, around 23rd December of that year. It was unknown for him to be so ill as to require hospital treatment. Perhaps he had been driving himself just that little bit too hard, keen as mustard to 'get on', and probably 'volunteering for everything'. Olive was now a very significant part of his life, and he wanted to present himself in the best light to Olive and her parents, to show he would make a 'good match' for her.

Alf sent the following 'group photograph' back home to Olive in England, showing himself standing, arm-in-arm, at the centre of a group of ten men. They were in highly varied dress, ranging from one PO. in double-breasted No.1 rig, with WW1 'Pip, Squeak and Wilfred' medals clinking, down to another man being just in a vest and shorts. Alf's card says, *"All seemed very pleased, dear - quite a mixed crowd."*, and one has to add that they certainly do look 'cheerily convalescent' in the photo.

---

[200] It does seem surprising that the sloops could not cope with this speed. Later events might suggest that it was mostly a question of the stokers not being able to keep up the high rate of work required of them. The Log of their sister-ship *Delphinium* quotes 10 knots as being her 'most economical speed' and shows that she could make a shade over 15 knots at 'full power'.

Authors inherited collection of family photographs.

Alf stands in the middle of the back row. Clearly, there is no set 'rig of the day'.

The Sanatorium stood on rising ground overlooking the quieter part of Simonstown Bay, away from the new docks. The shore-line was covered with a great many scattered rocks at this part of the bay, but there was a slipway and yard with a certain amount of activity to observe. Basically, it was a healthy location in which hospital patients stood every chance of making a good recovery.

Author's collection. An anonymous postcard, c.1925. The serial No. 8122 appears in the pre-printed frame for the postage stamp.

The sanatorium stood on rising ground, overlooking the Bay, as shown in this photograph. The sender of this postcard, evidently a young naval engineering officer, wrote home to his parents: "*This is a view of one end of the bay. Our main docks are at the other end of the town and it's my job to come through the town twice a day and draw the stores for the Engineering Department and have them sent by the lorry from the old yard to the new. My office is in the New Yard....*"

Author's collection of inherited family photographs.

A snapshot taken on 7th January 1923. It appears that Alf *(2nd from right)* and these men are now convalescent at the sanatorium, and are having a picnic at Smit Winkel Bay. Alf wrote to Olive on the back of this card: *"PO SYMONS, THORAGOOD, PINK, myself and Jack. I look awful, dear!" And, s*eeing the blonde peeping over his shoulder, Alf thought it wise to add a P.S. *("No connections with the family in the next cave!")*

Whilst Alf was at the sanatorium, preparations had been made to dock the ship, ammunition being disembarked and the boats taken to the West Yard, before the ship was shifted from the West Wall to the Dry Dock. The brows were taken in on the 11th December whilst pumping out of the dock began. During the next days small arms range-parties were landed, painting, refitting and re-provisioning continued, and the Fore-Topmast and Main Topmast were struck and later re-fitted. Christmas 1922 was spent quietly. Early in the New Year of 1923, Commander R.F.U.P. FITZGERALD, Lt B.F. JOHNSON and Midshipman N.J.CROSSLEY joined ship and the Rev C.G.C. PEARSON left ship for England. A Rake Party was sent to the tug *St Dogmael* for an experimental tow of a BP Target, returning the next day for a repeat tow, the sloops *Wallflower* and *Verbena* making gunnery practice at said targets on both days. On 19th January 1923 a Guard of Honour was landed to attend the Opening of Parliament by H.R.H the Governor-General of Capetown

It was not until the 29th January 1923 that the dock began to be filled, the ship being warped to the West Wall next day. On 31st January she embarked 600 tons of coal and five ratings rejoined from hospital, apparently not including Alf. Next day - and the next - she ammunitioned. Strangely, in view of the fact that she had just come out of dock, her divers were down examining her starboard propeller. Perhaps there had been some suspected little accident when the ship was being warped out of the dock. On 4th/5th February she re-provisioned, the painting of her messdecks and boats continuing the while. Five more ratings rejoined from hospital (probably including Alf), and a funeral party were landed for the burial of L. TRY, an AB of *Dublin*. This young man, aged only 20, had succumbed to enteric fever, malaria and fibrosis of the lungs, dying in the RNH at the Cape. He had clearly been very popular, and his death showed the risk of fevers which all the men on the Africa Station ran.

On the 7th January 1923 His Majesty's South African Ships *Sonneblom* and *Immortelle* arrived at Simonstown. Gunner F.R DOBSON joined ship, relieving Gunner W.A.R IMRIE, who later took passage for England in the S.S. *Gloucester* Castle. *Lowestoft* was warped to 'C' Wall, the Court Martial Flag was raised and the warning gun fired. The Court Martial lasted for five hours.

This was evidently the court martial of Charles Kingsley DAVIS AB, whose similarity of surname may have led the incident to stay in Alf's mind to some degree. Charles DAVIS AB was accused of six charges of theft of odd items of clothing, shoe-cleaning brushes and a Great War medal. The man's defence was well-conducted by the ship's chaplain, the Reverend Charles Edgar PAYNE, and, after perusing the evidence, and examining and cross-examining the witnesses, the case was found to be not proven. Able Seaman DAVIS was therefore exonerated.

There were some surprising aspects to the case, which can be read in the file ADM 156/61 at TNA (Kew). On mulling over them one gains the impression that some murky waters existed, and one wonders if this was a case of 'officialdom' trying to penetrate an area where the 'lower deck' normally and quietly 'sorted things out' by their own application of 'justice and retribution'. One suspects that Mr IMRIE, the Gunner, who had professed problems in being able to answer any verbal questions which might be put to him in the court, was in the difficult position where (having risen through the ranks), he knew, (or could shrewdly guess) what had really been going on, but had, to a considerable extent, to distance himself from that 'lower level', and to somehow uphold the rank of the officer which he had since become. He may even have felt that he had been 'set up' in some way, having possibly been used as a 'tool' by the Lower Deck, and felt that he needed to proceed very carefully to 'keep his own yard arm clear'. Perhaps the last thing he would have wanted would have been 'open questions', which might have led to him having to 'speculate' in some way, when responding verbally, as to the real facts of the matter, and immediately then putting himself at risk of being tightly cross-examined.

As it was, the court proceedings were later officially criticised because the questions put to Mr IMRIE were of '*a leading nature*', but it was said that Mr IMRIE felt unable to give his evidence unless the questions were put to him in that form. He may well have felt himself fortunate to be leaving the ship imminently, his relief, Gunner DOBSON having joined on the 7th January. One wonders how 'aware' Alf would have been about the 'insider' aspects' of all the goings on, especially as he was aspiring to rise to Warrant Rank and might well find himself in similarly difficult circumstances once he had '*managed to crawl up the hawsepipe*' from the Lower Deck.

It was general amongst Naval vessels that any articles left lying about would end up in charge of (say) 'The Buffer', and for a fine to be levied for any article accidentally lost and then, in all honesty, reclaimed.[201] It therefore seemed almost superfluous and heavy-handed that, arising from this case, an Admiralty Fleet Order was issued, stating that '*ship's orders should contain specific directives as to the disposal of all articles found lying about which are not the property of the finder.*'

---

[201] It was traditional for the fine to be paid in 'inches of soap', cut off from a large slab.

Still, back to *Lowestoft* and her 'normal occasions'. At 1600 on the 7th February the SS *Dunluce Castle* arrived and secured alongside the West Wall, *Lowestoft* sending a docking party to assist in her berthing, and *Lowestoft* landing a Beach party at about the same time on the following day to assist now in *unberthing* that Union Castle ship. *Lowestoft* herself came out of the basin and secured at No.1 Mooring in the bay, her boats returning from the Dockyard next day.

On the 13th they swung ship with the aid of *St Dogmael* to adjust compasses and carried out a Director Test, proceeding at 0600 on the 14th for Capetown, dropping one depth-charge as an exercise, whilst en route.

On the 17th they proceeded for St Helena, gradually working up for a Full Power Trial, and reducing to a 3/5ths Power Trial after running at F.P for six hours. When the ship was at 23° 49' S, 4° 41' E the hands rigged canvas baths in which to disport themselves, and then the ship began to suffer from 'condenseritis', the Port Engine having to be stopped for about 1½ hours in the morning of the 20th, and then again that afternoon. Meantime, she had a date to keep and ran at Full Power on the starboard Engine alone to 'keep up the pace'. Having run approximately 700 miles she came in sight of St Helena, coming to anchor five hours later, at 1600, and the C-in-C and his staff leaving to call on HE the Governor at 1650. *Lowestoft* saluted the Governor with 17 guns when he returned the visit at 1740. Next day they coaled (725 tons) and discharged 10 cases of perishable goods to the RN establishment ashore.

The ship was open to visitors on the 25th February, and they embarked fresh provisions next forenoon, before proceeding for carrying out Lyddite-firing at Barn Cliff. Now came an unsettling shock, for P2 Gun burst on firing its first round! Alf described it as a 'premature explosion'. He also referred to the gun as a Mk XII, whereas all other documentation the author has found refers to the ship's 6-inch guns as Mk XIs.[202] Owing to the ship's commitments, it would not be until 24th April that this gun would be unshipped for replacement. Meantime, it remained covered, but nonetheless a constant reminder of the dangers inherent in the Gunner's trade. Alf preserved a photograph of the gun in his album (See below). The crew had been extremely lucky, for it seems they had not suffered any casualties from this nasty incident.

Next day the ship proceeded from St Helena, heading slightly west of north to Sierra Leone. On the 27th they shifted to hand steering gear, and then to fore bridge steering. On the 1st March they took matters further, shifting to Engine Room steering, and then Lower Control Tower steering, before reverting to Bridge steering. Meantime, on the 28th February, after Divisions and Prayers, the Surgeon Lt Commander had given a lecture to one watch on the health precautions which should be observed on the West Coast on Africa. His lecture was clearly regarded as important, for it was repeated early on 1st March for the other watch, the ship having 'crossed the line' between times.

On 2nd March, there was a flurry of activity, exercising 'Action Stations', dropping a target for 1" aiming practice, picking up the target, letting go the port lifebuoy, followed immediately by 'Away port seaboat' to regather it, then 'Full Speed Astern Both', and then firing a rocket (found correct), before the seaboat returned with the lifebuoy. The seaboat was exercised again before midnight, and then again at 0300

---

[202] Various Marks of the 6-inch gun including a Mk XIA, and even ranging up to a Mk XVIII, were in use in the Royal Navy at one time or another.

and at 0530. Much the same lifebuoy exercise took place next day, ending with exercising Torpedo Stations.

The barrel of P II Gun after it had burst. Note the miles of wire-banding. Evidently the inner core of the barrel had remained intact and this had prevented the collapse of the main length of the barrel.

A snapshot from Alf's album.

At 0500 on 4th March the ship entered the Sierra Leone River, coming to anchor at 0550. The Colonel Commandant visited the ship, and the C-in-C returned the compliment. Next day the ship coaled, embarking 730 tons to make up for the 1,570 miles she had run since departing from St Helena. Her draught had increased by about 2 ft 3 ins forrard and by about 1 ft aft, or, say, one inch per 38½ tons.

The vegetation at Sierra Leone.

A snapshot from Alf small album.

On the 7th Ali Kali Mordu, Paramount Chief of the Lower Lokks visited the ship. Next day the company exercised 'Tow Ship Forward', and they proceeded for Bathurst on the 8th March, exercising their guns crews as they headed north up the coast for 480 miles and then sounding their way up the River Gambia, to come to anchor in 13 fathoms. On their way upriver the 710 ton gunboat HMS *Thistle* had saluted the C-in-C with 13 guns, *Lowestoft* replying with seven. The Governor visited the C-in-C during the afternoon, being saluted with 17 guns as he left the ship. The divers were down that day cleaning the ship's 'circulator discharge'. On the 14th she proceeded to Sierra Leone, the guns crews again being exercised and the hands put to physical drill. During the night of the 15th the lookouts sighted the glare of Sierra Leone, and the ship came to anchor at Freetown after a run of 926 miles, and taking in 655 tons of coal which increased her draught to 17 ft 9 ins f'w'd and 17 ft 6 ins aft, equivalent to about one inch per 36 tons.

On 19th March the ship landed a party of 150 officers and ratings for a day trip to Songo Town by rail. It is interesting to note that every man-jack of them wore a solar topee, for in those days it was believed that the greatest precautions needed to be taken against sunstroke caused by the sun striking the top of the head and the back of the neck. The Officers and men wore 'whites', but the men had an advantage in the great inland heat, for they wore shorts.

Two snapshots from Alf's small album.

Visit to Songo Town.

Native Dancers (*above*) and Native Musicians (*on right*).

Alf was one of those who went to Songo Town, and, as shown above, the album he left for posterity contains some snapshots of the native people they encountered. From Sierra Leone the ship now proceeded some 800 miles south and east along the coast to Sekondi, Ghana. On the way they again dropped a target and had two runs of sub/cal firing at it, before recovering the target and sponging out the guns.

They arrived at Sekondi early on the 23rd March, the Provincial and District Commissioner calling on the C-in-C and being saluted with 15 guns on his departure. That evening, the ship gave a searchlight display and fired two rockets and four Very Lights as an accompaniment to it. They proceeded later the same evening, arriving at Accra the following morning after a run of about 100 miles. The weather was very hot, at about 81 degrees Fahrenheit, though there was a gentle breeze off the sea to provide a little cooling.

On the 27th they proceeded east to Lagos, Nigeria, observing a tornado passing to the southward of them and experiencing a strong ESE wind but no rain. On arrival they were piloted to the harbour, HMS *Dwarf* saluting the C-in-C with 13 guns, and *Lowestoft* replying with seven. The C-in-C landed to call on HE The Governor, the visit being returned a little later. Next day, the 29th March, *Lowestoft's* Guard and Band were paraded as HE The Governor embarked in a Royal Mail Steamer for passage to England

A snapshot from Alf's album.

A view of Lagos from seaward.

That afternoon, a tornado passed over the ship, accompanied by a south-east wind and torrential rain. On 1st April a Party of Native Members of the Legislative Committee and Native Officers of Police visited the ship. Next day a Party were landed for a trip on the railway to Abba Konto. Heavy rain and a strong wind from the north-east soon led to Divisions being held below, on the Mess Deck. That evening a coal lighter came alongside and the ship embarked 975 tons, a heavy task in the heat and humidity prevailing.

Next day the C-in-C left the ship to inspect the 710 ton gunboat HMS *Dwarf* (a sister-ship of *Thistle*, built in 1898/99, with two four-inch guns, drawing only nine to ten feet of water, and having a complement of 90 men.) On the 5th *Lowestoft* gave another searchlight display as night came down. On 6th April, the Lt Governor of Nigeria came aboard and *Lowestoft* proceeded to sea. She was accompanied by *Dwarf,* towing a target against which *Lowestoft* carried out two runs of sub/cal firing. On ceasing fire, *Lowestoft* sent a boat to transfer the target, but *Dwarf* fouled the target wire with her port propeller. *Lowestoft* prepared diving gear, but *Dwarf's* propeller was cleared about 90 minutes later, apparently by her own efforts. However, the further gunnery practice which had been planned had to be abandoned, the Governor leaving the ship for *Dwarf* to return to Accra, whilst *Lowestoft* continued to Lobito Bay, Angola, 'crossing the line' *en route.*

On her way she had to stop her Port Engine for an hour to repair a condenser. She then encountered increasingly strong westerly winds and storms of heavy rain, and a moderate swell got up. Lobito was sighted at 0600 on the 11th April after a run of over 250 miles, the Port Captain, Intendent and British Vice-Consul all coming on board to visit the C-in-C as the ship came to an anchor. A seven-gun salute was fired as they left the ship.

Next day, *Lowestoft* proceeded to Walvis Bay. Friday the 13th lived up to its reputation for ill-luck, for the helm ran over to the hard-a'-port position and jammed there. The engines were worked to counteract the rudder, whilst efforts were made to change over to hand steering. However the helm continued in the jammed position for an hour, before the artificers managed to clear the problem. The ship's company continued to hand-steer, tension rising as the ship began to pass through a thick fog-bank. However, this cleared almost providentially as the whaling station hove into view, and the ship entered harbour at Walvis Bay, sounding her way in.

Next day, the 15th April, the C-in-C left the ship to continue by train to Simonstown, whilst the ship embarked 470 tons of coal to make up for the 790 miles run. During the third week of April the ship proceeded to Capetown, with a brief stopover at Luderitz Bay, reaching Capetown on the 21st. On the 23rd she coaled, using native labour and embarking 985 tons, before proceeding to Simonstown, and entering the Selborne Dock.

Whilst there, the damaged P2 gun was at last hoisted out. A new gun was hoisted in later the same day, Alf keeping a photographic image of the proceedings. (See next page.)

On the 27th April the ship was dressed overall throughout the day, and illuminated at 1900, in honour of the Wedding of the Duke of York to Lady Elizabeth BOWES-LYON.[203]

Lowestoft emerged from dock on 3rd May, and exercised at sub/cal firing and torpedo-firing with the cruiser *Dublin* and the sloops *Verbena* and *Wallflower* during the 7th, 8th and 11th May, following up with practice at the Dummy-Loader, and all preparatory to engaging in competitive shoots with each other. However, there was an embarrassing interlude at 1330 on the 11th, for *Lowestoft*, having picked up the flagship moorings at Simonstown, had an anchor drag which fouled those moorings. She therefore had to send down a diver to examine them. It took until 2000 for the anchor to be cleared and weighed. It also took a fair part of the next day for the wire to be unshackled from the moorings.

---

[203] Who would have guessed the enormously important role this Royal Couple would play in the future of the British Nation, as King George VI and Queen Elizabeth.

The damaged P2 Gun has been withdrawn and its shield is being removed for examination.

Come the 14th May the guns crews from the cruisers were at the Loader Competition, and, on the 15th, they were engaged in full/cal Competitive Firing, *Lowestoft* firing at a target towed by *Dublin*, and then reversing roles, the C-in-C and umpires transferring to whichever ship was in the shooting role. The towing wire parted when *Lowestoft* was returning to harbour with the target, at the conclusion of the exercise. However, the ever-faithful *St Dogmael* stepped in, and took the target in tow.

The day was not done, for a Court of Enquiry sat on board at 1800 to find the cause of death of Private P.T. BEAMS RMLI, who had been found dead in the GSW Heads at 1230 that day. Apparently he had committed suicide, for reasons unknown.

24th May saw the ship dressed overall for Empire Day, the Ship's Guard and Band being paraded and her Platoons landed. Next day the C-in-C came aboard and presented prizes for the Competitive Firing Competition. The ship was again dressed overall on the 26th May, in Honour of Queen Mary's Birthday, a 21-gun salute being fired. They ammunitioned ship on the 30th, and again dressed the ship overall on the 31st, for Union Day. Commander E.J. SPOONER DSO, RN joined ship that day, relieving Commander J.M MACRAVE, who had been the Navigator of *Lowestoft* since at least the start of the current commission, and who now returned to England. Ammunitioning continued on the 1st June. Come 2nd June the ship was dressed overall yet another time, in honour of the Birthday of H.M King George V, the Guard and Band being paraded and Royal Salute fired. A working party was sent ashore to berth, and later to unberth, the S.S *City of Agra*.

On 4th June, at 0800, there was a General Drill, followed by sending the field gun around the Basin anti-clockwise. Later, the Concert Party of the Ship's Company, who had been busily rehearsing, gave a concert on the Quarter Deck to entertain their friends and a great time was had by all, in a moderate temperature and calm weather.

On 5th June 630 tons of coal were embarked. Next day, a working party under the Gunner from *Lowestoft*, and augmented by men from *Dublin*, were landed to clean up the foreshore of the Dockyard. A further working party would be landed on the 8th. Meantime, exercises continued, such as sending away the cutter 'manned and armed', and landing the Marines and a Company of Seamen for military operations. Five signal rockets were also fired. Meantime the gun crews were kept at drill.

On the 20th the Officers held a small dance aboard, and on the 22nd the ship was dressed with masthead flags in recognition of the Anniversary of the Coronation. A Royal Salute of 21 guns was fired.

On 26th June the ship proceeded to Durban, dumping overboard over 800 rounds of redundant 12 pdr and other ammunition which had been received from the Ordnance Officer at Simonstown for deep-water disposal. Her company exercised Action Stations and tested alternative steering positions en route, and moored alongside 'E' Shed at Durban in the afternoon of 29th June, the ship being opened to visitors shortly afterwards. By now, the Ship's Log was being signed (as Navigator) by Commander (N) G.F. SPOONER who had joined ship on the 31st May.

On the 2nd July they coaled, using native labour and embarking 630 tons. On 4th July the C-in-C held a small dance aboard in Honour of Their Royal Highnesses the Prince and Princess Arthur of Connaught. The Prince was scheduled to make a tour of inspection of the harbour aboard the S.S *Harry Escombe* on the 12th July. *Lowestoft's* company now settled down to some serious training for the pending Fleet Regatta, and she had all her boats away pulling on the 16th. She also exercised 'Out Kedge Anchor' and 'Abandon Ship Stations', as well as continuing with gunnery drills.

On 23rd July she proceeded northwards from Durban to Lourenco Marques, exercising 'Action Stations' en route, and saluting the Flag of Portugal (21 guns), on her arrival at Lourenco Marques next day. On the 25th the British Consul General called on the C-in-C, receiving an 11 gun salute on leaving, and he was followed by His Excellency the Governor-General of Mozambique, who received 19 guns. On 26th July the Pulling Heats of the Regatta were undertaken, the ship being open to visitors that day and the next, when the American Consul and the French Consul each called on the C-in-C, both receiving 7-gun salutes. On the 28th the C-in-C and the Ship's Officers held an 'At Home' aboard.

The ship proceeded to Durban on the 31st, exercising General Quarters en route, and arriving on 1st August with 250 miles run. On 2nd August she landed a Party for the Wedding of Lt Commander JEPSON RN. On the 7th she coaled (750 tons) and landed her Field Gun crew for practice.

On 8th August the ship proceeded to East London, carrying out 1-inch aiming rifle practice, and also Maxim gun and 0.303 inch practice at a small target in 'Position 4', bearing 140 degrees from the Bluff Lighthouse. She subsequently picked up the target and, for practice, a lifebuoy.

On 9th August 1923 she struck the Flag of the C-in-C, and exercised General Quarters, later coming to her moorings abreast of 'E' Shed, with 200 miles run. At 0900 on the 10th August *Lowestoft* half-masted her colours together with the American Ensign in Mourning for President HARDING of the U.S.A, who had died in office on the 2nd August.[204]

Next day the ship was open to visitors. Surgeon Lt Commander F.C. WRIGHT left ship on passage for England. [Surgeon Lt HURST would join ship on the 18th, evidently as his replacement. Lt Commander SERVAES RN would also join ship on the 18th, relieving Lt Commander R.H. BEVAN RN who also then left ship on passage to England.] On the 13th, the Captain and Officers held a Dance aboard, and the following afternoon the ship proceeded to Simonstown. During the voyage they were subjected to a dummy air attack by two aircraft operating from East London, and that evening they exercised their searchlights, hoisted out their paravanes, went to Night Defence stations, streamed a fog buoy and exercised their seaboat's crew.

They secured at Simonstown next day, with 500 miles run, and embarked 600 tons of coal on the following day. On the 24th all the boats were away under sail.

Though not made clear in the log, it seems probable that the ship was now given a short refit, for there is a note on the 19th September that ladders were refitted to the foremast, with the hands working in the boats as requisite. Also, on the 20th, Blue Watch exercised 'Away Fire Engine' to the Pumping House. Otherwise, little of moment occurs in the log except for the 12th September, when the Marines and Nos 1 and 2 Platoons were landed, together with a Medical Party, for a combined landing exercise in conjunction with landing parties from *Dublin* and the sloops.

On the 20th the C-in-C inspected HMSAS *Sonneblom* and visited *Lowestoft*.

It was not until the 24th that *Lowestoft* was definitely active again, taking part in a torpedo practice that night in False Bay, using Star Shell illumination. On the 25th she repeated the exercise in daylight, coupled with sub-calibre firing at a target towed by *St Dogmael*. *Lowestoft* also conducted 1-inch aiming rifle practice with *Dublin* and then proceeded to a range taking exercise with her. This was all followed up by sub/cal firing exercises by night. The next day, in conditions of low-visibility, she carried out dummy torpedo attacks on a target line of *Dublin, Wallflower* and *Verbena*, and then took her place in the line whilst *Dublin* carried out an attacking run. Next day the C-in-C embarked, and *Lowestoft* carried out a full-calibre shoot of ten rounds per gun in False Bay, followed by the firing of a live torpedo at the shore in the vicinity of Pauls Bay.

Unfortunately, the torpedo failed to explode, so the ship's whaler was sent off in search for it, but without success. Meantime, further full/cal firing at a target towed by *St Dogmael* ensued, before the C-in-C disembarked and the squadron returned to Simonstown. The unexploded torpedo was a matter of considerable concern and, early next day, a demolition party was sent to search for it and to detonate its dangerous charge. (It is assumed that this mission was accomplished successfully.)

This was evidently not the only 'explosive matter' arising at that general time, for Sub Lieutenant C.K. ARBUTHNOT was admonished on 5th October *'for neglect of duty as OOD in not ensuring that the barge was sent alongside HMSAS 'Sonneblom' on anchoring, to disembark the C-in-C.'*

---

[204] This deference seems almost incongruous, for President HARDING had played a large part in naval disarmament. That is to say, he had called the Washington Naval Conference of 1921 to resolve conflicting British, Japanese and US ambitions in the Pacific. The treaties stemming from that Conference, though ostensibly stabilising international relations, were to the distinct advantage of the USA and to the considerable disadvantage of the UK.

On 11th October 1923 the C-in-C was aboard *Lowestoft* when she proceeded to False Bay for the Africa Station Torpedo Competition, six torpedoes being fired by each ship involved. Then, on the 15th, the Africa Station Pulling Regatta was held, in fine weather conditions, under blue skies with occasional passing clouds, and a pleasant temperature not exceeding 66 degrees Fahrenheit.

A snapshot from Alf's album.

Lowestoft had a long-standing reputation to maintain in pulling events, and the racing gig's crew were unbeaten during this commission. Seemingly, Alf played a full part in ensuring their success. In this photo of the gig he is *believed* to be the PO in the sternsheets.

On the 16th the Captain and Officers of the Africa Squadron were 'At Home' on board *Lowestoft* for the Regatta, but the weather became unsuitable for sailing as the light morning breeze faded right away. Hence, the events had to be postponed until the next day - and even then a sensitive touch was needed for the breeze was still very light. However, all the events were completed and the C-in-C presented the Regatta Cup and Prizes that evening. Thoughts now turned towards the Field Gun Competition and Naval Sports Day at Rosebank, Capetown.

The ship arrived in Capctown on the 19th October, having made 'Control Runs' with *Dublin* en route from Simonstown, and the C-in-C being embarked in *Wallflower*. The Field Gun was hoisted out on to the jetty at Capetown and the 22-man gun crew were disembarked next morning. They had been in training for many weeks, and they were now off to prepare the ground at Rosebank, ready for the Competition. As we shall see, Alf was among them.

In their absence, on Trafalgar Day, 21st October 1923, fourteen Officers and the Ship's Company were landed to attend a Memorial Service in the Cathedral. Next day they coaled ship (730 tons) and then cleaned ship. On the 25th a large number of local schoolchildren visited *Lowestoft*, followed by a visit by Kaffir schoolchildren next day. The ship was also open to visitors on the 27th October.

(Above) The Field Gun Competition at Rosebank, South Africa, 27th October 1923.
(Below) Lowestoft's winning team at a break during intensive training.

On that same day, the Naval Sports were held at Rosebank. With Alf as Gunner's Mate, and under a Lieutenant (presumed to be Lt HEAD), *Lowestoft's* twenty-man field-gun team won the 'Wolfe Cup' during the field-gun competition. This was a spectacular event, including the firing of blank charges and the generation of much spectacular smoke therefrom.

On the 29th the ship proceeded to Simonstown, securing in the Dry Dock. There her foul bottom was scraped clean and then painted. She undocked on the 2nd November, to secure to the West Wall of the Basin. There she de-ammunitioned, and got in other ammunition for transit to England. She also embarked 88 cases of clothing and boots from the V.S.O Simonstown for conveyance to England. Meantime, examinations for Educational Test Pt 1 were carried out aboard.

On the 7th November the hands were employed in rigging the Sail Loft in the West Yard for a dance which was given that evening by the C-in-C and the Captain and Officers of *Lowestoft*. On the 10th the C-in-C arrived on board for a photograph to be taken with the Ship's Company, and, next day, a Guard of Honour was landed to attend the Memorial Service to the Fallen of WW1. The ship's colours were half-masted and a 2-minute silence observed at 1100.

Two anon. studio portraits of 1923 from the author's inherited collect'n.

On the 13th November Alf had two studio portraits taken in his uniforms as a Gunner's Mate.

On 12th November 1923, a 21-gun salute was fired in honour of HRH Prince Arthur of Connaught, the Governor-General of South Africa, who was then in residence at Admiralty House Simonstown. [The ship would fire another 21-gun salute in his honour when the Prince departed from Simonstown on passage to England, on the 16th November.] In total contrast a, Private of the RMLI was sent to *Dublin* for trial by Court Martial. *Dublin* was soon to become the Flagship, and *Lowestoft* turned over the Admiral's Barge to her on the 16th.

Lowestoft now topped up her bunkers with a further 310 tons of coal, embarked further miscellaneous stores for passage to England, and was visited by the C-in-C on the 19th November, to bid the Ship's Company farewell. His Flag was then shifted to *Dublin*.

At 1130 on the 19th November *Lowestoft* proceeded for St Helena, her company manning and cheering ship in reply to the farewell cheers from *Dublin, Wallflower* and *Verbena*. They saluted the Flag of the C-in-C with 13 guns as they departed.

They arrived at St Helena on the morning of the 25th November, though their voyage had not been without incident for they had closed the SS *Ambridge* at 21° 57' S, 01° 50' E, after she had made a request for a Doctor. Her Boatswain, George NEONIS, had gone down with an acute case of Appendicitis, and *Lowestoft's* Surgeon Lt HURST subsequently carried out an emergency operation to remove the man's appendix. Mr NEONIS was subsequently discharged to the care of the hospital at St Helena.

On the 27th November 380 tons of coal were embarked, and the ship proceeded to Sierra Leone, arriving at 0800 on the 3rd December, having crossed the Line without ceremony on the 1st December, and having covered 1,657 nautical miles from St Helena. Using native labour she then embarked 1,000 tons of coal, increasing her draught to 18 ft 4 ins forward and 18 ft 4½ ins aft. HMS *Birmingham* was present at Sierra Leone, and *Lowestoft* discharged various stores into her, managing to lose one boathook in the process. She continued to transfer stores on the 6th and 7th, but landed a recreation party on the 6th and granted short leaves so her men could stretch their legs ashore.

On the 7th December Captain H.J.S BROWNRIGG, DSO, RN transferred to HMS *Birmingham* and assumed Command, and Captain G.H. KNOWLES, DSO, RN assumed command of *Lowestoft*. Commander R.F.P. FITZGERALD, Commander E.J. SPOONER, Lt Commander RM. SERVAES, Lts LATHAM, ARBUTHNOT and JOHNSON, Surgeon Lt HURST, Pay Lts FRANKLIN and TOWNSEND, and the Rev PAYNE all transferred to *Birmingham*. Thirty-one ratings joined from *Birmingham*, and 103 ratings were discharged to her.

The ship now coaled, using native labour, taking in 1,175 tons, and seeing the battlecruisers *Hood* and *Repulse,* and the light cruisers *Delhi, Danae, Dauntless* and *Dragon* arrive, before the water boat came alongside *Lowestoft*. Perhaps it was not surprising that the ship received no less than 28 bags of mail next day for passage to the U.K. She then proceeded to Las Palmas, with *Birmingham* in company, commencing OOW manoeuvres on the 10th, and being cheered by *Birmingham* at position 10° 08' N, 16° 42' W, with *Lowestoft* reciprocating before parting company.

Lowestoft then headed north for the Canary Islands, finding mist on the 13th December, and so having to drop her speed right down at times, stopping at 1215, and going 'Half-Astern Both!' at 1217, with a steamer passing the starboard beam about 2 cables away at 1218. It had evidently been a close shave! *Lowestoft* continued, but at only 7 knots until visibility began to improve!

The lookouts sighted the Mountains of Grand Canary at 0640 on the 14th, and *Lowestoft* came to anchor at 1100, promptly coaling from a lighter alongside. Her company embarked 253 tons to make up, to some extent, for the 1,370 nautical miles they had run. They proceeded that evening, in a moderate sea and swell, and a steadily declining temperature. The increasing chill would have been very apparent after their three years in more southerly climes. On the 18th they sighted Cape Finisterre, and on the 20th they sighted Beachy Head. The ship arrived at Sheerness at 0100 on the 21st December 1923, flying her long paying off pennant and coming to with the Port anchor in 12 fathoms in the Little Nore Anchorage. By 1000 ammunition lighters were alongside disembarking the ammunition they had transported from Simonstown. The lighters cast off at 2145, and at 0920 next day tugs secured alongside, and, taking *Lowestoft* in tow, proceeded with her to No.3 Buoy, where she secured alongside the cruiser HMS *Calliope*.

At 1300 the monthly payment was made together with an advance to men who were due Foreign Service Leave, and that leave was then granted to all but the minority who were required for 'care and maintenance' of the ship. Most of the men due Foreign Service Leave were thus 'home for Christmas'. Come 1st January the ship began to 'wind down', her guns being sponged out on the 1st January 1924 and victualling stores being disembarked, before she proceeded under tugs to Chatham Lock. There she disembarked further stores, coal, torpedoes, her ship's boats, her residual coal and her anchor cables. The 'skeleton ship's company' would have been working hard and it is to be hoped that they had some help in the interim from the companies of other ships in the basin. On 28th January the Ship's Company returned from their Foreign Service leave.

On 1st February 1924 the ship discharged 40 stokers to the RNB, and on the 11th her RM Band to the RM School of Music. She was still discharging the remnants of her stores, and her company was already dwindling, the consumption of meat having reduced from 250 lb/day to 165 lb/day, and of water from 20 tons/day to 5 tons/day. An inspection of the ship was carried out by the Captain of the Dockyard and his Staff on 28th February, baggage being disembarked to the RNB, messtraps being returned to the Dockyard, and a few 'Non-Chatham' ratings being discharged to Portsmouth and Devonport. Those men apart, the Ship's Company (including Alf) then marched off to the RNB Chatham at 1030 on the 29th February 1924, the ship having been paid off into Dockyard Control and the Pendant hauled down before the Officers, who were the last to leave, vacated the ship.

Officially, Alf's drafting to *Lowestoft* terminated on 28th February 1924. He would have learned a lot during this last commission. He was now given a draft chit for HMS *Pembroke* from the next day. On his return to England, he would have been given at least his basic entitlement of 21 days foreign service leave for his 2 years 8 months spell of service on the Africa Station - and hopefully an extension to that leave. He would remain at *Pembroke* for almost a year, partly to re-qualify to continue to hold his present non-substantive rating, and also, presumably, to provide instruction to men whose rank and experience was less advanced than his own. Hopefully he was given further spells of seven days leave every four months, perhaps with some week-end 'Friday While' leaves mixed in as well. At least *Pembroke* was in reasonably close proximity to Ipswich via the London Main Line Terminus, so Alf could have had frequent close contact with his beloved Olive.

Alf's previous voyages had taken him down the east coast of Africa, as far as Simonstown. This deployment in *Lowestoft* had extended his experience to the western coast, as far north as Bathurst, as well as refreshing his knowledge of the east coast as far north as Lourenco Marques. The return voyage had included a call at Grand Canary.

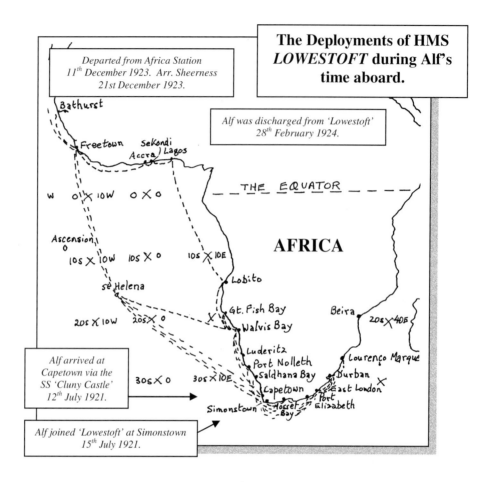

The Deployments of HMS *LOWESTOFT* during Alf's time aboard.

Departed from Africa Station 11th December 1923. Arr. Sheerness 21st December 1923.

Alf was discharged from 'Lowestoft' 28th February 1924.

Alf arrived at Capetown via the SS 'Cluny Castle' 12th July 1921.

Alf joined 'Lowestoft' at Simonstown 15th July 1921.

VOYAGES DURING DEPLOYMENT: Pers. RECORD of Alfred William DAVIS, RN					
Farthest North	Bathurst	14 N 13 W	*F/North (ever)*	Off Scapa Flow	59 N 02 E
Farthest South	Simonstown	34 S 18 E	*F/ South (ever)*	Simonstown	34 S 18 E
Farthest East	Lourenco Marques	26 S 31 E	*F/East (ever)*	Ras Asir	12 N 51 E
Farthest West	Bathurst	14 N 13 W	*F/West (ever)*	Atlantic Ocean	50 N 30 W

Alf had equalled his 'farthest south' record, actually off Cape Agulhas, the most southerly point of the Cape of Good Hope.

Crossings of the Equator to date:

Three times in HMS *Lowestoft*
Twice in HMS *Weymouth*
Once in the SS *Cluny Castle*

TOTAL: Six Crossings

Private Life

Alf had been admitted into the Phoenix Royal Arch Chapter 1860 of the Masonic Order at Simonstown on 10th November 1921, and he had been advanced to the degree of Mark Master Mason at Phoenix Lodge on 9th December 1921.[205] One suspects that Alf was finding various new contacts from this new side of his life, some possibly of potential use in furthering his career. One wonders how much some aspects of this may have been in conflict with his inner feelings of strong and unbending self-reliance and Spartan independence. Yet, he was also a 'team man' and a gregarious person, who would have enjoyed the ceremonies and 'togetherness'.

Olive was working on the cosmetics counter at Boots the Chemists in Ipswich. A first-cousin, Essie BISHOP, would later describe Olive, who had grey eyes and light-brown hair, as being 'One of the two prettiest girls in Ipswich.' (The other 'prettiest' girl, Jennie JESSOP by name, apparently also worked on the cosmetics counter. Seemingly, Boots had a very enterprising manager at that time!) In April 1923, Olive had sent Alf a photo of herself in semi-formal dress. In July 1923, she had sent him photos taken on the beach at Felixstowe, where she had gone for an informal day out with three of the 'Boots Girls' - apparently NOT including Jenny JESSOP - then, in September, one of herself in a semi-revealing bathing costume and frilly bathing cap.

(Above) Olive in a 'romantic' pose in the garden.
(Right) Olive, slightly 'revealed', with a 'Boots Girl' friend on the beach.

Judging by the photos which had been exchanged, things certainly looked as if they were proceeding well from Alf's 'courtship by letter'.

---

[205] Alf would go on to be 'acknowledged' (as Alfred *Vincent* DAVIS of the Royal Alfred Chapter No.103) in the Degree of *Excellent Master Mason* by the Supreme Grand Royal Arch Chapter of Scotland on 14th March 1922. At that time Alf was abroad, serving on the Africa Station. It is presumed that the document was forwarded on to him for his normal signature to be duly added at the bottom.

Although he had enjoyed his time in South Africa, Alf must have rejoiced to be back at home in England once more in December/January 1924, to be able to meet up face-to-face with his beloved Olive again, and to renew his active courtship of her. They were kindred spirits and their relationship was rapidly becoming an extraordinarily deep one. Indeed, Alf's steadily increasing bond with Olive somehow seemed to be emphasised by the intimate familiarity of that little word '*dear*' when, talking about his fellow-patients, he had written to her in December 1922 from the Sanatorium in Simonstown, "*All seemed very pleased, dear - quite a mixed crowd.*" Especially so when one remembers that their romance was then developing solely through such written correspondence as passed between them during the two years of his absence from England.

Alf was beginning to make a strongly favourable impression on her parents, too, and on some, at least, of the other family members. He began to work very hard at this, using the benefit of the uninterrupted spells of leave a sailor enjoys, as opposed to the more restricted times of weekend liberty normally available to a working-class civilian.

He had at least one strand in common with Olive's father, Joseph Walter GREEN, for 'Walter', as his wife called him, was a former Gunner, a fine man who had been in the Royal Garrison Artillery on the Western Front during the Great War. As already mentioned, like a great many others, his lungs had been permanently damaged by poison gas, leaving him with a constant cough - not helped by smoking a pipe which was having to be constantly re-lit by sulphurous 'Swan Vesta' matches. It is assumed that Alf was already a regular smoker by that time of his life. Whether he initially used 'ticklers' and rolled his own cigarettes is unknown. Certainly, by the mid-1920s, Alf favoured 'Senior Service' cigarettes, and, like most men of his day he was headed to become a chain-smoker. The incisive sound of Alf double-tapping the end of a 'tailor-made' cigarette on his gleaming gilt cigarette-case to tamp the tobacco away from the end he was about to put in his mouth would later become one of his hall-marks.

Whether Alf visited his siblings and father on any of his leaves is unknown. One suspects that contact may not have gone beyond the occasional exchange of letters and cards at this time - though Alf may have been becoming more than a little keen to 'show off' Olive to this or that member of his family. He may well have had Nellie in mind, for one. She and her husband were 'on the up' both in business and domestically. Their second child, a boy, Raymond, had been born at the Stonecross Hotel on 22nd March 1922, and, this time, praise be, everything had gone well.

By this time Alf had taken to calling Olive's parents 'Dad' and 'Mum', and one feels he had come to view them almost as if they were his true 'blood relations'. In return, they were beginning to admire him enormously.

CHAPTER NINE:

HMS *VERNON*, HMS *EXCELLENT* & HMS *DRYAD* (1924-5)

Alf was posted to HMS *Vernon* for a course which lasted from 17th January 1925 until 22nd February 1925. *Vernon* was the Royal Navy Torpedo School at Portsmouth, originally based on the hulk of an old 'wooden wall', but now 'brought ashore' as a building which stood on a former wharf. The courses at this establishment dealt with mines as well as torpedoes, and they had a strong involvement with the sciences of electricity and magnetism, linked with functional mechanics. Since the outbreak of the 1914-18 war there had been tight security and only a few 'internal' photographs found their way to becoming postcards in the public domain.

Author's collection. An anonymous postcard, c.1914.

The hulks which formed 'HMS *Vernon*'. This photo was passed by the Censor in December 1915. On 15th March 1914 'Harold' had written to his Uncle Tom on the back of a similar card (but of the main hulk only), to say: "*This is a photo of our ship and, as you will see, she is rather old, having been built in 1792. She was one of Nelson's older craft....*"

From *Vernon*, Alf was posted to HMS *Excellent* at Portsmouth, with effect from 28th February 1925. This was *the* training establishment for any man with aspirations to become a Gunner. It was an establishment where instant response to orders was expected, where a strong discipline was imposed, and where a high pride was fostered. Men moved from place to place at the double. Men who were trained here either came to love it - or to hate it passionately and forever. Alf, who, as we have seen, had a strong touch of the Spartan about him, dropped quite naturally into the former group.

As we have already seen with *Ganges, Impregnable* and *Vernon,* the training establishment HMS *Excellent* had originally been based on the hulk of an old 'wooden wall'. In fact, successive hulks had served over the years before, in 1891, the school had been transferred to Whale Island, a former mud flat. Over the years this mud flat had gradually been reclaimed from the river estuary, partly by natural changes which were occurring in the shore-line, but greatly aided by having large quantities of earth added to the increasingly large mud flat, to form much more solid ground.[206] During the ensuing years the buildings and facilities had been steadily expanded and extended on the reclaimed land. Small ships (such as gunboats and trawlers) had been attached to the island-based school, as necessary. As Alf had experienced back in 1911/12 when serving in *Impregnable* (when all her attached hulks had been renamed '*Impregnable II, III, etc.*'), all the gunboats and trawlers which were attached to the gunnery school were renamed '*Excellent*'.[207]

Author's collection. A postcard in the 'Wellington' Series by Gale & Polden. Postally used at Portsmouth, c.1910.

H.M.S. EXCELLENT   Guard House

The Guard House at HMS *Excellent*, photographed well before the outbreak of WW1. The facilities had increased during that war, with the installation of various defensive features including anti-aircraft guns. As can be seen, considerable efforts had been made over the years to convert the former mud flat into a well-stocked garden area, with shrubs and trees.

In addition to these small craft, and continuing past Alf's time at *Excellent*, destroyers and larger warships were attached to the training establishment for short periods. There is an inference that, in Alf's year of 1925, the monitor, *Terror*, with her two 15" guns, acted as Turret Drill Ship and the cruiser *Champion* was attached for a time. So, too, apparently, was the battlecruiser *Tiger*. No logs exist at TNA (Kew) for *Champion* or *Terror* for that year 1925, which would suggest they were either being used for training in a static mode only, or that they were 'laid up' somewhere in reserve. However, there *is* a log for *Tiger* at TNA (Kew), which confirms that she had a reduced complement of only 762 officers and men at this time (and was burning oil fuel only, so that she would have needed less stokers than if she had been burning coal as well. Re-fuelling would also have been less man-intensive.) In fact, she was equipped at that time as a '*Seagoing* Gunnery Training Ship' (author's italics).[208] During Alf's first spell at

---

[206] The book 'Whaley' by Captain J G WELLS provides much information on the detailed history of Whale Island, from 1830 to 1980.

[207] This renaming practice would later cease.

[208] In the normal way she would have had a complement of 1,480 officers and men, and would be burning both oil and coal.

Excellent, which ran from 17 Jan - 22 Feb 1925, *Tiger* was initially in Dry Dock at Portsmouth, but had prepared for sea on the 16th February. Four officers had joined for bombardment practices on that day, and these practices had been carried out at Spithead on the 17th and 18th Feb., whilst the ship was at anchor. Next day, further firing had been carried out with the ship under way.

Author's collection.. A postcard in the Real Photo Series by W H Smith, c.1925. Card postally used in July 1937. Card reproduced by courtesy of W H Smith Archive.

The battlecruiser HMS *Tiger*, of about 35,000 tons, with eight 13.5-inch guns and ten 4-inch. It is *possible* that Alf was aboard this ship for a short spell during his training at HMS *Excellent.*

On the 21st, *Tiger* had proceeded for Shoeburyness, where there was a 'bombardment range'. Officially the 22nd February was Alf's last day at '*Excellent*', and, if Alf had indeed been aboard *Tiger* during her gunnery practices at Portsmouth, he probably went ashore at Portsmouth before *Tiger* proceeded. Alf would then have continued to *Excellent*.

Alf was drafted back to HMS *Pembroke* on 7th March 1925, staying there until the end of the month. He was promoted to the rank of Acting Gunner on the 1st April 1925, initially being appointed as a Supernumary to *Pembroke*. His first assessment report still survives within the family. It says that Alf had conducted himself "*to my satisfaction*", the report having been signed by C. ROUND-TURNER, Captain (G), and countersigned by the Commodore, HMS *Pembroke.*

Alf's next appointment to '*Excellent*' was on 20th April, when he returned to serve 'under instructions' as Acting Gunner. On that day *Tiger* was at Portland. Her log shows that a class of 'Long Course' officers joined her there on 20th April.[209] A group of Portsmouth ratings also joined *Tiger* on that day and on the forenoon of that same day the ship had proceeded out to sea for three hours of AA Firings. Whether or not Alf was with either of these groups, or whether he remained ashore at *Excellent* is unknown. Somehow, one feels he had sailed with *Tiger*.

---

[209] The 'Long Course' lasted for six months, though only part of this time would have been in *Tiger.*

During the afternoon of 20th April, groups of Devonport and Chatham ratings also joined *Tiger* for firings, which were carried out next day and included 0.303" and sub/cal 13.5" firings. On the 22nd the groups of ratings were discharged to shore, and only the 'Long Course' officers remained, as the ship continued with 6" full/cal and 13.5" full/cal practice firings. The ship's log states that the Gunnery classes were then discharged.

However, *Tiger* continued with gunnery activities, carrying out 'Hot Gun Trials' on the 16th May, putting the HA gun crews to drill on the 18th May, exercising off Spithead on the 2nd June, working with multiple towed targets during exercises with the Battlefleet in mid-June, and carrying out further firing classes through into July. Whether or not Alf had been aboard for some or all of this time, he continued to serve nominally at *Excellent* until the 11th July 1925.

This would doubtless have been a very interesting and satisfying time for him, when his professional abilities were being well-honed and tested. He would also have felt that keen eyes would have been assessing his capabilities and powers of command. He was about to have further tests applied to his competence as a sea-going officer. That is to say, Alf's service at *Excellent* was immediately followed by the 'Pilotage Course for Warrant Officers on Promotion', held at HMS *Dryad*, the Navigation School at Portsmouth. Marks were awarded in the various subjects, and Alf was declared to have qualified.

His report survives, and reads as follows:-

SECTION	SUBJECT	FULL MARKS	MARKS OBTAINED
I	Compass	100	70
II	Astronomical Navigation	100	65
IV	Meteorology	50	50
VI	Tides	100	91
VII	Ship and Fleet Work	150	103
VIII	General Navigation	500	365
		TOTAL: 1000	TOTAL: 744

[The qualifying mark was 60% of the total, with a minimum of 50% in any subject.]

Alf had actually gained an overall mark of 74%. His lowest mark in any subject was 65% - that was in Astronomical Navigation - and his highest mark (100%) was in Meteorology. One suspects that he had done a lot of 'cramming'. He must have been very relieved and pleased at the outcome. Alf then returned to *Pembroke*. On behalf of the Commodore, Captain C ROUND-TURNER of HMS *Pembroke* issued another progress report on Alf, covering the period from 11th July 1925 to 21st July 1925, again saying that Alf had conducted himself as Acting Gunner *"to my satisfaction."* Alf then awaited his next appointment.

Fortunately, the rumours of pay cuts which had abounded in 1921 had eased to the extent that only newly-recruited personnel suffered from them, starting and continuing on a lower scale than that of the already-established men. (One imagines that this was a potential source of future problems and unhappiness with those individuals.) Alf was entering the marriage stakes and it would have been to his considerable relief when he found that he would not be *personally* affected by any pay-cuts.

Private Life

So far as his private life was concerned, Alf had proposed to Olive, her parents were more than agreeable, and she had accepted him. The natures of Alf and Olive were clearly very complementary. Although she was eight years younger than Alf, she was extremely capable and 'managed' him with love, subtlety, humour and ease. Alf was totally caught up in his career and in his courtship of Olive. Soon they would be beginning to formulate plans for their wedding ceremony. Whilst Alf was at *Pembroke* he could use 'Friday Whiles' to get to Ipswich to see Olive, and doubtless did so as frequently as he could manage it. The two of them evidently began to visit various friends and relatives of Olive and socialised at various 'GREEN Family' events.

Snapshots from Alf's album.

Alf is rapidly 'getting his knees under the table', and becoming very well-accepted in the GREEN Family. The GREENs currently live in Ipswich but have ideas of moving to Felixstowe, where they already have a beach hut. *(Top Left)* Olive with her father at the beach huts, Old Felixstowe. *(Right)* Alf with Olive's Dad, Joseph Walter GREEN, and Olive's young brother, George Neville. The men have broken off from an *impromptu* game of beach cricket and have had a 'bit of a laugh' in dressing the young lad up with his father's pipe clenched in his teeth and a newspaper on his arm. *(Bottom Left)* At home, Olive light-heartedly 'drives' her older brother's motor-bike on its stand, with young George Neville riding pillion. There is much humour and happiness in this family, much of it down to Olive and her Dad, who have a very close bond. Alf has brought an 'added dimension' to that happiness.

At this time, Alf was in contact with his sisters, but still not communicating directly with his father. On the other hand, there had clearly been some close contact between Alf's sister Nellie and their father, which had also involved Nellie's husband Wilf. One suspects that Nellie, now 27 years old, was still strongly influencing her father and had suggested to him that, since she and Wilf were vacating their pleasant pub in Midsomer Norton, he might like to take it over. She knew that her father had always had a measure of *wanderlust* in his soul, and she now probably dropped the hint that a change of venue away from Lincoln might well prove to be to his advantage. Maybe Nellie knew that her father had a yearning to move to the south-west of the Country, where, as we have seen, he had been born — though he might *still* have been carefully keeping that fact under wraps!

Perhaps, too, her father had detected that 'The Crown' was beginning to go downhill in certain respects, hastened by the car gradually taking over from the horse and the resultant steady decline of the once-celebrated Lincoln Horse Fairs. Certainly, the outcome was that, on 20th June 1924, Alf's father had sold up at Lincoln and had obtained a Licence to succeed his son-in-law, Wilfred PENNEY in the business of running the 'Stones Cross Hotel' at Midsomer Norton. Alf's two younger sisters were still living and working with their father, and had accompanied him to Somerset.

As indicated, Nellie and her husband Wilf PENNEY were doing well in business, and had taken over 'The Crown', in New Orchard Street, Bath. It would not be long before a second son, John, would be born to them.

CHAPTER TEN:

HMS *St CYRUS* (1925-26)

It was on an 'additional/temporary' basis that Alf was initially appointed to the Admiralty tug HMS *St Cyrus* on 22nd July 1925. She was a powerful, coal-fired, Saint Class tug, and had been built by Chrichton & Co. at Chester in 1919. Of 820 tons displacement, 143 feet long and with a beam of 29 feet, she could make 12 knots. Her most economical speed was 8 knots. She could accommodate about 250 tons of coal in her bunkers, giving her a range of about 5,500 miles between coalings.

Small as she was, as of 30th March 1926 she had the considerable draught of 11' 3" forward and 13' 6" aft which betokens the power within her vitals. She mounted one 12-pounder gun. She normally had a complement of just 12 officers and men - which, one hopes, Alf, as an 'additional', did not increase to a 'Jonah-like' thirteen! Events which transpired do lead one to wonder just a little about that! Be that as it may, Alf would cease to be 'additional/temporary' and would be appointed to be fully integrated into the company of *St Cyrus*, some four months later, on 10th November 1925.

If *Courageous* had been Alf's biggest ship, *St Cyrus* was certainly the smallest in which he had come to serve.[210] Let's see how she 'weighed in' against Alf's previous ships.

Name of Ship	Type Of Ship	Displace-ment (tons)	Year Completed	1st Year Alf srv'd (diff.)	Comple-ment	Max. Length (feet)	Max. Beam (feet)	Draught (feet)	Shaft Horse-Power	Max. Speed (knots)
Vanguard	Dreadnought	**19,250**	1910	1912 (2)	823	536	**84**	**31.75**	24,500	22
Russell	Pre-Dreadnought	14,000	1903	1912 (9)	718	418	75.5	28	18,220	19
Weymouth	Armour'd Cruiser	5,250	1911	1913 (2)	392	453	48.5	18	22,000	25.5
Courageous	Battle Cruiser	18,600	1916	1916 (0)	**829**	**786.5**	81	26	**90,000**	**35**
Lowestoft	Armour'd Cruiser	5,440	1913	1920 (7)	546	459.5	49.8	18.25	25,000	25.5
St Cyrus	Admiralty Tug	820	**1919**	1925 (6)	12	143	29	13.5	1,200	12

Name of Ship	Guns					Torpedo-Tubes		Armour			
	Main		Secondary		A.A			Deck	Side	Turr't	D.C.T
	Calibre	Number	Calibre	Number	Capability	Calibre	Number	(ins)	(ins)	(ins)	(ins)
Vanguard	12"	**Ten**	4"	Twelve	**2x3"**	18"	Three	1.5 - 3	**10**	**11**	**8 – 11**
Russell	12"	Four	6"	Twelve	-	18"	Four	2.5	3-4	6	12
Weymouth	6"	Eight	3"	One	1x3"	**21"**	Two	1-2	Nil	1	2
Courageous	**15"**	Four	4"	**Eighteen**	**2x3"**	**21"**	**Fourteen**	1-3	3	7-9	10
Lowestoft	6"	Nine	3 pdr	Four	1x3"	**21"**	Nine	1-2	3	1	2
St Cyrus	12 pdr	One	-	-	-	-	-	-	-	-	-

---

[210] Assuming that he was not one of the men drafted to one or other of the 'small ships' at the Rufugi River affair in 1915 - though those were, of course, temporary, *ad hoc*, transfers and not 'official draftings'.

As shown by the lone **bold** figure along the 'bottom lines', *St Cyrus*, completed just post-war, was actually the most modern ship in which Alf had yet come to serve, even though she was six years old by the time he reached her. The Battlecruiser *Courageous* remained the ship which had been the newest when he had reached her – in fact, still in-building at the time. Moreover, when compared with *St Cyrus*, only *Russell* (at nine years) and *Lowestoft* (at seven years) had been older than *St Cyrus*, when he first served in them.

Author's collection. A photograph by Wright & Logan, of March 1939, reproduced by courtesy of the RN Museum, Portsmouth.

The Saint Class Tug HMS *St Cyrus*, pictured in 1939, some thirteen years after Alf had served in her, but then still going strong.

It must surely be the case that 'discipline' aboard this small but powerful tug was far more relaxed than Alf had experienced on other ships, especially after the tight and formal discipline of the 'big ships', *Vanguard*, *Russell* and *Courageous*. Serving in cruisers, such as *Weymouth* and *Lowestoft*, would have opened his eyes to the fact that considerable differences in the level of formalised discipline could exist, but Alf probably still found some initial difficulties in finding the 'right' level of discipline to exert in this small tug, and in finding a reasonable balance between 'formality' and 'informality'. Was some God-like official, a civil servant at the Admiralty, deliberately pulling strings, perhaps in consequence of the confidential part of a report issued during a regular promotional evaluation of Alf? Be that as it may, this would have been a good test of Alf's abilities to cope with a new situation, in which officers, warrant officers, petty officers and men were living virtually 'cheek by jowl' in a small space. Yet, this small vessel was strong, reliable and robust, and, for reasons which will soon become apparent, one suspects that Alf developed a great deal of affection for her.

The logs of this ship survive at the Public Record Office for the period 22nd September 1925 to 3rd June 1926. They therefore cover nearly all the period of Alf's service in this ship, lacking only his first two months aboard.

On 22nd September 1925 *St Cyrus* was at Invergordon. There, she was mainly engaged on target-towing duties, working in conjunction with the tugs *Snapdragon* and *St Genny*. It is clear that the targets in use at that time were unstable if the wind got up, when they had a tendency to capsize. The wind playing on their tall vertical surfaces could also make them 'have a mind of their own'; when under tow, veering off in unexpected directions. Evidently for these reasons they were often towed alongside rather than being towed on a short cable in the more normal way. [This operation of towing alongside could of itself cause other complications, as when the main discharge pipe of *St Cyrus* became damaged on 30th September.]

Author's collection. A postcard in the 'National Series', published by 'M & L', c. 1935. Postally used 31st May 1943.

MIDDLE PIER, INVERGORDON

The Middle Pier at Invergordon c.1935, with two destroyers moored off-shore. This general scene was probably little changed from when the tug *St Cyrus* was based at Invergordon in 1925.

On reaching the target area, the targets would be veered to a long tow during the exercise itself, to give a safety margin should the gunnery be wide of the mark! Sometimes two tugs would operate together, each towing a target on the range, and close station-keeping on each other could then become vital. Sometimes the firing took place in twilight or at night, adding to the risks and problems involved.

When towing targets out to the firing range off Tarbat Ness, 'Marking Parties' drawn from the warships involved in the exercise, and intending to observe the accuracy of fire, would often come aboard the towing tugs before they left harbour. Around this time, it is known that one such party came from the battleship *Royal Oak*, and another from the battleship *Royal Sovereign*.

Wednesday 30th September 1925 would have been a big day for Alf, because, for the first time in his life, he was given the responsibility of acting as the Officer of the Watch (OOW), and, at 2000, he signed the log of *St Cyrus* in that capacity. Accepting this duty meant that he was responsible for the ship and to see that good discipline and order prevailed all the time that he was on duty. He had to ensure that the ship kept on her proper course. He also had to ensure that all signals from other ships were read and acknowledged as necessary, including proper conformance to signals from the Flag. In fact, the then current 'Manual of Seamanship, Volume II' devoted seventeen pages to the duties to be done!

He had the ability to call on the Captain for support if he felt he was 'getting out of his depth' in any situation which developed, but woe betide him if making such a request was not for 'good and sufficient reason'. And woe betide him if he failed to do so when the situation *did* warrant calling the Captain! In other words, he had to carry out standing orders faultlessly and exercise perfect judgement in all matters arising. He had never before had to carry so much responsibility.

During Alf's first ever stint as OOW the 2nd Battleship Squadron fired for six minutes at a target being towed by *St Cyrus*, also engaging a target being towed by *Snapdragon*, one cable astern. The course then had to be altered to keep station 2 cables on the port beam of *Snapdragon*. Here were key instances of the OOW having to respond exactly to orders from higher authority in other ships to ensure operational safety. (One suspects that the captain 'would have come to the bridge' during the critical time, but, even so….)

Being a small ship, the command of *St Cyrus* was vested in an officer who held a substantive rank no higher than that of Lieutenant. This meant that officers of higher rank, who were, to considerable degree 'total strangers' to the Ship's Company, came on board from time to time (usually in what seemed to be a rather cold-blooded way), to ensure that *St Cyrus* was being properly run and that she satisfied all the relevant regulations. Here was another aspect of naval life in a small ship which would have impinged on Alf's consciousness, possibly for the first time, though high-ranking officers had, in fact, come aboard *Weymouth* and *Lowestoft* during his time in them, either to inspect the Marine detachment, or to inspect the Engine Rooms.

Be that as it may, on 11th October the ship was inspected by the Captain of the Fleet, and, on the 24th October the ship's log was inspected by Captain E. WIGRAM, now Captain of the battleship *Ramillies*. He would have been familiar to Alf from his time at HMS *Ganges*, and one wonders if Captain WIGRAM might possibly have recognised Alf and, perhaps even have spoken to him. The Engineer Commander, the Surgeon Commander and the Paymaster Lieutenant of *Ramillies* also came aboard and each officer inspected the departments and books which were relevant to his branch of the Service. At 1100 that same day the ship's company was mustered for inspection by Captain WIGRAM. They may have been a small ship, but the Navy was going to ensure they 'kept up to the mark'. And, perhaps to make their own mark and show their independence and initiative, *St Cyrus* landed five men on 20th October to assist in extinguishing a fire on shore.

Another slant on the small size of *St Cyrus* was that her twelve-man company was insufficient for certain labour-intensive tasks, most notably, coaling. Hence, when re-fuelling became necessary on the 19th October, a working party from the battleship *Royal Oak* came aboard to help.[211] The company of *St Cyrus* had started at 0900, the working party arrived at 0915, and they had toiled together to 1430, with a short break for 'Up spirits' and a 45-minute lunch. By that time they'd taken in 60 tons.

---

[211] On 8th October a Marking party from *Royal Oak* had joined *St Cyrus* for a firing exercise, and this might have 'oiled the wheels' in regard to providing a Coaling Party to help the company of *St Cyrus*.

At her most economical speed (8 knots) *St Cyrus* consumed 1 ton of coal for every 24 miles travelled. [She was capable of only 18 miles per ton if travelling 'with all despatch', at the higher speed of 12 knots.] If she was going at her own most economical pace, 60 tons would give her about 1,400 miles of steaming. This was a consumption of only 37 cwt (0.33 tons) per hour. As already stated, with her bunkers full (250 tons) her potential range was about 6,000 miles. She proceeded from Invergordon for Sheerness on the 1ˢᵗ November, and by noon on the 2ⁿᵈ November she was at 52° 18' N, 01° 52' E, heading down the East Coast, and would soon be passing the estuary of the River Orwell, which led up to Ipswich where Alf's fiancée lived. *St Cyrus* arrived at Sheerness the same day, her Patent log indicating a distance safely traversed of 372 miles. (Author's Note: Surely a very large underestimate!) Her company then slightly 'blotted their copybook' by having an accident in hoisting the dinghy, resulting in the loss of its rudder, backboard and four oars.

On the 4ᵗʰ November, the order to 'clear lower deck' was given, and the Captain read out the report of the inspection of the ship which had been made by Captain WIGRAM of HMS *Ramillies*. [The contents of this report are unknown, but it is assumed to have been at the very least 'acceptable'.]

At this time the company was putting *St Cyrus* into reasonable condition, cleaning the bathrooms and heads, refitting ropes and taking in a 4½" FSW (Flexible Steel Wire) towing wire from a sister-tug, *St Genny*. They then proceeded into No.3 Basin of Chatham Dockyard, and, on the 9ᵗʰ November the ship paid off and her company (not including Alf) were discharged to the RN Barracks at Chatham.

On 10ᵗʰ November 1925 the ship was recommissioned for further service in the Atlantic Fleet, as a tender to the battlecruiser HMS *Repulse*. Next day the Captain, Lt TRILLO, paid a visit to the C-in-C. On the 11ᵗʰ the ship proceeded from Chatham Dockyard to Portland.

Author's collection. A postcard in the 'Seeward' Wessex series, dating from about 1925.

Portland Harbour on a dank day, with an aircraft-carrier, possibly HMS *Furious*, lying midway across the picture, just beyond the thin line of breakwater.

It was at Portland that, on the 21st November 1925, colours were flown at half-mast on the occasion of the death of Queen Alexandra, the Queen Mother, marking the end of a remarkable era.

On the 24th the ship made the return journey to Chatham, practising 'Fire', 'Collision' and 'Abandon Ship' on the way, and sighting *Furious* en route. Alf may have had some difficulty in recognising *Furious*, since this former battlecruiser had now been converted into a fully flight-decked aircraft-carrier. At midday *St Cyrus* was at 50° 33' N, 1° 56' W, on the longitude of Bournemouth, and well on her way to the east. Alf took over as OOD at 1600.

They were alongside at Sheerness by the 26th, and de-coaling into a lighter alongside. The company left next day for inoculation aboard the battleship *Royal Oak*, and then, despite what were probably already sore arms, they completed de-coaling and the lighter shoved off just before noon. On the 28th they disembarked all their fireworks on deposit to '*Lodge Hill*' after *St Cyrus* had been towed to No 26 buoy. Small they may have been, but they held Divisions and had Prayers on the Mess Deck on the 29th. The tug *Security* took them to No 25 buoy, on the 30th November and, though not mentioned in the Log, *St Cyrus* went into Dry Dock on or soon after that day. The company now became busy, ranging cable on the fo'csle, clearing out the after tank store, scraping and red-leading, drawing stores and re-provisioning ship. They checked that their fire service was correct, prepared for the storage of towing wires, arranged new wires and hemp towing ropes, cleaned and stowed the after tank room, and painted down aloft and alow. Meantime Lieutenant TRILLO paid a visit to the Captain (Supply) in the Dockyard, probably in an effort to hurry things along, and the 10th December saw Dockyard men working aboard, whilst the company kept right on scraping, red-leading and painting - to say nothing of stowing further wires (and returning one 4½" wire as unfit for use).

On the 12th December they coaled ship (2 tons), allowed one watch weekend leave, and had a welcome 'make and mend' as the ship was moved from the dock to the basin. The hands were still painting ship and drawing such items as shackles and boat covers. On 4th January 1926, they proceeded out of the basin in tow, then secured to No 18 buoy and swung ship to adjust compasses. Next day they coaled for a straight 6½ hours, taking in 98 tons, followed by a further hectic 4¾ hours, to bring the total to 230 tons! They must have been exhausted - to say nothing of being black-grimed from head to foot.

On the 7th January 1926 they put to sea for a trial, staying out overnight, before returning to harbour next morning. All seemed well.

At 1600 on the 12th January they slipped and proceeded for Gibraltar with the tug *Snapdragon* as leader, (and, though not shown in the log, accompanied by the tug *St Genny*) under blue sky with some cloud, but in a rising sea. By 1720 the ship was labouring badly and the upper deck was filled with seawater 'to the top of the gunwales'. Speed was increased to full power and the tug's head was turned into the sea 'to clear her upper decks'. Meantime, the wind, which had been coming from the south-east, had veered to full east, and it increased overnight from Force 5 to Force 7. By 0830 next morning Ushant was in sight almost directly to port, and course was altered at 0900 to 244°, to bring the sea more on to the quarter. By 1600, the ship was working so much that she had started to take in water on the port side of the stokehold, which was a most undesirable situation.

It was then found that the bilge pumps were choked with coal and ash, and perhaps also with the dunnage and rubbish which would have been swilling around almost everywhere. Sounding the well showed that the ship was carrying 4 ft of water where she should have been virtually 'dry'. Hence, at 2200 a bucket party was organised and set about baling manually from the after end of the Boiler Room. For a good two hours, they kept up this heavy and difficult toil in a vessel which was in violent motion.

The tug *Snapdragon* then ordered a further change in course, which brought some easing of the situation. Also, by this time the worst of the storm seemed to be over. However, it was not until 0700 the next morning that the baling party at last finished clearing the water from the bilges. It was estimated that 50 tons of water had already been on board when they had started! Repeated efforts had been made to clear the bilge pumps, but every time that had been done the pumps had rapidly choked again with coal and ash.

Now, as the weather continued to ease, the company could begin to get their doughty little ship back into some sort of order. By dint of their hard efforts they had survived a very dangerous situation. After that, the rest of the voyage to Gibraltar was 'child's play'. Partly because he had gone safely through this prolonged crisis in the Bay of Biscay in this small ship in company with two of her sisters, Alf carefully kept in perpetuity some amateur photographs of the huge seas and the little 'cork-like' ships in his small album).

A snapshot from Alf's photo album.

Huge seas are running in the Bay of Biscay. This shot, one of a series taken from *Snapdragon*, shows *St Cyrus*, and the mast of *St Genny* just visible under the 'X' marked on the photo. *St Cyrus* was in serious danger of foundering at one stage during this storm.

A snapshot from Alf's album.

Alf entitled this picture: "The Calm after the Storm!" Another picture from *Snapdragon* of *St Cyrus* and *St Genny*, the tugs now having the coast of Portugal abeam to port.

Whilst at Gibraltar they became heavily involved with *Snapdragon* in target-towing duties for ship and fleet exercises, sometimes carrying aboard marking parties from the ships concerned. Whilst so engaged on the 1st February the tow parted, the target capsized in the south-west breeze, and, although they initially recovered it with two grapnels, the grapnels both parted under the strain and, to the embarrassment of the Captain and company of *St Cyrus*, the target drifted down wind onto to the breakwater under the eyes of the Fleet.

They returned to harbour, but there were occasional squalls of rain, and the wind and sea continued to get up, so they set an anchor watch overnight. The 4th February was a typical day, starting with their repair of a target, following which they proceeded to sea for a night firing exercise by the 2nd Battleship Squadron. Before reaching the firing range, they went alongside the battleship *Resolution* and embarked her Marking party. They subsequently veered the target to a long tow, for the firing exercise, later hauling it to short tow, and then bringing it alongside for the return to harbour, where they secured alongside the tug *St Genny*.

During the ensuing days they carried out similar target-towing exercises, but, occasionally, they had other responsibilities, as when they stood by the battleships *Resolution* and *Ramillies* whilst 'shifting ship' was in progress. They also took part in an exercise, embarking landing parties from the battlecruiser *Hood* and another battlecruiser, proceeding outside the Detached Mole, and having secured, disembarking the men.

It seems that Alf made further friends whilst he was at Gibraltar, for his small photo album contains pictures of Alf in 'civvies', with a Mr and Mrs HADLEY, at some distance up the rock and having company from some of the famous baboons.

On *St Cyrus* they had to keep a constant watch on the condition of their towing wires, oiling and replacing them as requisite. And, of course, they had to embark coal from time to time, as on 18th February when a Coaling Party from the 2nd CS arrived on board and assisted them to embark 100 tons from a lighter alongside. This task took them the next 5½ hours. On 23rd February the hands were employed in rigging stages for painting the ship. The painting complete, which had included 'oxidising' the metal f'c's'le deck, it was back to target-towing. Meantime, the Atlantic Fleet had sailed, and the aircraft-carrier *Furious,* and the light cruisers *Centaur* and *Conquest* had arrived. They were accompanied by the 5th and 6th Flotillas of destroyers. These ships were followed in by the battleships *Royal Sovereign, Ramillies, Canada* and *Melbourne,* with the 2nd CS and further destroyers and submarines.

The 3rd BS sailed on the 12th March, *St Cyrus* embarking ratings (and a cot case!) from the Store Wharf and setting off 'in chase', securing to the *Empress of India* ten minutes later, and transferring her 'pierhead jumping' and impromptu passengers.

The final target-towing by *St Cyrus* at 'Gib' took place for the cruiser *Caradoc* later that week. Then, on the 23rd March, led by *Snapdragon,* and (though not stated in the log), evidently followed by *St Genny, St Cyrus* proceeded for Sheerness. Their course took them close to the Iberian Peninsula, followed by a direct line track across the Bay of Biscay (which was appreciably calmer than had been the case on their outward voyage) to round Ushant, and head straight up the Channel past Portland Bill. At this stage it was found that the rotator of their patent log, then showing 860 miles run, was fouled with waste. It had to be restarted from zero. And so on to Sheerness where they secured to No.25 Buoy on the 30th March. *St Genny* secured alongside. All told, they had run some 1,000 miles from Gib. In the afternoon of the 30th March they proceeded to the north-east corner of Basin No.3 at Chatham. One suspects that Alf managed to get at least a couple of days of leave almost immediately, though he would probably have asked special permission to 'spread' the days of leave to which he was now entitled.

The first days of April were quiet for the men remaining on board, but the tug was shifted to the south-east corner of the basin on the 5th and a working party from the RNB came aboard. One presumes that Alf requested an interview with his Captain around this time, asked for his formal permission to become married, and then asked his Captain if he would publish on board the ship on three successive Sundays prior to the 21st April, the banns of his (Alf's) forthcoming marriage, and subsequently issue a 'certificate of publication of banns' according to the Naval Marriage Act of 1908.

Meantime, scraping the ship, red-leading and returning stores to the Dockyard ensued. On 12th April Lt TRILLO left for *St Martin,* and Lt NORMAN took command of *St Cyrus.*[212] On 20th April 1926 the log shows that Mr DAVIS left the ship to join HMS *Birmingham,* presumably now armed with the certificate of publication of banns.

Seemingly, Alf, serving as Acting Gunner, had made a very good job of his duties in *St Cyrus.* His commanding officer's assessment report survives. It is signed by E J TRILLO, Lieutenant in Command, covers the period from 22 July 1925 to 10 April 1926, and reads:- "...*he has conducted himself entirely to my satisfaction. He has kept watch at sea and carried out his duties with care and attention. A reliable and trustworthy Warrant Officer.*" The report was countersigned by J REWOLD, Captain of the mighty HMS *Hood,* which ship was widely regarded as being the 'Navy's Darling'.

---

[212] Sad to relate, *St Cyrus* was fated to be mined and sunk off the Humber, nearly 16 years later, on the 22 January 1941. She would thus meet her end just eleven days after Alf would lose his own life.

Author's collection. A postcard sponsored c.1935 by the celebrated Naval outfitters Gieves Ltd. Image reproduced by courtesy of Gieves & Hawkes Ltd.

The 'Mighty *Hood*'. A truly beautiful battlecruiser, but one with potentially critical flaws in her armoured protection.

St Cyrus had carried Alf several thousand more sea-miles and he had stood a watch in her on a number of occasions. She had greatly expanded his experience of the control of discipline in a small ship and doubtless further 'rounded his character'.

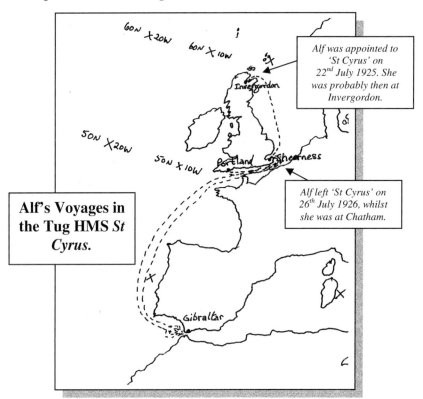

Alf's Voyages in the Tug HMS *St Cyrus*.

Alf was appointed to 'St Cyrus' on 22nd July 1925. She was probably then at Invergordon.

Alf left 'St Cyrus' on 26th July 1926, whilst she was at Chatham.

VOYAGES DURING DEPLOYMENT: Pers. RECORD of Alfred William DAVIS RN					
Farthest North	Invergordon	**58 N** 04 W	*F/North (ever)*	Off Scapa Flow	**59 N** 03 W
Farthest South	Gibraltar	**36 N** 05 W	*F/ South (ever)*	Simonstown	**34 S** 18 E
Farthest East	Sheerness	51 N **01 E**	*F/East (ever)*	Ras Asir	12 N **51 E**
Farthest West	Off Iberian Penin.	40 N **10 W**	*F/West (ever)*	*Atlantic Ocean*	50 N **30 W**

Alf had broken none of his 'farthest points' records, though he had come close to his 'farthest north' record, actually whilst target-towing off Tarbet Ness.

His 'Crossings of the Equator' remained unchanged at:

Three times in HMS *Lowestoft*
Twice in HMS *Weymouth*
Once in the SS *Cluny Castle*

TOTAL: Six Crossings

Private Life

One assumes that Alf was back with Olive as often as could be managed during his time aboard *St Cyrus*. Alf and Olive were clearly destined for each other, and highly compatible. However, *St Cyrus* was at Invergordon pre-September 1925 and throughout October that year, and it would have been difficult (though perhaps not impossible) for Alf to make the 600 mile journey back to Ipswich during that time. Perhaps the telephone was the primary link between the couple at this period of their lives, presumably with many loving letters also being exchanged.[213]

One imagines that, towards the end of October 1925, when Alf was stationed up in Invergordon, he would have been surprised to learn that his father, a widower since 1906, had suddenly married a widow, Ada DEAN, who had two grown-up sons, but who was twenty years his father's junior. One assumes that the move down to the West Country had suddenly brought romance into the life of Alf's father. The marriage of Alfred Wm and Ada DEAN née SMITH had taken place at Midsomer Norton Parish Church on 22nd October 1925, by Licence. At his first marriage in 1893, Alfred Wm had invented a father he called 'George', but this time he re-invented his father as 'Alfred DAVIS (Deceased)', and upgraded his occupation (from the previously conjured-up craft of 'Plumber') to have the rather more select status of 'Farmer'. For the benefit of the documentation, Alfred Wm had 'reduced' his true age of 58 down to 55, towards minimising the true age-gap with his 43 year-old bride. (At his previous marriage he had 'added' four years.) [214]

The Marriage Witnesses appear to have been friends. No photographs seem to have survived in-family. One wonders if Alf's sisters, Rose and Eva, were unhappy at their father re-marrying at this comparatively late stage of his life, when they had been working for him ever since they were youngsters, and presumably hoping to eventually inherit well from his estate. Was that inheritance now to be snatched away from them by this new and relatively young wife who had suddenly come on the scene? Would this new wife's two sons, now, in the eyes of the law, step-sons of Alfred Wm, also 'steal' some of the inheritance away? Did Nellie and her husband Wilf nurse rather similar feelings to those of Rose and Eva? Did Jack and his wife Kate have similar concerns? Could it just be that they all boycotted the wedding? Was it this remarriage which was the stimulus leading to the 27 year-old Rose shortly leaving home, later followed by Eva, now aged 25?

Alf, very much caught up with his fiancée and his career, probably kept at one remove from it all. This may not have been to the unmitigated pleasure of his siblings. Alf may also have heard at this time, from one or another of his sisters, that their father's health was not as good as one would have liked. The father was

---

[213] It is very unfortunate that none of the letters which would have passed between Alf and Olive have survived in-family. The best data that can be found are the few very brief notes written under the photos mounted in Alf's small photo album.

[214] This second marriage was in England, so Alfred Wm did not have to contrive a 'maiden name' for his mother, as he had been required to do for his first marriage in Scotland in 1893. (*Unlike Scottish certificates, English Marriage Certificates require no mention of the names of the mothers of Bride or Groom.*)

clearly well-informed that Alf was also now approaching marriage. The 'hurt rift' between son and father evidently continued unabated and unbridged, but the deep respect and underlying love remained between the two stiffly proud men. Indeed, one wonders if the father was experiencing the stirring of a wish to somehow heal the long-standing split before he departed this life.

As a token of this, a very strange event occurred as the bond between Alf and Olive deepened fast towards marriage. Olive's mother, Agnes Sarah GREEN, who was now due to become Alf's mother-in-law, used to describe this event much as follows: "*One day, I answered a knock at the front door, and found a gentleman standing on the lower step. He was very short in stature, but very smartly dressed, cocksure as a sparrow, and incisively well-spoken. "Good morning", he said, "My name's DAVIS. I understand that my son plans to wed your daughter!"* Invited in, he stayed but a short time, would not wait to be introduced to the bride or other family members, acted rather like a 'cat on hot bricks', and quickly departed. "*And that*", Nan would say, "*Was the only time we ever met Olive's father-in-law to be!*" [215]

Sure enough, Alfred Wm did not attend his son's wedding, which, as we shall shortly see, followed just a few months after his visit. And it seems that the bride-to-be was destined never to meet her father-in-law. One can only conjecture about all this. It certainly seems that Alfred Wm had a burning desire to know the sort of family which his son was marrying into, and that he simply HAD to make some sort of contact. Perhaps he was worried that he might inadvertently 'let a cat out of the bag' if he stayed too long and got into general conversation, especially if he were asked questions about his own parental family and the circumstances of his birth. He might have been very unsure what Alf might already have said on this subject, and been worried that whatever he, Alfred Wm, might say would not be compatible with Alf's own account of events, and might perhaps thus 'ruin his son's chances'.

One way or another we can only speculate as to Alfred Wm's motives. Nor do we know what Alf's reaction may have been, if, indeed, Alf ever came to know about the 'clandestine visit'. Had he done so, one fears that he might have strongly 'warned his father off'.

However, it does seem a great shame that Alfred Wm did not come to know Olive's family better, for one suspects that the GREEN family were already so besotted with Alf that a slightly disreputable family ancestry would have been only a trivial matter to them (especially as the GREENs had their own 'skeletons rattling in the closet'). Had they actually ever met, Olive and Alfred Wm might well have got on 'like a house on fire'. That is to say, Olive probably had many of the strong maternal qualities of Alfred Wm's first wife, and Olive would almost certainly have worked subtly, gently and cleverly to re-unite proud and unbending father with proud and unbending son, just as Eliza would have striven to do had she still been alive. [216]

It is even possible that Alfred Wm, whose days were now numbered, was somehow desperately hoping against hope that he would find Olive 'at home' on the

---

[215] Some versions of this family legend say that Alfred Wm went clandestinely to 'Boots The Chemists', in Ipswich, to sneak a look at Olive as she worked at the cosmetics counter. The Author feels this is *probably* a distortion of the facts.

[216] It is said that men usually marry women who epitomise their *psychological* image of a younger version of their mother. If Alf had chosen his wife-to-be in conformity with this 'expectation', the character of Olive might well have been something of a 'ringer' for that of Eliza, Alfred Wm's first wife.

one occasion when (it appears) he gave way to his emotions and curiosity and made his one call at the GREEN household. He had certainly made a long journey to do so, starting out from Midsomer Norton, and it is likely that he was already far from being a well man.

A faded snapshot from Alf's album.

A developing intimacy. Olive, masquerading in Alf's Gunner's Mate uniform. Photo evidently taken by Alf. Location: By the GREEN's beach hut at Felixstowe.

Olive is holding a mock-cigarette in casual imitation of her fiancé's 'cultivated mannerisms'. Alf had probably never had *anybody* who would gently mock him in such an outrageous way and prick the bubble of his vanity. He would normally become as hostile as any 'Torpoint Chicken' if his personal pride was pricked or if he felt that liberties were being taken with the King's Uniform. Yet, here was Olive, 'getting away with murder'. She really had Alf 'weighed off', and could bend him around her little finger just as she wanted. Her soft answers and calm manner always defused Alf's highly reactive temperament. He was falling head over heels in love with her.

So far as Alf's own courtship of Olive was concerned, well, he would have had a 'good window of opportunity' for short spells of leave at Ipswich in the first days of November 1925, and at times during the period from 1st December 1925 through to 6th January 1926. The above photo was evidently taken that November.

One feels that, during one or other of his leaves, Alf managed to take Olive to Bath and elsewhere around the south of England and to introduce her to his sisters. Some quite deep conversations would then have ensued, with wedding plans and bridesmaids to be agreed. Alf and Olive may also have called on some of Olive's 'distant' relations, such as Walter Lee BUSHBY at Hove, who was a first cousin of Olive's mother.

However that may have been, one can certainly visualise the engaged couple having had a great Christmas-time together at Olive's parental home. By now Alf was long into calling Olive's parents 'Dad' and 'Mum', and they had spontaneously formed what many people would have called a 'mutual admiration society'.

Post-Christmas Alf would have picked up his duties again, for, by the second week of the New Year *St Cyrus* was making sea trials prior to heading out to

Gibraltar on 12ᵗʰ January. Alf would have remained 'in the Med' until the 30ᵗʰ March 1926, when the ship at last came 'home' to Sheerness.

Somewhere along the lines the couple had 'set the date' for 21ˢᵗ April, which turned out to be exactly three weeks ahead of the day *St Cyrus* arrived back at Sheerness. One imagines that Alf had to leave it to Olive to set the reading of Wedding Banns in motion at the Church of St John the Baptist in Ipswich for three successive Sundays ahead of their Wedding Day, whilst (as previously described) he set about having the banns published aboard *St Cyrus*. Fortunately the Church of St John the Baptist lay within a stone's throw of the house where Olive was living with her parents. Alf certainly had leave in April 1926, probably a quick day or two to introduce himself to the Vicar and then further days of leave to attend to the myriad of pre-wedding matters arising, hoping that Olive, doubtless working in conjunction with her parents, had already sent out all the appropriate wedding invitations and fixed the bridesmaids and their dresses well in advance. Alf and Olive must have been corresponding about all this for months – and Olive would have been working to bring Alf's sisters 'into the fold'.

It would all have called for fine judgement on the part of Alf, for he needed to juggle his days of leave to give time for the wedding itself and for the ensuing honeymoon - and to get himself well-prepared for joining his next ship, HMS *Birmingham*, to which he had an immediate appointment. All too soon that ship would be heading off to the Africa Station for three years.

As matters turned out, Alf and Olive had a great wedding day. The Bride looked beautiful. Alf's sister Nellie was a Matron of Honour, and his youngest sister Eva was one of the Bridesmaids. (His middle sister, Rose, also attended. It is unclear as to why she was not also a bridesmaid.) Olive's sister Alice was a Bridesmaid, as was their young cousin Essie BISHOP and as was Olive's friend Millie NUNN. Dilys MORGAN, a tall and strikingly beautiful blonde Welsh-girl who was engaged to Olive's elder brother 'Joe', was another Bridesmaid, making six attendants in total. All these young women looked just fine as can be seen from the following pictures.

One of Alf's Naval friends, Sidney Pelham Harry MITCHELL, was Best Man, and the two of them, being of Warrant Officer status, wore impressive full dress uniform, including 'fore and aft Cocked Hats', their First World War medal ribbons and Dress Swords.[217] The Best Man acted as a marriage witness together with Alf's new in-laws, Joseph and Sarah GREEN. Olive's younger brother, George Neville GREEN, aged 10, was considered sufficiently 'grown-up' to be a part of the main family group. Olive was very popular, her parents had many relatives and friends, and a considerable number of guests attended the ceremony.

They had 'Howard' of Ipswich, a skilled professional photographer, to record the occasion 'for all time'. The Church of St John the Baptist was a modern but rather ugly structure in red brick, and the photographer cleverly used an adjacent church hall of more traditional 'ecclesiastical character' as a backdrop for the pictures which appear overleaf.[218]

---

[217] The author wishes he knew more about Sidney MITCHELL and where he and Alf had met.

[218] This completely foxed the author when, as a part of his research, he was looking around Ipswich for the church in which his parents-to-be had married – and initially 'discarded' the red-brick 'monstrosity' of St John the Baptist, because it was 'no match' at all for the wedding pictures.

From the author's collection of inherited family photographs.

It is the 21st April 1926, at the Church of St John the Baptist in Ipswich, Suffolk. Alfred Wm DAVIS, a Gunner in the Royal Navy and Olive Mabel GREEN, have just become man and wife.

From the author's collection of inherited family photographs.

The main wedding group. From left to right, seated, are Alf's sisters Rose and Nellie. Next comes Olive's elder sister Alice with their younger brother George Neville standing beside Alice. Olive and her mother complete the seated row. Standing behind, from left to right are Alf's younger sister Eva, then Olive's brother Joe and his fiancée Dilys MORGAN. Next come the Best Man and Alf, with Olive's father standing on Alf's left. The row is completed by the remaining two of the six bridesmaids, namely 'Essie' BISHOP, a first cousin of Olive, and a family friend, Millie NUNN.

One assumes that a sizeable reception followed, probably at Olive's parent's home, where her mother, formerly a skilled Cook/Housekeeper at Melford Hall, would doubtless have been cooking and preparing with great skill, as was her wont. Clearly, a fine time was had by all.

One supposes that questions might have been asked by the 'uninitiated' as to where Alf's parents might be, and whether he had any brothers to go with his three attractive sisters. But, as we have seen, his father did not attend (and may well not have been invited), his mother was long dead, Alf (so far as is known) had never met his brand-new step-mother, and he and his (now-married) brother John were 'out of touch' with each other.

The only real 'fly in the ointment' for Alf and Olive was that the honeymoon had to be a very short one, and it was heart-breaking to then have to part. However, Alf had already begun to think seriously of the possibility of having Olive join him out on the Africa Station, and move into married quarters, should this be possible. Seemingly, Olive would be only too willing. He had probably already begun to make 'official enquiries'.

During the interim, the only consolation was that Olive had her family and plenty of good friends around her. She would not be left all alone. But, all the same, parting was very bitter sweet. Such is too-often the lot of 'sailors' and those whom they marry.

CHAPTER ELEVEN:

HMS *BIRMINGHAM* (1926-28)

On 7th April 1926, Alf had been confirmed in the rank of Gunner, with seniority from 1st April 1925. It is believed that he was now being paid at the rate of 14/- a day, with the prospect of an increase to 15/- a day when he achieved three years in that rank.[219] [As a Petty Officer he had probably been receiving about 5/- a day two years earlier. Recently, as an Acting Gunner, he had probably been receiving about 7/- a day.][220] Should he achieve Commissioned Rank after the customary ten years as Gunner, he would probably attain 21/- a day. However, the whole question of pay was constantly 'in the air', due to continuing rumours of cut-backs in pay for all ranks being discussed 'in high places'.

Alf was appointed to HMS *Birmingham* on the 20th April 1926. That was the day the ship was re-commissioned by Captain R.H.L. BEVAN DSO, after her refit at Chatham Dockyard, a new company from the RNB coming aboard. During the next few days the ship received on board three months' stores, including oil, water, fresh provisions, canteen stores, and paint and timber. That is to say nothing of 13 cases of wine and a cask of wine, plus two motor-cars. Fires began to be lit in her boilers, and C-in-C Nore visited the ship to see that all was well, before she departed for Teneriffe.

Alf had clearly enjoyed his time aboard his last ship, *St Cyrus*. Some of the 'sharp corners' had evidently been knocked off his character and he had learned a lot aboard the sturdy little tug. However, it is fairly certain that he had come to feel that he was a 'cruiser man', and that he was glad to be bound for a 'real warship' once again. There he would find some of the ceremonial, smartness and formality into which he liked to fit. Now a married man, and keenly missing his young wife, at least he would have plenty to occupy his professional mind and to distract his emotional side to some degree.

Birmingham would have been very familiar to him, for she was a sister-ship of HMS *Lowestoft*, being a cruiser of 5,440 tons displacement, of length 450 feet and beam 50 feet. We will examine her details more closely a little further on in our story.

Birmingham had a distinguished history, for she had achieved instantaneous international fame in the Great War, when she was reportedly the first British ship to destroy a German submarine. This was the unfortunate U-15, which *Birmingham* destroyed by shellfire coupled with an attempt to ram which may have been effective in forcing the disabled submarine down into the abyss, though no actual contact seems to have occurred. Whichever way the damage was done, U-15 went down with all hands. The encounter took place on 9th August 1914, soon after an unsuccessful attack by several German submarines on a cruiser squadron of the main British Fleet.

Birmingham had been present at the Battle of the Dogger Bank in 1915, and then, as part of the 2nd Light Cruiser Squadron, at the Battle of Jutland in 1916. In May 1925, on her previous deployment to Alf's appointment to her, she had hit the local news in

---

[219] In those days, in 'Civvy Street', a salary of £5 a week was regarded as very good money indeed. Call it 19/- a day on the basis that most people worked 5½ day weeks.

[220] Balanced 'Comparisons' are difficult, because an officer had much greater expenses to meet from his own purse in regard to uniforms, dress sword and wardroom bills.

South Africa by being spectacularly lit overall when the Prince of Wales had paid her a night-time visit whilst she was in port at East London, South Africa.

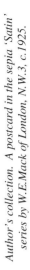

HMS *Birmingham*. The three port-side 6-inch guns on her FX Deck show up well. There was another 6-inch gun placed port-side on her Well Deck. The starboard side was similarly armed, and there was another 6-inch gun placed amidships on her quarter-deck.

She had been at the Equator on the 18th January the previous year, when King Neptune had come aboard and initiated a number of officers and men, including a Leading Telegraphist, Reuben E WILLOUGHBY.[221] She was now home in England, having returned from South Africa in the second week of April and landed the surplus ammunition and stores she had brought back.[222] *Birmingham* had entered No.2 Basin at Chatham on the 14th. She would soon be once again at the Equator, when she might well again be graced by a Neptunian visit.

As we have seen, Alf had just got married. It seems he had already set about securing married quarters on the Africa Station, and then had got a few days compassionate leave, in which to finalise his marriage arrangements, get through the ceremony on 21st April 1926 and squeeze in a quick honeymoon. That honeymoon must have been a short one. That is to say, having completed with stores and ammunition on the 21st/22nd April, and then having had C-in-C Nore come aboard to inspect the ship and the ship's company, followed by giving them a short address, HMS *Birmingham* had proceeded out of the Dock at Chatham on the 27th April. Alf would surely have had to join her by then. It is known that eight officers and 100 men had joined the ship on the 26th April from Chatham and Portsmouth for passage to Simonstown. Alf had probably come aboard at that time. (He might even have had to make something of a 'pierhead

---

[221] The author found Reuben's certificate, addressed "from Davy Jones' Locker", for sale at an antique fair in 2001. It just seemed a shame not to preserve Reuben's name.

[222] Such transporting of redundant ammunition and other stores from the Africa Station seemed to be the normal practice.

jump' on the 27th, though to leave matters so late would seem to have been alien to his highly self-disciplined character. The author therefore discounts this possibility.)

Let's break off for a moment to have a look at Alf's new ship. She was a sister-ship of *Lowestoft,* though she did embody a few minor improvements since Alf's last experience of her sister, such as permanently carrying depth-charge equipment for use against submarines. She also now had Gyro Compasses, which were a distinct improvement over the magnetic type. Her initial cost, back in 1913, had been £353,437. Her complement at that time had been of 400 officers and men. During the war it had risen well above that figure. It had now reduced again slightly, to a current total of 505.

Birmingham, built by the Elswick Yard, was driven by Parsons Combined Impulse Reaction Turbines 'Without Cruise', which had been installed in 1913. Her Boilers were by Hawthorne Leslie & Co., and were of the Yarrow Small Tube type. They had originally been installed in 1913 and renewed in 1922. Her propellers were by Hawthorne Leslie, three-bladed and made of manganese bronze. At Full Power she could do 24 knots (351 rpm), at which she would burn 24.25 tons of coal per hour. Her Most Economical Speed was 10 knots (135 rpm), at which she would burn 3.1 tons of coal per hour. Since she could carry 1,200 tons of coal (maximum), she had a potential range of 3,870 miles at her Most Economical Speed.[223] (Though only 1,188 miles at Full Power.) Her draught with Bunkers Full was 18ft 0 ins forward and 18 ft 6 ins aft. Her draught was increased by 1 inch for every 36.89 tons above her standard draught.

Name of Ship	Type Of Ship	Displace-ment (tons)	Year Completed	1st Year Alf srv'd (diff.)	Comple-ment	Max. Length (feet)	Max. Beam (feet)	Draught (feet)	Shaft Horse-Power	Max. Speed (knots)
Vanguard	Dreadnought	**19,250**	1910	1912 (2)	823	536	**84**	**31.75**	24,500	22
Russell	Pre-Dreadnought	14,000	1903	1912 (9)	718	418	75.5	28	18,220	19
Weymouth	Armour'd Cruiser	5,250	1911	1913 (2)	392	453	48.5	18	22,000	25.5
Courageous	Battle Cruiser	18,600	1916	1916 **(0)**	**829**	**786.5**	81	26	**90,000**	**35**
Lowestoft	Armour'd Cruiser	5,440	1913	1920 (7)	546	459.5	49.8	18.25	25,000	25.5
St Cyrus	Admiralty Tug	820	**1919**	1925 (6)	12	143	29	13.5	1,200	12
Birmingham	Armour'd Cruiser	5,440	1913	1925 (12)	504	459	49.8	18	25,000	25.5

Name of Ship	Guns					Torpedo-Tubes		Armour			
	Main		Secondary		A.A			Deck	Side	Turr't	D.C.T
	Calibre	Number	Calibre	Number	Capability	Calibre	Number	(ins)	(ins)	(ins)	(ins)
Vanguard	12"	**Ten**	**4"**	Twelve	**2x3"**	18"	Three	1.5 - 3	**10**	**11**	**8 – 11**
Russell	12"	Four	**6"**	Twelve	-	18"	Four	2.5	3-4	6	12
Weymouth	6"	Eight	3"	One	1x3"	21"	Two	1-2	Nil	1	2
Courageous	**15"**	Four	4"	**Eighteen**	**2x3"**	21"	**Fourteen**	1-3	3	7-9	10
Lowestoft	6"	Nine	3 pdr	Four	1x3"	21"	Nine	1-2	3	1	2
St Cyrus	12 pdr	One	-	-	-	-	-	-	-	-	-
Birmingham	6"	Nine	3 pdr	Four	1x3"	**21"**	Eleven	1-2	3	1	2

As can be seen from the general absence of **bold** figures along the 'bottom lines', *Birmingham* was not 'breaking any records' so far as Alf's experiences were concerned. Moreover, as can be seen from the fourth column, she was 12 years old when this

---

[223] Appreciably more than this if she also burned some of her 233 tons of oil.

commission started, making her the 'oldest-vessel-since-year-of-first-commissioning' in which Alf had served. None the less for that, she was going to be of considerable significance to Alf in various respects, both professional and emotional.

The ship's armament consisted of:

Stb and Port Side FX Deck,	B.L 6" Mk XII P VII Mtg:	6
Stb and Port Side Well Deck,	B.L 6" Mk XII P VII Mtg:	2
Quarter Deck Amidships,	B.L 6" Mk XII P VII Mtg:	1
FX Deck Amidships,	Q.F 3" HA Mk I P Mk II Mtg:	1
Stb & Port Side Well Deck	Hotchkiss Q.F 3 pdr Saluting:	4
Port Main Deck Passage	Hotchkiss Q.F 3 pdr Sub-Cal:	4
Stb Aft Seamen's Mess Deck	Hotchkiss QF Sub-Calibre:	2
Stb Side Fwd Well Deck, Field Gun,	8 cwt, 12 pdr, on carriage:	1

She also had:

2 submerged 21" Torpedo Tubes, one Port side and one Starboard,
(Both Beam Bearing.)
Nine 21" Mk II Torpedoes.
Two Hydraulically-operated Depth-Charge Chutes.
Six Depth-Charges.

She carried a large outfit of boats, namely:-

	No Persons/Craft	*Total*
2 x 35 ft Motor Boats	40	80
1 x 34 ft Drop Keel Cutter	66	66
2 x 30 ft Cutters	49	98
2 x 30 ft Drop Keel Gigs	26	52
2 x 27 ft Whalers	27	54
2 x 16 ft Skiffs	10	20
2 x Carley Floats (Large)	45	90
2 x Carley Floats (Small)	18	36
	TOTAL	*496*

This total would signify that she had just about sufficient 'boats' for her normal complement of 505 souls. However, had she suffered a need to abandon ship during her current voyage, she would have been hard set to find space in her boats for the further eight officers and 100 men whom she was taking out to the Africa Station, of whom the majority (68 ratings) had draft chits to join 'Wallflower'. One assumes that, had the worst happened, men would have been 'taking turns in the water' to prevent the boats from being dangerously overloaded.

The ship's company of 505 souls was comprised of 24 Officers RN, one Officer RNR, 160 Seamen, 17 Boys, 46 Marines, 209 Engine Room Establishment and 48 Non-Executive Ratings.

Her Commander was Captain R.H.L BEVAN DSO, and her Navigating officer was Commander (N) C.P. BOWEN. From the officers leaving the ship at various times during the ensuing months (and as their replacements joined ship in ones and twos after being appointed from the U.K), we can reconstruct the surnames of twenty out of the total of 25 officers and WOs whom Alf would have come to know in the early part of the commission, namely:-

Captain	R.H.L BEVAN DSO
Commander (N)	C.P. BOWEN
Lt Commander	GREY
Lt Commander	MORTON
Lt Commander	SWANSTON
Lt Commander	WALLER
Lt	DOWLING
Lt	FOX
Lt	FULLER
Lt	MITFORD
S/Lt	STEPHINSON
S/Lt	WARRAND
Major, RM.	BREWER
Major, RM.	YEO
Surgeon Commander	POOS
Surgeon Lt Cmdr	NEWMAN
Pay Lt Cmdr	E.A. SYMS
Commd Gunner	Mr GARDNER
Gunner	Mr A.W. DAVIS
Commd Signal Bos'n	Mr COOK

It would seem that some Midshipmen, together with one Gunner (T) and one Shipwright of warrant rank are missing from this list of names. One of the missing names may well be WEATHERLY, but the related rank and speciality are unknown.[224] Other 'missing' names would have been those of Engineering Officers and WOs, whose comings and goings seem to have seldom been recorded in the Logs of naval ships, rather as if they were something of a law unto themselves.

As already indicated, *Birmingham* was fitted with depth-charge chutes and carried depth-charges. Anti-submarine measures were by now an integral part of the equipment and function of RN cruisers.

However, it's time to get back to 27th April 1926, with *Birmingham* proceeding from Chatham. As matters turned out, a defect occurred in *Birmingham's* port engine (later found to be basically due to a misplaced indicator) as she passed Kethole Reach at Sheerness after undocking, and she was very fortunate that the sea was calm, and there was little wind, for she had the embarrassment of having to hoist an NUC signal until she

---

[224] See the names of persons who wrote to the family when they heard of Alf's death in 1941.

could secure to No.5 Buoy at Sheerness, whilst her engineers diagnosed and overcame the problem.[225]

Then *Birmingham*, her 'engine problem' quickly resolved, proceeded from Chatham for Teneriffe, having quickly exercised collision stations, and then headed for those more southerly climes, being at 50° 23' N, 00° 28' W, just west of the longitude of Greeenwich, and heading through the English Channel at noon on the 28th. However, there was another snag, for her young Stokers could not continuously 'shovel coal' fast enough to keep up the 155 revs required for 11 knots, and few of even the Leading Stokers and POs had any experience in coal-burning ships![226] Such was the price for going to sea in a ship built back in 1913, in a Navy which had since converted mainly to oil. [Many of the younger members of the ship's company had tasted the experience of 'coaling ship' *for the first time* on joining ship at Chatham, finding it a dirty and arduous experience. Alf was inured to it. Although the Navy had well over 200 oil-burning ships by this stage, only *Courageous* had provided the facility of oil in his *personal* experience of ships to date. He would have played his due part in coaling - but now with the advantage that he could wash off the grime under conditions of greater comfort, in the officers' bathroom.]

Next day *Birmingham* exercised her seaboat's crew and lowerers, and practised 'Prepare to Tow Aft', followed next day by 'Prepare to Tow Forward', with more exercising of her seaboat's crew. Her hands were at Gunnery and Torpedo duties the next day, and Alf was in the picture, signing as OOD. On Saturday 1st May the hands were given what should have been a relaxing 'Make and Mend', but the weather began to deteriorate, with the wind rising to Force 5 and a rough sea with a westerly swell getting up. The ship was rolling, the maximum being recorded as 23 degrees. This must have considerably aggravated the difficulties affecting the ability of the mainly inexperienced Stokers to 'shovel coal', and, indeed, probably led to much seasickness amongst the newly-joined company in all the departments. As has been said before, it seems that Alf did not suffer from this malady, and the Log would appear to confirm this, for he again did a stint as OOW at this time.

At 1452 on the 2nd May *Birmingham* passed the German steamship *Santa Theresa* of Hamburg, the two ships being on opposite courses about 4 cables distant. The German ship failed to dip her ensign, which Captain BEVAN took to be 'intentionally disrespectful', and would later report as much to his C-in-C.

By 3rd May life was falling into a pattern aboard, with rigging and sailmakers' parties at work, the gun's crews taking it in turns, day by day, to practice at the Loader, and painting taking place in the flats and wherever considered necessary. The paravanes were streamed for six hours on the 3rd. The weather had eased and the roll was down to 17 degrees. The sick list had grown to thirteen. Next day the ship arrived at Teneriffe, having quickly run 1,625 miles, and hoisting the Spanish ensign at the main as she came to anchor off Santa Cruz. The British Consul came aboard for a short informal visit and the Spanish Officer of the Guard for an even shorter informal visit. A water boat came

[225] NUC meant 'Not Under Control', signalling that the ship was a potential danger to herself and all and sundry.
[226] 'Shovelling Coal' required not just muscle power and endurance, but skill to 'trim' the furnaces as the coal was thrown in, using a deft twist of the wrists to fan the 'spray' of coal as it left the shovel, and thus to provide a smooth bed of flames which gave an even spread of heat to the boiler-tubes.

alongside, and a brief leave ashore was given to the 1st Class POs, a party of about 40 men going ashore. Next day the company coaled ship (904 tons), native labour filling the coal bags before they were hoisted aboard. The hands then cleaned ship and dressed the ship overall in honour of Accession Day. That day the official visits began, starting with the British Consul, then, (whilst the Consul remained on board), the ADC of the Spanish Military Governor, and then the Spanish Civil Governor.[227] A salute was fired as the Military and Civil Governors left the ship. The ship fired a noon-time salute of 21 guns in Honour of Accession Day, and this was returned by the Spanish shore battery. The British Consul left the ship during the mid-afternoon.

On the 8th May 1926 the ship proceeded for Monrovia, the temperature heading up into the 70s in degrees Fahrenheit, and the breeze stiffening though the sea remained quite calm. The sick list was still climbing for some reason, reaching 17 on the 10th May. On that day, at 11° 31' N, 17° 57' W the steering engine suddenly broke down, and *Birmingham* was obliged to hoist an 'NUC' signal for a while. She changed over to fore bridge steering whilst the problem was being resolved. Her Gyro Repeater then chose to stop, and steering had to be by magnetic compass until that second problem had been overcome.

At noon on 12th May she was at 05° 24' N, 10° 57' W, and she put her Guard of Honour to drill before arriving at Monrovia at 1300, with 1,487 miles run. She fired a 21 gun salute in honour of the country, and Mr SMALLBONES the British *Chargé d'Affaires* (who doubled as Consul-General) visited the ship accompanied by Mrs SMALLBONES. A 13-gun salute was fired as they left. Captain BEVAN went ashore with the Consul-General and they visited HE The President of Liberia, who officially thanked them for the present of two 6 pdr guns, free and gratis. Meanwhile the ship had landed fourteen 'packages' containing the two guns, complete with their carriages, pedestals and ammunition. The Captain then returned on board, and the ship proceeded south to St Helena.

On 13th May 1926 the ship ran through a very heavy rainstorm, but practised streaming and recovering her paravanes, and later, as the weather cleared, furling the fore part of her fo'csle awnings and rigging a screen and large canvas bath on the fo'csle deck as she ran ever more southwards towards the Equator. Sure enough, at 2100, H.M King Neptune, who had last set foot aboard this ship on 18th January 1924 and who was certainly no stranger to *Birmingham*, again came aboard accompanied by his Court. He met Captain BEVAN, said that there were men aboard who had not been 'introduced' to him, and claimed that these men should be made 'true seamen' next day. Captain BEVAN acquiesced.

Next day the ship exercised her seaboats' crews and lowerers, before holding Divisions and Prayers and sending her hands to General Quarters. Then, at 1400, H.M. King Neptune came aboard formally with his acolytes and held Court. By this time the canvas bath had been filled with water and a chair had been specially rigged overlooking the bath. One source says the ship was then at 00° 31' S, 09° 11' W, whereas another source claims 00° 00', 09° 23' W. Perhaps King Neptune had cast something of a spell over the mariners.

---

[227] The Spanish Captain-General had sent his ADC because, by regulation, he was not permitted to visit a foreign man o' war.

Be the truth of that as it may, this time there was no escape for Alf, and he was one of those who went through the necessary 'trials and tribulations', being sat in the chair, 'lathered' with a noxious mixture, and 'shaved' with a colossal 'razor' before being tipped unceremoniously out of the chair and headlong into the bath, to gain his 'Crossed the Line' certificate. This document, which was inherited by the author, earned Alf various nautical privileges and 'protection' from sharks, whales, eels, shrimps and whelks, to mention but a few of the fierce denizens of the Deep. It seems that much fun was had by all concerned - even those who, like Alf, were well and truly 'lathered, shaved and ducked'!

Then it was back to normality in the days which followed, unrigging the canvas bath, surviving "Captain's Rounds", and dealing with such excitements as exercising 'Fire in the After Provision Room' and 'Let Go Starboard Lifebuoy - Recover it by Whaler', before the lonely island of St Helena hove in sight on 18th May, glimpsed initially through a break in a series of heavy squalls. (Had they slightly provoked King Neptune, one wonders?) They came to anchor in 27 fathoms, with 1,378 miles run, and started to coal almost immediately from two lighters which promptly secured alongside. The officers and company would continue coaling next day, embarking, in total, 825 tons.

A snapshot from Alf's photo album.

Coaling ship. *"Alf, Ellis and 'The Sub'."*
Clearly, almost everybody 'pitched in' during
the arduous job of coaling ship.

They also took in 38 tons of fresh water, with more to follow. Their sick list was slightly reduced, now being down to 12 men, but with two of the sick men having had to be discharged to hospital ashore for more specialised treatment. The wind and sea were calm. The temperature was 70° F. The Fo'csle Awnings were spread. A Court of inquiry was held at the RM Barracks. Shore leave was given. *Tropical Helmets were 'Dress of the Day'.*[228]

On 22nd May 1926 the ship proceeded south-east to Capetown, with a swell getting up and the ship beginning to roll again, reaching a maximum of 20 degrees on the 23rd May. Despite the roll, she was regularly exercising her seaboat's crew, and putting her guns' crews to drill. She was having some difficulty with her Master Gyro, and taking steps to clear it. She also put her Guard of Honour to drill. Next day the ritual of 'Divisions' was held, but, unusually, with gasmasks, followed by gas mask drill and an inspection of gas masks by the Captain, before the gun crews were again put to drill. Further measures were being taken to clear the problem with the Master Gyro, and collision stations were also being practised. On the 27th the lower deck was cleared and Captain BEVAN addressed the Ship's Company before the ship came to anchor at Capetown with 1,690 miles run.[229] A Pilot came on board and the ship proceeded into the basin, where she secured in No.1 Berth alongside the South Wall.

Next day the ship landed her RM Guard of Honour for drill whilst the ship coaled, using Native labour. She discharged 1 WO, 5 POs, 1 CPO, and 1 AB to *Wallflower* and 1 PO to *Lowestoft*.[230] She also landed her Seaman Guard and Colour Party, gave leave to the off-duty watch until 0700 and landed a shore patrol of 1 PO, 1 LS and 4 ABs to keep order.

On 29th May 1926 *Birmingham* proceeded to Simonstown, dropping the Pilot at 0755, and later hoisting the flag of Sir Maurice FITZMAURICE KCVO, CB, before securing to No.1 Buoy at Simonstown just as a heavy downpour of rain began. Later, she discharged Lt DOWLING, S/Lts WARRAND and FOX and five Midshipmen to *Lowestoft* Next day the ship was dressed overall for Union Day, her Guard of Honour again being landed for drill. Her sick list had been holding at a round dozen, and she now discharged five ratings to hospital ashore. On 2nd June the ship again landed her Guard of Honour, this time to take part in dress rehearsals for a presentation on the next day. This was on 3rd June, when the ship was dressed overall in Honour of the Birthday of King George V, and the ship landed her Guard of Honour and a Party to witness the Presentation to the Africa Squadron of the King's Colour by H.R.H the Countess of Athlone. The presentation of a colour was a rare event, and *Birmingham, Lowestoft, Verbena, Wallflower* and *Delphinium* were all present, together with His Majesties South African ships *Protea, Sonneblom* and *Immortelle*. This was said to be a short but extremely impressive ceremony. A Royal Salute of 21 guns was fired, and the King's Colour was subsequently received on board *Birmingham*.[231]

---

[228] This note, extracted literally from the Log, is reminiscent of the legendary WW2 Tannoy message at Portsmouth which caused a lot of ribaldry, *"WRNS will wear Caps and Shoes. That is all."*

[229] Although no official record has been found of what was said, collateral evidence would strongly indicate that he was warning the men who had not served on this station before of the need to exercise great care against the strength of the sun, and also of the dangers of being violently robbed and possibly murdered if they wandered into certain native areas. Also of the very real dangers of catching sexually-transmitted diseases from the native women. He probably also reminded them that they were representatives of the Royal Navy and the British Empire, and must always uphold the 'Honour of the Flag'.

[230] One suspects that the Log had failed to record a much larger disembarkation a day or so earlier, since she was carrying a total of about 100 ratings for transfer to other ships when she left the UK.

[231] Only *Daffodil* was missing from this celebration. She was then lying at Luanda.

On the 4th *Birmingham* discharged to *Wallflower* 11 cases of rifles and other equipment from the ASO at Chatham, and two cases of WT equipment to *Lowestoft*. Eight 'Seedie' hands joined and were put to cleaning the ship's side.[232] On the 6th the hands were mustered by ledger for inspection by the C-in-C, and he arrived on board 10 minutes later to inspect the Ship's Company. Next day, *Birmingham* landed 10 cases of ammunition from St Helena for test, also 2 x 1-inch aiming tubes and one round of 3-pdr sub/cal ammunition. She also discharged one of her POs to *Lowestoft* under escort for Trial by Court Martial. On 8th June 1926 she fired the Court Martial Gun and broke the Jack at 0800, the Court Martial assembling on board at 0930, the President being Captain G.W. TAYLOR. The court adjourned at 1810, and sat again on Thursday 10th June from 0900 until it terminated at 1440. (*The charge and the decision of the Court are unknown to the author*.)[233]

The ship had landed a recreation ground working party on 9th June, and a Royal Marine Range Party on the 11th June. That day the ship received one field gun complete from the ASO together with stores and ammunition. On 14th June the ship carried out a Director Test of her starboard guns, had a Target party rigging a BP ('Battle Practice') Target, provisioned ship and exercised her Control Parties. Alf's name was pencilled-in as OOW on 27th May, but he had not over-signed it in ink, as seemed to be the usual practice. One assumes this was just an accidental oversight. Perhaps he was day-dreaming about his young wife Olive – or perhaps he was just extremely busy.

The C-in-C came aboard *Birmingham* on 15th June 1926 and she put to sea with *Lowestoft* and the sloops *Verbena* and *Wallflower* in company, carrying out manoeuvres at 10 knots, involving full-calibre firing with reduced charges by *Birmingham* and *Lowestoft* at a 100 ft BP Target towed by the tug *St Dogmael* which had a marking party from *Birmingham* aboard. Alf would have been busy with the gunnery aspects, but one wonders if memories of the problems of target-towing during his time aboard *St Cyrus* flitted through his mind as he watched the evolutions of *St Dogmael*. (See following photographs.)

The manoeuvres then continued with various evolutions of line ahead, line abreast, and 'exact' column and station-keeping. Searchlights were exercised by night. On the 16th June, *Verbena* and *Wallflower* parted company (to proceed to Port Elizabeth), and *Birmingham* and *Lowestoft* came to anchor in Mossel Bay.

The C-in-C had the intention of entertaining some of the local people on board, but this proved to be impossible due to frequent rainstorms and a heavy swell. His report to the Admiralty said that he felt this was very unfortunate, as the municipality showed much hospitality to the officers and ship's companies. On 18th/19th June, accompanied by a party of officers, he managed to get ashore on a visit to the City of George as a guest of the Mayor and Corporation, and attended a civic ball, but that had been the maximum possible.

---

[232] Seedies are understood to have been the naval equivalent of merchantile Lascar Seamen.

[233] The C-in-C mentioned the matter to the Admiralty in his Letter of Proceedings, saying, in effect, that the high quality of the men meant that Courts Martial were becoming increasingly rare events. Hence that any Junior Captain might find himself called upon to act as President of a Court without ever having had the valuable previous experience of sitting as Member of one. The C-in-C therefore recommended to Their Lordships that appropriate training should be added to Senior Officers Technical Courses.

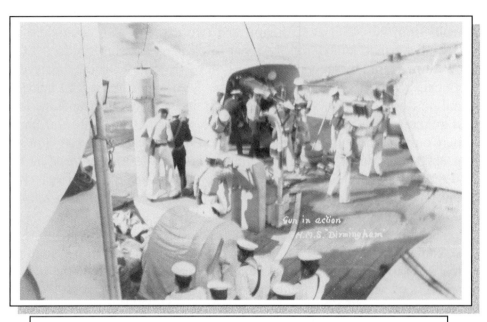

A 6-inch gun in action, HMS *Birmingham*. The officer standing by the tall ventilator, and observing the fall of shot, may well be Alf. Note the high level of exposure of all the men (except the few closed up in the gun-shield), to shrapnel or flying debris from any incoming shell-fire.

The C-in-C's Shoot. Shells from HMS *Birmingham* are causing splashes around the BP target, at a range of 13,000 yards (6½ sea miles).

On 21ˢᵗ June, now rejoined by *Wallflower* and *Verbena*, *Lowestoft* and *Birmingham* proceeded for East London, *Birmingham* rigging her paravanes, closing up her Blue Watch navigational party, exercising her searchlight crews and, later, carrying out a searchlight exercise with *Wallflower*. Aboard *Lowestoft* much the same exercises would have been going on.

On the 22nd June, the C-in-C took the opportunity to carry out an exercise in reporting the enemy and maintaining touch with a cruiser screen. He had previously arranged for the two South African naval ships *Sonneblom* and *Immortelle*, and four aircraft of the Union Air Force to co-operate in this exercise, the aeroplanes acting as reconnaissance for the 'Blue' (or retreating) cruisers. No strategical problems were set. The object was to refresh the memory of all concerned in the methods to be used. The aircraft made WT reports but were fitted with transmitters only, so they could not receive WT signals. The C-in-C hoped that this exercise might be the forerunner of more elaborate ones later.

Wallflower took station 7 cables off 'the Flag' (i.e. *Birmingham*) on a bearing of 138 degrees. Both ships were acting as a cruiser screen for their (imaginary) 'Red' Battlefleet, and steaming at 10½ knots, both streaming their paravanes. At 0700 they began what their log called their 'strategical' exercise, and increased to 11½ knots when they sighted the Blue 'Fleet' (the cruiser screen of that fleet being represented by *Lowestoft and Verbena*). At 0830 they exercised action, 15 minutes later engaging *Verbena* at 15,000 yards on a bearing of 086 degrees. Seven minutes later an unidentified and suspect aeroplane was sighted on very nearly the same bearing.[234]

Almost an hour later, *Birmingham* dropped two smoke floats to create some protection from view, and engaged *Lowestoft* 90 minutes later. At the conclusion of the exercise, one and a half hours later, *Birmingham* hauled her paravanes, a Pilot came aboard, and the ship secured alongside at East London late in the afternoon of that same day with 310 miles run from Mossel Bay to East London, including the extensive manoeuvring of the 'strategical exercises'. Her passage up the Buffalo River to East London was photographed. (See following photo.). The ship was immediately dressed overall in Honour of the Coronation of KGV and Queen Mary.

On 23rd June 1926 the hands worked the main derrick, hoisting out the gig and whaler and then the field gun. A shore patrol was also landed. Next day, the ship landed her RM. detachment for a route march which was badly-needed 'to stretch their legs', and her company went to Quarters at 1600. That evening a Ball was given by the Mayor and Mayoress in honour of the visiting ships, and the function was attended by a large number of the ships' officers.

On the 26th the C-in-C and the ships' captains were invited to dinner by the Mayor and Mayoress. That same day a motor outing was arranged for the ships' officers by the local branch of the Navy League of South Africa. On the 27th June the Captain Addressed the Ship's Company after Divisions and then the C-in-C, officers and men of the ship were photographed on the fo'c'sle, the ship subsequently being open to visitors. The Royal Marine Band was landed that evening to play in a very successful concert at East London City Hall, in a reasonable external temperature of 68° F. Various sporting events likewise took place. The final day at East London was a strenuous one, with a submersible pump being rigged early on, the order given 'Away all Boats under Oars',

---

[234] This would suggest that the Captains of the Red Fleet were unaware that the C-in-C had arranged for the use of aircraft by the Blue Fleet. Perhaps the C-in-C had just 'dropped a few clues' about being alert to all possibilities....

and the hands put to physical drill. Then a very elaborate party was given by the officers of *Birmingham* to about 200 of the local children, this being followed, for the hands, by 'cleaning ship' (i.e. dismounting all the slides, aerial rides, skittles and other 'amusements', and striking the equipment below.)

Author's collection. An anonymous postcard, c.1926.

HMS *Birmingham* making her way up the Buffalo River to East London. The hands are preparing the Admiral's barge for lowering. Five days of festivities will follow.

Next day a Pilot came aboard and tugs were employed to get *Birmingham* out to sea, proceeding for Durban. Again, physical drill was held aboard after the pilot had been dropped at the breakwater. (See photo below.) Once at Durban, they again used a Pilot to enter harbour, then coaled using native labour and embarking 475 tons.

The C-in-C's report to the Admiralty for this period refers indirectly to the Coal Strike which was ongoing back in England, as part of the General Strike, and which had meant that no collier had arrived from England to replenish the stocks of coal at Durban. The C-in-C had originally intended that, flying his Flag in *Birmingham*, he would visit Madagascar, but there was no Welsh coal available for *Birmingham* at the Madagascan ports either, and this plan had to 'go by the board'. Indeed, it was his understanding that the low stocks remaining at Durban were going to limit the onward cruise of the squadron to no further than Lourenco Marques. In the event, the stocks were even lower than he had anticipated, for *Lowestoft* had found only 900 tons, and not the expected 1,100 tons, when she had coaled just days before *Birmingham's* arrival. *Lowestoft* had taken a 'large half' of it. Seemingly, *Birmingham's* men had been obliged to 'sweep the dump' to get the last of the Welsh coal, and the two sloops had perforce to take on board only the Natal coal, which was poor stuff. To relieve the situation, the C-in-C authorised the burning of oil by *Birmingham* and *Lowestoft*.

Visits now began to be exchanged between the C-in-C and representatives coming aboard to see him, first the French and American Consuls and then the Portuguese

Consul, each being saluted with seven guns. Considerable hospitality was shown by the Durban Turf Club, The Royal Natal Yacht Club and the Durban Branch of the Navy League of South Africa. On 4th July the Governor-General and H.R.H Princess Alice, Countess of Athlone and staff attended Divine Service aboard, the ship being open to visitors during the afternoon.

Author's collection. An anonymous postcard, c.1926.

Physical drill on the f'c'sle of HMS *Birmingham.* Fifty men are working out, with four POs supervising them.

On the 5th July the Boys were landed for a Motor Drive to see the sights. The hands were exercised with all boats being away under oars and sail. Then provisions were embarked and the boats gear refitted as requisite. Whilst this was going on the wind sprang up very suddenly from the south-west, reaching Force 5.

On the 5th July there was a sailing dinghy race for all officers of the squadron held by the Royal Natal Yacht Club, which was won by the highly elated but duly modest C-in-C himself.[235]

Then, on 6th July 1926, all boats were away sailing for the Royal Natal Yacht Club Cup. This race, which was for seamen ratings, was won by a narrow margin by *Lowestoft's* 1st cutter, *Protea's* 2nd whaler being in hot contention right to the line.

The C-in-C, Captain and officers of *Birmingham* were subsequently 'At Home' to the Chairmen and Stewards of all the clubs mentioned. On 7th July a dinner and ball were

---

[235] Here and there in this narrative, the author has drawn upon the C-in-C's 'Visits of HM Ships 1925/26' as made to the Admiralty at that time. (See ADM116/4354/55 at TNA) The C-in-C's comments are often very informative and valuable. Whilst the general tenor is formally 'impersonal', human feelings do creep into the text from time to time, and Vice Admiral Sir Maurice FITZMAURICE's obvious pride in his achievement in winning the sailing dinghy race, albeit expressed with all due modesty, was one such personal note which the author of this book found to be very appealing. Well done, Sir! Bravo!

given by His Excellency the Governor-General and H.R.H Princess Alice to which many officers had the honour of being invited.

One presumes that Alf was involved in various of these activities. Certainly, he seems to have kept some photos which appear to relate to the various events, two of which are reproduced below.

Two snapshots from Alf's photo album.

HMS *Birmingham*, with *Lowestoft* lying outboard of her, is open to visitors. The lower picture shows *'Mr BIRD with Durban friends'*.

At 0600 on the 8th July the ship proceeded in company with *Lowestoft, Verbena* and *Wallflower*, heading northwards up the east coast for Lourenco Marques. On the way the ships assumed varying formations, carried out inclination exercises and manoeuvred in close order. *Birmingham* embarked a Pilot to enter harbour at Lourenco Marques on the afternoon of 9th July, after her 280 mile voyage, gave a 21-gun salute, and she proceeded to go alongside the 'A' Shed at St George's Quay, whilst the other three ships moored out in the harbour.

Mr PYKE, the newly-appointed British Consul General visited the C-in-C, Sir Maurice FITZMAURICE, being saluted with 11 guns.[236] He then accompanied the C-in-C as Sir Maurice called on HE the (Acting) High Commissioner of Mozambique, Colonel FERRAZ. The French, German and U.S. Consuls then visited the C-in-C, each receiving a 7-gun salute. The Governor-General received no less than 19 guns when he subsequently visited the C-in-C, bringing aboard and introducing to him the leading members of the British Colony. That afternoon squadron teams played Lourenco Marques at both Association Football and Rugby Football and, in the evening, the C-in-C and twelve senior officers dined at the Palace as guests of the Acting High Commissioner. A gymkhana had been arranged for the next day, but the weather turned so wet and cold 'as to make it a fiasco'. However, the Squadron played Lourenco Marques at Golf, losing by a narrow margin. On the 12th a large ball was given by the Portuguese authorities, at the Military Club, in honour of the visit by the Squadron, and various sporting events ensued, including tennis and football in aid of the funds of the Seamen's Institute. *Lowestoft's* concert party performed for the same cause. [*Joseph PYKE, the Consul-General, was inspired to write to the Admiralty on the very next day, saying that 400 ratings attended at the Seamen's Institute, and that the concert was a great success. The men were entertained afterwards at the Boat Club. He added that a race meeting was held, and a shooting party organised, as well as confirming that football, golf and tennis matches were played and dances held.*]

On the 15th July the C-in-C held a select dinner aboard *Birmingham*, to which the High Commissioner, the Bishop of Mozambique and Lebombo, the British Consul-General and the principal Portuguese Officers and Officials together with representatives of the British Colony were invited, followed by a Ball to which about 200 guests were invited, the ship spreading new awnings to create some welcome shade. That same day *Verbena* had been dispatched to coal and collect the squadron mails at Durban.

On the 17th July the C-in-C made a farewell call on the High Commissioner, whom he had found to be a person of high integrity and pleasant personality, with a good command of the English Language. [*The C-in-C would later report to the Admiralty that he had found Lourenco Marques to be a fast-spreading town whose British residents spoke highly of the efforts being made to enforce good sanitation and to stamp out malaria.*]

Then with the C-in-C's Flag still flying in *Birmingham***,** the two cruisers proceeded for Saldhana Bay, heading southwards around the Cape. On her way *Birmingham* carried out HA firing in conjunction with *Lowestoft*, and made rendezvous with *Verbena*, sending a boat to her for welcome mail. *Birmingham* exercised steering by hand wheel for a short spell.

Although not mentioned in *Birmingham's* Log, the C-in-C carried out an experiment on the 18th, stationing *Verbena* five miles off the starboard beam of *Birmingham*, and *Lowestoft* 5 miles off *Birmingham's* port beam, and ordering all three ships to use revs for 10 knots whilst they headed southward during their passage from

---

[236] At that time neither the C-in-C, nor Mr PYKE, were aware that the Foreign Office had recently authorised '13 guns' to be fired as the proper salute for a Consul-General.

Durban. *Birmingham* was ordered to maintain an offing of 20 miles from the coast as the other ships 'formed' on her. It was found that *Verbena* gradually drew ahead relative to *Birmingham* and *Lowestoft* gradually fell back. Over a period of six hours it was found that *Verbena* had averaged 1.9 knots faster than *Lowestoft* in terms of the actual distance they had traversed. *Verbena's* course had taken her one or two miles outside the 100 fathom line, and the C-in-C therefore believed that the maximum strength of the Agulhas Current was to be encountered just outside that 100 fathom line.

On the 19th the wind got up to Force 6 from the west, and continued to rise whilst the temperature fell to 48° F. The sloops were 'not comfortable' at the cruisers 'most economic speed' of 10 knots in the sea which was now running, and the C-in-C ordered the sloops to continue to Saldhana Bay at the best speed they could manage in tolerable comfort, whilst *Birmingham* and *Lowestoft* continued at 10 knots. Going ahead of the sloops in what was by now a full-blooded 'Force 8', allowed the cruisers time to head into Simonstown to land their sick cases at the RN Hospital, and to pick up the very latest mails. Meantime, the Senior Officer of the sloops had requested permission to seek shelter in False Bay, as he considered it unsafe to risk the sloops beam-on to the very heavy seas which were by then running. The C-in-C concurred, directed his two cruisers to stay in Simonstown overnight, and cancelled the proposed visit to Saldanha Bay because the westerly gale continued and he considered that bay too open to the west for the general drills and boatwork he had in mind.[237] Instead, on the 22nd, with the ships still at Simonstown, the order was given 'Out Kedge Anchor', and then, 'Raise by Hand', followed by 'Away All Boats, Pull Round the Fleet'. The C-in-C then left the ship for Admiralty House, followed by his staff. One imagines that the effort of raising her kedge anchor by hand, although presumably carried out with the aid of a three-fold purchase, was still a little too much for *Birmingham's* company to manage, with the ship pitching and rolling under the conditions prevailing. That is to say, according to her Log, she lost her kedge anchor at this time, together with six fathoms of manilla cable. She sent her divers down to recover the anchor next day, when the weather conditions had abated.

Come the 26th she was at sea, exercising, the practice including long range torpedo attacks against *Daffodil* and *Wallflower*, 3 pdr sub/cal firing against a target towed by *Wallflower*, the rigging of the hand capstan, the exercises 'Abandon Ship', 'Pull Round the Fleet', 'Out Bower Anchor', 'Out Kedge Anchor and Weigh By Hand'. Next day the P4 gun crew were practising at the Loader.

On the 29th July 1926 the ship landed her emergency battalion to support her RM Detachment, and, on the 30th, the C-in-C came aboard temporarily whilst the ship carried out a night encounter exercise with *Lowestoft* which involved the firing and recovery of a torpedo. On the 2nd August the ship was dressed overall to celebrate the Birthday of King George V, a Royal Salute of 21 guns being fired at noon. Then, on 5th August, the Annual Pulling Regatta was held, *Lowestoft* winning the Cruisers' event and *Verbena* the Sloops' event. *Birmingham* proceeded into the basin at this time, and embarked 902 tons of coal. Her sick list was by now down to the respectable level of just four or five men.

On the 9th she carried out sub/cal firing at a Pattern VII target towed by the tug *St Dogmael*. She also fired two torpedoes. Later, her gun crews were exercised at the

---

[237] This was a vicious gale, being accompanied by rain, hail and snow. The 21st was the coldest day that had been experienced in the Cape Peninsular for many years. There was snow on Table Mountain for the first time in seven years.

Loader, and the company exercised 'Action'. Subsequently, the ship moved out to sea and carried out night full-calibre firing and torpedo-firing at a BP Target.

During the next days she carried out a six-inch Director Test, put her Tubes and six-inch guns crews to drill, landed her Field Gun crew for drill, landed a mining party and a working party to draw stores, and sent a party to *St Dogmael* to lay a dummy minefield. On 10th August the seaboat crew had lost the pendant of No.1 mooring, so that the ship had proceeded to No.4 Buoy as an alternative. A diving party was now away (on 23rd August) sweeping for the No.1 moorings.

On 16th August Alf's wife, who had taken passage from England, had landed from the four-funnelled Union Castle ship *Windsor Castle* at Capetown, about 40 miles away from Simonstown by the direct railway line. One assumes that Alf would have been able to see to her installation in married quarters, and to be away from the ship from time to time to see to her welfare, at least whilst the ship remained based at Simonstown. [A *little further on in this narrative we will take a break to look at their 'Private Life' in South Africa*.]

On the 24th the C-in-C came aboard *Birmingham*, and the ship proceeded for combined full/cal gun-firing, followed by torpedo-firing, with *Lowestoft* and *Daffodil* in company. The C-in-C left the ship that evening. Next day there was a bombing exercise by aeroplanes on the ships. Later, the whaler was lowered but capsized and was damaged during the ensuing salvage operation. Fortunately, the accident, which took place in relatively calm conditions of wind and sea, caused no casualties, but the whaler was apparently damaged beyond repair and a replacement had to be drawn from the Dockyard later.

The 26th August saw the ship 'picking its way' through the dummy minefield which had been laid by *St Dogmael* a week earlier. The 27th saw the hands embarking 60 rounds of 6-inch practice shell, and the 30th saw the company cheering ship as *Verbena* proceeded to England to pay off. Then the submerged torpedo tubes crews were put to drill.

Rivalries between the ships in the Squadron were re-awakened in early September, with the 6-inch Loader competition, competitive torpedo and HA-firing against *Lowestoft*, and, on the 7th, with the 'C-in-C's Firing Competition' at a target towed by *St Dogmael*, umpires from both ships being used. On the 15th a demolition exercise was carried out in the Klaver Valley and, on the 16th a working party was landed to repair the Shark Net. (It is assumed that this was a public relations exercise, and that this net was one used to screen off a fairly small area of the sea close in to a part of the beach favoured by local swimmers.)

Two days later the RM Detachment was landed to practice on the firing range, and the hands were put to the heavy task of getting up and disembarking first shell, and, subsequently, cordite, before the ship was secured in No.1 Dock. Whilst she was dry-docked her bottom was chipped clean, her chain lockers were cleared out and painting began 'inside and out', as requisite. In the meantime, a working party had been landed to rig a boxing ring for the Squadron Boxing Competition, and the gig had been away to race in the Dockyard Regatta.

Alf signed the ship's log on 5th October 1926 after a long 'gap' in his entries. This may have reflected his involvement with the various firing exercises and competitions, but also, perhaps, his snatched spells of leave to travel back and forth to his young wife at

Capetown. The ship having been in dock from 23rd September would doubtless have been useful for him - and much yet remained to be done before the ship would emerge.

Author's collection. An anonymous postcard c.1919.

HMS *Yarmouth* in Selbourne Dock, Simonstown, in 1919. (*Yarmouth* was a sister-ship of *Weymouth*, in which Alf had served 1914-16.) HMS *Birmingham* would have looked very much like this as she sat in the *self-same* dock in 1926, similarly well-shored and with inclined brows to traverse. However, unlike *Yarmouth* or *Weymouth*, HMS *Birmingham* had the protection of a 3-inch thick armoured belt fitted along her side.

On that day he signed the log the ship was embarking provisions, cleaning out her boats and - still - had hands chipping her bottom. However, outside, 'life' was also going on, and she half-masted her colours on 10th October in Honour of the Delville Wood Ceremony.[238] On the 18th she also cleared Lower Deck and cheered *Lowestoft* on her departure for the U.K to pay off, and, on 21st October, she landed a party of officers and

---

[238] The South African Brigade had launched a very brave and determined attack on strongly-defended Delville Wood on 15th July 1916. In the two weeks which had elapsed since the opening day of the Battle of the Somme, this wood had already become one of the most horrific places in the holocaust along the Western Front. Where other units had totally failed, the attack by the South African Brigade on 15th July had half-succeeded, though only at the cost of very heavy casualties. The Brigade continued to take part in many desperate actions in the area, off and on, until at least the 18th of October, by which time the colossally-expensive Battle of the Somme was drawing to its close and Delville Wood was nothing but the stripped remnants of the trunks of the few trees still left standing in a mass of overlapping shell-craters. [Alf and Olive would both have 'identified' with the 'Delville Wood' ceremony, for Alf's brother Jack, serving with the Lincolnshire Regiment, had surely been involved in this battle and Olive's 2nd cousin, Walter Wilfred GREEN, a fine young Lance Corporal in the 8th Green Howards was one of the many 'missing' on the Somme. It seemed that Walter Wilfred had been killed in the general area of Thiepval on 6th October. Olive's mother's half-brother, George Wm ENGLISH, then a Private in the 8th East Surreys and a veteran of the Boer War had also been involved in the brutal fighting. And it is possible that Olive's father, Joseph Walter GREEN, then a Gunner in the Royal Garrison Artillery, had also been serving nearby. This sort of 'family involvement' was almost certainly echoed in other members of *Birmingham's* company and, indeed, pretty well endorsed throughout the length and breadth of Great Britain.]

ratings to attend the Trafalgar Day Service ashore. Meantime, she was landing successive parties of Marines and Seamen to practice at the rifle range ashore, and she also landed small parties (e.g. 1 PO and 3 ABs) on patrol and to be sentries. Then, on 29th October she landed a Royal Guard of Honour for HE The Governor-General, the 19 gun salute being fired by *Wallflower*. The 5th November 1926 saw a party being landed to extinguish a bush fire, the coincidence that it was Guy Fawkes' Day probably not escaping the attention of the wag of the party, and, by that stage, the bottom of the ship was being coated, her cables restored to the locker, and general refitting in full swing. This refitting was still on progress on 10th November which was the 23rd birthday of Alf's wife. One wonders if he managed to snatch a couple of day's leave to travel to Capetown to spend some time with her.

Flooding of the Dock was commenced on 18th November, the day of the Annual Cross-Country Race in which every officer and man who was free of a specific duty would have been expected to put in an appearance! *Birmingham* emerged from Dock on the 22nd, to secure alongside 'C' Wall, and provisioning, ammunitioning, coaling (350 tons), and the taking in of 188 tons of oil commenced. With the exception of embarking the oil, this was sheer hard work. The Log noted that the ship also received on board 264 Clarksons cases and 112 drill cartridges. [These were obsolete and redundant stores.]

Dublin arrived on 3rd December and saluted the C-in-C with 15 guns, *Birmingham* replying with 7 guns. On 6th December 1926 a trawler flying a flag of distress was sighted, drifting helplessly towards the rocky north shore of False Bay. *Birmingham* promptly raised steam, but she was pre-empted by the very alert water tank vessel *Chub* which proceeded to the rescue of the trawler and towed her into the basin. It was as well that this episode did not happen two days later, for the wind was rising and had increased to Force 7 by the close of day, reaching Force 8 by next morning and continuing through the 9th before easing.

On 14th December *Birmingham* proceeded to Capetown, again being afflicted by a breakdown of her steering gear *en route*, though the problem was quickly rectified. She took a Pilot aboard and subsequently secured to No.1 Berth, West Wall. She coaled next day using native labour (879 tons). One assumes that Alf was ashore as soon as he was reasonably able, to head for 'Nicholdene', his married quarters. The ship was open to visitors on the afternoon of the 16th. Perhaps Olive came aboard on what would surely have been her first-ever visit. One way or the other, it is assumed that Alf would have requested leave and spent the best part of the two days with Olive, whilst *Birmingham* was alongside at Capetown.

This may all have been quite hurried, for *Birmingham's* stay at Capetown was a short one, and she proceeded to Saldanha Bay late on the 16th, where she landed her rifle team to shoot for the Saldanha Cup, *Birmingham* winning the competition. Alf had a number of teaspoons with crossed-rifle stems amongst the souvenirs he left for posterity, including one engraved 'HMS *Birmingham*', and it seems probable that he was a member of the shooting team that day.

On 20th December 1926 the hands painted the Well Deck and guns P4 and S4 in the morning, before the boats' crews went away in a sailing race, in a good Force 4 breeze. *Birmingham* then sailed for Simonstown, after swinging her compass and streaming her paravanes. She was flying the flag of the C-in-C and came to anchor in 'A'

Berth. She was at Simonstown over the Christmas period, half-masting her colours on Boxing Day for the death of H.M. the Emperor of Japan.

Author's collection. An anonymous photograph on stiff plain card.

A photograph of *Birmingham*, secured in 'A' Berth at Simonstown during the Christmas period. Ratings, dressed in tropical white uniforms are active on her fo'csle. Her P2 gun is trained outboard. The C-in-C's flag is at her foremast.

    Lt Commander GREY joined *Birmingham* before she sailed for Port Elizabeth, where Lt Commander WALLER left the ship. Whilst she was at Port Elizabeth, her divers went down for an hour to clear the circulator inlet. The ship now proceeded to East London, taking a Pilot to guide her to No.2 Berth, where the ship was open to visitors on 3rd January, the Ship's Company being landed for a route march next day. Tugs later escorted her out of harbour, and she then returned to Port Elizabeth, where she landed a Battalion for a route march and discharged to shore three officers and 40 ratings of the RNVR (who had been aboard for training).

    On 10th January the ship proceeded the 387 miles to Table Bay to discharge Commander STRUBEN and S/Lt Von HOLDT of the RNVR, before proceeding from Capetown to Simonstown. She arrived there on the 12th January 1927, saluting HE the Governor-General on his arrival at the railway station (19 guns). The German cruiser *Emden* arrived at 1100 and she saluted the C-in-C with 15 guns, 15 guns being returned. The Captain of *Emden* later called on the C-in-C, Vice Admiral Sir Maurice FITZMAURICE KCVO, CB, CVO, who returned the visit. This, rather ironically, in view of the history of the *Emden's* predecessor, was evidently the last official act by the C-in-C, who was by then a very sick man. He now left *Birmingham* to attend the hospital ashore. He died on the 23rd January, at Admiralty House, Capetown. He was aged only 56, but had been suffering from *arterio sclerosis* which led to a stroke and respiratory failure. *Birmingham* landed a funeral party on the 24th for the burial ceremony, half-masting her colours at 1706.

In consequence of his illness the Admiral had stood down before going into hospital and *Birmingham*, having struck his flag at 1959 on the 22nd January, had hoisted the broad pennant of Commodore J.C. HODGSON. On the 25th Commodore HODGSON had transferred his broad pennant to *Flora*.

In the interim *Birmingham* had landed parties to fight bush fires, coaled ship (775 tons), landed parties for swimming proficiency tests and sent a small escort to proceed to Colesberg to apprehend two deserters. (The escort would subsequently return with one prisoner. The outcome in regard to the other deserter was not recorded.)

On 7th February, *Birmingham* landed a Guard for the reception of the new C-in-C, and hoisted the flag of Vice Admiral D.M. ANDERSON CMG, MVO, at 1037, *Flora* striking the broad pendant of Commodore J.C. HODGSON.

That same day, Captain A.E. EVANS and Pay Lt SATTESTHWAITE joined ship, Captain A.E. EVANS OBE assuming command of HMS *Birmingham* at Divisions (0900) on the 9th February 1927. Before he left the ship, Captain BEVAN had been busy, and his assessment report on Alf, covering the period 20th April 1926 to 7th February 1927, stated that Alf's conduct as Gunner had been "*...entirely to my satisfaction. A promising officer.*"

Alf now had a new Captain to please, and we shall subsequently see how Captain EVANS viewed him. In fact, Alf would come to have a yet harder target to satisfy, for Captain EVANS would later appoint him to be the Ship's Boatswain. As such he would be responsible for acting as a sort of 'monitor' over the men and seeing that all orders were executed promptly. He would also be responsible for seeing that the masts, ropes, chain cables, sails, etc., throughout the ship were maintained in good condition.

Brigadier General BRINCK called on the new C-in-C on the 7th February, a Guard being landed for his reception and a salute of 11 guns being fired. A strong, hot, breeze was blowing from the S.S.E that day. Over the next few days there now began a whole string of visits by Consuls General (or Consuls) on the new C-in-C, each visit calling for its own salute of guns of 11 (or 7) guns. The countries represented were, in order of visits, Sweden, Germany, Italy, Argentina, U.S.A., Belgium, France, Czechoslovakia, Brazil, Portugal, The Netherlands, Switzerland, Finland, Uruguay and Spain.

Whilst the various official visits had been in progress, a Court Martial had been held aboard *Lowestoft* (on the 18th February), and the sloop *Daffodil* had arrived, saluting the C-in-C with 15 guns and receiving 7 in reply. (She was going into dock, and a working party from *Birmingham* would be sent to assist in undocking her three weeks later, on 5th April.)

On 2nd March 1927 the field gun crew were landed for a display at Rosebank, parties were landed to deal with bush fires, and the hands were kept at physical drill. The divers were busy, for they were sent off to carry out underwater repairs to HMAS *Immortelle*, then to clear the propeller of *Birmingham's* steam launch and then to recover a lost tampion. On the 19th a working party were put ashore to carry out some work at the Union Jack Club, and, on the 21st, all the boats crews were away pulling.

The 30th March saw a dramatic event when the Master at Arms in charge of the Detention Quarters was taken into custody on board to await trial by Court Martial. One

Court Martial took place aboard *Lowestoft* on 4th April, being completed in just over six hours, and another took place aboard *Birmingham* on 7th April, with Captain A.E. EVANS as President. This lasted 10½ hours, and appears to have been the trial involving the MAA. The outcome is not known.

The heats of the Africa Station Athletic Sports were held on the 20th/21st April in the reasonable temperature of 65° F, and the finals were held on the 23rd. Meantime, *Birmingham* had topped up with 400 tons of coal, and she proceeded from Simonstown for Saldhana Bay on the 28th April, the C-in-C having come aboard. That evening she exercised her searchlight crews. Next morning the weather had "come on thick", and the ship began sounding every 5 minutes 'without a tube' and every ½ hour 'with a tube'.[239] Shortly after noon, in light airs, the ship had to suddenly alter course to avoid running down a fishing vessel which suddenly loomed up out of the fog. The murk dissipated slightly around 1600, and land was glimpsed to starboard - just sufficiently long for a quick bearing to be obtained. Then the fog descended thickly again, soundings now being taken every 10 minutes 'by tube', with the ship coming to anchor in Houtier Bay at 1830.

On Saturday 30th April 1927 the C-in-C inspected the messdecks, and he followed this up next day when General Drill was exercised, quickly followed by his succession of orders to 'Furl Awnings', 'Rig Hand Capstan', 'Tow Forward', 'Out Kedge Anchor and Fire Engine' and 'Away All Boats'. At noon the C-in-C inspected hammocks. One gains the feeling he was 'seeing' and 'wanting to be seen', so far as the men were concerned.

Author's collection. An anonymous photograph on card with a totally plain back.

The Africa Squadron Regatta of 1927. The 1st Seamen's Cutter Crew of HMS *Birmingham* were the Winners of the Final Pulls. So far as we know, Alf was not *directly* involved, but this photo is typical of the enthusiasm which such events generated.

On 3rd May 1927, the sailing race for coxswains of boats was held, the ship being dressed overall on the 6th May for the Anniversary of the Accession of H.M King George

---

[239] One assumes that the 'tube' collected a sample of the sand, shingle or mud, etc. of the sea bed for comparison with the map and as an aid to navigation.

V, and the C-in-C addressed the ship's company. That same day the opening heats of the pulling regatta were held, and, on the 10th May, the Finals of the Interport Regatta were pulled off.

Following the regatta, HMS *Birmingham* returned to Simonstown where the C-in-C left the ship. On 19th May 1927 the ship proceeded into dry dock at Simonstown, the usual business of scraping the ship's bottom and ranging the cables ensuing. The ship was dressed overall for Empire Day on 24th May, and again on 26th May, a Royal Salute also being fired this day in honour of the Birthday of H.M Queen Mary and yet again on 31st May in honour of Union Day.

Birmingham had come out of dock on the 30th May, being dressed overall on the 31st and the starboard guns crews being exercised on the Loader. The ship coaled on 1st June (617 tons), landing a gun's crew and funeral party that day and lowering her colours at 1400 for two hours. The funeral was for Stoker A.L. GARRETT, aged only 21 years. He had died of the dreaded scourge of Tuberculosis of the lungs, for which treatment in those days was prolonged rest in a sanatorium in an atmosphere of fresh air, a good outcome being far from sure. As Captain BEVAN had written to his C-in-C earlier, TB cases had been presenting a difficult problem, because homeward-bound steamers were almost invariably unwilling to take TB cases on board for evacuation to England, due to the risk of contagion (albeit slight) that they presented to other passengers. The ship was dressed overall again on 3rd June, and a 21 gun Royal Salute was fired in Honour of the King's Birthday, the hands cheering ship. Around this time Major BREWER and Major YEO of the Royal Marines were discharged to England.

On 8th June the ship proceeded for Port Elizabeth, in company with *Lowestoft,* carrying out torpedo-firing, exercising collision stations and carrying out OOW manoeuvres whilst en route. They arrived at Port Elizabeth at 0915 on 10th June after their 425 mile run, and the Mayor called on the C-in-C later that morning. On 14th June a party were landed for a motor trip. Next day the ship furled her awnings and proceeded for East London in a moderate sea with a W.S.W swell and a breeze which stiffened to Force 6. Alf signed the log that day. On 22nd June the ship was again dressed overall in honour of the Anniversary of Coronation Day, the ship proceeding next day for Durban. She arrived there on the 24th, the various consuls calling on the C-in-C and being saluted with 7 guns. The ship coaled (680 tons), increasing her draught from 15 ft 11 ins/17 ft 4 ins to 18 ft 1 in/ 18 ft 3 ins. From being down by the stern when low in coal, her trim had now improved considerably. Her new draught confirmed that it took about 37 tons to increase her draught by an inch.

Birmingham proceeded for Lourenco Marques on 11th July, with *Lowestoft* in company, *Birmingham* exercising her emergency searchlights at 0500 on the 12th. She saluted the national flag of Portugal with 21 guns on arrival at 1420, after her run of 250 miles, and fired a salute of 19 guns when HE the Governor-General called on the C-in-C shortly afterwards. He was followed by the German, French and American Consuls, who each received 7 gun salutes on leaving.

From Lourenco Marques, with *Lowestoft* in company, the ship furled her awnings and proceeded to Beira, which had become an important port, handling a large percentage of the produce of Northern and Southern Rhodesia, including heavy copper freights.[240] *Lowestoft* departed from Lourenco Marques on 18th July and arrived at Beira on the 20th,

---

[240] See Report by C-in-C Africa Station in ADM 116/2863 at TNA (Kew).

having sounded her way in every 15 minutes, starting at 0500, embarking a Pilot at 0745 and securing at 0900. At 0925 the British Consul and the Governor's ADC called on the C-in-C, and the C-in-C called on the Governor at 1100. On the 21st the 6 inch guns crews were practising at the Dummy-Loader and the hands were at physical drill. Her sick list had increased from 5 to now be 9 men. On the 22nd the German Consul called on the C-in-C (7 guns), and the ship was later rigged for a dance. On 27th July the hands were scrubbing out boats on the beach and, next day, all the boats' crews were away under sail. Alf signed the log on the 29th, after a long gap (and then again on the 31st).

A snapshot from Alf's album.

Alf in his full uniform as Officer of the Watch. Not only would he be impeccably turned out, but he would be looking for smartness in all the ratings coming on watch. Any 'sideboys' would receive his particularly close scrutiny.

On Saturday 30th July 1927 the ship proceeded for Durban, arriving at 1110 on the 12th with 265 miles run. She embarked 200 tons of coal from the collier *David Lloyd George*, taking just over five hours to do so. On the 5th August all the boats' crews were away sailing for the RNYC Cup.

On the 8th August the ship took a Pilot on board to see her out of harbour, and proceeded for Capetown, carrying out a 24-hour Full-Power trial en route, her hands going to physical drill as the trial began. (See photo below.)

They streamed paravanes for 5½ hours next day after reducing to their normal 10 knots, and arrived at Capetown on the morning of the 10th, following their run of 750 miles. It may well be the case that Alf managed a short 'long leave' at this time, for (say) three days. Certainly, his signature does not occur in the Log after 8th August, for some time ahead....More about this matter later.

Using native labour the company embarked 565 tons of coal on the 11th, to make up for the F.P Trial 'expenditure'. [This can be theoretically computed as having been 24 hours at the 'Full Power' of 25 knots (equivalent to a consumption of 24.25 tons/hour, and 24 hours at the 'most economical speed' of 10 knots (equivalent to 3.1 tons per hour) (i.e 24 x 24.25 = 582 tons, and 24 x 3.1 = 74 tons), making a grand theoretical total of

656 tons. This is 91 tons more 'theoretically consumed' than actually had to be 'replaced'. Perhaps a favourable current had provided some assistance during the trial, or perhaps the wizards in the Engine Room had managed to do some quiet 'coasting', and thus rest the stokers from their heavy labour just a wee bit. We shall never know.]

Inevitably, cleaning followed coaling, and the hands were also engaged in scraping down the funnels (which had doubtless become blistered from the prolonged F.P Trial), preparatory to painting them.

A snapshot from Alf's photo album.

A thrilling picture of the bows of HMS *Birmingham* during her full-power speed trials as she headed westwards around the Cape of Good Hope.

Come Friday 12th August the ship proceeded for Simonstown, with *Lowestoft,* following in single line ahead, and with *Birmingham* securing to the Flagship's moorings at Simonstown that same afternoon. On 15th August, *St Dogmael* secured astern and they carried out a Director Test. Meantime, the gun crews were practising at the Loader and a working party were rigging a BP Target. Next day *Birmingham*, with *Lowestoft* in company, and with a marking party aboard *St Dogmael*, carried out an FC shoot with her six-inch guns. She also fired three torpedoes. On 17th August a marking party embarked in *St Dogmael,* and, next day, an FC firing of *Birmingham's* six-inch guns was carried out. That evening she proceeded for night firing of her main armament and torpedoes, returning to harbour just before midnight. On the 19th she carried out a low-visibility torpedo exercise in company with *Lowestoft*, with the sloop *Delphinium* making smoke.

That night she fired two more torpedoes, one of which sank before it could be recovered. She dropped a Dan buoy to mark the spot, but searched in vain, subsequently lowering a seaboat to recover the buoy.

On the 20th her 1st Marine Range Party was landed. Lt Commander BENSON joined ship from England. On 26th witnesses were landed for a Court of Enquiry which was held on board *Lowestoft*.[241] Meantime, the guns crews of *Birmingham* were at a lecture.

On the 29th a north-west gale developed, rising from Force 5 to as much as Force 9 by noon, but then declining to Force 6 by 1600. A funeral party were landed on the 30th, and the colours were half-masted. This funeral was for Stoker J.A ANSELL, aged only 19, poor lad, another who had died of Pulmonary Tuberculosis. (See previous remarks concerning the related death of Stoker GARRETT. One imagines that their work in the stokehold had been detrimental to the declining health of these two very young men. One wonders if, by disposition, they were rather 'mole-like' and favoured the stuffy cosiness of either messdeck or stokehold, to their own detriment, rather than being out on deck in the fresh air whenever it could be managed.)

Next day the company was put to physical drill after Divisions and Prayers, and the submerged tubes crews were later at drill.

On 1st September 1927 preparations began for docking the ship, ammunition being returned. On 2nd September Lt Commander (E) HARRISON joined ship from England. Three days later, she proceeded into dry dock and the customary 'ritual' of scraping the ship's bottom then commenced, with her WT yards also being struck down. Lt STEPHINSON was discharged to England.

On the 11th September 1927 *Joan Olive DAVIS, infant daughter of Alfred William DAVIS Gunner RN and Olive Mabel DAVIS, was baptised on board by the Revd W.N. MARTIN RN assisted by the Revd A TURNER RN.* (See details in 'Private Life', which follows shortly.) Perhaps it was just as well that this pleasant ceremony had not been scheduled for the following day, for a north-west wind of Force 6 suddenly got up accompanied by a deluge of squally rain which lashed the dock and harbour, and, combined with the 'lop' which evidently got up in the harbour, somehow led to the ship's steamboat No.62 being swamped and foundering off No.14 steps. The divers had to be sent down later to salvage the craft, their efforts to do so continuing into the next day. Meantime the hands were bailing out the other ship's boats, which were all rainsoaked.

Come the 22nd September the Fleet Regatta was held, though no details of its outcome seem to have survived. Then Lts ORR-EWING, ELLIS and POWELL joined ship from England on the 26th (Lt FINTER joining a few days later), and Lt Commander SWANSTON and Lt MITFORD were discharged to shore for passage to England. On the 6th October the Marine Range Party returned on board from the range, and the kit of the late Stoker ANSELL was sold off.[242]

On the 11th the Dock was flooded to 11 ft over the blocks (i.e. to within about 8ft of floating the ship), and, on the 13th and 14th, whilst the gun crews were practising at the

---

[241] This may have been to do with the lost torpedo. No records seem to have survived at TNA (Kew).

[242] By Naval tradition the buyers would have 'bought generously' and the proceeds would have been sent home to his next of kin.

Loader, a Shark Net Party were landed. This was evidently as a public service to restore the net to good functional quality and protect the lives of local sea-swimmers.[243]

A snapshot from Alf's album.

Naval 'Brass'. The scene ashore at the Regatta. The 'X' denotes the feet of Olive, her person hidden behind a naval officer. Baby Joan is presumably in Olive's arms.

Meantime, provisioning of the ship continued. On the 15th Lt-Commander GREY was discharged to hospital.[244] Then, on Sunday 16th October, *David Edward SYMS infant son of Edward Amyns SYMS, Pay Lt Commander RN and Frances Margaret SYMS was baptised by the Revd Archer TURNER RN.* On the 18th the TS crew were at drill. Somehow or other a 'Gun Tampion, 6", Mk III' was lost overboard by accident on this day. [There may have been an effort by those involved to temporise about recording the loss, perhaps in the hope that the ship's divers would be able to salvage it, for the tampion would not be officially recorded in the Log as lost until 10th November.]

The 21st October 1927 was Trafalgar Day, and a party were landed at 0815 to attend the Memorial Service in Capetown, which lay over 40 miles away, but was readily reachable by road or rail. At 1115 the Mayor of Capetown called on Captain EVANS. This may have been to do with the annual Festivities at Rosebank, to which *Birmingham* sent her field gun crew to demonstrate, next day. Although not mentioned in her log, she had probably sent a working party ashore a little earlier to 'rig the showground', for, on the 24th October, which was a blustery day, with winds of up to Force 7, a working party was sent ashore to '*unrig* the showground'. Mr CROUCHER Warrant Shipwright joined ship from England the same day. That same day the Log tells us that the gig and 2nd whaler were hoisted in from the dockside. The ship was coming back to life.

Sure enough, next day the ship was floated out of dock and proceeded to No.1 Buoy. However, that buoy was found to be 'foul', and she came to anchor in 'A' Berth.

---

[243] A working party would be landed again on the 17th, evidently to complete the 'shark-net' task.
[244] He would not return to the ship until the 8th November.

St Dogmael secured astern and a Director Test was carried out. Meantime the hands were getting up ammunition. This was all preparative to intensive spells of sub-calibre firing by her main guns at towed targets and Director Tests right through to the end of the month, interrupted only when the wind increased to Gale Force 9 on the 27th, an anchor watch having to be set for a good four hours. The wind was still at Force 8 when competitors for the Squadron Cross-Country Running Competition were landed, so they must have had a hard time whenever they were heading into the gale. However, the weather soon settled down and awnings were spread against the heat of 67° F which returned on the 28th, night clothing being aired next day. The 31st saw a further Director Test and the 6-inch guns' crews having another drill on the Loader.

Clearly, Captain EVANS was working hard to prepare his gunnery teams for the 1st November, and undoubtedly looking to Alf to play his full part. Moreover, although not spelt out in the Log, it is believed that the C-in-C came aboard on the morning of this day, so that Captain and company were going to be directly under his keen gaze in whatever they did. All in all, the 1st November was a day of intensive competition, for umpires came aboard at 0800 and *Birmingham* proceeded for a full-calibre competitive shoot against *Lowestoft's* skills, each ship taking it in turns to fire at a BP Target towed by *St Dogmael*. The 'wind and wave' might have been telling factors in the results obtained (which are unknown to the author), and probably made the transfer of umpires from *Birmingham* to *Lowestoft* by seaboat a little 'uncomfortable' for, at 0800, the wind had again started to increase from Force 4, climbing to Force 6 or 7 by the late forenoon, when the exercise terminated. The wind would continue to increase, reaching Force 8 later in the day.

On 2nd November Lt Commander MORTON and Lt FULLER were discharged for passage to England. On the 4th the Marines were landed for a rifle competition, and the ship's divers were sent to examine the shark nets. One presumes that a shark had been observed within the area bounded by the net! Unusually, a rating was discharged to shore 'by purchase' at this time, evidently having 'bought himself out'. Perhaps he had come into an inheritance or found himself an heiress or a wealthy widow. (It was by no means unknown for men to 'go native' by marrying a local woman, sometimes deserting to do so, and thereafter being sheltered by her family from discovery and arrest.)

The ship proceeded the seventy miles by sea to Capetown on the 8th, to give a searchlight display. Whilst there she coaled, using native labour and taking in 680 tons. Three 'recovered' deserters rejoined ship under escort. On the 11th November *Birmingham* landed a ceremonial landing party at 1000, held Divine Service at 1045 and observed a 2-minute silence at 1100. The ship was then open to visitors from 1400 to 1600. One wonders if Alf's wife Olive came aboard, perhaps with Baby Joan who was then five months old, though the physical exertion involved might have been too much for Olive unless practical help could have been provided to her.

On the 12th November the ship proceeded for Walvis Bay, *Lowestoft* taking station astern, and both ships lifting rhythmically to a moderate southerly swell. On the 14th they streamed their paravanes for five hours and carried out an inclination test before reducing to six knots whilst their paravanes were recovered. They reached Walvis Bay on the 15th after a run of 681 miles, and embarked 280 tons of coal next day, followed by 30 tons of water on the next. On the 18th the guns crews and control parties attended a lecture, before the ship was opened to visitors. *Lowestoft* parted company. Alf's signature appeared in the Log as OOW, having been absent from it since 8th August. As well as being Ship's Boatswain, one imagines that he had been kept very busy with his gunnery duties, where, one feels, Captain EVANS was looking for high performance - as in everything to do with his ship.

Alf signed the Log again next day, when the ship proceeded for St Helena, rolling to a slight to moderate southerly swell as she did so.

Author's collection. An anonymous postcard. HMS 'Birmingham' inscribed in pencil on the back.

Sheets of spray are flung up and back as HMS *Birmingham* heads through a lively sea. The exact date of this photo is not known. However, the view must have been very familiar to Alf as one of the watchkeeping officers. Here we can see the voice-pipes, switch-boxes, binnacles and other bridge-furniture.

Lowestoft, who had joined up again temporarily, parted company that afternoon. Alf continued to sign the Log regularly during the ensuing days as the ship headed ever westwards, crossing the Greenwich Meridian on the night of 21st/22nd November, and progressively making her northing, to reach the lonely island of St Helena early on the morning of the 23rd, with 1,205 miles run. The ship had exercised her emergency searchlight crew on the way in, only to suddenly find her steering unsatisfactory and changing over the telemotor gear to overcome the problem. She coaled next day, taking in 310 tons over a period of eight hours and losing ten 2 cwt sacks overboard in so doing.

The ship did not linger at St Helena, but turned and proceeded for Sierra Leone on the 27th, at her customary and 'most economical' speed of 10 knots. She put her No.1 Platoon to drill on the 28th, and her No.2 Platoon to drill on the 29th. Next day the men were given a lecture on tropical diseases preparatory to their arrival at Sierra Leone, doubtless accompanied by the usual warnings about sexually-transmitted diseases. On 2nd December Night Defence stations were exercised and steering by hand. The latter may have been something of a precautionary measure, for the Master Gyro Compass had been wandering on the 28th November (perhaps affected by their informal crossing of King Neptune's territory at that time?), though it seemed to have settled down again. However, the Gyro Repeater started to wander again on the 3rd December, and steering was changed to use the magnetic compass, the Gyro not being put back in service until late in the day.

The Union Castle steamer *Arundel Castle* was sighted as they neared Sierra Leone, where they came to anchor at 0950 on the 4th December 1927, having run 1,576 miles. Next day HE The Governor-General called on the C-in-C, being given a 17-gun salute on leaving. The ship commenced coaling on the 6th, using native labour, and finishing 7½ hours later, by which time she had embarked 400 tons. The temperature was high, up to 86° F, with only light airs. *Birmingham* spread her awnings to provide a measure of welcome shade. On the 7th the ship discharged six ratings for passage to England in the SS *Aba*. On the 8th her hands were embarking potatoes and 9,200 lb of vegetables which had evidently been embarked from the newly-arrived RFA *Delphinula*.

At 0945 on the 12th *Birmingham* weighed and proceeded for Lagos, sounding her way out to sea after turning ship and stopping briefly at the fuel jetty where she had quickly embarked 85 tons of oil. Next day she carried out a rangefinder exercise. During the afternoon there was a problem with the starboard engine, which was shut down whilst the ship proceeded on the port engine alone, at 180 revs, for two hours, before the engineering staff pronounced all to be well again, when both engines reverted to the normal 147 revs for 10 knots.

At 1950 a heavy rain and south-easterly wind squall hit the ship, a swell having already got quickly up. The fo'c'sle awning was quickly furled to stop the ship 'paying off' in response to the high wind, and to help the helmsman in keeping *Birmingham* on course. Embarrassingly, the wheel chose to become jammed at this moment, both engines promptly being put to slow ahead and the NUC signal being quickly hoisted. Changing over the telemotor gears resolved the problem and, as the ship steadied back on her course, the NUC signal was struck.

On 16th December the ship exercised Night Defence stations and night action stations, and then her emergency searchlight's crew. [For some reason this was the last day on which Alf would sign the Log as OOW for some time to come.] At 0755 on the 17th *Birmingham* stopped off Lagos, after a run of 1,045 miles, embarked a Pilot and entered the harbour, securing fore and aft to No.1 and No.2 buoys.

HE the Governor-General called on the C-in-C within the hour, receiving a 17-gun salute on leaving.

At 0730 the next morning *Birmingham* landed a funeral party and her band, half-masting her colours at 0745.[245] The funeral party returned on board at 1015, and the collier *Uskhaven* secured alongside. Next day they embarked 550 tons from her, working for 13 hours in a temperature of up to 83°F, with a break in the hottest part of the day, from 1130 to 1530. At 1735, the collier cast off and proceeded alongside *Lowestoft*.

The company were allowed short runs ashore in the next five days, doubtless had the traditional early 'Pipe Down' on the 25th, Christmas Day, albeit in tropical heat far removed from the traditional English scene. Alf may well have had the feeling that he was 'so near, and yet so far' from his beloved wife, though, in truth, Lagos was a good 2,500 miles from Capetown. Christmas was a hard time for naval wives with their

---

[245] It is assumed that the deceased was from another ship, not *Birmingham*.

menfolk at sea, but Olive at least had their baby daughter to provide some sort of company and diversion.

A snapshot from Alf's album.

Native boats. [Alf had photographed these at Accra. Merchant shipping is moored alongside the wharf in the background. (See Page 302 *et alia*.)]

Meantime, at Lagos, the quarterdeck aboard *Birmingham* was rigged for a dance on the 27th, to which, one assumes, the more prominent members of local society were invited, before her men unrigged the awnings and screens at 0540 on the morning of the 28th, took a Pilot on board and proceeded to sea, heading for St Paul de Loanda. At this time their sick list was hovering around the half-dozen mark.

By 1010 on that first day out, they were proceeding on the starboard engine only, having had to 'stop port' to clean the condenser, then reversing the procedure, whilst the condenser for the starboard engine was cleaned. They then went to half-speed for a while to check that all was well, before reverting to their normal 10 knots. Meantime, the hands were stowing potatoes which had been embarked at Lagos just before their departure. *Lowestoft* was in company again and she took over as 'Guide of Fleet' for two hours so that *Birmingham* could steer various courses whilst adjusting her steering gear. Next day *Lowestoft* took station five cables on the starboard beam of *Birmingham* and rangefinder and inclination exercises were carried out. On the 30th December a night defence and searchlight exercise was conducted with *Lowestoft*, and, on the 31st the two ships alternated in the role of Guide of Fleet.

They reached St Paul de Loanda at 0700 on the 2nd January 1928, having run 1,110 miles and crossed the Equator. They saluted the flag with 21 guns, which the fort returned in full. Strangely, however, the Portuguese sloop *Republica* returned only 13 guns.

H.M. Consul-General visited the ship, being saluted with 13 guns as he departed. Leave was then given to the Chief Petty Officers until 1900. The Consul-General was followed by HE The Governor, who received a 17-gun salute on leaving. Next day they coaled (260 tons), in a temperature of 80°F, under blue skies with a few fleecy white clouds. The sea remained flat calm, with just a slight swell. The POs were given leave until 1900.

At 0713 on the 4th January, Alf's spirits lifted as they proceeded for Capetown, in single line ahead, at 10 knots. They exercised their TS and Control parties and HA guns crews as they went, later exercising Night Defence stations, going to Engine Room steering for 45 minutes, then to Fore Bridge steering for half-an-hour, before reverting to normal steering. On 5th January *Birmingham* carried out a sub-calibre throw-off shoot on *Lowestoft* from her port 6-inch guns, then streamed a fog buoy for practice and put the hands to physical drill. Next day, it was *Lowestoft's* turn to carry out a sub-calibre throw-off shoot on *Birmingham*, before *Birmingham's* port guns had a second go. By that time the sea had increased to a moderate 4 or 5, the wind was blowing at Force 5 to 6 and the skies clouded over for a while, before reverting to blue.

The weather had calmed by the 9th January, a gunnery training class was at instruction, and an HA gun practice was subsequently carried out, aiming at smoke shell bursts. On the 10th the ships streamed their paravanes and conducted a night signal exercise. Next morning they arrived at Capetown, and *Birmingham* secured alongside the new coaling jetty, whilst her hands cleaned ship. They holystoned the deck next morning, the 12th, before embarking 805 tons of coal - and then had to clean ship, and then themselves, and then their clothes, once again.

Ratings of HMS Birmingham, many of them *'as black as spades'*, after coaling ship in 1926. Exact time and place unknown.

The preceding photograph cannot be *definitely* attributed to this incident, but the heavily begrimed appearance of the men would certainly match how one might have expected them to look after embarking 805 tons with a working party numbering perhaps 400 to 450 men. One hopes that the 'new coaling jetty' had equipment in place which was of significant assistance – even if the coal was the 'dusty stuff' of Natal origin, spreading grime everywhere, to which Roy STRUBEN had referred during Alf's time aboard HMS *Lowestoft*!

It is just possible that Alf managed to squeeze in a short period of leave at this time, for matters were not going well for Olive. More on this in a moment.

On the 13th January 1927 they proceeded to Simonstown, where the King's Harbour Master came aboard before, and, followed by *Lowestoft*, they proceeded into the basin. Leave was promptly given to the port watch. Next day, Lt ORR-EWING was discharged to the RN Hospital. [246] Also, three offenders were discharged to the detention barracks. On the 22nd Mr PERCIVAL Commissioned Gunner and Pay Midshipman ANGUS joined ship from England, accompanied by five ratings. [On 3rd February Mr GARDNER Commissioned Gunner would be discharged to shore for passage to England.]

On the 24th the hands were employed 'painting down aloft', and next day the ship landed her Marines for drill and had a swimming class under instruction. On that day Lt ORR-EWING returned from hospital after his sojourn of ten days there. On 3rd February, Mr GARDNER Commissioned Gunner was discharged to shore for passage to England. One rating was also discharged, but he was under escort, for passage to England in the *Balmoral Castle*. Two ratings rejoined from the detention barracks. Meantime, a Gas Chamber Party had been landed, together with a Range Marking Party for the Rifle Range, and the marines had been landed for drill and exercise. A Recreation Ground working party had also been landed.

Throughout the first half of February, almost every day, Diving Parties and Gas Mask Parties were landed for exercises, and the Marines were also landed, for drill.

On the 7th February a rating had joined ship from St Helena. *Birmingham* had called there on the 24th/27th November and it *may* be that this rating had somehow been left behind, perhaps in medical care. However, the Log does not say '*re*-joined ship', and it may be that the rating was joining *Birmingham* for the first time ever.

On the 22nd February, a Rake and Target-Marking Party for *St Dogmael* were landed, and a Sail Floor Working party were landed next day. The ship was twice rigged for dances and dressed overall on the 25th, in Honour of the Birthday of H.R.H The Princess Alice, a 21-gun salute being fired.

Come the 28th, the Gunner's party were drawing and returning ammunition, a Target-Marking Party being landed that day and again on the next, whilst painting ship continued, the divers were at their 'monthly dip' and the submerged tubes crews were at drill. The Field Gun crew were landed on the 5th March and again on the 9th, for drill.

On the 13th March the ship proceeded for Port Elizabeth, the Mayor of Port Elizabeth calling on the C-in-C in the late morning of their arrival. The Field Gun crew and their gun were again landed for exercise that afternoon, and the reason for all their practice became clear on the 14th March, when they were again landed, but this time to

---

[246] One assumes he may well have been related to the Scottish family for whom Alf's parents had worked in and about 1892/4.

give a demonstration ashore. A Concert Party were landed at the same time – so one assumes that some of the hands had been practising hard in this form of entertainment in the run-up to this time.

Author's collection. An anonymous postcard.

A Gas Mask Party, possibly at Simonstown, date unknown, but representative of the conditions described in the text. Overwhelming gas attacks were being widely predicted for the 'next world war'.

Meantime, on board HMS *Birmingham*, the 6-inch gun crews were busily practising at the Loader. On the 17th, the ship was open to visitors during the daylight hours, but furled her quarter-deck awnings at 1700 and proceeded for Simonstown at 2115. Alf signed the Log next day, the ship having been making a steady 10 knots until a fog bank was encountered, which she eventually broke through. She stopped off Simonstown at 1615, after her run of 430 miles, the KHM came aboard, and *Birmingham* proceeded into the basin. She coaled next day, and the Field Gun crew were again landed for practice.

On the 21st March the ship carried out a 6-inch Sub/Cal throw-off shoot at *Lowestoft*, and, next day, carried out a low-visibility torpedo practice and made a paravane run through a dummy minefield. A Funeral Party was at drill, and, next day, after the ship had carried out a 6-inch reduced charge shoot at *Lowestoft*, this party was landed for the funeral of the late C.L.BRISTOWE, an ERA, the colours being half-masted at 1400. The late ERA had suffered a fractured skull at the Royal Naval Recreation Rooms, cause unknown. [No enquiry appears to have been held, which suggests this was regarded as an unfortunate accident.]

That evening, the ship proceeded for a night encounter exercise, firing two torpedoes. Next morning, the 25th, the Field Gun and its crew were landed and made their way to Bloemfontain, to participate at a public function. They would be away from the ship for six days. One suspects that Alf may well have been in immediate charge of the men, with a lieutenant or other officer in overall charge.

Meantime, on the 28th, the ship sent Target and Marking Parties to *St Dogmael*, and then proceeded out to sea with *Lowestoft*. It seems probable that the gunnery exercises also involved other ships, for *Verbena, Wallflower, Sonneblom* and *Immortelle* were all around at this time.[247] On 29th March, the hands were preparing for competitive torpedo-firing, which took place at 1100, *Lowestoft* being the target ship. *Birmingham* then returned to the basin. On 4th April she proceeded into the Dry Dock, where she was quickly staged and her company began to scrape her bottom, and, in the following days, to paint it. They also ranged her cables for examination. Now her various 'Range parties' began to leave the ship, in turn, for their musketry courses at the Simonstown range. Meantime, the dock was part-flooded on the 17th April, and, all appearing well, the dock was fully-flooded and the ship undocked and secured to the West Wall on the 19th. The Sloops Regatta was held on the 24th, and the ship's Guard and Band paraded on the 7th, a 21-gun salute being fired and the ship dressed with masthead flags. She was dressed overall again on the 24th May to celebrate Empire Day, and again on the 26th, in honour of H.M Queen Mary's Birthday. A 21-gun salute was fired that day.

A Court Martial was convened on board on the 2nd June. The C-in-C inspected *Delphinium* next day, and his inspection continued into the next, which was the Birthday of King George Vth. *Birmingham* was dressed overall, the hands manned and cheered ship and a 21-gun salute was fired at noon. On 6th June, Mr FLYNN Commissioned Signal Bos'n joined ship on the 6th, as did Surgeon Lt GRAFF, the latter replacing Surgeon Lt Commander NEWMAN who left the ship for passage to England.

Having inspected *Delphinium* the C-in-C now inspected *Birmingham's* mess decks and flats, followed next day by the upper deck, then storerooms, etc. In the middle of this HE The Governor-General arrived to inspect the ship's company.

On 14th June the ship proceeded from Simonstown for Capetown, carrying out long-range torpedo-firing during her short passage. On arrival, Mr COOK, Commissioned Signal Bos'n was discharged for passage to England.

As we shall see in the following section on 'Private Life', the health of Alf's wife had by now become a cause of major concern to him. It was fluctuating, and had temporary 'remissions', but was definitely trending downwards. Olive returned home in this month of June 1928 to seek expert medical aid in England. If Olive had not actually left as of the 14th, it is just possible that Alf might have been able to overnight with Olive in their married quarters, and to say his sad farewell to her, though there was the consolation that the end of *Birmingham's* commission was almost in sight and he could expect to be back in Home Waters well before the Autumn in England would yield to Winter. Meantime, he would have the melancholy task of winding down 'Nicholdene' ready for its next tenant, and packaging the various items of furniture and other possessions that he and Olive had bought, and shipping them home to England. [*We'll take a break at this point to check what had been happening in Alf's Private Life, starting off with Olive's arrival at Capetown, back in 1926.*]

---

[247] *Sonneblom* and *Immortelle* were 'small ships armed with single 12-pdr guns', according to the C-in-C's report filed in ADM 116/2863 at TNA (Kew).

Private Life

As we have seen, whilst he was in England, Alf had been confirmed in the rank of Gunner on 7th April 1926. He may have awaited that confirmation before finalising his marriage arrangements. He was appointed to HMS *Birmingham* on 20th April 1926, and, as we have already seen, he may have had some brinkmanship to perform in finalising his marriage arrangements. That is to say, in getting through the ceremony on 21st April, and in spending a short honeymoon with Olive before his ship HMS *Birmingham* sailed for the Africa Station on 27th April. During that period of leave he would also have had to prepare himself and his kit for a spell of foreign service, ensure that everything was 'on top line' in regard to his duties and preparation aboard ship, and confirm that his bride would be willing and prepared to follow him out to the Africa Station. It is assumed that he managed to obtain free passage for Olive within a matter of weeks.

As already indicated, quite soon after his arrival on the Africa Station in 1926, Alf had managed to obtain married quarters at a house called 'Nicholdene', in Capetown. Olive had obtained a passport on the 12th July 1926 and taken passage in the Union-Castle Line Royal Mail Steamer 'Windsor Castle', which had left England on 30th July 1926. The ship had arrived at Capetown on 16th August, having called at Madiera en route.

Author's collection. A postcard in the W.H. Smith 'Kingsway Real Photo Series', S.15188, c.1930. Image reproduced by courtesy of W.H. Smith Archive.

(Left) RMS Windsor Castle. (Below) Olive, standing, second from left, making friends with fellow-passengers on the outbound journey.

From a snapshot in Alf's album.

Soon Olive and Alf were well established at 'Nicholdene', with a rather irascible parrot called 'Polly' and a friendly terrier dog called 'Binkie'. They had also quickly begun to create a circle of friends, some made up from people Olive had met on the outward voyage as fellow-passengers, some coming from people Alf already knew, and some from neighbours they met when they came to live at Capetown. Amongst the names were Mrs EVANS, the WOODLANDS family and the HURCHER family at Capetown. Alf evidently also had friends at Durban and Simonstown to whom he would have wished to introduce Olive.

Snapshots from Alf's album.

Alf and Olive living a very happy life together at Capetown. (*Above*) On the beach with Binkie their dog. Alf, unusually, is smoking a pipe. (*Right*) Olive, who was an excellent needlewoman, quietly working in the morning sun on the '*stoep*' of their house, '*Nicholdene*'.

On 4th June 1927, some nine and a half months after Olive's arrival, baby Joan Olive had been born to Alf and Olive. The beautiful blond-haired baby had been baptised in the ship's bell on board HMS Birmingham, at Simonstown, on 11th September 1927. The ceremony had been performed by the Reverend W. N. MARTIN, RN, assisted by the Reverend A. TURNER, RN. Alice Agnes GREEN (proxy Mrs C. S. EVANS), Mrs Dilys GREEN (proxy the Mother), and Joseph Albert GREEN (proxy the Father) were the Godparents. As we have already seen, the details had been entered in the ship's log. [The selection of Godparents was interesting, Alice being Olive's elder sister, Joseph Albert ('Jim') being Olive's elder brother, and Dilys being Jim's wife. That is to say, Jim and Dilys, his beautiful blonde Welsh-girl, had been married just five days![248] One assumes that their prior agreement to be Godparents had been obtained by letter or cablegram. It will be noted that there were no 'DAVIS' godparents – Alf was certainly throwing in his lot with his wife's GREEN Family.]

This whole period of the lives of Alf and Olive must have been as near to 'heaven' for the pair of them as one could possibly imagine.

---

[248] Jim and Dilys had been married at St John's Church, Skewen, Glamorgan on 6th September 1927.

Author's collection. A Valentines postcard of the mid-1920s, reproduced by courtesy of St Andrews University. Library.

The main street in Capetown, which contained the Post Office and Railway Station, and where Alf and Olive would have often come shopping for their more major items.

A snapshot from Alf's Album.

A delightfully happy picture of Olive with Baby Joan and friends at the Naval Regatta of 22nd September 1927, held at Simonstown.

As symbolised by the four above pictures, the shared life of Alf and Olive was a great mix of 'domestic life', and 'naval occasion', both of which were burgeoning and bringing Alf and Olive the greatest happiness.

They went on all kinds of interesting outings from which they began to amass various souvenirs, such as a tea set (milk jug, sugar bowl, etc.) in native silver with Durban town crests, a piano stool in the form of an elephant carved in black wood, a set of smaller ornamental black elephants with ivory tusks, candlesticks in crested native silver, an ostrich egg, some ostrich plumes, a coconut complete with its outer casing of copra, and so on and so forth.

It would probably not be putting things too much into hyperbole to say that the couple were besotted with each other. Indeed, the author has come to believe that Alf and Olive were so closely involved with each other that their new-born infant soon began to instinctively pick up on those vibes and to try to compete with her father for her mother's attention by becoming fractious and given to much weeping and wailing when her father was around, somewhat to her parents' despair. That is to say, the child received the best of their attention and care, but it was much more fun for Alf and Olive to be making love or going out and about sightseeing and exploring whenever Alf could be home from his naval duties, rather than to be driven to distraction by a child who wanted to be rid of her father and constantly cuddled and consoled by her mother at his expense. Yet, somehow all was managed and Olive's calm composure, though often tested, generally kept matters on an even keel. Having a young native servant living-in was also a great help. Her husband's love became ever-deeper for Olive, and their domestic love-life together was a tremendous joy as they continued to 'feather the domestic nest' by building up material things of all kinds for their home. They also eagerly looked forward to hearing 'the patter of more little feet'.

However, this idyllic period would last for less than two years, for, sad to relate, Olive's overall health had not recovered well after the birth of baby Joan in mid-1927. Olive's vitality and strength fluctuated, but was definitely trending downhill. Clearly, something was seriously adrift and needed to be put right.

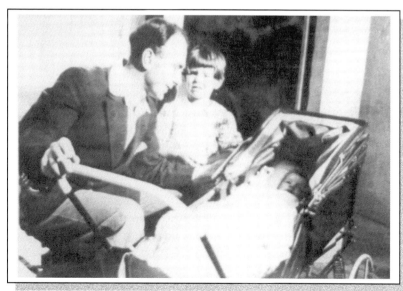

A snapshot from Alf's album.

Alf, in mufti and cigarette in hand, checks that all is well with Baby Joan. (The young girl is presumably a neighbour's child.)

It seemed best that Olive should return home to England where diagnosis of her problem and treatment for it might be best carried out. Most unhappy and distressed at having to leave 'Nicholdene', the home at Capetown where she and Alf had known almost enchanted happiness, Olive took ship back to England in June 1928 in the hope of obtaining expert medical advice and aid, and thus of somehow recovering her strength.

Alf was extremely worried about her, and desperately missed her loving presence. He also missed having their one year-old daughter in the family home.

On the return voyage Olive's strength had continued to fluctuate. She wrote to Alf to say that Baby Joan *"was too heavy for me dear"* when the time had come for a commemorative photograph to be taken on the day of the Children's Fancy Dress Ball. Instead, the baby had been held high aloft in her basket by a robust member of the British Olympic team who were also passengers in the ship. [*See following photo, with Baby Joan in the basket (just visible at Top Right) and Olive in top R H corner.*]

Luckily, the voyage home had been a relatively calm one, which Olive had survived quite well.

Photographs from Alf's album, showing (above) the Children's Party and (right) Olive with Baby Joan on the return voyage. It is clear that Olive's strength was variable, virtually from day to day. She had lost weight.

For the moment, Olive had returned to the security of her parents, now in a large new house at Felixstowe, whence they had moved from Ipswich early in 1928. There Olive could expect help from her parents and her still-unmarried elder sister, Alice, in looking after the infant, and, indeed, herself.

We can gain an idea of the renewed family relationships and living conditions from the photographs which follow overleaf.

Olive's parents would have been desperately worried about her clearly declining though variable condition of health, and hoping that restoration to the English climate would somehow improve matters once again. One imagines that her mother would have been making all kinds of nourishing dishes, such as gelatine-rich 'pork brawn', and gelatine-rich fruit 'jellies', and pressing them on Olive.

Meantime, however, the parents had to get on with their busy business lives, the father at his painting and decorating and the mother with her shop and tea-garden, for which two attractive old bus-hulks were now about to be purchased and set up in the garden at the side of the shop.

(Above) 'Nan' GREEN's brand new shop at Old Felixstowe – a part of the newly-built family home, which incorporated outbuildings at the rear for her husband's painting, decorating and carpentry business. *(Top right)* In 1929, Alice takes charge of toddler Joan in her push-chair, to relieve Olive of the physical work. *(Bottom right)* In 1928, 'Nan' GREEN is pleased as Punch to hold her first grandchild, but very worried about Olive's slowly deteriorating condition. [Identity of young girl (a neighbour's daughter?) not known.]

In regard to the wider DAVIS family, Alf's father, Alfred Wm, had clearly worked hard to establish himself well at Midsomer Norton. On 23 June 1924 and again on 19 June 1925, the 'Somerset Guardian and Radstock Observer' newspaper had carried items concerning the AGMs of the Welton Rovers Football Club, in each of which a hearty vote of thanks to Mr DAVIS, licensee of the 'Stones Cross Hotel', had been carried, expressing appreciation for the excellent accommodation provided for the club.[249]   Clearly, the hotel was thriving and Alfred Wm had achieved the financial success and status for which he had always longed and toiled. As would later become apparent, he had also made some wise financial investments in recent years. However, at the pinnacle of his success, at age 58, and now with a younger wife at his side, he was struck down with a very distressing illness which was to quickly prove fatal. He bore it stoically. He had achieved his self-set life's target by coming from nothing to achieve at least a measure of status and recognition in the community.

Meantime Alf continued on the Africa Station, probably remaining unaware until a late date that his father was dying of cancer of the larynx, to pass away in what must have become an extremely sad condition for all concerned, on the 27th September 1926. Obituaries for Alfred Wm appeared in two successive issues of

---

[249] These items are reproduced by kind permission of The British Library.

the local paper, singing his praises for the way he had run the Stones Cross Hotel since his arrival in Midsomer Norton, and extolling the way he had helped the local community. The obituary correctly stated that Mr DAVIS was a *'much-travelled man'*, but did not say from whence he had started out. Alfred Wm would have regretted having to leave the world so soon, but he would have treasured his obituaries. He would also have appreciated the fact that they gave nothing away concerning his humble roots – indeed he may never have 'let on' about them.[250]

Alfred Wm had died a comparatively wealthy man. He left a comprehensive Will. He had stood by his children, leaving precious little to his new wife and nothing to his step-sons by the new marriage. He had appointed Alf and Alf's elder brother, 'Jack', to be his co-executors.

However, the Will (as the solicitors later wrote to Alf) had been *"proved by your brother, Mr John DAVIS, alone, power being reserved to you to take out a like grant if it should be necessary."* Seemingly, this had been done without informing Alf of the situation, and, who knows, *perhaps* with the idea of somehow cutting Alf out from his entitlement under the Will. Certainly, Alf seems to have formed that low opinion when he was 'tipped off' as to what was going on. [The 'whistle blower' may well have been his youngest sister, Eva, who evidently still idolised Alf.] There are two surviving letters written by the solicitors involved, who, after being contacted by Alf, may possibly have "seen the Law Society looming on the horizon", and who were clearly 'back-pedalling' very fast and apologetically in regard to Alf's enquiries. (Apparently, the solicitors had *"...understood from your sister Mrs Nellie PENNEY that she was in constant communication with you and that you had requested her to watch your interests in the matter."* Clearly, this had not been the case. The solicitors were probably indeed 'liable' for not having verified the situation for themselves by making direct confirmatory contact with Alf.)

IF – and it is a big 'IF' - the other siblings had indeed resolved to diddle Alf of his inheritance, one can see that, from a purely emotional standpoint, they had a point, for they had slaved for their father to their own detriment and had helped to secure the eventual success of his public house enterprises, whereas Alf had escaped from all the drudgery after he reached the age of 15, and, in a sense, 'had left his siblings to get on with it'. It could well be said that the support that Jack, Nellie, Rose and Eva had given to their father had eventually led on to Alfred Wm becoming a wealthy hotelier, and, by and large, the more senior and strong-minded amongst them probably felt that they each richly deserved a full '25%' (i.e. rather than just 20%) of whatever estate their father had happened to leave, whereas, in their opinion, Alf really did not.

Alf had also been still, overtly, 'brass rags' with his father, and it may have been the case that his siblings could not perceive the love and respect of the one for the other which forever lurked beneath the surface of the proud and unbending father and proud and unbending son - nor, presumably, did they know of the rather clandestine visit which Alfred Wm had made on Alf's in-laws to be, perhaps in the vain hope of some kind of reconciliation.

Clearly, (that 'IF' prevailing) what Alf's siblings had apparently set out to do was quite illegal. It was up to the testator to decide how his legacy should be

---

[250] These quotations from The Somerset Guardian and Radstock Observer of 01 and 08 October 1926 appear by kind permission of the British Library. The author imagines that the obituaries were drafted by Nellie and her husband Wilf, but confirmation had not proved possible.

apportioned, and his decisions were sacrosanct. No matter what the level of 'perceived justification' might be, it was not up to one co-executor, aided and abetted by such other siblings as might be so inclined, to temper that division as he or they saw fit. Indeed, one might well believe that the father had deliberately made Alf a co-executor to ensure that straightforwardness, balance and honesty would prevail in the precise execution of his Will. After all, the father may well have reasoned that he *could* have had Alf back in 1911, when the lad had begged to be bought out from the Navy, and that it was *the father's* decision not to go ahead which had decided the issue.

The upshot was that Alf ultimately received his 'equal share' (i.e. 20%) from the solicitors - a very significant sum of money- and, so far as is known, he never communicated with his brother ever again.[251] However, perhaps rather surprisingly, Alf did not break up with any of his three sisters. Perhaps he felt that 'Jack' had dominated and bullied them into passive acquiescence over the handling of the Will. Bearing in mind the strength of personality of Nellie, the fact that the solicitors letter clearly stated that *"...we understood from your sister Mrs Nellie PENNEY that she was in constant communication with you..."*, and the manner in which Nellie had clearly 'managed' their late father, the apparent forgiveness of Nellie by Alf seems rather extraordinary. Was she, perhaps, still very important to him in the dual role of sister and 'family matriarch'. Was he, perhaps, almost too much prepared to always 'play the gentleman with the ladies'? Did the fact that Nellie was pregnant around this time affect the issue with Alf? (She would give birth to her second son, John, in 1927.)

It may well be the case that Alf did feel a measure of guilt over his 'abandonment' of the family when he was 15 years old - though some solace in that his father had turned down the chance to 'buy him out' from the Navy and thus had turned away from the chance to bring Alf back into the family business to help out in a major way. In retrospect, it was a shame that Alf's decision to permanently sever his connections with Jack would lead to his own children having no contact with the seven fine daughters that Jack and Kate would procreate - and to Alf's children never even meeting Jack himself.[252]

Be that as it all may be, Alf's inheritance was a positive God-send for him, for naval pay was low (and would actually become even lower in 1931), and it looked as if he might have a 'rocky hill to climb' in regard to Olive's poor state of health. This was an on-going cause of the gravest concern. It would not be long before Olive's

---

[251] Alf received about £670. It is hard to equate that with a modern cash equivalent. A civilian in a good, well-salaried job might expect to be paid £4 or £5 a week in 1926. So £600 represented well over two year's wages – perhaps £120,000 to £150,000 in today's values. In 1928, £600 would have bought a newly-built three bedroom semi-detached house in a good London suburb. One might hazard that it would therefore be worth £320,000 in today's money. However, house prices have gone 'through the roof' relative to other commodities, and a more reasonable 'general equivalent' might be £150,000. However one looks at it, Alf's legacy was a very large sum of money indeed. (His siblings had each inherited the same large sum, too, though Jack actually received only about £470, rather than £670, since he owed his father's estate some £200 from a loan he had previously received from his father.)

[252] The author eventually managed to trace and make face-to-face contact with some of them, but not until the 1990s! By that time Jack, Kate and their second-oldest daughter Joan Priscilla had all three unfortunately passed away.

illness was diagnosed and she would then be on a treadmill of having to travel up to one of the large London hospitals at regular intervals for tests and such palliative treatment as might be available.

A very happy picture of Olive with Baby Joan, then aged about 18 months. Baby Joan had her mother's undivided attention and was content. However, Olive's condition was fluctuating markedly. There were distinct remissions, but they were becoming shorter and with ever-longer time-periods between them. At least Alf, having received his inheritance, could begin to cast about for high-grade medical assistance for Olive

(Above) Nellie's son Ray, in a London Park, c.1927. He now had a new baby brother, John. *(Right)* Alf's sister Rose. Clearly, Alf was keeping in touch with his sisters, despite the upsets arising over the 'admin' of his father's will in 1926/7.

There was another benefit for the wider family from Alf's inheritance, for he lent a substantial part of it to his mother-in-law, Agnes Sarah, to help her in expanding her business. This was developing a lending library as well as the tea-rooms in the garden adjacent to the shop, and Agnes Sarah may have been at risk of over-extending her working capital. The author suspects the loan was by way of an informal business deal, where Alf may have expected some sort of return on his money in due course, but this was probably all fixed by a 'kiss and a handshake' and never put down on paper. (Though see his Will, made in 1937 and proved in 1941.)

A snapshot from Alf's album.

A happy picture of Baby Joan taking some of her 'first steps' in life, with her mother, Olive, in the background, egging Joan on, but keeping a careful eye on her safety. Olive's pose is very reminiscent of the posture her own mother, Agnes Sarah, would sometimes adopt. The fine shop in the background belongs to Agnes Sarah.

There was one other matter, for Alf had enquired through the solicitors about a silk waistcoat, and they replied that the garment was in the possession of Alf's brother, *"waiting to be handed to you on your return to England."* As we shall see, Alf would leave this heirloom to his eldest son when the time came for Alf to write his own Will in 1937.

Jack was living and working in Bristol, but now as a Licensed Victualler. [It is known that Alfred Wm had previously made a loan of £200 to Jack, and that had seemingly helped Jack to take over a small pub in Bristol. Jack's inheritance from his father's Will would now have been invaluable in supporting the business. The pub in question was the 'Bricklayer's Arms', which was apparently an old-fashioned pub with low oak beams and sawdust on the floor. [At around the time that Jack took over the pub his wife Kate had been expecting their second daughter, Joan Priscilla, who was born on 18th April 1926.]

We must now return to Alf in South Africa, where we had left him on 14th June 1928, Alf having (we assume) just said goodbye to Olive as she had stepped aboard the SS *Windsor Castle* to make her sad and tiring way back to England, carrying Baby Joan with her.

HMS *BIRMINGHAM (Continued)*

Assuming that he did manage to get to Capetown briefly to see Olive and the baby safely on their way to England, Alf would surely have had to be back on board at Simonstown by next afternoon 15th June 1928, when *Birmingham* paraded her Guard and Band and dressed ship with masthead flags. The 6th Cruiser Squadron (i.e *Birmingham* and *Lowestoft*) then proceeded at 1600, taking station one on either bow of the inbound Royal Mail Motor Vessel *Carnavon Castle* which was flying the flag of HE the Governor-General, arriving from England to take up his new appointment. The two warships turned inwards together 180°, saluted His Excellency with 19 guns, and then *Lowestoft* proceeded out to sea whilst *Birmingham* came to anchor, and undressed ship as the C-in-C landed for a short while to take the Oath as High Commissioner. The C-in-C was back on board at 1850, the time at which *Birmingham* proceeded for Port Elizabeth. Alf was on then on duty, for he signed the Log at 2000 on coming off watch. Shortly after he did so, the ship began to encounter very heavy rain which, fortunately, had held off for the ceremonials which had lasted throughout much of the day.

Verbena took station on *Birmingham* early next day, and the two ships anchored at Port Elizabeth on the 17th June, after their run of 400 miles from Capetown.

The C-in-C was active, inspecting first the Boys and then hammocks of all the company on the 18th, before the two ships proceeded for East London on the 19th, which they reached on the morning of the 20th. The temperature was a warm 80°F, with a slight westerly wind. The C-in-C moved on to inspect *Verbena* on the 24th, by which time *Birmingham's* 6-inch Control Parties were at drill and her small arms companies had been landed for a route march. On the 26th a photograph of the Ship's Company was taken after divisions and prayers. On the 28th it rained in torrents in the early morning and went on to rain and rain through the whole day and deep into the night. However, the next morning dawned bright and clear, as *Birmingham* proceeded at 0715, crossing the bar at 0732 and heading for Durban in a stiff south-westerly wind which was setting up a moderate sea. *Birmingham* embarked a Pilot at 0824 next morning to take her into the harbour, where she secured briefly next to 'C' Shed, hoisted out the C-in-C's car, and then proceeded further upstream.

The Cup Competition of the Royal Natal Yacht Club was due to take place on the 12th July, and *Birmingham* now had all her boats away pulling and sailing as often as could reasonably be managed. She was also drilling her Band and her Royal Marines in ceremonial duties at this time. The ship was open to visitors on the 8th July. On the 10th she coaled (160 tons), before landing her Rifle Team for a competition.

Following the Cup Competition of the RNYC on the 12th, *Birmingham's* company rigged the Quarterdeck and Waist for a dance next day, followed by opening the ship to visitors on the 14th and 15th. Come the 16th, however, the ship proceeded downriver to 'C' Shed, where the C-in-C's car was hoisted back on board, before the ship proceeded for Simonstown. Once more, the Gyro Compass started to wander, and the standard magnetic compass was brought back into use for two hours, until repairs could be effected. Things had settled down by the time Alf came on watch, signing the Log at 1800. He stood the same watch on the next two days as the ship continued towards Simonstown. In the small hours of the next day the ship exercised her emergency searchlight crews. At 1350 she embarked the King's Harbour Master, proceeding into the harbour and securing to 'C' Wall. She then discharged Midshipman McCLURE and three ratings to the Royal Naval Hospital, and two offenders to the RN Detention Quarters.

Birmingham embarked 875 tons of coal on the 20th, and began to return 'out of date' ammunition to the store, drawing new in its place. She also returned the field gun to the depot. Frequent afternoon leaves began to be given at this time, whilst the hands on watch went on cleaning, holystoning and provisioning ship. On 6th August *Birmingham* proceeded into dry dock. Next day she landed a funeral party and half-masted her colours for a time.[253] Come the 8th, the King's Colours were formally transferred to *Lowestoft* under escort, with appropriate ceremonial, and the C-in-C's flag was transferred to *Lowestoft* next day. Meantime, the dock had been part-filled, and the hands were painting the water-line.

On the 10th the paying-off pendant was broken at 0800, and the C-in-C left the ship at 1015. *Birmingham* then proceeded for St Helena, stopping before clearing the harbour to permit the KHM to leave. Alf stood a dog watch as the ship settled on her track, and continued to stand a dog watch on each of the next five days as the ship steamed steadily to the north-west. She reached St Helena on the early morning of the 17th August, with 1,670 miles run, and coaled for over eleven hours, embarking 405 tons. Next day she continued, taking in a further 175 tons before a short leave was given to the Port Watch. On a day of passing showers of rain, the Starboard Watch had their turn next afternoon, but only after the ship had been visited by HE The Acting Governor.

Next day, the 20th August 1928, the ship proceeded for the Ascension Islands, the hands being put to physical drill once the ship was out at sea, and a training class being held for the emergency searchlight crew. Alf stood a watch, and did so again on the next day - and the next. On the 23rd the ship came to anchor at Ascension after her run of 700 miles, landing her hockey team for a match against a local side and giving leave to the POs until 1800. It may well be the case that Alf participated in the match, though no records survive.

On the 24th the ship proceeded for Las Palmas, a gunnery training class being held on the 27th, the emergency searchlight crew being exercised on the 29th, and so on. On 2nd September Gran Canaria was sighted soon after dawn, and, having embarked a Pilot, and saluted the Spanish Flag (21 guns), the fort replying in kind, *Birmingham* came to anchor in La Luz Harbour of Las Palmas at 1300. The Spanish Officer of the Guard came aboard an hour later. The ship had run 2,190 miles from Ascension Island and had crossed the Equator for the fourth time of this commission. She now embarked 700 tons of badly-needed coal, increasing her draught to only 17 ft 2 ins forward and 17 ft 10 ins aft, demonstrating the considerable consumption of water and provisions which had transpired. Leave was given on a watch by watch basis over the next two days to give the ship's company a badly-needed chance to stretch their limbs ashore. Then, at 0715 on the 5th September *Birmingham* proceeded for Sheerness, Alf being on watch from 1600-1800 next day and again on the next, when the hands were set to sponging out the guns –

---

[253] It is assumed that the funeral was of a man who had been serving in another ship of the squadron - not *Birmingham*. (The only *Birmingham*-related death known at this time was that of A.D. MITCHELL, a PO aged 32, who had been invalided home on 4th July and had unfortunately died at Chatham RNH on 11th July, of Pulmonary TB.)

presumably following their use for saluting on the 5th. The sick list had crept up again, and was now running at 14 men. There was just a slight north-westerly swell running.

They passed Cape Finisterre early on the morning of the 9th, and spoke the destroyer HMS *Venemous* at 1730, during Alf's watch on that day. The sea was now less calm, being graded as 4 to 5, and the ship having to alter course to avoid a small fishing fleet. The Ushant Light was raised at 2012 on the 10th, the wind now freshening a little, with a slight swell and sea running, but still with blue skies and just occasional clouds.

Alf was on watch again on the 11th, going below shortly before the Royal Sovereign Lighthouse came abeam and the patent log was hauled in, showing 1,573 miles run from Los Palmas. Wind and sea had eased, but the temperature was declining into the mid-60s Fahrenheit. By the early morning of the 12th they were passing through the Downs, and the hands were set to getting up ammunition. By 0912 *Birmingham* had secured to No.2 Buoy at Sheerness, and, within 30 minutes, an ammunition lighter had secured alongside with the hands already beginning to 'de-ammunition' ship. Eight ratings were now discharged to the Naval Hospital at Chatham. Then, de-ammunitioned, *Birmingham* proceeded upriver to secure in No.2 Basin at Chatham, alongside the cruiser HMS *Calcutta*, a Cardiff-Class ship with a so-called 'trawler bow'.

The final process of returning stores of all kinds now began, including her torpedoes and provisions of all sorts, landing her boats and cleaning ship generally. Short Leave was given on a watch by watch basis during the ensuing days. The hands were mustered and paid on the 17th September, and, come Sunday the 18th, at 0745, 21 ratings were discharged to the RN Barracks at Devonport and Portsmouth.

Though not so stated in the Log, it is assumed that the great majority of the 'Chatham' men were also discharged that same day, for, as the Log *does* record, at 0830 the Reserve Company joined the ship and she was paid off into the Reserve.

A further assessment report was issued on Alf on this day. Signed by Captain A E EVANS, and covering the period 8th February 1928 to18[th] September 1928, it stated that Alf had conducted himself "*...to my entire satisfaction. He has carried out his duties as Boatswain of the ship most efficiently. He has been in charge of a watch at sea.*" Clearly, this was a very good report, even if it seemed to understate the amount of watchkeeping Alf had done. Perhaps, for some reason, Alf had not initially figured in his new Captain's watchkeeping list, although he had done so from the start with the previous Captain.

No Log exists at The National Archives (TNA) for the next period of time, whilst *Birmingham* was a part of the Reserve Fleet at the Nore. Evidently, no logs were maintained by ships in reserve. However, reports continued to be issued about the performance of the officers serving aboard them, and the third assessment report issued about Alf during his time aboard *Birmingham*, signed by Commander P HOWDEN, for the period 30th November 1928 to 30th December 1928, stated that he had carried out his duties"*...very satisfactorily.*" The fourth assessment report, signed by Captain HOLBROOK, and covering the period 31st December 1928 to 14th February 1929 stated that Alf had carried out his duties "*to my entire satisfaction*", and the fifth, signed by Captain MACKINESS (Senior Officer Home Fleet at the Nore), and covering the period 15th February 1929 to 4th March 1929, stated, "*Entirely to my satisfaction.*"

Alf's appointment to *Birmingham* ended in February 1929. Apart from the 'idleness' of 'swinging at a buoy' in a Reserve Ship with what amounted to only a skeleton company to keep the ship in a reasonable state of repair, Alf would have appreciated being within a comparatively short distance of Olive and 'home'. Under the prevailing domestic circumstances, his next appointment was as near to an ideal one as could well have been.

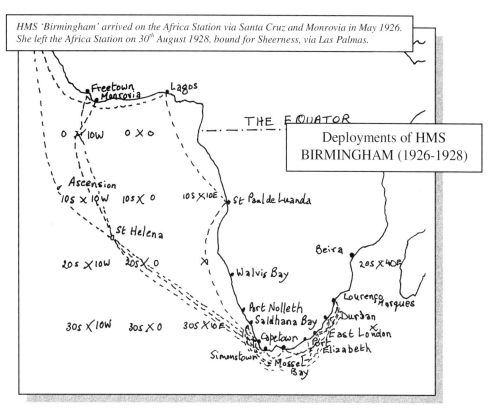

HMS 'Birmingham' arrived on the Africa Station via Santa Cruz and Monrovia in May 1926. She left the Africa Station on 30th August 1928, bound for Sheerness, via Las Palmas.

Deployments of HMS BIRMINGHAM (1926-1928)

VOYAGES DURING DEPLOYMENT: Pers. RECORD of Alfred William DAVIS RN					
Farthest North	Lagos	**06 N** 03 E	*F/North (ever)*	Off Scapa Flow	**59 N** 03 W
Farthest South	Simonstown	**34 S** 18 E	*F/ South (ever)*	Simonstown	**34 S** 18 E
Farthest East	Lourenco Marques	26 S **31 E**	*F/East (ever)*	Ras Asir	12N **51 E**
Farthest West	West of Ascension	09 S **14 W**	*F/West (ever)*	Atlantic Ocean	50 N **30 W**

Alf had broken none of his 'farthest points' records, though he had again reached his 'farthest south' point.

However, his 'Crossings of the Equator' had now jumped up:

Four times in HMS *Birmingham*
Three times in HMS *Weymouth*
Twice in HMS *Lowestoft*
Once in the SS *Cluny Castle*

TOTAL: Ten Crossings

Private Life

As soon as his ship had returned to the Nore in September 1928, and his leave came up, Alf set about seeking skilled medical advice concerning his wife Olive. Thanks to the inheritance from his Father's Will, Alf was also now able to take out a mortgage to purchase a newly-built house in Looe Road, Felixstowe for her and Baby Joan.[254] All this duly took place during his periods of leave from HMS *Birmingham* as the ship continued in the Reserve Fleet at the Nore.

As already mentioned, Alf had also used some of his inheritance to make a loan to his mother-in-law, to help her expand the lending library, general stores and tea-room which she had started in the large new property she and her husband had purchased in the nearby High Road. Her husband continued to be active in his carpentry and decorating business, and the joint business thrived. Alf and his in-laws got along very well, and Alf began to play a very large part in their lives, meeting many new relations and friends on his wife's side of the family and forming friendships, some deep, with them. Most people found him to be an extremely attractive, dashing and charming man with the romance of the sailor and the sea about him, and the freedom of action and leisure which is the due of the naval man on long leave followed up by the long weekends given by sundry 'Friday Whiles' (as compared with the endless 'treadmill' which was then the normal weekly lot of the average civilian worker, with its hurried 'one-and-a-half' day weekends.)

There is no doubt that Alf made many a female heart flutter. However, he was almost blind to this, for the distressing matter was that Olive was definitely in decline, and, for a couple who were so well-suited, so full of life and fun, and so very much in love, this was a total disaster. The only good thing was that Alf could get home quite often from the Nore to spend some quality time with his wife and child.

Alf would be appointed to HMS *Ganges* early in 1929. This would be a very welcome appointment for him, for it would bring him even nearer to his new home in Felixstowe East, and thus he would frequently be able to see his wife and infant daughter, and to get to know his parents-in-law ever more deeply.

Despite his wife's general decline, she had phases where her health improved, and their second child would be conceived in or around August 1929.

---

[254] The house in Looe Road was situated within three minutes walk of the large house, shop and workshop called *Surrey House*, whence Olive's parents had moved from Ipswich in 1928, taking their elder daughter and young son with them. Olive's mother's half-brother, 'Uncle Bill', an old soldier and a Builder's Labourer by civilian trade, also moved in. A young live-in maid was employed to help with the domestic chores.

CHAPTER TWELVE:

HMS *GANGES* (1929-31)

Alf was appointed to HMS *Ganges* on 1st March 1929. He was now near to his new home in Felixstowe East, and thus he would have frequently been able to see his wife and his 20 month-old daughter, and to further enrich his relationship with his parents-in-law and other family members.

From the point of view of getting to Felixstowe, it was sometimes possible to take passage in a naval boat from Shotley directly across the broad estuary which formed the joint outlet of the Stour and the Orwell Rivers, and thus reach Felixstowe Dock. Alternatively, one could head across the Stour from Shotley Gate to Parkestone Quay. From Parkestone Quay, which was a terminal for Rail Ferries from 'Harwich to the Hook of Holland', there was a small motor-boat ferry which plied back and forth across to Felixstowe Dock. From that point Alf could continue the short journey to Felixstowe East by bus. Alternatively, Alf could catch naval or civilian transport going into Ipswich from Shotley, and take a train or bus from Ipswich into Felixstowe. This took rather longer, but was still a very 'viable' journey.

During 1930 the messes which housed the nominal 1,000 or so Boys at Shotley were grouped, for the first time, into a number of 'divisions', each named after a famous British Admiral. Alf was attached to 'Hawke' Division.

Author's collection. A postcard by Edith F. Driver, probably c.1929/30.

This photo was probably taken in or about 1930 and thus may well have coincided with Alf's service at HMS *Ganges*. As we will see, there is a very similar photo of Alf leading out an armed platoon which was taken some five years later. A pencilled comment on back of this card says that the ratings are in a Sunday March-past.

To keep fit, Alf played hockey, at which he had become well-skilled. In September 1930 he obtained the certificate of the Royal Lifesaving Society for having proven his skill *'in rescuing and breaking the clutch of a drowning person, and in resuscitating the apparently drowned'*. The award of this certificate would have greatly pleased him. (It started a rumour around the family elders that Alf had rescued somebody from accidentally drowning, but the author believes this rumour was in error.)

Author's inherited collection. A postcard By Edith F Driver of Ipswich c.1930.

A Game of Hockey at Shotley. Alf, clad all in white, brushes past two men as he goes 'all out' in enthusiastic chase of the ball.

Author's collection of inherited family photographs.

A group photograph of the Officers and Instructors at HMS *Ganges* c.1931. Alf is 3rd from the right in the seated row. Has his eagle eye perhaps spotted some misdemeanour going on away to the photographer's right, thus distracting Alf's gaze? It is assumed that Captain F.W. AUSTIN is the central figure amongst these thirty-nine men (and probably the tall man second from left in the upper photograph.)

Reports were issued on Alf's conduct at *Ganges*, the first running from 1st March 1929 to 7th May that year, and signed by Captain W T R FORD. This said that Alf had conducted himself '*entirely to my satisfaction. A keen and capable officer.*' The second report, dated from 8th May 1929 to 10th March 1931, and signed by Captain F W AUSTIN, said Alf had conducted himself '*to my entire satisfaction and with zeal, ability and success. Has taken much interest in the general activities of the establishment and been a very efficient WO and 2nd OOD of Hawke Division.*' Clearly then, Alf had done very well, and made a very favourable impression on his superiors in rank. It may be worth reminding ourselves that the United Kingdom, in common with other parts of the developed world, especially the U.S.A., was entering a terrible financial depression at this period of time. We shall see a number of repercussions of the depression, which caused many businesses to crash and led to a great many cuts-back in all those activities, large and small, which required any sort of financial backing. The Navy was far from being exempt from this situation.

Surgeon Captain P.L. CROSBIE's Journal for the year 1931 tells us that Shotley had an average daily numerical strength of 878 Boys at this time, which was appreciably lower than had been the figure when Alf had been there nineteen years previously. Currently, there was an average of 40 Boys sick daily. There had been no large-scale epidemics in the year, only two cases of TB., ten cases of appendicitis, and one case of Gonorrhoea (caught from a prostitute by a Boy on leave! One really does feel for this unfortunate lad.) There had been 765 new entries and 634 Boys had been drafted to ships in that year. [The surgeon also reported that some 240 rats, always liable to infest the drains and other parts of establishments where large numbers of humans live together, had been destroyed. As we have seen, rat-infestation was a long-standing problem at *Ganges*.]

NOTE. Picture (ii) in Appendix J, page 749, is an impressive photograph of Alf leading a column of Boy Seamen from HMS 'Ganges' with a Field Gun and Limber in Tow. This was evidently taken at one of the Public Displays given at Ipswich.

As we shall shortly see, Alf was appointed to HMS *Delphinium* from 8th March 1931. This appears to have overlapped his service at *Ganges*, and it would seem that Alf had to do something of a 'pierhead jump' in setting off to join *Delphinium* on the Africa Station. One imagines that it was virtually a matter of shoving his gear into a suitcase and catching the first available Union Castle Line steamer to head for Capetown or perhaps a more appropriate port on the western coastline of Africa. Luckily, by now he was well-practised in packing his gear neatly, and in never accidentally 'leaving anything of importance behind'.

He was also well-practised in taking his farewells of loved ones. However, to have to say goodbye to Olive under the present circumstances must have rent Alf in twain. But more of that in a moment.

Private Life

Olive's illness was one which had remissions. She had rallied to some degree during Alf's stint at *Ganges*. So much so that they had created another little life during Alf's time at the training establishment, their son Neville Alfred being conceived in August 1929 and born at 'Seaforth', Looe Road, Felixstowe, at around 11.00 am on 17th May 1930. 'Little' Neville, so-called to distinguish him from his 14 year-old uncle (who thereafter came to be called 'Big Neville'), was generally a contented baby. This happy nature was unlike that of his elder sister, who (according to what the family elders would say in later years), had always cried a lot.[255]

Picture kindly loaned by the author's elder sister, Mrs Joan GOODMAN. Snapshot originally taken by an unknown photographer.

Olive holding her son, 'Little Neville', aged 2½ months. He is dressed in his christening robe. This picture was taken in the back garden of 'Seaforth', the new house which Alf had bought at Looe Road Felixstowe. Judging by her petulant expression, young Joan, aged three, scarcely seems pleased to have a little rival for her Mother's affections now suddenly on the scene. (*It is clear that this picture was not taken by Alf, for he was away on the high seas well before the 27th July 1930, the day when this image was created.*)

---

[255] As we have seen, this 'persistent crying' probably started during Joan's earliest days in South Africa, as an instinctive effort to obtain full attention from her lovely mother. This in a situation where little Joan had often been spoilt by having her lovely mother's *undivided* attention for long periods of time, but in a domestic scene in which her mother and father were besotted with each other, and where her father was quite often able to get home for short spells of leave. Little Joan would surely have seen him as an 'intruder' at such times, taking away far too much of her mother's attention. The arrival of a baby brother, naturally also demanding much attention from her mother, would certainly have heightened Joan's own attention-seeking behaviour. As we shall see, instinctive thoughts of finding one means or another to eliminate her 'rivals' from the domestic scene and thus regain 100% of her wonderful mother's love and time would doubtless have dominated little Joan's thoughts and behaviour.

Olive's relations soon came around from nearby Ipswich to inspect the new infant, and we know that his second cousin, young Joyce, daughter of Arthur Vernon BISHOP, herself only a very young child, was allowed to hold the baby the day after he had been born - a privilege she never forgot. Little Neville was baptised at the Parish Church in Old Felixstowe on 27th July 1930. (See photograph of his godparents on Page 396).

However, Olive's health had again been a matter of concern whilst she had been pregnant, and it was now the medical diagnosis that she had 'Hodgkinson's disease. This was a form of cancer of the lymphatic glands which would have periods of remission, but would inevitably be fatal within a few years. In those days, very little could be done to delay the progression of the illness, let alone to cure it. This was desperately sad news.

There was an understandable emotional reaction amongst some family members, who were deeply distressed at the 'injustice' which was taking the life of this fine young wife and mother. That is to say, they cast the new baby in the role of 'scapegoat' for his mother's condition. In point of fact, Olive had contracted her illness well before the new baby was conceived. Indeed, in the light of knowledge available today, it may well have been the change in climate, from England to South Africa that had adversely affected her immune system and triggered the condition.

Faced with the fatal diagnosis, the reaction of Alf and Olive, who continued to be forever very much in love, would be to continue to procreate life, for they would start *yet a third child*, about seven or eight months after the arrival of the baby, 'Little Neville'. Understandably, every moment of their lives may well have attained huge significance for the couple. Their emotional involvement with each other, always high, evidently reached even greater heights and they were perhaps also making too much of this very amenable new baby, 'Little Neville', for their daughter Joan, by then rising four years old, quite understandably became increasingly jealous of her parent's consequentially reduced devotion to her. Bearing in mind the considerable attention her baby brother was receiving, she therefore did her best to feed him to the irascible family parrot, which (luckily) retained its vegetarian principles! It seems probable that she did this 'feeding' after Alf had left 'Ganges', and was away at sea in his next appointment. In her later years Joan would always tell this story in a very honest and self-deprecating way. She implies that her attempt at the elimination of her little brother remained undetected. And, somewhat against the odds as time went by, the life of 'Little Neville' somehow continued long enough for him to be able to research and write this book.

Olive's sister Alice always claimed that Baby Neville was quite happy if left to play under the kitchen table or the kitchen sink, so long as he had a couple of metal saucepan lids to bang together. One would not be surprised to learn that some of the adults thought the little fellow to be rather simple-minded.[256]

---

[256] This coign of vantage under the table gave the author his first sight of the young family maid Florrie's very black stockings and knickers and, in stark contrast, her intensely white thighs. That vision of the family maid is one which he has never forgotten. He was instinctively interested in romantic sex from a very early age. Having since learned something of the highly-sexed DAVIS and HOPKINS genes, his promiscuous 'attitude' seems highly understandable. Perhaps it was little wonder that, as he grew up, he often felt like 'a fish out of water' when living in the highly 'reserved' household of his GREEN grandparents, aunt and uncle.

In the lead-up to the birth of his baby son, Alf would have learned of the marriages of his two younger sisters. That is to say, Rose had married Alfred WOOLFREY, a Plumber, at the Church of St Peter, Hammersmith, on 20 June 1929, and Eva had married Frederick THORNE, a Postman, in the parish church of Widcombe, Bath, on 26 December 1929. Eva had acted as a Witness at Rose's marriage, as had their elder brother John *alias* 'Jack'.[257]

Anonymous photograph kindly donated by Raymond PENNEY Esq.

Frederick THORNE, a Postman, marries Eva DAVIS at the Parish Church of Widcombe, Bath, on Boxing Day, the 26th December 1929. The donor of this print, Raymond PENNEY, is the seven year-old lad with the happy smile who is standing on the extreme right. His father, Wilfred PENNEY, who was a marriage witness, is the tall man standing between the bride and her matron-of-honour. It is assumed that the other witness (an 'E G THORNE') is the man standing on the extreme left – presumably an already-married brother of the bridegroom.

Both Rose and Eva would take over and run public houses with the aid of their new husbands, each woman presumably well-funded by her very substantial inheritance from her late father's Will.

Being stationed at Shotley, Alf would probably have been in a position to have attended both these marriages. However, due to the bad blood between Alf and Jack, it seems unlikely that Alf and Olive would have attended Rose's marriage if they had previously been made aware that Jack was going to be a significant presence. There may have been a greater chance that they would have attended Eva's wedding. However, the surviving photograph of the latter occasion shows no sign of their presence.

Most unfortunately, it seems that Alf's brother Jack had lost his Victualler's Licence by early 1929, apparently for allowing gaming to go on at his pub, the

---

[257] Rose and Berty John (alias 'Jack') got on quite well together, and, in much later life, Rose would visit Jack at Bristol and play cards with him on quite a 'sharp' basis, money being involved. They would also have a flutter 'on the horses', both seeing themselves as experts 'on form'.

'Engineer's Arms', which Ray PENNEY remembers as being a cosy old-fashioned one of the 'spit and sawdust' variety. Ray also remembers that, perhaps as a publicity 'gimmick', Jack had the embryo of a horse on display. It was about 8 inches in length, and preserved in formaldehyde in a glass jar. One supposes that this might have been a 'souvenir' gifted to him by his father, probably originally obtained from a 'Vet'. The loss of his pub must have very nearly broken Jack's heart.

He was now a 'Beer Retailer', presumably running an 'Off-License'. He and Kate now had a third daughter, Kathleen, born on 6th March 1929, and Kate would soon be pregnant again, for she would bear a fourth daughter, Margaret Lillian on 28th February 1931. By that time Jack would have become a Retail Grocer, still living in the Bristol area.

At this time, Alf's whole focus and preoccupation in life outside the Navy - and probably often intruding even into that - was his beloved Olive. He had been extremely fortunate in being able to spend so much time with her and Joan, now a toddler, and the new baby, little Neville. Could such luck in his appointments possibly continue? Certainly not! Alf's appointment to *Delphinium* in early March 1931, out on the Africa Station, must have come like a bolt from the blue. The 'Sword of Damocles' had fallen at last - and with a heavy crash at that.

Olive's periods may have been becoming a bit erratic by now, due to onset of Hodgkinson's disease, but she would have 'missed' twice at about the time that Alf received his new appointment, *perhaps* signalling that she was pregnant again – though this was not confirmed until later on. All ends up, Alf may well have considered making an appeal on compassionate grounds not to have to go to a 'foreign station'. If so, one imagines that Olive persuaded him not to imperil his career by so doing. She would have told him that she was in good hands with her parents close by and with Alice providing practical help whenever it was needed. Alf must have had nightmare memories of the similar situation which had arisen over his own fatally-ill mother in 1905/6, when various pressures had led his father to abandon his wife to the care of her elder sister. The parallels might well have been quite overpowering for Alf.

However, he packed his kit - embraced his beloved wife and children - and went. Things were not going to be simple and straightforward when he got to Africa, for *Delphinium* had commissioned in England, with a ship's company from Portsmouth, and they would have 'shaken down' during the three months which had already elapsed. As a Chatham man, Alf might well find himself being treated as a 'bit of a stranger' - at least until he had 'proved' himself. This would be the first experience he would have had of that sort of situation, for, apart from one small draft many years before, all his former ships had been made up with ship's companies drawn from Chatham.[258]

---

[258] There are old stories which used to go the rounds in the Navy about low-down behaviours by groups of sailors from a rival port, as contrasted with the 'gentlemanly' behaviour of the 'heroes' from one's own home port. One of the more legendary tales concerns an innocently romantic sailor who 'clicked' with a legless lady who was sitting in a wheelchair in a pub, treated her to a number of drinks, wheeled her home through a park after 'chucking out time', and ended up, somewhat to his surprise, by making ardent love to her after (at her suggestion, it may be said) he'd hung her most conveniently on the park railings by utilising the shoulder-straps which normally held her in her wheelchair. As he was tenderly tucking her back into her wheel-chair after lifting her down again from the railings with such strength as he had left, she asked what port he was from, and when he told her, she said, "*I thought as*

For the next three years after leaving Felixstowe Alf would have to rely on letters and snapshots sent from home to keep 'up to date' with everything. His receipt of a copy of the following snapshot would have been a token that 'life goes on at home', notwithstanding. That is to say, one family ceremonial which Alf would have missed by leaving England in March was the baptism of Baby Neville, which took place at Felixstowe Parish Church on 27th July 1930, with Olive's younger brother, George Neville and a friend called Tommy WINKWORTH being the godfathers and Olive's first-cousin Essie BISHOP being the godmother. One does wonder if Olive had proceeded with this ceremony 'whilst the going was good', fearing that her downward spiral into increasingly long periods of debility might prevent her from being present if she were to await Alf's return from the Africa Station.

Author's collection of inherited family photographs.

All smiles in the back garden at 'Seaforth', Looe Road. Cousin Essie holds her godson, Baby Neville, dressed in his christening robe. The godfathers stand beside her, Tommy on the left, and 'Big' Neville (aged 14) on the right. Baby Neville, aged 2½ months, and looking here (rather uncannily) as if he were already starting to 'take an interest in what was going on', would grow up to become the author of this book.

Receipt of the following studio photo would have confirmed to Alf that his children were being well cared-for, and smartly dressed. Already they were looking older than he would have remembered them, for the photograph was taken about eight or nine months after Alf left Felixstowe. It will be noted that Joan looks more

---

much! You're a really decent Jack Tar! - Those unkind boys from 'X' always leave me hanging there all alone and helpless!" [Said sort of tale, with the appropriate name of a rival port slipped into place as 'X', is reckoned to start a good old fight in any place where sailors from two different ports come together - and could just have been indicative of the rivalry, 'atmosphere' and back-biting which Alf, as a man from Chatham might have expected to find in a ship with a 'Pompey' complement, albeit that his rank would have offered him a considerable measure of face-to-face protection.]

settled emotionally, probably through her mother's careful maintaining of a close bond with her, involving young Joan in some of the household activities, and trying not to over-do the amount of attention given to the new baby. Joan's eyes have a rather strange expression, which is probably manifest of the short-sightedness which would later be diagnosed.

Author's collection of inherited family photographs.
Studio portrait by James W Howard of Ipswich.

Baby Neville (18 months) and his sister Joan (4½ years).

Alf would have been anxious to remain in constant touch with Olive's condition, and the regular arrival of mail from home would have been of the utmost importance to him.

Let's see what was happening to Alf out on the Africa Station...

CHAPTER THIRTEEN:

HMS *DELPHINIUM* (1931-33)

Alf was appointed to the sloop HMS *Delphinium* (Captain A.M.PETERS) from 8th March 1931. As has already been implied, she had recommissioned with a Portsmouth company. This had taken place at Sheerness, on 9th December 1930.

Delphinium had then undergone a very bad crossing indeed of the Bay of Biscay, but was now already well-established on the Africa Station. Prior to Alf joining her she had been at Calabar, Duala, Sierra Leone and various other places along the north-west coast. [These had included Lagos, where she had taken over the duties of SNO West Coast of Africa from her near-sister *Daffodil*, on 31st January 1931.]

Seemingly Alf had travelled out individually by intermediate steamer. It must have been extraordinarily difficult for him to take his leave from his ailing wife and little family. Once again, his solace would have been that Olive's sister, Alice, was a positive help, and that the parents of Alice and Olive were near at hand and highly caring and supportive.

It would be interesting to know what Alf's joining instructions had been. If he had been landed initially at Capetown he would have had to do quite a lot of 'chasing around' to catch up with *Delphinium*. However, Union Castle ships did call at various ports on the way south, and Alf may have been primed to disembark at Freetown or the nearest available port to that place.

Be that as it may, *Delphinium's* Log shows that Alf joined her at Freetown on 3rd April 1931, nearly a month after receiving his appointment. His arrival aboard *Delphinium*, perhaps slightly ominously, coincided with *Delphinium* discharging an ERA and an AB to the cruiser HMS *Calcutta*, for return home to England as invalids.[259]

Delphinium was a small but very attractive 'Flower-Class' sloop. She had been launched at Glasgow in March 1916. It will be remembered that the cruisers, such as *Lowestoft* and her sisters, patrolled much of the seaboard of the Africa Station, their patrol area stretching from a most northerly point on the east coast (at Beira, in Mozambique), then southwards around the Cape of Good Hope, and then as far north up the west coast of Africa as Lobito in Angola. The cruisers seldom continued further north up the coast than Lobito, and it was there, on the west coast, that the sloop *Delphinium* and her consorts took over, continuing northwards at least as far as Accra on the Gold Coast, their shallow draught suiting this coastline. They evidently worked to a fairly detailed programme set out in advance by their Captains, presumably following general instructions given by the Admiralty and the C-in-C Africa Station, and organised to comply with various pre-set fleet exercises and regattas, and to make other points of rendezvous for special events and celebrations tied in with events which were, essentially, land-based.

---

[259] One of these men had bacillary dysentery and another had contracted climatic bubo and subterian malaria fever (the latter, probably, in the surgeon's opinion, from having unprotected sexual intercourse with black prostitutes). Both men had been surveyed by a medical board and invalided from the service.

Delphinium had been made by Napier and Miller. She had been designed to act either as a sloop pure and simple, or as a minesweeper. [For the latter reason her designers had specified that these ships should have multi-walled fore-parts to their hulls, with the intention that these ships might be able to withstand severe damage to the outermost 'layers' of the bow area, probably leading to a certain amount of flooding of the 'intercellular space', and yet hopefully still stay afloat.]

Author's collection of inherited photographs. This image taken from a Ship's Christmas Greeting Card sent home by Alf in 1931.

HMS *Delphinium* dressed overall. Photographed at Lobito in Angola.

In terms of Alf's particular interests, *Delphinium* had single four-inch Quick-Firing Guns fitted with partial box-like shields, mounted fore and aft, on the centre-line, one being sited on the F'c'sle and one at the after end of the boat deck. She also had one 2 pdr Pom-Pom amidships and 4 x 3 pdr Hotchkiss Q.F Guns on the Quarter Deck. The latter were used as her saluting guns, but could also be used in anger should need arise.

Her log shows that the Most Economical Speed of *Delphinium* was 10.4 knots, at which she consumed 0.97 tons of coal per hour. At Full Power she could do just over 15 knots, at which she would consume 2.68 tons of coal per hour. It appears that she normally carried 200 tons of coal (say 220 tons max.). With 200 tons her range at 10 knots would have been about 2,080 miles.

There is a report by Surgeon Lt J.B. PATRICK (of whom more presently, and who served for at least a part of this 1931/33 commission), that he found this little ship to be generally very well-ventilated and comfortable for the ratings, even in tropical conditions.[260] The officers' quarters in the wardroom flat were also good on the whole, but had the disadvantage that the scuttles had to be closed when the ship was at sea. This led to the port side cabins becoming rather airless, because they lacked any efficient

---

[260] The POs and CPOs were rather less well-served by the ventilation in their part of the ship.

artificial ventilation.[261] The surgeon reported that *Delphinium* was a good seaboat, and, though rather 'wet', had stood up extremely well to her terrible crossing of the Bay of Biscay in January 1931.[262]

Let's see how *Delphinium* compared with Alf's previous ships. The increasing height of these tables is a measure of the ever-growing scale of Alf's naval experience.

Name of Ship	Type Of Ship	Displace-ment (tons)	Year Completed	1st Year Alf srv'd (diff.)	Comple-ment	Max. Length (feet)	Max. Beam (feet)	Draught (feet)	Shaft Horse-Power	Max. Speed (knots)
Vanguard	Dreadnought	**19,250**	1910	1912 (2)	823	536	**84**	**31.75**	24,500	22
Russell	Pre-Dreadnought	14,000	1903	1912 (9)	718	418	75.5	28	18,220	19
Weymouth	Armour'd Cruiser	5,250	1911	1913 (2)	392	453	48.5	18	22,000	25.5
Courageous	Battle Cruiser	18,600	1916	1916 (0)	**829**	**786.5**	81	26	**90,000**	**35**
Lowestoft	Armour'd Cruiser	5,440	1913	1920 (7)	546	459.5	49.8	18.25	25,000	25.5
St Cyrus	Admiralty Tug	820	**1919**	1925 (6)	12	143	29	13.5	1,200	12
Birmingham	Armour'd Cruiser	5,440	1913	1925 (12)	504	459	49.8	18	25,000	25.5
Delphinium	Sloop	1,250	1916	1931 (15)	80	267.5	33.5	11.75	2,200	15

Name of Ship	Guns					Torpedo-Tubes		Armour			
	Main		Secondary		A.A			Deck	Side	Turr't	D.C.T
	Calibre	Number	Calibre	Number	Capability	Calibre	Number	(ins)	(ins)	(ins)	(ins)
Vanguard	12"	**Ten**	4"	Twelve	**2x3"**	18"	Three	1.5 - 3	**10**	**11**	**8 – 11**
Russell	12"	Four	**6"**	Twelve	-	18"	Four	2.5	3-4	6	12
Weymouth	6"	Eight	3"	One	1x3"	**21"**	Two	1-2	-	1	2
Courageous	**15"**	Four	4"	**Eighteen**	**2x3"**	**21"**	**Fourteen**	1-3	3	7-9	10
Lowestoft	6"	Nine	3 pdr	Four	1x3"	**21"**	Nine	1-2	3	1	2
St Cyrus	12 pdr	One	-	-	-	-	-	-	-	-	-
Birmingham	6"	Nine	3 pdr	Four	1x3"	**21"**	Eleven	1-2	3	1	2
Delphinium	4"	Two	3 pdr	Four	**2x3"**	-	-	-	-	-	-

As indicated by lack of **bold** figures in the 'bottom-lines' in the above tables of comparatives, *Delphinium* was easily the smallest, least well-armed (except, interestingly, in anti-aircraft capability), and the 'least well-protected-by-armour' warship in which Alf had yet served (That is, *if one discounts the tug 'St Cyrus', which was not a warship in the usual sense of the word*). *Delphinium* also had *by far* the smallest complement of the warships in the table, and carried only a dozen or so officers on her books. As a 'war machine', however, *Delphinium* did have one important advantage, for she had the smallest draught, and this enabled her to traverse quite shallow shoals and 'river-bars', and to penetrate up estuaries and river-systems where her deeper-draught consorts dare not venture. She thus had a potential tactical advantage under certain circumstances.

---

[261] The ventilation to the forward port cabins via cowls on the upper deck was said to be 'singularly ineffective'. On the plus side for the officers, the wardroom was 'cool, comfortable and well-ventilated'.

[262] Her 'electrics' had suffered to some degree, one serious problem being that the motor for her refrigerating equipment had been put out of action. (See Admiral's Letter ADM 116/2863, filed at the TNA.) In the surgeon's opinion, the dampness throughout the ship in the extreme weather may have also contributed to the death of one rating from lobar pneumonia.

Delphinium actually had a maximum full-load draught of around 13' 9",
appreciably more than her designed draught, but a good 4' less, as can be seen from the
table, than that of cruisers such as *Birmingham* and *Lowestoft*.[263]

One other thing that might be said about *Delphinium* was that she had first been
commissioned in 1916, which (*discounting little 'St Cyrus', which had been completed in
1919*) made her virtually equal, 'in year of completion', to the most 'modern' warship
which Alf had yet joined (i.e. HMS *Courageous*, which ship Alf had joined whilst she
was still in-building in 1916.) Ironically, however, due to the flow of time, *Delphinium*
had now become the *oldest* ship in which Alf ever served, for this was now her 15th year
of service. (See bracketed figures in the fifth column of the upper table.)

In spite of any latent 'home port' rivalries, Alf probably settled in quite quickly,
and it seems likely that he would soon have found that the said Surgeon Lt PATRICK
was very 'go-ahead', and keen to keep malaria and diseases of all kinds under tight
control. In fact, it was during Alf's early days aboard that extra lengths of mosquito-
netting were embarked, the surgeon having obtained special permission from the C-in-C,
Vice Admiral TWEEDIE, to increase the netting-allowance for each man.[264] As OOW,
Alf would have found that his duties included a regular check, whenever the ship was
lying near a 'malarial' shore, that each man was properly covered by his net, and did not
have his knees pressed vulnerably up against the mesh.[265]

On 7th April 1931 *Delphinium* coaled (183 tons), her draught afterwards being
12 ft 7 ins forward and 13 ft 9 ins aft. (This suggests a ratio of about 21 tons per inch of
draught, though this figure is evidently much too high.) Alf was OOW from 1600 -1800.
Later that same day the ship proceeded for Takoradi, where she secured alongside the
coaling wharf at 0840 on the 11th. Prophylactic quinine was issued against the risk of
malaria while they were alongside at Takoradi. Alf was OOW on the 14th, and *perhaps*,
as a 'new broom', it was Alf who was '*the alert officer*' who (as Lt Surgeon PATRICK
reported in his journal) found several ratings without their nets spread, leading to
disciplinary action being taken and matters being tightened up generally. If this was
indeed Alf's work, it would have been typical of him, and he would have felt he had
'made his mark'. There would have been a certain special added 'spiciness' for him in
having done so as a Chatham-based man in a Portsmouth-commissioned ship.

Cricket and football matches were played against local teams, and one shooting
match, the ship being successful in all events. Leave was given, but only until the late
afternoon to avoid risks of mosquito-bites, for the mosquitoes became more active at
dusk and nightfall. The ship took in water during her stay, her company chlorinating it as
an added precaution. She proceeded for Lagos on the 17th. The hands were employed in
various maintenance tasks during the short voyage, especially in renewing the boats'

---

[263] As we shall later see, even a draught of 13 ft was enough to be something of an embarrassment
when attempting to cross one of the river-bars on her planned routes.

[264] Vice Admiral TWEEDIE (accompanied by Mrs TWEEDIE) had arrived at Capetown in the
RMS *Balmoral Castle* on 23rd February 1931, and taken over from Vice Admiral BURMESTER as C-in-C
Africa Station on the 26th. Admiral TWEEDIE was flying his flag in the cruiser *Carlisle.*

[265] It is a pity that no surgeon's logs have survived at TNA (Kew) for the other ships in which Alf
served on the Africa Station. This means that we have no readily available way of measuring the
effectiveness of the initiatives which Surgeon Lt PATRICK introduced with the aim of minimising tropical
diseases, etc.

falls, the work including the falls of the surf boat which she carried. The temperature was high at 80 degrees Fahrenheit and the relative humidity was around a sweltering 70%.

Whilst at Lagos, games of football and hockey were played against local sides. The company coaled ship on the 24th, using native labour and embarking 146 tons. They also embarked more water, again chlorinating it. They then proceeded for Victoria on a sea which remained calm, and arrived there on the 26th April. There they encountered very light airs and a sweltering heat of 85 degrees Fahrenheit. However, a large party of officers and men were landed to make their way to Buea, a Hill Station, for four enchanted days in the cool and invigorating air at 4,000 ft altitude, and in beautiful surroundings. Sports were played and pleasant walks enjoyed. A second party followed them. Whether Alf got away with one or other of these parties is unknown. The ship lay far out from the shore as a precaution against malaria, and, although the opportunity was taken by some of the company to visit the flourishing Botanical Gardens which the Germans had initiated at the start of the century, leave was again restricted to daylight hours. Despite all the precautions being taken, two ratings fell sick, and were subsequently diagnosed as having contracted malaria.

Delphinium then proceeded to the Sao Thome Islands which she reached on the 5th May after a run of 250 miles. The ship again lay off the coast. By that stage their draught was down to 11 ft 6 ins forrard and 13 ft 5 ins aft, due to the provisions consumed by the men and the coal and water consumed by the ship's engines. The 6th May was Accession Day and *Delphinium* was dressed with masthead flags. Next day *Delphinium* saluted the National Flag of Portugal with 21 guns, the salute being returned. Then, whilst the hands painted the hammock flat, Captain PETERS paid a special call on the Governor, which the Governor officially returned in the afternoon, receiving a 17-gun salute on leaving. The Portuguese were very hospitable and took a party of *Delphinium's* officers on a scenic tour of the beauties of the Island by motor boat.[266]

On the 8th May the ship proceeded southwards for Loanda, being at 0° 06' N, 6° 57' E at noon, stopping as she entered the Southern Hemisphere at 2040, and then being boarded by King Neptune and His Court, before continuing her voyage with the salty King aboard, proceeding at 2045. At 1015 next morning, as the Log put it, *'numerous persons were admitted into King Neptune's Domain, with the usual rites and ceremonies'*, and it seems that a good time was had by one and all. Alf, regularly standing watch, had the 'graveyard' midnight spell this day.

On 10th May the ship stopped at 1000, long enough for a balloon ascent to be made, apparently in relation to observations of a meteor, and, next day they arrived at the fine natural harbour of Loanda, which was the seat of government of Angola. *Delphinium* then came to anchor in 14 fathoms about 4 cables off-shore, saluting the

---

[266] As already indicated, the author is indebted to Surgeon Lt J.B. PATRICK who maintained a very interesting journal of this commission of HMS *Delphinium*. The journal is preserved at TNA under ADM 101/528. Whilst much of the journal is devoted to matters medical, concerning the treatment of specific cases, and the status of the various hospitals and medical facilities at places visited ashore - and therefore not relevant to the gamut of this book - other parts of Surgeon Licutenant PATRICK's journal contain a fascinating insight into the life led by the ship's company, their sporting engagements, interactions with the local people at various points of call, prophylactic measures taken to protect the men from tropical and sexually-transmitted diseases, and, at times, give an estimation of the physical condition of the men and the state of their morale. As deemed relevant to Alf's life, sundry aspects have been drawn from this to 'colour' the generally rather bare and necessarily terse statements made in the Ship's Log.

Portuguese Flag with 21 guns, and with Fort Miguel responding in kind. *Delphinium* remained at Loanda until 17th May (Alf's baby son's first birthday so quickly come around), the prophylactic doses of quinine being maintained for the company during those days. The ship then proceeded for Cape St Bras, 100 miles distant from Loanda. This place was uninhabited, but some good shooting of wild game was enjoyed by the officers, and the ship's company managed some fine fishing. From Cape St Bras the ship proceeded for Lobito on the 22nd May, where they coaled with native labour, embarking 120 tons. Although not mentioned in her Log, it is possible that the ship was dressed overall, probably for Empire Day (the 24th), whilst there, for a Christmas Card was issued for 1931, showing the ship so dressed at Lobito. During their stay at Lobito the company worked hard practising for the imminent West Coast Regatta. They also managed to get in some games of football against local sides. Again, a daily dose of quinine was maintained.

On 1st June the ship proceeded southwards for Walvis Bay, Alf signing the Log at 2400. Next morning, after passing cautiously through a fog bank, a target was dropped at 0935 and 1-inch aiming practice and Lewis gun firing was carried out, the target being picked up at 1215. The 4th June was Alf's daughter's 4th birthday. At 1515 that day, the ship passed the Bell Buoy and entered the Channel to secure alongside the Wharf at Walvis Bay at 1400, after her run of 710 miles. On 5th June *Daffodil* arrived and, next day, a Pulling Regatta between the two ships was held. The final result was that *Delphinium* took the honours, but only by the narrow margin of 20 points to 17, and that only after a terrific struggle. *Daffodil* then took over from *Delphinium* the duties of SNO West Coast of Africa. Walvis Bay was regarded as healthy and virtually free from malaria, so a final dose of quinine was given to the company on the 6th June, and no more was issued. On the 10th, *Delphinium* exercised her landing parties, and the hands worked on the falls for the whalers, turning them end for end. Meantime, the Kroomen were painting the ship's side.

On 11th June the ship proceeded for Simonstown, exercising Action Stations and again carrying out 1-inch aiming practice at a target dropped beforehand. Then, having picked up the target, the hands prepared the Oropesa Sweep for running, which was exercised next day for two hours.[267] On the 13th the ship began working up for a 3/5ths Power Trial, which lasted from 0800 to 1600, Alf being OOW for the last two hours.

Intermittent fog patches seriously delayed the ship twice next day, but she entered harbour at Simonstown at 0712 on the 15th, after her voyage of 730 miles from Walvis Bay. She promptly landed a young stoker with acute malaria, to be taken into the RNH at Simonstown.[268] At 0800 the ship saluted the Flag of the C-in-C, Vice Admiral H.J. TWEEDIE CB, with 15 guns. Already present at Simonstown were the cruisers *Cardiff* and *Carlisle* (Flag), and the sloops *Cyclamen* and *Verbena*. On the 16th *Delphinium* began to spruce herself up, re-spreading her awnings after her hands had scrubbed them, as well as scrubbing her already snowy decks. Shore leaves were granted. Then, on the 17th, the Africa Fleet Regatta was held, under light airs and perfect blue skies, but in the very reasonable morning temperature of 55°F which had climbed to only 72°F by noon. The ship's surgeon felt that the ship's company were not very

---

[267] The Oropesa Sweep was related to minesweeping activities. (Also see photo on Page 415.)

[268] He would be released back to the ship a fortnight later, regarded as 'cured', and put on light duties.

enthusiastic about the fleet competition, since the real contest in their minds had been the regatta against *Daffodil*, and the Fleet regatta came almost as something of an anti-climax. However, all the events were completed, and the prize-giving ceremony was held on schedule, at 1630. This was a halcyon period and *Delphinium's* sick list had fallen to 'Nil'. During the ensuing days general leave of four days was given to the ship's company in two watches, and a considerable amount or ordinary shore leave was also given.

On 22nd June 1931 the ship was dressed overall in Honour of 'Coronation Day' and a Royal Salute was fired. *Delphinium* then began to be taken in hand for a refit, stores and ammunition being discharged, the hands chipping and painting the ship's side, and so on. On the 3rd July she was shifted to the Selbourne Dock and entered Dry Dock, her draught by then having been reduced to 10 ft 3 ins forrard and 12 ft 6 ins aft - the lowest in Alf's time aboard. 'Life' went on at Simonstown, however, and a succession of parties left the ship for musketry courses on the Rifle Range at Simonstown, which is on the same general site as the sanatorium where Alf had been 'incarcerated' for a while during his service in HMS *Lowestoft*. The ship's surgeon felt that this respite away from the ship was greatly enjoyed by the ratings and that the results could be seen in the bearing and morale of the men. Indeed, the stoker who had been treated for malaria and released from Simonstown Hospital on 29th July, was sent off on one of the range parties for five days, and it clearly did him good. That same day of 29th July, a football match was played, and a stoker received a broken forearm. He was sent to the RNH at the Cape. He had company during the journey, at least, for another stoker had gone down with syphilis and went off for treatment (presumably in a quite different ward!) at the Cape Hospital.[269]

The standard Educational Test Part 2 was held on board around this time. Meantime, the ship's cables were being ranged on the bottom of the dock for surveying and the ship's bottom was being coated. By the 9th August, stores were being embarked and refitting was in progress. The cables were also being restored to their lockers, suitably oiled. Some of the boats' falls were being renewed and painting was in progress, especially of the after screen and battery. Indeed, the painting was now becoming a work of art, with the quarter deck and after superstructure being enamelled to bring these areas up 'just so'. The hands also 'blacked down aloft'. The pulling boats were subjected to their annual buoyancy tests, and the ship came out of dry dock and was shifted to the berth by 'A' Wall, where ammunition was embarked. Those of her boats which had been landed were hoisted in. Her refit was virtually complete - and Alf had stood his watch for a great deal of the time. Perhaps he found it easier to be almost constantly on duty rather than to be idle and moping about Olive.

On 20th July 1931 the ship carried out another 3/5ths 'Power Trial With Despatch', running at 11.8 knots and consuming 1.21 tons of coal per hour. She coaled on the 3rd August (200 tons), restoring her draught to 12 ft 6 ins forrard and 13 ft 6 ins aft,

---

[269] The first man would rejoin ship, fit for duty, on 15th October. The second man had returned to the ship on 18th August, fit for duty. However, his long-term prospects were unclear. [Vice Admiral TWEEDIE's report to the Admiralty for January/February 1931 had stated that the health of the men on the Africa Station was generally good, but that V.D. was still a problem. Men who contracted it *'would not be accepted as volunteers for a further commission on the Station.'* This was an interesting statement, implying that ratings could, under certain circumstances, elect to switch to a newly-arrived ship when theirs was soon to return to England. (See ADM 116/2863 at TNA.)]

then dressed ship with masthead flags and fired a 21 gun salute. Further 'touching up' of the paintwork ensued, before, on the 10th, she exercised her 4 inch gun crews whilst the other hands tested their gasmasks in the anti-gas chamber. On the 11th, *Delphinium* unbasined and the ship was swung to adjust her compasses.

Then the tug *St Dogmael* put to sea towing a Pattern VI Target, and *Delphinium* carried out four runs of 1-inch aiming practice at it. She then picked up the target and returned to harbour. During the ensuing days *Delphinium* carried out further firings at a BP ('Battle Practice') Target, including night-firings, and firing in local control. She also exercised her pom-pom crew. In between times her 1st and 2nd whalers managed to get away under sail for practice.

Delphinium coaled on the 13th August, and, next day the ship was brought to action stations and inspected in that condition by the Fleet Gunnery Officer, who surely put some very searching questions to various officers and men, those officers surely including Alf. On the day after it was the turn of the Fleet Engineering Officer - and the Fleet Medical officer - and then the FAO. Short shore leaves were being given at this time. On the 17th the C-in-C inspected the ship and the ship's company after Divisions, and the hands exercised Action, Fire and Collision Stations under his eagle eye. He left the ship at 1140 and *Delphinium* proceeded for 1-inch aiming practice at a Pattern VI Target in False Bay. The other sloops had been assembling and practising in much the same way, and, come the 18th August, *Cyclamen, Delphinium* and *Verbena* proceeded to Kogel Bay for the Sloop Competitive Shoot, with full/calibre ammunition at a BP Target, 12 rounds being fired per gun.

They were back in harbour at Simonstown that afternoon, when the storeship SS *Halita* arrived. Next morning the hands were busily embarking frozen meat and potatoes, and *Delphinium* proceeded at 2036, heading for Lobito. They arrived there on the 24th, having carried out Lewis Gun and Pom-Pom firing at Captive Balloons during the passage. On the 31st they coaled ship, using native labour and embarking 110 tons. The surgeon's log reported that: "*There was not much shoregoing by the ship's company, but a football match was played and the officers got in a little shooting.*"

In fact, the 31st August was the day when Alf, the 'Pilot' (viz Lt J.P HUNT) and two other officers named McIVER and MACKSEY (the latter described by Alf as '*a very good hunter of wild game*') donned their solar topees or slouch hats according to individual preference, put on their shorts or breeches, collected their 0.303 rifles and went off on a shooting trip from Lobito, travelling in a large open car with a native driver and evidently enjoying their adventure and freedom. It was evidently only a one or two-day excursion, for Alf was OOW on nearly every other day of their eight-day stay at Lobito. The chance to go off 'on safari', even briefly, and to test his marksmanship in a 'real life' way, would have been very satisfying for Alf. Unfortunately, as two photos which survive tell us, their 'bag' of game was nil and they returned to the ship empty-handed. (One of the photos is reproduced on the next page.)

Seemingly, on the morning of 2nd September, Captain PETERS decided to liven everybody up, and a rapid string of orders was suddenly issued, 'Exercise General Drill', 'Point Ship', 'Away All Boats - Pull Round the Oiler', 'Out Kedge Anchor', 'Land Fire Engine', 'Weigh the Kedge Anchor'. Then, at 1140, *Delphinium* proceeded for Lagos. Next day, the patent log was hauled in and the Orepesa sweeps were hoisted out and run for nearly three hours. On hauling them in, it was found that the port float was missing, and, despite a considerable retracing of their course, no sign of it could be found.

They crossed the Equator again on the 5th September at about 2100, increasing speed to an average of 11.3 knots on the 7th, to save a tide and to be able to enter Lagos Harbour in daylight. The ship occupied a berth off the marine wharf. The prophylactic doses of quinine had been restarted on 31st August. The ship coaled next day, embarking 165 tons by native labour. They also watered ship. The temperature was a sweltering 80°F, but the hands were cleaning the sides and funnels, and commenced to paint the batteries next day. Shore leave was granted during the daylight hours. Games of football and hockey were played and there was some swimming at the Police Bathing Pool. On the 15th they landed the ship's rifle club members, but one rifle was somehow lost overboard. Happily the divers managed to retrieve it. Seemingly Alf did not compete on this occasion, for he was OOW all day. (Yet Alf surely participated in one serious marksmanship competition during 1931, for he left behind an attractive silver trophy-teaspoon of which the haft consisted of miniature crossed rifles, and the head bore a small shield engraved *'Delphinium* 1931'.)

Author's collection of inherited family photographs.

Alf, fag in one hand and rifle in the other, looking very comfortable in himself, with officers McIVER and MACKSEY, on a shooting trip from Lobito, in Angola. In sending this card home to Olive, Alf wrote: *"Note the Bottle."* - perhaps to back up some comments on the *safari* which he had put in an accompanying letter to Olive.

Next day a provision lighter came alongside and the hands struck down frozen meat embarked from it. They also again took in water, which they chlorinated. On the 18th, *Daffodil*, which had arrived from Kotuna on the 8th, proceeded for England, and the company of *Delphinium* cheered ship at 1100 as *Daffodil* sailed. *Delphinium* proceeded for Accra at 1400 that same day, coming to anchor in Accra Roads at 1307 on the 19th, after a run of 225 miles. Captain PETERS wished to check the draught of his ship, but the scend of the sea was so pronounced that no accurate reading of the loading marks could be taken. The following day, and the next, the 20th, the surf and sea, always likely to be a problem at Accra, were still running strong. However, it was found possible to land parties for football and hockey, presumably demanding considerable skill by the boats' crews to avoid possible upsets. Maybe their surf boat came into its own! If anything, on the morning of the 22nd, the scend was even stronger, but the hands scrubbed decks as normal and carried out some hand-enamelling of the ship's paintwork.

This outwardly peaceful scene was illusory. The alertness and seamanship of the Officer of the Watch was about to be challenged. As it happened, that Officer was Alf. Suddenly, at 1500, the weight of the port cable came off the brake and full on to the Blake's Slip, which bent under the strain. The spare screw stopper was quickly shipped in lieu. One imagines that Captain PETERS was informed of the situation, but the Log is uninformative on that point.

Just over an hour later the port cable parted under the strain. Perhaps the company were anticipating this, for, within two minutes, the starboard anchor was let go, and veered to four shackles. At least the ship was back under control and secure for the moment. The port cable was weighed and a fractured link was found 64 links from the inboard end of the 3 inch shackle. The anchor, lengthening piece and 2½ shackles of cable were lost.

Clearly, the situation was still dangerous. If the starboard anchor should fail or the cable part, they had no immediate recourse to another anchor. It was advisable to find a less exposed position. Just over an hour later they shifted berth, coming to with the starboard anchor in 5 fathoms, veered to four shackles. An anchor watch was set. As a further precaution, steam was ordered at immediate notice. Indeed, it seems a little surprising that this precaution had been left so late.

Next morning, the 23rd September, *Delphinium* proceeded to sweep for her lost cable. She made three passes over the ground, without success. She anchored overnight, again setting an anchor watch and with steam still at immediate notice.

Next day she tried again. After three and a half hours of sweeping she hooked an obstruction. She promptly anchored. Somehow, at this stage, her sweeping wire became fouled in her propeller. [Now they were in a position where, should need arise, they could no longer ease the strain on the anchor-cable by using their engines! Matters were going from bad to worse.] An hour later, despite their efforts, the wire was still foul. As a further precaution they now shackled the kedge anchor to the port cable. They then continued for a further five hours before eventually succeeding in freeing the wire. This must have been a considerable relief! It was now long past sunset. Again, an anchor watch was set, and steam ordered at immediate notice.

Next morning, at 0815, they tried yet again. At 0950, they at last hooked the lost cable. They anchored immediately. At 1200, to the huge relief of the officers, the ship's company recovered the port anchor and 2¾ shackles of cable. Soon, all was made shipshape, with the kedge anchor unshipped, and the port anchor and cable re-shipped with a new link, and at 1620 *Delphinium* proceeded from Accra for Axim.

Perhaps to prove to themselves that all was well, it was with the port anchor that the company came to anchor at Axim, at 1100 on the 26th September, with 137 miles run. Axim was found to be a small town with few Europeans. Football and cricket matches were played against mixed teams of Europeans and Africans. Whilst they were there a party of Native Chiefs came aboard in their finery, before *Delphinium* proceeded for Takoradi, arriving there on the 29th. On the way they had exercised General Quarters, and, after arrival, the hands washed the ship's side and painted aloft after securing to No.6 Buoy. Although *Delphinium* was lying out in the harbour the local Medical Officer of Health still considered that mosquito nets should be used by the company. [The daily dose of quinine was also being maintained.] During the next few days the hands extended the painting to cover the funnels and ship's side. The inhabitants were very hospitable, and, considerable shore leave was granted, several football and hockey games also being played. Shooting matches and sailing competitions were also held and enjoyed by all. Water was taken on board and chlorinated. It was probably with some regret that, on the 10th October 1931, *Delphinium* headed out past the breakwater and proceeded for Lagos.

Now, whilst the ship had been at Takoradi, Alf's third child, a daughter had been born. She had arrived in the world on the 3rd October. Whether a cable was sent to Alf is unknown, but likely. How quickly it would have reached him is unclear. However, he would have known that the due date was approaching, and probably on tenterhooks to know all the details and, especially how his wife was bearing up. It would have been with huge relief that he would have heard that mother and child were doing as well as could be expected. Olive had come through a very demanding time and she was still alive.

Delphinium reached Lagos at 0800 on the 12th October, securing alongside No.3 Marine Wharf, where she embarked 160 tons of coal. Whilst there she ranged and re-marked her starboard cable, before, evidently as a goodwill gesture, her hands painted a Pattern VI Target which was in the custody of the Nigerian Marine. At 1000 the German warship D.K. *Emden* arrived *'looking very smart and businesslike'*.[270] *Delphinium* returned her 21-gun salute, before changing berth and securing to No.5 and No.6 Marine Buoys with her head north-west. Next day the Captain of *Emden* paid an official call on Captain PETERS, who returned the call in the afternoon. A visit was also made by wardroom officers of *Delphinium*, including the surgeon, to the officers of *Emden*. Whether or not Alf was there is unknown, but one suspects that he may have been very keen to meet and weigh up the type of men who had been trying to kill him from 1914 to 1918 and whom some people were already beginning to think might ere long be resuming that activity.

Generally, the English officers seem to have been very impressed by the smartness and keeness shown by the Germans, albeit that they may have had some afterthoughts about the mechanical way in which the German sailors were fallen in to swallow their quinine tablets to order, and the fact that every German sailor going ashore had to carry 'an outfit' for the prevention of venereal disease. Also to learn that catching V.D was regarded as a crime in the German Navy.[271] Alf may well have reflected that the German sailor of 1931 was a very different prospect to the defeated German Sailor of 1918, when the German ships had entered Scapa Flow for internment. Clearly, they had

---

[270] It may be recalled that, back in January 1927, the *Emden* had visited Simonstown briefly, and her Captain had called on the C-in-C, Admiral BENTNICK. However, no contacts had apparently been made on a 'ship-to-ship' basis at that time.

[271] The Captain of the cruiser *Cardiff* reported to the C-in-C on 14th November 1931, "*....I was very favourably impressed with the ship's company of the Emden. They were smarter and healthier-looking than our men - might well be athletes fallen in for the Olympic Games, in fact! Their universal rig of white shirts, singlets and bare feet lends itself to this impression. Their rig is spotless, the men being made to wash and change before the midday meal.*" (See ADM 116/2863 at TNA.)

recovered their pride and, if that turned to arrogance, it could become a serious problem for the Royal Navy in the years to come.

The C-in-C Africa Squadron had arrived during the afternoon of the 13th October, flying his Flag in the cruiser *Cardiff*. *Delphinium* then transferred the duties of SNO West Coast to *Cardiff*, and paraded a Guard of Honour for the C-in-C next morning. A sailing race took place in the afternoon. Next day a provision lighter and water-boat came alongside, and, late that afternoon, *Delphinium* proceeded for Warri. At 0148, whilst sounding her way, the sounding wire parted and the lead and its associated brass tube were lost. At 1240 *Delphinium* came to anchor in the stream off Warri, with the banks of the creek no more than 100 yards away on each beam. The heat was considerable, being up to 90° F, and with no air moving. The men were kept on quinine, and mosquito netting was carefully spread over himself by each man at night. Shore leaves were given, but generally only in daylight hours. Again, the local native chiefs came aboard on a visit.

On the 20th they proceeded for Koko, the hands overhauling the minesweeping wires before, at 1000, *Delphinium* entered Chanoni Creek, continuing up the Escravos River, then via Nana Creek. At 1404 they let go the port anchor underfoot for five minutes, to assist the ship in making the tight turn at the fork in the stream, then quickly weighed and proceeded at 10 knots, entering the Benin River at 1455 and coming to anchor in the stream off Koko. They had covered 82 miles of the intricate river system of the Delta of the River Niger, and the temperature was now hovering around 82° F. The air seemed lifeless. On the 21st they proceeded for Sapele, where the temperature was two degrees higher, and the land lying close to each beam. Quinine was maintained and nets again spread against malarial mosquitos. A large party, consisting mainly of CPOs and POs, was taken on a visit to Benin City, where the men had an audience with the 'King of Benin'. That evening, the 'Oba' of Benin (presumably the King's right-hand man) and his retinue visited the ship. Meantime, a cricket match was played by *Delphinium* against the local Europeans.

On the 24th *Delphinium* proceeded for Forcados, stopping briefly off Koko, retracing their course past the river-fork, proceeding down the Escravos River to Chanoni Creek and coming to anchor off Forcados on the evening of that same day. Strangely, although Forcados was swampy and low-lying, it was said to be healthy. The European population was very small - probably less than a score in all - but they were reported to be almost free from sickness. The ship was lying ½ mile off shore and it was considered unnecessary to issue mosquito nets. At 1500 on the 26th October *Delphinium* proceeded down the Forcados River, passed the bar at the river-mouth at 1700, increased to 10 knots and set course southwards for St Paul de Loanda.

At 0745 next morning they began working up for another 3/5ths Power Trial which lasted from 0800 until 1600. They had aired the men's bedding as they proceeded over a quiet sea with a slight SSW breeze and a still air temperature of 78° F. Alf came off watch at 2400, and the ship, heading ever south, re-crossed the Equator soon afterwards. On the 28th they held Divisions, followed immediately by 'Action Stations', and the men were then exercised at their Fire, Collision and Breakdown stations. On the 30th the ship was noisy at 1030 as fire was opened on 'towed balloons', first with the Pom-Pom gun, and then the Lewis gunners had a go. Alf came off watch at 1600, and *Delphinium* came to with her port anchor at St Paul de Loanda at 2227. She was anchored well out in the bay, and mosquito nets were not used. The daily dose of quinine was restarted, but at only five grains (i.e. half the dosage formerly employed).

The Portuguese warship *Republica* (1,683 tons) was in the harbour and *Delphinium* fired a 21-gun salute at 0800, after which the captain of the *Republica* paid an official call on Captain PETERS. This visit was followed by visits by the British Consul-General, who received 13 guns on leaving, and then by HE the Acting Governor-General of Angola, who received a 9-gun salute. Leave was given to the company in daylight hours and games of football were played against local teams in the days which followed.

[In later years, Alf once talked about a memorable football match against a Portuguese team, and it may well have been that it was a match played during his time in *Delphinium* to which he was referring. That is to say, (in Alf's account) this was a Portuguese team whose supporters looked as if they were going to 'cut up rough' after the Britishers, greatly enjoying the match up to that point, had eased into a comfortable lead. The game was taking place on Portuguese soil, hot Latin pride was on the line, and a 'diplomatic incident' might well have been in the offing. Standing orders had been given by the British authorities that the greatest attention was to be paid to maintain friendly relations with the Portuguese. Alf would later tell his family that the wise decision was taken to lose the game as gracefully and narrowly as possible, but to make absolutely sure that it was indeed lost. And all ended very well. Overhearing Alf's yarn, and becoming aware of the 'messages' that it contained, made a deep impression on the author of this book, then aged 9, with a mind-set (from having started to play organised football) of the sporting ethic of 'fair play and keenly-contested competition' and clearly with a great many 'scales' about 'tact' yet to 'drop from his innocent eyes.']

The Captain sharpened the men up by General Drill on 2nd November, 'Change Booms', 'Out all Wire Hawsers', 'Out Bower Anchor', 'Abandon Ship!' Next day the Educational Test Part One was sat by six candidates, in a comfortable temperature of 78° F with just a gentle zephyr of a south-west breeze blowing.[272]

On the 4th the Articles of War were read out and the Court Martial Returns (for the Quarter ended 30th June!) were also notified to the company. On Guy Fawkes Day the ship coaled, using native labour and embarking 180 tons. This increased her draught by 1 ft 4 ins, thus indicating that her draught was increased by 1 inch for every 11¼ tons embarked. The ship's whalers were sent ashore for washing out this day. Alf was OOW for the whole of the next day, and the ship sailed at 1130 on the 7th, proceeding for Walvis Bay.[273]

At 0930 the ship exercised Action Stations, repeating the Alarm to Arms at 2000. Simultaneously a Target was dropped overboard and aiming rifle practice was carried out at it as the ship continued on her course until the target was virtually out of sight. She then reversed her course, to re-gather the target. However, no signs of it could be found in the dwindling daylight and the search was abandoned at 2208.

Alf was OOW twice on the 10th November, which was his wife's 28th birthday. In view of her sad condition and his inability to be at her side, he may have been particularly glad to be able to lose himself in his duties on this day of all days. He may, perhaps, have also been glad to be a 'listening ear' to the intense conversation between Captain

---

[272] Ratings wishing to advance in rank were required to pass these Educational Tests, Pts 1 and 2.

[273] The surgeon's log called this place Walfish Bay, which has a certain charm in its own right.

PETERS and Lt J.P. HUNT, the Navigating Officer, which led to the 'Economical Speed' being exceeded for a while, during the night of 10th/11th November, to permit the ship to reach Walvis Bay in time to participate in the Armistice Day ceremony.[274] In fact, their ship secured alongside the jetty at Walvis Bay at 0730, having run 900 miles from St Paul de Loanda.   They cleared lower decks at 1045 and the Guard and Divisions were fallen in on the jetty for prayers, followed by the emotionally very moving two minutes silence at 1100, in tribute to the fallen.   One suspects that a signal gun was used to mark the beginning and end of this period of silence, which would have added to its poignancy.[275]

The surgeon reported that 'the ship's company were most hospitably entertained by the local people, and that the stay was much enjoyed by all.' There was much visiting to the ship by the local people, including those who were of German origin, who were friendly *and got along well with the ratings'*. The issue of quinine was re-started. Water was embarked - and chlorinated.   On the 12th the ship landed her rifle team for competition. We know that Alf did not compete on this occasion, for he was OOW all day.

Next day the ship proceeded for Saldanha Bay.   The Log for 14th November contains a short note by Captain PETERS stating that he had cautioned a (named) Lieutenant for negligence of duty as mail officer in failing to ensure that a bag of mails from HMS *Cardiff* (with regard to which special instructions had been given) was sent by the shortest route with the ship-mail. [One assumes that a complaint from HMS *Cardiff* about late-delivery had just reached the Captain's ears by WT.]

On the 15th they were forced to alter course to avoid a fog bank, but they arrived safely at the fine and well-protected anchorage of Saldhana Bay at 0800 on the 16th, and came to anchor. This place had received only limited development due to the general lack of water. Consequently, apart from the landing of the ship's rifle team for practice, there was no shore-going. The main relaxation for the company was boat-sailing. For example, the racing whalers being away under sail on the 16th, busily practising. Quinine was issued only until the 16th November.

On the 17th, 'night action' was exercised, including 1 inch aiming rifle practice at a target towed by the ship's motor boat. Twenty rounds were fired by each of the two 4 inch guns. Next day, after Divisions, a bombardment exercise was carried out, then the whalers were away again practising, and the rifle team were landed to compete in the Saldhana Cup Competition. Alf was OOW all day. That night the ship again carried out aiming 1-inch rifle practice at a target towed by the motor boat.

On the 19th November *Delphinium* proceeded for Simonstown, exercising action on the way in a sea which had suddenly become quite lively, with moderate waves and swell and a Force 6 wind from the south-east. She came to anchor off Simonstown at 1900, and kept steam on her engines against any emergency which might develop overnight. Next morning calm conditions prevailed and *Delphinium* proceeded into harbour, securing alongside 'B' Wall. It was probably well-known that the unusually limited rainfall had led to water supplies at Simonstown becoming a matter of concern.

---

[274] This action was subsequently approved by the C-in-C Vice Admiral TWEEDIE.
[275] The Log shows that a gun was sponged out on the 15th.

One well was being deepened to try to improve the supply. Ships such as *Delphinium* had been ordered by the C-in-C to reduce their expenditure by one-third.[276]

Alf was OOW over the next two days. During that time the hands launched a Pattern VI Target and exercised a Bush Fire Landing Party. Next day, the 25th, *Delphinium* proceeded into Simon's Bay in the morning to carry out a Sight and Director Test and went out again in the late evening for 1-inch aiming rifle practice at a Pattern VI Target which had been launched earlier and towed out. *Delphinium* anchored offshore. Next day Alf made out a signed report: *"Lost overboard by Accident, during Night Full Calibre Firing, three Cartridge Cases, Empty, 4-inch, Mk VI Gun."*

At 2020 *Delphinium* proceeded, and carried out 4-inch full/cal firing, 6 rounds per gun, and 3 pdr firing, at the Pattern VI Target. She again anchored overnight offshore, returning to harbour early next morning and hauling in the Target. At 1240 on the 28th a small fire was discovered in the Gunner's After Store, which was extinguished almost immediately. The cause of this slight fire is unknown: it may well have been electrical in origin.

Two assessment reports were issued on Alf during his time aboard *Delphinium*. The first, running from 8th March 1931 to 30th November 1931, and signed by A M PETERS, said that Alf's conduct had been '*to my entire satisfaction. An officer who is thorough and efficient in all his duties, and who displays great energy in promoting the efficiency and welfare of the ship's company*'. This last phrase is very interesting, and one wonders if the stimulus for Alf's drive in regard to the 'efficiency and welfare' of the troops might have had quite a lot to do with the hard conditions in which he and his shipmates had suffered during the monotony and oppressive heat of their long struggle to contain and then eliminate the *Konigsberg* in and around the Rufuji River on the east coast, sixteen years earlier. Alf was certainly becoming increasingly 'impressive'.

It may also be that his extrovert and perhaps almost extravagant behaviour was in some part a reaction which had as its roots the strong feelings then running throughout the Navy against the cuts in pay which had been announced by the Admiralty in September 1931, at the time of the great World Depression. By these cuts in pay Alf, as a Warrant Officer, would have been scheduled to a considerable reduction in his pay (of perhaps as much as 20%). The Naval Warrant Officers Journal for October 1931, published at Portsmouth, had contained a long article about this matter. It started off very reasonably and sensibly to the effect that the financial situation in Great Britain demanded all-round sacrifices from its nationals - including higher taxes, scaling back of certain allowances and taxes upon commodities. It said that the officer of and from Warrant Rank should bear his share with the civil population. However, it then went on to point out in detail that the Warrant Officers and Commissioned Officers from Warrant rank were being unfairly hit in relation to both other officers and the ratings. (One telling factor seemed to be that these very experienced WOs had been treated as *"junior officers"* in the 'pay tables', and thus unthinkingly categorised as if they were young and unmarried, with no family responsibilities - the very converse of the truth for these men, who were mainly married, with children, and approaching the ends of their careers.) One assumes that a copy of this excellent and moderate article would eventually have reached Alf. This must have been a difficult period for Alf to maintain his motivation. On a

---

[276] Vice Admiral TWEEDIE had reported to the Admiralty about this situation. He had ordered his cruisers to distil their own fresh water until matters improved. (See ADM 116/2863.)

personal basis he must have felt himself to be extremely fortunate that his inheritance under his father's will had been considerable, but his fellow-feeling for those warrant officers who were without any other private means and who were going to suffer serious financial hardship must have been very keen indeed.

The cuts for ratings, as initially proposed, would have led to them being extremely hard-hit, with a reduction of about 25%. The widely-reported 'unrest' amongst companies of naval ships at Invergordon - which virtually amounted to a mutiny - ultimately led to huge pressure on the British Government and the reductions in pay were actually held at only 10%, but the sour taste remained. [It would not be until 1934 that the 10% cut in pay was rescinded.]

It was around this time, actually on 14th November 1931, that the C-in-C Africa Station, Vice Admiral TWEEDIE, had been moved to write to the Admiralty (with very well-expressed tactfulness) that he had found that the Admiralty Telegram which ordered the local allotments of married pay at Simonstown, had specified that they were to be paid at the current (low) rate of Sterling exchange. This had meant a reduction of their local value by 20%. Not surprisingly, the men affected aboard his flagship, the cruiser *Cardiff*, had expressed their anxiety about this adverse situation to their Captain, and explained that the loss of £1 a month or more was putting their wives in an impossible situation.[277] The same telegram had inferred that pay would also be dealt with in local currency at current rates of sterling exchange instead of at par. This was causing great anxiety amongst all the men, married and single. One assumes that similar feelings prevailed in the companies of all the ships on the Africa Station, and that Alf would have been affected in just the same way. It would have been with considerable relief to ratings and officers alike that the difficulty was later resolved.[278]

On 1st December 1931 Commander R.B. WILMOT-SITWELL joined the ship and took command. Captain A.M. PETERS DSC left the ship for *Cyclamen* which was due to proceed to England on the 7th December. [Though Alf could not have known it at the time, he would come to serve under Captain PETERS again, often in highly demanding circumstances, a few years hence.]

It is difficult to 'reconstruct' the ship's officers and warrant officers whom Commander WILMOT-SITWELL would have found serving, since almost all of them lived out the commission 'anonymously', only one being replaced. Hence, the ship's logs are more or less 'mute' on the topic. [Three officers, though still 'anonymously', would continue to serve at the end of the commission, being transferred to the books of HMS *Victory* for accounting purposes.] The best that the author can manage out of the dozen or so who would have served in the commission is therefore:-

Captain	Commander R.B WILMOT-SITWELL
Navigating Officer	Lieutenant J.P.HUNT
Officers[279]	Lieutenant (?) Mc IVER
	Lieutenant (?) MACKSEY

[277] In those days, a well-paid civilian job commanded about £5 per week – say the equivalent of at least £600 p/w now. On that basis a loss of £1 a month was the equivalent of a loss of about £120 a month now.

[278] The Admiralty subsequently remedied this situation, and decided that compensation for loss on exchange would be paid, to Admiral TWEEDIE's 'great sense of relief' and appreciation.

[279] Most of these names have been garnered from notes incorporated with Alf's photographs.

Lieutenant (E) W. T. KIRKLAND
Surgeon Lt. J B PATRICK
Warrant Officers   Mr A.W. DAVIS, Gunner

During the next few days the ship refitted her boom gear and cleaned her cable lockers, later cleaning and bringing up her woodwork and brightwork. Parties also began to leave the ship for practice on the rifle range at the sanatorium. The ship's sick list was now down to nil. During the rest of December the hands were chipping rust and flaking paint and red-leading. Meantime, the hands were exercising the boats under oars and sails. Warrant Engineer F.C WALLINS joined ship and Engineering Lieutenant W.T. KIRKLAND left the ship. To keep the men fit, physical drill and doubling round the deck were ordered, and 'Out Fire Engine' was practised.[280]

Come the 29th December de-ammunitioning began. All the boats were landed on the 4th January 1932, the mine sweeping wire was unreeled and condemned, and all the guns were cleaned. Next day the ship was secured in dry dock, and the hands began to clean her bottom. On the 11th the cables were ranged for examination and the cable locker was scraped and painted. By now the hands were painting the ship's bottom, and, on the 13th they were applying 'boot topping' to her water line. The Portuguese sloop *Republica* arrived at this time, and her captain was saluted by *Cardiff* with 7 guns.

On the 18th, flooding of the dock was commenced, cable was restored to the locker, the aerials were refitted, the final stages of chipping preparatory to further painting were carried out and re-provisioning began. The cruiser *Carlisle* sailed for the U.K. on the 25th. Refitting of the rigging and checking the boats' falls continued, together with blacking down aloft, and matters continued in this general vein throughout the month of January. Alf may well have been out of the ship for some of this time, but he was present as OOW on the 6th and 7th January 1932, and then again throughout the third and fourth weeks of the month.

Delphinium emerged from the dry dock on the 6th February, and commenced coaling on the 9th, continuing at intervals for two days, by which time she had swept 'A' Shed and eventually embarked 220 tons, her full capacity. She also began to re-ammunition, having to break off due to heavy rain on the 11th, and drew her outfit of boats the next day, including a skiff to replace her surf boat. (This latter had been invaluable for communication with the shore at Accra.) *Delphinium* now began in earnest the enamelling and finishing of her paintwork first the gun battery and then, after rigging stages, for the painting of her upperworks. Meantime, her Tattoo Party were rehearsing and the ship's non-swimmers were being prepared for their provisional tests in the pool, preparatory to their full tests.

The Fleet Engineering Officer came aboard on the 23rd and inspected the Engine Room Department, and, on the 26th, *Delphinium* unbasined and proceeded into Simon's Bay for windlass trials, followed by swinging ship to check her compass variation, before proceeding for Capetown. During this short voyage she acted as a target ship for a

---

[280] It is a great pity that Lieutenant Surgeon PATRICK's Journal ceases at the end of December 1931. His diary has been most informative and we shall miss his contributions from here on. The survival of Surgeon's Journals in TNA records is sparse and seemingly random. So far as this book is concerned, we have only one other journal yet to come which is relevant for Alf's ships, and only two which relate to the training establishments in which Alf was involved.

dummy torpedo attack by the cruiser *Cardiff*. *Delphinium* then continued on her course, and secured alongside the coaling jetty at Capetown on the 26th.

Alf had frequently been OOW during recent days, and he was again on duty on the 27th when the ship was open to visitors from 1330 until 1730. She was again open next day too. The following day the ship landed her already perspiring Tattoo party for a full dress rehearsal in temperatures ranging from 85° F to 91° F, followed by another rehearsal on the morning of the 2nd March, prior to the full performance of the Capetown Tattoo that evening, when, fortunately, the temperature was a little more modest. Between-times, *Delphinium* had carried out yet another 3/5ths Full Power Trial at 11.5 knots.

On 3rd March *Delphinium* proceeded for Kynsa, exercising her 'Action', 'Fire' and Repair' parties as she did so. On the 4th she streamed her starboard sweeping wire and rewound it, before, at 1300, she slowed right down to attempt to pass the bar at Kisma Heads. This was found to be impossible that day, so *Delphinium* sheered off and sheltered overnight in Plettenberg Bay. At noon next day they tried again, still, however, finding the bar impassable, and again over-nighting in Plettenberg Bay. However, 'persistence hath its own reward', and, at 1540 on the 6th they managed to ease their way over the bar and secured alongside the jetty at Kynsa about twenty minutes later. The divers were exercised next day, somehow losing a 'woollen frock', evidently whilst making sure that no damage had been suffered by the ship in crossing the bar.

Author's collection of inherited family snapshots.

Minesweeping. Alf is standing right in the stern of the ship, closely supervising operations. He is marked with an 'X' in this snapshot. Brother officers watch closely.

The gun's crews were exercised on the 8th and 9th, Alf being OOW on both those days, the hands being occupied in refitting the minesweeping wires and preparing the ship to be open to visitors. Alf was again OOW on the 11th, when platoon and section drill was carried out before the hands were sent to bathe. The ship was open again to visitors on the 13th, before, early on the following morning, *Delphinium* proceeded for Simonstown. Her departure was not quite trouble-free, for she had to let go her starboard anchor and stop in mid-channel to clear river-weed which had become trapped in her starboard inlet. She dropped the Pilot before crossing the bar, and, as she gained the open sea her hands prepared the sweep for running.

After Divisions, and just before 1000, they commenced mine-sweeping. However, before the hour was out the bridle of the starboard float was wrenched out and it took some time to sort out the raffle and bring the sweeps back inboard.

After lunch, 1-inch aiming rifle practice was carried out with the RNVRs.[281] Then the Pom-Pom and Lewis Guns teams were exercised, firing at Balloon Targets. At 0730 on the 15th March *Delphinium* carried out a one-hour Range and Inclination exercise with the cruiser *Cardiff* as they closed Simonstown, before coming to anchor there at 1130. A stiff breeze was getting up from the south-east, and steam for slow speed was raised as a precaution. A 2/5ths Power Trial was carried out later this day. On the 16th a Sight and Director check was made, and, next day, the ship landed a Bombardment Observation Party before carrying out the related dummy bombardment. Next day she laid out a target and conducted a 1-inch aiming rifle bombardment practice on it for nearly three hours. On the 20th the ship again raised steam for slow speed as the wind increased, but the weather improved next morning and both 3 pdr and 1-inch aiming rifle practice was carried out with the ship moored fore and aft with a brake on the cable.[282] Next day, the 22nd, the Bombardment Observation Party was again landed, and the ship carried out 4-inch FC firing against a moored target, firing 16 rounds per gun. An aeroplane carried out spotting duties, perhaps reminding Alf of the action against the *Konigsberg* in 1915.

Next day they coaled (159 tons), washed down, and set about some more painting. This brought the ship up clean and fresh, and the Captain sent all available men for a route march on the 29th, to keep them 'freshened up' too. Next day (and the next) *Delphinium* sent rake parties to *St Dogmael*, presumably to assist in firing exercises by *Cardiff* or the other naval ships at Simonstown at that period, including *Verbena*.

The hands were detailed for vaccination on the 1st April, the whalers were away under oars and sail on the 3rd, and every available man was landed for a route march on the 7th. This march took nearly four hours to complete, and the company was fortunate that the temperature was a reasonable 78° F and that a gentle south-east wind was blowing. On Monday the 11th April a christening service was held aboard, and, on the 14th, yet another route march was carried out. Well, at least it broke the monotony of a spate of cleaning and painting. Next day the cruiser *Carlisle* arrived from England, and one AB joined ship from her. The 19th April was the day of the Fleet Rifle Meeting, and both Rifle and Revolver Teams left the ship in the morning to compete at the Klaver Valley range. Leave was given to spectators in the afternoon, and it seems that considerable enthusiasm was shown. Alf was on watch all day.

---

[281] Although scarcely mentioned in this account, it was evidently the usual practice for every ship on the Africa Station to take men of the South African RNVR aboard for short periods of time, to give them basic training in seamanship, gunnery, etc.

[282] This would suggest that the ship could be 'spun' on its own axis through a few degrees, bringing the bow forward as the stern was 'eased', or letting the bow fall back as the stern was brought forward. In this way the 'lie' of the guns on their targets could be assisted towards the optimal bearing.

Indeed, he was standing a great many watches at this period and one certainly again gains the impression that he was trying to lose himself in his duties rather than reflect too deeply about his wife, whose health continued to be a 'switchback ride', but was still trending ever-downward causing her to be weaker and weaker. Come the 20th, the Ship's Company 'passed through the Gas Chamber', as the Log expressed it. Then they endured another route march on the 21st, and had a rest on St George's Day, (when the ship was dressed overall), before the Seamen's Platoon were landed for field exercises on the 28th.

[The men would have found some changes going on at Simonstown, with a new road to the Sanatorium having been completed and brought into use, and the aerial ropeway 'mothballed'. The abundant rains which had fallen in 1932 had eased the water-supply situation, though a local scheme to impound water in the Dido Valley still seemed likely to go ahead.]

There now began a series of gunnery-related exercises which would have kept Alf on his toes. It started off on Accession Day, 6th May, when the ship was dressed overall and a 21-gun salute was fired at noon. Next morning *Delphinium* proceeded in company with the cruiser *Cardiff*, both ships anchoring in Simon's Bay and exercising their searchlights that evening. Next day they proceeded for exercises, *Delphinium* taking station ahead of *Carlisle* and carrying out Range and Inclination exercises and conducting 1-inch aiming rifle and 3 pdr firings at a Pattern VI Target. They then moved on to night-firing in the same vein and again anchored overnight in Simon's Bay. Early the next morning, the 11th May, they again proceeded, conducting 1-inch aiming rifle practice with the Officer of Quarters in local control. Then, having anchored in the middle part of the day, they again proceeded and carried out aiming rifle, 3 pdr and Pom-Pom firings at a Pattern VI Target. Yet again, they came to anchor in Simon's Bay.

Next day the hands were submitted to a dental inspection, and the Articles of War were read out. The 6th Cruiser Squadron had sailed for exercises on the 11th, but the C-in-C had stayed on at Simonstown, and he now exercised the sloops. His consecutive orders to 'Let Go Bower Anchor', 'Weigh by Hand', 'Exercise Collision Stations' and then 'Fire Stations', followed by his order to 'Send All Boats Away Under Sail', and then 'All hands to Physical Drill' continued relentlessly throughout the morning of the 13th. The ship proceeded at 1415, and 'Action Stations' was sounded at 1545. There then followed a 4-inch Full/Calibre shoot of eight rounds per gun, with GCO and OOQ combined control, followed by 4-inch, 3 pdr and Pom-Pom firings at night at a BP Target, four rounds being fired per 4-inch gun.

On 21st May Dockyard officials came aboard and a long meeting was held with the ship's officers concerning the ship's pending refit. The ship was dressed overall on the 24th and again on the 26th (for Empire Day and the Queen's birthday, respectively), and the C-in-C carried out his annual inspection on the 27th, having the men mustered by 'open list', then exercising 'General Quarters', 'Fire Stations' and 'Breakdown'. It seems that the C-in-C's beady eye had become attracted to a howitzer gun. The duty watch cleaned it, and the crew who had been told off for it started to drill with the howitzer on the 28th May and again on the 30th. Meantime the hands were preparing the ship for docking, chipping rollers and scraping the waterline. The ship entered the dock and was docked down on the 31st. The hands began to scrape her bottom straight away, and continued next day, Kroomen helping. On 2nd June they began to apply anti-fouling paint to the ship's bottom. They also returned 30 fathoms of IMS cable to the NSO. Meantime the howitzer crew were busily exercising. They had their reward on the 3rd, when they went to the Cricket Ground at Simonstown for the King's Birthday Parade, where the salute was taken by HE the Governor-General. A company of the South African Permanent Garrison Artillery participated, against whom the display by the *Delphinium's* howitzer team could be compared. Both displays were warmly received by the large crowd, despite the heavy rain which fell more or less continuously throughout the whole performance.[283] That day *Delphinium* flew masthead flags, but, being in dry dock and up on blocks, she was ordered not to participate when, at noon, a 21-gun salute was fired by the remainder of H.M Ships in harbour.

Alf had been OOW on every third day or so throughout the month of May, and he was OOW again next day, the 4th June, which was his elder daughter's 5th birthday. He would have been able to expand on the note in the Log for the 6th June, which said that a boat's badge had been lost overboard by accident that day. This seemed strange, for the ship herself was still in dry dock, with her hands returning cable and painting her funnels and bottom. One would not have expected the ship's boats to have been 'in the water'. It was not until the 9th that *Delphinium* was floated out, to secure to 'A' Wall.

The duties of the howitzer crew were by no means over, for they were now due to give a display at Durban, and they were landed for more drill on the 14th. Next day, the 15th June was the day of the Fleet Pulling Regatta, on a calm sea with a Force 3 south-east breeze to give the rowers a little relief from the heat, as they toiled away under skies which varied from azure blue to being slightly overcast. The regatta was held a little later in the year than usual due to the late arrival of the cruiser *Carlisle* from recommissioning. Vice Admiral TWEEDIE reported to the Admiralty that *"the event was a great success, the ships' companies of both cruisers and sloops displaying great keenness on behalf of their respective ships."*[284]

Alf had been OOW that day, as he was the next, when the divers of *Delphinium* and *Verbena* were exercised at deep sea diving, evidently without difficulty. Two days later the C-in-C shifted his flag to *Verbena*, and the cruisers *Cardiff* and *Carlisle* sailed for the East Coast of the Station. That same day, one Head Krooman, one 2nd Krooman and ten 'ordinary' Kroomen joined ship. (These were evidently the African equivalent of Indian 'Lascar' seamen. They carried out some of the labour-intensive tasks aboard, especially scraping and painting.)

On 20th June *Delphinium* proceeded into Simon's Bay for Windlass Trials, and then proceeded for Durban. Strangely, her Log shows that she lost overboard by accident 'one boat's badge', and one cannot but feel that the earlier entry, on 6th June, was this same event, but recorded retrospectively and erroneously.

On 22nd June the ship was dressed with masthead flags in honour of Accession Day, the flags whipping smartly in a Force 4 west-sou'-westerly wind, and the bows of the ship sending sheets of spray flying from time to time as *Delphinium* thrust her way through a moderate sea on which a slight swell was running. Next day, after Divisions and exercising Action Stations, *Delphinium* picked up the Pilot and secured alongside 'G' Shed at Durban, finding the cruiser *Carlisle*, back from the East Coast, and now in

---

[283] In his report Admiral TWEEDIE also saw fit to mention the racial tension between the Afrikaans-speaking people and the English, which could mar events.

[284] See ADM 116/2863 at TNA.

harbour. On the 24th *Delphinium* coaled (115 tons), embarked a Pilot and proceeded up-harbour to secure at Maydon Wharf.

On the 29th, in the trying heat of 90° F, the hands landed the howitzer and limber, together with its crew, so they could head for the Agricultural Show at which they were scheduled to make their display. This event proved to be very popular with the public. [Men from *Cardiff and Carlisle* were also competing.] Next day, they repeated the exercise, Alf being OOW on both days. He continued to be OOW during the opening days of July, while *Delphinium* lay alongside *Carlisle* and *Cardiff*, whilst the Fleet Sailing Race took place (on the 4th July), whilst frequent shore leaves were given, whilst *Delphinium's* Orepesa Floats were hoisted out for painting and, subsequently refitted, whilst the 2nd Whaler drew sand, and whilst the ship provisioned. Her sick list was now down to almost nil again.

On the 1st July she coaled again, embarking just 87 tons, before passing through the breakwaters to proceed to East London, where she arrived next morning, and spread her awnings. Whilst there her hands refitted her minesweeping gear, and, on the 27th, she proceeded for Port Elizabeth where she arrived on the 29th. On the 1st August she dressed ship in honour of the Birthday of H.M. the King, and fired a 21-gun salute after parading her guard. On the 4th *Delphinium* landed her Rifle Team, and next evening, she burnt her searchlights for exercise. On the 6th she proceeded for Simonstown, going to Night Action Stations at 2015, darkening ship and commencing a Night Encounter Exercise at 2030.[285] The exercise was completed at 2100, and *Delphinium* continued to Simonstown where she arrived on the 8th. For some reason her sick list had suddenly increased, and she discharged three ratings to the RNH at Simonstown on the day of her arrival. On the 15th she was exercising her boats under oars and sail. On the 15th she exercised General Drill independently. That day the cruiser *Cardiff* sailed for the West Coast flying the Flag of the C-in-C Africa Station. During the next few days *Delphinium* carried out a Sight and Director Test, proceeded out to sea to conduct 1-inch aiming rifle practice, then again put to sea for Pom-Pom, 3 pdr and more 1-inch aiming rifle practice, and also practised minesweeping for two hours. She carried out further rounds of AR practice on the 29th and 30th. This intensive gunnery practice was probably all a lead-up to the Sloops Competitive Firing Competition, which was held on the 31st, each ship embarking umpires and firing 10 rounds per gun.[286]

[Whether or not it was exercises such as these that inspired him, it is a fact that on 28th December 1932, in one of his annual 'Letters of Proceedings' to the Admiralty the C-in-C, Vice Admiral TWEEDIE, was moved to write generally about gunnery: *"It is possibly out of place for me from such a small Station as this to generalise on gunnery practices, but, as others have come to similar conclusions, it appears worth while saying what has been in my mind perhaps since I was Captain of HMS Marlborough and Director of Training and Staff Duties, when I read through many reports of firings of different natures. These conclusions have been very much confirmed while on this Station, viz:-*

Commanding Officers and Gunnery Officers appear to be very happy if the shots fall near the target. Hitting the target does not seem to be expected. Sir John (sic)

---

[285] This exercise probably involved the cruiser *Cardiff* and perhaps other ships on the Station.
[286] *Daffodil* and *Verbena* were evidently involved.

FISHER's tag of "Hit Quick and Hit Often" appears to be out of fashion and more often than not a perfectly unblemished target returns to harbour after what has been described as a very satisfactory shoot.

The teaching which persuades the gunner that 'to go near is good enough' seems to me to be radically wrong. The experts probably say that at the distance that modern firings take place and with the small size of a battle practice target at that distance, direct hits cannot be expected. If that is so it is considered that the distance should be reduced until hitting is reasonable and that nothing but direct hits and the time factor should count.

But it is seriously suggested that in spite of hundreds of thousands of pounds spent on fire control instruments and general mechanical aids to hitting the enemy by gunfire, the hits remain as scarce as ever. Either it would seem that our standards are low or we are setting out to accomplish the impossible. It appears worthwhile to emphasise that shells which fall in the sea even fifty yards away from the enemy, and, which from the firing ship look tremendously close, do no harm and even have a reverse effect on the morale of the company of the ship which is missed - whereas a direct hit, even by a comparatively small shell may do vital damage to personnel or material and in any case makes a terrific racket which has its moral effect....." [287]

One wonders if Rear Admiral TWEEDIE's remarks somehow 'touched a nerve'. Overtly at least, the Admiralty Chiefs were not impressed by the C-in-C Africa Station's remarks and seem to have set out to debunk them. The main comment on the docket ran: *"The C-in-C's remarks are open to considerable criticism. The importance of early hitting is stressed in the Gunnery Text books and except for the fact that spotting officers look for 'straddles' when correcting salvoes, there appears to be no ground whatever for the C-in-C's statement that 'The teaching which persuades the gunner that to go near is good enough'. The progress and development of the fleets in gunnery is left in the hands of the Cs-in-C, and if the ships on the Africa Station require more practice in short range shoots, the remedy is in the Flag Officer's hands. Fire Control instruments and general mechanical aids have increased the ranges at which our ships can open fire with a reasonable chance of hitting. Thus, a well-trained ship can obtain a great advantage over a less efficient adversary before <u>decisive</u> range is reached. Gunnery is not and never will be an exact science, but we cannot relax in our endeavours to give our ships every instrumental aid for obtaining hits at long range. Training to obtain efficiency under these conditions is therefore essential. The C-in-C quotes 'Hit Quick and Hit Often'. The instruments are provided for hitting 'Quick', the training must aim at hitting 'Often'.*

The DCNS endorsed this by adding: "The opinions expressed about Gunnery appear to be based on a general impression rather than a study of policy and progress during recent years. Examination of results, particularly of Competitive Firings, in the important fleets would show that the obvious functions of ships' armaments are not lost sight of either by the Commanders-in-Chief or the Admiralty. If the two cruisers on the Africa Station failed to show the efficiency he expected the remedy lay in the hands of the Commander-in-Chief. It is at his discretion to arrange their training at such ranges and under such conditions as he thinks fit."

---

[287] This particular report is filed at TNA under ADM 116/2863.

To the author this seems to miss the point raised by Admiral TWEEDIE, who was referring back to his general experiences, and not just as C-in-C Africa Station. Surely, what was needed was the ability to hit accurately *at long range*. Constantly straddling a hostile ship was no good. Direct hits *were* the need. This was the whole ethos of Admiral FISHER's famous dictum and, indeed, the *raison d'être* of the fast-moving battle-cruisers he had initiated. To have to 'get in close' to obtain hits against an enemy who could hit hard and accurately at both long and medium range was tantamount to suicide for battle-cruisers (and most certainly so for lesser warships), and came close to self-immolation even for the most heavily armoured of battleships. Further, for an Admiralty chief to say that "*Gunnery is not, and never will be an exact science*" was surely a statement that was simply begging to be challenged and refuted. [As WW2 would teach us, the Germans were very conscious of this whole matter and always went all-out to hit with their very first shots in any engagement, having excellent rangefinders and associated gear, very accurate and consistently-performing guns, and coming very close indeed to making gunnery an 'exact science'. One has only to consider the catastrophic loss of HMS *Hood* to the opening rounds of gunfire in her WW2 battle with *Bismark* – where the very sensible Admiral HOLLAND was urgently *trying* to close the range because he knew *Hood* was vulnerable to plunging fire at long range and much less so to flatter-trajectory fire close-in. He also knew that the accuracy of his own gunnery would be better closer in.]

One wonders if any of this high-level debate, particularly the dissatisfaction of Admiral TWEEDIE with the gunnery of his two cruisers, ever reached the ears of Alf.]

On 1ˢᵗ September *Delphinium* coaled (85 tons), and carried out a certain amount of maintenance over the next few days, scraping, scrubbing, cleaning and painting, holystoning her decks, renewing the fore and main pole halliards, rigging stages for painting, getting out the sweep wires for return to store and so on. Alf was OOW almost every day, including the 10ᵗʰ, when *Verbena* sailed for the West Coast and England to pay off, and *Delphinium's* company manned and cheered ship.

On the 24ᵗʰ the 1ˢᵗ Range party were landed to attend the Annual Musketry Course at the Sanatorium, Alf again being OOW. The 2ⁿᵈ Range Party left on the 4ᵗʰ (after the 1ˢᵗ Party had returned on board), and Alf went with them, for his name does not appear again as OOW until 20ᵗʰ October, by which time the 2ⁿᵈ Range Party had returned on board. Indeed, the following snapshots, which he retained in his album, indicates that he was in charge of that party.

This change of scene would surely have done him good both for health and morale. He may well have been *too* consistently on board, near-constantly as OOW, always trying to bury his deep anxieties about his greatly-beloved wife in sheer hard work, for far too long.

Author's collection of inherited family photographs.

Delphinium's Range Party at Simonstown in October 1932.
Alf is the Warrant Officer in the centre of the middle row.

Author's collection of inherited family photographs.

On the Range at Simonstown. Rifle-firing from a prone position. Alf,
who was observing and instructing, has marked his image in this snapshot
with an inked 'X'. He would have been in his element in this activity.

On the 19th October *Delphinium* had entered dry dock, and the usual tasks of scraping and painting her bottom had begun, her cables had been ranged for examination and blacking-down had begun aloft. On the 24th, her mining winch was hoisted out. Work continued in this vein whilst, on the 27th, the ship's platoon were landed for a field exercise, their arms being cleaned next day after their return. They were lucky to be back, for a nasty south-east wind got up on the next day, increasing to Force 7.

Come the 1ˢᵗ November, *Delphinium* undocked and promptly coaled (88 tons). Next day her hands cleaned the guns and provisioned ship, then cleaned the ship before a photograph of the ship's company was taken on the 3ʳᵈ November.[288] The ship underwent basin trials next day, and, on the 6ᵗʰ November, she temporarily hoisted her paying off pennant. This would have lifted Alf's heart a little, with the prospect beginning to loom of at last being back in England near to his greatly beloved and ailing wife. However, a considerable programme still remained to be gone through before *Delphinium* would be heading past Gibraltar and crossing the Bay of Biscay.

On the 7ᵗʰ the hands were busy embarking frozen meat, before, in a strange apposition, the ship's company donned their gas masks and passed through the gas chamber. At 0800 on the 8ᵗʰ November *Delphinium* again hoisted her paying off pennant, and the C-in-C Vice Admiral TWEEDIE came aboard at 1100 to say farewell. At 1134 the ship proceeded for Walvis Bay, hauling down her paying off pennant at 1300. At noon on the 10ᵗʰ November *Delphinium* was at 26° 02' S, 14° 33' E.

At 0810 on the 11ᵗʰ she entered the dredged channel at Walvis Bay and secured alongside the wharf at 0820. She had run 755 miles. At 1100 a 2-minute silence was observed in honour of the fallen of WW1. On 12ᵗʰ November *Delphinium* landed her Rifle Team for a competitive shoot against the local club, Alf remaining aboard as OOW. Next day a 2-minute silence was again observed at 1100, and the ship was open to visitors at 1400. They left Walvis Bay on the 17ᵗʰ, proceeding for Loanda.

During the next days they practised various techniques to do with steering, changing to hand control on the 18ᵗʰ, and reverting to the normal steam-assisted method after a half-hour. On the 20ᵗʰ they dropped three marker buoys and exercised handling ship and responding to new steering orders. During the early morning of the 21ˢᵗ they began sounding every hour as they approached Loanda, firing a 21-gun salute at 0840 as they closed the port, the fort returning in full. They anchored at 0850, after their voyage of 910 miles, and, at 1500, HE the High Commissioner for Angola paid a visit to the ship, receiving a 19-gun salute on leaving. Next day, at 1130, the Acting Governor-General of Angola paid a visit, receiving a salute of 13 guns.

On the 24ᵗʰ they 'weighed the ship's company'. The Log does not reveal what the weight was estimated to be.[289] Next day they coaled ship (152 tons). They also sent the boats inshore to scrub out. On the 26ᵗʰ *Delphinium* weighed, turned and proceeded for Butica. They were nearing the Equator, and the temperature had climbed to 86° F. Down in the engine room, the stokers were finding the going hard. So the Engine Room Windsail was rigged at 1500 in the hope of providing a little air for the men. As another

---

[288] Unfortunately no copy of the resultant print has survived in-family.

[289] One assumes this was done by taking a day when the water was flat calm, clearing the ship of every man-jack aboard, and then carefully checking the draught-marks. Then having everybody file gently back aboard and space themselves more or less uniformly throughout the ship, before the draught-marks were carefully re-checked. It was known that a load of about 11.25 tons would increase the draught by 1 inch. The company was 115 in number, and, if we assume an average weight of (say) 11 stone, that is equivalent to 17,710 lbs or 7.91 tons. So 7.91 tons would have increased the draught by [1 x 7.91 ÷ 11.25] = 0.70 inches - just about detectable and back-relatable to about (say) 'eight tons'.

sign of the tropical conditions and their closing with the land, a daily issue of quinine was commenced on the 30th November.

At 0330 on the 1st December *Delphinium* reduced to 7 knots and began to sound her way in to the estuary, taking measurements every half-hour. She came to anchor at 1000 at the end of her 680 mile run from Loanda. At 1430 she weighed and proceeded gently up the River Muni, initially at 8 knots, reducing to seven knots at 1610 and coming to anchor off Butica, in 5 fathoms, at 1800. The temperature was just short of 90° F: they were now just a few degrees north of the Equator, having crossed the Line during the previous night. On the 2nd December the Captain paid a call on the Delegate Governor of the Southern District of Spanish Guinea at Kogo.

On the 4th *Delphinium* proceeded down-river and, an hour later, came to off Ukoko, where the Administrator of French Sub-Division of the Gaboon of Coco Beach paid a call on the Captain, which was returned. Next morning the ship proceeded for Victoria coming to off Victoria in the British Cameroons at 0700 on the 6th, after a run of 185 miles, and spreading her awnings in the sweltering temperature of 86° F, scarcely relieved by the light airs which prevailed. Alf was OOW for much of this onerous time.

The company had accidentally lost a 60 lb. anchor at Butica: they now lost by accident a brass stanchion with a brass swivel and tube guard with cap, followed by a crowfoot spanner and a shifting spanner. Perhaps the heat and effort were 'getting at them'. However, relief was to hand, for, on the 11th December the first party left the ship for the peace of Buea Camp, with its refreshing coolness at 4,000 ft altitude, and, after their return, the second party left, not returning until the 17th. Seemingly, Alf did not go with either party, for he was OOW for much of this overall period of time. (His Spartan nature may have driven him to declare that '*He was fine*' and that others should go in his stead.)

Innoculation was carried out, and the galley flat was painted whilst the second party were absent. On the 19th December the ship proceeded from Victoria for Lagos, altering course four hours later to investigate a drifting boat, and then continuing her voyage. On the afternoon of the 20th she dropped a target and her Gunlayers and men recommended for Gunlayer carried out 1-inch aiming practice for a good hour, before the target was picked up and the ship proceeded. At 0800 on the 21st, she stopped, picked up a Pilot, and continued up-harbour to come to anchor, letting go both port and starboard anchors and securing her stern to No.5 Marina Buoy, stemming the flood. They had run 420 miles, the temperature was 91° F and a water boat was coming alongside.

Alf was OOW for much of the time they were in harbour at Lagos. He was OOW when the Rifle Team were landed on the 27th, a day when the temperature relented slightly to a more modest 85° F, though the humidity remained high. On the 29th the hands provisioned ship with frozen meat and potatoes from the S.S *Apapa*, and Alf was again OOW on the 30th, when the ship proceeded by tug to the *Apapa* at 0753 for further provisions. She then proceeded at 0830, again by tug, to the coaling wharf, where they coaled with native labour. A Water Boat came alongside during this process, until, coaled and watered, at 1700 a tug again took them in charge and towed them to the Marina where they secured as before, stemming the flood. Next day an ash lighter came alongside. The scend of the sea had been too great on the 19th for the ship's draught to be taken. Now, however, this procedure was possible, and her draught was checked as 11 ft 6 ins fore and 12 ft 7 ins aft before loading, and 13 ft 6 ins fore and 13 ft 3 ins aft after coaling and provisioning. (Probably equivalent to some 250 tons total lading, though her change in trim complicates matters.)

On 2nd January 1933 the ship proceeded northwards and westwards for Takoradi, which she reached in the afternoon of the 3rd. A waterboat was alongside on the 4th and canteen leave was given on the 8th, Alf having been OOW all day on the 5th, all day on the 8th and again on the 9th. He also stood a trick on the 14th, when the ship proceeded for Freetown. On the 16th the ship stopped at 4° 50' N, 9° 04' W for a balloon ascent to be made, and she came to anchor at Freetown at 0700 on the 18th, having run 885 miles. Captain's Rounds were held on the 21st, Alf having been OOW all the previous day, as he would be on the 23rd and 24th. During that latter day, shore parties were landed to load stores in a lighter from the 'Lay-Apart Store', a lighter being hired to come alongside bringing sweep wires and stores which were duly loaded aboard. Next day a water lighter secured alongside and water was embarked. On the 27th they coaled, using native labour and embarking 120 tons. That day the Log records that a Money Chest Pattern 1464 and another of Pattern 1480 were 'burst open beyond repair' by order of the Captain, presumably to get at the contents and thus to be able to pay the native stevedores. One can visualise a certain joy in the hearts of the POs and ABs undertaking the 'break-in', perhaps enlivened by a traditional 'reluctance' on the part of the Pusser's Mates who evidently could not furnish the necessary keys.

On the 30th January 1933 a further quantity of water was embarked from a lighter which came alongside and the ship then proceeded for Bathurst, where she arrived in the afternoon of the 1st February after a run of 440 miles over a gentle sea and in a quiet breeze. At dawn on the 4th January they then proceeded up the River Gambia, coming to with their port anchor off Balingho, at 1649, before weighing and proceeding at 0633 on the 5th, coming to with their port anchor off Kunta at 1416, in eight fathoms. They had covered 130 miles from Bathurst.

The day for the biennial buoyancy test on the 2nd skiff was now due. Such tests on the ship's boats would have been occurring regularly, but the Log did not normally record them. Exceptionally, it did record this particular one. [*The relative calm of the upper reaches of the Gambia River was presumably favourable for the operation, in which the skiff would have been weighed with all its equipment in place, and with its barricoes full of water, and then lowered in the sea. The falls would be left hooked on, but slack. The skiff would then have its plug withdrawn and water allowed to enter the skiff until the level of water in and outside the skiff was equal. The skiff would then have ballast applied progressively and in such a manner that the skiff was maintained on an even keel, and ballast would continue to be added until water was just pouring in over the topsides. The amount of ballast which had been added to bring the boat to this just-sinking condition would then have been carefully totalled up mathematically as it was removed. It was required to be more than one-tenth of the total weight of the skiff.*

Normally, it would have been expected that all would be well, and the weight would exceed the 10%. However, if it were not, then extra buoyancy was necessary. This could now be computed. Suppose, for example, the weight of the skiff was 1.5 tons. Ten per Cent of this weight would be 0.15 tons. If the weight of ballast required to submerge the skiff was (say) only 0.10 tons then a further 'buoyancy' of [0.15 - 0.10] = .05 tons (i.e. 112 lb.) would be required. One Cubic Foot of Sea Water weighs 64 lb. and the air-volume required is therefore assessed as [112 ÷ 64] = 1.75 cubic feet. Permanent buoyancy tanks to contain that volume of air would have to be fitted to the skiff. Having checked the buoyancy, the skiff would have had to have its plug refitted in place and then to have been baled out before re-hoisting, to prevent possible straining of the hull of the skiff and to ease the load on the falls and davitts, etc.]

Delphinium continued up-river as far as Deer Island, anchoring overnight off the western end of the island, in mid-stream. She had covered 150 miles from Bathurst. Next morning she turned and proceeded back down-river at 6½ knots. She anchored below Balingho at 1620, and sent her skiff and whaler away surveying. In the course of so doing they somehow lost two elliptical floats in the river.

On the 10th February the ship proceeded from Bathurst for Santa Cruz, Teneriffe, rounding the Gambia Fairway Buoy at 1127 and stowing away stanchions and ridge ropes. Next day her company returned all sun helmets to store. They were heading away from the tropics. A moderate swell was getting up. At 0900 on Sunday the 12th they passed the latitude of Cape Blanco, the Northern Limit of the Africa Station. At 1930 the company sloped and frapped the Q.D Awning.

On Valentine's Day, Tuesday, 14th February, at 0830, they stopped and embarked a Pilot to guide them into harbour at Santa Cruz, firing a 21-gun salute to the Spanish Flag as they did so. The salute was returned. They had run 920 miles. H.M. British Consul paid an official visit, being saluted with seven guns on leaving. The weather conditions were temperate (72° F) and calm. The hands began to red-lead the ship's side where necessary. Next day they washed the funnels and embarked potatoes.

On the 17th they proceeded for Funchal in a Force 4 breeze, and on a moderate sea and swell. The temperature had dropped to 65° F. They were approaching 30° N. By 0840 next morning they were closing Funchal, firing a 21-gun salute to the Portuguese Flag (which salute was returned), and coming to anchor at 0854. H.M.British Consul visited the Captain (7 guns), and the Captain's visit on the Civil Governor was returned that afternoon, the Guard being paraded (13 guns).

Alf was OOW all day on the 19th February. Next day they coaled (170 tons), and watered on the 23rd. There were heavy rain squalls that day, and, as the wind had got up to Force 5, they let go an extra anchor and raised steam for slow speed at 1 hours notice.

On the 23rd February they embarked water from a lighter alongside, and, on the 24th February *Delphinium* proceeded for Gibraltar, her hands washing the Carley Float and cleaning ship generally on the 26th. At 0715 the ship secured to No.9 Buoy at Gibraltar, after her 600 mile run. Next day, Alf was OOW all day. The Mediterranean was calm with only light airs. The temperature was 67° F. The sick list was running at just one man. On 1st March Pay Lt Commander C.S.B HICKMAN joined ship from *Warspite*. On the 2nd they slipped from the buoy at 0730 and proceeded for Portsmouth

Heavy rain squalls swept the ship on the 4th March, the wind being variable and still up to Force 7. Then it veered four points and freshened further to gale force from the north-west. The sea was getting up too, and *Delphinium* was beginning to roll and pitch in a lively fashion. Then, on the 6th, the weather moderated, and *Delphinium* returned to Portsmouth on 7th March 1933 with a long paying-off pennant trailing from her yard-arm. Her hands promptly began to de-provision and de-ammunition ship.

On 18th March at 0900 the ship's officers and company were discharged to HMS *Victory* for Foreign Service Leave. Just four officers and six ratings were retained on board, being borne on the books of HMS *Victory*, for closing the accounts.

Author's collection. A photo on card by Wright & Logan in 1933. This print appears by courtesy of the Royal Naval Museum, Portsmouth.

HMS *Delphinium* returns to Portsmouth on 7th March 1933. The body-shape and posture of the officer standing right in the bows of the ship suggest that he may well be Alf himself, doubtless desperately keen to hurry back to Felixstowe and his little family.

Alf now received a second assessment report covering his service in *Delphinium*. It covered the period from 1st December 1931 to 18th March 1933. The report was signed by Commander WILMOT-SITWELL, and it says that Alf's conduct had been '*to my entire satisfaction. An extremely loyal and trustworthy officer who possesses marked ability and common sense. A most efficient Warrant Officer who, in addition, 'fits' excellently in the Ward Room.*'

Here was high praise indeed. Clearly, Alf's ability to mix well with persons of all status levels, where he had a head start as a child living on large estates, further developed at his father's pub, and honed by many years in the Royal Navy where he had steadily become ever more closely involved with officers, had all borne fruit. His Masonic connections may have also added positively to this scenario. One suspects that he had set himself body and soul to better himself to the highest degree he could achieve, burying himself in work so as to shut out, so far as humanly possible, his pervading fears that he might well be about to lose his darling Olive to an illness against which he was powerless to intervene, despite the best medical attention which he could possibly call upon.

Author's collection. A photograph by Wright & Logan taken at Portsmouth in March 1933. This print appears by courtesy of the Royal Naval Museum, Portsmouth.

A view from astern as HMS *Delphinium* comes home to Portsmouth on 7th March 1933. She looks extremely neat despite her long voyage from South Africa.

The author has come to believe that this deployment had been of great significance for Alf. That significance is typified by the photograph of Alf standing right up in the eyes of the ship whilst demonstrating to other officers and warrant officers his mastery of the art of using an Orepesa Sweep. By this time Alf had acquired a tremendous range of knowledge and skill in the many aspects of seamanship. He had also developed great self-confidence, and he evidently loved to demonstrate his high level of proficiency and efficiency in finding the 'right and proper' way of dealing with any situation arising in his field of expertise. His 'naval side' was revelling in such matters, which were greatly boosting his ego.

There was, however, a down-side to the situation. As we shall see, when carried to extremes under the pressure of war, Alf was all-too-liable to be adopted as a 'father-figure' by the younger officers, especially those recently joined, and then he might well come to feel that he was often 'carrying the whole weight of the ship on his back'. In the longer term this could become very draining indeed, and thrust a huge level of personal responsibility upon his shoulders.

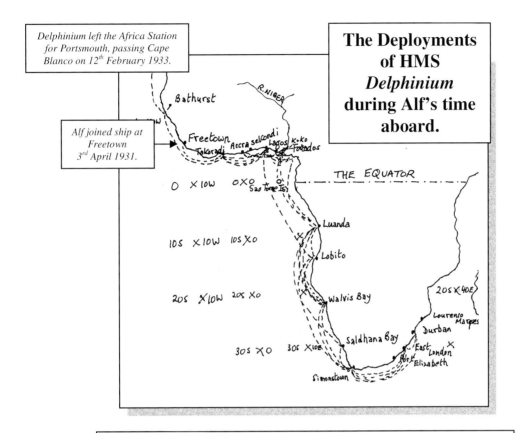

Delphinium left the Africa Station for Portsmouth, passing Cape Blanco on 12th February 1933.

Alf joined ship at Freetown 3rd April 1931.

The Deployments of HMS *Delphinium* during Alf's time aboard.

During this deployment Alf had crossed the Equator four more times, making ten crossings in all. He had also equalled his farthest South (ever) position.

VOYAGES DURING DEPLOYMENT: Pers. RECORD of Alfred William DAVIS RN					
Farthest North	Cape Blanco	**21 N** 17 W	*F/North (ever)*	Off Scapa Flow	**59 N** 03 W
Farthest South	Simonstown	**34 S** 18 E	*F/ South (ever)*	Simonstown	**34 S** 18 E
Farthest East	Durban	26 S **31 E**	*F/East (ever)*	Ras Asir	12N **51 E**
Farthest West	Cape Blanco	21 N **17 W**	*F/West (ever)*	Atlantic Ocean	50 N **30 W**

Alf would soon be able to head off home to inspect his new baby daughter and to see at first hand how his wife was faring. He must have been 'champing at the bit' for months on end to achieve just that target.

__Private Life__

Alf and Olive's third child, Jessica Agnes, had been born on 3rd October 1931, eight months after Alf had been appointed to HMS *Delphinium*. Perhaps her conception had been a part of the heightened emotions sparked by Alf's impending departure for an absence which would be of at least two years duration.

Like her brother Neville before her, Baby Jessica was baptised in the Parish Church in Old Felixstowe, her godparents being 'Dolly' BISHOP (a first cousin of Olive's), and Edgar WAITE, a soldier-friend of Olive's parents.

Photograph kindly loaned by the author's elder sister, Mrs J.O. GOODMAN. Original photographer unknown.

A lovely study of Olive with Baby Jessica, her third-born.

Jessica's birth had followed hard on the heels of young Neville. In later years, Alf's mother-in-law, Agnes Sarah GREEN, said, on more than one occasion, that, had Alf not been at sea so much, and, had Olive's health held up, there would have been *many more* DAVIS children born. Certainly, Olive was a natural mother, who raised her children with ease, seeming to seldom, if ever, to have any need to reprimand them. They just naturally did as she wished. There were absolutely no 'ructions' in the house such as might have lived on as harmful little traumas in the children's memories.

In fact, the children were raised under almost ideal circumstances whilst Olive retained a reasonable level of strength. Sadly, this would not endure for long, but, for the moment, Olive was just about managing, with some assistance from her elder sister Alice, in looking after her children and in running the home in Looe Road which Alf had bought.

When Alf's appointment in *Delphinium* terminated, evidently on 18th March 1933, he would have quickly returned home on Foreign Leave. Little Neville and baby Jessica would retain no memories of their father's return, but it is probable that Joan, now rising six, would carry some memories of the happy event.

Author's collection of inherited family snapshots. Date c.1933.

Olive's sister Alice with Neville, aged 3 years.

Joan aged 6 years. A blond, with 'peach and roses' skin.

As we are about to see, Alf would have had only about a week to renew his relationships at home and to assess how his wife was coping with her illness, before he was off on his next appointment, which was at Chatham. By now, he would have found that, increasingly, Alice had to step in to care for the children. Happily, all three children were thriving.

CHAPTER FOURTEEN:

HMS *PEMBROKE* & HMS *GANGES* (1933-35)

Before being appointed to HMS *Ganges*, Alf spent two months on a course at the Gunnery School, HMS *Pembroke,* from 26th March to 28th May 1933. Unfortunately, we have no details of this course. One assumes it was an up-dating in the latest equipment and techniques. It may also have been in the nature of a 're-qualifying' course, for Alf was in the running to be promoted to Commissioned Rank in 1935.[290]

Alf was appointed to HMS *Ganges* on 29th May 1933. One wonders if this might have been a compassionate posting, for, with his wife now in a very poor state of health, it was so very convenient for Alf to be near home.

Be that as it may, Alf did not allow events at home to deflect him from his naval duties and responsibilities. The photograph below shows Alf as a senior instructor of a division of young boys who have clearly won a lot of trophies in competition with other divisions at *Ganges*. The mixed nature of the trophies makes one recognise the very varied skills which are required of a qualified seaman. There is no doubt that Alf thoroughly enjoyed being an instructor, though he was undoubtedly a stickler for discipline and expected the very best from the men and boys he commanded.

Author's collection of inherited family photographs.

Hands on his kness, Alf is seated next to the Captain of the Division. The boys seated on the grass are holding at least a dozen trophies and what appears to be the overall cup-winners cup stands proudly in front of the Captain and Alf. The Division actually contained about twice the number of Boys who appear in this photograph.

---

[290] In 1941, Captain (G) G H G ACKLAND of the R N Gunnery School at Chatham would write to Alf's widow to say that 'Mr DAVIS was an officer for whom we all had the greatest regard'.

At the start of Alf's new spell at *Ganges*, the establishment could accommodate 1,290 Boys, in four so-called 'double-decker' messes, 29 ordinary messes and one 'special' mess. This was an increase in capacity since Alf's previous service there, in 1929-31, when (albeit operating somewhat below capacity) there had been an average of 878 boys accommodated.

Eight hundred cubic feet of space was allocated per boy. Currently, about 1,000 Boys were under training at any one time in the surroundings which had become so familiar to Alf.[291] The boys were organised in six Divisions, each of about 190 Boys, and, as noted earlier, each Division bore the name of an Admiral. Plans were afoot to increase the number of Boys to eight divisions, still of 200 Boys each, making a total of about 1,600.[292] As we shall see, this expansion was more than realised during Alf's stint.

To train the boys, some 26 Officers were required at the period when Alf arrived on the scene. There was accommodation for only 20 officers, so some of the married ones slept out. It is understood that there were also about 50 Warrant Officers (Gunners, Signal Boatswains, Warrant Telegraphists and Schoolmasters), and some 45 CPO Instructors, 40 CPOs and 60 PO Instructors. (Apparently, it was a 'rule of thumb' estimate that there should be at least one PO Instructor per 22 Boys, which would indeed imply a total approaching 60 POs.) Over and above these were the 'Ship's Company' of Supply, Cook and Writer Ratings and a small number of Pensioner Civilians. The pensioners included men with tailoring and shoemaking skills who worked in two hutments on the east side of the laundry. There was also a hut where a barber operated.

All these officers and men were commanded by Captain E.P. HARDMIN-JONES OBE. The planned expansion would increase the numbers of all these officers and men, by four Lieutenants, sixteen Warrant officers, thirty CPOs/POs and perhaps some 80 ratings. This was a very considerable expansion.

Further accommodation would have to be built, including a PO's mess. So far as gunnery equipment was concerned, there were four six-inch guns in the battery, three being of the obsolescent Mk VII type and only one being of the modern Mk XII type. (There were aspirations to change the guns to five Mk XIIs as the expansion proceeded.)

In 1933, Alf led a platoon of young sailors to the British Legion Fete at Ipswich. The platoon, bearing arms with bayonets fixed, and standing proudly in well-dressed line, were inspected by Admiral Sir Reginald TYRWHITT (Retd). This officer and gentleman had commanded the Harwich Force throughout the war with the greatest distinction, and Alf would have been delighted to have been able to lead the platoon for the Admiral's appraisal.

For his part, Admiral TYRWHITT would probably have been quite interested to see how HMS *Ganges* was getting along, for, as Commodore of the RNB at Chatham, he

---

[291] To the visitor, at least, the great mast at Shotley, rising over 140 ft in the air, always looked a terrifying sight. Sure enough, around this time, at least one Boy had fallen, in his case some 30 ft off the lower platform of the mast and into the safety-net below. Although he had fallen less than one-quarter of the full height, he was concussed and badly shocked. It was only stage by stage, over some months, that he was returned to normal duties. (See ADM 101/530). In 1931 there was an average daily sickness of 35 Boys. Infestations of rodents always posed problems at large establishments, and 240 rats had been destroyed that year.

[292] The idea was to close down *St Vincent*, a smaller Boys training Establishment, and thus to realise a cost saving. However, there would have to be related (albeit lower) expenditure in expanding the accommodation and staffing at *Ganges*, where only a limited amount of 'spare capacity' then existed.

had been rather non-committal two or three years earlier, when reporting to an Admiralty Committee examining possible changes to the training establishments. These proposed changes had involved the expansion of *Ganges* and the elimination of certain other establishments.

Author's collection of inherited family photographs. A postcard by Edith F Driver of Ipswich.

Sword at the present, Alf escorts retired Admiral Sir Reginald TYRWHITT as he inspects the men at the British Legion Fete in Ipswich. The display by the platoon included the ceremony of 'Colours'. Admiral TYRWHITT well merited great honour, for "*his conspicuous ability had gained him the unique distinction of retaining the Harwich Command throughout WW1.*"

Author's collection. A postcard by C. W. Faulkner c.1914.

Admiral Sir Reginald Y TYRWHITT KCB, DSO photographed when still a Commodore. He had played a distinguished part in the action in the Heligoland Bight and other operations during the First World War. In the lead up to his retirement he had been Commodore of the Royal Naval Barracks at Chatham.

Probably choosing his words to the Admiralty Committee very carefully, Admiral TYRWHITT had said that the proposed changes would have little, if any, effect on the RNB. Now that those changes had begun to come into operation, he would probably have been asking some pertinent questions of officers like Alf, and closely studying the demeanour of the boys under training.

In fact, by 1934, *Ganges* had already grown considerably. There is a Medical Officer's Journal for the year 1934, written by Surgeon Captain Thomas CREASER RN, which survives at TNA under reference ADM 101/544. It shows an establishment of 446 Officers and men and 1,729 Boys under training.[293] On average, 83 Boys were sick daily, mostly due to colds and sore throats, but with over 2,000 cases of Scarletina during the year. That implies that nearly every man-jack (boy-jack?) and many members of the training staff must have gone down with the (then) truly horrid illness. Rubella, Laryngitis, Catarrh and Mumps were also a significant problem. There had been three cases of TB.

There had been a host of minor injuries, many from boxing and field sports, some from gymnastics, and some from accidents in boat handling. Several Boys had been scalded whilst carrying hot water (generally whilst proceeding down the covered way to reach their various messes), whilst others had hurt themselves in slipping on the highly polished wooden floors in the messes. The fact that boots had to be removed before treading on the wooden floors, so that those floors were always crossed in stockinged feet, must surely have heightened the risk of such skating, sliding and slipping-over.

In total, over 300 'operations under anaesthetic' had been conducted. In a quite different but related field of hygiene, some 220 rats had been exterminated. (Much the same number as three years earlier, despite the expansion.) It may be recalled that infestation by rats had been an on-going problem right from Alf's earliest experiences of the training establishment, going back to 1911 and beyond.

A report on Alf by Captain H H ROGERS MVO, MBE, covering the period from 29th May 1933 to 22nd August 1935, said that Alf had conducted himself 'as Gunner and Commissioned Gunner', *entirely satisfactorily. A very able and reliable officer with a good power of command and plenty of image.* Another report, by Captain C. O. ALEXANDER, for the period 23rd August to 9th December 1935, said Alf had conducted himself 'as Commissioned Gunner', *to my complete satisfaction. He has shown zeal, ability and considerable personality in his work with the boys'.*

When one considers that his greatly beloved wife had finally succumbed to her wasting illness and that Alf had laid her to rest in February 1935, the achievement of such glowing reports by his successive commanding officers is truly remarkable. One can add to his grieving the matter that he also had the 'guardianship' of his three children to consider, and that this was an issue with urgent and competing difficulties to resolve.

Perhaps Alf was burying himself in his work in order to forget the pain and complications of his domestic situation. If so, he would almost certainly have been following the example of his own father, twenty-nine years earlier, immersing himself in work to bury the pain of immense private grief, and perhaps even being somewhat 'in denial'.

On 2nd June 1936 Alf had been appointed to the rank of Commissioned Gunner, with seniority from the 1st April 1935. [His warrant was signed by King Edward VIII who had come to the throne in 1936, but who was fated never to be crowned.] This confirmation of his promotion must have been a source of great satisfaction to Alf. He would surely have regretted the fact that it came too late for Olive to have been a part of

---

[293] By 1935 the total under training was approaching 2,000 Boys.

it. Nonetheless, it was a milestone in his career, and something he had been working towards for a long time. (Again, this was an echo of the life of Alf's father, with the death of Alf's mother occurring just as his father's life had taken an upturn towards its zenith.)

Author's collection of inherited family photographs.
A postcard by Edith F Driver c.1933

Despite the misty weather, Alf, in formal dress, with white gloves, sword and winged collar, leads an armed platoon, bayonets fixed, swinging smartly out of Shotley Barracks. One can almost hear the rhythmic 'tramp, tramp, tramp' of those gaitered boots and sense the unison of the swinging arms.

Author's collection of inherited family photographs.
A postcard by Edith F Driver c.1933.

Alf might have (nearly) given up playing hockey himself, but it certainly appears as if he knew how to support his Instructor-Lieutenant and to coach winning teams at the game.

Alf was now 40 years old. He had *almost* given up hockey, and taken up golf as a sporting recreation. He would soon be heading far to the north of the United Kingdom on an exciting new naval venture, but he would have many serious problems to take with him concerning his private life.

We'll just add a final picture as a reminder of one of the mental images Alf would have retained of his days at HMS *Ganges*. He had served there on various occasions in his service life, and it was very familiar territory to him – but, after this year of 1935, he would never see it at close hand ever again.[294]

Author's collection. An anonymous postcard c.1934, postally used on 9th July 1937.

'Hubert', the sender of this postcard, was a Boy under training in 12 Mess at *Ganges*, in 1937. He wrote home: "*I thought you would like this card of a Sunday Parade. It is not a new photo because in the space on the right a huge swimming bath is being built, and, instead of the black shed, some 'tin messes', like the New Annexe. The tallest man on the Bridge is the Captain, still here. The Band is also bigger now....There is a destroyer in here...*". There appear to be about 1,200 boys on this parade. Whether Alf was somewhere in this scene, or whether he had moved on shortly before, is not known. However, this is surely an image of the regular Sunday Parades which Alf would have long retained in his mind's eye. Perhaps it is little wonder that he had started to apply '*Ganges* principles' (rather prematurely!) in the raising of his own son, aged 5 when Alf left Shotley.

NOTE. Picture (iii) in Appendix J, page 750, shows that Alf DAVIS was still playing Hockey for HMS 'Ganges' at age 39, and Picture (iv) shows that he was on the 'Nozzer Staff' for at least a part of the years 1933-35.

---

[294] It is interesting to note that Alf's path must have crossed to some extent with that of the then Boy Seaman Harry WARDLE, who was in training at *Ganges* during 1935, and who later wrote the book "From Forecastle to Quarterdeck". (See Bibliography.) Like Alf, Harry WARDLE rose through the ranks, surviving much action during WW2, doing exceptionally well professionally throughout his career, and retiring with the rank of Lieutenant Commander RN, in 1958. This leads one to wonder whether Alf, too, had he survived the early years of WW2, might have gone on to achieve significantly higher rank.

Private Life

A programme for a Masonic 'Installation Festival' which was held at the impressive Felix Hotel, in Felixstowe, on 1st May 1935 by the Felix United Service Lodge No.3833 has been carefully maintained within the DAVIS Family. It contains the pencilled signatures of H.T.ABLETT, G.H. EDWARDS and E. DICKINSON. These names mean nothing to the author – unless the 'G.H. EDWARDS' was the General Practitioner of that surname who looked after the medical needs of the DAVIS Family - but the careful retention of this programme suggests that Alf may well have been present at the installation festival, presumably as a guest of a fellow-Mason.

This ceremony may quite well have been Alf's last experience of formal Masonic ceremony, for family rumour suggests that Alf had become increasingly disillusioned with the Masonic Movement. Certainly, he had obtained a 'Certificate of Clearance' from the Essex United Service Lodge No. 3804, at Harwich, on 30th September 1935, *'declaring off after settling all his dues'*, and it seems that he never joined another lodge.[295] One wonders if this was simply a matter that his ensuing naval appointments prevented him from settling long enough at any place to be drawn to join another lodge, or whether his mental orientation was to deliberately 'take a break' for a while, or even permanently. Maybe the loss of Olive in February of that year (*q.v.*) had totally 'thrown him'. Perhaps his attainment of his goal as Commissioned Gunner may have somehow precipitated his leaving the Masonic movement. One suspects that a large part of his independent nature would have always rebelled against the main concepts of Freemasonry - though his 'other side' carefully preserved his regalia and certificates, perhaps just as memorabilia, but perhaps in case he changed his mind.

Back in 1934, whilst Olive was in a period of remission from her illness, Alf had hired a small car, and, packed within it the family had gone off on trips into the countryside. Although a driving licence was required, no formal testing arrangements existed in those days regarding a person's fitness and abilities at driving. However, sailor-like, Alf seemed to cope with no problems whatsoever, and one wonders if he had perhaps been shown how to drive when out on safari in Africa, earlier in his career and perhaps, later, when on short spells of shore-leave, using hired cars. Alf took Olive, her parents, and the children to visit elderly 'Uncle Albert' and 'Aunt Lucy' in their country cottage at Twinstead, Essex, which was crowded with fragile porcelain ornaments and stuffed animals in glass cases.[296] Water was obtained from a pump in the kitchen, fed by a well, or from the communal pump on the nearby village green. The cottage toilet was a two-holer earth closet redolent with garden lime. The toilet paper was neatly torn squares of newspaper. For

---

[295] The author is very grateful to the Masonic Movement for confirming that their records show no further entries for Alf.

[296] 'Uncle' Albert ENGLISH, born in 1858, was the eighth of a round dozen children, of whom the second oldest, George ENGLISH, had become the father of Alf's mother-in-law, Agnes Sarah GREEN née ENGLISH. Following family tradition, both George and Albert were Carpenters by trade. See ENGLISH Family Tree in Appendix F. (As a matter of interest, Albert's wife, 'Aunt Lucy', had a sister, Jessie GEDYE née HUME, a housekeeper who, late in life, had married her employer, a widowed solicitor. Jessie would go on to long outlive her husband, and would eventually attain the great age of 106 years.)

reading material whilst one 'contemplated' in the loo there was a massive old family bible. For a young child this rural cottage was a fascinating place. A lot of Nan's and Uncle Bill's ENGLISH-named forbears lay at their eternal rest in the nearby churchyard, the graves well tended by Uncle Albert.

The family also went to see a buxom and rosy-cheeked cousin of their grandmother. This cousin was cheerful 'Aunt' Beatrix MAYNARD (née ENGLISH). She and her gardener-husband, lived in a small house at Stisted, Essex, which had small but beautifully-trimmed hedges of Box dividing off the various areas of immaculate garden-patches.

A snapshot by Alf.

Relatives. A visit to 'Uncle' Albert ENGLISH, aged 76, and 'Aunt' Lucy, aged 74, at their cottage in Twinstead, Essex. Joan, aged 7, stands between the old couple and their nephew, 'Uncle' Bill, aged 53 and their niece, Agnes Sarah, aged 60. Agnes Sarah is the grandmother of Joan and Young Neville, aged 4, who is wandering off to explore this strange old world – so new to him.

These trips, coupled by Alf with excursions to see naval events at Shotley, formed unforgettable and delightful memories for the children. Such naval events included firework displays with an enormous effigy of Guy FAWKES carried round the sports field by a platoon of sailors led by a marching band, before the effigy was cast on a huge bonfire, and enormous free-standing 'portraits' of King George V and Queen Mary being beautifully picked out in multi-coloured fireworks showering streams of sparks. There was also a huge firework 'elephant' (the main emblem of the Badge of HMS *Ganges*) which appeared to 'march'. All these items created wonderful images and impressions that the children would each carry forever in their mind's eye.

Alf also took the children to stay with a former school-friend of Olive, Nell BOOBY, who had married a Farmer, Eddie ROBERTS. There were two ROBERTS children, of ages akin to the DAVIS children, and much fun (and some mischief when the children were unsupervised) was had at Great Wratting Farm, which was situated near Haverhill, Suffolk. Alf soon had his children getting used to the horses, and put them in the saddle of a docile pony, though under his careful control.

Author's inherited family collection of (slightly faded) snapshots.

(Above) All three of Alf's children seem very composed with their mother, Olive, and their grandparents standing protectively behind them. *(Right)* The group is less composed with Alf having replaced Olive, whilst she takes the photo. Maybe just a small token of the disruption which Olive's impending death is going to bring about within this group.

Author's inherited collection of family snapshots.

Alf, a natural horseman, has the full confidence of this horse as he sits three boys, including his 4 year-old son, on its back. His elder daughter Joan prefers to stay safely on the ground, and his younger daughter, Jessica, aged three, shows every sign of reluctance to be lifted aboard. She would come around to the idea later.

Alf would also take the children on the beach at Old Felixstowe, going in the sea with them, encouraging them to build sand-castles and 'motor-cars' made of sand to sit in, and teaching them how to play 'French Cricket', the 'fielders' bowling tennis balls and the 'batsmen' using small wooden beach-spades as 'bats' with which to defend their legs, which acted as the wicket. The children loved all this

Alf, wanting to give his son confidence in the water, would load him on his back and swim well out to sea. The boy would cling on like a limpet, with one part of his mind rejoicing in the sheer animal power of his father's enormously strong back and shoulders, but with the other part of his mind knowing that his father urgently wanted him to learn to swim, and terrified that his father would simply unload him far out from the shore and sternly order him to swim back on his own, for the boy was sure he would drown. His mind could not accept that his sailor father, always something of a stranger to him, loved him dearly and would never let any harm actually happen. And the more the boy failed to respond to 'the test', the more he felt his stern father's love would evaporate away. The boy felt very cowardly and unworthy. How could he ever meet the high targets his father was setting for him?

Author's collection of inherited family snapshots.

A lovely shot of Olive with her three children, enjoying boiled eggs for breakfast at the grandparents' beach hut. Young Jessica and Neville are 'tucking in' busily, but Joan is looking quizzically at the photographer – perhaps a sign of her increasing myopia – or is she just trying to imitate and echo her greatly beloved mother.

Alf's nephew Raymond PENNEY, then aged about 14, came down to Felixstowe on at least one occasion. In later life Ray would say that he had great respect for his Uncle Alf, who always took Ray and his brother John out to interesting places when he came up to London to visit Ray's parents' home. Ray greatly appreciated such visits, because his own father was always busily engaged in the unremitting toil of running their big public house, and seldom seemed able to 'find the time' to take his two sons on outings. Ray felt that Alf and his mother Nellie always got on well together as brother and sister.

Alf with his nephew Raymond PENNEY, then aged about 14, and young Jessica, aged about four. Alf's face is quite 'drawn' and sunken, showing signs of the emotional drain on his physical resources as his wife's illness approaches the inevitable end. The heat of the tropics to which he has recently again been subjected may have also played a part in that physical reduction. However, he is putting a brave face on things, although he is soon going to have some very difficult decisions to make.

The 'Happy Time' for the Children. *(Left)* Olive with Jessica, her youngest child, aged three. *(Right)* Alf reads a comic to his three children, with Jess in the middle, young Neville paying full attention, and Joan looking 'gripped' and almost horrified. Perhaps some dreadful fate awaited one of the characters in the comic, and Alf was heavily dramatising it!

Whenever he was home, Alf took over many of the household chores, and he paid close attention to the state of health of his children. Thus he would check that they were drying between their toes after they had been in the sea (then said to prevent the onset of Athlete's Foot). Whenever they were out in the sun he would smear the children with a special white grease from a tall and cylindrical tin, by then gone quite rusty, which he had once obtained from 'Savoury & Moore' (then a large London department store). He would make the children wear their sun-hats to keep risks of sunstroke to a minimum.[297] He would also see that their nails were kept cut, clean and the quicks pushed down, their ears clean and wax-free and, most of all, ensure that their bowel habits were regular and that the children remained free from constipation. 'Syrup of Figs' was doled out frequently - probably too often and too liberally for their future internal health. Sometimes Alf would hire a boat, and row the children out to sea, once, thrillingly for the children, when Landguard Fort had its red flag flying and its nine-inch guns were firing at a target offshore.

Amongst the family friends on Olive's side of the family were veteran soldiers from the Great War, such as Billy MILLER (who'd lost his right arm in battle) and Sammy DYER (who had a talent similar to that of the actor-comedian Stanley HOLLOWAY in declaiming humorous monologues, including the night-watchman's lugubrious lament called "A'guarding the 'ole in the Road'). There was also Ben SCRIVENER, a retired Police-Sergeant from Ipswich, invariably accompanied by his gentle wife, and both chatting away in the most attractive of soft Suffolk accents. Various siblings and nieces of Joseph Walter, with their spouses and children, would visit on occasion. Such visits had been going on ever since Agnes Sarah and Joseph Walter had first moved from Ipswich to Felixstowe, back in 1928.

Highpoints would also arise when 'Uncle Jimmy', the older of the two brothers of Alice and Olive, would suddenly arrive with his beautiful tall, elegant and blond-haired wife Dilys and their young son, Colin.[298] Agnes Sarah often used to tell the children how narrowly their Uncle Jim had survived an attack of typhoid fever whilst he had been working with the Anglo-Iranian Oil Company (later B.P.) in Persia in the early 1920s. Uncle Jimmy always seemed to have a new car, for he was doing well in his career in the oil industry, and he and his little family would have driven all the way from South Wales to make the visit. In those days the route was a winding one that ran through town-centres and took many hours to accomplish. Uncle Jimmy seemed incisive and clever and drove faster than other family members, though evidently just as safely. He was, one felt, always on the verge of being acerbic in conversation. However, the author had come to like his Uncle Jim and respected him.

Tragically, Olive's strength was trending ever-downward, as she came out of ever-shorter periods of remission, and her elder sister, Alice, increasingly took charge of the children. By the time that Joan was seven, Neville was four, and Jessica was three, the whole family had moved out of their small house in Looe Road and had begun to live at their maternal grandparents' house in High Road East, so that Olive could be more readily cared-for. It was around this time that Olive was making journeys up to St George's Hospital in London for on-going medical assessments and the very limited treatment which was available in those days for a condition which was inevitably going to prove be fatal in a very short number of years. To reach the hospital Olive travelled direct to the terminus at Victoria by the

---

[297] A close family friend, Doctor EDWARDS M.D., had evidently died from sunstroke and was held up to the children as a 'dire warning' of the need for protection from the sun, especially for the nape of the neck.

[298] The adults may have known Jimmy and Dilys were coming, albeit that the children did not.

countrywide 'grey-green' long-distance coaches. The coaches had a pick-up point at the end of Garrison Lane, Felixstowe, and Joan well remembers accompanying her mother on some of these long journeys up to and down from the Metropolis.

As they grew bigger and became increasingly conscious of the world around them, Alf's children gradually came to recognise these older people and something of their backgrounds and worthiness. Another 'old soldier' who had a considerable influence was Agnes Sarah's half-brother, 'Uncle' Bill, who'd fought both in the Boer War and then against the Germans in the 1914-18 affair. All these relations and friends were useful factors in broadening the children's development.

Author's collection of inherited family photographs.

Alf's children, growing up. However, their mother is increasingly absent, and they are showing signs of that loss. On the left, Joan looks very withdrawn, and young Neville appears very resigned. Jessica is always sucking her thumb for consolation. The children are fortunate that their Uncle Neville has a vibrant girl-friend called Con, and she takes the children for walks along the sea-front, thus getting them out of a house of tension and near-despair.

At Christmas-time the family group would sometimes consist of as many as thirteen people sitting at table, with everybody bearing a hand in making the 'paper-chain' decorations on Christmas Eve, in helping in the kitchen and mixing drinks. Then in making their own 'music and song' evening to follow, or in playing card games, with a few low-value coins on the table, such games usually being 'Newmarket' or 'Rummy'. (The wireless played some small part in people's lives, but was still in its infancy from the point of view of providing 'entertainment').

The house at 21 Looe Road, which Alf and Olive had bought in such high hopes, was evidently rented out early in 1935 with some of the household goods being put into store. It was decided that the children should be spared the sad sight of their mother's physical deterioration, and that she should be kept free from their possibly boisterous and demanding presence. She was therefore installed on the first floor of 'Surrey House', above the shop. Her accommodation was in the former drawing room at the front of the house, which now became a sick-room. This room had a dark and heavy wooden door. That door was suddenly kept closed, and the children were thereafter prevented from ever seeing their ailing mother again. They were also enjoined not to make a noise anywhere near their mother's room. Only the adults of the household, and a professional nurse who came to live in, were allowed to go in and out through that heavy door.

The children's aunt and grandparents did their best to keep the children distracted and to see that they had toys and games to keep them entertained. Their grandmother was particularly effective at this, making each child feel as if their grandma had a special affection for him or her alone, as an individual, over and above the others. Whether, in the long run, this was a good or bad thing is hard to judge. Indeed, everything that the elder family members did was intended for the best - but, as later events were to prove, the children were all heavily and permanently traumatised by the shutting of that dark, heavy door (of which they were given no advance warning) and by the loss of their mother to them from that moment on.

Author's collection of inherited family photographs. A studio portrait c.1930.

Olive, who had become the dearly beloved wife of Alf, and superb mother to Joan, Neville and Jessica. The magnitude of her loss to the family was truly colossal and had near-catastrophic consequences.

Joan does remember - perhaps just before the door was closed - being in the room just the once, with its large double-bed and heavy wardrobe, each made in ominously dark wood with prominent wreath-like carvings. Joan also remembers her mother had knitted some baby socks with very attractive embroidered floral decoration, and was keeping them neatly folded in a piece of tissue paper. Were these intended for baby No.4? There does seem to be a hint of a rumour that, despite her ailing condition, Olive was pregnant yet again – but, if so, miscarried with this child at a fairly early stage.

Weeks later, their mother's death on 13ᵗʰ February 1935 (and funeral a week later) were also screened from the children, though they were regularly taken to see the grave thereafter. The thought of their lovely mother becoming a skeletal corpse greatly troubled at least one of the youngsters (the author), who had nightmarish fears about the grave opening up. In the years which followed, their grandmother constantly lauded their late mother to them in the most glowing terms – probably very much to their future step-mother's disadvantage.

As for Alf, there is not the least doubt that the death of Olive came as a terrible blow. He aged visibly as she declined and finally passed away. He looked like a man torn apart, and, so close had been their loving relationship, that this was probably very much how he felt in his very soul. It is highly likely that Olive's death also brought back to him all the trauma and sense of loss and isolation he had gone through at the time of his own mother's sad death. How much he perceived that the 'shutting away' of their mother had 'damaged' the children is hard to say, though one would have thought that their sense of loss, which would have mirrored his own when *his* mother had been shut away from him 29 years earlier, ought to have somehow 'come through' to him. Presumably, he had weighed everything up and had decided that no other course was open. Moreover, 'psychology' was pretty much a closed book in those days. People who followed the theories put forward by Sigmund FREUD and his like were regarded as rather dangerous cranks.[299]

Author's collection of inherited family photographs.

Olive's grave in Felixstowe Churchyard, where she was laid to rest after her death on 13ᵗʰ February 1935. Alf now had three young children to be cared-for, when he was in the impossible situation of being liable to be sent to sea at any time, perhaps many thousands of miles away.

Olive's funeral was very well-attended, with all her close family being present, including her brother Joe who had come up from South Wales. Olive's cousins Ada CASTELL and 'Willy' GREEN were also there, Willy being accompanied by his attractive blonde-haired wife Violet. Olive's aunts Alice BARHAM and Dolly BISHOP attended, as did Alf's three sisters, Nellie, Rose and Eva. A distant relation, Mrs Beatrice MAYNARD, also made the journey to be present. Long-standing family friends included Nell ROBERTS of Great Wratting Hall, Miss FROST, Tommy WINKWORTH, and Mr and Mrs Ben SCRIVENER. (We have

---

[299] A decade later, hard-bitten Yorkshiremen would still be saying, deprecatingly, "*Anyone who goes to see a psychiatrist 'needs his head examined'!*", and something of that attitude prevails to this day.

already encountered most of these people in our story. Some will appear or re-appear later.) All did their level best to provide some sort of comfort under the very difficult circumstances.

Through his intense grief, somehow or other, Alf had to maintain a hold on real life and practicalities. Thus, unbeknown to the children, various options were being considered as to their future guardianship. Clearly, as a serving Naval Officer, Alf was likely to be absent at sea for much of his time. Short of resigning from his career, with consequent sacrifice of income and pension, there was no way that he could take care of the children himself.

Author's collection of inherited family photographs. An anonymous studio portrait c.1933

The children that Olive had left motherless. Alf had to decide who was now going to look after them whilst he was away at sea.

One idea which was mooted around the wider family and which later 'evidence' suggests Alf may have very seriously considered, was to have Joan, his elder daughter, informally adopted by Nellie, Alf's eldest sister. [Nellie and her husband Wilf had two fine sons, but no living daughter, and it seems that they would have been very amenable to the idea.][300] Rose and her husband Alf, who had no children at all, would consider taking young Neville, and Eva and her husband Fred, who likewise had no children, would consider taking baby Jessica. It may even be that the three of Alf's sisters actually promoted this concept, though it is clear that none of the couples wished to take the massive step of individually adopting all three children as one composite family unit. One would scarcely have expected this of any of them. Thus, any such 'adoptions' would have involved the raising of the

---

[300] It may be recalled that Nellie had sadly lost her first child, a baby girl, at birth.

three young DAVIS siblings as separate entities, as well as Alf probably losing all control over them forever afterwards. Alf would also become a 'loner' once more.

However, a different option existed in respect of Alice, Olive's elder sister, who, at age 35, was still unmarried. As we have seen, she had frequently stepped in to take care of the children during Olive's recurring periods of weakness and debility. Here was a possible step-mother for the children, a person whom they knew well enough, and a woman who was a part of the wider family in which they were already living. Moreover, the siblings would be kept together as a single family unit if they came under her care. Further, instead of losing parental control over his children, Alf would remain as their father, in every sense of the word.

Yet it has to be said that, although they were sisters, Alice was a very different person to Alf's late wife Olive. Alice had strong opinions, met people head-on, and had been born with a quick, hot temper and considerable self-pride. Moreover, whilst still a young woman, she had become very embittered, and she still nursed that strong sense of bitterness. This all had come about a decade earlier, when Alice had fallen deeply in love with a young man. Unfortunately, her parents had perceived her belovèd to be a hopeless n'eer-do-well. In those days parents had real powers over the wishes of daughters, and, in the belief that they were looking after Alice's best interests, they had stopped the potential marriage in its tracks.

Author's collection of inherited family photographs. An anonymous studio portrait.

Alice, as a young woman, with her fine eyes and near-classic beauty.
It was a great shame that Alice had been made very bitter when her parents had prevented her marriage to a young man. This had sharpened her tongue and warmed-up her fiery temperament. She had many good qualities, including total honesty and straightforwardness, and a strong sense of duty, but was Alf going to be the right man to bring her best qualities to the fore?

With the benefit of hindsight, one feels that Alice might well have been able to make a go of that projected marriage, for she was of a strong and determined character and would probably have 'brought the young man into line'. Indeed, she may well have needed the sort of husband that she could have worked upon and moulded and mastered. However, the marriage having been irretrievably stopped by her parents, she had quickly become very bitter and disillusioned. Her bitterness and hot temper sometimes flared out when she was serving 'awkward' customers in her mother's shop and tearoom, to her mother's chagrin and potential loss of custom and *clientèle*.

Winnie BISHOP, one of Alice's first cousins, was in much the same boat as Alice, for Winnie had also fallen in love with a young man, and had desperately wanted to marry him. However, the man was deformed and handicapped, making him hunched and lame, and Winnie's parents had also taken it into their heads to stop the marriage. One has to remember that the generation in which Alice and Winnie were seeking husbands had lost a high proportion of its young men in WW1 combat. The chances of these girls finding other husbands was thus quite small – for there were simply not enough men to go round. Winnie, who was another overtly tough character, had become even more embittered than Alice. These two spinster cousins were friends and the one fed off the other in their extreme bitterness at having been denied their 'true loves'.[301]

Having weighed up matters, Alf decided that he wanted to keep his children together and to remain as their father, rather than have them off his hands and fostered out individually. Alice had always had a high regard for him and she was indeed a woman of high principle with a strong sense of duty. And, as already speculated by the author, over the 14 years he had known her, Alf may often have idly wondered what kind of love-partner Alice might make, for she had a good figure and lovely eyes, even if a rather exciting nuance of the 'taming of the shrew' might be involved for her lover. Who can say? Perhaps Alf felt he was well up to that sort of task.

The long and short of it was that Alf proposed marriage. *Once again, Agnes Sarah, the mother of Alice (and also of the late Olive) wished to prevent a marriage of Alice from going ahead.* Agnes Sarah, alias 'Nan', foresaw that two strong-minded people with hot tempers would not make for a happy marriage. It was Olive's good, calm, humorous approach to life, and her innate ability to lovingly cushion, absorb, deflect (and gently steer, usually just in the direction she desired!) her husband's quick temper and high pride, which had made their marriage work so well. A marriage with Alice would be a straightforward clash of wills as husband and wife each strove for mastery. They would surely 'knock lumps off each other'.

Agnes Sarah also considered that Alice was not very maternal by nature, she was already showing signs of her quick temper with the children, and, following (say) an argument with Alf, might well work off her resentment on those young children. However, Joseph Walter GREEN, the husband of Agnes Sarah, a man slow to anger but who was always mightily impressive when he did finally let rip,

---

[301] To see the by then widowed Alice and still-spinster Winnie in slightly later life, both knitting furiously, drawing heavily on their 'Craven A' cigarettes, and tearing the world apart in intense and vituperative conversation is an image which haunts the mind of the author to this day. Nor is he the only one, for little Essie, Winnie's sister (and the author's godmother) who had herself taken the enormous risk in 1938 of running away willy-nilly and penniless from a faithless husband to set up a totally new life far away (eventually taking a lover of her own), used to say in her 'widowed' dotage: *"Winnie - Oh, she was so BITTER! And, my goodness, how she 'fumed' as she smoked!"* In *hindsight*, the author finds Alice and Winnie *quite magnificent*, and loves them both dearly – though he would find the smoking a real 'off-put'.

refused to back up Agnes Sarah in her objections and said, *"No! I supported you when you turned down Alice's first marriage, and just look what unhappiness and bitterness that created! I'm damned if I'll stand in her way a second time! Let the girl have her chance at happiness."* So, Agnes Sarah, although very much the 'family matriarch', had to unwillingly concede defeat to the now thoroughly-aroused 'master of the house'.

It is quite possible that Alf perceived certain features in Alice which had existed in his birth-mother, for the respective birthdays of the two women lay only 12 days apart, both having been born under the sign of Leo. There is no doubt but that both women shared high ideals of duty and were strong personalities, and both had been headstrong in their youth, creating conflict and causing serious heart-searching problems for their parents. A tense time was surely going to lie ahead for Alf and Alice once they were bound together by marriage. There would have to be an enormous amount of 'adjustment' by one or both of them.

Author's collection of inherited family snapshots.

Alf's three children, Neville aged 5, Joan aged 8 and Jessica aged 4. Alice is standing behind them, smoking the inevitable cigarette. She has a hand placed discreetly behind Jessica in view of the nearness of the water behind them. Alice is not yet their step-mother, but soon will be. Neville is responding to the photographer. Joan looks despondent, though she does have her arms around her siblings. Did she just want to walk the three of them away from Alice forever? Jess is observing her brother. Her hands suggest that she is working some tactic out in her mind.

In the meantime, young Neville had started to attend 'Highclere School', run by Miss MULLINS. Sure enough, it had been Alice who had taken him along on his first day (though he had escaped and run back home all on his own later in the day!)

Neville and his two sisters were very fortunate that they had grandparents and others around them to cushion the blows to their *psyches* which would increasingly fall about their ears. They had lost their mother and the trauma of that was beginning to impinge on their consciousness, shielded though they may have been from it, to a significant degree.

Seen in retrospect, the two elder children were very fortunate that they were of an age to have some positive, very happy and comfortably secure memories of their mother. These would stand them in good stead in the difficult years ahead. The youngest child, Jess, still having been only three years old when her mother was secluded away, would have had only 'fringe memories'. However, their grandmother would constantly tell all three children how wonderful their mother had been, and these 'conditioned memories' would certainly reinforce such 'direct' memories as each of the children already possessed, Joan's memories naturally being the strongest by virtue of her greater age.

Author's collection of inherited family photographs. Photo taken by Alf.

Mobility. Kids and their Bikes. Neville, seen pulling a strange but quite rumbustious face, is doing well at school. He rides his faithful 'Fairy' bike the mile there each day. He has performed in a successful school play, as 'Jill', of the 'Jack and Jill' nursery rhyme. In fact, the girls are wearing pink gingham dresses made up from the same material as had been used for Nev's costume. Jess looks well enough, but Joan appears, so far as can be seen, rather solemn. (*Alf had pencilled a note on the back of this snapshot almost apologising for having 'cut off Joan's head'!*). Joan is attending a Convent School in Felixstowe, and Jess will follow suit in due course.

So far as one imagines Alf would have seen, the interrelationships of the children were good at this stage, Neville and Jess being close in age and often playing well together, such as when on the beach and making sand-model cars in which each would sit and 'drive' companionably. Joan was slightly distanced from her siblings due to her greater age, but Alf would have thought that the two girls would doubtless go on to develop shared interests in dresses, dolls and certain toys, even if only by virtue of their femininity. Alf would have perceived all three children as being basically in a good state together at this stage of their young lives. He and Olive had brought them up very well, and squabbles between the children had been almost unknown. He cherished ambitions to turn the boy into being more of a 'man', but it was still 'early days' in that regard. He would make Alice his ally in this.

Alf would have seen that there were some signs of unhappiness being displayed by the children now that Olive was no longer present, though that was *'only to be expected'*. Hopefully, matters would soon settle down again now that Alice would be taking over completely in Olive's stead.

We must leave 'matters domestic' here for the moment to return with Alf to his naval career, which was about to become extremely interesting, challenging and rewarding.

Strange to reflect that, when he was a boy, there had been no prospect at all of any man who had entered the Royal Navy as a Boy or Rating ever to rise above Warrant Rank to reach Commissioned Rank. This restriction had applied no matter how well-bred, intelligent, courageous and charismatic the man may have proved himself to be in either peace or war. This had all been quite different to the situation in the Army, where a man of reasonable breeding who showed good 'martial qualities' had for long stood a fair chance of gaining promotion from NCO to commissioned rank, especially when under conditions of 'active service' – indeed, so-called 'battlefield promotions' were relatively frequent. Matters had changed in the Royal Navy in recent years, but the climb to commissioned rank was still an extremely difficult one to achieve and Alf was thrilled to have done so. He would have been actively looking forward to this new appointment.

CHAPTER FIFTEEN (a):

HMS *SOUTHAMPTON* (1935-38)

It was on 10th December 1935 that Alf was appointed to HMS *Pembroke* 'for HMS *Southampton* on commissioning for acceptance trials'. The radically new light cruiser HMS *Southampton* was being built in John Brown's large shipyard at Clydebank, where her keel had been laid on 21st November 1934. Thus, for over a year before Alf came on the scene, the hull of what would become HMS *Southampton* had been taking shape. Alf would have just three months to familiarise himself with the developing structure of the new cruiser whilst she was still on *terra firma*, before the hull would be sliding down the ways and floating on the River Clyde ready to be 'fitted out'. Alf would not have been alone, for various specialist and experienced officers and WOs had already come on the scene, and more would arrive during those next three months, to work with the John Brown personnel in checking on every aspect of the construction of the new cruiser, to be involved in the carrying out of certain tests, and to learn all they could about her from the viewpoints of functional use, maintenance, damage-control and repair.

As a matter of interest, *Southampton* was being built in a berth near to where the red funnels and white superstructure of Cunard's great transatlantic ocean liner the RMS *Queen Mary* were dominating the landscape. *Queen Mary's* vast hull had been launched on the 26th September 1934 and the huge ship was now nearing spectacular completion. [Indeed, this magnificent leviathan was due to leave the yard fully fitted out on 24th March 1936. The launching of HMS *Southampton* would pre-empt the departure of the RMS *Queen Mary* from John Brown's yard by just two weeks.]

Although she was designed to meet totally different criteria to those of the vast ocean liner, *Southampton* was another fine ship in the building by John Brown's. She was the leader of what would become a class of eight ships, herself being of 9,100 tons displacement, 591½ feet in length, and with a beam of 61¾ ft. In comparison with Alf's earlier ships, she would be rated only fourth in terms of displacement - but in terms of length she would be second only to the battlecruiser *Courageous*.

In terms of her specific category as a cruiser, she would be 140 ft longer than the 'long and lean' cruisers *Weymouth*, *Lowestoft* and *Birmingham*. At 9,100 tons, *Southampton* had a much greater displacement than those three older cruisers with their 5,250 to 5,440 tons.[302] She was also 13 ft broader in the beam than they had been, and would turn out to have a 2ft greater draught than they had drawn.[303] It might therefore have been supposed that she would pitch and roll less than had the now-retired *Weymouth*, *Lowestoft* and *Birmingham*.[304] However, she had more superstructure and armour-plating than those cruisers had carried, and such factors (which would influence

---

[302] Her displacement was less than that of the County Class or of the Hawkins ('Improved' Birmingham) Class. (The County Class were also beamier.) However, Alf had not served in any of those ships.

[303] It appears that her designed draught was originally only 17 feet, but, in practice, she drew over 20 feet.

[304] The first-named had been scrapped in 1928 and the other two in 1931.

her metacentric height and the effects of windage) would need to be put into the equation. In the event, the *Southampton* class of ships would prove to be stable gun-platforms and to perform well in heavy weather - though they were certainly not immune from considerable rolling under certain sea states.[305]

Here is a basic overall comparison of *Southampton* as compared with Alf's previous ships:-

Name of Ship	Type Of Ship	Displace-ment (tons)	Year Completed	1st Year Alf srv'd (diff.)	Comple-ment	Max. Length (feet)	Max. Beam (feet)	Draught (feet)	Shaft Horse-Power	Max. Speed (knots)
Vanguard	Dreadnought	**19,250**	1910	1912 (2)	823	536	**84**	**31.75**	24,500	22
Russell	Pre-Dreadnought	14,000	1903	1912 (9)	718	418	75.5	28	18,220	19
Weymouth	Armour'd Cruiser	5,250	1911	1913 (2)	392	453	48.5	18	22,000	25.5
Courageous	Battle Cruiser	18,600	1916	1916 (0)	**829**	**786.5**	81	26	**90,000**	**35**
Lowestoft	Armour'd Cruiser	5,440	1913	1920 (7)	546	459.5	49.8	18.25	25,000	25.5
St Cyrus	Admiralty Tug	820	1919	1925 (6)	12	143	29	13.5	1,200	12
Birmingham	Armour'd Cruiser	5,440	1913	1925 (12)	504	459	49.8	18	25,000	25.5
Delphinium	Sloop	1,250	1916	1931 (15)	80	267.5	33.5	11.75	2,200	15
Southampton	Cruiser	9,100	**1937**	1936 (-1)	700	591.5	61.75	20	75,000	33

Name of Ship	Guns				Torpedo-Tubes		Armour			
	Main		Secondary		A.A			Deck	Side	Turr't	D.C.T
	Calibre	Number	Calibre	Number	Capability	Calibre	Number	(ins)	(ins)	(ins)	(ins)
Vanguard	12"	Ten	4"	Twelve	2x3"	18"	Three	1.5 - 3	**10**	**11**	**8 – 11**
Russell	12"	Four	**6"**	Twelve	-	18"	Four	2.5	3-4	6	12
Weymouth	6"	Eight	3"	One	1x3"	**21"**	Two	1-2	-	1	2
Courageous	**15"**	Four	4"	**Eighteen**	2x3"	**21"**	**Fourteen**	1-3	3	7-9	10
Lowestoft	6"	Nine	3 pdr	Four	1x3"	**21"**	Nine	1-2	3	1	2
St Cyrus	12 pdr	One	-	-	-	-	-	-	-	-	-
Birmingham	6"	Nine	3 pdr	Four	1x3"	**21"**	Eleven	1-2	3	1	2
Delphinium	4"	Two	3 pdr	Four	2x3"	-	-	-	-	-	-
Southampton	6"	**Twelve**	4"	Eight	**8 x 4"**	**21"**	Six	2	3-4	1-2	4

The **bold** figures in the above tables represent the 'maximum' for each column of

---

[305] The degree to which a ship will roll is dependent upon many factors involving her design and construction, the effectiveness of any keels and 'stabilisers' with which she may be fitted, her state of lading and trim at the time in question and her response to the particular combinations of external factors which may come into play at that given time. [Such factors include the variables of the strength of the wind, sea and swell, both in relation to each other and also in relation to the course and speed on which the ship is steering (or involving a whole raft of associated factors if she is at single anchor or otherwise without steerage way, when she may swing and even broach-to, greatly increasing her roll.) Other matters, such as the presence of nearby land masses and the depth and variability of the sea-bottom, especially in fairly narrow channels, may also be key factors.] However, to take just one example, *Southampton's* Log would show her as passing through a fairly stormy period in the Western Approaches from 19th to 23rd January 1939. The ship reached a roll of 19° as the storm began to get up, reaching an uncomfortable 35° by the time the wind was at Force 8. Then, as the wind eased to Force 5 and thence down to Force 3, the ship's roll reduced through 21° down to 12°. When anchored off Bilbao in 1937, she would show a considerable roll almost solely due to the heavy 'Biscay' swell which prevailed that day. The worst roll ever recorded in her log would be of 43° (almost half-way to being on her beam-ends!), due to a combination of very rough sea and a wind of near-hurricane force experienced in the Atlantic Ocean in May 1939.

'characteristics' (e.g. *Vanguard's* '**19,250** tons' still being the maximum entry for the 3rd Column ('Displacement').

As we can see, *Courageous*, at 786 ft., still remained easily the longest ship in which Alf had ever served. Yet, at just over 590 ft, *Southampton* would be about 55 ft longer than the Dreadnought battleship *Vanguard* and no less than 175 ft longer than the pre-Dreadnought battleship *Russell*. Of course, the 19,250-ton *Vanguard*, the 18,660-ton *Courageous* and the 14,000 ton *Russell*, had been much beamier than *Southampton*, and of considerably greater draught, armour and calibre in guns than *Southampton* would possess. Their respective behaviours in heavy weather had thus been quite different to the behaviour which this new cruiser would display.[306]

The appearance of only two (*uniquely*) **bold** figures in the 'bottom-lines' makes clear that it was only in her newness, in her anti-aircraft defences (*inadequate though they would prove to be in 'modern warfare'*) and in the *number* of her main guns that *Southampton* excelled over the other ships, though it has to be said that the *calibre* (and hence 'hitting-power') of those main guns was comparatively low. Yet, her *shaft horsepower* was considerable and, in the event, she probably rivalled that speedster, the 'battlecruiser' *Courageous*, in racking up the knots. Unquestionably, she was larger, faster, better-protected and harder-hitting than any of the other 'light cruisers' on which Alf had served to date.

Southampton's main guns were of the well-proven 6-inch Breech Loading Mk XXIII type mounted in triple turrets, two turrets on the centre-line forrard, and two aft. Their fire was controlled by a large Director Control Tower (DCT) mounted above the bridge. The guns were fed by ammunition hoists sheltered by protective trunking. These hoists brought up projectiles and cordite charges through flashproof doors from the shell room and magazine, the latter compartments being placed well below the waterline. It was considered that the relatively low weight of the 6-inch shell (about 100 lb. - the limit for manual handling) would facilitate a sustainably high rate of fire with which to 'saturate' a target - higher than would have been achieved with the much heavier weight of (say) an 8-inch shell weighing 250 lb. and requiring mechanical aids in handling.[307] [Despite such reasoning, later experience would show that the ammunition-supply handling for the 6-inch shells would never completely achieve the desired high volume for emergency combat conditions.]

Southampton also had eight 4-inch High-Angle dual-purpose guns, in shielded twin mountings carried amidships, four on the port beam and four on the starboard. The fire of the 4-inch guns was controlled by two High Angle/Low Angle (HA/LA) Director Control Towers (DCTs) mounted one each side of the bridge structure.[308] The principal

---

[306] Of these three ships, *Courageous* had been drastically restructured in 1927/28 and then re-commissioned as a fully flight-decked aircraft-carrier, *Vanguard* was no more since the catastrophic explosion which had suddenly torn her apart in 1917 with the immediate and tragic loss all but two of the 800 men aboard, and *Russell* had been lost after striking two mines off Malta in 1916, the resultant fire causing the partial detonation of one of her magazines as she began to founder.

[307] Alf's views on the counter-argument concerning the greater destructive effects of even single hits by 8" shells are not known. It was notable that the new Japanese and American cruisers were being fitted with 8" guns and that guns of even heavier calibre were being considered by those countries for their very latest cruisers.

[308] Ships of this Class which were built subsequent to *Southampton* and *Newcastle* had a second HA/LA DCT mounted aft, on the superstructure above 'X' gun deck.

function of these 4" guns was to defend against air-attack, to fire 'star-shell illumination' for the six-inch guns in night actions, and to provide offensive/defensive capability in surface actions at close range. Each dual mounting had a crew of sixteen men, and each gun could attain a rate of fire of ten rounds per minute. In total, therefore, the port and starboard batteries could fire off up to 80 rounds per minute when they were in full action.

Unlike the 6-inch guns, which had separate Cordite charges to propel the shells, the ammunition for the 4-inch guns came in one piece, as a brass cartridge, the whole shell weighing about 60 lb. The guns were dual-mounted and had armoured shields of 1 inch thickness. The frontal shields had box-like 'shoulders' and were part-roofed, to provide some forward, side and limited overhead protection. However, the guns were very open at the rear. There were adjacent ammunition boxes to supply each gun with ready-use ammunition, but further projectiles had to be collected by a handling party from a hatch on the centre-line of the ship. This 'hatch' was fed by an ammunition hoist from the 4" magazine deep down inside *Southampton's* vitals.

Because the gun-shields and the ready-use boxes provided only limited protection for the ammunition handling parties using these hatches, the men were vulnerable to the flying splinters of a 'near miss' of shell or bomb exploding in the sea close to the ship, or to shrapnel or flying *débris* caused by shells or bombs bursting overhead, let alone a shell or bomb direct hit anywhere near their vicinity. In his rank of Commissioned Gunner, it was the starboard battery of these secondary guns for which Alf would become Officer of Quarters (OOQ), reporting to a Gunnery Lieutenant. (The port battery would be manned by the Royal Marines, as was the normal custom.)

Southampton also mounted six 21-inch torpedo tubes, three on the port beam and three on the starboard. So far as is known, she would never actually come to fire these 'tubes' in action although much practice would be carried out with them - to say nothing of the subsequent painstaking efforts to find the torpedoes 'down-range' after practice firings, and, so far as possible, to recover every one of these expensive weapons for reconditioning and re-use.

As indicated in the Table, her armour consisted of a belt of 3 to 4 inches, with 2 inches of deck-armour increasing to 3 inches over some parts of her magazines. Her main turrets had armour of 1 to 2 inch thickness. Her Director Control Tower for the 6" guns had armour of 4 inches thickness.

Southampton had twin aircraft hangars which formed part of the bridge structure, one on each side of the foremost funnel. These hangars, which had steel roller-shutter doors, provided protection against sea and weather for her two '*Walrus*' aircraft, familiarly called 'Shagbats'.[309] Each aircraft was held on a handling trolley which ran from hangar to catapult in a slot in the deck. The aircraft were launched into the air by discharge from the catapult, which was mounted athwartships in a position just abaft the hangars. The catapult had a wheeled trolley (the 'bogey') to which the aircraft was transferred from its handling trolley. The aircraft 'sat' on the bogey-trolley which had

---

[309] She sometimes carried a third aircraft, it being just possible to store two aircraft, with wings folded, in each hangar. When the hangars were empty of aircraft, it was found that they made good 'churches' for divine service in adverse weather (an alternative venue being the officers' bathroom flat). [On ships of this class the hangars also doubled as informal cinemas in which to screen various 'Hollywood epics', often many times around. Such films could provide a welcome break in the tedium when the ships were anchored in remote places, such as Scapa Flow.]

special 'forward releasing gear'. The trolley was propelled along the run of the catapult by means of a clever system of ropes and pulleys which created high acceleration, the motive power being provided by compressed air.[310] Aided by the power from the aircraft's engine at high revs, delivered through its four-bladed 'pusher' propeller, this catapult hurled the *Walrus* forward over the catapult track for a distance of about 90 ft., dramatically accelerating it from inertia to a forward speed of about 65mph at the moment of release. The launch was always a 'hairy moment' and it would be normal practice to have a sea-boat manned on the falls, ready to be slipped immediately on 'search and rescue', should the aircraft and its crew come to grief. (The same safety measure would be applied when an aircraft was being recovered after a flight.)

The aircraft were intended principally for scouting ahead of the fleet, for 'spotting the fall of shot' in a naval engagement, for anti-submarine duties and, sometimes, for transferring ranking personnel from ship to ship, or between ship and shore. [They could carry a small load of bombs or anti-submarine charges for offensive purposes.]

The '*Walrus*' aircraft were amphibious. They were designed to land on quite rough seas, but, if sea conditions were adverse the ship would steam in a tight arc to 'create a slick' of flatter water to assist the aircraft to put down safely. If the aircraft did land on the sea, it would be recovered by means of one or other of two cranes.[311] These cranes were mounted one on each side of the ship's second funnel and were also used to lift the aircraft on to the catapult trolley for the next launch.

The cranes also did general duties in lifting stores aboard, and in hoisting the ship's boats outboard and inboard. (When not in use, these boats were stowed just abaft the second funnel. Even there, it would be found that they were by no means immune to damage in severe gales and they had to be very well secured.)

Single sets of four-barrelled 2-Pdr. Mk M multiple pom-poms were mounted near the aft corners of the hangar roofs, one on the port side and one on the starboard. [In 1941 two Boy Seamen (of whom more later) were amongst the men who had their Action Stations on the starboard mounting. From that lofty position they could observe Alf at his 4" guns on the deck below and forward of them, and would still remember him, some sixty years later.] The ship also mounted two quadruple 0.5 inch machine-guns, one on the port side and one on the starboard.

Southampton was given turbines totalling 75,000 shaft horse-power, and four propellers, giving her a designed speed of just over 32 knots. The ship was powered by four Admiralty-type three-drum water-tube boilers. Each boiler was fitted with superheaters and had a safety load of 350lb per square inch. The superheated steam drove the turbines in Engine Rooms which were adjacent to each Boiler Room, each turbine producing nearly 20,000 shaft horsepower. There was a forward Boiler Room and linked Engine Room which drove the two outer propeller shafts, and an After Boiler Room and Engine Room which drove the two inner shafts. Each of the propulsion units

---

[310] *Southampton's* Log states that she embarked 'catapult ammunition' at one stage. This probably referred to compressed-air 'bottles', but may have related to a 'controlled explosive' alternative.

[311] If putting down at an airfield, the pilot had to remember to lower his landing wheels. Otherwise, significant damage to the '*Walrus*' (and perhaps to its crew) was liable to occur. So far as is known, no such accident through 'lapse of memory' ever befell the aircraft of *Southampton*, but not all the pilots of all the ships of the class could make the same claim. It could become the cause of a lot of 'leg-pulling' for the unfortunate pilots concerned. [As we shall see, every '*Walrus*' aircraft led a quite busy and dangerous life even if its pilot flew it 'by the book' and with the greatest skill and attention.]

received its superheated steam through its own ahead and astern control throttles and consisted of one High-Pressure (HP) turbine working in series with one Low-Pressure (LP) turbine, each driving through a gear-box on to its propeller shaft. The astern turbine was incorporated into the LP turbine, and, for economical speeds, a cruising turbine was also fitted. It was estimated that 32 knots would be attained at 300 shaft rpm.

The ship would carry nearly 2,000 tons of fuel oil. Her economical cruising speed was designed to be 15 knots, to give her a range of 7,350 sea miles.[312] In practice, her most economical speed would be found to be 13.5 knots, at which she consumed only 2.3 tons of oil fuel per hour and thus had a potential range of over 11,000 miles. This would compare with a consumption of 23.7 tons per hour at 'Full Power' (32.86 knots), at which, if maintained throughout the voyage, she would have had the hugely reduced range of only 2,700 miles! [No wonder that (in peacetime) the details of every time-period during which a naval ship ran at significantly more than her 'Economical Speed' had to be entered in a special page of her log, for the signed 'concurrence' (or otherwise!) of a senior Engineer Captain and then for the overall signed 'concurrence (or otherwise!) of the Rear-Admiral of the squadron, and then for forwarding to the Admiralty.[313]]

Southampton had originally been intended to be much smaller - namely a 5,220 ton Arethusa class cruiser, the *Polyphemus*. Similarly, the next of her sister-ships, the *Newcastle*, already nearing completion at Vickers-Armstrong's on the Tyne, was once to have been the *Minotaur* of that same Arethusa class. However, the original building programme had been greatly revised following the overall tonnage restrictions of the London Naval Treaty of 1930. In effect, these two 9,100 ton ships, *Southampton* and *Newcastle* had now replaced what would have been three 5,220 ton Arethusa class ships.

The London Treaty had been secretly flouted by the U.S.A and Japan for some time, and, by 1935 this deception had become an open secret. It was then obvious that the international agreement was virtually in tatters, and, in any case, about to expire. Germany was also disguising the full displacements of its new warships, and it was clear that these three nations were gearing up for the next World War which was already threatening. Consequently, the British were also now ditching the Treaty, which was due for review, they'd already ordered two more Southampton-class ships and four more were now planned, and with at least two more of a modified Southampton class (later to be called the 'Belfast' class) to follow hard on their heels. [It was said that the finished cost of a Southampton-Class ship in 1937 was about £2 million. The post WW1 reductions in defence expenditure were suddenly 'going out of the window' with a vengeance.]

Some critics held that cruisers of the lower displacement of 7,500 to 8,000 tons would have been better for operational reasons. Others held that the new cruisers should have mounted eight 8-inch guns rather than twelve 6-inch. Others claimed that twelve 6"

---

[312] Some authorities quote much the same range at a higher speed. Throughout this book the author has used the ship's logs as his 'primary source'.

[313] *Southampton's* log for July 1937, when she was taking part in some 'war games' exercises with other naval ship and RAF units, would show the exceptional number of 13 days throughout the month where her 'Economical Speed' was exceeded. The 'exceedings' ranged from one hour to 23 hours in duration, at *average* speeds in such intense periods ranging from 13.8 to 23.4 knots. (The overall averages *during these periods* were of 12 hrs at 17.2 knots.). In January 1938 she would display an even greater intensity of 'exceedings'.

were inadequate and that sixteen 6" should have been mounted.[314] However, whatever their critics may have said, the unusual outlines of the *Southampton* class ships, caused by their amidships aircraft hangars and neatly raked funnels and masts, would soon become very familiar in the Navy and their ship's companies would become very proud of them.

Doubtless Alf's previous experience of the Elswick Shipyard on the Tyne, when *Courageous* had been in-building twenty years earlier, stood him in good stead as he arrived at John Brown's Shipyard on 10th December 1935 and picked up his duties as a Commissioned Gunner for Job No.542, soon to become named as HMS *Southampton*. One factor which Alf might well have noted almost immediately was that he could often 'hear himself speak', albeit that he was frequently in danger of being temporarily 'blinded' if he failed to avert his gaze when a 'sizzling sound' was heard. For, unlike in the case of the old *Courageous*, throughout much of her assembly the construction of *Southampton* used arc-welding instead of riveting. This saved hundreds of tons in weight.

Seemingly, relations between 'The Navy' and the John Brown personnel were very good. Perhaps there was the matter that the yard men were appreciative of the fact that shipbuilding was once more on the move, and beginning to accelerate, whereas there had been a terrible financial depression and unemployment in the late 1920s/early 1930s, and many a shipyard man and his family had been suffering considerable deprivations for lack of work. Work on the RMS *Queen Mary*, for example, involving thousands of men, had been stopped in 1931 - with the men being 'laid off' and unpaid - and work had only resumed after an interval of well over a year.

In any case, there was a tradition of good relations between John Brown's and the Royal Navy. Over the years John Brown's had built a goodly share of Britain's dreadnoughts and battlecruisers, including *Inflexible* laid down in 1907, *Australia* in 1910, *Tiger* in 1912, *Barham* in 1913, *Repulse* in 1915 and *Hood* (which since had gone on to become 'the darling of the Navy'), in 1918. [One could also mention that John Brown's had also built the Cunard liner *Lusitania* in 1906 as a forerunner to the splendid RMS *Queen Mary*, now being fitted out.] Throughout, John Brown's had maintained its reputation for building ships of high quality.

Southampton was launched by Countess HADDINGTON on 10th March 1936, with the sparkling mass of the virtually completed RMS *Queen Mary* forming a great background to the celebrations. [Crowds had flocked to see the still boyish-looking and controversial King Edward VIII when he had made a three-hour visit to the *Queen Mary* on the 5th March, just five days earlier and an air of public excitement still prevailed. The superb liner, with her black hull, contrasting white superstructure and black-topped bright

---

[314] Trials had shown that quadruple turrets were unsatisfactory, as the high level of turbulence caused by the close proximity of discharge of the four guns caused the shells to 'wobble' and deviate in flight, and there was a distinct risk of them actually hitting each other. In fact, experience showed that, even with *triple* turrets firing broadsides, 'sensitively-fused' HE shells sometimes exploded immediately on exiting the gun barrels. Hence, 'volley firing' of HE., alternating the firing of the two outer guns with firing the central gun (and having the turrets firing 'out of phase' with each other, so as to deliver equal-sized salvoes) was preferable to 'broadsides' being fired by all three guns of each turret at greater intervals of time. Interestingly, this was in line with old Jacky FISHER's maxim of keeping on hitting the opponent 'as often as possible' during an engagement. Yet, as we shall see, in 1940, at the Battle of Spartivento, *Southampton* and her consorts would fire *AP shells* in full broadsides, insofar as each of them was able.

red funnels, would leave the yard on the 24th March. However, she would not do so without some difficulty, for, despite the extra river-dredging which had been specially done, there was little room for manoeuvring her great length and she touched ground twice before the attendant tugs managed to get her clear and away.* Her maiden voyage from Southampton to New York would take place in August, and, for a time, she would hold the coveted and hotly contested 'blue riband' for the fastest 'international' crossing of the Atlantic. Perhaps her greatest triumphs would take place during the war to come when, time and time again, she would carry thousands upon thousands of troops across the Atlantic Ocean in perfect safety.] *Picture (v) in Appendix J shows her departure.*

Author's collection of inherited family photographs.

A fine shot of the Launching of HMS *Southampton* at John Brown's Shipyard. Note the newsreel cameraman busy on the improvised scaffolding and some of the many men who had been employed in her construction watching closely as she accelerates gently down the slipway to taste the brackish water of the River Clyde.

Southampton was officially completed almost a year after her launching. By that time the basic tests of her equipment would have been sufficiently advanced and acceptable for her Captain to 'sign for her' on her commissioning on 6th March 1937 (of which more presently), but a great many more tests and familiarisation trials of various degrees of sophistication would yet remain to be done and both she and her first-ever company would need to be 'shaken down'. Various members of her complement had been 'standing by' the ship over the months 'from her keel being laid' in 1935 up to early March 1937, just specialist officers of various departments initially, but building up during the second year with officers, WOs and key ratings of varied skills and experience. By the time of her launching it would appear that the officer and WO 'element' of the full team, under her Captain, consisted of at least a Commander (N), a Commander (E), a Lt Commander, two Lieutenants, a Lieutenant (E), a Lieutenant (A), a Pay Lieutenant, a Surgeon Lieutenant, a Commissioned Gunner (*namely, Alf*), two Gunners, a Warrant Engineer, a Warrant Electrician, and a Warrant Telegraphist. The number of experienced ratings would have increased considerably in mid to late February, to 'flesh out' the Navigating Party. However, as the ship sailed from Greenock to Chatham, the company was still 'skeletal' in numbers, being at rather less than 60% of her full complement. It was at Chatham that the great majority of the remainder of her complement would join on her arrival, and the rest soon thereafter. This would make her full complement in excess of 700 men, and her company would increase further in numbers as new items of equipment were added. By late 1939, with the coming of War, she would have over 800 officers and men serving aboard, making her full complement almost the equal of the two largest ship's companies Alf had ever experienced (i.e. around 825 officers and men in 1912 in the Dreadnought *Vanguard* and much the same number in 1916/19 in the (then) battlecruiser *Courageous*.)

Southampton's pre-commissioning speed trials were run off the Isle of Arran.

Author's collection of inherited family photographs.

HMS *Southampton* at high speed during her trials off the Isle of Arran. The men of her Lower Deck aver that she attained over 40 knots, but say the vibration at such a speed was 'terrific'.

Her trials showed that she could cut through the water at considerably more than her designed 32 knots. It was whispered that she actually attained over 40 knots, though the vibration was terrific at that speed, with everything 'trying to jump off the board', much crockery smashed, and so on. If true, this would have been Alf's 'fastest-ever' experience of travelling on a ship through water - the equivalent of about 47 mph on land.

Southampton never attempted to reach such a speed again, though she was no stranger to 33 knots and sometimes attained 35. Her company aver that the other ships of her class simply could not match her speed.[315] One way and another, John Brown's had certainly excelled themselves.

Alf was given a basic report on his personal development, countersigned by L.S.HILL, the Commander Superintendent of Contract Built Ships, which covered the period from 15th December 1935 to 1st November 1936. This simply stated that Alf (incorrectly referred to as '*Albert* W DAVIS') had conducted himself as Commissioned Gunner, '*to my satisfaction*'. It seems convenient to break off for a moment, shortly after the time of issue of this official progress report on Alf's career, to review the changes going on in Alf's *private life*, before resuming the story of Alf and this fine ship, as she was commissioned and entered her naval service proper.

---

[315] In Ronald BASSETT's fine book on HMS *Southampton's* sister ship, entitled 'HMS *Sheffield: The Life and Times of 'Old Shiny''*, it is said that *Sheffield* once attained 38 knots in an emergency, though she suffered some material damage in doing so, aggravated by the adverse sea state at the time.

Private Life

When the time for launching HMS *'Southampton'* drew near, Alf arranged for Alice to come up to Scotland to join him. In the ordinary way of things, one might have expected that he would have arranged for young Neville, as his son, to accompany her. The six year-old boy was of an age to have been thrilled by it all, and the three of them being alone together at such a major event might have developed and improved relationships all round.

However, in the event, Alice took neither Neville nor his elder sister, Joan, but elected to take four-and-a-half year-old Jessica, to whom the launching meant comparatively little. It is *possible* that Alice simply turned up with Jessica, taking Alf completely by surprise. It is more likely that they had a debate about it by telephone beforehand, with Alice refusing point-blank to take young Neville along, for he had been rebelling against her supervision and she would not have wanted to 'reward' him when he had been so disobedient. Moreover, Neville seemed to be going physically downhill in various respects since the death of his birth-mother. Much the same could be said for Alf's elder daughter, Joan, who was also strongly 'rebellious' against Alice's supervision. However, Alf's younger daughter, little Jessica, looked much more amenable and attractive for public display, and it is possible that Alf, perhaps wishing to preserve a 'best image' from a career point of view, simply conceded to the strongly-put arguments of his wife-to-be.

One suspects that Alf may already have experienced at least one quarrel with Alice, which, if she felt she had lost, may well have led her to sulk for a long time afterwards. Long periods of sulking would have been only too familiar to Alf from the past, for a similarly unfortunate trait lurked in his elder sister, Nellie.[316] Both women used this behaviour as a means of exerting power and control. Alf was probably almost desperate to avoid the risk that Alice might sulk and be deliberately ungracious at the launching ceremony, possibly to the detriment of Alf's career.

The author can certainly *still* remember the strong feelings of 'rejection' and disappointment which, as 'Young Neville', he nursed at the time, from his younger sister being taken to the launching and not him. It was a real slap in the face which served to deepen his feelings of loss and estrangement from Alice and his father.[317]

The author has a distant memory of somehow hearing that, almost from the start of his appointment to 'Job No.542', Alf had developed a friendship with a young secretary who worked at John Brown's Shipyard. The secretary was sufficiently young and attractive (if the author's half-memory is correct) to have been the cause of some underlying jealousy and suspicion when Alf's wife-to-be arrived on the scene at the time of the launch, and was duly introduced. (The lady is believed to have been a Mrs Margaret MAYO, who lived in Hillhead, Glasgow.) Outwardly, everything was very friendly between the three of them, but having to leave Alf and return home once the launching was over would surely have added to Alice's fears that Alf, who was very attractive to the female sex in general, was becoming much

---

[316] The author was spontaneously informed of this by Nellie's elder son, Raymond, during a conversation about Ray's memories of Alice.

[317] 'Old Southampton' and former SBA, the late Jack HAWKINS, just took it for granted that the author, then aged 6, would have been at the launching ceremony for his father's ship – and was utterly dumbfounded to learn that this had not been so.

too 'close' to this 'other woman'. Seemingly Alice's suspicions were groundless, but such matters sometimes fester with time and can resurface in future arguments on 'other things'.[318]

The Launching of HMS *Southampton* by Countess HADDINGTON on 10th March 1936. Little Jessica, aged 4½, wearing a white woolly hat and Alice, in black, stand at the extreme left of the above picture. (See close-up picture on left.) As might be expected, Little Jessica appears to be taking little interest in the hymn-singing and the blessing of her father's ship.

The marriage of Alf and Alice Agnes went ahead as planned. Alf's three children were only told about it 'after the event'. They had absolutely no say in the matter whatsoever. The marriage was a discreet affair which took place at Kirton Church, near Martlesham, Suffolk, on 18th July 1936. Alice had chosen this church because it was a favourite of hers and it was located far enough away from Felixstowe to avoid gossip and the unwelcome attendance which might otherwise have transpired from uninvited and curious neighbours.[319]

---

[318] Having been so prompted by Alice, perhaps out of curiosity, Joan (the author's elder sister), who was by that time serving in the WRNS, and on a posting to Scotland, went to see this lady in 1951, finding her to be an attractive woman by then in her early forties.

[319] Although it had become legal for a man to marry his deceased wife's sister as far back as 1908, many people still 'looked snootily sideways' at such a union - perhaps because, all down the years, it had been the accepted thing for an unmarried sister of a dying wife to move in to help in caring for the children of the marriage, and, when the wife passed away, such adult partnerships had often grown far deeper.

<u>Body Language</u>. Nan and Alice seem to be 'far apart'. Perhaps feeling that young Neville is being too harshly treated by Alice, Nan has put an almost defiantly protective arm around him, as she stares at the photographer. Joan (who, in far later years, had a vague memory that she might have just been kicked 'accidentally-on-purpose' by Jess as this picture was being taken) seems to look askance at Nan's arm being round Neville (i.e. rather than it being round herself). Jess, sitting apart, is the only one with any sort of smile for the photographer, who may well be 'Big Neville' (Nan's younger son). Alice, sitting even further apart, looks like the 'odd one out'. The daffodils are in bloom, and Alice and Jess have evidently just recently returned from the launching of HMS *Southampton*, for Jess has the same white hat, and Alice the same coat with dark fur collar and the same dark hat with contrasting white feather, that were worn at the ceremony. This photo was taken shortly before Alice and Alf were married. The stresses were soon going to increase sharply.

Alice's father Joseph Walter attended the wedding and her mother, Agnes Sarah, who still held strongly to her view that Alf and Alice were 'wrong for each other', positively did not. Some friends were invited but, seemingly, none of Alf's sisters or other GREEN family members attended. Indeed, the author's cousin, Raymond PENNEY, has a firm memory that his mother Nellie (Alf's eldest sister) was totally opposed to the union on moral grounds, and, as usual, her two sisters, Rose and Eva, went along with her strong opinion.[320] This may have been a cause of the antipathy which later developed between Alice and Nellie, whereas Olive and Nellie had always got on very well together. It may also have been the case that

---

Clearly, this was very natural, but *totally illicit in the eyes of the Church*, which had forbidden such liaisons. (See the 'Table of Affinities' in the Book of Common Prayer). Any children who were created by such a loving couple were therefore doomed to be illegitimate, at least until the law was changed to permit the parents to marry - and public 'hard nosed' attitudes always die hard even after a relevant change in the law *has* occurred. Indeed, as indicated above, Alf's sisters had very much that same 'conservative' attitude 28 years after the law was changed, and did not attend the wedding.

[320] One also wonders if Nellie might have been quite keen on the idea of adopting Joan, and upset that Alf had chosen to make Alice become Joan's step-mother.

Alice and Nellie were simply too much alike in too many ways, both being very strong-minded women, and both prone to sulk as a means of 'getting their way'.

This lack of relatives attending the wedding hardly seems to have been 'propitious', even if it was conventional in that era for second marriages to be 'low-key' affairs. The marriage witnesses were Alice's father, Joseph Walter GREEN and a certain B.M. MAYHEW, who was possibly the naval officer friend of Alf's, who acted as the Best Man and is probably the smart-looking chap in the following photo who is touching his hat to the bridal pair.

Author's collection of inherited family photographs.

Alfred William DAVIS and Alice Agnes GREEN are man and wife, at Kirton Parish Church, Suffolk, on 18th July 1936. The people here all appear to be friends rather than relatives, though Alice's father did attend and he signed the marriage register as a witness.

There is no question but that Alf would have found that Alice was a very different woman from Olive, his first wife, in a great many important respects. Not that Alf and Alice were strangers to each other. In fact, as stated in an earlier chapter, Alf had first met Alice sixteen years earlier in time. We do not know how far their pre-marital courtship had proceeded following Olive's death. If it had not gone 'all the way', Alf, who was both impetuous and highly sexed, might have been 'buying a bit of a pig in a poke'. Be that as it may, Alf was certainly now committed, and he was about to experience married life with this remarkable woman - already an aunt who was closely involved with caring for his three children and now 'legally formalised' in the role of being their step-mother.

Alice was indeed fine-looking, but she was also a proud woman who nursed that bitterness to which reference has already been made. She was headstrong and she would argue with Alf to get her own way, sulking if she failed. (In the author's opinion Alice's parents had made a bad mistake in stopping her previous wish to marry, for Alice had great strength of character and she was no fool. She may well have seen 'latent promise' in her first true love, which was simply not apparent to others. She may not have felt such a degree of 'romantic love' with Alf, but felt that a 'call of duty' to her dead sister was paramount, and believed all would work out for the best.)

Her parents' earlier attempt to put Alice into a nursing career had totally failed.[321] She had then become a worry to her mother because, although Alice was prepared to act as a shop-assistant in her mother's general stores, Alice could be very impatient, quick-tempered and sharp-tongued to customers hovering around the goods on display 'trying to make their minds up', and Alice's pithy 'urgings' (on the frank principle of *If you don't want the goods don't muck 'em about*") sometimes led to a real risk of upsetting clients and consequent loss of future business as word spread locally about *the rude and surly young woman at the General Stores*'.

Like many women of her day, it was clear that Alice perceived sex in a rather prurient and lavatorial way.[322] Lovemaking would involve her having to 'surrender herself' to Alf.[323] She might therefore have been highly resistant to him at times - whereas Olive had clearly been a warm and willing partner. Sometimes, one suspects, Olive had been quite the 'saucy seductress' and generally she had been very good-humoured, capable, warm and maternal. That maternal nature, one feels,

---

[321] Had Alice been involved in caring for wounded men in a war situation, her strong sense of duty might have carried her through. However, the war was over, and her temperament was not suited to a career in peacetime nursing, for she would have reacted adversely against the overbearing discipline of the traditional Hospital Matron of the 1920s. She would also have been very caustic-tongued to any patient she perceived to be a malingerer and her prurient nature would have given her difficulty in bringing herself to deal with the bodily functions of patients and with such things as infected injuries. It was hardly surprising that Alice and the nursing profession had soon parted company.

[322] In 1942 Neville had a 12 year-old schoolfriend. Around that time this friend had become very ill indeed, and it happened that the friend's mother and Alice were keeping vigil over the boy's bedside. The two women (both by then widows) had fallen into a deeply confidential conversation, both women strongly agreeing that they had not liked having sex with their late husbands. They were blissfully unaware that their young patient was only *feigning* to be deeply asleep, and that he was utterly fascinated and hanging on to every word which was said. The substance of the conversation between the two women was subsequently fed back to the author by his friend. Despite all that was thus reported, the author always felt there was a sort of defiant 'yearning' in Alice, which was evidently never satisfied. Perhaps her young lover had stimulated something in Alice that Alf never really re-awakened. [As a follow-up to this adverse report of 'frigidity', the author had been hugely relieved when Mrs McCLELLAND, a biology teacher at his school, had reassured him that women had the capability to enjoy sex even more than men, and that their climaxes were far more 'earth-moving'.]

[323] Alice died of cancer in 1972. Weeks before she passed away she had told the author and his wife that Alf, dead for almost 30 years, had suddenly appeared to her to and made clear that she would soon be reunited with him in another time and place. The family were called back to the hospital just before her end. When 'Old Man Death' finally came to take her she was far gone from consciousness with only the final citadel of heart and lungs still striving to function. The author and Alice's son Richard were each holding one of her near-lifeless hands. The author is a little 'fey' at times, and he had an overwhelming impression that, despite being *in extremis*, Alice, chest heaving, was still fighting Death 'tooth and nail', as if Death were a lover to whose fatal embrace she was resolved not to yield her body or her mind or soul. [It has to be said that the author's much more prosaic and down to earth younger half-brother Richard evidently had no such impression and, somewhat to the author's astonishment simply wrote in her obituary that his mother 'had died peacefully'. The author, perhaps unwisely, would have written 'fighting heroically to the last gasp'.]

had reminded Alf of his own late mother, and had surely been a large factor in his great and very romantic love for Olive.[324]

Being 'maternal' did not come naturally to Alice, though, to do her justice, work hard at it she did. She also struggled to become a cook, another task for which she was not naturally suited and in which she had to fight for a niche in the wider family household. That is to say, her mother, Agnes Sarah, was a highly skilled cook who had been professionally trained and took great pride in the meals she lovingly prepared with the invaluable but subservient helping hands of her young housemaid Florrie.[325] The mother did not want to 'let go of the reins one little bit', and thus lose a measure of the tight matriarchal control she exerted over the whole family. Hence, the mother always expressed impatience with Alice's efforts and belittled them. This was unfortunate, for Alice's mother would become highly stressed with doing the cooking for eight people (and sometimes for as many as a round dozen), whilst still attending to her busy shop, and was, 'sure as eggs are eggs', a prime candidate for a heart-attack. Deferring some of the cooking load to Alice would have been good for both of them - though it did not even begin to come to pass until the inevitable heart-attacks were running their course with Agnes Sarah years later.

However, before and after Alice's marriage to Alf, there was one weekly task in which Agnes Sarah, Alice and Florrie would all become involved, because it was so labour-intensive and such physically hard work. That was, in doing the family laundry for three children and at least five adults. In those days, to do any 'family wash' was a Herculean task, which always took place on a Monday. The larger the family, the greater the labour.

All the cotton garments, sheets, towels, etc., of the household had to be boiled in a galvanised steel 'copper', the women poking the material around in the sudsy, steaming water with stout wooden sticks, before transferring the washing to a Butler sink to drain and to be rinsed and part-wrung by hand, before putting it through the 'mangle'. This large piece of ironmongery had to be turned by hand, and considerable effort was often required to do so. Woollens and silks, etc., had to be washed by hand in soapy water before being rinsed and gently squeezed. This was all very hard on the hands.

Alice used to wear an unflattering bandana on her head, because, otherwise, the steam always made her hair go 'frizzy'. Hanging out the washing was the next stage, using one-piece wooden pegs bought off the gypsies at that time, because factory manufacture had yet to come into its own. Wire-sprung pegs were still years away. Household soap came in large, long blocks, from which one cut off 'chunks' or 'flakes' according to purpose. Improvements in producing 'soap suds' (the forerunners of detergents), 'Lux' flakes for gentle washing of woollens and silks, etc., etc, had yet to come. An *impression* of 'whiteness' was achieved by 'Reckitt's Blue' bags added to the wash, which otherwise tended to become rather yellowed. Bleach was used as a last resort

---

[324] It may not be a coincidence that their ('Goat/Rabbit', 'Cancer/Scorpio') union was very well-aspected in Astrological terms. [It was not without justification that Agnes Sarah used to say that Olive and Alf would have had 'dozens' of children, had Olive retained her health. Indeed, bearing in mind the little garments which Olive had knitted, the author and his sister Joan wonder if Olive might not have even been pregnant with a *fourth* child but had lost it in the run-up to her death.] In contrast, the ('Goat/Rat', 'Cancer/Leo') union of Alf with Alice, was not well-aspected astrologically.

[325] Prior to her marriage in 1899, Agnes Sarah had been 'in service' as a Cook/Housekeeper at Melford Hall, the seat of the HYDE-PARKER family – a family strong in naval traditions.

Once dried on the line, the sheets and clothes had to be ironed, using heated solid cast-iron 'irons', and then aired, using wooden 'clothes horses', which were left to stand around the house in front of the fires and the oven. This was all a major operation, and there was no time for cooking on 'washdays'. It was therefore 'cold commons' for the family, utilising the remainder of the 'Sunday Joint', perhaps with some pickles and even some boiled potatoes, if one was lucky. That was all part of the laborious domestic scene in the mid-1930s.

Once married, since both Alf and Alice were strong-minded and impatient, both liked to get their own way, and both had quick tempers, arguments could suddenly flare up between them over all kinds of issues. Alf had some redness in his fair hair, and, as often goes with red hair, his temper was one which flashed out but was quickly gone once the crisis was past. As already said, Alice's quick temper, on the other hand, could result in a long period of sullen silence if she were to lose out. (This reserve and sulkiness - almost a melancholia - seemed to be a strong trait found in some individuals of her GREEN family. As a child, and later, as a young teenager, being subjected by Alice and other members of the GREEN family to 'moods' such as this, and sometimes being 'sent to Coventry' for days at a time by Alice, made the author feel like a 'changeling', for his emotions seemed so lively and different from those of the highly reserved elders around him.[326])

Certainly, Alice was proud of Alf, and of the status which he had given her by their marriage. Like Alf, she had a very high sense of duty and she admired and loved him after her own fashion, though it was not the melting and warm love that his first wife had given him - more a contest between two worthy antagonists who, the author believes, sometimes did metaphorically "knock lumps off each other'.

It is more than possible that both Alf and Alice may have derived considerable stimulation from their 'sparring and sparking' of each other, leading to the eventual pleasures of the 'kiss and make up' phase. However, so far as the elder children were concerned, the change in relationship of those who had power over them was daunting. Everything was so different from their past experience, for all had been smooth and even under the subtly clever management of their birth-mother.

The author certainly remembers that he feared he would receive some of the aftermath and 'flak' from the aggression he remembers as being on display, following fierce arguments between Alf and Alice and the 'slamming about' between them. His elder sister's memory does not concur in this regard, and he wonders if her mind has deliberately erased such traumatic and desperately frightening matters for the young children within a family. His younger sister seems to him as if she looks back on it 'with romanticised rose-coloured glasses', again, *perhaps* as an 'escape' from such trauma. (As we shall see, she avoided the punishments her elder siblings often drew upon themselves and this could also have 'coloured the memories' for her.)

---

[326] 'Sent to Coventry' signifying that the person who had 'taken umbrage' would refuse point-blank to talk in any way to the person or persons, who, wittingly or unwittingly, had caused the 'offence' which had been taken. One sometimes literally had no idea why or how the 'offence' had been caused, and, by definition, no explanation would be forthcoming during the period that 'silence' was being moodily imposed. Family members would whisper to each other, asking, "Who's upset her now? Do YOU know why she's giving us all a hard time?", and a blight would be cast over the household until Alice gradually eased back towards normality. It was, of course, a way of imposing selfish power and control over the family. Happily, Alice's moods of deep depression greatly eased as she entered her late middle age.

Alf, photographed at Caldwell Golf Course on Sunday 9th August 1936, and hardly looking like a happily re-married man of three weeks standing. Has he just had a row with Alice? Was he thinking, *"Was Agnes Sarah right to try to stop the marriage? Oh God, have I done the right thing?"*

As so often happens when children are 'fostered', the two elder children resented the new step-mother, all the more so because she had been imposed over them without any form of debate or warning. To have her as an 'aunt' was one thing: to have her as a 'mother' with absolute power over them was something else. As already indicated, they had already started to rebel against Alice, and she now harshly asserted her authority over them, punishing the girl by telling her she was 'useless' and would never amount to anything, and by 'grounding her', and so on, and literally punishing with a heavy hand so far as the boy was concerned: not holding back when she slapped his bottom, on the 'six of the best principle', for his naughtiness and disobedience. As already suggested, it may be the case that Alf had said outright to Alice that he felt that Young Neville had been receiving far too much 'mollycoddling' and needed to be strongly disciplined by her in Alf's absence, to 'pull Young Nev back into line'. Be that as it may, Alice looked to Alf to 'endorse' her punishments, retrospectively, immediately he came home on leave, which he duly did (and with an even heavier hand than hers so far as the boy was concerned).

The elder children therefore had one punishment 'in hot blood', followed weeks or months later by their father's punishment 'in cold blood'. This meant that Alf's homecomings were regarded by his two elder children with mixed feelings, on the one hand with dread of retribution and on the other with excitement at the gifts they might subsequently receive and the wonderful and inspirational excursions they might be taken on by their charismatic and all-powerful father. This was a very 'mixed' message to be giving to young children, the two eldest of whom would each *still* carry in their septuagenarian memories the distinctive sound of their father deliberately and swiftly tapping the end of his 'tailor-made' Navy Cut cigarettes on his smart gilt-metal cigarette-case (to tamp the tobacco down), before putting a cigarette to his lips ready to be lit. The tempo with which he tapped the cigarette could be an indicator of his mood - and perhaps an indicator to his progeny of a punishment soon to come.

There is no doubt that Alf was concerned that young Neville was falling far short of the manly qualities and high standards of honesty and integrity which he desperately wanted to inculcate into the boy, and, as already indicated, Alf did not hesitate to punish his son with a thrashing when he misbehaved or when Alice reported the boy's childish 'crimes' to him. Everything became frantically condensed into Alf's periods of leave: punishment, correction, personal example, motivation, evaluation and modification. All these things in a truly loving but desperate yearning to make his son into 'a perfect man' and to lift him from the deterioration under 'petticoat government' [and 'mollycoddling' by his grandmother] which (Alf believed) each time led the (then) six year-old boy to 'fall back' since Alf's previous period of leave and discipline.

Alf's own hard upbringing, in which he had been expected to help his father in caring for horses and carriages and running errands from an early age, and then, in the aftermath of his own mother's death, and in his spare time from school, having to help out his father in running the Lincoln pub, from age 11 until he 'ran away to sea' at age 15 (initially to an even tougher life), may have added to Alf's frustration with his own son, now rising seven, and considering the 'easy ride' that Alf thought the boy was having. The boy was not responding well to either Alice's or Alf's discipline (Alf's being based on *'Ganges'* lines), and the lad was visibly changing from the bright, cheerful, outgoing five year-old that he had been under his natural mother's loving care to become, under his step-mother's reign, a nervous, rather craven seven year-old child, now wearing unflattering spectacles with magnifying lenses to correct a squint and to rectify his long-sightedness. Alf was also worried about his elder daughter Joan, for she too was by now having to wear spectacles (for short-sightedness in her case) and was also showing physical signs of her unhappiness under her new step-mother. *[Her 'escape' lay in going off in solitary walks along the beach and in reading books and totally 'losing herself' in them. Indeed, the grandmother, who was a natural teacher, encouraged all the children to read books. In many ways this stood them in good stead - but it probably did no good to Joan's eyesight, especially when she read by torchlight at night - and perhaps did no favours to the author's either, in the longer run.]*[327]

Certainly, Alf tried his best to mitigate his punishments and injunctions to these children by bringing them very thoughtful and loving presents when he came home on leave, but the elder children regarded him with ever-greater uncertainty, both being quite alone in their individual fears that his love would suddenly evaporate away in view of his very stern and strict reactions to their misbehaviours. Their earlier and uninhibitedly reciprocated love for him had changed and they now loved, feared and respected him in almost equal proportions.

Only the youngest child, little Jessica, seemed to have bonded with her step-mother and to be confident about her father's love, though Alf, if he had thought hard about it, may well have wondered if this bonding was 'genuine' or simply for 'self-preservation'. Jess scarcely remembered her natural mother. There seems to be little doubt that, as the youngest child, she was desperate to escape from the sort of retribution that she could see the rebelliousness of the older two children was drawing upon themselves. Overtly, she bonded with her step-mother, though she would also seem to side with her elder siblings when Alice was not around. As a boy

---

[327] The author's optometrist considers that the change in the author's eyesight from *long-sightedness* in infancy *to short-sightedness* by age 14 was due to 'hysterical effects' prompted by his father's sudden death, rather than to physiological changes *per se*. (In old age the author's distance vision has greatly improved again.)

the author was of the firm belief that Little Jess had quickly developed amazingly clever skills at turning the tables on her elder siblings and (he believed) in betraying to her step-mother incidents of her siblings' naughtiness, thus gaining Alice's approbation. If the author was correct in that assumption, Little Jessica 'ran with the hare' and 'hunted with the hounds' with the greatest aplomb and impunity. Indeed, if true, clever little Jess! But what high risks of discovery she would have run! This would have created huge stresses in the mind of the very young girl that she then was.

One suspects that Alf and Alice were simply glad that Little Jess was 'responding', no matter how or why, and becoming increasingly desperate to 'pull the other two children round'. Alf was just thrilled that his younger daughter shrieked with pleasure, ran to him and threw herself unreservedly into his arms whenever he arrived home on leave. If only the elder children could be brought back to once again behave in a kindred manner to their little sister.

Now, it was probably in or just before 1937 that little Jessica created a great fuss and panic in the family by claiming that she had accidentally swallowed a little decorative metal ring which had once come from a Christmas cracker. Probably to her great surprise, medical aid was promptly sought. There were no signs that the object had lodged in her mouth, wind-pipe or oesophagus. Medical advice was that little Jessica's stools should be examined day by day, probing them with a small stick as they lay in the small 'white enamel' potty that she was told to use, until such times as it should be found that the object had made its way through the child's alimentary canal and finally emerged into the light of day (so to speak). Jessica's memory is that Florrie, the family maid, was charged with this unenviable task. However, it is strong in the author's memory that Alf was home on leave at the time, and that it was Alf who shouldered this duty, though, clearly, somebody else – perhaps Florrie - would have had to pick up the duty after Alf's period of leave had expired. *If* the author is right about Alf being involved, little Jessica was gaining her magnificent father's devoted watching over her, and that in a <u>big way</u>! [328] The repugnant 'stool-search' went on for many days before being eventually and uneasily abandoned. The object was never found.[329] One wonders if Alf ever began to suspect that he might have been 'had' by his youngest child. His high pride might well have made him outwardly reject any such idea, but internally it might have been a

---

[328] Nev and Jess are agreed that Alice avoided this rather unpleasant task. Indeed, she may well have refused point-blank to do it. As suggested earlier, dealing with human functions was not a matter which she enjoyed.

[329] There can be but little doubt that all three of Alf's elder children were psychologically damaged by the loss of their birth-mother and that the damage was aggravated by the need to adjust to a step-mother of a totally different personality. Certainly, the author is deeply conscious of the adverse effects which were wrought in his own *psyche* throughout this difficult time. In 1937, the author (who was then rising 8 years old) had the impression that his younger sister had just been 'flying a metaphorical kite' and attention-seeking when she said that she had swallowed the little ring. At that moment it seemed to him that Jess was taken totally aback by the extreme reactions of Alf and Alice, and by their immediate calling in of the Doctor. The author had felt at the time that Jess had wanted to 'come clean' but simply did not dare to say it was all a big fib. To do so would have been to risk the sacrifice of her privileged position with Alice as the only 'non-troublesome' child, and she might well have lit the 'blue touch-paper' so far as the 'rocket-reactive' temperament of her father was concerned. He did NOT like being made to look a fool, especially where his relationship with somebody of standing, such as a G.P. was concerned. IF the author's childhood memory is anywhere near correct, the traumatic effects on young Jess's *psyche* at having to hold her nerve in such a terrible crisis during her most formative years can only be imagined.

different matter. He certainly did not lack for shrewdness and common sense: after all, he had decades of experience of matelots long-skilled at 'Shooting a Line'.[330]

Overall, it is scarcely surprising that, as time went on, the two elder children were finding their step-mother increasingly oppressive and explosive, almost as if she were desperate to bring them under total control so that she could demonstrate her success to Alf in at least one area of their lives, when he next came home on leave. Neither child was old enough to appreciate the difficulties with which their step-mother was beset. Lost in their own individual traumas of the breakdown of all that had been happening to their formerly wonderful world, and unaware even of the 'fellow-suffering' of their siblings, each child suffered in lonely isolation.[331]

The two elder children and perhaps little Jessica, too, (albeit that she might nowadays deny it) perceived their step-mother more or less as an avenging 'Troll' at that stage of their lives. It would take many years for that perception to radically change, and for sympathy for her to well up (despite some more bitterly 'hard knocks' from her), *eventually* turning to genuine love in the case of the author of this book and possibly for others of his siblings. However, that was all in the future.

At this early period of their lives, to a considerable extent, the three children turned to their maternal grandparents for the love and attention they naturally craved.[332] As has been said, Agnes Sarah, their grandmother, generally known as 'Nan', was love personified, making each child feel that she was there for him or her alone. Agnes Sarah's own birth-mother had died in 1875, when Agnes Sarah was only 15 months old, and her step-mother had been cold and non-maternal. The one son by the second marriage had been passed on to Agnes Sarah, as soon as she, his elder half-sister, was anywhere near old enough to care for him, and she was still

---

[330] Telling tall stories, often to try to get out of trouble.

[331] It was only in late middle age that the author discovered that his elder sister was going through parallel emotions to his own. This came about when he read a very evocatively-worded short story written by his elder sister, who, though as yet 'unpublished', has the great gift of story-writing. In the story she was describing the state of abject terror in which she had found herself one evening in 1937, whilst awaiting the return home of her step-mother. That is to say, she knew she was inevitably going to be severely punished for some little childish 'sin of omission', regarding a duty not done. In the story, little Jessica is playing happily and unconcernedly, and little Neville, aged seven, is calmly scoffing his 'Force' cornflakes, whilst she, in stark contrast, is suffering in lonely mental torment.

The only thing that the 'grown-up Neville' found wrong with his elder sister's short story was that it was not so much his elder sister who had been in the state of abject terror, *but he himself*, for some 'crime', not of omission, but one that he had 'inevitably' *committed*. (Thinking particularly of when he and a school-friend had egged each other on to devour 'a couple' of the simply scrumptious 'fairy cakes' which his grandmother had pulled out from the oven and set aside to cool on an open baking tray. The first illicit cake had led to the next, and then to the next, and so forth, until far too many had 'disappeared'. By no means unjustifiably, Neville had been memorably thrashed by both his step-mother and later (in 'cold blood') by his furious and even heavier-handed father, for that particular crime of greed.)

[332] They also looked to Florrie, the young Domestic Maid, for a certain sort of 'understanding and comradeship'. She occupied a little corner of the heart of Young Neville (who, as stated earlier, from a very early age had lusty feelings and vivid memories of seeing flashes of Florrie's white thighs, contrasting vividly with her black knickers and black 'Lisle' stockings.) A little later in his young life he was very disturbed and upset to find the stark poverty and primitive conditions in which Florrie was by then living as the wife of a rural labourer - so different for her from working and living in his grandmother's well-appointed home. This situation, and then, when he was six, hearing a small crowd gathered around the holiday residence at Felixstowe of the woman whom King Edward VIII madly adored, all lustily singing "*Hark the Herald Angels Sing - Old Ma SIMPSON's pinched our King!*", were young Neville's first real brushes with matters 'socio/political'.

doing so nearly 50 years later, for he (by then an unmarried 'Old Soldier') was back living in the matriarchal household which she had so lovingly and painstakingly maintained after her marriage. She had managed to create this matriarchal haven by marrying a half-starved young carpenter from a poverty-stricken young family, and backing her talented young man to the hilt in setting up a carpentry and decorating business.

[The household from which the young carpenter had come had been fortunate indeed to have its own determined 'Little Mother', called Alice Annie GREEN. She was a devoted elder half-sister of the young carpenter, and she was desperately struggling against the odds to run a greengrocery business, their artistically talented and 'house decorator turned beer-house keeper' father having simply 'given up on life' after he had suffered the second of his life's appalling 'hammer-blows'. That is, his first wife, Susannah, had (it is believed) gone utterly insane after bearing three fine children and had apparently been put into an asylum, and then his second union, with young Maria HANNANT had ended prematurely, after she had rebuilt his life and given him four fine children. Her terrible death from cancer of the eye-socket and mouth, ending with three long days of convulsions, finally 'broke his heart' and took away his will to live, leaving his eldest daughter to struggle on through the 1880s in raising all the other children as best she could under extremely deprived conditions.]

Agnes Sarah not only encouraged all her grandchildren to read books, but she would tell them romantic tales of ancestral family figures, clearly well-based on fact, even if somewhat garbled in the telling. [Indeed, since 1985 the author has used the little of what he still remembers of these 'family legends' as the initiating bases for much of his extensive family history research.]

The grandfather, a veteran gunner from the Great War, had a comfortingly soft Suffolk accent and language which was rich in both Suffolk dialect and in an "Old Soldier's" slang. When some delicate piece of carpentry split as he worked to chisel it to shape, he could swear better and longer than any man the author has ever met, not using 'basic terms' so much as ripe old rolling Suffolk swearwords from centuries back in time. Like his Uncle Neville before him (who was Agnes Sarah's youngest surviving child, by then turned 20), 'Little Neville' would creep quietly up to the open doorway of the old man's shed to listen in the greatest admiration to the colourful invective pouring forth on such occasions.

Grandpa GREEN, as he was called, taught the children to play Cribbage, and, to the children's delight, he would use WW1 'military phrases' such as '*A soldier's breakfast*' (when he had 'nothing' to declare as his score), and he would also slip in rather corrupted French phrases, often somehow linked with a half-sung, '*Mademoiselle from Armentieres, Parlez-Vous?*' He also taught the children to play Dominoes, puffing his pipe the while and coughing gently in a sort of mutter nearly all the time, due to the lung-damage he had received from German gas during WW1. The air was always full of the pungent whiff from the 'Swan Vestas' matches he was forever striking to re-light his pipe. He would sometimes doze off with the pipe in his mouth and the children were always fascinated that it never fell from his mouth, even when he would begin to snore gently.

He was a very fine, handsome man, who taught young Neville how to use carpenter's tools, provided him with small-sized versions of his own man-sized ones and made a handsome wooden tool-box for the boy to keep them in. Indeed, in a way he became a 'surrogate father' as well as grandfather to the boy, showing by quiet example that a gentler version of 'fatherhood' could exist than the more ambitious and quick-tempered 'parenting and disciplining' that Alf used. The boy's grandmother augmented Neville's collection of tools by adding old items from her side of the family, for her father had also been a carpenter, as had his forbears, and the boy thus began to develop practical woodworking and decorating skills and knowledge from an early age.

As indicated earlier, the grandparents used to have 'musical soirées' with their friends, when Old Soldiers, some disabled, who had somehow survived the holocaust and carnage of the trench warfare of WW1, used to have sing-songs and give recitals of lugubrious monologues, such as a night watchman's tale called *"A'Guarding the Hole in the Road"*, and the celebrated *"Albert and The Lion"*. These evenings were invaluable for the children's understanding and relationships with wonderful people of an older era.

Their uncles on their maternal side were important figures. As stated earlier, Uncle Joe and his wife Dilys, who had been the godparents (by proxy) at Joan's baptism in Capetown in 1927, had an only son called Thomas Colin Hannant GREEN. And, as already said, Joe and Dilys used to make the long drive from Swansea to Felixstowe every year or so. Their visits were always important occasions. Agnes Sarah had great admiration for her clever son Joe who was having a very successful career with the Anglo-Iranian Oil Company. His son, 'Young Colin' and 'Young Neville' got on well during these fleeting visits.

Uncle Neville, who was one of Young Neville's godparents, was 16 years younger than his sister Alice and still single. He seemed to be on a quite different emotional and mental wavelength to the children, being very reserved, trying to impress rather 'loftily', with his 'book learning', and, outwardly, quite unemotional. At base, however, he did try very hard to be something of a 'surrogate father' when Alf was absent. Uncle Neville had a lively auburn-haired girl-friend from his school days. He would marry this girl in 1941, bringing an 'Auntie Constance' fully into the family circle. She would have a profoundly balancing and good influence on the children. Indeed, she was already taking the three children out for walks along the 'prom', and at age just 19, somewhat to her chagrin and embarrassment, was often being congratulated by passing elderly ladies on 'her three lovely children', the oldest aged eight!

Alice would always remain as 'Auntie' Alice and never became 'Mummy' or 'Mum' to the three children - that term was considered to be just too sacrosanct and special. Interestingly, Alf never rebuked the children for not calling Alice their 'Mother' - and one might add that the mother of Olive and Alice positively fostered Alice being called just 'Auntie' by her step-children. The whole situation was rather hard all round. In retrospect, the children *should* have been gently coaxed to call Alice 'Mum', for that expression has colossal significance in life. It is also sad that Alice never managed to create a *foyer* in which any of her step-children – not even young Jessica - were inspired to spontaneously call her 'Mum' or 'Mother'.[333]

From an adult perspective one can feel much sympathy for Alice. The fact that the memory of her deceased sister was raised to almost saint-like levels by the children's grandmother must have been extraordinarily difficult and frustrating for Alice, though she always 'did her duty' as best she could, even if sometimes through a mist of hot temper and bitterness. She too would have needed to grieve for her

---

[333] Though, very happily, the fond name *'Nanny Felixstowe'* did come about, for some of the next generation (the author's children), in the late 1960s.

dead younger sister, for they had clearly been good friends, going out together to social events, shopping together and so on. In their youth, Olive's loveliness, light-heartedness and popularity would have bonded well with Alice's classic good looks and almost chaperone-like and protective presence. Olive's loss must have deeply undermined Alice's life. Yet matters conspired to keep cutting across Alice's needs to reflect upon and to come to terms with her sister's sad demise, let alone the whole psychological business of having married her late sister's charismatic husband - and clearly finding the marital relationship so very different to the wonderful affair that she had surely perceived her sister's union with Alf to have been. Things were not working well.

Increasingly, though he remained dominant and inspirational to the whole family circle whenever he was home on leave, the author has come to believe that Alf was turning to his naval life as his main solace. Here Alf was confident of his own position and responsibilities in a controlled world, where people would faithfully follow orders - or stand to be severely punished should they fail to do so. He still looked forward to going home, but the complexities of the human relationships at home were so great that, before his leaves were up, it is believed he was often keenly looking forward to getting back to the straightforwardness and comradeship aboard his brand-new ship and to playing his full part in the interesting tasks she was being called upon to perform. Then, whilst he was at sea, the more idealised aspect of his family would gradually reform itself in his mind, and his innate love for them would surface strongly by the time of his next leave. He would cast about for interesting and loving gifts to buy for them, he would talk enthusiastically about them with his shipmates, and the whole cycle would then recommence.[334]

Ever since the unhappy business over the late Alfred Wm's Will in 1926, all contact with Alf's brother Jack was now terminated. However, it should be recorded that Jack and Kate had continued to bring daughters into this world, with Barbara, born 31st October 1932, Shirley, born 2nd February 1935 and Patricia, born 15th March 1937. Seven daughters and still not a son in sight! One wonders if Jack blamed Kate for not giving him a son, as would have been the thought-process in those days.

Over this period of time from 1930-37, Jack's occupation had been initially that of Pricing Clerk, then a Shop Assistant, then a Tobacco Worker. In later years he would become a Docker. It would seem that he was not good at holding down jobs and perhaps his gambling proclivities were against him, though he did keep his family fed and a roof over their heads. One suspects he would always suffer from his hard upbringing and, especially, his traumatic experiences in the 1914-18 war. One notable fact was that he brought his daughters up 'with a rod of iron'. Both he and Alf clearly believed in 'tight discipline'.[335]

---

[334] It was at about this period that Alf persuaded one of *Southampton's* sailmakers to provide a new suit of sails for a rather large model yacht. (This yacht had generously been handed down to Young Neville by his Uncle Neville, ready for being taught to sail her on the fine Yacht Pond at Felixstowe, where model vessels were sailed by the young in heart of every age.) The sailmaking job was extremely well done, with beautiful ribbing on the two jibsails, the topsail and the mainsail, and with new blocks for the yards. The re-rigging of the yacht was a loving and sensitive gift for the boy by his charismatic father.

[335] It is a matter of great regret to the author that Jack had passed away by the time that the author had traced the family, so that the author never met his Uncle Jack face-to-face.

Perhaps this was a 'throw-back' to the way in which they had been raised by their father, Alfred Wm., probably greatly augmented by the tightly disciplined lives that Jack and Alf had each led in the armed services, and not least by their respective leadership roles as Sergeant and Gunner.

Meantime, Alf's three sisters continued to run their London pubs, each with the aid of her husband. These three ladies were swiftly becoming 'Londoners' in manner and accent, as if 'to the manner born', and showing few signs of their earlier raising in Ireland and Lincolnshire. Nellie was still the dominant sister, and becoming quite "well to do" in her style of living and mannerisms.

HMS *Southampton* (1935-38), continued.

Southampton was commissioned at Greenock on the River Clyde at 1620 on 6th March 1937 for service with the 2nd Cruiser Squadron, Home Fleet, under the command of Captain A.M. PETERS DSC RN. [It may be recalled that Captain PETERS had been Alf's captain when he had served in HMS *Delphinium* from 1931 to 1933.]

A postcard by Sellicks of Plymouth, dating from 1937, and inherited from Alf's collection.

On the back of this card Alf had written: "HMS *Southampton* commissioned for service March 6th 1937." It appears that the barge and its crew in the foreground are part of *Southampton's* complement. The two-badge 'Stripey' has a proud half-smile on his face.

Southampton weighed and proceeded later that same day of 6th March for Chatham, reaching Sheerness on 9th March and entering No.3 Basin at Chatham at 1045 on the 10th, after a run of 850 miles. During that run she had practised various evolutions, such as swinging the ship (for adjustment of her DF gear), steering from all possible conning positions, dropping a Dan buoy and manoeuvring the ship to re-embark it, then going on to steering by hand, and so on. Much more was now to come by way of 'shaking down' exercises.

A bag of mail for the Commodore's office was embarked on the 11th, being something of a token that the ship was coming into full service. She now began to expand her company, and, on that same day of 11th March, one CPO, 21 POs, 158 ratings and 4 ERAs joined the ship. So, too, what must have been virtually her full complement of Royal Marines, consisting of Captain YOXHAM and Lt TWEED RM, and 54 of their men, accompanied by one Band Major and 15 Marine bandsmen. [Moreover, Lt-Commander TINLEY RN and Lt-Commander SHATTOCK RN would join during the next week. They would be followed by Lt-Commander BROCK, five Midshipmen, and 14 more ratings before the month was up.]

This totals 278 men, and signifies that her 'navigating party' had formed only about 60% of her standard complement when she made her initial run from the Clyde to Chatham. Her company, including Alf, albeit doubtless proud of that responsible 'status', might have been feeling just a little hard-worked in the run up to commissioning.

Author's collection. An anonymous postcard c.1936.

HMS *Southampton*, photographed at Chatham, probably on her arrival there for the first time on 10th March 1936. She has the elegant appearance of being 'brand new'.

On the 15th March the C-in-C made a short official visit to HMS *Southampton*. Then the Admiralty 'Ventilation Committee' were led on board by Admiral CUNNINGHAM on the 19th March, and stayed for an hour and a half.[336] Meanwhile, provisioning of the ship was in progress and torpedoes were being embarked. Ten cases of 'catapult ammunition' were also embarked at this period.

There was a flutter of excitement on the 28th March when the Foremost Funnel Cover was found to be on fire and the Fire Party were mustered on the Pom-Pom Deck to deal with it.

On 1st April, 6,000 gallons of petrol was embarked from a lorry, all ports forward of 53 Bulkhead on the Port side being closed for safety reasons whilst this refuelling was in progress. At 1700 Quarters was exercised and this was followed by the routine of practising Fire Stations. The latter would have been done under Alf's eagle eye, as he

---

[336] It seems that the great importance of proper ventilation in ships had begun to be taken seriously – some might have said 'at long last'. The fact that a warship has to be 'closed down' into watertight sections when going into action, and the need not to reduce the strength of transverse bulkheads by 'piercing' them for the passage of ventilating ducting, meant that each main section needed its own separate system of ventilation, and separately powered fans, to take in and drive fresh air throughout the related ducting – and to collect and vent out the stale air.

was OOW from 1700 that day, apparently for the first time since the ship had been commissioned. This would have been a very proud day for him.

On 4th/5th April, aircraft stores were embarked, the hands were employed on the flight deck for equipment trials (presumably of the catapult and related mechanisms), and two LACs and three ACs temporarily joined the ship from the RAF, all in preparation for the embarkation and flying of her aircraft.

On 6th April the ship topped up her bunkers with oil, ready for going to sea. On the 7th Admiral Superintendent Rear Admiral C.F.S DANBY CB, RN inspected the ship and the ship's company, (perhaps, in part, to reassure himself that his dockyard had done a satisfactory job and to familiarise himself with this new type of cruiser) and, on 8th April at 0800, momentously, the flag of Rear Admiral T.F.P. CALVERT CB, CVO, commanding the 2nd Cruiser Squadron, was broken. Since the ship's complement was now virtually up to strength, we should take a look at the officers and warrant officers who would serve on the flagship during the opening phase of Captain PETER's command, and who by now included most of the following:-

NAME	RANK	MONTH JOINED	MONTH LEFT
PETERS, A.M.	Captain	Mar 1937	Dec 1938
Le MESURIER	Commander	Mar 1937	January 1938
DIXON	Commander	Jan 1938?	Jul 1938
NICHOLS, R.F.	Commander (N)	Pre-Mar 1937?	Dec 1937?
EDMONSTONE	Lt Commander	Pre-Mar 1937?	Apr 1940
BROCK	Lt Commander	Mar 1937	1938
COLLEY, D.B.	Lt Commander	Pre-Mar 1937?	Dec 1938
SHATTOCK	Lt Commander	Mar 1937	?
TILNEY	Lt Commander	Pre-Mar 1937	Dec 1939
TINLEY, C.B.	Lt Commander	Mar 1937	DoW, Jan 1941
BARLOW, N.A.H.	Surg Commander	Mar 1937	Dec 1939
YOXHAM	Captain RM	Mar 1937	?
NICHOLLS, P	Lt (N)	Mar 1937	April 1939
BLISS, P.M.	Lt	Pre-Mar 1937?	Jun 1939
CAIRNS	Lt	Pre-Mar 1937	Jul 1938
ELLMERS, P	Lt	Mar 1937	?
FEARFIELD	Lt	Pre-Mar 1937?	Dec 1938
MOWLAM	Lt	Mar 1937	Dec 1937
NICKOLAY	Lt	Mar 1937	?
BENNETT	Lt (A)	Pre-Mar 1937?	Sep 1938
BEST	Lt (E)	Pre-Mar 1937?	Aug 1940
BOTT, A.H.	Lt (E)	Pre-Mar 1937?	Sep 1938
THOMSETT	Lt (E)	Pre-Mar 1937?	Aug 1940
DUNN	Pay Lt	Pre-Mar 1937?	Jun 1939
SILVESTER, H.G.	Surg Lt	Pre-Mar 1937?	Sep 1938
TWEED, D.W.	Lt RM	Mar 1937	Oct 1938
MADDEN, C	S/Lt	Mar 1937	Jun 1938
GRAHAM, R.H	S/Lt	Mar 1937	1937
HOATH	S/Lt (A)	Pre-Mar 1937?	Apr 1939
HALL	Midshipman	Mar 1937	Dec 1937
HEIGHTON	Midshipman	Mar 1937	Dec 1937
JOHNSON	Midshipman	Mar 1937	Dec 1937

KEYES, The Hon R.G.B	Midshipman	Mar 1937	Dec 1937
RABAN-WILLIAMS, J	Midshipman	Mar 1937	Pre-Jan 1939
SHANNON	Midshipman	Mar 1937	Dec 1937
STEINER, O.S.J	Midshipman	1937	c.1938
DAVIS, Mr A. W.	Commissioned Gunner	Pre-Mar 1937	KiA, Jan 1941
PLAYER, Mr H C	Commissioned Gunner	Mar 1937	KiA, Jan 1941
SEMMENS, Mr	Commissioned Gunner (T)	Mar 1937	Aug 1937
KOESTER, Mr L	Gunner	Pre-Mar 1937?	DoW, Jan 1941
ALEXANDER, Mr	Gunner?	Pre-Mar 1937?	?
TURNER, Mr R.D.	Gunner	Mar 1937	Dec 1937
REES, Mr F.P.	Bandmaster RM	Mar 1937	Jan 1941
NOAKES, Mr	Warrant Electrician	Pre-Mar 1937?	May 1938

Names with 'Pre-Mar 1937?' against them were never shown in the ship's log as 'joining'. It is assumed they were officers and WOs who, like Alf, were appointed to the ship for her 'acceptance trials' *before* she was commissioned.

The above list is almost certainly short of two Warrant Engineers, a Warrant Telegraphist, and maybe three or four others. This would make the true TOTAL about 50 officers and WOs. [See also the lists on pages 534, 628 and 661 showing the officers and WOs serving in the ship under her future captains, and also the Master List in APPENDIX C, page 700, for the names of all officers and WOs known to have served aboard at some period during the life of the ship.]

In the normal manner of naval procedures in regard to transfers and promotions, etc., most of the officers and WOs shown in the above table would leave during the next year or two, but five (shown in **bold** type) were *still* serving aboard *Southampton* when the ship was lost, on 11th January 1941. During the four years which had by then elapsed, those five men would have come to know each other very well indeed. Extremely close ties certainly developed between the three long-serving 'Gunners', Alf DAVIS, Harry PLAYER and Lewis KOESTER. Note that Bandmaster REES was the only one of this five who would survive the traumatic end of the ship, in January 1941. A further four 'long-stayers' appear in the next list on Page 534.

It seems appropriate to mention at this stage that during her early life *Southampton* was given a ship's badge of a castle of gold out of which appears Her Imperial Majesty Queen Elizabeth I, holding in her right hand the Sword of Justice and in her left the Balance (or scales) of Equity. The associated motto was: "*Pro Justicia - Pro Rege*". [The badge had been derived, with appropriate permissions, from the Heraldic Civil Armorial of the Port and Town (later city) of Southampton, this award having been originally granted to the ancient town by the Monarch of the Realm way back in the Year 1575.][337]

Later on the 8th April 1937, Rear-Admiral CALVERT of the 2nd Cruiser Squadron (generally referred-to in her Log as 'CS 2') having come aboard, hands fell in for leaving harbour and the ship then proceeded downstream, securing to No.1 Buoy. Whilst she was there, a succession of lighters came alongside and much ammunition was embarked over the next two days, together with further provisions - to say nothing of the car of Admiral CALVERT. The troops had by now nicknamed their new admiral as '*Tubby*' CALVERT. (They had presumably done so well behind his back for he was reckoned to be quite a martinet for discipline.)

Later still on the 11th, the tug HMS *Firm* secured astern, and the ship was 'swung' to check her 'Magnetic Variation'. On 12th April the ship proceeded to Spithead, dummy aerial attacks being made on her on the following morning as an exercise, with 'Torpedo-

---

[337] The Author is indebted to the late Lt-Commander Freddie DANCE RNR for this information.

Bombers', striking at 0800 and again at 0920.[338] The ship varied her speed and course, and increased from 13 to 20 knots at times, to avoid their 'assaults'. At 1100, on arrival, the ship saluted the Flag of the C-in-C Portsmouth with 17 guns, then carried out a further DF calibration exercise and moored overnight, having run 183 miles since they left Chatham. Next day they proceeded the 95 miles to Portland, exercising 'Abandon Ship' stations and 'Out Collision Mat', whilst *en route*. Next morning they put their 4" fuse-setters to drill. *Southampton's* newly-commissioned sister-ship, HMS *Newcastle*, arrived early that evening and, at 1828, saluted the Flag of CS 2 with 13 guns, *Southampton* replying with 7 guns. *Newcastle* then became a part of 2nd CS. A smaller cruiser and another 'sister-ship' of *Southampton* would be joining the 2nd CS ere long.

During the next few days *Southampton* and *Newcastle* conducted various exercises, making the relatively short runs from Portland to Torbay, from Torbay to Weymouth Bay, back to Torbay, back to Portland and sometimes going for some distance out to sea between-times. The two cruisers exercised their searchlight and HA armament, exercised Collision stations, carried out Turning Trials, and, on the 26th April, whilst out at sea, they carried out manoeuvres which included a sub-calibre shoot with their 6" guns, the ships taking it in turn to fire and to mark the fall of each other's shot.

Whilst at Portland, on 30th April, the hands were busy painting ship, concentrating on the turrets and screens to bring them up to a state of glossy perfection, whilst the ship landed her special 'Guard' and her 'Royal Marine Platoon'. The latter were busily rehearsing that day for the impending Coronation of Their Majesties King George VI and Queen Elizabeth, for, whilst *Southampton* had been in her fitting-out stage, the Nation had been going through a long period of debate and divided loyalties surrounding the romantic activities of the as yet uncrowned King Edward VIII, who had inherited the title (amongst others) of 'Defender of the Faith' but scarcely seemed to understand the need to 'set an example of being a man of overt Christian morality and sobriety'.

As indicated in an earlier note, his reign had been brought to a crisis by his relationship with a married American woman, Mrs SIMPSON, and his ardent desire to marry her, which had overshadowed many other important world events. The *"King's Moll"* had now been *"Reno'd in Wolsey's Home Town"*, as an American newspaper so pithily put it.[339] However, marriage of the 'Defender of the Faith' to a divorced woman was not acceptable to the majority of Parliament and the nation, and this eventually forced Edward VIII's Abdication from the throne. Now, with relief in many hearts, and a sense of loss of what (they believed) the 'might have been' in others, the Nation looked to a new and little-known replacement King who was handsome enough but had none of the 'boyish charm' of his elder brother. Instead, King George VI had a severe stammer in his speech when he broadcast to his people and he looked embarrassingly *gauche* when he appeared on a newsreel film of a Scout Jamboree, miming and singing *'Under the Spreading Chestnut Tree'*. Still, at least this King and his Queen, and their two young princesses looked refreshingly 'normal' as a family unit.[340]

---

[338] It is assumed that the entry 'TB planes' in the Ship's Log signifies 'Torpedo-Bomber' aircraft.

[339] i.e. Divorced in Ipswich, which is why she had been temporarily resident in nearby Felixstowe.

[340] The Author can well remember listening intently to Alf and other family members having quiet 'adults only' discussions of some of the rumoured 'goings-on' amongst other members of the wider Royal Family, and of the apparently indiscreet relationships of various of 'The Royals' with Hollywood Film Stars and other celebrities. The other adult DAVIS/GREEN family members generally deferred to Alf's superior information and 'service knowledge' of such matters.

Meantime the World appeared to be heading inevitably towards a second World War and general expenditure on defence was beginning to increase, though the strong 'Pacifist Movement' was still strongly opposed to any such action. A certain Winston CHURCHILL was regarded by many of the British population as a dangerous warmongering antediluvian, refusing to let sleeping dogs lie, being alarmist, interfering with the proper processes of government and stirring up problems quite unnecessarily.[341] Yet there were many others, including a goodly proportion of Naval Officers, who were ardently hoping that 'Winston' would somehow be able to get back into a position where he would have a strong hold towards increasing Defence expenditure and improving matters to do with the Admiralty in general.

Still, let's revert to Alf and the ship. The rehearsals of *Southampton's* Guard and RM Platoon were continued ashore on 3rd May. The night of 3rd/4th May was fogbound, and the ship's Fog Bell was rung continuously from midnight to mid-afternoon as a warning to other shipping of their presence. The rather mournful and monotonous sounds of other ships' bells would have been heard faintly all around. Evidently the fog was patchy but lingered around, for the Port After Ladder was damaged by *Osprey's* steam launch at 1970, and *Southampton's* 1st Motor Boat had to be hoisted inboard at 2315 following damage it had received from accidentally hitting a buoy. [In these days of Radar and 'Clean Air Acts' it is sometimes hard to remember the stresses and strains put upon ships' companies as they fumbled their way blindly around in thick blankets of fog years ago.]

At 0731 on 6th May, *Southampton* took station six cables ahead of the 2nd Battleship Squadron, and the ships proceeded to Gravesend, joining the Home Fleet visit to the Thames as part of the Coronation festivities for King George VI and Queen Elizabeth. By arrangement on that day of departure from Portland, there was an 'aircraft exercise' (evidently consisting of further dummy attacks on the ships), commencing at 1000 and continuing until 1830. The ships reached Gravesend in the darkness of night at 0050 on the 7th. Whilst at anchor at Gravesend, on Saturday the 8th, a Fog Watch had to be set from 0150 to 0245, but the day improved and the ship was open to visitors from 1330 until 1800. Wednesday the 12th was Coronation Day, the assembled ships being dressed overall from 0800, firing a Royal Salute of 21 guns at noon, and celebrating by taking Dinner and 'Splicing the Mainbrace' at 1210.

The hands were then set free for the rest of the day (to 'Make and Mend Clothes' as Naval Tradition has it), the ship being opened to visitors from 1330 to 1800, and then darkened but with her outlines brightly illuminated by 'festoons' of lights, from 2130 to midnight. [The rest of the assembled ships did likewise with their lights, making a very spectacular scene.]

---

[341] *At that time*, whilst feeling that CHURCHILL usually had good points to make, adult conversations in the DAVIS/GREEN ménage always seemed to revolve around CHURCHILL's celebrated and successful dash for freedom after being captured by the enemy in the aftermath of the 'Armoured Train Affair' in the Boer War of 1899-1902. The question always asked was whether or not he had given the Boers *his parole* not to try to escape. i.e. Was he or was he not 'a true gentleman'. This was regarded as an important question, for how much trust, the family asked, could one place in any man who *might* have once broken his solemn word? The question never seemed to be answered, one way or the other. However, events yet to unfold, would prove answer enough for the family to savour from the immensely brave and spirited 'Old Bulldog'.

Next morning, the 13th, the hands unrigged the illuminating circuits, the Coronation Guard and Band returned from shore, the awnings were furled and the ship proceeded to sea at 1430, bound for Spithead. At 1155 she took her allotted station five cables astern of HMS *Furious*. [Alf had probably glimpsed *Furious* off Portland on 24th November 1925, but this would have been his first chance to study at close quarters what was now a 'full-blooded' aircraft-carrier rather than the strange battlecruiser with just one massive aft-mounted 18" gun and a small hangar and flying-off deck mounted forrard, which he would have remembered from the 1918-1919 period.] Now, as the fleet neared the end of its 200 mile run, the lines of its ships 'shaped course and speed', and each ship navigated to take up its 'Review Billet' at Spithead.

Author's collection. An anonymous postcard of c.1937.

HMS *Southampton* dressed overall and busy with her men. The rough-looking cordage 'overhead' belongs to the sightseeing vessel from which this photograph was taken, probably off Gravesend. The complete weather-protection provided for *Southampton's* aircraft by her box-like twin hangars, placed one on each side of her forward funnel, can be readily observed.

Soon *Southampton* was one ship in the many columns, gay with bunting, which lay off Portsmouth for the pending Royal Review. Almost 300 ships were assembled, representing 17 different nations. Early next morning the elegant lines of the new German 'pocket-battleship' *Graf Spee* were to be seen as she moored in her allotted billet near to *Southampton*. (See photo on next page.) Doubtless, many eyes were fixed upon her, surely including Alf's, all calculating and discussing her potential in combat. However, it is hard to conceive that any sailor, British or German, could have forecast the strangely ignominious fate which awaited *Graf Spee* at Montevideo, just two years ahead, after what would become known as the 'Battle of the River Plate'.

On the 18th May *Southampton* cleared her Lower Deck, and officers and men assembled whilst Lady HADDINGTON, who had launched the ship in 1936, kindly presented a fine model of the 4th *Southampton* to her new successor, the 5th *Southampton*.

(The 4th had been the cruiser which, amongst other achievements had scouted quite splendidly at the Battle of Jutland under Captain GOODENOUGH's command.)[342]

The German 'Pocket Battleship' *Graf Spee* lies off to the right of this photo, near to HMS *Revenge*, which is in the centre of this photo. All the ships are dressed overall to honour the Royal Review by King George VI and Queen Elizabeth.

Next day, Wednesday the 19th May, the ship was dressed with Masthead Ensigns from 0800, and dressed overall from 1745, in honour of the arrival of their Majesties King George VI and Queen Elizabeth at Portsmouth. Alice joined Alf at the 'Admiralty Ball to Commissioned and Warrant Officers' held at the Royal Naval Barracks in Portsmouth at 9.30 p.m. that evening. Mess Dress and Decorations were worn. We note from a programme card still held in-family that Alice danced a 'Foxtrot' with Mr ALEXANDER and a 'Bradford Barn Dance' with Mr H PLAYER. As previously indicated, it seems that Alf and Harry PLAYER, who was also in the Gunnery Branch, were not only colleagues but already becoming good friends as well. Harry lived at Maidstone. Perhaps his wife, Kitty Caroline, was present, but this remains an unknown.

In 1994, Lt-Commander Jocelyn RABAN-WILLIAMS (Rtd.), would write to the author in regard to Alf: *"I had the privilege of being shipmates with Mr DAVIS in 1937 when I joined Southampton as a Midshipman, my first ship in the Navy. One of the, if not the finest ship in the Home Fleet, and flagship of the 2nd Cruiser Squadron, flying the flag of Rear-Admiral CALVERT. It was due to men like Mr DAVIS that she was such a happy and efficient ship. My contact with him was at Quarters with the battery of 4-inch HA*

---

[342] It is good to know that, to everybody's surprise and pleasure, an 'Old Southampton' from the 4th ship of that name, then aged in his nineties, turned up at the first 'informal inaugural meeting' of the 'Old 5th/6th Southamptons', held aboard the 6th *Southampton*, in the early 1980s.

guns. He gave me a very good start and taught me so much - I used to call him 'my Gunnery Sea-Daddy'. We all liked and respected him - he was strict - fair - and very kind to us 'Snotties'. If only we had more of his like today, England would be a better country."

On the 20th May the ship was again dressed overall, taking her place amongst many others for the Royal Naval Review held to celebrate the Coronation, her company manning ship at about 1500, being one of the many firing a Royal Salute of 21 guns, and then giving three cheers as H.M. King George VI passed by in *The Victoria and Albert*, the veteran and stately Royal Yacht. Then, at 2145, *Southampton* was darkened and played her full part in the impressive Coronation Review Searchlight and Firework Display. On Friday 21st May, the ship was again dressed overall, Divisions were held at 1115, and H.M. King George VI arrived on board at 1135 to carry out a quick inspection, including a visit to one of her six-inch gun-turrets, before leaving the ship at 1215. Their Majesties would go on to pay quick visits to other ships, the Royal Yacht subsequently disembarking them at Portsmouth for their return to London.

Next day the ship was open to visitors from 1300 to 1850, and Alice came aboard *Southampton* with other wives and sweethearts that day, seeing more of the conditions under which Alf lived aboard, and his business-like and neat little cabin aft on the starboard side of the Lower Deck. The cabin had a tiny pull-down wash-basin cum writing desk, shallow storage cabinets and a narrow bunk.

Author's collection. A pair of inherited family photographs.

Visitors. Evidently the wives of the Commissioned Officers are here, including Mrs SEMMENS, the wife of the Commissioned Gunner (T), standing with her back to the camera and masking Alice. The deck-planking looks near-perfect.	Alice is present as the 5th lady from the left. The group is standing beside 'X' Gun Turret. As shown by the bunting aloft, HMS *Southampton* is dressed overall, as is the ship in the distance. *(The photographer is standing with his back near to Alf's S2 gun.)*

However, all too soon it was time to say 'Goodbye', and it was 'back to business' for *Southampton* on the 24th. That is to say, her three '*Walrus*' aircraft had arrived at last. Catapult trials began at once with a tug towing the ship's stern round to a position where maximum advantage could be taken of the wind, which happened to be only a south-easterly zephyr that day. Not that such flying activity prevented the ship from again being dressed overall, this time in honour of Empire Day.

On 26th May the ship proceeded to a position off Culver Cliff, where DF Calibration Trials were conducted, gunnery drills continued and (yet again!) the ship was dressed overall from 1100 to 2100, this time in Honour of H.M Mary the Queen Mother's Birthday. These DF Calibration Trials were continued next day, and again on the next (after an early morning delay due to fog), and yet again on the next, by which time the ship was on passage from Spithead to Portland. Apart from patches of fog, the weather had been charitably kind nearly all the time since her commissioning. On this day, however, a south-westerly swell got up for a while.

During the early part of June the ship carried out intensive exercises of firing (and regathering) her torpedoes. She also streamed her paravanes, zig-zagged under full helm and speed, and, after her paravanes had been hoisted back inboard, carried out further demanding 'turning trials'. On the 4th June she moved on to carry out sub-calibre 6" shoots in 'Area M', and also had a 4" HA (High Angle) shoot. She oiled (taking in 1,100 tons), and hoisted out one of her aircraft which took off for Lee on Solent, returning after having 'swung compasses'. Aircraft were also catapulted from the ship during a voyage to Spithead, being hoisted back inboard after very short flights and landing on the sea, to be hoisted back aboard and re-catapulted, time and again. Altogether, the ship was being thoroughly 'worked up' in many aspects.

On 10th June, *Southampton* weighed and proceeded from Spithead, her sister-ship *Newcastle* taking station three cables astern. The two cruisers were bound for Rosyth, and conducted various exercises on the way north, including streaming paravanes for three hours, and carrying out Range and Inclination exercises.[343] Then came the stressful operation for *Southampton* of the taking of *Newcastle* in tow (succeeding only at the second attempt!). These exercises were followed up on the next day by catapulting and recovering aircraft (having practised at turning the ship to make 'slicks' to aid the aircraft in landing). During this time, one '*Walrus*' aircraft 'broke away' when being hoisted in, and capsized, seriously damaging its port upper and lower wings. The 'crash boat' was immediately sent away to salve the aircraft.

During the day, the company also exercised Action Stations, had their night action control parties closed up, again streamed paravanes for a time, and then reversed the previous exercise, by having *Southampton* taken in tow by *Newcastle*. That night they conducted a night encounter exercise, *Southampton* sighting the dark shape of *Newcastle* at 2325, (perhaps at the same time that they were themselves spotted), so both ships fired starshell and opened the shutters of their searchlights at much the same moment, suddenly and spectacularly 'turning night into day'. Next morning, having run some 630 miles since leaving Spithead, they passed under the great steel bulk of the huge railway bridge over the Firth of Forth, which was such a familiar sight to Alf from 1917/1919 - almost like a homecoming.

A further programme of exercises now began in the Firth, concentrating at first on 6" sub-calibre firing by day and night, then moving on to torpedo-firing (including a dummy shoot at *Newcastle*), and then on to 4" High Angle firing at a sleeve target towed by an aircraft, and then on to Pom-Pom and 0.5" MG firing, this time at a 'flag target' towed by an aircraft. Then they went to full-calibre 6" firing by night. Accompanying

---

[343] 'Range' relates to the distance of another ship from one's own and 'Inclination' is the angle of her line of bearing from one's ship and one's own course. It is measured in degrees from 0 to 180, and right or left of the line of bearing.

these exercises were practices for the 6" and 4" Control parties, plotting exercises, range and inclination exercises, spotting exercises, going to Defence Stations and, again, the catapulting and recovery of their 'Walrus' aircraft. Interspersed with these drills were 'seamanship' exercises, such as 'rigging and weighing an anchor by hand', hoisting in and out boats, and streaming paravanes. And, now and again, for relaxation and stimulation of the stout-hearted, there was the optional 'Hands to Bathe' in the chill waters of the North Sea.

On the 19th June the ship was open to visitors (1330 to 1830) and on the 21st they put to sea for further exercises, including a 4" full-calibre shoot for over an hour at an aircraft-towed drogue target. Alf would surely have been involved in this exercise. CS 2 raised his Flag in Leander that day (the latter being a smaller and older cruiser of 7,270 tons displacement which had now joined the 2nd CS). Soon afterwards one of Southampton's aircraft was launched to spot for a 6" full-calibre shoot by Leander. The squadron then anchored briefly at North Berwick before proceeding to sea for 6" full-calibre night firing by all three ships. On the morning of 22nd June the squadron proceeded from Largs Bay to Spithead, carrying out 4" HA firing at sleeve targets towed by one of their Walrus aircraft, followed by Pom-Pom and 0.5" MG firing, again at an air-flown 'flag target'. Again, they streamed paravanes and carried out plotting exercises. Southampton also took Leander in tow for a while, only to have the tow part after 15 minutes with the necessity to stop to recover the wire. Inclination and other exercises were carried out next day. They arrived back at Spithead during the evening of the 24th, with 795 miles run at an average speed of 14 knots.

On 28th June a so-called 'TDX' (or 'Trade Defence Exercise') was started. This nominally extended through to the 7 July 1937. It consisted of Parts I and II, during both of which Southampton was acting in the role of a Commerce Raider. During Part I, the 27th June found her heading for Ushant in a slight breeze and a moderate sea. She was operating in conjunction with the Fleet Oiler Prestol, to which Lt NICKOLAY and some ratings had been temporarily transferred, evidently to maintain coded communications. Prestol was operating as a disguised and armed commerce raider, being generally out of sight of Southampton.

Southampton was up against defending forces consisting of her sister-ship Newcastle, the aircraft-carrier Glorious, and the destroyer Brazen. 'Sunderland' flying boats of the RAF, some based at Plymouth and others at the Isles of Scilly, also aided the 'defenders'. To capture a 'prize', Southampton had to stay with her 'victim' for 45 minutes, sending out 'raider warnings' on her WT (i.e. as if they were emanating from her 'victim'). She took her first prize (the SS Cordillera) at 0605 on the 28th June, 'sank' the SS Bronte at 1140, and another ship, the Southern Prince at 1400. Southampton then increased to 26 knots to get clear of the area. However, at 1715 she observed two defending aircraft which spotted and shadowed her, and, at 1917 a squadron of 20 aircraft which had evidently been 'called up' by the spotter planes was sighted by Southampton. This squadron, which had flown off from Glorious, promptly 'attacked' her, very skilfully indeed, and she was deemed to have been disabled and, effectively, 'sunk', bringing Part I of the 'TDX' to a conclusion so far as Southampton was concerned. [Her 'fate' seems to have been a remarkable and somewhat prescient conclusion by the referees, for no warship *under way* at sea had ever been sunk by aircraft up to that date.][344]

On 30th June, *Southampton* exercised hand wheel steering, and suddenly sounded the electrifying 'Call to Arms', subsequently carrying out Lewis and Pom-Pom firing exercises. The 'TDX' was still in progress, and 'Part II' began on 1st July. At noon on that day *Southampton* was at 47° 19' N, 14° 24' W, roughly 400 miles to the west of Brest, and, by 2000 she was shaping her course and speed for 'capturing' the SS *Nollington Court*, which she duly accomplished. Next day, at 2231 she closely followed the SS *Tunis*. However, on Saturday 3rd July at 1855 she sighted the 'enemy' destroyer HMS *Brazen* off to the north, *Southampton* promptly increasing speed to 22 knots and opening fire, with *Brazen* racing away to the north-east and *Southampton* in chase until 2013, when she ceased fire. By that time the wind had freshened from Force 3 to Force 6 or 7, and the sea from State 2 to State 4, with a steadily mounting swell.

Next day, having headed north-west into the Atlantic, *Southampton* closed the MV *Shropshire*, ordering her to heave-to, and sending a prize crew aboard at 0613. Seventeen minutes later DF reported a flying boat in the vicinity (This was evidently an RAF 'Sunderland' from Plymouth), but, (probably astutely when seen in retrospect), the aircraft gave no appearance of having spotted them. *Southampton* therefore set off in chase of a tanker, but, believing that she was approaching the area in which the 'enemy' aircraft-carrier *Glorious* was operating, forbore to continue in chase and veered away. At 1215, when cruising at about 49° 34' N, 7° 30' W, some 100 miles south-west of Lands End, *Southampton* sighted the 'enemy' cruiser *Newcastle*, and shaped course and speed to intercept and come to action with her. However, (probably 'whistled-up' by earlier signals from the flying boat) a heavy aerial torpedo and bombing attack was made on *Southampton* as she tried to bring *Newcastle* to action, and, although *Southampton* took avoiding action from the well-synchronised aerial attacks, the referees decided that she had once again been completely 'disabled'. All in all, this was a very significant exercise (for those with open minds) of the ever-growing strength of 'air-power' over warships.

On the 5th July *Southampton* flew off and subsequently hoisted-in both her aircraft before coming to anchor at Torbay. It was there, whilst Alf was OOW, that Lt NICKOLAY and the ratings who had accompanied him rejoined ship, their communications duty in *Prestol* done. Apparently *Prestol* had managed quite well, having 'captured or sunk' several merchant ships 'off her own bat', before being judged, somewhat controversially, to have also been 'destroyed' twice by aerial bombing, following 'Referee Decisions' made during the two exercises.

On the 12th July the Parliamentary Secretary for the Navy visited the ship and she departed next day to play her part in a 'CDX' (Coastal Defence Exercise), commencing with preliminary manoeuvres. Unfortunately, a Life Buoy was almost immediately and accidentally 'lost overboard', complete with one wire, one Kelvin Sounding Machine, one Sinker, one Guard Tube and Swivel and 240 fathoms of wire. The CDX proper began at 1500, with *Southampton* streaming her paravanes, making 22 knots and adopting a zig-zag course at times. Both amphibious and land-based aircraft were sighted, and speed was increased to as much as 25 knots now and again. By 0430, *Southampton* had

---

[344] This may be felt to disregard the feat of the American Colonel Billy MITCHELL in successfully bombing and sinking an obsolete battleship in 1926. However, the battleship was unmanned and moored. She was thus an unresisting, helpless and stationary target, and so scarcely representative of 'real life' conditions.

launched one of her aircraft and 'had her hands full', for she was engaging 'enemy' destroyers off Portsmouth, fending off attacks by aircraft and going on to 'bombard' Portsmouth. She then proceeded to Portland where she made another 'bombardment', commencing at 1410 and concluding 15 minutes later, before heading out to sea again. Next day she again closed Portsmouth, where she commenced a second 'bombardment' at 0422, subsequently opening up on the battery based on the Needles. The CDX was completed at 0800, and the ship returned to Portland. There, almost incongruously, she was open to visitors from 1300.

From Portland she proceeded to Southampton Docks on the 19th July, where she was open to visitors from 1600 to 1800 as part of a short 'Navy Week'. On 20th July Rear-Admiral CALVERT called on the Mayor of Southampton, who made a reciprocal visit at 1105. The ship *Southampton* remained at the City of Southampton until the 24th, being open to visitors for much of the time, and rehearsing for Navy Week at Chatham. It is understood that the authorities and people of Southampton took her to their hearts, virtually adopting her during this period, and the groundwork of much useful future liaison was laid.

The Rear-Admiral took formal leave of the Mayor on the 24th July, and *Southampton* immediately proceeded through the Irish Sea to Stranraer, carrying out an exercise whilst en route. This involved a 'night encounter' with *Newcastle*, which ship subsequently took station astern. However, *Southampton's* steering failed seven hours later and she had, perforce, to hoist a 'Not under Control flag'. She reverted initially to steering from the LCT and, later, went to hand-wheel steering. It was over three hours before the problem was resolved. (It turned out that the Gyro-Repeater which automatically controlled the steering had been switched the wrong way.) In the interim, Newcastle had taken station 4 cables ahead, as the lead ship. At 0842 on the 26th July the 5th Flotilla of Destroyers was sighted at the set rendezvous and the destroyers subsequently took station astern of *Newcastle* with *Southampton* now again leading. The cruisers anchored briefly in Belfast Lough, where they practised 'Manning Ship', just preparatory to meeting up with the Royal Yacht and its escort and providing a Royal Escort for HM the King on his formal entry to Loch Ryan and Stranraer on 27th July. Whilst there, *Southampton's* motor-boats commenced patrolling around the Royal Yacht. Clearly, no chances were to be taken in protecting the life of HM the King against terrorists of any complexion.

Next day the Royal Yacht and its escort departed for Belfast Lough, *Southampton* and her consorts keeping station as requisite, anchoring on arrival and firing a Royal Salute of 21 guns at 0835 as their Majesties landed. Later that afternoon they again fired a Royal Salute as their Majesties re-embarked aboard the Royal Yacht, and *Southampton* covered their return to Loch Ryan. Anchoring overnight, *Southampton* and *Newcastle* departed at 0910 next morning, conducting a brief rehearsal for the pending Navy Week, and then an Inclination Exercise which lasted for nearly an hour, before *Newcastle* was detached to join the Home Fleet. *Southampton* continued the 637 miles round the west and south coasts of England, to reach Chatham early on Friday the 30th July.

Next day the Lord Mayor of London came aboard at 1400 and, accompanied by the C-in-C Nore, Sir Edward EVANS, officially opened Chatham Navy Week. For the next six hectic days the ship was open to visitors for two hours each afternoon and the various 'parts of ship' put on various 'Navy Week' displays. *Southampton* looked particularly attractive on the 4th August when she was dressed overall in honour of the Birthday of the attractive Queen Elizabeth. [*Who then would have guessed the times through which the Consort of King George VI would live and the great age to which she would survive?*]

During the remainder of August 1937, a Seamanship Board convened on board for candidates for higher ratings, a representative from HMS *Vernon* (The Navy's Torpedo and Sea-Mine Training School) arrived for a specialist test on *Southampton's* paravanes, and a Court of Enquiry sat aboard. Mr SEMMENS, Commissioned Gunner (T) was discharged to HMS *Vernon*, Lt (N) MUERS joined ship, and HMS *Sheffield*, which had recently joined the 2nd CS, entered the Lock at Chatham.

During the first week of September, *Southampton* embarked aviation spirit, ammunition and fuel oil. She proceeded from Sheerness to Invergordon on the 9th, sighted *Newcastle* around noon, and commenced range and inclination exercises with her in a freshening breeze. The two ships continued in company, aircraft being sighted at 2050, flying around the ships. Next morning, about forty miles off Sunderland, two 'Anson' aircraft were sighted. *Southampton* then carried out a 'Dummy Run' of 6" firing against *Newcastle*, coming to anchor at Invergordon after a run of 555 miles. On the 13th The First Lord of the Admiralty visited the ship, and the aircraft-carrier *Courageous* (once the battlecruiser in which Alf had served 1917-1919) then left with the C-in-C aboard.

Author's collection. A postcard Ref 307 by 'M. & Co.', probably dated c.1937.

HMS *Courageous*. One wonders if Alf would have recognised the lines of his old ship, now, like *Furious*, totally transformed into a 'flat-top', with a flight-deck extending over three-quarters of her length. She had certainly undergone the most radical transformation. *Courageous* now operated nearly 50 aircraft and her complement had grown to over 1,200 officers and men.

Southampton hoisted in a *'Queen Bee'* target aircraft and her Arbuthnot Trophy Team was landed.[345] The ship put to sea on the 14th, exercising with her Pom-Poms and

---

[345] Admiral Sir Robert ARBUTHNOT had led the 1st Cruiser Squadron at Jutland. Unfortunately he drew upon his ships the fire of the German battle squadron, and the *Defence*, the ship in which he was

0.5 inch MGs against targets towed by her aircraft. She then closed up her 4" and 6" gun crews for exercise, together with the Transmitting Station parties. Having re-embarked her aircraft, she then carried out a 6" SC throw-off shoot with *Newcastle* before returning to Invergordon. Next day, the 4" gun crews and HA TS crews were closed up by 0815, when a Range and Inclination Exercise was begun in company with the battleship *Rodney* and *Newcastle*. *Southampton's* torpedo control parties, 'Y' Turret crew, Pom-Pom and 0.5 MG and ADO parties were then closed up in preparation for a 'night encounter exercise' with *Rodney* and *Newcastle* in which, at 2020 *Southampton's* searchlight and starshell gun-crews were closed up, and *Southampton* turned to make a dummy torpedo-attack on *Rodney*, subsequently recovering the two torpedoes she had fired.

Now followed hectic days of exercises against air-attack, in which her Action Air Look Outs, her 4" HA guns (and their Control Parties), her Pom-Poms and her 0.5 MGs were closely involved in 'action' against aircraft towing sleeve targets. Her 'A' Turret was also involved at one stage.[346] The exercises were continued by one in which the ship came into action in a Full Calibre throw-off surface shoot against *Newcastle*, whilst also being in action against aircraft towing sleeve targets. Next came more gunnery drills.

Former Shipwright the late 'Dusty' MILLER (of whom much more later), well remembered that, as part of their shakedown, the company of *Southampton* practised the repetitive catapulting of *'Queen Bee'* aircraft, which were wireless-controlled by specialist 'QB' Operators temporarily being carried aboard.[347] The company of *Southampton* shot at these aircraft with their 4" guns (controlled by the HA Transmitting Station), followed by the recovery of any shot-down aircraft from the water with one of the ship's cranes. It was, in fact, at this time in the history of the ship that all this action happened, over a period of a few days. In his position as Commissioned Gunner of the starboard battery of the 4" High Angle guns, Alf would have been heavily engaged in the training of the gun crews involved in the exercises, and in discovering the optimum way of arranging every detail for 'best practice' on the guns themselves. *Newcastle, Rodney and Fleetwood* all took part in this particular day's QB exercise. Next day it was back to a 4" HA shoot against aerial sleeve targets, these being fabric sleeves of 5 ft diameter and some 20 ft in length, towed about 100 yards behind the aircraft. The ships also carried out torpedo-firing and a 6" surface shoot against a target towed by *Guardian*, before

---

flying his flag, was severely hit and blew up, with the loss of all hands. Sir Robert had captained the Navy at both Rugby and Cricket, and he had been an enthusiast for physical training and a great endurance runner. It was in memory of her husband that, post-war, the Arbuthnot Trophy was presented by his widow for a Marathon race. This was competed for annually by every squadron in the Royal Navy.

[346] The main armament could only elevate to about 50°. However, it would become recognised practice to fire air-burst salvoes of 6" HE shells to break up any formations of enemy aircraft approaching the ship at relatively low-level - as might be done by torpedo-bombers - catching them whilst 'still some distance off'.

[347] As early as 1924 the Admiralty had begun experiments with pilotless aircraft for gunnery practice, initially working with the Royal Aircraft Establishment. (See ADM 116/2430). Their Lordships said they were looking for something for HA firing which was analogous to the 'target ship' HMS *Centurion* for LA firing, i.e. They wanted a large WT controlled aircraft capable of being catapulted from ships and suitable for use as an aerial target at long ranges and heights of up to 10,000 feet. Trials had continued until at least 1935, and were now bearing fruit. The aircraft were expensive, at some £1,150 each. At this stage no suitable means of simulating torpedo-attacks had been evolved. Efforts had been made to see how the Americans were doing in this latter field, but the USN would only respond on a 'reciprocal' basis – *'You tell us, and we'll tell you'*. This was regarded as unacceptable.

returning to the anchorage (the return being made slightly more complex for *Southampton*, due to a breakdown in the Upper Steering Position, with the need to change to LCT steering). Such practice gunnery exercises against aerial targets would prove to be of the greatest importance in the desperate years soon to come.[348]

At 0055 on the 23rd September the urgent signal 'Man Overboard' was repeated from *Rodney*, whereupon the Night Searchlight crew were closed up to play their beam on the waters. The man, who must surely have subsequently considered himself as very fortunate, was picked up ten minutes later. At 0835 *Southampton* proceeded in company with *Newcastle*, both manoeuvring for a special 4" gun drill. Then, at 1100, they began carrying out exercises to avoid a dummy submarine attack mounted on them by the 2nd S/M Flotilla, which had preceded them out of harbour by some 30 minutes. On the 27th September they were again at sea, this time carrying out Full/Charge 6" firing at a target towed by *Guardian*, then making a Wireless Trial followed by a Paravane Trial. On arriving back at their moorings, *Southampton's* picking up wire parted, fortunately without damage to ship or company. Her men therefore had to make a second attempt before they could secure the ship.

Three hours later the tug *St Cyrus* berthed alongside, and one wonders if Alf felt any nostalgic affection on seeing again, at close quarters, this little but powerful ship in which, years before, he had endured a seriously fierce Biscay Storm during which they had been at considerable risk of foundering, and also in which he had kept his first-ever watch at sea.

Next day, the 29th September 1937, they were again at sea, and again at barrage firing practice with their 4" armament against remote-controlled *'Queen Bee'* aircraft launched from the ship. As 'Dusty' MILLER would recall over 50 years later, and still with a measure of glee, during the afternoon Alf's starboard battery comprehensively shot down the aircraft, only the wreckage of it being recovered from the sea. Apparently a little 'miffed' by the total loss of their aircraft, the 'QB' personnel then left aboard the drifter *'Shower'*. At 1918, as dusk descended, 'Action Stations' were ordered, and night firing was carried out at a target towed by *Guardian*.

Next day was both noisy and spectacular, for they proceeded to sea at 0825, went to Action Stations at 0920, and opened fire on the 'Target-Battleship' HMS *Centurion* with their six-inch main guns, whilst engaging an air-towed sleeve target with their four-inch secondary guns and, for good measure, also firing two torpedoes at the 'enemy' *Newcastle* which was steaming hard on their port beam. Subsequently (having recovered the torpedoes), *Southampton* carried out so-called 'WPLO' (understood to signify 'wireless-jamming') exercises at the high speed of 30 knots, shortly before sighting the 'enemy' battleship *Rodney* on her port bow, just as *Rodney* 'opened fire' on *Southampton*, the dummy attack continuing for 30 minutes, before *Newcastle* took station

---

[348] PO George HOBLEY, (of whom more later) went on to serve in the cruiser HMS *Kenya* in the Korean War which followed shortly behind WW2. As a CPO he had the 'Fuse-Setters' on *Kenya's* 4" HA guns helping the 'Ammunition Handlers', so not a Fire Buzzer was sounded before the guns were loaded. He also routed the 'Ammunition Supply' ratings so that they did not have to cross behind the guns whilst the hot empty shell-cases were being ejected. Presumably Alf was also checking ways and means of this sort, to facilitate, speed up and control the working of the guns to best advantage. Though to what degree Alf would have departed from 'best practice as laid out in the handbook' remains unclear. It can be very difficult for a stickler to the rules, who has been on a course at Whale Island, to take 'unauthorised initiatives' - and gunners have strict rules for very good safety reasons.

astern of *Southampton* for another wireless jamming exercise which lasted for 90 minutes. On completion of the day's work they followed Alf's old ship the *Courageous,* now (as we know) a large 'flat-top' aircraft-carrier, into Cromarty Firth and re-entered harbour.

The oiler *Petronel* secured alongside early next morning to fill their bunkers. Late that afternoon the ship's team had a notable success in winning the King's Cup Soccer Match. [The Arbuthnot Trophy had been returned on board earlier that day.][349]

Author's collection of inherited family photographs.

Southampton firing a torpedo whilst manoeuvring at speed. This picture gives a frontal view of Alf's battery of four four-inch guns, located on the starboard side. (The port-side guns were manned by the Royal Marines.)

Then it was back to work, the ship being darkened at 1965 for an anti-aircraft exercise. Over the next days working parties were sent to *Centurion* to make good some of the damage their six-inch shells had done. This was evidently 'standard practice'. The *Centurion* 'took a lot of stick' in her lifetime, and performed her role nobly. A photograph of her appears on the next page, with her attendant destroyer, HMS *Shikari*.

Southampton was open to visitors on the 3rd October, which was Alf's younger daughter's sixth birthday. It was on this day that Alf signed his last Will and Testament, on a *proforma* purchased from H.M.S.O and witnessed by Thomas Joseph DOYLE and Herbert John BONGOURD, both of the Royal Navy. (The author suspects these men may well have been 'Ship's Writers'.) We will examine the wording of this Will at the next section on Alf's 'Private Life'.

---

[349] It would appear that the Squadron had managed to retain the trophy.

During the next days *Southampton* had further exercises in which a QB party came aboard to launch another *'Queen Bee'* aircraft against which *Southampton* opened fire with her close-range Pom-Pom and MG weapons, lowered her motor boat for acceleration trials, proceeded to the west of the Orkneys for night-firing against the much-battered *Centurion*, streamed paravanes, launched and regathered her *'Walrus'* aircraft, and practised depth-charge firing.

Author's collection. A post card issued by the RN Photographic Section, HMS 'Chrysanthemum', c.1936. Formerly in Crown Copyright.

A comparison in ship's beams. The ship's company of the target-battleship HMS *Centurion* are transferring to the destroyer HMS *Shikari,* which will stand off at a safe distance and manoeuvre *Centurion* by wireless. *(During that time of WT control, Centurion will be subjected to bombardment by the warships involved in the exercise.)* Both these ships have a few knots of way on, whilst the transfer is taking place, as betokened by the flash of white water at the stern of *Shikari,* the slight wave breaking near the port bow of *Centurion,* and the slight wash being left behind by both vessels. The men needed to be agile and adept during such transfers, but it had been found necessary to keep *Centurion* under way for the change-over to 'remote control' by wireless to be effective. Note how the upper works of *Centurion* have been stripped down to the 'bare essentials' to minimise the amount of repair work which will be necessary after each bombardment that she will experience during her long career.

These exercises over the preceding many months all had carried considerable point, for Rear Admiral EDWARD-COLLINS (*who, as we shall see, took over from Rear Admiral CALVERT in June 1938*) would issue his Annual Gunnery Report in November 1938, addressed to the C-in-C Home Fleet, and detailing the practices which had been carried out by his squadron (*Southampton, Glasgow, Newcastle, Sheffield* and *Cornwall*). His report made various analyses to do with the accuracy and spread of the 6-inch broadsides and salvoes which had been fired (which, to the author, as a 'lay reader', were far from impressive), and discussed some of the problems arising in fire-control, etc. As one major point, it seemed that the DCTs of the *Southampton* class were too small to accommodate Spotting Tables.[350] Hence, the Tables had been installed in the TS, necessitating improvements in the related communication systems.

So far as Alf's HA/LA 4-inch guns were concerned, a batteryless telephone had been under trial in *Southampton* with promising results, particularly in the Air Defence Group (whereas communication by ordinary 'phone was definitely impossible when the guns were in action). The report said that the present system of HA control was dependent on one heightfinder controlling four guns, the instrument being a normal short-base RF of the coincidence type *'with all the usual disadvantages'*. Blame for lack of improvement of the HA gunfire of the squadron had, by inference, been blamed on the guns' crews. However, Rear Admiral COLLINS believed that no improvement was likely to be made until at least three rangetaking instruments became available for HA control, their readings being *'meaned'* to improve accuracy. He held that the present tendency to elaborate the control systems and gun mountings was likely to interfere with efficient ammunition supply and to be ineffective in relation to the most vital information - range - which was still left to one man to control, using an instrument the adjustment of which varied daily and even hourly. Clearly, everything in the garden was far from being rosy.[351]

Following her depth-charge firing, *Southampton* then ran southwards in a brisk westerly breeze and a moderate sea to secure at No.2 buoy at Sheerness on the morning of the 8th, promptly oiling, ammunitioning and provisioning ship. By mid-morning of the 9th she was heading for Quiberon Bay, passing four German destroyers at 2215 and speaking to the German pocket battleship *Admiral Scheer* at 0107 on the 10th. At 0620 that day *Southampton's* Air Lookouts were closed up for an Air-Shadowing exercise in mid-Channel which lasted for two hours. At midday she was at 50° 16' N, 01° 50' W, and at 0605, having passed close to Belle Isle, she spotted the 25,750 ton battleship HMS *Resolution* heading for their pre-arranged rendezvous. At 0920 *Southampton* transferred correspondence to *Resolution*, and, following his orders, CS 2 assumed the duties of 'Senior Naval Officer (North Spain)'. *Southampton* then proceeded to St Jean de Luz, just on the French side of the Franco-Spanish border, by which time she had run 744 miles since leaving Sheerness.

Southampton was heading into some danger by approaching close to the coastline of Spain. Her company would have been only too well aware that the Spanish Civil War had broken out earlier in 1937, and that ships of the Royal Navy had immediately become involved in protecting the interests of British merchant shipping around the Spanish coastline. Some of the ships they were being required to protect did not have exactly 'lily-white' hands in the various activities, sometimes of a nefarious nature, which were going on to sustain one side or the other. Isolated incidents of reprisals by opposing factions and of casualties arising, some fatal, had affected a number of the British merchantmen and a few ships of the Royal Navy. A few British lives had been lost when ships had struck sea-mines, and various of our naval vessels had been near-missed by torpedoes fired by Italian submarines.

Indeed, one reason why the Spanish Reds were being defeated was that the Spanish Fascists were being actively supported by the Germans and the Italians, both of

---

[350] This would appear to have been a shortcoming which really ought to have been picked up at the design stage, and surely by the gunnery staff whilst the ship was still in-building.

[351] See ADM 116/3904 at TNA.

whom had élite units of soldiers and airmen in the field, and who were testing out various of their new tactics and weapons in readiness for the World War which now seemed certain to come, perhaps imminently but more probably in the 1940s. The Royal Navy were observing what they could of the tactics and weapons of the 'Axis Powers'. The Reds had widespread support from hundreds of European individuals, many of them idealists who had extreme socialist or communist leanings, and who were prepared to give their lives in the conflict. However, there was little material or financial support for these idealists from the governments of their countries. Atrocities were rife on both sides, and the town of Guernica would become world-famous after it was bombed to destruction by the aircraft of the German 'Condor' Legion, with heavy loss of civilian life. [*This was just a tiny foretaste of the aerial bombing due to hit Europe in 1939/45.*]

Now, *Southampton*, under CS 2, had been given the task of patrolling off the coast of Spain. This was sometimes going to pose very difficult problems and would require careful negotiations with the Spanish authorities and the companies of their warships. The British sailors were going into a brutal war-situation but were not, themselves, at war. The whole of the Iberian Peninsula was a potential powder-keg, and there was the underlying issue that Britain needed to ensure the security of her large naval base at Gibraltar, which base would be of colossal strategic significance in the now-anticipated second world war. The fighting in Spain, with the possibility of an overland *coup-de-main* by the Spanish military to seize Gibraltar, coupled with possible incursions into Portugese territory, were latent threats against Britain's continued ownership of that vital naval base. Moreover, the Italian dictator MUSSOLINI was bragging about '*mare-nostrum*' in connection with the Mediterranean, and was being backed-up by his fine, modern fleet. This aggravated the risks to Gibraltar, to say nothing of the associated threat to the excellent British facilities on the Island of Malta, which lay so close to the heel of Italy.

In addition to playing her part in protecting British interests and 'showing the flag', *Southampton* was also occupied in rescue work, picking up men and women who had been fighting on one side or the other in the Spanish Civil War, and who, having been cut off and pushed back to the coast, had found whatever boats they could and put out to sea. For those who failed to find a boat, the alternative was death, for neither side was interested in the taking of prisoners, and those who laid down their arms were often put to death in the most cruel manner.

There is nothing in *Southampton's* log to indicate that Admiral CALVERT or Captain PETERS addressed the company on the eve of their setting about their allotted duties off the Spanish Coast, though it is hard to believe that some sort of 'briefing' would not have been done. The risk of a wrong approach being taken by a junior officer or rating at a critical face-to-face moment between naval men of the two nations would surely have prompted the senior officers to brief their men to some degree.

However, all the log tells us is that the men's gasmasks were inspected, and that an exercise was then held in preparing for a gas attack, perhaps to emphasise the seriousness of the general situation.[352] A file preserved at TNA, under reference

---

[352] There was strong and widespread belief in many quarters that enemy aircraft would immediately bomb British towns and cities with massive quantities of poison gas as soon as the next war began. Indeed, gas masks would be issued to every individual, man, woman and child early on in 1939. Ways of creating a semi-gasproof room in every household were promoted by instruction leaflets issued by

ADM116/3680 refers to the 'Proceedings of H.M. Ships in Spanish Waters 1937/39', and states that the *'wearing of steel helmets is recommended in Air Raids, for ship's personnel exposed on deck, such as heightfinder's crews and signalmen.* It added a rider, however, that *'steel helmets have been issued (as standard) only to the Royal Marines, so far as the 3rd CS is concerned, at least'.* So, whether Alf and his gun and ammunition crews were ever issued with steel helmets seems unlikely. None of the few contemporary photographs shows naval men in helmets.

Southampton also landed an 'embarkation patrol'; she lowered her whalers and sent them away under sail; her paravanes were streamed and her men practised at 'Action Stations'. Next day, the 16th October, they spoke the Spanish cruiser *Admiralte Cervera*, taking the precaution of going to Action Stations 'for real' as they closed to do so.

Later that day they spoke the British merchant ships *Bramhill* and *Hillfern* and, at dusk, they set course to seaward to proceed on their night patrol line. At 0600 on the 17th they set a course to again close the land, passed a message to the Spanish warship *Admiralte Cervera* and later came across the French merchant ship *Sens*, hove to after being captured by the Spaniards, presumably for carrying a contraband cargo intended for the insurgents. Her they had no power to help.

However, on the 18th *Southampton's* Log recorded that they sighted and identified three French destroyers in the early morning light, and 'talked with them'. [File ADM 116/3680 (see above) refers to this matter, for it encloses a letter to the permanent Secretary to the Admiralty, which had originated from the French Ministry of Marine, *"...presenting their sincere appreciation and best thanks for the information given by HMS 'Southampton' to the French 10th Destroyer Division when searching for the cargo ship 'Sens' off the Spanish Coast. The information greatly helped our ships in their task."* From the scrawled margin notes one has the impression that this fulsome praise caused something close to embarrassment within the rather starchy higher realms of the Admiralty!]

Southampton continued her patrol and next passed a warning to the British merchant ship *Stanhope* that at least one Spanish warship was in the vicinity. *Southampton* again spoke to *Stanhope* next evening, and also to the *Stanleigh* which was in the proximity of *Stanhope*. An hour later they spoke to the *Hillfern* for a second time that day.

These ships were still in the same area (nominally about 3 sea-miles off Gijon) next morning, which had started off by being fitfully misty. *Southampton* again spoke with them. The tenor of the dialogue is unrecorded, but it is fairly certain that Captain PETERS would have been aware that the Spanish were seeking to impose an increase (to seven miles) of the internationally understood 'three-mile limit' for territorial control by a nation of its coastal waters, and one therefore suspects that he was warning these ships that they should proceed away from the dangerous area. However, his advice was being 'stonewalled' by the skippers of the merchant ships, who were probably in a 'Catch 22' situation. That is to say, these ships were hovering about to rescue so-called 'Red Refugees', whose Army had been getting the worst of things in the land-fighting in

---

HMSO. Boards coated with a pale-green reactive emulsion which would change colour to pink (as a visible warning) in the presence of gas were mounted on stands at intervals along every road. People were expected to carry their gasmasks at all times once the war began. The gas exercise aboard *Southampton* would therefore have had much greater significance for her men than people of today would recognise.

Northern Spain, and who had the stark choice of getting away by sea or staying to be butchered. To haul off to seven miles from the coast would render the refugees already slim chances of getting out to them even slimmer - probably almost impossible of achievement.

At 1500 the Lookouts spotted a merchantman being 'escorted' by a Spanish warship, which some accounts identify as the cruiser *Baleares*. HMS *Southampton* immediately went to Action Stations and closed the two vessels, whereupon Captain PETERS demanded the release of the merchantman, which was the *Stangrove*, a British ship, and a sister of the *Stanhope*. Indeed, though not shown in *Southampton's* log, it is said that, at one stage, *Southampton* interposed herself between the Spanish and some small craft with refugees which were desperately trying to reach the British merchantman. This 'shutting-out' manoeuvre succeeded, even if it was hardly 'diplomatic'. Nettled, the Spanish captain dubbed *Southampton's* Captain as "*Black PETERS*" and said he was a '*pirate*'.

Southampton subsequently escorted the *Stangrove* well away from the coast, *Southampton's* Lookouts doing well to sight the *Admiralte Cervera* at 2230 that night, despite that ship having 'darkened herself'. *Southampton* then went to the high speed of 25 knots as she raced back to close the *Bramhill* and the *Hillfern*, both by now crowded with refugees, and to shepherd these ships further out to sea and to safely.

On Friday 22nd October *Southampton* arrived back at the French port of St Jean de Luz, in the angle of land where the north Spanish Coast meets the west coast of France. The weather, from having been quiet and calm now suddenly changed, a breeze springing up from the SSE and a considerable swell, graded as 5 and worsening towards 6, then also arose. Consequently, for safety's sake, the Admiral's Barge, the Pinnace and the 2nd Motor Boat, which had all been hoisted out earlier in the day and were in use, were signalled to stay ashore for the night. Next day, the wind veered to the NE and intensified, and the swell was still running strongly. Nevertheless the Pinnace and the 2nd Motor Boat made it back to the ship, and were hoisted in. The Admiral then boarded his Barge and it fought its way back to the side of the ship.

It seems best to let the then Able Seaman GORMAN pick up the story at this point, for he was Bowman of the Admiral's barge at that moment in time. The crew of the barge had taken Admiral CALVERT ashore to see the Spanish Consul, and the sea had greatly got up by the time that they neared the ship on their return voyage. In fact, the barge *"was going up and down 'like a lift', and getting themselves and the barge safely back aboard was always going to be very tricky. Eventually the starboard crane was lowered with a breeches buoy hanging from its hook. Somehow, the Admiral managed to climb into the breeches buoy and was hoisted aboard. The barge was then directed to head back to shore until the weather improved."*

Like a true 'old salt', the 1st Coxswain of the Admiral's barge always claimed to have a girl in every port. Sure enough *"he reckoned he 'had a bit ashore' at St Jean de Luz, so he was pleased to 'lose himself', whilst the crew of the barge awaited events at the Café de Paris, not exactly stinting themselves."* As it happened, the sea-state remained bad, *Southampton* left port, and some days elapsed before she returned. In the interim the crew of the barge *"stayed on contentedly at the Café de Paris"*, and CPO GORMAN (as he later became) – then the PO bowman of the barge, said that the

Admiral ("*who could become very fierce*") was not best pleased at the considerable bill they had run up by the time that *Southampton* was able to put back in to collect them!

An anonymous photograph from Alf's collection, Oct 1937.

Yes, she could roll. Alf wrote on the back of this photo: *"St Jean de Luz: Sea quite calm but very heavy long swells."* One suspects the sea was rougher than this when the Admiral's barge was directed to 'head back to shore until the weather improved'.

A ship's log makes no reference to such 'financial affairs', but *Southampton's* log backs up the veracity of this yarn, for the log certainly confirms that it was not until 25th October, a full five days later, that *Southampton* would have been back in the vicinity of St Jean de Luz to recover the barge. [Indeed, it is not until the 29th that the Barge is specifically mentioned as being in use again, by which time the ship was at La Pallice, 150 miles to the north.] Here then, was a rather light-hearted happening in the midst of a very unpleasant overall situation, and it would seem that the Lower Deck considerably enjoyed the tale told by the crew of the barge, who were doubtless good at '*swinging the lamp*'. There seems to have been no envy of the fact that AB GORMAN and the other members of the crew of the barge had been enjoying their hedonistic pleasures whist their shipmates were enduring a fair amount of trauma.

What had happened was that the company of *Southampton* had started to pick up refugees themselves, some of whom were in a parlous state. On the 24th they had rescued 49 refugees from the drifter *Aurora*.

Anonymous 'official' photograph from Alf's collection.

'Red' Refugees being rescued in the Bay of Biscay in November 1937. Their boat, the *Aurora*, is receiving a heavy pounding against the side of *Southampton*, and transferring the refugees is clearly a very hazardous undertaking. Alf, marked with an 'X' on his white cap, stands near to the farthest group of officers and men.

Next day they had picked up 29 men and two women from a small boat, well out into the Bay of Biscay off Santander. They had fed all these refugees, tended their wounds and subsequently dropped off their 80 passengers, offering them the choice of being landed at either at St Sebastian or at Biarritz, to one being just in Spain and the other on the much safer French side of the border.

The Navy were finding that many of the boats the fugitives were pressing into service were barely in seaworthy condition, usually short of the necessities for survival, and often greatly overloaded with people who were desperate to make their escape. The Navy tried its best to be impartial in what it did, for the British Government was anxious to avoid the creation of any sort of 'diplomatic incident'. However, it was obvious that the 'Reds' were getting the worst of things, and it was almost invariably 'Red Refugees' that the Royal Navy were rescuing from the elements, and nourishing, before putting them ashore in some safe haven, usually at St Jean de Luz.

If a sea was running, or if there was a heavy swell, transferring the refugees to a large ship out at sea, such as *Southampton,* could be a difficult and dangerous operation. Indeed, there was a high risk of fatalities, for, despite the best efforts of *Southampton's* seamen, who often put their own lives at risk in aiding the transfers, people who were debilitated by defeat and unused to being at sea were sometimes prone to miss-time their 'stepping across' and to slip down between the two vessels. These vessels would often be pounding together, despite such cushioning as fenders could provide, and anybody falling between them was likely to be crushed to a bloody pulp before being washed away by the sea.[353]

Anonymous 'official' photograph from Alf's collection.

Picking up refugees from a ship's lifeboat. Putting his own life at risk, an officer has gone down into the lifeboat to take charge. He has put a bight of rope around this woman's waist and, by tension placed on the rope from above, she is being assisted to climb the rope-ladder to safety aboard *Southampton*. Alf, his cap marked with an inked 'X', is overseeing operations. The ship's crane has been turned outboard, in case it may be needed to aid in the recovery.

The lifeboat shown in the above photo was eventually recovered by being hoisted inboard. However, most of the small craft, once the refugees had been removed, (sometimes by then severely damaged from being buffeted whilst alongside, especially when a Biscay swell was running) were left drifting and thus immediately became 'derelicts'. To prevent them from becoming a hazard to navigation, they had to be sunk. This was accomplished by means of shellfire (see next photos) or by exploding a depth-charge in them. At least these operations made useful practice for the ship's secondary armament and its gun crews, or for its depth-charge personnel.

What is not really apparent in the photographs of the Spanish Civil War which appear here is the constant tension that the officers and men would have been operating under. To pick up refugees, who were in a highly stressed and desperate state was one thing, and often hazardous enough in its own right, but to know that one's ship was at significant risk from simply being in a war zone where mines, torpedoes, bombs and shells were all being used, and that 'overs', 'misses' or cynical 'aiming off' might lead to *Southampton* herself being struck, was quite another matter with which to conjecture.

---

[353] The author can remember overhearing his father talking in graphic descriptive detail to other adults of just such an event.

Two anonymous snapshots from Alf's collection, dating from Nov 1937.

Alf wrote on the back: *"Nice Roll!"* The refugees having been taken off the *Aurora*, the battered derelict was then sunk by shellfire from Alf's 4-inch guns, a direct hit being shown in the right-hand photograph, with the little ship being *"near its end"*, as Alf wrote down. If one considers the roll of the ship at this time, the ability to score a series of hits on a target which is also in erratic motion, reflected very well on the skill of the gunlayers and trainers.

Writing to the author in 1994, the late Rear-Admiral Colin MADDEN, CB, CBE, LVO, DSC, (Rtd.), would say: *"I was born in Bilbao where my father was British Consul at the time, and it was on this slender basis that I was made the unofficial and unpaid Spanish Interpreter for 'Southampton' during the Spanish Civil War. I took photographs of Mr DAVIS and other officers on 25 October 1937, when we were lying off Bilbao on the North Spanish Coast.[354] That was at the time of its evacuation. I remember Mr DAVIS as being a very nice man, always cheerful, much liked and a great person. I believe that he was President of the Warrant Officers Mess at that time. For my part, I was the 'Sub-Lieutenant of the Gunroom'.[355] I was present from the Commissioning of HMS 'Southampton' until mid-1938, when I was promoted to lieutenant and left the ship, later joining one of her sisters....."*

To continue our saga, on the 26th *Southampton* was again at sea, and investigated two small ships. These were allowed to proceed, but they then stopped the *Mary Tere*

---

[354] See photographic portraits of Alf in the frontispiece and three pages on from here.

[355] i.e. President of the Gunroom, and thus in a similar role to Alf. The Gunroom and the Warrant Officers' Mess were situated on the Lower Deck, directly opposite each other.

registered at Gijon, embarking the 283 men and eight women who had been crammed aboard this small coaster.

An anonymous 'official' photograph from Alf's collection, dated Novemebr 1937

Red refugees being rescued from the *Mary Tere*. There were no less than 283 persons aboard this small coaster. Alf, again marked with an 'X', keeps an eye on events. At least three of *Southampton's* ratings have gone aboard the *Mary Tere* to assist refugees to make the dangerous climb up *Southampton's* steep side by rope or rope-ladder. One refugee is being helped over the rail near Alf and another man is in mid-climb.

These people were evidently fleeing from the collapse of Bilbao. Once the refugees had been taken aboard, *Southampton* sank the derelict with a depth-charge at 44° 28' N, 02° 56' W, in the outer reaches of the Golfe du Gascogne. *Southampton* anchored late on the night of 26th October at a point of rendezvous with the fleet oiler *Celerol*. The oiler duly arrived and *Southampton* oiled from her. Unfortunately *Celerol* collided across the stem of *Southampton* on proceeding, though the damage was slight and both ships remained fully operational.

Again, *Southampton* disembarked her refugees (all 291 of them), and proceeded back to her patrol area, finding and hoisting-in a small refugee boat the *Emile Robin* on the 27th. On 28th October *Southampton* was at La Pallice, where she hoisted in her aircraft (flown off several days earlier) and *Celerol* again secured alongside, topping up *Southampton's* bunkers.

Next day, Alf did a spell as OOW. All leave was suddenly cancelled and, next day, 1st November 1937, they left the troubled Spanish waters and proceeded to Portland in a moderate wind, sea and swell. Soon it was 'Out Paravanes', and, whilst the paravanes were streamed, the ship made a four-hour Full Speed Trial, which helped to 'gobble up' the distance to Portland. They catapulted an aircraft to go ahead of them, and secured at B1 Buoy, Portland at 1540 on the 2nd November. The price they had to pay for their quick voyage was to have to scrape and paint their blistered funnels next day.

It is to be supposed that the whole company of *Southampton* were relieved to be back in home waters, for a Civil War is a dirty and degrading business to observe at near hand. It is very distressing to see the human victims it creates, whose disrupted lives are unlikely ever to return to 'normal'. No wonder that France soon accumulated a considerable population of sad left-wing Spanish *émigrés*, many of whom never really settled down. At the same time the ship's company were anxious about a quite different matter for a rumour had spread that the reason they had headed fast for England was that their much-respected Rear-Admiral was suspected to be seriously ill with cancer.

Be that as it may, on the 8th November Rear-Admiral CALVERT made a thorough inspection of the ship and her company. He started at Divisions, then inspected the Upper Deck, followed by the Store Rooms and Messdecks. The next day he inspected the company as they went to Action Quarters, oversaw the catapulting of an aircraft and the landing of the Royal Marine Emergency Party and a Demolition Party. 'X' and 'Y' Shore Patrols were also landed. On the 10th, after landing the ship's Royal Marine Detachment and Band for inspection by the FRMO, followed by Divisions and Prayers, *Southampton's* Captain really put the company through their paces (presumably at the suggestion of the Rear-Admiral), and the orders came thick and fast:-'Exercise General Drill', 'Furl Awnings', 'Out Kedge Anchor', 'Change Over Booms', 'Let Go Sheet Anchor on 6½ Inch Wire', 'Muster Emergency Platoon of Seamen', 'Exercise Fire Party'.

Captain PETERS put them through the same drills next day, plus having the 1st and 2nd whalers away under sail, though the two minutes silence of Armistice Day was carefully preserved. Next day wasn't so bad - just cleaning ship, followed by 'Exercise Gas Alarm' and 'Repel Aircraft'. And the next day was just a matter of getting half a ton of stores aboard and stowed away. However, come the 15th November, the Rear-Admiral really put the whole Squadron through the mill, setting ship against ship as he oversaw a 'Competitive Inspection of General Drill', followed by the competitive orders 'Furl Awnings', 'Point ship with Stream Anchor', 'Exchange Sheet Anchors', 'Land RM Emergency Platoon', 'Out Carley Floats', 'Down Ensign Staff', 'In Stern Boom', 'Scandalise the Gaff', 'Boats Away Under Oars', 'Replace Guy', 'Secure for Sea', 'Hoist Out Aircraft', 'Hoist Boats' and so on..

The company may well have groaned and wondered about their 'Martinet Admiral'. If he was going on sick leave he was certainly about to depart from them in some style.

Nor was the ship's day yet done, for at 1330 she proceeded from Portland to Sheerness in a calm sea, with little wind, having to close up her Fog Lookouts at 2300, soon thereafter reducing to 6 knots and starting her siren. Fortunately, the fog began to clear and at 2345 she was able to increase to 11 knots. Thus it was that at 0858 next morning she came to with her port anchor at Sheerness, in 12 fathoms, lowering her 1st whaler and 'sounding out round ship' to be on the safe side. At 1200 she hooked on to No.2 Buoy and thereafter began to de-ammunition. As the ammunition began to pile up on deck sentries were placed to ensure security.

It was not until 0955 next day that four ammunition lighters came alongside and the ammunition began to be disembarked. It took until 2015 for the operation to be completed. During that time an oil lighter which had come alongside at 0845 had cast off. Next day, *Southampton* was hauled round by tug and proceeded up to Chatham where she secured in No.3 Basin. Whilst there, a sale of a 'run man's' effects took place, a 'Board for the Examination of Candidates for Higher Ratings' assembled on board, and Captain W.P. MARK-WARDLOW, the Commander of HMS *Sheffield,* visited the Rear Admiral of CS 2.

Sheffield, a sister-ship of *Southampton,* had been commissioned on the 25th August. She had been adopted by the Mayor and Board of Commerce of the City of that name, and would be forever known as the 'Shiny Sheff' because, through the generosity of the City of Sheffield, much of her brasswork had been replaced by stainless steel, which requiring far less polishing. Already, *Sheffield* had been fitted with the highly secret so-called 'R/DF', Type 79X, for the detection of aircraft. This would probably have been one of the matters on the agenda of the meeting.

Author's collection of inherited family photographs. This photograph was taken by the then Sub Lieutenant Charles MADDEN (Later Rear Admiral C. D. MADDEN CB, CBE, LVO, DSC.) Photograph taken off Bilbao in November 1937.

Alf, standing by 'X' Gun Turret, cigarette in hand and looking very urbane and at ease. The experience he had gained in childhood, from watching his father coping comfortably with people of every status in life, had undoubtedly helped Alf to respond appropriately to officers of every level as he rose through the ranks. Then, once he had gained his commission, to be able to mix well with officers when off duty just as much as when on it. By this time Alf was enormously experienced in 'Naval Life', be it on the human or the seamanship side of things. His service career was at a peak.

On 1st December 1937 the company were occupied in storing ship, 'Tilt Test Parties' were mustered for the 6" and 4" guns, and the Rear-Admiral left ship to inspect the ship's Royal Marines on the range at Sheerness, whence they had departed a week earlier. On 3rd December the ship was warped into Dry Dock, shores were put in place to keep her stable, and the company began to scrub the ship's bottom. That Sunday it poured with rain, and Divine Service was held in the Officers' Bathroom Flats to provide weather-protection.

During the next few days, further parties left for practice at the range, including a pistol party, whilst painting and provisioning ship continued, together with some training and exercises, the latter including the mandatory 'Fire Stations'. On the 11th the ship came out of dock and was immediately dressed overall on the anniversary of the accession to the throne of King George VI. Three days later she was dressed again, this time in honour of the King's Birthday. The ship had oiled on the 13th, the air temperature was falling (it was below freezing on the 22nd) various changes in personnel were taking place, and Christmas was almost upon everybody. Lt MOWLAM, Midshipmen HALL, HEIGHTON, KEYES, JOHNSON and SHANNON and Mr TURNER, Gunner, all left the ship, and Lt WISE and Mr HARDING, Gunner, joined. Lt (N) P ELLMERS signed the log for the month of December, but Lt (N) P NICHOLLS was back in place for the ensuing month.

Now, during January 1938, the ship's economic speed would come to be exceeded no less than eleven times - and all due to exercises in one way or another. Rear-Admiral CALVERT would 'concur in the necessity' of every instance. However, as the month opened the ship was still re-provisioning, and embarking ammunition, aircraft stores, aviation spirit and petrol. Some more of the faces in her company were also changing, Commander Le MESURIER leaving, and Lt Commander BROWN, Lt BULL and six Midshipmen joining, together with Lt WRIGHT of the Royal Marines. Five CPOs, 4 POs, 2 ERAs and 54 Ratings also left the ship and were replaced by others, including 12 RNVR Ratings. Eight RAF 'Ratings' (as the Log called them) also joined the ship.

In fact, it was not until the 17th January that *Southampton* slipped from the jetty, being moved by tug to the North Lock, before proceeding under her own power to Sheerness. There she received on board her '*Walrus*' aircraft K8546 and K8556, and, next day swung ship for adjustment of her compasses before proceeding to Portland, making rendezvous with the 4th Destroyer Flotilla and HMS *Ramillies* and participating in an exercise with them whilst *en route*.

At 0700 next morning, the 19th January 1938, aircraft commenced dummy attacks on the ships, and one of *Southampton's* own aircraft, which should evidently have been launched on anti-submarine duties, fouled the bogey and was damaged. Accordingly, the ship was more limited than she might have been, when making her 'response' to the dummy submarine attack which was the final phase of the exercise.

As *Southampton* neared her anchorage at Portland, where the Home Fleet was assembling in preparation for the so-called 'Spring Cruise', *Sheffield* saluted the Flag of the Rear-Admiral, 2nd CS with her guns, *Southampton* replying. Early next morning CS 2 left the ship and hoisted his flag in *Sheffield*, the squadron proceeding to Gibraltar less than an hour afterwards, and almost immediately beginning a series of exercises which would continue for days to come. These exercises were initially made more tense and realistic by the presence of sea fog as *Southampton* took her station for reporting of 'enemy' warships believed to be closing in. Action Stations and, later, Night Action Stations were practised as fog buoys were streamed and the quartermasters and forward lookouts on each ship strained to follow the dim light of their 'next ahead' in line.

Despite the persistent fog, the 4th Destroyer Flotilla were sighted next morning as another phase of the exercise opened and the 6" gun crews were closed up to counter the destroyer attack which developed towards midday. Then, in the early evening the company went to Night Defence Stations and commenced another so-called "Trade Defence Exercise". Next day there was a 'Wireless Trial' with *Sheffield*, and at 0600 the following day, they commenced a 'dawn encounter' exercise, starting the plot immediately and going to Action Stations an hour later. The exercise concluded at 0830, followed by further manoeuvres. By this time they were at 38° 30' N, 10° 01' W (i.e. some 50 miles off Lisbon). They stopped to lower and recover both seaboats, then proceeded again, conducting a signalling trial and exercising Night Action. Next morning they exercised the refuelling of *Boadicea* 'by trough', then cast off the tow and went to 20 knots for a time. Indeed it was during this passage to Gibraltar that they exceeded the ship's economical speed virtually every day as the various exercises unfolded. Those exercises were primarily to do with 'Trade Defence', reflecting the Admiralty's preoccupation with their belief that the forthcoming war would see German surface warships and armed raiders penetrating into the Atlantic and striking at Britain's supply lines worldwide.

It should be mentioned that, in great secrecy, British warships had now been fitted with 'Asdic' (i.e. The Anti-Submarine Detection System which was later called 'Sonar'.) Following that installation, it seemed that the risk of such roving attacks into the Atlantic being made by submarine had been virtually discounted. *Just how wrong can one be?!*

During the morning of the 25th, whilst *Southampton* was stopped to lower her boats, the Rear Admiral re-hoisted his flag in *Southampton*, and she proceeded to No.46 berth at Gibraltar, *Sheffield* and *Newcastle* entering harbour 15 minutes later. The ships promptly oiled, *Southampton* taking in 573 tons. Meantime, her company cleaned their guns which had evidently been in action in at least one of the exercises, then they washed the ship's side and they touched up her paintwork. But, during the two days of 26th/27th January most of her company had the chance for at least one run ashore, sampling the delights of 'Gib' and joining the flood of Jolly Jack Tars swarming all around the port from the combined Home and Mediterranean Fleets.

Two days leave were the absolute maximum for any of the men, before the Combined Fleets put to sea for joint exercises. For her part, *Southampton* proceeded at 0740 on Friday the 28th, heading for the firing range in 'Area A' and launching her aircraft as she went. By 1015 she was engaged in sub-calibre firing at a Pattern VI target which was being towed by the tug *St Omar*, a sister-ship of Alf's former ship the *St Cyrus*. Recovering her aircraft, *Southampton* transferred correspondence to *St Omar* and later launched and subsequently recovered her other '*Walrus*'. That evening *Southampton* carried out another sub-calibre shoot, before returning to No.46 Berth.

Next day she provisioned ship and sent a diving party to assist the company of the destroyer *Tenedos*. She also granted some of her men a further chance for a quick run ashore. But she proceeded early next day, exercising 'Air Alarm', streaming her paravanes, commencing another exercise and HA firing at an aerially-towed sleeve target. Subsequently she stopped to carry out a Wireless Trial DF test, pointing ship as necessary, launched her two aircraft in turn, recovered them, and went on to carry out a Night encounter exercise, before returning to harbour at midnight. Next morning she proceeded to Palma, again launching her two aircraft and recovering them nearly two hours later. She then set her Torpedo Control Parties to drill and carried out a short exercise in which her Pom-Pom crews fired at balloons. This was followed by a further WT 'DYT' trial, before, in the small hours of the new day, her S1 HA guns crews were exercised. These were Alf's particular charge and one imagines he would have been present to check that all went well. (One wonders if by now, stimulated by the 'Spanish War patrols, steel helmets would have been embarked and issued as standard to men exposed on deck.). The torpedo crews then came into the action, firing off two torpedoes, both of which they recovered. More firing of the short-range armament, against balloons, followed, after which the ship transferred correspondence to *Newcastle* by fog buoy, exercised at streaming and recovering paravanes, and came to anchor at Palma on the morning of 3rd February, after a run of 851 miles. The battlecruiser HMS *Hood* and the County Class cruiser HMS *Shropshire* sailed just before noon, two Spanish armed trawlers sailed at 0715 next morning and *Newcastle* arrived soon thereafter, departing after only an hour's stay.

That morning, at 0600, *Southampton's* company had cleared away their HA armament to make it ready for near-instant use with live ammunition. They would continue to do so every day they were at Palma, for the port was being used by Spanish and Italian as well as British warships and the possibility of a sudden bombing attack on the harbour by one or another faction caught up in the continuing Civil War was a real possibility.

The weather continued to be very kind, but there was just enough breeze for all the ship's boats to be away under sail on the 7th, in blue skies and bright sun. Two Spanish destroyers sailed that day. They were followed by the *Baleares* next day - the Spanish cruiser whose captain had called Captain PETERS a pirate on the 19th October of the previous year. Meantime, *Southampton* had oiled the destroyer *Beagle* by means of an oil hose as she towed astern. Her Pom-Pom crews had been put to drill, a torpedo class put to instruction and hands told off to paint 'turrets and screens'. On the 9th *Southampton* half-masted her colours as a mark of respect for a rating who had died in an accident aboard the Italian destroyer *Francesco Nullo* and then watched as three Spanish destroyers sailed - and later returned. That day *Southampton's* B Turret and Pom-Pom gun crews were at drill.

On Thursday 10th January 1938 *Southampton* and *Newcastle* proceeded in company for exercises, streaming their paravanes, and engaging in an 'encounter exercise' with the County Class cruiser *Cornwall*. On completion, *Cornwall* joined company, and the three ships commenced manoeuvres, after which they hoisted in their paravanes and came to anchor, sending all their boats away under sail. They then exercised their 'Concentration parties', before transferring mails to and from the destroyer *Beagle* which had just arrived.

The Spanish minelayers *Volcano* and *Jupiter* arrived just after midnight, as a tangible reminder of the need for paravanes in certain areas, and of the risks being run, especially for merchant shipping of every nation using the waters around Spain. Come the dawn, *Southampton, Newcastle* and *Cornwall* again proceeded in company, streaming their paravanes and commencing manoeuvres, followed by another 'Trade' exercise. This took 2½ hours, after which *Cornwall* parted company, the remaining ships then coming to anchor in the mid-afternoon and lowering their pulling boats to practice for the forthcoming Fleet Regatta.

An anchor watch was set early the following morning for the wind was getting up and the glass was still falling, with occasional squalls of rain. At 0900 the battleship HMS *Nelson* arrived flying the flag of the C-in-C Home Fleet and exercises would soon begin in earnest which would not conclude until the end of March. They would be combined with competitions and regattas of the keenest nature. For the moment, however, ships of the squadron continued at Palma practising the crews of their pulling and sailing boats, marching past CS 2 by divisions, exercising their guns crews and clearing away their HA armament at 0600 every day, 'just in case of trouble'. Meantime, the 770-ton Italian destroyer *Francesco Nullo* sailed and the 1540-ton flotilla leader *Augusto Riboty* arrived. HMS *Newcastle* also arrived, as did the battleship *Royal Oak*.

On the 17th *Southampton* and *Newcastle* proceeded to Gibraltar, sighting three Spanish destroyers soon after setting out and, later, commencing signals trials. They also spoke two British merchantmen. Next day, at around 36° 20' N, 02° 30' W, they commenced another exercise, *Southampton* opening 6" FC 'Throw-off' fire on *Newcastle* for 5 minutes, and *Newcastle* subsequently replying. *Newcastle* then took *Southampton* in tow for two hours. Later, they exercised their night guns crews followed by a two-hour wireless trial.

They arrived at Gibraltar after a run of 490 miles, and oiled from *Celerol*, taking in 840 tons. On the 21st *Southampton* provisioned ship, taking in 8,700 lb of meat, 3,200 lb of butter and 5½ tons of vegetables. Meantime the gun crews were put to drill on the Dummy-Loader.

Further squadron exercises followed, some in conjunction with destroyers, starting off with another trade defence exercise, then 6" sub-calibre firing at a splash target, kite-flying (to provide a target for *Glasgow's* Lewis guns), the firing and recovery of three torpedoes, two 6" full-calibre shoots at a BP target, HA firing at a sleeve target (evidently towed by their own aircraft), and so on. They also practised at coping with a steering breakdown. Meantime further warships were arriving at 'Gib', including their sister-ship *Sheffield*, and the battleships *Nelson*, *Rodney*, *Ramillies* and *Revenge*. The impressive German pocket-battleship *Admiral Scheer* also arrived and would doubtless have been the subject of much circumspect scrutiny.

On 1st March 1938 the squadron proceeded to sea, and commenced manoeuvres. These included the laying of 'lachrymatory floats' for a gas alarm practice, WT trials, sub-calibre 'concentration' firing, yet further 'trade defence' and 'encounter' exercises, the launching and recovery of their aircraft and so on. In the midst of these exercises they passed the *Admiral Scheer* and two German destroyers heading east, perhaps, in their turn, having something of a look at what the British combined fleets were up to. Alf was OOW after the squadron had secured again at Gib.

In the early hours of 2nd March Gib was 'blacked out' when a dummy attack was made on the vast port by four destroyers. The lights came on again, only to be quickly extinguished when a second dummy attack was mounted. *Southampton* weighed by hand and proceeded on another exercise, involving the use of her aircraft and boats and the firing of torpedoes, 6" full-calibre firing at a BP target, live bombing, and another encounter exercise, testing her lookouts to the full. She returned to No.65 berth after a run of over 200 miles.

Next day she re-provisioned with vegetables after an early morning exercise involving 'darkening ship'. The submarines, *Narwhal* and *Porpoise*, which had apparently been involved in the exercise, secured alongside.

On 5th March *Southampton* half-masted her colours for the funeral of Boy Seaman BELL of the signals division. The circumstances of his death are unknown to the author, but he seems to have been a very popular young man. Next day things began to really hot up, with the 2nd CS at sea, spread on a screen ahead of the battleship *Nelson*, all streaming paravanes and involved in an 'enemy reporting exercise'.[356] Later, having slipped through the Straits of Gibraltar, they carried out another trade defence exercise, before forming up on the starboard beam of *Nelson* overnight. Next morning they commenced manoeuvres with the Battlefleet out in the Atlantic off the west coast of Morocco, before a dummy destroyer attack was mounted on them and they spread on a screen and started the plot for a further battle practice exercise with *Nelson*. Further exercises followed in succession over the next three days, some involving their aircraft, one involving working in company with *Galatea*, one in taking station on the battleship *Warspite* and one in having the 2nd CS acting as starboard wing column for the deployment of the Battlefleet. During one of these exercises they increased to as much as 25 knots.

They were at No.37 Berth, with their bows facing south for the two days 11th/12th March. The berths were crowded, for the Combined Home and Mediterranean Fleet was now at Gib., and it is not surprising to find that the destroyer HMS *Fearless* was berthed alongside *Southampton* for part of those two days, whilst *Southampton* took in another ton of vegetables and 40 rounds of starshell, some being for Alf's 4" guns.

Further Code-named exercises, one coming hard on the heels of another, ensued for the next week. The 2nd CS were operating in conjunction with *Nelson* and *Rodney* out in the Atlantic well off the coast of Morocco, spreading on a 'line of search', coming into action, being assessed as '*sunk with many casualties*' at one stage, moving on to the next exercise, being night-attacked by destroyers, being subjected to a 'massed air attack', going on to a 'strategical exercise', making a 'day approach exercise', 'using smoke', and so on.

Back at Gib to refuel and re-provision (taking in 8¾ tons of flour, 8 cwt of margarine, 5½ tons of potatoes...). The ship's hockey and tug-o'-war teams were put ashore to compete on the 20th, and the 1st football team and their supporters were landed next day. The Captain of *Sheffield* had visited CS 2 for the best part of an hour, before taking his ship back to England. The First Lord of the Admiralty had departed from *Nelson*. On the 25th March the C-in-C visited *Southampton*.

Soon afterwards *Southampton* and *Nelson* proceeded, rejoining the 2nd CS at sea and starting a further series of exercises, initially working up to a full speed trial for 3½ hours. *Southampton* and the 2nd CS were then involved in manoeuvring at 28 knots to avoid a series of torpedo attacks mounted on them, before reducing to 20 knots, with *Southampton* bringing her 6-inch guns into action with a 10 minute full/calibre throw-off shoot, *Glasgow* reciprocating. The 2nd CS then rejoined *Nelson*, and another exercise started in which depth-charges were fired, followed by other exercises of manoeuvring at speed in close company, such as 'opening and closing on a constant bearing'. They were still exercising as the glare of Cape Finisterre was sighted at 2030 on a bearing of 107° and the fleet began to cross the Bay of Biscay through the darkness of night.

At first light the 2nd CS shook out into their day screening positions for the next exercise, launching and recovering their two aircraft, passing the German seaplane carrier *Westphalen* and sighting the glare of Ushant as darkness descended. By morning they were entering the English Channel, and a final spate of exercises immediately started,

---

[356] These exercises were all code-named and carried out against written instructions, evidently with the senior officers present having the responsibility to adjust the timings and details of implementation and to control the movements of each squadron or unit by visual or WT signals.

Southampton taking station on *Nelson*, zig-zagging on a set mean line of approach at 14 knots, engaging 'attacking' aircraft, lining up for a 'steam past', and re-forming as further 'air attacks' developed, before Beachy Head light hove in sight.

Next morning *Southampton* secured to No.4 Buoy at Sheerness. The battleship Ramillies arrived later and secured to the adjacent buoy. By that time *Southampton* was discharging ammunition into two ammunition lighters which were alongside, and the destroyers *Electra, Encounter, Escort, Firedrake* and *Foxhound* had already proceeded upriver to Chatham. *Southampton* followed them next forenoon.

She would remain at Chatham until the 11th May 1938. During that time from late-March to mid-May, *Southampton* spent some of the time in dry dock for scrubbing and painting of the ship's bottom. During the rest of the time her hands were cleaning, painting and provisioning ship, checking her wire hawsers, renewing her boats falls as requisite, etc. Forty bales of clothing were embarked. A new quarterdeck awning arrived on board. 'Tilt tests' were conducted in her turrets. Shore leave was given, and some long leaves. Alf did the odd stint as OOW, but got in some leave as well.

Various people visited the ship, including the Captain of the *Royal Sovereign*, an Italian Naval Attaché, Class 305 from the RNB, a class from the Gunnery School, Boys from the training ship *Arethusa*, and signalmen and telegraphists from the Signal School at the RNB. A press photographer also visited the ship, perhaps taking the photo reproduced below.

Author's collection. A photograph reproduced by courtesy of the IWM. (Neg No. FX 8878.)

HMS *Southampton* photographed in March 1938, evidently whilst she was moored off Chatham. Two of her boats, one being the Admiral's barge, lie under her falls.

Various members of *Southampton's* company were discharged to other ships and courses, including Mr NOAKES Warrant Electrician and 35 ratings. New faces arrived on board, namely Lt CHANTRILL, S/Lt PEEVER, Midshipmen COLE-BLOOMER, HAMILTON, HARDEN and MASON, Mr FORD Warrant Telegraphist, and 67 ratings from the RNB.

Let's take a break to see how Alf's private life was progressing.

Private Life

As has already been mentioned, Alf had made a Will, which he had signed on the 3rd October 1937. He had appointed Alice to be his sole executrix, and he wrote *"I give and bequeath to my dear wife Alice Agnes DAVIS all my property viz: money owing to me by Mrs Agnes Sarah GREEN.....House at 21 Looe Road Felixstowe is to be sold off and after mortgage has been paid off balance is to be paid to my dear wife; insurance when realised is to be paid to my dear wife; furniture, etc., is to be used in a home which I hope my dear wife will take for our three children and herself.*

He then made individual bequests of *"...the waistcoat which has been in my family for years"* to his son Neville, *"....her Mummy's sewing machine – it was my darling's wish."* to his *eldest (sic)* daughter Joan, and *"...To Jessica, our baby girl, I would like her Mummy's jewellery and ivory hairdressing set given to her."*

Alf continued, *"If my decease should take place on land and within reasonable distance of Felixstowe I would like to be buried with my darling Olive. Funeral arrangements to be as simple as possible with minimum trouble to everyone concerned.*

Should my dear wife Alice remarry and our children Joan, Neville and Jessica not be of age I pray consideration will be given to them until they are of an age in that they will be cared for and loved as they have been accustomed to all their lives."

The Will is interesting in several regards, especially in Alf's repeated use of *'darling'* when referring to his first wife Olive, and *'dear'* when referring to Alice. This would seem to endorse the author's belief that Olive had been Alf's true romantic love and that, whilst he had genuine love and respect for Alice, the relationship was never going to attain the same extraordinary and climactic heights that his first marriage had achieved.

There is also the matter that Alf thought it necessary to spell out his wish that his three children by Olive should be cared-for until they came of an age. Was this just a wise legalistic precaution (bearing in mind the strong rights of husbands over wives in those days – including second husbands) – or did Alf have underlying feelings that all might not be plain sailing if he passed away? As we shall see, Alice did later try, at times, to 'disembarrass' herself, certainly of her two very difficult elder children and possibly, a little later, of Jessica too. [Indeed, as we shall see, because of the continuing friction between Alice and the two elder children, it seems that Alf himself made an attempt (albeit an unsuccessful one) to get them off her hands in 1940.]

The Will also seems to endorse the total trust and confidence Alf had placed in his mother-in-law, Agnes Sarah, with the implication that Agnes Sarah would come forward with exactly and unquestionably whatever moneys were due to be repaid from the loan which Alf had previously made to her.

Alf had spells of home leave soon after the ship returned to Sheerness at the end of her service off the Spanish mainland. During that time (late April/early May 1938) Alf's second son was conceived. It is to be supposed that Alf had a further spell of leave during the ensuing month of June. [The author's elder sister Joan has a memory that Alf was also home during the mid to late term of his second wife's pregnancy, for, (refusing to let other people see what was to her an embarrassing and humiliating 'bump'), Alice would not go out by day, but did grudgingly permit Alf to walk her out after dark in an attempt to give her at least some measure of exercise. As we shall see, *Southampton* was at Sheerness in September, and Alf getting home at this time would have 'twinned' with Alice being 'five months gone' and her 'bump' beginning to show.]

As we have already seen, Alf's son Neville was attending a preparatory school at Leopold Road, Felixstowe. It was around mid-1938 that Alf persuaded Neville to ask the headmistress, Miss MULLINS, if she would be receptive to the idea of his father coming along to give a talk to the children about the Royal Navy. Miss MULLINS proved to be more than acquiescent, and so the talk quickly came to pass. To young Neville's delight, the schoolchildren were enthralled by the masterful and superbly-pitched lecture his father delivered, standing square before the schoolchildren in his immaculate naval uniform. All the teachers were present, headed by the formidable and stately Miss MULLINS.[357] She was accompanied by the middle-aged and outwardly tough Miss HARRIS and the young, clean-smelling and sterile-seeming Miss HERBERT. All three teachers simply *drooled* over Alf.[358] Young Neville's reflected *kudos* shot sky-high with pupils and teachers alike for many weeks thereafter. Whether Alf's talk eventually led to any of the children being motivated to join the Royal Navy or the WRNS is unknown. One would not be one whit surprised to learn that it did.

It still gives the author a thrill when he remembers that fantastic day at school with his charismatic father, who was totally 'in control'. It was about this time that, in his art class at Prep School, the author drew and painted in watercolours, a childish picture of HMS *Southampton* at speed in a rough sea. It was flat and uninteresting - until Miss HARRIS asked for his consent to work on it at her home - bringing it back the next day with a few deft brush-strokes added, which had added highlight, shadows and movement and brought the whole thing to near miraculous 'life'. Neville suddenly realised there was a quite different dimension to 'tough' Miss HARRIS, and she stole a little bit of his heart forever after.

Miss HERBERT presenting him with a Prize 'for neat work' also greatly touched him. The prize took the form of a book called 'Tommy's Trek', and dealt with the adventures of a lad caught up in the comings and goings of the fighting in the Boer War of 1899-1902. Neville's grandparents had already given him the privilege of dipping, whenever he wished, into a very large leather-bound volume called 'With the Flag to Pretoria'.[359] This book graphically covered the fighting in the Boer War, and the little form prize 'twinned' nicely with the far larger 'official' tome. It may also be remembered that the author's oft childhood companion, his great-uncle Bill,

---

[357] Miss MULLINS, tightly-corsetted, heavy-busted and upright as Queen Mary, did her best to teach tone-deaf young Neville how to play the piano on the principle of 'whack him on the fingers with an ebony ruler if he plays a wrong note'. A part of Neville still regrets that he did not persist with her. Perhaps the ebony ruler was just that bit *too* heavy a weapon.

[358] The author sometimes finds Miss HERBERT's unique and evasive aroma stealing gently into his nostrils. This important woman of his early life laid the foundation stones of his education and he treasures these memories.

[359] This large book had been presented to the Author's grandfather circa 1910, ostensibly by his (then) three children, though, in actuality, surely inspired by Agnes Sarah, his much-beloved wife.

had fought in the Boer War and would often tell him tales about it. Perhaps young Neville had prattled about the Boer War and Miss HERBERT had remembered...

There were still stresses and strains on the domestic scene, but Alice, now pregnant for the first time at the relatively advanced age of 38, perhaps had a lot on her mind, probably felt that she had less to prove to Alf, and, maybe, that she had a convenient 'refuge' into which she could withdraw from his lovemaking advances by the very fact that she was in a 'delicate condition'.

Although the author can remember being well-thrashed at least once around this time, there was a rather less punitive air around generally.

We have already seen a picture of Alf reading a 'comic' to his children. The influence of comics such as 'Dandy' in encouraging children to read and in opening their eyes to humour, and the skill of the cartoonists in bringing movement, emphasis and drama to the story being told, was a very important factor in their development. Comics imported from the U.S.A. were quite different in concept to the British ones – with 'Tarzan' and 'Superman'-like characters, tough and ruthless 'untouchable' detectives, and so forth – and added further overall interest. Space travel and robots began to feature, too.

By now, another factor had entered the lives of the children. That is, they had begun to attend the cinema at Felixstowe. The author can well remember the magic and excitement of being taken to see the Hollywood child-actress Shirley Temple in *"Rebecca of Sunnybrook Farm"* and a swashbuckling film of heroic British soldiers in India called *"The Drum"*. There was also the fantastic cartoon film by Walt DISNEY, called *"Snow White and the Seven Dwarfs"*. All these films were in breathtaking 'Technicolor', which had suddenly burst on the scene, leaving 'black and white' film to be used for documentaries and the more sombre subjects generally. It was also used for 'Gaumont British' and 'Pathé' newsfilms. The broadening of the minds of the children, and the increase in their awareness of current events from seeing these films was tremendous, and 'going to the flicks' was speedily becoming an almost weekly institution across the whole country.

The quality of programmes on the 'wireless' was improving, but rather ponderously and slowly. And a man by the name of James Logie BAIRD was working towards broadcasting pictures by means of something called 'television' – though only the rich were going to be able to afford to pay the high prices for the receiving sets. Sure enough, Alf's sister, Nellie, would soon be in the running to own one.

HMS *SOUTHAMPTON* (1935-38) Continued.

Sunday 8th May 1938 was exceptionally cold at Chatham, and Divisions and Divine Service were therefore held in the shelter of the Officers' Bathroom Flat. Next day the lower deck was cleared and 'everybody' was set for a final flurry of painting and for embarking refrigerated stores and medical supplies. The maximum possible workforce was also set to 'ammunitioning ship' the day after that. On the 11th they embarked petrol and aviation spirit and were towed out of the North Lock, before swinging ship to adjust the standard compasses and then proceeding to Portland where they arrived on the 12th, firing a 17 gun salute to the C-in-C Home Fleet as they did so, *Nelson* replying to CS 2 with 13 guns. They then dressed ship and fired a 21 gun salute at noon to honour the first anniversary of the coronation of KG VI. The 4" control parties were then closed up for a height-finding exercise. Captain HAWKINS and Commander BREWER joined ship temporarily and *Newcastle* arrived. Next day the C-in-C made a short visit to the ship, after which she proceeded for Asdic trials, subsequently lowering her 1st whaler to convey Admiral CALVERT to *Glasgow*. He subsequently raised his flag in that ship.

Author's collection. A postcard by Wright & Logan, c.1938, reproduced by courtesy of the Royal Naval Museum, Portsmouth.

HMS *Southampton* flying the flag of the Rear-Admiral, 2nd CS. Depending on the exact date, this may have been the flag of either Rear-Admiral CALVERT, or of Rear-Admiral EDWARD-COLLINS. (The latter hoisted his flag in *Southampton* on 13th June 1938.)
[Note: Captain KENT, who wrote the Foreword to this book, has told the author that CS 2's flag would normally have been flown from the foremast. By custom the mainmast is reserved for the flag of a C-in-C only. The reason for this exception remains unknown.]

During the next days they put their 6" Director Test Party and TS crews to drill, then their 4" HA guns, first P1 and P2, the charge of the Royal Marines, and then S1 and

S2, which were in Alf's 'special charge'. They then made further tests of their Asdic. And further tests of the crews of their 6" and 4" guns and the associated TS and DCT operators, also of their pom-poms. They launched their aircraft for height-finding exercises, went to action stations, engaged aircraft which were 'attacking them' with torpedoes, carried out sub/cal shoots by day and night, and went through further 'trade exercises'. They were in company with their sister ships *Glasgow* and *Newcastle*, the Admiral flying his flag in *Glasgow* until the 17th May, when Admiral CALVERT's flag was struck at the conclusion of the ceremony of 'Sunset', he having been taken to hospital shortly beforehand. It seems that Admiral CALVERT was by then a very sick man. (It was evidently the absence of Admiral CALVERT from the Squadron which led to *Southampton's* log for April being countersigned by Captain W.P. MARK-WARDLOW, the Commander of *Sheffield*, as being the Senior Officer 2nd CS.)

From the 18th May *Sheffield* was present and exercises continued with torpedo bombing attacks on the ships, 6" sub/cal shoots, a night encounter 'trade defence' exercise, firing concentration drill, Asdic trials, an inclination test, streaming paravanes and then passing through a minefield at 18 knots, using their 4" guns to fire at sleeve targets, making a torpedo attack on *Sheffield*, embarking a man from the Shambles Light vessel, making an overnight landing exercise with men of the Lincolnshire Regiment (repeated two days later) and so on.

Anonymous 'official' photograph from Alf's collection.

This photograph is believed to relate to the landings, with troops of the Lincolnshire Regiment who had been carried aboard *Southampton* going down into a cutter. The cutter has steel sheets mounted in her bows to provide some protection from any defensive fire coming out to sea as the cutter nears the beach during the assault-landing exercises.

On 1st June *Southampton* proceeded from Weymouth Bay to Portland, in company with *Glasgow, Newcastle,* the old Ceres Class cruiser *Coventry* and the Arethusa Class cruiser *Aurora*. The squadron increased to 18 knots and carried out a full '*Queen Bee*' firing exercise under increasingly difficult conditions for the weather was rapidly worsening, the wind increasing from Force 4 to 8 to 10 to 11, with a sea and swell of 3 to 4, as they fought their way back to Portland harbour, setting an anchor watch and sending the 2nd motor boat inshore for the night rather than risk hoisting her on board. Next day the weather had moderated and they put to sea again, for more QB firings, accompanied by balloon firings and, later, by more practice landings of men of the Lincolnshire Regiment. On the Sunday the ship was open to visitors, and, come the Monday it was back to a further landing exercise, again with men of the Lincolnshires. Next day, the 7th June, *Southampton* proceeded to sea, detected the surfaced submarine *Narwhal* at an agreed rendezvous, and then, in conjunction with the destroyer *Exmouth*, commenced an exercise of tracking and 'attacking' *Narwhal* by Asdic after she had submerged. The following day they drilled at gunnery and exercised being taken in tow forward, before proceeding with the 2nd CS for 6" practice firings, their aircraft acting as spotters, and the squadron coming to anchor at Torbay. The 10th June was the Squadron Regatta Day there, with all pulling boats engaged. The 12th June saw the ship open to visitors, and Monday 13th June saw *Southampton* hoist the flag of Rear-Admiral G.F.B. EDWARD-COLLINS CB, CVO, RN, returning *Sheffield's* 13 gun salute with 7 guns. The captains of *Sheffield, Cornwall, Newcastle* and *Glasgow* then formally visited the new CS 2, and he repaid their visits. Meantime, 6" gun turrets 'A' and 'B' and their gun houses were put to drill.

On 14th June the 2nd CS proceeded, and each ship gave the poor old target ship *Centurion* a pounding with their 6" guns, their aircraft spotting aloft. *Southampton* and *Glasgow* then carried out two 6" concentration shoots, following up the first one with a torpedo attack. The squadron reformed and proceeded to Weymouth Bay, saluting the C-in-C with 17 guns and *Nelson* replying with 13. Next day they squeezed in a rehearsal for the pending visit of King George VI, before carrying out another landing exercise with men of the Lincolnshire Regiment. On the 16th they again put to sea as part of the 2nd CS, for firing exercises with their 6" and 4" guns against '*Queen Bee*' target aircraft. There was quite a cheer from those aboard when *Southampton's* 'run' so damaged an aircraft that it crashed. Before rejoining the squadron, and returning to Weymouth Bay, they carried out another Asdic exercise.

On 20th June the ships were dressed overall, saluting the King with 21 guns at 1817, when the Royal Standard was hoisted in the Royal Yacht, *Victoria and Albert*. Next day the Home Fleet put to sea under the command of H.M. King George VI aboard *Nelson*, *Southampton* taking station 6 cables astern of the battleship *Ramillies*. During the rest of the day the fleet 'performed'. For her part, *Southampton* steamed past *Nelson* to starboard at 25 knots, flying off one of her aircraft before taking station 5 cables ahead of *Nelson*. Destroyers then carried out a torpedo 'attack', which was followed by a '*Queen Bee*' shoot, *Southampton* and *Glasgow* sharing the honours of one which crashed. The 6" armament was closed up at 1410 for another crack at *Centurion*, but fog unfortunately closed down and that final phase had to be abandoned. How much new

Admiralty decisions about changes in manning in the Gunnery Branch were beginning to affect the ships (and Alf) by this stage is unclear.[360]

Author's collection. A postcard by Valentines, series ref. 388-8. Card reproduced by courtesy of St Andrews University Library.

388-8

Southampton dressed overall and neatly manned by her ship's company.

Back they went to Weymouth Bay after a run of 107 miles, and it was there that King George VI came aboard at 1445 to watch 'drill and evolutions', and to see the launching of both aircraft before he departed. The hands manned ship and cheered the King as he subsequently passed through the lines of ships in *Victoria and Albert*, and they fired a 21 gun salute as he disembarked from the Royal Yacht. The order was given

---

[360] Around this period of time the Admiralty were reorganising the Gunnery Branch of the Royal Navy and the Royal Marines. (See ADM 116/4437 at TNA.) The essence of the reorganisation was to divide the gunnery ratings into four branches, 'Gunnery Quarters', 'Fire Control', 'Gunlayers' and 'Anti-Aircraft'. Ratings attaining the top grade in their branch would be promoted to become, 'officer substitutes' in such duties as 'Ratekeeper', or 'Spotter' (in Main Armament Control Teams in major units of the fleet), or 'Ratekeeper' in charge of a gun-turret (in cruisers and destroyers), or 'Controller' (of long-range A.A. Fire), or 'Controller' (of a Mk M Pom-Pom Gun for shorter-range A.A.). The current Leading Rate would become the equivalent of the 2nd Class Grade of the new sections of the Gunnery Branch. The new 1st Class grade would receive an increase in pay, as would Gunner's Mates and Gunnery Instructors. The principle need was seen as being to restrict the employment of officers to stations which involved leadership in emergency and the maintenance of morale on a large scale, or the application of a high standard of general knowledge - and to entrust specially trained ratings with stations which called for leadership on a lesser scale or highly specialised knowledge in a restricted field. The increased complexity of modern weapons and the increasing development of A.A gunnery called for special measures if ratings were to 'remain as efficient as formerly'. In view of the possible substitution of officers, the committee provided for (a) 'Air Defence Officers', (b) a further officer on the bridge in action (in addition to the navigator, in battleships, cruisers and aircraft-carriers), (c) for ships in full commission to have their full complement of officers, and not to have to rely on additional officers being sent out to them on the outbreak of war and (d) that midshipmen in action should not have to carry out duties other than those appropriate to their status as officers. [The author believes that the effect was to keep the number of officers and WOs of *Southampton* but little changed, despite the large increase in her overall complement as her weapon-systems, etc., were improved and increased.]

'*Splice the Mainbrace*', spirits being issued, and the day ended with a spectacular searchlight display by the fleet.

Author's collection. A postcard by Photomatic Ltd. Photograph taken c.1938.

A fine stern view of *Southampton*, wearing the flag of Rear-Admiral EDWARD-COLLINS, dressed overall and with an awning spread over her quarterdeck.

On 23rd June 1938 they proceeded from Weymouth Bay to Portsmouth, exercising at torpedo firing and making acceleration trials (up to 28 knots) on the way. They saluted the C-in-C Portsmouth with 17 guns on arrival, and received a 13 gun reply. Next day colours were half-masted on the anniversary of the death of Alexandra the Queen Mother.

Come the 23rd, an Army advance party consisting of 60 men (all ranks) arrived on board as a rehearsal and the hands went to their Combined Ops (COX) stations. They did so again in the afternoon of the 28th, as the ship proceeded to Spithead, and No.2 COX Beach Party practised a landing. The troopship *Lancashire* arrived and sailed at 0655 next morning. *Southampton* followed her out, proceeding in company with *Revenge*, *Sheffield* and the 5th Destroyer Flotilla to come to anchor in Sandown Bay two hours later, then proceeding to Stokes Bay. There they sent the hands to their COX stations and exercised manning the boats

They secured, but then went through the same practice after dark, sending the boats to shore, and back to the ship where they were hoisted in. HMS *Centurion* sailed, followed by all the ships involved in the COX exercise to come to anchor in Sandown Bay. Next day they proceeded to sea again for a COX rehearsal lasting 2½ hours, *Revenge*, the 5th DF and the TS *Lancashire* all then sailing, followed by *Sheffield* and *Southampton*, heading to Portsmouth.

There now followed a sad interlude, for Rear Admiral CALVERT had died in hospital only six weeks after leaving the ship on 17th May. It was remarkable to have witnessed the determination with which he had so doggedly kept going, for so long. The rehearsals for his funeral took place on 3rd July. *Southampton* was honoured to be providing pallbearers for his coffin and a Guard. Her Colours were half-masted from

1400 to 1700. Next day she proceeded to Spithead where her funeral party left the ship, her colours were again half-masted, she manned ship, and began to salute the late Rear Admiral with 13 guns fired at one minute intervals, their solemn notes resounding around the anchorage.

Author's collection. A postcard by Wright & Logan reproduced by courtesy of the Royal Naval Museum Portsmouth.

HMS *Southampton* with her Jack and Ensign flying at half-mast, possibly during the day of the funeral of Rear Admiral CALVERT, 3rd July !938. A long signal hoist, yet to be broken, appears to be climbing her foremast halliards.

That evening 11 ratings joined the ship for the forthcoming COX exercise.[361] Amazingly, this was said to be the first such 'combined' exercise of any scale at all since Gallipoli, in 1915. Brigadier Bernard Law MONTGOMERY ('Monty'), who was in command of the 9th Infantry Brigade at Portsmouth, had been pressing for this divisional exercise for eight or nine months, and wanted all three services to be involved in the planned amphibious assault on Slapton Sands. 'Monty' had organised the exercise in conjunction with the Admiral of the Fleet Lord CORK AND ORRERY, who was the Naval C-in-C at Portsmouth. However, 'Monty' saw it as 'his baby' and he was determined to head the whole show. As the 'Senior Service' one feels that it would have been scarcely surprising to find that the 'Navy' cherished somewhat different and rather more independent ideas. Moreover, Lord CORK AND ORRERY wasn't nicknamed '*Ginger*' BOYLE for nothing!

Be that as it may, as a part of the meticulous preparations (which had involved a prodigious amount of written orders and paperwork), a 15ft model of the Slapton beaches had been constructed for study by the invaders, heralding one of the measures which would be adopted for future military assaults. The object of the exercise was summed up as being "*an investigation of the tactical and technical aspects of an approach from*

---

[361] It is assumed that these rating were specialists – perhaps additional signalmen.

seaward, and the landing of a force on an enemy coast; the provision and distribution of fire from ships in company supporting the landing force; and the co-operation of aircraft."

The naval ships in the exercise included the battleship *Revenge*, the cruisers *Southampton* and *Sheffield,* and the aircraft-carrier *Courageous.* A flotilla of destroyers and some minesweepers were also involved. The troopships *Clan McAlister* and *Lancashire* both carried men, vehicles and equipment, further troops being carried on some of the naval ships.

So far as *Southampton* was concerned, the exercise proper started early next morning, 5th July, when she commenced her zig-zag at 1045, and increased to 25 knots to investigate a report of 'enemy' destroyers, opening fire on them three times, at 1546, 1600 and 1608. At 1615 she fired on a surfaced submarine and, 30 minutes later she 'fired on', and 'sank' a destroyer. She then returned to help to cover the assault convoy.

It was unfortunate that the weather, which had been calm for days past, now chose to deteriorate, the wind rising to a Force 6 and the sea to state 3, with a state 4 swell for some time, though the conditions did moderate before midnight. Unfortunately, there had been considerable sea-sickness amongst the troops by that time. The force came to anchor in Start Bay in the darkness of 0105, all boats were hoisted out and the business of landing the Troops involved in the exercise was begun.

Author's collection. A photograph sponsored by 'Wayfarer Tailored Clothes', c. 1937.

An unopposed landing. The assault waves are already ashore and the main infantry force is now coming ashore from ship's lifeboats, preceded by a sailor and with the third soldier carrying a 2-inch mortar. A 'Beach Party' of four naval officers stands in the shallows, directing the landings. A score of soldiers have already disembarked and many more are arriving. An official photographer strides purposefully along the shoreline. At this stage the exercise is going extremely well.

The troops consisted of three battalions of Brigadier Bernard Law MONTGOMERY's 9th Infantry Brigade, comprising men of the 'East Yorks', the 'Kings Own Scottish Borderers' and the 'Lincolnshire' regiments. They were carried ashore in Naval cutters and whalers, and in lifeboats from the troopships, the last 'assault wave' being landed by about 0400.[362] Guns, tanks, lorries, stores and further troops were landed from flat-bottomed craft after first light using landing piers and tracks up the beach which were being rapidly constructed by army engineers.

The 'Wessex' defenders were taken by surprise as, under Monty's personal command, the 'East Army' fought its way inland supported by gunfire from the battleship, cruisers and destroyers, and also by twelve 'Swordfish' aircraft from HMS Courageous which were bombing ahead of the troops.

In the meantime, the naval ships put to sea to carry out a bombardment of the enemy defences, Southampton launching her aircraft as a spotter, and streaming her paravanes against the risk of mines having been laid.

It was planned that the ships should return to Stokes Bay at dusk to re-embark the troops. However, by 2100 the weather had again deteriorated, was expected to get worse still, and would have possibly led to swamping of the boats with risk of casualties by drowning. It had also left the naval ships dangerously exposed on a lee shore. The re-embarkation part of the exercise was therefore abandoned, somewhat to the Army's dismay, the assault ships coming to anchor in Start Bay. (As a token of the roughness of the sea, the lone motorised landing craft broke adrift from the Lancashire at 0300 and sank.) The troops were thus left isolated ashore and ere long they were wet, tired and hungry. [In consequence, there were some 'ruffled feathers' throughout the ranks of the 'Pongoes'. However, the Royal Navy did manage to come to the assistance of the Army, even if somewhat indirectly, by feeding and sheltering the troops in the Royal Naval College at Dartmouth. It was found that the troops existed in such large numbers that they could only be accommodated by 'packing them in like sardines' in every nook and cranny that could be found. It all made an interesting experience for the naval cadets to cope with.]

Despite the anticlimax with which it ended, there can be little doubt that Brigadier Bernard L MONTGOMERY mentally absorbed practical lessons from this combined exercise which would have borne fruit when, as a Field Marshal he became involved with the Amphibious Landings in Sicily in 1942, in Italy in 1943, and then in the enormously complex 'Operation Overlord', in Normandy, on D-Day 6 June 1944.[363]

---

[362] Some authorities 'could not see the wood for the trees' and seized on the fact that there was only one elderly landing craft proper available for the operation, heavily criticising the 'open wooden boats' which were employed. They failed to appreciate the great surprise and success achieved, and the comparative rapidity with which the landings were made. They also failed to absorb the many lessons which emerged so far as the planning and logistics of future seaborne assaults on enemy coastlines were concerned.

[363] Information concerning the 'Army' side of this exercise can be found in the book 'Monty. The Making of a General' by Nigel HAMILTON, published by Hamish Hamilton Ltd., 1981. Alan MOORHEAD made some mention of it in his book 'Montgomery', published by Hamish Hamilton in 1946. Brian MONTGOMERY's book, 'A Field Marshal in the Family', published by Javelin Books in 1973, says rather more and makes the point that Lt-General Sir Frederick MORGAN KCB (then a colonel and GSO 1 of the 3rd Division), who was the architect of the original planning for operation 'OVERLORD' in 1944, was also present at Slapton Sands. Surprisingly, Monty's own book, 'The Memoirs of Field Marshal Montgomery', makes no mention of the exercise. However, one has to remember that Monty was probably operating on 'autopilot' at that time, as he had just suffered the appalling blow of losing his dearly beloved wife Betty to a fatal illness. [Whilst writing of amphibious operations, it is interesting to note that Betty had been the sister of Major-General Percy

Even more immediately, Admiral of the Fleet Lord of CORK AND ORRERY, and those involved in *Southampton*, at widely varied levels of command, would doubtless have learnt practical lessons for the landings of troops in Norway in which they were to become engaged in mid-1940, less than two years later. [At that stage the *landings* would be effected well enough, but the sequence of loading of the assault *matériel* in the associated ships would be said to have been in serious error due to the unsuitable *disembarkation* sequence thereby imposed – though it has to be said that there were 'mitigating circumstances' due to the confusion and changes of plan which had prevailed at the highest levels of command.]

The minesweeping flotilla sailed (to Portsmouth) at 0630 in a gale which reached Force 7 at times. They were followed by the 2nd CS, and the remaining naval ships. The destroyer *Escort* was evidently one of the last to leave and arrived at Portsmouth at 1845 returning 'COX' personnel - presumably a Beach Master and his party - to *Southampton*.

Captain HAWKINS and Commander BREWER left the ship, which then proceeded to Whitby, *Sheffield* taking station astern. On the way they conducted further exercises, using their aircraft for shadowing, carrying out HA exercises, using their close-range weapons to open fire, in turn, on balloons released by one ship for the other to engage, closing up their 6" control parties and so on. At 1942 they passed the Sunk lightvessel, and Alf may have thought of his wife and children living at Felixstowe, then just a few miles off the port beam of the ship. At 2215 they started a night action, and came to anchor at Whitby at 0934, launching their aircraft to land shortly ahead of them as a 'herald' of the two 'Navy Days' to come. However, the wind had got up from the north-west, rising to Force 6, with frequent flurries of rain. They set an anchor watch and rode out the gale overnight, the weather moderating on the next day, and the ship being opened to visitors that day and the next. They put to sea at 1700 that day for another 'trade defence exercise', conducting DF trials (which continued overnight) with their own aircraft, going to action stations at 0640, streaming paravanes, going to 18 knots, and, in the pre-dawn darkness of the 21st July launching their spotter aircraft and 'opening fire' on Sheerness, before 'fleeing' south-east towards Ostend. Early on the 22nd they shaped course to make rendezvous with the C-in-C, exercised Action Stations, streamed paravanes, zig-zagged for several hours and then headed northwards to the latitude of the Firth of Forth, making frequent changes of course, 'ducking and weaving' to avoid the dummy air-attacks to which they were subjected. By 0830 on the 23rd they were well on their way southwards again, passing Flamborough Head, and *Southampton* came to anchor at Sheerness at 2029.

They de-ammunitioned and secured to the south wall of Basin No.3 on 26th July, Navy Week opening on Saturday 30th and the ship being open to visitors 1230 - 1915. It was on this day that a professional photographer captured her image for use as a postcard. The author believes that it was at about this time that he was taken to see *Southampton* for the only time in his life, about ten weeks after his eighth birthday. He remembers her as being utterly beautiful. In his memory (which may of course be inaccurate) the ship was painted light blue rather than battleship grey, with white rope-work and upper masts,

---

HOBART, the iron-willed military genius who devised the 'Funnies' (specialised armoured fighting vehicles – including 'swimming tanks'), which drove ashore on 6th June 1944 and performed a multiplicity of assault tasks which saved the lives of a great many men who might otherwise have been trying to cope by the desperate use of 'massed human flesh and blood'.]

and with brasswork polished to an unbelievable brightness. The family sat down to lunch in the Warrant Officers Mess, where his father presided like a Lord, and deferential white-jacketed stewards seemed to attend unobtrusively to his father's every whim. The roast potatoes which accompanied the meal were exquisitely prepared - probably flash-cooked with superheated steam - and of a flavour he has never yet found equalled. He remembers his father's little cabin, and being shown around the ship, especially the 6" and 4" guns. [It was a wonderful day out, which he has never forgotten and always treasured. He thus had the fantastic privilege of seeing the 'part of ship' in which his father was fated to lie after *Southampton* later became his tomb. The author can still see it in his mind's eye, and this helped him to create the drawing on Page 668 of this book.]

During this month and just into the next, Commander DIXON and Lt CAIRNS left the ship and Lt BENNET, Instructor Lt PETERS, S/Lt (E) SLADE, Midshipmen COLLIER and R.L. CUNNINGHAM and Mr HURRELL Senior Master joined. Also (on the 28th August) the Lower Deck had been cleared and CS 2 had presented an OBE to Sick Berth Attendant MACHIRE of the destroyer HMS *Kempenfelt*.

The ship was dressed overall on the 4th August in honour of HM the Queen's birthday. By 31st August the ship had emerged from the basin, re-provisioned, re-ammunitioned, and taken in 1,053 tons of oil. A crane lighter had come alongside and hoisted out the After Rangefinder. A new one was fitted on the 1st September when No.6 crane lighter secured alongside. That same day 4,000 gallons of aviation spirit, 485 gallons of petrol and further stores of ammunition were embarked.

On 7th September *Southampton* sailed for Invergordon, exercising on the way Action Stations, Abandon Ship, and Night Action Stations, also dropping lifebuoys and recovering them with her boats, coping with a steering breakdown, running her two pairs of paravanes, 4" HA firing at smoke bursts, and so on. Again, Alf, who would have been involved on the 4" guns, may have thought about his family as the Sunk lighthouse had come abeam at 1436 on the 7th. The 'Munich Crisis', with the risk that it would spark the now clearly impending war, may well have sharpened his thoughts about the family and the threats which might be hanging over it. He may have drawn consolation from the thought that none of the 'protagonists' yet seemed quite ready to commit themselves. The British Prime Minister was still totally set on 'appeasement' and pacifism - but the senior officers in the British Admiralty were sure that war was bound to come sooner or later and were intensively training their ships and companies, and disposing their forces around the globe, for just that eventuality.

At 0617 on the 9th *Southampton* was securing to No.21 Buoy at Invergordon after her 500 mile run and other ships of the Home Fleet were following her in, such as the battleships *Nelson, Royal Sovereign* and *Revenge*, the aircraft-carrier *Courageous, Southampton's* sister *Newcastle*, the destroyer *Wren* and the sloop *Bittern*. Gunnery drills of one sort or another followed daily until 13th September when *Southampton* proceeded in company with *Newcastle*, heading into the Moray Firth for various exercises which included inclination tests, 6" sub/cal firing at Patt II and, later at Patt VI targets, towed by the tug *Bandit*. Twelve RAF 'ratings' joined (brought alongside by HM Drifter *Shower*), and the cruisers came to anchor overnight off Tarbet Ness.

Next morning anti-submarine exercises followed, working with *Newcastle*, followed by height-finding exercises with aircraft, followed by manoeuvring to avoid dummy torpedo-bombing attacks by aircraft. *Southampton* embarked a third '*Walrus*',

No.712, and Lt Commander (A) E H SHATTOCK, Acting S/Lt (A) P.R.E.WOODS and Lt Commander TILNEY joined the ship. She then exercised 'concentration drill' and then exercised her Lookouts in repelling a dummy MTB attack mounted by the ship's own motor boats, pinnace, 1st cutter and gig. The following day there was 4" firing at a sleeve target, more 6" sub/cal firing at two Pattern VI targets towed by *Bandit*, OOW manoeuvres, torpedo-firing at *Newcastle* and further 6" sub/cal firing as dusk descended. They anchored overnight in the Cromarty Firth, just 4 cables from the light on the tragic and melancholic wreck of HMS *Natal*, riven by internal explosion and lost with heavy casualties in December 1915. Perhaps it would be more correct to say 'the light on what the scrap-metal salvagers had left of *Natal*'.

Southampton arrived back in 26A berth at Invergordon on 16th September 1938, half-masting her colours in honour of the funeral of HRH Prince Arthur of Connaught, whom Alf would have remembered seeing during his days in HMS *Lowestoft*, on the Africa Station. Next day, *Glasgow, Sheffield, Cornwall* and *Coventry* all arrived, and, two days later, on the 19th, *Southampton* proceeded 97 miles to Domoch Firth in company with *Newcastle* and *Sheffield* on an anti-submarine exercise. They then searched for an aircraft which was reported to have crashed, but gave up the search at dusk, moving on to a night encounter exercise in which they fired starshell and fired one torpedo. They anchored overnight in Domoch Firth, proceeding next morning for a range and inclination exercise and yet more 6" sub/cal firing at two Pattern VI targets towed by the faithful *Bandit*.

A photograph kindly donated by Brian Player Esq, the son of the late Commissioned Gunner Harry PLAYER.

Commissioned Gunners Alf DAVIS and Harry PLAYER on the quarterdeck of HMS *Southampton*. It is clear that these two men had become close colleagues and firm friends.

On the 20th they sailed 106 miles to Burghead, exercising 'placing collision mat' and conducting a night lookout exercise, again anchoring overnight and continuing to Cromarty Firth next day, acting as a target for dummy torpedo-bomber attacks in company with ships of the 2nd CS, and moving on to another night encounter exercise, before mooring overnight at Cromarty Firth. Whilst there, *Southampton* embarked 1,020 gallons of aviation fuel and S/Lt M.J.A. KEYWORTH RN joined ship. Lt (A) R.J.T. BARRATT RN joined a little later.

On the 23rd *Southampton* proceeded in close company, with the cruiser *Coventry*, with the 2nd CS, with the battleship *Nelson* and the 2nd BS Squadron, the aircraft-carrier *Courageous*, the destroyer *Wren* and the 6th Destroyer Flotilla, and with the 1st Minesweeping Flotilla, all the ships streaming paravanes, zig-zagging and heading for Scapa Flow. They came to anchor at 1800 after a run of 108 miles.

On Friday the 30th the squadron put to sea, leaving by Hoxa Sound, and, in *Southampton's* case having two runs of full/cal firing by their 6" guns. Back at Scapa Flow, they embarked provisions and Lt Commander the Hon. R.D. COLERIDGE, Mr A.G. SCROGGINS Warrant Engineer and three ratings joined ship. Lt (A) BENNETT, Surgeon Lt H.G. SILVESTER, Lt (E) A.H. BOTT and three ratings were discharged.

On 3rd October, the Diving Party were carrying out their quarterly deep dive in a freshening wind. This rose to Force 6, and a second anchor was let go to secure the ship. Meantime training classes and gunnery drills continued.

Southampton proceeded for Invergordon on the 6th October, taking station astern of *Nelson* and then acting as target ship for a torpedo-bombing attack mounted by aircraft from *Courageous*. She sent her company to Action Stations and carried out range and inclination tests before entering Cromarty Firth and securing to 25A berth at Invergordon, after a run of 112 miles. Gunnery drill and torpedo drill followed.

Come the 11th, *Southampton* proceeded to Cromarty, *Glasgow, Newcastle and Sheffield* being in close company. *Southampton* then engaged in 6" and 4" FC firing at 'Queen Bee' aircraft wireless-controlled by *Newcastle*. Later that day they would repeat the exercise, and add their short-range weapons to the barrage, ending by shaping a course to salvage the wreck of a 'Queen Bee' which they had shot down. Sandwiched between these two shoots, they had carried out a range and inclination exercise with *Sheffield*, then exercised 'Action Stations' and gone on to 'repel aircraft' stations. Nor was their day yet done, for they moved on to a 6" FC shoot at a BP Target towed by *Bandit*, and then torpedo-firing at HMS *Anson*, as well as marking the torpedo-firing at HMS *Anson* by *Newcastle*.[364] *Southampton* came to anchor at Invergordon at 2310

Next morning *Southampton* embarked 340 tons of oil fuel, 3,000 lb. of beef, 1,129 lb. of bacon, 2,246 lb. of butter and 73 cwt of fresh vegetables. During that day and the next Captain (E) G.L.G. SEBASTIAN, Lt G.H.R. MADDEN RM, and Mr W. RUMSEY Warrant Engineer joined and Lt Commander the Hon R.D. COLLINGE and Lieutenant D.W. TWEED RM were discharged. The 19th October saw the ship taking an HS BP Target in tow (from HMS *Buccaneer* off Whitley Bay) and towing the target at 6 knots whilst firing runs were made at it, first, by *Glasgow* and *Nelson,* and then by the battleships *Revenge* and *Royal Oak*. This must have been quite a sight for those in positions to observe the firing ships. Having duly handed over the target to *Buccaneer*, *Southampton* secured again at Invergordon.

---

[364] This HMS *Anson* was an obsolete warship, not the WW2 battleship of that name, which was launched in 1942.

She was at sea again on the 26th with *Glasgow* and *Sheffield* in company (for an air defence exercise), and again on the 27th/28th, taking station on *Nelson*, for engaging destroyers in a Night Action, and securing at Rosyth..

On 1st November *Southampton's* hands, presumably wearing their gas masks, exercised stations for repelling a gas attack by aircraft before proceeding (to Largs Bay), performing an anti-submarine exercise with HMS *Swordfish* en route, and a night encounter exercise with *Glasgow*, before coming to anchor after a run of 96 miles. Next day, *Southampton* acted as a target for a high-speed destroyer attack, exercised Action Stations and commenced another anti-submarine exercise with HMS *Swordfish*. She then participated in squadron manoeuvres and moored at Rosyth after a run of 107 miles. During the month, as usual, she had frequently flown off and hoisted her aircraft back aboard. It would appear they were mainly in use in the spotting and communication role at this stage, rather than being on Anti-Submarine (or 'A/S') duties.

Whilst at Rosyth, *Southampton* landed her RM detachment for a rehearsal of a ceremonial parade, which was carried out to honour Armistice Day, took in petrol and fresh water, and left the Firth of Forth by the North Channel on the 14th November, *Newcastle, Sheffield* and *Cornwall* being in close company. She prepared to refuel the destroyer *Fortune* as soon as she got out to sea, and catapulted all three aircraft she had on board. These flew to the RAF Base at Lee-on-Solent Aboard those aircraft were Lt Commander E.H. SHATTOCK, Lt Commander G.A. TILNEY, Lt (A) R.J.T. BENNETT, S/Lt (A) P.R.E. WOODS and six ratings.

The cruisers now started squadron manoeuvres at 19 knots for nearly two hours, after which *Southampton* refuelled *Fortune*, exercised gunnery drills, carried out range and inclination tests with *Newcastle*, and, as night came down acted as an outer screen for the battlefleet during a destroyer night attack exercise. Subsequently, the 2nd CS and *Coventry* formed into single line ahead screened by the 5th Destroyer Flotilla, and 10 miles from HMS *Nelson*. Next morning *Southampton* lit her A1 and A2 boilers and later carried out a Full Power Trial for two hours, followed by a Range and Inclination exercise with *Newcastle* and *Sheffield*, followed by gunnery drills. By noon on the 15th they were at 55° 15'N, 3° 58'E, on the latitude of North Shields but far out in the North Sea, in good weather conditions. *Sheffield and the destroyers Brilliant, Bulldog, Electra, Encounter, Escort, Firedrake, Fortune and Kempenfelt* were all in close company and, whilst a few proceeded elsewhere, the majority of this fleet arrived at Sheerness in the morning of 16th November. *Southampton* almost immediately began to de-ammunition, cleaned the ship's side and embarked 420 tons of oil fuel. Next day she entered No.3 Basin. Whilst there she half-masted her colours on the death of Kemal ATATURK

The ship now underwent a boiler-clean, her after Rangefinder was again hoisted out for attention or replacement, her RM Detachment went off for a 6-day musketry course at Sheerness Range, and she struck the flag of Rear-Admiral G.F.B. EDWARD-COLLINS.

Painting and provisioning went on through December, the colours being half-masted on the 8th December on the occasion of the funeral of Queen Maud of Norway, the ship being dressed overall on 11th December in honour of the King's Accession, and on the 14th in honour of his Birthday. During this period, Lt Commander F.M.G OLIPHANT, Lt A.D. ROBIN, Lt I.LT. HOGG, Lt (E) F.A. GUEST, and Major H.E.F. SHACKLETON RM joined ship and Lts BULL and WRIGHT rejoined from hospital.

The ship lost Lt Commander D.B. COLLEY and Lt Commander (E) E.D.H BRIGGS who were discharged to *Pembroke* and *Ivanhoe* respectively. Lts J.R. FEARFIELD and H.C.G. BULL were also discharged.

On 1st January 1939 Alf signed his name in the log as Captain F.W.H JEANS RN joined ship and took command. Lt Commander H.W.S. SIMS-WILLIAMS RN and Lt-Commander A.H. COPEMAN also joined ship. Captain A.M. PETERS relinquished command and left the ship later the same day.

However, before leaving the ship, Captain PETERS had signed a report on Alf which covered the period from 2nd November 1936 to 1st January 1939, and in which he said that Alf had conducted himself "*to my entire satisfaction. A very keen and efficient officer, whose loyalty, smartness and high ideals of service are a splendid influence in the ship.*" Here was an excellent testimonial. As previously said, one suspects that Alf was throwing himself 'hook, line and sinker' into his service life. This was to be the last formal report which would survive for posterity. Alf's copies of any later ones which were issued evidently went down with the ship just over two years later, for none of them ever reached Alf's home.

As we shall shortly see, *Southampton* would remain at Sheerness until 17th January. However, it seems convenient to break off at this point to have a further look at Alf's 'private life', before resuming his 'service life' under a new Captain and Commander.

Private Life

The author's memory agrees with that of Joan, his elder sister, that Alf was again home on leave during the time that his second son was born in the cottage hospital in Felixstowe, on the 14ᵗʰ January 1939, and that Alf remained at home for a day or two immediately following the birth. The movements of the ship would suggest that their memories of the situation are accurate, though Alf would have had to rejoin his ship on the 16ᵗʰ January at the latest. If his wife was already a little feverish, he would probably have done so in a worried state concerning her health, but he would have been powerless to help her at first hand. Such can be the lot of the naval man. He was reliant on the hospital authorities. Assuming that all continued well and that she was released from hospital, he would have to rely thereafter on his wife's parents to do their best to care for Alice. He also had, perforce, to look to Alice's parents to aid her in caring for the new-born babe and, until Alice regained her strength, also in caring for the older children, now aged 11, 8 and 7.

Alice, was 38 years old at that time - a considerable age at which to have one's first child. Many years later she would tell the author's wife that her pregnancy had well exceeded the normal nine months, and the delivery, although it was successful, had to be by Caesarean section. Unfortunately, puerperal fever then promptly set in, and Alice very nearly died from it. Somehow, she managed to pull through, though it took her a long time to recover.[365] The pioneering surgery was not as sophisticated as it later became in general surgical practice, and Alice suffered adverse effects from the weakening of her abdominal muscles which meant that she needed to wear a corset for the rest of her life and her physical condition caused her some permanent problems.

On the plus side, she had a fine baby boy, Richard Paul - the Paul coming from the name of the surgeon who had delivered her child. Apparently the surgeon had said that when he helped children into the world he always expected the mothers to call them after his forename - Paul for a boy and Paula or Pauline for a girl-child. It is remarkable that Alice, normally so strong-minded and self-opinionated, had actually consented to the surgeon's whim. If the author's memory serves, Alice had a strong measure of admiration for this surgeon, perhaps because he had strong charm and maybe a powerful personality as well as being a good exponent of his craft. Undoubtedly Alice was also in a weakened and perhaps somewhat emotional state, post-delivery, which may have affected the issue.

The choice of the name Richard is interesting, as it has no antecedent on Alice's side. It seems most probable that it was a totally free choice.

However, the use of the name Richard *may* have been Alf's idea. As described in Chapter One, Alf's father, Alfred Wm, seems to have been neglected from birth by his mother, and had evidently been very fortunate to be fostered and raised by his mother's parents, Richard and Ann DAVIS, i.e. Alf's maternal great-grandparents. There may thus have been some veneration shown to this long-dead gentleman, particularly if the late Alfred Wm, who had normally been so evasive about his illegitimate birth, had revealed 'everything' to Alf at some stage. If so, any

---

[365] Antibiotics were unknown at that time, though a scientist named Alexander FLEMING was one of a number who were striving to produce something effective in that field.

such 'levelling' could have opened up quite 'a can of worms', one way and the other! [There is also the aspect that Alf's putative HOPKINS grandfather was called Richard, and the possibility that he took some sort of interest in Alfred Wm as the lad grew up. Hence, there is a chance that this was the inspiration for the use of the forename. This may not be too far-fetched either.]366

In a strange way the weakness of Alice after the operation led to the first light of a dawn of a measure of sympathy and potential reconciliation in the hearts of her elder children. When their father took them to her bedside in the cottage hospital at Felixstowe, it was a surprise (to young Neville at least) to see how feminine, weak and soft she looked, compared with his mental precept of her brittle harshness and toughness. The strains between the two of them had not yet reached the extreme 'make or break' crisis point that lay two years ahead, but she touched something in his young heart that would never go away again.

There was also the matter of the healthy-looking infant in the cot beside the bed. Baby Richard was now a member of the family. He was much more than a half-brother, but just that bit less than a full brother. This would make for certain complications in 'relationships' and 'rights', and in 'recognition', and the accompanying 'acceptance' and 'rejection' of certain facets of his developing personality as he grew up. Although his siblings would set out to protect the infant, his being that little bit less than a full brother might well give them grounds for 'ducking out' from relating to him on some uncomfortable future issues – and *vice-versa!*

Author's collection of inherited family photographs. A studio portrait by Emmeny of Felixstowe, c. July 1939.

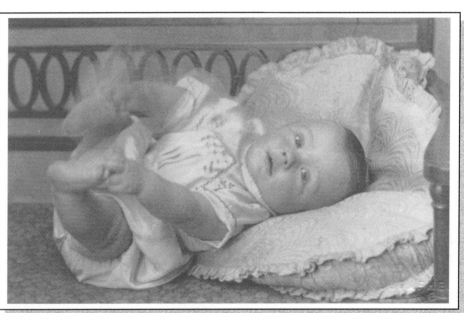

Playing with his toes. Baby Richard Paul DAVIS, the only child of Alice. To his siblings he was *"...much more than a half-brother, but just that bit less than a full brother."* This would make for certain complications *" in ' relationships' and 'rights"*.

366 Richard himself seems to have no idea as to whom, if anybody, he was named after. It should also be noted that 'Richard' is the earliest known ancestral name of the DAVIS Family. (See Appendix F.)

There was also the matter that Baby Richard had a full birth-mother, which his siblings now did not. He was nine years younger than his older brother Neville - a considerable age-gap to be bridged between the two boys. As he grew up, would his mother favour him - maybe even spoil him – to the disadvantage of her step-children?

Whether Alf reflected on such potential 'sibling' issues is unknown, but he would surely have been fretting about Alice and her well-being as he caught the train from Felixstowe to travel back to Chatham and rejoin his ship. He would probably have been aware that Alice was running a temperature, but he would not then have known that puerperal fever was about to set in. That issue apart, he would have been greatly 'bucked' that he had a second son and his fourth child.[367]

---

[367] We have discussed the Will which Alf drew up in 1937. Even though a second World War was clearly brewing up, it seems that he never drew up another Will, to cover the fact that he now had a fourth child. If he did, it went down with the ship in 1941. It was Alf's Will of 1937 which would be probated after his death.

CHAPTER FIFTEEN (b):

HMS *SOUTHAMPTON* (1939-41).

From the 1st January 1939, *Southampton* had come under the command of a new Captain. The officers and warrant officers under this Captain were as follows:-

NAME	RANK	MONTH JOINED	MONTH LEFT
JEANS, F.W.H	Captain	Jan 1939	Jun 1940
SEBASTIAN, G.L.G.	Captain (E)	Oct 1938	Pre-Jan 11 1941?
BROWN, H.N.S	Lt Commander	Jan 1938	Jun 1939
COPEMAN, A.H.	Lt Commander (T)	Jan 1939	Jan 1941
EDMONSTONE (Rtd)	Lt Commander	Pre-Mar 1937?	Jan 1941
OLIPHANT, F.M.G.	Lt Commander	Dec 1938	Pre-Jan 11 1941?
SIMS-WILLIAMS, H.W.S.	Lt Commander	Jan 1939	Pre-Jan 11 1941?
TILNEY, G.A.	Lt Commander	Sep 1938	Feb 1940?
TINLEY, C.B.	Lt Commander	Mar 1937	DoW, Jan 1941
BARLOW, N.A.H.	Surg Commander	Mar 1937	Dec 1939
SHACKLETON, H.E.F.	Major RM	Dec 1938	KiA, Jan 1941
MUERS	Lt (N)	Aug 1937	Pre-Jan 11 1941?
BULL, C.H.G.	Lt	Jan 1938	Pre-Jan 11 1941?
CHANTRILL	Lt	May 1938	Dec 1938
HOGG	Lt	Dec 1938	Pre-Jan 11 1941?
ROBIN, A.D.	Lt	Nov 1938	April 1939
WISE	Lt	Dec 1938	Pre-Jan 11 1941?
BARRATT, R.J.T.	Lt (A)	Sep 1938	Pre-Jan 11 1941?
BENNETT-JONES	Lt (A)	Jul 1938	May 1940
CASSON, J	Lt (A)	Pre-Mar 1937?	1940
WRIGHT	Lt RM	Jan 1938	Post-Dec 1938
MADDEN, G.H.R.	Lt RM	Oct 1938	1939
BEST	Lt (E)	Pre-Mar 1937?	Aug 1940
THOMSETT	Lt (E)	Pre-Mar 1937?	Aug 1940
GUEST, J.A.	Lt (E)	Dec 1938	KiA, Jan 1941
PETERS	Instr Lt	Jul 1938	Pre-Jan 11 1941?
PEEVER	S/Lt	May 1938	Pre-Jan 11 1941?
KEYWORTH, M.J.A.	S/Lt	Sep 1938	May 1940
SLADE	S/Lt (E)	Jul 1938	?
WOODS, P.R.E.	Acting S/Lt (A)	Sep 1938	Apr 1940
HOATH	S/Lt (A)	Mar 1937?	April 1939
ANTREBUS, F	Midshipman	Jan 1938	Jan 1939
BOWER	Midshipman	Jan 1938?	Jan 1941
COLE-BLOOMER	Midshipman	May 1938	Pre-Jan 11 1941?
COLLIER	Midshipman	Jul 1938	Apr 1940
CUNNINGHAM, R.L.	Midshipman	Jul 1938	Apr 1940
HAMILTON	Midshipman	May 1938	Pre-Jan 11 1941?
HARDEN	Midshipman	May 1938	Pre-Jan 11 1941?
MASON	Midshipman	May 1938	Pre-Jan 11 1941?
McINTOSH, J.	Midshipman	Jan 1938	Jan 1939
RUCK-KEENE, T	Midshipman	Jan 1938	1941
REES, Mr F.P.	Bandmaster RM	Mar 1937	Jan 1941
HURRELL, Mr	Senior Master	Jul 1938	Pre-Jan 11 1941?
DAVIS, Mr A. W.	Commissioned Gunner	Pre Mar 1937	KiA, Jan 1941
PLAYER, Mr H.C.	Director Gunner & Boatswn	Mar 1937	KiA, Jan 1941

KOESTER, Mr L	Gunner	Mar 1937?	DoW, Jan 1941
HARDING, Mr	Gunner	Dec 1937	Apr 1939
FORD, Mr F.	Warrant Telegraphist	May 1938	Pre-Jan 11 1941?
RUMSEY, Mr W.	Warrant Engineer	Oct 1938	Pre-Jan 11 1941?
SCROGGINS, Mr A.G.	Warrant Engineer	Sep 1938	Pre-Jan 11 1941?
SHELLEY	Acting Warrant Tel	?	Aug 1940

TOTAL: 49 Officers and Warrant Officers. This list is probably lacking a Commander, a Commissioned Gunner (T), a Pay Lt, a Warrant Electrician, etc. The TRUE TOTAL is probably about 57 officers and WOs.

On 17th January 1939 *Southampton* proceeded down the River Medway, *Sheffield* taking station astern. As they got out to sea, the two ships closed on the battleship *Royal Sovereign* and continued in station on her, carrying out Range and Inclination exercises and closing up their Air Lookouts. They arrived at Portland in the early morning and set an anchor watch, for the sea was getting up. *Southampton's* 6" guns crews and control parties were put to drill and she proceeded to Gibraltar at 1317, the 2nd CS and other ships of the Home Fleet being in company.

It was customary for the Home and Mediterranean Fleets to come together at this time of year to enable large-scale war-games to be carried out. The manoeuvres also served to act as a considerable deterrent to competing warlike nations, by demonstrating the huge concentration of warships which could be assembled by Great Britain.

The cruisers of the Home Fleet streamed paravanes and took station ahead of the battlefleet during the daylight hours of the 17th. As dusk descended *Southampton*, with *Glasgow* in company, took station as a night screen. By now the wind was coming from the south west at Force 5 and a swell graded as 4 was running. The ship was rolling up to 12° from the vertical as they passed the Lizard, the conditions worsening and the roll reaching 16° by noon on the 19th as they headed south. It was clear that they were in for a real 'Biscay' blow. *Nelson, Royal Sovereign* and *Sheffield* were all in company and beginning to make heavy weather of it. By now there were a great many very seasick men in the fleet, some beginning to pray that the ship might sink and put them out of their misery.

Southampton closed up her guns crews and control parties at 1345 and set off to search for a reported 'enemy' ship, her 'maximum roll' by now at 19°. Although the swell had apparently abated, the waves were by now up to 10 ft high and had 'taken over' as the predominant element of the two. The ship reduced to 8 knots. The storm was unrelenting and by noon on the 20th, when they were at 48° 20' N, 5° 30' W (off Ushant), the ship's roll was up to 27°, and had increased to no less than 35° by 2000. This was becoming very uncomfortable indeed, throwing people about and a significant risk to life and limb. The squadron had begun to lose visual contact with the battlefleet, though *Rodney* had been sighted six miles off at 0955.

It was not until 2000 on the 21st that, to everybody's relief, the wind and sea began to ease. By that time one of *Southampton's* lifebuoys and a sounding boom had been swept away, and *Southampton* had been forced to alter course and virtually heave-to whilst her seamen wrestled, ultimately successfully, at the dangerous task of making secure her bower anchor. This had been showing signs of breaking loose with the potential of then causing havoc up in the bows.[368] *Southampton* was still rolling 29° as she got back on course.

As the weather became a little calmer some manoeuvres were possible in the latter part of Sunday the 22nd, when, as ordered by the C-in-C, *Southampton* had reached the rendezvous point off Cape St Vincent. She streamed her paravanes and commenced throw-off sub/cal firings with *Newcastle*. The two cruisers then took station astern of *Rodney* for fleet manoeuvres in what was now only a low breeze but on a sea which was still lively, before both cruisers were detached for anti-aircraft practice, launching their own aircraft as 'targets', and later recovering them, before taking station on *Nelson*, and darkening ship overnight. Next morning *Southampton* again launched and recovered her aircraft before securing 'by 46 berth' of the South Mole at Gibraltar, having run 1,832 storm-tossed miles from Chatham. The rest of the 2nd CS, plus the battleships *Nelson*, *Rodney* and *Royal Sovereign*, the cruiser *Aurora*, and the 5th and 6th Destroyer Flotillas (which must have had a torrid time) followed them in to Gibraltar. *Southampton* spread her quarterdeck awning in a comfortable temperature of 60°F and 'let the ship dry out'.

Next day *Southampton* carried out a Director Test, exercised her control parties and the crews of her torpedo tubes, and her captain paid an official visit on the C-in-C. The following morning the commanding officers of *Glasgow*, *Newcastle* and *Sheffield* paid official visits to CS2, followed by the Fleet RM Officer. *Southampton* launched and recovered her aircraft and put her HA Director and 4" and 6" TS Crews to drill. She embarked 760 tons of oil, increasing her draught from 18' 9" forward and 20' 2" aft, to 20' 1" fwd and 21' 1" aft. (This would indicate that it took about 40 tons to increase her draught by one inch.) Her hands painted ship.

On the 30th January she put to sea, in company with *Glasgow* and *Sheffield*, for sub/cal firing followed by Range and Inclination exercises, flew off and recovered her aircraft, dropped lifebuoys and exercised her seaboats. She made torpedo attacks in low visibility, then, using star-shell from her 4" guns for target-illumination, she carried out a night sub/cal shoot, and later anchored overnight at Gibraltar.

Next morning, Rear Admiral EDWARD-COLLINS (CS2) left the ship, his flag being struck, and *Southampton* put to sea for an 'R and I' exercise with *Glasgow*, the two ships then participating in an anti-submarine exercise, a gunnery exercise and, later, a night encounter exercise. Once they were back at 'Gib', CS2 returned on board and re-hoisted his flag.

The month of January 1939 was over. Midshipmen J.McINTOSH and F. ANTREBUS now left ship to join *Nelson*. During that month Alf had been OOW at least nine times. Now the father of a fourth child, as soon as *Southampton* had reached 'Gib' he must have been hungry for every bit of news he could gather as to how his wife was doing following her dangerous operation and fever, and to hear if his second son was thriving.

However, he had to keep his mind on his naval duties, for, on 2nd February *Southampton*, with *Sheffield* and the submarine *Porpoise* in company, proceeded on an official visit to Lisbon. Regarded as 'Britain's Oldest Ally', Portugal was in an increasingly difficult position as the Republican forces began to collapse in Spain and the

---

[368] One assumes that the seamen had secure lifelines attached but still only completed this dangerous task by 'putting their bodies on the line'.

possibility of aggressive incursions into Portugal by the Dictator Franco's victorious Fascist forces became more pronounced.

Naval Power. A panoramic view of the crowded anchorage at Gibraltar, with the Home Fleet and the Mediterranean Fleet both gathered there. The ships of the Mediterranean Fleet are readily distinguishable by their lighter grey. Six battleships, a battlecruiser, two aircraft-carriers, four County-Class cruisers, three Southampton-Class cruisers, and about a dozen destroyers are present – to say nothing of numerous supporting craft.

Southampton encountered a mounting Atlantic swell (of up to grade 5) whilst on passage, which induced a maximum roll of 18°. Embarking a pilot next morning, she proceeded up the River Tagus to Lisbon, firing 21 gun salutes to the President of Portugal at 0800 and then to the Portuguese National Flag, the shore batteries replying and with the thunderous noise rolling around the port area. The Portuguese C-in-C then added to it by saluting the Flag of CS2, *Sheffield* replying.

The British vessels spread awnings and cleaned ship as CS2 landed on his first official visits. The Guard and RM Band were paraded as CS2 returned to *Southampton*, and the round of official visits to the ship by sundry dignitaries began. The ship was open to the public on the 5th February, and, next day, she landed a Seamen's Guard and the RM Band to attend a Cenotaph Service at which CS 2 was present in a leading role.

An 'At Home' was held aboard during the evening, with many different uniforms and colourful evening dresses on display. On 7th February some Portuguese Officers visited the ship, followed by representatives of the Portuguese League of Combatants (many of whom would have fought in the holocaust of the trench warfare of France and Flanders in the War of 1914/18). The ship was open to the public later in the day.

Other British naval vessels were present, including the modern Tribal Class destroyer *Somali* and the submarine *Starfish*. The visit proved to be a very popular one, the ships all being packed with visitors on the 'open days'.

During this period the crews of the British ships were allowed a welcome run ashore in unfamiliar but very friendly surroundings, and it seems that a good time was had by all. It was probably with a sense of regret that the British ships proceeded to Gibraltar on the 8th February, *Southampton* following *Sheffield*, *Starfish*, *Porpoise* and *Somali* down the Tagus to the open sea. Whilst on passage *Southampton* conducted R & I and anti-submarine exercises, before making 'recognition' trials with *Sheffield*. It is to be supposed that Alf would have been busy, for HA firings at smoke bursts and at sleeve targets were also being carried out. *Southampton* then made torpedo attacks on *Sheffield*, unfortunately losing 'one torpedo Mk IX, No.760 in deep water'. She moored alongside the South Mole at Gib after a run of 409 miles, in which she had made her navigational 'fixes' by star sights, and, as usual, had repeatedly flown and recovered her faithful aircraft.

On St Valentine's Day, the ship put to sea for sub/cal firing of her main guns, and an exercise with the military defences of Gibraltar. At one stage *Sheffield* took *Southampton* in tow, *Southampton* carrying out OOW manoeuvres after the tow had been cast off. *Southampton* then proceeded for night sub/cal firing practice, before returning to her moorings. The rest of the night was none too comfortable, for a nasty Mediterranean squall sprang up with the wind increasing to Force 8 at one stage, an anchor watch being set and steam maintained for slow speed should it become necessary to ease the strain on the cables.

Three days later the two cruisers were at exercise again, HA firing at a sleeve target, launching their aircraft for bombing practice, carrying out depth-charge 'attacks' (including the spectacular discharge of one live charge), and proceeding to a full/calibre shoot at a BP Target with their main armament by night, accompanied by the firing (and recovery) of a torpedo, before coming to anchor. On the 18th *Southampton* was at sea again, this time having *Glasgow* and *Newcastle* in company, and conducting FC firing at a BP Target, torpedo-firing, hoisting out the barge to transfer CS 2 and his flag temporarily to *Newcastle*, and herself speeding back to Gib at 24 knots.

20th February saw the motor boats hoisted out for exercises with the 'Rock Defences', and they would also be involved in making dummy attacks on the Mole entrance four days later. In the interim CS 2 had raised his flag temporarily in *Glasgow* and then in *Newcastle*.

Combined Fleet exercises began on the 27th February and continued at Gibraltar to 13th March. These Combined exercises were very involved. For her part, *Southampton* sometimes operated as a screen for the main battle fleet, running up to 10 miles ahead of it, conforming to its changes of course (sometimes drastic ones) and engaging other warships which were making dummy attacks on the fleet. Some of the attacks were by night. In doing such defending she was once deemed as having been 'sunk' by her opponents. Sometimes she herself was engaged in making dummy attacks on the battle fleet, be it with her main guns or her torpedoes. She exercised her 4" HA armament, flew her '*Walrus*' aircraft in various roles, closed on individual battleships at various times (such as *Barham, Malaya, Warspite* and *Revenge*), usually to give them increased AA protection, investigated Asdic contacts, encountered the enemy battlefleet (and was again deemed 'sunk'), was attacked by dive-bombers - and herself counter-attacked destroyer flotillas which were coming in for the kill at the same time. She also played her part in two runs of a pre-planned 'deployment and fire-distribution exercise', carried out a night search and attack exercise (part of the time at the high speed of 23 knots), and so on. During the opening period the ship ran 1,329 miles, and embarked 480 tons of welcome oil fuel from the Oiler *Prestol* on arrival back at Gib on 3rd March. On 11th March, after the final phase of the Combined Fleet exercises, she would take in 454 tons more. The C-in-C Mediterranean visited CS 2 for 90 minutes on 10th March and they presumably had some discussion on the outcome of the exercises before making their formal farewells.

On 13th March the Home Fleet proceeded to Portland, exercising as they went – height-finding, night encounters with firing of star shell, night shadowing (of *Rodney*) , 6" Full/Cal firing (at *Newcastle*), R & I (with *Sheffield*), firing short-range weapons at smoke bursts, conducting anti-submarine exercises, and so on. On 16th March 1939 *Southampton* secured to 'A' Buoy in Portland Harbour after the long run from Gibraltar. She was back in home waters Her ship's company painted ship for the next two days before proceeding to Dover, with *Rodney*, the 2nd CS and 5th Destroyer Flotilla in company. The wind was getting up, reaching Force 6 west by north, and *Southampton* set an anchor watch on arrival at Dover.

She sailed from thence on the 23rd, (with *Sheffield* in company), manning ship and, as she left Dover, firing a National Salute of 21 guns to President Albert LEBRUN of the French Republic (who was making a state visit to England, 'to strengthen the ties'). She secured to No.5 buoy at Sheerness on the 24th March. Alf must have heaved a great sigh of relief, for leave was now looming in which he would be able to get home and see his wife, who had been desperately ill, and their new infant son.

On 3rd April *Southampton* entered No.3 Basin at Chatham, cleaning, painting and provisioning of the ship began, and 'travelling leave' began to be given. Alf was off on leave just as quickly as he could manage it. A little later on we will discuss what he found on this leave. For the present, however, we will stay with *Southampton* and her activities.

Though Alf was probably not there to see it, by the 14th April, *Southampton* was 'docking down', and scraping of the ship's side had already begun which would continue on her bottom as the water drained from the dry dock. On 17th April Commander R OLIVER RN joined the ship and became her new Navigating Officer and thus the signatory of her Log, in place of Commander R.O. NICHOLS RN. At this time, Lt ROBIN, S/Lt (A) G. HOATH and Mr F. HARDING Gunner, were also discharged from the ship. (Ten Fleet Air Arm Ratings joined at this time.)

As can be seen from the following map and the table, Alf had already covered a great many miles in 'Southampton'. However, he had not yet broken any of his earlier globe-ranging records in other vessels. (As we will see, that record-setting situation was soon to change in a major way, and further maps of the deployments of HMS 'Southampton' follow on – see Pages 555, 640 and 655.)

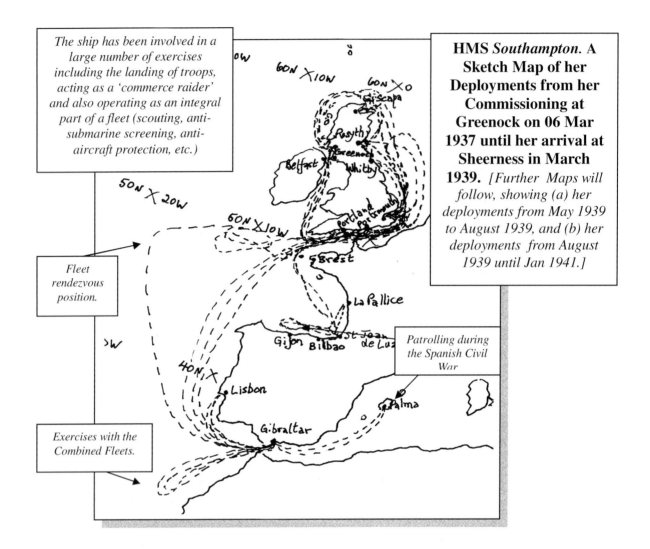

The ship has been involved in a large number of exercises including the landing of troops, acting as a 'commerce raider' and also operating as an integral part of a fleet (scouting, anti-submarine screening, anti-aircraft protection, etc.)

HMS *Southampton*. A Sketch Map of her Deployments from her Commissioning at Greenock on 06 Mar 1937 until her arrival at Sheerness in March 1939. *[Further Maps will follow, showing (a) her deployments from May 1939 to August 1939, and (b) her deployments from August 1939 until Jan 1941.]*

Fleet rendezvous position.

Exercises with the Combined Fleets.

Patrolling during the Spanish Civil War

VOYAGES DURING DEPLOYMENT: Pers. RECORD of Alfred William DAVIS RN					
Farthest North	Orkney Islands	**59 N** 03 W	*F/North (ever)*	Off Scapa Flow	**59 N** 03 W
Farthest South	Off Morocco	**31 N** 13 W	*F/ South (ever)*	Simonstown	**34 S** 18 E
Farthest East	Off Palma	40 N **05 E**	*F/East (ever)*	Ras Asir	12N **51 E**
Farthest West	Atlantic Ocean	48 N **18 W**	*F/West (ever)*	Atlantic Ocean	50 N **30 W**

By the 27th April *Southampton* was embarking ammunition. And on Friday 28th April, with Alf back on board, she proceeded from Chatham to Portsmouth, exercising General Quarters, briefly streaming her paravanes and carrying out 4" HA firings at 'smoke burst' targets whilst on passage. She came to with her starboard anchor after a run of 162 sea miles in a little under 15 hours. The aircraft-carrier *Ark Royal* (which was fated to achieve considerable fame in the next two years) sailed, and *Southampton* promptly began to spruce herself up by cleaning and adding further touches of paint to make herself just as 'spic and span' as possible. She also began to embark what her log called 'special stores'. Her crew remember that these 'anonymous' stores were embarked and struck below under conditions of the highest security, and the Lower

Deck quickly began to form a shrewd idea as to what they might actually be. (The operation of loading took three days to complete.)

On 2nd May the C-in-C Portsmouth paid a very quick visit to Rear Admiral EDWARD-COLLINS (alias 'CS 2') whilst the stores were being embarked. Next day Captain J W H JEANS 'cleared Lower Deck' at 0830 and addressed the whole Ship's Company about the importance of their pending mission. That is to say, *Southampton* and *Glasgow* had been given the honour of being escorts for the liner *Empress of Australia*, in which the King and Queen would sail for the impending Royal Tour of Canada, Newfoundland and the U.S.A. Once there, the King and Queen would undertake a strenuous travel programme towards cementing the expected enthusiastic accord of Canada to the now anticipated conflict with Nazi Germany, and the hoped-for, but by no means certain accord of the North American Continent to the cause of Britain, in that increasingly tense European situation.

Whether Captain JEANS also gave a 'nod and a wink' that the ship might be carrying gold bullion across the Atlantic remains unclear. Perhaps it was more a matter that the crew had already guessed what the 'special stores' might be, and nobody in authority saw fit to deny it, but took the line about '*If you really think so, fair enough. I really can't comment whether you're right or wrong - but keep your private thoughts under your hat all the same, for we do not want dangerous rumours flying about all over the place, do we?*'. Perhaps it was only with the precious gift of hindsight that the penny fully dropped.

The liner RMS *Empress of Australia* arrived at Portsmouth that same afternoon. Although not relevant to the main action in which *Southampton* was now involved, drama was somehow added to the day by the half-masting of the colours at 1100 for the funeral of the late Admiral Sir R G H HENDERSON, the cruiser *Curacao* sailing at 1300 for his burial at sea. [Few would have believed that, suddenly riven in twain by high-speed collision, *Curacao* herself would follow him down to the depths three and a half years later, on 2nd October 1942, taking most of her crew down with her - see footnote three pages ahead.]

Next day, *Southampton's* sister-ship *Glasgow* arrived at 0900, and both ships proceeded from their berths at 0930, each briefly exercising 'Manning Ship', and then dressing ship with masthead flags. Together with the battlecruiser *Repulse*, the two cruisers, now forming the 'Royal Escort Squadron', then hove-to outside the harbour awaiting the departure of the RMS *Empress of Australia* with Their Majesties the King and Queen aboard, *Southampton* and *Glasgow* firing a Royal Salute of 21 guns and taking station on the liner as she emerged from harbour at 1616. The liner stopped briefly to disembark both the Pilot and a ceremonial band, and then the squadron passed at the majestic speed of 12 knots between the imposing lines of the Home Fleet as further Royal salutes thundered out. The four ships thus had a 'royal' send off as, led by the two cruisers and followed by the battlecruiser, the *Empress of Australia* sailed down the lines.

At that time the Home Fleet included the strangely-profiled battleships *Nelson* and *Rodney*, completed in 1927, and the older battleships *Ramillies, Revenge, Royal Oak* and *Resolution*, with their more traditional outlines. There was at least one aircraft-carrier present, and two of *Southampton's* sister-ships, *Newcastle* and *Sheffield*. Altogether, the Home Fleet presented a most imposing sight (see following photograph.)

Anonymous photograph from Alf's collection.

HMS *Southampton* and HMS *Glasgow* lead the *Empress of Australia*, bearing their Royal Majesties King George VI and Queen Elizabeth, through the Lines of the Home Fleet off Portsmouth at the Start of the Royal Tour to Canada and the U.S.A., on 4th May 1939. The weather already looks slightly ominous.

If the liner was carrying one precious cargo in the shape of the King and Queen, *Southampton* was carrying another precious cargo, for she definitely had a considerable amount of gold bullion aboard, being transported under conditions of great secrecy and security. This gold formed a large part of the gold reserve of the country, and it was going for 'safe storage' at Fort Knox, U.S.A. Once there it would be available as collateral should Great Britain need to pay for any war *matériel* which might later need to be produced on her behalf in the vast factories of the U.S.A. – indeed some manufacture was already under way as Britain began to urgently try to catch up from her former idleness and preoccupation with 'disarmament'.

The Squadron increased speed as the Fleet parted company at 1820. Various 'Dispersion Patterns' had been agreed beforehand, and the squadron now shook out into shape, adopting 'Cruising Dispersion 2', and further increasing speed to 17 knots as twin-engined RAF flying boats roared overhead in a low altitude salute and the last of the motor cruisers and tugs hired by the Press began to fall astern. The crews of the cruisers and battlecruiser darkened ship and went to Night Action Stations at 2040. Clearly, no chances were being taken.

At 0042 the squadron stopped engines and the destroyer *Codrington* closed the *Empress of Australia* to collect dispatches and run them back to Portsmouth for onward transmission. At 0352 Wolf Rock lighthouse lay 5 miles off their starboard beam, and, as the day drew out the Atlantic was not looking welcoming, the wind rising from the south west and ten-foot waves running by dusk, as the squadron navigated its way carefully through a fishing fleet. The visibility was becoming poor, and the ships had come down to 12 knots and were streaming fog buoys by 0400. Happily the visibility improved early on the 8th, but the wind was still increasing, touching Force 7 at times, and a swell was also getting up.

Exercises continued aboard, including abandon ship drill - though the hands must have wondered what would happen to the gold if the ship went down, and this may well have sprung the odd pity comment, naturally VERY quietly spoken.

Up to this time the battlecruiser *Repulse* had been in company, but she departed at 1400 after closing the *Empress of Australia* and cheering ship. By now the Atlantic was showing her teeth, the south west wind coming at Force 10, waves recorded as 15 ft high, and a heavy swell running. *Southampton* was rolling 25° by 1600 and, as the barometer continued to fall, the roll had increased to 43° by 1655, at which time the port seaboat was stove in by a huge wave sweeping aboard.

An anonymous photograph from Alf's collection.

On the back of this photo Alf wrote, "*Atlantic Gale during passage to Quebec: 'Glasgow' seen from 'Southampton's Signal Deck.*" In fact, at the time this picture was taken, it was HMS *Southampton* which was in worse case, for she was rolling about 25° to *Glasgow's* 10°, at that precise moment. Matters would become much worse for both ships before they became better.

Her ship's company had only to glance at the gyrations of *Glasgow* to see how frightening things were looking to an external observer of their own ship.

In the midst of the near-bedlam of the storm *Southampton* had to alter course to avoid a merchant ship. The cruiser came down from 14 knots to 12 knots, and 'hove to' in the Last Dog, so that urgent repairs could be carried out to a stove-in port in the wardroom area. By now, the glass was rising slightly, and the ship's roll was easing to some degree. By 0300 on the 10th May they were able to steam at 17 knots, and the squadron began to pick up its skirts a little, to try to catch up on lost time and to stay on schedule, increasing to 20 knots by 1015.

During the 10th May *Southampton* conducted Inclination trials with *Glasgow*, then closed the *Empress of Australia* (*E of A*) and conducted under the eyes of their Majesties an HA full/calibre shoot using smoke bursts as targets. Alf would doubtless have been heavily involved in this. As night fell, the two cruisers conducted a night encounter exercise, before *Southampton* took station 7 cables ahead of the *Empress of Australia*, the squadron reducing to 15 knots through the hours of darkness and *Southampton* setting an Asdic watch for icebergs rumoured to be in the vicinity. (One wonders if this was also a subtle means of detecting any submarines which might have been prowling about, possibly with evil intent.)

However, the next three days would prove to be very trying indeed, for thick swirling fog came down as the wind and sea eased, and the ships began to sound their sirens from 0600 on the 11th, *Southampton* sometimes stopping her engines to try to pinpoint by sound the exact location of the '*E of A*' and to do her best to keep in close touch with her. However, to 'overcook' this was to run the risk of a serious collision, and at 1722 the '*E of A*' suddenly came into sight on a bearing of 055° at the frighteningly close distance of only 400 yards. At 2248 she appeared on a bearing of 100° at the comparatively short distance of only 900 yards. Such short distances left precious little margin for error when taking avoiding action.[369]

The voyage became very 'stop/start'. Indeed, there would be one period when they were stopped for almost eight hours. At noon on the 11th they had been at 44° 55' N, 45° 00' W. At noon on the 12th they were still only at 44° 57' N, 45° 17' W. The 13th gave them short periods when the fog lifted, giving visibility of as much as 10 miles, only for the fog to come down again as thickly as before. Nonetheless, they fired off a royal salute of 21 guns at noon on the 12th on the Anniversary of the Coronation of the King and Queen, and illuminated ship at 2100.

The fog they were experiencing was a result of a tepid air flow over a very cold sea, and betokened the likely presence of ice. Sure enough, at 1230 on the 12th an iceberg was sighted by the 'E of A' off her starboard bow.

The squadron hove to for a while, but proceeded at first light on the 14th, only to find that sludge ice was visible right across their course and about 5 miles off. At 0830 they entered the field ice at creep speed, finding the ice intermittent, and being able to increase speed at times as leads opened, even to as much as 15 knots, but then having to come right down again. The atmosphere was chill, at a recorded temperature of 33°F to 39°F even out of the wind.

Well before this phase, duffle coats had become treasured possessions. Indeed, the Queen was seen to be wearing one at around this time, backed up by a thick fur wrap, as the King, clad in a long camel-hair coat took photographs of the ice-fields, climbing on the roof of a deck house of the '*E of A*' to do so.

---

[369] It may be recalled by certain readers that the liner *Queen Elizabeth* was fated to accidentally run down the 4,190-ton light cruiser HMS *Curaceo* during a high-speed Transatlantic troop-carrying crossing in 1942, when the cruiser was said to have '*zigged when she should have zagged*'. The vast liner scarcely even trembled, as she knifed her way through and on, whilst *Curaceo* plunged straight on down into the depths - there one moment and gone the next, with most hands lost. [Clearly, the E of A and her escorts were not at high speeds at this fog-bound pre-war period, but a 'mid-Atlantic' collision would still have been a matter of the greatest gravity and danger - let alone the whole matter of 'national prestige' if *Southampton* had accidentally rammed the liner carrying the King and Queen, or had herself been rammed, with the consequential loss of *Southampton* herself *and* the 'hush-hush' precious gold bullion.]

An anonymous snapshot from Alf's collection.

The iceberg sighted by the *Empress of Australia*. (The first of many according to Alf's inscription on the back of the original photo.)
The weather had turned extremely cold and it will be seen that these men, standing in the exposed 'eyes' of the ship, are wearing hooded duffle coats.

The sea temperature had declined as they neared the ice field, coming down to 31°F on the 13th, and dropping to a near-freezing 30°F on the 14th, before reverting to 39°F next day and 44°F on the day after that. It was not until the dog watches of 14th May that the squadron cleared the ice field and worked up to 18 knots and it was not until the forenoon of the 15th that the ships were able to shake out once more into their pre-agreed cruising dispositions. The weather conditions were now calm and *Southampton* launched both her aircraft for 'height-finding exercises'.

She also dropped one depth-charge - perhaps to serve notice on any hovering submarine that she had 'teeth'. These were times of great international tension, and there was always the possibility of an attack on the King and Queen by submarine or even by a surface vessel, or should the secret have somehow got out, of efforts being made to sink the precious gold bullion which was being transported by at least one of the ships in company. (It is possible, though unlikely, that *Glasgow* was also carrying some bullion.)

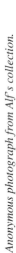

The *Empress of Australia* leading the squadron through the ice floes. Alf wrote on the back of the card that *"The sailors are interested in a large piece of ice passing the ship!"*

As a visible token to the crews of the British ships that they were nearing Quebec, and could now expect further protection, three Canadian flying boats flew over the ships at 1300. By that time they were a little past 46° 23'N, 55° 51'W and heading into the Cabot Strait. To get some air into the lungs of the crew and generally pep up the men, hands were ordered to double round the upper deck at 1600 after completing the heavy task of placing the collision mat at Station 80. (Again, this was probably a 'long-stop' precaution against potential hazards.)

On 16th May, at 0800, *Southampton* fired a 21 gun salute as Rear-Admiral EDWARD-COLLINS saluted His Majesty The King. *Southampton's* crew dressed ship, *Glasgow* doing likewise. By noon they were at 49° 15'N, 65° 59'W and entering the mighty St Lawrence River. They picked up a pilot and followed the course of the river up towards Quebec, coming to anchor overnight, before proceeding through the St Lawrence Traverses to reach No.26 berth at Quebec at 0630 on 18th May, with 4,295 miles run from Portland. During that final leg, on 17th May, a small fire had broken out on the bridge and promptly been extinguished by the Fire Party. The ship had given a searchlight display as night fell, then undressed and illuminated ship.

Southampton again dressed ship and fired a 21 gun salute as their Majesties left the *Empress of Australia* to begin their Royal Tour of Canada. They were now virtually three days behind schedule, due to the thick fog and the icebergs and field ice they had encountered. The programme of events and visits had required considerable last-minute emergency revisions.

An anonymous photograph from Alf's collection.

Another photograph of the icefields, with *Glasgow* following astern of *Southampton*. Alf is the nearest of the three officers who can be seen in the stern of *Southampton*. He has marked a cross to confirm the fact. His battery of 4-inch guns is nicely prominent.

The visit was indeed a momentous one, for this was the first occasion in history that a reigning British Sovereign had ever set foot on Canadian soil. Indeed, only India of the five Dominions had been so honoured. Nor had a reigning British Monarch ever set foot anywhere at all on the Continent of America. The King and Queen were going to enjoy a great welcome, far more informal and uninhibited than they were used to in England. The first person to greet them as they came down the brow at the Quebec quayside was the Prime Minister of Canada, Mr Mackenzie KING who was wearing full dress uniform, his cocked hat under his left arm.

After making various visits in Quebec, their Majesties would embark on a 'whistle-stop' train tour of Canada, running west across the continent from Quebec in the east to Vancouver and Victoria in the west, lying on the coastline of the mighty Pacific Ocean, which they were due to reach on 29th May. Their Majesties would return east by a slightly more northerly overland route, visiting Toronto on 22nd May, and crossing the border with the U.S.A., to reach Washington and New York in the time period 8th to 11th June, and then heading back north again, and then east, to reach the port of Halifax, Nova Scotia on 15th June.

This is not the place to follow all the functions which their Majesties attended, nor to talk of the many famous places and events they would have seen. Suffice to say that Alf and his shipmates would have been generally aware of them, but not specifically a part of them. There would, however, have been a realisation that this was 'showing the flag' in a big way, that the 'French Connection' was being 'soothed and wooed', and the people of British and Scotch descent reassured (be they from the East, mid-West or Pacific Coast), whilst the Hurons and other Indian tribes were also given recognition, and, direct contact was made with the American people through President ROOSEVELT and his wife, who were shown great respect by the British Monarchs. This was all about winning people over to one's side for the pending European Conflict - and 'The Navy' was expected to play its full part in backing-up their Sovereigns' lead.

First-off, however, as their Majesties began their long and arduous tour on the North American Continent, *Southampton* had fallen in her Special Store Party and they were quietly, competently and swiftly disembarking the 'special stores' (i.e. gold bullion), which (according to eye-witness reports by crew members) were loaded into armoured lorries waiting on the quayside, the movement being guarded by massed ranks of tough-looking and well-armed security guards. By 1305 the disembarkation was complete, all seemed to have gone well, and the lorries had driven off direct to Fort Knox. It was subsequently learnt that the gold bullion had arrived there safely. This must have been a huge relief to Captain JEANS who had been loaded with a truly massive responsibility.

Whilst the task of disembarking the 'special stores' had been on-going, the Brigadier-General and Mayor of Quebec had visited CS 2 and the ship had oiled, taking in no less than 999 tons. At 1600 the ship was clean and ready to receive the many happy and curious members of the Canadian public, who poured aboard in droves. Next day, the two cruisers sailed direct to New York, U.S.A., in a stiffish SW wind, but a calm sea. It was here, rather than in Canada, that 'Jack' was expected to bring his maximum charms to bear - and it was here, in the U.S.A that the greatest need existed for them to win over the American Public to provide support for the British should war with Germany break out. This might take some doing, as there was strong anti-British feeling amongst some of the descendants of the former German and Irish immigrants.

There was also the aspect that if the American Navy was going to play any part in, say, protecting future trade convoys as they began the Atlantic crossing to England and France, it would be as well for the 'friendly working contacts' which had existed between the armed services in 1918/19 to be renewed and updated.

Whilst en route to New York *Glasgow* fired a 13 gun salute on the occasion of the promotion of Rear-Admiral EDWARD-COLLINS to the rank of Vice-Admiral, *Southampton* replying with 7 guns. Later, *Southampton* launched her aircraft for a height-finding exercise to be carried out by her 4" Control Parties. There was then drama, for it was reported that her aircraft had crashed, and *Southampton* altered course to recover it, finding (to everyone's relief) that the crew were safe, and it was only a matter that the port float had been smashed in making a forced landing on the open sea. However, there was a sombre moment during the dog watches that evening, for an AB had unfortunately died aboard *Glasgow*, and the ships stopped whilst the hands went to Divisions and his body was reverently committed to the deep at a point to the south of Halifax, Nova Scotia.

The weather subsequently turned foggy but the cruisers continued on course at reduced speed to sight the Ambrose Light vessel at 0915 on the 23rd May. They then picked up a pilot who guided them to anchor in New York Harbour. Here, Rear-Admiral T WOODWARD U.S.N paid an official visit to CS 2 aboard *Southampton*, the ship firing a salute of 11 guns as he left. The next day being Empire Day, the ship was dressed overall, and some of the crew managed to hear the address which King George VI broadcast to all the countries of the Empire. (By that time their Majesties had reached Winnipeg on their outward train journey, and it was from the Canadian Broadcasting

Service that the King's world-wide message was transmitted.) He was struggling hard, with the aid of pioneering speech therapists, to overcome a serious stammer in his speech, and most of his listeners were sympathetic to his halting delivery. What he had to say was regarded as very important in terms of the critical state of world affairs.

CS 2 made a return official visit on R/Admiral WOODWARD U.S.N on 24th May, and *Southampton* paraded her Guard and RM Band. At 1550 she proceeded with a Pilot to secure to Pier 90, North Side. Next day the ship was again dressed overall (in honour of the Argentine National Holiday.)[370] She was open to visitors from 1600. She was also dressed overall on the 26th May, in honour of Queen Mary's Birthday, her Guard and Band again being paraded and the ship being open to visitors at 1615. She was also open next day.

Just as the public flocked to see the ships of the British Navy, so the ships' companies themselves sallied forth to sample the delights of the Port and City. The New York World's Fair was in full swing, and Alf duly made a visit to this very impressive event, dominated by its symbolic 'Trilon' and 'Perisphere', the Trilon soaring 700 feet into the sky. (The King and Queen would visit the New York World's Fair on or around 12th June, but, as we shall shortly see, *Southampton* and *Glasgow* would leave that vicinity long before their Majesties arrived.)

Various contrasting pavilions had been organised by such nations as Great Britain, France, Italy, Japan, Rumania, Russia and, of course, the U.S.A. There were many attractions, including an aquascade, a lake and spectacular fountains, and many relevant souvenirs to be bought. Alf, thinking of his family, made a number of interesting and thoughtful purchases, and took some snapshots with a newly-bought Kodak Folding 'Autographic' camera.

Alf sent a postcard of the British Pavilion to his brother-in-law, George Neville GREEN, saying: *"My Dear Neville, I paid a visit to the World's Fair yesterday, it is a wonderful show – exhibits and pavilions are first-class – you would have enjoyed seeing the Acquascade – a magnificent water spectacle – New York is very thrilling – enjoying sight-seeing and doing things very much – Love to Constance and all, Yours Alf."*

Come the 30th May, the ship half-masted her colours for Memorial Day, otherwise known as 'Decoration Day'. By that time competition had apparently grown amongst local towns for British Naval Officers to grace their various parades on that important commemorative day. Somehow or other Alf came to be made Marshal of the Decoration Day Parade in the town of Kent, in Connecticut, presumably having travelled there by train northward. The parade included the Kent County Volunteer Fire Brigade of Connecticut and the Kent School Band, all being in full uniform. Alf was mounted on a white horse, which he rode with confident skill. A splendidly turned out and hefty pipe-major of the Canadian Black Watch, a Mr F M CHUD, presumably a veteran of the fighting on the Western Front of 1917/18, was one of the leading lights. He liaised very well with Alf, and the day was clearly a great success. Alf would have been in his element, coping, sailor-like with whatever social challenge was flung at him, and being a splendid ambassador for the UK. He would receive a fine commemorative fully-signed photograph in due course, which is still held in-family and is shown below.

---

[370] The Argentine was another country of huge potential significance, for Great Britain would certainly need to continue receiving huge imports of meat from that country should war break out with Germany.

550

The commemorative photograph which was sent to Alf as Honorary Marshal of the 1939 Decoration Day Parade, 30th May 1939, by the Kent Fire Department of Connecticut, U.S.A. Pipe-Major CHUDD stands proudly at centre-stage.

Alf wrote: *"Our last view of New York when leaving, Skyscrapers in foreground* (sic.), *and 'Glasgow' astern of us. May 31st 1939"*. New York would turn out to be the most westerly point that Alf would ever reach.

The two cruisers left New York next day, at 0600 on 31st May, in murky weather, and headed northwards around Cape Cod, being scheduled to reach Boston the day after, and there to attend a further reception.

On their way they conducted R & I exercises, launched aircraft and set their 4" Control Parties to height-finding exercises. They also carried out ship handling trials. Then, having closed up her 6" Control Parties, *Southampton* carried out a sub/cal throw-off shoot against *Glasgow*. She again launched and recovered her aircraft and exercised her seaboat's crew, before sighting the Nantucket light-vessel as midnight approached. Around this time, *Glasgow* parted company to pursue her own separate duties for several days. She would rejoin on the 9th June.

By 0455 next morning Cape Cod Light was visible to port at 1.9 miles, and Boston Light-Vessel came in sight at 0720. A pilot came aboard and the ship secured alongside West Side No.1 Line at Charleston Navy Yard at 0900. They had run just under 400 miles from New York. The official visits began almost immediately, the Consul-General being first to arrive, followed by the Rear-Admiral commanding the 1st Naval District, then the Officer Commanding the 1st Army Corps. CS2 then made his official calls in response, the Guard and Band being paraded. Later, the Mayor of Boston made an official call. Alf was OOW for a part of this day. For the next three days, 2nd to 4th June, the ship was open to visitors as the daytime temperature climbed to 80° F.

On the 7th June, after Divisions, the ship held a Memorial Service for the men who had been so tragically lost in Liverpool Bay in trials of the new British submarine HMS *Thetis*. On 8th June *Southampton* proceeded to Halifax, Nova Scotia. An hour after leaving harbour they sighted the U.S.N Battleship Training Squadron, *New York*, *Arkansas* and *Texas*. As the two squadrons closed on a calm sea with blue skies, *New York* saluted the flag of CS 2 with 15 guns and *Southampton* replied with an identical number as she continued on her way, later launching her aircraft and carrying out height-finding and other exercises.

Very early next day she sighted *Glasgow*, who had been operating separately since 31st May, and took station on her. Both ships closed up their 6" Control Parties at noon, and then conducted a sub/cal throw-off shoot for about 40 minutes. At 1435 they secured alongside No.22 berth at Halifax, the capital of Nova Scotia, and believed by the Canadians to be the 3rd largest harbour in the world at that time.[371] *Southampton* was under 8 hours notice for steam. Official visits began at once, starting with the Officer of the Guard. The Commander-in-Chief also arrived. The ship's Guard and Band were paraded as CS 2 made a visit on the Lt-Governor.

Next morning the Lt-Governor made his official return visit and the ship fired a salute of 15 guns as he left. His visit was followed by that of the Prime Minister of Nova Scotia and by the C-in-C Halifax, a salute of 11 guns being fired as they left. Meantime, the ship was given a lick of paint here and there, and embarked 516 tons of oil, before being opened to a flock of enthusiastic visitors during the afternoon and over the next two days.

At 0600 on the 15th June *Southampton* and *Glasgow* proceeded and anchored off George Island. There they dressed ship overall and fired a Royal Salute of 21 guns as their Majesties arrived in Halifax. (Having left the U.S.A., the King and Queen had

---

[371] Halifax Harbour would become of enormous importance during WW2 as a port where Transatlantic convoys assembled in comparative safety before 'running the gauntlet' to Great Britain.

passed through the Canadian Provinces of New Brunswick, Nova Scotia, St John's, Newfoundland and Prince Edward Island. They had then headed back to the mainland of Nova Scotia, landing at Pictou and arriving at Halifax on 15th June.) As the white-hulled *Empress of Britain*, flagship of the Canadian Pacific Line, by now carrying their Majesties, proceeded out of Halifax harbour, the cruisers fired another Royal Salute before undressing ship, weighing and taking station on the liner, and with all three ships increasing to 20½ knots as they got out to the open sea. At 1900 on the 16th June they made rendezvous with the County-Class cruiser *Berwick*, who fired a 21 gun Royal salute on joining as an additional escort.

The squadron then proceeded to Conception Bay, where they anchored in the early morning of 17th June and dressed ship overall, the Guard and Band being paraded at 1000 as their Majesties left the *Empress of Britain*, and *Southampton* firing a 21 gun Royal salute as they landed to a great reception. The cruisers then undressed ship and proceeded the short distance to Holyroad Bay, where they anchored. They fired another Royal salute as their Majesties left shore, by barge, at 1745, and *Southampton* held Divisions and paraded her Guard and Band as their Majesties arrived on board and formally inspected Divisions. At the same time, Rear Admiral G. F. B. Edward COLLINS, CB, CVO. now promoted to Vice Admiral, was knighted by the King on the Quarter Deck.

It is difficult to be certain now, but the memory of the late Mr 'Dusty' MILLER, a shipwright since the time of *Southampton's* building and a colleague of Alf, is that Alf was in charge of the side party which welcomed their Majesties aboard. This conforms with a vague memory from the author's childhood. If true, Alf would have been as pleased as Punch to have been given the privilege of that duty. [See the reactions of the late Boy Seaman 'Freddie' DANCE on joining the ship in January1940.]³⁷²

The members of the crew were each given a commemorative certificate on behalf of their Majesties, incorrectly bearing the date of 7th June rather than the 17th. As his elder son, Alf's certificate is still retained by the author. In similar vein, the certificate of Marine Band Corporal Frederick P. REES has been retained by his son Barrie REES. That particular certificate has the signatures of the eighteen members of the then Marine Band inscribed upon its reverse side. These were talented men, most of whom could play at least two different instruments. Indeed, one of them, Bandsman L.B. COOMBS is remembered to this day by some of the Marines and the 'old salts' for his delightful and evocative rendering of the song 'Lucy Long' on his bassoon. We shall hear more of Corporal REES later.

Having knighted Admiral EDWARD-COLLINS, their Majesties departed to rejoin the *Empress of Britain* ('*E of B*'), and the squadron sailed for Portland, England that evening, *Berwick* parting company at 2116, the squadron by then proceeding at 24 knots in a pre-arranged disposition. Surely to the chagrin of the Vice-Admiral and her Captain, *Southampton* was forced to drop out of formation at 2305, so that her engineers could examine and adjust her condensers, which were running hot. By 0050, however,

---

³⁷² Later Lt-Commander 'Freddie' DANCE, RNR (Rtd). Freddie was the first person to respond to the author's request for information about his father, which had been broadcast on the TV 'Service Pals' teletext service. Freddie very kindly introduced the author to the 'Old Southamptons' Organisation and gave the author the most invaluable 'foundation' towards the writing of the related parts of this book.

the problem had been resolved and she was steaming at 28 knots to rejoin, resuming her station on the '*E of B*' by 0117.

An anonymous photograph in Alf's collection. (It may be the case that all the officers and WOs had access to copies, because, in 1999, former Shipwright 'Dusty' Dusty' MILLER also kindly gave the author a copy.)

Naval Pomp and Circumstance. Having inspected the impeccable Royal Marines, King George VI advances towards the side party and the accommodation ladder down to the barge, as the pipes start to shrill. The King is followed by the Queen and the newly-knighted and promoted Vice Admiral Sir William COLLINS. Can that be Alf flinging up what may well be the smartest salute of his whole life?

The air had been becoming chill, not helped by a stiff breeze so far as her lookouts and other members of her crew who were exposed to the elements were concerned. The sea temperature was quickly falling, and reached as low as 31°F. It was scarcely surprising that an iceberg was sighted abeam in the darkness of 0425, and then another quickly came in sight, and yet more, with the ships trying to skirt to the south of them, and a number of smaller bergs and growlers being abeam by 0600, and more small bergs again at 0930. By 1130, large bergs were visible at 6 miles, and smaller ones at 3 miles distance. The squadron was now at 48° 56' N, 47 ° 09' W, about 250 miles out from St Johns. The sea was becoming very rough, with a considerable swell running - and the ship had begun to roll, reaching a maximum of 22° on the 18th June. Compared with what had happened on the outward journey this degree of roll was not too frightening, but it was still uncomfortable enough. The presence of the icebergs had also been disturbing in its own right. Luckily, a large iceberg which they passed at a distance of 3 cables at 1317 on the 18th seemed to be the last - though they encountered fog at 0600 next morning which persisted on their course for 25 minutes, so it was hard to be sure that there were no other large bergs about.

Exercises continued aboard, including gunnery-related ones on the 19th, followed by physical drill for all hands. This despite the further patches of fog they encountered, the brisk temperature and the moderate sea and swell which were running. That patchy fog persisted into the 20th, but lifted enough to permit R & I exercises to be conducted, and for speeds of 18 to 20 knots to be sustained as a safeguard against any possible hostile attacks. By noon on the 21st they were at 50° 25' N, 11° 02' W, and at 2333 they sighted the Wolf Rock light. They were entering the English Channel. On the 22nd June they again had fog, but dressed ship with masthead flags, and, the fog clearing at 1110, they manned ship, and, running astern of the 'E of B', they fired a 21 gun Royal Salute, before parting company, their escort duty done. By 1830 they were secured at C.3 berth, Portland, and by 1940 the oiler *Montenol* was alongside. They had run 2,111 miles from Conception Bay, and they needed 996 tons of oil to replenish their depleted bunkers. [The 'E of B' continued safely to Southampton, where a reception was given by the Mayor for their Majesties, on the occasion of their arrival back in England. Ex-servicemen of the city were invited, being expected to wear their medals.]

Whilst at Portland *Southampton's* crew provisioned ship. CS 2 promptly left ship to pay an official call on the cruiser *Cumberland*, the Guard and Band being paraded. This County-Class cruiser had now joined the 2nd Cruiser Squadron, and CS 2 would fly his flag in her temporarily on 25th June, presumably to 'get the feel'. Various ships were arriving, including *Newcastle* and *Coventry,* and others were leaving, including *Nelson, Rodney* and *Sheffield.* It seems that these three ships were bound for the Firth of Forth where the Home Fleet were about to host a visit by some powerful new French naval units, including the modern battleships *Strasbourg* and *Dunkerque.* Seemingly, the strategists were beginning to contemplate the optimal dispersal of Allied units in a war.

On 27th June *Southampton* proceeded for Sheerness, securing to No.5 Buoy after a run of 200 miles in reasonably calm conditions. She was about to go into No.3 Basin at Chatham for maintenance which would last into July. Alf would have been looking forward to a solid spell of leave. He had acquired a lot of souvenirs and gifts for his loved ones and he would have been keen to get away. However, he was OOW on 29th June, so he was evidently not amongst the first of the crew to go on leave.

During the last days of June the ship disembarked ammunition, and began to be 'refitted', cleaned and painted. Though not clearly spelt out in her log, it seems likely that she was also docked to have her bottom scraped and painted.

Come 28th July, she was in the basin at Chatham and began to re-ammunition, also taking in 795 tons of oil. On the 29th, she came out of the basin, proceeded down the Medway and came to anchor in the Thames Estuary. The sea temperature was a reasonable 61°F, the sea was calm, and she sent her hands to bathe. She also sent a seaboat to *Sheffield* to collect her mails. During the month, Lt Commander D.L. RAYMOND, Pay Lt HEATHCOTE and Mr R.D.WADE Warrant Engineer joined ship, and Lt Commander H.N.S. BROWN, Lt P.M. BLISS and Pay Lt DUNN were discharged. We shall hear more about Lt Commander RAYMOND (who became Alf's Gunnery Officer) and Roy WADE later.

An anonymous postcard in Alf's collection.

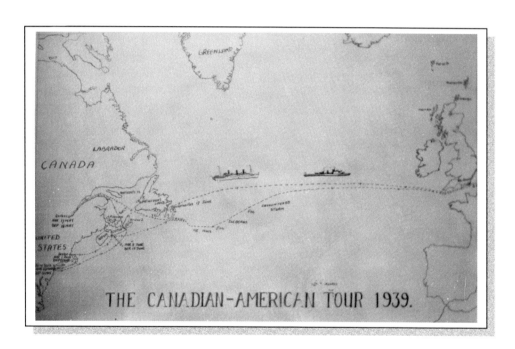

The Canadian-American Tour had taken Alf to New York, which was much further west that he had ever been before. Since May 1939 he had travelled extensively up and down most of the seaboard shown on the east side of the above map, actually ranging from Chatham on the east coast of England to Gibraltar in the south of the Iberian Peninsular. He had also taken in Lisbon and the River Tagus, which would have been 'firsts' for him. But it was the voyage across the Atlantic Ocean to the American Seaboard which had made the greatest impression on him. His 'Farthest Points' had now become as shown in the following table:

Alf's Voyages in HMS *Southampton* since May 1939.					
Farthest North	Sheerness	**51 N** 01 E	*F/North (ever)*	Off Scapa Flow	**59 N 02 E**
Farthest South	Gibraltar	**39 N** 05 E	*F/ South (ever)*	Simonstown	**34 S** 18 E
Farthest East	Off Sheerness	51 N **01 E**	*F/East (ever)*	Ras Asir	12 N **51 E**
Farthest West	New York, U.S.A.	41 N **74 W**	*F/West (ever)*	New York, U.S.A.	41 N **74 W**

Alf had made no further crossings of the Equator, as yet. But he had set a greatly increased personal record for his 'farthest West'.

On the 30th July 1939 *Southampton* proceeded in company with *Sheffield* for Invergordon, departing from Sheerness in a slight to moderate sea and a Force 4 south-west breeze. We shall leave her here for the moment as she starts to carry Alf northwards, whilst we take a look at what Alf would have found on the 'domestic front', when he went on his two latest leaves, the one prior to the Royal Tour of Canada and the U.S.A., and the one following that major event.

NOTE. Pictures (vi), (vii) and (viii) in Appendix J, pages 751 and 752, offer some further views of the departure of the Escort Squadron at the outset of the Royal Tour to Canada and the USA, and have particular relevance to the 'Empress of Australia'.

Private Life

Alf would surely have hurried home for a short leave at some time in the first three weeks of April, to check on the well-being of his wife and baby son, and to verify that all was well with his three elder children. [Certainly, around this time, Alf brought back an attractive set of Portugese stamps for his elder son, who was being encouraged and aided by his 'Uncle Neville' to compile a stamp collection. This collection already featured stamps from Gibraltar taken from envelopes franked *Gibraltar the Travel Key to the Mediterranean*' which had been presumably been used to convey letters despatched to various family members when Alf was in the Med.]

Alf would have found Alice considerably changed, both physically and emotionally. Whereas she had hard-disciplined her two elder step-children, and kept young Jessica on a tight rein, she was tending to indulge her new-born son and to look to her own mother to 'hush' him when he cried. He was being bottle-fed on 'Cow & Gate' baby food, which was then all the rage for building weighty, so-called 'bonny babies' (It was only by post-WW2 standards that fat babies became taboo.)

The older children were bewildered by Alice's behaviour. She may have had post-natal depression. She was not the hard woman that she had been, nowadays being more 'moody' than 'sharp' with them. On the positive side, she still tried her best to do her duty by them, so far as keeping them and their clothes washed and presentable. They were got off to school punctually every day on their bikes.

Physically, however, Alice was very worn down, depressed about the abdominal scarring from her Caesarean section, and the need to wear a corset forever afterwards to support her badly damaged abdominal muscles. As has been said, before her pregnancy she had clearly been very proud of her slim figure. Now, all that had changed. It is probable that she would not have welcomed Alf's amorous but 'unprotected' advances. This would have been the first time that Alf had found a wife who was not prepared to make love freely with him and to happily bear any children who happened to come along. In fact, Alice was almost certainly very well decided in her own mind that she did not want any more children – indeed, she had nearly died having Richard and she may well have been medically advised to avoid any such future risk.

The question of contraception would therefore have reared its head, surely for the first time, and Alf, whilst by no means uncaring about Alice's well-being, would probably have been instinctively very much opposed to the whole idea. The condoms available in those days were not the 'high-sensitivity' ones of today, but relatively thick as well as being dangerously weak and liable to tear. It was almost certainly left to Alice to go through the considerable embarrassment, for a woman such as herself, of having to discuss the subject of contraception with a doctor.[373] It is virtually certain that she was advised to use a fitted diaphragm and spermicidal

---

[373] When the family moved to Harrow in 1941, Alice registered herself and her children with a certain Doctor Lucy PARKER. It may well be that, back in 1939, Alice had somehow also managed to find a lady doctor (i.e. in preference to a man), with whom to discuss matters concerning contraception. It should be remembered that there were not many lady doctors to be found in those days in what was almost exclusively a 'male profession'.

cream, which was the most favoured 'woman's method' at that time.[374] Overall, this was probably a difficult leave-period for both Alice and Alf.

The author does well remember that, whilst Alf was absent on the Royal Tour which followed this particular leave, the submarine HMS *'Thetis'* failed to surface after a practice dive during her acceptance trials in Liverpool Bay, on 1st June 1939. The whole nation followed her dramatic fate, but the DAVIS and GREEN families did so particularly closely, feeling the 'naval' link very strongly. A salvage ship had managed to get the stern of *'Thetis'* out of the water, and (if memory serves) a wire cable and an air hose attached, and it seemed so frustrating to know that the crew inside the hull were so near to safety - and yet so far away from it. The weather was deteriorating and it was not long before the submarine could no longer be supported by the salvage vessel, and *Thetis* slipped back down to the seabed. Only her captain, bent on providing advice in her salvage, one other officer and two ratings had managed to escape. Surely, the DAVIS and GREEN families thought, further men should be able to escape by the 'Davis Escape Apparatus' we had all heard about. But no, seemingly not. The knocking sounds heard by divers in response to their tapping on the hull (whilst the divers were subsequently trying to secure lifting cables) faded away as the residual air in the submarine grew more and more laden with carbon dioxide, and the men suffocated and tragically died.

The author, aged just 9, followed the whole proceeding with fascinated attention and dread, feeling that, surely, SOMETHING could be done. In a strange parallel, he had a fine toy 'Sutcliffe' clockwork model submarine, which failed to surface one day whilst being run in the deep dark waters of the massive water-butt, from which his grandfather used to fill the garden watering-cans. After a day or two his grandfather came to young Neville's rescue (as seemed to happen so often) and 'salvaged' the submarine with a big shovel which he plunged down into the depths.

---

[374] Small wonder that Western women clamoured for 'The Pill' when, a generation later, scientists, seriously bent on reducing the 'economically insupportable' high birthrate in South America, came up with a biologically risky 'hormonal' alternative to the condom or the diaphragm. This was an alternative method which required no *'breaking off from foreplay for preventative preparation'* (which had long been a real 'turn-off', *'especially for passionate Latins'*, when thoughts of romantic and natural lovemaking were in full and ardent flow). The so-called 'withdrawal method' had often been employed as a more 'natural' way of lovemaking, but this was desperately unreliable even if well-practised, and required great self-control by both parties as well as being a potential cause of great frustration for the woman.

As a further thought on all this, a rather unreliable spermicidal pessary (a form of suppository), used by women shortly before intercourse, had come into a short vogue in the U.S.A circa 1940. This led to a 'shaggy dog' story going the rounds in 1942/3, when the (as yet) unblooded G.Is began to arrive in England. The yarn was about a U.S Major who fell into conversation with three hard-bitten British officers, and the talk somehow veered towards the *'longest moment'* which each man had lived. The British Army Officer talked of the dread of waiting for the colossal artillery barrage to start at El Alamein, when he knew he would have to go out into the open and lead his men by night through a minefield to attack the heavily defended German positions. The RAF Officer talked of the dread after having been 'coned' by German searchlights over Berlin, and risking ripping the wings off his heavily bomb-laden aircraft in desperate 'corkscrewing' to get out of the blinding light before a German night-fighter or ack-ack blasted him to 'Kingdom Come'. The RN Officer talked of the *Hood* blowing up with the immediate loss of all but three of her 1,400 men, and his dread as time seemed to creep by so slowly whilst he waited for the big guns of the massive German *Tirpitz* to train round on to his ship, the *Prince of Wales*, herself already part-crippled due to several of her guns being out of action. The eyes of the three veterans then turned to the Yank. He blinked , then drawled: *"Say, have any of you guys ever had to wait for a pessary to dissolve?!"*

The submarine came up dented, with its conning-tower ripped open and draped with foul-smelling slime. The boy couldn't get the stench out of his nose for days thereafter, and his mind somehow equated it with what would be found in the 'real submarine' when she was, eventually, raised from Liverpool Bay.

Alf came home on leave two or three weeks after the *'Thetis'* tragedy had hit the headlines.[375] The excitement of Alf's homecoming *almost* banished that stark tragedy from the forefront of the minds of the family.

Indeed, the family were greatly taken with the souvenirs Alf brought back from the New York World's Fair and his shopping expeditions in the U.S.A. He had purchased lovely silk kimonos from the Japanese Pavilion for his daughters and a fine little illustrated book on the Indian Tribes of North America for his elder son, which came together with a feathered Red Indian head-dress, imitation 'buckskin' clothing, toy weapons and other items. The children and adults were each given small plastic viewers with magnifying eyepieces, which, when held up to the light, showed transparent photographic views of the New York World's Fair.[376] These images were made on short strips of ciné film, which could be wound through, image by image, by means of a small knurled knob. The little viewers were a great hit. The adults also had other, more sophisticated gifts. Alf was in his element in talking about his experiences in the States and the family clung to his every word.

Alf had taken a number of photographs with his own Kodak Folding Autographic size 120 camera – which he had evidently purchased in the States. [His children had earlier been bought Kodak 127 'Box Brownie' cameras, moulded in black plastic, which were a great success with them. The hobby of amateur photography was taking off in a big way by this era, the films being wound on spools with protective 'duplex' backing papers which were printed with 'exposure numbers' on the back to provide 'metering', visible through a red window in the camera back, showing where to stop winding ready for the next exposure to be made.]

Alf also had more yarns to tell. One (possibly apocryphal) was of being taken on a conducted tour of a meat-canning factory and seeing all the live pigs going in at one end of the factory – to emerge as fully-processed tins of pork at the other end of the production line. *"They can everything except for the squeak!"* he had been told – *"And they're working on that!"* (Alf also told that story to his sister Nellie and her family, for his nephew Ray PENNEY also still remembered it 67 years later.)

It was probably around this time - just possibly, but improbably, on his previous leave - that Alf, who always lifted the spirits of the family by the sheer force of his charismatic and vibrant personality, played a practical joke on one of the older members of the family. The victim of the joke was 'Uncle Bill', whom we have

---

[375] It will be recalled that a Commemorative Service for the men lost in HMS *Thetis* had been held aboard *Southampton.*

[376] It is probable that 'Bakelite' was the plastic used in making these little 'viewers'. 'Plastics' were then in their infancy. Children's tea-sets were already being produced from 'Bakelite' (Alf's daughters had been given one). [Another pending plastics revolution in the U.S.A was the development of 'nylon' stockings, which were to prove to be utterly irresistible to women in WW2, with huge prospects of 'bribery and seduction' for enterprising travelling men - to say nothing of U.S. servicemen arriving in Europe, or Britishers returning from convoy escort duty to the States! As the author well remembers (by 1943 there was a USAAF Camp next door to his boarding school), U.S. 'WAACs' wore nylons, which made their legs look fantastic as compared with the lisle-stockinged legs of the British servicewomen. The WAACs were also very much more relaxed and 'tolerant' than British servicewomen, tolerant and kind even to him, by then a starry-eyed and sex-starved 13 year-old from a single-sex boarding school.]

met before in this narrative. 'Bill' was a half-brother of Agnes Sarah, Alf's mother-in-law. Then aged 60, 'Bill' was an old soldier who, as the reader will by now be well aware, had served as an infantryman in the Boer War and then throughout the Great War in France and Flanders. He was unmarried and he was regarded by the adults in the family as being 'a bit slow and simple'. In their eyes he was also too inclined to spend his days slowly supping ale and yarning with other grizzled old veterans outside the 'White Horse' pub in Church Road, rather than working as a Builder's Labourer. [Alf's son young Neville was not of the same impression about his Uncle Bill, for the boy had by now started to go early-morning beachcombing with Uncle Bill, who'd tell him fascinating stories of his experiences in fighting 'Brother Boer' and 'Old Fritz'. Uncle Bill was a survivor, only pretending to be slow. He was well aware when it was his duty to 'man the parapet', but he also knew the virtues of 'digging deep in Mother Earth' and 'when to keep his head well down'. He was a shrewd 'Old Soldier' and in many ways as sharp as a tack. Near-prophetically, in 1937 Uncle Bill had told the then seven year-old Nev, *"We ain't finished wiv' 'Old Jerry' yet, Young Nev, I reckon YOU'll have to finish orf wot we started in that larst scrap!"*.]

Alf *may* have been just a tiny bit jealous of the close, happy and easy relationship which was building up between his elder son and this grizzled old veteran, and the fact that they had so much enchanting 'idle time' to spend together, whereas Alf only had access to 'mould' and to get to know the boy during his occasional periods of leave.

Be that as it may, on the day of the practical joke, Alf had quickly brought Alice, her mother Agnes Sarah, and her father Joseph Walter into the plot. The seat of a dining chair was lifted out of its supporting framework, and a thin perforated board was slipped into the frame. A well-dampened sponge was placed above this board, and the seat was restored to its normal place, inevitably sitting just a mite higher than usual, but 'not so as you'd notice'. A chinaware chamber pot was placed discreetly beneath the chair. When Uncle Bill returned from the pub, he would be ushered to sit down on the chair, whereupon, due to the weight of his body, the sponge would be crushed and the water in it would cascade down through the perforated board into the chamber-pot. The adults all thought this would be an apt and great joke to play, and entered into it with highly amused enthusiasm. However, young Neville and young Jessica, both sternly told to stay silent when 'Uncle Bill' arrived, were highly disturbed by the joke. Neither child knew of the other's feelings. Independently and unknowingly of each other, both children desperately wanted to warn Uncle Bill of the plot against him, but neither dared to go against the adult conspirators.

The joke took place as planned immediately Uncle Bill arrived home from the pub. The water from the sponge promptly 'piddled' into the chamber-pot amidst such cries from the adults as, *"Oh, dear! Couldn't you wait!"* and *"My goodness, how that Cobbold's ale does go through one!"* There can be little doubt but that a point was being made by the 'joke'. However, the 'victim' took it all quite equably and in good part, and all the adults probably forgot the whole episode in no time.

However, Alf probably never realised the effect his joke had caused on his two middle children. In fact, although some might have seen these children as being 'priggish', they had deeply felt it was unworthy of their splendid father to lead the other adults to behave in that way against a well-intentioned old man. In their eyes their grandparents, whom they greatly loved and respected, had also let themselves down. The children were traumatised in that they had felt themselves to be very cowardly for not speaking out against the adults and trying to stop what they perceived as the humiliation of an old man that they loved. Interestingly, their feelings about Alice's part in the conspiracy were null. [377]

Gas masks had been issued to the whole civilian population around this time, stimulated by the generally tense international situation, but probably accelerated after the 'Munich Crisis'. The author can remember the horrible stench of the rubber which was used for the face-piece, and the way the clear plastic of his eyepiece quickly became steamed up with his breath. Baby Richard, just a few months old, had to be put into an all-enclosing bag-like 'suit', and a concertina-like pump had to be operated by his mother to filter the external air before it was passed through into the baby's air space. The baby was visible through a clear plastic window of the suit. He looked very strange inside that 'tent-like' enclosure. In a way Little Jessica looked even stranger, for she was issued with a weird travesty of a 'Mickey Mouse' respirator which had a ghastly pink face-mask and an ornamental blue flip-flap nasal projection sited above the conventional black-painted air-filter drum. Seeing the two smaller children inside these strange devices caused considerable half-scared merriment amongst the two elder siblings.

Indeed, there was a semi-realisation amongst Alf's children that a serious threat to their lives hung behind the issue of these gas-masks. Some of this 'came through' to them from the concern mirrored in the faces and behaviour of the adults. Some 'came through' from the official publicity, by which all people were sternly told that their gas-masks must accompany them everywhere, slung by tapes in their neat cardboard cases. And, as further back-up, lectern-like boards supported on waist-high wooden posts began to appear at intervals along the roadsides. These boards had been painted with a pale green chemical emulsion. In the event of a gas-attack it was said that the emulsion would change colour, and that gas-masks should then be immediately donned. The children kept looking at these boards, waiting in fascinated and unbelieving dread lest they should colour-change without warning.

The introduction of Identity Cards nationwide stimulated further tension in the family elders when an official called round to take down the family details and to issue the actual cards. Other warlike signs were evident in the increasing presence of soldiers at nearby Brackenberry Fort, and military vehicles, such as bren-gun carriers with steel-helmeted drivers and passengers, cavorting along the High Road, rocking back and forth on their well-sprung tracks. One night, an open-topped fifteen-hundredweight truck pelting along the High Road crashed into a heavy-duty metal pylon on the corner of Church Road, probably killing the two men aboard, the rumour being that one of them had been decapitated. This 'human evidence' was gone by daylight, with just the shattered and half overturned truck with its heavily blood-spattered seats remaining under the public gaze - including the eyes of the author, then eight years old.

---

[377] It was not until the year 2000, over sixty years later, that the author found out that Jessica, his younger sister, still shared this traumatic childhood memory and still retained identical feelings to his own. Both Nev and Jess were pretty well put off practical jokes for life by the incident. [However, Neville does have to put his hand up for at least one elaborate practical joke he played on a work-colleague in later life. The joke worked brilliantly and the victim took it all in very good part. The memory still sends Neville into guilty hysterics. Thinking about it, Neville now realises that his playing of this trick was in revenge for this person having been granted a privilege that he (Neville) had coveted. Was Alf in similar case?

The general belief was that the anticipated war would start with a devastating and overwhelming gas-attack on the population of the British Isles. Yet, there was a strange feeling of unreality about the situation. Few people seemed to believe that war was inevitable. Most people applauded Neville CHAMBERLAIN's attempts to bring 'Peace in our Time'. The swing towards general disgust with his 'softly-softly' approach was subtle - but very sudden when it did come. People then felt a sense of shame and a feeling that we had been weak and spineless - also that we had become terribly 'let down' and weakened by the reduction of our defences all through the peacetime years.

The whole family always looked to Alf as being their strength in all this critical uncertainty, and felt that somehow he and his naval colleagues would 'see us through', no matter what befell.

However, Alf was off to sea again (His ship was now being sent north, to Invergordon.) So long as he was at that distance, further leaves were most unlikely to occur. The family would somehow have to survive without his physical presence - the lot of so many servicemen's families, but especially the families of naval men.

A photograph from the extensive archive of the author's 1st Cousin, Colin GREEN. Note: This late-arriving photograph is not recorded in the List of Illustrations, nor has it been indexed in Appendix B.

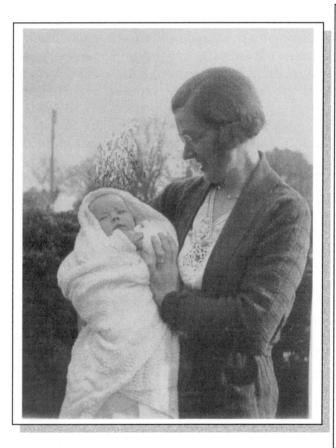

A pleasant picture of Alice with her son, Richard Paul, aged about six weeks. Alice had survived a life-threatening 'post-operational' attack of puerperal fever. She was still convalescent and looking thin and frail when this photo was taken. Alice now had four children to look after, ranging in age from new-born to eleven years old. The emotional response of each child to Alice differed widely from one to the next. The impending war would heighten those differences and add great complications.

HMS *SOUTHAMPTON* (1939-1941) (Continued):

B y 30th July 1939 *Southampton*, still flying the flag of Vice-Admiral Sir Frederick EDWARD-COLLINS, had re-joined the Home Fleet and now proceeded in company with *Sheffield* for Invergordon, departing from Sheerness in a slight to moderate sea and a Force 4 south-west breeze. On 31st July she launched one of her aircraft for an hour, as part of a height-finding exercise, and, when recovering it, stayed hove-to whilst she aided a seaboat from *Sheffield* which was in difficulties. *Southampton* subsequently proceeded, again with *Sheffield* in company, and later conducted an R & I exercise with her as they headed north, both ships streaming their paravanes whilst a sizeable force began to assemble around them.

Author's collection. An anonymous photograph, originally marked 'Passed for Transmission only (not for publication.)' This postcard was probably in Crown Copyright for 50 years.

A '*Shagbat*', officially known as a Supermarine '*Walrus*' aircraft, is catapulted from a 'Southampton' class cruiser. This was an exciting event which always drew a small crowd of off-watch 'goofers'. [In the original photo, taken c.1940, the censor had 'inked-out' the then-secret 'Unrifled Anti-Aircraft Projectiles' (UAPs) mounted on the hangar side. In this modified 'print' the ugly ink-markings which were at bottom-centre have been erased and replaced by means of computer-aided 'sea-wavelets'.]

Southampton later attempted to recover mails dropped virtually alongside, from an aircraft launched by *Revenge*. Unfortunately the float came away from the mail packet during recovery, and the mail sank and was lost. Mail is always eagerly awaited by sailors, and it is all too easy to imagine the considerable disappointment and sense of loss that this unfortunate accident would have cast over the ship's company.

Following this mishap, *Southampton* took station on the battleship *Revenge* and various manoeuvres ensued with *Sheffield* and the battleships *Royal Oak* and *Rodney* as the assembled force maintained a mean course northwards up the East Coast. However, there were considerable 'deviations' from this mean course, with the cruisers taking their positions on the night outer screen at dusk, and their crews going to Night Action Stations.

On 1st August, further Fleet manoeuvres followed, plus launching and recovery of aircraft, before the force came to anchor at Nairn at the end of their 700 mile run. That evening they exercised their searchlight control parties.

Next day, *Southampton* put to sea for a sub/calibre shoot, for 4-inch firing at a sleeve target, for torpedo-firing and recovery, and for more R & I tests. The ship also practised 'making slicks' - and CS2 (namely Vice-Admiral Sir Frederick EDWARD-COLLINS) held a meeting with the captains of the 2nd CS, presumably to discuss the likelihood of war soon breaking out, the tasks which would then lie ahead and the further training and preparation to deal with those tasks which must now be undertaken.

The morrow saw more of the same intensive training; viz, launching and recovery of aircraft and the 4-inch Control Parties closed up. Next day, both the 4-inch and the 6-inch Control Parties were closed up, and then *Southampton* practised taking her sister-ship *Glasgow* in tow. On the 5th August *Southampton* embarked oil and fresh water. On the 6th, by way of a slight diversion and to ease the tension, she landed her Hockey Team and Boys' Football Team for matches, evidently in competition against other ships' teams. On the 7th her hands painted ship - and a 'Catapult Structure' arrived from *Rodney*. As an odd note, on Thursday 8th August, a Royal Marine was brought off from shore suffering from head-injuries received in a car crash, and was tended in the Sick Bay.

Next day, the 9th, it was back to intensive training with a vengeance, and *Southampton* proceeded for full/calibre firing and torpedo-firing, also dropping and recovering her lifebuoys for exercise. She remained under 4 hours notice for steam after she had at last secured. Alf would have been busy next day, for she exercised her 4-inch gun crews in firing at a sleeve target. He was also OOW around this time. Although he had not been specifically shown in the log as having joined ship, another Commissioned Gunner, Mr L. KOESTER (of whom more later), was also now sometimes appearing as OOW.

Southampton, still flying the flag of Rear Admiral Sir Frederick EDWARD-COLLINS, and accompanied by *Glasgow, Sheffield* and *Cumberland*, now proceeded to Grimsby, the detachment streaming their paravanes and, around midnight, carefully feeling their way through a fishing fleet which had its gear out. Early next morning *Southampton* exercised Action Stations, and then Cruising Stations, watch by watch.[378] The force came to anchor at Grimsby at 2030 on the 11th, having run just 330 miles from Nairn, (The shortness of this direct voyage being in marked contrast to the 700 miles of their outward voyage on the 31st July/1st August, with its many 'deviations for manoeuvres').

On the 12th August the newly commissioned *Edinburgh*, a 10,260 ton 'Modified Southampton-Class' cruiser, joined the Squadron, firing a 15 gun salute to CS 2 as she did so, and *Southampton* replying with 7 guns. Many eyes must have studied *Edinburgh's* strange profile, which was very long and lean, being considerably 'stretched' in comparison with *Southampton* and her 'full' sisters (such as *Sheffield*), for this 'half-sister' *Edinburgh* had a long space between bridge and fore-funnel. It was here

---

[378] Her log describes the 'defence' watches at this time as being, 'Green', 'Red', '1st Miscellaneous', '3rd Miscellaneous', and 'Part'.

that her cranes were placed, instead of being between the two funnels. She also had her mainmast sited ahead of her after-funnel, and her 'X' and 'Y' gun-turrets placed one full deck higher than on the 'original' *Southamptons*, thus bringing her rear turrets to a level with her 'A' and 'B' turrets.

Author's collection. An anonymous postcard of French origin.

HMS *Edinburgh*, a modification of the 'Southampton-Class', nearly 1,000 tons heavier than *Southampton*, being 22 feet longer, and with increased armour protection. Her belt was about one-inch thicker and she was more robustly-built internally. Her anti-aircraft armament had also been improved, for she had 12 four-inch HA/LA guns mounted in six turrets. [*She was lost in May 1942 in defending a convoy to Russia, giving a good account of herself against German destroyers, but becoming damaged and later being fatally torpedoed by a U-boat whilst under tow in the Barents Sea. She went down with a large consignment of gold bullion still aboard. Fifty years later her wreck would be torn apart to gain access to the gold, in deep-sea operations which over-rode the protests of people who held that the wreck was a Commonwealth War Grave and should remain inviolate.*]

One can imagine that considerable discussion ensued between Alf and his colleagues about the probable merits and de-merits of these changed arrangements, and about the increased turning-circle that would be inherent from her greater overall length, as compared with the original 'Southampton Class'. However, from Alf's point of view one suspects that the most significant feature of all was the fact that *Edinburgh* had port and starboard batteries of no less than six 4-inch guns, as compared with *Southampton's* meagre four – and Alf would have been in no doubt about the merits of that arrangement. Whether it would have become immediately apparent to the watchers that *Edinburgh* also had an up-scaled armoured belt is unknown. Experience in operating at sea in conjunction with *Edinburgh* would probably have indicated to Alf and his fellow-officers that her maximum speed was very comparable to that of *Southampton* herself.

The five cruisers now became a part of the so-called 'Humber Force' - a detachment of the 2nd Cruiser Squadron which operated in the Pentland Firth and North Sea area. The Captain of *Southampton* talked to the crew at Divisions about the difficult tasks which would surely lie ahead of them, and it seemed almost incongruous that the ship was subsequently open to visitors, from 1400 to 1821. However, the country was not yet committed to war, and a touch of 'normality' was doubtless good for the morale of servicemen and civilians alike - to say nothing of the potential value for Naval recruitment in the current rapid expansion. Indeed, at this time reservists were already being called back, rather discreetly, for further service against what one might call 'eventualities'. Ultimately, this move would prove to have been invaluable in up-dating these men in the use of the latest equipment and techniques.

The 14th saw the ship, with *Glasgow* and *Sheffield* in company, proceeding to sea. They were playing the part of a German Squadron in offensive action against Great Britain, and were up against the defence of a so-called 'Red Force'. As darkness descended *Southampton* and her consorts 'sharpened up' their Lookouts (and frayed the nerves of their Watchkeeping Officers) by setting themselves to follow the shaded and dim blue stern lights of the 'next ship ahead', and straining to keep carefully to the stipulated distance of separation. As morning came they streamed paravanes, conducted R & I exercises, and closed up the 6-inch gun crews. At noon on the 15th, as part of these 'war games' exercises, they were at 54° 54' N 4° 47' E, off the Dutch Coast and about 70 miles west of the large and 'sensitive' German base of Wilhemshaven. Two hours later a German aircraft flew overhead and the crew went to Action Stations, mainly for 'live' practice but perhaps also just to be on the safe side - whether they were 'pretending to be German' or not.

During the remainder of that day and on through the night they steered well north, before making their easting, hoping thereby to outwit and break through the lines of the 'red' force which had been deployed against them. However, at 0647 a 'red' flying boat was sighted, flying at 7,500 ft. They suspected that the 'jig was up', and it soon became apparent that this aircraft had not only sighted them, but that it had called up a strike force, for, at 1145, they were dummy-attacked by twelve 'red' torpedo-bombers. By noon next day they were at 62° 03' N, 3° 36' E, at the latitude of the Shetland Islands, having continued a long way northward towards Norway, and still being quite close to its shores, having, as yet, veered but little eastward.

Then, later that day, *Southampton* and her consorts ran almost due eastward, and quickly closed the Scottish coast, the force passing with care through a Dutch and German fishing fleet during the evening of the 17th. Changing course again, they now ran southwards past Whitby. On the 18th *Southampton* exercised Action Stations with the ship speeding along at 27 knots, and then, with *Glasgow* in company, carried out dummy coastal bombardments, (simulating what the battlecruisers of the German High Seas Fleet had done 'for real' in WW1). Having reached the latitude of the Humber by midnight, the cruisers turned about and increased to nearly 28 knots once they had cleared an early-morning patch of fog. They now practised 'making smoke' for 10 minutes, the ships heading north until the 19th, when they turned about again, closing the coast as the exercise finished and securing at Rosyth on the 21st, having run nearly 1,000 miles around the North Sea. By that time the destroyers *Express* and *Encounter* were in company, and the cruiser *Cumberland* had joined early that morning. *Southampton* now oiled (1,061 tons), and embarked fresh water and petrol. She also took in provisions. As a precaution, her divers went down to examine her starboard screws, apparently finding nothing amiss.

Next day the force proceeded to sea for further exercises, streaming their paravanes and exercising their 6-inch and 4-inch Control Parties, before securing at Invergordon. On the 23rd August the Captain of *Belfast*, a sister-ship of *Edinburgh*, called on CS 2, and the renowned battlecruiser *Hood* arrived in harbour. Next day, Vice

Admiral L.V. WELLS, CB, DSO, commanding aircraft-carriers, called on CS 2. The aircraft-carrier *Ark Royal* proceeded that evening.

Southampton herself proceeded some time later, heading for Scapa Flow where she arrived on the 25th, after a run of 150 miles, and promptly topped up with oil. Next day her captain again addressed the ship's company, keeping them updated on the tense international situation by then prevailing, for Germany had just taken the governments of England, France, Poland and other countries totally aback by suddenly signing a 'non-aggression pact' with Russia. This had deep significance, for it meant that HITLER had no need to keep large military forces on the Eastern borders of Germany, and could hurl the majority of his Army and Air Force westward against France and Belgium, or maybe more northward, against Poland.

By now, pensioners as well as reservists were being recalled for Naval Service, and it looked as though Alf's looming retirement would be going 'on the back burner' for the time being.

Lt GRENFELL, Mr F.J.WHITE Warrant Engineer and 38 ratings joined ship. The ship's company tested their anti-gas respirators. Alf was OOW from time to time - so, too, Mr L KOESTER, Commissioned Gunner.[379]

On the 28th August the highly impressive Sir Max HORTON KCB, Vice Admiral Northern Patrol, and Rear Admiral H. BLAGROVE Rear Admiral 2nd BS Squadron, called on CS 2.

Next day, the mighty 33,950 ton battleship *Nelson* arrived and anchored next to *Southampton*. Evidently considering discretion to be the better part of valour, the 9,100 ton *Southampton* subsequently shortened in her anchor cable to four shackles 'to allow *Nelson* to swing clear'. Later, *Southampton* proceeded, streaming her paravanes as she cleared the Hoxa boom, with *Glasgow*, the destroyer *Matabele* and one of *Matabele's* sisters in company. They were heading out into the North Sea on patrol, noon on the 30th finding them at 59° 37' N, 01° 46' W, to the east of the Orkney Islands, the ships zig-zagging and the crew aboard *Southampton* being given physical drill. One imagines that the frequent changes of course would have added an additional test of balance to the normal PT 'evolutions'.

The ship subsequently turned about and headed south, to arrive at Grimsby at 0646 on the 31st August, with 570 miles run, the 4-inch guns crews and control parties later being closed up and practising at 'clearing away for action'. Next day they embarked oil and petrol, touched up paintwork and proceeded to sea at 2000.

Southampton was still patrolling in company with *Glasgow*, but now with eight destroyers, including the J-class *Jervis, Javelin, Jackel, Jersey, Jupiter* and a smaller E-class destroyer, *Echo*, in company. By noon on the 2nd September the force was at 53° 12' N, 03° 48' E, some 40 miles off Texel on the Dutch Coast, but then headed northward, so that they were off the south-west tip of Norway at 1100 next day when, momentously, the peace-loving Prime Minister Mr Neville CHAMBERLAIN showed some steel at long last, by broadcasting to the British nation that, because the Ultimatum

---

[379] Unfortunately, the 'signatures' of the OOWs generally consist only of freely-written and overlapping initials, and the author has found it hard to decipher and match them against the full names of Officers and Warrant Officers known to be aboard. Most 'signatures' have therefore remained 'anonymous' to him. However, Mr KOESTER's signature was clear and distinctive. (He was a married man aged 37. He and Alf had become good friends over the last couple of years.)

of Britain and France had been ignored, and no undertaking had been received from Germany to withdraw their troops from Poland, "*a state of war now existed between Great Britain and Germany.*"

Considerable tension had arisen on board, and, at 1300, what sounded heart-stoppingly like gunfire was heard ahead. It was with relief and slight embarrassment that this was soon found to be nothing worse than a distant thunderstorm breaking over the unquiet sea, with the wind soon rising to a stiff Force 6.

As would now become virtually 'standard wartime practice' whilst at sea, at 0500 on 4th September, as daylight broke, the ship increased to full speed and her crew went to Day Action Stations, not reducing to a lower 'State of Readiness' (be it of 1st, 2nd or 3rd Degree) until 0800. It was to the 3rd degree of Readiness that she went on this opening day of the War. *Southampton* later came down to 25 knots in speed, the other ships in company conforming.

At 1148 the destroyer *Jersey* was sent to investigate a vessel which the lookouts had sighted. This turned out to be a merchant ship, the *Johannes Mecklensberg*, which was wearing the Norwegian flag. She was boarded and was about to be cleared by CS 2 to proceed on her way, when one of the returning boarding party just '*happened to mention*' that, although disguised by a masking coat of paint, he had discerned swastika emblems on the ship's boats.

This caused quite a '*furore*', and Vice-Admiral EDWARD-COLLINS immediately ordered the *Johannes Mecklensberg* to be re-boarded, whereupon her crew, their bluff called, promptly opened the sea-cocks to scuttle her. The destroyer *Jaguar*, straight from the builder's yard and a striking sight because she was covered in pink 'red-lead paint', was ordered to sink her by gunfire. Being incomplete, *Jaguar* had to lay her guns in manual control, but her shots were quickly effective, and red flames appeared in the German merchantman's side as she slid beneath the waves.

Southampton's career might well have come to a sudden halt on the third day of the war. That is to say, visibility was hampered by fog-patches, and she suddenly had to go hard to starboard and full speed ahead to avoid a torpedo attack made on her at 60° 10' N, 00° 24' E, to the east of the Shetlands. This underwater attack was mounted on *Southampton* at 1225 by a very brave and determined U-boat captain, just ten minutes after *Jervis* had attacked an 'Asdic submarine contact' with a depth-charge, but without result. Whether this attack was made by the same submarine, or whether two or more were operating in the same area remains an unknown.[380]

Having run 850 miles on that patrol, *Southampton* was at Rosyth on 6th September - where she embarked fresh water, petrol and ammunition - leaving on the 8th and proceeding to sea on renewed patrol, with the same ships in company. That day *Jervis*

[380] It seems that the Admiralty had no idea that the U-boats were now strong enough to dive to depths much greater that the deepest depth at which the British depth-charges could be set to explode at that period. (See more detailed note about U-boat capability on Page 576.) It should be noted that, at this stage of the war, ASDIC (or 'Asdic') could give the bearing and range of a 'contact', but it would be two years and more before technological development would lead to ASDIC/SONAR equipment capable of giving the vital factor of the *depth* of the target as well. It would also be found that the operational range of the U-boats was much greater than British Intelligence had believed. (Early in 1942 the Germans would stupefy the U.S. Navy by sending some of their larger U-boats on long offensive patrols directly off the eastern seaboard of the U.S.A.) Clearly, German submarine technology had been streaking 'ahead of expectation' in various fields.

questioned and inspected a merchant ship, and, next day, *Jupiter* attacked a submarine, before the force put into Grimsby, having sailed 650 miles.

Author's collection. A photographic postcard by Valentines, c.1939. Image reproduced by courtesy of St Andrews University Library.

HMS *Jervis*, a destroyer of 1,696 tons displacement, speed 36 knots, armed with six 4.7-inch guns and ten 21-inch torpedo tubes, completed in 1939. She was the class leader of the five 'J-Class' destroyers which were operating with HMS *Southampton* around this time.

On the 10th they proceeded south for Sheerness, streaming their paravanes and going to 2nd Degree Readiness, with the ships making 24 knots as the new day broke. At 1050 *Southampton* fired her Pom-Poms for exercise, hauled her paravanes and passed through the South Edinburgh Channel (confusing title that!) to secure at No.7 Buoy, Sheerness. The C-in-C Nore visited CS 2 for an hour. It seemed that some sort of 'scare' was in progress, for, having embarked petrol, *Southampton* proceeded to sea briefly, with her crew held at 1st Degree Readiness, before returning to her berth at Sheerness. Whilst there she took in 300 tons of oil and a supply of fresh water, before heading back to Grimsby. She had a dramatic and thunderous departure from Sheerness, for she left her destroyers carrying out a depth-charge attack on a possible Asdic contact.

Nor was this the only excitement, for, whilst *Southampton* was running northward at 24 knots, a fire was detected in her after funnel uptakes. However, the fire was quickly extinguished, and she arrived safely at Grimsby on the 14th September after a run of 570 miles. Next day, the wind steadily increased, reaching Force 7 from the north-west at one stage, and an anchor watch was set. Ten minutes later it was deemed wise to drop a second anchor underfoot, and, sure enough, after an oiler had come alongside, both of *Southampton's* anchors began to drag. She therefore slipped the oiler and re-anchored, still in her original position, but this time anchoring successfully, perhaps aided by an easing in the wind.

Having been relieved on her station by *Edinburgh* on 15th September, *Southampton* left the Humber on the 16th September and arrived at Rosyth the next day, securing to the A1 Buoy after her run of 320 miles. She oiled (260 tons) took in fresh water and, in view of the adverse weather, held Divisions and Divine Service in her Starboard Hangar. During the next two days she embarked petrol and ammunition and landed a working party under the Boatswain to rig a Jury Mast ashore, purpose unknown.

Some sources say that she had a three-day boiler clean at this time, completed on the 19th. The log makes no specific reference to this but the shipboard events could fit. It thus might just be that a part of the crew could have had a snatched period of leave from the 17th to the 19th inclusive at this time. They would not have had much time, for *Southampton* proceeded to sea for sub/cal and full/cal practice shoots on the 20th, and was out again on the 21st on anti-submarine trials and height-finding exercises. Between times she also topped up with oil and provisioned ship, discharging 'boarding parties' to *Jervis* and *Jupiter* to boost their manpower for a forthcoming task.

That is to say, on the 22nd September *Southampton* departed Rosyth as a part of the 2nd CS to make a raid on the Skaggerak. However, for tactical reasons this raid was abandoned and the force returned to Rosyth on the following day, the cruisers altering course as they closed the Firth of Forth to avoid a possible submarine contact. Unfortunately the destroyers *Jersey* and *Javelin* had been in collision after darkness fell on the 22nd, putting them temporarily out of action.

Two days later, *Southampton* (having oiled to make up for the 680 miles she had run, and re-embarked the boarding parties she had 'lent' to the destroyer force for the earlier-projected raid), joined *Sheffield, Glasgow,* the 5,270-ton cruiser *Aurora* and six destroyers of the 1st Flotilla, which had all put to sea to escort home the badly-damaged submarine N69 (HMS *Spearfish*). This submarine was unable to dive, and the intention was to bring her back to Rosyth from the greatly 'exposed' vicinity of Horn Reef, Heligoland. The movement was covered by the Home Fleet, *Southampton* sighting *Nelson, Rodney,* the aircraft-carrier *Ark Royal* and attendant destroyers at 0810 on the 22nd. The weather conditions were initially poor in terms of visibility, but *Sheffield* and *Aurora* located the British submarine and the 2nd CS began to withdraw with her.

Meantime, the weather had cleared, and, early on 26th September, the Home Fleet was subjected to accurate bombing by four German Ju 88 aircraft, which near-missed the aircraft-carrier *Ark Royal* and actually hit the battlecruiser *Hood*. It was very fortuitous that the bomb was a dud and bounced off harmlessly. At the same time, nine He 111 aircraft of I/KG 26 attacked the 2nd CS, though without any hits being made. The naval ships were defending themselves vigorously, with explosions pock-marking the sky, empty brass shell cases from the 4" HA guns spilling across the decks, and the pom-pom guns hammering away. Alf would have been busy in seeing that his 'beloved battery' of four 4" guns mounted in two pairs on the starboard side of the ship was performing to peak capacity, all the more so when one aircraft seemed to select the ship as its own special target at 1210, though neither side managed to cause damage to the other. At that time they were at 57° 30' N, 03° 34' E about half-way home on their return passage. The objective had been accomplished, for *Spearfish* was being assisted to safety. *Southampton* secured to the A1 Buoy at Rosyth at 2050, having run 820 miles. Next day she oiled, cleaned ship, embarked petrol and put her hands to physical drill to get some air in their lungs and 'freshen them up'.

During the next week *Southampton* put to sea for exercises of one kind or another virtually every day - sub/cal and full/cal firing, concentration shoots with her main armament and torpedo-firing. On the 29th the 'Alarm to Arms: Repel Aircraft' was suddenly sounded, the crew securing eighty minutes later, by which time the aircraft had been confirmed to be friendly. However, as we shall see, the authorities were right to expect possible German attacks. *Southampton* and her consorts were also doing the correct thing in closing up their HA Directors and TS crews for an exercise with the shore searchlights on the 2nd October. Anything which tightened the liaison with the land-based anti-aircraft defences was going to prove useful - as was any exercise of the HA armament and related Control Parties, such as *Southampton* conducted on the 4th October, and again on 8th October, when she exercised her 4-inch gun crews in firing at a sleeve target towed by her '*Walrus*' aircraft.

It may be an idea to review how Alf's 4" guns were operated. The men manning the starboard HA Director, high up abaft the bridge, would maintain vigilant observation for any aircraft visible (or audible) around the 360° of the horizon, and promptly get their sights on to any aircraft spotted. (Lookouts on duty at various positions around the ship would be doing likewise, reporting their findings by phone to the delegated officer, to be immediately passed to the appropriate HA Director.) With the aid of his specialised equipment, the officer in charge of the HA Director would estimate Enemy Course and Speed, and an AB would estimate the height of the target. (Hence all those 'height-finding' exercises we have been recording.) The Layer would elevate the sights vertically on to the target and hold them on it, and the Trainer would train the sights horizontally and hold them on target, all men thus 'following' the aircraft on its (or their) course.

All the information thus being obtained (plus any information being input from the port HA Director) would be automatically and continuously fed to the HA Control Position, deep down in the ship, protected by heavy armour plate. There, 'corrections' would be applied to 'predict' the necessary 'aiming-off' to cause the shell which was about to be fired to reach the same position in space as would the aircraft itself moments later (if it maintained a steady course), and a fuse-setting would be calculated to cause the shell to explode just as it reached the right altitude. This information would be relayed both to the HA Director crew, and also to the guns crews, who would press their 'Gun Ready' buttons when the shells were appropriately fused and loaded. The Trainer's task was to press his 'trigger' to fire the 4" guns in unison, immediately after the Fire Hooter sounded.[381]

Clearly, the situation became more complex, and difficult decisions had to be made, should an approaching formation of enemy aircraft split up in order to make co-ordinated attacks from different points of the compass, thus seeking to divide the defensive fire being put up by the ship. For this reason, an 'Action Information Room' with an elaborate 'plotting table' and greatly aided by air and surface RDFs (Radars) would come into being in the Royal Navy as the war went on. However, as matters stood in 1939, the vulnerability of ships to aircraft attack was still not fully realised. Few ships had RDF. Where it was fitted, many of the officers considered it 'new-fangled' and unreliable, and, generally, tactical decisions against air-attack rested in the heads of such 'Air Defence Officers' as the Captain might decide to nominate.

---

[381] A down-to-earth account of his naval service by former CPO George HOBLEY, who was a PO Trainer of *Southampton's* 4-inch guns around 1939/40, endorses these arrangements. He says that 'Charlie', who took over his duty when George was drafted to a gunnery course, was one of the men killed on the 11th January 1941. (Also see later note about George.)

On 6th October *Southampton* launched her aircraft and then proceeded to sea, streaming her paravanes and going to Action Stations. *Edinburgh* was in company, and took station for a range finding exercise which lasted for an hour.

On the 8th and on the 9th *Southampton* was again at sea on exercises, heading out towards the Skagerrak, with her crew at Day Action Stations, making 28 knots and opening fire on a German reconnaissance plane at 0800 and again at 1816. At 1001 she opened 'deterrent' fire at the aircraft again for a couple of minutes, investigated the source of distant smoke (finding it to be a Norwegian steamer), and was soon thereafter subjected to a bombing attack by German aircraft attacking from fine on the port bow, their bombs falling 70 yards away from the ship, abreast the bridge. An hour later further aircraft were sighted overhead, and the ship's HA guns opened fire at them for one minute, no attack developing.

By that time the ship was at 58° 56' N, 04° 03' E, and turning for home. During her return passage she was harried from the air by numerous bombing attacks to which she replied with her HA guns and her Pom-Poms. At 1500 she changed course to avoid passing under a heavy patch of cloud (lest aircraft should make sudden attacks from its protection), maintained a zig-zag course, and lost sight of the last enemy 'shadowing' aircraft at 1745. *Southampton* arrived safely at Scapa Flow at 1230 on the 10th October, able to report "no hits, no damage and no casualties". None the more for that, Alf and his gun crews would have had a busy and stressful time of it.

Unsurprisingly, her crew were soon hard at work fusing more 4" shell. She also embarked 610 tons of oil, ammunitioned and cleaned ship. Scapa Flow was busy, with *Royal Oak, Repulse, Newcastle, Aurora* and the destroyers *Foxhound, Mashona, Matabele, Sturdy* and *Eskimo* all coming or going. On the 12th there was an 'Air Raid Red Warning', followed by a sudden 'Alarm to Arms', but no attack developed.

On October 13th *Southampton* left Scapa Flow shortly before noon, the Hoxa boom being lowered to allow her to proceed in company with her escorting destroyers *Matabele, Janus, Jervis* and *Jupiter*. Those of *Southampton's* crew who were on deck would probably have noted that the old battleship *Royal Oak* was still moored inshore, within the protection of the boom, as *Southampton* moved out eastward into the North Sea. Off to port the sky became ablaze with the flickering lights of the *Aura Borealis* as darkness began to fall. The OOW was so impressed with its majesty (and perhaps mindful of its possibly adverse effects on wireless signals) that he recorded the fact in the log, just before *Jupiter* was detached to investigate a Merchant Ship.

Early next morning, a boarding party from *Janus* decided that the Norwegian ship *Bonda* might be carrying a contraband cargo, and a prize crew were left aboard to bring her into Kirkwall in the Orkney Islands, for fuller investigation. Six hours later a submarine contact was reported by one of the destroyers and the force went to full speed to clear the area. Later in the day, *Jervis* put a prize crew aboard the Swedish tanker *Instoffe Rentol* to bring her into Kirkwall. The force joined up with a convoy during the night of 14th/15th October, receiving air cover from 0800 to 1730 on the 15th, the force parting company with the convoy at 2030 and heading for Rosyth. At 0725 on 16th October *Southampton* secured to A1 Buoy, just downstream from the immense steel structure of the famous railway bridge. She was under 4 hours notice for steam, and she oiled immediately after her run of 170 miles.

To go back two days in our narrative, on the night of 14th October, whilst Southampton was out on her patrol, the German submarine U-47 (Lt-Commander Gunther PRIEN), running on the surface, had very boldly and skilfully penetrated the anchorage at Scapa Flow, and had torpedoed the battleship Royal Oak, which had sunk with heavy loss of life. U-47 had managed to escape scot-free, again running on the surface.[382]

Perhaps piqued by this 'Kreigsmarine success', it is said that Hermann GOERING, the Reichmarshal of the Luftwaffe was furious at the failures of the German aircraft to strike much more serious blows than they had achieved thus far against the ships of the Royal Navy. Hence, when a high-flying German reconnaissance aircraft spotted a British battlecruiser - which its crew (correctly) believed to be the 'Hood' - at sea on 15th October, and which was seen by a second reconnaissance plane to enter the Firth of Forth on the 16th, an attack was promptly set in hand. This was to be carried out by Ju 88 aircraft of I/KG 30, based at Westerland on the Island of Sylt, in North Germany, under Captain POHLE. However, POHLE was given a direct order from the Fuhrer himself that, should the 'Hood' already have docked, she was NOT to be attacked. This came about because, at that stage of the war, Adolf HITLER was still hoping for a negotiated laying down of arms by the UK, and would not allow any British civilians to be killed. Every German aircraft crew was briefed accordingly. Incidentally, they were also told that there were no 'Spitfire' fighters stationed in Scotland, 'since they had all been drawn to the south of England or were out supporting the BEF in France'.

When Captain POHLE arrived over the target area in the afternoon of 16th October, he saw that Hood was by the sluice gate leading to the dock, and that bombing her might conceivably result in 'civilian casualties'. So, as 'alternative targets of opportunity', he attacked the cruisers and destroyers in Rosyth Roads. One of those ships was 'Southampton', who was still moored to the Admiral's telephone buoy ('A1'), near the Firth of Forth Railway Bridge.

As we have seen, *Southampton* had oiled on that morning of 16th October, and the activity of German aircraft overhead had caused her to sound the 'Alarm to Arms' at 1030, followed by an 'All Clear/Secure', only for a further 'Alarm to Arms' to be sounded at 1057, followed by another 'All Clear/Secure' at 1115. These alarms were probably related to the activities of the various German reconnaissance aircraft mentioned above.

There was yet another 'Air Raid Warning/Alarm to Arms' at 1430 and the ships in the anchorage were promptly attacked by the German air striking force. At 1435 *Southampton* was struck by a bomb which (according to her log) *"passed from Flag Deck Port side and finally through the ship at No.84 station, 5 ft above the water line. One rating was killed and three seriously injured."*

---

[382] When they later returned to Scapa Flow, the crew of *Southampton* found that the channel near to the exit they had used on October 13th had been sealed with a blockship filled with concrete, as a further defensive measure against any subsequent attempts at 'submarine penetrations'. Grieving about the men lost in *Royal Oak*, it seems that there was a strong feeling amongst *Southampton's* crew that this was rather in the nature of 'shutting the stable door after the horse had bolted'.

Aboard *Southampton*, Shipwright 'Dusty' MILLER had seen a German aircraft (presumably Captain POHLE's) initially heading inland and observed it as it turned around and dived towards the Firth of Forth Railway Bridge, dropping its bomb-load as it did so. *Southampton* was hit a glancing blow by one of the bombs, a 500 kg one, which had been dropped from a height of 3,000 ft. This bomb passed through two decks of *Southampton*, hit the armoured deck of the Royal Marine's Mess, passed through the ship's side and emerged on the waterline. It exploded as it sank in the water immediately under the Admiral's barge, which was alongside.[383] Tragically, 18 year-old Boy Seaman 1st Class Herbert BRADLEY was ascending the mess deck ladder when the bomb struck, and it is understood that a flying shard of metal decapitated him. The following photograph shows how the German airmen saw this scene unfolding far below them.

This incident gave *Southampton* the unfortunate distinction of being the first British warship to be hit by aerial bombing in the vicinity of Rosyth during WW2.

Boy Seaman BRADLEY was the only fatal casualty. Nevertheless, his untimely death shocked the crew deeply, and made them realise how vulnerable they were.[384] [The log confirms that three other ratings, all with significant wounds, were discharged to the Royal Naval Hospital at Port Edgar at 1650.]

It has been estimated that *Southampton* was near-missed by no less that twenty other bombs which rained down from the German aircraft which were led by Captain POHLE. As evidenced by the following photograph, it is not surprising to learn that *Edinburgh* also suffered slight damage from bombing by aircraft of POHLE's I/KG 30. Moreover, the destroyer *Mohawk* (which is not visible in the photograph) had no less than 25 casualties from a very near miss.

Captain POHLE of the 'Luftwaffe' paid a heavy price for the damage he had inflicted on the naval ships. Contrary to the pre-briefing information he had been given, fighter aircraft were not only present in Scotland, but they were there in significant numbers. In fact, the RAF. had two squadrons of 'Spitfires' at Turnhouse aerodrome near Edinburgh, and a 'Hurricane' squadron at Drem airfield, on the Firth of Forth. The second of the high-flying Luftwaffe reconnaissance planes had been detected by RAF Fighter Command, and they had deduced that a bombing raid might well follow. They therefore had aircraft from the two 'Spitfire' squadrons (Nos 602 and 603) up on patrol when the German bombers arrived.

Captain POHLE's Ju 88 aircraft was 'bounced' by the three 'Spitfires' of Red Section of 603 Squadron, led by Squadron-Leader E.E. STEVENS. The 'Spits' dived down and fired in succession in a text-book attack, raking the German bomber along its length. Squadron-Leader STEVENS was subsequently credited with the 'kill' of POHLE's aircraft, which was seen to 'be shot down into the sea'.

In fact, POHLE managed to recover control of his badly shot-up aircraft just sufficiently to be able to 'ditch' it rather than plunging straight on down into the depths. However, he was the only one of his crew who survived, being pulled out of his wrecked and sinking plane by British fishermen who happened to be nearby. He lay unconscious for five days in Port Edwards Hospital on the north bank of the Firth of Forth, later

---

[383] The Admiral's Barge sank but was later salvaged.

[384] The author can remember overhearing his father Alf talking about it quietly with his father-in-law, Joseph GREEN.

spending the rest of the war as a PoW. One other aircraft of I/KG 30 was also shot down, none of its crew members surviving. The RAF had only claimed this aircraft as 'damaged', so it either fell into the sea out of sight of land somewhere on its way back, or it ditched and its crew (if they got out into a dinghy) perished of exposure and/or their dinghy eventually foundered. [The above information is a composite of factual information as given in various books, including 'The Luftwaffe War Diaries' and 'Spitfire', but 'reconciled' with such things as Southampton's Log and interviews with her then ship's company.]

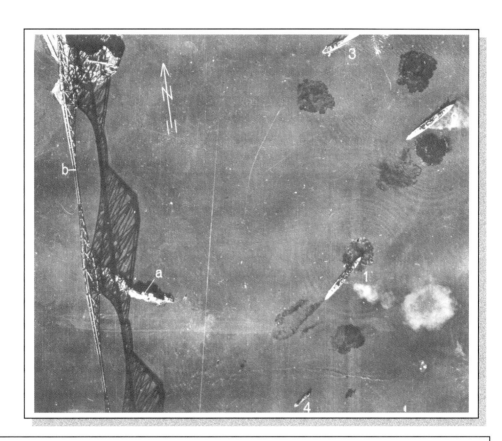

Author's collection. A photograph from German sources, originally seen by the author in 1940, in an American magazine. This copy of the photograph appears by courtesy of the Imperial War Museum, London. Neg No.C5643.

The German airmen's view of things from a height of 3,000 ft. At '1', the bomb which has struck and damaged *Southampton*, is now exploding as it sinks beside *Southampton's* bows, causing the Admiral's barge, which was alongside, to founder. *Edinburgh*, lying about six cables to the north-east of *Southampton*, is being near-missed. In fact, at least six bombs are currently bursting in the vicinity of the two cruisers. Smaller vessels are shown at '3' and '4'. The Firth of Forth Bridge is indicated by 'b', and is well-defined by its strong early-afternoon shadow. The letter 'a' indicates Inchgarry Islet under the bridge.

According to 'Dusty' MILLER (who was then a Shipwright), the damage to *Southampton* was superficial, electrical power being lost only temporarily, and the hole in the exterior of the hull being quickly repaired by the ship's own artificers. These skilled men collected a steel plate from the nearby dockyard when the ship went alongside, and welded the plate in place themselves.[385] Although it does not detail the repairs made, the log generally supports this account, for it states that the ship proceeded upriver to secure alongside the north wall in W Berth at Rosyth and did not proceed out until 2020 on the 23rd. During that week there were several series of Alarms to Arms followed by All Clears, though no more bombs fell.

On 23rd October *Southampton* had proceeded from Rosyth to Sullom Voe, hauling her paravanes after a run of 320 miles and following a Pilot Drifter which led her to her anchorage. There she oiled. She departed from Sullom Voe that same night for a patrol off south-east Norway, encountering a chill wind which was now of Force 7 from the NNW, and having to come down from 20 knots to 10 knots in the lee of the Faroe Islands to secure her anchors. These may not have been properly 'catted', had come somewhat adrift, and were at risk of causing damage as they thrashed about. She made them secure during a brief spell when the wind relented, and it was as well that her seamen managed this demanding task, for the wind soon increased to gale force.

Southampton was now heading into the notorious Denmark Strait, her patrol area being at 67° 26' N, 20° 30' W. This was the farthest north that Alf had ever been, on the rim of the Arctic Circle. On the 27th *Southampton's* Asdic picked up a submarine echo, on which she dropped two depth-charges without effect.

On the 28th she investigated a ship which proved to be the armed merchant cruiser (AMC) HMS *Transylvania,* and on the 29th another ship, which proved to be the AMC HMS *California.* [These ships were clearly the 'adjacent links' in the chain of cruisers and AMCs which the Admiralty had stretched across the Denmark Strait to detect and report the movements of any German commerce raiders trying to break out into the Atlantic Ocean. It was to be expected that some of those German raiders would be heavily-armed 'pocket battleships', and the task of scouting for them, often in very poor visibility, was a dangerous game of 'nip and tuck' for the speedy cruisers - and a near-suicidal 'game' for the relatively slow AMCs, which were merely small converted liners sketchily armed with antiquated 6-inch guns. These ships were invariably commanded by retired Royal Naval Officers of senior rank who, as the war went on, would be found to show the very greatest leadership, courage and resolution when suddenly faced with the most appalling and usually fatal odds.]

On the 30th, *Southampton* detected another probable submarine, and dropped three depth-charges on the contact area, without any evidence of a 'hit'.[386] At least the gale

---

[385] Not only this data, but also other matters as indicated on these pages, were given to the author in 1994 by former Shipwright the late 'Dusty' MILLER.

[386] It seems that the greatest depth-setting for our depth-charges at this early part of the war was about 500 feet, and they had to explode very close alongside a U-boat to cause her disablement or destruction. The Admiralty seems to have been unaware that the newer German U-boats could go as deep as 700 feet and that they would even venture below 800 feet if they found themselves in serious danger from depth-charge attacks - despite the nerve-stressing and frightening creaks and groans due to the compression of the pressure-hull and the heart-stopping effect of the odd rivet yielding under the enormous strain and ricocheting about in the submarine like a bullet! The depth of water in the Denmark Strait north of Iceland, and across the Iceland-Faroes Ridge to the south of it, was between 600 and 1,500 feet, and it was even deeper between the Faroes and the Shetlands, so the U-boats being attacked by *Southampton* certainly had scope to 'run deep' when breaking out into the Atlantic, and probably got nothing worse than 'a slight shaking and a mild headache' from the deepest and most well-laid of the depth-charges fired by *Southampton* and her consorts at that period of the war. [Also see books such as the classic 'Walker RN' (Britain's Ace U-Boat Killer) by Terence ROBERTSON, Pan Books, London, 1958.]

had abated by then, and there was a breeze of only Force 5, with waves and swell rated as only 'rough' rather than 'high'. However, when she set about streaming her paravanes *Southampton* still had to shape her course to keep the heavy seas astern. *Southampton* continued her patrol, investigating the occasional trawler plodding her lonely way to or from the Icelandic fishing grounds, finding another AMC which had come on to her patrol station, finding another submarine echo and steering clear of it at increased speed, finding the Norwegian ship *Eikaug* travelling in ballast, and so on. One night, having sent her crew to Action Stations, and with everybody on the *qui vive*, she used her searchlights to suddenly illuminate a suspect ship she had been stalking - only to find the anti-climax of 'just another lonely trawler'.

There was considerable relief when her patrol time was up and she could head back to Scapa, passing through the Hoxa boom defence at 0900 on the 6th November. Once the ship was moored, her divers were soon sent down to examine the port side at No.74 station for storm-damage.[387] Lt Commander BARKER-HAHLO (of whom more later) and Lt PARNALL joined ship that day. (Lt R.O. de STACPOOL of the Royal Marines would join at Immingham, a few days later.)

By the time *Southampton* entered Scapa she had run 4,740 miles on patrol, without re-fuelling. She now took in some badly-needed oil, half-filling her bunkers and partially restoring her draught from the exceptionally low figures of 18ft 0 ins fwd, 19 ft 10 ins aft, to become 19 ft 2 ins fwd and 19 ft 11 ins aft. Clearly, she was then still 'travelling light', which might well have been a reflection of the pressure on British stocks of oil at Scapa, at that period of the war.

Southampton proceeded the 250 miles to Rosyth late the same day, passing upriver beneath the great railway bridge just before 0900 on the 7th, and taking in more needed oil to 'complete her fill'. This oil brought her draught to 20 ft 5 ins fwd, 20 ft 10 ins aft. She was thus *still* riding a little high, evidently not yet having been replenished with provisions, fresh water, aviation fuel, etc.

The battleships *Nelson* and *Rodney* were already present and *Belfast*, another modified Southampton-class cruiser, and a full sister of *Edinburgh*, arrived at Rosyth on the 9th. On the 10th there was a pre-arranged 'fly-by' of 'friendly' aircraft from 0900 to 0945, to give 'the Navy' the chance of familiarising themselves with British aircraft silhouettes, in a non-threatening situation. The increasing intensity of German bombing of ships and the increasing realisation amongst ship's crews of their extreme vulnerability to aerial attack, were generating 'twitchy trigger fingers' amongst ship's crews. Indeed, throughout the war the Navy would receive a measure of scorn (from the land-based RAF and Coastal Command men) for 'firing at anything which flew' - and the Navy did not always miss their target! 'Friendly Fire' was just as deadly as 'Hostile Fire'. Thus, any measure which improved aircraft recognition by the Navy was to be praised, and this 'fly-by' was a good idea by the authorities.

A strike force was formed at Rosyth on the 10th. It consisted of *Southampton,* her sister *Glasgow*, the Edinburgh Class cruiser *Belfast*, and the Arethusa Class cruiser *Aurora*.[388] They were accompanied by ten destroyers. Departing Rosyth at 0317 on 11th November, they proceeded to Immingham, going to Action Stations at 0745, and then

---

[387] One wonders if this examination was related to checking the repairs to the bomb-damage which the ship had received in the Firth of Forth on 16th October, which was allegedly at Frame 74, port side.

[388] The 'Edinburgh' Class were usually called the 'Modified Southampton' Class at that time.

staying at 2nd or 3rd degrees of readiness during the passage. They practised forming into various pre-set 'screening diagrams' as they went. The ships were streaming paravanes, and passed a floating mine which tended to 'emphasis the need', nuisance though paravanes could be. The force arrived at Immingham at 1700, *Southampton* securing alongside in the dock at 1710, with *Jervis* later securing alongside her.

The force had three relatively quiet days, *Southampton* using them to land her marines for drill and to close up her HA armament for practice. She also had one 'Alarm to Arms' when an air raid warning was given, though without any attack developing. On the 16th the force proceeded, anchoring at Rosyth at 0800. They were officially listed as '2nd CS Home Fleet' from that day, Vice-Admiral Sir Frederick EDWARD-COLLINS leaving *Southampton* with his flag flying for a quick visit to the 'newcomer' *Belfast*, but returning within the hour. On Sunday the 20th November, due to the miserably inclement weather, *Southampton* held Divisions (followed by Divine Service) in the welcome shelter of the Starboard Hangar. At noon there was an 'Alarm to Arms', but, again, no air raid materialised.

The squadron departed from Rosyth on 20th November to exercise at a sub/cal shoot in the Firth of Forth, running down-river beneath the Forth Bridge at 0930 and passing the Boom Defences at 0940. The ships then streamed paravanes, and Southampton flew off aircraft G9A (Lt CASSON), ready to spot the fall of shot in the exercise. *Southampton*, by now travelling at 17 knots, was leading *Belfast* out into the Forth when (*according to veterans of her crew*) *Southampton* 'pinged' a magnetic mine with her Asdic. Again according to her crew, she promptly took drastic avoiding action, but *Belfast*, perhaps caught slightly by surprise and known to be slightly less manoeuvrable (due to her 22 ft greater length), could not match *Southampton's* tight turn and ran over a mine - perhaps not even the same one. The mine exploded under *Belfast*, virtually breaking her back. It was said that only her armoured deck kept the two halves together. With her 4" magazine and boiler rooms flooded, *Belfast* came back to Rosyth under tow.[389] [*Southampton's* log does not spell out any 'Asdic ping' or avoiding action being taken, but merely reports that *Belfast* was hit by a believed enemy mine at 1050, and that *Southampton* went to full speed ahead for returning to harbour, passing the boom at 1145, still streaming her paravanes. The log also confirms that *Belfast* returned to harbour in tow, entering at 1630.][390]

On 23rd November *Southampton* exercised 'Collision' and 'Abandon Ship', before embarking ammunition. That afternoon there was another Air Raid Warning, but, yet again, no attack developed. She therefore stood her men down from Action Stations at 1425.

However, early on that day of the 23rd November, the Armed Merchant Cruiser '*Rawalpindi*' had been overwhelmed and sunk by the powerful German battlecruisers '*Scharnhorst*' and '*Gneisenau*' whilst she was about half-way between the Faroes and Iceland, on those infamous Northern Patrol duties. Only 32 of the crew of '*Rawalpindi*' had survived the grossly uneven contest. The two German warships, under the command

---

[389] Once there she was patched up, leaving Rosyth in June 1940 for a full refit at Devonport. She would be out of action until early December 1942.

[390] In view of her near-sinking at this time, it is slightly ironic that *Belfast* is the only cruiser of the Southampton or Modified Southampton Class which is still in existence. (As of 2005, she is preserved as an historic museum-ship, being moored on the River Thames, near Tower Bridge.)

of Vice-Admiral MARSCHALL, had been trying to break through the thin line of the British Northern Patrol cruisers and AMCs, and thus hoping to be able to *débouche* into the Atlantic, and to range freely to attack British shipping all around the Atlantic. However, *'Newcastle'*, which was on patrol in the vicinity of the Fair Isle Passage, had spotted and reported *'Scharnhorst'*, and had tried to shadow her. *'Newcastle'* had been disappointed to later lose contact, though it was perhaps almost inevitable in the murk and gloom of a wet and stormbound November day.[391]

Now urgent orders had come in for the diminished 2nd Cruiser Squadron, now consisting only of *Southampton, Edinburgh, Aurora* and three destroyers, to proceed from Rosyth to hunt for the German ships. Her log shows that *Southampton* (evidently accompanied by her consorts and escorts) proceeded to sea at 1900 on the 23rd, streaming her paravanes, and heading at high speed for her search area. Seemingly this search was to be centred at 61° 35N', 04° 20' E, a little to the east of the Shetland Islands, perhaps in case the German ships turned back for home, rather than continuing to try to break out into the Atlantic against the other forces stationed out there by the Admiralty. By midday on the 24th *Southampton* and her consorts had reached 60° 00 N', 02° 15W', having made most of their northing but with a good many miles yet to proceed east around the south of the Shetlands.

The weather was deteriorating, the wind reaching Force 6 on the 25th, with a rough sea and swell running. *Southampton* had to reduce speed at 0110 to allow her first aid party to recover an injured man from the ship's waist and to get him down to the Sick Bay in any sort of safety, and at 1150 she had to alter course temporarily to secure her port-side torpedo tubes which were working loose of their stays. Next day the weather was even worse, the wind coming from the south-east at Force 7 and the swell becoming 'high', with crests towering up to 15 ft. Luckily, the storm abated somewhat on the 27th, when *Southampton* closed to investigate a merchant ship. However, the abatement in the weather was of only limited duration, and, on the 28th, it was necessary to keep the ship's head to wind when they hauled and re-streamed their paravanes. On the 29th they went to General Quarters when a hostile aircraft was sighted, opening and keeping up fire on this aircraft for 10 minutes – and pumping a great many shells at it, her gun crews queuing up in short but 'endless' lines, toiling hard to insert the rounds into the breeches, swiftly banging each round home with a deft and quick blow of a clenched fist as the breech began to quickly close, and sometimes stumbling over the succession of hot shell-cases which were tumbling out of the guns from the shots fired instants before (to say nothing of the hazards from the cooling-down shell-cases from earlier shots already rolling haphazardly about on the deck under the influence of the rolling and pitching of the ship) – the loaders who'd inserted the latest rounds already moving away fast from the guns to collect a fresh round and rejoin the line.

Southampton later investigated the Swedish merchant ship *Oxclosund*, subsequently sending her into Kirkwall for closer appraisal. On the 30th they sighted *Suffolk* astern of them and, 15 minutes later they spotted her escorting destroyers. Next

---

[391] As would become apparent post-war, *Newcastle's* 'sighting message' to the Admiralty had been picked up by German intelligence, and (so far as the British were concerned) this had created a useful 'deterrent effect' on the breakout attempt by the German battlecruisers. The 'secret war' of intercepting radio messages and breaking codes, well practised by both sides, often had the strangest repercussions. Despite her disappointment, *Newcastle* had actually been highly effective - and that without any spilling of the blood of her men.

day, 1st December, they went to 1st Degree Readiness just before sighting a convoy, later altering course to ease the motion of the *Southampton* as much as possible to aid the task of her engineers who were struggling to repair a defect in the Forward Engine Room. It took the engineers 2¼ hours to complete the job, but they evidently mastered the problem, for, later in the day *Southampton* increased speed to no less than 30 knots. She did so to investigate an unidentified warship, going to Action Stations as she did so, and hearts beating faster. However, tension was eased 15 minutes later, when the ship was identified as friendly. As midnight approached *Southampton* again altered course, working up to 30 knots once more, this time to investigate a possible submarine contact.

By now they were returning to Rosyth, and the ship had run 4,250 miles by the time they closed the boom defences and secured to their buoy. They were running short of the 'essentials', so they re-fuelled and took in provisions almost at once, 'clearing the lower deck' to put everybody available on the job of provisioning, lest the ship might suddenly be required to put straight back out to sea again.

However, a little later it was later established by the Admiralty that the German battlecruisers, after initially heading north on the 24th November, had given up the idea of a breakout, had reversed their course (in fact, had probably passed the 2nd CS's search area well before the 2nd CS had themselves reached it), and had since reached the safety of the Jade Estuary.

Southampton remained in harbour for a few days, exercising her crew at 6-inch turret drill, and conducting 'concentration exercises'. Further air raid warnings came and went, still with no bombs being dropped. Captain (E) H.H. WILSON joined the ship. Alf signed the log now and again, as did Mr H. PLAYER (Commissioned Gunner) of whom we have already heard and of whom we shall later hear more. On 13th December *Southampton* launched her aircraft G9A, piloted by Lt (A) CUSSON and carrying Lt Commander TINLEY and Lt Commander BARKER-HAHLO. All leave was cancelled at 1630, libertymen being immediately recalled. The ship sailed at 2235, heading for Scapa Flow, sighting the cruisers *Delhi* and *Cardiff* whilst *en route* and securing at Scapa at 1356. At 1455 her HA armament was closed up as the ship took up her duty as HA Guard. There was an Alarm to Arms at 2345, but the All Clear went an hour later, no attack having developed.

Next day, *Edinburgh* took over at 0800 as HA Guard, and, the following day, Sunday 17th December, the Admiral's Communications Staff transferred to that ship, CS 2 transferring his flag to *Edinburgh* in their wake. On 18th December *Edinburgh* and *Southampton* proceeded out on patrol, maintaining intermittent visual contact with each other in the same general area where the 2nd CS had been during the *'Scharnhorst' and 'Gneisenau'* scare of late November, and again with very stormy weather developing, the waves becoming 'very high' and the wind reaching Force 7 at times. It was also very cold, with the air temperature dropping to 35°F at times even when right out of the wind. Aircraft, each identified as friendly after tense moments of doubt, passed overhead from time to time. On 21st December four 'friendly' destroyers were sighted, and a 'friendly' submarine was spotted on the surface soon afterwards. On 22nd December *Southampton* sighted and, as ordered, began to screen a convoy, taking station astern of *Edinburgh*. Almost immediately *Edinburgh* obtained a submarine contact, swiftly followed by a second one. Both cruisers increased to 20 knots to avoid possible submarine attack.

On 23rd December, in a wind which was again increasing to gale Force 7, both cruisers conducted 6-inch full/cal shoots before *Southampton*, which had evidently suffered significant storm damage, was given the order 'Proceed independently'. She headed for Newcastle-on-Tyne, hauling her paravanes and forming astern of minesweepers as she entered the River at 1030 on 24th December, taking a pilot aboard and securing fore and aft to buoys in Long Reach. . At 1830 her Port Watch proceeded on long leave, being the first watch to depart and overjoyed to be home (just) in time for Christmas. Alf did not go with them, for he signed the log at 1800. A considerate and relaxing 'Pipe Down' was ordered at 0900 on the 25th, so the men could enjoy a little Christmas fare in comfort, but the heavy work of de-ammunitioning proceeded on the 26th, and the ship proceeded into the Middle Dock on the 28th. Her repairs were not completed until 23rd January 1940, and, from the absence of his signature as OOW from 25th December to 5th January, it seems fairly certain that Alf managed to get away on a 'long' leave - perhaps of seven days - during that period. We will follow him home to see what he would have found.

Author's collection of inherited family photographs.

Alf photographed at the rear of X-Turret, with a Carley Float at his heels. He is showing signs of the mental and physical effects caused by the hard war that the officers and men of HMS *Southampton* are having to endure. Seeing at close hand the effects of German aerial bombing and mining of our ships has been hard. Going on patrol in the bitter weather of the notorious Denmark Strait, with the constant tension due to the risk of meeting a powerful German unit desperate to break out into the Atlantic, has added to the toll on his reserves. Yet, as a 'father-figure', he is keeping himself under close control and doing his best to present a calm and relaxed attitude to sustain and boost the morale of the younger men around him.

Private Life

Prior to this period of leave, Alf had experienced being bombed several times and, indeed, of his ship being hit and suffering its first casualties, including the one sad fatality. He had also seen, at close hand, the devastating effects of a magnetic mine on a cruiser, and learned of the casualties that had caused. So, Alf may have begun to think hard about his own mortality and the possible consequences of his death on his family. Though his son Neville was still short of his tenth birthday, young Neville would have to become the 'Man of the Family' should the worst happen to Alf. Young Neville somehow needed to have his self-confidence boosted accordingly. At present Alf considered it was at far too low an ebb in the boy (See following photo.)

It is probable that Alf talked with Alice about improving the boy's confidence, though their conversation may have been heavy going. It is likely that she would have told Alf that she was desperate for him (Alf) to survive, come what may. She would probably have shut her mind to 'eventualities', and refused to discuss the 'ridiculous' matter of young Neville and his possibly having to be *in loco paternis* in any shape or form - though Alf's words may have nestled somewhere deep down in her proud being. (Her instinct would have been to turn to her younger brother, the boy's 'Uncle Neville', though he, too, would soon be caught up in the war, no longer his own master, and perhaps far away from home.)

Such considerations of 'the effects of his possible death' apart, Alf would have found that life at home was not greatly changed by the war to date, except in regard to (a) the 'blackout', which made getting about very difficult after dark, especially on moonless nights, and which was promoting many traffic accidents, (b) the gross overcrowding on trains and (c) the rationing of food. Although the system of control was a fair one for the civilian population, the size of the rations of key commodities like butter, sugar, tea, meat, etc., was very small, and there were already shortages and rationing of many other items such as clothing, shoes and sweets. The situation regarding food was in marked contrast to the generous (if rather monotonous) supply of food provided for the Royal Navy and the other fighting forces, and the Navy's 'plenty' sometimes caused some heart-searching when a serviceman returning home on leave saw the comparatively 'short commons' his family was subsisting on.

Earlier fears of 'overwhelming' bombing of England, and, especially, of the widespread use of poison gas, had receded to some extent. [On the day that war had been declared, the gut-melting sound of the wailing roar of the air-raid sirens rising and falling several times over had caused considerable fright amongst the civilian population, but nothing had followed this 'warning', which had soon been followed by the continuous noise of the 'All Clear'.] Nevertheless, everybody still carried a gas-mask about with them - not only because it was a regulation strictly enforced by the Police and ARP Wardens, but also 'just in case' a potentially death-dealing gas-attack really did come about.

Indeed, people were still concerned to some degree about the possibility of being bombed, be it with poison gas, high-explosive, incendiaries, or whatever. Gummed paper tape, which was stuck criss-cross fashion on the windows of houses and offices, and netting pasted with a sort of 'Isinglass glue' across the inside of the windows of buses, trams and trains (to minimise the amount of flying shards of glass from bomb-blast) and the strictly-enforced 'Black-Out' at night, were constant reminders that bombing might yet become a real threat.[392] There were very few civilian cars and motor-bikes on the roads, as restrictions on the use of petrol had long been introduced. A 'black-market' was creeping in, especially in obtaining petrol illegally (usually from 'military sources').

Author's collection of inherited family photographs. A studio portrait by Emeny of Felixstowe.

Alf's children in the early Spring of 1940. Neville (very nearly 10 years old) looks nervous and insecure and his slight squint is apparent. Joan (aged nearly 13) has a very odd smile – almost a grimace. Jess (aged 8½) has switched on, actress-like, an especially bright face for the photographer. Baby Richard (15 months) looks bonny and well enough, even if perhaps a tad wilful. The lives of the two emotionally-disturbed and be-spectacled elder children are soon to go through a further shock to their systems.

Uniforms and military vehicles were now more frequently seen and there were fewer young men around in civilian clothes (the exceptions being men in 'reserved occupations' and men who were seriously handicapped). One reason that

---

[392] The Isinglass 'glue' used to affix the netting to the glass distorted the view, and the netting usually had a clear, diamond-shaped, central section to permit passengers to look out for their alighting place. Human nature being what it is, people were often guilty of peeling back the netting to extend their range of vision. Later, a tubby little cartoon character dressed in neat pinstripe business suit and bowler hat, and called 'Billy Brown of London Town', would be developed for propaganda purposes in the metropolis. One extensively-used poster showed him gently reprimanding one such 'peeler back', saying: *"I trust you'll pardon my correction - that stuff is there for your protection!"* Almost invariably there would be a piece of graffiti beside it: *"Thank you for the information - But I can't see the bleedin' station!"* People smiled - and appreciated both points made.

the trains were so crowded was that many of the passengers were soldiers, sailors and airmen being posted here and there all around the country and abroad.

The Navy were suffering some losses in ships, the tragic loss of the AMC *Rawlpindi* being one case in point, and Alf's former ship the *Courageous* had gone, succumbing to a torpedo from a U-boat on 17th September, with heavy loss of life. However, the Royal Navy was also having some victories (The morale-boosting destruction of the German 'pocket-battleship' *Graf Spey* at Montevideo being a classic example). Overall, people were fairly confident, and believed that the BEF and their French comrades, helped by the 'impregnable' Maginot Line of deep-dug concrete fortresses, would be able to hold the Germans at the French and Belgian borders, so that fighting would go with both sides 'dug-in', rather as it had in World War One.

It was widely believed by the civilian population that the ground-fighting would not come near enough to seriously threaten the shores of England. The Navy would protect our Empire and merchant ships and ensure an adequate supply of imported food so that we would stay sufficiently fed, even if a little slimmer. Overall, people believed we were in a reasonable state and we would grow stronger as our factories turned out increasing quantities of war matériel and we began to draw on the vast arsenals of the U.S.A.

On the emotional front at home, little had changed, with the stresses and strains between Alice and the two elder children continuing, though, increasingly, Alice's mother was acting as a cushioning buffer for all three children. There was much love between this older woman, 'Nan' (alias Agnes Sarah), and the children. As has already been touched upon, Nan had the gift of being able to make each child believe that he or she was *uniquely* loved by her, in a special way which transcended her love for their siblings. Nan had lost her own mother when she was only 15 months old, and Nan had suffered by having a cold step-mother imposed on her, back in the 1880s. That step-mother was not maternal by nature and it seems that little Nan was often 'farmed out' to the families of her father's brothers, especially to her kindly Uncle Daniel ENGLISH and his wife Hannah, and probably sometimes to Jane BUSHBY, the married sister of her late birth-mother. Then, after Nan's step-mother had borne a son, she had soon put Nan (by then aged about ten years old), to look after her little half-brother, as if she were just a servant-nurse.

It was therefore not surprising that Nan had subsequently fashioned her own marriage and child-raising with great care, almost like building a human citadel. Nor one whit surprising that Nan had a natural sympathy with her grand-children in their current predicament regarding 'motherhood', and that a sort of 'accommodation' had now begun to exist within the family.

For his part, Alf's elder son, Young Neville, had crept into the Pier Pavilion at Felixstowe where an anti-war propaganda *cum* refugee-relief film of the vicious fighting in the Sino-Japanese conflict was being shown at that time. [*This savage war had broken out in mid-1933 and was receiving little public attention in England - though it was having significant effects on British interests, and was already affecting the British Naval Base at Wei-Ha-Wei and British navigation along the Yangtze River.*] In the Pier Pavilion Young Nev saw films which were surely intended for 'adult eyes only' - close-ups of mutilated bodies of men, women and children, parts of bodies thrown up on to telephone wires and carelessly draped on the leaf-stripped branches of rail-side trees after a crowded train had been heavily bombed, and so forth. He had also seen close-up camera shots of the weeping and wailing of naked toddlers with their clothes blown off by blast desperately trying to prod the torn and blood-smothered bodies of their mothers back to life, and similar horrors which would vaguely haunt his memory for the rest of his life.

He had thus seen something of the reality of war as opposed to the clean 'Cowboys and Indians' film images (with lots of bullets fired but precious little blood spilt) which was so often purveyed to his generation. However, Young Nev, then nine years old, kept these distressing 'aerial bombing revelations' to himself. He knew that his womenfolk, be they old or young, should be screened from seeing such horrors, and he did not talk to the menfolk lest word might somehow get back to his father of what he had seen. He did not want to risk being punished by his father for going where he had no right to enter.

So Alf remained unaware of the 'realities of war' that the boy had seen, which had opened Neville's young eyes further than would have been the case for most other boys of his age. Alf, was, however, well aware that the boy was going beachcombing with his great-uncle, and that he was seeing the jetsam being cast ashore from the many merchant ships of all nationalities being mined and sunk off Felixstowe. It just seemed amazing that young Neville had yet to see a corpse or two washed ashore. Alf sincerely hoped that it would remain so.

All ends up, Alf probably returned from his leave more concerned about his own immediate future and that of his ship, than about the physical state and safety of his nearest and dearest. The emotional problems at home would have to 'go on the back burner' for the present. They were not a matter of life and death. Keeping 'his' 4-inch guns and their crews 'on the top line' would be.

HMS *Southampton* (1939-41) (Continued):

A Boy Seaman named 'Freddie' DANCE had joined *Southampton* at South Shields on 11th January 1940. He could not possibly have known, but he would have *exactly* one year in which to serve in her. In 1994 he would write to the author to say: "*When in harbour, we lads were detailed as Side-Boys, to act as Messengers under the jurisdiction of the Officer-of-the-Watch, which was a duty carried out by Mr DAVIS, your father. I might add that, whenever we boys reported to him, we knew we would get a thorough dress inspection before we would be allowed to proceed to the Quarter-Deck to go on Watch.*"

In a subsequent conversation Freddie would say that he admired 'Mr DAVIS' but that, naturally, there was a tremendous gulf between them due to 'Alf's' hard-won senior rank as Commissioned Gunner and his vast and encyclopaedic knowledge and experience of all things naval from 'Lower Deck to Wardroom' on the human scale, and from 'truck to keel' on the shipboard scale. One might add to this Alf's pride in the traditions and customs of the Service, which he fully upheld, his wide-ranging experience in the War of 1914-18 and now in this Second World War, and his considerable age in a ship's company composed of generally far younger men. And all this, as compared with Freddie's inexperience and youth. Freddie said he would never have dared to make a comment or broach a conversation, unless Mr DAVIS had happened to speak to him first. [We shall hear more from the late Freddie as this account continues. He was a very fine person and he is greatly missed.]

Whilst on this topic of Alf's personality, it somehow seems appropriate to mention that a young rating had evidently tried to be a bit of a 'Jack the Lad' in front of his mates when, on joining *Southampton,* he had given Commissioned Gunner Mr DAVIS a bit of 'familiar lip'. This rating still remembered, fifty years later, the frigid 'ticking off' he had received for his impertinence in not respecting *the uniform*, and the firmness with which he was very firmly put 'back in his place'. He never 'tried it on' with Mr DAVIS ever again - though 'Albert' was *still* clearly a bit of an irrepressible 'Jack the Lad' even when deep into his seventies, bless his heart.[393]

Southampton was still under the command of Captain F.W.H JEANS, CVO and, on 1st January 1940, had become a part of the 18th Cruiser Squadron, Home Fleet, under Vice Admiral LAYTON, flying his flag in *Manchester.* Surgeon Commander N.A.H. BARLOW reported in his journal that the weather whilst in dry dock at South Shields had been exceptionally trying, very cold conditions having been experienced and a considerable amount of snow. Internal condensation on the ship's sides and on some of the natural-air fan trunks was causing some problems, especially during the 'Black-Out' hours when the ship was, effectively, 'sealed'. Turning the steam off at 'pipe down', and not turning it on again until the hands were called the next morning had helped to reduce the overnight stuffiness, but the ship then quickly became very cold when daylight operations commenced with doors and hatches being opened. The lowest temperature

---

[393] This little episode was as told by 'Albert' to the author's daughter Rosalind DAVIS, who was deputising with a man-friend and her brother Robert for her (then) hospitalised father at the ceremony to commemorate the 60th Anniversary of the loss of the *Southampton.*

experienced at South Shields had been 14° F. The ladies of easy virtue at South Shields may have been very appealing and hard workers, but they had done *Southampton* no good turns at all when 'granting their favours', for 15 cases of gonorrhoea had been contracted there, and a further lone one at Sunderland. Worse, there were two cases of chancroid which had been contracted at South Shields. As the late Jack HAWKINS, then a Sick Berth Attendant, would comment sixty years later, all such severe cases were put in what the hands ironically called the '*Rose Garden*' aboard ship.

As a general point, the surgeon was experiencing problems in treating his various cases due to the shortage of certain drugs. Apart from sexually-transmitted diseases, he was having to deal with nine cases of rubella which had arisen, requiring isolation of the men affected. On a lesser scale in severity, but a much larger one in incidence, there had also been an outbreak of common colds and laryngitis. As what sounds like a rather unpleasant attempt to attack this widespread infection, the messdecks were being sprayed twice daily with Formaldehyde (which the author remembers from school biology lessons as being used to preserve dead animals, and as having a truly foul aroma). A little Formaldehyde was also being put into the fan trunking at the source of the air supply, once daily. The ship's company were also mustered twice a day in their messes for throat spraying. One suspects that none of the 'remedies' would have been at all effective.

On 24th January the hands were clearing up the decks and preparing for sea. That afternoon, the ship left the dock and came to moorings off the Timber Yards. Here she oiled from lighters and began to take in ammunition. This ammunitioning continued for three days, perhaps slowed down a little because, as we have seen, the company was being ravaged by illness, with the Ship's Log showing 31 on the sick list and the number still going up. The air temperature was around freezing and the chill factor far higher due to the bitter east coast wind which was blowing.

Cable was ranged for examination at this time, both watches being employed at the very chilly task - and the F'c'sle Sentry was put under close arrest at 0530 on the 30th, for 'deserting his post', probably to find a spot more out of the wind. If so, one can find a measure of sympathy for him - but deserting one's post in time of war is a very serious offence.[394] Whilst he was under arrest another air raid warning was sounded off, though no attack developed.

At 1045 on 1st February, Southampton left the dock in South Shields, and proceeded for Scapa Flow. She dropped her harbour pilot when she got as far as the breakwater, then moved out to sea, streaming her paravanes as she did so. Her HA personnel were already closed up against possible surprise air attack, and she settled down to a steady 20 knots northbound, her company at 2nd Degree Readiness. Later she increased to 24 knots, but soon had to reduce to 22 knots due to a problem which developed with the starboard outer turbine. At 0901 on the 2nd February she passed the Hoxa boom at Scapa after a voyage of 390 miles. She oiled, closed up her HA defence

---

[394] The author can identify with this for soon after the German surrender in May 1945, when he was aged 15, he needed precious little persuasion to simply abandon his boring and isolated sentry post at a Summer Camp of his Army Cadet Unit, to go off with his enthusiastic mates on what the Navy might have called a 'poodle-faking' expedition, seeking 'popsies' - and, Boy! His feet 'hardly touched the ground' when he was later arrested and subsequently given one hell of a 'bottle'. He'd simply never been properly briefed and had never even considered all the *possible* implications of being absent from his post in the great rural quiet of the countryside.

watches, which had not long been stood down, and quickly proceeded to sea again, streaming her paravanes as she did so and closing up her night defence watch.

She was about to go on the Northern Patrol, and would continue to operate out from Scapa Flow for some time to come. Noon on the 3rd saw her at 61° 10 N', 00° 40' E, with visibility at 7 miles, on a moderate sea with a south-east breeze. At 1302 the distinctive shape of a '*Sunderland*' flying boat was sighted. Next day, travelling ever north-east, she was at 67° 26' N, 11° 14' E, approaching the north coast of Norway and sighting two fishing boats as she closed the land. Next day, the 5th, she was off the North Cape at 71° 15' N, 27° 37' E, and the next day at 71° 50' N, 29° 50' E off Kirkenes and approaching Murmansk. It was reported that this put her further north than any British warship had ever been up to that date. (To put a more human bias on that statistic, Alf's 'furthest north' had been the Denmark Strait, at about 67° N, 20° W, until that time.) The weather remained bitterly cold and *Southampton's* sick list had now reached 42.

On the 5th she had sighted a destroyer on her port beam and had gone to General Quarters until the destroyer had been identified as Norwegian and thus, at that time, neutral. *Southampton* had also taken avoiding action when a possible submarine echo had been detected ahead. Next day she had sighted two Norwegian aircraft flying away from the ship, and subsequently had a strong submarine Asdic echo. *Southampton* promptly made a large change of course to avoid the area. That evening, *Southampton* closed a small neutral passenger ship, which she identified by searchlight.

On the 8th she launched her aircraft G9A (Lt CUSSON) on a reconnaissance flight, recovering it three hours later, before sighting and investigating a destroyer and then a merchant ship. Next day, at 0505, she investigated another merchant ship, then two more the following day and sighted a Norwegian destroyer close inshore on the 11th. On that day she was well to the east, virtually off Murmansk, being at 71° 21' N, 31° 34' E at noon. The still air temperature was a freezing 28°/32°, and the sea was rough at times. Yet her sick list had at last begun to decline, with only 21 now ill.

She now began her long haul for home, sighting two trawlers at 0630. These turned out to be Norwegian, one hoisting the Norwegian flag and her company coming over in a small boat for a friendly visit. *Southampton's* log says they were later 'returned to the trawler' (possibly, dare one suggest, a little the worse for drink, probably having been gently 'primed and pumped' for information?) Somewhat in contrast, *Southampton* sighted *Glasgow* next day, accompanied by one captured trawler. *Southampton* kept station on this trawler, and later took her in tow. Then began a near-pantomime, with the towing cable 'stranding' and having to be replaced, then the new tow parting at the trawler, with *Southampton* then having to keep station astern of the trawler in the darkness of night, then sending a whaler to restore the tow, then slipping the tow and keeping station again, then the trawler stopping to repair an engine defect, then both ships proceeding together, then parting company, then rejoining - only to have *Southampton's* 'A' Boiler Room report a defect, slowing them both down. In the meantime they had voyaged the many miles from 70° 31' N, 18° 20' E to 65° 11' N, 05° 33' E.

Next day, the 16th, a wave which might have been caused by a submarine was reported astern, *Southampton* immediately increasing to 25 knots to try to out-run any torpedo which might have been launched at her. Nothing ensued and within the hour her Special Sea Dutymen were closed up for entering harbour, and she came to anchor at 1433, inside the Hoxa boom. She had travelled 4,560 miles on her patrol, and oiled immediately. An irregular pattern was being set whereby, usually operating alone, *Southampton* would normally be out ten to fourteen days on patrol and would then have four days or so at Scapa Flow to dry out, clean ship, repair minor storm-damage, refuel and replenish her stores. On such occasions a visit by Vice Admiral LAYTON (CS 2) was likely, to hold discussions with Captain JEANS. Meantime, the ship would hone her skills by conducting height-finding exercises, sub/cal shoots, MG and Pom-Pom firing, starshell and searchlight practice, by sending away her boarding whalers' crews and by going to Action Stations. Then she would take in ammunition, fuel, and provisions. Meantime, other ships, such as *Arethusa* and *Edinburgh*, would be arriving from patrol and departing anew.

Alf was present as OOW every other day during this first lull between patrols, Lt Commander TILNEY leaving ship for HMS *Daedelus* at Lee-on-Solent, and Lt MANNING joining. [The company would always be wishing that damage to the ship, or a breakdown, might be just bad enough to need a 'dockyard job' at Rosyth, or wherever else there might be a possibility for 'long leave'. Chance would be a fine thing!]

Southampton's next patrol started on 23rd February and would take her to the area of sea between the Faroe Islands and Iceland. She proceeded from Scapa at 0830, and had a one-hour HA shoot starting at 0950 at a pre-arranged target towed by an aircraft, before heading out past the famous rock-feature called the 'Old Man of Hoy'. She later sighted the incoming destroyer *Kimberley* which was escorting a prize vessel and she then passed a naval trawler on patrol. During the night, heading ever north, *Southampton* investigated three vessels, using her searchlights to illuminate the third. At 0810 *Manchester* was sighted and *Southampton* commenced her patrol, releasing *Manchester* to return to Scapa. *Southampton* was now at 62° 41' N, 12° 18' W, 380 miles from her base at Scapa.

A strong breeze was blowing from the north-east, the sea had waves 4 ft high, and there was a variable swell, sometimes attaining 15 ft. The temperature was chill, the sky cloudy, but sometimes with patches of clear blue, and daytime visibility varied from 4 to 7 miles. The cruiser investigated the lone vessels she found, becoming suspicious about a Swedish freighter bound from New York to Gothenberg and escorting her in to the Faroes on the 27th. *Southampton* then went from Cruising Stations to Defence Stations when sending a boarding party to investigate the Norwegian freighter *Norne* bound for New York to Trondheim. On the 28th at 0355 *Southampton* sighted a darkened ship, going to Action Stations as she challenged her, only to find she was the AMC *Cilicia*, and, at 0729 challenging another ship which identified herself as the cruiser HMS *York*. At 0955 *Southampton* investigated yet another ship, finding her to be the Norwegian ship *John Babke*, bound from Valporiso to Trondheim with general cargo. This ship she told to alter course and escorted her through the hours of darkness, handing her over to the trawler *Northern Skye* at 0600 on the 29th.

On the 1st March she investigated two more Norwegian ships, the *Tigne* and the *Haflergh*, herself being challenged by *Newcastle* at 0730, the two cruisers being near the junction of their respective patrol lines, and grasping the opportunity to exchange their navigational fixes, *Southampton* then recording hers as 62° 53' N, 13° 58' W at noon.[395]

---

[395] The further north (or south) the latitude, the greater the risk of errors in navigation. A cross-check of positions was always useful, especially when a ship had been travelling by 'dead-reckoning' in

She was again challenged by *Newcastle* next morning, and herself challenged a very similar silhouette the following morning, finding this to be *Manchester*, coming on station on the 3rd March to relieve *Southampton*.

This relief was very welcome and *Southampton* now 'lifted up her skirts', going from 10 to 20 knots, as she began her passage southwards, streaming her paravanes, with her company at cruising stations, and investigating two ships as she did so. She passed the Hoxa gate at 0902 on the 4th March, her screws having driven her another 3,200 miles since 23rd February. She promptly oiled. *Newcastle*, also just relieved, came in from her patrol almost immediately afterwards.

Though not shown in *Southampton's* log, Surgeon Commander W.P.E McINTYRE joined ship on the 5th and Surgeon Commander N.A.H BARLOW was discharged to shore. As we shall see, Surgeon Commander McINTYRE would later become a busy man. During the next few days *Southampton's* company tidied up, in various respects. The sick list was down to six, but the working complement was just slightly reduced because two ratings had to be discharged to Greenwich to go to prison. On the material side, it seems that the rough weather encountered, though not exceptional in those climes, had damaged the Asdic dome and *Southampton's* diving party worked on it on the 7th. It was the turn of *Southampton* to be AA Guard ship that day, Alf signing the log when he came off watch at 1800. Next morning the Cable Party and Special Sea Dutymen closed up at 0855, and *Southampton* proceeded for a Sub/Cal shoot.

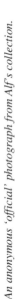

An anonymous 'official' photograph from Alf's collection.

Shoot! A pre-war photograph of HMS *Southampton* at high speed and firing a practice broadside from her 6-inch guns. Bearing in mind the distinct possibility of suddenly encountering a German 'pocket-battleship' or heavy cruiser almost anywhere whilst at sea, the assets of *Southampton's* high speed and manoeuvrability , combined with her reasonably heavy guns, were a positive reassurance for her men. However, it was her 'secondary' dual-purpose 4-inch guns, in their AA role, which were going to be of greater significance in the impending campaign in northern waters.

open seas, with no confirmatory 'sun' or 'star' sights having been possible for days on end due to overcast skies.

She made three runs of Sub/Cal firing on the nearby range. She then practised making 'slicks' for her aircraft, and subsequently followed *Newcastle* out of the Flow to carry out a Full/Calibre shoot, opening fire at 1345.

Southampton's newly-repaired Asdic was evidently now functioning well, for she obtained a 'Hydrophone Contact' at 1402 and promptly increased to 20 knots, losing the contact. *Newcastle's* shoot was immediately abandoned and the two cruisers shaped course to return to harbour, only to find the Hoxa Gate closed - presumably due to the 'submarine scare'. They therefore had to divert to use the northerly gate.

On the 9th two watches of 'the troops' were given a brief run ashore. Whilst they were out of the ship an Air Raid Warning was sounded and the HA armament was closed up, though nothing developed. At 1030 the battleship *Rodney* and the battlecruisers *Repulse* and *Renown* arrived, as a token of the heavy units which might be called upon by the Admiralty should *Southampton* or any of other cruisers and AMCs in the defensive screen placed across the Atlantic wastes from the Orkneys to the Denmark Strait happen to detect and report a heavy German unit trying to break through the cordon.

Then, as a more immediate and rather ominous portent to the company of *Southampton*, their sister-ship *Newcastle* sailed for her patrol area, just to the north of theirs. They followed her out the next morning, passing through the Hoxa Gate at 0755, sighting a friendly trawler escorting a Danish ship at 1330 and themselves then investigating the *Elise*, which they later handed over to the trawler *Northern Sun*. At 0957 on the 11th they challenged and then relieved *Manchester*, and commenced their Patrol at 1244, with the hands at cruising stations and the ship on a zig-zag course.

At noon on the 12th, at 63° 36' N, 11° 14' W, they challenged a cruiser with a familiar silhouette, receiving no reply in the poor visibility, but assuming her to be *Newcastle* on her adjacent patrol 'beat'. On the 15th, when at 63° 24' N, 12° 12' W, *Southampton* challenged *Newcastle* again, this time with immediate response, and then carried out a Range and Inclination test on her, parting company at 1524. Four hours later, *Southampton* sighted the mast of a vessel hull down on the horizon, and assumed it was again *Newcastle*.

The temperature was hovering around freezing point, sometimes as low as 27° F. The sea was almost deserted, *Southampton* having sighted only one other vessel before she again closed with *Newcastle*, this time on the afternoon of the 17th. However, on the next day *Southampton* did sight, and next day challenged and exchanged signals with the AMC *Circussia* at 63° 09' N,14° 02' W (evidently she was on the adjacent patrol beat to the south) and also investigated the Norwegian ship *Toulouse*, bound westward. Having investigated two small ships on the morning of the 19th March, *Southampton* was herself challenged by the *Circussia*, which seemed to be very much 'on the ball' as befitted an AMC with no armour and only limited speed. For her part, *Southampton* challenged *Manchester* a little later as that ship came on patrol to relieve her. *Southampton* then wasted no time in heading south for Scapa, investigating the Swedish *Sverige* as she did so, and later having to come down to 20 knots because of the low visibility. She passed through the Hoxa Gate at 0746 on the 20th March, closed up her HA crews, as the 'preparative' of an Air Raid Warning had been given, embarked oil to fill her bunkers after the 3,201 miles she had steamed, but gave a short 'Canteen Leave' to such of her company as she could spare. By 1715 she had her company at General Quarters, for an Air Raid Red warning had been issued.

Just before midnight her former cruiser squadron, the 2ⁿᵈ, proceeded. The next days saw constant air raid warnings, with the HA armament being closed up each time, and Alf with them, giving him little rest. They embarked their aircraft (Lt WOODS) whilst an air raid warning was in being, and painted and provisioned ship. The sick list was down to five, when *Newcastle* put to sea on the 26ᵗʰ, as a harbinger of their own departure a few short hours later.

Ominously, the glass had been falling. Two hours out from Scapa they had a 4-inch HA shoot at an aircraft-towed sleeve target and at two remote-controlled aircraft, following which they sighted and identified three destroyers travelling in company, and investigated a Swedish merchant ship. At 0600 on the 27ᵗʰ they challenged *Birmingham*. By now the sea was rough, with a wind of Gale Force 7 at times, and occasional flurries of snow, the air temperature hovering around freezing. Speed had to be reduced at 0620 to repair a broken scuttle through which the sea was making inroads. At 1535, as they were investigating the Swedish tanker *Lionel*, they sighted *Glasgow*. They sighted and identified her again next morning, when *Southampton* was at 63° 11' N, 4° 26' W, in a bitterly cold E.S.E wind of Force 8 with a 15ft swell running.

An anonymous 'official' photograph from Alf's collection.

Glasgow in stormy conditions, and with a heavy swell running. Mid-Atlantic photograph taken from *Southampton* during the Royal Tour to Canada in 1939.

In these conditions *Southampton* investigated a Norwegian ship the *Emily Maarsk* bound for Denmark, and, being dissatisfied with her, began to escort the *Emily Maarsk* to the West Faroes. Next day, whilst escorting this ship, *Southampton* challenged and identified the cruiser *York*, and was challenged in her turn by *Glasgow*. Having investigated a Swedish tanker, the *Atlantides*, and the weather having moderated slightly, *Southampton* sent a boarding party to the *Emily Maarsk*. Using her searchlights, she then investigated and cleared two other merchant ships. Tempers became a little frayed the next day, the 30th March, when the Norwegian ship *Ruth* was investigated at 0543 and ordered to Heave-to, whilst a boarding party went aboard from *Southampton's* 1st whaler. *Ruth* was then ordered to proceed into Kirkwall for closer examination and the destroyer *Vanoc* was signalled to escort her in. However, at 1445, the Master of *Ruth* refused to navigate his ship and an armed guard was put aboard to back up the command. *Ruth* then proceeded as ordered, but, (if the author's memory of a long-past conversation is valid, Captain JEANS admired and respected the Master's spirit), and, as the log shows, *Ruth* was soon released to go about her business after only a token period of 'arrest'.

On the 31st March *Glasgow* was again glimpsed in the severe weather, and challenged when sighted at 0555 the following morning. *Southampton* took station astern of her, breaking away for an 'R & I' practice, before again taking station and, later, marking the fall of *Glasgow's* throw-off shoot at her. The two cruisers then continued in station together through the early hours of the night, *Southampton* later being released by *Glasgow* (at 0035) to proceed independently to Scapa. One imagines that these throw-off shoots not only served as useful practice, but were also a good way of easing the tension of being in constant anticipation of suddenly running into a heavy German unit. *Southampton* arrived at Scapa at 0810, having been challenged by *York* in the darkness of 0400 (probably yet another heart-stopping moment as the winking light suddenly started to make its challenge), but otherwise uneventfully.

Anonymous 'official' photograph from Alf's collection.

Glasgow, 'shipping a big 'un', as Alf wrote on the back of the original print. This photo was taken in 1939, during the Royal Tour to Canada and the U.S.A. One imagines that, following the outbreak of war, *Glasgow's* white yards would long have been dulled down by 'crabfat' grey paint – but the seas breaking aboard in heavy weather were probably not greatly changed – except in being even colder by being further north.

Southampton's 1st cutter which had been stranded on Flotta returned and was now hoisted in and *Southampton* embarked her aircraft (S/Lt WOODS). Again, her HA armament was frequently closed up, as Warnings Yellow were still proliferating. Alf would doubtless have been heavily involved: he was also OOW from time to time. On the 3rd April an anchor watch was set, the wind having risen to Force 6 from the S.S.E. There was also heavy rain. On the 4th the 2nd Cutter, which had also been stranded on Flotta, returned to the ship waterlogged, and was hoisted in. [*The story behind the cutters having been stranded sounds darkly interesting but is unknown to the author. For some reason it evokes memories of a moving and rather moralistic tale by 'Taffrail', set in those waters in WW1, about a hair-raising piece of sailing and seamanship by a small boat to avoid being driven catastrophically on to a rocky lee shore in a severe gale. The moralistic point to the story was that the midshipman or any other officer in charge should never allow himself to be persuaded by his Senior Rating to take a 'soft option', but always to have his boat 'on the top line' for any and every eventuality.*]

On the 5th Midshipmen COLLIER and CUNNINGHAM left the ship for *Excellent*, and, on the 6th, the hands were busy provisioning ship, with the HA armament closed up yet again. *Cairo, Sheffield* and *Penelope* arrived that day. The destroyer *Mohawk* had arrived the previous day. During those two days, *Renown* and the destroyers *Gloworm, Ilex, Imogen, Janus* and *Mohawk* had put to sea. *Southampton* would proceed next day.

It was about this time that a report by the ship's new medical officer, Surgeon Commander McINTYRE, was issued, covering the period of March. He had several concerns, such as the continuing shortage of certain medical supplies, the absence of any green vegetables for a month, the enforced and prolonged drinking of condensed water (rather than fresh water), the 'darken ship routine' at night (which prevented proper ventilation), and the fact that no leave had been given for nine weeks, (apart from a very small number of canteen leaves at Scapa). He went on to say that the ship had been at sea since 6th March (apart from 6 days at Scapa), and that the men were getting no rest and relaxation when they did put in to Scapa, due to the continuous air raid warnings when they were there. Indeed, he said, the men preferred to be at sea rather than endure the endless warnings of air raids at Scapa. He wrote: "*As chief censor, and from enquiries the men are making, they are suffering from sexual starvation. 90% of the letters show it. Unless something is done to give the men shore leave, such as a '48 hours' every two months, I fear nervous trouble and unnatural offences, etc., are to be expected. These observations are being brought to the attention of the Squadron Medical Officer.*"[396] Even if he was doing so on a logical and argued basis, the surgeon was really saying: 'Scapa, bloody Scapa!', just like the countless thousands of Naval men who had gone before him, ever since the base had been opened at Scapa Flow at the start of the first World War. Soon, though, as we shall see, the Surgeon Commander was going to have a completely different set of tasks and pre-occupations, which would wipe 'Scapa' and all these frustrating matters right out of his mind.

Come Sunday the 7th April *Southampton* was off again, following *Manchester* out through the Hoxa Gate at 0737, but then taking station ahead of her, as paravanes were streamed and the HA armament closed up to 2nd Degree Readiness. (The LA armament closed up to only 4th Degree). Soon, the two ships were zig-zagging at 27 knots, later

---

[396] See ADM 101/571 at TNA.

sighting two aircraft, subsequently identified as friendly, but *Southampton* then getting an Asdic contact at 1320, signalling *Manchester* immediately and dropping three depth-charges on the contact area.

By 1500 they had joined the Norway-bound Convoy ON 25 which was already being escorted by the destroyers *Eclipse, Grenade, Janus* and *Javelin* who were proceeding with it at 7½ knots in a very stiff breeze which reached gale force at times. At noon on the 8th April *Southampton* was at 61° 08' N, 00° 51' W, sighting the Shetlands two hours later, and rejoining *Manchester* at around 1600. Although not made clear in the log, information had been received from the Admiralty that the Germans were invading Norway, and Convoy ON 25 was now recalled to the UK. For their part, *Manchester, Southampton* and the five destroyers were ordered to join the Home Fleet at sea, 100 miles to the south-west of Bergen, on 9th April. Things were suddenly hotting up. The Germans were already invading neutral Norway. The Allies were about to do the same!

The log shows *Southampton* investigating a merchant ship at 0530 that day, and, at 0550, sighting first *Sheffield* on her port bow, and then the battleships *Rodney* and *Valiant*, together with their escorting destroyers. At 0605 *Southampton* ordered the SS *Halder* (presumably a ship bound for Norway) to return to the U.K. *Southampton* was ordered to take station astern of *Sheffield*, with *Manchester* following. At 0835 *Southampton* opened fire at long range with her 6-inch guns at an aircraft, which disappeared, and she then sighted cruisers and destroyers ahead, just before opening up with her 6-inch and 4-inch armament at distant aircraft. The detachment then met up with French units, and was subsequently ordered by CS 18 to take up a position on the port flank of the battlefleet.

Enemy aircraft were still overhead, and *Southampton* opened fire with her 4-inch HA at them. At this stage, *Manchester, Southampton, Sheffield, Glasgow, Aurora* and the destroyers *Afridi, Gurkha, Mohawk, Mashona, Matabele, Sikh* and *Somali* were detached from the Home Fleet and ordered to attack the German invasion assault shipping at Bergen and Stavanger. The force was under the command of Vice-Admiral Geoffrey LAYTON. At noon they were at 61° 18' N, 03° 08' E, and thus about 80 miles out from their target. However, the attack was called off at 1400, by which time they had probably closed to within 30 miles of their target, and the ships headed back to rejoin the fleet.[397] However, the Home Fleet had been observed and reported by German reconnaissance planes which were already operating from swiftly captured Norwegian airfields, and from 1430 that same afternoon, for three hours, heavy attacks were made on the Home Fleet by 47 Ju 88 aircraft of the 'Eagle' Geschwader KG 30 and 41 He 111 bombers of the 'Lion' Geschwader KG 26.

Southampton and *Glasgow*, though homing in fast on the Home Fleet, were still out to the east of it when the attacks started. Both escaped with only minor damage, although *Glasgow* unfortunately had two ratings killed. Midshipman Thomas RUCK-KEENE, who was *Southampton's* Air Defence Officer, says that one stick of bombs dropped close alongside *Southampton*, heeling her over and carrying away her wireless aerials. Her log confirms that, at 1442, a large bomb near-missed on the starboard side

---

[397] It seems that the Admiralty called off the attack because aerial reconnaissance had reported two heavy German cruisers in the harbour. Their presence there indicated to the Admiralty that the Germans had already taken over the Norwegian shore batteries.

and says that the DCT went out of action. The cruisers now formed into single line ahead, ceasing fire at 1740. *Rodney* and *Valiant* were then in sight.

In fact, *Rodney* had been hit by a 1,000 lb. bomb which had failed to penetrate her armoured deck. On the other hand, the destroyer *Gurkha* had been sunk west of Stavanger after she was hit by four bombs, dying hard. Aboard *Southampton* Alf would have been very busy at his 4" guns during this time, the expenditure of shells from the port and starboard batteries probably amounting to some 700 rounds. One German aircraft was seen to crash into the sea, and there were three 'probables'. (*Author: The 'value' of shooting those rather expensive 'Queen Bee' aircraft out of the sky during pre-war practice was now becoming apparent.*) On 10th April, *Southampton* was at 60° 30' N, 04° 10' E, sighting a friendly aircraft, and obtaining a suspicious contact on her Asdic soon afterwards. At 1920 she sighted a French cruiser and two destroyers, and she passed the Hoxa Gate at 2003. She embarked ammunition almost immediately, being in urgent need of it for her 4-inch guns.[398] She also needed general replenishment and to transfer Commander TINLEY, who needed treatment for lumbar fibrositis, into the hospital ship *Annapurna*. Lt Commander EDMONSTONE was also transferred, suffering from lumbago. The ship was now temporarily bereft of two very senior men. Interestingly, her complement had increased from 700 in 1936 to 790 men by this time. By the 22nd July it would further increase to 816 men - all signs of the extra and more complicated weaponry and systems being carried as the war went on. Finding accommodation for those additional 116 men would be no easy task and would call for much tolerance, particularly but by no means solely by the Lower Deck.

Scapa looked different, for both French and Norwegian warships were now at anchor there. Moreover, as *Southampton* had learned on her way in, although few outward scars were visible, the Germans had mounted a heavy bombing attack on the shipping and harbour installations at 2100. It was very fortunate for the Navy that little serious damage had resulted, for some of the ships had been in a very highly vulnerable state, having been caught in the act of taking in fuel, ammunition and stores. The raid had cost the Germans six of their aircraft shot down by heavy anti-aircraft fire combined with land-based fighter opposition.

Next day, *Southampton* proceeded from Scapa at 1211 with General MACKESEY (C-in-C Norwegian Expeditionary Force) and 350 troops aboard, including an advance party of two companies of Scots Guards. Captain L.E.H. MAUND had come aboard as Naval Chief of Staff to the Expeditionary Force, and a young Norwegian-speaking naval officer called Patrick DALZEL-JOB had also come aboard, as a part of the small staff which was to accompany Captain MAUND. Following shortly behind came *Manchester*, *Sheffield*, *Glasgow* and *Aurora*, which were also carrying troops, and they, together with half-a-dozen destroyers, escorted the convoy bearing the main part of the Allied Expeditionary Force during their voyage to Norway. The troopships included the *Empress of Australia*, whose profile would have been familiar to Alf from the Royal Trip to Canada and the U.S.A in 1939, though she would now have been painted mainly dull-grey, perhaps with some camouflage touches, instead of her mainly white peacetime

---

[398] The high expenditure of 4-inch shell in the anti-aircraft mode was already a matter of some concern when the matter that the ship might be *under continuous attack at sea, for day after day*, was considered.

colours. She was accompanied by the two sister-ships *Batory* and *Chobry*, and the liners were completed by the *Monarch of Bermuda* and the *Reino del Pacifico*.

The original intention was that all the soldiers being transported should be landed at Harstad, a small island town to the north of Narvik. However, part of the convoy, including the *Empress of Australia* and the *Chobry*, and some of the escorts were diverted to make a landing at Namsos. The remainder pressed on.

According to Patrick DALZEL-JOB and others there seemed to be a total lack of understanding by the planners and higher command of the snowbound and icy conditions which would be encountered in Norway at that still-early time of year. It was clear that the whole operation had been put together in a hurry. Indeed, at 1645 on the 13th *Southampton* was passing charts and instructions to her escorting destroyers, before she cruised off Stadtlandet, searching unsuccessfully for German warships. Though not mentioned in her log, it appears that around this time she was attacked by the German submarine U-38, off Harstad, the torpedoes missing.[399]

At 0600 on the 14th, having launched her 'Walrus' aircraft to scout ahead of her, *Southampton* passed through Topsundet Fiord, and hauled in her paravanes off Harstad. At 0700 she heaved-to, whilst three 'Swordfish' aircraft, presumably from the aircraft-carrier *Furious* passed overhead, and her 1st Motor Boat went into Harstad, signalling back at 0730 that there were no enemy forces there. In addition to its naval party this boat was carrying Norwegian-speaking Patrick DALZEL-JOB.[400] He had some debate with the local people, including a few Norwegian Army officers, which apparently would subsequently lead to the first intimation to the Norwegian Army Headquarters on the mainland that Allied troops had landed in response to the German invasion which was already in progress.

Patrick DALZEL-JOB communicated back with the staff on *Southampton* by signal-lamp, and a small ship carrying a number of Norwegian representatives, including a local Pilot, put off to *Southampton* at 0910 for further discussions. Meantime the destroyers kept up an anti-submarine sweep, and *Southampton* kept one of her aircraft in the air scouting. At 0920 the local Norwegian Chief of Police and the Mayor came aboard from the steamer *Salangen*. The outcome was that *Southampton* went on to land the two companies of Scots Guards at the hamlet of Selangensverket, at the head of deep-water Salangen Fiord, though General MACKESEY and his staff remained aboard *Southampton*. A vital signal from Lord CORK AND ORRERY, which would have led to this landing being made 40 miles further south, at Narvik, was received too late to be implemented. Wireless reception in the mountainous areas of the fiords was notoriously difficult and unreliable. [*The Germans had suffered serious losses in two hard-hitting naval battles which had recently taken place in Narvik Fiord. The Germans had thought these battles had presaged an immediate landing in force by the Allies at Narvik, and the small German garrison had abandoned the port. Now, the Germans were hurrying to re-occupy Narvik, and time for the Allies to beat them to it was fast running out. The failure*

---

[399] Some sources say she was also attacked unsuccessfully by U-51, just days later, on 18th April.

[400] He was wearing a handsome and impressive-looking brassard which had been made up for him by courtesy of *Southampton's* Pay-Commander and fashioned by her signalmen. It had the initials 'RNLO.' (indicating Royal Navy Liaison Officer) and was adorned with miniature British and Norwegian flags. 'Bunts' had excelled himself. So long as Lt DALZEL-JOB wore heavy clothing to disguise his quite lowly substantive rank, he found his brassard, if accompanied by an incisive manner and loud voice, met with considerable respect from most people, regardless of nationality or rank.

of the wireless message to be received promptly by General MACKESEY thus had the most highly adverse results, for Narvik could probably have been readily captured by a resolute 'coup de main' at that time.]

On 14th/15th April *Southampton* had re-fuelled her attendant destroyers *Electra* and *Escapade*, and supplied them with water. She also received aboard Ernest PLANT, an AB from *Escapade*, who was lucky to be alive, for he had been swept along *Escapade's* deck by a heavy wave but had somehow had the good fortune not to be carried clean overboard. As it was, he was suffering from shock and was generally weak. He was subsequently transferred from *Southampton* to the hospital ship. At 0758 a rating fell overboard from the ship's aircraft, and a whaler was quickly slipped to rescue him, for a swimmer could not last long in these very cold waters. As the whaler was being hoisted in, *Southampton's* lookouts sighted the Allied troop convoy, and *Southampton* proceeded to close *Aurora, Valiant,* eight destroyers and the troopships, *Monarch of Bermuda, Batory* and *Reina del Pacifico,* each carrying about 3,000 troops. *Southampton* now became AA Guardship, for which Alf may well have 'felt the weight'.

General MACKESY and Captain MAUND RN transferred from *Southampton* to *Aurora* at 0945, evidently for tactical discussions with Admiral of the Fleet Lord CORK AND ORRERY who was flying his flag in *Aurora*.[401] *Southampton* stopped in Topsundet Fiord to take station astern of the convoy, and there was a sudden 'Alarm to Arms' at 1020 when an unidentified aircraft swept quickly overhead and as quickly disappeared. *Southampton's* own aircraft G9A was hoisted in, and the ship proceeded, following the convoy into Vaagsfiord.

At 1210 depth-charges were dropped by the destroyers on a suspicious contact. Two friendly aircraft passed overhead, plus one distant and unidentified one. At 1320 *Southampton* hove-to and disembarked the GOC's staff to Harstad, the Norwegian pilot leaving the ship soon afterwards by the 1st Motor Boat. *Southampton* then proceeded at 25 knots to Bygden Fiord and anchored there overnight. At 0830 The Admiral of the Fleet Lord CORK AND ORRERY (otherwise known as 'Ginger' BOYLE) came aboard from *Aurora*, and was subsequently flown off in aircraft G9A (S/Lt WOODS), the plane returning with the Admiral at 1120, and the Admiral going back on board *Aurora*. Sadly, one young Scots Guardsman, George JOHNSTONE by name, after going through an irrational and wild phase, had died peacefully at 2020, probably of meningitis, and his body was respectfully transferred to the destroyer *Electra* to be taken ashore for burial at Harstad.[402]

At 1420 the bugler sounded the Alarm to Arms as two hostile aircraft closed on the anchorage, and the HA armament opened fire as bombs fell around the ship, but clear of her. At 1600 she was attacked again by two aircraft, the bombs again falling clear. Despite the risk of further bombing, at 1800 the destroyer *Amazon* came alongside to re-fuel. The skies were blue, and weather conditions were calm, but the air temperature was scarcely above freezing.

---

[401] 'Ginger' BOYLE was a man who liked to take swift and decisive action. MACKESEY was cautious by nature – and was under orders to be prudent. The debates between these two men were evidently 'not of the best'.

[402] Commonwealth War Graves Commission records confirm the Guardsman George S JOHNSTONE of Rigside, Lanarkshire, died on 15th April and was buried in the cemetery at Harstad.

Despite the previous successful advance landing of the 350 Scots Guards at Salangensverket, 'higher powers' had decreed that it was at Harstad that the follow-up force of about 10,000 soldiers would be landed. And it was at Harstad that Admiral of the Fleet Lord CORK AND ORRERY and the French General BETHOUART would set up their headquarters. The troops were being landed by local fishing boats, properly called *skøyter*, but nicknamed 'puffers' by the naval forces after the 'equivalent' Scottish boats. The anchorage at Harstad was becoming overcrowded and there was a need to continually disperse vessels to alternative nearby fiords.

At 0357 on the 17th April *Southampton* proceeded astern of the three now unladen troopships, leaving Bygden Fiord through Vaagsfiord and Topsundet Fiord, streaming her paravanes as she passed out of Topsundet Fiord, keeping station on the convoy and increasing to 10 knots.

At 1530 she left the convoy, which continued back to the UK. Intermittent snow flurries were seriously interfering with visibility. At 2100 her Asdic had a contact and she dropped three depth-charges, finding another contact which faded as she closed on it, finding another at 2120, but losing that one too as she closed on it. She made a drastic alteration of course and closed towards the land, finding another submarine contact at 0025, again altering course and increasing to full speed, sighted land, passed through Topsundet and Vaagsfiord fiords and entered harbour at Harstad at 0530. She then sent her Motor Boat to *Aurora* for signal ratings, hoisted the M.B back in and proceeded to Bygden Fiord where she anchored at 0835. Two hours later she moved back to Harstad to occupy the berth just quitted by *Aurora*. Half an hour later the Alarm to Arms was sounded and two hostile aircraft dropped two salvoes of bombs which missed the ship. The Admiral of the Fleet came aboard as the aircraft departed and hoisted his flag. The HA armament went to defence watches. Alf would have been active in keeping everything on top line, ready for the next attack.

Some reports state that *Southampton* had sustained one casualty from the near-misses of the various bombs by this time. The surgeon's journal does not support this, though it does show that Alf might have been one loader or handler short, because AB ATKINSON had seriously injured his left thumb due to a 4-inch projectile falling on it. He was discharged to the hospital ship. Meantime, the damage to the ship was accruing, although it was still officially classified as 'superficial'. Whether it was 'superficial' or not, there was flooding in the cable locker, paint shop and a storage area, due to the shrapnel penetrating the thin plating of the ship's side forrard of her armoured bulge. The ship's artisans plugged these holes by driving in wooden spikes between the bombing raids. Up to this time the weather, albeit chill, had been kind, with blue skies and calm seas. Now this gave way to intense cold sometimes accompanied by flurries and blizzards of snow, gradually clearing again.

Brigadier PHILLIPS (in command of 146th Brigade) and his signals staff were still aboard. Next day there was an Alarm to Arms at 1150 but no attack developed. Meantime, there were comings and goings of other warships, including *Ardent* and *Enterprise*. The repair ship *Vindictive* also arrived. The Admiral of the Fleet and L/O MANNING embarked in aircraft G9A (S/Lt E. WOODS) and were flown for discussions with Army Commanders, returning at 2035. At 0945 on the 20th April, a Norwegian flying boat landed, the officers visiting *Southampton* for discussions with F.O. Narvik. Meanwhile the aircraft was secured astern of *Southampton*. The destroyer *Codrington* arrived and D1 visited F.O. Narvik (Admiral of the Fleet Lord CORK AND ORRERY). At 2245 F.O. Narvik transferred to the newly-arrived cruiser *Effingham*. Other destroyers were arriving, *Acasta, Electra* and *Fortune*. *Southampton* oiled. On 21st April she proceeded from Harstad, heading for Bygden Fiord. Whilst en route, *Southampton* sighted *Warspite* and her five attendant destroyers, not long from the Narvik Battles, and waiting to communicate with her in Bygden Fiord, which was duly accomplished.

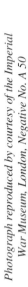

Photograph reproduced by courtesy of the Imperial War Museum, London, Negative No. A 50

Southampton photographed whilst in Topsundet Fiord. She is wearing camouflage paint, intended to confuse her image as observed in enemy rangefinders. The wartime censor has erased a feature in the vicinity of her aircraft hangar. It is believed this feature related to UAP weaponry – which, in the event, proved to be virtually useless and was soon abandoned. The installation of such weapons as Oerlikon AA guns would have been vastly preferred. Note the snow of this mountainous region, which seriously hampered movement on land.

Southampton then proceeded to Harstad, bringing her 4-inch guns into action against a hostile aircraft directly overhead. No bombs were dropped and no hits were obtained on the enemy aircraft. *Warspite* had followed *Southampton* to Harstad, and she promptly fired on an aircraft in sight. Ships were coming and going at the small anchorage, *Acasta* and *Electra* had left an hour before midnight on the 20th, and *Ardent* and *Codrington* had proceeded at 0500 on the 21st. Now, late on the 21st, *Codrington* had returned, and *Foxhound* had put to sea. The weather was freezing cold, but the skies often had generous patches of blue, and there was good visibility. At 2030 on the 21st Lt Commander 'T' and eight ratings left the ship on special duties (probably to do with demolitions): seemingly they returned sound and safe for they were off again the next morning. Meantime, another Norwegian flying boat had landed and its officers had gone aboard *Effingham* for discussions with F.O. Narvik. The aircraft was hoisted aboard *Southampton*.

Southampton proceeded at 0855 at 18 knots, obtaining an echo and heading away from it at full speed, contact being lost 5 minutes later. She came to anchor in 27 fathoms in Bygden Fiord, later taking in provisions from the *Franconia*. Her diving party returned on board.

On the 23rd she proceeded to Harstad, where one platoon of her Marines was transferred to *Effingham*. The carrier *Furious* arrived and her Captain visited *Southampton*. Apparently, *Effingham's* aircraft had been damaged and it was hoisted aboard *Southampton* for repair.[403] *Effingham* then sailed.[404] Next day, headed by Lt Commander 'T', the Torpedo Party again left the ship. The weather remained bitterly cold with blue skies alternating with snow squalls. Ships came and went and the crews of the HA armament were kept at defence watches, lest further air attacks suddenly developed. *Effingham* came to anchor at Harstad and *Southampton's* Marine platoon returned aboard. Just after they did so there was an 'Alarm to Arms', twenty aircraft being seen, though no attack developed. *Furious* sailed, perhaps to seek a position less exposed to aerial attack, one aircraft identified as hostile being seen later, though out of range. *Southampton* again headed for Bygden Fiord, where an oiler secured alongside in the 'twilight' of the 'Arctic' night. This generally tense situation continued until 27th April, with the ship standing to arms when individual aircraft were sighted, and with ships coming and going, such as the destroyers *Acasta, Ardent, Delight, Diana, Electra* and *Wren*. Captain JEANS visited *Effingham* for tactical discussions. Despite the considerable tension, no air attacks actually developed. However, this suddenly changed on the 27th, after Lt Commander 'T' had left the ship, and had embarked in the trawler *Loch Fin* with his Torpedo Party. *Southampton's* aircraft had just brought F.O. Narvik back to the ship, when there was an Alarm to Arms, and two bombs fell close to the ship. This was typical of the tense situation now prevailing, where bombing aircraft could sweep in over the steeply mountainous terrain totally unseen and unheard until virtually the last moment.

Fame and the French troop transport *Flandres* arrived at 2200, and the Captain of *Fame* called on 'Southampton'. At 0230 *Southampton* landed a beach party at Skoenland, and then sent away her powerboats and both cutters to assist in landing the troops from *Flandres*. At 1705 the French transport *President Paul Drumur* arrived, escorted by *Fame* which had departed earlier. Southampton proceeded in order to pick up her 2nd Motor Boat which was carrying her Torpedo Officer and his party. She then returned to Hardstad and sent her 2nd Motor Boat in there. There were some comings and goings by destroyers, and *Bedouin* arrived at 1205, carrying Lt Commanders PETTY and BULFORD with five ratings who all joined ship. Mail, which would have been very welcome, was also sent over from *Bedouin*.

On the 29th *Southampton* passed through the Maelstrom to proceed up Vestfiord, and oiled, proceeding next day to Skjed Fiord, challenging and identifying *Sheffield* and then forming up with the 18th C S.

---

[403] Unlike *Effingham*, *Southampton* had hangars in which the aircraft could be worked upon 'out of the weather'.

[404] She was still carrying *Southampton's* Marines, and was bound for Narvik where, accompanied by other warships including the battleship *Warspite*, she would participate in a bombardment, followed, if propitious, by an armed landing by Marines and some troops who were being carried in the *Vindictive*. For various reasons the operation was a fiasco and the force returned to Harstad.

On the night of 30th April/1st May, *Southampton* joined up with the cruisers *Arethusa, Galatea, Sheffield* and six destroyers, together with the small troop transports *Ulster Prince* and *Ulster Monarch*, in evacuating 2,500 troops from Andalsnes, which lay 500 miles south of Narvik. Thomas RUCK-KEENE says these troops were *'the weary and harassed remains of the Sherwood Foresters and other regiments'*. This evacuation took place under continuous night-bombing, though this was 'night' almost of the 'midnight sun' variety being that far north in midsummer. Alf would have been busy, for the 4 inch guns put up a heavy barrage, necessitating the replacement of their worn-out gun-barrels at Rosyth, during the end of the first week of May.

The log shows that *Southampton* was hove-to in Rombacksfiord at 0140 on the 1st May, the destroyer *Wanderer* coming alongside and transferring 160 troops. *Southampton* then crossed Rombacksfiord at 28 knots, with her Action HA closed up, and with *Galatea* keeping station astern. At 0345 three aircraft attacked the convoy, *Southampton's* HA opening fire. The bombs fell ahead of the ship and no damage was done. At 0500 three friendly aircraft were sighted astern, but at 0705, when a Dornier aircraft was sighted on the horizon, the company were brought back from 3rd degree to 1st degree readiness and the 6-inch LA armament opened fire on the Dornier. There was relief when *Arethusa* was sighted at 0808, then *Sheffield* at 0955 and then *Manchester, Birmingham* and three destroyers to add to the AA defences of the convoy. The destroyers *Walker* and *Westcott* were sighted at 1045, and also joined. Meantime, hostile aircraft probed around the flanks of the convoy but kept discreetly out of range.

At 1245 the reassuring shape of a friendly 'Sunderland' flying boat was sighted and the HA armament was reduced to 2nd degree readiness. *Southampton*, becoming low on fuel, was detached from the convoy at 1830, with the destroyers *Walker* and *Westcott* in company, and headed for Sullom Voe, anchoring outside the port whilst *Wescott* secured port side and took off the troops. Some of these men were wounded. They had been very well treated before coming on board, mostly by Norwegian doctors, but all their wounds had been re-dressed on arrival in *Southampton*. The great majority were not wounded, but, to the last man, they were utterly exhausted. A hot meal had cheered them up remarkably well, and they had slept during most of the return journey. The men who were wounded came mostly from the King's Own Yorkshire Light infantry, the Yorks and Lancs., and the Sherwood Foresters. There was also one Green Howard, one Gunner, one RAF Corporal and one Norwegian soldier.

Southampton subsequently entered Sullom Voe and took in a supply of oil. She proceeded almost at once, passing the net defences at 2120, streaming her paravanes and sighting *Codrington* and two ships she was escorting at 0325, and then *York* and the convoy on *Southampton's* port bow at 1506. A few minutes later an unidentified aircraft was in sight, the Action HA being immediately closed up. By 1700 the ship was in station astern of *Devonshire*, when a hostile float plane was sighted right on the horizon. One round of 4-inch HA was fired at it, whereupon it flew off.

At 0425 on 4th May, three 'London' flying boats were sighted, then three Lockheed 'Hudson' aircraft assumed air patrol over the convoy, then three 'Blenheim' aircraft took over. Despite their comforting presence, a German submarine may have been assessing its chances of a torpedo shot, for a contact was reported and investigated by *Acheron* and *Antelope* at 1625. At 2130 the HA was put to 1st degree readiness as the air escort left, being reduced to 2nd degree as the convoy neared Scapa Flow. At 0440 on the 5th May *Southampton* passed through the Hoxa Gate. She came to anchor at 0532, and, at 0800, hoisted the Flag of Rear Admiral M.L. CLARKE 2nd in Command of the 18th Cruiser Squadron. At 0920 Commander C.B. TINLEY rejoined the ship from the hospital ship *Annapurna*, having missed a lot of the 'fun'. *Southampton* began to embark ammunition, petrol and more oil, and watched as *Kelly* and *Imperial* left, escorting three troop transports. She took in more ammunition and provisions next morning, and launched L2294 (S/Lt WOODS) which flew off to Rosyth carrying Lt MANNING and others. The Rear Admiral visited *Devonshire*. Next day, the 7th, *Southampton* proceeded to Rosyth at 0435, altering course at 0607 and going to full speed to avoid a floating mine her Asdic had detected.

Soon after her arrival she hoisted in her '*Shagbat*' (i.e. '*Walrus*' aircraft) L2294 (S/Lt WOODS), later taking on board a harbour pilot and proceeding into the lock, securing alongside. Here she remained for several days, making repairs of the many holes in her side, painting ship, embarking Carley Floats, being twice visited by the Admiral Superintendent to check on her status and needs, and on the repairs which were going on.

Some of her men were in need of 'repairs', too. One Marine virtually ran amok with a bayonet at this time, was talking to himself unintelligibly when restrained, and was said by his messmates to have been 'shaky' ever since the air raid at Rosyth on 16th October, when Boy Seaman BRADLEY had tragically been killed. This Marine was discharged to the RN Hospital at Port Edgar. Other men were also becoming affected by 'nerves', at least one other being discharged to the hospital at this time with 'anxiety neurosis'. Seeing the number of times that the ship had been 'near-missed' and the constant tension the men were under all the time they were at sea, these cases were hardly surprising. At least the ships' surgeons seemed to take a sensible view of all this and to treat the men sympathetically, rather than berating such men and marking their record as having a 'lack of moral fibre', as happened all too often in other of our fighting forces.

The two cases were accompanied to hospital by a Telegraphist who'd been knocked down by a taxi in Edinburgh. He appeared to have concussion, for he thought he'd been treated by an Army M.O, but he was in something of a daze and could not be sure. He was evidently one of a number of men who had been given a short run ashore at Edinburgh. Some of them appear to have indulged themselves a little too liberally, for eleven cases of gonorrhoea and three of chanchroid were subsequently treated by the ship's surgeon, two of the latter having to be put ashore for hospital treatment. (It has to be said that the ship had also called in at Glasgow, where some of the 'blame' might have lain, but Edinburgh seemed to be the 'prime suspect' in the mind of the surgeon.)

Although not directly spelt out in the log, it is clear that *Southampton* was fitted with 'de-gaussing' gear whilst she was at Rosyth, to 'neutralise' the ships magnetic field and thus protect her against magnetic mines. The log makes no mention of it, but Thomas RUCK-KEENE's account says that the ship's 4-inch guns had new barrels fitted at about this time, which would doubtless have demanded Alf's close attention, and this probably coincided with the fitting of de-gaussing gear. It was just as well that the guns were being brought 'on top line', for the ship was soon going to have great need of them.⁴⁰⁵

---

⁴⁰⁵ Thomas RUCK-KEENE was a Midshipman who joined HMS *Southampton* in May 1938 and survived her sinking in 1941. In 1993 Thomas RUCK-KEENE had very kindly written to the author about his memories of Commissioned Gunner Alfred Wm DAVIS, whom he had called his 'Sea-Daddy'. Thomas

Some sources say that *Southampton* was also equipped with Type 279 Air-Warning Radar at this time, but, if this was the intention, it seems that, though the relevant aerials *may* have been fitted to her mastheads, the full equipment appears never to have been carried through to actual installation and manning. Perhaps the urgency of the time prevented it.[406] This would prove to be a very great pity indeed.

Divisions were held on the jetty on the 12th, and the Admiral walked round the ranks of men, having a word here and there to boost morale. S/Lt DIGBY-RYEBACK joined ship and Lt KEYWORTH left. Lt BENNETT-JONES left ship three days later. French ships were becoming increasingly evident at Rosyth, including the depot ship *Jules Verne*, which would quickly be followed by the submarines *Circe* and *Amazon*.

On the 15th May a violent thunderstorm broke in the afternoon and five barrage balloons were spectacularly destroyed by lightning. It looks as if the company managed to get in some sport at this time, probably going a little madly at it as a reaction to the general stress they had all been labouring under. Perhaps the consequences were inevitable. Leading Stoker PHILLIPS and Stoker PRATER were both injured whilst playing football, PHILLIPS having fallen on his left hand, and PRATER on his wrist, the latter suffering a Colles fracture. They were treated aboard ship, rather than being discharged to hospital.

They were not the only ones injured at sport. That is to say, on the 18th May, the log shows that Alf left the ship for the Royal Naval Hospital at Rosyth. It would not be until the 1st August that the log would register his return! The reason for his very long absence was (initially at least) that he had '*overstretched himself*' when he had been playing 'organised hockey' in the afternoon of the 17th May, and he had '*felt something give in the small of his back*'. On the 18th May he was unable to move without great pain and it appeared that he had ruptured some of the fibres in his lumbar muscles. He was sent to the Garthdene Nursing Home, Dumferline for treatment. A 'hurt certificate' was granted by the ship's surgeon. According to his younger daughter it is *possible* that the opportunity was taken to remove Alf's tonsils at this time, which had evidently been causing him some trouble and reducing his 'operational effectiveness'. The author feels that his sister may well be correct in her assumption, for Alf would be sick and 'convalescent' for an appreciable period to come.

In fact, Alf was now going to miss some desperate and tense periods of action in which *Southampton* would be involved during the next 2½ months. Although he would not be present, it seems worthwhile to quote a synopsis of those events in this narrative, for, becoming aware, after his return to duty, of the many dangers which he had thus escaped may have had a very significant effect on Alf and on his subsequent behaviour.

---

had maintained a journal of the ship's movements and incidents affecting her. Leonard E WELLS, BEM, had joined Southampton in November 1939 as a Supply Assistant and also survived the sinking. The two men met up 50 years later, and, after Thomas' death, by prior agreement, Leonard wrote a foreword to Thomas' journal, adding supplementary text and a supporting article by former Midshipman JERRAM (another survivor), which were all bound together and formally presented to the 6th HMS *Southampton* in 2003. [Leonard WELLS very kindly presented the author of this book with a copy, which has been drawn upon to a limited but invaluable extent, to add flashes of further 'colour' to this account of *Southampton's* movements.]

[406] A photo which the author has seen, allegedly of *Southampton*, and allegedly taken on 10th October 1940, shows the Type 279 Air-Warning aerials in place on the ship's topmasts. Yet the author has been assured by members of her company that Radar was never fitted, and the Court of Enquiry following her sinking in 1941 also stated that no RDF was fitted.

It is just possible that he may have had to endure a certain amount of gentle leg-pulling (or for some reason come to believe that people were 'talking behind his back'), and this might well have 'touched a sensitive nerve and pricked his high pride'.

During his absence then, on 21ˢᵗ May 'Southampton' carried out 12 runs on the 'DG' (de-gaussing) Range, and practised new 'Defence' and 'Action Stations'. One suspects that the latter were influenced by the heavy air-attacks to which our ships were being subjected. 'Southampton's DG Trials were protracted, and she continued them next day. At around this time her badly-needed and overdue supplies of medical stores arrived. Of particular concern to Surgeon Commander McINTYRE had been supplies of M & B 693. These had now arrived, and he was going to find them invaluable in the three months to come.

'Southampton' put to sea on the 23ʳᵈ May, heading northwards and then east of north, to be at 67° 29' N, 01° 32' E at noon on the 24ᵗʰ, having put her HA armament to practice that morning. By 1825 she was nearing the Norwegian Coast, having investigated two Norwegian trawlers as she did so, and being attacked by an enemy aircraft at 1840, three bombs falling astern. This was just a little foretaste of what was to come.

That night she passed through Topsundet Fiord and Vaagsfiord to arrive again at Harstad. She oiled from the tanker 'British Governor', and then started to shuttle back and forth between Harstad and Vaagsfiord, using the latter when enemy aircraft were sighted, to obtain greater room for evasive manoeuvring. On the 25ᵗʰ one or more enemy aircraft were frequently overhead, and by 1130 her HA guns were in action, having to divide their fire on the different aircraft attacking the shipping. At 1230 a salvo of bombs fell close alongside, causing three casualties and damage in the Messdecks. Three small holes were punctured in the Flour Store, below the water line. Alarms to Arms became almost continuous, five bombs being dropped astern at 2025, causing three more casualties. These six men, Petty Officer GADD, ERA POTTER, ERA PRESTON, AB ROWELL, AB PEARSON and Stoker WARD were seriously wounded and were sent ashore to hospital at Harstad.[407] The ship's Commanding Officer, Captain JEANS, received two shrapnel wounds just above his right ankle, but carried on for a day before, reluctantly, he had to consent to being discharged to the General Hospital at Harstad.

Stoker WILES was slightly wounded in the knee. [He 'carried on', but this wound would continue to cause him problems and he would be discharged to the hospital ship 'Annapurna' in late June. He would be accompanied by a Stoker who had become very nervous and was discharged for observation and treatment.] It seems appropriate at this point to refer to the Surgeon's journal for the period 1ˢᵗ April-30ᵗʰ June 1940, where he said that fifteen casualties had been caused by enemy bombing attacks during that period. He considered that the number was remarkably low in view of the extensive albeit 'slight' material damage caused in the ship itself. He attributed the small number of human casualties to the fact that ratings below decks, if not required for other duties,

---

[407] The log states that AB Robert PEARSON unfortunately died next day, the 26ᵗʰ May. The records of the Commonwealth War Graves Commission state that AB PEARSON aged 30, of Newcastle-on-Tyne is buried at Harstad. No records of burials of the other men listed above are shown in CWGC records. The inference would be that they survived and were almost certainly repatriated in the hospital ship *Atlantis*, arriving back in the UK in early June 1940 after a 'narrow squeak'. (See later events.)

were under strict orders to lie flat on the deck during raids. The casualties which had occurred related to ratings who had to work in exposed places or in positions where they were insufficiently protected by armour plating. The shrapnel from the bombs which were dropped passed right through ordinary ships' plates, and some of the plates looked 'just like a sieve afterwards'. The pieces of shrapnel varied enormously in size, but all were very jagged. One of the worst features was the suddenness with which the attacks occurred, often without any warning, as was almost bound to occur in narrow, mountainous fjords. The absence of darkness in northern Norway in the summer months meant there was no time of night or day when an attack might not happen. All this put a severe strain on the nervous system, though 'the ship's company were standing up to it remarkably well and were quite cheerful afterwards'.

Let's return to the 25ᵗʰ May. It had been fortunate that 'Vindictive' had been present to add her close-range HA fire to the defences for most of that day, when 'Southampton' suffered her largest batch of casualties. 'Vindictive' had left late on the 25ᵗʰ, though the destroyers 'Walker' and 'Delight' arrived next morning and could add their light weapons. Further aerial attacks soon developed, four bombs falling astern of 'Southampton' at 1430. At 1925, as indicated above, Captain JEANS left the ship for treatment in the hospital ashore, Commander C.B. TINLEY assuming command in his absence. At 2125 there was yet another 'Alarm to Arms', but to everyone's relief this time six 'Hurricane' fighters swept protectively over the shipping. They were very welcome, for an ammunition lighter came alongside very soon afterwards, bringing much-needed 4-inch shells for 'Southampton'. The destroyer 'Eskimo' left at this time, under tow. Although not mentioned in the log, the cruiser 'Curlew' was sunk this day, by German bombers, off Skaanland. ['Effingham' had been wrecked, and had therefore been destroyed by other ships of the RN on the 21ˢᵗ May.]

On 27ᵗʰ May, patrolling off Harstad and in Vaagsfiord, 'Southampton' stopped to pick up a message from a boat. It is probable that this message was a plea from the survivors of the cruiser 'Curlew'. These men were now sheltering ashore in harsh conditions. 'Southampton' closed Harstad and transferred supplies to these men, before continuing her patrol. By 2100 she was proceeding to Narvik, joining up with the cruisers 'Cairo' and 'Coventry', with their escorting destroyers, and carrying out a bombardment of the small towns of Adjansenes and Fagnenes in support of an attack overland on Narvik conducted by the French Legionnaires. At 0130, 'Southampton' opened fire on German machine-gun posts as advised by the destroyer 'Firedrake', ceasing fire on instructions from shore, then opening fire at 0302 on other targets as advised.

Eye witnesses talk of 'Southampton', in company with the cruisers 'Cairo' and 'Coventry', bombarding Narvik in support of a night-attack by French Legionnaires. Narvik was taken on 27ᵗʰ May after heavy fighting. Thomas RUCK-KEENE says that Southampton had poured 'a barrage of 600 six-inch HE shells into the town, only ceasing fire when all targets were invisible behind smoke columns which rose hundreds of feet into the air'. [Intense as this bombardment was, it is a tribute to its accuracy that the number of civilian casualties from it happily remained very low. It should also be noted that a large proportion of the civilian population of Narvik, by now well experienced in being bombarded by warships, had probably melted away into the neighbouring mountains before the firing on the port began.]

Meantime, further aerial attacks were developing on the British ships, and 'Cairo', now flying the flag of Admiral of the Fleet Lord CORK AND ORRERY, and with the Allied Army Commanders, General AUCHINLECK (who had replaced General MACKESEY) and General BETHOUART (now in charge of all the French and Polish troops) also aboard, suffered some casualties from near-misses. For her part, 'Southampton' was near-missed astern at 0402, and then close on her port side at 0512. Her HA guns continued in action but she had taken two more casualties, one being serious, and damage in her 'Contamination' store. The latter problem necessitated a reduction in speed when she was ordered to return to Harstad at 0630, passing through Tielsundet and Vaagsfiord to heave-to off Harstad. Whilst stopped there she transferred her two casualties to the shore hospital.[408] She then proceeded to Telsundet Fiord communicating with 'Coventry', and returning to Narvik on patrol duties on the 29th.

This proved to be hazardous in the extreme, for, although 'Hurricanes' and Gloster 'Gladiators' were sighted at 0827, enemy aircraft attacked 'Southampton' at 1115, 1550 and 1554, the bombs near-missing and causing damage in the main central store. This was quickly tackled by the damage control parties. Though not mentioned in her log, various sources say that a further bombardment was carried out by 'Southampton' at this time, in support of a Polish force, which had a tough task on its hands, attacking Narvik across the Ankenes Peninsular. [One wonders if this relates to the attack already mentioned as taking place on the 26th/27th.] Be that as it may, so heavy were the attacks by German aircraft that Southampton was forced to break off her supporting salvoes of 6-inch gunfire for a while, to get under way in a hurry and make evasive manoeuvres, whilst she concentrated on the use of her secondary weapons in the anti-aircraft role against a tremendously fierce attack from out of a glaring sun. [It is worthy of mention at this point that Thomas RUCK-KEENE says that the 'German aircraft, which were operating from Trondheim, 200 miles away, gave the ship no peace for the whole of the five weeks she was in Norwegian waters'. Petty Officer HOBLEY who was the Trainer in the starboard HA Director tower at the time, says that the ship had so many holes in her side that she 'could hardly move, let alone make turns to dodge bombs'.][409] Meantime, the destroyer 'Beagle' had come alongside to transfer a field gun's company, with 'Beagle' and 'Firedrake' later acting as an anti-submarine screen.

On 1st June, 'Southampton' oiled, and, next day, patrolled off Harstad, five enemy aircraft bombing the ships and seeming to concentrate on the destroyer 'Echo'. The destroyers 'Ardent', 'Acasta', 'Delight' and 'Havelock' arrived on the 3rd June, followed by 'Campbell' with a small convoy'. 'Havelock' and 'Walker' sailed just before midnight. At 1715 Captain JEANS had left the ship for further attention to his leg wound. It seems probable that Commander C.B. TINLEY again took over for some of the ensuing period, though Captain JEANS did struggle back on duty as the month of June continued.

---

[408] Strangely, her Surgeon's Journal makes no mention of these men. Perhaps this was a sign of the severe stresses the whole ship's company were labouring under. One assumes these men were also evacuated to England on the hospital ship Atlantis, making a party of seven 'Southamptons' in all.

[409] Later CPO HOBLEY. He left Southampton in 1940, to attend a Gunnery Course, and to go on from there to serve in various ships. Post-war, he produced a very interesting and 'salty' typescript of his wartime experiences.

Narvik had been taken on 27th May after heavy fighting.[410] *Certainly, the capture of Narvik had satisfied Allied military honour, but it was to prove to be little more than a token and slightly morale-boosting victory, for the Allied Higher Command now decided that the campaign in Norway could no longer be sustained.* [This hard decision was taken because the German Army in France and the Low Countries had poured irresistibly through a huge breach they had made in the Allied Line near Sedan. Their *blitzkrieg* tactics had proved to be devastating, relentless and unstoppable. Under heavy and sustained German bombing, the British Expeditionary Force in France had started to be evacuated through Dunkirk on 27th May, and the last men had got away on 4th June even as the German ground forces closed in. Several Allied destroyers had been lost and others badly damaged. The French Government was about to capitulate. Italy was expected to enter the war at any moment. Regrettably, Norway must now be abandoned to her fate.] *The evacuation would begin on 7th June, troopships being sent out from the UK. for that purpose.*

There were further arrivals and sailings amongst the destroyers at Harstad on the 5th June. Evidently in preparation for the evacuation, the oiler 'Oleander', which had been damaged and beached on the 26th May was now scuttled.[411] *A damaged lighter was also sunk. On the 6th June the cruiser 'Coventry' arrived, and five 'Walrus' aircraft from the cruisers present took off on anti-submarine patrol. At 2200 'Southampton' embarked eight cars and 20 motorbikes from shore. At 0345 on the 7th 'Southampton' closed up her HA crews and went to Action Stations at 0352, having heard that Narvik, which had been heavily bombed and virtually burnt to ashes on the 2nd June, was again being bombed. At 0800 'Southampton' hoisted the flag of Lord CORK AND ORRERY (F.O. Narvik), and struck the flag of Rear Admiral CLARKE of the 18th CS. Four hours later the faithful troopships 'Ulster Prince' and the 'Ulster Monarch' arrived, and 'Southampton's two aircraft returned, evidently having been part of the escort for the empty troopships during the final leg of their journey out from the UK. Meantime, 'Southampton' was embarking stores from the shore. Flag Officer Narvik and his staff came aboard at 1740.*

At 0420 the destroyer 'Vanoc' came alongside 'Southampton' briefly, apparently to transfer the last of the demolition and other parties leaving Harstad. The port was now in ruins, partly from bombing and partly from Allied demolitions intended to deny its use by the enemy for some time ahead. Though not shown in 'Southampton's log, it is said that she also took aboard a party which put out from the jetty by motor-boat. Included amongst them was Captain L.E.H MAUND, the Naval Chief of Staff [who was fated to later command the famous aircraft-carrier 'Ark Royal' from 19th April 1941 until she was torpedoed and lost on 14th November 1941.] Probably the very last of all to leave Harstad was Patrick DALZEL-JOB, who had apparently been half-hoping that the last Allied ship would have left by the time that he got back from his mission, so that he could

---

[410] The Germans issued special commemorative plaques boldly inscribed 'NARVIK' to their fighting forces which were worn with pride by their veterans. They had taken many casualties in the campaign.

[411] One is filled with admiration for the officers and men who formed the ship's companies of the almost defenceless oilers and other supply vessels, some carrying ammunition and other explosives, amidst the depredations of the *Luftwaffe*.

carry on the fight alongside the Norwegians. As matters stood, he was exhausted by his huge exertions and slept solidly for a great many hours once he was aboard.[412]

At 0445 'Southampton' proceeded from Harstad, switching on her DG gear as she entered Vaagsfiord, reaching Topsundet Fiord at 0520, and stopping at 0631 whilst destroyers were disembarking troops to the transports. The HA armament was closed up, the crews restraining their taut nerves and witholding their fire as six 'Skuas' swept over at 0757, but going into action at 0930 as the anticipated German response began, some twenty bombing attacks being made on the assembled ships. At 1015 there was a lull, during which the destroyer 'Campbell' came alongside and 8 officers and 80 troops of the French Foreign Legion came aboard.

By 1425 'Southampton' was in station on the assembled convoy which consisted of the troopships 'Arandora Star', 'Duchess of York', 'Oronsay', 'Ormonde', 'Royal Ulsterman', 'Ulster Prince' and 'Ulster Monarch'. The escorting ships were 'Southampton' (9,100 tons, 6" guns), the smaller cruiser 'Coventry' (4,190 tons, 6" guns), and the destroyers 'Beagle', 'Delight', 'Fame', 'Firedrake' and 'Havelock' (ranging from 1,300 to 1,400 tons, 4.7" guns). The weather had been clear for days, but, providentially, a heavy snow-cloud appeared quite low in the sky above Harstad as the

---

[412] The late Patrick DALZEL-JOB (alias 'JOB') was an inspirational, fearless and very self-reliant young man. His book, "From Arctic Snow to Dust of Normandy" makes fine reading. The author is indebted to Patrick's son, Major I E DALZEL JOB, and to 'Pen and Sword Books', for permission to use relevant parts taken from the text of that book. The author feels that that he has a 'link' with Patrick, because, during the mid-1950s the author was privileged to play Rugby Football with a wonderful character named Vladmir GRENFELL, and kept in touch with Vladmir until his death forty-five years later. During 1944/5, Vladmir had been in a small unit commanded by Patrick DALZEL-JOB. This unit was one of Ian FLEMING's so-called '30 AU' teams. They were independent and highly mobile, often operating 'discreetly' by means of by-roads, often well *in front* of the Allied Lines as they advanced across France and Germany. Vladmir, justly described by 'JOB' as a 'very unusual bespectacled young RNVR sub-lieutenant of studious appearance', had a Russian mother and an Irish father. 'JOB' called him 'Bob', but, certainly in his later years, he was more usually called 'Vlad'. He spoke a most perfect 'public school' English and, at one time, he had played Rugby Football for Bath at a high level. One reason that 'Vlad' was with JOB's team was that he had the ability to speak fluent German.

In the immediate aftermath of the German capitulation in May 1945, the irrepressible General HORROCKS personally led his 51st Division into Bremen. JOB's team followed immediately behind the General's jeep, and promptly swung off into the dock area as the General led the main column onward to the city centre. There were many 'targets' for JOB's very limited team to deal with, pending the arrival of more powerful 'regulation' forces. JOB therefore gave 'Vlad' the job of securing the 'gold mine' of secret signal documents in a fully commissioned German 'Narvik Class' destroyer which had been on the point of leaving the harbour. JOB could only give 'Vlad' (alias Sub-Lieutenant GRENFELL) a team of three ratings to undertake the highly dangerous task of checking right through the destroyer, to ensure there were no scuttling charges placed, to make the guns safe and to disarm the ship's company, whose morale varied from sullen near-suicidal hysteria to vicious anger and a desire to 'fight to the death'. It was largely though the ability of 'Vlad' and his determined but pleasant manner, that the delicate and fraught situation remained under control. JOB later gave 'Vlad' high tribute for his calm handling throughout. It should be added that the German Captain of the ship also acted very honourably in an extremely difficult situation.

Although the situation barely draws comparison, the author, too, had the most lively respect and admiration for 'Vlad'. As 'pack-leader' and 'hooker', right in the heart of the action, 'Vlad' would lead us fearlessly into the toughest Rugby situations, swearing terrible oaths in the most perfect and incongruous of English accents. He later became one of the most loved, progressive and urbane Chairmen that the Kodak Rugby Club ever had the privilege to elect. Typically, when quizzed by the Author of this book, Vlad was very modest about JOB's praise of his 1945 exploits. Overall, the situation is somehow a 'small world' link back to some of the finest of men, to the cruiser *Southampton* and thus to the author's late father.

convoy left, so that German aircraft which could be plainly heard overhead were thwarted from sighting and bombing the British ships.[413] [A convoy consisting of the British cargo ships, 'Acrity', 'Blackheath', 'Conch', 'Coxwold', 'Cromarty Firth', 'Harmattan', 'Oligarch' and ' Theseus', and the French cargo ships 'Enseigne Maurice Préchac', 'Paul Emile Javary' and 'Vulcain', under an escort of destroyers and armed trawlers had left the previous day, and made a safe crossing. Such materièl as the ships had been unable to embark had been burnt or sunk, with surplus food being distributed to the Norwegian inhabitants who were remaining behind.]

Two French officers, *les chefs* FAURE and COCHE, of the *Chasseurs Alpins*, who had come aboard HMS *Southampton* for the return voyage to the U.K. The troopships of the convoy are assembling in the near distance. Providentially, a snow-cloud is forming overhead, shielding the ships from being shadowed and bombed by the *Luftwaffe*.

On 9th June, near midday and when the convoy was at 69° 37' N, 05° 45' E, a body was sighted in the water and 'Southampton' altered course to investigate, her log stating that she quickly found three more bodies and sped back to rejoin the convoy in her charge. Eye witness reports say that, on reaching the area, the body of a Royal Marine officer wearing a green life-jacket was observed in the water, passing down the ship's side, and the look-outs could see other bodies in the water further off. Clearly, there had been a recent naval battle in the vicinity. This was worrying, especially as no report of an engagement had been received, thus implying that one or more of our warships had been suddenly overwhelmed before being able to get off a sighting report.

---

[413] This could sometimes be a definite disadvantage, for the ships' mastheads could sometimes project above low-lying banks of cloud, making them *visible* to aircraft, whilst the aircraft themselves remained *invisible* to the lookouts on the ships below. Everything depended on the actual thickness and altitude of the clouds at the particular time.

That enemy force, which was likely to be a powerful one, might still be in the vicinity. Great unease prevailed.

An hour after Southampton had rejoined the convoy 'Firedrake', evidently having had an Asdic contact, dropped a depth-charge 12 cables astern. At 1648 'Southampton's lookouts sighted the aircraft-carrier 'Ark Royal', and, at 2215 the battleship 'Valiant'. At 2300, one enemy aircraft was sighted and 'Ark Royal' and 'Coventry' both opened fire on it.

Throughout this time, Southampton had been carrying the important personages of the Admiral of the Fleet, Lord CORK AND ORRERY (F.O. Narvik), plus the military commanders General AUCHINLECK and the French General BETHOUART. Now, aboard 'Southampton', at 2400 the Flag of Admiral of the Fleet F.O. Narvik was struck and the Flag of R.A 18 (Rear Admiral CLARKE) broken. [It had been on the direct instructions of the new British Prime Minister, Winston CHURCHILL, that General AUCHINLECK had relieved General MACKESEY. However, it had all been too late to restore a situation which was, in any case, being overridden by the shattering events in other theatres of war. For his part, General BETHOUART had shown exceptional leadership, commonsense, honour and resolve amidst an Allied politico/military climate where the higher authorities had shown much dithering and irresolution. It seems to have been a great tragedy that General BETHOUART (by then a member of the Vichy French Forces in North Africa but with strong sympathies for the Allies), was later to be badly used by the British and the Americans at the time of the landings in North Africa in late 1942. (Operation 'Torch'). Virtually betrayed, he was lucky to not to have been shot by his own countrymen for treason at that very difficult period of negotiations.][414]

At 0100 on the 10ᵗʰ June, a Dornier flying boat was sighted shadowing the convoy, and was driven off by three 'Skuas' launched from 'Ark Royal'. The cruisers 'Newcastle' and 'Sussex' were sighted and joined the convoy for a while, the battlecruiser 'Repulse' also taking station. Their presence was very welcome, not only against possible threats by German surface forces, but also because heavy air raids were being mounted by the Germans in the west of the North Sea. Indeed, the convoy was being routed around the North of Scotland to avoid them. At 2255 'Firedrake' reported another Asdic contact, but lost it as she began her attack.

By now the convoy was heading round the north of the Faroe Islands before making its southing. At 0720 on the 11ᵗʰ a 'Sunderland' flying Boat was sighted, providing anti-submarine escort, and at 1004 'Repulse' began a practice shoot at a smokescreen, presumably to 'get her eye in' in case any major German units were lying in wait. The weather, which had been calm and clear, with good visibility, now began to break up, the wind swiftly rising to a Force 7 south-westerly, with a moderate sea running. At 1920 'Southampton' lost her port paravane, being forced to slow to 8 knots for 10 minutes to make repairs before being able to re-stream her paravanes. At 2100 she left the convoy and headed down the west coast of Scotland for the Clyde, where she had been launched four event-packed years earlier. She was just about 'operational' but badly in need of repairs from the many shrapnel wounds she had suffered, some below

---

[414] The author was pleased to learn that General BETHOUART had been carried in the cruiser HMS *Bellona* as a guest of the Royal Navy to attend a ceremony held under Admiral Wm WHITWORTH to honour those who had fallen at the Battle of Narvik. This commemoration took place at Narvik on 28ᵗʰ May 1946.

the waterline and only temporarily plugged. Her company would have been heavily stressed and hugely tired by now.

On 12th June the comforting sight of a 'Lerwick' flying boat was seen on the port bow, and at 1330 'Southampton' switched off her DG and came to anchor. Less than an hour later F.O. Clyde came aboard as she began disembarking her troops. Her two 'Walrus' aircraft P567 and L2294 (Lts WOOD and MANNING) were flown off for overhaul on the mainland, Admiral of the Fleet the Lord of CORK AND ORRERY and his staff left the ship and, at 1930, the French troops began to disembark into a transport which had secured port side. Their future was now very much in question, for their country was about to capitulate to Nazi Germany. Most of them were concerned for the safety of their families if they fought on, and the majority probably believed that the British, now standing virtually alone against Germany, would also soon be seeking some sort of honourable surrender terms. Hence, most Frenchmen would choose to return to their native France.

At 2305 the cruiser 'Coventry' and the destroyers 'Echo', Firedrake', 'Delight', 'Fame', Beagle' and 'Havelock' arrived with the troop transports. 'Southampton' and her consorts had run 1,139 miles from Harstad. They had delivered home safely those troops who had survived the land-fighting in Norway.

[To a considerable extent, the safe arrival of the 25,000 troops and their commanders, can be attributed to the attention of the Germans having been distracted by other actions taking place in the North Sea. Sadly, one of these other actions had resulted in the loss of the aircraft-carrier *Glorious* and her escorting destroyers *Acasta* (H09) and *Ardent* (H41) to gunfire from the *Scharnhorst* (11" guns). There was attendant heavy loss of life. In fact, only one man had been saved from the *Acasta*. She had died hard, attacking through a smoke-screen she had cleverly laid and managing to hit *Scharnhorst* with a torpedo, before finally succumbing under a hail of shot and shell. The torpedo had hit near *Scharnhorst's* after-turret and caused significant damage below her waterline, killing two German officers and 46 men.

It may be that *Acasta* had thus saved the troop convoy, for the damaged *Scharnhorst*, accompanied by *Gneisenau, Admiral Hipper* and their escort, had headed away for temporary repairs at the port of Trondheim. Had *Scharnhorst* not been damaged by *Acasta*, the German warships might have continued north-east, and they might well then have come across the large convoy being escorted by *Southampton* and her consorts, which had left Narvik 12 hours after *Glorious* and her escorting destroyers. It was said that an unidentified cruiser and its escorting destroyers (possibly *Southampton* but much more probably *Devonshire*, which was carrying the King of Norway and the leading members of his Government) actually sailed westbound, close by the position where *Glorious* and the two destroyers had gone down - near enough to be seen by the survivors in the water, who were already in the most desperate straits through exposure, but seemingly not near enough for the lookouts of the ships to spot the many men then surviving in the water. It was only on the 11th, two days later, that the little Norwegian ship *Borgund* came across what was by then left of those survivors, picking up just 46 men from the thousand or more who had gone into the water.

The ships sunk had included the Norwegian tanker *Oil Pioneer* (5,660 tons), which was in ballast and was being escorted from Tromso in North Norway across the

North Sea by the trawler *Juniper*. This action had taken place early on the 8th June, when, being uncertain of the identity of two warships which were closing them from dead ahead at 67° 20' N, 04° 09' E, a little way inside the Arctic Circle, *Juniper* (530 tons, 11 knots, one 12 pdr gun, complement of 35 men) had semaphored to the leading ship in plain Morse, "What ship?". It was somehow galling to learn that, *Gneisenau*, closing fast, had replied "HMS *Southampton*" as a deceptive ruse, just minutes before *Admiral Hipper*, (8" guns) which was the ship in company with *Gneisenau* (11" guns), had opened overwhelming fire, quickly sending little *Juniper* to the bottom. Twenty-nine of *Juniper's* company were picked up by the Germans. *Gneisenau* had then turned her secondary armament on to the *Oil Pioneer* (after the ship's company had humanely been ordered to abandon her), promptly turning the tanker into a blazing wreck, which was finished off by a torpedo fired by one of the escorting German destroyers.

To the credit of the commanding officers of *Gneisenau* and *Scharnhorst*, although they sank the 19,500 ton troopship *Orama* (which was fortunately empty of Allied troops), they did not fire on the *Atlantis*, a hospital ship. (*Atlantis* had likewise obeyed the rules of war and had not attempted to forewarn by radio other Allied shipping of the presence of the German warships.) *Southampton's* log shows that *Atlantis* had sailed from Harstad on 4th June, and it is almost certain that she would have been evacuating those of *Southampton's* wounded men who had been landed at the shore hospital there prior to that date, evidently a party of at least seven men.]

On 13th June a harbour pilot came aboard and 'Southampton' proceeded upriver, a tug securing forward and taking them on the final leg into the K.G. V Dock. White watch were then given four days leave. Red Watch would follow White on 'long leave', then Blue would go. According to Thomas RUCK-KEENE, 'Southampton' was put alongside in Glasgow to repair the 200 holes in her side caused by German bombing. (Seemingly, the worn-out barrels of her 4-inch guns were again replaced at this time.) Tom goes on to say that: "Four days leave was given to both watches - and how we needed it after weeks of standing-to as the first crash of bombs came - for RDF ships were scarce then." [N.B. Tom's last remark confirms that 'Southampton' had no RDF.]

Midshipmen ELGAR and COCKBURN of the Australian Navy Volunteer Reserve joined ship at this time, reflecting the involvement of their Dominion in the War, and eleven ratings were discharged to the Royal Naval Hospital ashore for treatment of one kind and another. A CPO would follow them to Hospital three days later.⁴¹⁵ Thirty other ratings were discharged to the RN Barracks at Chatham.

An armed guard consisting of a PO and nine ratings under Lt JACKSON were sent to the 'Monarch of Bermuda' on the 14th June, to deal with trouble which had broken out aboard.

[British tactical and strategic planning now assumed further dimensions, as Italy had entered the war on 10th June and France signed surrender terms with Germany on

---

⁴¹⁵ The Surgeon's Journal appears to make no mention of these men, though it does show that one Ordinary Seaman RNVR was discharged to the Hospital Ship *Vasma* after being found 'very nervous' during a bombing attack on the ship on 6th July. This poor man had evidently reached 'the end of his particular tether'. Clearly, for the sake of the morale of the other members of the ship's company, it was best that the few men showing extremes of fear and instability should be removed from the ship as soon as practicable. The accidents reported below may also have been tokens of the extreme stresses under which the company had been working, now only half-relieved and making for a strange emotional state.

25th June. The British and their Empire now stood virtually alone, supported only by such relatively few men from the conquered countries as had been able to escape to England and had decided to throw in their lot with her. It was indeed fortunate that the arsenals of the U.S.A were prepared to sell armaments to Great Britain under the so-called 'Lend-Lease Scheme'. One subject of great immediate concern was the matter as to whether or not the French Navy would sail its ships away from Metropolitan France and join with the British Navy in continuing the struggle, or whether they would allow themselves to be taken over by Nazi Germany.]

On 18th June Captain B.C.B. BROOKE RN joined the ship and assumed command, replacing Captain JEANS who, as we have seen, was carrying a leg wound after the operations in Norway. Only ever used 'sotto voce' and 'behind his back', Captain BROOKE would later acquire the nickname "Beer, Charlie, Beer" after the (then) Morse code names for those initial letters. [The 'Baker, Charlie, Baker' of today would have had less 'appeal'.]

'Southampton' completed oiling, provisioning and cleaning ship, hoisted in her aircraft, and proceeded to sea on the 22nd, experiencing a minor fire in the fo'c'sle when her DG was switched on, which was quickly extinguished and the fault rectified, only to have a calcium fire break out in the port hangar one hour later, perhaps from a damaged flare. However, by 1425 on the 23rd 'Southampton' had come to anchor at Scapa Flow. Next day she emerged from harbour for a practice shoot in the Flow, after BC 1 had called on CS 18. She emerged again on the 27th and again on the 29th for further shoots with her 6-inch guns, then with her 4-inch guns. Petty Officer THOMSON was injured during the practice shoot with the 6-inch guns on the 27th, by being caught a blow by the rammer, in his left side, and ending up in the Sick Bay. The ship then practised 'slick' landings with her aircraft, the second aircraft making a heavy landing and having to be towed back alongside. On the 30th Captain BROOKE addressed the Ship's Company on the Quarter Deck, and RA Destroyers called on RA 18

During the first five days of July 'Southampton' continued her 'working up' exercises in this vein, interrupted by Air Raids Warning Red, though no bombs were dropped. As a sort of 'confirmation' that the 4-inch guns had fired during this period, Boy Seaman KEENAN complained to the surgeon of deafness whilst he was employed on the 'A.A Guns'. It was recommended that some form of ear-protectors should be employed as a safeguard.

On the 6th July the ship proceeded from Scapa to Rosyth, in company with the Cardiff Class cruiser 'Coventry' and several destroyers, to make rendezvous with the submarine 'Shark', which had been damaged and was unable to dive. 'Southampton' had to go to Action Stations at 1042 and open fire on an enemy aircraft at 1120, three others being out of range. At 1230 she again opened fire, five bombs falling astern. At 1245 the destroyer 'Fume' in company was hit aft, and 'Maori' was near-missed astern by a salvo of bombs. At 1443, another wave of aircraft appeared, seven bombs falling astern of 'Fume' and a salvo near-missing almost alongside 'Fortune'. A 'Hudson' aircraft appeared soon afterwards, though one enemy aircraft still remained, shadowing the ships at a respectful distance - until three 'Hurricane' fighters showed up. Nor were aircraft the only threat, for 'Cossack' (of 'Altmark' fame), which had joined with 'Fortune', obtained a submarine contact (and dropped depth-charges on it).

Task fulfilled, 'Southampton' arrived at Rosyth at 0128 on the 7th July after this run of 450 miles. She quickly oiled and embarked ammunition, and proceeded back to Scapa at 2030, exercising her HA armament in a shoot at a towed target whilst on passage. She oiled again after a run of 727 miles, painted ship and put her torpedo crews to practice. Gas mask inspections, DG trials, and further practice shoots with her 6-inch guns ensued in the following days, with RA 18 paying a visit to 'Glasgow' on the 14th and to 'Rodney' on the 15th, 'Southampton' having had yet another practice shoot that morning.

These practice shoots under a new Captain were certainly advisable, to keep everybody on 'top line', for, come the 16th July, the squadron of which 'Southampton' was a key part came under orders to intercept German warships which were making a sortie into the North Sea. She attempted to proceed from Scapa at 0830, 'Glasgow', 'Sussex' and 'Shropshire' being in company. However, thick fog descended, and it was not until 1015 that the squadron was able to get to sea, the eight destroyers of Flotillas D3 and D4 scouting ahead.

At noon they were at 58° 26' N, 02° 40' W, off Rattray Head, heading south-east. At 1530 'Cossack' opened fire on a shadowing Dornier which had ventured too close for comfort. That aircraft would already have radioed back to its base a sighting message, and this may have been the cause of the German ships putting back to their base early that afternoon. News of their heading back east soon came to the ears of the Admiralty, who terminated the operation. At 1540 the 2nd CS and 8th D.F parted company with 'Southampton' and her consorts, the latter squadron receiving orders at 1557 to return to Scapa.

As they were doing so, zig-zagging at 20 knots, 'Shropshire' opened fire on another shadowing aircraft at 1605, and 'Southampton' changed from 2nd to 1st degree readiness for her HA armament, which promptly went into action as bombs were dropped astern. Her Action HA was kept closed up as she rounded Rattray Head, learning that an Air Raid Red Warning was in operation at Scapa Flow. Patches of thick fog persisted in the darkness, and 'Imogen' and 'Glasgow' were reported in collision at 0045 the next morning. Visibility was virtually nil as 'Southampton' felt her way to her berth at Rosyth at 1125.

[It was subsequently learned that, whilst negotiating the Pentland Firth in the thick fog which had prevailed, *Glasgow* (9,100 tons),whilst zig-zagging at twenty knots, had unfortunately collided with the destroyer *Imogen* (1,370 tons). *Imogen*, severely struck, had soon foundered. *Glasgow* was slightly damaged, though she would be quickly repaired.]

On the 18th, whilst 'Southampton' was exercising her aircraft, the one piloted by Lt WOODS capsized on its second take-off of the day, and sank. Lt WOODS, S/Lt HERRING and three F.A.A ratings were all saved, due to prompt action by a drifter. However, Lt WOODS and A/Mech JOHNSON had come off rather the worse for wear, Lt WOODS being unconscious 'though easily roused'. Both men were transferred to the hospital ship 'Vasma' for observation.

[Although, since mid-October 1939, the ships of the Home Fleet had been withdrawn from the Firth of Forth and Rosyth to the West Coast of Scotland and to Scapa Flow, to keep them out of range of the German bombers, it was now decided to take the considerable risk of sending *Southampton, Birmingham* and *Manchester*, with three escorting destroyers, south to the Humber or even to the Thames as a counter to possible German invasion of the south-east coast.]

Thus it was that, on 19ᵗʰ July, 'Southampton' proceeded to Sheerness, opening fire on one enemy aircraft at 2015, which veered away, just before three 'Spitfires' came on the scene. At 0058 she passed a northbound convoy which had 'Sheffield' and destroyers as escort, and she had the comforting presence of 'Hudson' and 'Blenheim' aircraft overhead at 0500. Despite their presence, however, at 0630 an enemy aircraft boldly attacked, and 'Southampton' quickly opened fire on it, the bombs falling astern. She fired at another attacking aircraft at 1302. At 1740 'Southampton' anchored at Sheerness, but maintained an HA watch closed up all the time she was there, having the ship secured for sea and steam for full speed at ½ hour notice. She also had her Asdic Cabinet crew closed up.

At that time the ship had green and brown camouflage paint (See earlier photograph taken in Topsundet Fiord.) On 22ⁿᵈ July this was now painted out and replaced by the conventional grey – called 'Crabfat' by her troops. That day CS 18 paid a call on Captain BROOKE before returning to 'Birmingham', and the ship embarked ammunition. Next day, at dawn, there was an Air Raid Warning Red, as the ship proceeded upriver to Chatham, keeping her HA and close range weapons closed up and the ship at short notice for steam. She later cleaned her guns, took in stores, oiled, and embarked petrol and water. Surgeon-Commander MACKINTYRE left the ship, Surgeon Lieutenant W.C. SLOANE RNVR having relieved him. In his final report, covering the period 1ˢᵗ-21ˢᵗ July 1940, Surgeon Commander McINTYRE, whose account has added invaluable 'colour' to this book, said that on one occasion in the Norway Campaign the ship had been bombed continuously by waves of aircraft over a period of ten hours, putting a severe nervous strain on the personnel. Several other bombing attacks had occurred. There had been no men killed or wounded, but two ratings had requested treatment for their 'nerves', one of whom he had discharged to the hospital ashore. No ports had been visited and only one man had fallen ill.

On the night of 27ᵗʰ July a barrage balloon was observed to fall in flames, perhaps shot down by a German aircraft. Next morning the damaged destroyer 'Brilliant' was towed in, and 'Southampton' proceeded down river, anchoring at B Berth. She closed up her 4-inch Director Test party, held an anti-gas exercise and catapulted one of her aircraft, No.2294, piloted by Rating Pilot HARRIS with Lt MANNING as Observer. 'Southampton' completed with oil on the 31ˢᵗ.

[In the meantime the RAF was bombing, seemingly with some effect, the invasion ships, tugs and barges that the Germans were busily assembling at the northern French ports. Some daring but successful bombardments were also carried out by ships of the Royal Navy. The Luftwaffe, as we have seen, was very active around the coasts of Great Britain, trying to sink our merchant ships and cripple our warships. As we have also seen, German U-Boats were active. A cataclysmic struggle to achieve dominance of the skies was beginning between the German *Luftwaffe* and the Royal Air Force. Invasion by both airborne and seaborne assault was expected at any time. The situation was extremely tense.]

As the then Midshipman RUCK-KEENE later said: "Always at short notice and with little leave, it was a tiresome business which dragged on into August, with nothing to do but wait and wait." Yet, as we shall see, there were certain compensations, such as the provision of fresh fruit and vegetables which had been lacking for some time and had led to minor physical complaints such as boils and, the surgeon thought, to the many common colds amongst the company.

On 1ˢᵗ August, the hands continued to embark stores and clean ship, and, as the log says, *"Mr DAVIS Commissioned Gunner, rejoined ship from Sick Leave."* Alf was back after an absence of 2½ months. He evidently had convalescent home leave immediately prior to rejoining and we'll have a look at that next, before resuming our narrative of his service life.

Before we do so, it may be useful to recapitulate, in broad brush terms, what Alf had missed due to his enforced absence on sick leave.

- A great many bombing attacks, which had left the ship with some 200 holes in her side and a number of casualties, one fatal. These attacks had caused considerable nervous strain, to the extent that a few men had broken down completely. (The damage to the ship had only recently been repaired.)
- Captain JEANS had been wounded and he had now been replaced.
- Three shore-bombardments had been carried out, one under such intensive aerial bombing that it had been necessary to break off from the bombardment for a while to seek a less exposed position.
- About a dozen depth-charge actions had been necessary to protect the ship from possible submarine attack.
- The 'homeward-run' of 'their' troop-convoy from Norway to the UK had been carried out successfully, but at great risk of attack by powerful German units. *Southampton* had passed through floating bodies and wreckage which betokened the fact that a 'sister-convoy' had been utterly destroyed, hugely adding to the tension on board.

One suspects that Alf would have been very concerned to have missed out on playing his full part in defending the ship from all these manifold hazards, and above all from the many aerial attacks. Due to his age and enormous experience and to the respect he commanded generally, he had long begun to see himself as something of a 'father-figure' in the ship, and this enforced absence could have played on his mind to a very significant degree.

Private Life

In the Spring of 1940, probably when he was given convalescent home leave towards the end of his 2½ months of 'sick leave' in the hospital ashore, Alf had bought two fine books for his elder son, which he dedicated on the fly leaf as, *"To Dear Neville, From Daddy, Easter 1940"*. These books were Volumes II and III of "Her Majesty's Navy", of which the full set of three volumes describes the history of the Royal Navy in some detail, from the Saxon ships of King Alfred's time, right through until the 1890s.[416] This was a very thoughtful and loving gift. It also represented something of a contradiction in terms, for Alf had once said that he did not want Neville to go into the Navy (perhaps thinking that the boy would not be suited to the life), yet here, potentially, was strong motivation for the boy to do just that.

When Alf did manage to get home, two months after his previous leave, he would have found that a 'sea change' had transpired within the land, the transformation being most notable in the south-east of the country. The 'Fall of France' and the evacuation of Dunkirk, with the British Expeditionary Force having to leave nearly all its tanks, transport and ordnance behind, had rocked the nation to its core. The need for the evacuation of the Allied troops from Norway was regarded as just another proof of how amateurish, ill-equipped and poorly-organised we were. The only comfort people drew was that the Royal Navy had handled both of the evacuations very well, although at a terrible cost in ships and men. It was clear that the anti-aircraft defences of our ships were woefully inadequate against the power of the *Luftwaffe*. Cover by our fighter-aircraft had been regarded as 'generally absent and usually ineffective'.

Invasion of the south-east of England by the Germans was expected imminently. There had been hope that the French Air Force and Navy would come over to our side, and that both our nations would be able to utilise French bases outside Metropolitan France, such as in the French colonies in Africa. However, this was not to be.[417] In certain quarters of England panic was not far away. Some eminent people were talking of surrender on the best terms which could be obtained. Some wealthy people had been actively seeking to leave the country for the U.S.A. (The general reaction of 'ordinary' people to this was to say: *"Goodbye and good riddance' - and we don't ever want you back!"*)

All around the country, families had huddled around their wireless sets and listened, half fearfully, half with a defiant pride, as the new leader, Winston

---

[416] These books by Lt Charles Rathbone LOWE F.R.G.S. and printed by J.S. Virtue of London have achieved almost heirloom status within the family. They not only give the author warm thoughts of his father, but they have proved to be a most useful source of reference many times over.

[417] British people tended to forget that the parents, wives and children of French fighting men were nearly all located in Metropolitan France, and hence now either directly under the German yoke, or under the control of a puppet government which was hostile to the English. The counter-measures which might be taken against these innocent civilians if their menfolk were known to be fighting as 'Free French' (and that after their country had surrendered to the Germans, so that some would say they were 'renegades'), were a powerful disincentive for the French soldiers to carry on the struggle. Although the British would perceive the matter as grossly unfair, there were also voices in France which claimed that the British Army had fled precipitately through Dunkirk, leaving the French soldiers in the lurch.

CHURCHILL, had growled, "*We will fight on the beaches; we will fight on the landing grounds; we will fight in the fields and in the villages; we will fight in the hills and in the towns. We will never surrender!*". People felt, "Well, we're on our own now, but at least we no longer have dubious allies to worry about, fretting that they may let us down when it comes to the crunch. Now we all talk one language, surely we can rally behind this new leader, and, as one nation, we can rely on one another."

Yet, all along the east, south-east and south coasts of England, if perhaps not quite so much elsewhere, people knew only too well that, despite Winston CHURCHILL's fine words, there was actually precious little left with which to fight back. Weapons of all categories, including vitally-needed anti-tank guns, were few in number. As poor substitutes, 'Molotov Cocktails' made from petrol-filled glass bottles and each with a wick torn from an old bed-sheet, were being stock-piled for use against German tanks. 'Pill-boxes' hastily made in brick, and barbed-wire entanglements, were being erected frantically, almost everywhere along the coast and in its hinterland, and gaps had been blasted in seaside piers to hinder their use as landing stages. Good stocks of anti-personnel and anti-tank mines did exist, and had been hastily planted on those beaches which were regarded as possible disembarkation points for the German invasion forces, the mine-mapping often being far too vague by normal standards.[418]

What was not well-known was that significant numbers of the soldiers who had been brought back from the Dunkirk beaches were so demoralised and mentally affected by their experiences that they would never again be capable of front-line service.

Rumours, perhaps deliberately inspired, had been circulating concerning the '*smoke-blackened and scorched bodies of German soldiers*' being washed ashore on the south-east coast of Kent, where, it was alleged, we had secret equipment which could '*set the sea ablaze*'. If only it were so, and on a wide scale at that.[419] As a sign of the desperate state of things, a 'Local Defence Force' of old men and 17 year-olds had been urgently formed to man static defences in England and to sell their lives as dearly as possible against the crack German assault troops. This would hopefully buy time for the regular soldiers, held in reserve, to be brought into action in the most tactically effective and organised manner, rather than being sucked piecemeal into a jumble of 'immediate response' 'fire-fighting' actions on beaches and air-landing grounds.

Overall, such hopes as there were amongst the general population of successfully defending our Island existed mostly in the people's implicit faith in the Royal Navy. The Royal Air Force was still an unknown quantity, though, as the summer had worn on, the RAF had begun to show its teeth. Alf's family knew that, at Bawdsey Manor, near Felixstowe, (and apparently at other places around the south coast), there was a mysterious framework of tall metal towers that local people believed could somehow help our aircraft by means of 'wireless waves', though few people knew exactly how. It was an open secret on the East Coast that, pre-war, a large German airship, evidently equipped as a sort of 'flying research laboratory', had once snooped along close in to the coast, trying to probe the secrets of this 'hush-hush' place at Bawdsey, though apparently with little success. As we have seen,

---

[418] They would prove to be very difficult and dangerous to clear years later.

[419] Experiments *were* made in this direction, with 'erratic' results, but far too late to be seriously considered.

Alice's younger brother, George Neville, had a vibrant auburn-haired girl-friend named Con, who worked at 'hush-hush' Bawdsey Manor. However, Con had signed the Official Secrets Act, and never breathed a word to the family about what went on there.[420]

All that had happened in France in regard to the performance of the RAF was that their obsolete Fairy 'Battle' Bombers had been shot out of the sky, in gallant but near-suicidal attempts to destroy bridges over which the German 'Panzer' Divisions, which were well-equipped with AA weaponry, were pouring almost unopposed by the Allied land forces. As for our fighters, well, they seemed to be inferior to the German Me 109s in combat, where it was rumoured that violent manoeuvres (such as when rolling off the top of a 'loop' and, generally. when the 'control stick' was pushed hard forward), often led to the carburettors of our planes failing temporarily. This would cause the engine to splutter and sometimes cut out, before the effect of air-resistance on the idling propeller would build up (due to the acceleration as the plane fell though the sky) and this would increase the speed of rotation of the propeller to the point where it would (normally) restart the engine. This 'cutting-out' could occur just at the vital moment in a 'dog-fight', whereas the injection-fed German engines just kept going, regardless of whatever so-called 'g-forces' came into play.

It was rumoured that we'd already lost not just semi-obsolete Fairy 'Battle' bombers in France, but also large numbers of our fighter aircraft. Would we have anything like enough aircraft now left to defend our homeland? It seemed likely that our RAF lads were going to have to face very heavy odds. Would our planes and pilots to be good enough to hold their own against the massed aircraft of the 'Luftwaffe'? Yet, in what was becoming called 'The Battle of Britain' our *'Hurricanes'* and *'Spitfires'* did seem to be holding their own, having the advantage that if the pilots were forced to 'bale out', they stood a good chance of landing on home ground, ready to be given a new plane and to fight again, whereas any Germans baling out were taken prisoner or died in the seas around the British Isles. Yet the Luftwaffe seemed to have endless waves of aircraft to send against us.

In the meantime, the Germans had begun to build up a huge fleet of invasion barges in the northern ports of France and Belgium. Once they'd won the war in the air the German forces would soon be heading across the Channel. Rumours of German airborne troops disguised as nuns and landing everywhere simply abounded. There was much talk of German spies and of a treacherous 'Fifth Column' of English people with German sympathies who would stir up trouble.

This, then, was the sort of confused 'civilian' climate in which Alf would have found himself whilst making his journey south in crowded trains, wondering what he would find when he arrived home and earnestly hoping that the Germans were not about to unleash their assault. Stitched through this 'miasma' would have been his own privileged knowledge of events from his position as a naval officer. Mentally, he would have been able to confirm and extrapolate on some aspects, but where this was so, his information would have been of a confidential nature, preventing him from saying a word. Doubtless, he would also have heard some

---

[420] A great many years later it emerged that she had been a personal secretary to Robert WATSON-WATT and other key scientists working on 'Radio Location', later to be called RDF ('Radio Direction-Finding') and, later still, RADAR. In 1941 she would move home and workplace, and become a secretary at the secret headquarters of RAF Fighter Command at Bentley Priory, in Middlesex.

worrying rumours and disturbing items of news which were totally new to his experience and more or less incapable of his evaluation.

When he did finally reach home, Alf quickly found that, although the main family were still there, his elder son and daughter were no longer living in Felixstowe. Following the Dunkirk evacuation, in common with other schoolchildren aged 10 and above who had been living in the invasion-threatened coastal areas, they had been grouped together at short notice, loaded into trains and sent off, more or less 'willy-nilly', into the interior of England, the children identified only by luggage labels giving their names and home addresses, tied to the lapels of their raincoats or jackets. Whether Alf had received any advance warning of this evacuation by a letter from Alice is unknown. Alf and Alice *may* have communicated by telephone once he was in hospital, but he may well have held back from telling her he was incapacitated, for fear of alarming her in the tense situation which prevailed. Knowing how mail often took a long while to 'catch up' with the ships to which it was directed (let alone being forwarded from there to a hospital), and the speed with which events had been happening on the 'Home Front', such matters as the recent evacuation of his children may well have come as a total shock to Alf.

We do know that his younger daughter Jessica, then aged 8, was still at home. Over sixty years later, she would still retain a clear memory of running towards her father in delight as he made his entrance into the house. The eight year-old was preparing to immediately throw herself bodily into his loving arms, as was her wont, and she says that she was greatly surprised when he stopped her as she went to do so, Alf stepping back from her enthusiastic approach with his hands held forward defensively, palms and fingers outspread. It then dawned on her that, currently, he was physically incapable of absorbing the impact of her flying body, and, somehow or other, she soon came to suspect that he was nursing a war-wound on his body. As we have seen, she was not quite right. His disabling 'wound' was of a sporting origin but he may have been quite content, tactically, that she had this misunderstanding.

Despite the enforced evacuation of her two elder siblings, little Jessica would have been only slightly comprehending of the general situation regarding an invasion, though it was certainly true that she was well aware that her Daddy had been away at sea fighting the Germans. On the other hand, there is no doubt that her step-mother and her grandmother were only too well aware of the dreadful potential consequences of the invasion threat hanging over them, and of the seriousness of what was going on. Indeed, they were both badly frightened by the whole situation, which might well put them in the middle of a fighting zone at any moment.

Their fear had been magnified when Alice's father, then aged 63 and, as already recounted, a veteran Gunner of the First World War (to say nothing of being the grandson of a hardened infantryman of Napoleonic times), had arrived home after joining the 'Local Defence Volunteers'. He had volunteered immediately the 'LDV' was initiated in the immediate aftermath of the Dunkirk Evacuation. He had walked home from the recruiting centre carrying a Short Lee-Enfield rifle, which he had put down on the wooden kitchen table with a memorably solid 'thump' which still rings in the ears of the author, sixty-five years later. Joseph Walter had then taken an 'LDV' brassard out of his pocket.[421] This had been followed by a clip of five rounds of .303" ammunition, and he had then declaimed to the family in a heavy and depressed voice, *"That's all the ammunition that they could let me have. There were not enough weapons to go round, so some of the men will have to pick up a rifle when another man gets badly hit. As for me, I'll take four Germans with the first four of those rounds, but the fifth one's reserved for me - for there's no way I'll ever surrender to the bloody Huns."*[422]

It was crystal-clear that the old man meant every word that he had said. So, here were desperate life and death straits indeed, and it was evident that the lot of any women and children caught up in the fighting were going to be dreadful to contemplate. No wonder Alice and Agnes Sarah were frightened - and they had the new baby Richard, aged just 16 months, as well as young Jessica to worry about.

It takes little imagination to realise that Alf would have walked into quite a scene of weeping and wailing and appeals for remedies and assistance, none of which he could really provide - certainly not in the short term. Even to find words of reassurance would have been hard. The best he could do would have been to place a consoling arm around the shoulder and to say something like *"Don't fret too much - the Navy'll stop them ever setting foot ashore!"*, though, with *Southampton* having just come through so much bombing by the *'Luftwaffe'* off Norway leading to casualties and some loss of ships, and probably knowing something of the losses and damage our destroyers had suffered to aerial bombing off Dunkirk (to say nothing of the loss of *Glorious, Ardent, Acasta, Gloworm* and other naval shipping to German surface ships off Norway, which he had probably learnt about already), he may have found difficulty in making the sound of his voice really convincing.

Making love to Alice might have been hugely important for them both under the highly stressful circumstances. However, she may have been simply too overwrought to be able to actually respond to him. And on his part, his back-injury may have inhibited him physically, and the thought of risking further physical damage to his back may have been too overwhelming to contemplate. He could hardly risk having to inform his ship that he was unfit to continue on active service, when he had already missed weeks of hectic combat. He must have already felt deeply that he had 'left his colleagues in the lurch', when he should have been there to secure the very best possible performance out of the 4-inch guns in the anti-aircraft role, protecting his ship as best he could. So, both he and Alice may well have been looking for an excuse not to have to make 'physically-ardent' love.

---

[421] The Local Defence Volunteers (or 'LDV') were the fore-runners of what became the 'Home Guard'.

[422] The author well remembers this scene, which became deeply ingrained in his memory. The great fear in the minds of the women was very manifest. As a boy of ten, greatly excited by it all, and still with only fragmentary knowledge of what war was really like, he thought the women weak and pathetic. He wished he had a rifle. He'd already helped his Grandpa to dig a large and deep sand-bagged bomb-shelter in the garden, roofed with earth-covered corrugated iron and soundly based on WW1 gun-site principles. Now he'd like to fight beside Grandpa, though he feared Grandpa wouldn't let him. On the morning of 22nd November 1939 he'd seen the mined wreck of the broken backed destroyer 'Gipsy' lying just off Felixstowe with her 60 drowned sailors and the great black jellied masses of fuel oil which had come ashore from her, lying everywhere along the beaches. For months now, during their beachcombing activities, he and Uncle Bill had been collecting the jetsam from mined merchant ships of various nations lying half-drowned on the fringes of the fairway. There seemed to be a mighty lot of mastheads and funnels sticking up in the water there already. The boy was collecting spent bullets scattered around from the aerial 'dog-fights' high over Felixstowe. He was *beginning* to grow up - fast.

Obviously, stating that he had an injury or was somehow unfit would have been a 'way out' of this for Alf. However, he undoubtedly had tremendous self-pride, and it is more than likely that he would not have wanted to confess to Alice that he had missed some of the fighting due to a mere 'sports injury'. On the other hand, he would certainly not have wanted to create the false impression that he had suffered a 'war wound'. Apart from his natural reluctance to claim a credit which could not be justified, he would also have wanted to tone down any idea that his life might have been at undue risk. The womenfolk were already too highly keyed-up for that notion to be permitted to surge forward to add to their woes. So he may well have simply spun a little yarn to the effect that he had a slight internal health problem. Alice certainly seemed to end up with the impression that he was mildly unwell with some slight abdominal condition.[423]

In terms of general life-prospects, one way and another, it is clear that Alf resolved that the family would have to leave their home and move inland away from the area threatened by German invasion - Alice and the children first, with the elders guarding the property from looters 'pro tem', and trying to lease it or possibly sell it off, if only they could find somebody who was interested. [The elders were also rather loath to leave behind their younger son, George Neville, then aged 23 and in a semi-reserved occupation in the Tax Office at Felixstowe, but awaiting possible call-up to the armed services. For his part, George Neville also wished to stay near his girl-friend, Con, who (as stated earlier) was working at 'hush-hush' Bawdsey Manor. George Neville and Con would soon be becoming engaged to marry each other.]

Before becoming too committed in regard to moving Alice and the two children, Alf's next care was to see how his elder daughter and elder son were faring, following their recent evacuation to people who were total strangers and of unknown character and status. Anything could have been happening to them. The billeting officers had taken records of the address where each schoolchild had been housed, and this had been supplied to the parents of every evacuated boy and girl. Alf's first reaction may well have been surprise, when he discovered that his two children had ended up in quite different parts of the same Midlands district, on the outskirts of Birmingham. It is believed he would have expected them to have stayed together if they could. This separation was going to make the final part of his journey, which would inevitably be by overcrowded and unreliable wartime trains, just that little bit more complex and time-consuming.[424]

---

[423] The author and Alice chatted about Alf in their later lives, when she talked of Alf as being generally tired and unwell at this time. (At that time the author was completely unaware of Alf's inhibiting 'sports injury' – and Alice was long dead by the time the author had carried out that piece of research in the records at TNA.)

[424] In fact, Joan, a natural blond with a peach and roses complexion, then rising 13 years old, had been one of the first children selected for fostering by the tide of would-be 'foster-parents' arriving on the desolate station platform where the children had all been 'unloaded' late one evening. Joan, doubtless traumatised and very relieved to find a motherly person willing to 'adopt' her, had gone off without even a backward glance at her young brother. He, on the other hand, had been the very last child left – a half-craven bespectacled 'Ugly Duckling' and 'Hobson's Choice' rolled into one for the few late-coming 'adopters'. The boy was not one whit surprised. It just went to show how far his natural mother's death and his step-mother's harsh rule had pulled him down in morale and appearance. He had not the least idea where his elder sister had ended up. He was on his own. So be it. He didn't greatly care. Joan would only have tried to boss him about and there was no way he had wanted that to happen.

In the event, to his considerable relief, Alf found that Joan was reasonably well housed with a lady of quite acceptable respectability and status, who already had a son, and had been longing to 'adopt' a daughter.[425]

Neville's foster-parents, however, were a 'quite different kettle of fish'. They lived in a poor urban district and it seemed that their main reason for having an evacuated child under their roof was simply that they had several mouths of their own to feed, and that they badly needed the billeting allowance to help the family finances. They were not abusing Neville, but merely treating him as if he were one of their own, with a sort of casual, relaxed, semi-indifference. Like their other children, the boy was fed and bedded after a fashion, but, basically, the kids were all running wild, living on a pittance of 'pocket money', but mainly on their wits, 'nicking' oddments of fruit off market stalls, and pinching such little luxuries as they could. [For example (as Alf would soon discover), by sneaking into cinemas via the emergency exit doors at the rear of the building (of which the crash bars had been surreptitiously opened from the inside by one of the gang who'd paid for a ticket to get in)]. At present their behaviour was more or less in the nature of 'misdemeanours', but Alf considered that it might well soon lead on to a life of petty crime or maybe worse. Basically, Alf was appalled.

[*The fact of the matter was that the toys that young Neville had taken with him had long been smashed in warlike games, perhaps inspired through envy, (because none of the gang had ever had such toys of their own), but also as a sort of 'ad hoc' initiation test of Nev's suitability and 'toughness' to join the gang. Somehow, Nev, then aged just 10, had bit his lip and held back his emotions at the wanton destruction of some of his favourite playthings - even joining in to a degree - and only shedding a few quiet tears later, under cover of the darkness of the night. He had managed to hold back his tears because he really did want to 'belong' to the gang. He was delighted to be freed from his step-mother's harsh regime and he welcomed the careless, but never carping or unkind way in which his 'foster-parents' kept just a minimal eye on his well-being. He was indeed quickly growing up and revelling in new experiences and independence. Since his birth-mother had died he had been feeling increasingly like an 'ugly duckling' and an 'oddball' and he was just pleased to be among people who had 'accepted him', rough and ready though they might be.*]

For his part, looking at his son face-to-face, Alf was utterly dismayed. The boy was filthy dirty, his clothes grubby, his shoes badly scuffed. A few well-phrased questions served to show that the boy was leading a disreputable life, almost certainly learning bad habits which, in Alf's view, would only end in delinquency and crime. This was the very antithesis of the fine, honest, upright, smart and gentlemanly image which Alf yearned for his son to adopt.

And yet, as Alf could clearly see, the boy was happy as he was, and he was showing a new independence of spirit. The boy did not want to return home. Alf was livid with him, though he kept his emotions in check. This situation could not be allowed to continue. The boy must be removed to a more suitable environment as soon as could possibly be managed.[426] But, Alf could stay no longer, and quickly

---

[425] Joan says that the lady had what amounted to a 'cocooned pink nest' of a bedroom all ready to receive a girl-evacuee. In psychological terms, that might have been found slightly worrying to '21st century' eyes'.

[426] For his part, the boy looked at his father, who had arrived 'out of the blue' so far as he was concerned. His father was more of a stranger to him than ever. It dawned, almost subconsciously, on the

returned to invasion-threatened Felixstowe. *Neither father nor son knew that they would never lay eyes on each other ever again.*

Once back at Felixstowe, Alf promptly set the wheels in motion to have Alice move into lodgings in Buckinghamshire, taking Jessica and Baby Richard with her. When Alice was established there, Neville and Joan could perhaps be collected and taken to join her, though it was just a little worrying to think of them being exposed to Alice without the comforting 'buffer zone' and emotional support of their grandparents, for Alice would be under considerable emotional and functional pressure, and Alf recognised that she might be highly volatile and reactive.

In the meantime, rather than allow Neville to stay where he was for a moment longer, Alf would ask his London-based middle sister, Rose, to put up young Neville for a week or two. Perhaps she and young Neville would bond with each other, and, if Rose's husband, Alf, was agreeable, *maybe* the 'adoption arrangement' (previously once mooted) could become a permanent one. Whilst this was going on, perhaps he, Alf, would ask his elder sister Nellie and her husband Wilf to put up Joan for a while, to see if that bond might also work. Both Neville and Joan were clearly happier and less stressed when away from their step-mother, and these fostering alternatives might be for the best, much though he would hate to lose direct contact and control of these two rather difficult children. Oh, how much simpler life would have been had Olive survived! Young Neville had been such a rumbustious, confident and happy child in those days - so different from his present low image - and young Joan seemed so 'negative' nowadays.

All too soon, his short leave having quickly expired, Alf went back to South Shields and his 'other life' with his ship and the war. At least he had the satisfaction as he said his goodbyes of 'having set the wheels in motion'. He had long been attuned to the inevitability of having to let go of one 'life' to go back to the other, turn by turn. But this time, above all others, it must have been very disturbing for him to have to leave the womenfolk and the two youngest children still in the threatened invasion zone, where they could be in mortal danger. At least Alice and the children should be heading away from that danger point very shortly, as the arrangements fell into place. Alf could do no more except to play his full part in combating the German forces and in inspiring the men under and around him to do likewise, whilst bolstering those above him.

Neither Alf, nor Alice, knew that this was the last time they would see each other ever again, and that ere many months were past, the four children would be fatherless. For good or ill, before his eleventh birthday dawned, *and if he did not run away from home in the interim,* Young Neville was fated to become the surrogate 'Man of the Family'. And what a tremendous example was being set for him by his fantastic father.

---

10 year-old boy's brain that this being who had total control over him was looking much older and more haggard than formerly. Yet, his father was as decisive and incisive as he had ever been. The boy had cherished hope against hope that his father would see that his son had 'come through the fires', discern how his independence of spirit and self-confidence had grown, and so be pleased with him rather than critical. The boy was desperate not to have to go back to his hectoring step-mother *ever again.* Yet, looking at his father's set face, he saw that his father was once again dissatisfied with him, and that his hopes of staying clear of his step-mother were surely about to be dashed. His former miseries now seemed likely to be renewed very soon and, at that moment, *he rather wished that his father hadn't come to see him at all.*

The Author's last mental image of his father conforms well to this photographic study of Alf. This father was suddenly showing the stresses of a hard war and the physical effects of his hospitalisation – but he was still immaculately turned out despite everything, and quick and incisive in taking hard and difficult decisions.

HMS *SOUTHAMPTON*, (1939-41) *continued:*

On his return from sick leave Alf would have learnt of the happenings to *Southampton* in the second part of the Norway Campaign, and during the evacuation. He would have learnt of the casualties they had suffered, including the fact that Captain JEANS had been wounded and replaced by Captain BROOKE. If the author's memory is correct, Alf had always expressed great admiration for Captain JEANS. Somewhere deep inside the mind of the author there is a feeling that Alf's first impressions of Captain BROOKE (perhaps piqued by the enforced move of the wounded Captain JEANS away from *Southampton*) were not too favourable. However, if a letter which would be written to Alf's widow by Captain BROOKE in 1941 is anything to go by, an excellent understanding quickly built up.

There was considerable movement of destroyers in and out from Sheerness in August escorting East Coast convoys and on various other duties. There were many air raid alarms, yellow flares being seen overhead on the night of 4th/5th August and bombs seen to fall on or near Margate. During the following night the 1st Motor Boat was made fast to the Quarter Boom for any 'anti-flare duties' which might become necessary (though, rather embarrassingly, the Motor Boat was not 'made fast' *enough*, so it broke loose and had to be returned to the ship by tug!). Later that day *Southampton* proceeded with her DG switched on, and anchored off Southend evidently as an extra AA defence for the town, her searchlight crews closing up at 2320, an Air Raid Warning ensuing, and an Alarm to Arms being given, though no bombs were dropped. Much the same happened at noon. On the night of the 9th a white flare was dropped on the port beam, and, at 0530 on the 10th the dead body of a man drifted past the ship. People were getting a little jumpy and Rear Admiral CLARKE's Messdeck Rounds that forenoon, probably with an apt calm and matter-of-fact word here and there, may have helped to steady the company a little. That night *Southampton* returned to Sheerness.

There were now near-constant Air Raid Warnings in this area where the full weight of the German assault landing was expected to fall, but 'normal' shipboard life still continued, with Sunday Divisions being held, RA 18 inspecting the company, naval stores being embarked and re-fuelling and embarkation of petrol continuing. The ship's company also exercised 'Abandon Ship'. On 12th August, Alf lost one of his gunnery team, when AB FULLER severely injured a finger. This had become jammed between a 4-inch drill cartridge and the loader-mechanism, the top joint being almost severed.

On the 13th August *Southampton* opened fire on six enemy aircraft which 'broke ranks' from the massed formations flying inland high overhead. No bombs were, however, dropped. Again, on the 16th, *Southampton* opened fire on enemy aircraft, no bombs falling.

During this period Mr MARTIN (Gunner) left the ship, as did Lt (E) THOMSETT, and Lt (E) BEST and Midshipman JENKINS, RNVR joined. Mr SHELLEY (Acting Warrant Telegraphist) was discharged to RND Chatham a few days later.

It seems appropriate to take a look at the officers and warrant officers being commanded by Captain BROOKE as in early September 1940. New technology and weaponry of various kinds were being installed, and, to meet the new operational requirements, the ship's complement was increasing in size, especially in the number of ratings. Perhaps a further half-dozen officers/WOs were now in evidence.

NAME	RANK	MONTH JOINED	MONTH LEFT
BROOKE, B.C.B	Captain	Jun 1940	Jan 1941
WILD	Captain (E)	Nov 1939	Pre-Jan 11 1941?
OLIVER, R.	Commander (N)	Apr 1939	Nov 1940
FYFE, R.W.	Commander (E)	?	KiA, Jan 1941
McINTYRE	Surg Commander	Dec 1939	Jul 1940
BARKER-HAHLO, J.F.C.	Lt Commander	Nov 1939	KiA, Jan 1941
BULFORD	Lt Commander	Apr 1940	Pre-Jan 11 1941?
EDMONSTONE (Rtd)	Lt Commander	Pre-Mar 1937?	Jan 1941
COPEMAN, A.H.	Lt Commander (T)	Jan 1939	Jan 1941
FAWCUS, Sir P.	Lt Commander	Apr 1940	Jan 1941
PELLY, C.S.	Lt Commander	Apr 1940	Jan 1941
RAYMOND, D.L.	Lt Commander (G)	Aug 1939	Jan 1941
TINLEY, C.B.	Lt Commander	Mar 1937	DoW, Jan 1941
FIDO	Lt Commander RNR	?	Nov 1940
SHACKLETON, H.E.F.	Major RM	Nov 1938	KiA, Jan 1941
BARRATT, R.J.T	Lt	Sep 1938	Pre-Jan 11 1941?
GRENFELL	Lt	Aug 1939	Pre-Jan 11 1941?
JACKSON	Lt	Pre-Jun 1940	Pre-Jan 11 1941?
PARNALL	Lt	Nov 1939	Pre-Jan 11 1941?
THOMSETT, E.	Lt	?	Aug 1940
JACKSON	Lt RNVR	?	Nov 1940
MANNING	Lt (A)	Dec 1939	Pre-Jan 11 1941?
CASSON, J.	Lt (A)	Pre-Nov 1939	1940
BEST	Lt (E)	Aug 1940	Pre-Jan 11 1941?
GUEST, J.A.	Lt (E)	Nov 1938	KiA, Jan 1941
de STACKPOOL, R.O.	Lt RM	Nov 1939	Jan 1941
HEATHCOTE	Pay Lt	Aug 1939	Pre-Jan 11 1941?
RICHARDS, N.L.C.	Pay Lt	?	KiA, Jan 1941
PETERS	Instr Lt	Jul 1938	Pre-Jan 11 1941?
OLIVER, J.E.	Temp Instr Lt	?	KiA, Jan 1941
FAIRWEATHER, D.J.	Surg Lt (D)	?	KiA, Jan 1941
SLOANE, W.C.	Surg Lt RNVR	Jul 1940	1940
DISNEY-ROEBUCK	S/Lt	May 1940	Jan 1941
HERRING	S/Lt (A)	Pre-Sep 1940	Jan 1941
STEVENSON	S/Lt	?	Nov 1940
POITRIE	S/Lt (A)	Pre-Sep 1940	Pre-Jan 11 1941?
STEVENSON	S/Lt RNVR	?	Nov 1940
ALFORD, I.F.O.	Midshipman	1940	1940
BOWER	Midshipman RNR	Jan 1938?	Jan 1941
COCKBURN	Midshipman RANVR	May 1940	Pre-Jan 11 1941?
DAVIDSON, G.V.	Midshipman	Sep 1940	KiA, Jan 1941
ELGAR, J.M.	Ty Midshipman RANVR	May 1940	1940
JENKINS, G.	Midshipman RNVR	Aug 1940	Pre 11th Jan 1941
JERRAM, F.R.	Midshipman	1939	Jan 1941
KENT, B.H.	Midshipman	Sep 1940	Jan 1941
LEARMOND, P.A.	Midshipman	Sep 1940	Jan 1941
MOCATTA, J.M.	Midshipman	Sep 1940	KiA, Jan 1941
RUCK-KEENE, T	Midshipman	Jan 1938	Jan 1941
SMITH, P.R.G.	Midshipman	1939	Jan 1941
TURNER, G.T.	Midshipman	Sep 1940	Jan 1941
BEASLEY, B.R.	Chaplain	1939	Jan 1941
DAVIS, Mr A. W.	Commissioned Gunner	Pre Mar 1937	KiA, Jan 1941
PLAYER, Mr H. C.	Commissioned Gunner	Mar 1937	KiA, Jan 1941

KOESTER, Mr L	Gunner	Mar 1937?	DoW, Jan 1941
MARTIN, Mr F.	Gunner	?	Aug 1940
REES, Mr F.P.	Bandmaster RM	Mar 1937	Jan 1941
WADE, Mr R.D.	Warrant Engineer	Aug 1939	Jan 1941
WHITE, Mr F.J	Warrant Engineer	Aug 1939	KiA, Jan 1941
SHELLEY, Mr	Acting Warrant Tel	?	Aug 1940

TOTAL: About 59 Officers and Warrant Officers. (Also see Master Table of Names in Appendix C, page 700.) The names of personnel who were still serving in January 1941 are shown in **bold** type.

The invasion threat was still very live, and it seemed almost anti-climactic when, on the 17th August, *Southampton* slipped and proceeded to Rosyth, *Birmingham* being in company. Not that her company were being let 'off the hook' – far from it in fact – they were just being withdrawn for reasons of tactical dispersal and concentration. At 2125 an aircraft was sighted, magnesium flares were dropped overhead and the rattle of machine-gun fire was heard. Later that night they passed a northbound convoy escorted by *Sheffield*, and, later still they passed five RN trawlers. As the daylight grew they passed a southbound convoy, and they entered the Firth of Forth at 1225, coming to anchor at Rosyth at 1325. They oiled immediately and were at 2½ hours notice for steam. They stored ship and the Captain of the new cruiser *Fiji* (another product of John Brown's Shipyard) called on Captain BROOKE.

A dive-bombing exercise was carried out by aircraft on the 22nd. The battlecruiser *Hood* was present, and there were considerable 'comings and goings' by the always-busy destroyers, of which, post-Dunkirk and post-Norway, there were now significantly fewer to cover the manifold duties required. *Manchester* and *Birmingham* arrived on the 30th August, and RA 18 visited the former ship. Next day the wind got up with a vengeance from the south-east, and an anchor watch was set.

On the 1st September the weather moderated and *Southampton* proceeded out to sea with *Manchester* and *Birmingham* in company, returning to Rosyth, taking in oil and water, and securing for sea at 2000. Meantime, Captain BROOKE had made an official visit on the Captain of *Manchester,* and Midshipmen DAVIDSON, KENT, LEARMOND, MOCATTA and TURNER joined ship from the RN College at Dartmouth. We shall hear much more of Midshipman KENT (later Captain KENT) before the end of this account.[427]

On the 4th September *Southampton* proceeded southwards for Immingham, opening fire for exercise with her close-range weapons as she got out to sea. Perhaps the Admiralty knew that events were conspiring so that the key German decision to invade immediately was perforce about to be made. Otherwise, the invasion would have to be stood down *pro tem.* Once at Immingham, *Southampton's* aircraft 2204, piloted by Rating Pilot BLACKWELL, with S/Lt POITRIE (O) and A/G BELL, returned to the ship, and *Southampton* provisioned and took on board engineer's stores from a drifter, oiling and embarking further provisions on the 6th September. On the 11th the coastal minelayer HMS *Plover* put to sea for the burial of the Captain of the destroyer D20. RA 18 paid an official call on CS 18. At 1115 a man fell overboard port side and was rescued. Next day, aircraft L2336 was lowered into the water and taxied 20 miles

---

[427] Captain B H KENT very kindly checked this book throughout for errors, including those relating to appropriate 'naval usage', and he also wrote the foreword.

upriver, piloted by Lt WOODS (who had recovered well from his crash and near-drowning on the 18th July.).

Lt Commander HARTMANN of the U.S.N joined ship this day, 17th September 1940, as an observer of British naval procedures.[428] Alf had been busy, having signed the log as OOW no less than five times since 2nd September. He would sign further times as the month went on. Short leaves were granted all through the month, and four ratings came back from *long leave* on the 21st September, but, although his pattern of signing the log would have 'permitted it', so far as is known, Alf had no further long leave at this period. All kinds of practices and exercises were going on, especially of the HA armament and HA Control Parties, and of the searchlight Crews and Control Parties, against a 'backdrop' of 'Yellow' status Air Raid Warnings which were occurring almost every day.

All though this period from Alf's rejoining and before, the role of the squadron of which *Southampton* was a part would have been to attack the eastern flanks of the streams of barges and light coastal craft expected to be carrying German assault troops towards the south-east coast of England. The squadron might have inflicted huge losses on these German troops - but they would have had to do so in the face of very heavy German aerial bombing, coupled with fire from long-range coastal batteries and possible torpedo attacks by light, high-speed, German craft. There would also have been lines of U-boats stationed at the eastern and western fringes of the invasion sea-lane that the Germans proposed to use, the orders for which had now been issued.

Losses would probably have been heavy on both sides – in fact, the situation might well have become *'Gotterdammerung'*-like. It was a desperate situation to contemplate, even though the thought of defending one's own family, one's way of life and one's country were the most powerful of motivators.

However, in mid-September, as is now well-known, the struggle between the German air force and the Royal Air Force for the mastery of the skies over England, had reached its peak. The desperate fighting in the air became known as 'The Battle of Britain', and it ended in what amounted to defeat for the *Luftwaffe*. The whole affair had been a fantastically close-run thing. Prime Minister Winston CHURCHILL had been absolutely correct when he later said that, *"Never before, in the field of Human Conflict had so much been owed by so many to so few"*, and it is true that the German *Luftwaffe* had suffered severe and unsustainable losses in air combat. However, at one point the RAF had been reduced to a state where there were no reserve squadrons left to put into the air, and its pilots were becoming physically, emotionally and mentally exhausted. Quite apart from the continuous losses incurred in attacking the fighter-escorted German bomber streams, this exhaustion had been brought about by a mixture of German tactical dive-bombing, conventional bombing and low-level straffing, which had all but knocked

---

[428] The US Navy knew it was only a matter of time before they would be at war with Japan. They also knew that it was highly probable that they would soon have to start escorting convoys as they set out on their transatlantic voyages to England, and, sooner or later, to escort the ships of those convoys as they voyaged around the coastline of the U.S.A to the convoy assembly-points. The more they could learn of British tactics in modern warfare the better it would be in their struggles yet to come. In the event, the US Navy came into combat with the German U-Boats months before their country officially declared war on the Axis Powers. [That *official* declaration of war by the USA did not come about until the Japanese suddenly made a pre-emptive and very nearly overwhelming air-strike against Pearl Harbour, on 7th December 1941.]

out both the usability of the southern RAF airfields and also some of the English 'Radio Location Stations' (later called R/DF and later still RADAR Stations). These stations were vital in terms of getting our aircraft into the air at just the right time to meet each German thrust and their loss would have been devastating. Had Hermann GOERING better understood their crucial importance to the RAF, and sent concentrated attacks against them, the scales would have swung overwhelmingly in his favour.

Thus, at one stage, the RAF was almost like a boxer 'hanging on the ropes' under the continuous German assault, and it was the switching of the German bombing assault to London (in gross Hitlerian revenge for a few RAF bombs which fell on Berlin - that paltry bombing itself being a Churchillian riposte for a few German bombs which had *accidentally* fallen on London) which had eased the pressure at the very climactic and allowed the RAF to go on to win the battle for daylight air supremacy. The German Air Marshal Hermann GOERING's fatuous boast *"No enemy aircraft shall ever fly over the German Reich"* had been the nucleus for a storm of Germanic protest when RAF bombs DID fall on Berlin, and must have been a big factor in the change in German tactics to heavy and protracted bombing of London and other cities before the extinction of the RAF aircraft and its airfields, and of the RDF (Radio Direction Finding) stations in southern England was tactically 'complete'.

It seemed utterly uncanny when the daylight skies over southern England in the third week of September remained clear of the massed hordes of German aircraft which had been coming over remorselessly day by day, week by week and month by month.

Clearly, the signs were already there that the citizens of London and other major British cities would have much severe day and, especially, night-time bombing yet to undergo, but, suddenly, the most immediate and urgent crisis was past. Without mastery of the skies, and without clear dominance at sea, the Germans dared not risk an invasion of England. Autumn was now well advanced. It was now unlikely that there would be any large-scale invasion of England at least until the spring of 1941. In the meantime, the British could expect heavy bombing raids on both civilian and military targets in an effort to break their will, and attacks by submarines and surface vessels on their supply lines to 'starve them out'. The British would also need to protect their Empire and Commonwealth and to transport and maintain British forces engaged in the various theatres of war overseas.

However, British naval ships that had been on anti-invasion duties could now mostly be stood down from that task and prepared for these other roles. [It could well be said that the Allied warships, especially but by no means solely those of the Royal Navy, had 'done their bit' in staving off the invasion, because several German warships had been sunk or sufficiently damaged to prevent their use during those vital months, so that the remaining naval forces available to Germany for protecting the flanks of any seaborne assault had been seriously reduced. This would have been a factor in the decision of the German Higher Command, endorsed by HITLER, to postpone the invasion at least *pro tem*. It was also a key fact that HITLER had 'other fish soon to fry', especially 'Operation Barbarossa' (the then still-secret pre-emptive invasion of Russia), though that operation would be crucially postponed because the Army of his ally Benito MUSSOLINI would get in a terrible pickle in fighting the Greeks, who had strong British military and naval support, and the Italian Army was already in a dreadful mess against General WAVELL in North Africa. These situations would each require intervention by both the *Luftwaffe* and the *Wehrmacht* – and all this would buy vitally important time for the retreating Russians when 'Barbarossa' was unleashed, with the German offensive doomed to peter out in the bitter winter snows of 1941, just as the 'sticking point' arrived and the Germans were *almost* at the point of clinching their victory.]

Southampton continued at Immingham into October, conducting intensive training of the crews of her main armament, including sub/cal firings. The Captain of *Glasgow* visited RA 18 and the Captain of *Southampton*, and some of the exercises were made in conjunction with *Glasgow*. *Manchester* proceeded on the 3rd October, and *Southampton* reverted to 4 hours notice for steam - a sign of a slight easing in the tension. On 5th October the Lower Deck was cleared and RA 18 (Rear Admiral M.L. CLARKE) addressed the company, to say his goodbyes, to express his appreciation of their conduct under very trying circumstances and to wish them well. He might have considered quoting Winston CHURCHILL's words at that time: "*This is not the End, it is not even the beginning of the End, but it may be the End of the Beginning.*" The Captain of *Glasgow* paid yet another visit and Rear Admiral CLARKE struck his flag, the last of his staff leaving the ship next day. As if to say things were not yet over, there was another Air Raid Warning and the HA armament went to 2nd degree readiness that night.

It seems appropriate to say that a report had been issued by Surgeon Captain SLOANE, covering the period 22nd July to the 30th September. There had been facilities for limited shore leaves and the opportunity to play sports and get in some exercise. This, plus the general reduction in tension, the reduction in the number of air raids, the reduced need to 'batten down the ship', (thus improving the overnight ventilation), and the improved supply of fresh fruit and vegetables, had all done much to restore the company. However, the surgeon did point out a number of negative factors, such as the overcrowding in the mess decks due to the additional one hundred men being carried (as compared with the pre-war complement), the blanking out of the scuttles in the lower mess deck, and the reduction to only one scuttle in the other messes, all of which cut down on the fresh air and light. He 'condemned' such modifications and certainly did not want to 'condone' them. The surgeon was highly critical of the ventilation of the ship, being most critical of the galley, where the average temperature was no less than a debilitating 120° F.

In terms of illness, individual cases had occurred of appendicitis, of a perforated gastric ulcer (which, sadly, ultimately proved fatal after the man was transferred to hospital ashore), of pulmonary TB, and of severe bronchial catarrh. A large proportion of the cases treated on board were victims of the common cold, of boils, and of injuries to fingers and toes which had subsequently turned septic. The number of cases of venereal disease had fallen sharply. This was probably influenced by the low amount of shore leave granted, but aided, he believed to the increasing use of sheaths. Lectures given to the company on various matters, including V.D, seemed to be having some good effect. One hundred and thirty-four officers and ratings had volunteered to be blood donors if so required. Blood grouping was being carried out on board.

Not mentioned in the Surgeon's Journal, the wartime 'Black-Out' was responsible for many accidents, especially during moonless nights, and people who were disorientated and lacked balance due to a heavy bout of drinking were particularly vulnerable to such accidents. This was probably the cause of *Southampton's* duty SBA being called at 0305 to attend a casualty who had fallen in the Dry Dock on the 6th October, unfortunately only to be found to be dead.

Further gunnery exercises continued, and the ship embarked further provisions and ammunition, and topped up with oil. Perhaps to relieve boredom in a 'constructive' way, a rifle range was opened on the jetty on the 11th. The detachment of Royal Marines was landed to stretch their limbs and sharpen up their drill. *Manchester* returned to harbour on the 16th and Captain BROOKE paid an official visit on her Captain.

As a part of the sea-change in reactive tactical thinking following the Battle of Britain, *Southampton* was withdrawn from the Humber on that day, switching on her DG at 1655 and proceeding for Scapa Flow at 1718. She passed the Humber boom defence at 1814, slowed to stream her paravanes, and increased to 24 knots as she got out to sea. At 2050 she passed a northbound convoy, sighting a southbound one at much the same time, and, just before midnight she passed minesweepers engaged in sweeping. At 0250, heart-stoppingly, she was suddenly challenged by a darkened trawler which was clearly keeping a very sharp lookout, and which identified itself as British. At 1050 *Southampton* was making 26 knots over a moderate sea when she sighted several fishing vessels one mile distant, just before entering a fogbank. She hauled her paravanes at 1253 closed up her Close-Range Weapons crews and passed the Hoxa boom at 1230, coming to anchor at Scapa at 1255 and switching off her DG. She oiled almost at once, from two oilers, embarking 250 tons. At 1530 the Captain of the new Dido-Class cruiser *Phoebe* visited Captain BROOKE. Alf was OOW and there may have been some covetous glances at the main armament of *Phoebe*, which consisted of ten of the excellent 5.25 inch dual-purpose guns paired in five turrets, which could be elevated to comparatively high angles against aircraft attack.[429]

Next morning *Southampton* embarked 2,000 gallons of aviation spirit and she then underwent two weeks of intensive gunnery practice. This included 6-inch day and night sub/cal firing in the Flow, the latter whilst burning search-lights, and closing up her close-range weapons crews, drilling her 4-inch crews, acting as 'flank marker' for the new Fiji-Class cruiser *Nigeria* as she carried out an HA shoot with her 4-inch guns at a sleeve target (and then exchanging roles) and opening fire with 6-inch and then 4-inch LA guns at a target. Most of these exercises involved multiple runs.

This period of training was twice interrupted due to 'scares' which were evidently linked with residual fears of a German assault on England of some kind The scares came to nothing, but were typical of the very understandable 'jitters' which prevailed at that time. The first took place on 23rd October, when *Southampton* was ordered, at 1407, to join CS 2 in pursuit of a reported enemy unit. By 1504 she had joined the cruisers *Arethusa* and *Norfolk* and they had formed into line ahead at 28 knots. At 1945 her hands were in Night Action Stations at 2nd degree of readiness. At 2035 'F' coil of the DG fused, and the DG was switched off, leaving the ship vulnerable to magnetic mines. At 2102 the 'M' and 'Q' coils of the DG were switched on. As midnight arrived the company went to 1st degree readiness as they drove on to the east and north of the Shetlands. It would have been about this time that the mission was aborted by the Admiralty. At 0715 the squadron was challenged by destroyers, before, at 0810, a part of

---

[429] Of the 11 ships of this 'Dido' Class, four were lost during the war. However, none of the losses was due to air-attack, whereas, of the eight ships of the 'Southampton' Class, both *Southampton* herself and *Gloucester* would succumb to aerial bombing.

Southampton's port paravane broke adrift. By 1015 they were following in the wake of CS 2 due to the broken paravane, and matters grew worse by 1265 due to a communication error between the Bridge and the Lower Steering Position, causing the ship to be astern of station. Captain BROOKE was probably fuming with rage by that time. Thus it was probably with relief that the company hauled their paravanes at the end of this particular voyage and came back to their berth at Scapa, the DG being deliberately left ON. As the ship oiled the entry being made in the log recorded the loss of *'one Paravane Mk VII, one Space Bar, one Roller Cutter, and two Shackles'*.

More gunnery practice followed immediately. This included the familiar height-finding exercises for the 4-inch Action Control Parties, and the 6-inch Control Parties were also drilled, before the ship put to sea for 6-inch barrage-firing.

An innovation came at this time. German E-Boats, fast and well-armed craft with determined and resourceful commanders had been attacking our East Coast convoys, especially at night and sometimes with dire results for our merchant ships and their escorts. Gunnery drills now included 'anti-E-Boat procedures' for both the 6-inch and 4-inch LA guns, and included firing of 4-inch starshell whilst searching for a fast-moving target representing an E-Boat.

Then, on 28th October, topped up with oil, petrol, water and ammunition, *Southampton* proceeded in company with *Hood, Repulse, Dido and Phoebe* in adverse weather conditions, the wind coming from the south-east and increasing to Force 8, and the waves getting up to rather rough, with a very high swell running. The ships were forced to reduce from 24 knots down to 16 knots and on further down to 14 knots. At 1530 on the 29th *Southampton's* port lifebuoy was lost overboard, and at 2043 the ship was forced to heave-to in the severe southerly gale which had by now developed. At 0100 on the 30th October the Sounding Boom on the starboard side was smashed by the heavy seas. However, they were moving again, and were well to the north of the Faroe Islands when, at 0445, a light was sighted. This proved to be the Finnish merchant ship *Boré X*, with a cargo of lorries. She was ordered to stay in company. Seemingly a message was received about that time ordering a return to Scapa. At 0755 the port paravane recovery wire was lost. The ships of the squadron were losing touch with each other, and, at 1258 *Southampton* challenged a warship in the poor visibility prevailing, which identified herself as *Phoebe*. At 1705 the paravane towing wire parted, but the starboard paravane was recovered. At 1900 *Southampton* switched on a shaded stern light for *Boré X* to follow, and so made her way back to Scapa, *Boré X* following faithfully astern.

At Scapa she quickly oiled (250 tons), embarked fresh water and took in beef from a drifter. Then, on the 2nd November it was yet more 6-inch, 4-inch HA and close-range weapons gunnery practice, anti-E-boat gunnery practice at a fast-towed target, including more star shell illuminated night-firings, acting as a target ship for *Dido*, torpedo firing, R & I exercises with the destroyer *Eskimo* and undergoing dummy torpedo attacks by '*Swordfish*' aircraft. Once again *Southampton* had a fire on the fo'c'sle caused by the DG, which had to be switched off. On 4th November aircraft L2287 (Lt WOODS) with S/Lt HERRING, Lt-Cmdr HARTMANN USN and a Tel/AG took off, presumably in a spotting role, and the rigmarole of gunnery practice resumed as on the 2nd November, but this time including a dummy bombing attack by '*Swordfish*' aircraft. Meantime, *Southampton's* DG had been repaired and was in use again.

That evening the ship took its turn as AA guardship, and the Lookouts and the "ADO's Mate" were closed up. This is the first specific reference in the log to an ADO (Air Defence Officer) - a role which, as we know, was being fulfilled by Midshipman Thomas RUCK-KEENE (possibly amongst others) by the second phase of the Norway Campaign, if not before. On 5th November the ship proceeded for further exercises in the Flow. These took a new twist, consisting of 'General Breakdown' drills, with the ship being 'conned from aft', 'towed forrard' and 'towed aft', followed by 'Abandon Ship' drill and 'Gas Alarm' practice. By 1318 *Southampton* was back at A2 Berth, being kept at one hour notice for steam. *Nelson* and *Rodney* and the destroyers *Punjabi* and *Phoebe* arrived at much the same time. At 2350, *Hood* and *Repulse*, the cruisers *Bonadventure* and *Niaid* and the destroyers *Eskimo*, *Mashona*, *Matabele* and *Punjabi* proceeded. It looked as if some sort of scare was in progress.

Thus it came as no surprise to her company when, at 0635 on 6th November *Southampton* also proceeded, and accompanied the battleships *Nelson* and *Rodney* on patrol duties off Iceland. *Southampton's* departure was just a little embarrassing, for they had a foul anchor which took almost 20 minutes to clear. They thus kept everybody waiting to some extent, including the escort of six destroyers assembled outside the Hoxa Gate. Captain BROOKE was probably quietly fuming again - or perhaps not so quietly!

In fact, their detachment was a part of a widespread hunt by RN ships for the German battlecruiser *Admiral Scheer*. [The previous day this German warship had sunk the AMC *Jervis Bay* and five of the ships she had in convoy, though *Jervis Bay's* gallantry had given time for most of her charges to scatter sufficiently widely to escape.] At 1010 *Southampton's* log shows that the detachment passed an eastbound convoy of twenty-five ships. *Southampton's* HA armament was at 2nd degree readiness, when, at 1035 a Ju 88 was sighted. This flew right over the ship, hotly pursued by an intrepid Lockheed 'Hudson'. The ship's Action HA armament was quickly closed up, and the ship started to zig-zag. Another aircraft was sighted at 1625, but this proved to have the friendly and unmistakable shape of a 'Walrus'. At 2325 *Rodney* parted company, and *Southampton* took station astern of *Nelson*, zig-zagging.

The next three days were frustrating ones, investigating various ships in the area lying to the west of the Faroe Islands, which proved to be innocent trawlers and lone merchant ships. *Southampton* parted company with *Nelson* at times, being warned at one such time by the C-in-C that aircraft, believed to be hostile, were in a nearby sector. On the 8th *Southampton* ordered the Swedish ship *Hera* to keep in company, and fired a round of 4-inch across her bow when she refused to alter course, *Hera* subsequently signalled that she had clearance papers, and was allowed to proceed. On the 9th a swell began to get up as *Southampton* put into Reykjavik, having sent her 'Walrus' on ahead the previous day. By the afternoon the wind was rising rapidly, and the ship let go a second anchor. The wind was now Force 10, and slight damage was done to the Quarter Deck when an oiler tried to come alongside. Both anchors came out of the ground and *Southampton* proceeded to an anchorage more sheltered from the gale, setting an anchor watch once she had secured. She proceeded within the hour, streaming her paravanes as she went.

The wind had eased marginally, and was now Force 8, but bitterly cold as it was coming from due north. The swell was high and, by midday was gauged as 'tremendous'. *Southampton* was rolling with a vengeance, up to 40° to starboard. She'd had to reduce speed more and more as the swell mounted, and from 20 knots she was by now down to 8 knots. At 1350 the port Whaler started to come adrift and was damaged. Men risked their lives to secure it. That was the peak of the storm. Conditions began to ease, but with further flurries of wind and heavy rollers.

The company continued at 2nd Degree Readiness, and *Southampton* challenged a ship at 2300, finding her to be a trawler 'making a living' under appalling conditions.

An anonymous 'official' photograph from Alf's collection.

Southampton in a severe storm, with her bows crashing down into a heavy sea. This photo was probably taken on the Royal Tour in 1939, but serves to give an idea of the 'forces of nature' and something of an understanding of ship's boats, sounding booms and other items being carried away by the sea, despite having been well 'lashed down'.

By 0020 on the 11th November *Southampton* was back at 20 knots. At 0540 the Butt of Lewis was sighted, and two ships hove in sight, identifying themselves as *Bonadventure* and the destroyer *Mashona*. An aircraft also identified itself as friendly, and, at 1600, a destroyer with an unusual profile identified herself as *Montgomery*. She was one of the fifty near-obsolete destroyers obtained on Lend-Lease from the U.S.A., but badly-needed to cover our destroyer losses during the evacuation of Dunkirk and in the Norway campaign.

Southampton switched on her DG as she began to close the coast, hauled her paravanes at 1800, and came to anchor at Bangor Bay at 2100, setting an anchor watch because, although the sea had greatly moderated, hurricane blasts of wind were still coming at irregular periods. During the patrol, though not spelt out in the log, it seems that the extremely heavy weather had damaged *Southampton's* Asdic equipment. The exact nature of the damage is unknown, but could have been due to her heavy plunging and rolling causing the sea to break into, or partially unship, the Asdic dome, which was located on the ship's bottom, near the keel.[430]

There was a short Air Raid Warning next day, and on the 13th November *Southampton* was piloted, with tugs fore and aft, into Alexander Dock, Belfast. She remained in Dry Dock until the 15th, whilst repairs were made to her Asdic equipment and the ship's foul bottom was scraped. Midshipman RUCK-KEENE said that the C-in-C's visual message: "Docking is advisable *before proceeding abroad*" (which had been read all over the ship) had led to some 'tenseness' when it was announced that Belfast was the place chosen for the repair work. For months past the whole ship's company had been speculating about docking at Rosyth or some other place where there was at least a chance for some home leave. It was also customary for a period of home leave to be granted before proceeding abroad. By no stretch of the imagination did Belfast qualify as 'home'.

There might therefore have been some envy of Surgeon Lt/Cmdr FIDO RNVR, Lt JACKSON RNVR and Sub/Lt STEVENSON RNVR, who were all discharged to shore at Belfast to make their way back to England for courses.

At midday on the 15th Southampton was out of the dock, and by 1430 she had re-fuelled, had turned in mid-stream, hoisted in aircraft L2333 (Pilot PO BLACKWELL) and L2211, and ammunitioned. At 1900 the company switched on their DG (only to turn it off again ½ hour later, following the cancellation of the 'Purple Warning'), closed up their close-range weapons crews at 2135 and closed up their Special Sea Dutymen as a preparative to proceeding.[431] Now came a problem, and White Watch of the Royal Marine Detachment were called upon to provide brute strength to clear the backhaul which had become foul of the cathead. It took them just five minutes, and the ship proceeded for Gibraltar, heading down the west coast of Ireland and shaping a course well out into the Atlantic. Ominously, the glass was dropping.

At 0740 on the 16th November *Southampton* made rendezvous with the aircraft-carrier *Furious* and took station on her, sighting the cruiser *Cairo* at 0812. At 1705 they sighted the newly-built sloop *Black Swan*, and by 1830 they had taken station astern of a convoy which consisted of the three fast troopships, *Clan Forbes*, *Clan Frazer* and *New Zealand Star* with attendant destroyers. Later, though not specifically shown in the log, they were joined by *Southampton's* sister-ship *Manchester* and the 5,450 ton anti-aircraft cruiser *Dido*, escorting the troopship *Franconia*, which was carrying 1,500 RAF and military personnel. The glass went on dropping. There were passing showers of rain and a considerable swell was running on a rough sea. By the morning of the 17th, all the ships were making heavy weather of it. In fact, though again not made clear in the log, the weather quickly became so bad that the destroyers had to heave to, and subsequently

---

[430] It is known that *Sheffield's* ASDIC dome was carried away completely in a terrible storm in February 1943, *possibly* due to the towing wires of the paravanes she was streaming accidentally crossing and passing close under the ship's keel in the manner of scissors. (Shades of *Courageous* and her paravane problems in WW1.)

[431] Some sources say that *Southampton* had embarked 500 RAF personnel for Malta and some troops for garrisoning Gibraltar. However, her log makes no reference to this and the author has therefore discounted it. (It might well be true that *Manchester* had such personnel aboard.) The fact that it was *Southampton* which was sent off on 'lone errands' away from the convoy, to check out this or that suspicious sighting or contact, would suggest that she was travelling with only her normal complement of 800 men aboard, and that she was not burdened with a large number of airmen and troops.

return to port, no longer able to continue their protective anti-submarine role for the convoy. This screening task had to be taken up by the cruisers, although, fortunately, the chances of submarine attack in such heavy weather were fairly remote.

For her part, *Southampton* was rolling 40° to port by 1300, having to put some of her best seamen to the dangerous task of securing the preventer chain on the fo'c'sle at about that time, and having to heave-to for 15 minutes at 1520 to secure the starboard whaler which was coming adrift in the seas crashing inboard. The soldiers and airmen in the transports were having a torrid time.

Photograph reproduced by courtesy of the Royal Naval Museum, Portsmouth.

A 'Southampton-Class' cruiser, probably HMS *Sheffield*, with her forward turrets trained abeam to reduce the risks of damage and flooding from the force of the heavy seas breaking aboard. Doubtless, this mirrors the conditions often experienced by HMS *Southampton* during her northern patrol duties and now being experienced by her in mid-Atlantic.

A ship was sighted at about 1600 and, now lacking any destroyers for the task, the escort commander ordered *Southampton* to investigate. *Southampton* soon found that the stranger was accompanied by another ship, half-hidden in the prevailing conditions. Initially these two ships failed to respond to the identifying challenge, and, as their silhouettes were unfamiliar, *Southampton's* company were promptly sent to Action Stations. However, the strangers turned out to be two frigates, the newly-built *Anenome* and *La Malouine*, the latter having been 'acquired' by the RN after the Fall of France.

At 1716 *Southampton's* port lifebuoy was swept away overboard as the ship made its way back to rejoin the convoy, and at 1015 next morning the Sounding Boom had to be secured on 'B' Gundeck - a token of the manner in which *Southampton* had been taking it 'green over the bows'. By noon on the 18th they were at 47° 58' N, 19° 04' W, that is, at the latitude of Lorient, but some 620 miles to the west of it. The weather was beginning to moderate and the speed of the convoy had risen progressively, now attaining 17 knots and more.

Southampton had been keeping in visual touch with *Manchester* as part of the screen for the convoy, but, at 1218, *Southampton* parted company to search for an enemy tanker which had been reported, sending her hands to Action Stations when smoke was sighted on the horizon, and going to 28 knots when the smoke resolved itself into two ships steaming at high speed. However, an exchange of signals soon identified the two ships as the aircraft-carrier *Furious* and the cruiser *Dido*. (These two ships had left the convoy and were now westward bound for the Azores. The *'Hurricane'* aircraft being carried on *Furious* were being flown from the Azores to the British Desert Air Force in Egypt via a refuelling and 'staging' post in a French Colony in Central Africa which General de GAULLE, now leading the 'Free French Forces', had organised.)

At 1715 *Southampton* sighted another ship, closing up her 6-inch Defence Watch as she challenged the stranger, and establishing that she was the AMC *Marsdale*. It was not until 1100 on the 19th that *Southampton*, heading back to rejoin the convoy, sighted *Manchester* and was able to resume her place in the screen an hour later, coming down to 17 knots after a considerable period of hard steaming.

A merchant vessel was sighted at 1550, subsequently identified by *Manchester* as the *Clan McNab*. *Manchester* and the SS *Franconia* now parted company with the convoy to head straight on for Gibraltar. *Southampton* then took station ahead of the convoy. The sea was now calm, the risk of submarine attack was thus at an increased level, and it was now that the absence of escorting destroyers might really begin to make itself felt. The convoy began to zig-zag, and *Southampton* exercised at making emergency turns. Her Asdic Cabinet Crew was closed up. The Zig-zag pattern was changed. Tension was mounting, especially when an Asdic Contact was made at 1525, *Southampton* immediately changing course to the bearing indicated but losing the contact despite a search. She went back to her screening position. The convoy and its escort were now on the latitude of Cape St Vincent, but still far out at sea.

At 0850 on the 21st November *Clan Frazer* suddenly hoisted 'Not Under Control' signal balls, her steering gear having jammed. Happily, she hauled down her worrying signal just five minutes later. The convoy had now almost arrived at its rendezvous position, and speed was reduced to 8 knots, with a new zig-zag pattern. A warship was sighted at 1217, when the convoy was at 38° 34' N, 19° 06' W, and the hands were sent to Action Stations. However, the ship was speedily identified as *Sheffield,* heading for the rendezvous.[432] At 1335 *Southampton* was able to hand over the convoy to *Sheffield's* charge.

Southampton then sped to Gibraltar at 29 knots, sighting two lone merchantmen and the destroyer *Wishart*, before entering harbour by the North Gate to secure in Berth 3 at about 1400. She was indeed badly in need of fuel, and embarked 1,275 tons from 1530 to 2015. At 1845 the admiral commanding 'Force H' (Vice Admiral SOMERVILLE) came aboard for a quick visit before returning to *Renown*. On the 23rd November the aircraft-carrier *Argus* went into dry dock, and the destroyers *Faulknor* and *Despatch* arrived. By way of light relief and adding a touch of normality the 2nd whaler went away

---

[432] Some accounts put the convoy further west at 38° 50' N and 18° 27'W, and say they continued to circle for two days before destroyers arrived at the rendezvous to relieve *Sheffield,* and escort the convoy into Gibraltar, *Sheffield* racing ahead of them.

sailing in the blue, sunblessed waters. However, there was a 'worm in Paradise', for there was a Yellow Warning at 1715, and six rounds were fired by the 4-inch guns at an unidentified aircraft on the port side. At 2010 a lighter secured alongside and the embarkation of baggage began.

At 0930 on the 24th CS 18 came on board from *Manchester* and inspected the Ship's Company, having a quiet and encouraging word here and there, before addressing the Ship's Company as a whole. Divine Service followed, and, bearing in mind what has been said, it is to be believed that the prayers were generally heartfelt.

It seems convenient to review Alf's voyaging to date, now that a new phase is about to start.

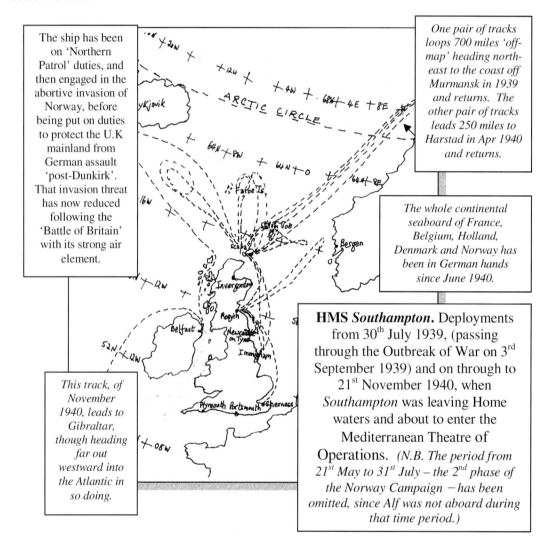

The ship has been on 'Northern Patrol' duties, and then engaged in the abortive invasion of Norway, before being put on duties to protect the U.K mainland from German assault 'post-Dunkirk'. That invasion threat has now reduced following the 'Battle of Britain' with its strong air element.

One pair of tracks loops 700 miles 'off-map' heading north-east to the coast off Murmansk in 1939 and returns. The other pair of tracks leads 250 miles to Harstad in Apr 1940 and returns.

The whole continental seaboard of France, Belgium, Holland, Denmark and Norway has been in German hands since June 1940.

This track, of November 1940, leads to Gibraltar, though heading far out westward into the Atlantic in so doing.

HMS *Southampton*. Deployments from 30th July 1939, (passing through the Outbreak of War on 3rd September 1939) and on through to 21st November 1940, when *Southampton* was leaving Home waters and about to enter the Mediterranean Theatre of Operations. *(N.B. The period from 21st May to 31st July – the 2nd phase of the Norway Campaign – has been omitted, since Alf was not aboard during that time period.)*

Alf's Voyages since 30th July 1939 in HMS *Southampton*.					
Farthest North	Off Murmansk	**72 N** 30E	*F/North (ever)*	Off Murmansk	**72 N** 30E
Farthest South	Gibraltar	**39 N** 05 E	*F/ South (ever)*	Simonstown	**34 S** 18 E
Farthest East	Off Murmansk	72 N **30E**	*F/East (ever)*	Ras Asir	12 N **51 E**
Farthest West	Atlantic Ocean	38 N **19W**	*F/West (ever)*	New York, U.S.A.	41 N **74 W**

Alf had now crossed the Arctic Circle – another first for him, and he had gone on to cross that line three more times. He was thus now well-qualified as a 'Bluenose'. In fact, he had been much further North than ever before, reaching about 72° N (just 18° from the North Pole). This latitude was evidently a northern record for a British warship.

Photograph reproduced by courtesy of the Imperial War Museum, London, Negative No. A 2.390.

HMS *Southampton,* possibly photographed on the instance of her leaving the convoy at speed, to head into Gibraltar for badly-needed fuel. Note the barrels of the Multiple Pom-Pom of the near ship silhouetted against the sky and creating a part-frame for the picture.

To return to 24ᵗʰ November at Gibraltar, Aircraft L2333B was disembarked after the Divine Service was completed. Piloted by PO Pilot BLACKWELL, the plane was taxied to *Manchester* and officer, crew and machine joined that ship.

Southampton embarked 67 bags of mail for passage, and took in more baggage. At 2157 *Sheffield* entered harbour after her stint of guarding the convoy. In the darkness at 0545 *Southampton* began to embark RAF and Military personnel. There were 1,370 RAF personnel in total, destined from Gibraltar for Alexandria. *Southampton* embarked 600 of them, the remainder being embarked in *Manchester*. This was all a part of the highly complex 'Operation Collar'. *Southampton* proceeded at 0732, passing the mole two minutes later and forming up with the 18ᵗʰ C.S and a destroyer screen. *Ark Royal, Renown, Sheffield* and *Despatch* also left harbour and formed up with the Fleet. They were heading into the Mediterranean on a course just slightly south of due east, zig-zagging as they went....

In the year 2001, former Wireless Operator Bernard DEEKS, who was one of the RAF men in the convoy, would write to the author, *"Our voyage had started on HMT 'Franconia' which departed Glasgow on 15th November 1940. We were transferred to HMS 'Southampton' in Gibraltar Harbour at around 0400 on 25th November. The transfer was by lighter, with full kit. I heard that someone missed his footing and went in the drink, though he was pulled out O.K."*

"We sailed at 0500 and quickly built up a good head of steam. On allocation to a mess, I think I was first to make for the 'heads' as the ship's motion at speed and zig-zagging was something quite different from my RAF marine craft days, and different again from the slow roll of the 'Franconia'. However, 'Jack' made us most welcome. We must have been a pain in the neck to the company, having so many extra bods getting in the way. In regard to messing, well food was brought to the mess by, I suppose, designated orderlies. Sleeping arrangements another matter. I found a hangar aft and dossed down there, but as the water got into my 'ration' of deck I moved therefrom to the benches, where I lashed myself on to some boxes of tools. I've had worse. I don't know how the officers fared, as I was only 'lower deck'."

"You mention something you've heard about RAF bods possibly helping with the ammunition when the ship came to action stations, but this is news to me. I can only remember some on the bridge doing aircraft recognition, and RAF cooks helping out in the galley - the latter heralded by a 'pipe' which we learnt was 'RAF Cooks to the Galley!' I can only speak for those of us who were on Southampton - I have no knowledge of those on Manchester. I do remember coming on deck one morning and finding a sight to behold, for there were ships all around as far as one could see. That is one of many sights still very clear in my mind."

Part of 'Force H' had accompanied the troopships of the convoy in from the Atlantic through the Pillars of Hercules into the Mediterranean Sea, and *Renown, Ark Royal, Southampton, Manchester,* and their attendant destroyers, which, as we have seen, had put out from Gibraltar, joined them at sea that same day, and the whole force, proceeded eastwards towards Malta and Alexandria, keeping close to the North African coast. *Ark Royal* was operating her aircraft from time to time. At 1715 on the 26th, *Manchester, Wishart and Encounter* parted company. (They were going to escort the convoy, which was on a slightly different course from the Fleet.) The weather remained good.

Next morning, Wednesday the 27th, a vessel was sighted ahead which was identified as *Manchester* with the convoy, and *Southampton*, accompanied by *Firedrake*, set an interception course to join *Manchester*, lowering her Asdic Dome as she closed and taking station ahead of CS 18. At 1000, *Southampton* executed an emergency turn, for a destroyer on the starboard beam had a submarine contact. *Southampton* set a Listening Watch on her Asdic and took station astern of *Manchester*. At 1055 her hands were sent to Action Stations, for aircraft from *Ark Royal,* scouting ahead of the Fleet, had spotted and reported enemy surface ships.

The cruisers were almost immediately ordered to take up positions in the van of the Fleet, and parted company with the convoy. It was at about this time that the Fleet was joined from the eastward by *Newcastle*, the County-Class cruiser *Berwick*, and the old battleship *Ramilles*, which had all come through the Sicilian Narrows. The total force, led by Admiral SOMERVILLE in *Renown*, was now coming together, though the ships arriving from the east would need to reverse their course before becoming an integral part of the oncoming fleet. They were about to do so and the assembled ships would then be a considerable force. The visibility was extreme, the sea was smooth and there was a slight south-east wind of Force 3.

At 1155 *Berwick* and *Newcastle* joined the van, and *Ramillies* completed her turn and joined *Renown*, steaming behind the cruisers in the van of the Fleet. Masts were sighted above the horizon almost dead ahead at 1205, and, by 1215, these had resolved into an array of Italian cruisers and destroyers bearing from 343° to 013°, the fleets closing very rapidly on each other. At 1216 the enemy opened fire, and the British ships began to reply two minutes later at a range of about 23,000 yards.

At 1222 the enemy turned away, their Admiral having apparently lost his nerve. *Southampton* concentrated her fire on the destroyers, shifting to the cruisers eleven minutes later, and continuing in chase, not ceasing fire until 1308, by which time the enemy ships, travelling at extreme speed, were out of range. All this can be reconstructed from the log of *Southampton*. However, from various sources it is possible to widen the story of what had happened.

[*The combined British Fleet had proved to be more powerful than the Italian Admiral CAMPIONI had been led to believe, as he headed south from Sardinia to intercept it, leading his fleet of two battleships, seven 8" cruisers and sixteen destroyers. Following the serious losses suffered by the Italian Fleet during the recent Fleet Air Arm raid at Taranto, CAMPIONI had been given orders not to risk his two battleships unless he were confronted by a 'decisively' inferior force. It was known to the Italians that 'Force H' was inferior in ships to Admiral CUNNINGHAM's force in the Eastern Mediterranean, and it was therefore Force H which CAMPIONI had decided to attack. He had also asked for bombing support from the Italian air forces in Sicily and Sardinia.*]

Luckily for the British, as we have already seen, aircraft flying from *Ark Royal*, (and also, it seems, a Short '*Sunderland*' flying boat, flying on air-patrol out from Malta), did an excellent job in spotting and reporting both parts of this Italian force (at that time in two separate groups about ten miles apart from each other) doing so whilst the nearer of those two groups was still some 60 miles north of SOMERVILLE's ships. The Italians were reportedly closing at about 15 knots.

This interception by the aircraft gave Admiral SOMERVILLE time to organise the formation of his ships, with the cruisers *Sheffield, Manchester, Newcastle* and *Berwick* leading the way in line abreast at about 30 knots, supported by the battlecruiser *Renown*. [Some accounts put *Southampton* in an intermediate position, shielding the aircraft-carrier *Ark Royal,* and the destroyers in rear. However, this placement of *Southampton* is clearly incorrect. She was in the van with her sisters.[433]]

---

[433] The log of *Southampton* simply shows her as being in the van with the other cruisers. In his evidence to the subsequent Court of Enquiry, Captain LARCOM of the *Sheffield* said the British cruisers were in echelon, *Manchester* leading, then *Southampton, Newcastle, Sheffield* and *Berwick*   Captain BROOKE of *Southampton* criticised *Newcastle* and *Berwick* for 'failing to take up their proper stations in the line', which had perforce led to undue bunching by *Manchester, Southampton* and *Sheffield*. Captain BROOKE said that the bunching "*risked the danger of blanking each other's fire and took a disproportionate part of the Captain's attention*". Clearly, all the cruisers were in slight echelon, virtually in line abreast, with *Manchester* (Flag) just ahead, and *Berwick* well out on the starboard wing of the line.

The *Ark Royal* had already launched further planes to observe and report the movements by the Italian Fleet. Admiral SOMERVILLE sent the troopships away to the south-east, to keep them clear from the impending action. They were escorted by the elderly cruiser *Despatch*, 4,850 tons.

Photograph reproduced by courtesy of the Imperial War Museum, London, Negative No. A 2347.

Two of the four Southampton-Class cruisers engaged in the action, most probably *Newcastle* and *Sheffield*, with their 6-inch 'A', 'B', 'X' and 'Y' turrets in action, firing at the fleeing Italian Fleet. Just visible out on the horizon is the 8-inch cruiser *Berwick*, with her distinctive 'humped back', due to her aircraft hangar being sited well aft.

Midshipman Thomas RUCK-KEENE in *Southampton* was critical of the fact that Admiral SOMERVILLE did not order his ships to haul in the paravanes which they were streaming (to increase their speed by the knot or two which, Tom said, *'would have made so much difference'*).[434] Tom RUCK-KEENE was also critical that the relatively slow *Ramillies* did not start her 180° turn into line until she was abeam of the first line of SOMERVILLE's quickly oncoming ships, thus falling well behind them. He said it would have been much better had she turned at once, and allowed herself to be overhauled from aft. As it was, she was never able to enter properly into the action, which became known as 'The Battle of Spartivento', after the nearby cape of that name in the extreme south-east of Sardinia.

As we have seen, the Italian cruisers, in the van of their fleet, opened fire at 1222, at 26,000 yards, straddling *Manchester* with their very first salvo.[435] Some accounts say that the Admiral then ordered the British cruisers to fall back upon *Renown*, before the Italian battleships, then looming up on the distant horizon, entered the action. However, after firing two broadsides, the Italian cruisers, and the remainder of the Italian fleet,

---

[434] He was probably unaware the *Berwick* had previously told Vice-Admiral HOLLAND that she could only do 27 knots - though she must have well exceeded that speed during the action.

[435] Midshipman Thomas RUCK-KEENE gives quite different times, running about 80 minutes later. Captain BROOKE's times seem to run just slightly later than the 'official' ones.

turned away to the north-east, heading back to their base at Naples. Admiral CAMPIONI had decided that the British looked too resolute and that the odds were too great against him. The British cruisers therefore continued in the van at around 29.5 to 31.5 knots, with *Sheffield* (flanked by her cruiser-consorts) five cables ahead of *Renown* (Flag), and a stern-chase developed, in which the 15" guns of the 'X' and 'Y' turrets of the fast-fleeing Italian battleships *Vittorio Veneto* and *Guilio Cesare* quickly became engaged in support of the fire of their cruisers.

Author's collection. An anonymous postcard. Note that the image has been 'reversed' for 'artistic reasons'.

HMS *Renown* at high speed, and rigged for running her paravanes. (The twin cables which run down to her forefoot - and which show here as a dark vertical line coming down from the eyes of the ship - relate to paravane-towing.) So this picture gives an idea of how *Renown* might have looked at the Battle of Spartivento. However, her guns would have been at high elevation to reach the great range required, and she would have been fully 'cleared for action'. *[That is far from being the case in this picture, which was evidently taken pre-war. In fact, her decks are crowded with men and her jackstaff has not been unshipped. (Unusually, she is wearing the Union Flag at her jackstaff whilst at sea, denoting that she is actually 'dressed overall'.)]*

The Italians seemed to be concentrating most of their fire on *Manchester* (the leading British cruiser), which was flying the flag of Vice-Admiral Lancelot HOLLAND. That fire was accurate, and *Manchester* was soon being further straddled, not only by 8" shells from the cruisers, but now by 15" shells from the distant battleships. *Berwick* was also receiving a good share of attention from the Italians, and the other cruisers were also being straddled at times.[436] By now it was obvious that the British cruisers would bear

---

[436] Vice Admiral HOLLAND's report to the subsequent Board of Enquiry said that the Italian fire was remarkably accurate for range and believed this was due to their use of stereoscopic rangefinders (as opposed to the less-effective British coincidence rangefinders.) The French used stereoscopic rangefinders and had tipped him off about the Italians' use of them. Interestingly, Admiral HOLLAND referred to 'RDF rangefinding', for which high hopes were nursed (and with which some British battlecruisers were already

the brunt of the action and Vice-Admiral HOLLAND (C.S 18) was ordered to take overall command since *Renown* and *Ramillies*, strive for speed as they might (and did) were only going to be able to play minor roles.[437]

The British ships were replying, with their forward 'A' and 'B' turrets constantly in action, and their 'X' and 'Y' turrets aft, trained round on extreme forward bearings, coming into action whenever either or both would bear. The 6" guns of the cruisers were at high elevation, with the breeches sunk deep in their wells, for they were firing at their maximum range. *Berwick,* fitted with longer-reaching 8" guns, was in slightly better case.

Photograph reproduced by courtesy of the Imperial War Museum, London, Negative No. A. 2349.

Two of the cruisers, believed to be *Newcastle* and *Sheffield* driving forward at over 30 knots, with heavy shells from the retreating Italian Fleet falling between them. Both cruisers have their main guns at almost full elevation, with their 'X' and 'Y' turrets trained round as far forward as possible. Once again, the wartime censor saw fit to obliterate a feature on the side of the '*Walrus*' Hangar.

Renown, struggling to keep up the fast pace, came into action with her long-range 15" guns, mainly concentrating on the Italian cruisers, for she scarcely had the range to hit the Italian battleships so far were they ahead. (A '*Walrus*' aircraft, launched by *Sheffield*, was spotting for her.) *Ramillies*, labouring even harder and falling further and further astern, only got off a couple of salvoes, as compared, for example, with the total of 86 salvoes fired by *Renown*.

As we shall see in a moment, each of the cruisers in the forward line had expended much more ammunition than the 86 of *Renown* - say an average of 240 salvoes per ship. That had involved a great deal of hard and exhausting work by the ammunition

fitted.) He suggested that firing triple salvoes in line would be the best method to use with it, for 'end-on' engagements.

[437] *Renown* was rated at a maximum speed of 29 knots and *Ramillies* at a maximum of only 21 knots. The Italians were evidently fleeing at something approaching 33 knots.

parties. There were large numbers of empty cordite cases to be cleared away from the turrets afterwards. (See photograph on the following page.)

Hits were certainly scored on the Italian ships, a fire being started in one of their cruisers, and a destroyer, which had appeared to be laying a smoke-screen, being severely damaged, set on fire, and quickly retiring behind the other ships. The destroyer was later discovered to be the *Lanciere*. However, the superiority in speed of the Italian ships enabled them to draw steadily away, and by 1246 they were beyond the horizon, heading for Sardinia and sanctuary.

Manchester had been frequently straddled during the action, and she had been very fortunate not to have been hit. *Berwick*, out on the right wing, had not been so lucky, as she had received two hits from 8" shells, one of which had disabled her 'Y' turret. There had been casualties, including some fatalities. *Southampton* had been straddled eight or nine times, and hit once, though, luckily, the shell had failed to explode.

Southampton had fired 271 salvoes (totalling 750 rounds), of which 188 (approx. 70%) had been from her 'A' and 'B' turrets. *Manchester* had done incredibly well, getting off no less than 912 rounds, of which 62% had been from her forward turrets. *Southampton's rate* of firing salvoes was evidently well up with her other sisters, with all the cruisers firing armour-piercing shells to maximum capacity, i.e. nominally all three guns in each turret, every time that the turret bore on a target.

However, rather than the 'potential maximum' of $(271 \times 3) = 813$ rounds, *Southampton* had fired only 750 rounds. The saturation effect of her gunfire *per salvo* would therefore have been rather less than that of her sisters. It is clear from this that *Southampton* had problems, the main one being that the right gun of 'A' Turret had a shell jammed in the breech right from the start of the action. A few salvoes were also missed by that turret when the cordite hoist jammed until the secondary (manual) supply was established. The centre gun of 'B' Turret also missed a few salvoes when the centre cordite hoist became jammed, though this was soon rectified when it was found that the lower door had not been quite closed. (Author: Seemingly, a manual supply was established in the interim - see below.) And 'Y' Turret missed two salvoes due to slow loading.[438]

The slight 'jinking' of the British cruisers, which was left to the individual captains to conduct as they saw fit, plus rather larger deviations from the direct line at times, to open up the 'A' arcs and thus to bring the 'X' and 'Y' turrets into the action, seems to have had the beneficial effect of generally leading the cruisers to steer away from successive well-laid enemy salvoes.

The main problem experienced during the action was that of keeping the line correct. This was attributable to several factors, (a) The fine inclination, (b) The frequent alteration of enemy course at high speed, combined with the long time of flight of the shells at such extreme range, (c) The large number of salvoes fired by two turrets only, (d) Canted trunnions due to frequent alterations of course which caused a list when firing

---

[438] Captain BROOKE's report of the action made this all clear. The jamming of the shell in 'A' turret gun was due to a testing tube which had been accidentally dropped in the loading tray and rammed into the chamber with the shell. This shell could not be withdrawn until an ejector was used after the action. Towards the end of the action there was also a problem with the left guns of 'A' and 'B' turrets, which failed to run out until put to full depression. The jamming of the cordite hoist to 'A' Turret was due to the bottoms of charges having fallen off and built up in the floor-well.

on extreme forward bearings, (e) The inexperience of the Rate Observer, who needed to be coached by the Control Officer in the early stages of the action. The difficulty of obtaining co-operation between the Rate and Spotting Groups, which had become increasingly obvious when, later in the action, the inclinations became very fine and the range extreme. Generally, the rangetaking was good and the spread was under 250 yards for most of the action.[439] [One might add that, as Captain BROOKE's report makes clear, that there was a high 'degree of difficulty', for the Italian ships were mostly hull-down on the horizon, at times with only their mastheads showing and frequently obscured by smoke.]

Photograph reproduced by courtesy of the Imperial War Museum, London, Negative No. A 2416.

Aboard *Sheffield*, her gunners are removing empty 'Cordite' Cases , re-capping them and sending them down for subsequent return to the Ordnance Stores ashore. The same process would have been going on aboard *Southampton* and the other ships engaged. It was the build-up of empty cases like these during the action which had caused some of the problems aboard *Southampton*, reducing the volume of her salvoes.

Bernard DEEKS, who, as we have seen, was one of the 760 RAF personnel embarked in *Southampton*, would write to the author a half-century later, "*We were accommodated in the torpedomen's mess on the starboard side of the ship, under the forward 6" gun turrets. When the battle opened I have to say I was a bit frightened, having been 'battened down' with all the watertight doors closed. When the guns opened up I think the word 'terrified' would be more to the point. The noise was horrendous and the motion of the ship keeling over a bit worrying. After each salvo the lights went out,*

---

[439] The appendix to Captain BROOKE's report shows that the TS made two mistakes when applying the spotting rules.

except for some pale blue ones, which gave just a little illumination. Also, water trickled slowly on to our deck. It was believed to have come from the cooling system for the guns."

"The running commentary given by the Damage Control Officer over the ship's P.A. system was reassuring, though, and, when it was all over, the Navy lads said it was a good job we had not seen the near-misses! Eventually, in their time-honoured way, the Italians turned and ran....and that was the Battle of Cape Spartivento. The only casualty on Southampton was a torpedoman from our mess deck who had a watertight door swing back in his face. It did not improve his looks, but at least he survived - for that action at least."

Bernard DEEKS had said that he did not remember any of the RAF lads helping to handle ammunition, but Shipwright 'Dusty' MILLER recalled that the ammunition hoist to 'B' gun turret broke down during the action, and some of the RAF members on board manned the hoist and passed up the ammunition. Subsequently, the commander of HMS *Southampton* (Commander TINLEY), congratulated them, and said he believed this to have been the first naval action fought by members of the Royal Air Force.

One other point worth mentioning is that just after 1300 two large liners flying Vichy French tricolours were sighted to the NNE, when the British cruisers were some 30 miles from the Sardinian coast. Their presence was ignored by the opposing fleets.

Soon after 1300, Vice Admiral SOMERVILLE withdrew, and set a south-easterly course at a somewhat reduced speed, to rejoin the troop transports and their escort. He would thus renew their protection, which was in line with his standing orders to 'ensure the safe and timely arrival of the convoy'.

But let's get back to *Southampton's* log, at 1559, when she and her consorts had closed *Renown*, and the cruisers and battlecruiser were heading back to rejoin the convoy. Perhaps, to put a sort of seal on the surface action, it is worth mentioning that Mr S.B. COBB Commissioned Gunner (T) of *Southampton*, made out a report after the battle concerning Depth-Charges Type D, 3 in number: Pistol Mk IV, 3 in number: Keys, Depth-Charge, 3 in number; *'Dropped when Engaging Italian Surface Force'*. Captain BROOKE's narrative of the action, as given to Vice-Admiral HOLLAND, makes clear that the depth-charges on deck were jettisoned before battle was joined and this was clearly a reference to that order. The same report by Captain BROOKE states that *Southampton's* 'Walrus' aircraft was readied, but not flown off as *'it could have served no useful purpose'*.

At 1630 *Southampton's* Action HA was closed up and *Renown* and *Ark Royal* opened fire on ten enemy aircraft. At 1646 *Southampton* also opened fire. *Ark Royal* was near-missed by bombs minutes later, the Italian bombers then withdrawing, but the Fleet was still being shadowed by several seaplanes. At 2215 a listening watch was set on the Asdics, but at 2245 the dome was housed.

At 0137 on the 28th a heavy underwater explosion was heard and the ship went to 1st Degree Readiness as the Fleet neared Pantellaria. At 0730 ships soon identified as *York, Glasgow* and *Gloucester* were sighted ahead as the HA Alarm to Arms was sounded, fortunately a false alarm, as the aircraft were *'Swordfish'*, presumably from *Illustrious* and scouting ahead for the Fleet from Alexandria. The destroyer *Hotspur*, evidently living up to her name, drew alongside at 0820 to pass dispatches to *Southampton* by line, and the Fleet from Alexandria hove in sight ten minutes later, *Warspite and Valiant* being readily identifiable, as well as the great aircraft-carrier *Illustrious*. By 0904 the combined Fleets were assembled, still heading east. At 0945 a destroyer in the port side column reported a mine in sight, and opened fire on it.

Southampton closed on *Manchester* at 1000, just before the *Clan Frazer* and *Clan Forbes* parted company and headed in to Malta, evidently escorted by *Glasgow*. The ships *Manchester, Southampton* and *New Zealand Star* continued through the Sicilian Narrows with *Warspite, Valiant* and *Illustrious* providing protection, the battleships of the Mediterranean Fleet and their attendant cruisers and destroyers parting company at 1120 to return to Alexandria by a parallel but slightly more northerly 'protective' route.

At 1155 *Southampton's* lookouts reported *Glasgow* being bombed by aircraft off Malta and *Southampton's* Action HA were closed up. At 1217 *Illustrious* flew off aircraft and at 1710 *Southampton* took up her screening position in the pre-arranged pattern. The convoy speed was 15 knots. There were signs that submarines were about, *Southampton* commencing an A/S Sweep at 1800 and hearing two depth-charge explosions at 2115. A 'fused key' led to the sweep being discontinued at 2235, but it was resumed at 2300.

At 0647 on the 29th a destroyer reported an Asdic Contact, and the convoy, which was already zig-zagging, took further avoiding action. A mine was sighted at 1057 and gunfire was opened on it, this fire being supplemented with Bren-gun and rifle fire five minutes later, probably relieving quite a lot of tension for those whose fingers were on the triggers. Fourteen minutes later the A/S reported an underwater explosion which was believed to be the mine detonating as it sank. At 1350 *Southampton* was ordered to join the C-in-C (flying his flag in *Warspite*), sighting the Battle Fleet at 1450, proceeding at 29 knots and taking station astern.

At noon of the 30th November *Southampton* was coming alongside at Alexandria, and, at 1255 the RAF Units fell in for leaving the ship. A Draft for the battleship *Barham* followed them off the ship, and the Army Units left at 1330.[440] *Southampton* immediately oiled to make up for the 1,325 miles she had run, and embarked ammunition. She would now have to get back to normal, clean ship and paint her scorched gun-barrels.

Here, at 30th November 1940, is the last surviving log-record for HMS *Southampton*. Alf will have been very busy at his 4-inch gun battery. His signature has not appeared as OOW during this hectic voyage. This last log was signed by Lt Commander (N) ROSS, then by Captain BROOKE, but countersigned by Vice-Admiral L.HOLLAND (as 18 CS) on 4th March 1941, eight weeks after *Southampton's* demise.[441]

---

[440] Many, perhaps most of the men in this draft were surely fated to lose their lives when the *Barham* was torpedoed by a U-Boat in the Eastern Mediterranean on 25th Nov 1941, quickly turned on her beam ends over to port, and blew up with an enormous explosion. Having seen newsreel film of the colossal explosion it seems incredible that well over 200 men of her ship's company somehow managed to survive.

[441] Sadly, Vice-Admiral Lancelot HOLLAND, who was evidently a very sensible and able commander of naval forces, was fated to lose his life when in command of the battlecruiser *Hood* which

Photograph reproduced by courtesy of the Imperial War Museum, London, Negative No. A 2459.

The aircraft-carrier *Ark Royal* being near-missed by a stick of bombs from a high-flying Italian aircraft. A Southampton-Class cruiser is half in view on the right.

The 'official accounts' of the voyage state that, after the Italian surface ships had fled out of range, the Italian bombers at last appeared and bombed *Ark Royal*, near missing her. (See above photo.)

At much the same time a strike force of aircraft from *Ark Royal* attacked the Italian battleships, pretty well out of sight of SOMERVILLE's ships, though the smoke of the Italian HA fire was just distinguishable to the Control Officers. However, the aerial attack was apparently without effect. Admiral SOMERVILLE then handed the three troopships over to the protection of Admiral CUNNINGHAM's force, which had sailed from Alexandria on 25th November, and which *Southampton* and *Manchester* now joined. Admiral CUNNINGHAM's augmented force then escorted the troopships through the Sicilian Narrows and on to Alexandria, which was reached safely on 30th November. This had been a highly successful operation by the British Navy and had demonstrated some weaknesses in the Italian Naval and Air forces at that time

It seems a great shame that the Admiralty saw fit to arrange a Board of Enquiry *"to enquire into the reasons why: (i) Admiral SOMERVILLE broke off the action at 1310, and (ii) why a second TSR flight from Ark Royal did not attack the enemy battleships."* The Board duly sat under the Presidency of the Admiral of the Fleet Lord CORK AND ORRERY, on 4th December 1940, at Gibraltar. Admiral SOMERVILLE was subsequently exonerated - but the whole affair 'left a nasty taste in the mouth', and hit naval morale in and around 'The Med' at a time when the Royal Navy had 'got its tail up' after seeing the Italians run at Spartivento, and, all unknowingly, was about to begin to

---

blew up on 24th May 1941 in the opening salvoes of a dramatic encounter with the mighty battleship *Bismark*.

need careful shepherding through a period of the greatest stress and loss. It must have re-awakened memories of men like Alf of the wretched 'stink' and undeserved shattering of reputations which had been associated with the *Goeben* and *Breslau* affair 26 years previously. Was the Admiralty going to launch into similar witch-hunts throughout WW2?[442]

Thomas RUCK-KEENE said: "*I think the RAF lads were mildly relieved to set foot on land again. It isn't everyone who meets the enemy's battle fleet on their first voyage. However, their conduct had been exemplary, especially in the case of those who helped to supply ammunition when a shell-hoist broke*". [Tom thus confirmed 'Dusty's' story, and, as we have seen, Captain BROOKE's report on the action said that a '*cordite hoist was fouled by the bottom of charges which dropped off*', and, '*Secondary supply by hand through the messdecks was begun at once*'.]

Southampton was at Alexandria briefly, being still listed as a part of the Home Fleet (CS 18), but attached to the Mediterranean Fleet. Whilst based at Alexandria she assisted to guard the Vichy French warships, where an uneasy 'truce' prevailed. Seizing this opportunity, Alf managed to send a Cablegram to his wife Alice which was date-stamped at London on 4th December 1940. It read, "*Am quite alright. Hope all well at home. Christmas Greetings You and Kiddies. Alf DAVIS*".

The ship then proceeded to Suez, which she reached on the 1st December. Whilst she was there, she discharged Midshipmen ALFORD, MOORE and HALIFAX, who were returning to England.[443] She then passed through the Canal to Aden, to gain the Red Sea. On the way through the Red Sea *Southampton* headed through a huge convoy carrying reinforcements and equipment for the Western Desert Force. Then she continued south past Somaliland, which was then held by the Italians, crossed the Equator and, as ordered by C-in-C East Indies shelled German tankers and Italian shipping at the strongly fortified port of Kismayu which stands at 0° 23' S.

This turned out to be a dangerous undertaking, as the defences had been 'stirred up' by an attack made by the South African Air Force an hour earlier, and the enemy shore batteries 'fired first' as *Southampton* closed in, carrying away her wireless aerials and battle ensign with their first salvo![444] Ranging on the shipping in the port was difficult as the ships had been moored in line ahead, with only 'one hull' but a 'dozen pairs of masts' visible in the viewfinder. Worse, *Southampton* had been ordered to fire only HE.[445] This meant that, due to risk of premature detonation on leaving the gun-muzzles, only four-gun salvoes could be fired from each pair of turrets, instead of the six-gun 'broadsides' possible with CPBC shells. After firing six salvoes it was found that the opposing shellfire was becoming 'a little hot', and *Southampton* quickly 'made smoke' and withdrew behind her own smokescreen. Air reconnaissance later established that at

---

[442] One positive outcome from the Author's point of view is that the witness statements do help to clarify the positioning of *Southampton* and her consorts during the Battle of Cape Spartivento, and generally do add 'colour'. (See ADM 116/4309 at TNA.)

[443] This is inferred from the Diary of Midshipman Barrie KENT.

[444] Captain BROOKE, probably wisely as it turned out, had deferred his attack for an hour, until sunset, but due to the need for security, had been unable to warn the Air Force by wireless of his decision.

[445] An apology was later received from C-in-C E.I. that he had no Gunnery Officer on his staff. "*Incredible but true*", commented Midshipman RUCK-KEENE.

least one ship had been severely damaged by the bombardment and was in a sinking condition.

Next morning the ship arrived at Mombassa, where the heat was described as 'appalling' by Midshipman RUCK-KEENE, who added that, *'the heat and shortage of beer apart, everyone liked the place and a good time was had by all'* during the week they spent there. One supposes that memories of being at this place in 1915 may have come flooding back to Alf, and even more so when *Southampton* arrived at Zanzibar on the morning of the 17th December. Here they stayed only long enough to pick up the Sultan of Zanzibar and the Governor Delegate of Aden, Mr HALL, before continuing southwards to 22° South of Latitude.[446]   Here *Southampton* made rendezvous with a large Allied convoy having the code WS 4B, which had come up from the Cape of Good Hope and Durban, escorted by the County Class cruisers *Shropshire* and *Devonshire,* and which was bound for the Middle East. On meeting the convoy, *Southampton* heaved to and transferred mails to *Devonshire,* which having been relieved by *Southampton*, then headed back to Durban. 'Dusty' duly noted that *Devonshire's* company were in cool tropical rig, whilst he and his shipmates were still in blues.

The convoy, which consisted of ten large liners carrying about 20,000 troops, headed northwards, soon crossing the Equator and maintaining a speed of 17½ knots over the next six days. These days proved uneventful, despite a navigational error which took the convoy within ten miles of Italian-held Eritrea. This occurred on Christmas Day, and Midshipman RUCK-KEENE wondered if that *'time-of-festivities'* was the reason for the apparent lack of response to their appearance off the Italian coastline. The convoy and its escort arrived safely at Alexandria.

Southampton had regained Suez on the 28th December having travelled 18,000 miles in less than eight weeks, of which 45 days had been at sea. During that time they had travelled from the Arctic Circle to at least 20° South, *'a most remarkable feat'* as Midshipman RUCK-KEENE pointed out. On arrival at Alexandria she became a unit of the 3rd Cruiser Squadron of the Mediterranean Fleet, of which *Kent* and *Southampton's* sisters *Glasgow,* and *Liverpool* had all been damaged by torpedoes, and the bridge of another sister, *Gloucester*, had been carried away by a bomb. The auguries for ships operating in the Mediterranean did not look good.

Alf had managed to send off a Christmas card (probably whilst he was at Alexandria on 30th November) *"from Daddy, with Love to All"*. This, and the cablegram already mentioned would prove to be Alf's last communications with his family. As always happened in the war, the prevailing need to maintain security and the matter of censorship, prevented any information about his condition and experiences being transmitted. One imagines, however, that Alf would have been pleased to be back in his 1913-15 'stamping grounds', and away from the fearful cold of Arctic waters.

---

[446] 'Dusty' MILLER and others say they actually continued south until they were off Durban, which lies at latitude 30° S. If so, even more memories would have come back to Alf, evocative of his late and greatly beloved first wife.

Southampton at speed in a rough sea, with the destroyer *Jaguar* laying a protective smokescreen. When he was at Alexandria in December 1940, Alf sent a copy of this fine photograph home to his family, enclosed as an integral part of a handsome Ship's Christmas Greeting Card

We'll now have a quick look at Alf's globe-trotting record up-to-date. Having done that (as shown overleaf), it seems appropriate to break off to consider what had been happening to his wife and children on the 'Home Front', before resuming the story of Alf's life on active service.

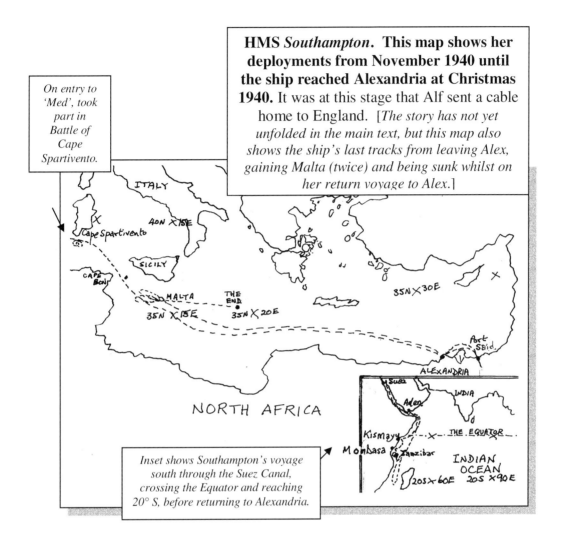

HMS *Southampton*. This map shows her deployments from November 1940 until the ship reached Alexandria at Christmas 1940. It was at this stage that Alf sent a cable home to England. [*The story has not yet unfolded in the main text, but this map also shows the ship's last tracks from leaving Alex, gaining Malta (twice) and being sunk whilst on her return voyage to Alex.*]

On entry to 'Med', took part in Battle of Cape Spartivento.

Inset shows Southampton's voyage south through the Suez Canal, crossing the Equator and reaching 20° S, before returning to Alexandria.

Alf's Voyages since 30th October 1940 in HMS *Southampton*.					
Farthest North	Cape Spartivento	**38 N** 10 E	*F/North (ever)*	Off Murmansk	**72 N** 30E
Farthest South	Off Madagascar	**20 S** 34 E	*F/ South (ever)*	Simonstown	**34 S** 18 E
Farthest East	Off Ras Asir	12 N **51 E**	*F/East (ever)*	Ras Asir	12 N **51 E**
Farthest West	Gibraltar	36 N **05W**	*F/West (ever)*	New York, U.S.A.	41 N **74 W**

Alf had equalled his farthest east position, off the Horn of Africa. He had also crossed the Equator twice more, making 12 crossings in all in his lifetime.

He had now ranged from 72° North to 34° South (i.e. 106 degrees out of a possible 180 degrees. (Say 59% of the max. vertical circumference of the globe).

And he had ranged from 51° East to 74° West (i.e. 125 degrees out of a possible 180 degrees. (Say 69% of the max. horizontal circumference of the globe).

This concludes Alf's travel-record, his final days all being in the 'Med' and thus well inside the above parameters.

Private Life

Alf's cablegram had been addressed to Mrs DAVIS at 'Orpington House, Bellingdon, Chesham, Bucks'. Clearly, then, he had received mail from his wife which had kept him reasonably up-to-date with the family situation.

Sure enough, in mid-1940 Alice had managed to get away from invasion-threatened Felixstowe, taking her baby son Richard and her younger step-daughter Jessica with her. Alice's elder step-children, Joan and Neville, had been withdrawn from their respective 'evacuee' homes, as arranged by Alf, and had eventually been taken to join Alice in the Buckinghamshire countryside, where she had found 'digs' in a pleasant, though small, and low-ceilinged bungalow with a large garden. It was owned by an old lady. The family were living in a couple of rooms in this bungalow, under very crowded conditions.

'*En route*', the two older children had stopped for a while in London, Joan staying with Alf's eldest sister, Nellie, and Neville with Alf's middle sister, Rose. Exactly what had transpired here will probably never be known, but, if adoption by these aunts was ever really in the wind, it had not gone ahead. Neville would, however, always remember his stay, and the way that his Aunt Rose had bought fine model soldiers and a die-cast model of a motorised gun-team for him. Rose, who was now very much a 'Londoner', was comfortable to be with and he had genuine affection for her. Aunt Nellie was pleasant enough, but very much Rose's elder sister, more acerbic, more well-to-do, kind, certainly, but determined to be 'in charge'. Nellie's sons, John in particular, had been generous to Neville during his short stay with Aunt Rose, giving him some of their old but high-quality toys. John and Ray were now grown-up, and would be serving in the Forces before too long. They took young Neville to the mews where the family horses were stabled, and took him riding in Rotten Row, which was a never-to-be-forgotten thrill for him.

An interesting thing had happened to Joan whilst she was staying with Nellie, for Joan had met a cousin, Joan Priscilla DAVIS, who was about her own age and the second daughter of Alf's brother, Jack, from whom Alf had parted 'brass rags', fourteen years previously. This was the only known encounter between any of the total of eleven children of the two brothers in Alf's lifetime.[447]

It might just be that NOT being 'adopted' by Rose and Nellie saved the lives of Neville and Joan, for the German Blitz caused colossal devastation all around the public houses occupied by the two ladies and their husbands. And, as previously mentioned, their younger sister Eva, to whom young Jessica might once have gone, would later have to be dug out of the wreckage of her pub at Clapham. Eva survived but she suffered head-injuries for which she later needed several operations, and never recovered fully.

It would be wrong to say that Joan and Neville had been happy to be restored to the charge of their step-mother. Considerable strains still remained, but the experiences the children had gained from being evacuated, and the elapsed time, meant they had 'grown up' to an extent. Also, other people and children (who were

---

[447] It took the author a huge amount of diligent research to track down these cousins in his later life. Their subsequent input has been fundamental to building up the history of the family and its interpersonal relationships.

not family members) were around, and this moderated the situation to some extent. Alice was still short-tempered, but she had mellowed to some degree. After a short time, Alice and the children moved on to Orpington House at Bellingdon, on the heights above Chesham. This was a large house, into which Alice's mother and father also moved from Felixstowe, her younger brother George Neville sometimes also staying there. It is assumed that the sale of the fine house, shop and workshop at Felixstowe (which probably 'went for a song' due to the expected German invasion) helped to pay for the purchase of Orpington House. A married couple also moved in as paying lodgers.

In the early days of their habitation there, all three of the elder children suddenly went down with the mumps or some such childhood illness, all approaching the feverish crisis at the same time of night of the same date. Jessica was taken into Alice's bed for comfort and reassurance, and Joan was taken into her Nan's bed. Thus, Neville, aged 10, had no 'mother' figure left over to give him comfort, desperately ill and frightened though he felt. Whereupon, his grandfather said, *"I'll take him in with me"*, and, strange as it felt to be 'mothered' by a man, Neville, initially very scared by his high fever, still cherishes the memory of the wonderfully secure feeling he had that night as he drifted off to sleep with the old man's strong carpenter's arm round his shoulders - weird though it was at first to feel the old man's striped flannel nightshirt against him and the odour of pipe tobacco in his nostrils.

Soon, as organised by her grandmother, Joan went off to live with a couple called the STANDRINGS who were school-teachers and who had a physically attractive and mentally 'brilliant' daughter of Joan's age. Unfortunately, this did nothing for Joan's already rather low self-esteem, especially as she was treated like a 'poor relation' by the STANDRINGs, though she did have the benefit of attending Dr Challoner's School, which had an excellent educational reputation. Neville attended the Council School in the valley, at Chesham. His education there was fairly rough and ready, though he does have a good memory of a master who was helpful and sensible in a very down-to-earth way. The country boys perceived Neville as a snob because his previous education (at Miss MULLINS' academy at Felixstowe) had been superior to theirs, and his speech had a different country accent to theirs. However, Neville experienced no bullying. Perhaps the independence of spirit he had gained from being evacuated somehow manifested itself in his bearing.

The children's lives were jogging along. They greatly missed the sea and the beaches of Felixstowe. But Neville and Jessica had a large garden to play in, with apple trees to pretend to 'parachute' out of, and chalky banks behind which to lie in ambush and to pretend to 'snipe' at people passing along the road outside – for Neville had found the rusted metal remains of a WW1 rifle in the garden and he had improvised a butt, a stock and a sling for it. Neville had also sat in the tight-fitting cockpit of a German Me 109 fighter which had been brought down almost intact, and was being displayed in a 'War Savings Week' exhibition in a park at Chesham. He thought of the men who were fighting and dying and wanted to 'do his bit' against the German bombers. The RAF had become the heroes defending Britain, and seemed to be gradually gaining the ascendancy. Neville had begun to make flying models of aircraft out of balsa-wood and doped tissue-paper. Non-flying, but accurate pre-fabricated 1/72nd scale model kits, some in wood but others in pioneering moulded plastic form, would soon be becoming available in the shops. The house often smelt of glue and dope.

The children's grandmother was cooking for the assembled family again, finding the best ways to improvise and 'stretch' meals from the still-reducing wartime rations. The chalky garden was full of stinging-nettles and Nan cooked them to make a spinach-like vegetable. The creamy layer on top of the milk was taken out of the bottle and beaten laboriously by hand into the tiny butter ration, to make the butter smoother and thinner to spread, so it would go further. Alice often worked at that hard task. Food-rationing made life difficult, but Alice also regularly contrived lunchtime sandwiches for the children, which were usually made from 'National Loaf' bread and a pickled 'sandwich spread'.

Alice was raising Little Richard, but unfortunately spoiling him. That is to say, when he made some unacceptable demand or other, Alice would initially say 'No', but if he kicked and yelled or screamed, rather than hold out against him, she would say *"Oh, if you really must"*, and give way to him. He thus became a rather spoiled and petulant child. His mother's raising of him seemed to be in strange contrast to the hard and determined way in which she had gone on with her elder step-children, and possibly signified that she was in a rather low physical and mental state. Her condition was probably seriously borne down by her concerns about Alf's safety, and the steadily increasing length of his unrelieved absence away at the war, coupled with continuing fears of German bombing and possible invasion.

The latest communications from Alf, showing that he was at Alexandria, had been rather alarming, for the war news was beginning to show that the Royal Navy was taking some serious losses in the Mediterranean. 'Lord HAW-HAW' (James JOYCE, the Irishman who broadcast from Germany and who was a skilled propagandist), kept claiming that the *Ark Royal* had been sunk, and, judging by his past form, one day he would be right. All too often, his claims about the sinking of naval vessels and suchlike presaged what the Admiralty or other authorities sooner or later had to admit was true. People detested Lord HAW-HAW, but they listened to him so that they might pick up the earliest news regarding possible harm coming to their loved ones. It was all very stressful.

Nevertheless, the family could only see Alf as being immortal. He was such an extrovert, resourceful and strong character, and powerful swimmer, that it was impossible to visualise him as drowning, even if his ship should, by some calamity, be sunk. It was all a matter of 'hanging on' and 'hoping against hope', until Alf came striding up the garden path of this large house, which he had never seen.

HMS *Southampton* (1939-41), continued:

O n the night of 5ᵗʰ/6ᵗʰ January 1941, *Southampton* departed from Alexandria for the Aegean Sea, carrying 500 troops for Malta, by a roundabout route which was intended to mask her intentions. She made rendezvous in the Aegean with CS 3 in *Gloucester* and the destroyers *Ilex* and *Janus,* and the four ships reached Malta safely on 8ᵗʰ January, where *Southampton* secured at Parlatorio Wharf and disembarked her troops. 'Dusty' says they tied up alongside HMS *Penelope*, by then familiarly known as HMS 'Pepperpot', because of the numerous shrapnel holes in her sides and superstructure sustained from continuous bombing in Malta. The 'Southamptons' probably 'identified' quite strongly with the 'Pepperpots', because *Southampton* had been in rather similar case after the Campaign in Norway.

The ships then proceeded westwards minus *Janus*, (*Southampton*, when travelling at 28 knots, just missing an impact with a floating mine) and meeting up by arrangement in the Narrows with the new Dido-Class cruiser *Bonaventure* and the destroyers *Hasty, Hero* and *Hereward,* who were escorting an eastbound convoy bound for Malta, the ships in the convoy being heavily loaded with ammunition, crated *'Hurricane'* fighter aircraft, foodstuffs, etc. Admiral SOMERVILLE's Force H, consisting of the battleship *Malaya,* the aircraft-carrier *Ark Royal,* and the cruiser *Sheffield,* had been escorting this convoy during its eastward voyage from Gibraltar, during which it had been bombed unsuccessfully by Italian *'Savoia 79'* aircraft. At 0800 on the 9ᵗʰ *Southampton* had opened fire on a shadowing float-plane. On the evening of that day, its escort duty done, Force H had turned back for Gibraltar, all the ships then being under high level bombing attacks. All these naval movements were parts of another complex operation going under the name of 'Excess'.

On 10ᵗʰ January, the merchant ships, now being escorted through the Narrows by the Dido-Class cruiser *Bonaventure,* plus *Southampton, Gloucester* and four destroyers, encountered the Italian destroyers *Circe* and *Vega* at 0730. (One presumes that *Bonadventure* had initially detected them on her RDF.) *Southampton's* 'A' and 'B' turrets had a very accurate shoot and *Bonaventure's* much less so. Between them, they badly damaged *Vega* by gunfire, her company fighting valiantly back with the one gun they still, by then, had in action, before *Bonadventure* closed in and raked *Vega* from stem to stern. *Vega* was then finished off by a torpedo fired by *Hereward*, the resultant explosion causing a huge mushroom cloud to rise thousands of feet up into the air. By that time a misty dawn had broken, and the rocky outline of the Island of Pantelleria was distinguishable as a backdrop to the dramatic scene. The other Italian destroyer, *Circe*, escaped at extraordinary speed, but later gallantly returned to pick up the few members of *Vega's* company who had survived.

The convoy the British ships were escorting reached Valetta Harbour, Malta, without loss, that same day, where they were accorded a tremendous welcome by the thousands of Maltese people crowding every available vantage-point. There was a strange after-the-battle reaction among *Southampton's* company who felt that *Bonaventure's* poor shooting had caused a quite unnecessary level of carnage on the *Vega*.

Southampton and *Gloucester* had not themselves entered Valetta Harbour, but had headed west, accompanied by the destroyer *Diamond*, to meet up with the destroyer *Mohawk* who was towing the damaged destroyer *Gallant*. The latter had lost her bows at 0830 on the 10th due to striking a mine whilst still about 100 miles out from Malta, and was being towed there stern-first. The two cruisers, with *Bonadventure* and *Griffin* in company, were tasked by the C-in-C Mediterranean with escorting both destroyers to the dubious safety of the Island, which was duly achieved. Aboard *Gallant* was Sub-Lieutenant Robin GRAHAM, who had served aboard *Southampton* as a Midshipman, in 1937.[448] He would forever treasure memories of *Southampton* coming to their aid. Shortly after this event three Ju 87 aircraft attacked *Southampton* at very low level, one bomb bursting close alongside. The aircraft that dropped it was itself hit by one of *Southampton's* pom-poms, and *'wobbled away over the horizon with most of his tail shot away.'* Midshipman Barrie KENT reported in his dairy that this damaged aircraft had made its attack at such low-level that it had flown through *'its own bomb-splash'*.

Author's collection. An anonymous postcard c. 1939.

HMS *Gallant*. This destroyer had lost her bows due to striking a mine. She had suffered many casualties, and was being towed stern-first into harbour at Malta under grave risk from aerial bombardment. Serving aboard was Sub-Lt Robin GRAHAM, who had previously served in HMS *Southampton*, and he was thrilled and comforted to see his former ship coming to provide anti-aircraft cover. This aid was something that he would never forget.

Both *Mohawk* and *Gallant* were units of Admiral CUNNINGHAM's main force. As we have seen this force had headed in towards Malta from Alexandria, and had now turned about to escort merchant ships in passage from Gibraltar to Alexandria, and having an element bound for Suda Bay, Crete.

Italian torpedo-carrying aircraft had been attacking CUNNINGHAM's ships without success, and the Fairy *'Fulmers'* which were flying from his aircraft-carrier *Illustrious* had shot down one of the Italian reconnaissance planes. However, whilst the

---

[448] Later Captain R H GRAHAM, MVO, .DSC, RN (Rtd)

two 'Fulmers' on air patrol were vainly chasing after two further Italian planes which had unsuccessfully made a low-level torpedo attack, a large swarm of enemy aircraft flying at high level were sighted by the British ships. The *Illustrious* quickly began to launch more fighters, but it was clearly going to take them too long to gain the necessary altitude to tackle these oncoming enemy aircraft.

Until now, the hostile aircraft had been almost exclusively Italian. *But this large swarm was of German aircraft.* They were from Fliegerkorps X, which had constantly attacked British ships in and around Norway in April, May and June 1940, but with only limited success. However, since the Allied evacuation of Norway, the aircraft of Fliegerkorps X had been undergoing intensive training in attacking ships, and 150 Ju 87 dive-bombers, 120 long-range bombers, 40 fighters and 20 reconnaissance aircraft had been transferred to airfields in Sicily on 12th November 1940, to bolster up the Italian efforts.

On 10th January 1941, information had been received by the Germans that a British supply convoy with a large escort of warships was headed for Malta. Hauptman Werner HOZZEL had led his I/St.G1 Stuka force against the British ships, the aircraft diving down from 12,000 ft to 2,000 ft into the concentrated fire of the British ships to plant their bombs into the most important target, the *Illustrious*.

The German dive-bombers quickly obtained six direct hits and caused near-mortal damage to the aircraft-carrier, which soon had fires blazing at many places over her entire length and a pall of black smoke rising thousands of feet into the air. By dint of great efforts, *Illustrious* was nursed over 400 miles into harbour at Malta, where she was further bombed, time and again. [Nicholas MONSARRAT brilliantly and compassionately described the terrible condition of the interior of this great vessel, and the carnage of so many of her company, in his book "The Kapilan of Malta".][449]

Alf would have been well aware of her suffering, and one presumes that, in common with the appropriate anti-aircraft weapons of all the assembled warships, during the evening and overnight 'his' 4" guns would have been involved in putting up barrage fire to protect the damaged *Illustrious*, as did the other ships in the dockyard and harbour area, and the many shore anti-aircraft installations.

During the brief pause of *Southampton* at Malta it seems apt to consider the officers and WOs now under Captain BROOKE (or only very recently posted elsewhere). Those shown in **bold** type are all believed to have been serving up to 11th January 1941.

NAME	RANK	MONTH JOINED	MONTH LEFT
BROOKE, B.C.B	Captain	Jun 1940	Jan 1941
FYFE, R.W.	Commander (E)	Post-Nov 1940?	KiA, Jan 1941
ROSS, T.D.	Lt Commander (N)	Nov 1940	Jan 1941
RAYMOND, D.L.	Lt Commander (G)	Aug 1939	Jan 1941
COPEMAN, N.A.	Lt Commander (T)	Jan 1939	Jan 1941
BALFOUR, S.H. (Rtd)	Lt Commander	Post-Nov 1940?	KiA, Jan 1941
BARKER-HAHLO, J.F.C. (Rtd)	Lt Commander	Nov 1939	KiA, Jan 1941
BULFORD	Lt Commander	Apr 1940	Pre-Jan 11 1941?

---

[449] She would eventually manage to limp away from Malta after temporary repairs and make her way to the U.S.A for major repairs which would keep her out of the war for a long time to come

EDMONSTONE (Rtd)	Lt Commander	Pre-March 1937	Jan 1941
PELLY, C.S.	Lt Commander	Apr 1940	Jan 1941
TINLEY, C.B.	Lt Commander	Mar 1937	DoW, Jan 1941
FAWCUS, Sir P	Lt RNVR	Apr 1940	Jan 1941
SHACKLETON, H.E.F.	Major RM	Nov 1938	KiA, Jan 1941
BARRATT, R.J.T	Lt	Sep 1938	Pre-Jan 11 1941?
GRENFELL	Lt	Aug 1939	Pre-Jan 11 1941?
JACKSON	Lt	Pre-Jun 1940	Pre-Jan 11 1941?
PARNALL	Lt	Nov 1939	Pre-Jan 11 1941?
PEMBERTON, R.H.S.	Lt	Nov 1940?	Jan 1941
MANNING	Lt (A)	Dec 1939	Pre-Jan 11 1941?
CASSON, J.	Lt (A)	Pre-Nov 1939	Pre-Jan 11 1941?
WOODS, P.R.E	Lt (A)	Sep 1938	Jan 1941
GUEST, J.A.	Lt (E)	Nov 1938	KiA, Jan 1941
GRIFFIN, E.G.	Lt (E)	Post-Nov 1940?	Jan 1941
MARSHALL	Lt (E)	Post-Nov 1940?	Jan 1941 (W)
TUFFILL	Temp Lt (E)	Post-Nov 1940?	Jan 1941
de STACKPOOLE, R.O.	Lt RM	Nov 1939	Jan 1941 (W)
SLOANE	Surg Lt Commander RNVR	Post-Nov 1940?	Jan 1941 (W)
FAIRWEATHER, D.J.	Surg Lt (D)	Post-Nov 1940?	KiA, Jan 1941
GOTHARD, H.W.	Surg Lt	Post-Nov 1940?	Jan 1941
MORTON, T.J.	Surg Lt RNVR	Post-Nov 1940?	KiA, Jan 1941
HEATHCOTE	Pay Lt	Aug 1939	Pre Jan 11 1941?
RICHARDS, N.L.C.	Pay Lt	Post-Nov 1940?	KiA, Jan 1941
PETERS	Instr Lt	Jul 1938	Pre-Jan 11 1941?
OLIVER, J.E.	Instrr Lt	Nov 1940?	Jan 1941
PEMBERTON, R.H.S.	Acting Lt	Post-Nov 1940?	KiA, Jan 1941
LLOYD-SMITH, V.B.	Temp Pay Lt RNVR	Post-Nov 1940?	KiA, Jan 1941
OLIVER, J.E.	Temp Instr Lt	Post-Nov 1940?	KiA, Jan 1941
DISNEY-ROEBUCK	S/Lt	May 1940	Jan 1941
HERRING	S/Lt	Pre-Sep 1940	Jan 1941
MUTTRIE	S/Lt (A) RNVR	Nov 1940?	Jan 1941
POITRIE	S/Lt (A)	Pre-Sep 1940	Pre-Jan 11 1941?
GRAY, C.K.	Pay S/Lt	Post-Nov 1940?	KiA, Jan 1941
LLOYD-SMITH, V	Pay S/Lt RNVR	Post-Nov 1940?	Jan 1941
PAGE, L.F.	Prob Temp S/Lt RNR	Post-Nov 1940?	KiA, Jan 1941
CUTLER, J.L.	Midshipman RNR	Post-Nov 1940?	Jan 1941
DAVIDSON, G.V.	Midshipman	Sep 1940	KiA, Jan 1941
JENKINS, W.G.	Midshipman RNVR	Post-Nov 1940?	Jan 1941
JERRAM, F.R.	Midshipman	1939	Jan 1941
KENT, B.H.	Midshipman	Sep 1940	Jan 1941 (Sl/W)
LEARMOND, P.A.	Midshipman	Sep 1940	Jan 1941
MOCATTA, J.M.	Midshipman	Sep 1940	KiA, Jan 1941
PHILLIPS, R	Midshipman RCN	Post-Nov 1940?	Jan 1941
RUCK-KEENE, T	Midshipman	Jan 1938	Jan 1941
SMITH, C.G.	Midshipman RCN	Post-Nov 1940?	Jan 1941
SMITH, P.R.G.	Midshipman	1939	Pre Jan 11 1941?
TURNER, G.T	Midshipman	Sep 1940	Jan 1941 (Sl/W)
BOWER, R.G.	Midshipman RNR	Jan 1938?	Jan 1941
HOLMES, A.B.	Pay Midshipman	Post-Nov 1940?	KiA, Jan 1941
ROYNTON-JONES, E	Pay Midshipman	Post-Nov 1940?	KiA, Jan 1941
BEASLEY, B.R.	Chaplain	1939	Jan 1941
DAVIS, Mr A. W.	Commissioned Gunner	Pre Mar 1937	KiA, Jan 1941
ELLIOTT, Mr	Warrant Shipwright	Nov 1940?	Jan 1941
JARROLD, Mr	Warrant Schoolmaster	Nov 1940?	Jan 1941
PLAYER, Mr H.C.	Director Gunner & 'Bosun'	Mar 1937	KiA, Jan 1941
KOESTER, Mr L	Commissioned Gunner	Mar 1937?	DoW Jan 1941
COBB, Mr F.A.	Commissioned Gunner (T)	Jan 1941	Jan 1941
REES, Mr F.P.	Bandmaster RM	Mar 1937	Jan 1941

SIMMONDS, Mr	Warrant Ordnance Officer	Nov 1940?	Jan 1941
WADE, Mr R.D.	Warrant Electrician	Aug 1939	Jan 1941
WHITE, Mr F.J	Warrant Engineer	Aug 1939	KiA, Jan 1941

TOTAL: Approx 70 officers and WOs, of whom about twelve would leave the ship before the fatal 11th January 1941. The true running total was probably about 57 officers and WOs. (N.B. The last surviving ship's log ended on 30th November. There was surely a large 'draft' after that, probably in early December whilst *Southampton* was at Alexandria before heading for Zanzibar, or at Alex again on 5th/6th January.) A tabulation made up by Midshipman KENT around that time has been invaluable in adding new names, etc.

We can see from a glance at the fourth column the very high rate of attrition which was to come in a very short while. It actually accounted for 22 out of (say) 57 officers and WOs, or about 39% - a very high rate of fatal casualties. Officers with a '(W)' are known to have been wounded. More on all this later.

On the 11th January, *Gloucester*, flying the flag of Rear Admiral RENOUF, *Southampton* and the destroyers *Diamond* and *Jaguar* left Malta escorting eight unladen merchant ships to meet up with a Piraeus-bound convoy. By 1530 they were about 150 miles out from Malta, and some 180 miles from the Sicilian airfields from which the enemy aircraft were operating. The last shadowing aircraft had been sighted at 1000. The sky had since been clear. It was considered that they were now out of range of the Ju 87s which had caused such havoc to HMS *Illustrious*. Consequently, the ship's company, who had been closed up at 'Action Stations' for many, many hours had gone into two watches, so one watch could 'get their heads down' for a while. This had become essential, for the ship's company was almost exhausted and their efficiency, especially in keeping a sharp lookout, was deteriorating markedly. Aboard *Southampton* (and evidently aboard *Gloucester* too), many of the officers and warrant officers had now gone to relax in the after-part of the ship. Specifically, *Southampton* was at 'Day Defence Stations'. That is to say, (according to the Court of Enquiry which ensued) the following were closed up:

> 6" Director and TS (Reduced Crew)
> One 6" Gun in each Turret
> Two HA Directors and HA TS's
> (Reduced Crews)
> One 4" Mounting each side.
> The Starboard Pom-Pom
> The Port 0.5" machine-gun
> The Air Defence Officer
> The Air Defence Officer's Mate
> Six Air Look-outs)　One
> Four Submarine Look-outs)　PO
> One Masthead Look-out)　in Charge
> Nucleus Fire and Repair Parties
> in each Section
> Depth-Charge Numbers

The Look-outs had been told to keep a very good look-out. The ADO and PO in charge of Look-outs paid frequent visits to these men. The Pom-Pom's crew had been warned to keep a particularly good look-out in the direction of the sun and one man armed with a sun-glass was doing so.

Unfortunately, the British ships, *none of which had RDF*, were unaware that the additional fuel tanks which had been fitted to the Ju 87s gave them a range in excess of 300 miles. Now, led to their target by a Heinkel 111 twin-engined bomber, twelve *'Stukas'* from Major ENNECCERUS's II/St.G2 made a surprise attack at about 1530, six peeling off in turn and diving down out of the sun on *Southampton* and six diving down in turn on *Gloucester*.

As recounted to the author in 1994, Boy Seaman 'Freddie' DANCE, at his 'Readiness' position by the multiple pom-pom on the starboard side of the hangar deck of *Southampton*, could hear the Stukas diving down on the ship, but they were hurtling down from right out of the sun's eye, which was incredibly bright, and it was impossible to pick them out from the harsh glare. Most 'official accounts' state that two bombs hit the ship. However, Freddie avers that *three* bombs hit *Southampton* in quick succession, one forrard, then one aft, then one amidships. Another Boy Seaman, John EVANS, was also stationed on the poms-poms on the starboard side, near Freddie DANCE.[450] These young men were very fortunate that they were stationed on the *starboard* side, for the bomb which Freddie said 'hit amidships' had entered via the port *'Walrus'* hangar, just on the other side of the funnel from them. (The subsequent Court of Enquiry heard that this bomb, allegedly the *first* to hit the ship, hit between the port Pom-Pom and the Ready Use Magazine, passing through the hangar and bursting either in the vicinity of 'A' Boiler Room or in the ERA's Mess. A second bomb narrowly missed the ship abreast of the Port Hangar, splinters from its explosion penetrating the ship's side and causing casualties amongst the HA personnel in the Hangar Mess before they could get to their Action Stations.[451] A third bomb hit the ship aft, just before 'X' Turret and burst in the vicinity of the Main WT Office, killing a large number of officers and men who were on their way to their Action Stations.[452]

In fact, the delayed action bomb which had 'hit aft' was of 250 kg and had incendiaries attached.[453] It smashed its way through 'X' gun deck, then down through the wardroom and into the gunroom flat, and there burst by the hatch to the main WT office. All watertight doors in the vicinity were shattered and intense fires broke out in the aft superstructure and wardroom flats. Tragically, a large number of officers, warrant officers and petty officers had been relaxing there, and many were killed outright. The

---

[450] The late John EVAN's position atop the hangar overlooked the starboard battery of 4"guns 30 yards aft of it. He was accustomed to seeing 'Mr DAVIS, the Commissioned Gunner', at those guns, and, fifty years later, he could still recall Alf's image to mind. [John survived the attack on *Southampton*, also the sinking by aircraft of his next ship, the monitor *Terror*, off Derna on 24th February 1941 and then the sinking by aircraft of a tug, which swiftly capsized and from which he was extremely lucky to fight his way to the surface. (It is believed that this was the *St Issey*, sunk off Benghazi on 28 December 1942.) Thereafter, apparently in line with a fairly well-established procedure for men 'sunk thrice', the Admiralty had the consideration to find him a *shore-based* job. Post-War John emigrated to Australia, never losing his lovely West-Country accent. He passed away in the year 2000.]
[451] The author suspects that these were mainly Royal Marines from the P1 and P2 mountings. Five Royal Marines are listed amongst the men who lost their lives.
[452] It would seem that Alf's friend and colleague Commissioned Gunner John PLAYER was one of the men killed here, and Commissioned Gunner Jack KOESTER was severely wounded by shrapnel. (Sadly, he died after being transferred to *Diamond*.)
[453] The Board of Enquiry considered it possible that there might have actually been two bombs which hit at almost the same point. (Midshipman KENT also gave this as his opinion when writing his diary.)

heavy armoured hatch leading to the main WT office was welded shut by the explosion, and, tragically, nothing could be done to extricate the men trapped in that office. According to Midshipman Barrie KENT, the force of the explosion had *'blown the bulkhead just aft of the gunroom bodily backwards against 'X' barbette, wiping out the cabins just behind it'*.

In fact, as Barrie KENT would later write in his diary, in rapid response to the sounding off of Action Stations, he had quickly mounted from the Gunroom Flat to the Wardroom flat above it, he had passed the short run of cabins leading away from the wardroom flat, and, followed by other officers, he had just started to ascend the ladder to the 4-inch gun deck when this bomb exploded *'with a terrific flash and crash'*, blowing him off the ladder. Wreckage and dirt fell all around him and *'something hot – possibly a steam pipe'* - hit him *'on the back of the neck'*. Everything *'seemed pitch black'* but he made his way up the ladder, minus his cap and with his uniform absolutely filthy and with his hair and face covered in dust and small splinters. It was *'difficult to see out of one eye'* which was bruised and dust-seared. A dazed-looking man at the top of the ladder seemed more or less all right, but *'everybody's nose was bleeding'*. *"The 4-inch guns and crews seemed all right but everything was covered in dirt and bits of wreckage. I noticed that most of the bows of the motor cutter (my boat) had been knocked to pieces and there was a large piece of the port hangar lying on the crane."*

Soon, smoke would be pouring out of every door and hatch aft of the torpedo tubes, and it would not be long before the After Engine Room would have to be abandoned due to the spread of the intense fire.

The bomb which had 'hit amidships' was also of 250 kg with incendiaries attached. It smashed its way through the port hangar, penetrated the ERA's pantry, and exploded on the protective armoured deck above 'A' boiler room. This protective deck split, a superheater pipe was blown off the boiler, and the compartment had to be immediately abandoned. Casualties were caused by the escaping steam, a thick cloud of which immediately poured up through and around the port hangar, masking the forward view. The Boiler Room caught fire, all power and water-supply was lost, and the fire quickly began to rage, out of control. Thick smoke began to pour out of the forrard funnel and the paint on its sides began to blister. Soon it would become red-hot and the paint would be falling off it in great, heavy, flaming masses.

The crash of the first bomb hitting the ship and the sounding of the "Alarm to Arms" on a bugle were almost synchronous. For most of the company they were the first intimation that the ship was under attack. Indeed, eye witnesses say that the bugler had started to sound off the normal routine 'Cooks to the Galley' before stopping momentarily and starting the 'Alarm to Arms'.

The Gunnery Report given at the Court of Enquiry confirmed this. It says: *'The attacking aircraft appear to have approached quite unseen and dived from the direction of the sun. At the time the ship was under rudder for a zig-zag turn. Aircraft were almost simultaneously sighted by the ADO and the 0.5" Crew, who saw aircraft diving on 'Gloucester' who was on the starboard bow. The sun was on the starboard beam or quarter. The order "Alarm Starboard" was passed and Action Stations sounded. Almost at the same moment aircraft were heard and seen diving on 'Southampton'.*

As far as can be determined, the aircraft dived out of the sun from astern and from the starboard quarter. The Starboard Pom-Pom opened fire on one aircraft attacking from about Green 130, and continued to fire at it until it pulled out of its dive, having dropped a bomb. S1 Gun went into local barrage firing and fired about eight or ten salvoes.' (Author's Note: It is known that Alf was at his 'beloved guns' when the attack started, and he may well have had a hand in getting off these 4" salvoes.)

The Germans aver that no gun fired from either ship as they dived down to the attack. This is probably true, in a literal sense. As we have seen, when the attack opened *Southampton* had only one 4" mounting manned and one close-range mounting manned, on each of the port and starboard sides. *Gloucester* was probably in much the same state. The 4" guns evidently came into action only in time to fire as the last aircraft were pulling out of their dives, and with no observed effect.[454]

The bomb-hit which penetrated the port hangar would have been about 140 ft ahead of Alf at his 4" guns, and on the other side of the ship to him. The point of entry of the bomb which penetrated 'X' deck, would only have been about 80 ft directly aft of him. He would therefore have been more conscious of the latter one, and, as a Gunner, he would have been acutely aware of the risk it imposed to the magazines if it had made a deep penetration. The flames and smoke immediately welling up would have been a major concern to him. Initially, however, one assumes that, as his first priority Alf would have stood to his four guns and supervised such members of the crews as had survived the bombs, as they rushed to man the guns (one of which was already semi-manned) and come into action against the dive-bombers. And that Alf would have remained there at least until the supply of ready-use ammunition dwindled, and the drastic situation in the Magazine began to unfold.

In fact, the supply of 4" shells from the Magazine would probably have stopped immediately after the bomb-hit aft, and communication with the handling party below may well have been cut off. (These unfortunate men were evidently entombed.) Alf may have quickly foreseen that his S2 gun position would have to be abandoned (as it subsequently was) if the fire spread forward to any degree. In any case, the guns would be useless once the supply of ammunition ceased. Alf was the OOQ and presumably the senior man present. (As we will see, Lt Commander RAYMOND was off-watch.)

The Gunnery report continued: *'After the forward explosion the ADO Position and the HA Directors were obscured in steam from 'A' Boiler Room and the guns continued to fire in local control for a few minutes whilst the dive bombers were in the vicinity. Fire was then ceased and the order given to check receivers. These were found to be correct except that one gun was 5 degrees out for training. This was lined up.*

Following the dive bombing attack several single aircraft carried out high level bombing attacks. The exact number of attacks cannot be stated with any certainty but it is thought that there was one from the Port side and two from the Starboard side. The aircraft were difficult to see against the bright blue sky at a height of about 12,000 to 15,000 feet. The fire of the starboard battery appeared to be particularly accurate. (Author's Note: Perhaps Alf's steadying influence again, coupled with a ballistic height adjustment which had been carried out the previous day - see below.) *Two or three*

---

[454] The Germans say they lost no aircraft in the attack. The then Leading Seaman Les MOSS, who, in common with most of the ship's company had become exhausted by being continuously at Action Stations, was asleep on a table in the Mess Deck when the Alarm was given. Les says that he moved fast, but by the time he reached S1 gun and it came into action, the German aircraft had already done their worst and were gone.

bombs were dropped but all fell very wide. The ship at this time was still able to manoeuvre at a fairly high speed.

In his evidence, Lt Commander RAYMOND (Alf's senior gunnery officer) said he had been lying down on a camp bed in the Admiral's Charthouse when the attack started. He heard the whistle of a bomb as he was putting on his coat and cap, and threw himself down on his face. There were two loud explosions which he knew were either hits or near misses. He then went to the ADO Position, another loud explosion occurring while he was on the ladder.

When he arrived at the ADO Position he found everything enveloped in steam. Going forward to the Compass Platform gave him a better view, and, as aircraft still appeared to be flying round both ships he ordered the 4-inch guns to go into local barrage firing. When it appeared that the aircraft had retired he ordered "Cease Firing" and told the Gunnery Officers to check receivers to see if all was correct.

Shortly after receivers had been checked and found correct single aircraft began high-level bombing attacks on the ships from about 12,000 to 15,000 ft. He could not be certain but believed there were three attacks, two from the Starboard side and one from the Port side. On the previous day it had been found that the 4-inch guns were shooting short and as a result of this experience and a subsequent calibration, it had been decided to apply a ballistic height correction of about 1,200 feet at 45 degrees angle of sight. He remembered on this occasion thinking that the 4-inch fire, particularly on the Starboard side, was very steady and accurate.

For a short period during these high-level bombing attacks the director firing circuits failed and firing was done by lanyard. During a lull in the firing the director and local circuits were again tested and found correct.

While the bombing attacks were being made, Midshipman BOWER RNR., came up to report to Lt Commander RAYMOND that the 4-inch ammunition hoists had jammed and that they could not get in touch with the Magazine. The Lt Commander therefore sent Sub-Lt DISNEY-ROEBUCK and Chief Gunner's Mate CHAPLIN to organise a supply of ammunition by secondary hand method. After a while the Chief Gunner's mate came back to report to him that the hoists were jammed: a fierce fire was raging in the Gunroom Flat and Cabin Flat above: that it was impossible to enter the Magazine and that it would probably be necessary to flood the Magazine. Lt Commander RAYMOND reported this to the Captain who then went aft.

Lt Commander RAYMOND learned subsequently that Mr DAVIS, the Commissioned Gunner of the Ship and 4-inch OOQ, had gone down the hatch from the Galley Flat to try and flood the Magazine from the position just outside his cabin and he had not re-emerged. The citation for his subsequent M.I.D refers to Alf *"advancing into the after flats, when filled with fire and smoke, in an attempt to flood the 4" magazine. He was not seen again."*[455]

One assumes that Alf would first have tried to flood the 4-inch Magazine by use of the controls in the nearby 4-inch Flooding and Spraying Cabinet on the Upper Deck, only to find (or perhaps to have already had reported to him) that the controls were smashed and not responding. (They were situated exactly where the bomb had initially

---

[455] These were the words of the Citation of the Posthumous Mention in Despatches which he was subsequently awarded.

668

struck and penetrated the Upper Deck.). Then, he would have thought of the manual flooding controls located just outside his cabin on the Lower Deck, in territory which would have been almost as familiar to him as the back of his hand. In the event, there was a fair chance that those controls were not actually smashed. That is to say, it seems likely that the bomb had not fallen vertically, but at an angle, smashing the 4-inch spraying cabinet, penetrating the Upper Deck, probably bouncing on the armoured Lower Deck, before exploding nearer the far side of the flat, away from the flooding controls on that deck-level. (The explosion of the bomb at the aft end of the Gun Room Flat would have accounted for the watertight hatch to the Main WT Office, which was on the far side of that flat, being 'welded shut' – see following drawing. Also for the aft bulkhead having been blown backwards against X gun barbette, as reported by Midshipman KENT.)

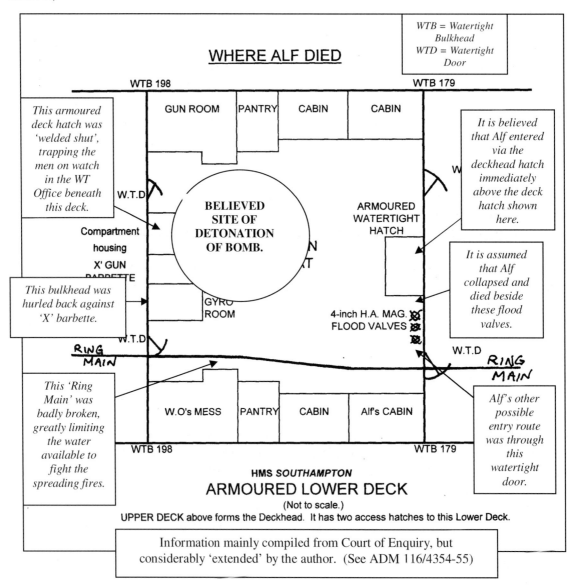

Whether Alf matter-of-factly weighed up his chances of getting out alive if he descended to the Lower Deck, or whether he just went ahead 'regardless', seeing it as his responsibility as OOQ and 'the man on the spot' to flood the magazine, and to do that just as quickly as was humanly possible, we shall never know. However, he was dashing and gallant by nature, he was imbued with a great many years of naval discipline, and he was perceived as a 'father-figure' within the ship. The author suspects Alf just 'went for it'. If he emerged from the inferno, he would be very fortunate. He would strive his hardest. If he failed – well, the magazine would probably detonate and that might well set off 'X' and 'Y' magazines and write *finis* to the whole ship anyway…

Access to the Gun Room Flat via the watertight hatch in the deck of the Ward Room Flat would have been quick and direct for Alf, but the problem was the fire and smoke venting up through the hole the bomb had smashed through the Upper Deck, and the fumes and heat from the secondary fires springing up all around the Ward Room Flat and the Gunroom Flat below it. Speed would have been of the essence.

The sight that would have met Alf's eyes would have been utterly appalling, for, in addition to the welling flames and smoke, there had been absolute carnage of a score or more of officers in the Ward Room Flat immediately above and of warrant officers and other men in the Gun Room Flat at the seat of the explosion.

From the fact that the 4" Magazine never blew up, despite the fires which raged around it, one feels that Alf probably accomplished his self-set task of turning on the flooding valves in the Gun Room Flat, but collapsed from his exertions in the intense heat from the nearby and increasing fire, and from his inevitable inhalation of the fumes and smoke, before he could make the short return journey to the hatch and near-safety.

IN A SENSE, IT IS AT THIS POINT THAT THE STORY OF COMMISSIONED GUNNER ALFRED WILLIAM DAVIS COMES TO AN ABRUPT END. HIS SPIRIT WILL HAVE FLED FROM THE MORTAL SCENE.

However, it seems more appropriate to finish this part of the book with the now-impending death of the fine ship which became his tomb, and to consider the actions, many heroic, which ensued as the ship went to her end. Also to list the men, some already dead and others still living but trapped and now doomed to die, who went down in her, accompanying Alf's body to the floor of the Ionian Deep far below.

By 1605 *Southampton* had lost steerage way and was drifting to a halt, dead in the water.

Freddie DANCE told the author that there was some confusion in the immediate aftermath of being hit, and as the fires began to break out. As a Boy Seaman he looked to the older and more senior men around him for guidance as to what to do, but found some of the people he had previously looked to for instruction and decision now to be shocked almost out of their wits, and irresolute. The 'chain of command' now had serious 'missing links', for it was quickly apparent that many senior personnel had been caught by the bomb which had exploded in the Wardroom Flat. Normally, each man looked to his next senior in rank, when a crisis occurred which was beyond his level of ability. Now, in many cases, the 'next senior man', and, indeed 'the next senior man after that', were both dead.

In fact, 22 out of the sixty or so officers and warrant officers were dead or dying, including the vital figure of the lone Commander (E), one of the two Lts (E), one of the two Warrant Engineers, and two of the ship's six Lt Commanders. All three of the Commissioned Gunners were also dead. And, although Commander TINLEY had been apparently 'functioning' in leading 'damage control operations', due to his head-wound he had been doing so in a highly erratic and ineffective fashion.[456]

Whereas the officers and WOs had suffered the terrible attrition rate of about 40% fatal casualties, the ratings had suffered much less badly in percentage terms, with about 8% fatalities. Hence, it was not so much in terms of sheer manpower, but far more in terms of the loss of command and experience, particularly in Engineering and Damage Control personnel, that the effectiveness of the fire-fighting operations was floundering.

One very serious source of confusion lay in the fact that Commander TINLEY, *appeared* to be rational, and men were obeying his orders, strange though those orders often seemed. [It only slowly dawned on them that this tall and magnificent-looking man was no longer *compos mentis*, and that the bloody bandage round his head disguised a massive wound. In fact, the bandage was all that was preventing his brains from protruding through a hole in his cranium.[457] It was beyond comprehension that he was still on his feet at all.] It was some time before Captain BROOKE became aware that Commander TINLEY was not handling damage control in his normal competent way, but actually most irrationally. Thus, as told to the Board of Enquiry, it was only when the Captain himself went aft, some time after the bomb-hits, that he assessed Commander TINLEY to be "*utterly insane*".

It did become apparent early on that there was little or no water in the ring main, with which to fight the fires, the main breach being deemed to have probably occurred immediately outside Alf's cabin.[458] 'Y' magazine was successfully flooded, but attempts to use the remote system for flooding 'X' magazine failed (though this was kept quiet to prevent possible alarm from spreading). Nor (as we have already seen) could the 4" magazine be flooded automatically - though, as we have observed, it is *possible* that Alf's manual efforts to do so had been successful. One way and another, with the fires growing worse and spreading, there was now great risk of catastrophic explosion.

---

[456] It is not inconceivable that Alf had reported to Commander TINLEY, who was in charge of Damage Control, that he (Alf) was making an attempt to manually flood the magazine, not recognising that Commander TINLEY was no longer *compos mentis*, and in no position to oversee and organise any necessary extrication of Alf via the watertight hatch, should Alf manage to operate the flooding controls and make his way back to the hatch set in the deckhead. This thought process is almost too awful to contemplate.

[457] The bandage had been applied by Midshipmen PHILLIPS and TURNER, who appear not to have realised that this great man was mentally disabled by his gross head wound. Perhaps there had been so much blood and matting of his hair that they had failed to see his skull had been penetrated and the dura broken, so that a part of his brain was protruding through the wound. The fact that, amazingly, the Commander had stayed on his feet may also have been a telling factor in the two young men simply 'patching him up to carry on'. It is probably another tribute to the strength and fitness of this magnificent man that he did not die until 17th January, six days after he had suffered this grievous wound. Midshipman Barrie KENT wrote in his diary that Commander TINLEY was '*about 2ft behind me, just coming out of his cabin, when the bomb exploded*'. '*The Commander's cabin was destroyed*'. It is worthy of note that the officers immediately following Barrie KENT were also wounded in the order in which they were moving, Midshipman TURNER with burns and bruises, Lt de STACPOLE RM with cuts in the face and a damaged arm, and Lt (E) MARSHALL with wounds in an arm and leg.

[458] The author has come to believe the break was actually displaced a little further aft.

It is not mentioned in the reports given to the Court of Enquiry, but some accounts say that when Alf failed to return, Lt Commander J. F. C. BARKER-HAHLO, who had presumably been in his (now redundant) action station in the after director tower for the 6" guns (which were now unusable), and who had descended to the quarter deck, took the incredibly courageous decision to follow Alf down, and also failed to reappear. It is hard to know whether this really happened. The balance of probabilities would suggest not. The absence of Lt Cdr BARKER-HAHLO's name from Captain BROOKE's reports would seem to discount the matter. And a letter written by Captain BROOKE to Alf's widow would also appear to run counter to the idea.

That is to say, Captain B.C.B. BROOKE would write to Alf's widow later in 1941, saying *"Of all the gallant acts of heroism done that day, I have heard of none greater than your husband's. Your husband was a great and splendid character whose memory we have in our hearts. We are desperately sorry for you, for Mr Davis was a very great man and a much beloved man."* Lt Commander Duncan L RAYMOND would also write, at about the same time, to say, *"I have never had the luck or the pleasure to have in my department such an able, willing and reliable officer as Mr DAVIS. He was always at work, always to be relied upon, and always so very pleasant and cheerful to work with. You can understand therefore that I feel that I too have lost a friend who has always given me his most loyal support"*. And Captain (G) G. H.G. ACKLAND would write from the RN Gunnery School at Chatham : *"....Mr DAVIS was an officer for whom we all had the greatest regard...."*.]

Whilst these efforts to flood the magazines were in progress, the fires were growing worse. Down in the Gun Direction Room, Royal Marine Band Corporal Frederick P. REES would always remember how the paint on the bulkhead blistered as the fire raged against its other face.[459] There would have been great relief to him and his men when the order was eventually given to abandon their compartment.

Warrant Electrician Roy D. WADE survived the bombs. He was a friend of Alf's, and he wrote a long letter to Alf's widow, Alice, in 1941. In this letter, which clearly sought to give Alice as much comfort as possible, he recounted how Alf had *'dropped a rope down through the flames to rescue men trapped in the Shell Room, and got two out by his own efforts'*, before, *'whilst trying to rescue the Corporal of Marines, whose legs were trapped by the fallen shells, the ammunition racks collapsed on them and they were killed.'* It seems that this well-meaning letter was written from hearsay, and it was clearly in error. It is unfortunate that it led Alf's widow to quickly pass it with great pride to a national newspaper who published it under the headline 'Deserved a VC.'[460] The author, his elder son, to whom a cutting was sent at his boarding school, wept proud tears over it many times over. (His sisters may well have done likewise.) But the author, right from his then age of 11 and on into his adult life, wondered how his Dad could have been attempting to perform the critically urgent task of flooding the magazine by one, 'official', account and rescuing men by the other, highly 'personalised' account. Especially so when weight appeared to be given to Roy WADE's account, because he talked of being proud to have been Alf's friend, said how much he was missing him, and

---

[459] As written to the author by Corporal REES' son, in 1994.

[460] It is a strange fact that the only 'lesser alternative' to a VC was a humble 'Mention in Dispatches'.

referred, knowledgeably and correctly, to the deaths of other mutual friends, such as Commissioned Gunner Harry PLAYER and Warrant Engineer Mr WHITE, both of whom had been direct victims of the bombs, and also to Commissioned Gunner Lewis KOESTER, who had died of his wounds. No wonder the author's step-mother had preferred to believe Roy WADE's letter rather than the official account.[461]

Seemingly, the consoling account assembled by Roy WADE, obviously with the best of intentions, was a distorted version of another great act of bravery which took place that day. This was by Acting Corporal Horace JONES of the Royal Marines. According to a shipmate, Corporal JONES had made his perilous way down into a damaged compartment in which some of his men were trapped with fire around them, to see if he could effect their release, only to himself become trapped. Amazingly, the 'Navyphone' was still working, and by this means he managed to contact one of his close friends who was in a safe part of the ship, requesting him to go to see his wife and family when he next had home leave, tell them what had happened and of how much he loved them and regretted having to leave them. The friend faithfully carried the message as soon as he was able to do so. However, rather as in Alf's case, the 'official' account states that '*Corporal JONES was seen working in the vicinity of 'X' Turret: he too disappeared into the flats to get to the Magazine Floods Valves and was not seen again.*'[462]

The Corporal JONES' story does not tie in entirely with Roy WADE's account, and it is even possible that Roy's story disguises yet another brave and self-sacrificial act, the secret of which has long since been lost to posterity. As Captain BROOKE wrote to Alf's widow, "*.....of all the brave deeds which took place that day....*"

In that context, Midshipman Tom RUCK-KEENE states that the Torpedo Officer '*worked above 'X' magazine with a party for 1½ hours, knowing that the magazine might blow up at any moment*'. He also recounts how a stoker '*managed to extricate three men from the inferno of 'A' Boiler Room, carrying the third one up the hatch on his own back to get him to safety.*'

According to Freddie DANCE, there was a very real feeling amongst the surviving members of the company that *Southampton* could still be saved, if only they could persuade another ship to come alongside and rig her hoses for them. Some of the men still trapped in damaged and fire-threatened compartments might then be have been able to be cut free. However, it was the survivors' understanding, from their unprivileged

---

[461] In 1994, former Shipwright 'Dusty' MILLER and former Boy Seaman 'Freddie DANCE, by then a Lt Commander RNR (Rtd), [both having recognised that the author had been 'part-raised' on Roy WADE's letter], had considerable mutual debate and soul-searching before breaking the news to the author that the letter had been in serious error. Freddie did this in the most gentle and careful manner imaginable, checking step by step that the author did truly prefer the 'unvarnished truth' to the 'glorious myth'.

[462] The son of Corporal H JONES contacted the author in the year 2000 and, by putting together what they knew about their respective fathers' deaths, they reconstructed this version between them as being the likely scenario. However, the thought does occur that the shipmate might have been doing a 'Roy WADE', and giving the widow and family a story of 'saving lives' , and 'dying with others', rather than telling of him advancing alone into a terrible environment of fire and smoke to try to flood 'X' magazine, and dying all by himself. The Navyphone conversation might have been a white lie, told with the very best and most humane of intentions. [Just as in Alf's case in regard to the 4-inch Magazine, Corporal JONES received a posthumous Mention in Despatches for his great gallantry in attempting to manually flood 'X' Magazine. It is *possible* that he succeeded in that task, though at the cost of his own life. Certainly, 'X' Magazine did not blow up before the ship was abandoned.]

position as 'Lower Deck', that Rear-Admiral RENOUF, flying his flag in *Gloucester* would not hear of it.[463] Barrie KENT's diary states that, after *Southampton* had drifted to a halt *"hands then prepared to tow forward, it being intended that 'Gloucester' should take us in tow"*. However, the fires got worse and orders were given to flood the magazines. A, B and Y were flooded successfully, but , reported Barrie, *"the flooding valves for X were useless as the spindles were all bent and twisted and just broke."* (He was unsure about the situation in the HA Magazine.)

Gloucester had also been hard-hit in the same attack by six of the other Stukas from the same 'Gruppe' that had set *Southampton* afire. A 250 kg bomb had burst apart on *Gloucester's* bridge causing great devastation, killing 14 men, including her Captain, and wounding 16 others, though, miraculously, it had not exploded. (Barrie KENT's diary states that this bomb had passed straight through the DCT and had ended up in the WT Office, failing to actually detonate because it had glanced off an open WT Door which had neatly knocked away its fuse. Another bomb had *'gone through the Marines barracks and out through the side...'*). Perhaps Rear-Admiral RENOUF, who would have just seen at first hand the dreadful effects of a bomb bursting on the ship flying his flag, including the instant death of the ship's captain who was probably standing virtually alongside him, could not face the prospect of *Southampton's* 'X' magazine exploding, possibly leading to other sympathetic detonations, and maybe causing irreparable damage to any ship alongside her. Perhaps he feared more air-attacks at any moment. (As Tom RUCK-KEENE rightly says, there had been follow-up high-level attacks by Ju 88s, with bombs exploding harmlessly on the port side of the ship, before *Southampton* had lost steerage way.) Perhaps Rear-Admiral RENOUF could simply not contemplate any rescue attempt which might delay the withdrawal of his surviving ships to Alexandria and safety. His decision may well have been the correct one to take, but it clearly went sorely 'against the grain' for many of the survivors.

Be that as it may, Admiral RENOUF insisted that *Southampton* be abandoned. All the company were told to assemble on deck. Boy Seaman Freddie DANCE was ordered to go below with another Boy Seaman, to see that all the compartments in a particular area were clear.

This seems to have been a hard order to give to young lads, but perhaps it was considered that they would be more quick and nimble than older hands. Perhaps it was also felt that they might be more devoted in their search than an experienced 'Jack the Lad', who would have been more conscious of the physical dangers of going below in semi-darkness to areas which might have had battle-damage resulting in missing companion-ways, holes torn in the deck, ripped open bulkheads and sides with projecting shards of sharp metal, warped watertight doors, and other potentially lethal hazards - to say nothing of the fact that the pipe 'Abandon Ship' might be given at any moment.

The conscientious search made by Freddie and his young shipmate took them near to 'A' Boiler Room, and they came across a severely wounded man in that vicinity.

---

[463] There is a poster at the Royal Naval Museum, Chatham, which was presumably issued during the war as a dire warning to the other ships of her class. This poster claims that *Southampton* could have been saved if the various pumps supplying her 'ring main' had been kept switched on at all times and other precautions adopted. However, that situation would have had to exist *before* she received any damage from the bombs.

Since the passageway was in semi-darkness they never knew who he was. He may well have been unrecognisable, even in a good light, for, when they went to pick him up, his surface skin came away in their hands like wet blotting paper and he slipped down again to the deck. He was part-naked and he had been parboiled, presumably by the superheated steam escaping from the broken pipe in the Boiler Room. With the greatest generosity of spirit he said, in a hoarse voice, *"It's O.K. Leave me, lads. I'm done for. Save yourselves, off you go! Get back on deck for the Abandon Ship!"* And, reluctantly, away they went - but Freddie would be haunted by this traumatic incident for the rest of his life and always wondered in vain if anything *could* somehow have been done. Midshipman Tom RUCK-KEENE was another who instigated and led a search, in his case of the forward part of the ship, finding nobody left alive, so far as could be ascertained.

The destroyer *Diamond* came alongside at 1900 ("right forward and bow to bow", as 'Dusty' later said, to be as far away as possible should *Southampton's* magazines decide to explode) and *Southampton's* survivors lifted their wounded aboard, followed by the walking wounded (amongst them, incredibly, the mortally-wounded Commander C.B. TINLEY, *who was still on his feet*) and then the uninjured. By then, Captain BROOKE, his resolve probably beginning to falter with relief, was telling them to hurry lest 'X' magazine explode.

Barrie KENT recorded in his diary that two POs and twenty-four volunteers were kept behind as the transfer to the destroyer *Diamond* began. These brave men opened up all the accessible watertight doors in *Southampton* to speed her sinking. During that process, Leading Seaman Les MOSS, who was the captain of S1 gun, remembers that he and another eleven volunteers manned S1 gun lest another air-attack developed. (They subsequently got away in a Carley float, and were later picked up by a destroyer. Les remembers this as being on the following day.)

Whilst the main transfer to *Diamond* was in progress, some warships were seen approaching, and were at first thought to be enemy. Barrie reported that *"Gloucester gallantly declared that she'd fight them first and then rescue us"*. (Note that this seems to be in total apposition to the 'Lower Deck' opinions of the prevailing mood in higher command, as expressed by Freddie DANCE.) Luckily, these ships turned out to be the 7th CS, *Orion, Ajax* and *Perth*.

The destroyer *Diamond* was grossly overloaded with 800 extra men aboard, and the living (save for the Commander and nine very severely wounded men) were all subsequently transferred to *Gloucester* at a safe distance from the now-abandoned and fiercely-burning *Southampton*. Les MOSS remembers her as being ablaze from *"stem to stern"*. Admiral CUNNINGHAM's main force reached the scene at about 2100, and the higher officers decided that it was impractical to tow the vessel, even if the fires might possibly be subdued. It was therefore decided to sink *Southampton*, to prevent any possibility of her falling into enemy hands.

She died hard. It took one torpedo from HMS *Gloucester* and four torpedoes from HMS *Orion* to finish her. 'Freddie' told the author that he felt dreadful at this time, as if a part of him was being torn apart too, and that many of his shipmates would have felt just the same. One of *Southampton's* magazines finally exploded (Barrie KENT thought it was her X Magazine – perhaps the only one which was not flooded) and she went down, a blazing, tortured wreck, at 2030 on 11th January in position 35° 54'N, 18° 24' E, about 200 miles south-east of Cape Spartivento, which is the most southerly point of the 'toe' at the foot of Italy. The author was once shown photos which were at that time in the possession of Lt Cmdr Freddie DANCE RNR, showing *Southampton* at her spectacular and sad end.

The bodies of Alf and many of his shipmates, most but not all yet dead, went down with her. Their remains lie there still, undisturbed, in the Ionian Deep, some 2,000 fathoms (12,000 ft) below the waves of what is often the most beautiful sunlit deep blue sea.

R.I.P

CHAPTER SIXTEEN:

HMS *Southampton.*

Battle Honours: Norway 1940
Spartivento 1940
Malta Convoy 1941

The Roll Of Honour of her Ship's Company is as follows
(The following eighty-one men were killed or died during the following days
from wounds received in the action of 11th January 1941.)

Officers

Lieutenant Commander S H BALFOUR RN
Lieutenant Commander J F C BARKER-HAHLO RN
Midshipman G V DAVIDSON RN
Mr A W DAVIS Commissioned Gunner RN
Surgeon Lieutenant (D) D J FAIRWEATHER RN
Commander (E) R W FYFE RN
Paymaster Sub Lieutenant C K GRAY RN
Lieutenant (E) J A GUEST RN
Paymaster Midshipman A B HOLMES RN
Mr L C KOESTER Commissioned Gunner RN
Temporary Paymaster Sub Lieutenant V B LLOYD-SMITH RNVR
Midshipman J M MOCATTA RN
Surgeon Lieutenant T J MORTON RNVR
Temporary Instructor Lieutenant J E OLIVER RN
Probationary Temporary Sub Lieutenant L F PAGE RNR
Acting Lieutenant R H S PEMBERTON RN
Mr H C PLAYER Commissioned Gunner RN
Paymaster Lieutenant N L C RICHARDS RN
Paymaster Midshipman E ROYNTON-JONES RN
Major H E F SHACKLETON RM
Commander C B TINLEY OBE RN
Mr F J WHITE Warrant Engineer RN

Ratings

Acting Engine Room Artificer (5th Class) J W B ANDERSON
Able Seaman W BETTS
Cook (O) W J BRERETON
Acting Engine Room Artificer (4th Class) V BRIDGE
Mechanician A F BRUNDLE
Marine C T CATLIN
Able Seaman G T CHAMBERLAIN
Able Seaman C J CHEW
Steward (RNSR) W E CLARKE   (Continued overleaf)

Ratings *(Continued)*

Acting Engine Room Artificer (4th Class) W H CLARKSON
Stoker (1st Class) C H CLEMENTSON
Chief Engine Room Artificer A G COY
Ordinary Seaman R D CURRY
Assistant Cook (O) L S DEAN
Stoker (1st Class) H H S DRURY
Engine Room Artificer C E DUNT
Ordinary Telegraphist R J DURRANT
Assistant Steward A EAMES
Temporary Petty Officer Writer R EBSWORTH
Telegraphist J EDGE
Acting Leading Seaman B R McL EDMUNDS
Petty Officer C B EMERY
Ordinary Seaman N GILBERT
Able Seaman K C GRAY
Petty Officer Steward J W Q GRAVES
Ordinary Seaman J G HARDY
Stoker (1st Class) W A HARRISON
Ordinary Seaman R H HIMSWORTH
Able Seaman R K HUNT
Acting Corporal H JONES
Cook (O) (2nd Class) L KENNARD
Marine W G LEE
Assistant Steward D R LEEDING
Leading Seaman W A M D LILLEY
Ordinary Telegraphist S McCALLUM
Stoker (2nd Class) T McMAHON
Stoker (2nd Class) S A MARDLING
Telegraphist R W L MINION
Chief Stoker (Pensioner) S D MUSPRATT
Engine Room Artificer (1st Class) F W NORRISS
Stoker (2nd Class) C H NORTHRIDGE
Chief Petty Officer Telegraphist A O'SULLIVAN
Marine C PENFOLD
Marine M F PINN
Supply Assistant E J POTTER
Stoker (1st Class) A RUSSELL
Assistant Steward G W L SCRIVEN
Ordinary Seaman H L SELLERS
Chief Engine Room Artificer A SHAW
Stoker (1st Class) J SHIELDS
Chief Stoker W A SKUDDER
Able Seaman R E SMITH
Able Seaman G A E STRATFORD
Ordinary Seaman T W SULLIVAN
Stoker (1st Class) P J TAYLOR
Ordinary Telegraphist J J THOMPSON
Marine R WATSON
Canteen Manager A J WEST
Stoker R C WILLIAMS

A further nine ratings were seriously wounded. Seventy-one officers and ratings were non-seriously wounded. This makes a total of 160 casualties.

Earlier in her career, the ship had suffered other casualties in action, including:

Boy Seaman 1st Class H M BRADLEY killed in action on 16th October 1939, at Rosyth, Scotland, nine other men being wounded and sent ashore to hospital.

Able Seaman R P PEARSON died of wounds on 25th May 1940 at Harstad, Norway. A further eight ratings had been seriously wounded, and had also been landed at Harstad, Norway on 25th/27th May 1940. (These men evidently survived and it is believed that they were safely evacuated to England in the hospital ship *Atlantis* on 4th/5th June 1940.) Captain JEANS and at least ten ratings were non-seriously wounded off Norway between 25th May and 7th June 1940 and returned to England aboard *Southampton*.

AWARDS

Of the men who lost their lives on 11th January 1941,
Mr A W DAVIS Commissioned Gunner RN
and Acting Corporal H JONES RM
each received a Posthumous Mention in Despatches
for their attempts to flood the 4-inch and 'X' Magazines, respectively.

Of the men who survived the sinking, the following each received a Mention in Despatches coupled with a Commendation for the Services Rendered.

Officers

Lieutenant (E) E G GRIFFIN
Surgeon Lieutenant H W GOTHARD

Ratings

Chief ERA L A HOLBROOK
Mechanician J DOWELL
Stoker J R FUDGER
Stoker J JENKINS
Leading Stoker W B MOORE
Shipwright H E G PEPPERALL
ERA J S WINGFIELD

Able Seaman W C MURRAY was also strongly recommended by Captain BROOKE for recognition, but did not receive an actual award.[464]

---

[464] Details of the actual recommendations and witness statements regarding the sinking and the subsequent actions in the desperate attempt to save the ship can be found in ADM 116/4354 at TNA. Reading these documents filled the author with great admiration for Chief ERA HOLBROOK, who seemed to be quite outstanding in a ship where many fine feats were being accomplished.

All these awards are very interesting, for they reflect the great shortage of officers and warrant officers following the carnage in the Wardroom Flat.

Taking them in order, Alf and Corporal JONES RM each received an award for their heroic and self-sacrificial attempts to save the ship from instant immolation. Alf's award may also be a reflection that all three Commissioned Gunners (G) lost their lives. Similarly, Corporal JONES' award may reflect the heavy casualties amongst the Royal Marines, where the lone Major and six of his relatively small squad of about 15 bandsmen and 55 Marines had perished. (Say, 10% of them.)

Presumably, official thoughts then turned to the efforts which had been made to save the ship from the fires which were raging. In that context, Lt (E) GRIFFIN was the most senior engineering officer left, for the lone Commander (E) was dead, as was Lt GRIFFIN's only brother-officer (E), Lt GUEST. Ironically, Lt GUEST had just returned from a very long course in fire-fighting and damage-control and his services would have been utterly invaluable. One of the two Warrant Engineers was also dead, and evidently about twenty of the artificers, mechanicians and stokers under them. Chief ERA HOLBROOK played a huge role in filling the void which was left and he was nobly supported by the other ranks around him. They fully deserved their awards.

Surgeon Lt GOTHARD was evidently the *only* medical officer still on his feet, with his senior officer wounded in the head and his two brother-officers dead. Lt GOTHARD would have been heavily dependent on his SBAs and such help as he could elicit from those ratings who had no specific duty left to perform in the aftermath of the ship being hit. These men would have been particularly useful for evacuating and transhipping the casualties when the 'Abandon Ship' pipe was given. Barrie KENT reported that every wounded man had his wounds properly dressed before the transfer to *Diamond*. Most of them were unrecognisable, since they had bandages covering flash or burns wounds on their faces, which proved, wrote Barrie, '*the necessity of wearing anti-flash gear*'.

One cannot help wondering whether the ship could not have been saved, particularly if the bomb had not killed quite so many of the senior engineering officers and if Commander TINLEY had been more quickly recognised to be performing erratically when key 'damage control' operations were totally under his supervision. One can understand the frustration of Freddie DANCE and his 'oppos' that no ship spontaneously came alongside to lend her hoses and pumps to suppress the conflagrations – and that Admiral RENOUF did not see fit to order one of his squadron to do so. A lot came down to the strength of the probability as to whether or not X Magazine – and maybe the HA Magazine too – was/were going to blow up. Dare another ship be risked in the attempt? Whichever way Admiral RENOUF decided, it was going to be a bitter pill to have to swallow.

Saving the ship would have made no difference to Alf, or to Corporal JONES and the other officers and men already dead or dying of wounds, but men then still alive although trapped in compartments by the bomb-damage and fires, might have ultimately been rescued. The Royal Navy desperately needed every cruiser and every experienced man it could lay or keep hands on at that stage of the war. Desperately hard times lay just ahead for its ships and men, especially in the

Mediterranean. There were an enormous number of human sacrifices yet to be made and great tragedies to be wrought on the vast number of 'next of kin' and their close relations. The ultimate victory would come at a terrible cost to all the protagonists.

-oOo-

CHAPTER SEVENTEEN:

"KiA": The Immediate Aftermath, back in England

Ten year-old Neville was at school in Chesham on 17th January 1941. A dreadful foreboding stole over him as the day went on. It became worse and worse as he came out of school and climbed the steep slope up Hivings Hill towards home. Long before he reached the front door of Orpington House, he was in near-torment with the tremendous and incomprehensible mental forces which had come down 'out of the blue' to press on him. He had never known anything remotely like them before.

So, when he stepped into the house to find his family in the most appalling state of grief, with the women weeping and wailing, tears streaming down their faces, and almost prostrate with grief, he knew, before a word was spoken, that the most terrible thing that could have happened had happened, and that his father was dead. The force of the grieving and distress of the women had somehow reached out to him telepathically, 'through the ether', far down into the valley.

He learnt that the telegram boy had arrived at the house that morning, bearing the dreaded orange-yellow envelope that everybody with a son, brother or husband (or, indeed, daughter) away at the war was constantly terrified of receiving. The telegram was addressed to Alice, with the message inside: *"From Admiralty; Deeply regret to inform you that your husband Mr A W DAVIS Commissioned Gunner RN has been killed in action."*

A letter followed, dated hard on the heels of the telegram, but incorrectly addressed to Alice's former address at Felixstowe, and forwarded on from there: *"In confirmation of the Admiralty's telegram of 16th January (sic), I am commanded by My Lords Commissioners of the Admiralty to state that they have been informed that your husband, Mr Alfred William DAVIS Commissioned Gunner RN, lost his life on 11th January 1941 during the course of an enemy air attack upon HMS SOUTHAMPTON, in which he was serving. My Lords desire me to express to you their deep regret at receiving this intelligence and their personal sympathy in the great loss which you have sustained. I am, Madam, Your Obedient Servant, H.R.MARKHAM."*

A further letter followed, dated 31st January, still wrongly addressed, which said: *"I am commanded.....to inform you that a report has been received that your husband........who was killed in action on 11th January....was buried at sea."*

None of the family could take in the fact that Alf was dead. Surely, it was a mistake and, somehow, he MUST have survived. He was such a charismatic and vital man, he must surely have cheated whatever hazards had confronted him. Perhaps he would yet be picked up out of the sea alive.

Nan encountered one of her spiritualist friends, and Nan told her the sad news, including the last letter from the Admiralty, saying that Alf had been 'buried at sea' "*Agnes*", said her friend. "*I was on my way to see you because I have been very troubled. You see, Alf 'came to me' in spirit the other night, and I clearly saw him surrounded by flames and smoke, and very distressed indeed. I think that is how he met his end, dear. I do not believe he was 'buried at sea' in the conventional sense that the Admiralty would like you to believe, albeit with the best of intentions. I do not think there is the least chance that he is still alive, dear Agnes. He has already gone on into the next world to join his beloved Olive.*"

Letters of sympathy began to flood in as news of Alf's death percolated around relatives and friends. They told a lot. One came from Nell KOESTER, sister of Commissioned Gunner Lewis KOESTER, following hard on the heels of a postcard she had rushed off to Alice saying, "*So sorry to tell you my brother has died of wounds*", her letter now adding, "*I am so sorry I wrote not knowing you were also bereaved. Mother is being very brave. Lewis was her best beloved, and I have lost my dearest 'Pal'*"....and ending, "*Your sister in sorrow.*"

Nan's half-brother, the old soldier 'Uncle Bill', wrote from Colchester to express his love and deepest sympathy, saying, "*I always looked up to Alf as a fine fellow - so good to everybody. I bet he was respected on his ship...*". Another letter came to Alice from Phyllis KNIGHT of Looe Road, Felixstowe, to say, "*My husband and I, and all at Old Felixstowe, will remember your husband's kindness to all around him...*': another came from H and M WEATHERLEY of Plymouth, saying, "*Having heard of the bombing of 'Southampton', we had kept wondering about Alf. He was such a great friend, and we well remember your visit to Glasgow with us.*"[465] Warrant Officer F Maurice CHILD of No.4 Manning Depot at Quebec, Canada, was another who wrote, saying, "*We cannot recall ever entertaining anyone that we liked as well as your husband - nor one that was as grateful as he...*"[466] Bert BURROWS wrote from Natal, South Africa, expressing his condolences. He had heard the news from a fellow-officer of Alf's whom he had run into in Alexandria. Bert had "*met Alf whilst serving in 'Birmingham', back in 1926, and twice since then*", and had clearly regarded him as a real friend.

Signing herself '*your loving Aunt*', Mrs Jessie GEDYE wrote to Nan from Grange-over-Sands to say, "*I am so grieved for your dear daughter*".[467] Walter Lee BUSHBY, signing *himself 'Your Loving Brother Walt'* wrote to Nan from Hove, to say, "*Alf endeared himself to us years ago when he used to visit us.*"[468] Like various of the others who wrote, in an effort to 'identify' with the grieving, Walter Lee (who ran a greengrocer's shop at Hove) talked a little about his own problems, saying, "*There is nowhere safe for us to go, unless it is Dora's people. Business is very difficult now*

---

[465] This was presumably the visit to attend the launching of *Southampton* at John Brown's Shipyard in 1936.

[466] This was evidently to do with the escorting duties of *Southampton* during the Visit of KG VI and Queen Elizabeth to Canada in 1939.

[467] Jessie, née HUME was then aged 78. She would live on until the great age of 106 years.

[468] He was actually one of her 1st cousins, and (probably originally prompted by his mother Jane BUSHBY née SKINNER) had clearly always identified strongly with Nan, who, it may be remembered, had lost her own mother (Jane's older sister) at a very early age, and then had a rather cold step-mother set over her.

...there is little to sell. I am very sorry, Dear Aggie - I quite believe that you miss your house so much...."[469]

All the letters poured out deep sympathy, and numbers of them resembled Walter Lee's, such as one from 'Millie' of Hampstead, talking of *'bombs all round us'*, and Amy HOOPER née ENGLISH of Wimbledon Park, who talked of her nephew Peter who had *'only just got out from Dunkirk'*, and referred to his father, who had been tragically killed on the Western Front late in 1918, as the end of the First World War was approaching. 'Billie and George' wrote to say, *"Like us, you've had some knock-out blows.."* and went on to report that *"There is little left of Portsmouth now and thousands are out of work.",* and 'Phyllis' wrote from Bury St Edmunds to say, *"Our baby son was born in November. Liverpool was rather bad before we left..."*

Great Aunt Alice wrote from Ipswich to say that, *"Elsie and Mrs MAWMANN do not like sleeping in the shelter...",* and Margaret McFADYEN wrote letters from the Admiralty Office at Clydebank and from Helensburgh to express her great sympathy and to add, *"The last Blitz here was terrific."*

A typically well-worded letter came from young Neville's former Head Mistress, Miss MULLINS, saying she would *"always remember the kindly interest Mr DAVIS took in the school - how he appreciated all we tried to do for Neville. How Neville will miss his father."*

Seemingly, Alice had still been casting about as to what to do with her 'difficult' older step-children (it will be remembered that Alf had arranged for them to be withdrawn from their evacuee status in the Midlands and returned to her care), for her aunt Ethel BISHOP now wrote to Alice to say, *"If this were not such a bad area* (she meant from the bombing point of view), *I'd say send Joan here...."*

All told, Alice and Nan heard from over eighty people over Alf's death, some more than once. As indicated above, the letters make quite a mosaic of the stresses and strains of the life going on in the UK at that time of the war. Although not detailed above, the letters were interesting at a lower level too, for they told of the childhood diseases being endured around the wider family, of deaths from natural causes, of displacements of people from their normal homes, of worries about sons serving in the armed forces, of lads not quite of call-up age serving in 'Home Defence' *pro tem*, and so on. They also told of the bonding in adversity which took place between family, friends and neighbours during the war. A great deal of love and sympathy was on view.

The toll on Alf's children, on Alice, on Alf's in-laws and other family members due to Alf's death cannot be quantified. There is no doubt that it was of massive degree, especially, of course, on the 'nearest and dearest', but the ripples also ran wide. When one reflects that this was just one man - that eighty were lost in *Southampton* alone, and that thousands of others had already lost their lives on land, sea or in the air, with *millions* yet to come, the true cost of war just *begins* to dawn.

---

[469] It may be remembered that Nan and Grandpa GREEN had been forced to sell their fine house and businesses at Felixstowe, and to get away from the immediate danger of invasion by moving inland with Alice and the younger children and buying a property there. It is not surprising to thus learn that Nan had confided to Walter Lee that she was greatly missing her previous excellent and much-loved home.

CHAPTER EIGHTEEN:

Some Reflections on Alf's Premature Death

Had not the war cut his life short, Alf might have lived to be a comparatively old man. That is to say, his siblings all went on to live to considerable ages. His brother Jack lived to age 77, his sister Nellie to 89, Rose to 80 and Eva to 78. (As already recounted, these three 'girls' had pubs in London, and Death had come very close to them, too, during the German bombing 'blitzes'. There was colossal devastation around Nellie's pub in South Kensington, some of it due to a huge 'land-mine' explosion. Rose's pub in Victoria was also in the thick of it, and the heavy rescue services actually had to dig poor Eva out of the rubble of her severely damaged Clapham pub. She had received serious head injuries from which she never fully recovered, despite four surgical operations over the years.)

Jack died in 1971, of prostate cancer, after a difficult life. His wife, Kate, lived on to 1979, though allegedly somewhat 'borne down' by the vicissitudes of her married life. There seems little doubt but that Jack had given her a 'hard time', though he certainly mellowed as he aged and their relationship became a happier one. The author's cousin Kath WALLER is positive that her father Jack had never hit Kate or any of his daughters, but agrees that he had certainly suffered from extreme frustration and anger at times, and that he then used to vent his powerful temper rather spectacularly by bashing his fist against some inanimate object, such as the kitchen table. One assumes that much of his frustration had arisen from the way his life had turned out, probably not one whit helped by his hard wartime experiences. (He had been of the type of 'Old Soldier' who never talked at all about the war and had evidently always kept things tightly 'bottled up' in his *psyche*.)

There was no 'son of Jack', to carry on the DAVIS name. Jack had raised his seven daughters with an iron hand. All the girls married, and nearly all of them had children and have since become grandparents. Five of Jack's seven daughters are still alive (as are four of their seven husbands). That is, only Joyce and Joan Priscilla have departed this life. Joan's late husband, Wilfred Desmond "Bill" GUEST, was a natural 'Mr FIXIT' who worked in the aircraft industry. Bill had been kindness personified in acting as a 'go-between' when, late in life, the author was trying to contact the 'girl-cousins' he had never met. He eventually 'stumbled across' Bill by 'near-serendipity', and Bill more or less 'did the rest'.

Neville (the author) has remained in quite close contact with one of his girl-cousins, Kath, and her husband Maurice. Kath somehow reminds him of 'Aunt Rose', who was once in the running to adopt him.[470]

Nellie died in 1986, having outlived her Publican husband, Wilf, by some 45 years. Wilf had died of natural causes in 1941, but constant 'hosting, drinking and

---

[470] The author is profoundly grateful to Kathleen and her husband Maurice for reading through what had been drafted about 'Jack', and suggesting two or three amendments which have been included in the foregoing text. (It is interesting to note the coincidence that Nellie's second son, John PENNEY, had been an officer in Maurice's unit of the Royal Tank Regiment towards the end of WW2.)

entertaining' as a publican had evidently taken a serious toll on his health. Sadly, this meant that his two sons had lost him whilst they were still only in their teens.

Those fine sons of Nellie and Wilf were well-educated and both had successful 'civilian' careers post-war, after serving as officers in the armed forces, the elder son, Raymond, having become an officer in the Royal Marine Commandos in time to take part in the bitter fighting against the desperate Japanese around the Pacific Rim in 1945. Both sons married and had children, and have since become grandparents. The elder son, Ray and his wife Dorothy are not in good health, but have been very helpful and generous to the author in his investigations of 'their side' of the family history. Both Nellie's sons have a great love of horses, and a good ability at handling and judging them, doubtless inherited from their father and their DAVIS grandfather. These horsemanship traits also run strongly in Ray's daughter.

Alf's widow, Alice, had inherited only £175 from Alf's estate, his Will having been proved on 30th May 1941, in the Principal Probate Registry which had been evacuated from London and was then based at Llundudno. The Will bore an Admiralty stamp, dated 31st December 1941, confirming that it had been *"examined in the Office of the Inspector of Seamen's Wills and admitted as available for the receipt of Naval Assets."* The sum of £175 was probably the equivalent of only about £8,000 in the values of today and would not have lasted long with four children to clothe and care for, and a house to maintain in co-operation with Alice's aging parents.

Alice never remarried but worked as a clerk in an international industrial concern to supplement her incredibly meagre war-widow's pension. She always did her duty by Alf, constantly preserving and trying to pass on to his children the high moral standards, integrity and discipline by which Alf had lived. She became a full-time housekeeper to her family after her mother died in 1951, her mother being shortly followed to the grave by Alice's father. Alice was later involved in 'charitable work' with the Women's Institute at Harrow, in Middlesex. She eventually retired to Felixstowe at the age of 65, continued there with her charitable work, and died in 1973, aged 72. The author had gone through many vicissitudes and crises with Alice since Alf's death.[471] However, aided by his young wife (who got on with Alice 'like a

---

[471] The crises included a spontaneous but desperately-serious attempt by the author, then aged 11, to run away in mid-1941 after yet another 'confrontation' with Alice. To his amazement, Alice caught up with him, her desperation 'giving her feet wings'. If she had hit him, he would have run again, in a more controlled and planned way. However, she merely wept and pleaded with him not to go, and he warmed to the vulnerable, distressed and 'feminine' side she had suddenly revealed. There was no way he could run away after that. There was also one particularly terrifying 'crisis' night in 1944, when they drew strength from each other as they shared a 'Morrison' shelter whilst a seemingly unending succession of V1 Flying Bombs roared ear-shatteringly low overhead, literally vibrating the house, and with the two of them desperately hoping that the motors would not cut out as each 'Buzz-Bomb' approached. Luckily, they didn't and Neville was thus destined to become the 'Man of the Family' in his late father's stead – helping Alice, especially through the difficult post-war years, by raising hens for eggs and rabbits for much-needed meat, and by producing vegetables from the garden. He also did the house-maintenance, as well as getting a permanent job after leaving school in 1947 at age 17 and thereafter paying into the family budget. He sustained this supportive but emotionally fraught role of being 'a husband-without-conjugal-or-administrative-rights' until 1961, when he was supplanted by Alice's own maturing son, Richard, who took over the upstairs part of the house as a flat for himself and his new wife. 'Encouraged to leave', Neville initially felt rejected by mother and son, but Alice had done him a favour and he was a 'free man' at last. He was married within two years of leaving the family home.

house on fire'), the author had come around to love Alice deeply and there were happy occasions when he, his wife Liz and their two young children stayed with Alice for seaside holidays, and where Alice became a loved 'Nanny Felixstowe'. The author was also proud that Alice came to find refuge and to spend the final weeks of her life with him and his family before entering hospital, by then fatally afflicted with cancer of the brain.[472] Alice left a Will, the terms of which left equal shares to all four of Alf's children.

Alf's children by his first wife, Olive, had varied lives. Perhaps, bearing in mind the early loss of their birth-mother, followed by Alf's re-marriage to a very different woman, followed so soon by Alf's own death, too much should not have been expected of his children, who were all emotionally crippled to some extent.[473] The semi-orphans were, however, fortunate in receiving good educations, partly aided by the charity of the Masonic Movement, and partly (in the case of Alice's son Richard) by the charity of the trustees of Christ's Hospital Bluecoat School.

Alf's elder son, Neville (the author), worked in industry for 43 years, becoming a technologist. He had tried to 'follow in his father's footsteps' by entering the Royal Naval College at Dartmouth, initially scraping through the written exams and initiative tests, but only to be subsequently turned down for naval (and military) service on medical grounds. However, disregarding repeated medical advice about the risk of heart failure, he became a keen amateur Rugby Player for many years, and 'racketed around socially' to some degree, hard-drinking with Rugby-playing war-veterans, and sometimes being deeply involved with women much older than himself (probably working out psychological problems to do with the early loss of his mother – and maybe to do with Alice, too). He was fortunate, for these affairs proved to be highly beneficial learning and maturing experiences for him though they also brought heartbreak, mainly to others, sad to say. He ultimately settled down with Elizabeth SAKLATVALA, a considerably younger woman, by whom he had three children, two of whom, a son and a daughter, survived. (These children each married but are now divorced.) Neville and his wife have recently celebrated their 42nd wedding anniversary. Their son, a graduate in building and construction, seems to have inherited the DAVIS strong love of horsemanship. Their daughter, who has very good PR skills, worked as a Secretary and PA in the City of London for 16 years, and has since been working in the Home Counties, nearer her home, in a demanding PA role.

Alf's elder daughter, Joan, served in the WRNS (as a 'Marine Wren') and, later, worked in industry. She married John GOODMAN, a naval man, *Ganges-*

---

[472] She had been a heavy smoker for much of her life, which may well have accelerated the development of her cancer.

[473] Following team-building exercises at Kodak Ltd., industrial relations consultant Harold GOULDING (who was a survivor of Japanese Prisoner of War camps, and the author of '*Yasme*'), became the author's psychological 'guru'. Harold once told Neville that he saw great suppressed violence in his (Neville's) character. Perhaps that was why the author loved the spice of 'physical combat' and played Rugby in the front row until the advanced age of 60 years. Nev's guru also expressed amazement that the author had not 'dropped out' and even contemplated suicide as a very young man - for it is traditional to expect a son to out-do his father, and how on earth does a son aspire to out-perform an inspirational father like Alf, who had 'died a hero's death'. Perhaps such generalisations do not take sufficient account of the human factors of sheer 'bloodymindedness' and 'in-built obstinacy'? Interestingly, the author married a girl who had survived a very difficult childhood by very much the same natural characteristic of stubbornness and near-defiance. At least it leads to a strong measure of mutual understanding and caring.

trained, who had served as a Torpedoman in the destroyer *Dainty* amongst other ships, and, in true Naval Tradition, had taken to boxing as his sport.[474] He gained electrical skills from his naval training, and worked in manufacturing industry post-war. Joan's husband died of coronary problems in 1978. They had two sons, who both grew up to have a 'country bent'. The younger son, a Farm Manager, is married and has three sons.

Alf's younger daughter, Jessica, married Eric FORD, an electronics engineer who later moved into the marketing side of his profession. Husband and wife emigrated to Canada, where they had two sons, but then divorced. One of the sons is married.

Alf's son by Alice, Richard Paul, was arguably the most successful of the siblings profession-wise. As a young man he did National Service, obtaining a Commission in the Royal Corps of Signals. In his subsequent professional career, he became a Company Secretary. However, he has had the misfortune to be married and divorced three times. He has no personal memories of his father whatsoever – which lack he says was a most grievous loss to him as he grew up. For example, he did not know how to behave on visitors' days at his boarding school when the other boys were chatting comfortably with their fathers. However, unlike his siblings, he did have a reasonably long-lived mother. (The author, nine years Richard's senior, strove to be not only an 'older brother', but also something of a 'junior surrogate father' to Richard, to try, as best he could, to make up for Alf's irreparable loss. This was an echo of his Uncle Neville's earlier kind behaviour towards the author. The author can identify with Richard's problem 'of having no father', because he always felt odd at school after age five 'from having no mother' when virtually all the other children did. To subsequently lose a father just intensified what was already a disaster. His sisters were, of course, in much the same boat.)

All of Alf's four children are still alive, the older three now being well into their seventies. All four now have serious health problems.

What Alf would have made of it all is hard to know. Currently, there is only Robert DAVIS, son of Neville, to carry on the DAVIS name in which Alf always expressed such pride and for which he always expected such high standards of behaviour by his children. However, Robert is divorced and, in any case, seems disinclined towards fatherhood. Be that as it may, the twists and turns of fate never cease to amaze one.

Perhaps, posthumously, on some astral plane or other, the author may meet up in spirit with his father Alf, and be able to mull it all over with him, soul to soul. A lot of water has flowed under the bridge since Alf was born on 9th July 1895. The author hopes the spirit of his lovely Mum will then be around too, and Alice, and Nan and Grandpa and Uncle Bill, and Con and Neville, and Jimmy and Dilys - to say nothing of the beloved baby daughter whom the author and his wife lost in 1965 - and many others to whom he has referred, including various 'Old Southamptons'. Might be quite a party! He hopes he won't get too many hard kicks for what he has exposed in his writing.

---

[474] Apparently John had survived three sinkings during WW2. He had gained prize-money whilst serving in *Dainty*.

Alf and all the other members of the ship's complement who were lost on 11th January 1941 are not forgotten. The 6th HMS *Southampton* has visited the site from time to time over the years and services of commemoration have been held with the destroyer hove-to, floating high above the wreck of her cruiser predecessor. The latest time the destroyer hove-to above the wreck is believed to have been as recent as the 11th November 2004.

Before he cast a handsome wreath of red poppies into the sea at one such commemoration in 1993, the late Lt Cmdr Freddie DANCE RNR, who had been a Boy Seaman aboard *Southampton* at the time of the sinking, was thrilled, moved and honoured to have the privilege of reading the liturgy, "*They shall not grow old as we that are left grow old, age shall not weary them, nor the years condemn. In the morning, and at the going down of the sun, we will remember* them". He broke down part-way through, and it took him a few moments to recompose himself. He was subsequently told by the Captain that his (Freddie's) eyes were far from being the only ones filled with tears.

Other services of commemoration have been held at ports and other venues in England. At such gatherings, the author and his family have been pleased and proud to have the honour to meet surviving 'Old Southamptons', all now 'Grand Old Men', and, through them, to reach back in time to 'touch base' with Alf, dead these sixty-four years and more, but never forgotten.

THE END

APPENDIX A

AS ALREADY STATED, GRATEFUL THANKS AND ACKNOWLEDGEMENTS ARE DUE TO MANY ORGANISATIONS AND PEOPLE. SOME DETAILS CONCERNING THE PRIMARY 'NATIONAL' SOURCES ARE GIVEN BELOW.

DOCUMENTS FROM WHICH FACTUAL INFORMATION BEARING ON ALF'S LIFE HAS BEEN DRAWN. THE REFERENCES AND TITLES ARE THOSE USED BY THE REPOSITORY CONCERNED. Where titles cover a wide range and/or mask the relevant 'connection' with Alf's career**,** supplementary data has been added [*in italics, and in square brackets*] to indicate the particular 'aspects', sections and/or dates which have been drawn upon.

a) THE IMPERIAL WAR MUSEUM (Department of Documents)

Misc 164 (2541)   Diary of an Unidentified PO Stoker in HMS *Weymouth* 1914-18 [*Period 1914-16*]
Box: 86/60/1   Diary of Commander RFC STRUBEN RN [*esp. Pt 1, Chapter 9, 'The Cape Station' .*]
Box: 71/29/1   Diary of Vice Admiral D B CRAMPTON [*when Captain of 'Weymouth', 1914-16*]
Box: 99/34/1-3   Records of NAPIER, Vice Admiral Sir Trevelyan, KCB MVO [*For the Period 1917-18*]

The author is very grateful to the IWM for making these documents available for study. Only factual data has been extracted from Admiral NAPIER's records, but a number of quotations have been taken from all of the three diaries. Two quotations, both taken from Roy STRUBEN's diary, are large ones, viz. a 225-word quotation, dramatically describing the hive of activity on the upper decks of a large WW1 warship when she was getting under way, and a 300-word quotation describing the conditions in gun-turrets and associated action stations when the same ship was cruising at night, in a 'moderate' sea. Other quotations from the three diaries are far shorter – often just a couple of words – but all have been invaluable for adding 'colour'. It is understood that copyright has lapsed, but, should that understanding be in error, the author would always be pleased to hear from any relatives of these diarists, and to credit the relatives appropriately, should any further editions of this book be made.

b) THE NATIONAL MARITIME MUSEUM

HTN/219: 'The Hamilton Papers'. [A Section of date c.1911, re the armour/armament of HMS *Vanguard*.]
DEY/29: 'The Papers of Sir James D'Eyncourt.' [A Section c.1916 re structural failures, HMS *Courageous*]

The author is very grateful to the National Maritime Museum, Greenwich, for permission to use the quotations which have been taken from these two documents.

c) THE NATIONAL ARCHIVES (Formerly the PRO) (Admiralty Section)

ADM 1/8380/151   The Empire's WT Communications, 1914.
ADM 1/8391/286   Cruiser Engagement in Heligoland Bight 28 AUG 1914: New Gun Sights prop'd 1914.
ADM 1/8402/416   Blockade of German Warship *Konigsberg* off German E/Africa 10 NOV 1914: 1914
ADM 1/8676/50   Operations & Destruction of German Cruiser *Konigsberg*: 1925
ADM 101/528   DELHI-DIOMEDE 1931.   [*Medical Officer's Journal for Delphinium 1931*]
ADM 101/530   GANGES-GODETIA 1931.   [*Medical Officer's Journal for Ganges 1931*]
ADM 101/544   GANGES-GUARDIAN 1934.   [*Medical Officer's Journal for Ganges 1934*]
ADM 101/571   SOMALI-SPARTIATE 1940.   [*Medical Officer's Journal for Southampton 1940*]
ADM 104/103-04   SHIPS 1910-1918/ SHIPS 1919-1930.   [*Deaths of 'shipmate' Ratings (Non-War)*]
ADM 104/110-11   SHIPS 1910-1918/ SHIPS 1918-1930.   [*Deaths of 'shipmate' Ratings (Non-War)*]
ADM 104/126   Registers of Reports of Deaths 1919 Aug - 1941 Oct   [*Deaths of 'shipmates'(War)*]
ADM 116/1615A   Loss of HMS *Vanguard* 9th July 1917. 1917   [*Believed spontaneous detonation.*]

c) THE NATIONAL ARCHIVES (Admiralty Section), Continued

ADM 116/2258	Married Allowance for Officers 1924.
ADM 116/2348	Ships Magazines - protection of 1920-1927.
ADM 116/2430	Air Targets for Gunnery Practice: WT Controlled Aircraft. 1924-1932
ADM 116/2458	Refits of HM Ships: Lengthening of Periods between. 1925-1928
ADM 116/2863	Africa Station: Report of Proceedings. 1931-33
ADM 116/2887	Commissioned Warrant Officers & Lieutenants ex Warrant Rank - Pay Cuts. 1931-32
ADM 116/3171	Africa Station: visits of HM Ships: visit of HRH Prince Of Wales, etc. 1925-1926
ADM 116/3337	Boys Training Establishments: accommodation, education, staff, etc. 1931-1936
ADM 116/3909	Fleet Gunnery Practices 1938-1939
ADM 116/4017	Royal Visit to Canada & USA: arrangements. 1937-1939
ADM 116/4037	Anti-Aircraft Re-armament of the Navy. 1937-1939
ADM 116/4041	Armament of HM Ships - Improvements 1919-1939
ADM 116/4309	Termination of Action between Force 'H' and Italian Forces. 1940
ADM 116/4354-55	Loss of HMS *Southampton*: Board of Enquiry. 1941
ADM 116/4437	Reorganisation of RN & RM Gunnery Branches: Revised Substantive Pay. 1938-1939
ADM 12/1512	Index T-Z 1913 *[Correspondence ref 'Weymouth']*
ADM 12/1524	Index T-Z. 1914 *[Correspondence ref 'Weymouth']*
ADM 12/1571A	Index C 1917 *[Correspondence ref 'Courageous']*
ADM 137/3105	Pursuit of *Goeben & Breslau* by *Gloucester*; Mediterranean 1914.
ADM 137/702	Paper No. H.S. 702 *[Adm KING-HALL: Reports of Proceedings at Cape Stn, 1915.]*
ADM 137/3608	Loss of HMS *Natal* 1915 Dec 30 - 1916 Feb 29 *[Believed spontaneous detonation.]*
ADM 137/3680	Loss of HMS *Vanguard* 1917 July 10 - Sep 10. *[Believed spontaneous detonation.]*
ADM 137/3727	Loss of Kite Balloons 1917 Sep 23 - 1918 Mar 11 *[and Hazards involved in their use.]*
ADM 137/3834	Projectiles: Types in use in HM Fleet 1917 Feb 17 - Mar 17
ADM 137/3835	Projectiles: capabilities and improvements 1916 Dec 9 - 1917 Jan 13
ADM 137/3836	Projectiles: remarks in C-in-C's letters, 1917 Jan 3 - Feb 3 *[Hurrah ADM BEATTY!]*
ADM 137/3837	Projectiles: Types in use in HM Fleet 1917 Feb 17 - Mar 17
ADM 137/3838	Trials with various explosives in APC shells 1917 Mar 8 - Mar 13
ADM 137/3839	Reports compiled...of dmge done to ..German High Seas Fleet 1917 Jan 13 ['*Jutland*']
ADM 137/4173	Anti-submarine equipment 1916-1918 *[Hydrophones, Depth-charges, etc.]*
ADM 137/4702	Req'ts to allow movement of German Personnel at Scapa *[Implicit restraints,1918/19]*
ADM 137/4822	Extract of gunnery practices, Grand Fleet Battleships & B/cruisers 1914 - 1918, 1922
ADM 137/4823	Extract of gunnery practices in Grand Fleet Light Cruisers 1914 - 1918, 1922
ADM 156/61	Confident'l Adm F/Order: Theft by Finding: AB E, C.K., HMS *Lowestoft*, 1923
ADM 156/76	Forbearing to Chase German Warships *Goeben & Breslau* 1914-1915.
ADM 156/110	Forbearing to chase German Warships *Goeben & Breslau*, etc. 1914 - 1919
ADM 156/159	Chase of German Warship *Goeben* in Mediterranean: Acquittal, etc. !914 - 1917
ADM 156/182	ADM Sir Berkeley MILNE 1918 *[Concerning chase of 'Goeben' and 'Breslau']*
ADM 156/184	Admiral Sir Berkeley MILNE *[Concerning chase of 'Goeben' and 'Breslau']*
ADM 178/158	Admiral Sir Berkeley MILNE retirement 1918-1919 *[Concerning chase of 'G' & 'B']*
ADM 53/31471	*Vanguard* 1912 Mar 28 - 1913 Mar 29 *[Ship's Log as relevant to Alf.]*
ADM 53/25846	*Russell* 1913 Jan 1 - 1913 Aug 31 *[Ship's Log as relevant to Alf.]*
ADM 53/68440-55	*Weymouth* 1913 Oct 11 - 1916 May 29 *[Ship's Logs as relevant to Alf.]*
ADM 53/43057	*Gloucester* 1914 Feb 10 - 1915 Jan 31 *[Ship's Log ref chase of 'G' and 'B']*
ADM 53/38781-808	*Courageous* 1916 Nov 4 - 1920 Nov 21 *[Ship's Logs as relevant to Alf.]*
ADM 53/79944-47	*Lowestoft* 1920 Sep 20 - 1923 Feb 29 *[Ship's Logs as relevant to Alf.]*
ADM 53/85649-52	*St Cyrus* 1925 Sep22 - 1926 Jun 3 *[Ship's Logs as relevant to Alf.]*
ADM 53/87561	*Tiger* 1924 Dec 20 - 1925 Nov 25 *[Ship's Log when Alf at 'Excellent'.]*
ADM 53/71403-05	*Birmingham* 1926 Apr 20 - !928 Sep 18 *[Ship's Logs as relevant to Alf.]*
ADM 53/75663-87	*Delphinium* 1931 Mar 1 - 1933 Mar 18 *[Ship's Logs as relevant to Alf.]*
ADM 53/106151-72	*Southampton* 1937 Mar 6 - 1938 Dec *[Ship's Logs as relevant to Alf.]*
ADM 53/110655-66	*Southampton* 1939 Jan - 1939 Dec *[Ship's Logs as relevant to Alf.]*
ADM 53/113248-58	*Southampton* 1940 Jan - !940 Nov *[Ship's Logs as relevant to Alf.]*

[NOTE: The author is very grateful for having been permitted to use factual information from relevant parts of the above documents. Quotations have been used from a minority of them. Generally those quotations are brief, but rather longer quotations have been taken from the main findings of Courts of Enquiry and Courts Martial, etc., such as exist in ADM 116/4354/55, ADM 137/3680, and ADM 156/76.

It is clear that many documents have not survived. To take the ADM 101 series as one example, Surgeon's Journals relevant to Alf's service in ships other than those shown above and/or at other dates to those shown above, no longer exist. Thus there thus are no Surgeon's Journals at all for *Birmingham, Courageous, Lowestoft, St Cyrus* or *Vanguard* during periods when Alf was serving on them. This is a great shame, for Surgeon's Journals usually convey a considerable amount of 'peripheral' information.]

d) THE NATIONAL ARCHIVES (Formerly The PRO) (General Register)

Piece No.	Fol No.	Pp.	Place of Census & Year	[*Key Name(s) of Interest Age(s).*]
HO107/1839	236	18	Market Lavington, Wilts (1851)	[*Richard/Eliz DAVIS 43/3m*]
RG9/1291	98	12	Market Lavington, Wilts (1861)	[*Richard/Eliz DAVIS 54/10*]
RG9/1291	111	8	Market Lavington, Wilts (1861)	[*Richard HOPKINS 24*]
RG10/1911	28	15	Market Lavington, Wilts (1871)	[*Richard//Alfred DAVIS 64//4*]
RG10/1911	38	6	Market Lavington, Wilts (1871)	[*Mrs Elizabeth HOPKINS 33*]
RG10/1911	58	15	Market Lavington, Wilts (1871)	[*Caroline DAVIS 24*]
RG10/1928	26	7	Bratton, Westbury, Wilts (1871)	[*Richard HOPKINS 34*]
RG11/2042	91	1	Market Lavington, Wilts (1881)	[*Richard HOPKINS 45*]
RG11/2042	87	3	Market Lavington, Wilts (1881)	[*Eliz 'HOPKINS'(DAVIS) 25*]
RG11/2042	92	14	Market Lavington, Wilts (1881)	[*Ann/MaryAnn DAVIS 67/35*]
RG11/2063	17	5	Tilshead, Wiltshire (1881)	[*Alfred DAVIS 14*]
RG12/1601	60	1	Market Lavington, Wilts (1891)	[*Richard HOPKINS 54*]
RG12/1601	73	3	Market Lavington, Wilts (1891)	[*Elizabeth DAVIS 38*]
RG13/1928	64	3	Market Lavington, Wilts (1901)	[*Richard HOPKINS 64*]
RG13/1928	78	10	Market Lavington, Wilts (1901)	[*Elizabeth DAVIS 43*]
HO107/621/10	8	10	Potterhanworth, Lincs (1841)	[*John ATKINSON 30*]
HO107/2104	182	18	Potterhanworth, Lincs (1851)	[*John ATKINSON 48/20*]
RG9/2356	45	10	Potterhanworth, Lincs (1861)	[*John ATKINSON 29*]
RG9/2356	46	11	Potterhanworth, Lincs (1861)	[*Eliza ATKINSON 1*]
RG10/3367	64	10	Potterhanworth, Lincs (1871)	[*John/Eliza ATKINSON 39/12*]
RG11/0099	125	24	76 Eaton Square, Middx. (1881)	[*Elisa ATKINSON 23*]
RG13/3058	137	25	Metheringham, Lincs (1901)	[*Mary HICKS 46*]
HO107/621/10	8	1	Potterhanworth, Lincs (1841)	[*William DAYKINS 40*]
HO107/621/10	8	2	Potterhanworth, Lincs (1841)	[*Emma DAYKINS 10*]
HO107/2104	184	22	Potterhanworth, Lincs (1851)	[*William/Emma 52/20*]
RG9/1138	81	4	Hengrave, Suffolk (1861)	[*James/Sarah SKINNER 44/14*]
HO107/1019/8	7	8, 9	Somersham, Suffolk (1841)	[*Jos/Jos/Joseph GREEN 70/50/5*]
HO107/1799	201	12	St Nicholas, Ipswich, Sfk (1851)	[*Joseph GREEN 15*]
RG9/1130	107	24	St Peter, Sudbury, Suffolk (1861)	[*Joseph GREEN 25*]
RG10/1730	95	4	Mildenhall, Suffolk (1871)	[*James SKINNER 54*]
RG10/1716	111	7	All Saints, Sudbury, Sfk. (1871)	[*Joseph GREEN 35*]
RG11/829	82	27	Wimbledon, Surrey (1881)	[*Geo/George ENGLISH 58/39*]
RG11/1828	82	17	St Peter, Sudbury, Suffolk (1881)	[*Joseph/Joseph W GREEN 45/4*]
RG11/1825	122	7	Twinstead, Sudbury (1881)	[*Dan'l/Agnes S ENGLISH 32/4*]
RG11/1442	26	7	Sudbury, Suffolk (1891)	[*George/Geo W ENGLISH 49/8*]
RG12/1442	6	6	Sudbury, Suffolk (1891)	[*Joseph W GREEN 14*]
RG12/842	80	16	South Berstead, W.Sussex (1891)	[*Robt/Walter L. BUSHBY 37/5*]
RG13/1744	110	15	Sudbury, Suffolk (1901)	[*Joseph W/Agnes GREEN 24/26*]
RG11/3061	86	21, 2	Nuneaton, Warwickshire (1881)	[*STUBBS Family Household*]
RG12/2445	137	19	Nuneaton, Warwickshire (1891)	[*STUBBS Family Household*]
RG13/2902	115	31	Nuneaton, Warwickshire (1901)	[*STUBBS Family Household*]

d) THE NATIONAL ARCHIVES (General Register) (continued)

RG11/164	13	19	Marylebone, London	(1881)	[*LEON Family Household*]
RG12/1149	81	2	Great Brickhill, Bucks	(1891)	[*DUNCOMBE Family Household*]
RG13/1359	71	7	Great Brickhill, Bucks	(1901)	[*DUNCOMBE Family Household*]
RG12/582	45	4, 5	Caterham, Surrey	(1891)	[*WHITE Family Household*]
RG12/1443	86	14	Melford, Suffolk	(1881)	[*HYDE-PARKER Fam Household*]
RG13/1745	80	14	Melford, Suffolk	(1901)	[*HYDE-PARKER Fam. Household*]
RG12/2591	125	24, 5	St Mary Wigf'd, Lincoln	(1891)	[*Public Houses & Trade, Brayford*]
RG12/2591	129	32	St Mary Wigf'd, Lincoln	(1891)	[*Public Houses & Trade, Brayford*]
RG13/3061	167	37	Brayford Street, Lincoln	(1901)	[*'The Crown & Woolpack' P.H*]

Notes: The author is very grateful for having been permitted to use information from relevant parts of these documents. As so often happens with Family History Research, various 'gaps' in the derived data still exist, e.g. Alfred Wm DAVIS and Eliza ATKINSON are both believed to have been separately 'in service' at the time of the 1891 Census, but their actual whereabouts have not yet been discovered. Alfred Wm's mother, Elizabeth DAVIS, has not yet been found in the 1871 Census (though Alfred Wm's *putative* father *has* been located, living apart from his lawful wife and legitimate children).

A great many records (not listed above) have been probed in vain, providing only 'negative information', such as 'persons not present in their normal home environment'. Census records of 'sibling' and other 'collateral' families (not recorded in the above listings because not specifically named in the book), have had value in a 'general background' context. [Further Note: TNA records state that the 1841 Census records for Market Lavington have been lost to posterity. Hence there are no DAVIS or HOPKINS entries above for the year 1841.] [Yet Further Note: Very limited, but nevertheless important reference has also been made to Scottish Census Records of 1891 and Irish Census Records of 1901. Both of Alf's parents are believed to have been in Ireland at the time of the 1901 Census (by then married and with five children), although they have not been found. N.B It is probable that their elder son has been located in Ireland, living separately from the family, albeit somewhat 'disguised'.]

e) B, M, D CERTIFICATES

A considerable number of Birth, Marriage and Death Certificates have also been used in researching the story. Copies of some certificates had been preserved in family archives, but many have been purchased from TNA after tracking down likely-looking entries as found by probing through the indexes available within the Family Record Centre at Islington (Formerly housed at 'St Catherine's House', and before that at 'Somerset House'). The use of these documents is indicated where appropriate within the text, but they are not specifically listed either in this Appendix or elsewhere in the book. (Civil Registration of Births, Marriages and Deaths commenced in September 1837. Prior to that date, the Researcher is thrown back upon Parish Records of Baptisms, Marriages and Burials, such as are to be found in the County Record Offices for the related districts – See below. [N.B. Some reference to Scottish records has also been made.]

COUNTY RECORD OFFICES, The PROBATE OFFICE, etc.

a) PARISH RECORDS

Parish Records have been examined for appropriate baptisms, marriages and burials, in the counties indicated in the family trees set out in Appendix F, mainly Lincoln, Norfolk, Suffolk, Surrey and Wiltshire. [The author would like to express his appreciation of the work of amateur and professional researchers and various indexers, who have compiled such guides as the I.G.I., the 'Nimrod' index for Wiltshire, the Suffolk F.H.S. index of baptisms, marriages and burials, and the Lincolnshire F.H.S. index of marriages, all of which have provided some assistance in leading towards certain parish record entries. See various footnotes in the text and the appendices]

b) WILLS & TESTAMENTS

Where appropriate the Wills left by various individuals have been consulted. Copies of some, such as that of Alf (proved in 1941) and that of his father (proved in 1926), were already preserved in family archives, but copies of others have been traced and purchased from the Probate Office authorities or from the appropriate County Record Offices, and used as general 'background' material. See footnotes in the text.

c) MARRIAGE LICENCES

County Record Office records have been consulted, and Marriage Licences have been used in the few cases where they have been found to exist. (See individual Family Trees.)

THE SOCIETY OF GENEALOGISTS

The records of the Society of Genealogists have been probed to find information bearing on the history of the families shown in Appendix F. For example, various volumes of Boyd's Marriage Index and Phillimore's transcriptions of parish registers have been consulted and found very helpful. Research has also been conducted using (i) microfiche copies of the IGI (to which reference is made elsewhere in this book), (ii) the surname indexes to certain censuses, (iii) copies of indexes to Scottish Birth, Marriage and Death certificates and so forth. Much of the information is of the type which requires verification 'at source' (e.g. within the original parish registers), but the works held by the SoG provide invaluable 'finding aids'.

THE NEWSPAPER MUSEUM (Now Part of the BRITISH LIBRARY)

a) NEWSPAPERS

Newspaper cuttings preserved within the family archives (usually bereft of the title and exact date) have been used as background. Newspapers at the Newspaper Museum at Colindale have been consulted for further data concerning family members. It has been rare to find relevant entries, though certain family-submitted obituaries have been helpful. The 'ace' finding was Alfred Wm's advertisement when he was opening his pub in Lincoln in December 1906. The author is indebted to the British Library for permission to use the above information. (See individual footnotes in the text.)

APPENDIX B

'COPYRIGHT AGREEMENTS' for REPRODUCING IMAGES FOR THIS BOOK

i) Grateful thanks are due to each of the following organisations for their help and advice, and for allowing the author to reproduce images from their photographic collections:

> **The Imperial War Museum (Fifteen images**, reproduced on pages 93, 172, 173, 181, 187, 218, 226, 512, 575, 600, 641, 644, 646, 648, 651.)
> **The National Archives (Formerly the PRO) (Five images**, 22/83, 82, 194, 195)
> **The Royal Naval Museum, Portsmouth (Four images**, on pages 138, 261, 322, 638.)
> **The Warwickshire County Record Office (Two images**, on pages 35, 36.)
> **English Heritage: National Monument Record (One image**, on page 25.)
> **The Royal Commission on the Ancient and Historical Monuments of** Scotland **(One image**, on page 47.)
> **The Lincolnshire County Council, Education and Cultural Services** Directorate **(One image**, on page 50.)
> **ECPAD (Etablissement de Communication et de Production Audiovisuelle de la Défense), France. (One image,** on page 610.)

> **Total: 30 images** (One repeated)

ii) Grateful thanks are also due to each of the following 'copyright-holders' for their help and advice, and for allowing the author to reproduce copies from related postcards in his own collection.

a) **Businesses still in-being.**

> **W.H.Smith**: Agreement received from **W. H. Smith Archive** to use **six** 'WHS' postcards dating from 1913 to 1930. (Images on pages 63, 65, 141, 206, 317, 374.)

> **Gieves Ltd**: Agreement received from **Gieves & Hawkes Ltd**. to use **one** 'Gieves' postcard dating from c.1935. (Image on page 330.)

b) **Businesses which have ceased trading, but where some or all of the relevant Stock and/or** Copyright is known to have been Passed On.

> **James Valentines & Co**: Agreement received from the **University of St Andrews Library** to use **eleven** postcards dating from 1887 to 1937. (Images on pages 33, 51, 62, 69, 72, 89, 205, 245, 376, 520, 569.)

[It should be noted that the major archive of monochrome topographical views by the firm of Valentines is held by the University of St Andrews Library. For further details of this collection please contact the Library, or refer to http://speccall@st-andrews.ac.uk .]

Wright & Logan: Agreement received from the **Royal Naval Museum Portsmouth** to use **four** postcards dating from 1939. (Images on pages 427, 428, 517 and 522.)

[It should be noted that the major archive of ship-portraits by Wright & Logan is held by the RN Museum, Portsmouth. For further details of this collection please contact the Museum Library.]

Abrahams: Agreement received from the **World Ship Society** to use **two** postcards, dating from c.1914 and c.1924. (Images on pages 198 and 219.)

The Pictorial Newspaper Co. (1910) Ltd: Agreement received from the **British Library** to use **one** postcard dating from c.1915. (See page 204.)

Sub-Total: 25 images. Cumulative Total: 55 images

iii) This leaves other postcards where it has not been found possible to obtain formal agreement for reproduction.

c) **Well-known Businesses which have been sold off, with the stocks of negatives being divided into separate sales lots, each carrying a segment of the copyright forward under the new owner's business name.**

The Photomatic Company: (Stocks of certain subjects (e.g. 'Railways' and 'Aircraft'), were sold off separately years ago, each with their own copyright, but it is understood that there were insufficient 'Naval' postcards to form a viable sales category, so the 'Naval' segment of copyright apparently lapsed.)

1 'Naval' card used, the image originally dating back to 1937. (Image on page 521.)

d) **'Anonymous' Postcards.** (It seems unlikely that copyright ever existed for these 'unattributable works'.)

50 postcards used dating from 1904 to 1931. (See pps 51, 52, 56, 57, 58, 68, 70, 80, 111*, 125, 133, 147, 154, 165, 168, 170, 176, 212, 220, 228, 231, 232, 237, 243, 246, 253, 258, 259, 260, 271, 277, 278, 296, 315, 348*, 350, 351, 356, 358, 360, 367, 372, 437, 479, 484, 565, 645 and 660. (154 was issued anonymously on behalf of the *Deutches Marineheim*. 243 bears the hand-inscribed initials 'FWS' within the photograph.)

A single asterisk indicates two images per page: two would indicate three images.

Sub-Total: 51 images. Cumulative Total: 106 images.

e) **Well-known Businesses which have ceased trading, evidently with no Copyright Passed on, and/or with the Inheritor(s) of the Copyright having allowed it to lapse**

Note by The Author:

No register of either 'active or terminated copyrights' exists, and it is clear that one is often in the position of trying to 'prove a negative', where, like 'Old Soldiers', the copyright-owners have simply 'faded away'. *Where no 'revival' of copyright was made and formally recorded*, it is understood that, *prior to 1945*, the duration of copyright for British-made postcards lasted for 50 years after the production of the work. That being so, such images which have been reproduced in this book will all have been out of copyright since the 1980s, and most far earlier in time.

As already indicated by paragraphs (a), (b) and (c), I have made substantial enquiries to trace every copyright-holder, but my searches have led to 'dead ends' in regard to the following postcards and the related businesses. I apologise if I have failed in any way in my researches for copyright owners. [For every illustration I have striven to quote the original source and other potentially 'identifying details' beside the image.]

<u>Gale & Polden Ltd</u>: **21 postcards** used in this book, dating from 1904 to c.1915 and therefore between 90 and 100 years old. (See pages 70, 74, 75, 81, 94, 97, 105, 110, 116, 126, 132, 134, 136*, 144, 167, 175, 182, 234, 242, 316.)

<u>Edith F Driver of Ipswich, Suffolk</u>: **7 cards** used in this book, dating from c.1920 to c.1930. (See pps 259, 260, 389, 390, 434, 436*.)

<u>The Rotary Photographic Company</u>: **5 postcards** used, dating from 1913 to 1918. (See pps 86, 99, 128, 159*.)

<u>Beagles & Co.</u>: **2 postcards used,** dating from c.1915 to c.1918. (See pages 207 and 280.)

<u>C.H.R. Tunn of Ipswich, Suffolk</u>: **2 cards** used, dating from c.1918 to c.1920. (See pages 67 and 257.)

<u>J. Welch & Sons of Portsmouth</u>: **2 postcards** used, one dating from c.1911 and one from c.1913. (See pages 120 and 274.)

<u>Cozens</u>: **2 postcards** used, probably dating from around 1913 (See page 92, 130.)

<u>Raphael Tuck</u>: **2 postcards** used, dating from 1937. (See pages 149 and 485.)

<u>Levy et Fils, of Paris</u>: **1 postcard** used, dating from c.1914 (See page 163.)

<u>Russell & Sons</u>: **1 postcard** used, dating from c. 1913 (See page 155.)

Sub-Total: 45 images. **CumulativeTotal: 151 images.**

f) **Postcards from less well-known Firms: 20 'singleton' cards used,** dating from 1909 to 1919.

Brain (See Pp.31), Grinstead (31), Jones (37), Swinton (53), Sankey Photo (85), Davidson (107) *Empire* Series (114), W.N *Real Photos* (115), Bean, Malin & Co. (118), Ettlinger (123),

Elliott & Fry (153), Photochrom (156), A. Montiero (171), Pollingee (180), T.Kent (250), Ive & Lowe (255), 'Seeward' Wessex Series (325), W.E. Mack (339), Faulkner (434), Sellicks (478).

g). Postcards bearing 'initials' but no full name (of which initials only 'WHS' has been identified by the author– see W H Smith, above): 10 postcards used, dating from 1905 to 1935.

K& S (See Pp 49), G.D & D (91), F.T.W.D *'Dainty'* Series (100 and 101), W.R & S (122), Ala 44 (164), T.I.C (270 and 370), M & L (323), M & Co (491).

h) Miscellaneous Photographic Images: 2 items used, viz a Trade Card (See 193) and a Publicity Advertising Image (See 523). Neither of the sponsoring companies appears to be still in business.

Sub-Total: 32 images.   **Cumulative Total: 183 images.**
[Also see following Totals.]

One hundred and thirty-four of the other reproduced images come from 'family sources', all but nine of them coming from the author's own collection of inherited family photographs.

The great majority of these images, dating from the 1920s onward, are amateur 'snapshots' of very varied quality, but with a few approaching professional standards. Where known, the name of the amateur photographer has been added to the detail around the individual reproduced image. (See pages 10, 29, 257, 269, 272**, 273, 283*, 284, 285*, 287, 296, 297, 300*, 301*, 302, 304, 307, 308*, 313*, 319**, 327, 328, 334, 345, 352*, 362, 363, 365, 369, 374, 375*, 376, 377, 378* 379**, 382**, 383, 392, 396, 406, 415, 422*, 431*, 439, 440**, 441, 442**, 444*, 446, 450, 451, 465, 466, 470, 486*, 503*, 506, 527, 545, 550*, 581, 626.)
Sub-Total: 89 (amateur pics.)   **Cumulative Total: 272 images**

Of the photographs in the author's inherited collection which his father, Alf, had left behind, twenty-three appear to have been taken more or less 'professionally and officially', under naval auspices. Some of these were probably in 'Crown Copyright' after they were taken, though the related 50-year expiry limit has long been passed. (See 399, 460, 461, 464, 494, 500, 501, 502, 504, 518, 537*, 542, 543, 546, 547, 553, 555, 590, 592, 593, 636, 654.) [In recent years the author has also purchased two postcard-sized photographs which were clearly taken under 'official' naval auspices c.1939 (See 495 and 563.)]
Sub-Total: 25 ('official' pics.)   **Cumulative Total: 297 images**

A further twenty-one of the 'inherited' images were 'commissioned' by members of the DAVIS or GREEN Family, and then taken professionally as studio portraits. Where the studio is known, the detail has been quoted against the reproduced image. (See 27, 77/78, 185, 261, 267, 289, 309*, 336*, 390, 394, 397, 430, 432, 445, 447, 448, 532, 583.)
Three early *Carte de Visite* photographs are also included (See 40, 42 and 44.)
Sub-Total: 24 ('Studio' and 'C de V')   **Cumulative Total: 321 images**

Finally, the author has included his own hand-drawn Maps of the Deployments of the ships in which Alf served. (See 105, 135, 188, 189, 248, 312, 330, 387, 429, 540, 640 and 655).
Using TNA documents, he has also developed a Drawing to show 'Where Alf Died' (See 668.)

<u>Sub-Total: 13 ('Maps & Drwgs')</u>   **Cumulative GRAND TOTAL: 334 images**

<u>NOTES</u>: Of the Grand Total of 134 'inherited' photographs, five were in the possession of the author's cousin, Mr R PENNEY (See 40, 42, 44 and 77/78), two were in the possession of the author's sister, Mrs J GOODMAN (See 392 and 430), and one was in the possession of the author's cousin, Mr C GREEN (See 269). A further snapshot (See 527) was in the possession of Mr B PLAYER, the son of one of Alf's close friends, Harry PLAYER. The author is extremely grateful for the very kind contributions and assistance provided by all these people.

(Note: Not included in the total of 134 are two postcard-sized photographs inherited from Alf, which both bore the identity of 'Edith DRIVER' (the professional photographer) and have therefore been included in Section 'e', above. They have the page numbers 389 and 390.)

<u>Further to the above, and NOT included in the totals,</u> APPENDIX J contains eight photographic images inherited from Alf. Of these, one is from a postcard by Edith F DRIVER, one is a snapshot (probably taken by Alf himself) and four are from anonymous postcard-sized or larger prints. The latter were almost certainly taken 'officially' under naval auspices and copies made available to at least some members of the ships' companies. No copyright holder related to Edith DRIVER has been found, and it is assumed that any copyright for the 'official' photographs will have long elapsed.

INCLUSION OF THESE EIGHT IMAGES BRINGS THE GRAND TOTAL OF ILLUSTRATIONS UP TO 342.

<u>GENERAL NOTE ON REPRODUCED IMAGES</u>

Sometimes the subject of the photograph on the face of the card, or its title on front or back, indicates the *precise time and place* when the photograph was taken, so that it has been possible to enter the image at exactly the appropriate part of the narrative in the book.[475] Where this degree of 'exactitude' is missing, potentially suitable cards which have been *postally used* sometimes exist. 'Used' cards normally bear a decipherable date of postage – which thus shows the '*very latest* date' by which the photograph on the face of the card must perforce have been printed, and this can be fundamental to its relevance to Alf's story.[476] Hence, the year of postal use is always recorded beside the image of any 'used' postcard reproduced in this book. It has also occasionally happened that the personal message written to the addressee by the sender of this or that photographic postcard has provided relevant information about the time, event and place of the scene portrayed. A précis of such valuable information is also reported, either right beside the image reproduced in this book, or quoted in the surrounding narrative.

---

[475] As a help towards such dating, the University of St Andrews Library, who are the copyright holders of Valentine's postcards, market an index which relates any serial number appearing on a Valentine's card against the year of production of that card.

[476] The *earliest* date of printing is quite a different matter! That is to say, it is clear that individual postcards sometimes remained in retailers' stocks for many years before being bought by a customer and postally used. <u>NOTE</u>: The printing of photographic postcards began c.1890. The earliest postcard image in this book dates from about 1887, but it is an exception. There are several from the early 1900s.

N.B. The images which have been reproduced all appear in the book in '256 greyscale', and not as the 'black-and-white', 'sepia-toned' or 'hand-tinted' photographic images of the original postcards concerned. This has been done to maintain uniformity and to maximise 'photographic authenticity'. Some of the images have also been 'cropped', generally to add 'focus' to the subject matter of interest, but also sometimes to 'clean up' physical edge-damage which had occurred to the original postcard during its very long history 'out in the marketplace'. Further, in a very few instances, certain unwanted and 'distracting' parts of the overall photograph have been suppressed to enhance and add 'focus' to the object of primary interest.

For all these reasons the image in the book, though almost certainly 'recognisable' against the face of any postcard of that same series number, will not always tally exactly in 'spread' and dimensions, nor perhaps in graphic presentation and nor perhaps in titling, with the original image as shown on that run, despite having 'fully matching details' of Publisher's Name and Series No. (if any).

It will be noted that the photographic quality of the images in this book improves 'as the years roll by', with some of the early postcard images (and early snapshots, see below) being of quite low quality.

It has often been possible to conceal physical damage, 'foxing', fading and other defects by computer-means, but there are limits as to what can be achieved in terms of improving definition, contrast, etc, etc.

APPENDIX C

A MASTER LIST of
Officers and Warrant Officers known to have served in HMS *Southampton*.

Those names which are in **bold** type are of officers and WOs known to have been serving in January 1941, at the time of the ship's loss.

Midshipman B.H. KENT's Diary contains a list of officers and WOs who were serving at the time of the loss of the ship. This has been most useful for filling in gaps in names and the related joining/leaving dates. Those gaps had been caused by the loss of the ship's last log, and the fact that a number of officers and WOs had joined the ship, or been discharged from her, subsequent to the last *surviving* log which was dated in November 1940.

Names in italics relate to Officers and WOs (or their relatives) who are, or have been, listed amongst the sometime membership of the 'Old Southamptons'. This data has also been drawn upon, and a few names have been found to be listed *only* in the 'Old Southampton' files and not recorded at all in the ship's logs preserved in the National Archives. (They are distinguishable by appearing only as YYYY *sans* MMM.)

It is clear that the following list may still have a small number of minor deficiencies. The author would be very pleased to hear 'chapter and verse' of any suggested additions or modifications.

NAME	RANK	MMM/YYYY JOINED	MMM/YYYY LEFT
ALEXANDER, Mr	Gunner?	Pre-Mar 1937?	Pre-Jan 1941
ALFORD, I.F.O	Midshipman	1940	Dec 1940
ANTREBUS	Midshipman	Jan 1938	Jan 1939
BALFOUR, S.H. (Rtd)	Lt Commander	Post-Nov 1940?	**KiA, Jan 1941**
BARKER-HAHLO, J.F.C.	Lt Commander	Nov 1939	**KiA, Jan 1941**
BARLOW, N.A.H.	Surg Commander	Mar 1937?	Dec 1939
BARRATT, R.J.T	Lt	Sep 1938	Pre-Jan 1941
BEASLEY, B.R.	Chaplain	1939	Jan 1941
BENNETT, R.J.T	Lt (A)	Pre-Mar 1937?	Sep 1938
BENNETT-JONES	Lt	Jul 1938	May 1940
BEST	Lt (E)	Aug 1940	Pre-Jan 1941
BLISS, P.M.	Lt	Pre-Mar 1937?	Jul 1939
BLOOMER	Midshipman	May 1938	Pre-Jan 1941
BOTT, A.H.	Lt (E)	Pre-Mar 1937?	Sep 1938
BOWER, R.G.	Midshipman RNR	Jan 1938?	Jan 1941
BROCK	Lt Commander	Mar 1937	1938
BROOKE, B.C.B	Captain	Jun 1940	Jan 1941
BROWN, H.N.S	Lt Commander	Jan 1938	Jul 1939
BULFORD	Lt Commander	Apr 1940	Pre-Jan 1941
BULL, C.H.G.	Lt	Jan 1938	Dec 1938
CAIRNS	Lt	Mar 1937?	Jul 1938
CASSON, J	Lt (A)	Pre-Nov 1939	1940
CHANTRILL	Lt	May 1938	Pre-Jan 1941
COBB, Mr F.A.	Commissioned Gunner (T)	Jan 1941	Jan 1941
COCKBURN	Midshipman RANR	May 1940	Pre-Jan 1941
COLE	Midshipman	May 1938	Pre-Jan 1941
COLERIDGE, The Hon R.D.	Lt Commander	Sep 1938	Oct 1938
COLLEY, D.B.	Lt Commander	Pre-Mar 1937?	Dec 1938

COLLIER	Midshipman	Jul 1938	Apr 1940
COPEMAN, A.H.	Lt Commander	Jan 1939	Jan 1941
CUNNINGHAM	Midshipman	Jul 1938	Apr 1940
CUTLER, J.L.	Midshipman	Post-Nov 1940?	Jan 1941
DAVIDSON, G.V.	Midshipman	Sep 1940	**KiA, Jan 1941**
DAVIS, A.W.*	Commissioned Gunner	Pre-Mar 1937	**KiA, Jan 1941**
DISNEY-ROEBUCK, M.W.	S/Lt	May 1940	Jan 1941
DIXON	Commander	Mar 1937	Jul 1938
DUNN	Pay Lt	Mar 1937?	Jul 1939
EDMONSTONE (Rtd)	Lt Commander	Pre-Apr 1940	Jan 1941
ELGAR, J.M	Temp Midshipman RANR	May 1940	1940
ELLIOTT, Mr	Warrant Shipwright	Nov 1940?	Jan 1941
ELLMERS, P.	Lt	Mar 1937	Pre-Jan 1941
FAIRWEATHER, D.J.	Surg Lt (D)	Post-Nov 1940?	**KiA, Jan 1941**
FAWCUS, Sir P.	S/Lt RNVR	APR 1940	1941
FEARFIELD	Lt	Pre-Mar 1937?	Dec 1938
FIDO	Lt Commander RNVR	?	Nov 1940
FORD, Mr	Warrant Telegraphist	May 1938	Pre-Jan 1941
FYFE, R.W.	Commander (E)	Post-Nov 1940?	**KiA, Jan 1941**
GOTHARD, H.W.	Surg Lt	Post-Nov 1940	Jan 1941
GRAHAM, R.H.	S/Lt	Mar 1937	1937
GRAY, C.K.	Pay S/Lt	Post-Nov 1940?	**KiA, Jan 1941**
GRENFELL	Lt	Aug 1939	Pre-Jan 1941
GRIFFIN, E.G.	Lt (E)	Post-Nov 1940?	Jan 1941
GUEST, J.A.	Lt (E)	Nov 1938	**KiA, Jan 1941**
HALL	Midshipman	Mar 1937	Dec 1937
HALIFAX	Midshipman	?	Dec 1940
HAMILTON	Midshipman	May 1938	Pre-Jan 1941
HARDEN	Midshipman	May 1938	Pre-Jan 1941
HARDING, Mr	Gunner	Dec 1937	Apr 1939
HEATHCOTE	Pay Lt	Aug 1939	Pre-Jan 1941
HEIGHTON	Midshipman	Mar 1937	Dec 1937
HERRING	S/Lt (A)	Pre-Sep 1940	Jan 1941
HOATH	S/Lt (A)	Pre-Mar 1937?	April 1939
HOLMES, A.B.	Pay Midshipman	Post-Nov 1940?	**KiA, Jan 1941**
HURRELL, Mr	Senior Master	Jul 1938	Pre-Jan 1941
JACKSON	Lt RNVR	Pre-Jun 1940	Nov 1940
JARROLD, Mr	Warrant Schoolmaster	Nov 1940?	Jan 1941
JEANS, F.W.H	Captain	Jan 1939	Jun 1940
JENKINS, G.	Midshipman RNVR	Aug 1940	Jan 1941
JERRAM, F.R.	Midshipman	1939	Jan 1941
JOHNSON	Midshipman	Mar 1937	Dec 1937
KENT, B.H.	Midshipman	Sep 1940	Jan 1941
KEYES, The Hon R.G.B.	Midshipman	Mar 1937	Dec 1937
KEYWORTH, M.J.A.	S/Lt	Sep 1938	May 1940
KOESTER, Mr L	Gunner	Mar 1937?	**DoW, Jan 1941**
Le MESURIER	Commander	Mar 1937	Jan 1938
LEARMOND, P.A	Midshipman	Sep 1940	Jan 1941
LLOYD-SMITH, V.B.	Temp Pay Lt RNVR	Post-Nov 1940?	**KiA, Jan 1941**
MADDEN, C.D	S/Lt	Mar 1937	Jun 1938
MADDEN, G.H.R.	Lt RM	Oct 1938	1939
MANNING	Lt (A)	Dec 1939	Pre-Jan 1941
MARSHALL	Lt (E)	Post-Nov 1940	Jan 1941 (W)

MARTIN, Mr	Gunner	Post-Nov 1940?	Aug 1940
MASON	Midshipman	May 1938	Pre-Jan 1941
McINTOSH, J.	Midshipman	Jan 1938	Jan 1939
McINTYRE*	Surg Commander	Dec 1939	Aug 1940
MOCATTA, J.M.	Midshipman	Sep 1940	**KiA, Jan 1941**
MOORE	Midshipman	?	Dec 1940
MORTON, T.J.	Surg Lt	Post-Nov 1940?	**KiA, Jan 1941**
MOWLAM	Lt	Mar 1937	Dec 1937
MUERS	Lt (N)	Aug 1937	Pre-Jan 1941
MUTTRIE	S/Lt (A)	Nov 1940?	Jan 1941
NICHOLLS, P	Lt (N)	Mar 1937	Apr 1939
NICHOLS, R.F.	Commander (N)	1937	Apr 1939
NICKOLAY	Lt	Mar 1937	Pre-Jan 1941
NOAKES, Mr	Warrant Electrician	Pre-Mar 1937?	May 1938
OLIPHANT, F.M.G.	Lt Commander	Dec 1938	Pre-Jan 1941
OLIVER, J.E.	Temp Instr Lt	Post-Nov 1940?	**KiA, Jan 1941**
Oliver, R.	Commander	Apr 1939	Pre-Nov 1941
PAGE, L.F.	Prob Temp S/Lt RNR	Post-Nov 1940?	**KiA, Jan 1941**
PARNALL	Lt	Nov 1939	Pre-Jan 1941
PEEVER	S/Lt	May 1938	Pre-Jan 1941
PEMBERTON, R.H.S.	Acting Lt	Nov 1940?	**KiA, Jan 1941**
PETERS	Instr Lt	Jul 1938	Pre-Jan 1941
PETERS, A.M.	Captain	Mar 1937	Dec 1938
PELLY C.S.	Lt Commander	Apr 1940	Jan 1941
PHILLIPS, R.	Midshipman RCN	Post-Nov 1940?	Jan 1941
PLAYER, Mr H.C.*	Commissioned Gunner	Mar 1937	**KiA, Jan 1941**
POITRIE	S/Lt (A)	Pre-Sep 1940	Pre-Jan 1941
RABAN-WILLIAMS, J	Midshipman	Mar 1937	Pre-Jan 1939
RAYMOND, D.L.	Lt Commander (G)	Aug 1939	1941
REES, Mr F.P.	Bandmaster RM	Mar 1937	Jan 1941
RICHARDS, N.L.C.	Pay Lt	Post-Nov 1940?	**KiA, Jan 1941**
ROBIN, A.D.	Lt	Nov 1938	April 1939
ROSS, T.D.	Lt Commander (N)	Nov 1940	Jan 1941
ROYNTON-JONES, E.	Pay Midshipman	Post-Nov 1940?	**KiA, Jan 1941**
RUCK-KEENE, T.	Midshipman	Jan 1938	Jan 1941
RUMSEY, Mr W.	Warrant Engineer	Oct 1938	Pre-Jan 1941
SCROGGINS, Mr A.G.	Warrant Engineer	Sep 1938	Pre-Jan 1941
SEBASTIAN, G.L.G.	Captain (E)	Oct 1938	Pre-Jan 1941
SEMMENS, Mr	Commissioned Gunner (T)	Mar 1937	Aug 1937
SHACKLETON, H.E.F	Major RM	Nov 1938	**KiA, Jan 1941**
SHANNON	Midshipman	Mar 1937	Dec 1937
SHATTOCK	Lt Commander	Mar 1937	Pre-Jan 1941
SHELLEY	Acting Warrant Tel	?	Aug 1940
SILVESTER, H.G.	Surg Lt	Mar 1937?	Sep 1938
SIMMONDS, Mr	Warrant Ordnance Officer	Nov 1940?	Jan 1941
SIMS-WILLIAMS, H.W.S.	Lt Commander	Jan 1939	Pre-Jan 1941
SLADE	S/Lt (E)	Jul 1938	Pre-Jan 1941
SLOANE, W.C.	Surg Lt RNVR	Aug 1940	Jan 1941 (W)
SMITH, C.G.	Midshipman RCN	1939	Jan 1941
de STACKPOL, R.O.	Lt RM	Nov 1939	Jan 1941 (W)
STEINER, O.S.J.	Midshipman	1937	1938
STEVENSON	S/Lt RNVR	?	Nov 1940
SWATTON, Mr	Warrant Engineer	Post-Nov 1940	Jan 1941

THOMSETT, E	Lt	?	Aug 1940
TILNEY	Lt Commander	Mar 1937?	Dec 1939
TINLEY, C.B.	Lt Commander	Mar 1937	**DoW, Jan 1941**
TUFFILL, H.C.	Temp Lt (E)	Oct 1939	Jan 1941
TURNER, G.T.	Midshipman	Sep 1940	Jan 1941 (Sl/W)
TURNER, Mr R.D.	Gunner	Mar 1937	Dec 1937
TWEED, D.W.	Lt RM	Mar 1937	Oct 1938
WADE, Mr R.D.	Warrant Engineer	Aug 1939	Jan 1941
WARD SMITH	Pay Commander	?	Oct 1940
WHITE, Mr F.J	Warrant Engineer	Aug 1939	**KiA, Jan 1941**
WISE	Lt	Dec 1938	Pre-Jan 1941
WOODS, P.R.E.	Lt (A)	Sep 1938	Jan 1941
WRIGHT	Lt RM	Jan 1938	Post Dec 1938
YOXHAM	Captain RM	Mar 1937	Pre-Jan 1941

TOTAL: approx. 150 Officers and Warrant Officers, of whom 57 were evidently serving at the time of the Ship's Loss.

Note: The asterisks against the 2 Commissioned Gunners who were KiA on 11th January 1941 (Mr A W DAVIS and Mr H C PLAYER) signify that their sons represent them in the membership of the 'Old Southamptons'.

Some of the officers went on to have distinguished careers. For example it is known that:-

Lt Commander BROCK became Rear Admiral BROCK CB, DSO, RN
S/Lt C.D. MADDEN became Rear Admiral C.D. MADDEN, CB, CBE, LVO, DSC
Midshipman O.S.J. STEINER became Rear Admiral O.S.J. STEINER CB, RN
Midshipman R.H. GRAHAM became Captain R.H. GRAHAM MVO, DSC, RN (Rtd)
Midshipman B.H. KENT became Captain B.H. KENT RN (Rtd).[477]

---

[477] Captain KENT, who is the author of '*Signal: A History of Naval Signalling*', very kindly wrote the foreword to this book.

APPENDIX D

Appendix D

A BIBLIOGRAPHY

Title	Author	Pb/Hb	ISBN No.	Publisher	Date
"Action Stations!" The Royal Navy at War	Rear Admiral H G Thursfield	Hb	-	Adam & Charles Black, London	1924
A Dictionary of Ships of the Royal Navy of the 2nd WW	John Young	Pb	0 85059 332 8	Patrick Stephens Ltd., Cambridge	1975
A Sailor's Odyssey	Viscount Cunningham	Hb	-	Hutchinson & Co., Ltd., London	1951
A Seaman's Pocket-Book B.R.827	Anon.	Hb	-	H.M.S.O	1943
Air Power in War	The Lord Tedder, G.C.B.	Hb	-	Hodder and Stoughton, London	1948
Alston's Seamanship	Commander T.P. Walker, R.N.	Hb	-	Griffin & Co., Portsmouth	1893
'Ark Royal'	Kenneth Poolman	Pb	-	William Kimber & Co. Ltd	1956
Battleship, Cruiser, Destroyer	Gregory Haines & B.R. Coward	Hb	1 85648 174 3	The Promotional Reprint Co., Ltd	1994
Battleship Warspite	V.E. Tarrant	Hb	0 85368 971 7	Arms and Armour Press, London	1990
Best Stories of the Navy	(Collected Stories of 'Taffrail' et alia)	Hb	-	Faber and Faber, London	1941
Britain's Glorious Navy	Admiral Sir Reginald H.S. Bacon	Hb	-	Odhams Press, London	1944
Britain's Wonderful Fighting Forces	Captain Ellison Hawks, R.A.	Hb	-	Odhams Press, London	1940
Britain's Wonderful Fighting Forces	Captain Ellison Hawks, R.A.	Hb	-	Odhams Press, London	1941
Cruiser. A History of British Cruisers from 1889 to 1960	S.L. Poole	Hb	7091 1344 7	C. Tinling & Co. Ltd., London	1970
Cruisers	Anthony Preston	Hb	0 86124 064 2	Bison Books Ltd., Greenwich, U.S.A.	1982
Cruisers	Bernard Ireland	Hb	0 600 34975 6	The Hamlyn Publishing Group, London	1961
Dreadnought: (Britain, Germany & the Coming of WW1)	Robert K. Massie	Pb	0 224 03260 7	Jonathon Cape	1991
Dreadnoughts in Camera 1905-1920	Roger D. Thomas & B. Patterson	Hb	1 84015 108 0	Sutton Publishers Limited	1998
East of Malta, West of Suez	Anon.	Pb	-	H.M.S.O.	1941
Untitled Document: Parts relevant to HMS *Southampton*	Former C.P.O. Royal Navy, Mr G. Hobley	-		(Typescript Autobiography: 11 Pp.)	1982
Diary: Parts re. Operations against SMS *Konigsberg*, etc.	Commander R.F.C. Struben R.N.	-		(MSS Autobiography held in I.W.M.)	1920
Diary: Parts re. Operations against SMS *Konigsberg*, etc.	Anon. P.O. Stoker of HMS *Weymouth*	-		(Anonymous MSS Diary held in I.W.M.)	1915
From Arctic Snow to Dust of Normandy	Patrick Dalzel-Job	Hb	0 85052 901 8	Pen & Sword Books	1991
History of the Royal Navy	Robert Jackson	Hb	0 75256 698 9	Parragon, Bath	1999
History of the Royal Navy	Anthony Preston	Hb	0 86124 121 5	W.H. Smith & Son Ltd.	1985
HMS Ganges: 1866-1966: 100 yrs Training Boys for R.N.	Instr. Lt. D.L. Summers, R.N.	Hb	-	W.S.Cowell Ltd., Butter Mkt, Ipswich	1966
HMS *Sheffield*: The Life and Times of 'Old Shiny'	Ronald Basset	Hb	0 85368 911 3	Arms and Armour Press, London	1988
HMS *Southampton*	R.H. Osborne, R. Nailer, R. Lumb	-	-	(Typescript: 5 Pp.)	1975
HMS *Southampton* of W.W.2	An Anon. Group of 'Old Southamptons'	-	-	(Typescript: 5 Pp.)	1988
HMS *Southampton*, 1937-1941	Anon.	-	-	(Typescript: 1 Pp.)	1987
HMS *Southampton*, 1937-1941	Former Shipwright R.N., Mr W.J. Miller	-	-	(Typescript: 7 Pp.)	1987
Home from Sea	Godfrey Winn	Hb	-	Hutchinson & Co., Ltd., London	1944
Jane's Fighting Ships of World War 1	John Moore	Hb	1 85170 378 0	Butler & Tanner Ltd., Frome & London	2001

Title	Author		ISBN	Publisher	Year
La Saga de Narvik: Printemps 1940	Jean Mabire	Pb	2 258 03147 8	Presses de la Cite	1990
Last Days of the German Fleet	Ludwig Freiwald (Translated by Moore)	Hb	-	Constable and Company Ltd., London	1932
Malta Convoys	David A Thomas	Pb	0 85052 6639	Redwood Books Ltd., Trowbridge, Wilts	1999
Man o' War 5: Town Class Cruisers	Alan Raven and John Roberts	Hb	0 85368 135 X	Arms and Armour Press, London	1975
Manual of Seamanship 1937	Anon.	Hb	-	H.M.S.O.	1938
Manual of Seamanship, Vol 1, 1951	Anon.	Hb	-	H.M.S.O.	1951
Memories	Admiral of the Fleet, Lord Fisher	Hb	-	Hodder and Stoughton, London	1919
Modern Military Series: Warships	H.P. Willmott	Pb	0 7064 0356 8	Octopus Books Ltd., London	1975
Narvik	Jaques Mordal	Pb	-	Presses de la Cite	1960
Naval and Overseas War 1914-1915	Trevor Nevitt Dupuy	Hb	-	Franklin Watts Inc., New York	1967
Naval Aviation in the First World War (Impact & Influence)	R.D. Layman	Hb	1 86176 007 8	Chatham Publishing, London	1996
Naval Battles of the First World War	Geoffrey Bennett	Hb	0 330 23862 0	B.T. Batsford Ltd.	1968
Naval Ratings Handbook 1951	Anon.	Hb		Naval Training Dept., Admiralty	1951
Navy and Army Illustrated	Cmdr Charles N. Robinson, R.N.	Hb		Hudson and Kearns, London	1896
Nine Vanguards	Lt-Cmdr. P.K. Kemp, R.N.	Hb		Hutchinson & Co., Ltd., London	1951
Operation Sea Lion	Peter Fleming	Pb	0 330 42057 7	Pan Books Ltd., London	2003
Operations against the *Konigsberg*	C-in-C at Cape of Good Hope	-	-	The London Gazette of 8th Dec., 1915	1915
Our Navy	Anon.	Hb	-	Ward, Lock & Co., London	1941
Plain Yarns from the Fleet	Charles Owen	Hb	0905 778 219	Sutton Publishing Limited	1997
Prologue to a War: The Navy's Part in the Narvik Campaign	Ewart Brookes	Hb	-	Jarrolds Publishers (London) Ltd	1966
Royal Navy Ships' Badges	Peter C. Smith	Hb	-	Photo Precision Ltd., Huntingdon	1974
Salvo: Classic Naval Gun Actions	Bernard Edwards	Hb	1 86019 959 3	Arms and Armour Press, London	1995
SEA: Twentieth Century War Machines	Christopher Chant	Hb	-	Chancellor Press Ltd.	1999
Service Most Silent	J.F. Turner	Hb	85617 070 4	George G Harrap & Co. Ltd	1955
Ships and the Sea	Pay-Lt E.C. Talbot-Booth R.N.R.	Hb	-	Sampson Low, Marston & Co., London	1936
Ships of the Royal Navy	Oscar Parkes, O.B.E., M.B., Ch.B.	Hb	-	Sampson Low, Marston & Co., London	1926
Ships of the Royal Navy	Anon.	Hb	-	Hutchinson & Co., Ltd., London	1942
(Southampton Class Cruisers)	R.G.R. Robison	-	-	(Ships Monthly Magazine)	1984
Spitfire	John Vader	Pb	345 09757 2	Pan/Ballantine	1969
Stuka at War	Peter C. Smith	Hb	7110 0197 9	Ian Allan Ltd., Shepperton, Surrey	1971
Sub-Lieutenant: A Personal Record of the War af Sea	Ludovic Kennedy	Hb	-	B.T. Batsford Ltd.	1942
The Battle for the Mediterranean	Donald Macintyre	Pb	0 330 02525 2	Pan Books Ltd., London	1964
The Battle of Malta	Joseph Attard	Pb	0 600 20548 7	Hamlyn Paperbacks	1980
The British Navy from Within	"Ex-Royal Navy"	Pb		Hodder and Stoughton, London	1916
The Devil's Device: The Story of the Invention of the Torpedo	Edwyn Gray	Hb	0 85422 104 2	Seeley Service & Co., Ltd., London	1975
The German Navy in World War Two	Edward P. Von der Porten	Pb	0 330 23235 5	Pan Books Ltd., London	1969

Title	Author	ISBN	Hb/Pb	Publisher	Year
The Great Gunnery Scandal: The Mystery of Jutland	Anthony Pollen	0 00 216298 9	Hb	William Collins Sons & Co., Ltd., London	1980
The 'Handy-Man': Training of a Lad for the British Navy	W.M. Crockett	-	Pb	Doidge's Western Counties Illust. Annual	1912
The Life and Death of a Cruiser (Supplementary Pers. Notes)	Lt-Cmdr. Frank Jerram, R.N. (Rtd)	-	-	(Typescript: 3 Pp.)	1999
The Life and Death of a Cruiser in WW2: HMS *Southampton*	L.E. Wells & T. Ruck-Keene	-	-	(Typescript: 18 Pp.)	1991
The Life and Letters of David, Earl Beatty	Rear Admiral W.S. Chalmers	-	Hb	Hodder & Stoughton	1951
The Luftwaffe War Diaries	Cajus Bekker (Trnslt'd. by Frank Zeigler)	-	Hb	Macdonald & Co., London	1964
'The Month': The Royal Navy in the Mediterranean 1939-41	Rowland Langmaid	-	Hb	The Batchworth Press, London	1948
The Month at Sea (Navy Magazine Vol XLVI, Feb. 1941)	Rear Admiral H G Thursfield	-	-	(Wightman & Co., Ltd., Hitchin, Herts.)	1941
The Narvik Campaign	Johan Waage (Tranltd, by Ewan Butler)	-	Pb	George G Harrap & Co. Ltd	1964
The Navy	Admiral Sir Herbert W. Richmond	-	-	William Hodge & Co., Ltd., London	1937
The Navy and Defence	Admiral of the Fleet, Lord Chatfield	-	Hb	William Heinemann Ltd., London	1942
The Navy and the Y Scheme	Anon.	-	-	H.M.S.O.	1944
The Navy at War	Captain Stephen Roskill R.N. (Rtd)	1 85326 697 3	Pb	Wordworth Editions Ltd., Ware, Herts	1998
The Navy of Britain	Michael Lewis	-	Hb	George Allen and Unwin Ltd., London	1948
The Royal Navy	Lieutenant D. Wilson MacArthur	-	Pb	William Collins Sons & Co., Ltd., London	1940
The Royal Navy in Focus 1930-39	Mike Critchley	0 90771 04 1	Pb	Maritime Books, Liskeard, Cornwall	1981
The Royal Navy Today	Frank H. Mason	-	Pb	Odhams Press, London	1942
The Sea Cadets at Shotley (Navy Magazine XLIII, Oct. 1938)	Anon	-	-	(Wightman & Co., Ltd., Hitchin, Herts.)	1938
The Seafarers: The Dreadnoughts	David Howarth	7054 0628 8	Hb	Time-Life Books, Inc., New York, U.S.A.	1979
(The Sphere Magazine for 25th January 1941)	Anon.	-	-	(The London Illustrated News and Sketch)	1941
The Story of HMS Dryad	Vice Admiral B.B. Schofield	0 85937 087 9	Hb	Kenneth Mason Publications Ltd., Hants	1977
The True Glory: The Royal Navy	Max Arthur	0 340 62301 2	Hb	Hodder and Stoughton, London	1996
The War: Second Year	Edgar McInnis	-	Hb	Oxford University Press, London	1941
The Wonder Book of the Navy	Harry Golding	-	Hb	Ward, Lock & Co., London	1930
Three Years of War in East Africa	Captain Angus Buchanan, M.C.	-	Hb	John Murray, London	1920
(Training Ship Memories)	Patrick O'Keefe	-	Pb	(The Nautical Magazine)	1917
Vickers: A History	J.D. Scott	-	Hb	Weidenfield and Nicholson, London	1962
War at Sea	Aiden Chambers	-	Pb	Macmillan Education Ltd., Hants.	1978
War at Sea in the Ironclad Age	Richard Hill	0 304 25273 X	Hb	Cassell, London	2000
War in a Stringbag	Charles Lamb	-	Pb	Arrow Books Ltd.	1977
Warships	Norman Polmar & N. Friedman	0 906320 07 0	Hb	Octopus Books Ltd., London	1981
We Joined the Navy: Traditions and Customs of the R.N.	R. Burgess & R. Blackburn	-	Hb	Adam & Charles Black, London	1943
Whaley: The Story of HMS *Excellent* 1830-1980	Captain John G. Wells, R.N.	-	Hb	Linneys of Mansfield	1980

NOTES: (A) 'Tracing Your Naval Ancestors', by B.Pappalardo, published by the P.R.O, ISBN 1 903365 37 6, 'arrived' very late in the author's ken, but it is a fine work for aspiring researchers.

(B) A quotation has been taken from the authentic novel "The Passing of the Flagship" by Major W.P. Drury, published by A.H. Bullen of London, in 1902. (C) The author has gained much 'feel' from of a lifetime's reading of:- 'Bartimus', Brian Callison, C.S. Forester, Alexander Fullerton, Max Hennesy/John Harris, Alistair Maclean, Nicholas Montserrat, Douglas Reeman, 'Taffrail', *et alia*.

APPENDIX E

(Author's Note on the research on which Chapter 1 of this work is based)

All four of my father Alf's siblings – born from 1894 to 1900 - had passed away by the time that I embarked on the formal research for this book (and subsequently managed to trace them), and Alf had no known cousins. I therefore turned to my own siblings and first cousins – born from 1921 to 1939 – for information on the origins of the DAVIS Family. My cousins took a deal of finding, for some were long-lost and others never-before-met. However, when that very pleasant task of 'reunion' had pretty well been accomplished and celebrated, and the information of all and sundry had been pooled, it was surprising to find how very limited was the amassed knowledge of our DAVIS forbears.

Running throughout that amassed knowledge, albeit not articulated at all by the more discreet of the individuals, there was a strong implication that some sort of serious scandal must have existed in an earlier generation. That is to say, a 'cover-up' had clearly taken place, commencing in the mid-19th Century. This had apparently made Alf's generation, born from 1894 to 1900, also 'clam up' and pass little by way of 'family legends' on down to us, their children.[478] The fact that a long-enduring 'schism' between Alf and his brother 'Jack' had riven the family in twain from 1926 onwards had complicated the whole issue. Subsequent 'personality clashes' between my step-mother and Alf's elder sister, Nellie, and other divisions within our parents' generation had driven in further wedges which had increased the 'distances' dividing the family groups.

Yet, as was later found, some invaluable clues had emerged from the pooling of the pieces of the 'jigsaw' of memory and memorabilia of the newly 're-united' living kin – above all the fact that Alf's parents – despite (correctly as it turned out) being believed to be English-born - were apparently living in Scotland around 1890/95. Certainly, their son 'Jack' had been born there – "at a castle", as he later used to boast mysteriously to his seven daughters, but only to then refuse point-blank to be drawn any further about the family history – and to become extremely angry if 'pressed' on the matter. [I already knew that, apart from my 'Uncle Jack', Alf and the other three children of that generation had been born in one place or another in England – on fine estates as it later turned out - but certainly not in 'castles'. And, when later tested, my Uncle Jack's boast didn't entirely 'hold water' either, even though 'the castle' proved to be an invaluable clue in my investigations – and it led, at last, to my discovery of the (Scottish) marriage record of Jack and Alf's parents.]

I had already begun to make formal research in official records in the national repositories of England. Now, aided by the fragments of new and supporting information from my cousins, I extended and intensified my research to track down the appropriate birth and marriage certificates in Scottish records too, and I then combined them with census records in both England and Scotland, plus death certificates, 'last wills and

---

[478] This was very different to the *maternal* side of the author's family, where legends of the past, some quite astounding, simply abounded – mainly thanks to stories he 'learnt at grandma's knee'- or from his 'Auntie Kitty DANIELS' (actually née Kathleen Mary MOONEY, a 1st cousin once removed - see Appendix F, GREEN Family Tree.) [The more astounding of these 'GREEN' legends have been investigated and the interesting outcome will be reported in a different book.]

testaments', etc., to compile a narrative of the family history. It was far from easy to track the relevant records down, for elaborate 'smokescreens' had indeed been laid by Alf's parents. It was eventually proved that the reason for the central smokescreen was to disguise the awkward circumstances surrounding the illegitimate birth of Alf's father, way back in 1866/7. Moreover, other untruths had been told in the period 1885-1901, to secure jobs and to facilitate subsequent job-promotions for the growing lad who would later become Alf's father. Quite independent untruths had been told to aid Alf's mother in her early career too, both mother and father having been individually 'in service' to the gentry from a young age. Those job-related untruths had perforce been amalgamated and carried forward on to their Scottish marriage certificate of 1892, because a man who was clearly the Domestic Butler to their then joint employer was present, and the Butler signed as a marriage witness. There was therefore a crucial need to 'stick rigidly to the fibs which had been told to gain employment' – or to run the risk of discovery of their falsehood, which would probably have led to 'dismissal without a reference'. That would almost certainly have quickly brought them right down 'into the gutter' and utterly destroyed their lives.

Thus it was that the Scottish marriage certificate of 1902 was a tissue of lies and half-truths in almost every respect of age, occupation and parentage, save for the names of bride and groom, and (wonderfully for the author as the researcher!), the correct maiden name of the bride's mother! It was <u>only</u> this maiden name which provided confirmation that the marriage certificate was the 'right' one – for 'Alfred DAVIS' is a commonly-occurring name and the link to an 'Eliza ATKINSON' (ATKINSON being another quite common name) might have been sheer happenchance, especially as the ages were not in good accord with other evidence, those ages actually having been deliberately falsified!

However, given that 'fix' from the correct 'bride's mother's maiden name', the very fibs that were told 'in the vestry' held hidden 'clues' which proved to be absolutely vital to the research – and the odd fragments of what turned out to be the 'bits of truth' which remained, albeit sometimes distorted, eventually proved to be invaluable 'clinchers'. [NOTE: A <u>quite different set of untruths</u> had been told in regard to Alf's father's age and parentage, when, after a long period as a widower, Alf's father had re-married, in England, in 1925. Those <u>'highly convincing'</u> untruths, too, provided latent 'clues', <u>though ONLY once their TOTAL FALSEHOOD had at last become apparent!</u>]

The upshot of all this was that the research led the author to follow various 'red herrings' up many 'blind alleys' in both English and Scottish records, and the desired outcome required a considerable number of years, and the occasional aid of highly skilled professional researchers, to resolve. Even then, it was only through the 'happenchance' of several 'lucky breaks', combined with much dogged persistence, that the miasma of fibs could be unravelled sufficiently for the author to arrive at an approximation of 'the truth'. Certain 'confirmatory' statements (and donations of very old photographs) kindly made to him by his cousin Raymond PENNEY were invaluable at that stage. Those photographs evidently include a portrait of Alf's 'putative' paternal grandfather in company with his natural son, Alf's father. It is a great shame that the names were not recorded. Even now, that grandfather's identity is not 100% certain and a certain level of 'informed conjecture' has been necessary to fill in that void and a few other gaps amidst the now known facts.

The reconstructed and complicated 'yesteryear' of Alf and his family runs as laid out in Chapter 1 of this book. This starts off with Alf's birth and generally works forward through his life, though with a few backward glances at times, to see how the past had heavily influenced the lives of Alf's parents, enormously changing and 'volatilising' the careers of each of them from the highly stable and rustic lives of the direct-line ancestors who had gone before each of them since the mists of time – until, on Alf's father's side, the young teenage girl who would become Alf's unmarried paternal grandmother had 'gone off the rails' in 1866.

A decade later events concerning totally unconnected, but equally stable ancestral roots, were unfolding in a totally different part of England where the man who was destined to become Alf's <u>maternal</u> grandfather had re-married. This had indirectly led to the eviction of his 'rebellious' teenage daughter from the family home, setting her off 'into a life in service' and thence to her eventual marriage with Alf's father, each of them being by then several hundreds of miles away from their respective parents' homes. As can be seen in the book, the quite revolutionary influences of the Victorian and Edwardian eras, and the vicissitudes of the lives which Alf's near-penniless and yet wide-ranging and highly ambitious parents led together, [both whilst 'in service' and thereafter], fundamentally affected the relationships of those parents with all their five children.

The author was born in time to see and learn something of the relationships which had developed between the five children, and that personal knowledge certainly aided the formal research from that point onwards in time. He hopes that all he has written is a fair representation of the facts which have evolved.

APPENDIX F

(Notes by the author on the Family Trees which follow.)

The trees which are shown here are abbreviated ones. Moreover, to make them 'fit on the page', they have had, perforce, to be reproduced in a small scale.

Appendix E has recounted something of the particular difficulties experienced in developing the DAVIS Family Trees which form the first two pages of this appendix. Happily, the GREEN, HOPKINS, ATKINSON, DAYKINS and ENGLISH Families, though not without their own 'skeletons rattling in the cupboards', were a lot more honest about the data they passed to 'officialdom'. These lines therefore created fewer difficulties for the researcher from that sort of aspect. *However*, the very high frequency of the HOPKINS name in Wiltshire and of the GREEN name in Suffolk, each presented its own difficulties in deciding which persons amongst various possible choices from the different generations were the correct ones.

That said, the research was conducted by the well-established methods used by all skilled genealogists, and to be found in various textbooks which set out the techniques to be employed. Basically, one works backwards into time, heading, elucidated fact by elucidated fact, from the known into the believed, then on to the rumoured, and to the stuff of legend, and onwards into the totally unknown, using logic and reasoning, combined with the latest evolved facts, every step of the way. Then taking 'time out' to see how everything is 'hanging together', especially in 'cross-compatibility' of dates.

Suffice to say that the findings illustrated in the trees come from an amalgam of human memory/old family legends/civil records of births, marriages and deaths/parish records/census returns/last Wills and Testaments/newspaper cuttings/and so forth. The increasing availability of indexes of all types also greatly helped, especially the indexes to the 1881 and 1901 censuses, and the renowned IGI itself.[479] Where found possible, the establishment of contact with fellow-researchers of the same 'clans' in the same areas was tremendously useful. And, where the author was 'stymied', and/or where he was dealing with distant places, recourse to the services of a skilled professional researcher, working within well-defined and mutually-agreed parameters, was often of major assistance.

Survival (or loss) of old records, possible absence of baptisms (due to poverty or 'non-conformity'), possible absence of marriage records (perhaps where the poor had merely 'jumped over the broom-stick') and other factors – especially 'migration', and the confusion arising over people with common names, birthplace and age – all make for something of a lottery as to the ability of the researcher to trace the origins of a family. Further, the English Civil War of the mid-17th Century led to the destruction of many old parish records, mainly due to the loathing of the church clergy for the puritan clerks who

---

[479] The 'International Genealogical Index' – a computerised listing of baptisms and marriages compiled by the Church of Latter-Day Saints from parish records. Coverage is less complete for certain counties in the U.K. than others, but it is an excellent index to search for potential 'short-cuts' to the discovery of ancestors. The author's ENGLISH-named Family is particularly well-covered by the IGI – some of 'his' other families hardly at all.

replaced them during the Commonwealth period, and *vice-versa* following the Restoration of the Monarchy. Hence, many parish records extend back only as far as the Restoration in 1666 or have 'missing years' around the time of the Commonwealth. Degradation due to damp, rodent-attack, theft, outbreaks of fire, etc., have caused other losses over the centuries.

These effects are to be seen in microcosm in regard to 'my' families. That is to say, it has been possible to trace two of the above-named families back into the 16th Century, another family as far back as the 17th, two back as far as only the 18th, and one only as far as the early 19th. Happily, all the families have been traced sufficiently far back for their influences on the subject of this book and on his wives and children to be reviewed and analysed.

As a small boy the author had been inspired by the old family legends which his maternal grandmother used to tell to him, and, after the deaths of his mother and his father, both his grandmother and his step-mother gave him old family photographs to put into a large album, and encouraged and coached him to 'write them up', and to become the 'Family Historian'. Thereafter the author kept copies of all significant new photographs, 'writing them up' in albums, as his life unfolded. However, it was not until 1985 that he suddenly found the need and inspiration to investigate the past history of his family in detail. One of the outcomes, of what became more of an obsession than a hobby, is this book on his father's life.

To save badly-needed space on the following sheets bearing family trees, various symbols have been employed to 'abbreviate' the statements made. Most (but not all) of these symbols are 'conventional' ones, and will be readily understood from the context. However, some may be less familiar, and a (hopefully) complete list is therefore included after the last of the following trees, should the reader require clarification.

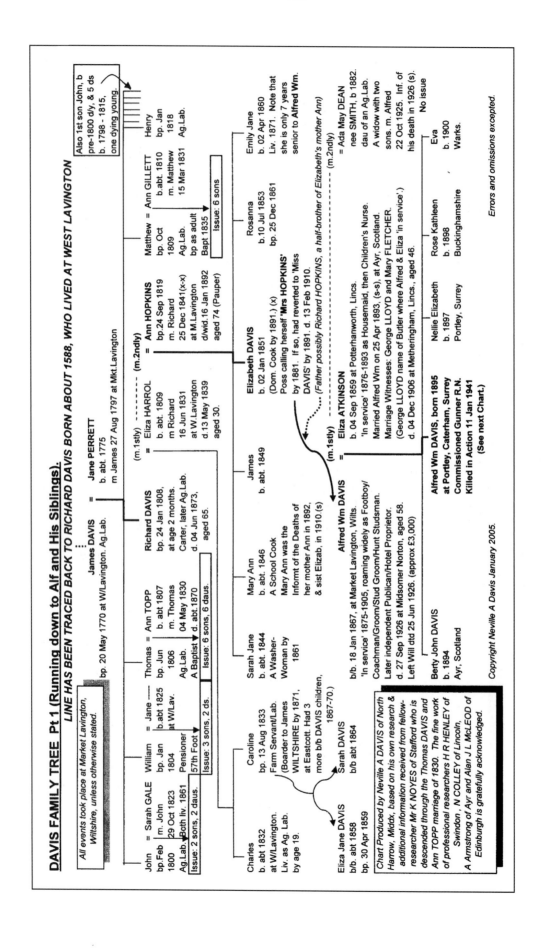

DAVIS FAMILY TREE Pt 1 (Running down to Alf and His Siblings).

LINE HAS BEEN TRACED BACK TO RICHARD DAVIS BORN ABOUT 1588, WHO LIVED AT WEST LAVINGTON

All events took place at Market Lavington, Wiltshire, unless otherwise stated.

James DAVIS = **Jane PERRETT**
bp. 20 May 1770 at W/Lavington. Ag.Lab.   b. abt 1775
m James 27 Aug 1797 at Mkt.Lavington

Also 1st son John, b pre-1800 d/y, & 5 ds b. 1798 - 1815, one dying young.

(m.1stly) — — — — — **(m.2ndly)**

Richard DAVIS = **Eliza HARROL**
bp. 24 Jan 1808,   b. abt 1809
at age 2 months.   m Richard
Carter, later Ag.Lab.   16 Jun 1831
d. 04 Jun 1873,   at W/Lavington
aged 65.   d. 13 May 1839 aged 30.

= **Ann HOPKINS**
bp.24 Sep 1819
m. Richard
25 Dec 1841 (x-x)
at M.Lavington
d/wid.16 Jan 1892
aged 74 (Pauper)

Matthew = **Ann GILLETT**
bp. Oct   b.abt 1810
1809   m. Matthew
Ag.Lab.   15 Mar 1831
bp as adult
Bapt 1835

Issue: 6 sons

Henry
bp. Jan
1818
Ag.Lab.

John = **Sarah GALE**
bp.Feb   m. John
1800   29 Oct 1823
Ag.Lab.   Both liv. 1861
57th Foot
Issue: 2 sons, 2 daus.

William = **Jane ——**
bp. Jan   b.abt 1825
1804   at W/Lav.
Pensioner

Thomas = **Ann TOPP**
bp. Jun   b. abt 1807
1806   m. Thomas
Ag.Lab.   04 May 1830
A Baptist   d. abt.1870
Issue: 6 sons, 6 daus.

Issue: 3 sons, 2 ds.

Elizabeth DAVIS
b. 02 Jan 1851
(Dom. Cook by 1891.) (x)
Poss calling herself 'Mrs HOPKINS'
by 1881. If so, had reverted to 'Miss
DAVIS' by 1891. d. 13 Feb 1910.
(Father possibly Richard HOPKINS, a half-brother of Elizabeth's mother Ann)

Rosanna
b.10 Jul 1853
bp. 25 Dec 1861

Emily Jane
b. 02 Apr 1860
Liv. 1871. Note that
she is only 7 years
senior to **Alfred Wm.**

James
b. abt. 1849

Mary Ann
b. abt. 1846
A School Cook
Mary Ann was the
Informt of the Deaths of
her mother Ann in 1892,
& sist Elizab. in 1910.(s)

Caroline
bp. 13 Aug 1833
at W/Lavington.
Farm Servant/Lab.
Liv. as Ag. Lab.
by age 19.
(Boarder to James
WILTSHIRE by 1871,
at Eastcott. Had 3
more b/b DAVIS children,
1867-70.)

Alfred Wm DAVIS = **Eliza ATKINSON** **(m.1stly)**
b/b. 18 Jan 1867, at Market Lavington, Wilts.   b. 04 Sep 1859 at Potterhanworth, Lincs.
'In service' 1875-1905, roaming widely as Footboy/   'In service' 1876-1893, then Children's Nurse.
Coachman/Groom/Stud Groom/Hunt Studsman.   Married Alfred Wm on 25 Apr 1893, (s-s), at Ayr, Scotland.
Later independent Publican/Hotel Proprietor.   Marriage Witnesses: George LLOYD and Mary FLETCHER.
d. 27 Sep 1926 at Midsomer Norton, aged 58.   (George LLOYD name of Butler where Alfred & Eliza 'in service'.)
Left Will dtd 25 Jun 1926. (approx £3,000)   d. 04 Dec 1906 at Metheringham, Lincs., aged 46.

= **Ada May DEAN** **(m.2ndly)**
nee SMITH, b 1882.
dau of an Ag.Lab.
A widow with two
sons. m. Alfred
22 Oct 1925. Inf. of
his death in 1926 (s).
No issue

Eliza Jane DAVIS
b/b abt 1858
bp. 30 Apr 1859

Charles
b. abt 1832
at W/Lavington.
Liv. as Ag. Lab.
by age 19.

Sarah Jane
b. abt 1844
A Washer-
Woman by
1861

Sarah DAVIS
b/b abt 1864

Alfred Wm DAVIS, born 1895
at Portley, Caterham, Surrey
Commissioned Gunner R.N.
Killed in Action 11 Jan 1941
(See next Chart.)

Berty John DAVIS
b. 1894
Ayr, Scotland

Nellie Elizabeth
b. 1897
Portley, Surrey

Rose Kathleen
b. 1898
Buckinghamshire

Eva
b. 1900
Warks.

*Chart Produced by Neville A DAVIS of North
Harrow, Middx, based on his own research &
additional information received from fellow-
researcher Mr K NOYES of Stafford who is
descended through the Thomas DAVIS and
Ann TOPP marriage of 1830. The fine work
of professional researchers H R HENLEY of
Swindon, N COLLEY of Lincoln,
A Armstrong of Ayr and Alan J L McLEOD of
Edinburgh is gratefully acknowledged.*

Errors and omissions excepted.

Copyright Neville A Davis January 2005.

DAVIS FAMILY TREE Pt 2 (Overlapping and Going On to show Alf's Descendants.)

Alfred Wm DAVIS
b/b. 18 Jan 1867, at Market Lavington, Wiltshire. 'In service' 1875-1905 successively as Footboy/ Coachman/Groom/Stud Groom/Hunt Studsman. 'Independent' Publican/Hotel Proprietor post-1905. d. 27 Sep 1926 at Midsomer Norton, @ 58. Left £3,000 Will dtd 25 Jun 1926 (Equal shares to all 5 children)

(m.1stly) = Eliza ATKINSON
b. 04 Sep 1859 at Potterhanworth, Lincs.. dau of a Carpntr & Joiner. 'Evicted' after father's re-marriage. 'In service' 1876-1893 as Housemaid, then Children's Nurse. Married Alfred Wm on 25 Apr 1893, (s-s), at Ayr, Scotland. Marriage Witnesses: George LLOYD and Mary FLETCHER. d. 04 Dec 1906 at Metheringham, Lincs., aged 46.

(m.2ndly) = Ada May DEAN nee SMITH
b 1882, dau of an Ag Lab. A 43 year-old widow with two teenage sons. m 58 yr-old Alfred Wm 22 Oct 1925 at Midsomer Norton. (s-s). No issue. Informant of Death of Alfred Wm in 1926 (s). dsp

---

Berty John DAVIS
b. 17 Mar 1894 at Newark Castle, Maybole, Ayr, SCO. Put to work at a very young age to support his family, losing much schooling. Yet achieved rank of Army Sergeant in Linconshire Regt. in WW1. Post-War became Publican but 'lost licence'. Later became a Docker. d. 25 Dec 1971 at Knowle, Bristol @ 77.

= Kate HOOPER
b. 02 Oct, 1898 at Bristol, dau of a Mason's Labourer. Married John alias 'Jack', (then a Mill Worker), at the P/Church of St James, of St.James, Bristol, on 27 Aug 1921, after Banns. d/wid in 1979, at Bristol, aged 81, cared-for by her daughters but rather worn-down by her hard life.

Alfred Wm DAVIS
b. 09 Jul 1895, at Portley, SRY. Messenger Boy for GPO. Ran away from home and joined RN as Boy II. Served in First World War. Promoted to Gunner in 1925 and to Commissioned Gunner in 1936. Served in 2nd World War. Killed in Action 11 Jan 1941, gaining posthumous M.I.D. Went down with his ship HMS *Southampton*, which is now a Commonwealth War Grave. Left Will dated 03 Oct 1937, proved 30 May 1941 at Llandudno, S/Wales.

(m.1stly) = Olive Mabel GREEN
b. 10 Nov 1903 at Sudbury, Suffolk, dau. of a Carpenter & Decorator Olive worked at Boots (Chemists), in Ipswich. Married Alf at Parish Church of St. John the Baptist, Ipswich, 21 Apr 1926. In South Africa with Alf 1926/8, where 1st child born. Rtrnd home nr-invalid, with fatal wasting illness, but bore 2 more children. d. 13 Feb 1935, aged 31. bur. Old Felixstowe, SFK. Also see GREEN Tree.

(m.2ndly) = Alice Agnes GREEN
b. 16 Aug 1900 at Sudbury, Suffolk. (Elder sister of Olive.) Helped in her mother's shop. (Clerk for Kodak Ltd in her middle age.) Married Alf at Parish Church of Kirton, Sfk., 18 Jul 1936, becoming step-mother to Olive's children. d 25 Jun 1973. Cremated at Ipswich. Will pvd Sheffield 1973. (Alice's younger brother George Neville GREEN was the Executor.) Also see GREEN Tree.

Nellie Elizabeth
b. 11 Jan 1897 Portley, Surrey Barmaid (Linc.& LON.) m. Wilfred Geo. PENNEY, 24 Feb 1918, at Chiswick. ('Wilf' then a Pvte in the RNAS.) He & Nellie ran P/Houses. SOM '20?, LON fr.'25. [Issue: 1 d died/inf & sons Raymond (1922) & John (1926) both m & issue. Nellie d/wid 29 May 1986 at Cambridge, @ 89. Will dtd 06 Jul 1979.

Rose Kathleen
b. 29 May 1898, Bletchley, Bucks. Former barmaid to her father's business. Married Alfred Thomas WOOLFREY, a Plumber, 20 Jun 1929, at Hammersmith. They ran a P.H. at Victoria, Ldn., for many years. They had no issue. Rose d/wid 05 Mar 1979, at Worthing, @ 80. Will dated 1978.

Eva
b. 16 Sep 1900 Nuneaton, WKS. Former barmaid in her father's public house. m. Frederick J. THORNE, a Postman,.. at P/Church of Widcombe Bath, 26 Dec 1929. They ran a P.H. at Eltham, SRY d/wid. 07 Feb 1979, @78, at Worthing. Will dtd 1975

Seven Daughters (b.1921-1937)
Namely, Joyce, Joan, Kathleen, Margaret, Barbaba, Shirley and Patricia, all born in Bristol. All these daughters married, and all had issue under their different married names. (There was no DAVIS son to carry on this part of the line.)

Joan Olive DAVIS
b. 04 Jun 1927 at Capetown, S/Africa. bpt on bd HMS *Birmingham* on 11 Sep 1927. m.19 Sep 1953 John GOODMAN an Electrician (A/Craft Factory) & former Torpedoman RN. Issue: 2 sons (1955/59), one married, with issue. Joan was widowed 1978.

Neville Alfred DAVIS
b. 17 May 1930 at Felixstowe, SFK. Bpt 27 Jul 1930 at Felixstowe P/Church. A Technologist (with Kodak Ltd. for 43yrs) (Member of Institution of Qual. Assurance.)

= Elizabeth Anne SAKLATVALA
b. 30 Apr 1943 at Rayners Lane, Middlesex. A Secretary at Kodak Ltd. Married Neville at Harrow Register Office, 19 Oct 1963. Issue: 1 dau d/newbrn (1965), 1 DAVIS son (1966), (m&div).
Issue: 1 dau d/newborn (1965) & one surviving dau (b. 1968) & 1 DAVIS son (b.1968), (m&div).

Jessica Agnes DAVIS
b. 03 Oct 1931 at Felixstowe, Suffolk. A Secretary with B.E.Airways. Married Eric FORD on 04 May 1957 at Harrow Weald. Divorced in Canada 1970. Issue: 2 sons (1 married), both b in Canada, 1963/65.

Richard Paul DAVIS
b. 14 Jan 1939 at Felixstowe, Suffolk. A Company Secretary. (A 2nd Lt. in the Corps of Signals during Nat'l Service.) Married Angela BICKELL in 1961. Divorced. Married Lynne BARON in 1982. Divorced. Married Carole McCAHERY in 1986. Divorced (No issue by any of these marriages, but has a step-daughter by the 3rd marriage.)

Errors and Omissions Excepted.

GREEN FAMILY TREE Pt 1
Location: East Suffolk (Somersham, etc.)

Isaac GREEN = **Anne BEAUMONT**
b abt 1730. (Ag.Lab?.) 'Of Great Blakenham' prior to his marriage.
m Isaac at Ringshall 13 Feb 1758.
Witnesses: Wm, Thos & Elizb GREEN.

Isaac's father may have been Wm GREEN of Somersham who had m. Sarah TAMPION at Gt Bricett 28 Sep 1731.

(All bpt at Lt Blakenham.)

John bpt 1758. dsp (?)	
Ann bpt 1761	
William bpt 1761, married Sarah RICH. & had issue.	
Robert bpt 1763, m Amy GARRARD.& had issue.	
Thomas bpt 1765. dsp(?)	

(m.1stly) = **Sarah ARCHER** b abt 1768?
-------- (m.2ndly?) --------
Mary HILL(?) b. 1767 at Bricett *(sic)*. bpt Offton, 08 Jul 1767? A 'Mary GREEN' was living with Joseph GREEN in Somersham, in 1841. (She is believed to be the Mary HILL who married Joseph GREEN (a wid) at Barking, SFK, on 20 Dec 1801.) Mary 'made her mark 'x' on a 'note' added to (step-son?) Jos' Death certificate. d/wid and a Pauper 24 May 1851 @ 84.

Joseph GREEN
Bpt 13 Mar 1768, at Elmsett. An Agricultural Labourer, living at Somersham with a Mary GREEN (a 2nd wife?) at the time of the 1841 Census. d 11 DEC 1846, 'aged 77', and bur at Somersham.

Married Joseph at Nedging, 03 NOV 1785? She and her husband drawn to Baptist faith post Apr 1788. Believed to have died pre-1801.

James bpt 08 Jul 1770 at Elmsett m. Charity RICH at Nedging. 19 Oct 1785. Had issue at Elmsett, 1 s & 2d

Saul bpt 31 Jan 1773 at Elmsett bur at Elmsett 10 Jul 1774 **aged 1.**

Samuel bpt 15 May 1774 at Elmsett m. Hannah —— and poss. had GREEN issue at Ringshall, incl. Abraham & Elizb.

Samuel GREEN
bpt 19 MAR 1786, at Gt Bricett An Ag. Lab. Apparently he was 'the' Samuel serving in the Wminster Militia with his bro' Joseph. *Maybe* married Sarah (ANDREWS?), by whom a d, Maria. b. 1836. If so, Samuel prob. d pre-1841, leaving 'wid & d' in Joseph's care by 1841.

Joseph (alias Jonas) GREEN
b 23 Jan 1788, at Gt Bricett. Bpt 13 APR 1788 at Gt Bricett? b recorded at Wattisham Baptist Meeting House. An Ag Lab who was also in the Westminster Militia. Joined 24th Regt of Foot in 1807 and served for 16 yrs, mainly in India. Became an Out-Pensioner of Chelsea Hospital in OCT 1823. Returned to civilian life as peripatetic Dealer and Jobber. Evidently a Lay Baptist Preacher. d. 16 MAY 1845 at Somersham, SFK., aged 57. bur. in prominent position nr Somersham Baptist Chapel. Headstone extant 2004.

= **Elizabeth (CLARKE?)**
b. 02 Apr 1792 at 'Bassen' (Barsham?), NFK Married Joseph after his discharge from the Army. (Marriage probably at Elmsett, 05 APR 1825, (s-s) by Banns, If so, her maiden name was CLARKE. Witnesses: George & Elizabeth GREEN.) d. 24 AUG 1855 at Ipswich, aged 63. bur nr Somesh'm Bpt Chapel, with husband.

Joshua
b 17 Jan 1791 birth recorded at Wattisham Bapt Chapel. Mother's name shown as Sarah GREEN nee ARCHER (he is alternative possibility for father of Maria b. 1836 - See entry under his bro. Samuel. More probably, he died young.)

William GREEN
b 19 JAN 1826 at Needham Mkt. Lab in Iron Foundry A Fitter (Engineer) A Machinist, etc.

= **Susan HARVEY**
b 29 MAY 1827 at Bricet (sic), SFK.

David GREEN
b 23 JAN 1828 at Willisham, SFK. Dealer/Jobber/ Dealer & Beershop Keeper/Farmer/ Cattle Dealer.

= **Lucy STOLERY**
b 19 FEB 1828 at Ipswich, SFK.

Emma GREEN
b 05 MAY 1831 at unknown place in SFK. d 28 JUN 1839, aged 8 bur near Somersham Strict Baptist Chapel, next to her parents.

(m.1stly) ------ **Susannah WEBSTER** b abt 1836 at Sudbury.
Joseph GREEN
b 04 OCT 1835 at Somersham. Painter/House Decorator/Inn-Keeper/Painter Glazier.
('m'.2ndly) = **Maria (Potter) HANNANT** b SEP? 1840 Worstead, NFK

(See next Chart) (See next Chart)

Line of Descent to Neville A DAVIS and siblings. (See next Chart.)

Copyright Neville A DAVIS Jan 2005.
E and O.E.

Chart produced by Neville A DAVIS of North Harrow, Middx, mainly on the basis of his own research though fine work by fellow-researchers Mrs June GREEN (late husband Peter descended through Wm GREEN b 1826) and Mrs Jennie King (descended thro' David GREEN b 1828) is most gratefully acknowledged. As is the vastly helpful family data provided by the late Peggy COLEMAN, and the late Elsie Harvey GREEN (both descended through Wm GREEN b 1826): also key fragments by the late Geo Neville GREEN and Geoffrey CASTELL, both descended through Joseph GREEN b 1835. Prof indexer Pam PALGRAVE has also provided help. Tracing GREEN pedigrees in Suffolk is extremely difficult due to the many persons having that surname who were of similar ages and living-areas and who bore the same forenames. Non-conformity was strong, and, as revealed by comparison with census records from 1841 onwards, numerous people never appeared at all in C of E records. Several other amateur researchers of 'GREEN in Suffolk' have been consulted, but with no success in finding 'further links'.

GREEN FAMILY TREE Pt 2 (O'lapping & Continuing.)   Joseph alias Jonas GREEN = Elizabeth CLARKE(?)

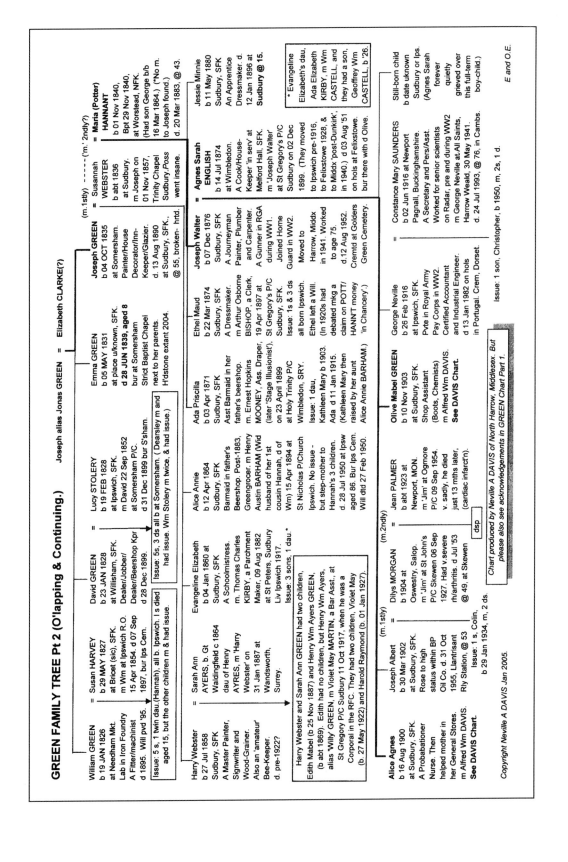

William GREEN b 19 JAN 1826 at Needham Mkt. Lab in Iron Foundry A Fitter/machinist d 1895. Will pvd '95.
= Susan HARVEY b 29 MAY 1827 at Bricet (sic), SFK. m Wm at Ipswich R.O. 15 Apr 1854. d 07 Sep 1897, bur Ips Cem.
Issue: 5 s, 1 twin dau. (Hannah), all b. Ipswich. 1 s died aged 15, but the other children m & had issue.

David GREEN b 23 JAN 1828 at Willisham, SFK. Dealer/Jobber/ Dealer/Beershop Kpr d 28 Dec 1899.
= Lucy STOLERY b 19 FEB 1828 at Ipswich, SFK. m David 22 Sep 1852 at Somersham P/C. d 31 Dec 1899 bur S'sham.
Issue: 5s, 3 ds all b at Somersham. (Dearsley m and had issue. Wm Stolery m twice, & had issue.)

Emma GREEN b 05 MAY 1831 at place u/known, SFK. d 28 JUN 1839, aged 8 bur at Somersham Strict Baptist Chapel next to her parents. H'dstone extant 2004.

(m.1stly) ----- (m.' 2ndly?)

Joseph GREEN b 04 OCT 1835 at Somersham. Painter/House Decorator/Inn-Keeper/Glazier. d. 13 Aug 1890 at Sudbury, SFK.. @ 55, broken- hrtd.
= Susannah WEBSTER b abt 1836 at Sudbury. m Joseph on 01 Nov 1857, Trinity Chapel Sudbury. Poss went insane.
= Maria (Potter) HANNANT b 01 Nov 1840, Bpt 29 Nov 1840, at Worstead, NFK. (Had son George b/b 16 Mar 1864.) (*No m. to Joseph found.) d. 20 Mar 1883, @ 43.

Harry Webster b 27 Jul 1858 Sudbury, SFK A Master Painter, Signwriter and Wood-Grainer. Also an 'amateur' Bee-Keeper. d. pre-1922?
= Sarah Ann AYERS, b. Gt Waldingfield c 1864 dau of Henry AYRES, m 'Harry' Webster on 31 Jan 1887 at Wandsworth, Surrey.

Evangeline Elizabeth b 04 Jan 1860 at Sudbury, SFK A Schoolmistress. m. Thomas Charles KIRBY, a Parchment Maker, 09 Aug 1882 at St Peters, Sudbury Liv Ipswich 1917. Issue: 3 sons, 1 dau.*

Alice Annie b 12 Apr 1864 Sudbury, SFK Barmaid in father's Beershop. Post-1883, Greengrocer. m Henry Austin BARHAM (Wid husband of her 1st cousin Hannah, d of Wm) 15 Apr 1894 at St Nicholas P/Church Ipswich. No issue - but step-mother to Hannah's 3 children. d. 28 Jul 1950 at Ipsw aged 86. Bur Ips Cem. Will dtd 27 Feb 1950.

Ada Priscilla b 03 Apr 1871 Sudbury, SFK Asst Barmaid in father's beershop. m. Ernest Hopkins MOONEY, Ass. Draper, (later 'Stage Illusionist'), St Gregory's P/C Sudbury, SFK. Issue: 1s, 3 ds all born Ipswich.

Ethel Maud b 22 Mar 1874 Sudbury, SFK A Dressmaker. m Arthur Osborne BISHOP, a Clerk, 19 Apr 1897 at St Gregory's P/C Sudbury, SFK. Issue: 1s & 3 ds all born Ipswich. Ethel left a Will. (In 1920s had debated mkg a claim on POTT/ HANN'T money 'in Chancery'.)

Joseph Walter b 07 Dec 1876 Sudbury, SFK A Journeyman Painter, Plumber and Carpenter. A Gunner in RGA during WW1. Joined Home Guard in WW2. Moved to Harrow, Middx in 1941. Worked to age 75. d.12 Aug 1952. Cremtd at Golders Green Cemetery.
= Agnes Sarah ENGLISH b 14 Jul 1874 at Wimbledon. A Cook/House-Keeper 'in serv' at Melford Hall, SFK. m 'Joseph Walter' at St Gregory's P/C Sudbury on 02 Dec 1899. (They moved to Ipswich pre-1916, to Felixstowe 1928, & to Middx 'post-Dunkirk', in 1940.) d 03 Aug '51 on hols at Felixstowe. bur there with d Olive.

Jessie Minnie b 11 May 1880 Sudbury, SFK An Apprentice Dressmaker. d 12 Jan 1896 at Sudbury @ 15.

> * Evangeline Elizabeth's dau, Ada Elizabeth KIRBY, m Wm CASTELL, and they had a son, Geoffrey Wm CASTELL, b '26.

> Harry Webster and Sarah Ann GREEN had two children, Edith Mabel (b 25 Nov 1887) and Henry Wm Ayers GREEN, (b abt 1869). Edith had no children, but Henry Wm Ayers, alias 'Willy' GREEN, m Violet May MARTIN, a Bar Asst., at St Gregory P/C Sudbury 11 Oct 1917, when he was a Corporal in the RFC. They had two children, Violet May (b. 27 May 1922) and Harold Raymond (b. 01 Jan 1927).

Alice Agnes b 16 Aug 1900 at Sudbury, SFK. A Probationer Nurse. Then helped mother in her General Stores. m Alfred Wm DAVIS. See DAVIS Chart.

Joseph Albert b 30 Mar 1902 at Sudbury, SFK. Rose to high status within BP Oil Co. d. 31 Oct 1955, Llantrisant Rly Station, @ 53
(m.1stly) **= Jean PALMER** b abt 1923 at Newport, MON. m 'Jim' at Ogmore P/C Skewen 06 Sep 1954. v. sadly, he died just 13 mths later, (cardiac infarct'n). dsp
(m.2ndly) **= Dilys MORGAN** b 1904 at Oswestry, Salop. m 'Jim' at St John's P/C Skewen 06 Sep 1927. Had v.severe rh/arthritis. d Jul '53 @ 49, at Skewen Issue: 1 s, Colin, b 29 Jan 1934, m, 2 ds.

Olive Mabel GREEN b 10 Nov 1903 at Sudbury, SFK. Shop Assistant (Boots, Chemists). m Alfred Wm DAVIS. See DAVIS Chart.

George Neville b 26 Feb 1916 at Ipswich, SFK. Pvte in Royal Army Pay Corps in WW2. Certified Accountant and Industrial Engineer. d 13 Jan 1982 on hols in Portugal. Crem. in Cambs.
= Constance Mary SAUNDERS b 02 Jun 1916 at Newport Pagnall, Buckinghamshire. A Secretary and Pers/Asst. Worked for senior scientists on Radar, pre and during WW2 m George Neville at All Saints, Harrow Weald, 30 May 1941. d. 24 Jul 1993, @ 76, in Cambs.
Issue: 1 son, Christopher, b 1950, m, 2s, 1 d.

> Still-born child b date uknown Sudbury or Ips. (Agnes Sarah forever quietly grieved over this full-term boy-child.)

HOPKINS FAMILY TREE

Location:: Market Lavington,WILTSHIRE

LINE HAS BEEN TRACED BACK TO RICHARD HOPKINS OF URCHFONT b abt 1650, WHO MARRIED MARY GYLES ON 06 APRIL 1678, at MARKET LAVINGTON AND HAD ISSUE THERE...

It is notable that illegitimacy had become rife in various parts of the wider family during the 19th C.

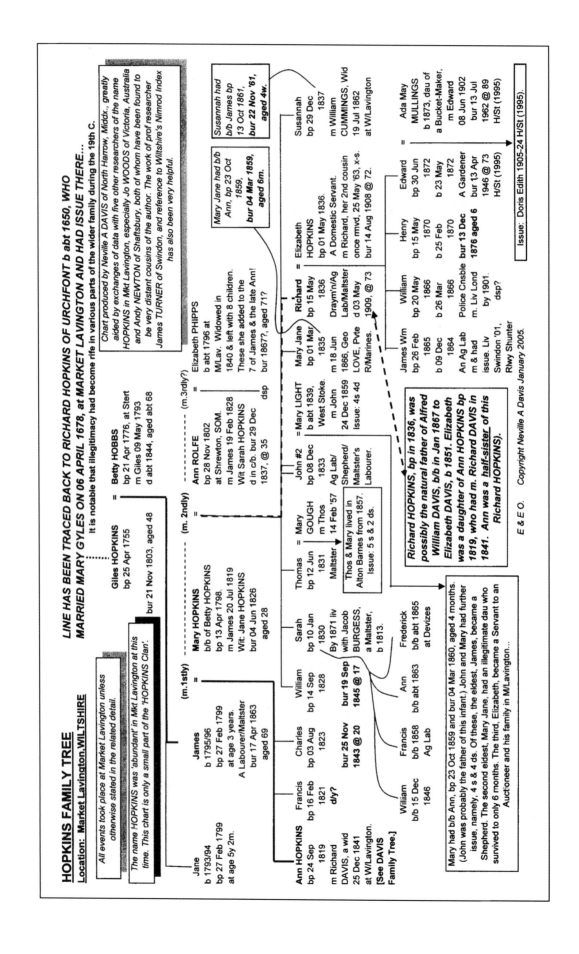

Chart produced by Neville A DAVIS of North Harrow, Middx., greatly aided by exchanges of data with five other researchers of the name HOPKINS in Mkt Lavington, especially Jo WOODS of Victoria, Australia and Andy NEWTON of Shaftsbury, both of whom have been found to be very distant cousins of the author. The work of prof researcher James TURNER of Swindon, and reference to Wiltshire's Nimrod Index has also been very helpful.

All events took place at Market Lavington unless otherwise stated in the related detail.

The name HOPKINS was 'abundant' in Mkt Lavington at this time. This chart is only a small part of the 'HOPKINS Clan'.

Giles HOPKINS bp 25 Apr 1755 = **Betty HOBBS** bp 21 Apr 1776, at Stert m Giles 09 May 1793 d abt 1844, aged abt 68

bur 21 Nov 1803, aged 48

Jane b 1793/94 bp 27 Feb 1799 at age 5y 2m.

(m.1stly) =

James b 1795/96 bp 27 Feb 1799 at age 3 years. A Labourer/Maltster bur 17 Apr 1863 aged 69

Mary HOPKINS b/b of Betty HOPKINS bp 13 Apr 1798. m James 20 Jul 1819 Wit: Jane HOPKINS bur 04 Jun 1826 aged 28

(m. 2ndly) =

Elizabeth PHIPPS b abt 1796 at M/Lav. Widowed in 1840 & left with 8 children. These she added to the 7 of James & the late Ann! bur 1867?, aged 71?

-------- (m.3rdly) =

Ann ROLFE bp 28 Nov 1802 at Shrewton, SOM. m James 19 Feb 1828 Wit Sarah HOPKINS d in c/b. bur 29 Dec 1837, @ 35 dsp

Susannah had b/b James bp 13 Oct 1861, bur 22 Nov '61, aged 4w.

Mary Jane had b/b Ann, bp 23 Oct 1859, bur 04 Mar 1859, aged 6m.

Susannah bp 29 Dec 1837 m William CUMMINGS, Wid 19 Jul 1862 at W/Lavington

Richard bp 15 May 1836 Draym'n/Ag Lab/Maltster d 03 May 1909, @ 73 = **Elizabeth HOPKINS** bp 01 May 1836. A Domestic Servant. m Richard, her 2nd cousin once rmvd, 25 May '63, x-s. bur 14 Aug 1908 @ 72.

= **Ada May MULLINGS** b 1873, dau of a Bucket-Maker, m Edward 08 Jun 1902 bur 13 Jul 1962 @ 89 H/St (1995)

Mary Jane bp 01 Mar 1835 m 18 Jun 1866, Geo LOVE, Pvte R/Marines. Issue: 4s 4d

John #2 bp 08 Dec 1833 Ag Lab/ Shepherd/ Maltster's Labourer.

= **Mary LIGHT** b abt 1839, West Stoke. m John 24 Dec 1859 Issue: 4s 4d

Henry bp 15 May 1870 b 25 Feb 1870 **bur 13 Dec 1876 aged 6**

Edward bp 30 Jun 1872 b 23 May 1872 A Gardener bur 13 Apr 1946 @ 73 H/St (1995)

Issue: Doris Edith 1905-24 H/St (1995).

Thomas bp 12 Jun 1831 Maltster = **Mary GOUGH** m Thos 14 Feb '57 By 1871 liv with Jacob BURGESS, a Maltster, b 1813.

Thos & Mary lived in Alton Barnes from 1857. Issue: 5 s & 2 ds.

Sarah bp 10 Jan 1830

William bp 14 Sep 1828

James Wm bp 26 Feb 1865 b 09 Dec 1864 An Ag Lab m & had issue. Liv Swindon '01, Rlwy Shunter

William bp 20 Jun 1866 b 26 Mar 1866 Police Cnsble m. Liv Lond by 1901. dsp?

Charles bp 03 Aug 1823 **bur 25 Nov 1843 @ 20**

Francis bp 16 Feb 1821 **dly?**

Ann HOPKINS bp 24 Sep 1819 m Richard DAVIS, a wid 25 Dec 1841 at W/Lavington. [See DAVIS Family Tree.]

Richard HOPKINS, bp in 1836, was possibly the natural father of Alfred William DAVIS, b/b in Jan 1867 to Elizabeth DAVIS, b 1851. Elizabeth was a daughter of Ann HOPKINS bp 1819, who had m. Richard DAVIS in 1841. Ann was a half-sister of this Richard HOPKINS).

E & E.O. Copyright Neville A Davis January 2005.

Frederick b/b abt 1865 at Devizes

Ann b/b abt 1863

Francis b/b 1858 Ag Lab

William b/b 15 Dec 1846

Mary had b/b Ann, bp 23 Oct 1859 and bur 04 Mar 1860, aged 4 months. (John was probably the father of this infant.) John and Mary had further issue, namely, 4 s & 4 ds. Of these, the eldest, James, became a Shepherd. The second eldest, Mary Jane, had an illegitimate dau who survived to only 6 months. The third, Elizabeth, became a Servant to an Auctioneer and his family in M/Lavington....

ATKINSON FAMILY TREE

LOCATION: POTTER HANWORTH, LINCOLNSHIRE

All events took place at Potterhanworth (P/H) unless otherwise stated on chart.

Parentage of John ATKINSON is uncertain. He may spring from a brother, cousin, (or be the self-same man) of the John ATKINSON who, with wife Fewdy, had issue at P/H including Christopher bp 04 Feb 1775 and Anthony bp 30 Dec 1780, leading to collateral lines of descent to those shown here. It may be, however, that 'our' John originated from elsewhere.

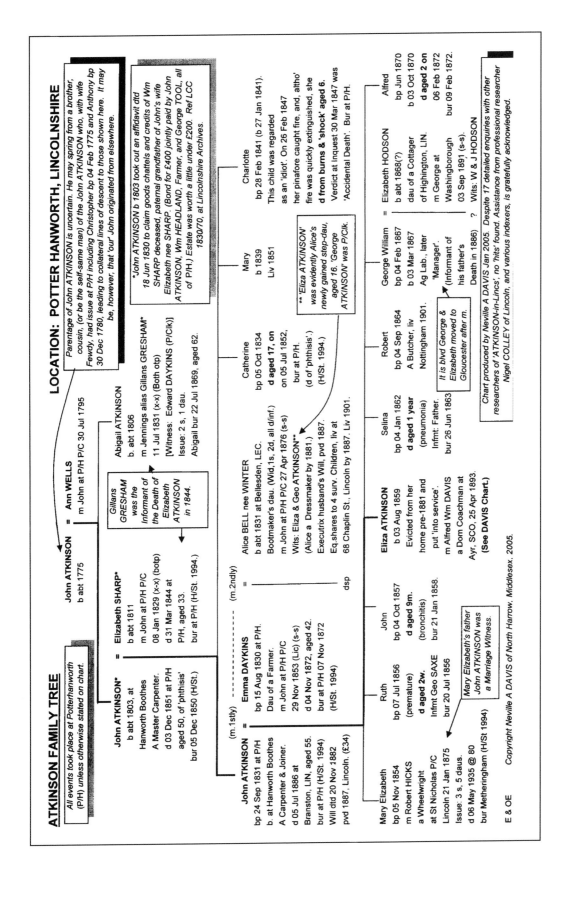

John ATKINSON
b abt 1775

= **Ann WELLS**
m John at P/H P/C 30 Jul 1795

"John ATKINSON b 1803 took out an affidavit dtd 18 Jun 1830 to claim goods chattels and credits of Wm SHARP deceased, paternal grandfather of John's wife Elizabeth nee SHARP. (Bond for £400 jointly paid by John ATKINSON, Wm HEADLAND, Farmer, and George TOOL, all of P/H.) Estate was worth a little under £200. Ref LCC 1830/70, at Lincolnshire Archives.

John ATKINSON*
b abt 1803, at Hanworth Boothes
A Master Carpenter.
d 03 Dec 1851 at P/H aged 50, of 'phthisis'
bur 05 Dec 1850 (H/St.)

= **Elizabeth SHARP***
b abt 1811
m John at P/H P/C 08 Jan 1829 (x-x) (botp)
d 31 Mar 1844 at P/H, aged 33.
bur at P/H (H/St. 1994.)

Abigail ATKINSON
b. abt 1806
m Jennings alias Gillans GRESHAM*
11 Jul 1831 (x-x) (Both otp)
[Witness: Edward DAYKINS (P/Clk)]
Issue: 2 s, 1 dau.
Abigail bur 22 Jul 1869, aged 62.

Gillans GRESHAM was the Informant of the Death of Elizabeth ATKINSON in 1844.

Charlotte
bp 28 Feb 1841 (b 27 Jan 1841).
This child was regarded as an 'idiot'. On 26 Feb 1847 her pinafore caught fire, and, altho' fire was quickly extinguished, she d from burns & 'shock' aged 6. Verdict at Inquest 30 Mar 1847 was 'Accidental Death'. Bur at P/H.

Mary
b 1839
Liv 1851

Catherine
bp 05 Oct 1834
d aged 17, on 05 Jul 1852, bur at P/H.
(d of 'phthisis'.)
(H/St. 1994.)

**"Eliza ATKINSON' was evidently Alice's newly gained step-dau, aged 16. 'George ATKINSON' was P/Clk.

(m.1stly) ———————————— (m.2ndly)

John ATKINSON = **Emma DAYKINS**
bp 24 Sep 1831 at P/H   bp 15 Aug 1830 at P/H.
b. at Hanworth Boothes   Dau of a Farmer.
A Carpenter & Joiner.   m John at P/H P/C
d 05 Jul 1886 at   29 Nov 1853 (Lic) (s-s)
Branston, LIN, aged 55. d 04 Nov 1872, aged 42.
bur at P/H (H/St. 1994) bur at P/H 07 Nov 1872
Will dtd 20 Nov 1882   (H/St. 1994)
pvd 1887, Lincoln. (£34)

= **Alice BELL nee WINTER**
b abt 1831 at Bellesden, LEC.
Bootmaker's dau. (Wid,1s, 2d, all d/inf.)
m John at P/H P/C 27 Apr 1876 (s-s)
Wits: Eliza & Geo ATKINSON**
(Alice a Dressmaker by 1881.)
Executrix husband's Will, pvd 1887.
Eq.shares to 4 surv. Children, liv at
68 Chaplin St., Lincoln by 1887. Liv 1901.

dsp

George William
bp 04 Feb 1867
b 03 Mar 1867
Ag Lab., later 'Manager'.
(Informant of his father's Death in 1886.)

= **Elizabeth HODSON**
b abt 1868(?)
dau of a Cottager of Highington, LIN.
m George at Washingborough
03 Sep 1891 (s-s).
Wits: W & J HODSON

Alfred
bp Jun 1870
b 03 Oct 1870
d aged 2 on
06 Feb 1872
bur 09 Feb 1872.

Robert
bp 04 Sep 1864
A Butcher, liv Nottingham 1901.

It is blvd George & Elizabeth moved to Gloucester after m.

?

Selina
bp 04 Jan 1862
d aged 1 year (pneumonia)
Infmt: Father.
bur 26 Jun 1863

Eliza ATKINSON
b 03 Aug 1859
Evicted from her home pre-1881 and put 'into service'.
m Alfred Wm DAVIS a Dom Coachman at Ayr, SCO, 25 Apr 1893.
(See DAVIS Chart.)

John
bp 04 Oct 1857
d aged 9m.
(bronchitis)
bur 21 Jan 1858.

Ruth
bp 07 Jul 1856
(premature)
d aged 2w.
Infmt Geo SAXE
bur 20 Jul 1856

Mary Elizabeth
bp 05 Nov 1854
m Robert HICKS a Wheelwright at St Nicholas P/C Lincoln 21 Jan 1875
Issue: 3 s, 5 daus.
d 06 May 1935 @ 80
bur Metheringham (H/St 1994)

Mary Elizabeth's father John ATKINSON was a Marriage Witness.

Chart produced by Neville A DAVIS Jan 2005. Despite 17 detailed enquiries with other researchers of 'ATKINSON-in-Lincs', no 'hits' found. Assistance from professional researcher Nigel COLLEY of Lincoln, and various indexers, is gratefully acknowledged.

DAYKINS FAMILY TREE

LOCATION: POTTER HANWORTH, LINCOLNSHIRE

The parentage of William DAYKINS is unknown. It seems likely that he was the eldest (or only) son of a DAYKINS Family, his sizeable farm presumably having been inherited under the rule of primogeniture. There were various DAYKINS families around the area and William even had a namesake, b abt 1792 and bur on 17 Jul 1853, aged 61, at South Scarle, Notts (just over the county border). Other, presumably collateral, DAYKINS families lived in P/H itself throughout this period.

Chart produced by Neville A DAVIS of North Harrow, Middlesex. No co-researchers found, except of DAYKINS families which may have been 'collateral' to the family in this chart. The author is indebted to prof researcher Nigel COLLEY of Lincoln, and to certain professional indexers, for positive assistance. (The author would also like to express his thanks to Kathleen BANGER of Ontario, Canada, who has provided useful local colour from childhood visits to a gt-aunt at Potter Hanworth.)

Basically, Alfred's Will of 1866 asked that his farm and possessions be sold off, and the proceeds used to make cash payments to his 'sisters', Viz £300 to Elizabeth TAYLOR, **£100 to Emma ATKINSON**, & £200 shared equally to the children of the late Eliza WOOLDRIDGE (as each reached the age of 21): the residue to be shared equally between Mahala and Priscilla, who were then both unmarried. The Executor was a local Farmer, William HEADLAND. (He had evidently also been a bondsman in 1830 - see ATKINSON chart.)

* Since Ruth RADFORD was under 21, and fatherless, a certain John BRIGGS, Farmer of P/H, had to swear on oath that he was her lawful guardian and that he gave his consent to the marriage. Ref MBs1819/458 & 459 at Lincolnshire Archives.

William DAYKINS = **Ruth RADFORD** ---- **(m.2ndly)** = **Sarah TAYLOR**

(m.1stly)

William DAYKINS
b abt 1797 at
Potterhanw'rth
A Farmer (of
240 acres, emp
2 n/f men by 1851.
d/wid. 27 APR
1861, aged 64.
(Heart Disease)
bur P/H. (H/St)

Ruth RADFORD
b abt 1801 at P/H
m William at
Potterhanworth
01 MAR 1819
By Lic and Oath*
d 1832, poss in c/b.
bur P/H aged 32,
13 Oct 1832

Sarah TAYLOR
b. abt 1802, of P/H
m William at
Potterhanworth
21 MAR 1836
by Licence (s–s).
d. MAR 1851
aged 50, bur
P/H 15 MAR 1851

John
bpt 19 Mar
1820, P/H
Farmer's Son
bur 21 FEB,
1857, a. 38.
d.s.p

Elizabeth
bpt 03 FEB
1822, P/H
m. John
TAYLOR
pre –1862

William
bpt 20 DEC
1823, P/H
Farmer's
son.
d. 28 MAY
1855 @ 31.
(Phthisis)
bur 31 MAY
1855
d.s.p

Robert
bpt 20 DEC
1824, P/H
d/y
**bur 27 Jun
1826, @ 1.**

Eliza
bpt 10 DEC
1826, P/H
m. a Mr
WOOL-
DRIDGE,
a Thresher,
& had issue
d. pre-1866.

Robert
bpt 18 MAY
1827, P/H
Farmer's
son.
d. 1849/50
aged 25
bur 18 JAN
1854
d.s.p

Emma DAYKINS
bpt 15 AUG
1830, P/H
m.John
ATKINSON,
a Carpenter,
29 NOV 1853
by Licence (s–s).
**(See ATKINSON
Pedigree).**

Mahala
bpt 07 MAY
1837, P/H
A Female
Labourer,
still un-married
in 1881 & then
living with her
bro-in-law,
John TAYLOR.
d.s.p?

Alfred
bpt 03 DEC 1838, P/H
b 05 Nov 1838 at P/H
A Farmer. Applied for
Admon of his father's
estate, rated at 195
acres in 1873. (£800)
Left own Will dtd 1866,
pvd 1870. (< £1,000)
(Copy ex Lin Prob Registry)
d 04 SEP 1870, a. 31.
(Rheum Inflmtn of heart)
bur P/H (H/St.) **d.s.p.**

Priscilla
bpt 20 DEC
1840, P/H
Post-1866, m.
Edw. NICHOLLS
of Brampton
Manor, Chester-
field. (Secretary
of a Tramway Co.)
Prisc. bur 12 Apr
1882, aged 41.
(H/St.) **d.s.p.**

b/b Henry
bpt 10 OCT
1841

b/b Anne
bpt 14 OCT
1838

Evidently raised as children of John TAYLOR.

Emma's later heart-problems would seem to stem from her father William's genes.

As can be clearly seen from the 'd.s.p' endings, etc., this Line of the DAYKINS clan terminated with Alfred's death in 1870.

E & O.E   Copyright Neville A DAVIS, Nth Harrow, Middx. 2005

ENGLISH FAMILY TREE

All events took place at Twinstead in Essex, unless otherwise stated in the detail. (Tw = abb 'n for Twinstead. WStP = abb'n for Wickham St Paul.)

LINE HAS BEEN TRACED BACK TO ROBERT ENGLISH, a WEAVER, bur 20 Jan 1564 at Gt. WALDINGFIELD, SFK.

Earliest finding is the WILL of 'Johannes ENGLYSSHE' of Gt W., dtd 11 Jun 1480.

Chart produced by Neville a DAVIS of North Harrow, Middlesex, greatly aided by several co-researchers, especially Audrey BUXTON (of Rutland), Doug WENT and Molly SPOONER (both of Essex), Jean-Paul THOMPSON (of Bergamo, Italy), Dennis and Joan HAMILTON (of E.Sussex), Robin HANSELL (of Hants) & others.
Also well-aided by various prof researchers & indexers.

Robert ENGLISH = **Alice DIXEY**

Robert ENGLISH
bp 22 Nov 1795, at Bulmer. A Carpenter, who moved to Twinstead after about 1818. d 22 May 1863, aged 68. bur at Twinstead. H/St (1998). Left Will (< £200) dtd 17 Feb 1858, pvd Ipswich 31 Oct 1863. (4 s to each inherit properties on d of relict.)

Alice DIXEY
b abt 1790, at Pebmarsh dau of John DIXEY. m Robert 03 Sep 1816 at Bulmer P/Church. d 16 Jan 1869, @ 79. H/St (1998) Called 'Ellen' in Robert's Will. (Rec'd rents of 4 propts for her lifetime)

William ENGLISH = **Mary Ann RAYMOND**

William ENGLISH
bp Bulmer 23 Mar 1817. A Carpenter in Twin'std, emp sons Charles and Albert & 2 men by 1881. Adv in Kelly's 1882. Carptr & Grocer by '91. Co-Exec of father's Will. d 04 Mar 1892 @ 78 bur Tw. H/St (1998)

Mary Ann RAYMOND
b Twinstead 1818, (dau of Peter RAYMOND, A Labourer.) m William 29 Oct 1838 at Twinstead P/Church ('Wits: Wm's bro Robt, and his wife-to-be Hannah HOLLAND) d. 10 May 1884, aged 65. bur Tw H/St (1998)

Robert ENGLISH = **Hannah Chickle HOLLAND**

Robert ENGLISH
b Twinstead 1819. A Shoemaker who moved into Sudbury. Blvd to be the 'Robert ENGLISH' who srvd on Coroner's Jury in Sudbury 10 May '69. d 06 Apr '91, @ 73

Hannah Chickle HOLLAND
b Sudbury 1818. A Dressmaker. m Robert 11 Feb 1839 at All Saints P/C Sudbury.

Issue: 2 s and 3 d (all b Sudbury).

George ENGLISH = **Sarah —**

George ENGLISH
b Twinstead 1823. A Carpenter in Tw until c.1855. Then set up a business 'near Wimbledon Common,' emplyg 4 men by 1881. died pre-1901.

Sarah —
b Hadleigh 1822. Pres-umed to have m George in Tw but no record found. Liv. wid, 1901.

Issue: 1 s 3 d (b Tw), 2 s (b Wimbledon).

Daniel ENGLISH = **Matilda ALSTON**

Daniel ENGLISH
b Twinsted 1829. A Shoemaker working in Friars St., Sudbury, near bro Robert. Co-Exec of father's Will. liv 1892.

Matilda ALSTON
b Wiggin End, Sudbury, 1828. A Hand-Loom Silk Weaver pre & post m. m Daniel 12 Dec 1848 at St Gregory's P/C Sudbury. Liv 1901.

Issue: 5 s and 4 d (all b Sudbury).

Ellen, b. 1839
d 21 Aug 1849 bur 23 Aug '49, aged 11. Informt of the Death, Mary Ann ENGLISH, (the mother). Father's name given as George ENGLISH (sic) on the death certificate.

Jane, b 04 Oct 1840.
Liv with her ENG g'rnts in 1841. d @ 2 (influenza).

George ENGLISH
b 13 Feb 1842. A Carpenter who moved to Wimbledon to work with his Uncle George, and m whilst there. Re-turned to Twinstead by 1881, where re-married. By then a Builder & Master Carpenter. d 09 Feb 1913, aged 70. bur Twins'd. H/St (1994)

(m.1stly) **Sarah SKINNER** ——————— (m.2ndly) **Eliza FISHER**

Sarah SKINNER
b Doddington, CAM 29 Mar 1847, dau of a Gardener/Beer-Shop Kpr. m George 02 Jun 1873 at P/C of St Mary, Wimble-don. (Wits: sis Jane SKINNER & Arthur ENGLISH, Geo's coz) d 28 Oct 1875 aged only 28. Bur near front porch of St Mary's. H/St (1994)

Eliza FISHER
b 01 Jun 1845 at Gt Henny, dau of James FISHER, a Shoemaker. Was a wid when she m George 06 Dec '81 at Gt Henny. d 29 Sep 1926 @ 81. bur Tw (H/St) Co-exec of hsbd's Will.

Issue: 1 s 2 d.

> Geo. left Will dtd 1906 (£2,410). Main inheritor: 2nd wife, but also properties to his son & dau.

George Wm ENGLISH
b 07 Jan 1883, at Twinstead. Pvte Soldier Boer War & WW1 (E.Srys). Labourer. d Colchester 24 Jan 1942. dsp.

Agnes Sarah ENGLISH, b Wimbledon 14 Jul 1874
A Cook/Housekeeper at Melford Hall. Married Joseph Walter GREEN, a House Decorator, 02 Dec 1899, at St Gregory, Sudbury. **See GREEN Tree.**

Walter b 1847
A Carpenter. m Mary Ann DIXEY at Twinstead P/Church on 26 Aug 1872. He died aged only 26 on 10 Aug '73 (of T.B), & she out-lived him only briefly. H/Sts (1994) dsp

Daniel ENGLISH b 1849
A Shoemaker, wkg in Twinstead m Alice WALFORD (b Tw 1849), on 07 Oct 1875 at Twinstd P/C. (Seven yr-old niece Agnes Sarah ENGLISH was 'visitor' at 1881 census, and may have often lived with Daniel, Alice and their children.) Daniel liv 1881, prob d pre-1891. Issue: 1 s 2 d.

Charles b 1851
A Carpenter wkg with his father & bro Albert at Twinstead. m Hannah PYE (b Gt Henny 1853) at Gt Henny on 13 Apr 1875. Hannah was lnft of Jane's death in 1890. Issue: 3 daughters. (Chas liv 1910).

William b 1855
Died (just 4 mths after his g/fthr died) on 01 Sep '63 @ 8. (scarletina) bur 15 Sep '63. H/Stone (1994)

Albert b 28 May 1858, a Carpenter wkg at Tw with his fthr & bro. By 1881, back with parents as wid & invalid. Died 1890. Issue: 1 s, Wm.

m Lucy A. HUME, (b WStP in 1859) at WStP P/C, on 21 Feb 1884. (She Laundress by 1891.) d 16 May '37, Wdn H/St (1994).

Matilda, b 1853. 'In service' Wit at her bro' Albert's m 1884. Liv '01, Dom Cook, at Halstead

Also Sarah b 1843 'in service', then Shopkpr by '71, Liv 1901, Shopkpr. **Jane b 1846.** m Wm SKIPPER in 1870, Norwich. By 1881, back with parents as wid & invalid.

> **NOTE:** A copy of the Will of 1480 is held in Bury St Edmunds C.R.O. Copies of the Wills dated 1858 and 1906 are held in the Principal Probate Registry, LON.

Copyright Neville A DAVIS, 2005. E & O E

Abbreviations used in the Family Trees

@ - *often means 'aged '(rather than 'at').*
abt - *about or approximately*
adv - *advertised*
Ag Lab - *Agricultural Labourer*
Ag Lab/Drayman/Maltster – *Job Titles separated by '/' imply jobs held consecutively – not concurrently with each other.*
b - *born.*
b/b – *'bastard-born' i.e. parents not joined in wedlock.*
blvd - *believed*
bp - *baptised*
bro – *brother (within a family)*
brokn-hrtd – *broken-hearted*
bur - *buried*
c – *about or approximately*
C - *century*
c/b - *childbirth*
crem – *cremated*
d - *'died' or' daughter', depending on context.*
(d) aged 3 – *Bolding of a phrase like this highlights (and 'eliminates') individuals who clearly had no chance of ' creating an ensuing generation'.*
DAVIS, Alfred Wm – *Any 'bolded' name signifies a direct blood-line relationship*
DAVIS/DAVIS – *All Surnames are capitalised throughout to distinguish them from forenames.*
d/inf – *died as an infant (or d/inf? - believed to have done so). N.B Prior to 1837, small infants of impoverished families were sometimes only' informally' buried, maybe in the 'back-garden'.*
dsp – *decessit sine prole, i.e. there were no children from this union.*
d/wid – *died as a widow (or widower)*
d/yng – *died young*
E & O E – *'errors and omissions excepted' (because the chances of being 100% correct are rather slim! – especially where outright lies had been told to 'officialdom'! – and to say nothing of the risks of 'human error' by the original clerk, cleric, transcriber or, indeed the modern family history researcher. Sometimes the choices between possible alternatives of people having virtually the same names, ages and locations are extraordinarily difficult to decide. It is all too easy to build an elaborate 'house of cards' just waiting for a fellow-researcher to 'blow it all down' – perhaps by the telling of a strong legend in their family line, or by making some new discovery in a remote archive, or by sheer weight of logical argument – or by finding two graves where only one was 'anticipated' (as recently happened to the author!!*
emp - *employing*
E/Srys – *The East Surrey Regiment*
fr – *from*
H/St (date) – *Decipherable headstone still extant at the date shown.*
husb - *husband*
inf - *infant*
infmt - *informant*

inflmtn - *inflammation*

Issue: - *number of children born [followed by (say) '1 s 2 d' for 1 son & two daughters.]*

Lic. – *Licence. (Marr by Licence often meant that the couple were of above-ave. status.)*

lines (bolded) – *indicate blood-lines*

lines (horizontal, with 'drop-lines') – *show the siblings of a marriage*

lines (vertical) – *when dropped from an '=' sign, shows the children of that marriage.*

lines, (vertical, <u>multiple</u>) – *show some of the children of a marriage (often the daus), grouped together in one column, as a device to save space on a crowded family tree.*

lines (wavy, plus arrow) – *when dropped down from a female to a child, show an illegitimate birth.*

liv – *the last 'sighting' of this individual (say, at a census.) A date is normally appended.*

m – *marriage or married (Absence of a marriage record may imply that the couple had only 'jumped over the broomstick' in an informal ceremony with friends & family.)*

m&div – *married and later divorced*

n/f – *non-family (as of men working for a Farmer, to show they were not his own sons.)*

otp – *man or woman of this parish (or 'botp' – both of this parish)*

phthisis – *the disease of Tuberculosis, sometimes related to the husbandry of TB-infected cattle.*

P/C – *parish church*

P/Clk – *Parish Clerk. When adult family members were lacking at the ceremony, or reluctant to come forward due to their illiteracy, this official often acted as a Witness for Marriages.*

P.H. – *public house (But 'P/H' – 'Potter Hanworth', a village in Lincolnshire.)*

propts - *properties*

relict – *widow and inheritor of deceased husband's estate*

RFC – *Royal Flying Corps (precursor of the Royal Air Force.)*

RGA – *Royal Garrison Artillery*

RN – *Royal Navy*

RNAS – *Royal Naval Air service*

s – *'son' or 'signed', depending on context*

shpwmn - *Shopwoman*

(sic) – *data directly preceding the bracket is as given in the original source, albeit miss-spelt or otherwise clearly erroneously.*

sis - *sister (within a family)*

(s-s) – *both parties signed (a marriage document) cf (s-x) – bridegroom signed, wife merely 'made her mark'.*

wcp – *with consent of parents (usually where person becoming married is aged under 21)*

wdn - *wooden*

will – *person left a will. ('dtd' – date will written and witnessed. 'pvd' – date will 'proved' and probate granted to the Executor(s).)*

WW1/WW2 – *First World War/Second World War*

(x-x) – *neither bridegroom nor bride signed, but merely 'made their marks'. (i.e. were probably illiterate)*

'=' - *marriage*

'1stly', '2ndly', '3rdly' (placed above an '=' sign) *shows the sequence of the marriages of a man married more than once. A dashed line - - - - is used to connect such entries.*

#2, #3, etc. – *literally No.1, No.2, etc., but used in these trees to denote the situation where a family has named a child (say) 'John'(or 'Jane'), only to have the child die as an infant. It was often the custom to give the same name to the next 'available' child of the same sex that was born, (though sometimes the first 'John' had lived long enough for one or more other children to arrive and be named* *differently, so the re- naming as (say) '#2 John' had to be held over until the <u>next</u> arrival of the <u>same</u> sex).*

Sometimes, if the first (deceased) child had been baptised, the new child was regarded as 'already covered' by baptism, even if it had arrived years later. This can lead to confusion when 'age at marriage', 'age at death as an adult', etc., is compared with the 'date of baptism'. It can therefore be useful for the family tree compiler to note and show where more than one child of the same name is 'listed' amongst the siblings. Hence, if (say)'John #2' appears in a tree in this work ,it signifies that there was a 'John #1' earlier – even if sometimes omitted from the tree to save space. (If so, there will normally be a <u>double</u> 'drop-down line' to the name which <u>is</u> recorded.)

It will sometimes be noted that the time elapsed between birth and baptism is recorded, especially if of a year or more.

APPENDIX G

This Index is in two main parts, the first part dealing with **Alf's** *Naval* **Life**, and the second part dealing with his ***Private* Life**. (There is also a short supplementary Index relating to the author's work in researching and writing this book.)

1ˢᵗ **INDEX (Alf's Naval Life)**

All index titles refer to the Forces of Great Britain, *unless otherwise stated.*

NOTE: In general, individual names are *specifically* indexed for naval officers of high rank only, under titles such as **"Commanding Officers of RN Ships and Training Establishments".** However, persons seeking the names of less senior officers or warrant officers, believed to have served in the ships whose names occur as the titles to Chapters 8 to 15, may well find those persons under **"Listings of Ship's Officers and WOs."** If so, there may well be notes about such matters as their joining or leaving the ship to be found *within the main text of the related chapter.* [N.B. Appendix C contains a full alphabetical tabulation of all the known names of officers and WOs who served in HMS *Southampton* from 1936-1941. This overall tabulation has been compiled mainly from the date-related listings within Chapters 15(a) and 15(b).]

Exercises (By Single Ship) (Cont'd):	Practice with Demolition Charges, 282, 355, 505 Range-Finding/Range-Taking, 218, 221 Repelling Aircraft Attack, sometimes involving Gas, 306, 481, 483, 489, 505, 507, 511, 527, 528, 538, 570, 571 Repelling Destroyer or MTB Attack, 101, 125, 287, 289, 415, 511, 527, 538, 539 Repelling Submarine Attack, 122, 507 'Rig Hand Capstan!', 360 Searchlight Operation, 102, 229, 231, 302, 306, 360, 361, 366, 367, 368, 384, 385, 419, 546, 627 Shore Signalling, 293 Streaming Paravanes, 121, 221, 229, 279, 306, 343, 344, 349, 357, 362, 366, 487, 488, 495, 498, 504, 508, 509, 525, 526, 540 Torpedo-Firing, sometimes by Night, 104, 121, 147-150, 218, 219, 236, 247, 281, 290, 372, 487, 509, 564, 570 Towing and being Taken in Tow, 231, 294, 343, 519 Wireless Communicat'n & Jamming, (See Exercises by Sqdn.)
Experts (&/or Inventors &/or Authors):	BERRY, W T, 211, CHATFIELD, Captain, later Adm, 195, 201-203, DALZEL-JOB, Patrick, Lt, RN, 596, 597, 608, 609, FLEMING, Sir Alexander, 531, GRAY, Edwyn, 202, HISLAM, Percival, 197, JELLICOE, J, Capt, 83, 100, 161, 206-208, 234, 241, 280, KELVIN, Lord, 100, POLLEN, Arthur, 201, 202, PRENDERGAST, R J, 211, 213, Prince Louis of BATTENBERG, 100, POOLE, S L, 195, 199, SCOTT, Captain Percy, 96, 97, 120. (Also see 'Bibliography', Appendix D)
Flotillas:	4th Destroyer, 507, 5th Destroyer, 329, 521, 529, 536, 539, 6th Destroyer, 329, 528, 536, 8th Destroyer, 615. (See also 'Squadrons' re Cruisers, etc.)
Fuelling Bases, Fortified:	**St Helena**, 276, 279, 284, 299, 300, 309, 310, 344-347, 367, 371, 385, **Sierra Leone**, 276, 299-302, 310, 367, 368, 398,
Fuelling Bases, Non-Fortified:	**Durban**, 168, 169, 174, 276, 290, 293, 305, 350-354, 361, 362, 384, 418, 429, 653, **Suez**, 179, 180, 186, 188, 652-655, **Walvis Bay**, 278, 284-286, 303, 366, 403, 410, 411, 423, **Zanzibar**, 164, 165, 168-174, 179, 653, 663
'Hill Stations':	Buea (Africa Stn.), 402, 424
Journals, Surgeons:	BARLOW, N A H, Surg Capt, 586, 590, CREASER, Surg Capt, 435, CROSBIE, P L, Surg Capt, 391, McINTYRE, Surg Capt, 590, 594, 605, 616, PATRICK, J B, Surg Lt, 399, 401, 402, 414, SLOANE, W C, Surg Capt, 616, 632
Land Engagements, Pre-WW1:	The Boer War, 76, 77, 106, 483
Land Engagements, WW1:	Battle of the Somme, 356
Land Engagements, WW2:	German Blitzkreig (in France 1940), 608
League of Nations:	Hopes of Peace, 256
Lifesaving Society:	Certificate of: 389
Listings of Ship's Officers and WOs:	HMS *Birmingham*, 342, HMS *Delphinium*, 413, 414 HMS *Lowestoft*, 291, HMS *Weymouth*, 173, 174 HMS *Southampton*, 480, 481, 534, 535, 628, 629, 661, 662 (Also see Appendix C)
Magazines, RN Ships (Spontaneous Detonation of):	HMS *Bulwark*, 112, 222, HMS *Natal*, 112, 133, 222, 527, HMS *Vanguard*, 111, 112, 222

Ships, Oilers and RFAs in Naval Service: *British Governor*, 605, *Burma*, 233, *Celerol*, 504, 510, *China*, 247, *Faun*, 239, *Griffin*, 224, 238, *Kite*, 237, *Limmerol*, 218, *Maggie Purvis*, 240, *Montenol*, 554, *Oleander*, 608, *Prestol*, 488, 489, 539, *Petronel*, 494, *Sea Nymph*, 231, *Teal*, 238, *Unio*, 235. (General), 569, 596, 608, 633, 635

Ships, Passenger, converted to AMCs and/or Minelayers in WW1: *Dunvegan Castle* (Union Castle Line), 174, *Kinfauns Castle* (Union Castle Line), 169-174, 288, 290, *Laconia*, 174-176, *Laurentic*, 176, *Princess Margaret*, 232, 233, *Tantallon*, 186

Ships, Passenger, converted to AMCs and/or Minelayers in WW2: *California*, 576, *Circussia*, 591, *Jervis Bay*, 635, *Marsdale*, 639, *Rawalpindi*, 578, *Translyvania*, 576

Ships, Purchased or Commandeered For Naval Service (E Coast of Africa): *Adjutant*, 170, *Blackcock*, 176, *Challenger*, 176, *Childers*, 176, 177, *Duplex*, 166-168, 174, *Echo*, 176, 177, *Fly*, 171, 176, 177, *Pickle*, 176, *Revenge*, 176, *Sarah Joliffe*, 176, *T A Joliffe*, 176

Ships, Supply, German: *Sperrbrecher*, 179, 222

Ships, Union Castle, (in Peacetime): *Arundel Castle*, 368, *Balmoral Castle*, 371, *Carnarvon Castle*, 384, *Cluny Castle*, 262, 267, 272, 277, 282, 312, 331, 387, *Dunluce Castle*, 299, *Gloucester Castle*, 298, *Kinfauns Castle*, 288, 290, *Windsor Castle*, 355, 374, 383. (Also see 'Ships, Passenger, converted to Armed Merchant Cruisers, AMCs')

Shipyards: Armstrong Whitworth, 194, 195, Chrichton & Co, 321, Elswick, 139, 195, 196, 340, 459, Harland & Wolf, 195, John Brown, 453, 459, 460-463, 629, 682, Napier and Miller, 399, Palmers, 116, Royal Dockyard, Devonport, 73, 75, Vickers, 80, 84, 86, Vickers-Armstrong, 458

Shore Establishments: HMS *Daedelus*, 589, HMS *Dryad*, 318, HMS *Excellent*, 315-318, HMS *Ganges*, 24, 60-69, 81, 84, 208, 256-262, 315, 324, 389-391, 432-437, HMS *Impregnable*, 24, 69-75, 84, 315, 316, HMS *Pembroke*, 23, 80, 81, 109, 110, 114, 126-129, 135, 136, 186-189, 222, 248-250, 255, 256, 262, 267, 311, 317, 325, 318, 432, 434, 453, 530, 613, HMS *St Vincent*, 437, HMS *Vernon*, 213, 315, 491, Detention Barracks, 185, 281, 371, 385

Squadrons (Pre-WW1): 2nd BS, 102, 147, 3rd BS, 102, 1st CS, 102, 2nd CS, 102, 2nd LCS, 138

Squadrons (WW1): 1st BS, 226, 232, 234, 2nd BS, 231, 5th BS, 230, 233, 243, 1st BCS, 226, 231-234, 1st CS, 156, 160, 225, 2nd CS, 280, 1st LCS, 226-233, 236-241, 2nd LCS, 235, 236, 338, 3rd LCS, 229, 230, 231, 235, 239, 6th LCS, 226, 227, 231-235, 7th LCS, 236

Squadrons (pre-WW2): 2nd BS, 324, 328, 483, 528, 329, 1st CS, 491, 2nd CS, 329, 478-488, 507-530, 535, 536, 539, 554, 564, 565, 570, 578-580, 615, 3rd CS, 498, 6th CS, 233, 384, 417, 2nd LCS, 338

Squadrons (WW2): 2nd BS, 567, 1st BCS 614, 2nd CS, 517, 567-581, 614, 633, 634, 3rd CS, 653, 18th CS, 586, 601-603, 608, 614, 629-632, 640641 (See also 'Flotillas' ref Destroyers.)

Straining of Ship's Hulls: HMS *Mersey* & HMS *Severn*, 178, 206, HMS *Courageous*, 205, 206, 209-213

Suicides: On Board Ship, 145, 146, 304

Surrender of German Fleet (WW1): 243-250 (Scuttling, 250-251)

Tests: Buoyancy of Boats, 404, 425, 426

Warships, Royal Navy (Cont'd):

2nd INDEX (Alf's Private Life)

NOTE: Certain supplementary information to be found in the Appendices, especially in the Family Trees, has NOT been specifically referenced in this index.

Supplementary Index of
Assistance Given to the Author

**ALSO SEE ALSO the COMMENTS regarding Assistance and Co-Operation as given in the
various Family Trees in Appendix F, and the invaluable assistance provided by relatives of
the Author.**

APPENDIX H

A GLOSSARY OF ABBREVIATIONS USED IN THIS BOOK

AB	Able Seaman
AG	Air Gunner
ADO	Air Defence Officer
AMC	Armed Merchant Cruiser
AP	Armour Piercing (a type of Shell)
AR	Aiming Rifle
ARP	Air Raid Precautions (Civil Defence Personnel)
BEF	British Expeditionary Force
BCS	Battlecruiser Squadron
BP	'Battle Practice' (a type of large towed Target)
BS	Battleship Squadron
CB	Companion of the Bath
CBE	Commander of the British Empire
CDX	Coast Defence Exercise
COX	Combined Operations Exercise
CPBC	Contact Percussion Ballistic Capped (a type of AP shell)
CPO	Chief Petty Officer
CVO	Companion of the Royal Victorian Order
CWGC	Commonwealth War Graves Commission
DCT	Director Control Tower
DF	Direction Finding or Destroyer Flotilla
DG	De-Gaussing Gear
DoW	Died of Wounds
DNC	Director of Naval Construction
DSO	Distinguished Service Order
ERA	Engine Room Artificer
FC	Full-Calibre
FRMO	Fleet Royal Marine Officer
GCO	Gunnery Control Officer
GOC	General Officer Commanding
GI	Gunnery Instructor
GL	Gunlayer
GPO	General Post Office
HA/LA	High Angle/Low Angle (dual-purpose gun)
HE	His Excellency or High Explosive (depending on context)
HO	Hostilities Only
IWM	Imperial War Museum
KiA	Killed in Action
LCS	Light Cruiser Squadron
KCB	Knight Commander of the Bath
KCVO	Knight Commander of the (Royal) Victorian Order
KHM	King's Harbour Master
LDV	Local Defence Volunteers (later the 'Home Guard')
LS	Leading Seaman

LVO	Licentiate of the (Royal) Victorian Order
MAA	Master at Arms
MBE	Member of the British Empire
MG	Machine-Gun
MP	Military Police
MVO	Member of the Royal Victorian Order
NMM	National Maritime Museum
NSO	Naval Stores Officer
NUC	Not Under Control
OBE	Order of the British Empire
OOD	Officer of the Day
OOQ	Officer of Quarters
OOW	Officer of the Watch
PO	Petty Officer
PoW	Prisoner of War
PRO	Public Record Office (now TNA)
PT	Physical Training
P1 HA/LA	(See S1 HA/LA)
QB	'Queen Bee' (a Target Aircraft, wireless-operated)
RAF	Royal Air Force
RF	Rangefinder
RFA	Royal Fleet Auxiliary
RDF	Radio Direction Finding (later called 'Radar')
RM	Royal Marine
RMLI	Royal Marine Light Infantry
RMS	Royal Mail Steamer
RN	Royal Navy
RNAS	Royal Naval Air Service
RNB	Royal Naval Barracks
RNH	Royal Naval Hospital
RNLO	Royal Naval Liaison Officer
RNR	Royal Naval Reserve
RNVR	Royal Naval Volunteer Reserve
S1 HA/LA	The 1st Starboard-side HA/LA Gun
SNO	Senior Naval Officer
TB	Tuberculosis
TBD	Torpedo-Boat Destroyer
Tel	Telegraphist
TNA	The National Archives
TS	Transmitting Station or Troopship, depending on context
VC	Victoria Cross
WO	Warrant Officer
WT	Wireless Telegraphy
UK	United Kingdom

APPENDIX J

'LATE-ARRIVING' PHOTOGRAPHS

GUNNERY OFFICERS AND STAFF. H.M.T.E. SHOTLEY. JUNE. 1921.

(i) Alf (marked with an 'X') is the Petty Officer standing on the extreme left of the back row of this photo of the Gunnery Officers and Staff at Shotley, taken in June 1921. (See page 262.)

(ii) A Naval Display at Ipswich c.1931. Now holding the rank of Gunner, Alf leads a column of sailors from *Ganges* with a field gun and limber. (See page 391.)

Collection of Richard Paul DAVIS Esq. An anon postcard.

(iii) The Hockey Team of HMS *Ganges* for 1934-35. Left to Right. Back Row, Lt WRIGHT, Mr SPRINGALL, RPO THOMAS, Lt BELOE, Mr DAVIS, Mr GILES: Front Row, Lt G. COLLET, Lt COCHRANE, Lt C. COLLET, Lt EWING, Lt CREASE. (See page 437.)

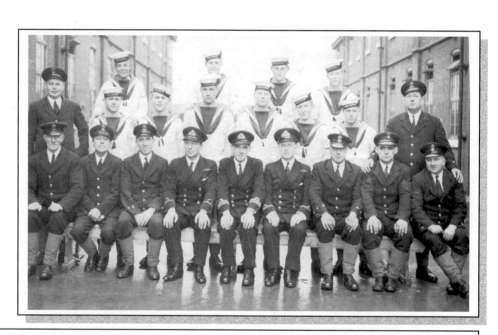

Collection of Richard Paul DAVIS Esq. An anonymous postcard.

(iv) "Nozzer" Staff, HMS *Ganges*, 6th June 1934. Back Row, Instructor Boys JEFFREY, WELLOW, HARKER, REID, Middle Row, POs WINK, MARSHALL, COWIE, MITTON, LAMBRICK, CLARKE, THOMAS and CPO MERRICK .
Front Row, PPO McFIGGANS, PO PAGE, CPO LOVEDAY, Mr DAVIS, Lt WILKINSON, Mr BALDERSON, CPO WEST, PO MILLS and PO HAINES. (See page 437.)